EDUCATIONAL MEASUREMENT

EDUCATIONAL MEASUREMENT
Third Edition

SPONSORED JOINTLY BY
NATIONAL COUNCIL ON MEASUREMENT IN EDUCATION
AND
AMERICAN COUNCIL ON EDUCATION

Edited by
Robert L. Linn

American Council on Education • *Macmillan Publishing Company*
NEW YORK

Collier Macmillan Publishers
LONDON

Macmillan Publishing Company
866 Third Avenue, New York, NY 10022

Collier Macmillan Canada, Inc.

Library of Congress Catalog Card Number: 88-17461

Printed in the United States of America

printing number
1   2   3   4   5   6   7   8   9   10

Library of Congress Cataloging-in-Publication Data

Educational measurement / edited by Robert L. Linn, National Council
   on Measurement in Education [and] American Council on Education. —
   3rd ed.
         p. cm.—(The American Council on Education/Macmillan series
   on higher education)
     Includes bibliographies and index.
     ISBN 0-02-922400-4 (Macmillan)
     1. Educational tests and measurements.   I. Linn, Robert L.
II. National Council on Measurement in Education.   III. American
Council on Education.   IV. Series: American Council on
Education/Macmillan series in higher education.
LB3051.E266   1988
371.2′6—dc19   88-17461
                    CIP

Contents

PART III: Applications 445

List of Figures

List of Tables

Foreword

We are pleased to present the third edition of *Educational Measurement*. The first edition, edited by E. F. Lindquist and published by the American Council on Education (ACE) in 1951, stimulated the development of quality assessment programs by collecting, structuring, and evaluating the practices and knowledge in the field at that time. The second edition, edited by Robert Thorndike and published by ACE in 1971, involved new authors who considerably reworked the contents in addition to updating the material. This edition, published in the ACE/Macmillan Series on Higher Education in cooperation with the National Council on Measurement in Education (NCME) and edited by Robert Linn, again draws on the expertise of outstanding authors and incorporates the accumulated research and practical knowledge since the publication of the last edition.

It is fitting that the professional association of researchers and practitioners in educational measurement (NCME) and the nation's comprehensive association of colleges and universities (ACE) have cooperated to produce this volume. Both organizations share the concern for fair and valid assessment of educational outcomes; both have been actively involved in working for improvements in the area for many years.

Comprehensive reference books such as this one serve to mark progress in the discipline as well as to guide the efforts of new generations of researchers and practitioners. Robert Linn has organized and shaped a book that will prove valuable in the classroom as well as in the workplace. Some of the nation's premier researchers have contributed to this volume. The conclusions and recommendations in this book are important to all levels of education and to nontraditional as well as traditional educational programs. NCME and ACE are indebted to the editor, authors, and reviewers for their contributions.

Robert H. Atwell, *President*
American Council on Education

Carol K. Tittle, *President*
National Council on Measurement in Education 1987–88

Editor's Preface

Initial discussion and planning for the preparation of the third edition of *Educational Measurement* began independently at the two sponsoring organizations in late 1982. The discussion at the American Council of Education was initiated by Douglas R. Whitney. Based on his review and discussion of the possibility with other specialists in the field, he proposed that work begin on a new edition. This proposal was approved, and negotiations with Macmillan were underway when Lorrie A. Shepard, the 1982–83 president of the National Council on Measurement in Education, contacted the American Council on Education to explore the possibility of initiating a project to revise the book under the joint sponsorship of the two organizations.

The two organizations quickly agreed to jointly sponsor the preparation of the third edition and appointed an editorial advisory committee in the spring of 1983. The committee advised on the selection of the editor and worked closely with him in the planning of the contents of the book and the identification of chapter authors. The members of the committee are Alexander W. Astin, University of California at Los Angeles; Nancy S. Cole, University of Illinois at Urbana-Champaign; Leonard S. Feldt, The University of Iowa; Richard M. Jaeger, University of North Carolina at Greensboro; Jason Millman, Cornell University; and Douglas R. Whitney, American Council of Education. The guidance and support of the advisory committee was of great value throughout the long life of the project, but it was of particular importance in the initial phases of the effort.

The decision to prepare a third edition was based on the belief that there had been substantial changes in the field of measurement since the publication of the second edition in 1971. Although the mathematical foundations of item response theory were clearly described in Lord and Novick's (1968) book, for example, the rapid explosion of research on and practical applications of the theory to a wide variety of testing problems began after the publication of the second edition. Consequently, the second edition gave hardly any attention to item response theory. Several issues such as computerized test administration and the fair use of tests with minorities, which Thorndike (1971) mentioned in his opening chapter, "Educational Measurement for the Seventies," but otherwise were given little attention in the second edition, proved to be important issues indeed. On the other hand, certain areas covered in the second edition underwent much more modest changes and did not seem to warrant the addition of new chapters.

From even a cursory comparison of the chapter titles in the second and third editions, it is apparent that there is far from a one-to-one correspondence. Some of the chapters (e.g., Chapter 2, "Validity") have obvious parallels in the second edition while others (e.g., Chapter 5, "Principles and Selected Applications of Item Response Theory") are clearly new topics. Chapter 8, "The Specification and Development of Tests of Achievement and Ability," on the other hand, covers topics that were found in several chapters of the second edition.

A large number of people contributed to the development of this book. In addition to the authors and the editorial advisory board, many people contributed time as reviewers. In addition to these people, many other reviews were solicited directly by individual chapter authors.

Chapter 2, "Validity," by Samuel Messick, Educational Testing Service, was reviewed by Lee J. Cronbach, Stanford University, and Robert M. Guion, Bowling Green University.

Chapter 3, "Reliability," by Leonard S. Feldt, The University of Iowa, and Robert L. Brennan, The American College Testing Program, was reviewed by Ronald K. Hambleton, University of Massachusetts at Amherst, and Nambury S. Raju, the Illinois Institute of Technology.

Chapter 4, "Principles and Selected Applications of Item Response Theory," by Ronald K. Hambleton, University of Massachusetts at Amherst, was reviewed by Ross E. Traub, The Ontario Institute for Studies in Education, and Wendy M. Yen, CTB/McGraw-Hill. The outline and plan for the chapter was also reviewed by Frederic M. Lord, Educational Testing Service.

Chapter 5, "Bias in Test Use," by Nancy S. Cole, University of Illinois at Urbana-Champaign, and Pamela A. Moss, University of Pittsburgh, was reviewed by Lloyd Bond, University of Pittsburgh, and Lorrie A. Shepard, University of Colorado at Boulder.

Chapter 6, "Scaling, Norming, and Equating," by Nancy S. Petersen, Educational Testing Service; Michael J. Kolen, The American College Testing Program; and H. D. Hoover, The University of Iowa, was reviewed by William H. Angoff, Educational Testing Service, and Richard M. Jaeger, the University of North Carolina at Greensboro.

Chapter 7, "Implications of Cognitive Psychology for Educational Measurement," by Richard E. Snow, Stanford University, and David F. Lohman, The University of Iowa, was reviewed by John B. Carroll, University of North Carolina and Chapel Hill, and Robert Glaser, University of Pittsburgh.

Chapter 8, "The Specification and Development of Tests of

Achievement and Ability," by Jason Millman and Jennifer Greene, Cornell University, was reviewed by William E. Coffman, The University of Iowa; Anthony J. Nitko, University of Pittsburgh; and Mauritz Johnson, State University of New York.

Chapter 9, "The Four Generations of Computerized Educational Measurement," by C. Victor Bunderson, Educational Testing Service; Dillon K. Inouye, Brigham Young University; and James B. Olsen, Wicat Systems, Inc., was reviewed by Garlie Forehand and William C. Ward, Educational Testing Service.

Chapter 10, "Computer Technology in Test Construction and Processing," by Frank B. Baker, University of Wisconsin at Madison, was reviewed by Delwyn L. Harnisch, University of Illinois at Urbana-Champaign, and Tse-chi Hsu, University of Pittsburgh.

Chapter 11, "The Effects of Special Preparation on Measures of Scholastic Ability," by Lloyd Bond, University of Pittsburgh, was reviewed by Anne Anastasi, Fordham University, and Donald E. Powers, Educational Testing Service.

Chapter 12, "Designing Tests That Are Integrated with Instruction," by Anthony J. Nitko, University of Pittsburgh, was reviewed by Peter W. Airasian, Boston College, and Thomas M. Haladyna, The American College Testing Program.

Chapter 13, "Administrative Uses of School Testing Programs," by Joy A. Frechtling, Montgomery County (MD) Public Schools, was reviewed by Joan Bollenbacher, Cincinnati Public Schools, and William A. Mehrens, Michigan State University.

Chapter 14, "Certification of Student Competence," by Richard M. Jaeger, University of North Carolina at Greensboro, was reviewed by Ronald A. Berk, The Johns Hopkins University; James C. Impara, Virginia Polytechnic Institute; George F. Madaus, Boston College; and W. James Popham, University of California at Los Angeles.

Chapter 15, "Educational Admissions and Placement," by Douglas R. Whitney, American Council on Education, was reviewed by Franklin R. Evans, Law School Admission Service, and Richard L. Ferguson, The American College Testing Program.

Chapter 16, "Counseling," by Lenore W. Harmon, was reviewed by John G. Darley, University of Minnesota; Carol Kehr Tittle, City University of New York; and Bert W. Westbrook, North Carolina State University.

Chapter 17, "Identification of Mild Handicaps," by Lorrie A. Shepard, University of Colorado at Boulder, was reviewed by Barbara K. Keogh, University of California at Los Angeles; Nadine M. Lambert, University of California at Berkeley; and Barbara M. Pedulla, Clinical Psychologist, Sudbury, MA.

Chapter 18, "Testing of Linguistic Minorities," by Richard P. Duran, University of California at Santa Barbara, was reviewed by Richard A. Figueroa, University of California at Davis.

Robert L. Linn

1

Current Perspectives and Future Directions

Robert L. Linn

University of Colorado, Boulder

A comparison of the current status of educational measurement with that in 1971, when the second edition of this book was published (Thorndike, 1971), or even with that in 1951, when the first edition appeared (Lindquist, 1951), yields a mixed picture. There are senses in which there has been tremendous change and others in which there has been relatively little.

Consider, for example, a computerized-adaptive test. It differs from its familiar paper-and-pencil counterpart not only in the mode of item presentation, but also in the response-contingent selection of items to present, the efficiency of measurement, the procedures used for estimating scores, and the precision of the estimates at different levels of ability. On the other hand, the same multiple-choice items may be used on both the paper-and-pencil and the computerized-adaptive versions of a test. Moreover, the two test versions can be used for the same purpose and be essentially indistinguishable in terms of validity. Thus, there is much that is fundamentally the same beneath the dramatically different surfaces.

On the other hand, measurement procedures that appear much the same can conceal important changes. For example, on inspection of three versions of a well-established, standardized achievement test battery, one published around the time of each of the three editions of this book, one might easily wonder if there had been any progress in the field of educational measurement since the early 1950s. The multiple-choice items, grade-equivalent scores, and percentile ranks would give quite a sense of constancy. Without detailed analysis, the efforts to represent minorities in stories, pictures, and references; to avoid gender stereotypes; and to achieve a gender balance might not be noticed by the reviewer. The item-bias analyses, which have become a standard part of the work of some pub-

lishers, might go unnoticed. Also concealed from a simple inspection might be the fact that the current test form is not an off-the-shelf form. It is a customized form produced to meet local or state specifications and linked to normative estimates through the use of items from the publisher's item bank that had previously been calibrated using item response theory.

In still other instances, modest changes would be seen. For example, if the reviewer of the three versions of a test battery focused on score-reporting systems rather than item formats, the differences between the three versions would appear greater. Today's school administrator is offered a bewildering array of optional, computer-produced score reports, including item-level, skill-level, total-score-level, and narrative reports. The administrator might even choose to obtain certain types of data on a floppy diskette for use in the school's personal computer. Many of these score reports were also available at the time of the second edition of this book, but the options were far narrower at the time of the first edition.

Some of the differences in score reports are simply a consequence of the availability of ever increasing electronic scoring and computer capability rather than of conceptual advances. The primary normative scores, percentile ranks and grade-equivalent scores, remain essentially unchanged. True, the Normal Curve Equivalent score was added to the list as the result of Title I evaluation requirements, but that is only a variation on a well-known theme of normalized standard scores. Other additions in score-reporting options, on the other hand, reflect conceptual developments. Possibly the most fundamental change of this type has been the increase in emphasis on skill-, criterion-, or objective-referenced score reports for small subsets of items. These added scores were more a response to the criterion-referenced testing movement inspired by Glaser's 1963 classic article, which flourished during the 1970s, than to the computer technology that made it easy to produce a multitude of scores.

Without belaboring the point, it is clear that there have been changes. Some are superficial, whereas others reflect more fundamental conceptual differences. The changes come from a variety of sources and could be classified in a number of ways. For convenience, the discussion in this chapter organizes them into three categories: (a) technological developments, (b) changes in the demands for and expectations of testing, and (c) changes in the social and legal contexts in which tests are used.

Focusing on changes provides a means of highlighting certain features that are important to an understanding of the current status of educational measurement and of setting the stage for more detailed accounts in the chapters that follow. It also provides the framework for exploring some of the implications of these changes for measurement in the 1990s and beyond.

Technological Developments

There have been many technological developments that affected testing in the 1970s and 1980s. Many analyses that used to require access to a mainframe computer can now be easily conducted on a microcomputer. So, too, can some analyses, such as confirmatory factor analysis and structural equation modeling, that were beyond our reach not long ago. Advances in exploratory data analyses and computer graphics enhance understanding and communication of the results. Empirical Bayes procedures have provided a means of using collateral information to improve predication systems and the handling of missing data problems. Meta-analysis has made it possible to find regularities and led to challenges of previous conceptions of the lack of generality of criterion-related validity. Each of these, and several other topics represents significant developments that would be worthy of detailed discussion. There are two developments, however, that seem to stand out from the rest in terms of their potential impact on educational measurement. These are item-response theory and computer technology.

Item-response Theory

One of the most significant technical developments of the 1970s and 1980s was the tremendous growth in the use of item response theory to deal with practical measurement problems. The first of the item response theory models, the normal-ogive, item-characteristic-curve model, was described by Lawley (1943) and used in theoretical arguments by some psychometricians (e.g., Brogden, 1946; Tucker, 1946) several years before the publication of the first edition of this book. But the model was far from being a practical tool at that time. Indeed, the Lindquist (1951) edition of *Educational Measurement* predated Lord's (1952) classic monograph by a year and was far ahead of any operational applications.

There were major theoretical advances in item-response theory between the first and second editions (see, for example,

Birnbaum, 1968; Lord & Novick, 1968; Rasch, 1960; Wright, 1968). Operational applications were yet to be seen, however, and, for most people concerned with measurement, item-response theory was nothing more than a theoretical possibility. But the potential was recognized. Henrysson (1971), for example, provided a brief description of the normal-ogive, item-characteristic-curve model in his chapter on item analysis, which he concluded as follows:

> Until now, item characteristic curves have had little practical application in test construction. However, as high-speed computing facilities become more common, their attractive statistical properties may result in wider use. (p. 148)

In a similar vein, Angoff (1971) indicated in his chapter on scales, norms, and equating that "A major hope of those using . . . [item response theory] is that the item constants . . . will in fact prove relatively invariant over populations and that inferred ability . . . will be relatively invariant over different sets of items" (p. 529). Angoff clearly recognized the potential importance of these invariance properties, noting that it was conceivable that they "could lead to some major innovations in mental measurement" (p. 529).

In the years since the second edition, much of the promise that was foreseen at that time has been realized. Item response theory has provided the means of dealing with problems that are intractable within the confines of classical test theory. It has been shown to provide a practical means of dealing with important problems such as the design of tests, the investigation of item bias, test equating, and the design and scoring of computerized-adaptive tests. Several major test publishers are now using item response theory as a routine part of their operational testing programs. Item response theory made it possible for the first time to report the 1984 and previous National Assessment of Educational Progress results in reading on a common scale for all three cohorts and years of administration. It is the basis of several state assessment programs and, as was previously mentioned, is being used with increasing frequency to create customized tests that are linked to a scale by precalibrated items in an item bank.

Because the theory and several of its applications are discussed in greater detail in other chapters of this book, no attempt will be made here to elaborate on these applications. Instead, the reader is referred to Hambleton's chapter for a discussion of the fundamentals of item response theory and some of its applications. Chapters dealing with equating (Petersen, Kolen, & Hoover), bias (Cole & Moss), and computerized test administration (Bunderson, Inouye, & Olsen) also provide discussions of item response theory within the context of those specific applications.

Although item response theory has gained fairly wide acceptance as a practical tool and has already had a substantial impact on practice, a number of questions and challenges remain for future research and development. Dimensionality of a test and applicability of a unidimensional model in a given circumstance remain important issues, especially in the use of item response theory with educational achievement tests. Some have challenged the appropriateness of the theory (e.g., Goldstein, 1980; Hoover, 1984; Traub, 1983), which was developed and initially applied within the context of tests of general ability such as the Scholastic Aptitude Test, when applied to educational achievement tests (also see Snow & Lohman, this volume). More needs to be known about the degree to which results for educational achievement tests are sensitive to the stages of learning represented in a calibration sample, to differences in instructional emphases, and to context effects (see, for example, Yen, 1980; Yen, Green, & Burket, 1987).

Work on group-level models (e.g., Mislevy, 1983) and the possibility of combining group-level and individual-level models as proposed in the *duplex design* (Bock & Mislevy, 1987) hold considerable promise for the design of improved assessment systems. Initial research on the duplex design suggests that the approach could simultaneously provide estimates of school or system performance for specific curricular areas and yield global achievement scores for individual pupils. This or related developments could provide a basis for the construction of flexible educational testing networks.

Computer Technology and Testing

Testing and electronic technology have been closely linked for decades. High-speed scoring machines have contributed greatly to the efficiency of the testing enterprise, as has the use of computers for analysis and reporting. As is clearly indicated in Baker's chapter, not only has efficiency in the scoring, reporting, and creation of item banks and test forms increased dramatically during the 1970s and 1980s, but also, with the availability of relatively low-cost microcomputers and desk top scanners, this technology is no longer the sole province of the large test publisher.

The more dramatic change in testing as a result of ready and inexpensive access to computers is one that has been discussed for a good many years, but it is just beginning to become a reality in more than a few isolated examples. That, of course, is the use of computers to administer tests. Computerized test administration is the focus of the chapter by Bunderson, Inouye, and Olsen. Hence, the present commentary will be quite brief.

In its most rudimentary form, test administration by computer involves simply putting the items of an existing paper-and-pencil test into a computer and programming the computer to administer and score the items. Even this type of computer-administered test, which Bunderson, Inouye, and Olsen dub the first generation of computerized-test administration, can change the nature of testing and raise new validation questions.

More substantial changes are anticipated with the movement toward computerized-adaptive testing. The selection of items based on the test taker's previous responses has intuitive appeal and has been shown to have psychometric advantages. Thorndike (1971) anticipated the major advantages of adaptive testing in his introductory chapter to the second edition of this book.

Basing the selection of each new item upon the individual's history of successes and failures up to that point will make it possible to bracket his ability level efficiently and to get the maximum amount of information from each additional item administered to him. (p. 6).

As Thorndike anticipated, the primary advantage of an adaptive test is a gain in efficiency: the reduction of testing time or the reduction of the magnitude of the errors of measurement within a fixed time (see the Bunderson, Inouye, & Olsen chapter for a discussion of these and several other potential advantages of adaptive tests).

Improved efficiency from the use of computers to administer tests would be welcome. The substantial reduction in testing time without loss in reliability or validity that adaptive testing can yield is nontrivial. The appeal of computers as testing devices is not limited, however, to doing what we already do with greater efficiency. Rather, the stronger appeal comes from the vision that computers can make it possible to effectively measure abilities that are not well measured by paper-and-pencil tests and that they can enhance the instructional value of measurement.

The longer term potential of computers as test-administration devices is largely unknown, though many would agree with Bunderson, Inouye, and Olsen that the potential is both exciting and vast. One thing that seems clear at this point is that the challenges for measurement specialists will be substantial.

As Millman and Greene (this volume) suggest, the development of response-contingent exercises with two or more related tasks makes it possible to construct test problems that mirror real-world criteria. For example, simulations of realistic problems can be produced by a computer that make intuitively appealing tests, but they pose a host of psychometric problems. This is evident from experience with the patient-management problem (e.g., McGuire & Babbott, 1967). Patient-management problems simulate the interaction of a physician with a patient. They have great face validity and have been used extensively in testing for some time, with or without the help of a computer. Psychometric sophistication of scoring, equating, and analysis lags far behind the substantive aspects of these tests, however, despite the fact that patient-management problems have been in use since the 1960s.

Will computers make it possible to enhance the instructional value of measurement? Will they provide the means of constructing better diagnostic tests? Will they lead to a real integration of testing and instruction? These are important, but as yet unanswered, questions. Computers appear to be well suited to the task of diagnostic testing and measurement, albeit not of the type that is done on current tests. Diagnosis is certainly a necessary component of an intelligent tutoring system. One can readily imagine the use of a computer to adapt the testing to cognitive and instructional hypotheses about student misconceptions and instructional needs. However, the design of such a test requires more than computer capability. It also requires a theory of instruction and a theory of knowledge (Ward, 1984).

Expanding Demands and Expectations

During the 1970s and 1980s there was considerable expansion in the demand for testing in education. Much of this growth in demand came from policymakers who were dissatisfied with the status of education and who sought ways of increasing accountability. This has led to new roles for educational measurement and to new expectations of tests as instruments of change.

In addition to the policymakers' top-down use of tests to affect education, there has been renewed interest in the potential uses of tests by individual classroom teachers to help students learn. Much of the impetus for renewed emphasis on instructional uses of tests comes from developments in cognitive psychology and artificial intelligence. This work has created the expectation that tests should do a better job of diagnosis and prescription.

Both the top-down accountability and the bottom-up instructional perspectives seek ways of improving education through measurement. The former perspective has already had a major impact on the use of tests in the schools, and the latter is largely a research and development agenda and a hope for the future. However, both perspectives have important implications for educational measurement.

Accountability

Educational policymakers have come to place greater reliance on measurement, both for purposes of evaluating education and as a major policy tool. The widely heralded decline in test scores, especially on tests used for admission to college, that occurred during the 1960s and 1970s provided much of the documentation that reformers used to make a case that the educational system was in trouble. The use of test results to monitor and evaluate educational progress, or the lack thereof, is neither a new nor an unexpected role for educational testing. What is somewhat more surprising is the increasing reliance on tests as major instruments of policy.

In the 1970s the major example of the use of testing as a mechanism of educational policy was the minimum-competency testing movement. During that decade, minimum-competency testing programs swept the nation. Though legislation implementing the programs varied greatly from state to state, the majority of states instituted some form of competency testing during that time (see Jaeger, this volume).

The competency testing movement was stimulated by concerns that large numbers of high school graduates lacked the basic skills needed to function in society. To remedy this perceived deficiency, test requirements were put into place. The legislative language made heavy use of "assure" and "guarantee," to indicate that future high school graduates would no longer lack essential skills.

Minimum-competency testing programs were created as a means of improving education. They frequently included funds for special remedial programs for students who failed the tests. But the test requirement was clearly the centerpiece of the program.

Competency testing focused the attention of educational measurement specialists on several issues, which, although not unique to that context, were made salient by this use of test results. Considerable attention was focused on the standard-setting problem and on issues of validity. Concerns about unintended consequences and legal challenges focused attention on relationships between what is taught and what is tested, on

adverse impact and possible bias against minorities, and on the availability and appropriateness of the tests for persons with handicapping conditions. These and other issues are addressed in some detail in Jaeger's chapter.

A second major expansion of testing as the result of concerns for accountability was the area of teacher testing. Teacher testing, albeit of a different kind than we see today, was common before the reforms of the 1920s and 1930s (Vold, 1985). After a brief demise, teacher testing was reintroduced with the creation of the National Teacher Examinations in 1940. However, the great upsurge in teacher testing is much more recent. Although the requirements are quite varied, a substantial majority of states now require teachers to pass some kind of test prior to certification. Tests for recertification, for merit pay, and for entry into teacher-preparation programs have also been introduced in some states.

The measurement issues raised by the increase in the testing of teachers are generally the same as those raised by the minimum-competency movement. Definition of the domain to be covered by the tests, procedures for obtaining evidence of validity, procedures for setting of standards, and identification and elimination of sources of bias are particularly salient.

A third major expansion in testing as the result of emphasis on accountability is in the area of assessment and public reporting. Although the National Assessment of Educational Progress (NAEP) has been conducting assessments since 1969, its role during the early years was relatively low-key. In recent years, however, expectations for NAEP have increased considerably. The labeling of reports as "The Nation's Report Card" is in keeping with this new emphasis. So, too, are the calls for a major redesign of NAEP.

The recommendations contained in the Alexander–James (1987) report called for a much more ambitious role for NAEP in the future than it has had in the past. The report was the result of work by a blue-ribbon committee chaired by Governor Lamar Alexander, with Thomas James serving as study director. The Alexander–James committee was commissioned by the U. S. Department of Education to provide a comprehensive review of NAEP and make recommendations regarding its future. The result was a call for the major redesign and expansion of NAEP.

One of the key elements in the proposed redesign was the call for collection of data that could be reliably reported by individual states. Also envisioned were options for local school districts to pay for expanded testing, so that district-level reports could be obtained. State-to-state comparisons, which were intentionally precluded in the original design of NAEP, are viewed as desirable by policymakers who see the reporting of such information as an important element of accountability and as a motivator for state educational agencies.

Use of test scores to compare schools, districts, or even states is not new. But, with the emphasis on accountability, such comparisons have been made with increasing frequency and have received increasing publicity. At the national level, comparisons among states have been highlighted by publication of the *wall charts* that were first introduced in 1983 by former Secretary of Education Terrell H. Bell. Although the wall charts contain information of several types, the majority of attention has been focused on "performance outcomes," which include the estimated graduation rate and the state average on either the American College Test (ACT) or the Scholastic Aptitude Test (SAT).

It is obvious that neither the ACT nor the SAT was designed for comparing the quality of the education that is provided in different states, and it hardly seems necessary to review the many criticisms of this use of these tests. The inadequacy of these indicators of student achievement for the states is even acknowledged by the Department of Education when the wall charts are released. The fact that they continue to be released because of a lack of better data comparing states in terms of the achievement of students attests to the hunger for such information.

The press at the national level for test results to encourage greater accountability at the state level is mirrored over and over again at each succeeding level of education. State reports of district-by-district performance on tests mandated by the state have become increasingly familiar, as has the listing of test-score averages for individual school buildings. In some instances, the process of comparing units based on the aggregated test performance of students is even carried to the level of individual classrooms.

The use of aggregated test results to draw inferences about the relative performance of classes (or teachers of those classes), schools, districts, or states raises a host of issues for the educational measurement profession. The evidential and consequential bases for test interpretation and test use that Messick (this volume) identifies as the facets of validity apply to the interpretations of aggregated test scores and the uses made of those results. The evidence that might be accumulated to support the interpretations and uses of the test scores for individual students does not necessarily support the interpretations and policy uses of the aggregate results. The validation requirements are neither less important nor less challenging in this new context than they are in the more familiar individual-differences context. To date, however, the former have received relatively little attention.

Instructional Uses

Unlike the demand for expanded use of tests for purposes of accountability, which has largely been the creation of legislators, administrators, and policy boards, the renewed interest in using tests by teachers and students to make better day-to-day instructional decisions comes from educational measurement specialists and cognitive psychologists. What is envisioned is testing that is an integral part of instruction. The focus in instructional uses of test results is not on the prediction of who will succeed or on the reporting of results to satisfy accountability demands; rather it is on helping the individual student gain the most from instruction.

The idea that testing should help students learn better is certainly not new. In the first edition of this book, Cook (1951) discussed the functions of educational measurement. He concluded quite simply that "all the functions of educational measurement are concerned either directly or indirectly with the facilitation of learning" (p. 4). In his chapter, Tyler argued forcefully that the facilitation of learning through measurement requires a close link between testing and instruction. In

his words, "educational measurement is conceived, not as a process quite apart from instruction, but rather as an integral part of it" (1951, p. 47).

Few would argue with these statements as important, though not necessarily the only, goals for educational measurement. However, a number of authors (e.g., Bejar, 1984; Glaser, 1981, 1986) have questioned the value of current testing for making instructional decisions, especially diagnostic decisions about which of several courses of action is most likely to facilitate the learning of an individual pupil. Educational tests currently do a much better job of predicting future achievement than of diagnosis and prescription. "At present, tests (with the exception of the important informal assessments of the good classroom teacher) typically are not designed to guide the specifics of instruction" (Glaser, 1986, p. 45).

As was suggested, and is elaborated on in the chapter by Bunderson, Inouye, and Olsen, computer technology may be a necessary tool to overcome some of the obstacles to integrating testing and instruction. In particular, the computer can help with the labor-intensive aspects of collecting enough information on a continuing basis to assist with day-to-day instructional decisions. But computers do not solve the problem of knowing what or how to measure, any more than printing technology determines paper-and-pencil tests. As the chapter by Nitko illustrates, the design of tests useful for the instructional decisions made in the classroom requires an integration of testing and instruction. It also requires a clear conception of the curriculum, the goals, and the process of instruction. And it requires a theory of instruction and learning and a much better understanding of the cognitive processes of learners.

The conceptual developments most relevant to these needs are those that have come from the field of cognitive psychology in the past few years. Cognitive psychology has made great strides in the past decade and promises to provide the basis of a theory of learning and achievement that can guide the future development of tests. The chapter by Snow and Lohman brings together much of that work and points to many of its implications for the possible improvement of educational measurement. As they acknowledge, however, the path to the creation of practical testing systems based on laboratory findings is largely unmarked and is likely to have many dead ends.

Social and Legal Contexts

The increased demand for testing has taken place during a period in which testing has also been the subject of considerable controversy. Although testing has frequently been a subject of public controversy (Cronbach, 1975; Haney, 1981), some of the current debates about it have sustained momentum for an unusually long time. More important, the actors in the debates are much more likely to be judges, legislators, and administrative agencies than was true in previous years.

Bias in Test Use and Interpretation

In his introduction to the second edition of this book, Thorndike (1971) wrote about the increased questioning of the fairness of using tests for certain minority groups. He noted that there was a lack of clarity in the definitions of fairness and a shortage of evidence relevant to the question. Because of the substantial amount of work on the problem that was underway at that time, however, Thorndike was optimistic that "clarification of concepts and expansion of the data base from which conclusions may be drawn can be expected in the near future" (p. 12).

Considerable research has indeed been accumulated since that time, and a great deal has been written about item bias, bias in test use, and concepts of fairness. As is clearly demonstrated in the chapter by Cole and Moss, however, clarity in definitions and evidence regarding the comparability of prediction systems cannot be expected to resolve the underlying value conflicts. Evidence, for example, that the regression of first-year grades in college on high school grades and test scores is essentially the same when based on data for black students as when based on data for white students is relevant to the decision of whether or not the test information should be used in the admissions process for black students. But a variety of other types of information regarding the likely consequences of using the prediction information in various ways is also needed. As Messick argues (this volume), test use needs to have both an evidential and a consequential basis.

Analyses of the consequences of alternative test uses pose serious challenges for the measurement profession. Although analysis of the likelihood of some consequences is well within reach, that of others can be done only with considerable effort and expense, if at all. For example, analysis of the degree of adverse impact that could be expected for alternative uses of a test can be conducted with relative ease, though even here there might be different perspectives on the appropriate base for the calculations. It is far more difficult, however, to evaluate consequences of a longer term and more global nature.

Consider, for example, an evaluation of the consequences of the decision of the National Collegiate Athletic Association (NCAA) to require that the combination of grade point average in core subjects and scores on the ACT or the SAT exceed a specified minimum in order for the athlete to be eligible to compete during his or her freshman year of college. Two major studies, one supported by the NCAA (Bartell, Keesling, LeBlanc, & Tombaugh, 1985) and one by the American Association of Collegiate Registrars and Admissions Officers and the American Council on Education (Braun, et al., 1984), were conducted to investigate a variety of issues related to the policy as it was initially proposed, as well as to several alternative policies. Issues of likely adverse impact, differential prediction of grades, academic progress, and graduation were addressed in the analyses. But many other issues considered relevant by supporters and opponents of the policy were not, and possibly could not have been, addressed. For example, the effects of the policy on the decisions of minority student athletes to take different courses in high school, on the guidance and support services (including test preparation courses) provided by high schools, on the likelihood that students who are not eligible their freshman year will still attend college, or on the actions of colleges to support athletes who are not eligible their freshman year, to say nothing of the long-term effects on the education and employment of minorities, were not investigated.

The NCAA example is not intended to suggest that all these consequences should have been investigated before any action was taken, or even to suggest that they are all part of a complete analysis of bias in test use and interpretation. Rather, it is intended to show that judgments about what is a desirable and fair use of a test depend on a host of considerations and on the values that are attached to various effects. The measurement specialist could appropriately define the absence of predictive bias in accord with the *Standards for Educational and Psychological Testing* (American Psychological Association [APA], 1985) by finding that "the predictive relationship of two groups being compared can be adequately described by a common algorithm (e.g., regression line)" (p. 12). However, it should be recognized that this definition neither corresponds to the meaning of the critic who charges test bias nor resolves the issue of how the scores of minority test takers should be used or interpreted.

Thorndike was correct in identifying the concern about the fair use of tests for minorities as a major issue of the 1970s. It has also been a major concern of the 1980s and will, in all likelihood, continue to be one in the years to come. If anything, the concerns are apt to expand, with issues related to the testing of persons from non-English-speaking backgrounds and of persons with handicapping conditions getting greater attention in the years to come.

Professional Standards

Although the involvement of the American Psychological Association in issues of standards for the publication and use of tests can be traced back at least to 1895 (Novick, 1981), the history of formally published test standards is much shorter. The original predecessors of the current *Standards,* the *Technical Recommendations for Psychological Tests and Diagnostic Decisions* (APA, 1954) and the *Technical Recommendations for Achievement Tests* (National Education Association, 1955), did not appear until the mid 1950s. The first standards to be developed by a joint committee of the American Educational Research Association, the American Psychological Association, and the National Council on Measurement in Education, the *Standards for Educational and Psychological Tests and Manuals,* published by the American Psychological Association, appeared in 1966. Since that time the *Standards* have twice been revised by joint committees of the three sponsoring associations (APA, 1974, 1985).

The standards reflect the evolution and refinement of the concepts that are fundamental to sound measurement practice (see, for example, Messick's discussion of the treatment of validity, this volume). Although there are clearly changes in the technical expectations the *Standards* have for test publishers, it is in the area of test use that the differences are most notable. The 1954 *Technical Recommendations* and the 1966 *Standards* were clearly targeted toward the test publisher. The stated goal of both those documents was that test manuals "should carry information sufficient to enable any qualified user to make sound judgments regarding the usefulness and interpretation of the test" (APA, 1966, p. 2). The critical importance of the user in determining the appropriateness of test use was recognized in the 1966 *Standards,* where it was noted that "primary responsibility for improvement of testing rests on the shoulders of test users" (APA, 1966, p. 6). However, it was not until the 1974 revision that the first standards for test users were introduced, and it was not until the most recent revision that the user became a major focus of the *Standards.* This expanded emphasis on the user is evident in the statement that "the ultimate responsibility for appropriate test use lies with the user" (APA, 1985, p. 3).

The changing social and legal context in which the *Standards* were developed is reflected in the differences among the several versions. The Equal Employment Opportunity Commission (EEOC) *Guidelines on Employment Selection Procedures* (EEOC, 1970) and related litigation concerning discriminatory test use had a substantial influence on the 1974 *Standards.* Consider, for example, Standard G4: "Test users should seek to avoid bias in selection, administration, and interpretation; they should try to avoid even the appearance of discriminatory practice" (APA, p. 60).

The 1985 *Standards* were equally dependent on the context in which they were developed. Chapter 13, "Testing Linguistic Minorities" and chapter 14, "Testing People Who Have Handicapping Conditions," for example, reflected the heightened awareness of these important, but difficult, uses of tests. Similarly, chapter 16, "Protecting the Rights of Test Takers," was stimulated by contemporary testing issues such as the rights of a test taker in cases of alleged cheating, informed consent, and the protection of privacy.

The *Standards* have been influential documents in a number of ways. The seriousness with which test publishers take the *Standards* was evident from the time and effort of the professional staff at several test development and publishing companies devoted to reviewing and commenting on each of the drafts of the 1985 *Standards.* The use of the 1974 *Standards* in court cases was very salient for personnel psychologists who had firsthand experience with this use. Nonetheless, some see the *Standards* as relatively ineffective in preventing test misuse and argue for the need to have the three professional associations take a more active role in monitoring compliance and in creating enforcement mechanisms and associated sanctions. Others question the appropriateness and feasibility of such activities by the associations. The resolution of these differences will be quite a challenge for the profession.

Litigation and Educational Testing

The influence of judicial decisions on testing has increased considerably since 1971. The early involvement of the courts in testing most frequently dealt with charges of discrimination in employment brought under provisions of Title VII of the Civil Rights Act of 1964. Discrimination has also been a central issue in the cases involving the use of tests in education.

The principle that evidence of disproportionate impact can be used to make a prima facie case of discrimination under Title VII of the Civil Rights Act of 1964 was established in 1971 by the Supreme Court in *Griggs v. Duke Power Company.* In *Griggs,* the Court also established the principle that tests "must measure the person for the job and not the person in the abstract" (p. 436). Thus, to refute the presumption of discrimination based on evidence of disproportionate impact, the employer must demonstrate that the test measures job-related qualifications. The Court did not, however, provide a clear indication of the evidence required to satisfy the job-relatedness standard. Though it is now obvious from subsequent court cases that "some sort of formal validation is necessary" (Wigdor & Garner, 1982, p. 105), there is still no clear way of determining whether the evidence of validity accumulated by an employer will be judged to be sufficient.

Although educational testing has not been affected by court decisions to the degree that employment testing has, the courts have played, and are continuing to play, an important role in shaping some educational-testing practices. As is true in the employment context, discrimination has been a central issue in most of the educational-testing cases. As noted by Wigdor and Garner (1982, p. 107), "most of the constitutional and statutory protections afforded to test takers in either setting relate to members of groups considered vulnerable to discriminatory practices based on color, race, ethnic origin, gender, or handicapping condition."

The use of individually administered intelligence tests in decisions to place children in special education came under sharp attack in the 1970s. In 1979, 7 years after plaintiffs brought suit, the use of standardized tests by the California State Department of Education for the identification and placement of black children in self-contained classes for the educable mentally retarded (EMR) was prohibited by the *Larry P. v. Riles* decision. In keeping with the *Griggs* decision, the disproportionate placement of black children in EMR classes established the prima facie case of discrimination. Judge Peckham concluded that the IQ tests in question were biased and found the evidence of validity presented by the defendants to be unacceptable.

"*Larry P.* defines an unbiased test as one that yields 'the same pattern of scores when administered to different groups of people' (p. 955)" (Bersoff, 1981, p. 1049). This definition obviously differs sharply from psychometric notions of bias. On the other hand, Judge Peckham's analysis of validity evidence was more sophisticated. He rejected the criterion-related evidence of validity, which was based on correlations of IQ scores with achievement test scores and school grades, using the following rationale:

> If tests can predict that a person is going to be a poor employee, the employer can legitimately deny that person a job, but if tests suggest that a young child is probably going to be a poor student, the school cannot on that basis alone deny the child the opportunity to improve and develop the academic skills necessary to success in our society (*Larry P. v. Riles,* p. 969).

This reasoning is consistent with that expressed by the National Academy of Sciences' Panel on Selection and Placement of Students in Programs for the Mentally Retarded, though the Panel was more explicit in defining the type of validity evidence that is needed.

> In the context of educational decision making it is not enough to know that IQ tests predict future classroom performance, nor would it be enough even to know that they measure general ability.

It is necessary to ask whether IQ tests provide information that leads to more effective instruction than would otherwise be possible. Specifically, is it the case that children whose IQs fall in the EMR range require or profit from special forms of instruction or special classroom settings? In the language of contemporary education research, is there an "aptitude–treatment interaction" . . . such that different instructional methods are effective for children with low IQs? (Heller, Holtzman, & Messick, 1982, p. 53).

The aptitude–treatment interaction requirement is clearly a much more demanding standard than one that would simply require the test to be correlated with a criterion measure. It is also more in line with the purposes of education. Whether, if satisfied, it would meet the requirements of a court, however, is not so clear.

Just 9 months after the *Larry P.* decision a similar case was decided in Illinois in which some of the same IQ tests, the Stanford Binet, the WISC, and the WISC-R, were ruled "not to discriminate against black children" (*PASE v. Hannon*, 1980, p. 883). The decision in *PASE* was based primarily on Judge Grady's personal inspection of the test items. Because he considered only a small percentage of the items to be potentially biased and the test was only one component of the decision process, he did not believe that the few questionable items were cause to conclude that the use of the tests discriminated against black children. Given what is known about the lack of consistency among judges in the identification of "biased" items and the poor agreement between such judgments and statistical indexes of item bias, the Grady judgment of no bias should be of little comfort to those who support the use of these tests and believe them to be unbiased. Certainly, the conclusion is no more in keeping with psychometric concepts of bias than is the conclusion of Judge Peckham, which seems to equate bias with differences in group performance. In any event, the implications of these decisions for future uses of tests for special education placement decisions in other jurisdictions remains problematic.

There are at least three other educational testing contexts where court actions deserve some comment. These are the use of minimum competency tests for the award of high school diplomas, the use of tests for teacher certification, and the use of tests for admission to professional school. In the first two instances, discrimination against minority test takers was again a central issue, whereas in the third instance, the most publicized case and the only one to be decided by the Supreme Court, the issue was that of reverse discrimination against a white applicant who was denied admission to medical school despite having higher test scores and previous grades than some black applicants who were admitted.

Although the Supreme Court decision in *Bakke v. the Regents of the University of California* did not lead to a clear resolution of the broader question of the use of race-conscious procedures to select minority candidates who would not be selected using strictly numerical criteria, it did find that it was legal to use race as one factor in admissions. The Court made it clear that selective institutions are not required to select only those applicants who have the highest academic qualifications as indicated by previous grades and test results. Rather, it was judged appropriate for institutions to seek diversity, along a number of dimensions, including race. Thus, although not providing any clear guidelines on affirmative action in admissions, the Court provided implicit support for the special admissions practices common to many colleges and graduate schools.

The most significant case to date involving minimum competency testing is *Debra P. v. Turlington* (1983). Florida's plan to require students to pass a test in order to receive a high school diploma, starting with the class of 1979, was delayed by a class action suit on behalf of all students who failed or would fail the test. Charges that the test was biased were dismissed by the trial court, and that decision was affirmed by the circuit court. However, the circuit court delayed implementation of the test requirement, partially on the grounds that the "State may not deprive its high school seniors of the economic and educational benefits of a high school diploma until it has demonstrated that the SSAT II is a fair test of that which is taught in its classrooms." Although the state of Florida was eventually successful in satisfying the court that the test was a fair measure of that which is taught, it did so only after conducting a large-scale survey of teachers as to whether the material tested had been taught.

The degree to which students are given an opportunity to learn the material on a test is apt to be a concern in future uses of tests for student certification. This requirement is suggested, not only by the court actions in the *Debra P.* case, but also by the 1985 *Standards for Educational and Psychological Testing*.

> When a test is used to make decisions about student promotion or graduation, there should be evidence that the test covers only the specific or generalized knowledge, skills, and abilities that students have had an opportunity to learn (APA, 1985, p. 53, Standard 8.7).

With the dramatic growth in the use of tests for initial certification of teachers and, in a few cases, for recertification, it is likely that the number of legal challenges will increase. The most notable case to date, however, involved the use of the National Teacher Examinations (NTE) by South Carolina. The Supreme Court provided a summary affirmation of the district court's ruling in favor of South Carolina (*U. S. v. South Carolina,* 1977). The court accepted the judgments by teacher educators that the test's content was included in the content of the state's teacher-training programs as sufficient evidence that the test was valid and therefore that the disproportionate failure rate of minority candidates did not imply unfair discrimination.

Decisons regarding other licensure and certification tests are also potentially relevant to teacher certification testing. So, too, might be the much publicized out-of-court settlement between the Golden Rule Insurance Company and the combined Illinois Department of Insurance and Educational Testing Service (ETS). Although out-of-court settlements obviously do not have the precedent value of court decisions, the participation of the testing giant ETS in the settlement contributed to the attention that the settlement has received and to the fact that it has been used as a model for legislation proposed in California, New York, and Texas and for another out-of-court settlement involving teacher certification testing (Faggen, 1987).

The feature of the Golden Rule settlement that is most controversial and that could have the greatest impact on educational measurement is the use of within-group item difficulties to classify items and the role of that item classification in the assembly of test forms. Pros and cons of the Golden Rule procedure are the subject of considerable debate (see, for example, Bond, 1987; Faggen, 1987; Jaeger, 1987; Linn & Drasgow, 1987; Rooney, 1987; Weiss, 1987), and the debate is likely to continue for some time. The appropriateness of the Golden Rule strategy for eliminating bias and the effects of the procedure on the validity and reliability of tests are issues of vital importance to the field of educational measurement.

Legislation and Educational Measurement

Historically, legislation at both the state and national levels has often contributed to the expansion of educational testing. The previous discussion of the expansion of testing as the result of state legislation intended to make education more accountable is a case in point. As Wigdor and Garner (1982) noted, federal educational legislation and policy have also frequently encouraged testing, whether indirectly, as in the form of evaluation requirements for federal programs, or directly, as in the support provided for NAEP.

Of course, legislation has been the basis of many of the court actions described. Title VI of the Civil Rights Act of 1964, Section 504 of the Rehabilitation Act of 1973, and the Education of All Handicapped Children Act of 1975 (PL 94–142) have all been important in providing a basis for litigation involving educational testing. But none of these acts was designed to restrict testing. On the contrary, the last two acts place considerable emphasis on the use of a variety of assessment techniques, including tests. They require detailed assessment prior to a placement decision and periodic reassessment.

The PL 94–142 regulation set high expectations for the value of measurement and for evidence supporting the use of the measures. It requires that tests "be validated for their intended use, given in the child's native language, and administered by trained personnel" (Heller, et al., 1982, p. 37). Reliance on a single source of information as the only basis for a placement decision is prohibited. These requirements are in keeping with good measurement practice and are consistent with those set out in the 1985 Standards (APA, 1985).

With regard to state legislation, considerable attention was focused on the LaValle Bill during the late 1970s. The LaValle Bill, which its proponents referred to as "truth-in-testing" legislation, was finally passed into law by the New York legislature in 1979. It requires the disclosure of college admissions tests administered to students in New York. The bill was fought by many test publishers and other specialists in educational measurement who expected that it would damage the technical quality of the tests and drastically increase costs. Although test disclosure certainly changed the ways in which certain steps such as test equating can be accomplished and greatly increased the number of new test items required each year, the law did not have as great an effect on admissions testing as many measurement experts anticipated. On the other hand, there is no reason to believe that the law has benefited economically disadvantaged or minority test takers, as many of its proponents anticipated.

Since the LaValle bill was passed, legislation to regulate some aspects of educational testing has been proposed at the federal level and in several states from time to time. Activity at the state level, however, increased substantially in 1986 and 1987. Much of the recent activity has incorporated features of the legislative agenda put forward by the National Center for Fair and Open Testing that would extend test-disclosure provisions, require collection and reporting of test and item-analysis results broken down by gender and racial–ethnic group, and, in some cases, implement procedures modeled after the Golden Rule settlement. Needless to say, the shape of educational testing could be substantially affected by the outcome of this ongoing legislative activity.

Conclusion

This brief recounting of some of the changes that have taken place during the 1970s and 1980s that have affected current practice and are likely to affect the shape of measurement in the 1990s and beyond was obviously selective in its coverage. Predictions of the future are always risky. The identification of challenges, however, is much easier.

In my view, the biggest and most important single challenge for educational measurement today is no different from what it was at the time the first edition of this book appeared; that is, to make measurement do a better job of facilitating learning for all individuals. However, to date, measurement has done a much better job of predicting who will achieve and of describing that achievement than of helping teachers adapt instruction to enhance the learning of individual students. The combined efforts of cognitive psychologists, measurement specialists, and educators will need to be devoted to this task if educational measurement is going to become, not "a process quite apart from instruction, but an integral part of it" (Tyler, 1951, p. 47).

REFERENCES

Alexander, L., & James, H. T. (1987). *The nation's report card: Improving the assessment of student achievement.* Washington, DC: National Academy of Education.

American Psychological Association. (1954). *Technical recommendations for psychological tests and diagnostic techniques.* Washington, DC: author.

American Psychological Association, American Educational Research Association, & National Council on Measurement in Education. (1966). *Standards for educational and psychological tests and manuals.* Washington, DC: American Psychological Association.

American Psychological Association, American Educational Research Association, & National Council on Measurement in Education. (1974). *Standards for educational and psychological tests.* Washington, DC: American Psychological Association.

American Psychological Association, American Educational Research Association, & National Council on Measurement in Education. (1985). *Standards for educational and psychological testing.* Washington, DC: American Psychological Association.

Angoff, W. H. (1971). Scales, norms, and equivalent scores. In R. L. Thorndike (Ed.), *Educational measurement (2nd ed.)* Washington, DC: American Council on Education.

Bakke v. the Regents of the University of California, 432 *U.S.* 265, 1978.

Bartell, T., Keesling, J. W., LeBlanc, L. A., & Tombaugh, R. (1985). *Study of freshman eligibility standards* (Tech. Rep.). Reston, VA: Advanced Technology.

Bejar, I. I. (1984). Educational diagnostic testing. *Journal of Educational Measurement, 21,* 175–189.

Bersoff, D. N. (1981). Testing and the law. *American Psychologist, 36,* 1047–1056.

Birnbaum, A. (1968). Some latent trait models and their use in inferring an examinee's ability. In F. M. Lord & M. R. Novick (Eds.), *Statistical theories of mental test scores.* Reading, MA: Addison-Wesley.

Bock, R. D., & Mislevy, R. J. (1987). *Comprehensive educational assessment for the states: The duplex design.* Technical Report No. 262. Los Angeles, CA: UCLA Center for Research on Evaluation, Standards and Student Testing.

Bond, L. (1987). The Golden Rule settlement: A minority perspective. *Educational Measurement: Issues and Practice, 6*(2), 18–20.

Braun, H., Broudy, I., Flaugher, J., Robertson, N., Maxey, J., Kane, M., & Sawyer, R. (1984). *Athletics and academics in the freshman year: A study of the academic effects of freshman participation in varsity athletics.* Washington, DC: American Association of Collegiate Registrars and Admissions Officers and American Council on Education.

Brogden, H. E. (1946). Variation in test validity with variation in the distribution of item difficulties, number of items, and degree of intercorrelation. *Psychometrika, 11,* 197–214.

Cook, W. W. (1951). The functions of measurement in the facilitation of learning. In E. F. Lindquist (Ed.), *Educational measurement.* Washington, DC: American Council on Education.

Cronbach, L. J. (1975). Five decades of public controversy over mental testing. *American Psychologist, 30,* 1–14.

Debra P. v. Turlington, 644 F. 2d 397, 5th Cir. 1981: 564 F. Supp. 177 (M. D. Fla. 1983).

Faggen, J. (1987). Golden Rule revisited: Introduction. *Educational Measurement: Issues and Practice, 6*(2), 5–8.

Glaser, R. (1963). Instructional technology and the measurement of learning outcomes. *American Psychologist, 18,* 519–521.

Glaser, R. (1981). The future of testing: A research agenda for cognitive psychology and psychometrics. *American Psychologist, 36,* 923–936.

Glaser, R. (1986). The integration of testing and instruction. *The redesign of testing for the 21st century: Proceedings of the 1985 ETS Invitational Conference.* Princeton, NJ: Educational Testing Service.

Goldstein, H. (1980). Dimensionality, bias, independence, and measurement scale problems in latent trait test score models. *British Journal of Mathematical and Statistical Psychology, 33,* 234–246.

Griggs v. Duke Power Company, 401 *U.S.* 424 (1971).

Haney, W. (1981). Validity, vaudeville and values: A short history of social concerns over standardized testing. *American Psychologist, 36,* 1021–1034.

Heller, K. A., Holtzman, W. H., & Messick, S. (Eds.). (1982). *Placing children in special education: A strategy for equity.* Washington, DC: National Academy Press.

Henrysson, S. (1971). Gathering, analyzing, and using data on test items. In R. L. Thorndike (Ed.), *Educational measurement (2nd ed.).* Washington, DC: American Council on Education.

Hoover, H. D. (1984). The most appropriate scores for measuring educational development in elementary schools: GE's. *Educational Measurement: Issues and Practice, 3,* 10–14.

Jaeger, R. M. (1987). NCME opposition to proposed Golden Rule legislation. *Educational Measurement: Issues and Practice, 6*(2), 21–22.

Larry P. v. Riles, 495 F. Supp. 926 (N. D. Calif. 1979).

Lawley, D. N. (1943). On problems connected with item selection and test construction. *Proceedings of the Royal Society of Edinburgh, 61,* 273–287.

Lindquist, E. F. (Ed.). (1951). *Educational measurement.* Washington, DC: American Council on Education.

Linn, R. L., & Drasgow, F. (1987). Implications of the Golden Rule settlement for test construction. *Educational Measurement: Issues and Practice, 6*(2), 13–17.

Lord, F. M. (1952). A theory of test scores (*Psychometric Monograph No. 7*).

Lord, F. M., & Novick, M. R. (1968). *Theories of mental test scores.* Reading, MA: Addison-Wesley.

Mislevy, R. J. (1983). Item response models for grouped data. *Journal of Educational Statistics, 8,* 271–288.

McGuire, C. H., & Babbott, D. (1967). Simulation technique in the measurement of problem-solving skills. *Journal of Educational Measurement, 4,* 1–10.

National Education Association. (1955). *Technical recommendations for achievement tests.* Washington, DC: author.

Novick, M. R. (1981). Federal guidelines and professional standards. *American Psychologist, 36,* 1035–1046.

Pase v. Hannon, 506 F. Supp. 831 (N. D. Ill. 1980).

Rasch, G. (1960). *Probabilistic models for some intelligence and attainment tests.* Copenhagen, Denmark: Nielson & Lydiche.

Rooney, J. P. (1987). Golden rule on "Golden Rule." *Educational Measurement: Issues and Practice, 6*(2), 9–12.

Thorndike, R. L. (Ed.). (1971). *Educational measurement (2nd ed.)* Washington, DC: American Council on Education.

Traub, R. E. (1983). A priori considerations in choosing an item response model. In R. K. Hambleton (Ed.), *Applications of item response theory* (pp. 57–70). Vancouver, British Columbia: Educational Research Institute of British Columbia.

Tucker, L. R. (1946). Maximum validity of a test with equivalent items. *Psychometrika, 11,* 1–13.

Tyler, R. W. (1951). The functions of measurement in improving instruction. In E. F. Lindquist (Ed.), *Educational measurement.* Washington, DC: American Council on Education.

U.S. v. South Carolina, 445 F. Supp. 1094 (D. S.C. 1977).

Vold, D. J. (1985). The roots of teacher testing in America. *Educational Measurement: Issues and Practice, 4*(3), 5, 8.

Ward, W. C. (1984). Using microcomputers to administer tests. *Educational Measurement: Issues and Practice, 3*(2), 16–20.

Weiss, J. (1987). The Golden Rule bias reduction principle: A practical reform. *Educational Measurement: Issues and Practice, 6*(2), 23–25.

Wigdor, A. K., & Garner, W. R. (Eds.). (1982). *Ability testing: Uses, consequences, and controversies: Part I. Report of the committee.* Washington, DC: National Academy Press.

Wright, B. D. (1968). Sample-free test calibration and person measurement. In *Proceedings of the 1967 ETS Invitational Conference on Testing Problems* (pp. 85–101). Princeton, NJ: Educational Testing Service.

Yen, W. M. (1980). The extent, causes and importance of context effects on item parameters for two latent trait models. *Journal of Educational Measurement, 17,* 297–311.

Yen, W. M., Green, D. R., & Burket, G. R. (1987). Valid normative information from customized achievement tests. *Educational Measurement: Issues and Practice, 6*(1), 7–13.

1

Theory and General Principles

2

Validity

Samuel Messick

Educational Testing Service

Validity is an integrated evaluative judgment of the degree to which empirical evidence and theoretical rationales support the *adequacy* and *appropriateness* of *inferences* and *actions* based on test scores or other modes of assessment. As will be delineated shortly, the term *test score* is used generically here in its broadest sense to mean any observed consistency, not just on tests as ordinarily conceived but on any means of observing or documenting consistent behaviors or attributes. Broadly speaking, then, validity is an inductive summary of both the existing evidence for and the potential consequences of score interpretation and use. Hence, what is to be validated is not the test or observation device as such but the inferences derived from test scores or other indicators—inferences about score meaning or interpretation and about the implications for action that the interpretation entails.

It is important to note that validity is a matter of degree, not all or none. Furthermore, over time, the existing validity evidence becomes enhanced (or contravened) by new findings, and projections of potential social consequences of testing become transformed by evidence of actual consequences and by changing social conditions. Inevitably, then, validity is an evolving property and validation is a continuing process. Because evidence is always incomplete, validation is essentially a matter of making the most reasonable case to guide both current use of the test and current research to advance understanding of what the test scores mean.

To validate an interpretive inference is to ascertain the degree to which multiple lines of evidence are consonant with the inference, while establishing that alternative inferences are less well supported. To validate an action inference requires validation not only of score meaning but also of value implications and action outcomes, especially appraisals of the relevance and utility of the test scores for particular applied purposes and of the social consequences of using the scores for applied decision making. Thus the key issues of test validity are the interpretability, relevance, and utility of scores, the import or value implications of scores as a basis for action, and the functional worth of scores in terms of social consequences of their use.

Although there are different sources and mixes of evidence for supporting score-based inferences, validity is a unitary concept. Validity always refers to the degree to which empirical evidence and theoretical rationales support the adequacy and appropriateness of interpretations and actions based on test scores. Furthermore, although there are many ways of accumulating evidence to support a particular inference, these ways are essentially the methods of science. Inferences are hypothe-

NOTE: Acknowledgments are gratefully extended to William Angoff, Walter Emmerich, Norman Frederiksen, Harold Gulliksen, Stanford von Mayrhauser, and Michael Zieky for reviewing the manuscript; to Lee Cronbach and Robert Guion for their thorough, sometimes humbling and often mind-stretching comments on the big issues as well as important details; and, to Warren Willingham for his suggested modifications, emendations, and illustrations. Special thanks go to Ann Jungeblut for her contributions to the entire effort, from refining the ideas and honing the phrasing to shepherding the manuscript through multiple drafts.

I also welcome this opportunity to acknowledge a long-standing intellectual debt to Lee Cronbach, whose seminal work on test validity has had a profound influence on my thinking about this topic, as has the work of Donald Campbell and Jane Loevinger. This chapter is dedicated:

In memory of Melvin R. Novick, who devoted what proved to be the last years of his life to the development and acceptance of scientifically based standards in testing; and,

In honor of Harold Gulliksen, whose prescient early paper on "Intrinsic Validity" made it clear that if you do not know what predictor and criterion scores mean, you do not know much of anything in applied measurement.

ses, and the validation of inferences is hypothesis testing. However, it is not hypothesis testing in isolation but, rather, theory testing more broadly because the source, meaning, and import of score-based hypotheses derive from the interpretive theories of score meaning in which these hypotheses are rooted. Hence, test validation embraces all of the experimental, statistical, and philosophical means by which hypotheses and scientific theories are evaluated.

This chapter amplifies these two basic points, namely, that validity is a unified though faceted concept and that validation is scientific inquiry. To be sure, validation occurs more and more frequently in a political context, which means not only that scientific judgments must be attuned to political considerations but also that political judgments may become more scientifically grounded. Before proceeding, however, we must first address some preliminary points about the nature of test responses and scores, as well as about the nature of evidence in general and validity evidence in particular.

The central issue is appraisal of the meaning and consequences of measurement. For example, what kind of evidence should guide the interpretation of scores on arithmetic word problems when simply rewording the problems changes what the test measures (De Corte, Verschaffel, & De Win, 1984)? Or, on multiple-choice arithmetic items, when moving from numerical distractors all of which are close to the correct answer to more widely spaced alternatives changes what the test measures (Messick & Kogan, 1965)? Or, on a syllogism item-type when the introduction of attitudinal or affective content evokes other response processes besides logical reasoning (Abelson, 1963; W. J. McGuire, 1960)? How do we know what an achievement test score means if different processes are engaged by alternative styles or strategies of performance or as a function of varying levels of experience or expertise (French, 1965; Chi, Glaser, & Farr, 1987)? As a final instance, should tests predictive of dire academic failure be used to place children in special education programs without explicitly assessing the intended and unintended consequences of such use (Heller, Holtzman, & Messick, 1982)?

Preliminary Points

The major concern of validity, as of science more generally, is not to explain any single isolated event, behavior, or item response, because these almost certainly reflect a confounding of multiple determinants. Rather, the intent is to account for *consistency* in behaviors or item responses, which frequently reflects distinguishable determinants. In contrast with treating the item responses or behaviors in question separately as a conglomeration of specifics, these behavioral and response consistencies are typically summarized in the form of total scores or subscores. We thus move from the level of discrete behaviors or isolated observations to the level of measurement. This is not to say that scores for individual items or discrete behaviors are not often of interest but, rather, that their meaning and dependability are fragile compared with response consistencies across items or replications.

The key point is that in educational and psychological measurement inferences are drawn from *scores,* a term used here in the most general sense of any coding or summarization of observed consistencies on a test, questionnaire, observation procedure, or other assessment device. This general usage subsumes qualitative as well as quantitative summaries and applies, for example, to protocols, clinical interpretations, and computerized verbal score reports. For example, the *Guidelines for Computer-Based Tests and Interpretations* (American Psychological Association [APA], 1986) makes reference to the nature of the evidence needed to support different types of computerized interpretations and to undergird diagnostic classifications and outcome predictions, indicating that the validation of computer-based tests and protocols does not differ in kind from the validation of tests generally (see also Green, 1987; Green, Bock, Humphreys, Linn, & Reckase, 1984).

Nor are scores in this broad sense limited to behavioral consistencies or attributes of persons. They refer as well to judgmental consistencies and attributes of groups, situations or environments, and objects, as in the case of solidarity, evaluative stress, and quality of artistic products. By and large, the principles of validity and validation discussed in this chapter may, and ordinarily should, apply to all of these instances. Henceforth, when the terms *score* and *test* are used, they are to be taken in this generalized sense.

Scores in Context

The emphasis is on scores and measurements as opposed to tests or instruments because the properties that signify adequate assessment are properties of scores, not tests. Tests do not have reliabilities and validities, only test responses do. This is an important point because test responses are a function not only of the items, tasks, or stimulus conditions but of the *persons* responding and the *context* of measurement. This latter context includes factors in the environmental background as well as the assessment setting.

As a consequence, the social psychology of the assessment setting requires careful attention, as do relevant aspects of the examinee's environmental background and experiential history. For example, is the presented task meaningful to the respondent in terms of prior life experience, or does it assume a special or different meaning in the assessment context? As a specific instance, a child might exhibit apparent lack of understanding of the preposition *on* when asked in an assessment task to "put the circle *on* the square," whereas in the classroom setting the same child readily complies with the request to "put the truck on the shelf" (Sigel, 1974).

We are thus confronted with the fundamental question of whether the meaning of a measure is context-specific or whether it generalizes across contexts. On the one hand, the impact of contextualization can be compelling because the very nature of a task might be altered by the operation of constraining or facilitating factors in the specific situation. On the other hand, we note that the use of multiple task formats along with the standardization of testing conditions contributes to convergent interpretations and comparability of scores across respondents and settings. Rather than opt for one position or the other, in this chapter we urge that the role of context in test interpretation and test use be repeatedly investigated or monitored as a recurrent issue. Thus, the extent to which a measure displays the same properties and patterns of relationships in different population groups and under different ecological conditions becomes a pervasive and perennial empirical question.

The possibility of context effects makes it clear that what is to be validated is an *"interpretation of data arising from a specified procedure"* (Cronbach, 1971, p. 447). The validated interpretation gives meaning to the measure in the particular instance, and evidence on the generality of the interpretation over time and across groups and settings shows how stable or circumscribed that meaning is likely to be. But it is important to recognize that the intrusion of context raises issues more of generalizability than of interpretive validity. It gives testimony more to the ubiquity of interactions than to the fragility of score meaning. Consider Cronbach's automotive example:

> The variables engineers use to describe automobile performance are functionally related to the octane rating of the fuel. What the functions will be depend upon the engine design, the cleanness of the engine, and the driving speed. These complications are matters for the engineer to understand, but the variation of the parameters does not per se call the validity of octane measurement into question. (in press, p. 11)

Thus, one might seek and obtain generality of score meaning across different contexts, even though the attendant implications for action may be context-dependent by virtue of interactions operative in the particular group or setting. If the meaning of scores does change with the group or setting, the scores might indeed lack validity for *uniform* use across the varied circumstances but not necessarily lack validity for differential use or even validity of meaning in specific contexts. These issues of generalizability will be addressed in more detail later, once some conceptual machinery has been developed to deal with the complexities.

Scores as Signs and Samples

Test behaviors are often viewed as samples of domain behaviors (or as essentially similar to domain behaviors) for which predictions are to be made or inferences drawn. Test behaviors are also viewed as signs of other behaviors that they do not ordinarily resemble and as indicants of underlying processes or traits (Goodenough, 1949; Loevinger, 1957). Tests often do double duty, however, as in the example of an essay examination on causes of the Civil War, which provides samples of writing and thinking as well as signs of analytical and critical skills. In educational measurement, the latter are usually acknowledged as *constructs* or inferences about underlying processes or structures, whereas the former often are not. This leads, as we shall see, to considerable contention over what makes for a valid score. In psychological measurement, behaviorists and social behaviorists usually interpret scores as samples of response classes; whereas for trait theorists (and cognitive theorists as well), scores are largely signs of underlying processes or structures (Wiggins, 1973).

A *response class* is a set of behaviors all of which change in the same or related ways as a function of stimulus contingencies, that is, a class of behaviors that reflect essentially the same

changes when the person's relation to the environment is altered. A *trait* is a relatively stable characteristic of a person—an attribute, enduring process, or disposition—which is consistently manifested to some degree when relevant, despite considerable variation in the range of settings and circumstances. A response class is a type of behavioral consistency. A trait is an enduring personal characteristic hypothesized to underlie a type of stable behavioral consistency. Another term widely used in contradistinction to trait is *state*. In contrast with connotations of relative stability and enduringness associated with traits, states are conceptualized as temporary conditions of mentality or mood, transitory levels of arousal or drive, and currently evoked activity or process (Messick, 1983).

Many psychologists interpret behavioral consistencies—whether on tests or in nontest situations—to be manifestations of traits, which serve to organize the behavior or otherwise produce response consistencies (e.g., Allport, 1937, 1961; Cattell, 1957). Others contend that behaviors, including test behaviors, are consistently interrelated because they are elicited and maintained by the same or related environmental conditions, especially reinforcement conditions (cf. Anastasi, 1948; Skinner, 1971; Tryon, 1979). In the latter view, related behaviors form a response class because they enter the same functional relationships with antecedent, concurrent, or consequent stimulus conditions; it is these environmental contingencies, not traits, that control behavioral consistencies. Many psychologists, of course, adopt intermediate views, attributing some behavioral consistencies to traits, some to situational factors, and some to interactions between them, in various and arguable proportions (K. S. Bowers, 1973; Ekehammar, 1974; Zuroff, 1986).

Whether test scores are interpretable as signs of trait dispositions or internal states, as samples of domains or response classes, or as some combination, are hypotheses to be validated. A major problem is that many investigators take one interpretation or the other for granted. Worse still, this presumption often determines the type of evidence deemed sufficient for validity. A troublesome complication is that the term *trait* is widely used as shorthand for behavioral consistency in general, from whatever source. One type of validity evidence is even called *"trait* validity." This is especially problematic because it implies a dispositional source of the observed consistency. Hence, the important validity principle embodied by this term might be mistakenly limited to the measurement of personal attributes when it applies as well to the measurement of object, situation, and group characteristics. Although we will try to maintain appropriate distinctions when these issues are discussed in detail later, the shorthand usage of "trait" is too convenient and insidious to be eliminated completely.

Sources of Evidence in the Evaluation of Scores

Different kinds of inferences from test scores may require a different balancing of evidence, that is, different relative emphases in the range of evidence presented. By *evidence* is meant both data, or facts, and the rationale or arguments that cement those facts into a justification of test-score inferences. "Another way to put this is to note that data are *not* information; information is that which results from the interpretation of data" (Mitroff & Sagasti, 1973, p. 123). Or as Kaplan (1964) states, "What serves as evidence is the result of a process of interpretation—facts do *not* speak for themselves; nevertheless, facts must be given a hearing, or the scientific point to the process of interpretation is lost" (p. 375). Facts and theoretical rationale thus blend in this concept of evidence.

Evidence takes form only in answer to questions.

> How we put the question reflects our values on the one hand, and on the other hand helps determine the answer we get. . . . [Through] a process of interpretation, . . . data have meaning, and this word "meaning," like its cognates "significance" and "import," includes a reference to values. (Kaplan, 1964, p. 385)

As Weber (1949) has emphasized, "Empirical data are always related to those evaluative ideas which alone make them worth knowing and the significance of the empirical data is derived from these evaluative ideas" (p. 111). Facts and values thus go hand in hand. Indeed, Vickers (1970) put it even more emphatically: "Facts are relevant only to some standard of value; values are applicable only to some configuration of fact" (p. 134). Hence, just as data and theoretical interpretation were seen to be intimately intertwined in the concept of evidence, so data and values are intertwined in the concept of interpretation. And this applies not just to evaluative interpretation, where the role of values is often explicit, but also to theoretical interpretation more generally, where value assumptions frequently lurk unexamined. Fact, meaning, and value are thus quintessential constituents of the evidence and rationales underlying the validity of test interpretation and use.

The basic sources of validity evidence are by no means unlimited. Indeed, if we ask where one might turn for such evidence, we find that there are only a half dozen or so distinct sorts. We can look at the content of the test in relation to the content of the domain of reference. We can probe the ways in which individuals respond to the items or tasks. We can examine relationships among responses to the tasks, items, or parts of the test, that is, the internal structure of test responses. We can survey relationships of the test scores with other measures and background variables, that is, the test's external structure. We can investigate *differences* in these test processes and structures over time, across groups and settings, and in response to experimental interventions—such as instructional or therapeutic treatment and manipulation of content, task requirements, or motivational conditions. Finally, we can trace the social consequences of interpreting and using the test scores in particular ways, scrutinizing not only the intended outcomes but also unintended side effects.

One or another of these forms of evidence, or combinations thereof, have in the past been accorded special status as a so-called "type of validity." But because all of these forms of evidence fundamentally bear on the valid interpretation and use of scores, it is not a type of validity but the relation between the evidence and the inferences drawn that should determine the validation focus. The varieties of evidence are not alternatives but rather supplements to one another. This is the main reason that validity is now recognized as a unitary concept. We will next examine the nature and limitations of the traditional "types" of validity and how these conceptions have evolved over the years. We will then present other ways of cutting evidence, and of reconfiguring forms of evidence, to highlight major facets of a unified validity conception.

Stage-Setting and Crosscutting Themes

To set the stage for a detailed discussion of validity in relation to current and prospective testing practice, it is important to review not only traditional approaches to validity but also some of the philosophy of science associated with past and current validity views. Philosophy of science has undergone radical changes in recent years, and it is illuminating to consider the evolution of validity theory in the context of these changes. Validity issues in relation to developments in the philosophy of science will be addressed in the last major part of this section.

Traditional Ways of Cutting Validity Evidence

At least since the early 1950s, test validity has been broken into three or four distinct types—or, more specifically, into three types, one of which comprises two subtypes. These are content validity, predictive and concurrent criterion-related validity, and construct validity. Paraphrasing slightly statements in the 1954 *Technical Recommendations for Psychological Tests and Diagnostic Techniques* (APA, 1954) and the 1966 *Standards for Educational and Psychological Tests and Manuals* (APA, 1966), these three traditional validity types are described as follows:

> Content validity is evaluated by showing how well the content of the test samples the class of situations or subject matter about which conclusions are to be drawn.

> Criterion-related validity is evaluated by comparing the test scores with one or more external variables (called criteria) considered to provide a direct measure of the characteristic or behavior in question.

> Predictive validity indicates the extent to which an individual's future level on the criterion is predicted from prior test performance.

> Concurrent validity indicates the extent to which the test scores estimate an individual's present standing on the criterion.

> Construct validity is evaluated by investigating what qualities a test measures, that is, by determining the degree to which certain explanatory concepts or constructs account for performance on the test.

These concepts survive in current testing standards and guidelines, with some important shifts in emphasis. They are presented here in their classic version to provide a benchmark against which to appraise the import of subsequent changes. By comparing these so-called validity types with the half dozen or so forms of evidence outlined earlier, we can quickly discern what evidence each validity type relies on as well as what each leaves out.

Content validity is based on professional judgments about the relevance of the test content to the content of a particular behavioral domain of interest and about the representativeness with which item or task content covers that domain. Content validity as such is not concerned with response processes, internal and external test structures, performance differences and responsiveness to treatment, or with social consequences. Thus, content validity provides judgmental evidence in support of the domain relevance and representativeness of the content of the test instrument, rather than evidence in support of inferences to be made from test scores. Test responses and test scores are not even addressed in typical accounts of content validity. Hence, in a fundamental sense so-called content validity does not qualify as validity at all, although such considerations of content relevance and representativeness clearly do and should influence the nature of score inferences supported by other evidence (Messick, 1975). To be sure, some test specialists contend that what a test is measuring is operationally defined by specifying the universe of item content and the item-selection process. But as we shall see, determining what a test is measuring always requires recourse to other forms of evidence.

Criterion-related validity is based on the degree of empirical relationship, usually in terms of correlations or regressions, between the test scores and criterion scores. As such, criterion-related validity relies on selected parts of the test's external structure. The interest is not in the pattern of relationships of the test scores with other measures generally, but rather is more narrowly pointed toward selected relationships with measures that are criterial for a particular applied purpose in a specific applied setting. As a consequence, there are as many criterion-related validities for the test scores as there are criterion measures and settings. This is in contradistinction to content validity, which is usually viewed as a singular property of the test relative to the particular domain for which it was constructed. Of course, if the relevance and representativeness of the test content were evaluated in relation to alternative perspectives on the same domain or to possibly different domains, content validity too might vary, as when the content of the National Teacher Examinations is appraised relative to various teacher-training curricula. In its pure form, criterion-related validity is not concerned with any other sorts of evidence except specific test-criterion correlations. This is not to say that a particular test use supported by criterion-related validity alone might not be seriously vulnerable to the absence of evidence, for example, about content relevance or adverse social consequences.

Construct validity is based on an integration of any evidence that bears on the interpretation or meaning of the test scores. The test score is not equated with the construct it attempts to tap, nor is it considered to define the construct. This is in stark contrast with strict operationism, in which each construct is defined in terms of a narrowly specified set of operations that becomes its sole empirical referent. Rather, the measure is taken to be one of an extensible set of indicators of the construct. Indeed, the construct is invoked as a latent variable or "causal" factor to account for the relationships among its indicators. Because the set of indicators is extensible and because indicators are often probabilistically related to the construct as well as to each other, constructs are not explicitly defined but, rather, are more like "open concepts" (Pap, 1953, 1958).

Almost any kind of information about a test can contribute to an understanding of its construct validity, but the contribution becomes stronger if the degree of fit of the information with the theoretical rationale underlying score interpretation is explicitly evaluated. This point is elaborated in more detail in a later section on strong versus weak construct validation. Historically, primary emphasis in construct validation has been placed on internal and external test structures, that is, on patterns of relationships among item scores or between test scores and other measures. Probably even more illuminating of score meaning, however, are studies of performance differences over time, across groups and settings, and in response to experimental treatments and manipulations. Possibly most illuminating of all are direct probes and modeling of the processes underlying test responses, an approach becoming both more accessible and more powerful with continuing developments in cognitive psychology (e.g., Lachman, Lachman, & Butterfield, 1979; Snow, Federico, & Montague, 1980).

Construct validity also subsumes content relevance and representativeness as well as criterion-relatedness, because such information about the content domain of reference and about specific criterion behaviors predicted by the test scores clearly contributes to score interpretation. In the latter instance, correlations between test scores and criterion measures, viewed in the broader context of other evidence supportive of score meaning, contribute to the joint construct validity of both predictor and criterion. In other words, empirical relationships between the predictor scores and criterion measures should make theoretical sense in terms of what the predictor test is interpreted to measure and what the criterion is presumed to embody (Gulliksen, 1950a).

Thus, construct validity embraces almost all forms of validity evidence. The only source of evidence not yet explicitly incorporated in a type of validity is the appraisal of social consequences. This comprehensive nature of construct validity has led some measurement theorists to argue unequivocally that "since predictive, concurrent, and content validities are all essentially *ad hoc,* construct validity is the whole of validity from a scientific point of view" (Loevinger, 1957, p. 636). This chapter goes further still. For reasons to be expounded later, it is here maintained that, even for purposes of applied decision making, reliance on criterion validity or content coverage is not enough. The meaning of the measure, and hence its construct validity, must always be pursued — not only to support test interpretation but also to justify test use (Messick, 1980).

In one way or another, then, these three traditional types of validity, taken together, make explicit reference to all but one of the forms of validity evidence mentioned earlier. This occurs in spite of the singularity of reference of both content and criterion-related validity, but because of the comprehensiveness of reference of construct validity. Only the social consequences of test interpretation and use are neglected in these traditional formulations. It is ironic that little attention has been paid over the years to the consequential basis of test validity, because validity has been cogently conceptualized in the past in terms of the functional worth of the testing — that is, in terms of how well the test does the job it is employed to do (Cureton, 1951; Rulon, 1946).

We will return to this issue of a consequential basis of test validity in later major sections of this chapter. There we will underscore the continuing need for validation practice to address the realities of testing consequences, including the often subtle systemic effects of recurrent or regularized testing on institutional or societal functioning. The key questions are whether the potential and actual social consequences of test interpretation and use are not only supportive of the intended testing purposes, but at the same time are consistent with other social values. Because the values served in the intended and unintended outcomes of test interpretation and test use both derive from and contribute to the meaning of the test scores, the appraisal of social consequences of testing is also seen to be subsumed as an aspect of construct validity.

Historical Trends in Conceptions of Validity

The theoretical conception of validity has gradually evolved over the years (Anastasi, 1986; Angoff, 1988). An early focus historically was on the prediction of specific criteria, as epitomized by Guilford's (1946) claim that "in a very general sense, a test is valid for anything with which it correlates" (p. 429). A subsequent focus was on a limited number of types of validity, as just discussed. A still later focus was on the meaning or interpretation of measurements or test scores. That is, increasing emphasis has been placed on construct validity as the essence of a unitary validity conception, pithily captured in Cronbach's (1980) conclusion that "all validation is one" (p. 99).

There are a number of important aspects to this evolution. One is the shift in emphasis from numerous specific criterion validities to a small number of validity types and finally to a unitary validity conception. Another is the shift from prediction to explanation as the fundamental validity focus, in the sense that the utility, relevance, and import of the prediction cannot be appraised in the absence of sound empirically grounded interpretation of the scores on which the prediction is based.

This transition in validity conception has not been an entirely smooth one, especially in regard to professional acceptance of the attendant implications for testing practice (Messick, 1988). Nonetheless, the gradual acceptance by the testing field of critical changes in the theoretical formulation of validity is noteworthy. A more detailed sense of this acceptance can be obtained from a brief look at historical trends in the professional standards for testing as well as trends in successive editions of widely used measurement textbooks, such as those by Anastasi and by Cronbach.

As previously indicated, the 1954 *Technical Recommendations* (APA, 1954) codified four types of validity—namely, content, predictive, concurrent, and construct validities. These were reduced by amalgamation to content, criterion-related, and construct validities in the 1966 *Standards* (APA, 1966). Both editions clearly linked these types or aspects of validity to particular aims of testing. These aims are, respectively, to determine how an individual presently performs in a universe of situations (content), to forecast an individual's future standing or to estimate her or his present standing on some significant variable different from the test (criterion), and to infer the degree to which the individual possesses some trait or quality (construct) presumed to be reflected in test performance. The 1966 edition also took a tentative first step toward unification by noting that: "These three aspects of validity are only conceptually independent, and only rarely is just one of them important in a particular situation. A complete study of a test would normally involve information about all types of validity" (p. 14).

Although the 1974 *Standards* (APA, 1974) perpetuated this distinction among validity types related to particular testing aims, it also characterized them as "interdependent kinds of inferential interpretation" and as "aspects of validity . . . interrelated operationally and logically" that can be discussed independently only for convenience (p. 26). The 1974 edition also described content validity in terms of how well "the behaviors demonstrated in testing constitute a representative sample of behaviors to be exhibited in a desired domain" (p. 28). This is in contrast with earlier editions, in which reference was made to how well test content samples the class of situations or subject matter about which conclusions are to be drawn. This reference to "behaviors" as opposed to the "content" of situations or subject matter implies that more than mere professional judgment of content relevance and representativeness is involved. It invokes the need for evidence of reliable response consistencies on the test as well as construct evidence that test and domain behaviors are similar or from the same response class. The major advance in the 1974 edition, however, was a long overdue first step toward codifying standards for test use, thus explicitly introducing concern for bias, adverse impact, and other social consequences of the uses and misuses of tests.

The 1985 edition (APA, 1985) greatly expands the formalization of professional standards for test use. This was accomplished by substantially increasing the number of applied testing areas treated in detail, including the use of tests in clinical, educational, and employment settings; for counseling, licensure, certification, and program evaluation; and, with linguistic minorities and handicapped individuals. Even more important, though inherently controversial, was the valiant attempt to incorporate sufficient behavioral specification to make it possible to judge whether or not the standards are in fact being satisfied. Along with this change in emphasis, there was also an important, though subtle, change in title. As opposed to the titles of previous editions which refer to standards for *tests,* the 1985 title refers to standards for *testing*.

With respect to its conception of validity, the 1985 *Standards* (APA, 1985) continues the march toward a unified view. This edition states flatly that validity is a unitary concept, referring to the "appropriateness, meaningfulness, and usefulness of the specific inferences made from test scores" (p. 8). The text no longer refers to *types* of validity, but rather to categories of validity evidence called content-related, criterion-related, and construct-related evidence of validity. Furthermore, this latest *Standards* document maintains that "an ideal validation includes several types of evidence, which span all three of the traditional categories, . . . [with emphasis on] obtaining the combination of evidence that optimally reflects the value of a test for an intended purpose" (APA, 1985, p. 9).

Similar and additional points emergent in tracking the differences in the various editions of the professional standards and federal guidelines for testing are summarized by Novick (1982). For a less official but no less influential perspective, let us next briefly examine changes in the treatment of validity in the five editions of Anastasi's (1954, 1961, 1968, 1976, 1982) *Psychological Testing* and the four editions of Cronbach's (1949, 1960, 1970, 1984) *Essentials of Psychological Testing.*

The presentation of validity in Anastasi's first edition (1954) is organized in terms of face validity, content validity, factorial validity, and empirical validity. Face validity, which refers to what a test appears to measure to the untrained eye, is discounted as not really being validity at all in the technical sense. However, whether the test is judged relevant to its objectives by respondents, users, or others can affect examinee cooperation and motivation as well as user and public acceptance of the results. Therefore, it is argued, face *in*validity should be avoided whenever possible—except, of course, when indirect or disguised measures are intended, as in some approaches to attitude and personality assessment. The treatment of content validity, also referred to as "logical validity" and "validity by definition," stresses judgment of content relevance and representativeness but also judgment that irrelevant factors have been excluded from the test. Empirical procedures for checking on content validity, now seen with hindsight to be instances of construct validation, were also proposed, such as demonstrating significant improvement between pretraining and posttraining measures of educational achievement. Factorial validity refers to the correlation between the test scores and a factor common to a group of tests or other measures of behavior. That is, factorial validity corresponds to the test's external structure, which is also now seen as an instance of construct validity. By far the bulk of the discussion was given to empirical validity, which essentially refers to the relation between the test scores and a criterion, the latter being an independent and direct measure of what the test is designed to assess or predict. Here, too, in an extended treatment of the criterion, the suggested use of age differentiation, contrasted groups, and correlations with other tests as criteria blurs the later distinction between criterion-related and construct-related evidence.

The account of validity in Anastasi's second edition (1961) was organized in terms of content, predictive, concurrent, and construct validities, as promulgated in the 1954 *Standards.* Under construct validity were included discussions of age differentiation, correlations with other tests, and factor analysis, along with consideration of internal consistency and score differences in response to experimental intervention. The validity framework in Anastasi's third (1968), fourth (1976), and fifth (1982) editions was in terms of content, criterion-related, and construct validities, with increasingly more space allocated to construct validity in successive editions. The headings in the fifth edition actually refer to content, criterion-related, and construct *validation* rather than validity, and the index lists "types of validation procedures" in contrast with the indexing of "types of validity" in previous editions. This modest endorsement that validity does not come in types is underscored by the appearance of a separate section in the fifth edition on "inclusiveness of construct validation."

The treatment of validity in the first edition of Cronbach's *Essentials of Psychological Testing* (1949) was organized in terms of logical validity and empirical validity, with problems of content validity being discussed in a later chapter on achievement measurement. Logical validity is based on judgments of precisely what the test measures. Empirical validity is based on correlations between the test scores and some other measure, usually a criterion known or presumed to tap some characteristic of importance. Logical validity "aims at psychological understanding of the processes that affect scores" (p. 48). It is judged by making a careful study of the test itself to determine what the scores mean, with special attention to the possible role of irrelevant variables contaminating test performance. As examples of contaminating variables, Cronbach discussed response styles as plausible rival hypotheses to account for performance consistencies on ability or attitude tests. Emphasis on the discounting of plausible rival hypotheses, as we shall see, is to become a hallmark of construct validation. Hence, this formulation of logical validity is one clear precursor of construct validity.

Cronbach's second edition (1960), like Anastasi's (1961), follows the four-part conception of validity given in the 1954 *Standards.* The chapter on validity has a main section devoted to predictive and concurrent validity and another to construct validity. Once again, however, treatment of content validity was relegated to a later chapter on proficiency tests, where there also appeared an additional extended discussion of construct validity. In Cronbach's third (1970) and fourth (1984) editions, content validation is moved to the major chapter on validation, joining criterion-oriented and construct validation as the three major types of validation, or methods of inquiry. But Cronbach (1984) emphasizes that these three types of validation are not to be taken as alternatives: "With almost any test it makes sense to join all three kinds of inquiry in building an explanation. The three distinct terms do no more than spotlight aspects of the inquiry" (p. 126). Cronbach (1984) concludes that "the end goal of validation is explanation and understanding. Therefore, the profession is coming around to the view that *all* validation is construct validation" (p. 126).

Hence, the testing field, as reflected in the influential textbooks by Anastasi and by Cronbach as well as in the professional standards, is moving toward recognition of validity as a unitary concept, in the sense that score meaning as embodied in construct validity underlies all score-based inferences. But for a fully unified view of validity, it must also be recognized that the appropriateness, meaningfulness, and usefulness of score-based inferences depend as well on the social consequences of the testing. Therefore, social values and social consequences cannot be ignored in considerations of validity (Messick, 1980).

Indeed, there is movement on this score as well. In his treatment of validation as persuasive argument, Cronbach (1988) stresses that *"the argument must link concepts, evidence, social and personal consequences, and values"* (p. 4). Furthermore, he maintains that the bottom line is that validators have an obligation to review whether a practice has appropriate consequences for individuals and institutions, and especially to guard against adverse consequences. You . . . may prefer to exclude reflection on consequences from meanings of the word *validation,* but you cannot deny the obligation. (p. 6)

But the meaning of validation should not be considered a preference. On what can the legitimacy of the obligation to appraise social consequences be based if not on the only genuine imperative in testing, namely, validity?

*Meaning and Values as Ways of Cutting
Validity Evidence*

Traditional ways of cutting and combining evidence of validity, as we have seen, have led to three major categories of validity evidence: content-related, criterion-related, and construct-related. However, because content- and criterion-related evidence contribute to score meaning, they have come to be recognized as aspects of construct validity. In a sense, then, this leaves only one category, namely, construct-related evidence. Yet in applied uses of tests, *general* evidence supportive of construct validity usually needs to be buttressed by *specific* evidence of the relevance of the test to the applied purpose and the utility of the test in the applied setting.

Relevance of test use may derive from a number of sources such as professional judgments of the relevance and representativeness of test content in relation to the content of the applied domain, evidence that the test validity reflects processes or constructs judged to be important in domain functioning, or significant test correlations with criterion measures of domain performance. Utility of test use is based on test-criterion correlations in relation to the benefits and costs of the testing. But note that even as specific evidence of relevance and utility in the applied setting complements general construct validity evidence vis-à-vis the particular applied purpose, it also contributes additional interpretive strands to the general construct validity fabric.

Thus, in general, content- and criterion-related evidence, being contributory to score interpretation, are subsumed under the rubric of construct-related evidence. Yet, considerations of specific content and selected criteria resurface, in addition to the general construct validity of score meaning, whenever the test is used for a particular applied purpose. Cutting validity evidence into three categories that are then folded into one does not illuminate these nuances in the roles of spe-

cific content- and criterion-related evidence as adjuncts to construct validity in justifying test use.

Furthermore, the continuing enumeration of three categories of validity evidence perpetuates, no less than did three types of validity, the temptation to rely on only one (or, worse still, any one) category of evidence as sufficient for the validity of a particular test use. Moreover, to speak of "kinds of validity analysis strategies" as opposed to kinds of validity, as Lawshe (1985) did, simply compounds the problem, especially when three types of analysis strategies are highlighted to match three familiar broad categories of inference based on test scores. What is needed is a way of cutting and combining validity evidence that forestalls undue reliance on selected forms of evidence, that highlights the important though subsidiary role of specific content- and criterion-related evidence in support of construct validity in testing applications, and that formally brings consideration of value implications and social consequences into the validity framework.

A unified validity framework that meets these requirements may be constructed by distinguishing two interconnected facets of the unitary validity concept. One facet is the source of justification of the testing, being based on appraisal of either evidence or consequence. The other facet is the function or outcome of the testing, being either interpretation or use. If the facet for source of justification (that is, either an evidential basis or a consequential basis) is crossed with the facet for function or outcome of the testing (that is, either test interpretation or test use), we obtain a four-fold classification as in Table 2.1 (Messick, 1980).

As indicated in Table 2.1, the evidential basis of test interpretation is construct validity. The evidential basis of test use is also construct validity, but as buttressed by evidence for the relevance of the test to the specific applied purpose and for the utility of the test in the applied setting. The consequential basis of test interpretation is the appraisal of the value implications of the construct label, of the theory underlying test interpretation, and of the ideologies in which the theory is embedded. A central issue is whether or not the theoretical implications and the value implications of the test interpretation are commensurate, because value implications are not ancillary but, rather, integral to score meaning. Finally, the consequential basis of test use is the appraisal of both potential and actual social consequences of the applied testing.

These distinctions may seem fuzzy because they are not only interlinked but overlapping. For example, social consequences redounding to the testing are a form of evidence, so the evidential basis referred to here includes all validity evidence except social consequences, which are highlighted in their own

TABLE 2.1 Facets of Validity

	TEST INTERPRETATION	TEST USE
EVIDENTIAL BASIS	Construct validity	Construct validity + Relevance/utility
CONSEQUENTIAL BASIS	Value implications	Social consequences

right. Furthermore, as we shall see, utility is both validity evidence and a value consequence. Moreover, to interpret a test is to use it, and all other test uses involve interpretation either explicitly or tacitly. So the test use referred to here includes all test uses other than test interpretation per se. The fuzziness—or rather the messiness—of these distinctions derives from the fact that we are trying to cut through what indeed is a unitary concept. Nonetheless, these distinctions do provide us with a way of speaking about functional aspects of validity that helps disentangle some of the complexities inherent in appraising the appropriateness, meaningfulness, and usefulness of score inferences.

Some measurement specialists maintain that test interpretation and test use are distinct issues, so that the two columns of Table 2.1 should be treated more independently. In this view, construct validity is usually accepted as the validity of test interpretation, but the validity of test use is appraised more in terms of relevance or utility or both. But judgments of relevance and utility as well as of appropriateness depend, or should depend, on the meaning of the item or test scores. Hence, construct validity binds the validity of test use to the validity of test interpretation, as is made explicit in Table 2.1.

Others contend that value implications and social consequences of testing are policy issues separate from test validity as such, so that the two rows of Table 2.1 should also be treated independently. But a social consequence of testing, such as adverse impact against females in the use of a quantitative test, either stems from a source of test invalidity or reflects a valid property of the construct assessed, or both. In the former case, this adverse consequence bears on the meaning of the test scores and, in the latter case, on the meaning of the construct. In both cases, therefore, construct validity binds social consequences of testing to the evidential basis of test interpretation and use, as will be made explicit shortly. Accordingly, the validity of test interpretation and test use, as well as the evidence and consequences bearing thereon, are treated here in the unified faceted framework of Table 2.1, because of a conviction that the commonality afforded by construct validity will in the long run prove more powerful and integrative than any operative distinctions among the facets.

The distinction between test interpretation and test use is similar to other common distinctions in the validity literature. For example, Cronbach (1971) distinguishes between using a test to describe a person and using it to make decisions about the person. He points out that

decisions generally are intended to optimize some later 'criterion' performance of the individual or group, hence the decision maker is particularly concerned with criterion-oriented validation. Descriptive use relies on content validity or construct validity. But the correspondence among categories is not so neat as this. (p. 445)

This untidiness is straightened out in the framework of Table 2.1. The validity of descriptive interpretation is based on construct-related evidence. The validity of decision-making uses is based on construct-related evidence as well, with the proviso that evidence be included bearing on the relevance and utility of the test for the specific decision. Thus, the validation of a descriptive interpretation versus a decision rule is viewed in

this framework as being more hierarchic or part–whole in nature than dichotomous.

However, on the face of it, a comprehensive validation of decision-making uses of tests should include an appraisal of social consequences and side effects of the decisions. This suggests that the unified validity framework embodied in Table 2.1 might better be translated as a *progressive matrix.* If this were the case, the upper left cell would include construct validity as it did before, while the upper right cell would include construct validity attuned to relevance and utility as it formerly did. But the lower left cell, to signal that score interpretation is needed to appraise value implications and vice versa, would now include both construct validity and its value ramifications. Similarly, the lower right cell—in recognition of the fact that the weighing of social consequences both presumes and contributes to evidence of score meaning, relevance, utility, and values—would now include construct validity, relevance, and utility as well as social and value consequences.

One advantage of this progressive-matrix formulation is that construct validity appears in every cell, thereby highlighting its pervasive and overarching nature. Furthermore, evidence of the relevance and utility of test scores in specific applied settings, and evaluation of the social consequences of test use as well as of the value implications of test interpretation, all contribute in important ways to the construct validity of score meaning. This makes it clear that, in this generalized sense, construct validity may ultimately be taken as the whole of validity in the final analysis.

The remainder of this chapter is organized in terms of the unified validity framework presented in Table 2.1. The next four main sections correspond to the four cells of the table, and the final main section refers to the marginals of the table. Before proceeding to a detailed discussion of the evidential basis of test interpretation, however, there is one aspect of stage-setting that still remains to be covered. This pertains to the philosophy of science underlying prior validity conceptions as well as the philosophy guiding, or at least consistent with, current and evolving formulations. Inevitably, the following discussion is a cursory summary of complex philosophical positions. On the other hand, it needs to be sufficiently extensive to permit critical points to be developed and linked to aspects of validity theory.

Philosophical Conceits

The term *conceits* in the title of this section is intended to underscore the point that the philosophy of science is more philosophy than science, that the philosophical principles at issue result largely from mental activity or conceptual analysis and not from scientific evidence. Secondary meanings of conceits as fanciful ideas or elaborate metaphors are not to be stressed here, but neither are they always to be denied. The intent is to introduce a modicum of cold caution with respect to the prescriptive, as opposed to the clarifying, uses of philosophy of science.

As we shall see, validity conceptions and validation practices have been roundly criticized for adhering too rigidly and too long to outmoded philosophical principles. But the import of this criticism depends on whether validity conceptions were ever uniquely tied to particular philosophical positions or whether they are congenial with multiple positions. This is an important issue because if construct validity is considered to be dependent on a singular philosophical base such as logical positivism and that basis is seen to be deficient or faulty, then construct validity might be dismissed out of hand as being fundamentally flawed. This issue is explored in depth here both to preclude such a rash conclusion and to make manifest some of the rich affinities between evolving validity theory and a variety of philosophical perspectives. Indeed, an appeal to multiple perspectives with respect to validity theory and validation methods will emerge as a crosscutting theme in the chapter generally.

As validity theory developed, the philosophy of science was turned to selectively to legitimize different points and procedures. As validity theory has become more unified, a key question is the extent to which the various philosophical rationalizations of the parts constitute a mutually consistent whole. More directly and more sensibly, however, we might ask what philosophy of science can be formulated to rationalize current validity thinking and practice in ways that are consistent with their scientific basis.

In addressing these issues, we will first briefly examine the early role of logical positivism as the philosophical foundation of construct validity. In its heyday, positivism focused on the logical structure, or even the axiomatic structure, of scientific theories and offered an attractive framework for addressing the role of constructs in psychological theory and measurement. We will next review some of the successive challenges and alternative views that led to the demise of positivism and stimulated a rising philosophical emphasis on actual scientific practice. Over time, we thus "see questions about 'the logical structure of scientific systems' replaced at the center of philosophy of science by questions about 'the rational development of scientific enterprises'" (Toulmin, 1977, p. 613). Along with this change in philosophical focus, there was a change in ontological perspective from instrumentalism to realism, or at least a shift in relative preference from the former to the latter. The implications of these philosophical changes for the conception of validity in general and of construct validity in particular are explored along the way. In addition, some concepts from the philosophical literature that are akin to concepts invoked in the subsequent treatment of validity theory are introduced here. Finally, we examine some philosophical positions stemming from epistemology that emphasize not theories of knowledge per se but, rather, theories of knowing or inquiry. Implications of different modes of inquiry for the garnering of evidence of validity, that is, for the process of validation, are then adumbrated here and elaborated periodically in succeeding sections of the chapter.

POSITIVISTIC CLIMATE FOR FLEDGLING CONSTRUCT VALIDITY FORMULATIONS

When notions of construct validity were first being systematized in the early 1950s, logical positivism was a prominent philosophical force in psychology, especially in methodological circles. As such, it offered a ready framework within which

to flesh out and legitimize the emergent validity ideas (Cronbach & Meehl, 1955). For these purposes, the salient themes of logical positivism were essentially epistemic ones: that logic and syntax are critical to structuring knowledge of the world and that meaning is factual verifiability.

The first theme centers attention on the logical structure of scientific theories, trading on the generality of mathematical logic for formalizing both mathematical and linguistic propositions, as previously demonstrated by Whitehead and Russell (1910–1913). For the logical positivists, scientific theories are subject to axiomatic formulation in terms of mathematical logic, whereby theoretical terms are linked to observational terms by correspondence rules. Correspondence rules are coordinating definitions or rules of interpretation that both define theoretical terms and specify the admissible experimental procedures for applying a theory (Suppe, 1977b). A special case of correspondence rules is the well-known *operational definition,* although its celebrated requirement of explicit specification was soon relaxed by construing correspondence rules as *reduction sentences* that only partially define theoretical terms (Carnap, 1936–1937).

The second theme focuses attention on the positivist criteria of meaning as embodied in the verifiability principle. According to this verifiability theory of meaning, something is meaningful if and only if it is logically true following prescribed rules of construction and inference or else is empirically verifiable. This contrasting of logical truth and empirical fact comprises the so-called analytic–synthetic distinction (Carnap, 1966), which in one form or another has been prominent in philosophical thinking at least since Kant. The intent of the verifiability principle was to undercut all recourse to metaphysics by insisting on the separation of sense from nonsense and meaningful propositions from pseudopropositions.

Yet there remain certain types of statements that are useful to science but are neither analytically or logically derivable nor unequivocally verifiable empirically. These include universal propositions or general laws that can never be fully verified by finite observations. Also included are hypothetical constructions that constitute essential steps in scientific inference but are inherently beyond the pale of direct verification. However, because both general laws and hypothetical constructs can potentially generate statements that have observable consequences, their meaning can still be addressed, though far from conclusively, within a verifiability framework. Two approaches can be distinguished within the positivist movement for dealing with such issues: One is an empiricistic approach in which meaning is a matter of factual reference; the other is a syntactical approach in which meaning is contingent only on the connection of statements with other statements (Turner, 1967).

In one line of development within the syntactical approach, the problem of conferring meaning on hypothetical constructs was addressed by formulating a theoretical system in terms of those constructs and then providing the system with an experiential interpretation (Hempel, 1952/1970). In this view, an adequate empirical interpretation transforms a theoretical system into a testable theory, because hypothesized relations involving terms that have been interpreted become amenable to testing by reference to observables, either directly or indirectly through a chain of derivative relations. A scientific theory is thereby likened to a complex spatial network in which constructs are represented by knots interconnected by strands, which corrrespond to definitions and to the fundamental and derivative hypotheses of the theory.

> The whole system floats, as it were, above the plane of observation and is anchored to it by rules of interpretation. These might be viewed as strings which are not part of the network but link certain points of the latter with specific places in the plane of observation. By virtue of those interpretive connections, the network can function as a scientific theory: From certain observational data, we may ascend, via an interpretive string, to some point in the theoretical network, thence proceed, via definitions and hypotheses, to other points, from which another interpretive string permits a descent to the plane of observation. (Hempel, 1952/1970, p. 688)

Such a theoretical network, or interlocking system of lawful relations, has been referred to as a *nomological network* (Cronbach & Meehl, 1955).

Interpreted theoretical networks, according to Hempel (1952/1970), provide both predictive and postdictive bridges from observational data to potential observational findings. But this cannot be accomplished in terms of observables alone, by mere inductive summaries generalizing observational results. Theoretical constructs and hypothesized relationships among them are needed to give the network deductive or predictive power (Glymour, 1980). Furthermore, it is important to recognize that there is feedback between the observational plane and the theoretical network. Data help to generate constructs, and new data serve iteratively to test and modify constructs. The interpretive strings are all-important here and, in subtle yet fundamental ways, are generated out of the theoretical or conceptual system (Margenau, 1950).

Although the interpretive statements clearly serve as rules of correspondence, they need not be operational definitions or even partially defining reduction sentences. Hempel (1952/1970) goes so far as to allow that they might simply link hypothetical states or processes to observable clues, thereby providing "indicators" that are tied to theoretical constructs by probabilistic relations. This is akin to Pap's (1953, 1958) notion of an "open concept," in which indicators are probabilistically linked to the construct, the meaning of which is a "promissory note" that, given adequate research, the factor or entity underlying these probabilistic linkages will gradually become stipulated (Meehl & Golden, 1982).

In this regard, Hempel (1965) subsequently extended the deductive–nomological model, in which relations follow logically or theoretically, to include statistical relations that hold only probabilistically. Collectively, the deductive–nomological and inductive–statistical models form the basis of what is known as the *covering-law model of scientific explanation*. The name derives from the fact that an event is explained by subsuming it under a law or set of laws that "covers" its occurrence. A controversial implication of the deductive–nomological model is that explanation and prediction are symmetrical, because advancing the explanatory argument prior to the event would improve the ability to predict it.

In the early theoretical development of construct validity concepts, heavy reliance was placed on these positivistic formulations. To illustrate, it was maintained that "a rigorous

(though perhaps probabilistic) chain of inference is required to establish a test as a measure of a construct. To validate a claim that a test measures a construct, a nomological net surrounding the concept must exist" (Cronbach & Meehl, 1955, p. 291). In other words, "a necessary condition for a construct to be scientifically admissible is that it occur in a nomological net, at least *some* of whose laws involve observables" (p. 290). Nor is this commitment to a nomological network formulation of construct validity limited to initial discussions of the topic (Meehl & Golden, 1982). In the second edition of the present volume, for example, Cronbach (1971) states that "construct validation is described formally in philosophy of science" (p. 475), making specific reference to the work of Hempel.

Indeed, descriptions of construct validity in terms of nomological networks still occur in the present chapter, as they did in precursors to it (Messick, 1975, 1980, 1981a, 1981b), but no longer as a requirement or defining feature of construct validation. Nomological networks are viewed as an illuminating way of speaking systematically about the role of constructs in psychological theory and measurement, but not as the only way. The nomological framework offers a useful guide for disciplined thinking about the process of validation but cannot serve as the prescriptive validation model to the exclusion of other approaches such as causal explanation or the modeling of operative mechanisms. In fact, it may be an overinterpretation to read Cronbach's identification of construct validation with Hempel's philosophy of science as prescriptive or delimiting —for example, as Norris (1983) apparently does. After all, the 1971 chapter repeatedly insists that theory takes many forms and is subject to a variety of validation techniques. Even the examples of nomological networks offered are reasonably interpretable as causal models, at least in the structural-equation sense.

Nevertheless, Cronbach (in press) maintains that "it was pretentious to dress up our immature science in the positivist language; and it was self-defeating to say . . . that a construct not a part of a nomological network is not scientifically admissible" (p. 12). But the positivist doctrines have been criticized on numerous grounds, beginning with attacks on the verifiability theory of meaning itself and on the distinction between theoretical and observational terms that is so central to the logical construction and empirical testing of scientific theories. Because the philosophical perspectives of the critics have messages of their own for test validation, we will next examine some of the successive rivals to logical positivism.

From Positivism to Relativism to Rationalism

Early on, the verifiability theory of meaning was seriously questioned by Popper (1935/1959) on the basis of Hume's critique of induction. Subsequently, the analytic–synthetic distinction at the very core of the verifiability theory was itself attacked, along with the associated doctrine of the reducibility of synthetic statements to statements about immediate experience (Quine, 1951). Popper argues that although general scientific propositions can never be verified by any possible accumulation of particular observational evidence, scientific theories can be empirically falsified. Specifically, deductions from general theoretical propositions can be tested by comparing observed findings with the deduced pattern. Failure to confirm the expectation can falsify the theory in question, but corroborative data only provisionally support the theory to the extent that no rival theory can account for the results. Even in this latter case, because of the ambiguity of confirmation, the theory is only considered to be "not yet disconfirmed." From this deductionist perspective, a statement is meaningful if it is falsifiable.

But according to Popper (1935/1959), statements are not falsified by findings or facts alone but rather by other statements, following logical conventions. Thus, theories are falsified by alternative theories in conjunction with discordant facts. This places an emphasis on the proliferation of plausible rival theories subjected to possible empirical falsification, which provides a clear message for validity theory, a message that is gradually being heeded. It is true that much of the writing on construct validation is verificationist in tone, as are the professional standards for testing. But, as we have seen, the notion of plausible rival hypotheses surfaced in incipient form at least as early as Cronbach's 1949 treatment of logical validity (see also, for example, R. Bowers, 1936). Shortly thereafter, plausible rival hypotheses were explicitly treated as threats to the validity of causal inference in experiments by D. T. Campbell (1957; Campbell & Stanley, 1963). Later, they were highlighted as guiding strategies for test validation (Cronbach, 1971; Messick, 1975) and, later still, the discounting of plausible rival hypotheses was dubbed the hallmark of construct validation (Messick, 1980).

Both the verifiability and falsifiability views of meaning are based on the distinction between theoretical and observational terms, a distinction that has become less clear over the years as well as more context-dependent (Glymour, 1980). Both views assume that observations can be sufficiently independent of presumptions in the theory to be useful in testing its validity. Eventually, however, there came a barrage of criticisms: Theories are not value-neutral; neither observations nor meanings are theory-independent, being influenced by the Weltanschauung, or worldview, of the theory; methodology itself is not theory-neutral and hence is incapable of generating a neutral set of facts for appraising competing theories (Feyerabend, 1975; Hanson, 1958; Kuhn, 1962).

For example, Hanson (1958) maintains that "a theory is not pieced together from observed phenomena; it is rather what makes it possible to observe phenomena as being of a certain sort, and as related to other phenomena" (p. 90). Kuhn (1962) views everyday or "normal" scientific research as occuring within a "paradigm" or worldview that comprises a strong network of conceptual, theoretical, instrumental, and metaphysical commitments. These paradigms determine the nature of the problems addressed, how phenomena are viewed, what counts as a solution, and the criteria of acceptability for theories. Paradigms thus have a normative or valuative component (Suppe, 1977a).

According to Kuhn, periods of normal science are punctuated by occasional scientific revolutions, which occur when a theory or paradigm is faced with intractable theoretical anomalies so that alternative paradigms must be sought. Because each paradigm has its own tailored standards of adequacy,

however, choosing among the alternatives proliferated during revolutionary episodes smacks of arbitrariness. Furthermore, these decisions are made even more difficult by the global and loose manner in which the term *paradigm* is used. In reaction to such criticism, Kuhn (1977) later distinguished between two aspects of paradigms that were formerly confused: exemplars, which are specific problem solutions accepted by the scientific community as paradigmatic in the conventional sense; and, disciplinary matrixes, which are professionally shared elements of communication, judgment, models, generalizations, and values. This relativity of observation and meaning to theory and of theory to paradigm or worldview is carried to an even more radical extreme by Feyerabend (1975). His argument is that not only does each theory possess its own experience but there may be no overlap between these experiences, thereby leading to a fundamental incommensurability of theories.

The import of these relativistic positions for validity theory depends on how extreme a version is deemed tenable (Garrison, 1986). For example, one relativist perspective is a form of idealism that holds that the mind and the world cannot be separated, that investigators and their instruments actually serve to construct reality. And if social reality is mind-dependent, it follows that the theories, values, and purposes of the investigator play a fundamental role in the construction process (Eisner, 1979; J. K. Smith, 1983a, 1983b, 1985; J. K. Smith & Heshusius, 1986). In this idealist framework, validity is a matter of agreement between the test and the version of reality it helps to construct, as attested to by those holding the common reality construction (conditioned by social place and historical time).

The mode of inquiry in this idealist tradition is mainly naturalistic or qualitative, and the associated criteria of validity apply more to the inquiry process than to the interpretive outcome, serving as relative standards for establishing agreement within the community of believers. Criteria of the trustworthiness of qualitative inquiry in this idealist framework include credibility in terms of the mind-constructed interpretation of reality, dependability, confirmability, and transferability to other settings (Guba & Lincoln, 1981). But note that these criteria support the trustworthiness of the qualitative inquiry process relative to a given worldview, not the validity of the interpretation itself, which in the final analysis is an accolade bestowed by intersubjective agreement.

In a detailed conceptual analysis of relativist approaches, Suppe (1977a) vindicated only the more moderate versions of the controversial claims. He concluded that while these relativistic theories "could be interpreted in such a way as to divorce science from a determination of the objective nature of things, they need not be so interpreted" (p. 217). In an earlier section of this chapter in which the nature of evidence was discussed, we have already embraced some of relativism's basic points, namely, that observations and meanings are theory-laden and that theories are value-laden (Messick, 1975, 1980). In some form or other, these points are simply not to be denied.

However, we do deny, along with Cook and Campbell (1979), any notion that observations are laden with only a single theory or paradigm. This is partly a reminder of the Duhem (1908/1954) hypothesis that since every test of a theory involves not only the focal theory but also the whole set of background theories and assumptions (about methods, equipment, uncontrolled variables, and the like), we can never be certain which of these assumptions is refuted in a falsifying experiment. It is also partly a recognition that observations are not only multiple-theory laden, but multiply laden to different degrees and in various ways. Thus, through the application of multiple operations in scientific research, convergent findings cumulate and "most of the facts and apparatus, as theory laden as they are, still remain available for comparative tests which help assess the relative merits of extant and new rival theories" (Cook & Campbell, 1979, p. 24).

Both the positivists and Popper focus on the deductive structure of scientific theories and portray scientific method in formal, general, yet relatively static ways. The approach is highly rational but not very relevant to the nature of either actual scientific thinking or the course of conceptual change in science. In contrast, Kuhn deals with conceptual change as alternations between normal science operating within a paradigm and revolutionary science in which different paradigms vie as potential successors. But the price paid by Kuhn and others for their relativism is that rationality is relevant only internally to a paradigm; there is no external rationality for appraising paradigms themselves or for choosing among them. This dilemma has been confronted in two ways: On the one hand, Kuhn's revolutionary version of scientific change is rejected in favor of a more gradual, evolutionary view; on the other hand, although it is accepted that facts are theory-laden and theories value-laden, the resultant relativism is tempered by reality testing (Gholson & Barker, 1985; Lakatos, 1970; Shapere, 1977; Strike & Posner, 1977: Toulmin, 1953, 1972).

Specifically, Lakatos (1970) has argued that conceptual change in mature science does not occur cataclysmically through the falsification of theories but, rather, occurs systematically in an ever improving series of related theories, which he calls a "research program." Research programs include methodological heuristics for determining problem shifts, negative heuristics signaling what to avoid and positive heuristics what to pursue. Research programs thus offer a rational basis for persisting in the face of ostensibly falsifying evidence. This is accomplished by the negative heuristic, which isolates a "hard core" of theory that is to be modified or rejected only as a last resort. The line of defense is provided by a "protective belt" of modifiable auxiliary hypotheses relating the hard core theory to the observed world. Since in this framework scientists face no logical constraint to reject a core scientific theory when confronted by seemingly obstreperous findings, neither Popper's falsificationism nor Kuhn's paradigm shifts provides a realistic account of scientific change. However, Lakatos (1970) identified only one of a variety of rational strategies for acquiring scientific knowledge and, by focusing exclusively on the modification of theories within a research program, left out other important ways of developing theories (Suppe, 1977c).

From among these other approaches to theory development, Shapere (1977) stresses the role of domain problems and the need to clarify the scientific domain itself. As a replacement for the old and unclear observational-versus-theoretical distinction, Shapere proposes the concept of a domain, which not only incorporates elements from both the traditional observa-

tional and theoretical categories but also recognizes their mutual interdependence. A scientific domain is "the total body of information for which a theory is expected to account. *A theory can, then, be judged complete or incomplete relative to that body of information*" (Shapere, 1977, p. 559). Shapere maintains that the content of science does indeed impose constraints on what constitutes a legitimate scientific concept or problem and, furthermore, that content influences the specific directions that science takes. That is, to some degree facts not only raise their own questions but also suggest solutions. Moreover, the study of scientific domains enables one to discern various characteristic patterns of reasoning as scientists cope with these constraints. By examining reasoning patterns in the course of actual science, Shapere hopes to illuminate what, for him, is the fundamental problem in philosophy of science, namely, making sense out of how science arrived in a justified way at its present beliefs about the world.

With respect to the objectivity of scientific knowledge, Shapere contends that the theory-ladenness of observation need not compromise objectivity. He argues that direct observation can be a source of knowledge, granted the background information used in the interpretation is also knowledge. Usually, even variant interpretations stemming from different theories rely in part on a mutual body of consonant background theory. In such cases, the problematic aspects of the interpretation can be "unloaded" to yield an interpretation or description that is common to the competing theories and thereby is epistemically noncontroversial. In the final analysis, science is objective for Shapere if it accepts into the domain only those knowledge claims rationally supported by evidence. But rationality alone is not enough to sidestep subjectivity or relativism, because an important part of scientific objectivity is concerned with establishing putative facts about the real world. Thus, Shapere openly embraces a metaphysical realism with respect to truth, along with a belief that patterns of good scientific reasoning can enable rational appraisal of the credibility of truth claims (Suppe, 1977c).

A central problem within the revolutionary view of scientific change is that all intellectual standards and evaluative criteria are contravened simultaneously in periodic massive upheavals. In contrast, Toulmin (1972) posits an evolutionary model of conceptual change in which any particular new departure can be evaluated against a relatively stable background of rational standards and explanatory ideals. From Toulmin's perspective, the problem with both the positivists and the relativists is that they erroneously assume that rationality is a property of a conceptual or logical system. Rather, "rationality is an attribute . . . of the human activities or enterprises of which particular sets of concepts are the temporary cross-sections" (Toulmin, 1972, p. 134). To avoid this defective equating of the "logical" with the "rational," he explicitly stresses not only the logical procedures for analyzing concepts in a given theoretical system but also the rational procedures for addressing conceptual problems in a developing science.

For Toulmin (1972), scientific objectivity rests not on the matching of hypotheses with facts, but on the reasoned evaluation of conceptual variants and explanatory ideals. In particular, objectivity derives from the fact that these conceptual and strategic judgments are subject to criticism in the light of experience, in ways that "involve prospective estimates of the consequences to be expected from alternative intellectual policies, and so amount to 'rational bets' . . . with the possibility of making the natural world itself a more intelligible object of human understanding" (Toulmin, 1972, p. 246). Hence, strategic evaluative judgments among conceptual rivals, including the evaluation of potential consequences, have a clear epistemic aspect. Toulmin (1977) saw philosophers of science moving away from the

> traditional, static, or "snapshot" view of *theoretical calculi* to a more "kinematic" view of *scientific enterprise.* . . . [In so doing, they must ask] how the concepts, and families of concepts, current in any one temporal cross-section of the science concerned *develop rationally* into those of successive later cross-sections. (pp. 613–614)

In this march toward the philosophical legitimization of rationalism in the scientific enterprise, there are a number of beats for validity theory to resonate to. For instance, Lakatos's (1970) distinction between hard-core theory and a protective belt of auxiliary hypotheses speaks to the issue of what constitutes negative evidence and what should be done about it. In construct validation, as we shall see, the construct and its indicant, the test score or measurement procedure, are intertwined. Positive evidence jointly supports both the construct and its measure, but negative evidence may impugn either the construct theory or the measurement procedure, or both. Positive and negative heuristics of the type discussed by Lakatos are used, often tacitly, to decide whether to revise either the construct or the measure, whether to modify both, or whether to try again with better control of irrelevant variables. These tacit heuristics need to be made an explicit part of validation methodology.

Other specific instances of ties to validity theory are Shapere's (1977) concept of a scientific domain and Toulmin's (1972) concept of a rational bet based on the evaluation of potential consequences of alternative intellectual policies. Notions of domain similar to Shapere's are invoked later in connection with the relevance and representativeness of test content vis-à-vis a construct theory. And evaluation of the potential consequences of testing policies are to be central to appraisals of the functional worth of testing. A more general point of contact between validity theory and the kinematic view of rationality in the scientific enterprise, however, is the long-standing recognition that construct validation is a dynamic process of continual revision and refinement of both construct theory and measurement over time. The basic message is that this process of moving from one snapshot of a construct and its associated measurement to a subsequent snapshot is not only dynamic but should be rational.

From Instrumentalism to Realism

Because the move away from a philosophical focus on the logical structure of scientific theories to a focus on the rationality of scientific enterprises entailed movement toward a metaphysical realism with respect to truth, we should be clear about the existential differences among the other philosophical positions discussed and what import these have, if any, for validity theory. With respect to the ontological status of theoretical entities, logical positivists view theoretical terms as logical constructions whose meaning is purely contextual. That is, the meaning of theoretical terms derives implicitly from their systemic relations to other terms in the theory and explicitly from their correspondence or reducibility to observables. Thus, theoretical terms are simply a shorthand manner of describing or speaking about a complex of observable phenomena and relations, conveying neither surplus meaning nor any implication of reified existence.

In regard to the nature of truth, positivists generally adhere to a coherence theory, although many find an instrumentalist theory of truth quite congenial as well. According to the coherence theory of truth, a statement is true if it is consistent within a system of other statements, that is, the logical consequences deducible from the statement and other statements in the system are in agreement. According to the instrumentalist theory of truth, a statement is true if it is useful in directing inquiry or guiding action. These two perspectives on truth are clearly compatible in that the deductions or predictions derived by logical positivists from coherent systems can be deemed useful for guiding action. The relativists are essentially instrumentalists too, although for them the usefulness of theoretical terms is itself relative to the theory, paradigm, or worldview adopted by the investigator. Thus, although logical positivism may be dead, instrumentalism is one aspect that survives the demise and, ironically, is shared by the relativists in a joint opposition to realism (Phillips, 1983).

Realists view theoretical terms as conjectures about existing, though presently unobserved, attributes of the world. Such terms carry surplus meaning along with the ascription of real existential status. Popper (1935/1959), for one, agreed that theories, albeit hypothetical, do ascribe reality to the world. Furthermore, although such theories are not in principle verifiable, they can be subjected to severe critical tests. That is, the hypotheses can be held to a correspondence theory of truth, wherein a statement is true (or at least not yet false) if what it asserts is indeed actually the case—in other words, if the hypotheses accord with the facts. For Popper (1956), "some of these theories of ours can clash with reality; and when they do, we know that there is a reality; that there is something to remind us of the fact that our ideas may be mistaken. And this is why the realist is right" (p. 117).

However, given the relativist manifestos, we can no longer seriously contend that there is a preinterpreted "given" or even any theory-neutral data, so the test of truth cannot be simply by correspondence with the "facts." As a consequence, a new realism has emerged (Bhaskar, 1978, 1979; Harré, 1970, 1972; Manicas & Secord, 1983), building on such arguments as Toulmin's (1972), which we have already examined. In this view,

> the practices of science generate their own *rational* criteria in terms of which theory is accepted or rejected. The crucial point is that it is possible for these criteria to be rational precisely because on realist terms, there is a world that exists independently of cognizing experience. (Manicas & Secord, 1983, p. 401)

That is, we might indeed be found to be wrong in the light of reality testing, but one must be an ontological realist in order to be an epistemological fallibilist. Such an approach has sometimes been called *critical-realist* because it posits that causal relationships exist outside the human mind, but that they are not perceived with total accuracy due to our fallible sensory and intellectual capacities (Cook & Campbell, 1979).

In this new realism, "scientific laws are *not* about events or classes of events, regularly or stochastically conjoined, but are about the causal properties of structures that exist and operate in the world" (Manicas & Secord, 1983, p. 402). The intent is to construct testable explanatory theories about such structures and their properties in terms of generative mechanisms or causal powers and their enabling conditions (Secord, 1986). In the realist view, things never operate in a closed fashion, which is why we are confronted by probabilities, patterns, and tendencies. Events always derive from a complex of multiple causes at many different levels. Through experimentation we attempt to create closure in an effort to test specific relationships, but we need theories about the operative structures and their causal properties in order to do this. Finally, because events derive from complexes of causal processes operating in open systems, the realist theory of science rejects the covering-law model of scientific explanation along with its instrumentalist implication that explanation and prediction are symmetrical, which holds only under conditions of closure (cf. Robinson, 1984). Scientific explanation for the realist is not subsumption under laws, but causal explication. That is, because it is unlikely that "systems of organized complexity exhibit simple, widespread noninteractive regularities, . . . [the aim] is the development of a sense of how some of these systems of organized complexity work" (D'Andrade, 1986, p. 39).

Once again, the message for validity theory is clear and straightforward. In the realist view, construct validation should develop representations of the processes that could reasonably underlie test consistencies and task performance. For example, this might entail the formulation and testing of alternative causal models that generate or account for the observed performance consistencies. As cognitive psychology in general and information-processing models of cognition in particular have advanced over the years, producing powerful experimental and quantitative techniques of task decomposition, this modeling approach has become much more salient in measurement circles. Although in one form it has only recently been incorporated into the validity literature under the rubric of *construct representation* (Embretson, 1983), the explicit probing of the processes productive of performance has long been part of the validation repertoire (Cronbach, 1971; Cronbach & Meehl, 1955).

The contrasting implications for validity theory of instrumentalist and realist views of theoretical entities or constructs become more illuminating if they are cast explicitly in terms of the relation between test and nontest indicants of the construct. Three ontological perspectives on the relation between test and nontest consistencies will be examined. First is the view that both test and related nontest consistencies are manifestations of real traits or else are attributable to real stimulus contingencies in the environment. The second view summarizes test and nontest consistencies in terms of a set of theoretical constructs and the relationships among them, with meaning grounded in the theoretical network rather than in the real world. Finally, in the third viewpoint, test and nontest consistencies are attributable to real trait or environmental entities but are only understood in terms of constructs that summarize their empirical properties in relation to other constructs in a theoretical system (Messick, 1981a).

A portrayal of a psychological realist position is presented in Figure 2.1. Some characteristic or trait of the person *causes* both the test and nontest behaviors, which are mutually related by virtue of common or related causes. Some adherents of this realist position would likely stop short of attributing causality to traits, which are viewed merely as dispositions to respond in certain ways under certain circumstances (Alston, 1975; Zuroff, 1986). Rather, consistencies in test and nontest behaviors are deemed to be *manifestations* of traits, which organize behavior or otherwise reflect potential for response regularities. At issue in relation to the focal test behaviors in the left side of the figure are both nontest behaviors and scores on nonfocal tests of related variables, as represented on the right side of the figure. The boxes enclosing the focal test behaviors and the nontest behaviors in the figure are darkened, as is the curved line of relationship between them, to emphasize that these are the primary observables that are available.

The nontest behaviors are surrounded by a situational context of environmental influences that can modulate empirical relationships, as can the measurement context surrounding the focal test behaviors. Furthermore, the focal trait is embedded in a personality structure implicating other related traits. Thus, one motive or need, for example, might operate in the service of another motive or need in a particular situation. Or, one characteristic of the person, such as defensiveness, might interfere with the measurement of other personal characteristics in a given measurement context. If for "trait" we substitute "response class" and for "personality structure" we read "focal stimulus contingencies," a behavioral–realist approach is thereby sketched. In this case, the test and nontest behaviors are related because they fall in the same response class, being elicited and maintained by the same or related reinforcement conditions. In realist formulations, theoretical entities, whether traits or otherwise, are referred to directly by constructs, which are themselves embedded in theoretical or causal models of personality structure and functioning or of task performance. The bottom circle in Figure 2.1 does double duty by representing both the real trait and the realist's direct construction of it as well as the real personality structure and the realist's causal model of personality.

The interpretation of test behaviors in terms of constructs that have no supposed reality outside the theoretical system of the investigator is schematized in Figure 2.2. The circle representing the nomological network in Figure 2.2 is drawn to overlap the situational and measurement contexts to signal the need to take account of these factors in construct interpretation, either through a unified theory of the construct-in-context or through collateral theories of context effects. The dashed lines represent three major ways that constructs are inferred: from consistencies in test behaviors, from consistencies in nontest behaviors, and from consistent relationships between the two. The double arrows on these dashed lines indicate not only that constructs are inferred from such consistencies but also that in other circumstances they imply or predict such consistencies.

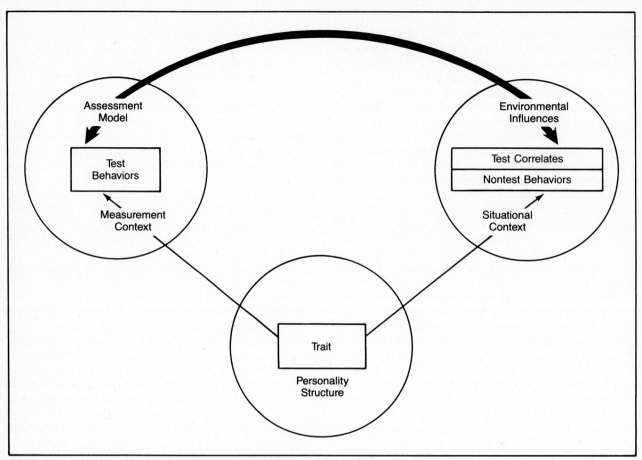

FIGURE 2.1 Realist view

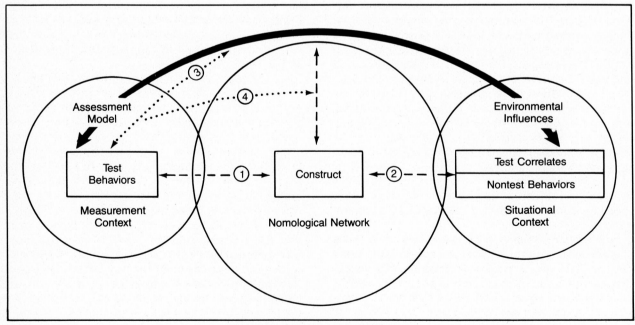

FIGURE 2.2 Constructivist view

The circled numbers in Figure 2.2 refer to some recurrent questions in construct validation that will be addressed in depth in the next main section (Loevinger, 1957, p. 643):

1. "To what extent does the test measure whatever is specified by a given construct?" Roughly speaking, this corresponds to what D. T. Campbell (1960) calls *trait validity.*

2. "To what extent does the construct embody a valid hypothesis?" By and large, this corresponds to what D. T. Campbell (1960) terms *nomological validity* and Embretson (1983) labels *nomothetic span.*

3. "To what extent does the test measure . . . [something] that 'really' exists?"—that is, in terms of observed consistency, not reified construct. This is the basic and prior question of behavioral consistency in test performance, which indicates that "something" is indeed being measured.

4. "How well does the proposed interpretation correspond to what is measured by the test?" Essentially, this amounts to what Loevinger (1957) calls *substantive validity,* which appraises how well the test interpretation captures the nature of that "something."

Question 3 examines the magnitude and consistency of relationships, both internal to the test and external to other measures, that is, the structural aspects of internal and external relationships. Question 4 examines the content and nature of internal and external relationships, that is, their substantive aspects. Internal aspects, both structural and substantive, are incorporated in Embretson's (1983) concept of *construct representation,* whereas external aspects are incorporated in her notion of *nomothetic span.* For Peak (1953), the structural consistencies entailed in Question 3 provide evidence of "functional unities," and the remaining questions bear on the validity of interpretation of those functional unities.

In this constructivist view depicted in Figure 2.2, the main function of constructs is to provide inductive summaries of observed relationships as a basis for elaborating networks of theoretical laws (Beck, 1950; Cronbach & Meehl, 1955). Constructs thus provide organized interpretations of observed behaviors, as well as a means of predicting previously unobserved behavioral consistencies from the theoretical implications of the nomological network. There is no implication that the constructs reflect existential reality but, rather, instrumental utility. This view has a mustiness of logical constructionism about it. It reflects the spirit if not the extent of Russell's (1917) "supreme maxim" of scientific philosophy: "Wherever possible, logical constructions are to be substituted for inferred entities" (p. 155).

A critical–realist, or more apropos, a constructive-realist approach to the interpretation of test and nontest behaviors is diagrammed in Figure 2.3. This perspective is realist because it assumes that traits and other causal entities exist outside the theorist's mind; it is constructive–realist because it assumes that these entities cannot be comprehended directly but must be viewed through constructions of that mind. By attributing reality to causal entities but simultaneously requiring a theoretical construction of observed relationships, this approach

aspires to attain the explanatory richness of the realist position while limiting metaphysical excesses through rational analysis. At the same time, constructive–realists hope to retain the predictive and summarizing advantages of the constructivist view. According to Beck (1950), in contrast to inferred real entities, "the function of constructs is to preserve and summarize; their virtue is metaphysical chastity, not scientific pregnancy" (p. 78). But the constructive–realists want to have it both ways.

An especially vigorous proponent of constructive–realism is Jane Loevinger, who argued that the term

> *construct* connotes construction and artifice; yet what is at issue is validity with respect to exactly what the psychologist does not construct: the validity of the test as a measure of traits which exist prior to and independently of the psychologist's act of measuring. It is true that psychologists never know traits directly but only through the glass of their constructs, but the data to be judged are manifestations of traits, not manifestations of constructs. (1957, p. 642)

By including both real traits and hypothetical constructs as mediating variables between test and nontest consistencies, this perspective makes explicit in Figure 2.3 a new line of relationship that was implicit in the realist schematic of Figure 2.1, namely, the relation between the construct and its referent trait. This relation between the trait and our current best understanding of it becomes important in our later deliberations —not so much because the construct might be completely off target, which is usually ultimately caught by reality testing, but because the construct might be biased in more subtle ways as a representation of the trait. A construct may be biased, as we shall see, by virtue of its inclusion in a particular theoretical network that is incomplete or tangential to the operation of the trait. Or, more problematic because more pervasive, a construct can be biased by an ideological overlay of value connotations. There is a big difference between claiming that the theory of trait X is false and being able to say that the theory is about trait X but what it claims is wrong or biased. Technically speaking, instrumentalists can state the former but not the latter, because according to them there is no trait X (van Fraassen, 1977).

Nonetheless, this treatment of the constructive–realist viewpoint is not meant to imply that for every construct there is a counterpart reality or cause in the person or in the situation or interaction (Leary, 1984; Messick, 1981a). On the contrary, many useful constructs, especially higher-order constructs such as "ego" or "self," are employed within this framework as heuristic devices for organizing observed relationships, with no necessary presumption of real entities underlying them. The attribution of reality to such constructs as "working class" and "middle class" or "childhood" and "adolescence" is similarly debatable. Rather, the constructive–realist position of Figure 2.3 might be thought of as an overlay of Figure 2.2 on Figure 2.1, in which some constructs have real referents while others do not. As an overlay, the circle surrounding "construct" should be considered to be enlarged to include not only nomological networks but also causal models and other ways of representing constructs and their measures.

A similar distinction between realistic and nonrealistic uses of constructs in science was drawn by Shapere (1977). He held that the argument between instrumentalists and realists over

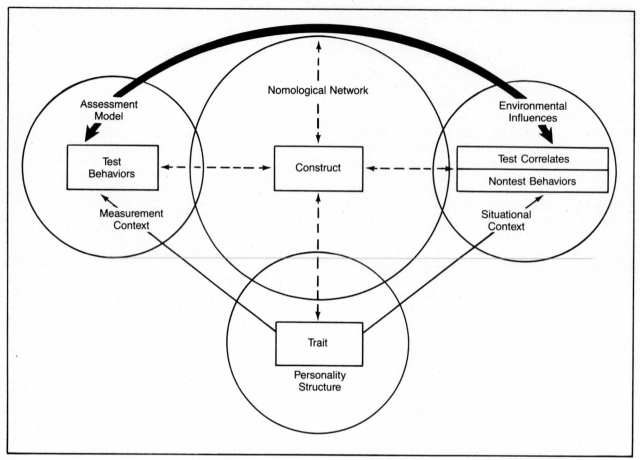

FIGURE 2.3 Constructive–realist view

the ontological status of constructs is based on the outworn theoretical-versus-observational distinction and must be reappraised in the light of his concept of scientific domains. In some of the patterns of scientific reasoning illuminated by the study of domains, Shapere discerns a distinction between whether or not a theoretical entity exists and whether or not it is convenient and useful to attribute to theoretical entities characteristics that they could not really have. The former constructs are referred to as *existence concepts* and the latter as *idealization concepts.*

The validity literature in general and the construct validity literature in particular has been severely criticized for being philosophically inconsistent (Norris, 1983). At one point or another, each of the criteria of truth has been either explicitly or tacitly invoked—whether coherence, correspondence, instrumentalist, or rationalist. At the same time, realist and instrumentalist interpretations of constructs occur side by side. But this melange is by no means inconsistent if some constructs refer to real entities while others do not, if the meaning of some constructs derives from theoretical relationships while others reflect causal properties of operative structures in the real world, or if realistic and nonrealistic uses of constructs occur in the same theory.

To be sure, at an intuitive level, many validity theorists

speak sometimes in instrumental and sometimes in realist terms, Cronbach (1971) being a case in point (Norris, 1983). But on reflection, Cronbach (in press) prefers instrumentalism on the grounds that the constructs in education and psychology seem "closer to common sense than to some presumed structure of Nature" (p. 14), and because validation is expected to follow the same path in both realist and instrumentalist frameworks. Yet, for reasons we have just examined in detail, this latter may not necessarily be the case—unless, of course, one systematically interprets causal explanations as merely useful fictions.

In this extended review of developments in the philosophy of science, we have seen that validity conceptions are not uniquely tied to any particular philosophical position but, rather, are congenial with aspects of multiple positions. Just as alternative philosophical views were articulated in reaction to the shortcomings of previous formulations, so validity theory also evolved over time, taking into account many of the same critical points. Before proceeding to our coverage of validity theory and methodology per se, however, we will briefly examine some prominent theories of inquiry. The intent is to illuminate the point that the philosophical foundations of validity and validation combine elements not only from multiple philosophical but also from multiple methodological perspectives.

From Formal to Recursive Systems of Inquiry

It will be recalled that in the fourth edition of his basic textbook, Cronbach (1984) referred to content, criterion-oriented, and construct validation as "methods of inquiry." This usage serves to highlight the fact that test validation is a process of *inquiry* into the adequacy and appropriateness of interpretations and actions based on test scores. We next examine five broad modes or systems of inquiry which, singly or in combination, afford multiple frameworks for guiding the conceptualization and conduct of validation procedures. These inquiry systems derive from the efforts of Churchman (1971) and his colleagues (Mitroff, 1974; Mitroff & Sagasti, 1973) to recast some of the major theories of epistemology in a way that makes them more directly pertinent to the knowledge-acquisition and model-building goals of the practicing scientist. Associated with each of these systems as an eponym is the name of the philosopher who, for Churchman, best captures the spirit of the corresponding system. Accordingly, these "inquiring" systems, as Churchman calls them, are labeled Leibnizian, Lockean, Kantian, Hegelian, and Singerian (Churchman, 1971; Singer, 1959).

Each inquiring system has its own building blocks or elementary information units for representing a problem, and each has a "guarantor" for ensuring the validity of the final information or problem representation. A *Leibnizian* inquiring system entails a formal or symbolic approach to problem representation. Starting with a set of primitive "analytic truths" and a system of rules or operations for generating theoretical propositions deductively, an expanding network of increasingly general "contingent truths" is developed. The guarantors or standards of validity of a Leibnizian inquiry system are the specification of what constitutes the proof of a derived proposition, along with such systems properties as internal consistency, completeness, and comprehensiveness. A *Lockean* inquiring system entails an empirical and inductive approach to problem representation. Starting with an elementary data set of experiential judgments or observations and some consensually accepted methods for generating factual propositions inductively, an expanding network of "facts" is produced. The standard of validity of a Lockean inquiry system is the consensus of experts on the objectivity, or lack of bias, with respect to the data and methods.

Both the Leibnizian and the Lockean approaches are best suited for attacking well-structured problems, that is, problems for which there is a sufficiently clear definition or consensus for them to be amenable to known methods. For ill-structured problems, where the major issue is to formulate the nature of the problem itself, or for ostensibly well-defined problems where the consensual basis is open to question, the three remaining inquiring systems are more apropos. In a Lockean system, agreement about problem solution is a signal to terminate inquiry. But in Kantian, Hegelian, and Singerian systems, agreement is often a stimulus to probe more deeply.

A *Kantian* inquiring system entails the deliberate formulation or identification of alternative perspectives on problem representation, each of which contains both Leibnizian and Lockean components. The Kantian approach thereby explic-itly recognizes the strong intertwining of theory and data. Specifically, a Kantian inquiring system starts with at least two alternative theories or problem representations, from each of which are developed corresponding alternative data sets or fact networks. Contrariwise, the Kantian approach might begin with an existing fact network, for which alternative theories are then formulated. The alternative perspectives, although to some degree complementary, are potentially divergent but not antagonistic. From these multiple alternative interpretations, the hope is that one of them might be identified that is best in some sense or several identified that are best in different senses. The standard of validity for a Kantian inquiry system is the goodness of fit or match between the theory and its associated data. The Kantian approach is suitable for moderately ill-structured problems, where diverse perspectives need to be examined in order to be able to conceptualize the issues, as in dealing with a complex social problem such as alcoholism or a complex theoretical problem such as the nature of achievement motivation.

A *Hegelian* or dialectical inquiring system entails the deliberate formulation or identification of rival or antagonistic counterperspectives on problem representation. Specifically, the Hegelian approach starts with at least two antithetical or contrary theories, which are then applied to a single common data set. It is hoped that this dialectical confrontation between rival interpretations of the same data will expose the contrary assumptions of the competing models to open examination and policy debate. The guarantor of a Hegelian inquiry system is conflict. Indeed, a number of rhetorical devices, such as critique and rebuttal, are often used in scientific debate to intensify conflict—not so much because the "truth will out," but because tacit assumptions and latent inconsistencies will be revealed. Perhaps even a creative synthesis of the opposing views can be brought about.

In the dialectical technology of the Hegelian approach, the debate is not between people but between ideas. The scientist is called upon to "identify with the enemy" and to make contrary conceptions look as good as possible in the formulation of the counterperspective—a psychologically demanding requirement, to be sure. By confronting this counterperspective, the scientist may come to realize not only that some of the arguments in support of his or her own position are open to serious question, but also that there are common as well as disparate assumptions on both sides of the debate offering grounds for agreement as well as disagreement (Churchman, 1968). Hegelian inquiry is best suited for "wickedly" ill-structured problems where there is intense disagreement over the inherent nature of the problem itself, as in dealing with a conflictful social problem such as abortion or a conflictful theoretical problem such as the determinants of intelligence. It often becomes apparent in such Hegelian inquiry that the intense disagreement arises not only because of contrary theoretical or scientific assumptions but also contrary value assumptions.

Some key differences among the last three approaches are succinctly characterized by Churchman:

The Lockean inquirer displays the "fundamental" data that all experts agree are accurate and relevant, and then builds a consistent story out of these. The Kantian inquirer displays the same story from different points of view, emphasizing thereby that what is put into the story by the internal mode of representation is not given from the outside. But the Hegelian inquirer, using the same data, tells two stories, one supporting the most prominent policy on one side, the other supporting the most prominent policy on the other side. (1971, p. 177)

As we shall see, the Singerian inquirer, by taking recursive perspectives on problem representation, transforms one mode of storytelling into another and tells stories not only about the other stories but about the other storytellers.

Singer (1959) contends that just as the reality of any aspect of the world depends on observation, so the reality of an observing mind depends on its being observed. So, too, the reality of an inquiring system depends on its being "observed" by another inquiring system. Indeed, he suggests that what is fundamental or "given" in one inquiring system is an issue to be deliberated by another inquiring system that is observing the first one in its problem-solving activities. Hence, a central feature of Singerian inquiry is that each type of inquiring system can be observed or processed by the methodologies of the other types in an effort to elucidate or disrupt the distinctive properties of the target inquiry process.

Another central feature of Singerian inquiry is its emphasis on explicit probing of the ethical implications of scientific models. The prominence of ethics in this system derives from Singer's (1959) insistence that science should be based not on a logic of indicatives but on a logic of imperatives. That is, in place of statements such as "X is P," Singer would substitute something like "X is to be taken as having property P plus or minus error." As Churchman put it,

> The "is taken to be" is a self-imposed imperative of the community. Taken in the context of the whole Singerian theory of inquiry and progress, the imperative has the status of an ethical judgment. . . . [Its] acceptance may lead to social actions outside of inquiry, or to new kinds of inquiry, or whatever. Part of the community's judgment is concerned with the appropriateness of these actions from an ethical point of view. (1971, p. 202)

Thus the perennial problem of how to go from "is" to "ought" is no problem at all for the Singerian inquirer. The system speaks exclusively in "ought" statements; any "is" statements, when they occur, are merely convenient stratagems for reducing uncertainty in the discourse.

In sum, then, a *Singerian* inquiring system starts with the set of other inquiring systems (Leibnizian, Lockean, Kantian, Hegelian) and applies any system recursively to another system, including itself. The intent is to elucidate the distinctive technical and value assumptions underlying each system application and to integrate the scientific and ethical implications of the inquiry. The guarantor of a Singerian inquiry system is progress, or improvement through successive approximation. The system is an exceptionally fertile source of methodological heuristics because the recursive feature of Singerian inquiry, by having each inquiring system process every other system including itself, generates a five-by-five table of research strategies, as seen in Table 2.2.

By far the bulk of educational and psychological research falls in the four cells in the upper left of Table 2.2. Historically, the research emphasis in these fields has been on theory devel-

opment and empirical fact finding, followed by the empirical testing of theoretical implications and the theoretical formalization of observed fact networks, that is, on Leibnizian and Lockean approaches and the interaction of the two. The remainder of the table, however, testifies to the richness of other modes of inquiry. But only recently have Kantian and Hegelian approaches been seriously or extensively assayed in education or psychology—for example, by explicitly testing alternative structural or causal models (Bentler, 1980: James, Mulaik, & Brett, 1982; Jöreskog & Sörbom, 1979), by statistically appraising plausible rival hypotheses (Cook & Campbell, 1979), or by jointly using multiple methods of data collection and analysis to complement each other and to compensate for the strengths and limitations or biases of each (Shadish, Cook, & Houts, 1986). And systematic attention to the ethical implications of scientific theories and findings as an integral part of the inquiry process is just beginning to emerge into view.

To undertake the Kantian and Hegelian approaches (as well as the Singerian approach when applied to these two inquiring systems) requires the existence or generation of alternative or antithetical theories, respectively. Furthermore, these theories must be amenable to being compared in some sense, and such comparisons are problematic to the extent that extreme relativistic positions are adhered to. Feyerabend (1975), for example, also adopted a dialectical approach, but it foundered because his strong view of the theory-dependence of facts meant that alternative theories were, in principle, incommensurable for him (Suppe, 1977d). Some sort of common meeting ground is needed, such as commensurate observational reports or an uninterpreted observation language or, as Shapere (1977) proposes, theoretical terms that are "unloaded" to the level of compatible background theory. For then we can come to the proving ground of reality testing.

In this regard, we hold with Cook and Campbell that the relativists

> have exaggerated the role of comprehensive theory in scientific advance and have made experimental evidence seem almost irrelevant. Instead, exploratory experimentation . . . [has] repeatedly been the source of great scientific advances, providing the stubborn, dependable, replicable puzzles that have justified theoretical efforts at solution." (1979, p. 24)

Once again, this appears reminiscent of Shapere's (1977) notion of the function of facts in a scientific domain. The point is that, because observations and meanings are differentially theory-laden and theories are differentially value-laden, appeals to multiple perspectives on meaning and values are needed to illuminate latent assumptions and action implications in the measurement of constructs (Messick, 1982b).

TEST VALIDATION AS INQUIRY PROCESS AND SCIENTIFIC ENTERPRISE

Test validation as a process of inquiry can legitimately call on any of these inquiring systems as well as on the research strategies derived from their interactions. The function of test validation is to marshal evidence and arguments in support of, or counter to, proposed interpretations and uses of test scores. Evidence and arguments derived from any of the inquiring systems and from any or all of the cells in Table 2.2 are fair game in this as in any other scientific enterprise. We should not wear a hair shirt or be defensive about the source of our evidence and arguments. After all, within loose limits of scientific respectability, the issue is not the *source* of the evidence and arguments but, rather, their nature and quality.

All of these sources of evidence have respectable foundations and, with the possible exception of the comprehensive Singerian approach, all have their limitations. The major limitation is shortsightedness with respect to other possibilities, which is at its worst if we stick with one inquiring system or with one cell or limited combination of cells in Table 2.2. Nor

should we be so shortsighted as to think that the five inquiring systems delineated by Churchman (1971) are exhaustive of the class of such philosophical systems. But an important cautionary note: This very variety of methodological approaches in the validational armamentarium, in the absence of specific criteria for choosing among them, makes it possible to select evidence opportunistically and to ignore negative findings (D. T. Campbell, 1960). Some form of disciplined thinking must be applied to forestall this. As we shall see, such discipline will stem partly from methodological maxims insisting on both convergent and discriminant evidence. But it will derive mainly from the construct theories themselves and the theoret-

TABLE 2.2 Taxonomy of Research Strategies from the Interaction of Inquiring Systems

INQUIRING SYSTEM	PROCESSED AS				
	LEIBNIZIAN	LOCKEAN	KANTIAN	HEGELIAN	SINGERIAN
Formal systems (Leibnizian)	Metatheory; theory for choice of specific model.	Empirical testing of theoretical implications.	Generation of ideas, of alternative constructs, of alternative theories. Brainstorming	Generation of conflicting or contrary ideas and theories.	Derivation of scientific and value assumptions underlying the theory; its ethical implications.
Empirical networks (Lockean)	Theoretical formalization of fact network; propositional basis for observed relations.	Data and inductive integration of fact network into higher-order fact networks; evidence on the nature of the empirical evidence (e.g., reliability).	Trouble shooting. Generation of alternative hypotheses, of alternative relationships, of alternative fact networks. Problem identification.	Generation of plausible rival hypotheses.	Derivation of scientific and value assumptions underlying the empirical model; its ethical implications.
Alternative perspectives (Kantian)	Detailed formalization of alternative perspectives (ideas, relationships, hypotheses).	Testing empirical consequences of alternative perspectives.	Alternative futures. Elaboration of multiple perspectives; higher-order perspectives; integration of alternative perspectives. Problem clarification.	Conflict generation. Conflicting futures.	Scientific and value bases of multiple perspectives; ethical implications of futuristic planning.
Counter-perspectives (Hegelian)	Conflict resolution or suppression on theoretical grounds (negotiation, persuasion, regulation, legislation).	Conflict resolution or suppression on empirical grounds.	Conflict management.	Conflict enhancement (debate, rebuttal, cross-examination).	Scientific and value bases of conflicting perspectives and their ethical implications.
Recursive perspectives (Singerian)	Scientific theories of ethical ideas and implications (simulations of consequences).	Empirical data and fact networks for ethical ideas and implications (data on empirical consequences).	Alternative perspectives on ethical implications (alternative viewpoints).	Conflicting perspectives on ethical implications (conflicting viewpoints).	Value basis of the value basis. Ethics. Inquiry into the process of inquiry. Modeling the art of building models.

Adapted from "Epistemology as General Systems Theory: An Approach to the Design of Complex Decision-Making Experiments" by I. I. Mitroff and F. Sagasti, 1973, *Philosophy of Social Sciences, 3*, p. 130. Copyright 1973 by Wilfrid Laurier University Press. Adapted by permission.

ical expectations about data patterns derived therefrom, which provide a rational basis for linking the specific inferences to be made to the forms of evidence needed to support them.

As we have already seen, test validation began historically with a Lockean emphasis on observed test-criterion relationships. Next added was a concern for Leibnizian–Lockean interactions as reflected in judgments of content relevance to a specified domain and in the empirical testing of construct implications. Kantian and Hegelian features then followed in connection with the discounting of plausible rival hypotheses. We turn next to an extended treatment of these topics as we consider the evidential basis of test interpretation and, later, of test use. We also invoke Singerian precepts for probing value implications as we examine the consequential bases of test interpretation and use. But the philosophical conceits of such labels aside, the major tasks remaining require an elucidation of problems and principles in assessing the meaning and consequences of measurement. The following quote from Margenau (1978) provides a fitting bridge between this discussion of philosophical frameworks for scientific inquiry—hence, for test validation—and the measurement issues addressed in the remainder of this chapter:

> If observation denotes what is coercively given in sensation, that which forms the last instance of appeal in every scientific explanation or prediction, and if theory is the constructive rationale serving to understand and regularize observations, then measurement is the process that mediates between the two, the conversion of the immediate into constructs via number or, viewed the other way, the contact of reason with Nature. (p. 199)

The Evidential Basis of Test Interpretation

As indicated in Table 2.1, the evidential basis of test interpretation is construct validity. And construct validity, in essence, comprises the evidence and rationales supporting the trustworthiness of score interpretation in terms of explanatory concepts that account for both test performance and relationships with other variables. Next, we will discuss some overarching requirements of construct validity and their function in discounting two general types of threat to interpretive meaning—namely, the role of convergent and discriminant evidence in protecting against both construct underrepresentation and construct-irrelevant variance in the test. Then we will examine content, substantive, structural, and external aspects of construct validity and how they are combined in the modeling of underlying processes and the appraising of construct implications. Finally, after a detailed account of types of data and analyses relevant to construct validation, we will explore the generalizability and limits of score meaning.

Evidence to Counter Threats to Construct Validity

In evaluating the adequacy of construct measurement, two closely connected points need to be disentangled. One is that tests are not only imprecise or fallible by virtue of random errors of measurement but also inevitably imperfect as exemplars of the construct they are purported to assess. Tests are imperfect measures of constructs because they either leave out something that should be included according to the construct theory or else include something that should be left out, or both. The second point is that two different kinds of evidence are needed in construct validation, one to assess the degree to which the construct's implications are realized in empirical score relationships and the other to argue that these relationships are not attributable instead to distinct alternative constructs.

CONSTRUCT UNDERREPRESENTATION AND IRRELEVANT TEST VARIANCE

Although there are a number of specific threats to construct validity, most of which are addressed in later parts of this main section, they all fall into two major classes or types (Cook & Campbell, 1979). In one type, referred to as "construct underrepresentation," the test is too narrow and fails to include important dimensions or facets of the construct. In the other type, referred to as "surplus construct irrelevancy"—or more pointedly as "construct-irrelevant test variance"—the test contains excess reliable variance that is irrelevant to the interpreted construct. Such construct-irrelevant test variance constitutes a contaminant with respect to score interpretation but not necessarily with respect to criterion prediction, because the criterion *measure* might be contaminated in the same way. A salient issue in a later section revolves around whether the so-called contaminant in the criterion measure is relevant or irrelevant to actual criterion performance.

There are two basic kinds of construct-irrelevant test variance. In the language of ability and achievement testing, these might be called "construct-irrelevant difficulty" and "construct-irrelevant easiness." In the case of construct-irrelevant difficulty, aspects of the task that are extraneous to the focal construct make the test irrelevantly more difficult for some individuals or groups. An example is the intrusion of undue reading comprehension requirements in a test of subject-matter knowledge. In general, construct-irrelevant difficulty leads to construct scores that are invalidly low for those individuals adversely affected (e.g., knowledge scores of poor readers).

In contrast, construct-irrelevant easiness occurs when extraneous clues in item or test formats permit some individuals to respond correctly in ways irrelevant to the construct being assessed. For example, a teacher may write multiple-choice items in which the longest options are most likely to be correct, and some students learn to capitalize on that clue. Or, respondents might endorse questionnaire items simply on the basis of their social desirability rather than by reflecting on the specific content of the items. Construct-irrelevant easiness can also derive from effective test-taking strategies such as those for guessing or time allocation. However, for some constructs— intelligence, for instance, at least in its planning aspects (R. J.

Sternberg, 1985a)—such sources of easiness may not be irrelevant.

Examinees who benefit from construct-irrelevant easiness in the test and thus attain improved scores are called "test wise" (Millman, Bishop, & Ebel, 1965; Sarnacki, 1979). In general, test-wiseness leads to construct scores that are invalidly high. But there are instances, as with effective time allocation, that are better characterized as forestalling the attainment of scores that are invalidly low, much as does test familiarity or low test anxiety (Messick, 1982a). On the other hand, ineffective test-taking strategies, which are tantamount to construct-irrelevant difficulty, often lead to construct scores that are invalidly low. It should be noted that both construct-irrelevant difficulty and construct-irrelevant easiness, when they occur, are important sources of invalidity with respect to construct interpretation.

In regard to construct underrepresentation, let us consider three separate measures of a complex construct having three facets, A, B, and C. Suppose the first measure taps facets A and B, along with some irrelevant variance X; the second measure taps B and C with extraneous variance Y; and, the third measure taps A, C, and Z. For example, the complex construct of general self-concept might embrace multiple facets such as academic self-concept, social self-concept, and physical self-concept (Marsh & Shavelson, 1985; Shavelson, Hubner, & Stanton, 1976). One measure (tapping academic and social self-concept) might be cast in a self-rating format where the major contaminant is the tendency to respond in a socially desirable manner; another measure (tapping social and physical self-concept) cast in a true-false format where extraneous variance stems from the response set of acquiescence; and, a third measure (tapping academic and physical self-concept) in a 7-point Likert format of "strongly agree" to "strongly disagree" where irrelevant variance derives from extremity response set.

By virtue of the overlapping components, the three measures will intercorrelate positively and appear to converge in the measurement of "something," presumably the overall complex construct. Yet, each measure is underrepresentative of some aspect of the construct. A composite of the three measures would cover all three aspects and, furthermore, the construct-relevant variance would cumulate in the composite score while the irrelevant variance would not. This is akin to increasing homogeneity by the control of heterogeneity, as advocated by Humphreys (1962).

Two points are to be underscored here, both of which will be addressed in detail in later sections. One is that the breadth of content specifications for a test should reflect the breadth of the construct invoked in score interpretation. The other is that we should strive mightily to avoid what Cook and Campbell (1979) call the "mono-operation bias": "Since single operations both underrepresent constructs and contain irrelevancies, construct validity will be lower in single exemplar research than in research where each construct is multiply operationalized in order to triangulate on the referent" (p. 65). This means that measurement research in general and construct validation in particular should, as a matter of principle, entail multiple measures of each construct under scrutiny. When a single test

score is employed, however, one strategy for triangulating on the referent construct is to incorporate multiple item or task formats in a total-score composite.

CONVERGENT AND DISCRIMINANT EVIDENCE

Now suppose our three tests, in addition to their unique irrelevant variance, each taps facets A and B but none includes facet C (e.g., academic and social self-concept but not physical self-concept). The three tests will still intercorrelate positively and appear to converge in the measurement of something, presumably the *total* construct. But now even the composite of the three is underrepresentative of the overall referent construct because facet C is nowhere assessed. Hence, we have a misleading instance of convergent evidence that the three tests indeed intercorrelate as expected from the construct theory. It is misleading unless the research is broad enough to note that some implications of the theory—namely, those derived from facet C—are not realized in data patterns associated with these three tests. Thus, when only certain convergent findings are forthcoming, one should also assess the possibility that other convergent findings equally expected from the theory might fail to obtain.

As a final supposition, assume that the irrelevant variance X (e.g., social desirability response set) is common to all of the tests in the two previous illustrations. The three tests will now intercorrelate partly (and in other examples that could be constructed, solely) because of shared construct-irrelevant variance. Therefore, convergent evidence, showing that measures intercorrelate as implied by the construct theory, is never enough. In addition, we need discriminant evidence that the tests are not related to some other construct that could account for the intercorrelations.

A rich source of such rival constructs is the measurement method itself. Each measure may be thought of as a trait-method unit or, more generally, a construct-method unit, that is, as a union of construct variance with procedural or method variance not specific to that construct (D. T. Campbell & Fiske, 1959). Method variance includes all systematic effects associated with a particular measurement procedure that are extraneous to the focal construct being measured. Method variance includes, for example, the effects of recognition on multiple-choice tests of recall or knowledge retrieval and of verbal ability on paper-and-pencil tests of mechanical aptitude. Further examples are halo effects and other biases on rating scales, response styles on questionnaires, and cognitive styles on information-processing tasks (Messick, 1983). As a consequence, convergent and discriminant data patterns for multiple measures or exemplars of a construct all based on the same procedural method, such as ratings or paper-and-pencil tests, might still be grossly misleading by virtue of shared method variance. Hence, to render method irrelevancies heterogeneous, one should avoid not only a mono-operation bias but a mono-method bias as well, that is, one needs not only multiple measures of the construct but also distinctly different methods of measurement (Cook & Campbell, 1979). Techniques for appraising the import of method variance will be discussed in a later section.

Convergent evidence signifies that the measure in question is coherently related to other measures of the same construct as well as to other variables that it should relate to on theoretical grounds. Discriminant evidence signifies that the measure is not related unduly to exemplars of other distinct constructs. Discriminant evidence is particularly critical for discounting plausible rival hypotheses to the construct interpretation (D. T. Campbell & Fiske, 1959). For construct measurement, *both* convergent *and* discriminant evidence are needed in order to be supportive or corroborative—which should be understood, following the admonitions of Popper and others, as meaning "not yet disconfirmed." Failure to produce *either* convergent *or* discriminant evidence after serious attempts to do so would be disconfirmatory. The reference to "serious attempts" is meant as a warning that test unreliability and small sample size offer plausible rival hypotheses that low convergent correlations (presumably disconfirmatory) might be mistaken, while low discriminant correlations (presumably corroborative) might similarly be mistaken. That is, low correlations, disconfirmatory for a convergent expectation and corroborative for a discriminant expectation, might in each case reflect instead merely unreliable measures and data.

The previous remarks are couched in correlational terms and might be interpreted as being limited to the testing of theoretical implications à la nomological networks. But the points about construct underrepresentation and construct irrelevancy, as well as the need for both convergent and discriminant evidence, hold with equal force in other approaches to construct validation such as causal modeling of process or of generative mechanisms (as distinct from the basically correlational structural equation modeling of conditional dependencies). The causal model might simulate only part of the construct, not its entirety, and might include components that are irrelevant to the construct theory. Furthermore, the causal model must be evaluated not only in terms of convergent predictions of test performance consistencies, but also by showing that it is distinct from and in some sense better than alternative models for predicting those consistencies.

While positive convergent and discriminant findings are provisionally supportive or corroborative of construct measurement, the implications of negative evidence are more complicated. Negative evidence may be interpreted in three or four ways: The test might not capture the construct very well, the construct theory might be faulty, the auxiliary hypotheses supporting the derivation of testable empirical consequences might be deficient, the experimental conditions might not sustain a proper evaluation, or any combination of these might be the case. As a consequence, some strategies or heuristics are needed to help us proceed.

For instance, in the second illustration, where all three tests measured both the *A* and *B* facets of the construct but not the *C* facet, the finding of certain convergent evidence with the failure to obtain other expected convergence might lead one to revise the measures first before modifying the theory. However, after repeated unsuccessful attempts to incorporate facet *C*, one might decide to make the construct theory less inclusive and to restrict the construct interpretation of the measures to only *A* and *B*. In other cases, given the puzzle of an entrenched construct theory confronted with negative empirical findings,

one might first attempt to modify and test different auxiliary hypotheses in an effort to explain the results via that route (Putnam, 1977).

The two types of threat to construct validity and the role of both convergent and discriminant evidence in construct validation should be kept in mind in what follows. These considerations serve as background for our discussion of content, substantive, structural, and external aspects of construct validity, to which we now turn.

Considerations of Content in Test Interpretation

Traditional considerations of content treat the test as a sample from some specified behavioral domain or item universe about which inferences are to be drawn or predictions made. The key issues of content involve specification of the nature and boundaries of the domain as well as appraisal of the relevance and representativeness of the test items with respect to the domain. A latent issue involves the nature of the item sample itself—that is, whether it is a content sample, a behavioral sample, or a process sample—especially in relation to the form of judgmental evidence offered to support relevance and representativeness.

Historically, the erstwhile notion of content validity has been conceptualized in three closely related but distinct ways: in terms of how well the *content* of the test samples the content of the domain of interest (APA, 1954, 1966), the degree to which the *behaviors* exhibited in test performance constitute a representative sample of behaviors displayed in the desired domain performance (APA, 1974), and the extent to which the *processes* employed by the examinee in arriving at test responses are typical of the processes underlying domain responses (Lennon, 1956). Yet, in practice, content-related evidence usually takes the form of consensual professional judgments about the relevance of item content to the specified domain and about the representativeness with which the test content covers the domain content.

But inferences regarding behaviors require evidence of response or performance consistency and not just judgments of content, whereas inferences regarding processes require construct-related evidence (Cronbach, 1971; Loevinger, 1957). According to the 1985 *Standards* (APA, 1985), "methods classed in the content-related category thus should often be concerned with the psychological construct underlying the test as well as with the character of test content. There is often no sharp distinction between test content and test construct" (p. 11). Indeed, one can make a strong case that the word *often* should be deleted from both of the quoted sentences—that as a general rule, content-related inferences and construct-related inferences are inseparable.

Thus, the heart of the notion of so-called content validity is that the test items are samples of a behavioral domain or item universe about which inferences are to be drawn. But these inferences are likely to invoke, even if only tacitly, psychological processes or behaviors rather than mere surface content. In a quite literal sense, "test behavior is always utilized as a sign of non-test behavior. . . . The very fact that one set of behaviors occurs in a test situation and the other outside the test situation introduces an instrument error which is ignored by the concept of content validity" (Loevinger, 1957, p. 656). For example, students could demonstrate the ability to solve physical equations and quantitative physics problems correctly in the schematized test situation but display naive views of the same physical forces when confronted with real-world events (Caramazza, McCloskey, & Green, 1981; McCloskey, Caramazza, & Green, 1980).

Because of such context effects or irrelevant method variance, among other reasons, content-related evidence must always be viewed as part of a broader set of construct-related evidence supportive of score inferences. Even if the test tasks are a direct sample of domain tasks as in a job-sample test, content-based inferences implicitly rely on conceptions of test and domain meaning and, hence, on construct validity. This is so because, even under the best of domain sampling conditions, where test tasks and job tasks are viewed as members of the same behavioral class, content-based inferences are threatened by context effects (such as an evaluative atmosphere) that influence the test but not the job, at least not in the same way, or by situational factors (such as interpersonal attraction) that influence the job but not the test (Guion, 1977).

Content-related evidence is thus treated here explicitly as part of construct validity because we share with Loevinger (1957) "the conviction that considerations of content alone are not sufficient to establish validity even when the test content resembles the trait, and considerations of content cannot be excluded when the test content least resembles the trait" (p. 657). This is not to say that considerations of content are not extremely important, because the nature of the test content and the extensiveness of content coverage influence and limit the specifics of score inferences supported by other evidence. We turn now to the central content issues of domain specification and of the relevance and representativeness of the test as an exemplar of the domain.

THE ROLE OF CONSTRUCT THEORY IN DOMAIN SPECIFICATION

The nature of the behavioral domain about which inferences are to be drawn or predictions made becomes especially important at two points in the measurement process: first, at the stage of test construction, where domain specifications serve as a blueprint or guide for what kinds of items should be constructed or selected for inclusion in the test; second, at the stage of test use, where the relevance and coverage of the constructed test must be evaluated for applicability to a specific, possibly different applied domain. The central problem at either stage, of course, is determining how to conceptualize the domain. This way of posing the problem also points to a strategy for solution, namely, ultimately delineating the boundaries and facets of the domain in terms of some conceptual or construct theory of relevant behavior or performance.

A particular test use, to be sure, often affords an *ad hoc* basis for domain specification. As an instance, if the intended testing purpose is to predict job performance or to certify minimal or desirable levels of knowledge and skill for occupational or professional practice, the nature of the particular job or profes-

sional specialty delimits the domain of reference—as determined, for example, through job or task analysis. Or as another instance, if the intended testing purpose is to certify minimal or desirable levels of knowledge and skill acquired through a course of instruction or to evaluate the effectiveness of the instruction, the nature of the curriculum or of actual classroom experiences similarly serve to delimit the domain.

The role of construct theory in developing test specifications is not abrogated in these applied instances but, rather, displaced to the level of rationalizing job and curriculum specifications or of justifying the often implicit links between the knowledge, skills, and other attributes measured by the test and those required on the job or fostered by the curriculum. The issues and methods involved in establishing test specifications —as well as item relevance and representativeness—with respect to a particular job, curriculum, or course of instruction will be addressed in a later section on considerations of content in test use. Here we focus on more general issues of domain specification, relevance, and representativeness involved in the interpretation of what the scores measure—regardless of whether or not particular job performance, curriculum learning, or other applied functions are entailed.

We are concerned with linking the contents (or behaviors or processes) reflected in test responses to those reflected in domain responses because we wish to generalize test interpretations to nontest domain interpretations. And if construct theory is critical for test interpretation, it should not be surprising that construct theory is also deemed critical for domain specification. It will be recalled that Shapere (1977) defined a scientific domain as "the total body of information for which a theory is expected to account" (p. 559). More specifically for present purposes, the domain of reference is the total body of information for which the construct is expected to account. The relevance and representativeness of the test can then be judged in relation to that body of information.

To illustrate, let us consider the domain of achievement motivation. A conceptual analysis of the construct of need for achievement and its relevant theoretical and research literature led Jackson, Ahmed, and Heapy (1976) to specify six distinct dimensions or facets: competitiveness, concern for excellence, status with experts, status with peers, acquisitiveness, and achievement via independence. In the standard content-oriented approach, items would be devised for each of these facets and assembled into a test where the total score is interpreted as achievement motivation. The relevance and representativeness of the test would be evaluated in terms of consensual judgments rationally linking the items to the facets and attesting to the adequacy with which the facets are covered.

But this is rarely if ever enough, even if we discount the possibility of irrelevant test variance. Just because the domain is specified in terms of the body of information for which the construct is theoretically expected to account does not mean that the construct empirically accounts for the domain information in a complete or generalizable fashion. To appraise the generality of the construct with respect to domain information, and hence the level of construct generality advanced in test interpretation, requires examination of test content in relation to not just domain content but also the structure of response consistencies to the test items or tasks. Such consideration of response consistency takes us beyond test content per se into the realm of substantive and structural aspects of construct validity, addressed in the ensuing two major parts of this section.

As an illustration of these points, let us consider once again the six facets of achievement motivation. Jackson et al. (1976) devised multiple measures of each facet and, in terms of the structure of response consistencies, provided convergent and discriminant evidence to support six salient dimensions in this domain. It would seem important, then, to include items covering each facet in any representative measure of general achievement motivation. Yet, although the six dimensions were variously intercorrelated, a single second-order dimension interpretable as need for achievement did not emerge. Rather, three relatively independent second-order dimensions appeared that were interpretable as entrepreneurial competitiveness, need for status, and autonomous striving for excellence. There was little evidence that the total score over all six facets was interpretable as general "need for achievement" or, indeed, that a unitary construct could account at all for the structure of the specified domain. Under such circumstances, it would be less misleading to develop a profile of scores across three higher-order or six first-order dimensions or else to focus attention on one or another of the more restricted constructs such as concern for excellence (Jackson, 1967b).

It is sometimes proclaimed that correlational evidence is completely extraneous to issues of content relevance and representativeness (e.g., Cronbach, 1971). But this is in the sense that a specified domain and its associated test may actually be highly heterogeneous, in which case high item correlations would imply inadequate sampling or coverage. However, it is not that correlational evidence is irrelevant to considerations of content, but that *low* correlations should not necessarily be taken as a failure of test content to fit domain specifications or as an automatic reason to eliminate items from the test. Rather, correlational evidence is highly relevant to appraising whether the degree of homogeneity in the test is commensurate with the degree of homogeneity expected from the construct theory of the domain.

Nor should *high* correlations between measures of ostensibly distinct constructs or domains, such as quantitative reasoning and mathematical knowledge, necessarily lead to collapsing them into a single measure or blurring the distinction between them in interpretation. There might be other important discriminant evidence—such as different levels of attainment, differential responsiveness to direct instruction, differential involvement in aptitude-treatment interactions, different courses of development, or different process components—for keeping the measures and the constructs separate (Messick, 1984a).

Because the acceptability of high or low item correlations depends on the nature of the construct, the degree of item homogeneity or internal consistency bears on the construct validity of score interpretation (Anastasi, 1982; Loevinger, 1957). For example, higher item homogeneity might be expected on a test of addition than on a test of arithmetical problem solving. Another way of putting this is that a longer test or larger item sample might be needed to confidently estimate performance in the broader domain of problem solving than in the more limited domain of addition. Similarly, very high internal consistency would be good news for a brief questionnaire measure of concern over excellence, say, or of headache proneness, but not necessarily good news for a brief scale of the broader domains of achievement motivation or of neurotic tendencies (Paunonen, 1984; Paunonen & Jackson, 1985).

It is not enough, however, that construct theory should serve as a rational basis for specifying the boundaries and facets of the behavioral domain of reference. Such specification must also entail sufficient precision that items or tasks can be constructed or selected that are judged with high consensus to be relevant to the domain. This raises the issue of *domain clarity* (A. R. Fitzpatrick, 1983), which in its strongest form holds that the domain should be sufficiently well described that different item writers working independently from the same domain specifications would produce roughly comparable or even interchangeable measures (Ashton & Goldberg, 1973; Cronbach, 1971; Jackson, 1975). Indeed, Cronbach (1971) went so far as to suggest that if the alternative measures derived from such a duplicate-construction experiment were administered to the same individuals, the two sets of scores should be equivalent within standard errors of measurement. Such a favorable result would imply that the test performance was fully captured by the domain specifications and the test construction rules. This latter reference to test construction rules is a reminder that not only domain specifications but also test specifications are important in determining item or task relevance and representativeness, topics we will next address in tandem.

CONTENT RELEVANCE

Judgments of the relevance of test items or tasks to the intended score interpretation should take into account all aspects of the testing procedure that significantly affect test performance. These include, as we have seen, specification of the construct domain of reference in terms of topical content, typical behaviors, and underlying processes. Also needed are test specifications regarding stimulus formats and response alternatives, administration conditions (such as examinee instructions or time limits), and criteria for item scoring (Cronbach, 1971; Millman, 1973). Such test specifications indicate what aspects of the procedure are to be standardized or controlled and what aspects left variable because they do not systematically influence a person's score. That is, aspects of the testing procedure that are likely to influence the test score should be controlled and thereby included in the operational specification of what has been called the "universe of admissible operations" (Cronbach, Gleser, Nanda, & Rajaratnam, 1972). The nature of these admissible operations affords provisional limits in generalizing from test interpretations to domain interpretations. For example, measures of decision making under stringent time limts with instructions to emphasize quickness of reaction should not, in the absence of additional information, be generalized in score interpretation to decision making that emphasizes accuracy of response with no time limits or to decision making more broadly.

To the extent possible, stimulus and response specifications for test items should be based on what is known about nontest stimulus and response properties in the behavioral or trait domain under scrutiny. Indeed, the 1985 edition of the *Standards* (APA, 1985) stipulates that an important task in test construction, as well as in test evaluation, is to determine the degree to which the format and response properties of the test items or tasks are germane to the specified domain. For example, a verbal paper-and-pencil test of machine operation would be less relevant to the specified performance domain than a hands-on manipulation test. But what about the following two tests of alphabetizing skill: one requiring the examinee to indicate which of five randomly presented names would appear third in strictly alphabetical order; the other requiring that a given name be appropriately inserted in an alphabetical list?

Despite their surface similarity and a consensus of expert judgment that both tests were clearly relevant to the filing of alphabetical material, the two tests (both reliable) were found to be uncorrelated with each other (Mosier, 1947). Even from a restricted content perspective, this lack of correlation raises serious questions as to which test, if either, is relevant to the specified skill domain—unless one wishes to contend that a specific and circumscribed skill such as alphabetizing constitutes a highly heterogeneous domain. Thus, although the relevance of item format and content to the specified domain of reference is traditionally based on consensual expert judgment, such judgment can be fallible and needs to be buttressed by construct-related evidence as to what the items measure. This need is clear enough when the domain specification refers to the *processes* involved in domain performance, as underscored by Lennon (1956). But even when domain specifications adhere to strict behavioral descriptions of stimulus content and of the response or result that the examinee is asked to produce, the ultimate need for construct-related evidence cannot be denied—as illustrated in the example of alphabetizing tests.

Nonetheless, expert judgment is clearly an important ingredient in attesting to content and format relevance. Although relevance judgments are routinely made as an ongoing part of the professional test-development process, systematic attempts to document the consensus of multiple judges are far from commonplace at this test-construction stage. However, quantitative methods for systematically summarizing relevance judgments have been proposed and are increasingly being applied in test-development practice (Hambleton, 1980, 1984; Tittle, 1982). For example, content specialists' judgments of whether or not each item reflects the content defined by each dimension or facet of the domain specification could be numerically summarized in a statistical index of item-domain congruence (Rovinelli & Hambleton, 1977). Or, content experts could rate each item (say, on a 5-point scale) for the extent to which it reflects the domain facet that the item was intended to measure. Or as a third instance, content specialists could match each item to the domain facet they think the item best represents, if any. Furthermore, factor analysis or multidimensional scaling of relevance ratings by multiple judges can serve both to document the nature and degree of consensus reached and to uncover any differing points of view about the relevance of specific domain facets or item content (Tucker, 1962).

At the same time that content relevance is being judged, it is often convenient to make a systematic appraisal of the *technical quality* of the items or tasks included in the test (A. R.

Fitzpatrick, 1983; Hambleton, 1980, 1984). Because ambiguous or otherwise flawed items are apt to elicit irrelevant sources of difficulty, the relevance of poor items to any content domain is suspect (Ebel, 1956). Although appraisals of technical quality rely heavily on empirical evidence about difficulty level and item-discriminating power, expert judgment also plays a critical role. These judgments should focus on such features as readability level, freedom from ambiguity and irrelevancy, appropriateness of keyed answers and distractors, relevance and demand characteristics of the task format, and clarity of instructions. Indeed, in a number of instances, helpful checklists and rating forms have been constructed to formalize this judgment process (Hambleton, 1980, 1984).

Thus, at the very stage of test development, explicit concern for irrelevant test variance could lead to item and format revisions, or to the introduction of experimental controls for method variance, that would render certain perennial rival hypotheses about score meaning much less plausible. For example, it has been previously noted that a plausible rival hypothesis for a subject-matter achievement test is that it might, by virtue of its advanced vocabulary level or prolix sentence structure, be in part a reading comprehension test in disguise. Contrariwise, a purported reading comprehension test might be merely a measure of recall, recognition, or feature matching between the question and the passage. Explicitly dealing with such possibilities in test construction could limit if not eliminate in advance these counterarguments to the intended test interpretation.

Before proceeding to the topic of content representativeness, the convergence of content relevance and construct relevance should be underscored once again. Although frequently tacit, what is judged to be relevant to the domain of reference is not the surface content of test items or tasks but the knowledge, skills, or other pertinent attributes measured by the items or tasks. There is an implicit *two-step rationale:* First, relevant knowledge and skill important in domain performance are delineated by means, for example, of job or task analysis or other sources of domain theory; second, construct-valid measures of the important knowledge and skill are selected or developed. Test items and tasks are deemed domain relevant because they are presumably construct-valid measures of relevant domain knowledge and skill or, more generally, of relevant domain processes and attributes.

CONTENT REPRESENTATIVENESS

A central focus of test specifications, as well as of test evaluation for particular applied purposes, is the representativeness with which the test covers domain content (or behaviors or processes). To achieve representativeness, however, one must specify not only the domain boundaries but also the logical or psychological subdivisions or facets of the behavioral or trait domain. Then the test constructor can systematically cover the subdivisions according to specified rules, such as equal or uniform coverage, according to frequency of ecological occurrence, or in proportion to judged life importance (Brunswik, 1947). The actual number of items representing each facet or subdivision could be made proportional to frequency or importance, or else weights could be applied to achieve the same effect (as long as the subdivisions to be weighted are measured with sufficient reliability).

This process of domain coverage is usually spoken of in sampling terms. For example, Lennon (1956) explains that a representative test is an item sample that "*re-presents* the universe—that is, one that duplicates or reproduces the essential characteristics of the universe, in their proper proportion and balance" (p. 301). Lennon goes on to stress an important aspect of domain clarity in sampling terms, that is, the sample and the sampling process should be specified with sufficient precision to enable a test constructor or test user to judge how adequately the test or sample performance typifies domain or universe performance. As used here, the terms *universe* and *domain* are closely related but not identical. The universe is the total set of possible items relevant to the domain, which in turn is the total body of information—relationships as well as instances—for which the construct is expected to account.

At the same time, the very notion of content sampling has been attacked in some quarters. This is mainly on the grounds that although there might be a definable domain of content, there is no existing universe of items or testing conditions. Under such circumstances, how can one talk about how well the test "samples" the class of situations or subject matter (Loevinger, 1965)? In point of fact, items are constructed, not sampled. However, this argument is countered by the claim that the important requirement is that the boundaries of the universe be sufficiently well specified to appraise whether any particular item is included or ruled out (Cronbach, 1971). In any event, we wish to make inferences from the test to the domain, to a universe of items or tasks *like those* constructed or observed, and the sampling terminology permits us to invoke sophisticated inferential models for doing this with considerable rigor (Cornfield & Tukey, 1956; Cronbach et al., 1972; Kane, 1982a). These models, of course, generalize not from sample content to domain content, but from sample performance to universe performance. They require response data of the internal consistency type that is technically not available in the traditional content-validity framework but becomes available in the substantive-validity framework to be discussed shortly.

There is a trivial sense, of course, in which one can speak conventionally of the sampling of items, namely, when a large pool of previously constructed items has been assembled and the test is comprised solely of items selected from that pool. But sampling from a large item pool is not sampling from the item universe, unless one may be assured that the item pool is coterminous with the universe. This would become nontrivial if the operative properties of all items that could possibly appear in the universe, and hence on the test, could be specified in advance, so the adequacy with which the pool covers the universe could be appraised.

One approach to such complete advance specification has been proposed by Guttman (1958). In this approach, the investigator delineates the logical dimensions or facets of a domain (in terms of content, form, complexity, and so forth) and then systematically crosses these facets in factorial fashion. The resultant Cartesian product yields a facet design of the domain, which in turn provides the basis for a mapping sentence or item-generation rule for determining the item universe (Gutt-

man, 1969). Items can then be constructed to cover the universe uniformly, or in proportion to life importance or frequency of occurrence, or in some other representative fashion (Brunswik, 1947; Loevinger, 1965; Stephenson, 1953). The facet design and mapping sentence fully specify the domain as well as the items or tasks that potentially appear in the item universe. Thus, this faceted item-generation process may be thought of as sampling from a *potential* item universe, one that might not actually exist at a particular time but that in principle could be produced.

Closely related notions have been employed by Osburn (1968) and by Hively, Patterson, and Page (1968) to generate what they call "universe-defined" tests. In this approach, a content area is conceptually analyzed into a hierarchical arrangement of item forms. An item form, for them, specifies a fixed syntactical structure containing one or more variable elements along with a list of replacement sets for those elements. Items are constructed in a given item form by systematically changing the variable elements until all of the possibilities are covered. Note that the direction of the argument flows not from a domain specification to an item sample but from an item form to an item universe, which is explicitly defined by the algorithmic playing out of the item-generation rule. Although once again this process may be thought of as sampling from a potential item universe, this universe is restricted to what follows from the particular item form. Guttman's (1969) mapping-sentence approach, being structured in terms of domain facets rather than specific item forms, is more generally applicable to broad domains. The use of item forms, mapping sentences, and other approaches to the technology of item writing is discussed in detail by Roid and Haladyna (1982).

Proponents of the item-form approach contend that since the item universe is completely specified therein and the test is a direct sample of that universe, nothing else is needed to claim validity. To wit, Osburn maintains that

> what the test is measuring is operationally defined by the universe of content as embodied in the item generating rules. No recourse to response-inferred concepts such as construct validity, predictive validity, underlying factor structure or latent variables is necessary to answer this vital question. (1968, p. 101)

But knowing that the test is an item sample from a circumscribed item universe merely tells us, at most, that the test measures whatever the universe measures. And we have no *evidence* about what that might be, other than a rule for generating items of a particular type.

Yet, ready acceptance of a strictly content basis of validity is widespread in current practice (Messick, 1975, 1988a), even though test construction is rarely as logical or systematic as in the item-form approach. As Cronbach lamented,

> ambiguity remains in many definitions of universes; . . . reviewing of draft items is an art not reducible to rules. . . . It is not at all uncommon, however, for the test developer to claim validity by construction, bolstering the claim with a detailed account of the construction process. (1971, p. 456)

We will next examine such one-sided content validity claims in more detail because they have a long history in educational and psychological measurement, arguing that they are at best only one-sided and at worst perverse.

LIMITATIONS OF CONTENT AS THE SOLE VALIDITY BASIS

Ebel (1961) has argued that "if the test we propose to use provides in itself the best available operational definition, the concept of validity does not apply" (p. 643). But Cronbach (1971) counters that "this language gives the game away, for the 'best available' definition is presumably not the best conceivable, and How good is the operation? remains a meaningful question" (p. 481). Thus, an operational definition does not necessarily yield a valid representation, except by definition (Mosier, 1947). Still, Ebel attempted, in one of his last publications (1983), to accommodate this criticism by adding to the basic requirement of operational definition a further requirement of rational justification. This formal rationale for the tasks used in test construction, especially if sufficiently compelling that other expert judges endorse it, provides the basis for what he called "intrinsic rational validity."

Specifically, Ebel's line of argument in support of content-based validity proceeds as follows:

> The evidence for intrinsic rational validity will consist of an explicit rationale for the test: a written document that (a) defines the ability to be measured, (b) describes the tasks to be included in the test, and (c) explains the reasons for using such tasks to measure such an ability. The explicit rationale indicates what the test is measuring. If that is what the user intends to measure, the test is a valid test for the user's purposes. (1983, p. 8)

This argument is riddled with references to the construct of "ability," and hence the proposed test rationales come close to being construct theories without appeal to construct-related evidence. However, Ebel might counter, as he has long contended (e.g., Ebel, 1974), that he uses the term *ability* merely to refer to a class of behaviors, not to an underlying trait, so neither constructs nor construct-related evidence are at issue. We will deal with this point shortly, but first let us take Ebel's defense of intrinsic rational validity at face value. Granted, the recommended development of explicit test rationales is an important aid not only in test construction but in test interpretation (Rapaport, Gill, & Schafer, 1945). Yet, surely such rationales embody the *hypotheses* underlying proposed test interpretation and use, not warranties of their validity. Remember, test validation is in essense hypothesis testing. Although rationales are essential to this process, so is empirical evidence (Gardner, 1983).

Nonetheless, many investigators, especially in educational and industrial contexts, take a stand similar to Ebel's. For example, Yalow and Popham (1983) claim that "content validity resides in a test and once the test is taken, that validity makes available an inference about the examinee's status on the performance domain of interest" (p. 11). But this inference relies on evidence of response consistency and score meaning, not on content rationales alone. Even as far back as the 1955 *Technical Recommendations for Achievement Tests* (American Educational Research Association, 1955), it was recognized that evidence of discriminating power in conjunction with content validity is needed for achievement tests of subject matter content and, more generally, that "construct validity is highly important in achievement testing" (p. 17).

Ironically, the manner in which Yalow and Popham (1983) phrase their position reveals its essential flaw. They contend that content validity "resides" in a test, whereas validity is a property of test responses and of the inferences based thereon. This point has long been recognized in psychometric circles. For example, Cureton (1951) states that "validity . . . applies to the acts evoked by the test materials in the test situation, and not to the test materials . . . as such. . . . It is the examinees' responses to the elements of the test situation . . . which possess . . . validity" (pp. 662–663). The major problem here is that so-called content validity is focused upon test *forms* rather than test *scores,* upon *instruments* rather than *measurements.* Though Cronbach (1971) allowed that it might degrade over time, with the test eventually becoming unrepresentative of evolving domains or curricula, content validity in its traditional guise gives every appearance of being a fixed property of the test (under its standard conditions of administration and scoring) rather than being a property of test responses. In traditional terms, "if the content is validly selected, the test is content-valid for persons of all kinds" (Cronbach, 1971, p. 453). This epitomizes the major deficiency of content per se as a prime basis for validity in educational and psychological measurement (Messick, 1975).

Strictly speaking, even from a content viewpoint, it would be more apropos to conceptualize content validity as residing not in the test, but in the judgment of experts about domain relevance and representativeness. The focus should not be on the test, but on the relationship between the test and the domain of reference. This is especially clear if a test developed for one domain is applied to other similar domains. Because a particular set of test items might be highly representative of one domain and only moderately representative of another, the test logically has a different content validity for each domain to which it is applied. Although content validity is usually considered in relation to the original domain for which the test was constructed and for which the item-selection process can be described, tests are frequently transported to ostensibly similar domains for which new judgments of content relevance and representativeness might not be quite the same as the original. Thus, even in traditional terms, content validity should not be viewed as residing in the test but, if anywhere, in the relation between the test and the domain of application.

Before closing the issue of content validity, it should be noted that some serious philosophical arguments in favor of the primacy of content have been propounded (Norris, 1983). The basic argument here is nominalistic in tone, holding that what is measured is operationally defined by specifying the behavior class of which the test is a sample. For nominalists, "classes are conventions by which objects are grouped according to perceived similarities" (Turner, 1967, p. 266). There are no universals or enduring laws or even generalizations apart from reductive convention; there are only convenient classes of particular entities. In this view, abilities or other attributes are defined as classes of behaviors. And to say that a test samples a specified class of behaviors is to say that the test measures the ability or attribute inherent in that class. As we mentioned earlier, this position is implicit in Ebel's (1983) notion of intrinsic rational validity. From this perspective, content validity is sufficient for justifying inferences about people's abilities or other attributes based on test responses.

However, even apart from the fundamental problem of irrelevant test variance, which should be discounted on the basis of empirical evidence before assaying such content claims, there is a deeper reason why this argument is specious. It will be recalled from the section on preliminary points that a behavior class is a class of behaviors all of which change in the same or related ways as a function of stimulus contingencies or, in less strictly behavioral terms, that share or are organized by common processes. The notion of behavior class, like the broader concept of domain, constitutes a hypothesis that particular behaviors or tasks are related in some way and, as such, it qualifies as a construct. In this instance we are speaking of a behavioral construct, to be sure, but a construct nonetheless. "Whenever one classifies situations, persons or responses, he uses *constructs*, . . . the latter term [emphasizing] that categories are deliberate creations chosen to organize experience into general law-like statements" (Cronbach, 1971, p. 462). In other words, to claim that a particular behavior or task is a member of a behavioral class or domain, or that a set of behaviors or tasks is representative of the domain, invokes hypotheses that might ultimately be rejected on the basis of empirical evidence (Shapere, 1977). The need for such evidence, which in actuality is construct-related evidence, gives further testimony to the insufficiency of traditional content validity as the sole basis for validity.

One final caveat about content-based inferences is that, at best, they are only *one-directional* in import (Messick, 1980, 1981b). That is, limited content-based inferences might be sustainable about high scorers on a test but not low scorers, and only then if the strict behavioral language of task description is adhered to. Otherwise, constructs are apt to be invoked and construct-related evidence required (Cronbach, 1971). Thus, one might infer that high scorers possess suitable skills to perform domain tasks successfully because they repeatedly succeeded on representative test tasks. Even here, however, the inferences implicitly rely on conceptions of test and domain meaning, because these content-based inferences are threatened by context effects and situational factors that influence test performance and domain performance in different ways.

But what kinds of content-based inferences can be sustained for low scorers on the test? The caution could not be colder on this score. In terms of content-related evidence, all that can be claimed is that low scorers did not perform the tasks successfully; they did not demonstrate domain or test competence or skill (Cronbach, 1971). There is no basis in the test performance per se for interpreting low scores as reflective of incompetence or lack of skill. To do that requires evidence to discount such plausible rival interpretations of low test performance as anxiety, inattention, low motivation, fatigue, limited English proficiency, certain sensory handicaps, and other sources of irrelevant test variance. And evidence discounting plausible rival hypotheses, as we have seen, is the hallmark of construct validation.

The intent of these cautionary remarks is to underscore, in no uncertain terms, that content judgments alone do not pro-

vide a sufficient evidential basis for the validity of inferences and actions based on test scores. Indeed, although typical treatments of test content may address item scoring, they rarely if ever mention test scores or the ways in which scoring models or procedures should be reflective of what is known about structural consistencies in the nontest domain of reference.

But nothing in these remarks should be taken to diminish the importance of content relevance and representativeness in supporting (and limiting) score-based inferences and actions sustained by other evidence. It is clear that content-related evidence cannot stand alone, but we need to examine how it functions in concert with construct-related evidence in a unified validity framework. The critical role of content in test validity becomes clarified by viewing it in conjunction with the structure of response consistencies, both internally to the test and externally with other measures, as part of the overarching concept of construct validity. This integrative effort is assayed in the next three major parts of this main section, which are labeled in turn the *substantive, structural,* and *external* components of construct validity. This terminology is followed in deference to Jane Loevinger, whose seminal 1957 monograph on *Objective Tests as Instruments of Psychological Theory* is organized in these terms.

Substantive Component of Construct Validity

Item and task content can be incorporated as an important feature of construct validity by considering content properties and response consistency jointly. Indeed, the substantive component of construct validity entails a veritable confrontation between judged content relevance and representativeness, on the one hand, and empirical response consistency, on the other. In the traditional content approach, items are included in a test solely on the basis of the domain specification. In strictly empirical approaches, items are included in a test solely on the basis of data, whether internal test data such as item homogeneity and factor loadings or external data such as item correlations with criteria and discrimination between criterion groups. In the substantive approach, items are included in the original pool on the basis of judged relevance to a broadly defined domain but are selected for the test on the basis of empirical response consistencies. The substantive component of construct validity is the ability of the construct theory to account for the resultant test content (Loevinger, 1957).

EXPANDING THE ITEM POOL FOR THEORETICAL LEVERAGE

In the substantive approach, the initial item pool is deliberately expanded beyond the domain specifically relevant to the target construct theory at issue to include items relevant to competing theories of that construct, if possible, as well as items relevant to other constructs. Item responses are then obtained and analyzed, and test items are selected from the pool on the basis of empirical properties that conform best to an appropriate structural model of the domain (as well as of the test scores). Unlike traditional content validity, the substantive validity component requires response analysis: not just facet design, but also facet analysis (Guttman, 1969); not just the generation of universe-defined tests (Hively et al., 1968; Osburn, 1968), but also the analysis of response consistencies to item forms to appraise their homogeneity as diagnostic categories.

The content of items retained in the test is then examined to see how well the selected items exemplify the theory of the construct being measured and whether they are distinct from exemplars both of competing theories and of other related constructs. In principle, every item included in the scoring key for the test should be rationally accounted for, while the exclusion of items should be explainable on theoretical or methodological grounds (Jessor & Hammond, 1957). Both convergent and discriminant evidence are thereby obtained at the very stage of test construction, and a miniature evaluation of the construct theory is afforded at the item level (Loevinger, 1957). This principle of combining theory testing and scale construction in terms of interpretable differential response consistencies in a broad empirical domain has long been recommended by factor analysts (e.g., Guilford, 1967; Thurstone, 1947).

The reason that the substantive approach is described as a confrontation between content coverage and response consistency is that the exclusion of certain items from the test, on the basis of poor empirical properties or lack of empirical fit to the construct theory, can distort the test's representativeness in covering the construct domain as originally conceived. If this occurs, efforts should be made to regain domain representativeness by replacing the faulty items with psychometrically sound ones meeting the affected content specifications.

But this might not be possible, and content coverage in terms of the original specifications may appear to be eroded. Such erosion may be justified on the grounds that the resulting test thereby becomes a better exemplar of the construct as empirically grounded in domain structure. This might occur, for example, because the eliminated items are unduly subject to response sets or other method distortions, and replacement items minimizing such contaminants could not be created. Or, because appropriately convergent and discriminant items for purported aspects of the domain could not be constructed after repeated attempts, suggesting that the original domain conception should be revised. That is, both the construct interpretation and the test content would be edited in the light of negative empirical evidence. This pinpoints another weakness of traditional content validity — namely, that the content representativeness of the test items should be appraised in terms of the empirical domain structure that underlies the final test form and ultimate score interpretation, not in terms of the ostensible domain facets originally conjectured.

These analyses of item response consistencies offer evidence for the substantive component of construct validity to the extent that the resultant content of the test can be rationally explained by the construct theory (along with collateral theories of test-taking behavior and method distortion). In Loevinger's (1957) words, the substantive component of construct validity is "the extent to which the content of the items included in (and excluded from?) the test can be accounted for in terms of the trait believed to be measured and the context of measurement" (p. 661).

A Combined Convergent–Discriminant Strategy for Test Construction

An efficient elaboration of the substantive approach is to develop measures of two or more distinct constructs at the same time. In this case, the combined item pool would be administered to respondents along with measures of anticipated method contaminants such as reading comprehension or response styles. Provisional test scores are then derived for each construct, based on responses to each construct's specific item pool. Items are retained on a given construct scale if they correlate more highly with their own purported construct score than with scores for other constructs or for response styles or other method influences. Thus, item selection is systematically based on convergent and discriminant evidence conjointly, while at the same time method contaminants are suppressed (Jackson, 1971; 1980).

The substantive approach in general and this convergent–discriminant extension in particular make explicit reference to test scores as part of the item-appraisal process. Content validity, as we have seen, has little to say about the scoring of content samples, and as a result scoring procedures within the content framework are typically *ad hoc* (Guion, 1978). Scoring models in the construct framework, in contrast, should be rationally attuned to the nature of the construct, an often neglected issue that is next on our agenda.

Structural Component of Construct Validity

In the construct validity framework, scoring models should be rationally consistent with what is known about the structural relations inherent in behavioral manifestations of the construct in question (Loevinger, 1957; Peak, 1953). Arguing that a theoretical rationale should determine the way in which items of observed behavior are summarized in the form of a score, Peak (1953) stressed that "the satisfactory determination of weights to be given items in a test and the manner in which they are combined to produce a score should rest on knowledge of how the processes tapped by the items combine dynamically to produce effects" (p. 273). Subsequently, Loevinger (1957) formalized the call for rational scoring models by coining the term *structural fidelity*, which refers to "the extent to which structural relations between test items parallel the structural relations of other manifestations of the trait being measured" (p. 661). The structural component of construct validity includes both this fidelity of the scoring model to the structural characteristics of the construct's nontest manifestations and the degree of interitem structure.

In regard to degree of interitem structure, it is assumed that, for any given construct or trait, there is a characteristic level or upper limit of intercorrelation among its manifestations. And as was previously pointed out, the degree of homogeneity in the test should be commensurate with this characteristic degree of homogeneity associated with the construct. For example, two manifestations of a circumscribed construct such as number facility should be more closely related than two manifestations of broader constructs such as reasoning or creativity. Furthermore, the nature and dimensionality of the interitem structure should reflect the nature and dimensionality of the construct domain, and every effort should be made to capture this structure at the level of test scoring and interpretation. For example, a single total score usually implies a unitary construct and vice versa; a profile of scores implies a differentiated construct such as literacy, for which separate scales for prose, document, and quantitative literacy have been developed (Kirsch & Jungeblut, 1986); and, a combination of both subscores and higher-order or composite scores implies a hierarchical construct such as intelligence (R. J. Sternberg, 1985a; Thorndike, Hagen, & Sattler, 1986; Wechsler, 1958).

MANY A SLIP BETWEEN SCORING MODEL AND SCORE INTERPRETATION

For present purposes, a scoring or measurement model describes the way in which item responses are combined to form test scores, along with any control procedures taking account of conditions of testing that influence score interpretation (Messick, 1981a; Messick & Ross, 1962). The most widely used scoring model in educational and psychological measurement is a cumulative quantitative model in which the number or frequency of manifestations indexes the amount of the construct or trait, that is, the test score is the number of items answered correctly or in conformance with a scoring key or some weighted combination thereof. Although the cumulative model is predominant for ability and achievement tests, it should not be taken for granted that cumulative scores are always appropriate. For example, in the measurement of attitudes by the endorsement of items previously scaled for favorability toward some attitudinal target (such as open education), wherein individuals agree with items that are close to their own position and disagree with items far removed in either direction, the appropriate score is not the number but the average scale value of items endorsed (Torgerson, 1958).

As another instance, it might not be the frequency but the intensity or quality of response that forms the basis of the desired construct score. Consider that two individuals are each asked to produce 10 creative products, with each response being judged on a 10-point scale of goodness. Suppose further that one individual receives 10 ratings of unity, whereas the other receives 9 ratings of 0 and a single rating of 10. With use of the traditional weighted summations implied in the ubiquitous cumulative scoring model, the two individuals would be assigned identical overall scores. But scores based on models that accommodate frequency and quality in noncompensatory ways, or one based simply on the highest rating attained, might better differentiate the two individuals with respect to the creativity construct at issue (e.g., N. Frederiksen & Ward, 1978).

Other potential competitors to the cumulative scoring model, depending on the nature of the construct, include class models, dynamic models, and ipsative models. Although cumulative models differentiate individuals in terms of degree, class models differentiate them in terms of kind (Loevinger, 1957). That is, in a cumulative model the higher the score, the more of some underlying characteristic the respondent displays; whereas in a class model the higher the score, the higher the probability that the respondent belongs in some class or diagnostic category. An example of a dynamic model is one in

which two or more manifestations of the same trait may be mutually exclusive or negatively correlated because they represent alternative expressions of the trait. For instance, if hostility is expressed as verbal carping, it might not also take the form of aggressive action. In an ipsative model (Cattell, 1944), scores serve to order a set of variables or traits for each individual, allowing comparisons *within* individuals in the relative level of each trait vis-à-vis other traits assessed. Ipsative models might be used, for example, to identify an individual's relative strengths and weaknesses, preferred interests, or salient traits. This is in contradistinction to the more typical normative scores in psychology and education, which serve to order individuals with respect to some attribute or variable. These scores are called "normative" because they provide the distribution of respondent's attribute values in any reference group and allow comparisons *among* individuals in levels of performance or trait (Messick, 1983).

In addition to interpreting a person's performance or trait level normatively in terms of how other individuals score on the dimension in question or ipsatively in terms of that person's relative scores on other dimensions or traits, scores may also be interpreted criterially in terms of performance standards or behavioral referents. Scores interpreted within this latter framework are called *criterion-referenced* or *domain-referenced*, typically in contradistinction to *norm-referenced* scores. A norm-referenced score interpretation indicates where the examinee stands relative to other people who took the test. A criterion-referenced interpretation treats the score as a sign that the respondent can or cannot be expected to satisfy some performance requirement in a situation unlike the test. A domain-referenced interpretation treats the score as a domain sample indicating what level of difficulty the person can cope with on tasks like those in the test (Cronbach, 1984). Both criterion-referenced and domain-referenced scores are widely used to place individuals above or below specific performance standards such as those associated with minimal competency or with mastery (Hambleton, 1980, 1984; Popham, 1978). In such applications, a categorical or class model is implied to underlie scoring and interpretation.

Sometimes two or more scoring or measurement models are combined, or one is overlaid on the other, so that one aspect of test interpretation derives from one model and another aspect from the overlay. This type of *model compounding* leads to confusion as to what construct theory to reference, as well as to confusion about the forms of evidence needed for the construct validation of the compound interpretation (Messick, 1981a). As an illustration, consider an interpretation of test scores in terms of minimum competency in reading comprehension. The primary measurement model, the one underlying test development, is a cumulative scale relating higher test scores to higher amounts of the measured reading proficiency. Overlaying this is a categorical model relating score levels above a specified standard to the demonstration of minimum competency and scores below that standard to failure. The two components of minimum competency and reading comprehension tap into different construct theories, thereby creating possible uncertainty as to what construct validity evidence is needed to support inferences and actions based on the test scores. It should be clear that compound score interpretations require compounded sources of evidence, bearing on both the meaning of the scores as measures of reading comprehension and the validity of the cutoff score as a standard of minimum competency.

Another type of confusion, which might be called *model slippage*, occurs when scores derived by one measurement model are interpreted in terms of a different measurement model (Messick, 1981a). For example, many scales of the Minnesota Multiphasic Personality Inventory (MMPI) were developed empirically by selecting items that significantly discriminated one or another psychopathological group from normal persons. This approach implies a class model linking scale scores to the probability of diagnostic placement. But that is not the way the test is typically employed; it is generally used instead to make inferences about the personality of the respondent. The implicit measurement model for the latter kind of interpretation is a cumulative scale linking scores to the amount of some personal characteristic or trait. Classification studies of the accuracy of patient assignment to diagnostic categories, along with construct-related evidence on the meaning of the categories, would bear directly on the validity of the scales as originally derived but only indirectly on the validity of individual personality interpretations. The latter interpretations, in terms of personality characteristics, require construct validity evidence vis-à-vis those characteristics. The validity of actual score interpretation and use should prevail over the validity of any original intentions, which suggests that MMPI scales as predominantly used should be appraised more in terms of construct validity than classification accuracy. It should be noted, however, that one person's inadvertent model slippage may be another's deliberate creative leap.

INTERNAL STRUCTURE AND SUBSTANCE IN CONSTRUCT REPRESENTATION

In the previous discussion of the substantive and structural components of construct validity, attention was focused on correlational structures of item responses and their interpretation in terms of construct theory. The resulting test, reflecting the obtained item structure, was evaluated substantively in terms of how well the construct accounted for the observed pattern of consistent individual differences in item performance. But as an alternative and complementary approach, the internal structure and substance of the test can be addressed more directly by means of causal modeling of item or task performance. This approach to *construct representation* attempts to identify the theoretical mechanisms that underlie task performance, primarily by decomposing the task into requisite component processes (Embretson, 1983). Being firmly grounded in the cognitive psychology of information processing, construct representation refers to the relative dependence of task responses on the processes, strategies, and knowledge (including self-knowledge) that are implicated in test performance. Nor are individual differences a necessary ingredient, because processes essential in task performance may be mastered to roughly the same degree by all persons under study.

Four general criteria for construct representations have been proposed by Embretson (1983). First, the relation between person performance and the stimulus characteristics of items should be clearly specified. Second, there should be an explicit method for comparing alternative theories of the constructs involved in item or task performance, preferably in terms of quantitative comparisons of the goodness of model fits to data. Third, the methodology should provide for quantification of these theoretical constructs, that is, parameters should be specified for each item on the constructs entailed in its solution. Finally, the methodology should yield person parameters measuring individual differences on the operative constructs. As approaches to construct representation, Embretson (1983) explicitly examines mathematical modeling of task performance, psychometric modeling of item responses, and multicomponent latent-trait modeling, but computer simulation modeling offers a promising alternative as well (e.g., Feigenbaum & Feldman, 1963; Tomkins & Messick, 1963). These modeling approaches are discussed in more detail in a later section on analyses of process.

External Component of Construct Validity

The external component of construct validity refers to the extent to which the test's relationships with other tests and nontest behaviors reflect the expected high, low, and interactive relations implied in the theory of the construct being assessed (Loevinger, 1957). Thus, the meaning of the test scores is substantiated externally by appraising the degree to which empirical relationships with other measures, or the lack thereof, are consistent with that meaning. That is, the constructs represented in the test should rationally account for the external pattern of test correlations. This might be demonstrated in terms of detailed theoretical rationales for the obtained patterns or, more quantitatively, in terms of factor analytic or structural equation models that attempt to reproduce the observed correlations in construct-consistent ways. Next, a brief comment, first, about what in the test provides the basis for the external correlations and, second, about what kinds of external measures should be included in the correlational pattern.

In regard to the first point, although individual item responses could be directly studied in relation to external variables, the external component of construct validity primarily concerns correlations with the test's total score and any subscores. Because such scores imply a commitment to some structural model, they constitute not observed data but intervening variables. A test score is an intervening variable in the technical sense that a measure of its amount can be derived directly from empirical laws or relationships among the item responses by grouping of terms (MacCorquodale & Meehl, 1948). The test score summarizes consistencies in item responses in an aggregated form specified by a particular scoring or measurement model and justified by the model's empirical fit to item data. The test score thereby functions as an intervening variable in relating response consistency across test items to any other measure. Hence, the structural scoring model chosen may influence the nature and size of external correlations as well as their interpretation.

In regard to the second point, the external correlational pattern could embrace the relationships of the focal test score to *test* measures of other constructs, as well as to *nontest* exemplars of both the focal and related constructs, as schematized in Figures 2.1, 2.2, and 2.3. Loevinger (1957) argued, and we tend to agree, that "it seems reasonable to require that complete validation of any test include a demonstration of some non-zero relationship with a nontest variable" (p. 675). Although in the interest of reality testing and generalizability it would indeed be desirable if the test were related to real-world behavioral variables, what is critical is that it relate appropriately to other construct scores based on distinctly different measurement methods from its own. Otherwise, shared method variance becomes a plausible rival explanation of aspects of the external relational pattern, a perennial threat that must be systematically addressed in making external validity claims.

The external component of construct validity emphasizes two intertwined sets of relationships for the test scores: one between the test and different methods for measuring both the same and distinct constructs or traits; the other between measures of the focal construct and exemplars of different constructs predicted to be variously related to it on theoretical grounds. Theoretically relevant empirical consistencies in the first set, indicating a correspondence between measures of the same construct and a distinctness from measures of other constructs, have been called *trait validity*; theoretically relevant consistencies in the second set, indicating a lawful relatedness between measures of different constructs, have been called *nomological validity* (D. T. Campbell, 1960). Trait validity deals with the fit between measurement operations and conceptual formulations of the construct, as schematized by the dashed line numbered 1 in Figure 2.2. Nomological validity deals with the fit between obtained data patterns and theoretical predictions about those patterns (Cook & Campbell, 1979), as schematized by the dashed line numbered 2. Trait validity is concerned with the meaning of the measure as a reflection of the construct, and nomological validity with the meaning of the construct as reflected in the measure's relational properties and implications. These two aspects of the external component of construct validity will now be examined in detail.

TRAIT VALIDITY AND THE MULTITRAIT–MULTIMETHOD MATRIX

D. T. Campbell (1960) distinguished between trait validity and nomological validity because he noted that many test-development efforts in education and psychology were oriented not toward clear theoretical constructs embedded in elaborated theoretical networks, but toward loose assemblies of concepts and implications or even toward more intuitive "folk constructs." These loose conceptions, which are often casual and typically incomplete, are sometimes referred to as "constructions" rather than "theories." Although they may not be sufficient for guiding any but the most primitive or initial nomological explorations, such constructions frequently prove adequate for guiding the collection of convergent and discriminant evidence needed to undergird differentiated construct measurement. This is so because even primitive constructions "suggest first-order questions to investigate and aspects of a situation to be observed or put under research control" (Cronbach, 1986, p. 89).

This brings us to the basic notion of trait validity, which is that constructs should not be uniquely tied to any particular method of measurement nor should they be unduly redundant with other constructs. Specifically, trait validity is the extent to which a measure relates more highly to different methods for assessing the same construct than it does to measures of different constructs assessed by the same method. Unfortunately, the label "*trait* validity" is an especially perverse misnomer because it implies that this important validity principle holds only for the measurement of personal characteristics. In point of fact, so-called trait validity applies with equal force to the measurement of object, situation, and group characteristics.

To demonstrate that a construct is not uniquely tied to any particular measurement method requires the convergence of two or more methods of measuring the construct. To demonstrate that a construct is not redundant vis-à-vis other constructs requires discrimination among measures of two or more constructs. In a sense, we are speaking of two types of redundancy: one a desirable redundancy of measurement as revealed in the convergence of methods for measuring the same construct; the other an undesirable redundancy or proliferation of indistinct constructs. Even here, whether two constructs are redundant or should be kept separate depends on the context. At an everyday level of discourse, for example, it might be fruitless to distinguish between "ability" and "achievement" (or between "mass" and "weight"), but precise distinctions become important to teachers and admissions officers (or to physicists and astronauts).

The need for simultaneous evidence about multiple traits measured by multiple methods was neatly addressed by D. T. Campbell and Fiske (1959) in their formulation of the multitrait–multimethod matrix, an example of which appears in Table 2.3. Such a matrix displays all of the intercorrelations generated when each of several constructs or traits is measured by each of several methods, thereby permitting one to gauge the relative contributions of trait and method variance associated with particular construct measures.

For discussion purposes, it is convenient to have labels for various segments of the matrix, as have been provided in the footnote to Table 2.3 following the somewhat precious terminology of D. T. Campbell and Fiske (1959). This kind of systematic comparative display of correlational data makes a number of points readily discernible. To begin with, direct convergent evidence is afforded by the coefficients in the bold-faced validity diagonals, which should be statistically significant and sufficiently large to warrant further efforts. Second, since the validity value for a trait measured by different methods should be higher than correlations having neither trait nor method in common, the entry in the validity diagonal for a trait should be larger than the values appearing in its column and row in the heterotrait–heteromethod triangles. Third, because two independent methods of measuring the same trait should correlate more highly than measures of different traits by the same method, the validity diagonal values for a trait should exceed correlations for that trait in the heterotrait–monomethod triangles. In Table 2.3, this is seen to be the case for the trait of Dependence with respect to method 1 but not method 2 (the correlation for A_2C_2 exceeds A_2A_1); for Sociability with respect to method 2 but not method 1 (C_1B_1

**TABLE 2.3 Hypothetical Correlations Among Three Traits
Each Measured by Two Different Methods**

	Traits	METHOD 1			METHOD 2		
		A1	*B1*	*C1*	*A2*	*B2*	*C2*
Method 1	A1 Dependence	(.85)					
Self-report	B1 Warmth	.20	(.91)				
	C1 Sociability	.30	.70	(.90)			
Method 2	A2 Dependence	**.35**	.18	.22	(.80)		
Peer ratings	B2 Warmth	.15	**.40**	.28	.30	(.50)	
	C2 Sociability	.20	.30	**.55**	.40	.50	(.90)

Note. Each "heterotrait–monomethod triangle" is enclosed by a solid line.
Each "heterotrait–heteromethod triangle" is enclosed by a broken line.
The "reliability diagonals" are the two sets of monotrait–monomethod values in parentheses.
The "validity diagonal" is the set of three coefficients in bold face, that is the monotrait–heteromethod coefficients.

exceeds C_1C_2) and, for Warmth with respect to neither method (both B_1C_1 and B_2C_2 exceed B_1B_2). Fourth, the same relative pattern of trait interrelationships should occur in all of the heterotrait triangles, both monomethod and heteromethod, as is the case in Table 2.3 despite gross variations in the level of the coefficients.

Further detailed perusal of the multitrait–multimethod matrix may reveal some plausible rival hypotheses for why some coefficients are inadequately low while others are disturbingly high. For example, in Table 2.3 the reliability of B_2 is substantially lower than that of the other measures. This suggests that the B_2 correlation coefficients are not generally comparable to the others and that in particular the convergence value of B_1B_2 might be too low, that is, attenuated by the larger errors of measurement in B_2. As a matter of course, then, one might better appraise the obtained convergent and discriminant evidence if all of the coefficients were corrected for attenuation using appropriate reliability coefficients. In the multitrait–multimethod formulation, the coefficients in the reliability diagonals are clearly monotrait–monomethod values, but whether test–retest, alternate form, internal consistency, or other types of generalizability estimates are used depends on the inferences to be made (Cronbach et al., 1972; Lord & Novick, 1968).

In regard to hypotheses about the nature of possible method variance in Table 2.3, the self-report measures of method 1 may share response-style consistencies such as the tendency to respond in a socially desirable manner. Because Dependence is less socially desirable than Warmth and Sociability, the response style might serve to reduce the correlations of A_1 with B_1 and C_1 but to increase the correlation between B_1 and C_1. Halo effects in the peer-rating measures of method 2 might tend to operate in the same direction, but perhaps to a different degree. These hypotheses suggest the need for certain refinements, such as additional experimental controls or the inclusion of response-style measures directly in the matrix, for an ensuing round of trait validation.

Lack of convergence across methods could indicate that one or more methods are introducing excessive specific variance or else that the methods are not measuring the same constructs. Hence, what is to be interpreted as method var-

iance is a major issue in its own right. One investigator's contaminant may be another's focal construct. In any event, whatever is viewed as method variance constitutes a phenomenon to be explained. In this regard, the history of research on response styles provides an illuminating example (Berg, 1967; Jackson & Messick, 1958). As a specific case in point, it is implied in the very construction of Table 2.3 that, for purposes of this validation exercise, self-reports and peer ratings were viewed as alternative methods for trait measurement, that the self and peers could serve as interchangeable observers and reporters. Hence, high validity diagonals were desirable for convergent evidence. Yet from another perspective, self-concept and reputation are distinct constructs, so that high correlations between the two would be problematic (Cronbach, in press).

As thus far discussed, the multitrait–multimethod matrix is a heuristic device, not an analytical procedure. But it is a tough (often humbling) heuristic device that forces the investigator to confront simultaneously both convergent and discriminant evidence, or the lack thereof. Indeed, the specificity of method thereby encountered is often so compelling as to engender not humility, but pessimism (Fiske, 1973, 1976). In this view, every effort should be expended to minimize method specificity because it is a prime reason that knowledge in social science is discrete and fragmented (Fiske, 1986). But one must be careful not to overreact to method specificity because some amount of it may be inevitable. The issue is not simply whether or not methods converge as interchangeable indicators of the same construct but, rather, which methods are usefully complementary in the convergent measurement of which constructs. That is, one must take into account the nature and degree of both method specificity and construct or trait generality, but these might not be easily discerned at the level of correlational patterns and might require the probing of deeper relational structures (Huba & Hamilton, 1976; Jackson & Paunonen, 1980).

The multitrait–multimethod matrix provides a standard routine for initiating construct validation that helps forestall the opportunistic selection of evidence and any tendency to ignore disconfirmatory findings (D. T. Campbell, 1960). But at the same time, it is vulnerable to inadequate sampling of individuals, to variations in reliability across measures, and especially to variations in restriction of range across traits, all of which pose serious hazards to interpretation. Although not technically an analytic procedure in itself, several powerful analytic methods have been appended to it (Jackson & Paunonen, 1980; Schmitt, Coyle, & Saari, 1977). These include nonparametric (Hubert & Baker, 1978), analysis-of-variance (Kavanagh, MacKinney, & Wolins, 1971; Stanley, 1961), factor analytic or principle component (Golding, 1977; Golding & Seidman, 1974; Jackson, 1969, 1975), confirmatory factor analytic (Kallenberg & Kluegel, 1975; Kenny, 1976; Werts, Jöreskog, & Linn, 1972), and path-analytic (Schmitt, 1978; Werts, Jöreskog, & Linn, 1973; Werts & Linn, 1970) models and techniques. Moreover, because method effects may be multiplicative rather than additive, some direct-product models have also been formulated (Browne, 1984; D. T. Campbell & O'Connell, 1967). In addition, the multitrait–multimethod matrix has been combined with Brunswik's (1956) representative design of experiments to appraise generalizability not only across measurement methods but across conditions or treatments more generally (Hammond, Hamm, & Grassia, 1986).

But whether as a heuristic device or an analytical technique, the use of a multitrait–multimethod matrix should be informed by the theory of the constructs under investigation, a nicety that the very cookbook nature of the procedure tends to subvert. For instance, since two or more traits are required by the technique, any two traits tend to serve, as when convergent and discriminant conclusions about multiple methods or sources of ratings (e.g., by supervisor, subordinates, peers, self) are mechanically produced without regard to the construct theories of the multiple traits rated (Kavanagh et al., 1971; Lawler, 1967). But discounting the redundancy of a construct is only powerful, or even sensible, in relation to closely related or rival constructs. Empirically distinguishing the construct of assertiveness from sociability provides discriminant evidence, to be sure, but it is not as pertinent as distinguishing assertiveness from aggressiveness. Thus, the judicious choice of constructs to include in a multitrait–multimethod matrix can afford provisional evidence bearing on the nomological validity of the constructs.

NOMOLOGICAL VALIDITY AND NOMOTHETIC SPAN

The basic notion of *nomological validity* is that the theory of the construct being measured provides a rational basis for deriving empirically testable links between the test scores and measures of other constructs. It is not that a proven theory serves to validate the test, or vice versa. Rather, the test gains credence to the extent that score consistencies reflect theoretical implications of the construct, while the construct theory gains credence to the extent that test data jibe with its predictions. Thus, corroborative evidence provisionally supports both the construct theory and the test interpretation, while disconfirmatory evidence undercuts either the theory or the measure, or both.

In nomological validation, it is often prudent to adopt a precept from trait validity, namely, that each construct should

be represented by more than one measure. Failure to do this leads to what has been called *nomological noise* (Messick, 1981a). Because no single test is a pure exemplar of the construct but contains variance due to other constructs and method contaminants, there is no solid basis for concluding that an observed score relationship stems from that part of the test variance reflective of the construct or from other parts. This leads to a beclouding inconsistency in nomological validation, which becomes even worse if different single tests are used to represent the construct in different studies. As an example, consider two tests long purported to tap aspects of the cognitive style of field independence versus field dependence (Witkin & Goodenough, 1981), namely, the embedded-figures test and the rod-and-frame test. Numerous investigations employ only one or the other test, not both. Yet, the variance shared with a third variable by either one of these tests singly might or might not be the same variance they share with each other (Wachtel, 1972). By using two or more tests to represent the construct in nomological or relational studies, one can disentangle shared variance from unshared variance and discern which aspects of construct meaning, if any, derive from the shared and unshared parts.

Moreover, because each test contains some degree of error variance, an additional source of noise derives from differences across tests in score reliability. These differences in reliability should be taken into account by corrections for attenuation or other means in studies of nomological validity just as they were in studies of trait validity. This is highly desirable because in any investigation in which correlation coefficients are appraised or compared, score unreliability provides a plausible rival hypothesis for observed lack of relationship.

An essentially similar concept to nomological validity is Embretson's (1983) notion of *nomothetic span*, which basically refers to the empirical network of relationships of the test to measures of other constructs and criterion behaviors. Technically speaking, nomothetic span is somewhat broader than nomological validity as ordinarily conceived because it explicitly includes correlations of the test with other measures of the same construct and with measures of the same construct obtained under different conditions. As indicated in the previous paragraphs, however, the inclusion of multiple measures of each construct is also recognized as an often felicitous addition to nomological validation, even though it blurs the distinction between trait validity and nomological validity. Both nomological validity and nomothetic span may include targeted predictive relationships between the test and specific applied criterion behaviors, thereby formally subsuming criterion-related evidence under the rubric of construct validity and making clear that criterion prediction is to be appraised in terms of empirically grounded predictor and criterion meaning.

In the context of Embretson's (1983) previously discussed approach to construct representation, which identifies the component constructs or theoretical processes underlying task performance, nomothetic span indicates the predictive importance of the test as a measure of individual differences. The stronger and more frequent the test's correlations with other variables that should correlate with the construct on theoretical grounds, the wider the nomothetic span. Furthermore, if the constructs operative in test performance have been previously identified in the construct representation phase, quantitative models that permit a priori construct specification may be applied to the correlational data. For example, path-analytic or structural equation models (Bentler, 1980; James et al., 1982; Jöreskog & Sörbom, 1979) may be used to appraise the extent to which the component constructs can account for the test's external pattern of relationships. Quantitative modeling of construct relationships constitutes an extremely strong approach to construct validation. In regard to more typical approaches, the important point is not so much that they are often less rigorous as that they vary enormously in their degree of rigor.

Strong Versus Weak Construct Validation

Construct theory as a guide to test construction provides a rational basis for selecting task content, for expecting certain consistencies in item responses, and for predicting score relationships. If one starts with well-grounded construct theory, the whole enterprise is largely deductive in nature, and the approach to construct validation can be well specified and relatively rigorous. But often one starts with a dimly understood test or set of tasks and attempts to induce score meaning from an assorted array of the test's empirical relationships. Unfortunately, this empirical miscellany is often all that is offered in the name of construct validity, and it is an extremely weak approach, indeed (Cronbach, 1988, in press). As anticipated by Peak, "a protest must be entered . . . against the proliferation of blindly empirical validities which are without the disciplined guidance of theory, for the increment of meaning from the accumulation of miscellaneous correlations may ultimately approach zero" (1953, p. 288).

However, this weak approach becomes considerably stronger if the miscellaneous correlational pattern, or various subsets thereof, can be rationalized in terms of induced construct hypotheses that could be subjected to subsequent empirical test. Thus, "it would seem more productive for a validity model to give investigators some guidance for a certain amount of inductive 'fishing' before moving to substantive hypothesis testing. At the other extreme, adopting a strictly inductive view throws away the power of hypothesis testing" (J. P. Campbell, 1976). This amounts to a call for an interplay between Leibnizian and Lockean modes of inquiry which, as we have seen, has long been informally practiced in validation efforts. This is a good thing because validation is "a continuous process that starts sometimes with a construct in search of proper measurement and sometimes with an existing test in search of proper meaning" (Messick, 1980, p. 1023).

At this point, construct validity has been cut a bewildering number of ways: in terms of content relevance and representativeness as well as criterion-relatedness; in terms of substantive, structural, and external components; in terms of trait and nomological validity; and, finally, in terms of construct representation and nomothetic span. Though grossly oversimplified, Figure 2.4 is offered as a graphic aid to conceptualizing the ways in which these various cuts fit together to constitute construct validity.

On the left side of Figure 2.4, under the label "Test Domain," appears an overlapping set of boxes, each one representing a different method of measuring the focal construct. Within each of these boxes corresponding to multiple construct measures, three test attributes are specified—content, item or task performance consistencies, and test scores—each being enclosed by dashed lines. On the right side of Figure 2.4, under the label "Nontest Domain," three sets of behavioral attributes are also enclosed by dashed lines: content-process consistencies in the domain of reference, performance processes or constructs underlying task performance, and measures of related constructs including applied criteria.

Within the test domain, the *substantive component* of construct validity links content judgments with item response consistencies. *Construct representation* combines substantive and structural aspects of test performance, the latter being schematized by the line linking performance consistencies or item structure to the structural model of test scores. Within and across domains, *trait validity* links substantive considerations to convergent and discriminant evidence revealed in relationships among multiple construct measures. Across test and nontest domains, content *relevance and representativeness* appraise test content in relation to the content (or behaviors or processes) in the domain about which inferences are to be drawn or predictions made. *Structural fidelity* appraises the extent to which items are combined into test scores in ways that reflect the structure of nontest manifestations of the construct, the latter being schematized by the line connecting content-process consistencies in domain performance to the constructs accounting for domain consistencies. Finally, *nomological validity* links test scores to measures of related constructs; *criterion-related* evidence connects test scores to measures of applied criteria; *nomothetic span* relates test scores (and component construct scores) to measures of other constructs and criteria; and, the *external component* of construct validity links test or construct scores to external variables generally.

Data and Analyses Relevant to Construct Validation

It was stressed earlier that different inferences from test scores require different blends of evidence and, furthermore, that the basic sources of validity evidence are not unlimited but fall into a half dozen or so main forms. The number of forms is arbitrary, to be sure, because instances can be sorted in various ways and categories set up at different levels of generality. But a half dozen or so categories of the following sort seem to provide a workable level for highlighting similarities and differences among validation approaches: We can engage in judgmental and logical analyses as is done in documenting content relevance and representativeness. We can conduct correlational studies to examine structure and variance components, both internally with respect to item or task consistencies and externally relating test scores to other variables. We can directly probe the processes underlying item responses and task performance. We can investigate differences in test processes and structures over time or across groups and settings. And we can see if test scores are appropriately altered in response to in-

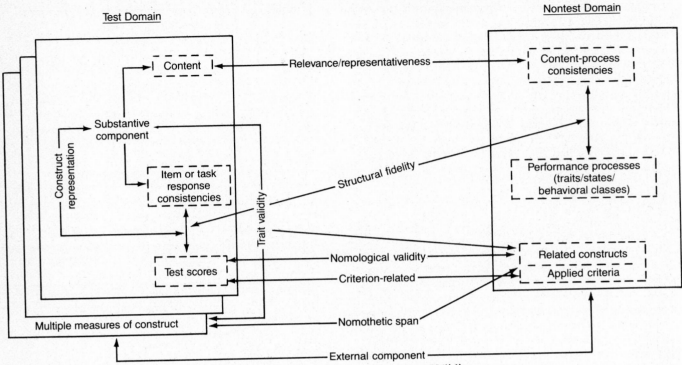

FIGURE 2.4 Components of Construct Validity

structional interventions or to experimental manipulations of content and conditions. We can also appraise the value implications and social consequences of interpreting and using the test scores in particular ways, but these form the consequential bases of validity, which are to be addressed as topics in their own right in later sections.

Within such categories of evidence, however, there exists a wide variety of data and analyses that are pertinent to construct validation (Cronbach, 1971). Of course, no one can realistically expect this vast panoply of data and analyses to be displayed in any single validation effort, or possibly even in an extended program of construct validation. Rather, data and analyses are to be advanced that are relevant to the score-based interpretations and decisions being made. The validation task is to accumulate a preponderance of evidence for or against the proposed interpretation or use. What follows is a discussion of possibilities of how to go about this. In practice, some selection needs to be made (or new alternatives created). But not just any selection will do; evidence should be sought to support and challenge the inferences to be drawn.

JUDGMENTAL AND LOGICAL ANALYSES

Technically speaking, judgmental and logical analyses can neither prove nor disprove validity claims. But such analyses frequently uncover plausible rival hypotheses that can be discounted, or at least rendered less plausible, by analysis of test data or by introduction of experimental controls to forestall the rival interpretation. We have seen how judgmental analysis of the content domain of reference can lead to expansion of the item pool to include exemplars of additional or alternative processes and structures. And how substantive analysis of hy-

pothesized domain facets in the light of item response consistencies can winnow out the merely plausible from empirically grounded versions of the construct measure. As an instance of experimental control, if acquiescent response style offers a plausible rival interpretation for questionnaire scores derived from a true-false or agree-disagree format, it can be effectively discounted by showing that results are the same with a multiple-choice or forced-choice format. Thus, judgmental or logical analyses of test or domain content and of test format could engender plausible alternative hypotheses as to score interpretation, but so could judgmental analyses of scoring models, administration procedures, and measurement contexts. The main point here is that if such judgments are made in advance of test use, any forthcoming rival hypotheses can be appraised by planned data analyses or possibly subverted by installing control procedures.

To illustrate, consider the following threats to the interpretation of a test purportedly measuring reading *comprehension*: The vocabulary level might be sufficiently difficult that the scores tap knowledge of isolated concepts rather than comprehension of connected discourse; the questions might require only recognition or recall of material presented in the passage; and, the time limits might be sufficiently stringent that the scores primarily reflect reading speed. These alternatives can be appraised via analyses of correlations between reading scores and vocabulary tests, of item difficulty as a function of indexes of feature matching between question and passage, and of the degree of speededness in test performance (Kirsch & Guthrie, 1980; Vernon, 1962). Or the rival interpretations could be experimentally precluded, or rendered less plausible, by reducing the vocabulary demands, by eliminating simple feature-matching questions, and by modifying the time limits.

Examples of rival hypotheses derived from judgmental and logical or mathematical analyses of scoring models include the following: Scores for acquiescent response style based on the total number of "true" or "agree" responses have been shown to confound the probability of responding "true" when at a loss to answer on any other basis with the number of items not known or found ambiguous (Cronbach, 1946, 1950; Helmstadter, 1957; Messick, 1961). Because these two components probably reflect different construct bases, the former purportedly tapping impulsivity or lack of ego-control and the latter skill in resolving verbal ambiguity, they should be measured separately or else one or the other source of variance should be controlled (Bentler, Jackson, & Messick, 1971: Jackson, 1967a: Messick, 1967).

As a final example, scores for empathy, insight, or interpersonal sensitivity based on the difference between a judge's prediction of a target person's self-description and the latter's actual self-description have been shown to reflect a number of components. These include real similarity between the judge's self-description and that of the target person, the judge's assumed similarity to the target as revealed in the difference between the judge's own self-description and his or her prediction of the target, the judge's ability to predict typical behavior in a class to which the target belongs (stereotype accuracy) as well as to predict how the target deviates from this norm (differential accuracy), and certain biases in the use of the response scale. It is clear that simple agreement between the judge's prediction and the target's self-description should not be interpreted as empathy or sensitivity without first disentangling these components through separate measurement or control (Cronbach, 1955; Gage & Cronbach, 1955).

CORRELATIONAL OR COVARIANCE ANALYSES

A wide variety of correlational analyses are relevant to construct validation, most of which have already been discussed in one form or another. The focus of these analyses is typically either internal to the test to examine interitem or intertask structure or external to the test to examine the structure of test or construct scores in relation to other variables. So as not to lose sight of its bearing on construct validation, let us begin by explicitly mentioning item homogeneity or *internal-consistency reliability*. This is relevant validity information because the degree of homogeneity in the test, as we have seen, should be commensurate with the degree of homogeneity theoretically expected for the construct in question.

Another basic notion central to most validation efforts is that persons who score high on the test should score high on other presumed indicators of the construct being measured. Or, more precisely, persons high on the construct should score high on a variety of indicators of that construct. This leads one to expect a *convergence of indicators*, although high correlations are not necessarily expected because of situational and method variables that might influence one indicator differently from others. For such reasons, it is usually desirable to take the notion of convergence of indicators quite literally and base inferences on some combination of several indicators, preferably derived from quite different measurement methods. "So long as each measure is subject to interactive effects, no one measure can be accepted as a standard" (Cronbach, 1971, p. 483). It should be noted, however, that convergence may be legitimately (though myopically) addressed by interrelating several construct scores based on the same measurement method, such as several different questionnaire scales of the same construct or several different observers rating the same target person. This amounts to a multimeasure, but not a multimethod, approach; all of the measures could be subject to the biases and perturbations that the particular method is heir to (Cattell & Digman, 1964; Messick, 1983).

In addition to convergent analyses, of course, we also need analyses of *discriminability from other constructs*. The construct as measured should be discriminable from measures of similar or related constructs to avoid substantive redundancy and from method contaminants to avoid artifactual score interpretations. This latter type of discriminability vis-à-vis method contaminants implies that construct scores should show *consistency across different methods of measurement or observation*. As previously noted, all three of these forms of correlational analysis—convergence of indicators, discriminability of constructs, and consistency across methods—can be powerfully and efficiently conducted through the vehicle of a multitrait–multimethod matrix.

Studies of discriminability across constructs sometimes reveal that theoretically distinct constructs are quite highly correlated. One possibility under such circumstances is that domain theory is being unnecessarily complicated by redundant constructs and that, in the name of parsimony, one or the other of them should be dropped or they should be merged into a single construct. Yet parsimony is not a rule or law, but an advisory guideline. Oftentimes, even highly correlated constructs, such as mathematical knowledge and quantitative reasoning, should be kept separate because they can be distinguished empirically on grounds other than correlation (Cronbach, in press; Messick, 1984a).

Indeed, high intercorrelations challenge the proponent of distinct constructs to locate or create the circumstances under which the variables in question are distinguishable, as was done by R. J. Sternberg and Weil (1980) for varieties of syllogistic reasoning and by Birenbaum and Tatsuoka (1982) for varieties of arithmetic tasks. The two constructs might entail some different component processes, for example, or develop experientially in different ways or in response to instructional programs. One possibility in this regard is to examine the *convergence of variables across groups*, because an across-group correlation provides different information from a within-group correlation. Mathematics knowledge and quantitative reasoning may indeed correlate highly within a group of individuals exposed to the same program of study. But if class averages for measures of the two constructs are correlated across several groups, the coefficient might be lower because different teachers or curricula may emphasize reasoning to different degrees (or might come to do so through the selective introduction of new or experimental curricula).

Another way of disentangling correlated but theoretically distinct constructs is to examine their patterns of *correlations with other variables*, because even closely related constructs may exhibit differential correlates. Contrariwise, even uncorrelated or negatively correlated indicators of the same construct may exhibit common correlates. This might be a signal that these indicators dynamically represent alternative expressions of the construct (Wittenborn, 1955). That is, if one mode of expression is employed, others need not or cannot be. Hence, even in the absence of the typical or direct form of convergent evidence, namely, a substantial correlation between two or more indicators, the demonstration of a common pattern of correlates for the indicators nonetheless provides indirect convergent evidence. As was previously noted, patterns of correlations of construct measures with other variables afford validity evidence to the extent that obtained data patterns conform to expectations deduced from construct theory. On the other hand, the mere unrationalized display of miscellaneous correlations provides weak validity evidence at best, although such unfocused empiricism may yield induced construct rationales having empirically testable consequences that could be the subject of subsequent strong validation efforts.

As the number of constructs and methods under study increases, it often becomes difficult to disentangle the threads of multiple influences by simply examining, however systematically, the surface pattern of correlation coefficients. Some method is needed for controlling certain variables while examining relationships among other variables. This can be accomplished by means of factor analysis or other multivariate techniques such as path analysis or structural equation modeling. *Exploratory factor analysis* attempts to derive from intercorrelations among items or tests a limited number of underlying component variables that, in weighted combination, would account for the observed covariation (e.g., Cattell, 1978; Harman, 1976; Mulaik, 1972). That is, if scores for these component variables (or factors) were available and were partialed out of relationships among the test variables, the residual relationships would be negligible.

The derived rotated factors are usually interpreted in terms of common processes cutting across the various tasks or tests aligned on the factor. These so-called "process" interpretations are inferences drawn from test outcomes about possible processes that might plausibly have produced the correlated results and, as such, they constitute provisional constructs. But factor interpretations, like all constructs, are hypotheses to be subjected to further empirical testing. Correlations, and hence factors, merely reveal the way that responses or performances covary in the culture from which the sample of respondents is drawn. Factors may reflect common performance processes, to be sure, but they may also reflect contiguous learning, positive transfer, common interests and experiences, or shared cultural exposure generally (Cattell, 1971; Ferguson, 1954, 1956).

Factor analysis has long been held to be a powerful tool in construct validation because the coalescence of multiple indicators of a construct into a factor provides convergent evidence; the simultaneous emergence of separate factors corresponding to different constructs provides discriminant evidence; and, the correlations among distinct factors, corresponding to relations among constructs, provides some nomological evidence (Carroll, 1980; Messick & Barrows, 1972; Royce, 1963). But it should be noted that discordant results — such as those showing that a test not deemed to be an indicator of the construct nonetheless receives a substantial loading on the factor, or that a purported indicator of the construct loads instead or in part on a different factor — are symptoms of impurity in construct measurement or signs that convergent and discriminant expectations have failed to be fulfilled in detail.

Such anomalies should be followed up empirically because they are frequently the source of new insights in science. For example, the repeated occurrence of discordant loadings on a factor might indicate that the construct is broader than originally conceived, that ostensibly separate constructs should be unified, or that a higher-order construct might be invoked to systematize the findings. On the other hand, when presumed indicators of a construct split off onto another factor, some new construct distinctions may be called for. For example, because of divergent factor loadings, flexibility versus rigidity was differentiated into spontaneous flexibility as opposed to perseveration and adaptive flexibility as opposed to persistence in the face of altered conditions (Frick, Guilford, Christensen, & Merrifield, 1959). As a general rule, the power of factor-analytic studies can be enhanced if they are designed to include marker variables for alternative or rival interpretations of the focal constructs or of the experimental tasks intended to tap them. If attempts to resolve the factor-analytic data in terms of conceivable counterhypotheses — such as, in the above instance, a single flexibility–rigidity factor or four separate factors representing spontaneous flexibility, adaptive flexibility, perseveration, and persistence — prove to no avail, then the proffered structure gains further credence.

In contrast with such exploratory factor analysis of correlated data, *confirmatory factor analysis* begins with an existing construct theory and derives a postulated pattern of item or test loadings on hypothesized factors. This theoretical pattern is then tested statistically for goodness of fit to data, preferably in comparison with competing theoretical patterns (Jöreskog & Sörbom, 1979). An example of the application of confirmatory factor analysis in construct validation is the fitting of four highly correlated factors (on the order of .8 or above) representing reading comprehension, antonyms, sentence completion, and analogies to data for the Scholastic Aptitude Test-Verbal (SAT-V), and two highly correlated factors (above .9) of regular mathematics and quantitative comparisons to data for SAT-M (Rock & Werts, 1979). Another instance involves the Graduate Record Examinations (GRE) General Test, which has three parts: Verbal, consisting of four item types; Quantitative, consisting of three item types; and, Analytical, consisting at the time of the study of three item types. A 10-factor model at the first-order level of item types fit the data quite well, but a higher-order 3-factor model (V, Q, A) fit somewhat less well than a 4-factor model separating reading, vocabulary, quantitative, and analytical factors (Rock, Werts, & Grandy, 1982).

Other multivariate procedures for clarifying the structure of intercorrelations among tests include *path analysis* and *structural equation modeling*, which are techniques used to assess the direct or so-called "causal" contribution of one variable to another in correlational or nonexperimental data. The word "causal" in this connection is not meant to imply any deep philosophical connotation of metaphysical realism beyond a shorthand designation for an unobserved hypothetical process. The general approach in these path or structural models is one of estimating the parameters of a set of structural equations (typically assumed to be linear) representing the cause–effect or antecedent–consequent relationships hypothesized in a particular theoretical conception. Several recent path models incorporate unobserved latent constructs or factors which, although not directly measured, have operational implications for relationships among observed variables (Bentler, 1980; Blalock, 1985a, 1985b; Jöreskog & Sörbom, 1979). In effect, by including factors as well as tests in the structural equations, this approach combines path analysis with factor analysis.

Another way of examining convergence and discriminability is to analyze response consistencies across a set of tests or testing conditions in terms of variance components derived from analysis of variance. Thus, the *analysis of variance components* of the type used in studies of reliability and generalizability (Brennan & Kane, 1979; Cronbach et al., 1972; Kane, 1982a; Shavelson & Webb, 1981; Webb, Shavelson, & Maddahian, 1983) is also pertinent to construct validation. Such analysis estimates the influence of various impurities in the test score and indicates how wide a domain or how broad a construct the measurement may be generalized to. The basic aim is to estimate the extent to which measurements or test scores belonging to one set of observation conditions can sustain inferences about behavior under other conditions. That is, to what degree can one legitimately generalize from one item sample to another, from one observer to another, from one testing time to another, from one test format to another, from one setting to another? Consider, for example, a study in which each of several students prepares six essays—two topics in a narrative mode, two in an expository mode, and two in a persuasive mode—with each essay being graded by three readers (Breland, Camp, Jones, Morris, & Rock, 1987; Godshalk, Swineford, & Coffman, 1966). Variance components would describe the extent to which the students' scores are affected by the topics, modes, readers, and various interactions, thereby indicating the degree to which the scores signify a general compositional skill rather than several skills varying with mode or topic or some combination.

Inherent in all of these correlational and variance-component approaches to construct validation is a search for convergent and discriminant evidence conforming to expected patterns derived from construct theory. If the propositions of the construct theory are sufficiently well developed and interconnected that a network of empirically testable consequences can be deduced therefrom, then one might proceed with a *formal testing of the nomological network* (Cronbach, 1971). But as is the case with strict operational definitions—"the closure that strict definition consists in is not a precondition of scientific inquiry but its culmination" (Kaplan, 1964, p. 77)—the testing of a nomological network seems more apropos in a mature construct validation program than in a beginning one. The reason for this is that a construct embedded in an articulated theory has systemic as well as observational meaning. "To discover what [a construct] is up to we must be prepared to send not a single spy but whole battalions. . . . What begins as the effort to fix the content of a single concept ends as the task of assessing the truth of a whole theory" (Kaplan, 1964, p. 57).

Construct validation by this nomological approach could proceed by methodically attempting to verify in turn the array of possible derivations from the construct's theoretical network. But this verificationist strategy might prove interminable and, after much investment, might yield discordant findings that cast the whole enterprise into question. A more efficient strategy is to direct attention from the outset to vulnerabilities in the network by formulating multiple counterhypotheses attacking the theory's soft underbelly. If repeated challenges from a variety of plausible rival hypotheses can be systematically discounted, then the original interpretation becomes more firmly grounded (Chamberlain, 1965; Popper, 1935/1959). In passing, it should be noted that nomological networks can be tested not only by means of correlational evidence, but also by evidence of experimental and naturally occurring performance differences, as well as by evidence bearing directly on the *processes* underlying nomological relationships. Accordingly, this topic provides a suitable bridge to the remaining types of analyses relevant to construct validation.

ANALYSES OF PROCESS

With the burgeoning of developments in the cognitive psychology of information processing (Lachman et al., 1979; Snow & Lohman, 1988), several promising techniques have emerged for the direct analysis of the processes underlying item or task performance, thereby affording multiple approaches to construct representation. Prominent among these methods is *protocol analysis*, wherein respondents are asked to think aloud during task performance or to describe retrospectively the procedural steps they employed, the verbal reports then being subjected to some form of discourse analysis (e.g., Bloom & Broder, 1950; Ericcson & Simon, 1984; C. H. Frederiksen, 1985; French, 1965; Newell & Simon, 1972). A frequently associated technique for formal construct representation is *computer modeling* of the processes identified in such protocol analyses or otherwise derived from task analysis or cognitive theory (e.g., Anderson, 1976; Dehn & Schank, 1982; Newell & Simon, 1972; Tomkins & Messick, 1963). Within computer modeling approaches, a distinction is often drawn between computer simulation models, which attempt to represent the processes actually entailed in human performance, and artificial intelligence models, which attempt to incorporate optimal processes of task performance (e.g., Dehn & Schank, 1982; Messick, 1963). Both protocol analysis and computer modeling are frequently employed in connection with extended tasks that require a few minutes or longer and that are at least somewhat accessible to introspection.

In contrast, tasks that are performed in a few seconds or less and are not readily open to introspection are usually more amenable to chronometric analysis and mathematical modeling (R. J. Sternberg, 1977). The study of task processes by means of *chronometric analysis*, or the analysis of response times, typically involves contrasts in reaction times for tasks or subtasks that differ in processing load (e.g., J. R. Frederiksen, 1980, 1982; Posner, 1978; Posner & Rogers, 1978; R. J. Sternberg, 1977; S. Sternberg, 1969a, 1969b). The obtained differences in response times provide a basis for inferences about stages of information processing and about the duration of isolated processes. With respect to construct representation, the *mathematical modeling* methods ordinarily applied to cognitive task performance are of two basic types, which have been dubbed the method of complexity factors and the method of subtask responses (Embretson, 1983).

In the former method of complexity factors, each item is rated or scored on the process (or structural) factors underlying task performance. As an example, Mulholland, Pellegrino, and Glaser (1980) identified two processing factors important in solving geometric analogies: encoding complexity, which is a function of the number of figural elements in the first stimulus presented in the analogy, and transformational complexity, which depends on the number of changes needed to convert the first stimulus into the second. Using an exponential mathematical model, these process scores were shown to be quite predictive of item difficulty in terms of both response time and accuracy. In an analogous but less formal approach, differences in item difficulty as a function of ability level (as derived from item-analysis data) are studied in relation to various item characteristics such as word frequency (Carroll, 1980).

In the latter method of subtask responses, the items are considered to be composites of subtasks, and item difficulty is modeled mathematically in terms of processes identified from responses to a complete series of the subtasks (e.g., R. J. Sternberg, 1977; Whitely, 1980b, 1981). The two methods of complexity factors and of subtask responses are by no means mutually exclusive and are sometimes combined to good effect, as was done by R. J. Sternberg and Turner (1981) in developing mathematical models of syllogistic reasoning.

Mathematical modeling of task performance usually employs measures of underlying processes to account for task difficulty, as reflected in response time, accuracy, or error rate. In contrast, psychometric modeling of item responses attempts to represent the probability of a correct response as a function of both item difficulty (as well as other item parameters) and the respondent's location on the construct or latent trait singularly tapped by the items (Hambleton & Swaminathan, 1985; Hulin, Drasgow, & Parsons, 1983; Lord, 1980). In addition, what are known as multicomponent models combine both types of modeling, usually in one of two ways. In one approach, a mathematical model relating complexity factors to item difficulty is combined with a psychometric model relating item difficulty and person differences to response probability (Fischer, 1973; Stenner, Smith, & Burdick, 1983; Whitely & Schneider, 1981). In the other approach, a psychometric model relating item and person differences on component processes to subtask outcomes is combined with a mathematical model relating subtask outcomes to the probability of correct item performance (Embretson, 1983; Whitely, 1980a). In addition, a general multicomponent model combining features of both approaches accommodates the modeling of task performance in terms of complexity factors and component outcomes simultaneously (Embretson, 1984).

As an indication of the generality of the approach, it should be noted in passing that mathematical modeling has been applied not just to cognitive task performance but also to self-descriptive questionnaire responses. As an instance, one model relates a person's item endorsement to the extent to which his or her interpretation of item content, in terms of internalized semantic schema (derived from multidimensional scaling), is consistent with the person's self-image and the impression to be made (Cliff, 1977; Cliff, Bradley, & Girard, 1973; DeBoeck, 1978). Another model relates the probability of agreement for a questionnaire item to the person's degree of discrimination among item desirability levels and the person's threshold on the desirability scale corresponding to an endorsement probability of .5 (Voyce & Jackson, 1977).

In one way or another, computer and mathematical modeling, as well as protocol and chronometric analysis, aim to represent item or task performance in terms of underlying information-processing components. In addition to such a cognitive components approach, another point of entry for studying underlying processes is to examine the *cognitive correlates* of test performance (Pellegrino & Glaser, 1979). In this approach, high and low test scores are used to form subgroups which are then compared on laboratory tasks tapping well-defined cognitive processes or information-processing skills such as memory scanning or attention allocation (e.g., E. Hunt, 1978, 1980a; E. B. Hunt, Frost, & Lunneborg, 1973; E. Hunt, Lunneborg, & Lewis, 1975). In essence, this is akin to asking how the test scores relate to well-defined marker tests of cognitive abilities or asking what the pattern of test loadings is on a set of reference ability factors (Ekstrom, French, & Harman, 1976; Guilford, 1982; Lansman, Donaldson, Hunt, & Yantis, 1982; Ward, Frederiksen, & Carlson, 1980).

A number of other approaches may also be used to illuminate the processes underlying test performance. For example, an *analysis of reasons* could be undertaken in which examinees are asked to provide a rationale for each response or, for multiple-choice items, to give their reasons for accepting one alternative and rejecting each of the others. Or one could conduct an *analysis of eye movements* in which the direction and duration of visual attention during task performance is recorded, possibly in parallel with the gathering of verbal reports about procedural steps (Newell & Simon, 1972; Snow, 1980). Inferences about information processing can then be derived from the fine structure of attentional behavior and from the consistency, or lack thereof, between visual attention and verbal report. Or, as a final instance, one could perform an *analysis of systematic errors* in task performance, deriving inferences about process from procedural bugs or from misconceptions or distortions in the respondents' problem representations or conceptual models (Brown & Burton, 1978; Caramazza et al., 1981; Stevens & Collins, 1980). In a sense, systematic errors represent pathologies in learning and performance (e.g., Pask, 1976a, 1976b), and it is a hallowed precept of abnormal psychology that one of the most useful approaches to the understanding of human functioning is to study the ways in which it breaks down or goes awry.

In numerous applications of these various techniques for studying process, it became clear that different individuals performed the same task in different ways and that even the same individual might perform in a different manner across items or on different occasions (e.g., Cooper, 1980; Embretson, Schneider, & Roth, 1986; E. Hunt, 1980b; MacLeod, Hunt, & Mathews, 1978; Snow, 1980, 1988; Snow & Lohman, 1984). That is, individuals differ consistently in their *strategies and styles of task performance* (Cooper & Regan, 1982; Messick, 1984b, 1988). This has consequences for the nature and sequence of processes involved in item responses and, hence, for the constructs implicated in test scores. For example, French (1965) demonstrated that the factor loadings of cognitive tests varied widely as a function of the problem-solving strategies or styles of the respondents. In a similar vein, C. H. Frederiksen (1969) found differential performance patterns in verbal learning as a function of strategy choice, which was in turn shown to be partly a function of strengths and weaknesses in the respondent's ability repertoire.

Thus, as a consequence of strategic and stylistic consistencies, test scores may mean different things for different people —not just for different population groups, about which we will speak shortly, but for different individuals as a function of personal styles and intentions. This being the case, the notion that a test score reflects a single uniform construct interpretation or that validation should seek to defend (or challenge) a single test-construct match becomes illusory. Indeed, that a test's construct interpretation might need to vary from one type of person to another (or from one setting or occasion to another) is a major current conundrum in educational and psychological measurement. It suggests that the purview of construct validation should include delineation of the alternative construct meanings of test scores as a function of stylistic and strategic differences and, if possible, the development of diagnostic heuristics for deciding when a particular interpretation applies.

This is not so different in spirit from the previously implied viewpoint that construct validation should include a delineation of the variety of contaminants that might distort a proposed score interpretation under different circumstances. Ultimately, of course, the particularities of score interpretation—that is, deciding whether or not method contaminants or stylistic differences should be taken into account in interpreting a given person's score—must be determined on the basis of local information about specific individuals in the specific setting.

ANALYSES OF GROUP DIFFERENCES AND CHANGES OVER TIME

Other kinds of data and analyses pertinent to construct validation include cross-sectional comparisons of the performance of different criterion groups and longitudinal comparisons of performance for the same group at two or more points in time. In the cross-sectional case, so-called criterion groups are identified that are expected to differ with respect to the construct being measured. In the longitudinal case, the relative stability of test scores, as well as the nature and degree of any developmental changes, are appraised in relation to the stability and developmental course theoretically expected for the construct under scrutiny.

In regard to criterion-group differences, one would expect on theoretical grounds that a measure of paranoia, for example, or of depression should significantly discriminate certain psychopathological groups from normal persons; that a scale of attitude toward war should discriminate theological seminary students from career military officers; and, that an educational achievement test in a subject-matter field such as American history should discriminate students who took a pertinent history course from those who did not. This last type of contrast

between experienced and beginning learners in a subject—or, more broadly, *comparisons between experts and novices* in a field— is a promising technique from cognitive psychology for identifying basic abilities and strategies underlying complex performance (Chi et al., 1987; Simon, 1976; R. J. Sternberg, 1981). The general thrust of this work for educational measurement is that experts in a variety of fields do not merely comprehend and cope with increasingly difficult and complex problems and materials, but they also process information in qualitatively different ways from novices, using integrated functional schemas that consolidate dimensions novices treat discretely. Therefore, to tap a construct of developing expertise in a subject field requires not just progressively more difficult achievement tests but also items and tasks that tie the sources of difficulty (or facilitation) to the cognitive processes and knowledge structures operative at successive levels (Messick, 1984c).

In regard to changes over time, the *test–retest reliability* of the scores should be commensurate with the degree of stability theoretically associated with the construct under investigation. Thus, just as was the case for internal-consistency reliability with respect to the homogeneity of the construct, high test–retest reliability would be good news for a measure of verbal ability in young adulthood but bad news for a measure of mood, where the scores would be expected to fluctuate on theoretical grounds even in the short run. Furthermore, again depending on the nature of the construct, changes over time might be investigated in terms not only of stability of the relative ordering of individual scores but also of theoretically expected *changes in score level and variability or in dimensional structure* (e.g., Keating & Bobbitt, 1978). For example, some construct scores (such as for general knowledge) would be expected to increase with age, whereas others (such as for impulsivity) would be expected to decrease. In some construct domains such as knowledge acquisition, new dimensions might be expected to emerge over time, whereas existing dimensions might become more differentiated or more hierarchically integrated, or both.

RESPONSIVENESS OF SCORES TO EXPERIMENTAL TREATMENT AND MANIPULATION OF CONDITIONS

The final type of data and analyses highlighted here as relevant to construct validation derives from attempts to alter test scores in theoretically predicted ways. For example, this might be accomplished through instruction, coaching, therapy, or other intervention or through systematic manipulation of test directions, item characteristics, or motivating conditions. The use of instruction or training to selectively improve component skills identified by task analysis is a technique becoming increasingly popular in cognitive psychology (R. J. Sternberg, 1981). To the extent that improving a component skill facilitates overall task performance, the task analysis gains some credence. And to the extent that the characteristics and duration of an effective training program are rationally based on an understanding of the construct to be trained, the construct theory gains some credence.

The relative effectiveness of instructional interventions should also be expected to vary as a function of the nature of the construct to be altered and the properties and duration of the treatment. For example, according to learning-and-transfer theories of cognitive ability development (e.g., Cattell, 1971; Guilford, 1967), verbal ability in adolescence grows gradually and experientially in response not to a specific curriculum but to a multiplicity of school and nonschool experiences. From this perspective, therefore, verbal ability should be affected only moderately by short-term coaching of, say, 20 to 30 hours or less, whereas achievement in a curricular subject such as history or chemistry would be expected to improve more strikingly (Messick, 1982a; Messick & Jungeblut, 1981). In some instances, however, test scores purported to measure verbal ability may prove more coachable than expected because of construct-irrelevant difficulty (such as unfamiliarity with specialized item types) or because of construct-irrelevant easiness (as in the case of inadvertent item or format clues that are amenable to test-taking tricks). On the other hand, if verbal ability scores that are not thus contaminated prove highly coachable in the short run, then the construct theory of verbal ability development becomes vulnerable.

In addition to treatment interventions designed to alter test scores in theoretically consistent ways, systematic manipulations of item characteristics and testing conditions can be employed to much the same end. For example, one construct theory of acquiescent response style links yeasaying to uncritical impulse expression and naysaying to cautious impulse control (Couch & Keniston, 1960; Messick, 1967). When the tendency toward impulsive reactions was heightened experimentally by systematically increasing the speed of item presentation, acquiescence scores were found to increase monotonically while an acquiescence factor shifted from fifth largest under longer exposure times to being the largest under fast presentation conditions (Trott & Jackson, 1967). As another example, manipulation of the semantic schemas embodied in arithmetic word problems—that is, whether the problem involves an event that causes a change in quantity, involves a combination of two quantities, or involves a comparison of two quantities—demonstrated that such schemas were strong determiners of task difficulty for second-grade students (Greeno, 1980).

These remarks conclude our treatment of data and analyses relevant to construct validation, but the discussion by no means covers all the possibilities. Remember, test validation in essence is scientific inquiry into score meaning—nothing more, but also nothing less. All of the existing techniques of scientific inquiry, as well as those newly emerging, are fair game for developing convergent and discriminant arguments to buttress the construct interpretation of test scores. We turn now to the question of the generalizability of score meaning across varying circumstances and to an examination of the limits or boundaries on the extrapolation of findings.

Generality of Construct Meaning

Because of numerous factors contributing to interactions and systematic variability in behavior and performance, generalizability of the construct meaning of test scores across various contexts cannot be taken for granted (Messick, 1983). Indeed, a perennial issue in educational and psychological measurement is the need for systematic appraisal of context effects in score interpretation, especially the degree of generalizability across different population groups, different ecological settings, different time periods, and different task domains or subdomains. The degree of generality of construct meaning across contexts may be appraised by any or all of the techniques of construct validation; for example, by assessing the extent to which test scores reflect comparable patterns of relationships with other measures, common underlying processes, or similar responsiveness to treatment across groups, situations, times, and tasks.

It should be noted that generalizability of score meaning explicitly does *not* require that all of the statistical relationships that a score displays with other variables in one group or context need be replicated in other groups or contexts. Indeed, the scores may interact with different variables in different contexts or with the same variables in different ways, as the earlier example of octane rating of fuel has illustrated. As other examples, correlation coefficients and regression systems, for purely technical reasons, must vary over population groups with different score ranges (Linn, 1983). And a group falling in a different region of an interactive regression surface from the group initially studied might not reproduce the original findings but, rather, might fit the original interactive regression function as appropriately extrapolated (Cronbach, 1968).

GENERALIZABILITY OF SCORE INTERPRETATION ACROSS CONTEXTS

Several aspects of generalizability of special concern in score interpretation and use have been given distinctive labels, such as "population validity." Granted that evidence of generalizability always contributes either to firming up or to undercutting construct interpretations, as they are discussed in the measurement literature these labels unfortunately invoke the sobriquet "validity" when the issue is more clearly one of "generalizability." In the interest of clarity, we will use the latter term in preference to the former (Messick, 1981b) or to other candidates more heavily loaded with surplus meaning, such as Cattell's (1964) "transferability." The extent to which a measure's construct interpretation empirically generalizes to other population groups is here called *population generalizability;* to other situations or settings, *ecological generalizability;* to other times, *"temporal generalizability;* and, to other tasks representative of operations called for in the particular domain of reference, *task generalizability.*

Emphasis on generalizability to and across types of persons, settings, and times was stimulated in measurement circles by the D. T. Campbell and Stanley (1963) discussion of what they called the "external validity" of experimental findings. Ever since, as applied to the properties and meaning of test scores as opposed to the results of experiments, the need for explicit generalizability evidence to support widespread test interpretation and use has become increasingly salient. In regard to *population generalizability,* the issue has long been recognized at a rhetorical level (Shulman, 1970) and is coming to be addressed with more and more sophistication at an empirical level. For example, a confirmatory factor analysis of SAT scores across random samples of American Indian, black, Mexican American, Oriental, Puerto Rican, and white test takers indicated that the test was measuring the same constructs in these population groups, in the same units, and with equivalent accuracy (Rock & Werts, 1979).

With respect to *ecological generalizability*, an extensive treatment of various sources of external invalidity has been given by Bracht and Glass (1968) as a guide for evaluating or controlling such threats to ecological and other forms of external generalizability. An important issue in ecological generalizability is that standardization of test materials and administration conditions could actually be a source of invalidity across cultural settings. That is, individuals from different cultural backgrounds might display their skills or engage task processes more optimally if the task conditions were altered to be more in line with the respondent's cultural context. This latter point mirrors M. Cole's dictum that "cultural differences reside more in differences in the situations to which different cultural groups apply their skills than in differences in the skills possessed by the groups in question" (M. Cole & Bruner, 1971, p. 847; M. Cole, Gay, Glick, & Sharp, 1971; M. Cole, Hood, & McDermott, 1978).

In regard to *temporal generalizability*, two aspects need to be distinguished: one for cross-sectional comparability of construct meaning across historical periods, say, or birth cohorts and the other for longitudinal continuity in construct meaning across age or developmental level. It should be noted that individual differences in test scores can correlate highly from one time to another (stability) whether the measure reflects the same construct on both occasions (continuity) or not. Similarly, scores can correlate negligibly from one time to another (instability), again regardless of whether the measure reflects the same or a different construct (discontinuity) on the two occasions. By combining indicators of test–retest reliability and construct meaning, it is therefore possible to disentangle the facets of stability versus instability and continuity versus discontinuity in measurement (Emmerich, 1964, 1968; Jöreskog & Sörbom, 1979; Kagan, 1971; Tucker, 1966).

Finally, with respect to *task generalizability*, Shulman (1970) focuses on the extent to which the responses a person is called upon to make in the assessment task are representative of what takes place in the external domain of reference or in other tasks derivable therefrom. This smacks of the kind of generalizability from item sample to task domain that is entailed in content representativeness, but it also includes for Shulman the generalizability of findings from assessment settings to educational applications.

When these important aspects of generalizability are referred to as types of validity, as has been customary in the measurement literature in general and the program evaluation literature in particular, this might be taken to imply that the more generalizable a measure is, the more valid. This is not generally the case, however, as in the measurement of such constructs as mood, which fluctuates qualitatively over time; or concrete-operational thought, which typifies a particular developmental stage; or administrative role, which varies by type of organizational setting; or delusions, which are limited to specific psychotic groups. Rather, the appropriate degree of generalizability for a measure depends on the nature of the construct assessed and the scope of its theoretical applicability.

The closely related issue of *referent generality* concerns the extent to which research evidence supports a measure's range of reference and the multiplicity of its referent terms (Snow, 1974). That is, the variables that are nomologically and empirically related to the construct as measured can be classified in terms of their remoteness from the pivotal processes underlying the construct — perhaps into a number of regions such as central, proximal, and distal, to use Brunswik's (1956) terms. Referent generality, then, refers to the range of variables potentially implicated with or affected by the construct as measured. It is similar in many ways to the concept of nomothetic span (Embretson, 1983) and to the distinctions made in factor analysis among general, broad, and narrow or specific factors (Coan, 1964). Differences among constructs in referent generality point to the need to tailor the level of construct interpretation to the limits of the evidence and to avoid both overgeneralization and oversimplification of construct labels. Nonetheless, construct interpretations depend not only on available evidence but on potential evidence, so that the choice of construct labels is influenced by theory as well as by evidence and, as we shall see, by ideologies about the nature of society and humankind that add value implications that go beyond evidential validity per se.

To summarize the main point of this section, the various degrees of generalizability of score meaning across different groups, settings, times, and tasks do not constitute types of validity but forms of validity evidence. Generalizability studies contribute to an evidential basis for judgments of the validity of uniform, as opposed to differential, test interpretation and use across varied contexts.

Threats to the Tenability and Generalizability of Research Conclusions

The evidential basis of test validity depends largely on empirical studies evaluating hypotheses about processes and relationships. Hence, we must be concerned about the quality of these studies themselves and about the extent to which any research conclusions derived therefrom are tenable or are threatened by plausible counterhypotheses to explain the results (Guion, 1980). Four major classes of threats to the tenability and generalizability of research conclusions are delineated by Cook and Campbell (1979), with primary reference to quasi-experimental and experimental research but also relevant to nonexperimental correlational studies.

These four classes of threats to the dependability and extendability of research inferences deal, respectively, with the following questions:

1. "Statistical conclusion validity" — whether or not a relationship observed in the sample might have arisen by chance (that is, from sampling error)
2. "Internal validity" — whether the observed relationship is plausibly causal from one operational variable to the other (that is, whether a difference between outcome measures in two particular samples was caused by differences in the way they were treated)

3. "Construct validity"—how the causal processes and effects may be labeled or explained (that is, whether one can generalize from operational measures to cause-and-effect constructs)
4. "External validity"—how generalizable is the (interpreted causal) relationship across population groups, settings, and times.

These four categories of threat to valid research inferences are an elaboration of the two classes of "internal" and "external" validity previously propounded by D. T. Campbell and Stanley (1963). The first two categories subdivide the earlier Campbell and Stanley notion of internal validity into conclusions about covariation, based on statistical evidence, and conclusions about causality, based on experimental or quasi-experimental evidence and causal modeling. The last two categories subdivide the erstwhile Campbell and Stanley external validity into generalizability of the causal relationship to and across alternate measures of cause-and-effect constructs and generalizability to and across different types of persons, settings, and times. Internal validity is considered atheoretical, being simply a demonstration that a complex treatment made a real difference at the particular place and time under scrutiny, that is, internal validity might be more aptly termed "local molar causal validity" (D. T. Campbell, 1986). In contrast, external and construct validities inherently involve theory or, at least, informal theorylike constructions.

Cronbach (in press), for one, lauds Cook and Campbell (1979) for giving proper breadth to the notion of constructs by extending the construct validity purview from the meaning of measures to the meaning of cause-and-effect relationships, for advancing "the larger view that constructs enter whenever one pins labels on causes or outcomes" (p. 6). At the same time, however, Cronbach (in press) insists that construct validity and external generalizability are inseparable: "The class of (for example) sites to which one generalizes is described in terms of constructs, and the indicated boundaries of the class are hypotheses to be evaluated" (p. 19). This is not a minor dissent because Cronbach is ultimately led to a position almost diametrically opposed to that of Cook and Campbell with respect to the priority of validity questions, at least in educational research (Mark, 1986). For Cook and Campbell (1979), "the primacy of internal validity should be noted for both basic and applied researchers" (p. 83). For Cronbach (1982), interactions are such a fact of life that the so-called causal or treatment variables are more likely than not to interact with population and site characteristics, as well as with observational conditions in the immediate research setting, to modify the meaning of the outcome or effect. As a consequence, the primary question for Cronbach becomes one of the external validity of interpretive extrapolations.

Cook and Campbell (1979) provide an extensive discussion of various threats to each of their four classes of validity inferences, along with a detailed explication of analytical procedures for countering their impact. Likewise, Cronbach (1982) discusses models for internal and external inference from his perspective, along with a detailed examination of both the controls that promote internal reproducibility and the limitations

of arguments that extrapolate research findings into expectations about different or future situations.

In addition, problems in generalizing from controlled research settings to naturalistic applied settings have been discussed by Snow (1974) and by Fromkin and Streufert (1976), among others. The latter authors invoke the concept of "boundary variables," which are critical differences, between the research setting and the applied setting to be extrapolated to, that limit the generalizability of research findings. A "critical difference" is a factor present only in the research setting and missing in the applied setting, or vice versa, that is essential to the unaltered occurrence of a relationship between variables. This formulation suggests that studies of the transportability of measures and findings from one context to another should focus on identifying all of the boundary variables that are a source of critical differences between the two contexts, as well as on gauging the potency and direction of the effects of these boundary variables on events in the two conditions.

Although the causal inference stressed by Cook and Campbell (1979) is not the dominant concern in construct validation, construct theories typically entail some causal claims. For example, the tenability of cause–effect implications is central, even if often tacitly, to the construct validation of a variety of educational and psychological measures such as those interpreted in terms of ability, intelligence, and motivation. Indeed, the causal overtones of constructs are one important source of the value implications of test interpretation, the topic that comes next on the agenda.

The Consequential Basis of Test Interpretation

As indicated in Table 2.1, the consequential basis of test interpretation comprises the value implications of constructs and their associated measures. By now, the vaunted battle cry of the relativists, that facts and theories are value laden, has become a celebrated cliché (e.g., Howard, 1985; Howe, 1985). Consequently, taking into account the role of values in scientific inquiry, and hence in test validation, is virtually mandatory. Max Weber's perverse ideal of a value-free social science is passé (Gouldner, 1962). The issue is no longer *whether* to take values into account, but *how*. On these points, we hold with Kaplan (1964) that "not all value concerns are unscientific, that indeed some of them are called for by the scientific enterprise itself, and that [in scientific inquiry] those which run counter to scientific ideals can be brought under control" (p. 373).

Values Intrinsic to Validity

As aptly phrased by Kaplan (1964), "all propositions . . . are judged on the basis of their implications, and not just in terms of what they entail but also in terms of what they make more likely" (p. 374). This is no less the case for score-based inferences with respect to their value implications. Indeed, it is difficult to isolate questions of the value implications of score interpretations from questions of the validity of those interpretations. Even the meanings of the words "valid" and "value" derive from the same Latin root, *valere*, meaning "to be strong." Furthermore, derivation of the term "value" from the old French *valoir*, meaning "to be worth," applies as well to modern uses of "valid," as in references to the functional worth of the testing. Hence, because validity and values go hand in hand, the value implications of score interpretations should be explicitly addressed as part of the validation process itself.

VALUES AS BIAS AND AS MATRIX OF MEANING

Values are important to take into account in score interpretation not only because they can directly bias score-based inferences and actions, but because they could also indirectly influence in more subtle and insidious ways the meanings and implications attributed to test scores, with consequences not only for individuals but for institutions and society. In this context, bias might be defined as the intrusion of ordinarily tacit extrascientific motives or beliefs into the fulfillment of scientific purposes, that is, as an "adherence to values of such a kind and in such a way as to interfere with scientific objectivity" (Kaplan, 1964, p. 373). But this view of bias by no means requires that science be value free or that the part values play in science be limited to that of bias. For example, values can serve as subject matter for scientific investigation, and are clearly salient in the professional ethics of science, without usually making for bias.

More equivocally with respect to bias, values form a basis for the identification and selection of problems and for the priorities and resources allocated to their solution. Bias is not inevitable here because "values make for bias, not when they dictate problems, but when they prejudge solutions" (Kaplan, 1964, p. 382). Everything depends on the way in which the inquiry is conducted and the conclusions are derived: "Freedom from bias means having an open mind, not an empty one. . . . [In any event,] science does not demand that bias be eliminated but only that our judgment take it into account" (Kaplan, 1964, pp. 375–376). The ways and means of taking bias into account are far from obvious, however, and whatever prescriptions do exist usually presume that the intrusive values have been identified. For example, the standard social science answer is that "*there is no other device for excluding biases in social sciences than to face the valuations and to introduce them as explicitly stated, specific, and sufficiently concretized value premises*" (Myrdal, 1944, p. 1043). But what if the value premises are subtle, unclear, or conflicting? Under such circumstances, we need comparative and dialectical strategies of the type embodied in the Kantian, Hegelian, and Singerian modes of inquiry to help expose operative value assumptions to open examination.

Among the most subtle and pervasive of value influences in scientific inquiry in general, and in test validation in particular, are those contributing to or determining the *meanings* attached to attributes, actions, and outcomes. In this case, it is not so much that values predetermine the results of inquiry as that they give form and flesh to the interpretation of those results. "What is at stake here is the role of values, not in our decisions where to look but in our conclusions as to what we

have seen" (Kaplan, 1964, p. 384). Once again, Kantian, Hegelian, and Singerian approaches should prove useful in helping to discern the underlying value matrices in which particular meanings or interpretations are embedded. The role of values as bias, especially in connection with the appraisal of action implications of score interpretations, will be discussed in more detail in a later main section on the consequential basis of test use. The remainder of this main section is devoted to the form-giving role of values in determining or distorting the meaning of score interpretations per se. As a consequence, emphasis is also given to the need for empirical and rational grounding of the value aspects as well as the substantive aspects of construct meaning.

Sources of Value Implications of Measures and Constructs

Whenever an attribute, event, or relationship is interpreted or conceptualized, it is judged—even if only tacitly—as belonging to some broader category to which value already attaches. For example, if a crime is viewed as a violation of the social order, the expected societal response would be to seek deterrence, which is a derivative of the value context of this way of seeing. But if a crime is seen as a violation of the moral order, expiation might be sought. And if seen as a sign of distress, especially if the distress can be assimilated to a narrower category like mental illness, then a claim of compassion and help attaches to the valuation (Vickers, 1970). Or as another instance, if overrepresentation of minority children in special education programs is perceived as a violation of equal protection under the law, strategies for reducing the inequality might be sought. But if seen as demographic differences in educational needs, then strategies for equitable provision of educational services would be stressed (Heller et al., 1982).

In Vickers's (1970) terms, the conceptualization of an attribute or relationship within a broader category is a process of "matching," which is an informational concept involving the comparison of forms. The assimilation of the value attached to the broader schema is a process of "weighing," which is a dynamic concept involving the comparison of forces. For Vickers (1970), the reality system and the value system are elaborated in concert. He uses the term *appreciation* to refer to these conjoint judgments of fact and values (Vickers, 1965).

In the construct interpretation of test scores, such appreciation processes are pervasive, though typically implicit. Constructs are broader conceptual categories than are test behaviors, and they carry with them into score interpretation a variety of value connotations stemming from at least three major sources: the evaluative overtones of the construct labels themselves; the value connotations of the broader theories or nomological networks in which constructs are embedded; and, the value implications of still broader ideologies about the nature of humankind, society, and science that color our manner of perceiving and proceeding (Messick, 1980).

THE VALUES OF CONSTRUCT LABELS

Let us consider first the evaluative implications of the construct label itself. As a case in point, envision a performance measure that, at one extreme, reflects continual changes of strategy in attacking successive problems and, at the other extreme, reflects the repeated application of a single strategy. The evaluative implications of score interpretations would be very different if the construct being measured were conceptualized as "flexibility versus rigidity," say, as opposed to "confusion versus consistency." Similarly, a construct and its associated measures interpreted as "inhibited versus impulsive" would have different implications if it were instead labeled "self-controlled versus expressive," and distinctly different yet if labeled "inhibited versus expressive." So would a variable like "stress" if it were relabeled "challenge." The point is not that we would convert a concept like stress from a bad thing into a good thing by renaming it. But, rather, by not presuming stress to be a bad thing, we would be more likely to investigate broader consequences, facilitative as well as debilitative (McGrath, 1976).

In choosing a construct label, one should strive for consistency between the trait implications and the evaluative implications of the name, attempting to capture as closely as possible the essence of the construct's theoretical import (especially its empirically grounded import) in terms reflective of its salient value implications. This could prove difficult, however, because some traits, such as self-control and self-expression, are open to conflicting value interpretations. These cases may call for systematic examination of counterhypotheses about value outcomes—if not to reach convergence on an interpretation, at least to clarify the basis of the conflict. Some traits could also imply different value outcomes under different circumstances. In such cases, differentiated trait labels might be useful to embody the value distinctions, as in the instance of "facilitating anxiety" and "debilitating anxiety" (Alpert & Haber, 1960). Rival theories of the construct might also highlight different value implications, of course, and lead to conflict between the theories not only in trait interpretation but also in value interpretation, as in the case of intelligence viewed as fixed capacity as opposed to experientially developed ability (J. McV. Hunt, 1961).

Apart from its normative and evaluative overtones, perhaps the most important feature of a construct label in regard to value connotations is its breadth, or the range of its implied theoretical and empirical referents. This is the issue, discussed earlier, that Snow (1974) called *referent generality*. The broader the construct, the more difficult it is to embrace all of its critical features in a single, or even a composite, measure. Hence, the broader the construct, the more we are open to what Coombs (1954) has called "operationism in reverse," that is, "endowing the measures with all the meanings associated with the concept" (p. 476). And the broader the construct, the more likely it is that hidden value implications will flourish unheeded.

In choosing the appropriate breadth or level of generality for a construct and its label, one is buffeted by opposing counterpressures toward oversimplification on the one hand and overgeneralization on the other. At one extreme is the apparent safety in using strictly descriptive labels tightly tied to behavioral exemplars in the test (such as Adding and Subtracting Two-Digit Numbers). The use of neutral labels descriptive of test tasks rather than of the processes presumably underlying task performance is a sound strategy with respect to *test* names,

to be sure (Cronbach, 1971). But with respect to construct labels, choices on this side sacrifice interpretive power and range of applicability if the construct might be defensibly viewed more broadly (e.g., as Number Facility). At the other extreme is the apparent richness of high-level inferential labels such as intelligence, creativity, or introversion. Choices on this side suffer from the mischievous value consequences of untrammeled surplus meaning.

Misaligned or tangential surplus meaning can be problematic even for more circumscribed variables. As an instance, labeling as "acquiescence" the probability of agreeing with items when at a loss to respond on any other basis helped to create a context in which investigators mistakenly expected this response style to correlate with such variables as conformity, submission, or persuasibility (Messick, 1967). In general, however, the surplus meaning of well-grounded construct labels often affords a rich source of research hypotheses for elaborating construct meaning. As Cronbach put it,

> surplus meaning is an advantage, insofar as it sends out shadowy lines connecting the systematic observations with situations and variables that have not been systematically studied, [constituting] an interim basis for judgments that would otherwise have to be made without any scientific guidance. . . . The disadvantage in surplus meaning comes when the tentative, speculative nature of the surplus is forgotten. (1971, p. 482)

At first glance, one might think that the appropriate level of construct reference should be tied not to test behavior, but to the level of generalization supported by the convergent and discriminant research evidence in hand. But constructs refer to potential relationships as well as actual relationships (Cronbach, 1971), so their level of generality should in principle be tied to their range of reference in the construct theory, with the important proviso that this range be restricted or extended when research evidence so indicates. The scope of the original theoretical formulation is thus modified by the research evidence available, but it is not limited to the research evidence available. As Cook and Campbell (1979) put it, "the data edit the kinds of general statements we can make" (p. 88). And debating the value implications of construct interpretation may also edit the kinds of general statements we *should* make.

THE VALUES OF THEORIES

Value implications derive not only from construct labels but also from the broader theories or models in which constructs are enmeshed. As we confront the different value implications of alternative theories of a domain, we are struck by the apparent cogency of one of the relativists' basic points, namely, that advocates of opposing theories appear to live in literally different worlds (Kuhn, 1962; Weimer, 1973). There appear to be "divergent rationalities" (Shweder, 1986) and diverse "ways of worldmaking" (Goodman, 1978), so that the boundary between subjectivity and objectivity is blurred and reality is not independent of the viewer's version of it. Consider the following, somewhat fanciful illustration from the history of science:

> Tycho sees the sun beginning its journey from horizon to horizon. He sees that from some celestial vantage point the sun (carrying with it the moon and planets) could be watched circling our fixed earth. Watching the sun at dawn through Tychonic spectacles

would be to see it in something like this way. Kepler's visual field, however, has a different conceptual organization. Yet a drawing of what he sees at dawn could be a drawing of exactly what Tycho saw, and could be recognized as such by Tycho. But Kepler will see the horizon dipping, or turning away, from our fixed local star. (Hanson, 1958, p. 23)

Disputes over substantive issues as well as value issues are joined when one theoretical perspective or worldview is confronted by another, and the tacit assumptions of each become explicitly clarified as territorial distinctions are defended. This is the main reason why Churchman (1971, 1979) has persistently invoked Kantian, Hegelian, and Singerian modes of inquiry when, as is usually the case in social science, a central issue involves ways of seeing or defining the issues themselves.

Let us play this scenario out in more detail with respect to theories of intellective abilities (Messick, 1981b). The various theories in this domain are dominated by different conceptions and attitudes about the origins and development of intelligence. They vary profoundly in their relative emphasis on different determinants of ability, ranging from generally genetic to entirely environmental, as well as in their attendant emphasis on the limits as opposed to the potentialities of learning. The theories also differ in preferred approaches to the study of intelligence, ostensibly reflecting in a number of ways various theoretical or methodological predilections, but simultaneously conveying tacit value commitments about the nature of the human being and of human perfectibility (Messick & Sigel, 1982).

Although the theory and measurement of intelligence as such is only a limited part of educational and psychological measurement, the three predominant issues in the history of criticism of the testing movement, according to Carroll (1978), have focused on this topic. Specifically, the three recurrent themes are as follows:

1. The question of whether intelligence is a valid concept, and, if so, whether it corresponds to a "single ability" that generalizes to all kinds of activities, or to a multiplicity of abilities. 2. The possible genetic basis of intelligence, and its modifiability. 3. The relevance of intelligence to scholastic success (p. 83).

These issues are not mutually independent, in that a firm position on one has important ramifications for the others. For example, a multidimensional conception of intelligence is cumbersome in connection with a genetic view or one that highlights innate determiners of intellectual functioning. It is just plain unwieldy to postulate innate mechanisms for the dozen or so primary mental abilities of Thurstone (1938, 1944), for the roughly two dozen first-order and half-dozen or so higher-order abilities of Cattell (1971), or for the upwards of one hundred faceted abilities of Guilford (1967, 1982). Although both Guilford and Cattell identify a few basic processes as innate, they gave equal or greater prominence to environmental influences, emphasizing the experiential development of differentiated abilities through learning and transfer. In contrast, those theorists stressing the predominance of heritability, like Jensen (1972) or Burt (1949, 1955), tend to stress as well a single overarching general factor of intelligence. Granted that the issues of heredity versus environmental impact are complex if not intractable, should we not by now have reached

some closure on the singularity versus the multiplicity of intelligence? One might have thought so were it not for the different-world syndrome.

In one camp, intelligence is conceptualized in terms of a single monolithic dimension of general intellectual prowess. As a consequence, the measurement of intellective ability tends to focus on general aspects of comprehension, reasoning, and judgment, using a limited range of relatively complex tasks that require these processes in various combinations. Scores on these complex tasks, by virtue of this overlap, then tend to correlate substantially with each other and to yield a large general factor when factor analyzed. The unity of this large average factor is emphasized in this approach, as is the average level of individual functioning across the related tasks, with variability in performance typically attributed to trivial specific factors or to error of measurement.

In the other camp, intelligence is conceptualized in terms of multiple discrete abilities. As a consequence, intellectual measurement tends to entail extensive batteries of diverse tasks focusing on distinct aspects of comprehension, reasoning, judgment, fluency, visualization, and the like. Scores on these disparate tasks then tend to correlate quite differently with one another and to yield sizable multiple factors when factor analyzed. The diversity of these multiple factors is emphasized in this approach, as is the pattern or profile of individual functioning across different types of tasks, with variability in performance typically attributed to individuality.

Each of these contending theories of intelligence carries its own construct system and influences in subtle or substantial ways the kinds of data collected, the types of analyses conducted, and ultimately the range and nature of conclusions drawn. And if this contrast of unitary versus differentiated theories of intelligence has elements of different-worldliness about it, one should note that the two conceptions are not that radically different in their theoretical frameworks. Indeed, both may be considered to reflect the same general theoretical orientation or metaphorical model of intelligence, namely, a geographic model that aspires to map the intellectual sphere using dimensionalizing techniques such as factor analysis.

But as R. J. Sternberg (1985b) reminds us, there are a number of other theoretical perspectives or metaphorical models of intelligence conducive to different techniques and outcomes. For example, in addition to the geographic model, Sternberg classifies existing intelligence theories as reflecting one or another of the following conceptual orientations: a computational model of intelligence as a computer program, an anthropological model of intelligence as a cultural invention, a biological model of intelligence as an evolving system, a sociological model of intelligence as the internalization of social processes, and a political model of intelligence as mental self-government. If two intelligence theories sharing a common metaphorical perspective — such as unidimensional and multidimensional conceptions within the so-called geographic model — can engender the different-world phenomenon of investigators talking past one another, as we have seen, just imagine the potential babble when more disparate models are juxtaposed. Yet it is precisely such mutual confrontation of theoretical systems, especially in attempting to account for the same data, that opens their underlying scientific and value assumptions to public scrutiny and critique (Churchman, 1971; Singer, 1959).

In speaking of the power and consequences of key scientific metaphors—such as the clockwork models of the 18th century, the organismic models of the 19th century, and the computer models of the 20th century—Kaplan stresses their invasive impact on the manner in which problems are formulated and solutions sought.

> Our own metaphors . . . are the ways of speaking which make sense to us, not just as being meaningful but as being sensible, significant, to the point. They are basic to semantic explanation and thereby enter into scientific explanation. If there is bias here it consists chiefly in the failure to recognize that other ways of putting things might prove equally effective in carrying inquiry forward. But that we must choose one way or another, and thus give our values a role in the scientific enterprise, surely does not in itself mean that we are methodologically damned. (1964, p. 384)

But must we choose one way or another? For if so, we become conceptually hamstrung in a scientific enterprise in which, as R. J. Sternberg (1985b) put it, "the model is the message." Before considering methodological alternatives that facilitate the taking of multiple perspectives, however, let us briefly examine another major source of value implications in measurement.

THE VALUES OF IDEOLOGIES

Value implications in educational and psychological measurement derive not only from construct labels and the broader theories that undergird construct meaning, but especially from the still broader ideologies that give theories their perspective and purpose. An ideology is a complex configuration of shared values, affects, and beliefs that provides, among other things, an existential framework for interpreting the world—a "stage-setting," as it were, for viewing the human drama in ethical, scientific, economic, or whatever terms (Edel, 1970). The fall-out from ideological overlays is hard to avoid in educational and psychological measurement. Ideologies influence theoretical conceptions and test interpretations in subtle and not so subtle ways, especially for very general and evaluative constructs like intelligence or competence, often in a fashion that goes beyond empirically grounded relationships in the construct theory (Crawford, 1979). Indeed, evidence for value implications is not the same as evidence for nomological implications. The former evidence appears sparse, very likely because it has not often been systematically sought.

Thus, ideological differences can lead to radically different perceptions of the value implications of test interpretation and use (Messick, 1981b). Consider the contrasting value assumptions of the following two social ideologies. One, which has been called an institutional–universalist paradigm, "assumes that learning is an apolitical and uniform process, measurable by universally applicable, objective criteria. It promotes human freedom by liberating people from the confining parochial ways of neighborhood, locality, myths, and the past" (Kelly, 1980, pp. 77–78). Adherents of the other, which has been called a participatory–selectivist paradigm, emphasize "subjective experience and individual perceptions as essential to learning. To them learning is political, diffuse, multi-fac-

eted, and individual. They believe it is impossible to measure individuals or groups fairly using universal, 'objective' criteria" (Kelly, 1980, p. 78).

The universalism of the former perspective admits the utility of standardized tests interpreted in terms of universal or general educational standards. The selectivism of the latter perspective balks not so much at testing per se as at being standardized. In the latter view, the objection is to universally applied tests interpreted in terms of uniformly applied standards. What is needed, according to this viewpoint, are selectively applied tests interpreted in terms of selectively applied standards that are attuned to individual or group needs and goals.

Given the pervasiveness and subtlety of impact of values and ideologies on test interpretation, we need to explore some ways and means of uncovering tacit value premises and of coping with their consequences for test validation. Let us turn next to a brief consideration of how this might be attempted.

Methodologies for Confronting Values and Value Biases

To the extent that scientific observations are theory-laden and theories are value-laden, both the objectivity of sensory experience and the logical distinctness of fact and value are undermined. Because scientific decisions are thus underdetermined by both experience and logic, the choices that scientists qua scientists make to accept or reject a theory or hypothesis are value judgments (Rudner, 1953). The point is that the epistemic principles guiding these scientific choices—such as predictive accuracy, internal coherence, external consistency, unifying power, fertility, or simplicity—are values, not scientific rules of inference (Howard, 1985). Moreover, although scientific decisions are ostensibly based on such epistemic values, they are also pervasively influenced by nonepistemic emotive and ethical values. In this light, value judgments become an integral if not routine part of science—especially social science, which is "*doubly value-laden . . .* [because] the very concepts social researchers employ are evaluative of human behavior" (Howe, 1985, p. 12).

From this relativistic standpoint, scientific judgments such as those involved in test interpretation *are* value judgments, so it is almost tautological to inquire into or appraise the value implications of scientific interpretations. But labeling scientific decisions as value judgments, as opposed to factual or theoretical judgments, does not absolve them from the need to be supported empirically or to be rationally defended against criticism. One need not go this far down the line with the relativists, however, to recognize that value implications cannot be ignored in appraising the validity of score interpretations. One need only ask, along with Singer (1959), what the consequences would be if a given scientific judgment had the status of an ethical judgment.

Exposing the value assumptions of a construct theory and its more subtle links to ideology—possibly to multiple, cross-cutting ideologies, is an awesome challenge. One approach is to follow Churchman's (1971) lead and attempt to contrast each construct theory with an alternative perspective for interpreting the test scores, as in the Kantian mode of inquiry. Better still for probing the value implications of a theory is to contrast it with an antithetical, although plausible, Hegelian counterperspective. Churchman (1961) contends that although consensus is the decision rule of traditional science, conflict is the decision rule of ethics. Because the one thing we universally disagree about is "what ought to be," any scientific approach to ethics should allow for conflict and debate, as should any attempt to assess the ethical implications of science. "Thus, in order to derive the 'ethical' implications of any technical or scientific model, we *explicitly* incorporate a dialectical mode of examining (or testing) models" (Mitroff & Sagasti, 1973, p. 133). This dialectical approach may be undertaken not only by two or more scientists with rival perspectives, but by a single scientist alternatively playing rival conceptual roles. The intent is to illuminate the scientific and value assumptions of constructs and theories so that they may be subjected to either empirical grounding or policy debate, or both.

The utility of dialectical and rhetorical methods in social science is becoming more widely recognized, as is the pragmatic value of a logic of practical judgment, that is, of the means–ends reasoning of practical deliberation among psychological and educational researchers and practitioners (Garrison, 1986). It will be recalled, for example, that Toulmin's (1972) "rational bets," by being subjected to criticism in the light of scientists' experience, led to prospective estimates of the consequences (including the value consequences) to be expected from alternative intellectual positions or policies. Thus, the rationality of the scientific enterprise, as revealed in the reasoning patterns of practicing scientists (Shapere, 1977), affords a pragmatic basis for deliberating value implications—provided, of course, that the collective practitioners of science (and of education) evince sufficient practical wisdom. The means–ends deliberation of value consequences of testing will be explored further in a subsequent section on the consequential basis of test use. But first, after a brief summation, let us examine the evidential underpinnings of testing applications.

In sum, the aim of this discussion of the consequential basis of test interpretation was to raise consciousness about the pervasive consequences of value-laden terms (which in any event cannot be avoided in either social action or social science) and about the need to take both substantive aspects and value aspects of score meaning into account in test validation. In particular, attention was centered on the value implications of test names, construct labels, theories, and ideologies, as well as on the need to take responsibility for these value implications in test interpretation. That is, the value implications, no less than the substantive or trait implications, of score-based inferences need to be supported empirically and justified rationally.

This is an important aspect of test validity because the value implications of score interpretation are not just a part of score meaning, but a socially relevant part that often triggers score-based actions and serves to link the construct measured to questions of social policy. In contrast, some argue that these are *only* issues of social policy and not of test validity per se (N. S. Cole, 1981; N. S. Cole & Moss, 1988). To be sure, the determination of social policy falls beyond the pale of validity theory. But the interpretation of test scores and, as we shall see later,

the use of test scores in the implementation of social policy falls well within the realm of validity inquiry, because the import of scores for action depends on the validity of their meaning and their value implications.

The Evidential Basis of Test Use

Returning to Table 2.1, we recall that the evidential basis of test interpretation is construct validity. In a fundamental and profound sense, the evidential basis of test use is also construct validity, but with the important proviso that the general evidence supportive of score meaning be enhanced by specific evidence for the relevance of the scores to the applied purpose and for the utility of the scores in the applied setting. Everything that has already been said about construct validity with respect to test interpretation holds with equal force in connection with test use. Implications for action based on test scores depend on meaningful score interpretations for their legitimacy. The justification of test use also depends on the relevance and utility of the scores vis-à-vis the applied purpose and context, as well as on the potential and resulting consequences of actual test use. The social consequences of test use and their bearing on validity are addressed in the next main section. Here we focus on the meaning, relevance, and utility of test scores as requisites for test use and on the range of evidence needed to support these claims.

At this juncture, no attempt will be made to reprise the various principles and procedures of construct validation that have already been covered. But all of these points should be kept in mind in what follows because construct validity is a sine qua non in the validation of test use, in the sense that relevance and utility as well as appropriateness of test use depend, or should depend, on score meaning. Using test scores that "work" without some understanding of what they mean is like using a drug that works without knowing its properties and reactions. You might get some immediate relief, to be sure, but you better ascertain and monitor the side effects. As will be maintained shortly, side effects or, more generally, the social consequences of testing contribute to score meaning but cannot substitute for score meaning in the rational justification of test use.

Especially important to keep salient, because of its pervasive and overarching impact, is the need for both convergent and discriminant evidence to discount the two major threats to interpretive meaning, namely, construct underrepresentation and construct-irrelevant variance. These threats jeopardize the construct validity of score interpretation, whether for domain-sample or predictor tests, as we have seen. But construct underrepresentation and construct-irrelevant variance must also be explicitly dealt with in the very delineation of applied domains and in the conceptualization and measurement of criterion variables, that is, in precisely those aspects of domain coverage and criterion prediction that are the heart of traditional content and criterion-oriented validity. Thus, we begin this treatment of the validity of test use by maintaining that the construct validity of score interpretation undergirds *all* score-based inferences, not just those related to interpretive meaningfulness but also the content- and criterion-related inferences specific to applied decisions and actions based on test scores.

Construct Validity as a Rational Basis for Test Use

The unified concept of validity integrates considerations of content, criteria, and consequences into a construct framework for testing rational hypotheses about theoretically relevant relationships, including those with an applied focus. The bridge or connective tissue that sustains this integration is the meaningfulness or trustworthy interpretability of the test scores, which is the goal of construct validation. In other words, the essence of the unified view of validity is that the appropriateness, meaningfulness, and usefulness of score-based inferences are inseparable and that the unifying force is empirically grounded construct interpretation.

Some major applied benefits derive from this unified validity perspective in that construct-valid score meaning provides a rational basis for hypothesizing predictive test-criterion relationships, for judging content relevance and representativeness, for claiming job or curriculum relatedness, for anticipating potential testing outcomes, and for detecting possible side effects of testing. It has been maintained from the outset that validation is scientific inquiry into score meaning, that score-based inferences are hypotheses and the validation of such inferences is hypothesis testing. In applied as well as scientific measurement, "the problem is not one of evaluating tests, it is one of developing and validating hypotheses" (Guion, 1976, p. 791).

A key question is, Where do these hypotheses come from? Or more pointedly, How may such applied hypotheses be rationally generated? The answer with respect to applied hypotheses is the same as for substantive or scientific hypotheses, namely, from the implications of construct theories. In applied instances, of course, these would typically be construct theories of performance domains as well as construct theories of the critical aspects of performance that it would be important to diagnose, certify, or predict in connection with applied decision making. Thus, domain constructs and criterion constructs—that is, the knowledge, skills, cognitive processes, personal attributes, or whatever that are entailed in successful domain performance—provide a rational basis for selecting attributes that are representative of the domain or likely to be predictive of criterion success. Construct theories of each identified attribute then serve to guide test construction and test evaluation. Furthermore, the construct theory of the performance domain also affords a rational basis for appraising the meaning and adequacy of the criterion measures themselves. Thus, empirical predictor-criterion correlations not only test the specific applied hypothesis of a relationship between them, but also contribute one more strand to the construct validity of both the predictor and the criterion measures.

In applied work, domain and criterion constructs as well as predictor constructs are typically derived from job or task analyses or from examination of extant curricula or training programs. Often the products of these analyses are described only in terms of job or lesson content or in terms of task behaviors. But knowledge, skills, and other attributes underlying domain performance are not only implied but acted upon in test construction as well as in validation design. By making construct theories of the performance domain and of its key attributes more explicit, however, test construction and validation become more rational, and the supportive evidence sought becomes more attuned to the inferences made.

On the other hand, it might be argued that construct theories have nothing to do with the certification of curriculum learning or the prediction of job success. The existing curriculum or job is the touchstone, not some theory. But the extant curriculum or job is an empirical realization of a theory as to what should be covered in the curriculum or how the tasks should be organized into the job. Although focus on the specifics of a given curriculum or job is often precisely on target in applied testing, this does not obviate the construct theory but, rather, makes it *ad hoc* to the particular circumstances. The need for construct theory becomes visible when one appraises the adequacy of the specific curriculum vis-à-vis the knowledge domain or the adequacy of the specific job structure vis-à-vis the performance requirements. In any event, the testing of rational hypotheses generated from a construct theory of the performance domain helps protect us from unsupported inferences whenever action implications are based, as they always ultimately are, not on the content of task performance or the size of predictive correlations but on the inferred meaning of the scores in terms of attributes and processes assessed.

Thus, just as it was argued earlier that traditional content validity alone does not provide a sufficient evidential basis for test interpretation and use, so it is argued here that traditional criterion-oriented validity alone does not provide a sufficient basis either. The traditional view of criterion-oriented validity holds that

> the information about validity is in the correlation coefficients and the regression equations on which they are based. . . . The nature of the measurement is not what is important to this statement. The important fact being reported is that these variables can be used to predict job performance within the limits of accuracy defined by the correlation coefficient. (Guion, 1974, p. 288)

This may be the case for some constrictive conception of predictive accuracy, but it is not enough for the validity of test interpretation and use. There is simply no good way to judge the appropriateness, relevance, and usefulness of predictive inferences in the absence of evidence as to what the predictor and criterion scores mean. It is not enough, for example, to show that a test significantly improves the prediction of freshman grades at a particular college. Whether it should be used in selection, or whether the criterion should be modified, depends on what the test scores mean. It is one thing if the scores reflect achievement striving, for instance, but what if they reflect docility?

It should also be recognized that judgments of the relevance and representativeness of domain coverage and judgments about which critical aspects of performance will serve as criteria, as well as decisions about which rational hypotheses to test, are all fundamentally value judgments. "If we examine values carefully and if we take them seriously, we may change the hypotheses to be tested" (Guion, 1974, p. 292) or the curriculum coverage promulgated or the criteria advanced (Messick, 1982b). As already indicated, such issues of value implications in test use are addressed in the ensuing main section. We proceed now to a discussion of the relevance of content and criteria and of the utility of test-criterion relationships in applied testing practice.

Considerations of Content in Test Use

As was pointed out in the previous considerations of content in test interpretation, issues of content relevance and representativeness arise in connection with both the construction and the application of tests. In the former instance, content relevance and representativeness are central to the delineation of test specifications as a blueprint to guide test development. In the latter instance, they are critical to the evaluation of a test for its appropriateness to a specific applied purpose. In the present section, the focus is on particular curricula, instructional experiences, or jobs as *ad hoc* targets for test construction and use. But it should be noted that one may go from a target job or curriculum to a test in a number of distinct ways.

In a test format, for example, one might present the stimulus or task conditions identified through job or curriculum analysis in roughly the same form and in the same relationships as they appear on the job (or in the curriculum). The intent is to elicit a response class of interrelated behaviors similar to that on the job, although not necessarily a precisely identical class (because of inevitable differences between the test and job settings). Such a *job-sample* test is tailored to the specific job (or curriculum) and should be highly predictive of specific job performance (Wernimont & Campbell, 1968). Or, one might present the identified task conditions more discretely to cover the major job components in some representative fashion but not in the combinations or contexts characteristic of the specific job. Such a *content-sample* test might not be as predictive as a job-sample test for the specific job, but it might have wider applicability across jobs containing various combinations of the task components. Or, as a final instance, one might infer from the categories of task requirements and associated response classes—that is, from what needs to be done and what typically is done—the processes and abilities suitable for job performance, and then develop or select tests to measure the relevant constructs or traits. The resulting *construct-referenced* test or battery might have still wider applicability across jobs or criterion settings calling for the measured abilities and constructs, even though specific criterion tasks qua tasks may vary considerably. Tenopyr (1986) views such examples as falling on a continuum ranging from "specific validity" to "general validity," but this dimension merely serves to confound validity with both generalizability and referent generality.

Although the previous discussion was couched in terms of prediction, its basic points apply to not only selection and placement uses of tests but also certification and licensure uses. On the face of it, the distinction involved here is between predicting subsequent levels of criterion performance and affirming the current attainment of performance standards. More fundamentally, however, the distinction is between constructs or traits that are predictive of a range of performance levels and those that are prerequisite for performance at a given level (Guion, 1976; Hedberg & Baxter, 1957). Prerequisite constructs or traits, although not generally predictive over the full range of task or job performance (or, more broadly, of occupational or professional performance), are nonetheless critical in the sense that their absence, or the absence of an adequate or minimal level, constitutes a severe limitation on domain performance (Kane, 1982b).

Thus, it would appear that it is not only the particular curriculum or job, but also the particular applied purpose, that should determine the target for test construction and test evaluation. For instance, the intended certification of minimal or desirable performance levels focuses attention on the discriminability of individual scores in the vicinity of the standard or cutting score, as we have just seen, rather than on discriminability over a wide score range as pertinent for criterion prediction. Such different test uses have important implications for both test construction and validation. Hence, the nature of both the target curriculum or job and the intended uses of the testing will be addressed in the current considerations of test relevance. But it should be kept in mind in what follows that representing the target curriculum or predicting the target job are merely *ad hoc* instances of more general and overarching measurement principles. In such applied testing, as in all educational and psychological measurement, one should strive to maximize the meaningfulness of score interpretation and to minimize construct-irrelevant test variance. The resulting construct-valid scores then provide empirical components for rationally defensible prediction systems and rational components for empirically informed decision making.

CURRICULUM RELEVANCE AND REPRESENTATIVENESS

Although a test could be constructed to reflect a *specific* subject-matter curriculum or training program actually being used or considered for use in particular localities, a more usual procedure in large-scale standardized testing is to construct a test that reflects the *generality* of extant curricula in the subject-matter domain. This is typically accomplished by having the test specifications set by a representative committee of subject-matter experts, preferably informed by timely curriculum and textbook surveys. Given the prescriptive prerogatives of the expert committee, its representativeness of viewpoint should be systematically appraised from time to time, perhaps by conducting a duplicate-specification experiment akin to Cronbach's (1971) duplicate-construction experiment. In this case, under the same rules for appointing members, two or more expert committees would be convened, each charged with the independent development of test specifications. The resulting specifications could then be evaluated for their degree of overlap and for salient similarities and differences. Any major differences might next be adjudicated to generate a consensual test blueprint, or perhaps each set of specifications could serve as the starting point for a duplicate-construction experiment.

In essence, the representative committee of experts is put in the position of taking a broad view and of specifying what the ultimate educational objectives are or ought to be for covering the given subject-matter domain at the particular grade or instructional level in question. To do this requires some working conception of the nature and structure of the domain — in our earlier terms, at least some provisional "construction" and at best an elaborated construct theory of the domain. That is, construct theories of subject-matter domain performance — for example, in terms of knowledge structures and information-processing skills — provide a rational basis for outcome measurement in education (Haertel, 1985).

The judged degree of fit between the test and the ultimate educational objectives for covering the subject-matter domain is an example of what Cureton (1951) calls "logical relevance." This notion may also be applied to the judged fit between a test and the ultimate performance objectives in a job domain. An example of test specifications for a high-school level reading test is given in Table 2.4. These specifications reflect committee judgments of relevant domain coverage, recognizing that no specific curriculum may match these specifications in detail. A remaining step is to specify the number of items, or the amount of testing time, to be devoted to each row and column or cell of this grid so that the test is judged to be representative in its coverage of the domain.

Alternatively, test specifications could be set to reflect the topical content and task requirements relevant to the immediate objectives of a *specific* curriculum. For a test targeted toward a specific curriculum, the judged fit of the test to the immediate objectives of that curriculum is called *curricular relevance* (Cureton, 1951). But note that in such instances, one

might also inquire as to the relevance of the immediate curriculum objectives to the ultimate objectives of domain coverage. In regard to job-training programs, for example, a test could be judged relevant to the training objectives, but its relevance to the job depends on the relevance of those training objectives to job performance. By targeting test construction toward a specific curriculum, the issue of what ought to be covered as opposed to what is covered is essentially finessed, in the sense that the relevance of the immediate curriculum objectives to the ultimate educational objectives has either been demonstrated or taken for granted. But this issue of ultimate relevance cannot be ignored over the long haul because, to modify Cronbach (1971), "the universe pertinent in summative evaluation [of student qualifications as well as of curriculum effectiveness] is the universe of tasks graduates are expected [by society] to perform" (p. 460).

In a number of applied instances, whether an existing test is constructed to reflect a broad perspective of domain coverage or the narrower perspective of immediate curriculum objectives, the test could subsequently be considered for use in connection with another curriculum having possibly different topical coverage or emphasis. For example, a test might be wanted to certify the minimal competence of graduates from various teacher-training programs in a state. Or a test might be sought that is sufficiently on target to be useful in evaluating the effectiveness of a curriculum that is different from, though in the same domain as, the curriculum guiding test construction.

In the process of professional test development, a number

TABLE 2.4 Committee Specifications for the Reading Test (National Educational Longitudinal Study)

	Literal Detail	Main Idea	Supporting Evidence	Sequence	Author's Purpose	Inferred Meaning	Audience/Tone	Author's Use of Language Irony, Loaded Words	Figurative Language Simile, Metaphor	Cause/Effect	Extension of Ideas	Seeking Relationships	Finding Faulty Logic	Fact/Opinion
EXPOSITORY														
1. Science passage (geological clock)														
2. Literary passage (Harlem Renaissance)														
3. Social Studies passage (transportation)														
PERSUASIVE														
4. Editorial														
POETRY														
5. Poem														
NARRATIVE														
6. American fiction														
7. Biography														
8. Fable														

of systematic review procedures are typically employed to increase, if not insure, the judged relevance and representativeness of the resultant test items with respect to the test specifications. Similarly, when a test is selected for a particular applied purpose, as in the instances just given, systematic appraisal of relevance and representativeness with respect to the specific domain of application also seems called for (Tittle, 1982). Once again, this need is often addressed by convening panels of experts, not to set test specifications but to gauge the degree of fit of the test specifications, as well as of the test items, to the particular applied context.

To illustrate, several studies have been undertaken to appraise the suitability of the National Teacher Examinations (NTE) for certifying the minimum amount of knowledge and academic skill needed for competent performance as a beginning teacher in a particular state (e.g., Faggen, 1984). These studies ordinarily employed two or three types of panels of expert judges. Of prime importance were content review panels, usually composed of teacher educators. Each panel member was typically asked to supply independent judgments of the content appropriateness of each test item to the specific state-approved curriculum or applied domain at issue. Each member was also asked to judge the relative emphasis of the test topics vis-à-vis the curriculum emphasis, to indicate any curriculum topics omitted from the test, and to provide an overall judgment of the similarity between the test and the curriculum.

When performance standards or cutting scores were to be recommended, knowledge estimation panels were also convened, preferably including classroom teachers and school administrators in addition to teacher educators. Each member of these panels was asked to provide independent judgments of the percentage of minimally qualified examinees who would know the answer to each of the test questions. These item judgments were then combined to estimate the score that a minimally qualified person would receive on the total test. This particular judgmental procedure is only one of several approaches that could be used to set passing scores (Livingston & Zieky, 1982).

Moreover, in some studies, the issue was the relevance of the test items to not only the immediate objectives of the teacher-training curriculum but also the more distal objectives or requirements of the job of beginning teacher. In such cases, job-relevance panels comprised of practicing teachers and school administrators were asked to judge, independently member by member, the degree to which the knowledge and skills tapped by each test item were relevant to competent performance as a beginning teacher in the state. To complete the circle, one might have also asked, of course, for judgments of the relevance of curriculum topics to the job of beginning teacher. But by at least judging the relevance of the test to both the curriculum and the job, one gains an important entry point for appraising the logical relevance of the teacher-training program to beginning-teacher performance requirements.

In regard to the consistency of results from such panel review studies, the usual approach is to divide each panel into equivalent half panels based on detailed information about the background of each panel member. The degree of agreement between the judgments of the two half panels can then be quantified in a variety of ways. But in some quarters, the judged relevance of the test to the curriculum, regardless of how reliably or consistently determined, has been deemed insufficient for claiming that a test is relevant for educational certification because the curriculum might not have been fully implemented for the students. What is needed, it is argued, is test relevance with respect to actual instructional experience.

INSTRUCTIONAL RELEVANCE AND REPRESENTATIVENESS

A well-intentioned but perverse concept called "instructional validity" has recently appeared on the educational measurement scene. As a putative form of validity, this concept is perverse because it is duplicative, vague, and refractory to appraisal. And it virtually invites confusion and interpretive slippage with respect to a fundamental aspect of measurement that is already overburdened by a bevy of specialized, quasi-legitimate validity labels (Messick, 1980). The confusion engendered by this concept stems from a number of sources. To begin with, there are at least two distinct versions in the literature. Furthermore, each version aspires to a form of validity when, instead, one conception deals with test relevance and the other with both relevance and utility. The objection to instructional "validity" here is as a form of test validity per se, not to the underlying notion that test scores should be specifically relevant to instructional experience for some educational purposes.

The version of instructional validity entailing both test relevance and utility applies to the appropriateness of pupil classification into different instructional programs. It holds that "the choice of a basis for classification should start with an examination of the differences between the instructional alternatives and the abilities they require; the examination of the child should focus on the abilities that are requisite for the instruction" (Wigdor & Garner, 1982, p. 175). The point is that tests used for planning student experiences ought to promise greater benefit to the student if the plan is carried out than if alternative plans are followed.

But it is not clear whether this version of instructional validity refers to the utility of differential instruction in effectively producing meaningful educational improvement, or to the relevance of identified student characteristics as indicative of differential educational needs, or to the construct validity of tests in assessing those characteristics and needs, or to some combination of any or all of these. In any event, it would appear that the central issues underlying this version of so-called instructional validity concern the test's degree of relevance to the classification or instructional decision as well as the test's utility in advancing instructional goals. However, it would seem more illuminating to address these clearly important issues by means of the already existing psychometric concepts of relevance, utility, and construct validity than to confound them in an amorphous conglomerate relabeled "instructional validity."

The other version of instructional validity is considerably less vague, especially if one jettisons the validity misnomer and labels it more in keeping with its essential properties, namely as "instructional *relevance*." The basic notion may be thought of as a further refinement of curricular relevance. As we have seen, curricular relevance refers to how well the test items represent the immediate objectives of the curriculum. Instructional relevance refers to how well the test items reflect the still more immediate objectives of actual instruction, that is, those objectives that students were actually exposed to (McClung, 1978). Both of these notions are in contrast to what has been called logical relevance, which refers to how well the test items represent the ultimate educational objectives of domain coverage, including generalization and transfer objectives (Cureton, 1951). The intent of this version of instructional validity or relevance is that tests used to certify student success, especially if sanctions are invoked, should assess what students have had a chance to learn in school.

The apparent straightforwardness of these conceptual distinctions belies the controversy and confusion surrounding their application (Yalow & Popham, 1983). Much of the controversy derives from operational difficulties in attempting to assess adequately and without bias a slippery concept like instructional relevance, especially because each of the three major approaches of teacher judgments, student reports, and classroom observations are either cumbersome or vulnerable to distortion, or both (Tittle, 1982). Proposing a standard of relevance that is impractical to appraise is another instance of the perverseness mentioned earlier. It should be clear, however, that it is not the appraisal of student outcomes in relation to opportunity to learn that is perverse but, rather, the implication that such fractious evidence signifies test validity.

Furthermore, much of the confusion about instructional validity results from an equating of so-called content validity with the logical relevance of the test items vis-à-vis domain coverage and possibly from a blurring of adequacy of exposure or opportunity to learn with adequacy of preparation as a basis for instructional relevance. For example, Yalow and Popham contend that

> content validity is present if the content of the test representatively samples the content of a desired performance domain. . . . When we test a high school student's knowledge of mathematics, . . . the "desired performance domain" is not mathematics that happened to be taught, but mathematics that should be known. (1983, p. 12)

This is a clear reference to the ultimate educational objectives of domain coverage. Yalow and Popham (1983) went on to claim that "adequacy-of-preparation is not a component of content validity, . . . it is not a form of validity at all" (p. 12).

Some of this confusion might also be dispelled not by making further distinctions within the realm of content relevance, but by discriminating more clearly between the constructs of educational achievement and competence. Educational achievement traditionally refers to what a student knows and can do in a specified subject area as a consequence of instruction. That is, "achievement constructs . . . are the intended consequences of planned instructional experiences" (Haertel, 1985, p. 42). Competence refers to what an individual knows and can do in a subject area however that knowledge and skill is acquired—whether through instruction, nonschool experience, or whatever. In terms of content relevance, educational achievement tests would be referenced to curricular or instructional objectives, whereas competency tests would be refer-

enced to representative coverage of domain knowledge and skill regardless of curriculum or instruction. In this framework, competency tests referenced to curricular or instructional objectives would qualify as misconstrued achievement tests, while achievement tests referenced to domain coverage would qualify as misconstrued competency tests (Messick, 1984c). Yet ultimately, it is not merely the test labels that need to be clarified but the purposes of the testing.

Instructional relevance was introduced in the first place because of concern over the potential unfairness of denying a high school diploma to students lacking skills, if those students had not had instruction adequate to develop those skills. However, Yalow and Popham (1983) argue that "such potential unfairness resides in the *use* of the score-based inference, not in the inference itself" (p. 13). But action implications *are* score-based inferences. So this certification use of tests, like all test uses, is a score-based inference subject to validation. Some of this confusion dissipates if we follow through on what has been maintained all along: that these issues of content are not issues of validity per se, but of relevance. The validity of test use requires additional evidence, not the least of which bears on score meaning and on the social consequences of use. What are the consequences of denying diplomas if students were not adequately exposed to pertinent instruction? Or what are the consequences of awarding diplomas if minimum competence is not demonstrated? Or, more fundamentally, is it fair to examine students on something that has not been explicitly taught and, if not, what about testing for generalization, transfer, and problem solving? As we shall see in the next main section, it is not that adverse social consequences render test use invalid but, rather, that the validation of test use should assure that adverse social consequences do not stem from any source of test invalidity, such as construct-irrelevant variance.

Nonetheless, Yalow and Popham (1983) have identified a critical problem in certification testing, one that might be at least in part resolved by focusing on the appropriate relevance question to be asked. Because relevance "is always a matter of relevance for some purpose" (Cureton, 1951, p. 672), this question should be determined by the proposed test use. Here, some advice from Cureton might help.

> As we move from ordinary unit and course and subject achievement tests to tests covering larger areas of knowledge and behavior, and from there to still more comprehensive tests which attempt to assess the general level of the students' educational development, the value of curricular relevance becomes progressively lower. The only safe standards of relevance for such tests are the standards of logical relevance developed on the basis . . . of the ultimate aims of education. Such tests should always measure genuine desired outcomes of the educational process rather than merely the outcomes to be expected from existing instructional materials and methods. (1951, p. 671)

Accordingly, if certification tests were constructed to represent ultimate domain objectives, as Yalow and Popham (1983) also desire, these should prove useful in evaluating the coverage and effectiveness of both the curriculum and the instruction, as well as in certifying student competence in terms of tasks that —by social or expert consensus—they should be able to perform. Then accountability for unsatisfactory student competence might impinge on the teacher and the curriculum developer and not wholly on the student.

JOB RELEVANCE AND REPRESENTATIVENESS

Another important *ad hoc* source of test specifications is the target job or set of tasks for which successful performance is to be predicted or minimum performance levels certified. In this regard, techniques of job and task analysis developed in industrial psychology, which are akin to techniques of behavioral analysis from experimental psychology and of process analysis from cognitive psychology, are often helpful in delineating critical job or task dimensions to guide both test construction and test evaluation. There are a variety of approaches to job and task analysis that variously emphasize such aspects of, or contributors to, job performance as work activities, worker functions, worker traits, and task characteristics (e.g., McCormick, 1976). For example, a *behavior description* approach focuses on what actually is done in the course of task performance; a *behavior requirements* approach focuses on what should or must be done for successful performance, as opposed to what is done; an *ability requirements* approach focuses on the human attributes required by the task, as opposed to the behaviors required; and, a *task characteristics* approach focuses on the stimulus conditions that elicit performance, as opposed to the activities triggered, the behaviors required, or the abilities called into play (Dunnette, 1976; McGrath & Altman, 1966).

From a measurement perspective, one of the main objectives of job or task analysis is to identify categories of important job behavior that might then be represented on a job-sample or content-sample test. Another main objective is to establish a link between categories or dimensions of job performance and the human attributes prerequisite to and predictive of that performance, as a basis for developing or selecting construct-referenced measures of job-relevant skills. The former objective stresses a behavior requirements approach while the latter stresses an ability requirements approach. Data relevant to both approaches are usually obtained in the form of expert judgments by job incumbents in response to job inventories.

A job inventory is a structured job-analysis questionnaire comprising a list of relevant tasks that might be performed within the occupational field in question. The set of tasks is usually constructed on the basis of direct observation or audio-visual recordings of job activities; on the basis of individual and group interviews with job incumbents; open-ended questionnaires, logs, or diaries completed by incumbents; or, critical incidents of worker behavior characteristic of very good or very poor job performance. The job inventory is then administered to job incumbents and sometimes job supervisors, who are asked to judge each task with respect to such rating dimensions as the relative time spent, the degree to which the task is part of the job, the frequency with which the task is performed, and the importance or criticality of the task to the job (McCormick, 1976). In addition, the ability or attribute requirements of the job can be identified by having each of the tasks or job components rated for the degree to which it requires each of several specified abilities or adaptive attributes (Dunnette, 1976; McCormick, 1976).

If one or more sets of task ratings such as those for importance or relative time spent are factor analyzed, the resulting dimensions of job importance (or of deployed time) can serve as test specifications. Items can then be constructed to represent the task behaviors that mark or load substantially on these dimensions, or to tap the knowledge and abilities judged to be requisite to the marker tasks. In this regard, an important finding supportive of this approach is that factor structures based on the rated importance of task elements for performing the job were basically similar to factor structures based on profiles of abilities and attributes judged to be operative in each of the task elements (McCormick, Jeanneret, & Mecham, 1972). Furthermore, in relation to observed consistencies in actual task performance, "results show quite conclusively that expert judgments of required abilities for task performance do accurately map the abilities shown factor analytically to be most important for performing those tasks" (Dunnette, 1976, p. 509).

Indeed, expert judgments of test-criterion relationships, at least for cognitive tests predicting criteria of training success, appear to provide more accurate estimates than do typical criterion-related validation studies, which are more often than not based on small samples with restricted ranges and deficient criterion measures (Schmidt, Hunter, Croll, & McKenzie, 1983). However, less experienced judges do not fare nearly as well, exhibiting about twice as much random error as the experts' estimates (Hirsh, Schmidt, & Hunter, 1986).

As a starting point, when an existing test is to be evaluated for its applicability to a particular job, judgments by job incumbents, supervisors, or other experts could be obtained for the extent to which the test specifications match the importance dimensions for the job. Better yet, at a more detailed level, each test item could be judged for the extent to which the knowledge and skills tapped are pertinent to the marker tasks that define the job-importance dimensions (Rosenfeld, Thornton, & Skurnik, 1986). At a more global or molar level with respect to the job, each test item could be judged as to whether or not it taps knowledge or skill that is essential to overall job performance; more globally with respect to an ability or skill test, each of the specific job tasks could be judged as to whether the tested skill is essential for that task performance (Lawshe, 1975).

The extent to which the knowledge or skill measured by a test item is judged to be essential to job performance has been quantified in industrial applications in terms of a statistical index that basically reflects the plurality of the judgments of "essential" over those of "not essential." Those items for which this index is not statistically significant for the given number of judges are then eliminated in the scoring of the test, and the average of the indexes for the retained items serves as a kind of content-relevance coefficient for the resultant test scores (Lawshe, 1975). However, the elimination of some items from the test scoring might erode content representativeness, so the match of the resultant test to the content domain should be reappraised. This approach could also be employed in educational applications to quantify the extent to which each test item (and the resultant "purified" test) is appropriate to a particular curriculum or subject-matter domain. These are important first steps in the test validation process but, as emphasized next, they are only first steps.

FROM TEST SPECIFICATIONS TO VALID TEST SCORES

Whatever the source of the test specifications—whether they be *ad hoc* to a particular job, curriculum, or course of instruction or derived from construct theories of domain performance or of ultimate job or educational outcomes—it is not enough merely to construct or assemble test items that are judged by experts to meet those specifications (Linn, 1980). As indicated earlier, these expert judgments are in actuality a two-step affair, with one of the steps often remaining implicit or taken for granted. That is, what the experts judge to be appropriate to the curriculum or essential to the job is the knowledge or skill represented in the test item, presuming that the item is a construct-valid measure of those attributes or processes. If the items are indeed construct-valid measures, then by expert judgment they may be deemed relevant and representative with respect to the job, curriculum, or subject-matter domain, as the case may be.

But whether the test items tap relevant knowledge, skills, or other attributes cannot be left to supposition or to expert judgment alone. Construct-related evidence is needed of the types delineated in the earlier section on the evidential basis of test interpretation, especially evidence to discount the operation of construct-irrelevant method variance. As outlined previously, a wide array of evidence supportive of the inferences to be drawn is pertinent to the construct validation of the test scores. This includes evidence bearing on interitem structure, fidelity of the scoring model, score homogeneity, theoretically expected convergent and discriminant correlational patterns, underlying processes, responsiveness of test performance to instruction or experimental manipulation, and the like. In brief, the setting of test specifications and the determining of item relevance and representativeness by expert judgment is only a starting point in test construction or test evaluation. Ultimately, the legitimacy of test interpretation and test use becomes ever more firmly grounded by taking subsequent steps in pursuit of construct validation.

Utility of Test-Criterion Relationships

Job or task analysis and construct theories of job or subject-matter domain performance, in addition to providing a basis for developing test specifications, also afford a basis for specifying criterion measures. That is, careful analysis and theoretical conceptualization of the criterion behavior and the situations in which it occurs facilitate the isolation of effective criterion dimensions and subdimensions. And as will be elaborated later, this disaggregation of criteria into multiple dimensions, each predicted by different variables, is central to clarifying the construct validity of the criteria themselves. Such analysis also helps one to discern the relative importance of the criterion dimensions and to formulate feasible approaches to their measurement. In other words, construct analysis of the criterion domain helps to determine what criterion elements or dimensions to measure, how each element is to be measured, and if

desired, how to combine them into overall criterion composites (Brogden & Taylor, 1950b).

Such systematic examination of criterion behavior is in contrast, as lamented by Brogden and Taylor in 1950, with the more usual first step in criterion development, which is to search for *available* criterion measures that are *apparently* suitable for the purpose at hand. Today's laments are little different:

> We continue to pour most of our resources and effort into measurement of predictors and into schemes for relating predictor scores to contaminated and deficient but convenient criterion measures. Far too little attention has been given to what it is we are trying to predict: to behavior, its causes, and its evaluation as effective or ineffective. (Hakel, 1986, p. 352)

The reference to "contaminated and deficient but convenient criterion measures" is an important one because it stresses what, indeed, is a major theme of this section, namely, that criterion measures must be evaluated like all measures in terms of their construct validity. That is, convergent and discriminant evidence must be forthcoming to counter the two major threats to criterion meaning: construct irrelevant variance (or criterion contamination) and construct underrepresentation (or criterion deficiency). In practice, the main sources of such evidence are criterion-oriented studies relating test scores to criterion scores.

Although the prime purpose of these studies is to evaluate the hypothesis of a relationship between tests and criteria, they afford as much information about the meaning of the criteria (i.e., the performance or outcome being predicted) as about the utility of the tests. This is clearly so when prediction of a real-world criterion is at issue, in which case the pattern of correlations with various (interpretable) predictor tests helps clarify what the criterion measure means. It is also the case when the meaning of particular test scores is at issue and correlations with relevant criterion measures are appraised to help clarify the test's meaning. That is, the information inherent in correlations between tests and criteria, as in all correlations, is a two-way street. "In fact, a test-criterion study may be seen as simply another examination of convergence of indicators, and its interpretation must be as careful as that of any study of convergence" (Cronbach, 1971, p. 488). One reason that such care in interpretation is needed is that typical criterion-oriented studies do not provide much, if any, discriminant evidence to discount the intrusion of rival constructs or method variance (Gulliksen, 1950a, 1976, 1986).

For example, suppose a job analysis indicated that an important aspect of the job of teaching was skill in diagnosing learning difficulties (construct C_1), which might be captured in a criterion measure (Y) such as supervisors' ratings of the teacher as a diagnostician. Suppose further that the ability to infer particular learning difficulties from patterns of incorrect student performance was deemed on theoretical grounds to depend on inductive reasoning (construct C_2), assessable by means of a paper-and-pencil test (X). Four relationships pertinent to construct validation can now be generated (Nunnally, 1978):

1. $Y = f(C_1)$, the construct interpretation of the criterion measure as a reflection of C_1;

2. $X = f(C_2)$, the construct interpretation of the test as a reflection of C_2;
3. $C_1 = f(C_2)$, the theoretical or nomological relation between C_1 and C_2; and,
4. $Y = f(X)$, the predictive hypothesis of a test-criterion relationship.

If both X and Y have a reasonable degree of construct validity, then (4) implies (3), along with the attendant action import stemming from construct meaning. If (3) is well-grounded in other evidence or is theoretically compelling, then (4) contributes to the construct validity of both the test and the criterion measure, relatively more so to whichever one is weaker in this regard. By itself, positive evidence for (4) supports all three of the other relationships but does not discount other constructs as a plausible basis for the finding—hence, the need for carefulness in convergent interpretation. On the other hand, negative evidence for (4) undercuts all three of the other relationships. But to the extent that one or two of them are well grounded, then the source of invalidity becomes circumscribed (along with the plausible rival hypothesis that inadequate control procedures were responsible for the negative evidence in the first place). Finally, if the construct tapped by the test is presumed to be another indicator of the criterion construct—in this example, say, a test of learning-error diagnosis—then C_1 equals C_2 and (4) contributes directly to the validity of the two remaining relationships, that is, provides evidence for the convergence of X and Y as measures of a common construct.

Before addressing further these issues of the validity and possible invalidity of criterion measures, let us consider some traditional distinctions among criterion-oriented studies in terms of the timing and function of criterion data collection.

TIMING AND PURPOSE IN CRITERION MEASUREMENT

As noted earlier in this chapter, criterion-related evidence takes two distinct forms, one comprising predictive relationships and the other concurrent relationships. Predictive evidence bears on the extent to which the test scores forecast an individual's future level on the criterion, whereas concurrent evidence relates the test scores to an individual's present standing on the criterion. This manner of phrasing the distinction stresses the issue of timing, that is, whether the criterion data are collected at a later time than the test data or at roughly the same time. A more fundamental issue, however, is that of the function or purpose of the testing—for example, whether the decisions based on test scores involve selection, classification, or readiness diagnosis (for which criterion data are inherently unavailable until a later date) as opposed to certification or remedial diagnosis (for which criterion data are, at least in principle, collectible at the time of testing).

In *selection* decisions, persons are either accepted or rejected for a given *treatment*, which is the general term customarily used to refer to any educational or training program, job assignment, counseling procedure, therapeutic intervention, and so forth. In *classification* decisions, there are two or more categories or treatments, and every person is assigned to some category. If the alternative treatments form an ordered sequence or continuum, as in elementary and advanced subject-matter courses, the decision is referred to as *placement*. An important type of selection or classification decision might be called *readiness diagnosis*, whereby individuals are predicted to respond favorably to the available treatment or more favorably to one among a set of alternative treatments. This is in contrast with *remedial diagnosis*, whereby current needs or disorders are identified (Snow & Lohman, 1988). Remedial diagnoses followed by prescriptions of treatment become readiness diagnoses. The point is that the identification of needs is separable from the prescription of treatments, and tests can be separately validated for the two purposes.

Where feasible, the utility of test scores for selection and classification decisions, including readiness diagnosis, should be evaluated by longitudinal studies that follow up treated individuals (after some period of exposure to the treatment) in order to collect measures of criterion performance. Tests useful in selection are those that are predictive of this subsequent criterion performance, whereas tests useful in classification or placement are those that predict subsequent criterion performance differentially in the alternative treatments (Cronbach & Gleser, 1965).

In contrast, for tests useful in the remedial diagnosis of, say, reading-skill deficiencies or behavior problems and in the certification of attainment of educational outcomes, the issue is not so much the prediction of future criterion performance as it is the relation of the test scores to concurrent criterion data—such as current reading performance, behavior ratings, course grades, performance standards, and the like. Another instance in which concurrent evidence is appropriate is in appraising the suitability of substituting a test for a longer, more cumbersome, or more expensive measurement procedure (now viewed as the criterion), as when a group-administered technique is to replace an individually administered one or a paper-and-pencil version is to replace a laboratory task.

In some instances, however, the need for predictive as well as concurrent evidence has become blurred, as in teacher certification or professional licensure. In such cases, assessment typically focuses on the attainment of performance standards for critical knowledge and skills, but most of these are deemed critical because they presumably have an effect on student or client outcomes. Evidence relating critical professional knowledge and abilities to client outcomes sounds as if it is criterion-oriented and predictive, to be sure, but it does not necessarily need to be in terms of predicting future performance of individuals. Such evidence might be based, for example, on the relationships between critical professional abilities and client outcomes averaged over large numbers of professionals and clients, as in clinical trials (Kane, 1982b, 1986), although this approach would be compromised by any tendency of the most skilled professionals to treat those clients in greatest need. Evidence of this type, along with other construct-related evidence and logical analyses supportive of a construct theory of critical professional abilities in a field, goes a long way toward justifying certification and licensure practice. But it does not obviate the ultimate desirability of criterion-oriented evidence if feasible (Madaus, 1986).

A straightforward example of predictive evidence for certification and licensing examinations would involve appraisal of the degree of agreement between the pass–fail dichotomy on the examination and a competent–incompetent dichotomy in subsequent professional practice (Kane, 1982b). However, there are numerous personal and circumstantial reasons, apart from critical knowledge and skills, why practitioners might fail to exhibit competence in the profession. Hence, although individuals who pass the examination should be more likely to fall on the competent than the incompetent side of the practice dichotomy, special attention should be paid to other factors in addition to test invalidity leading some certified practitioners to appear incompetent. Less equivocally, it is important to document that individuals who fail the examination are much more likely, if the test is a construct-valid assessment of critical knowledge and skills for them, to fall on the incompetent side of the practice dichotomy.

Such predictive studies of dichotomous states would suffer even more seriously than usual from the bane of most selection research, namely, that the test-criterion relationship cannot be well estimated in the absence of criterion scores for those who fail as well as for those who succeed on the test. There are also enormous political difficulties entailed in arranging for uncertified persons to enter a field—even on a probationary or experimental basis—just to facilitate validation studies, especially in fields where the public must be protected from serious adverse consequences. Nonetheless, efforts to obtain test scores for persons entering a profession newly contemplating certification or licensure, or to estimate the predictive relationship in fields already subject to entry standards, should not be forsaken simply because of political roadblocks.

Without such direct predictive evidence, the criterion-related support for certification and licensure tests is indirect, though possibly quite substantial. That is, the main purpose of certification and licensure is to ensure that professional knowledge and skills that are important or necessary for safe and effective practice have been acquired. However, because professions, unlike specific jobs, encompass a wide range of activities in a variety of settings, the predictive relationships between critical skills and actual professional performance may be both fragile and difficult to reveal amid this real-world complexity. An alternative, less direct, validation strategy argues that the knowledge and skills tested are critical by virtue of a relationship to client outcomes. As in the case of content relevance, the argument here also involves a two-step, construct-mediated approach: First, empirical evidence and logical or theoretical rationales are assembled affirming that critical professional knowledge and skills are related to client outcomes or potential outcomes and, second, that the test provides construct-valid measures of such knowledge and skills (Kane, 1982b, 1986).

In still other instances, *concurrent* evidence is used, with or without appropriate caveats, to provide an estimate of *predictive* relationships (Barrett, Phillips, & Alexander, 1981). In practice, rather than waiting for some time of treatment to elapse before collecting criterion data for accepted applicants, both test and criterion measures are often obtained concurrently for job incumbents or students already enrolled in educational programs. Although this is a convenient and sensible first step in criterion-oriented research, such concurrent data on incumbents should not be confused with or substituted for follow-up data on newly hired or admitted applicants, primar-

ily because concurrent designs sample the wrong population for the intended purpose (Guion & Cranny, 1982). On practical grounds, concurrent estimates of predictive relationships might be defended in instances where the applicant pool is changing so rapidly that follow-up data no longer apply to the selection circumstances or where it is infeasible to test and hire enough applicants to conduct a sufficiently powerful predictive study. Concurrent designs might also be defended on the strictly empirical grounds that the resulting test-criterion correlations differ little, on average, from those obtained in typical predictive designs (Barrett et al., 1981; Schmitt, Gooding, Noe, & Kirsch, 1984).

But in point of fact, incumbents differ from applicants in such important ways that applying inferences to the latter population that are based on the former is fraught with interpretive difficulties. To begin with, it cannot be assumed that incumbents are motivated for the test in the same way that applicants are. Furthermore, both age and experience could influence the criterion performance of incumbents, thereby contaminating test-criterion relationships vis-à-vis those for followed-up new hires. Moreover, experience has a different impact on performance than does age, but these effects are confounded both with each other and with attrition in concurrent studies of incumbents whereas they are separable in longitudinal designs (Giniger, Dispenzieri, & Eisenberg, 1983). Finally, corrections for range restriction due to selection and attrition are much less tenable, if possible at all, in concurrent than in follow-up studies (Guion & Cranny, 1982).

PROBLEMS OF CRITERIA AND THEIR MEASUREMENT

Among the standard requirements for criterion measures are that they should be relevant to the applied purpose, reliable, free from bias or distortion, and practical, in the sense of being plausible and acceptable to decision makers as well as available or attainable (P. C. Smith, 1976). More tendentious issues in criterion measurement include whether to address multiple criteria or a single criterion, whether the single criterion should be global or a weighted composite of several elements, whether the criterion domain is dynamic or stable, and whether the focus is on ultimate criteria inherent in the applied purpose or on immediate criteria embodied in applied practice. We begin this section by examining the latter distinction between ultimate and immediate criteria because it bears on the two fundamental issues of criterion measurement, namely, the relevance and meaning of criterion scores.

In Thorndike's (1949) words, "the ultimate criterion is the complete final goal of a particular type of selection or training" (p. 121)—in other words, the complete final goal of domain performance. In contrast, immediate criteria are the performance goals actually assessed in the applied setting for use in decision making, such as program completion or course grades in education as well as production records or supervisors' ratings in industry. This distinction between ultimate and immediate criteria is similar to Astin's (1964) distinction between conceptual criteria and criterion measures. For Astin, the conceptual criterion comprises the important or socially relevant outcomes inherent in the general purposes or aims of the decision maker. Given such distinctions, *criterion relevance* has been defined as the extent to which a criterion measure reflects the same knowledge, skills, and other attributes as are required for success on the ultimate criterion (Thorndike, 1949). The term *other attributes* is included in this formulation to signal, as Astin (1964) reminded us, that ultimate or conceptual criteria are not necessarily strictly psychological in nature but may, and often do, entail sociological or ecological interactions.

Unlike content relevance—which applies to a *test* in relation, for example, to the ultimate objectives of domain coverage (logical relevance) or to the immediate objectives of a specific curriculum (curricular relevance)—criterion relevance applies to a *criterion measure* in relation to the ultimate objectives of domain performance. In respect to content relevance, however, it will be recalled that the relation of immediate curricular objectives to ultimate domain objectives was indeed recognized as an important relevance question. Because the immediate objectives of the specific curriculum and the ultimate educational objectives of domain coverage are tantamount to criteria for judging the content relevance of the test, this relationship has now been formalized in the concept of criterion relevance.

Thus far, the discussion has sidestepped the critical question of how to delineate and assess the "complete final goal" that comprises the ultimate criterion. The answer to this question depends on the recognition that, in the final analysis, the ultimate criterion must be determined on theoretical or rational grounds (Thorndike, 1949)—that is, in terms of a construct theory of domain performance.

> The ultimate criterion can best be described as a *psychological* [or sociological, environmental, or other] *construct*. Thus, the process of determining the relevance of the immediate to the ultimate criterion becomes one of *construct validation*. That is, the assessment of the relevance of our measures of job performance involves determining the "meaning of the measurement." (Kavanagh et al., 1971, p. 35)

This brings us to a consideration of the major threats to criterion measurement which, since criteria are constructs, are basically the same as the threats to construct validity in general.

As previously indicated, the literature on criterion measurement treats the familiar validity threats of construct underrepresentation and construct-irrelevant variance under the rubrics of criterion deficiency and criterion contamination, respectively, as part of the general problem of criterion bias (Brogden & Taylor, 1950b). Other biasing factors include inequality of scale units on the criterion measure, which is a continual concern especially when ratings serve as criteria, and distortion due to improperly combining criterion elements into a composite. These forms of criterion bias may all be viewed as problems in the allocation of weights in criterion measurement: In criterion deficiency, zero weights are given to elements that should receive substantial weight; in criterion contamination, positive weights are given to elements that should receive zero weight; in scale unit inequality, different weights are assigned to different parts of a criterion continuum; and, in criterion distortion, inappropriate weights are applied to various elements in forming composites.

Sometimes these biasing factors primarily affect the estimates of test-criterion correlations, sometimes the estimates of criterion reliability, and sometimes both. Furthermore, these biases operate differentially on the three major forms that criterion measures typically take: namely, job samples, supervisors' ratings, and production records in industrial settings or achievement tests, teacher judgments, and career data in the case of educational outcomes. For example, an insidious form criterion contamination that must be controlled for when ratings serve as criteria is the possibility that the judgments might have been influenced by prior knowledge of the predictor data. Moreover, a major source of criterion deficiency stems precisely from the predilection of many investigators to rely on only one type of criterion measure to the exclusion of other types (Brogden & Taylor, 1950b). Thus, an appraisal of convergent and discriminant evidence derived from multiple methods appears no less valuable in criterion measurement than in trait measurement.

In the interpretation of criterion-related evidence, it is important to distinguish criterion bias that is correlated with the test scores from criterion bias that is unrelated to test performance. Consider the following example, taken from Guion (1976) as illustrated in Figure 2.5.

> Suppose a test of arithmetic reasoning is used to predict performance on a salvage and repair operation as rated by the supervisor. The total systematic test variance is principally due to some form of logical thinking, but some of it may be due to verbal ability. Suppose further that there are two main sources of systematic variance in supervisory ratings: (1) the intended variance, demonstrated salvage skill, and (2) contaminant variance stemming from the supervisor's erroneous tendency to equate salvage skill with verbal indications of superior intelligence—being able "to talk a good job." In these circumstances, the validity of the basic hypothesis (that test scores predict actual performance) is represented by the shaded area *a*, but the obtained validity coefficient is represented by the total of the shaded areas *a* and *b*. The obtained statement of validity is misleading because it represents to an appreciable degree the correlation between test scores and an irrelevant contaminant. (p. 790)

As another example, reading comprehension variance would be a contaminant in a paper-and-pencil *criterion* measure of mechanical knowledge if the job in question required little reading but not if the job required extensive reading. Reading variance in a *predictor* test—say, of quantitative aptitude— would contribute to the prediction of the criterion measure in either case, misleadingly so in the former but relevantly in the latter. Reading variance would be a contaminant, in any event, in the interpretation of scores on the purported quantitative aptitude test.

It is part of the traditional wisdom in the measurement field that "contaminating test variance has no influence on the predictions unless there is a correlated contaminant in the criterion" (Guion, 1976, p. 790). Furthermore,

> the introduction of bias having no relation to the predictor is . . . equivalent, in effect, to an increase in the error of measurement of the criterion, [attenuating] the relationship of all predictors to the criterion . . . [but leaving] the relative magnitude of the validities and the partial regression coefficients . . . unaffected. (Brogden & Taylor, 1950b, p. 163)

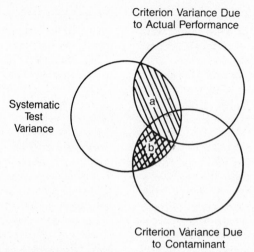

Criterion Variance Due
to Actual Performance

Systematic
Test
Variance

Criterion Variance Due
to Contaminant

FIGURE 2.5 Representation of Spurious Validity Due to Correlation Between Test Scores and Criterion Contaminants. From Robert M. Guion, "Recruiting, selection, and job placement," in *Handbook of industrial and organizational psychology,* ed. Marvin D. Dunnette. Reprinted by permission of John Wiley & Sons, Inc.

In summary,

> criterion bias due to omission of relevant elements or the inclusion of irrelevant elements is much less serious if these elements do not correlate with the predictors. The biases that enhance the apparent validity of one predictor while lowering the apparent validity of another are the ones that introduce systematic injustice into decisions. (Cronbach, 1971, p. 488)

But these remarks apply to the evaluation of tests for use in selection or for other applied purposes, not to the potential consequences of contaminants in the tests and the criteria, even if uncorrelated, when contaminated measures are used in practice.

Regardless of the correlation with test contaminants, irrelevant variance in real-world criterion measures actually used in decision making (such as course grades or supervisors' ratings) may engender adverse social consequences for some incumbent individuals and groups. Similarly, regardless of the correlation with criterion contaminants, irrelevant variance in the test—because of the possibility of differential irrelevant difficulty or easiness—may have adverse impact on some applicant individuals and groups. Granted, the problem is even more serious if the tests were erroneously chosen in the first place partly on the basis of correlated test-criterion contaminants. Indeed, it is precisely this problem of assuring that adverse social consequences of testing do not derive from any sources of invalidity, such as construct-irrelevant test or criterion variance, which forms the core of the next main section of this chapter. In this context, although much effort is assuredly needed to purge *criteria* of irrelevant variance and to clarify the meaning of criterion measures (P. C. Smith, 1976), enhanced efforts are also required to purge *tests* of irrelevant variance whether or not it is correlated with particular criteria.

We are thus confronted with a paradox: If criterion measures can be contaminated with irrelevant variance, how can they serve as the unequivocal standards for evaluating tests, as is intrinsic in the criterion-oriented approach to validation? The answer is that the criterion measures must be evaluated, along with the tests, in relation to the construct theory of the ultimate criterion. That is, it is not just a question of whether the tests relate to the criterion measures, but of whether both relate to the ultimate outcome sought by the decision maker. However, before considering construct validity as a rational basis for criterion prediction in particular and criterion-oriented validation in general, let us first examine two major aspects of criteria that should be taken into account in their associated construct theories—namely, whether the domain entails a single criterion or multiple criteria and whether they are dynamic or stable over time.

Historically, until rumblings to the contrary in the late 1950s and early 1960s, the measurement field attempted to capture the "complete final goal" entailed in the ultimate criterion in terms of a single global measure. For example, in characterizing the so-called ultimate-criterion model, James (1973) bluntly states that "the ultimate criterion approach to criterion measurement is based upon combining all criteria acquired for a particular job into one linear composite which reflects overall success" (p. 76). A single criterion, whether global or composite, was apparently sought because it was feared that multiple criteria were also only partial criteria (Wallace, 1965). Yet Thorndike (1949) maintained that "a really complete ultimate criterion is multiple and complex in almost every case" (p. 121).

Adherents of multiple criteria point to an overwhelming majority of analyses indicating that intercorrelations among criterion measures rarely yield a single general factor, as is implied in the use of a single criterion score, but rather yield multiple factorially independent dimensions (James, 1973; P. C. Smith, 1976). Nor does it make much sense logically to combine several relatively independent criterion measures, each having differential correlates, into a single composite as if they were all measuring different aspects of the same unitary phenomenon. On the contrary, the empirical multidimensionality of criterion measures indicates that success is not unitary for different persons on the same job or in the same educational program or, indeed, for the same person in different aspects of a job or program. Furthermore, because two persons might achieve the same overall performance levels by different strategies or behavioral routes, it would seem logical to evaluate both treatments and individual differences in terms of multiple measures (Cronbach & Snow, 1977; Ghiselli, 1956, 1960).

Moreover, it would also seem that the study of multiple criteria and the various dimensions along which they differ should illuminate, better than the use of a single criterion, the underlying psychological and behavioral processes involved in domain performance (Dunnette, 1963b; Schmidt & Kaplan, 1971; Wallace, 1965). As a consequence of such arguments and evidence, Hakel (1986) has declaimed that "we have reached the point where the 'ultimate criterion' should have been consigned to the history books. Our preoccupation with it has limited our thinking and hindered our research" (p. 352). But Hakel is speaking of the ultimate criterion as a single global measure, not as the "multiple and complex" conceptual criterion or construct theory guiding test and criterion measurement and validation.

Ironically, the use of measures of multiple criterion dimensions or components affords a workable approach to composite criterion prediction — not through the direct prediction of a single criterion composite of component measures (which yields the questionable correlates of a conglomerate average), nor through canonical analysis of the multiple test-criterion correlations (which merely yields the most predictable criterion composite), but rather by combining correlations between tests and separate criterion dimensions using judgmental weights that reflect the goals or values of the decision maker. For example, criterion dimensions or job components could be identified through job or task analysis, along with weights reflecting their relative importance in the particular setting; correlations between tests and job component measures could then be determined empirically; and, the component predictive information could be combined, using the importance weights for the job in question.

A related example from higher education is the modeling of the global criterion of "most successful student," which was originally based on faculty nominations (Willingham, 1985). Regression weights were determined for predicting these faculty judgments from such measures as college and departmental honors, elected and appointed leadership positions, and accomplishment in science, art, communication, and other areas. These weights were then used to construct a composite criterion of "most successful student" that proved to be more predictable than the subjective faculty judgment from which it was derived. Such a composite criterion has the advantage of being based on objective and routinely available measures but weighted according to the values that faculty place on different types of success.

The approach of using multiple dimensions in composite criterion prediction is akin to that of so-called *synthetic validity* (Lawshe, 1952; Mossholder & Arvey, 1984). As a general strategy, the notion of synthetic validity involves "the inferring of validity in a specific situation from a systematic analysis of job elements, a determination of test validity for these elements, and a combination of elemental validities into a whole" (Balma, 1959, p. 395). Thus, in this approach a single global criterion is not assessed in terms of overall or clinical judg-

ments of job performance, nor is it predicted directly by test scores. Rather, such a global criterion is analyzed into multiple dimensions or components which are each separately predicted, the test-component correlations then being combined into a composite prediction using weights reflective of applied goals.

Another important indication of the multidimensionality of criterion performance is that the relationships between tests and criterion measures tend to change systematically over time (Bass, 1962; Ghiselli, 1956; Prien, 1966). That is, ostensibly the same criterion measure displays a different pattern of test correlations or a different factor structure at different points in time or, more fundamentally, at different points in the experiential development of domain performance (Fleishman & Fruchter, 1960; Fleishman & Hempel, 1954; Ghiselli & Haire, 1960). This *dynamic* quality of criteria suggests that there may be a shift in the knowledge and abilities used in criterion performance or in the ways in which abilities are strategically organized for action, as in the qualitative differences in functional schemas observed between novices and experts in a number of fields (Chi et al., 1987; Messick, 1984c). An appearance of dynamics can also stem from changes in job requirements, expectations, or organizational demands as the length of time spent in a position or program increases (Prien, 1966; Seashore & Yuchtman, 1967). An example is the "honeymoon effect," wherein personality measures of achievement motivation and interpersonal orientation were unrelated to performance during the first 3 months on the job, but became significantly and stably related over the ensuing 6 months (Helmreich, Sawin, & Carsrud, 1986).

An important educational instance of dynamic criteria appears in the prediction of grades through the 4 years of college (Willingham, 1985). Several lines of evidence indicated that the joint action of departmental grading variations over the 4 years, combined with student migratory patterns from major to major, served to diminish grade-point average as a criterion of academic performance. Grades went up in the later years in some departments, especially those with weaker students, but not in others. Furthermore, students with poor freshman grades were more likely to change majors to a department with more lenient grading in the upper division. The overall effect was to systematically lower observed correlations between admissions tests and successive yearly grade averages — in this instance, not so much because the tasks changed or the academic abilities required were different, but because the criterion grade averages became contaminated as a measure of academic quality.

However, the dynamic nature of criteria should not be taken for granted. Evidence of criterion change must be evaluated carefully to assure that it represents a systematic shift and not merely instability resulting from multiple sources of criterion unreliability (Barrett, Caldwell, & Alexander, 1985). In any event, because the meaning of the criterion measure may vary depending on the level of training, experience, or exposure to treatment of the persons being measured, the time span covered in a criterion-oriented study is an important consideration that should be determined not by convenience or circumstance but in relation to the testing purpose (P. C. Smith, 1976; Weitz, 1961).

When multiple dimensions or components of criterion performance have been identified through job or task analysis, say, or through domain theory, it may be necessary to artificially *construct* tailored criterion measures to represent the separate dimensions—for example, in the form of situational or role-playing tests such as the in-basket procedure and patient-management problems (N. Frederiksen, 1962, 1966; C. H. McGuire & Babbott, 1967). Such narrowly defined criterion measures are likely to be more interpretable and probably more predictable than global or composite criteria, as was previously argued, but they are also only *partial* criteria. Hence, they need to be considered in the context of a comprehensive, representative, or critical set of partial criteria or else buttressed by more global measures of remaining criterion aspects (Cronbach, 1971). Such constructed criterion measures constitute intermediate criteria, both in the sense that they are less immediate than the criterion measures actually used in educational and industrial practice and in the sense that they are sometimes used not only as criteria for validating predictor tests but at other times as predictors of more ultimate criteria.

When the constructed criterion is to serve as an outcome measure in a validation study to appraise the utility of tests, it is often feasible and usually worthwhile to develop more elaborate *simulation* procedure than could be used routinely in mass measurement—although they are often practical in specialized measurement settings (N. Frederiksen, 1986b; Hubbard, 1971; C. McGuire, Solomon, & Bashook, 1976). That is, because a constructed criterion measure should elicit "behaviors that are as similar as possible to those . . . that occur in the criterion domain, [it] might best take the form of a simulation of situations that in real life elicit the performance one wants to assess" (N. Frederiksen, 1986a, p. 5). In a sense, any performance test may be considered a type of simulation, but we are here concerned with those that simulate the criterion situation with more comprehensiveness and fidelity than the typical paper-and-pencil test—such as a job-sample test, in which actual job tasks are presented under working conditions that are uniform for all examinees.

Unfortunately, for a given cost and level of control, there may be trade-offs in simulation between comprehensiveness (or the range of different situational aspects that are simulated) and fidelity (or the degree to which each simulated aspect approximates its real counterpart). What is important to simulate are the critical aspects of the criterion situation that elicit the desired performances, at a sufficient level of fidelity to detect relevant changes in the performance variable (R. Fitzpatrick & Morrison, 1971). Simulated criterion situations have the marked advantage over typical real-world criteria that individual performances can be compared to known standards under highly controlled and standardized conditions. However, this very control introduces a testlike atmosphere and elements of artificiality that serve to separate even highly realistic simulations from real-world performances (Wallace, 1965). Hence, the relevance and construct validity of simulated criterion measures should at some point also be appraised vis-à-vis ultimate goals.

In recognition that criterion measurement should ultimately delineate and assess the psychological and ecological constructs underlying criterion performance, some attempt has been made to model the criterion domain in terms of interactions among multiple person, task, organizational, and environmental dimensions (J. P. Campbell, Dunnette, Lawler, & Weick, 1970). This general criterion model also accommodates the dynamic nature of criteria by permitting task demands, expectancies, interests, behaviors, and so forth to change over time as a function of both performance feedback and a changing environment. This approach is strongly reliant on construct validity because the attempt to delineate and assess the ultimate constructs of performance effectiveness in specific task–person–environment settings can best be advanced by a sustained program of construct validation (James, 1973).

The present treatment of problems of criteria and their measurement has often been couched in the terms of industrial psychology, emphasizing job analysis, job criteria, and the like. This occurs because many of the pertinent analyses of criterion issues appear in the industrial psychology literature, and it is easier to discuss the relevant concepts and techniques in the context in which they were developed. Use of the original terms, rather than translations into educational descriptors, also affords a clear tie to this rich industrial literature. Nonetheless, all of the concepts and methods discussed in this section in terms of job criteria are, in principle, equally applicable to educational criteria (Anastasi, 1964).

CONSTRUCT VALIDITY AS A RATIONAL BASIS FOR PREDICTION

A construct theory of domain performance—or the less formal theoretical construction derived from job or task analysis—affords a rational foundation for delineating criterion and predictor constructs, for appraising the construct validity with which both are measured, and for discerning the meaning and not merely the statistical significance of the relationships between them (Guion, 1976). In regard to criterion constructs, priority should be given to those critical dimensions that differentiate good from poor performance or that are judged to be important in domain functioning or highly valued in the applied setting. In regard to predictor constructs, priority should be given to measures of the knowledge, skills, and other attributes that are embodied in the criterion constructs (i.e., to *samples* of behaviors and processes similar to those in the criterion dimensions) as well as to measures of those variables that should relate to the criterion constructs on theoretical grounds (i.e., to *signs* of the criterion dimensions). This approach is consistent with long-standing practice, as witness the following hoary quotation: "the tests . . . can be chosen only on the basis of some more or less plausible relationship between particular tests and the sort of duties performed in the job" (Kornhauser & Kingsbury, 1924, p. 47). But more stress is placed here on the predictive and summary power that comes from replacing the merely plausible with rationalized theoretical constructions.

In formulating and testing predictive hypotheses, it is of course important to assess the individual traits and processes that predict criterion performance. But it is also important to assess the stimulus variables that affect performance as well as the situational and subgroup characteristics that might influence or moderate predictor-criterion relationships (Guion, 1976). Individual traits may also moderate prediction in the sense that predictor-criterion correlations may vary systematically in accord with score levels on some psychological variable (Saunders, 1956), as when motivation influences the predictive correlations of aptitude measures (Ghiselli, 1968) or level of job or school satisfaction mediates the prediction of success (Betz, 1971). Situational variables such as organizational climate or work-group autonomy may also serve not only as possible predictors (or control variables) but as moderators as well (N. Frederiksen, Jensen, & Beaton, 1972). As a final instance, demographic or subgroup characteristics may function either as direct predictors or as moderators, the latter case sometimes involving subgroups for which quite different variables are predictive. With such qualitative differences in subgroup performance, a different predictor battery might be used with each group (Dunnette, 1963a, 1974), each battery representing a different hypothesis about the relationships between predictors and criterion performance. However, because of statistical and methodological problems such as the need for cross-validation, moderator variables should be invoked cautiously and appraised carefully in practice (Zedeck, 1971).

Thus, the rational basis for prediction provided by construct validity engages the full range of construct validity issues. The construct validity framework alerts us to go beyond concern over the mere convergence of indicators that is typical of traditional criterion-oriented studies. It leads us to address, as well, varieties of discriminant evidence essential in the construct validation of both predictor and criterion measures. In this framework, the generalizability of relationships, or the lack thereof, across population groups and environmental settings is also a perennial issue to be explicitly considered. Furthermore, the construct theory of domain performance should reflect analyses both of the job or tasks and of the applied context, because criterion and predictor constructs might appropriately embrace not only psychological attributes but sociological and ecological variables and interactions as well.

Implicit in this rational approach to predictive hypotheses, there is also a rational basis for judging the relevance of the test to the criterion domain. This provides a means of coping with the quasi-judicial problem of job-relatedness, even in the case where criterion-related empirical corroboration is missing. "Where it is clearly *not* feasible to do a study, the defense of the predictor can rest on a combination of its construct validity and the rational justification for the inclusion of the construct in the predictive hypothesis" (Guion, 1974, p. 291). This is another instance of two-step, construct-mediated reasoning: First it is argued from job analysis or domain theory that a particular construct is implicated in or related to job behavior and then, from convergent and discriminant evidence, that the predictor test is a valid indicator of that construct. The case becomes stronger if the predicted relationship has been documented empirically in other similar settings where a criterion-oriented study was feasible. Guion (1974), for one, maintains that this stance offers better evidence of job-relatedness than does a tenuous criterion-related study done under pressure with small samples, truncated variances, or questionable criterion measures. Furthermore, the mere demonstration of a statistical relationship between predictor and criterion scores in the absence of a cogent, empirically grounded rationale is a dubious basis for justifying test relevance or use (Messick, 1964, 1975, 1980).

Harking back to the four relationships inherent in predictor- and criterion-construct measures—$Y = f(C_1)$, $X = f(C_2)$, $C_2 = f(C_1)$, and $Y = f(X)$—the previous points mean that if one can rely on construct meaning as embodied in the first three relationships, one can forgo if need be the test-criterion prediction embodied in the fourth. Furthermore, criterion prediction without valid construct interpretation is a dubious basis for action. By this line of argument, construct meaning in the absence of criterion prediction is a defensible basis—but criterion prediction in the absence of construct meaning is a dubious basis—for justifying test relevance and use. Hence, construct meaning is not only extremely important but essential in applied testing. Granted, empirical test-criterion prediction alone often sustains test use in practice. But this is a strictly pragmatic basis, not necessarily a valid one. It is heavily contingent on acceptable side effects of the testing, because there is no accompanying theoretical rationale for justifying appropriateness of test use in the face of adverse testing consequences.

In sum, in the construct validity framework, the predictive hypothesis that test X is related to criterion measure Y—i.e., $Y = f(X)$—is the outcome of a rational process linking the domain theory to the choice of criterion and predictor constructs as well as to the empirically grounded construct interpretations of the criterion and predictor measures. The testing of the predictive hypothesis in a typical criterion-oriented study feeds back information that is either supportive or nonsupportive of the theoretical rationale, suggesting on the down side the need for possible modifications in domain theory, criterion or predictor measurement, experimental controls, or some combination of these. What is appraised in the criterion-oriented study is not the validity of the test, which depends on a mosaic of convergent and discriminant evidence, but rather the validity of the hypothesis of a relationship between the test and a criterion measure (Guion, 1976).

This view of construct validity as a rational basis for prediction is inverted in some quarters by claiming that prediction—i.e., $Y = f(X)$—is the prototype for validity (Landy, 1986). In other words, from this perspective, validation is viewed as hypothesis testing, consistent with the present chapter, but the generic hypothesis of a test-criterion relationship emerges as the fundamental validity concept. "Testing has no purpose if it is not used to draw an inference about future behavior (i.e., to predict)" (Landy, 1986, p. 1187). To support this precept, a number of additional points or side conditions reminiscent of construct-validity theory are appended, such as the following: "a criterion-related design is not the only, or possibly not even the best, way to support the [predictive] inference" (Landy, 1986, p. 1187), but rather the use of scores based on content and construct considerations can also have a predictive basis; the term "criterion should probably be interpreted to mean some independent measurement of the attribute in question . . . [so that] the extent to which the predictor and criterion jointly form a conceptual theory of performance" is appraised (p. 1189); and, "the better the evidence, the more alternative explanations for the relationship . . . can be ruled out" (p. 1191).

But apart from empirical serendipity, the effective entry point in test validation is not the predictive hypothesis, for which one then seeks construct-related evidence of its meaning and action import. The entry point is provisional construct meaning, which then serves as a guide for what the predictive hypotheses might reasonably be. Thus, as a general validation strategy, the order seems to be mixed up in Landy's (1986) line of development. Moreover, the elevation of prediction to validity prototype gives short shrift to validation approaches aimed at explanation—as, for instance, in causal modeling of process. Indeed, just as validity does not come in types, neither does it come in prototypes.

Within the framework of construct validity as a rational basis for prediction, a promising refinement has been proposed that examines the *construct similarity* of predictor and criterion measures (N. Frederiksen, 1986a). This approach could prove especially helpful in guiding the test development of predictors for use with applicant groups who have not yet acquired the specialized knowledge and experience that is instrumental to subsequent criterion performance, as in selecting medical students on the basis of predictions of their subsequently developed clinical problem-solving skills. Because the methodology can be initially applied to concurrent data, it provides validity information to guide test construction prior to the formal undertaking of any longitudinal or follow-up validation study.

The approach begins with the development of a theory of domain performance, on the basis of which criterion measures are selected or constructed. These might be in the form of situational simulations designed to elicit the criterion performances delineated by the theory—for example, the clinical problem-solving skills of fourth-year medical students. Then, on a sample of fourth-year students, the construct validity of the criterion measures is appraised, perhaps by examining the factor structure of their relationships with measures of relevant knowledge and cognitive abilities identified in the domain theory. Next, predictor tests are developed, possibly in the form of similar problem-solving simulations that do not entail specialized knowledge. These predictor measures are also administered to the fourth-year medical students, either simultaneously with the criterion measures or in sequence, and the factor structure of their correlations with the cognitive ability measures is ascertained.

One is now in a position to compare the two factor structures to gauge the degree of similarity entailed in the constructs tapped by the predictor and criterion measures. Because training and experience in medical problem solving could influence problem-solving performance in nonspecialized areas, as a final check the predictor measures and the battery of cognitive tests should be administered to applicants or, say, to first-year medical students. As a consequence, the construct similarity of the predictor measures for novice and experienced groups can be evaluated.

This construct-similarity approach, though it might appear arduous, is fairly straightforward and much more illuminating of the meaning of the measures than simply appraising concurrent correlations between predictor and criterion scores in the experienced sample (N. Frederiksen, 1986a). The notion of construct similarity is akin to Cureton's (1951) conception of *factorial relevance*, which holds that if two tests have a similar pattern of factor loadings and one test correlates substantially with a criterion measure, then the other test is also likely to display a comparable criterion correlation if the settings and groups are comparable.

FROM TEST-CRITERION RELATIONSHIPS TO DECISION-MAKING UTILITY

The usefulness of a test for selection or other applied purposes depends on the strength of the test-criterion relationship, to be sure, but it also depends on a number of other factors such as base rates, selection ratios, and the costs of testing. Hence, instead of speaking in the traditional terms of predictive or criterion-oriented *validity*, which classically refers to the size of the test-criterion correlation, we instead employ for this aspect of validity the more descriptive label of *utility*, which refers to the relative benefits derived from utilizing the test in decision making. In the present usage, the term *utility* is intended to embrace the general notion of scientific or applied usefulness (Cattell, 1964) as well as the specialized notion of benefits relative to costs expressed on a common scale of utility units (Cronbach & Gleser, 1965).

From a measurement standpoint, the usefulness of a test is typically appraised in terms of its accuracy in prediction or estimation, using some index of the average amount of error—but usually without regard to the type of error. One such index is the "coefficient of determination" or r_{XY}^2, which indicates the proportion of criterion variance associated with or "determined" by test variance, that is, the ratio of predicted criterion variance to observed criterion variance. Another is the now nearly defunct "index of forecasting efficiency" or $(1 - \sqrt{1 - r_{XY}^2})$, which indicates the percentage reduction in errors of prediction obtained by using the test. In both of these cases, the usefulness of the test scores is considered to be a function of r_{XY}^2 that is, a parabolic function of the test-criterion correlation coefficient.

From a decision standpoint, in contrast, different types of errors may be differentially important to the decision makers, so that the values of different outcomes in the applied setting need to be taken into account in gauging the utility of the test scores. Before considering some of the consequences of this shift in emphasis from accuracy to utility, however, let us first examine the advantages that accrue from treating the issues of both accuracy and utility in terms of regression equations rather than simply correlation coefficients.

To begin with, regression equations are preferable to correlation coefficients because they convey much more information relevant to accuracy and utility—not only information bearing on the strength of the test-criterion relationship but also on test and criterion variance, as well as on mean levels and standard errors of estimate. In addition, while the magnitude of correlation coefficients varies with the variance of the group studied, being large for highly variable groups and relatively small for more homogenous groups, regression slopes and errors of prediction are more stable across groups.

More fundamentally, regression coefficients are not subject, as are correlation coefficients, to the attenuating effects of criterion unreliability and restriction of range due to selection.

Indeed, correcting the regression coefficient (i.e., the slope of the regression line) for measurement errors depends only on the predictor or test reliability, not the criterion reliability (Cronbach & Snow, 1977; McNemar, 1969). Moreover, the assumption that the regression line will be the same in the selected or curtailed group as in the unselected or extended group forms the very basis for deriving corrections for restriction in range (Gulliksen, 1950b). This assumption is highly plausible for direct selection determined by the predictor itself, although less so for indirect selection in terms of other variables (Heckman, 1979). Another reason for preferring regression equations over correlation coefficients is that differential prediction studies (regression systems) typically exhibit more statistical power than do differential validity studies (correlation coefficients), both in detecting measurement nonequivalence or bias across population groups and in detecting consequent nonequivalent relationships with external variables (Drasgow, 1982, 1984; Drasgow & Kang, 1984).

To shift the emphasis from accuracy to utility, let us for the moment transform the prediction problem into one of predicting discrete criterion outcomes, such as success and failure in the program or job, as opposed to predicting individual criterion scores all along the criterion continuum (J. P. Campbell, 1976). By thus moving to a decision context in which only two or a limited number of options are predicted, we can then consider predictive accuracy in terms of the proportion of correct predictions, rather than in terms of average error in predicting criterion scores. If the criterion to be predicted constitutes a dichotomy, then the bivariate test-criterion distribution can be reduced to a four-fold classification in which four distinct outcomes may occur, as depicted in Figure 2.6: (a) correct prediction of success; (b) correct prediction of failure; (c) overprediction, or incorrect prediction of success; and, (d) underprediction, or incorrect prediction of failure.

It should be clear from Figure 2.6 that the proportion of correct predictions depends not only on the degree of predictor-criterion correlation, but also on the criterion split or base rate as well as on the predictor split or cutting score. The criterion *base rate* is the proportion of individuals in the potential applicant population who would succeed in the program or job. In connection with the predictor cutting score, the proportion of individuals in the applicant population scoring above this score — that is, the proportion of acceptable applicants — is called the *selection ratio*. In contrast, the proportion of individuals in the actual applicant sample who are admitted or hired is referred to as the admission or hiring rate (Alexander, Barrett, & Doverspike, 1983). It should also be clear that changes in the predictor cutting score or in the criterion base rate have differential consequences for the two kinds of errors (overprediction and underprediction). For example, increasing the predictor cutting score reduces the proportion of overpredictions while it increases the proportion of underpredictions.

Given this trade-off between the two kinds of errors as a function of the cutting score, Taylor and Russell (1939) determined the increases in the percentage of correct predictions of success as the cutting score increases, given a particular base rate and correlation coefficient. Rather than finding that predictive efficiency or utility is a parabolic function of the test-criterion correlation, as in the coefficient of determination or the index of forecasting efficiency, they noted that the correlation–utility relationship differs for different selection ratios. They further noted that low correlation coefficients afford substantial improvement in the prediction of success for accepted applicants when the selection ratio is low. On the other hand, if the cutting score is not properly determined, under some circumstances even a good predictor can prove less useful in maximizing the total correct decisions than simply predicting solely in terms of the base rate (Meehl & Rosen, 1955).

However, the Taylor–Russell tables are concerned only with correct and incorrect predictions of success for persons accepted on the basis of the test; rejected individuals are completely ignored. This concern with minimizing overpredictions, or the proportion of accepted individuals who prove unsatisfactory, is consistent with traditional institutional values of efficiency in educational and personnel selection. But concern with minimizing underpredictions, or the proportion

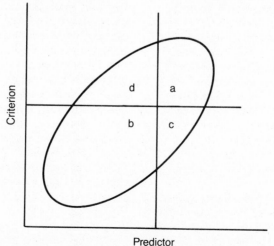

FIGURE 2.6 Continuous test-criterion distribution treated as a dichotomous prediction decision

of rejected individuals who would succeed if given the opportunity, is also an important social value in connection both with individual equity and with parity for minority and disadvantaged groups. Indeed, if one defines "benefits" as the proportion of unsuccessful persons screened out and "costs" as the proportion of successful persons missed, then raising the cutting score increases both the benefits and the costs (Berkson, 1947). Somehow the social values of both the hits and the misses must be taken into account so that the cutting score can be set to maximize expected utility for the decision maker (Cronbach & Gleser, 1965).

In contrast with the Taylor and Russell (1939) results for predictions of success, if predictions of both success and failure are included, then the proportion of correct predictions is a roughly linear function of r_{XY}, not r_{XY}^2 (Curtis & Alf, 1969). Furthermore, Brogden (1946) demonstrated that gain in average criterion performance resulting from selection by means of a test is linearly related to r_{XY}, regardless of the selection ratio. In other words, a test correlating .5 with the criterion yields 50% of the improvement that would obtain in perfect selection, that is, by using the criterion measure itself or a perfectly valid test. The apparent discrepancy entailed in viewing predictive efficiency or utility as a linear function of r_{XY}, as a parabolic function of r_{XY}, or as variable by selection ratio is explained by noting that errors are evaluated in different ways in these three instances.

In the coefficient of determination and the index of forecasting efficiency, errors are evaluated in terms of the discrepancy between the predicted and actual performance of individuals. But in the dichotomous prediction of success and failure, only errors of category placement degrade the utility of the decisions, that is, selecting a person who should be rejected and vice versa (Wesman, 1953). Overpredictions and underpredictions of individual performance are costly only when they cause decision errors. The Taylor–Russell and Brogden approaches differ in that the former assumes a discontinuous two-valued payoff (all persons in the successful group being assumed to make equal criterion contributions, as are all persons in the unsuccessful group), whereas the latter assumes a continuous scale of increasing payoff for increasing levels of criterion performance (Cronbach & Gleser, 1965).

Thus, for selecting individuals into a fixed treatment, the utility of the test score is linearly related to the test-criterion correlation coefficient. But for selection into an "adaptive treatment"—that is, one in which the treatment is adjusted to the quality of the persons accepted—the benefit from testing is once again a parabolic function of r_{XY}, although considerably more complicated than the simple parabolic functions (coefficients of determination and forecasting efficiency) previously encountered (Cronbach & Gleser, 1965).

In the case of classification or placement—that is, the assignment of individuals to different treatments—the gain in utility from using the test is a function of the difference in within–treatment regression slopes for the prediction of outcome from test scores (Cronbach & Snow, 1977). For example, one purpose of the College Board's Test of Standard Written English (TSWE) is to provide a dependable basis for assigning enrolled students to appropriate English instruction. The needed empirical justification for this is the demonstration of a statistical interaction between TSWE scores and the instructional options (an aptitude-treatment interaction) for courses in each college separately (Cronbach, 1971; Hills, 1971; Willingham, 1974). That is, when a uniform criterion measure of writing ability collected after exposure to the alternative courses of instruction is regressed onto the placement scores, regression coefficients should differ significantly from course to course (Cronbach, 1985). However, when such research was undertaken, several factors such as small within-college sample sizes led to weak results (Breland, 1977; Breland, Conlon, & Rogosa, 1976). "In a search for regression differences, only a modest fraction of the samples showed a pattern indicative of validity for routing freshman into remedial rather than regular English courses" (Cronbach, 1988, p. 9).

To derive the full power of decision-theory models of utility, both costs and benefits must be expressed on a single scale of utility units. Either the benefits of testing, such as gain in mean criterion performance, and the costs of testing must both be translated to a common scale of utility, or else criterion performance must be evaluated in the same scale as costs, namely, dollars. In particular, because the benefit due to selection depends on the value of individual differences in performance, the criterion standard deviation—which is a key parameter in utility models (Cronbach & Gleser, 1965)—must be estimated in dollars. Given the difficulty of this scaling problem, many investigators and decision makers shy away from applying utility models—but only at their peril, because such avoidance might prove tantamount to acting as if all types of errors have the same value or consequences. However, even when criterion performance cannot be evaluated in dollar terms, one need not forgo utility models completely. Important utility considerations can still be taken into account if at least the ratio of utilities for overpredictions and underpredictions or for correct predictions of success and correct predictions of failure can be reasonably estimated (Darlington & Stauffer, 1966; Rorer, Hoffman, & Hsieh, 1966).

Indeed, considerable progress has been made in the development of practical methods for estimating the criterion standard deviation in dollar terms since Brogden and Taylor (1950a) first elaborated cost-accounting approaches to the construction of the "dollar criterion." For example, if it is assumed that criterion performance evaluated in dollars is normally distributed, then supervisors' estimates of the dollar value of performance at the 15th, 50th, and 85th percentiles would provide two direct estimates of the criterion standard deviation in dollar terms (Schmidt, Hunter, McKenzie, & Muldrow, 1979). Modifications of this judgmental procedure, incorporating consensual feedback to reduce large variation in supervisors' estimates, appear to be reasonably accurate and practical (Bobko, Karren, & Parkington, 1983; Burke & Frederick, 1984; Reilly & Smither, 1985), as do procedures for estimating the standard deviation of criterion output as a percentage of mean output (Schmidt & Hunter, 1983).

UTILITY AND FAIRNESS IN DECISION MAKING

Because different social values may attach to the four outcome categories generated by the criterion dichotomy of success versus failure and the test dichotomy of acceptance versus rejection, decision-theory models afford illuminating heuristics not only with respect to utility but also with respect to fairness. This is especially true when different population groups display significantly different mean scores on predictors, or criteria, or both. Under these circumstances, group-differential prediction and potential selection bias exacerbate the issues of fair test use in selection (Linn, 1984; Linn & Hastings, 1984). Because fair test use implies that selection decisions will be equally appropriate in some sense regardless of an individual's group membership (Cleary, 1968; N. S. Cole, 1981; Dunnette, 1974; Guion, 1966; Thorndike, 1971), and because different selection systems yield different proportions of selected individuals in population groups displaying differential performance, questions of test fairness arise in earnest.

In response to this complexity, several distinct models of fair selection were formulated and contrasted with each other in good Kantian fashion (e.g., Clearly, 1968; N. S. Cole, 1973; Darlington, 1971; Einhorn & Bass, 1971; Linn, 1973, 1976; Thorndike, 1971). Indeed, some models proved to be mutually incompatible or even contradictory, thereby offering true Hegelian contrasts (Darlington, 1971; Petersen & Novick, 1976). Such models assume, either explicitly or tacitly, an unbiased criterion measure that is fairly and uniformly applied across groups. This then serves as the standard for evaluating potential bias in the predictor measures, such as the unanticipated but widespread finding of overprediction for minority groups in both academic and industrial settings (Breland, 1978; Hunter, Schmidt, & Hunter, 1979; Linn, 1982; Linn & Hastings, 1984; Schmidt, Pearlman, & Hunter, 1980). The notion of an unbiased criterion also facilitates the evaluation of various measurement artifacts—such as the effects of test unreliability, group differences in variance, and the inclusion or exclusion of a second predictor in the regression equations —that often mimic or exacerbate bias effects (Einhorn & Bass, 1971; Linn, 1983; Linn & Hastings, 1984; Linn & Werts, 1971; Reilly, 1973).

It soon became apparent, in comparing alternative models for fair selection, that each one accords a different importance or social value to the various subsets of selected versus rejected and successful versus unsuccessful individuals in the different population groups (Dunnette & Borman, 1979; Linn, 1973). Moreover, the values accorded are a function not only of desired criterion performance but of desired individual and group attributes (Novick & Ellis, 1977). Thus, each model not only constitutes a different definition of fairness but also implies a particular ethical position (Hunter & Schmidt, 1976). Each view is ostensibly fair under certain conditions, so that arguments over the fairness of test use turn out in many instances to be disagreements as to what the conditions are or ought to be.

With the recognition that fundamental value differences are at issue, several utility models were developed that require specific value positions to be taken (e.g., Cronbach, 1976; Gross & Su, 1975; Petersen & Novick, 1976; Sawyer, Cole, & Cole, 1976), thereby incorporating social values explicitly with measurement technology. But the need to make values explicit does not determine choices among them. At this point, it appears difficult if not impossible to be fair to individuals in terms of equity, to groups in terms of parity or the avoidance of

adverse impact, to institutions in terms of efficiency, and to society in terms of benefits and risks—all at the same time. In principle, a workable balancing of the needs of each of the parties is likely to require successive approximations over time, with iterative modifications of utility matrices based on experience with the consequences of decision processes to date (Darlington, 1976). In practice, however, such balancing of needs and values almost always comes down to a political resolution.

This concern with the social consequences of test-based actions, coupled with the recognition that outcome measurement and utility—or more generally, validity and values—are inseparable, broaches the topic of the next main section, which deals with the consequential basis of test use. Before we proceed, however, an important aspect of the evidential basis of test use remains to be addressed, namely, the generalizability of test-criterion relationships across population groups and applied settings.

Validity Generalization

It is part of the traditional wisdom in the field of educational and psychological measurement that context effects in general and situational variables in particular create inevitable situational specificity, so that local validation is needed to attune applied measurement to the particularities of the local setting. That is, such factors as level of motivation, style of teaching or supervision, and type of classroom or organizational structure affect the nature and operative requirements of what is ostensibly the same task or job in different settings or at different times. Given that mental measurement has strong roots in psychology, this sensitivity to specific sources and moderators of performance variability is not surprising. But mental measurement also has strong roots in statistics, so that sensitivity to sampling variability is equally understandable and, indeed, offers a plausible rival hypothesis to explain apparent situational differences.

The issue is joined: Are test-criterion relationships specific to local situations, or do they generalize across settings and times—as in the Cook and Campbell (1979) concept of external validity—because observed situational variability stems mainly from statistical artifacts? In discussing this issue of what is popularly called "validity generalization" as opposed to situational specificity, it should be kept in mind that we are speaking only of criterion-oriented validity generalization. There is much more to validity than a test-criterion correlation coefficient and the range of credible values it may assume when sampling across contexts.

SITUATIONAL SPECIFICITY AND THE NEED FOR LOCAL VALIDATION

The notion of situational specificity derives from the repeated observation that predictive- and concurrent-validity coefficients vary widely, not only across jobs and tasks but also across time, location, and type of organization, even for similar test–job combinations (Albright, Glennon, & Smith, 1963; Ghiselli, 1966, 1973). Because this observed variability appeared to be too large for sampling error alone to account for, Ghiselli (1966) concluded that "much of the variation results from differences in the nature of and the requirements for nominally the same job in different organizations, and in the same organization from one time period to another" (p. 28). A similar position was adopted by many measurement experts (e.g., Guion, 1965; Lawshe & Balma, 1966; L. E. Tyler, 1963), along with the corollary that predictor tests should be recurrently validated in local settings and possibly even for minor job variants.

The concept of local specificity actually combines two points that it is helpful to keep separate (Schmidt & Hunter, 1981). First, a test that is valid for a job or task in one setting might be invalid (or have a different validity) for the same job or task in a different setting, which constitutes *situational specificity* per se. Second, a test that is valid for one job might be invalid (or have a different validity) for another job albeit in the same setting, which is better described as *job specificity*. Adherents of validity generalization argue that much, if not all, local variability stems from sampling error and other statistical artifacts. Furthermore, they maintain that not only are criterion-oriented validity coefficients more generalizable than previously thought, but the importance of situational specificity has been grossly exaggerated. It is not that they deny that such factors as motivation or supervisory style affect job or task performance. Rather, they argue that these factors do not systematically affect the *correlations* between ability tests and job performance (Schmidt, Hunter, Pearlman, & Hirsh, with commentary by Sackett, Schmitt, Tenopyr, Keho, & Zedek, 1985).

This line of argument for validity generalization is buttressed by a formidable array of evidence that seems to run counter to situational specificity—an idea that has long been deeply entrenched not only in educational and personnel psychology but also in social psychology more broadly. Until the mid 1970s, at least, it has also been deeply entrenched in the test standards, as witness the following flat pronouncement: "Validity coefficients are specific to the situations in which they are obtained" (APA, 1974, p. 36). Let us next consider in more detail the nature and credibility of the validity-generalization challenge to established criterion-oriented validation practice.

BAYESIAN GENERALIZED VALIDITY VERSUS LOCAL VALIDATION

It is widely recognized in psychometric and statistical circles that the magnitude and variability of observed predictive- and concurrent-validity coefficients are affected by such statistical artifacts as sampling error and range restriction, as well as by criterion and test unreliability. What was needed was a consistent method for estimating these artifacts quantitatively and taking their impact into account. This groundbreaking step was essentially accomplished by Schmidt and Hunter (1977). Their breakthrough took the form of a mathematical model in which the mean and standard deviation of the "true validity" distribution are estimated from the distribution of observed validities adjusting for sampling error, range restriction, criterion unreliability, and, in the case of the standard deviation, for test unreliability as well (Schmidt et al., 1985). A number of revised and alternative estimation procedures are now available (e.g., Burke, 1984; Callender & Osburn, 1980;

Hunter, Schmidt, & Jackson, 1982; Linn & Dunbar, 1986; Linn, Harnisch, & Dunbar, 1981b; Pearlman, Schmidt, & Hunter, 1980; Schmidt, Gast-Rosenberg, & Hunter, 1980; Schmidt, Hunter, Pearlman, & Shane, 1979), which for practical purposes appear to yield similar estimates in empirical and simulation studies (Burke, 1984; Callender & Osburn, 1980; Callender, Osburn, Greener, & Ashworth, 1982; Linn & Dunbar, 1986).

These procedures were applied in extensive meta-analyses of criterion-related validity data. For various approaches to meta-analysis, which is the application of quantitative methods for combining evidence from different studies, see Glass, McGaw, and Smith (1981); Hedges and Olkin (1985); Hunter, Schmidt, & Jackson, (1982); Light and Pillemer (1984); and Rosenthal (1984). When these meta-analyses were completed, a number of startling findings emerged. For example, an average of 72% of the observed variance of validity coefficients was accounted for by the four artifacts listed earlier, and roughly 85% of this explained variance was due to sampling error alone (Schmidt & Hunter, 1981; Schmidt, Hunter, & Pearlman, 1981).

In addition, it was found that "there is no job for which cognitive ability does not predict training success . . . [and] that ability tests are valid across all jobs in predicting job proficiency" (Hunter & Hunter, 1984, p. 80). Furthermore, "for entry-level jobs there is no predictor with validity equal to that of ability, which has a mean validity of .53" (p. 72), as well as "a mean validity for training success of about .55 across all known job families " (Hunter & Hunter, 1984, p. 80). However, cognitive ability tests were not found to be superior to other types of predictors (such as assessment centers) in another, more variable meta-analysis (Schmitt et al., 1984). For job families established by level of complexity rather than by similarity of tasks, the criterion-related validity of cognitive ability tests decreased as job complexity decreased but never approached zero (.61 to .27), while the validity of psychomotor tests tended to increase with decreasing complexity (Hunter & Hunter, 1984).

In summarizing results based on validity distributions for 152 test–job combinations, Schmidt and Hunter (1981) stressed that true validities for cognitive ability tests are consistently positive and that "the validity of the cognitive tests studied is neither specific to situations nor specific to jobs" (p. 1133). In regard to the first point, for 84% of the 152 test–job combinations, even the validity value at the 10th percentile of the estimated true validity distribution (i.e., using the conventional Bayesian one-tailed 90% credibility interval) is positive and substantial enough to be practically useful. In regard to the second point, so much of the variance in observed validities is accounted for by statistical artifacts that to argue that even task differences in jobs serve to moderate the validity of ability tests is seen as a red herring (Schmidt, et al., 1981). Overall, Schmidt and Hunter (1981) conclude that "professionally developed cognitive ability tests are valid predictors of performance on all jobs . . . in all settings" (p. 1128).

With such a far-reaching conclusion, it is important to be clear about just what Schmidt and Hunter are claiming and what they are not claiming. They maintain that cognitive ability tests are valid predictors for all jobs, but not *equally* valid for all jobs (Schmidt et al., 1985). Their own research has repeatedly demonstrated reliable differences among jobs in the validity of most ability tests (e.g., Hunter & Hunter, 1984; Schmidt & Hunter, 1978; Schmidt et al., 1981). Furthermore, Gutenberg, Arvey, Osburn, and Jeanneret (1983) showed that the information-processing and decision-making dimensions of jobs generally moderated the validities of cognitive ability tests (in the positive direction) as well as the validities of manual dexterity tests (in the negative direction). Hence, job specificity is a red herring only if a moderator effect is conceived to mean that a test having substantial validity for one job has zero validity for other jobs, as opposed to having a significantly different validity for other jobs (Linn & Dunbar, 1986).

The major conclusion, then, is that validity is generalizable in the sense that most of the values in the distribution of estimated true validities fall in the positive range—that is, true validity is unlikely to be zero or near zero—although important situational and job specificity still occurs. This statement is more cautious than the typical Schmidt–Hunter rhetoric, and there are technical reasons why even more caution is needed. In particular, the statistical

> power of validity generalization studies to distinguish between populations of studies with zero true validity variance and studies with low-to-moderate true validity variance is inadequate by commonly accepted standards unless truly massive amounts of data are available (i.e., many studies having unusually large sample sizes). (Osburn et al., 1982, p. 120)

Unfortunately, however, in huge data files criterion measures tend to be nonuniform and criterion data generally poor.

Although the findings just described derive from meta-analyses of validity data for test–job combinations in industrial settings, similar results are obtained for scholastic ability tests in predicting success in educational programs. For example, in predicting first-year grades in law school, about 70% of the variance in observed validity coefficients was accounted for by sampling error, range restriction of Law School Aptitude Test scores, and criterion unreliability; nonetheless, situational specificity of validity remained as a function of the particular law school and the year the study was conducted (Linn et al., 1981b). Similar findings of both substantial validity generalization and important situational specificity were also obtained in the prediction of first-year college grades by SAT scores (Boldt, 1986b), but only moderate generalization was observed in the prediction of departmental graduate school grades by GRE scores (Boldt, 1986a).

EMPIRICAL-BAYES AND GENERALIZED REGRESSION APPROACHES

The Schmidt-Hunter approach to validity generalization attempts to estimate a variance component for population validities across studies, taking into account statistical artifacts. It is argued that if this variance component is small, then situational specificity is negligible and the validity in any specific situation is best characterized by the overall average validity (Schmidt, 1988). This extreme position is diametrically opposite to the equally extreme position that test validity is situation bound, that validity in one situation provides no information bearing on validity in other, even similar situations. Fortu-

nately, empirical-Bayes methodology affords a compromise between these two unlikely extremes when the data point to such an intermediate position (Braun, in press; Hedges, 1988; Raudenbush & Bryk, 1985). Empirical-Bayes methods estimate not only the mean population validity and the associated variance component, but also the size of effects due to situational specificity. Furthermore, estimates of the validity in any particular situation are improved by supplementing the single-situation data with validity information from other situations (borrowing strength).

Another issue is that the Schmidt–Hunter validity generalization procedures are applied to distributions of test-criterion correlation coefficients, which then need to be adjusted for such statistical artifacts as range restriction and criterion unreliability. This raises all of the perennial concerns about the assumptions, biases, and overall appropriateness of using such corrections, especially when the final sample is influenced by nonchance factors other than the predictors (Bobko, 1983; Heckman, 1979; Lee, Miller, & Graham, 1982; Linn, 1968; Linn, Harnisch, & Dunbar, 1981a; Lord & Novick, 1968; Murnane, Newstead, & Olson, 1985; Muthén & Jöreskog, 1983). The analysis of regression slopes, which are not as subject to the effects of range restriction and criterion unreliability, would partially ameliorate this problem. However, under some circumstances, namely, where there is selection on variables not included in the regression model—as, for example, in selective dropout (Heckman, 1979)—estimates of regression parameters may also be biased and need to be corrected (e.g., Linn & Hastings, 1984). In any event, serious roadblocks stand in the way of cumulating regression equations across studies. The main hangup is that if different tests and criterion measures are used in different studies, there is neither a common criterion metric nor a common test metric. Hence, neither the criterion standard deviations nor the test standard deviations would be comparable across studies, nor would the regression slopes and intercepts.

Nonetheless, there are a number of important situations, such as selective admissions into educational programs and training assignments in large corporations or the military, where a single test or battery is used across programs and where the criterion measure is arguably comparable, such as the ubiquitous 5-point grading scale. Under such circumstances, the cumulative analysis of regression equations is to be preferred, because there could be systematic differences across studies in regression slopes and intercepts even though the differences in correlation coefficients are minimal. Fortunately, for cases such as these, both fully Bayesian and empirical-Bayes estimation procedures are available for generalized regression analysis (e.g., Braun, in press; Braun & Jones, 1981; Braun, Jones, Rubin, & Thayer, 1983; Novick, Jackson, Thayer, & Cole, 1972; Rubin, 1980).

Furthermore, in situations such as professional school admissions, where there are students accepted by two or more schools and enrolled at one, it is possible to construct a universal criterion scale linked across institutions (Braun & Szatrowski, 1984a). It is also possible—because universal criterion scores become available both for students not choosing to attend and for those rejected by one institution but enrolled at another—to estimate institutional validities for groups of applicants, not just enrolled students (Braun & Szatrowski, 1984b). Hence, predictive validities can be estimated for extended distributions of scores without traditional corrections for restriction in range.

As an instance of the generalized regression approach, Dunbar, Mayekawa, and Novick (1986) estimated regressions of final course grades on relevant predictors from the Armed Services Vocational Aptitude Battery for training courses in three categories (clerical, electrical, and mechanical). They found complete generalization of predictor-criterion relationships to be tenable only for a carefully selected subset of courses in a given category and not for all groups included in the analysis. Once again, generalization of test-criterion relationships is found to have its limits, and situational specificity must also be taken into account.

BOTH VALIDITY GENERALIZATION AND LOCAL VALIDATION

In light of the validity generalization arguments about the impact of statistical artifacts and the need for adequate sample size and statistical power (Sackett & Wade, 1983; Schmidt, Hunter, & Urry, 1976), the value of undertaking a local validation study of typical proportions is questionable. Yet, given adequate power, a local study serves important specialized purposes, such as evaluating combinations of predictors, providing local norms pertinent to the setting of cut scores, and predicting locally specific criteria (Schmidt et al., 1985). Thus, fully adequate local validation studies are desirable apart from evidence of validity generalization. But even marginal (not inadequate) local studies are desirable in conjunction with generalized validity. Schmidt and his colleagues (1985) maintained that local validation studies are important because they provide the observed validity coefficients needed for validity generalization studies. But local studies afford considerably more than that. They provide the basis for addressing the situational specificity beyond generalized validity and for combining appropriately weighted local evidence with generalized validity evidence to characterize the applied setting, as in the empirical-Bayes strategy (Hedges, 1987; Rubin, 1980).

Another more cautious approach in defense of using a predictor test without local tryout is to conduct not a local validation study, but a local job analysis to identify relevant job dimensions; then tests can be identified that have been validated elsewhere as measures of those dimensions. This type of job-components study is in the tradition of synthetic validity (Colbert & Taylor, 1978; McCormick, Denisi, & Shaw, 1979). Basically, the notion is that if a job dimension is found to be common to different jobs, then the abilities and other attributes needed to perform that aspect of the jobs should be the same or similar as well.

Inherently, this strategy relies more heavily on construct validity evidence than does the validity generalization approach because, once again, a two-step, construct-mediated inference is entailed: First, abilities and processes important in local job performance are identified through job analysis, and then construct-valid measures of those processes are selected for the applied purpose. As indicated earlier, the proposed test use becomes more firmly grounded if the predictive validity of the test for a similar criterion and setting was documented elsewhere in an adequate validation study, or if a similar test-job combination exhibits generalized validity. But this appeal to nonlocal criterion-related validity data is supportive, not determinative, of the local test use.

Thus, within the construct validity framework, both situational specificity and generalized validity can be addressed in tandem even in the absence of a local criterion-oriented study. For example, from the conceptualization of the job derived from a local job analysis, a rational basis can be developed for including a construct measure in a predictive hypothesis of relationship to a particular criterion measure. Criterion-related evidence is then sought in support of this hypothesis, preferably by transporting relevant findings from adequate validation studies in similar settings with similar criteria, as well as in the form of generalized validity evidence. Yet fundamentally, the proposed test use is to be justified not only because cognitive tests are valid for all jobs or even because a similar test-job combination generally exhibits positive validity, but mainly because the abilities or other constructs validly tapped by the test are deemed relevant to this specific job in this particular applied setting.

Thus, generalization to the local context follows not only from sampling considerations across multiple validation studies, but from theoretical explanation that takes local interactions into account (Cronbach, 1982). As Cronbach advises,

> although a certain kind of test has worked well in some class of situations, users cannot logically apply that generalization until they check the fit of this instance to the class where experience accumulated. Beyond that, they may have to assess whether a court will be persuaded that particular features of this case did not matter. (1988, p. 12)

In sum, the construct validity of score interpretation must be attended to sooner or later—if not in justifying test use in terms of meaning and relevance in the first place, then in justifying it in terms of social consequences in the final analysis. Indeed, as we shall reconfirm in the concluding main section of this chapter, construct validity must be continually attended to in connection with inferences and actions that arise throughout each measurement enterprise.

The Consequential Basis of Test Use

Let us now turn to the remaining (lower right) cell of Table 2.1. Here we add to our concern with the meaning, relevance, utility, and value implications of test scores a formal concern with the social consequences of testing as an integral part of validity. The section on the consequential basis of test interpretation addressed the import or value implications of scores, not only as a part of score meaning but as a basis for social action. The present section addresses the functional worth of scores in terms of social consequences of their use.

Potential Social Consequences of Test Use

Judging validity in terms of whether a test does the job it is employed to do (Cureton, 1951; Rulon, 1946)—that is, whether it serves its intended function or purpose—requires evaluation of the intended or unintended social consequences of test interpretation and use. The appropriateness of the intended testing purpose and the possible occurrence of unintended outcomes and side effects are the major issues. The central question is whether the proposed testing *should* serve as means to the intended end, in light of other ends it might inadvertently serve and in consideration of the place of the intended end in the pluralistic framework of social choices (Messick, 1980).

It is not that the ends should not justify the means, for what else could possibly justify the means if not appraisal of the ends. Rather, it is that the intended ends do not provide sufficient justification, especially if adverse consequences of testing are linked to sources of test invalidity. Even if adverse testing consequences derive from valid test interpretation and use, the appraisal of the functional worth of the testing in pursuit of the intended ends should take into account all of the ends, both intended and unintended, that are advanced by the testing application, including not only individual and institutional effects but societal or systemic effects as well. Thus, although appraisal of the intended ends of testing is a matter of social policy, it is not only a matter of policy formulation but also of policy evaluation that weighs all of the outcomes and side effects of policy implementation by means of test scores. Such evaluation of the consequences and side effects of testing is a key aspect of the validation of test use.

Some examples of the broader social or systemic consequences of testing that might be monitored in the long-range appraisal of its functional worth include the following: the social mobility function of credit-by-examination or exemption tests like those of the College Board's College Level Examination Program (CLEP), where test utility depends partly on improvement of student progress and access to credentials; the curriculum enhancement function of such tests as those of the College Board's Advanced Placement Program, where the utility of the test resides partly in its effects on the quality of secondary school curricula and on improved articulation between secondary and higher education; the energizing effect of writing samples in admissions tests, where the utility of the writing test benefits from any consequent improvements in the teaching of writing; the accountability function of school-leaving examinations, where test utility depends partly on attendant improvements in learning and instruction to meet educational standards; the comparability and scaling functions of national standardized testing programs such as the SAT and ACT, where the long-term utility of the tests stems in part from their support of a wide range of academic standards while at the same time facilitating individual opportunity and free academic commerce; and, the signaling function of the National Assessment of Educational Progress, where utility derives in part from the timely identification of—and political as well as educational responsiveness to—performance changes in population groups. Contrariwise, adverse systemic consequences may also redound to test use, and these too should be weighed in appraising the functional worth of the testing.

ANTICIPATING SIDE EFFECTS AND BY-PRODUCTS OF TESTING

As an instance of unintended side effects, the occurrence of sex or ethnic differences in score distributions might lead to adverse impact if the test were used in selection, which would directly reflect on the apparent functional worth of the selection testing. But whether the adverse impact is attributable to construct-relevant or construct-irrelevant test variance or to criterion-related or criterion-unrelated test variance are salient validity issues in appraising functional worth and in justifying test use. If irrelevant sources of test and criterion variance are likely culprits in this regard, adverse impact through use of the test is an issue of test *invalidity*. However, if the sex or ethnic score differences reflect valid properties of the construct tapped by the test, they contribute to score meaning and thus are an issue of test *validity*. That is, if sources of invalidity, especially construct-irrelevant variance or criterion contamination, are not plausible—or can be discounted as the cause—then the adverse impact is an issue of political or social *policy*, whether deliberate or de facto. Hence, professional judgments of test use must accommodate both evidential and consequential determinants. Under such circumstances, it is likely that these "judgments embody tradeoffs, not truths" (Cronbach, 1980, p. 102).

As another instance of side effects, the use in educational achievement tests of structured-response formats such as multiple-choice (as opposed to constructed responses) might lead to increased emphasis on memory and analysis in teaching and learning rather than on divergent thinking and synthesis. This is an example of what N. Frederiksen (1984) called "the real test bias," but the direction that this bias is perceived to take depends on one's educational values. It is not that having tests drive instruction or the curriculum is always bad, but that it is a consequence to be evaluated for good or ill. On the positive side, for example, R. W. Tyler (1960) admonished that, with "a testing program that faithfully reflects the objectives sought by the school, . . . the influence of testing is to reinforce the other efforts of teaching" (p. 13). On the down side, if course and teacher evaluation as well as student evaluation are limited solely to those student-outcome variables that are conventionally tested, then the development of broad curricula is likely to be discouraged (R. W. Tyler, 1960). The point is that the functional worth of the testing depends not only on the degree to which the intended purposes are served but also on the consequences of the outcomes produced, because the values captured in the outcomes are at least as important as the values unleashed in the goals.

Once it is denied that the *intended* goals of the proposed test use are the sole basis for judging worth, the value of the testing must depend on the total set of effects it achieves, whether intended or not (Cook & Shadish, 1986). However, enumerating the potential consequences of test use to evaluate their social import is likely to be as interminable a process as attempting to corroborate in turn the possible derivations in a construct's theoretical network. And there is no guarantee that at any point in time we will identify all of the critical possibilities, especially those unintended side effects that are remote from the expressed testing aims. But once again, the construct interpretation of the test scores plays a facilitating role. Just as the construct meaning of the scores afforded a rational basis for hypothesizing predictive relationships to criteria, construct meaning provides a rational basis for hypothesizing potential testing outcomes and for anticipating possible side effects. That is, the construct theory, by articulating links between processes and outcomes, provides clues to possible effects. Thus, evidence of construct meaning is not only essential for evaluating the import of testing consequences, it also helps determine where to look for testing consequences.

PITTING THE PROPOSED TEST USE AGAINST ALTERNATIVE USES

There are few prescriptions for how to proceed in the systematic evaluation of testing consequences. However, just as the use of counterhypotheses was suggested as an efficient means of directing attention to vulnerabilities in a construct theory, so the use of counterproposals might serve to direct attention efficiently to vulnerabilities in a proposed test use. The approach follows in the spirit of counterplanning in systems analysis, in which the ramifications of one proposal or plan are explored in depth in relation to a dramatically different or even antagonistic proposal (Churchman, 1968). The purpose of the counterproposal—as in Kantian, Hegelian, and Singerian modes of inquiry—is to provide a context of debate exposing the key technical and value assumptions of the original proposal to critical evaluation.

As applied to a proposed test use, the counterproposals might involve quite different assessment techniques, such as observations or portfolios when performance standards are at issue. Or they might attempt to serve the intended purpose in a different way, such as through training rather than selection when productivity levels are at issue. As the latter illustration intimates, a particularly powerful and general form of counterproposal is to weigh the potential social consequences of the proposed test use against the potential social consequences of *not* testing at all (Ebel, 1964). This recommendation is not intended in the contentious sense of most attacks on testing, but in the rhetorical sense of providing systematic discourse on the potential risks and benefits of both the proposal and counterproposals. Thus, the potential consequences of proposed test use are appraised through means–ends deliberation contrasting the value outcomes of plausible alternative proposals. But choice among alternative test uses itself "rests on value assumptions, or, you might say, on beliefs about the long-run empirical consequences for society. Such assumptions or beliefs require diligent scrutiny" (Cronbach, in press, p. 5). One way to facilitate such scrutiny is to examine the value assumptions of the proposed test use in the context of multiple value perspectives.

The Values of Multiple Perspectives

Just as the development of multiple theoretical perspectives helps cope with the problem of subjectivity in science and the development of multiple assessment procedures helps cope with method contamination in measurement, so the construction of multiple value positions helps reduce the likelihood of parochial weighting of value assumptions (D. T. Campbell, 1960; Churchman, 1971; Cook & Shadish, 1986; Cronbach, 1986; Howard, 1985). To see how this occurs, let us consider a range of value premises bearing on a major type of test use: namely, testing for selection or classification, which we have already seen to be permeated by value issues both blatant and latent.

DISTRIBUTIVE JUSTICE IN SELECTION

The selection or classification of individuals according to their predicted criterion performance implies that enhancement of productivity and efficiency are the major social values being served. As with any sorting principle, there are questions of fairness or unfairness to those excluded from the desired program or job. But are problems of fairness substantially alleviated by other sorting principles, or are the sources of perceived unfairness simply shifted in light of changed value premises? Since different sorting or selection principles may serve different social values and bear on the vital issue of fairness in different ways, it is important to consider what some alternative selection principles and their attendant value bases might be and, in particular circumstances, what they ought to be (Messick, 1982b).

If desirable educational programs or jobs are conceived as allocable resources or social goods, then selection and classification may be viewed as problems of distributive justice (Nozick, 1974; Rawls, 1971). The concept of distributive justice deals with the appropriateness of access to the conditions and goods that affect individual well-being, which is broadly conceived to include psychological, physiological, economic, and social aspects. Any sense of injustice with respect to the allocation of resources or goods is usually directed at the rules of distribution, whereas the actual source of discontent may also (or instead) derive from the social values underlying the rules, from the ways in which the rules are implemented, or from the nature of the decision-making process itself. In selection systems, we are thus faced with multiple sources of potential injustice—injustice of values, of rules, of implementation, and of decision-making procedures—any one or combination of which may be salient in a particular selection setting (Deutsch, 1975). And it must be remembered that "the whole selection system is to be justified, not the test alone" (Cronbach, 1980, p. 103).

With respect to injustice of values, there are a variety of possible value bases for selection (e.g., in terms of ability, of effort, or of accomplishment). Regardless of the particular basis or combination chosen, there will likely be perceived injustice by those disadvantaged on that basis, as well as by those preferring some alternative basis. Even when there is agreement on a value basis, such as accomplishment, there may be perceived injustice of rules, depending on how accomplishment is measured (e.g., whether in terms of course grades or evaluated work products). Even when there is agreement about the value basis and the rules (such as course grades to reflect accomplishment), injustice might be perceived in the way in which the rules are implemented (as when course grades actually reflect another value basis, such as ability). Finally, there could be perceived injustice related to the decision-making process itself (as when students feel that they should have some say about which dimensions or types of predictive information are most appropriate for, or relevant to, them). As these examples illustrate, the value issues discussed here also apply broadly to the evaluation of students, whether by teachers assigning grades or by state-mandated minimum competency tests.

Granted that perceived injustice has many roots, let us now

concentrate on its most fundamental source, namely, injustice of values. In the literature on distributive justice, several key social values have repeatedly surfaced as alternative bases for selection or distribution. For example, as summarized by Deutsch (1975), justice has been variously viewed as the treatment of all people as follows:

1. according to their abilities
2. according to their efforts
3. according to their accomplishments
4. in terms of equity, so that all receive outcomes proportional to their inputs (i.e., in proportion to their ability, effort, accomplishment, time, or some combination of valued assets signifying merit)
5. according to their needs
6. in terms of equal opportunity, so that all may compete without external favoritism or discrimination
7. according to the supply and demand of the marketplace
8. according to the principle of reciprocity
9. according to the requirements of the common good
10. so that none falls below a specified minimum, or
11. as equals

It is apparent that these different values might often be in conflict: "The most needy may not be the most able, those who work the hardest may not accomplish the most, equal opportunity may not lead to equal reward, treating everyone as equals may not maximize the common good" (Deutsch, 1975, p. 140). Nor does any one value or small set of values appear to have natural or universal priority, except for the distribution of rights (as distinct from income or other barterable goods), where equality of entitlement generally prevails (Okun, 1975).

Conditions in which productivity is a primary goal tend to foster equity or merit as the dominant principles of distributive justice. But other conditions important to educational settings, as well as to the world of work, foster equality or need as dominant principles. Under circumstances where enhancement of solidarity or of mutually satisfying social relations is a primary goal, equality probably would emerge as the dominant and facilitating principle. However, when the enhancement of personal development and personal welfare is the primary goal, individual need would probably prevail (Deutsch, 1975). Under other conditions concerned not only with individual well-being but with group and societal well-being, other value bases such as equal opportunity or the common good might predominate.

The point is that in evaluating test use in selection or classification, one should not focus on one value basis—even the value perspective of the decision maker—to the exclusion of all others. To do so engenders too narrow a validation inquiry and reduces our sensitivity to side effects that are likely to be seen as adverse by other value positions. A familiar example here is the validation of employment tests by predicting criteria that the employer values, while ignoring impact on applicant groups disproportionately rejected by the tests. Such an employer-centered approach highlights sources of predictive validity but neglects the possibility that sources of test *invalidity*

may lead to adverse social consequences. Adverse social consequences associated with *valid* test interpretation and use are also important, to be sure. But as was previously noted, these are valid properties of the construct assessed and hence raise social and political issues as opposed to invalidity issues.

In the context of alternative and even rival value perspectives, "informed argument often ought not end in agreement, because substantive findings are equivocal and because participants weigh values differently" (Cronbach, 1988, p. 7). As was seen in an earlier section of this chapter, conflict and debate are instrumental to a dialectical mode of deriving and examining the ethical implications of scientific models or, in this case, of selection and validation models (Churchman, 1961, 1971; Mitroff & Sagasti, 1973).

MULTIPLE PERSPECTIVES TO OFFSET THE PREEMPTIVENESS OF VALUE COMMITMENTS

By giving primacy to productivity and efficiency, a selection procedure downplays the significance of other important goals in education and the workplace. Coordinately, by highlighting the polarity of individual equity and group parity and by calling for flexible decision rules to effect a tolerable compromise between the two (Wigdor & Garner, 1982), the resulting selection procedures deemphasize other bases for fairness and leave other value conflicts unattended. It is not that productivity and efficiency should not be paramount, for in many instances they are and should be. Nor is it that some other value, such as equality or need, should be given primacy or equal status, although this too seems appropriate on many occasions. Rather, no single value principle should systematically color our thinking about the functions of selection or of test use more generally, especially in education. Instead, we should evaluate test use in the context of multiple value perspectives to assure that a broad range of potential social consequences of the testing are addressed in the validation process.

The recognition and systematic application of multiple perspectives is beneficial in a variety of ways, because it tends to broaden the range of values, criteria, and standards deemed worthy of consideration (Messick, 1982b). In a worldview in which productivity and efficiency predominate, grade-point average and work output appear to be fundamental and natural criteria. In such a world, it is not surprising that challenges from competing values, such as equal opportunity and group parity, would be met by seeking balance and compromise, resulting in the suboptimal enhancement of the ostensibly basic productivity criteria (e.g., Hunter & Hunter, 1984; Schmidt, Mack, & Hunter, 1984). But if a multiple-perspectives approach or a more pluralistic worldview were adopted, with the criteria themselves in question, one would be likely to seek alternatives as well as compromises and to press the limits in search of extensions and reformulations.

In considering alternatives in educational selection, one usually thinks of alternative predictors to aptitude and achievement tests and to course grades. For example, one might consider interviews, biographical information, letters of recommendation, previous accomplishments in similar or related activities, portfolios, and work samples. But what about alternative criteria to be predicted? Would the range of predictive alternatives be changed if student satisfaction rather than student performance were the criterion? Or instead of grades per se, if academic growth or value-added improvement were the criterion, as the Commission on the Higher Education of Minorities argues (Astin, 1982)? And what of alternatives to selection itself as the route to program eligibility or job entry — for example, via prerequisite training or probationary appointment?

In sum, the very recognition of alternative perspectives about the social values to be served, about the criteria to be enhanced, or about the standards to be achieved should be salutary in its own right. This is so because to the extent that alternative perspectives are perceived as legitimate, it is less likely that any one of these perspectives will dominate our assumptions, our methodologies, or our thinking about the validation of test use.

Test Misuse and the Ethics of Test Use

The value implications of test interpretation and the potential social consequences of proposed test use derive largely from the test's construct meaning, but not entirely so. Other more political and situational sources of social values bearing on testing often assume equal or greater importance. In particular, critical value implications frequently emerge when the test is placed in the specific social context of a local applied setting, as when intelligence testing for placement in special education programs confronts the value conflict between disproportionate placement by race on the one hand and entitlement to needed services on the other (Heller et al., 1982). As a further complication, these context-specific value implications may differ depending on whether the test use bears on selection, instruction, guidance, placement, or other educational or applied functions. Because the test user is in the best position to evaluate these locally specific value implications, a heavy ethical burden thereby falls on the user.

The test user is also in the best position to evaluate the meaning of individual scores under the specific circumstances, that is, to appraise the construct validity of individual score interpretation and the extent to which the intended score meaning might have been eroded by contaminating variables operating locally. For example, verbal intelligence scores for Hispanic students should be interpreted in light of their English-language proficiency, and test scores for inattentive children and those with behavior problems should be interpreted with care and checked against alternative indicators (Heller et al., 1982).

Although the delineation of possible influences that might contaminate a test score from the standpoint of a proposed construct interpretation is part of construct validation, the user's task in this instance is not construct validation per se but to recognize which of the possible contaminants are operating in his or her particular situation. In the final analysis, as Cronbach early maintained,

> responsibility for valid use of a test rests on the person who interprets it. The published research merely provides the interpreter with some facts and concepts. He has to combine these with his other knowledge about the persons he tests and the assignments or adjustment problems that confront them to decide what interpretations are warranted. (1969, p. 51)

in the particular case. Thus, the test user bears not only a heavy ethical burden but a heavy interpretative burden as well. And this burden includes responsibility for the social consequences of invalid local score interpretation and use.

But the test user cannot be the sole arbiter of the ethics of assessment, because the *value* of measurements is as much a scientific and professional validity issue as the *meaning* of measurements. One implication of this stance is that the published research and interpretive test literature should not merely provide the interpreter or user with some facts and concepts, but with some exposition of the critical value contexts in which the facts are embedded and with a provisional accounting of the potential social consequences of alternative test uses (Messick, 1981b). The test user should also be explicitly alerted to the dangers of potential test misuse, because test misuse is a significant source of invalidity. That is, just as the use of test scores invalid for the specific purpose is misuse, so the misuse of otherwise valid scores leads to invalidity in practice.

The distinction between valid test use and test misuse is typically thought of rather superficially as a simple dichotomy, whereas in actuality there are complex gradations between two extremes. If compelling evidence exists that a proposed test use is not valid, then such use is misuse. But between this extreme and one in which compelling evidence supports the use, there lie a number of contentious positions about which measurement professionals often disagree. By and large, the contention stems from two related sources: one, disagreement about what constitutes sufficient evidence supportive of action; and, the other, divergent value perspectives about potential social consequences. As a result, test misuse is a topic demanding not only intensive study of actual and potential testing consequences under circumstances having various types and degrees of supportive validity evidence, but also continuing policy debate over value assumptions and the valuation of outcomes. That is, among other aspects of test misuse, we should investigate what kinds of potential testing consequences are protected against or rendered less plausible by the available validity evidence and what kinds are not, and we should attempt to clarify their respective importance from multiple value perspectives.

The Social Consequences of Test Invalidity

The consequential basis of test use addresses the functional worth of test scores by adding an appraisal of the social consequences of testing to our concern with meaning, relevance, utility, and value implications as integral aspects of score validity. As has been stressed several times already, it is not that adverse social consequences of test use render the use invalid but, rather, that adverse social consequences should not be attributable to any source of test invalidity such as construct-irrelevant variance. If the adverse social consequences are empirically traceable to sources of test invalidity, then the validity of the test use is jeopardized. If the social consequences cannot be so traced — or if the validation process can discount sources of test invalidity as the likely determinants, or at least render them less plausible—then the validity of the test use is not overturned. Adverse social consequences associated with valid test interpretation and use may implicate the attributes validly assessed, to be sure, as they function under the existing social conditions of the applied setting, but they are not in themselves indicative of invalidity.

In general, the best protection against adverse social consequences as threats to valid score interpretation and use is to minimize in the measurement process any potential sources of test invalidity, especially construct underrepresentation and construct-irrelevant variance. Thus, the watchword for educational and psychological measurement is to maximize the empirically grounded interpretability of the scores and minimize construct irrelevancy.

Evidence and Ethics in Test Interpretation and Use

Pervasive throughout this treatment of the content, criteria, and consequences of testing is the central and unifying role played by the construct meaning of test scores. Since construct-related evidence undergirds not only construct-based inferences but content- and criterion-based inferences, as well as appraisals of testing consequences, construct interpretation is the unifying force that integrates all facets of test validity. After all, constructs are the medium of exchange of ideas in scientific and social discourse, and their essential role in measurement gives a means of making or maintaining contact with those ideas and of embodying them in quantitative terms.

Theoretical and Value Contexts of Testing

The process of construct interpretation inevitably places test scores both in a theoretical context of implied relationships to other constructs and in a value context of implied relationships to good and bad valuations, for example, of the desirability or undesirability of attributes and behaviors. Empirical appraisals of the former substantive relationships contribute to an *evidential basis for test interpretation,* that is, to construct validity. Judgmental appraisals of the latter value implications provide a *consequential basis for test interpretation.*

The process of test use inevitably places test scores both in a theoretical context of implied relevance and utility and in a value context of implied means and ends. Empirical appraisals of the former issues of relevance and utility, along with construct validity, contribute to an *evidential basis for test use.* Judgmental appraisals of the ends a proposed test use might lead to, that is, of the potential consequences of a proposed use and of the actual consequences of the applied testing, provide a *consequential basis for test use.*

These four aspects of both the evidential and consequential bases of both test interpretation and test use constitute the four cells of Table 2.1, as we have seen. However, the interactions among these aspects are more dynamic in practice than is implied by a simple fourfold classification. A more sequential and interactive representation is needed to portray this dynamic quality.

FEEDBACK REPRESENTATION OF UNIFIED TEST VALIDITY

In an attempt to schematize the interdependence and feedback among the four validity aspects, a flow diagram is presented in Figure 2.7. The double arrows linking the box labeled "construct evidence" and the box for "test interpretation" in the diagram are meant to imply an iterative and interactive process that starts sometimes with a construct in search of valid measurement and sometimes with an existing test in search of valid meaning. The arrow linking "test interpretation" to "value implications" signifies appraisal of the degree to which the value connotations of score interpretation are both consistent and commensurate with the score's theoretical connotations. If there is a problem of inconsistency, the validation process recycles for further consideration of construct evidence. If consistent, the theoretical and value implications of the scores provide the import for action leading to proposed test use.

At this point, evidence is evaluated bearing on the relevance of the scores to the specific applied purpose and on the utility of the scores in the applied setting. If this evidence is not deemed to be a defensible basis for the pending action, the process recycles for reconsideration of the proposed use or to buttress the available relevance and utility evidence. If deemed defensible, the potential social consequences of the proposed use are appraised to anticipate adverse outcomes that might be forestalled by changed testing practices or by the introduction of safeguards and controls. If potential adverse consequences are not likely to be alleviated by control procedures, the process recycles for further consideration of the proposed use or for its justification acknowledging potential side effects.

This feedback representation also includes at the bottom of the diagram a pragmatic component for the continual evaluation of the actual consequences of testing practice. It is pragmatic in the sense that this component is oriented, like pragmatic philosophy but unlike the top of the diagram, toward outcomes rather than origins and seeks justification for test use in the practical consequences of use. The primary concern of this pragmatic component is the balancing of the instrumental value of the test in accomplishing its intended purpose with the instrumental value of any negative side effects and positive by-products of the testing. Most test makers acknowledge responsibility for providing general validity evidence of the instrumental value of the test. The terminal value of the test in relation to the social ends to be served goes beyond the test maker to include the decision maker, the policy maker, and the test user, who are responsible for specific validity evidence of instrumental and terminal value in their particular settings and for the specific interpretations and uses made of the test scores.

Intervening in the diagram between test use and the evaluation of consequences is a decision matrix, which is intended to highlight the fact that tests are rarely used in isolation but, rather, in combination with other information in broader decision systems. As we have seen, the decision process is profoundly influenced by social values, which need to be appraised and adjudicated as part of the decision matrix. Indeed, whether or not a test score proves useful often depends on

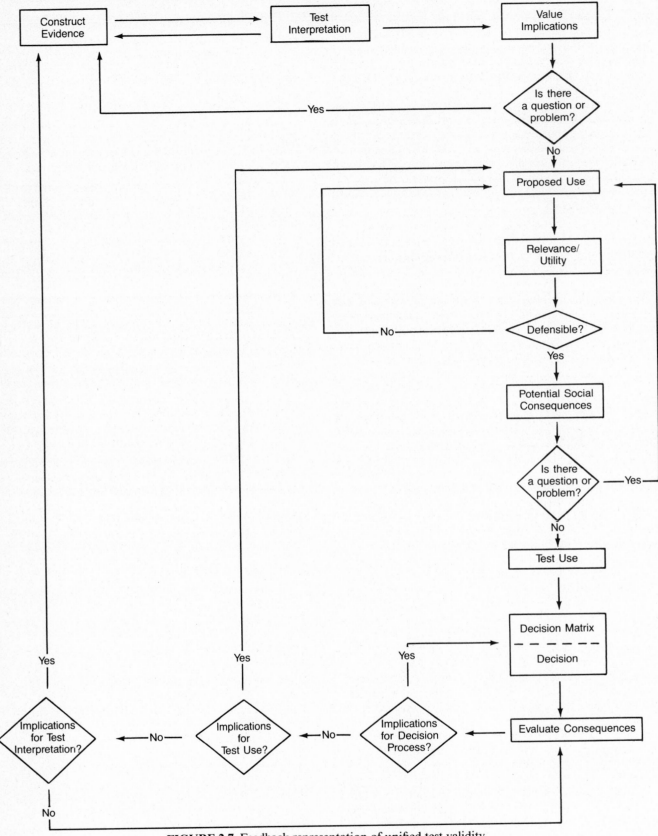

FIGURE 2.7 Feedback representation of unified test validity

90

what other information it is combined with and whether decision processes in practice actually follow policy intentions. For example, Willingham and Breland (1982) showed that the actual weights placed on measures in college selection decisions may be unwittingly quite inconsistent with those of prediction equations, as well as with the intentions of the institution. Thus, the actual consequences of using selection measures might be quite different from those normally inferred from the predictor-criterion relationships used to characterize predictive validity. This is because selection is often not based on strict application of decision algorithms. Hence, discrepancies in this regard in actual test use could limit test utility in much the same manner as does unreliability.

Finally, this feedback representation of unified test validity is portrayed as a closed or recycling system to emphasize the point that, even when testing consequences are evaluated favorably, they should be continually or periodically monitored to permit the detection of changing circumstances and of delayed side effects. The system is closed, of course, only with respect to the continuing nature of the validation process, not with respect to accessibility to new evidence and hypotheses.

Validity and the Politicization of Testing

The politicization of testing is hardly a new phenomenon, as witness Cronbach's (1975) review of 5 decades of public testing controversy. In many ways, politicization of testing is inevitable, not only because of incautious interpretations and misuses of tests, but mainly because testing serves multiple ends inherently embroiled with contending or conflicting social values. As a consequence, the interpretations and uses of tests need to be justified not only in scientific and professional forums, but in the public arena as well. "The public intends to judge specific test uses for itself, directly or through courts and legislatures" (Cronbach, 1980, p. 100). Whether these public judgments are fought through in the media, on issues of test bias and fairness or in the courts on issues of adverse impact on minority groups or in the legislatures on issues of test disclosure, fought through they will be. A major issue, however, is whether and how the professional measurement community will participate in the debate.

In any event, one aspect of the debate is becoming increasingly foreclosed, namely, the legal aspect. That is, legal restrictions are being placed on the ways in which tests are used or acceptably validated (Lerner, 1980). To illustrate, there are federal mandates, such as Section 504 of the Rehabilitation Act, regarding the use and validation of employment and admissions tests applied to handicapped individuals. It is important in ascertaining how to comply with the federal regulations (or in seeking to have them modified) that measurement specialists attempt to clarify in a timely manner how test validity for handicapped people should be defined and evaluated (e.g., Sherman & Robinson, 1982; Willingham et al., 1988).

When confronted with media controversy, judicial review, or legal dispute, test specialists are often thrown off balance and frequently filter evidence through their own social values without weighing alternative value perspectives. The impact of social values on the interpretation of evidence is difficult to

avoid in any event. However, the effect is less variable or idiosyncratic if the evidence is interpreted in the context not only of personal values and the values of others, but of technical standards to guide professional judgment as well. Because validity is the only essential justification for test interpretation and use, professional judgments about testing should be guided by validity principles in particular and by the broader testing *Standards* (APA, 1985) in general. However, to be credible, these validity principles and testing standards must be applied sensibly in practice and communicated sensibly to nonprofessional participants in the public debate (Kleiman & Faley, 1985). This strategy is predicated on the assumption that "scientific argument and political argument differ in degree rather than kind, science having a longer time horizon, more homogeneous participants, and more appeal to formal reasoning" (Cronbach, 1988, pp. 6–7).

Test Standards and the Politics of Compromise

Ironically, the testing *Standards* (APA, 1985) not only offer principles to guide professional judgment but also allow professional judgment to guide the application of the principles. This loophole, or principle of grace, occurs up front in the very definition of what constitutes primary standards. Specifically,

> *primary standards* are those that should be met by all tests before their operational use and in all test uses, unless a sound professional reason is available to show why it is not necessary, or technically feasible, to do so in a particular case. (APA, 1985, p. 2)

There is, indeed, a good rationale for why sound professional judgment should have veto power in practice: otherwise the standards would be completely prescriptive and, hence, unresponsive to compelling local exceptions. But in the absence of enforcement mechanisms, where is the protection against unsound professional judgment? And how could one tell the difference, if not on the basis of the validity principles and testing standards themselves? As one member of the *Standards* committee lamented, "it is with great sorrow that I have to say that they can be so broadly interpreted that almost anything goes" (Madaus, 1986, p. 14).

As a case in point, consider some of the official standards for validity. From the perspective of a unified view of validity, the *Standards* (APA, 1985) enunciate effective validity principles, but with sufficient qualification to permit considerable variation in practice. Much of this variation stems from appropriate allowance for sound professional judgment, as previously indicated. But the same allowance for professional judgment that facilitates flexibility in test validation also permits perpetuation of less desirable uses of the past. For example, the very first validity standard promulgated requires evidence for the major types of inferences entailed in the specific test uses recommended, along with a rationale supporting the particular mix of evidence presented. However, the accompanying comment may give the gain away, for it states that "whether one or more kinds of validity evidence are appropriate is a function of the particular question being asked and of the context and extent of previous evidence" (APA, 1985, p. 13). The perennial context in applied testing is one of limited time and resources for making decisions. Therefore, tests that give incomplete information are often used in practice, and validation findings that are incomplete have to guide these decisions as well as the next research steps in understanding the variables. But when tests are used in the face of incomplete information, it should matter what the nature and extent of the incompleteness amount to. In addition, the background material on validity also states that

> other things being equal, more sources of evidence are better than fewer. However, the quality of the evidence is of primary importance, and a single line of solid evidence is preferable to numerous lines of evidence of questionable quality. Professional judgment should guide the decisions regarding the forms of evidence that are most necessary and feasible in light of the intended uses of the test. (APA, 1985, p. 9)

These accompanying comments are cogent under circumstances in which, for example, knowledge and skills important in job performance are identified by content-related evidence and then assessed by tests deemed on the basis of prior results to be construct-valid measures of that knowledge and skill, even though it is infeasible to collect criterion-related evidence in the local circumstance. Indeed, the forgoing of one form of validity evidence when infeasible may be defended if heavy reliance can be placed on the other forms of evidence, especially (indeed, essentially) construct-related evidence and a construct-based rationale for the plausibility of the predictive hypothesis. But this is a far cry from selective reliance on any *one* sort of validity evidence. Yet, the comments accompanying the validity standard leave the door open for an interpretation that there exist circumstances under which only one kind of validity evidence — be it content-related, for instance, or criterion-related — may be not only feasible but also adequate for a particular applied purpose. This selective reliance on one kind of validity evidence, when it occurs, is tantamount to reliance on one kind of validity as the whole of validity, regardless of how discredited such overgeneralization may have become and of how much acceptance is voiced of validity as a unitary concept.

Other examples of the interpretive looseness of the testing standards are provided by Della-Piana (1986) and by Haney and Madaus (1988). The latter authors point to the increasing leeway afforded in successive drafts of the 1985 *Standards* as a consequence of political compromises effected by contending reviewers. Granted that the standard-setting process was political and that compromises were exacted, there are laudable as well as questionable features of the final document. The 1985 testing *Standards* take an enormous step forward, especially in regard to standards for test use. The final document puts forth scientifically based standards as principles to guide and legitimize testing practice — albeit accommodating, via the emphasis on professional judgment, the current and varied needs of educational, industrial, clinical, and research practitioners and sometimes setting standards with an eye toward the vulnerability of testers in the public arena.

The price paid in the politics of compromise is that the standards downplay principles that would lead the measurement field forward, that is, the formulation of desirable though challenging next steps toward improved testing practice. To be sure, the codification of current best practice is not an inappropriate role for scientific and professional standards. Yet it is also appropriate that this chapter not be limited in the same way. It is important, for example, that the 1985 *Standards* took the major step of maintaining that "validity . . . is a unitary concept" (APA, 1985, p.9). But the *Standards* stop short of asserting that construct validity is the unifying force and of addressing the scientific and ethical ramifications of the unitary validity view. The pursuit of such implications has redounded to the present chapter and to other treatments of validity issues. In particular, the *Standards* also stop short of stipulating the need to appraise the value implications of test interpretation and the social consequences of test use as integral aspects of unified validity. At some point, however, the official testing standards of the future must confront the value consequences of testing, because validity and values are one imperative, not two. Once more, we agree with Cronbach (1980) that "value-free standards of validity is a contradiction in terms, a nostalgic longing for a world that never was" (p. 105).

REFERENCES

Abelson, R. P. (1963). Computer simulation of "hot" cognition. In S. S. Tomkins & S. Messick (Eds.), *Computer simulation of personality: Frontier of psychological theory* (pp. 277–298). New York: John Wiley & Sons.

Albright, L. E., Glennon, J. K., & Smith, W. J. (1963). *The use of psychological tests in industry*. Cleveland: Howard Allen.

Alexander, R. A., Barrett, G. V., & Doverspike, D. (1983). An explication of the selection ratio and its relationship to hiring rate. *Journal of Applied Psychology, 68*, 342–344.

Allport, G. W. (1937). *Personality: A psychological interpretation*. New York: Holt.

Allport, G. W. (1961). *Pattern and growth in personality*. New York: Holt, Rinehart and Winston.

Alpert, R., & Haber, R. N. (1960). Anxiety in academic achievement situations. *Journal of Abnormal and Social Psychology, 61*, 207–215.

Alston, W. P. (1975). Traits, consistency, and conceptual alternatives for personality theory. *Journal for the Theory of Social Behavior, 5*, 17–47.

American Educational Research Association, & National Council on Measurements Used in Education. (1955). *Technical recommendations for achievement tests*. Washington, DC: National Education Association.

American Psychological Association. (1954). Technical recommendations for psychological tests and diagnostic techniques. *Psychological Bulletin, 51*(2, Pt. 2).

American Psychological Association. (1966). *Standards for educational and psychological tests and manuals*. Washington, DC: Author.

American Psychological Association. (1986). *Guidelines for computer-based tests and interpretations*. Washington, DC: Author.

American Psychological Association, American Educational Research Association, & National Council on Measurement in Education. (1974). *Standards for educational and psychological tests*. Washington, DC: American Psychological Association.

American Psychological Association, American Educational Research Association, & National Council on Measurement in Education. (1985). *Standards for educational and psychological testing*. Washington, DC: American Psychological Association.

Anastasi, A. (1948). The nature of psychological 'traits.' *Psychological Review, 55*, 127–138.

Anastasi, A. (1954). *Psychological testing* (1st ed.). New York: Macmillan.

Anastasi, A. (1961). *Psychological testing* (2nd ed.). New York: Macmillan.

Anastasi, A. (1964). Some current developments in the measurement and interpretation of test validity. *Proceedings of the 1963 Invitational Conference on Testing Problems* (pp. 33–45). Princeton, NJ: Educational Testing Service. (Reprinted in A. Anastasi [Ed.]. [1966]. *Testing problems in perspective* [pp. 307–313]. Washington, DC: American Council on Education.)

Anastasi, A. (1968). *Psychological testing* (3rd ed.). New York: Macmillan.

Anastasi, A. (1976). *Psychological testing* (4th ed.). New York: Macmillan.

Anastasi, A. (1982). *Psychological testing* (5th ed.). New York: Macmillan.

Anastasi, A. (1986). Evolving concepts of test validation. *Annual Review of Psychology, 37,* 1–15.

Anderson, J. R. (1976). *Language, memory, and thought.* Hillsdale, NJ: Lawrence Erlbaum.

Angoff, W. H. (1988). Validity: An evolving concept. In H. Wainer & H. Braun (Eds.), *Test validity* (pp. 19–32). Hillsdale, NJ: Lawrence Erlbaum.

Ashton, S. G., & Goldberg, L. R. (1973). In response to Jackson's challenge: The comparative validity of personality scales constructed by the external (empirical) strategy and scales developed intuitively by experts, novices, and laymen. *Journal of Research in Personality, 7,* 1–20.

Astin, A. W. (1964). Criterion-centered research. *Educational and Psychological Measurement. 24,* 807–822.

Astin, A. W. (1982). *Final report of the Commission on the Higher Education of Minorities.* San Francisco: Jossey-Bass.

Balma, M. J. (1959). The concept of synthetic validity. *Personnel Psychology, 12,* 395–396.

Barrett, G. V., Caldwell, M. S., & Alexander, R. A. (1985). The concept of dynamic criteria: A critical reanalysis. *Personnel Psychology, 38,* 41–56.

Barrett, G. V., Phillips, J. S., & Alexander, R. A. (1981). Concurrent and predictive validity designs: A critical reanalysis. *Journal of Applied Psychology, 66,* 1–6.

Bass, B. M. (1962). Further evidence on the dynamic character of criteria. *Personnel Psychology, 15,* 93–97.

Beck, L. W. (1950). Constructions and inferred entities. *Philosophy of Science, 17,* 74–86. (Reprinted in H. Feigl & M. Brodbeck [Eds.]. [1953]. *Readings in the philosophy of science* [pp. 368–381]. New York: Appleton-Century-Crofts.)

Bentler, P. M. (1980). Multivariate analysis with latent variables: Causal modeling. *Annual Review of Psychology, 31,* 419–456.

Bentler, P., Jackson, D. N., & Messick, S. (1971). Identification of content and style: A two-dimensional interpretation of acquiescence. *Psychological Bulletin, 76,* 186–204.

Berg, I. A. (1967). *Response set in personality assessment.* Chicago: Aldine.

Berkson, J. (1947). "Cost-utility" as a measure of the efficiency of a test. *Journal of the American Statistical Association, 42,* 246–255.

Betz, E. L. (1971). An investigation of job satisfaction as a moderator variable in predicting job success. *Journal of Vocational Behavior, 1,* 123–128.

Bhaskar, R. A. (1978). *A realist theory of science.* Atlantic Highlands, NJ: Humanities Press.

Bhaskar, R. A. (1979). *The possibility of naturalism.* Brighton, England: Harvester Press.

Birenbaum, M., & Tatsuoka, K. K. (1982). On the dimensionality of achievement test data. *Journal of Educational Measurement, 19,* 259–266.

Blalock, H. M., Jr. (1985a). *Causal models in panel and experimental designs.* New York: Aldine.

Blalock, H. M., Jr. (1985b). *Causal models in the social sciences* (2nd ed.). New York: Aldine.

Bloom, B. S., & Broder, L. J. (1950). *Problem-solving processes of college students.* Chicago: University of Chicago Press.

Bobko, P. (1983). An analysis of correlations corrected for attenuation and range restriction. *Journal of Applied Psychology, 68,* 584–589.

Bobko, P., Karren, R., & Parkington, J. J. (1983). Estimation of standard deviations in utility analyses: An empirical test. *Journal of Applied Psychology, 68,* 170–176.

Boldt, R. F. (1986a). *Generalization of GRE General Test validity across departments* (GRE Report No. 82-13P and ETS RR 86-46). Princeton, NJ: Educational Testing Service.

Boldt, R. F. (1986b). *Generalization of SAT validity across colleges* (CB Report No. 86-3 and ETS RR 86-24). New York: College Entrance Examination Board.

Bowers, K. S. (1973). Situationism in psychology: An analysis and critique. *Psychological Review, 80,* 307–336.

Bowers, R. (1936). Discussion of "A critical study of the criterion of internal consistency in personality scale construction": An analysis of the problem of validity. *American Sociological Review, 1,* 69–74.

Bracht, G. H., & Glass, G. V (1968). The external validity of experiments. *American Educational Research Journal, 5,* 437–474.

Braun, H. I. (in press). Empirical Bayes methods: A tool for exploratory analysis. In D. Bock (Ed.), *Multilevel analysis of educational data.* San Diego, CA: Academic Press.

Braun, H. I., & Jones, D. H. (1981). *The Graduate Management Admission Test prediction bias study* (GMAC Research Report 81-4 and ETS RR 81-25). Princeton, NJ: Educational Testing Service.

Braun, H. I., Jones, D. H., Rubin, D. B., & Thayer, D. T. (1983). Empirical Bayes estimation of coefficients in the general linear model from data of deficient rank. *Psychometrika, 48,* 171–181.

Braun, H. I., & Szatrowski, T. H. (1984a). The scale-linkage algorithm: Construction of a universal criterion scale for families of institutions. *Journal of Educational Statistics, 9,* 311–330.

Braun, H. I., & Szatrowski, T. H. (1984b). Validity studies based on a universal criterion scale. *Journal of Educational Statistics, 9,* 331–344.

Breland, H. M. (1977). *A study of college English placement and the Test of Standard Written English* (RDR-76-77, No. 4). Princeton, NJ: Educational Testing Service.

Breland, H. M. (1978). *Population validity and college entrance measures* (RDR 78-79, No. 2 and ETS RB 78-19). Princeton, NJ: Educational Testing Service.

Breland, H. M., Camp, R., Jones, R. J., Morris, M. M., & Rock, D. A. (1987). *Assessing writing skill* (Research Monograph # 11). New York: College Entrance Examination Board.

Breland, H. M., Conlon, G. C., & Rogosa, D. (1976). *A preliminary study of the Test of Standard Written English.* Princeton, NJ: Educational Testing Service.

Brennan, R. L., & Kane, M. T. (1979). Generalizability theory: A review. In R. E. Traub (Ed.), *New directions for testing and measurement: Methodological developments* (pp. 33–51). San Francisco: Jossey-Bass.

Brogden, H. E. (1946). On the interpretation of the correlation coefficient as a measure of predictive efficiency. *Journal of Educational Psychology, 37,* 65–76.

Brogden, H. E., & Taylor, E. K. (1950a). The dollar criterion: Applying the cost accounting concept to criterion construction. *Personnel Psychology, 3,* 133–154.

Brogden, H. E., & Taylor, E. K. (1950b). The theory and classification of criterion bias. *Educational and Psychological Measurement, 10,* 159–186.

Brown, J. S., & Burton, R. R. (1978). Diagnostic models for procedural bugs in basic mathematical skills. *Cognitive Science, 2,* 155–192.

Browne, M. W. (1984). The decomposition of multitrait-multimethod matrices. *British Journal of Mathematical and Statistical Psychology, 37,* 1–21.

Brunswik, E. (1947). *Systematic and representative design of psychological experiments.* Berkeley, CA: University of California Press.

Brunswik, E. (1956). *Perception and the representative design of psychological experiments* (2nd ed.). Berkeley, CA: University of California Press.

Burke, M. J. (1984). Validity generalization: A review and critique of the correlational model. *Personnel Psychology, 37,* 93–111.

Burke, M. J., & Frederick, J. T. (1984). Two modified procedures for estimating standard deviations in utility analyses. *Journal of Applied Psychology, 69,* 482–489.

Burt, C. (1949). The structure of the mind: A review of the results of factor analysis. *British Journal of Educational Psychology, 19,* 100–111, 176–199.

Burt, C. (1955). The evidence for the concept of intelligence. *British Journal of Educational Psychology, 25,* 158–177.

Callender, J. C., & Osburn, H. G. (1980). Development and test of a new model for validity generalization. *Journal of Applied Psychology, 65,* 543–558.

Callender, J. C., Osburn, H. G., Greener, J. M., & Ashworth, S. (1982). Multiplicative validity generalization: Accuracy of estimates as a function of sample size and mean, variance, and shape of the distribution of true validities. *Journal of Applied Psychology, 67,* 859–867.

Campbell, D. T. (1957). Factors relevant to the validity of experiments in social settings. *Psychological Bulletin, 54,* 297–312.

Campbell, D. T. (1960). Recommendations for APA test standards regarding construct, trait, or discriminant validity. *American Psychologist, 15,* 546–553.

Campbell, D. T. (1986). Relabeling internal and external validity for applied social scientists. In W. M. K. Trochim (Ed.), *Advances in quasi-experimental design and analysis* (pp. 67–77). San Francisco: Jossey-Bass.

Campbell, D. T., & Fiske, D. W. (1959). Convergent and discriminant validation by the multitrait-multimethod matrix. *Psychological Bulletin, 56,* 81–105.

Campbell, D. T., & O'Connell, E. J. (1967). Methods factors in multitrait-multimethod matrices: Multiplicative rather than additive? *Multivariate Behaviorial Research, 2,* 409–426.

Campbell, D. T., & Stanley, J. C. (1963). Experimental and quasi-experimental designs for research on teaching. In N. L. Gage (Ed.), *Handbook of research on teaching* (pp. 471–535). Chicago: Rand McNally.

Campbell, J. P. (1976). Psychometric theory. In M. D. Dunnette (Ed.), *Handbook of industrial and organizational psychology* (pp. 185–222). Chicago: Rand McNally.

Campbell, J. P., Dunnette, M. D., Lawler, E. E., & Weick, K. E. (1970). *Managerial behavior, performance, and effectiveness.* New York: McGraw-Hill.

Caramazza, A., McCloskey, M., & Green, B. (1981). Naive beliefs in "sophisticated" subjects: Misconceptions about trajectories of objects. *Cognition, 9,* 117–123.

Carnap, R. (1936–1937). Testability and meaning. *Philosophy of Science, 3,* 420–468; *4,* 1–40. (Reprinted as a monograph, [1950]. New Haven, CT: Whitlock's. Also reprinted in H. Feigl & M. Brodbeck [Eds.], 1953. *Readings in the philosophy of science* [pp. 47–92]. New York: Appleton-Century-Crofts).

Carnap, R. (1966). *Philosophical foundations of physics.* New York: Basic Books.

Carroll, J. B. (1978). On the theory-practice interface in the measurement of intellectual abilities. In P. Suppes (Ed.), *Impact of research on education: Some case studies* (pp. 1–105). Washington, DC: National Academy of Education.

Carroll, J. B. (1980). Measurement of abilities constructs. In *Construct validity in psychological measurement: Proceedings of a colloquium on theory and application in education and employment* (pp. 23–39). Princeton, NJ: Educational Testing Service.

Cattell, R. B. (1944). Psychological measurement: Normative, ipsative, interactive. *Psychological Review, 51,* 292–303.

Cattell, R. B. (1957). *Personality and motivation structure and measurement.* New York: Harcourt Brace Jovanivich.

Cattell, R. B. (1964). Validity and reliability: A proposed more basic set of concepts. *Journal of Educational Psychology, 55,* 1–22.

Cattell, R. B. (1971). *Abilities: Their structure, growth, and action.* New York: Houghton Mifflin.

Cattell, R. B. (1978). *The scientific use of factor analysis in behavioral and life sciences.* New York: Plenum.

Cattell, R. B., & Digman, J. M. (1964). A theory of the structure of perturbations in observer ratings and questionnaire data in personality research. *Behavioral Science, 55,* 341–358.

Chamberlain, T. C. (1965). The method of multiple working hypotheses. *Science, 148,* 754–759.

Chi, M., Glaser, R., & Farr, M. (1987). *Nature of expertise.* Hillsdale, NJ: Lawrence Erlbaum.

Churchman, C. W. (1961). *Prediction and optimal decision: Philosophical issues of a science of values.* Englewood Cliffs, NJ: Prentice-Hall.

Churchman, C. W. (1968). *The systems approach.* New York: Delacorte Press.

Churchman, C. W. (1971). *The design of inquiring systems: Basic concepts of systems and organization.* New York: Basic Books.

Churchman, C. W. (1979). *The systems approach and its enemies.* New York: Basic Books.

Cleary, T. A. (1968). Test bias: Prediction of grades of negro and white students in integrated colleges. *Journal of Educational Measurement, 5,* 115–124.

Cliff, N. (1977). Further study of cognitive processing models for inventory response. *Applied Psychological Measurement, 1,* 41–49.

Cliff, N., Bradley, P., & Girard, R. (1973). The investigation of cognitive models for inventory response. *Multivariate Behavioral Research, 8,* 407–425.

Coan, R. W. (1964). Facts, factors, and artifacts. The quest for psychological meaning. *Psychological Review, 71,* 123–140.

Colbert, G. A., & Taylor, L. R. (1978). Empirically derived job families as a foundation for the study of validity generalization. Study III. Generalization of selection test validity. *Personnel Psychology, 31,* 355–364.

Cole, M., & Bruner, J. S. (1971). Cultural differences and inferences about psychological processes. *American Psychologist, 26,* 867–876.

Cole, M., Gay, J., Glick, J., & Sharp, D. (1971). *The cultural context of learning and thinking.* New York: Basic Books.

Cole, M., Hood, L., & McDermott, R. (1978). Ecological niche picking as an axiom of experimental cognitive psychology. San Diego: University of California, Laboratory for Comparative Human Cognition.

Cole, N. S. (1973). Bias in selection. *Journal of Educational Measurement, 10,* 237–255.

Cole, N. S., (1981). Bias in testing. *American Psychologist, 36,* 1067–1077.

Cole, N. S., & Moss, P. A. (1988). Bias in test use. In R. L. Linn (Ed.), *Educational measurement* (3rd ed.). New York: Macmillan.

Cook, T. D., & Campbell, D. T. (1979). *Quasi-experimentation: Design and analysis issues for field settings.* Chicago: Rand McNally.

Cook, T. D., & Shadish, W. R., Jr. (1986). Program evaluation: The worldly science. *Annual Review of Psychology, 37,* 193–232.

Coombs, C. H. (1954). Theory and methods of social measurement. In L. Festinger & D. Katz (Eds.), *Research methods in the behavioral sciences* (pp. 171–246). New York: Holt, Rinehart and Winston.

Cooper, L. A. (1980). Spatial information processing: Strategies for research. In R. E. Snow, P-A. Federico, & W. E. Montague (Eds.), *Aptitude, learning, and instruction: Vol. 1. Cognitive process analyses of aptitude* (pp. 149–176). Hillsdale, NJ: Lawrence Erlbaum.

Cooper, L. A., & Regan, D. T. (1982). Attention, perception, and intelligence. In R. J. Sternberg (Ed.), *Handbook of human intelligence* (pp. 123–169). New York: Cambridge University Press.

Cornfield, J., & Tukey, J. W. (1956). Average values of mean squares in factorials. *Annals of Mathematical Statistics, 27,* 907–949.

Couch, A., & Keniston, K. (1960). Yeasayers and naysayers: Agreeing response set as a personality variable. *Journal of Abnormal and Social Psychology, 60,* 151–174.

Crawford, C. (1979). George Washington, Abraham Lincoln, and Arthur Jensen: Are they compatible? *American Psychologist, 34,* 664–672.

Cronbach, L. J. (1946). Response sets and test validity. *Educational and Psychological Measurement, 6,* 475–494.

Cronbach, L. J. (1949). *Essentials of psychological testing* (1st ed.). New York: Harper.

Cronbach, L. J. (1950). Further evidence on response sets and test design. *Educational and Psychological Measurement, 10,* 3–31.

Cronbach, L. J. (1955). Processes affecting scores on "understanding others" and "assumed similarity." *Psychological Bulletin, 52,* 177–193.

Cronbach, L. J. (1960). *Essentials of psychological testing* (2nd ed.). New York: Harper.

Cronbach, L. J. (1968). Intelligence? Creativity? A parsimonious reinterpretation of the Wallach–Kogan data. *American Educational Research Journal, 5,* 491–511.

Cronbach, L. J. (1969). Validation of educational measures. *Proceedings of the 1969 Invitational Conference on Testing Problems: Toward a theory of achievement measurement* (pp. 35–52). Princeton, NJ: Educational Testing Service.

Cronbach, L. J. (1970). *Essentials of psychological testing* (3rd ed.). New York: Harper & Row.

Cronbach, L. J. (1971). Test validation. In R. L. Thorndike (Ed.), *Educational measurement* (2nd ed., pp. 443–507). Washington, DC: American Council on Education.

Cronbach, L. J. (1975). Five decades of public controversy over mental testing. *American Psychologist, 30*, 1–14.

Cronbach, L. J. (1976). Equity in selection: Where psychometrics and political philosophy meet. *Journal of Educational Measurement, 13*, 31–41.

Cronbach, L. J. (1980). Validity on parole: How can we go straight? New directions for testing and measurement: Measuring achievement over a decade. Proceedings of the 1979 ETS Invitational Conference (pp. 99–108). San Francisco: Jossey-Bass.

Cronbach, L. J. (1982). *Designing evaluations of educational and social programs.* San Francisco: Jossey-Bass.

Cronbach, L. J. (1984). *Essentials of psychological testing* (4th ed.). New York: Harper & Row.

Cronbach, L. J. (1985). Review of College Board Scholastic Aptitude Test and Test of Standard Written English. In J. V. Mitchell, Jr. (Ed.), *The ninth mental measurements yearbook* (Vol. 1, pp. 362–364). Lincoln, NE: University of Nebraska Press.

Cronbach, L. J. (1986). Social inquiry by and for earthlings. In D. W. Fiske & R. A. Shweder (Eds.), *Metatheory in social science* (pp. 83–107). Chicago: University of Chicago Press.

Cronbach, L. J. (1988). Five perspectives on validation argument. In H. Wainer & H. Braun (Eds.), *Test validity* (pp. 3–17). Hillsdale, NJ: Lawrence Erlbaum.

Cronbach, L. J. (in press). Construct validation after thirty years. In R. L. Linn (Ed.), *Intelligence: Measurement theory and public policy* (Proceedings of a symposium in honor of Lloyd G. Humphreys). Urbana, IL: University of Illinois Press.

Cronbach, L. J., & Gleser, G. C. (1965). *Psychological tests and personnel decisions* (2nd. ed.). Urbana, IL: University of Illinois Press.

Cronbach, L. J., Gleser, G. C., Nanda, H., & Rajaratnam, N. (1972). *The dependability of behavioral measurements: Theory of generalizability for scores and profiles.* New York: John Wiley.

Cronbach, L. J., & Meehl, P. E. (1955). Construct validity in psychological tests. *Psychological Bulletin, 52*, 281–302.

Cronbach, L. J., & Snow, R. E. (1977). *Aptitudes and instructional methods: A handbook for research on interactions.* New York: John Wiley.

Cureton, E. E. (1951). Validity. In E. F. Lindquist (Ed.), *Educational measurement* (1st ed., pp. 621–694). Washington, DC: American Council on Education.

Curtis, E. W., & Alf, E. F. (1969). Validity, predictive efficiency, and practical significance of selection tests. *Journal of Applied Psychology, 53*, 327–337.

D'Andrade, R. (1986). Three scientific world views and the covering law model. In D. W. Fiske & R. A. Shweder (Eds.), *Metatheory in social science* (pp. 19–41). Chicago: University of Chicago Press.

Darlington, R. B. (1971). Another look at "culture fairness." *Journal of Educational Measurement, 8*, 71–82.

Darlington, R. B. (1976). A defense of "rational" personnel selection, and two new methods. *Journal of Educational Measurement, 13*, 43–52.

Darlington, R. B., & Stauffer, G. F. (1966). Use and evaluation of discrete test information in decision making. *Journal of Applied Psychology, 50*, 125–129.

DeBoeck, P. (1978). Validity of a cognitive processing model for responses to adjective and sentence type inventories. *Applied Psychological Measurement, 2*, 371–378.

DeCorte, E., Verschaffel, L., & De Win, L. (1984, April). The influence of rewording verbal problems on children's problem representations and solutions. Paper presented at the meeting of the American Educational Research Association, New Orleans.

Dehn, N., & Schank, R. (1982). Artificial and human intelligence. In R. J. Sternberg (Ed.), *Handbook of human intelligence* (pp. 352–391). New York: Cambridge University Press.

Della-Piana, G. M. (1986). The 1985 *Test Standards:* Where do they leave the teacher-as-test-user? Unpublished manuscript, University of Utah, Provo.

Deutsch, M. (1975). Equity, equality and need: What determines which value will be used as the basis of distributive justice? *Journal of Social Issues, 31*(3), 137–149.

Drasgow, F. (1982). Biased test items and differential validity. *Psychological Bulletin, 92*, 526–531.

Drasgow, F. (1984). Scrutinizing psychological tests: Measurement equivalence and equivalent relations with external variables are the central issues. *Psychological Bulletin, 95*, 134–135.

Drasgow, F., & Kang, T. (1984). Statistical power of differential validity and differential prediction analysis for detecting measurement nonequivalence. *Journal of Applied Psychology, 69*, 498–508.

Duhem, P. (1908/1954). *The aim and structure of physical theory.* New York: Atheneum.

Dunbar, S. B., Mayekawa, S., & Novick, M. R. (1986). Simultaneous estimation of regression functions for marine corps technical training specialties. *Journal of Educational Statistics, II*, 275–292.

Dunnette, M. D. (1963a). A modified model for test validation and selection research. *Journal of Applied Psychology, 47*, 317–323.

Dunnette, M. D. (1963b). A note on *the* criterion. *Journal of Applied Psychology, 47*, 251–254.

Dunnette, M. D. (1974). Personnel selection and job placement of the disadvantaged. Problems, issues, and suggestions. In H. L. Fromkin & J. J. Sherwood (Eds.), *Integrating the organization.* New York: Macmillan, Free Press.

Dunnette, M. D. (1976). Basic attributes of individuals in relation to behavior in organizations. In M. D. Dunnette (Ed.), *Handbook of industrial and organizational psychology* (pp. 469–520). Chicago: Rand McNally.

Dunnette, M. D., & Borman, W. C. (1979). Personnel selection and classification systems. *Annual Review of Psychology, 30*, 477–525.

Ebel, R. L. (1956). Obtaining and reporting evidence on content validity. *Educational and Psychological Measurement, 16*, 269–282.

Ebel, R. L. (1961). Must all tests be valid? *American Psychologist, 16*, 640–647.

Ebel, R. L. (1964). The social consequences of educational testing. *Proceedings of the 1963 Invitational Conference on Testing Problems* (pp. 130–143). Princeton, NJ: Educational Testing Service. (Reprinted in A. Anastasi [Ed.] [1966]. *Testing problems in perspective* [pp. 18–29]. Washington, DC: American Council on Education.)

Ebel, R. L. (1974). And still the dryads linger. *American Psychologist, 29*, 485–492.

Ebel, R. L. (1983). The practical validation of tests of ability. *Educational Measurement: Issues and Practice, 2*(2), 7–10.

Edel, A. (1970). Science and the structure of ethics. In O. Neurath, R. Carnap, & C. Morris (Eds.), *Foundations of the unity of science: Toward an international encyclopedia of unified science* (Vol. 2, pp. 273–377). Chicago: University of Chicago Press.

Einhorn, H. J., & Bass, A. R. (1971). Methodological considerations relevant to discrimination in employment testing. *Psychological Bulletin, 75*, 261–269.

Eisner, E. (1979). *The educational imagination.* New York: Macmillan.

Ekehammar, B. (1974). Interactionism in personality from a historical perspective. *Psychological Bulletin, 81*, 1026–1048.

Ekstrom, R. B., French, J. W., & Harman, H. H. (1976). *Kit of factor-referenced cognitive tests.* Princeton, NJ: Educational Testing Service.

Embretson (Whitely), S. (1983). Construct validity: Construct representation versus nomothetic span. *Psychological Bulletin, 93*, 179–197.

Embretson (Whitely), S. (1984). A general latent trait model for response processes. *Psychometrika, 49*, 175–186.

Embretson, S., Schneider, L. M., & Roth, D. L. (1986). Multiple processing strategies and the construct validity of verbal reasoning tests. *Journal of Educational Measurement, 23*, 13–32.

Emmerich, W. (1964). Continuity and stability in early social development, II: Teacher ratings. *Child Development, 35,* 311–332.

Emmerich, W. (1968). Personality development and concepts of structure. *Child Development, 39,* 671–690.

Ericcson, K. A., & Simon, H. A. (1984). *Protocol analysis: Verbal reports as data.* Cambridge, MA: MIT Press.

Faggen, J. (1984). *Report on a study of the NTE Core Battery tests by the state of New York* (rev. ed.). Princeton, NJ: Educational Testing Service.

Feigenbaum, E. A., & Feldman, J. (Eds.). (1963). *Computers and thought.* New York: McGraw-Hill.

Ferguson, G. A. (1954). On learning and human ability. *Canadian Journal of Psychology, 8,* 95–111.

Ferguson, G. A. (1956). On transfer and the abilities of man. *Canadian Journal of Psychology, 10,* 121–131.

Feyerabend, P. (1975). *Against method: Outline of an anarchist theory of knowledge.* London: New Left Books.

Fischer, G. H. (1973). The linear logistic model as an instrument in educational research. *Acta Psychologica, 37,* 359–374.

Fiske, D. W. (1973). Can a personality construct be validated empirically? *Psychological Bulletin, 80,* 89–92.

Fiske, D. W. (1976). Can a personality construct have a singular validational pattern? Rejoinder to Huba and Hamilton. *Psychological Bulletin, 83,* 877–879.

Fiske, D. W. (1986). Specificity of method and knowledge in social science. In D. W. Fiske & R. A. Shweder (Eds.), *Metatheory in social science* (pp. 61–82). Chicago: University of Chicago Press.

Fitzpatrick, A. R. (1983). The meaning of content validity. *Applied Psychological Measurement, 7,* 3–13.

Fitzpatrick, R., & Morrison, E. J. (1971). Performance and product evaluation. In R. L. Thorndike (Ed.), *Educational Measurement* (2nd ed., pp. 237–270). Washington, DC: American Council on Education.

Fleishman, E. A., & Fruchter, B. (1960). Factor structure and predictability of successive stages of learning Morse code. *Journal of Applied Psychology, 44,* 97–101.

Fleishman, E. A., & Hempel, W. E., Jr. (1954). Changes in factor structure of a complex psychomotor test as a function of practice. *Psychometrika, 18,* 239–252.

Frederiksen, C. H. (1969). Abilities, transfer, and information retrieval in verbal learning. *Multivariate Behavioral Research Monograph 69-2.*

Frederiksen, C. H. (1985). Cognitive models and discourse analysis. In C. R. Cooper & S. Greenbaum (Eds.), *Written communication annual: Vol. 1. Linguistic approaches to the study of written discourse.* Beverly Hills, CA: Sage.

Frederiksen, J. R. (1980). Component skills in reading: Measurement of individual differences through chronometric analysis. In R. E. Snow, P-A. Federico, & W. E. Montague (Eds.), *Aptitude, learning, and instruction: Vol. 1. Cognitive process analyses of aptitude* (pp. 105–138). Hillsdale, NJ: Lawrence Erlbaum.

Frederiksen, J. R. (1982). A componential theory of reading skills and their interactions. In R. J. Sternberg (Ed.), *Advances in the psychology of human intelligence* (Vol. 1, pp. 125–180). Hillsdale, NJ: Lawrence Erlbaum.

Frederiksen, N. (1962). Factors in in-basket performance. *Psychological Monographs, 76*(22, Whole No. 541).

Frederiksen, N. (1966). Validation of a simulation technique. *Organizational Behavior and Human Performance, 1,* 87–109.

Frederiksen, N. (1984). The real test bias: Influences of testing on teaching and learning. *American Psychologist, 39,* 193–202.

Frederiksen, N. (1986a). Construct validity and construct similarity: Methods for use in test development and test validation. *Multivariate Behavioral Research, 21,* 3–28.

Frederiksen, N. (1986b). Toward a broader conception of human intelligence. *American Psychologist, 41,* 445–452.

Frederiksen, N., Jensen, O., & Beaton, A. E. (1972). *Prediction of organizational behavior.* Elmsford, NY: Pergamon Press.

Frederiksen, N., & Ward, W. C. (1978). Measures for the study of creativity in scientific problem solving. *Applied Psychological Measurement, 2,* 1–24.

French, J. W. (1965). The relationship of problem-solving styles to the factor composition of tests. *Educational and Psychological Measurement, 25,* 9–28.

Frick, J. W., Guilford, J. P., Christensen, P. R., & Merrifield, P. R. (1959). A factor-analytic study of flexibility of thinking. *Educational and Psychological Measurement, 19,* 469–496.

Fromkin, H. L., & Streufert, S. (1976). Laboratory experiments. In M. D. Dunnette (Ed.), *Handbook of industrial and organizational psychology* (pp. 415–465). Chicago: Rand McNally.

Gage, N. L., & Cronbach, L. J. (1955). Conceptual and methodological problems in interpersonal perception. *Psychological Review, 62,* 411–422.

Gardner, E. F. (1983). Intrinsic rational validity: Necessary but not sufficient. *Educational Measurement: Issues and Practice, 2*(2), 13.

Garrison, J. W. (1986). Some principles of postpositivistic philosophy of science. *Educational Researcher, 15*(8), 12–18.

Ghiselli, E. E. (1956). Dimensional problems of criteria. *Journal of Applied Psychology, 40,* 1–4.

Ghiselli, E. E. (1960). Differentiation of tests in terms of the accuracy with which they predict for a given individual. *Educational and Psychological Measurement, 20,* 675–684.

Ghiselli, E. E. (1966). *The validity of occupational aptitude tests.* New York: John Wiley.

Ghiselli, E. E. (1968). Interaction of traits and motivational factors in the determination of the success of managers. *Journal of Applied Psychology, 56,* 270.

Ghiselli, E. E. (1973). The validity of aptitude tests in personnel selection. *Personnel Psychology, 26,* 461–477.

Ghiselli, E. E., & Haire, M. (1960). The validation of selection tests in the light of the dynamic character of criteria. *Personnel Psychology, 13,* 225–231.

Gholson, B., & Barker, P. (1985). Kuhn, Lakatos, and Landau: Applications in the history of physics and psychology. *American Psychologist, 40,* 755–769.

Giniger, S., Dispenzieri, A., & Eisenberg, J. (1983). Age, experience, and performance on speed and skill jobs in an applied setting. *Journal of Applied Psychology, 68,* 469–475.

Glass, G. V, McGaw, B., & Smith, M. L. (1981). *Meta-analysis of social research.* Beverly Hills, CA: Sage.

Glymour, C. (1980). The good theories do. *Construct validity in psychological measurement. Proceedings of a colloquium on theory and application in education and employment* (pp. 13–20). Princeton, NJ: Educational Testing Service.

Godshalk, F., Swineford, F., & Coffman, W. (1966). *The measurement of writing ability* (RM No. 6). New York: College Board.

Golding, S. L. (1977). Method variance, inadequate constructs, or things that go bump in the night? *Multivariate Behavioral Research, 12,* 89–98.

Golding, S. L., & Seidman, E. (1974). Analysis of multitrait-multimethod matrices: A two step principal components procedure. *Multivariate Behavioral Research, 9,* 479–496.

Goodenough, F. L. (1949). *Mental testing.* New York: Rinehart.

Goodman, N. (1978). *Ways of worldmaking.* Indianapolis: Bobbs-Merrill.

Gouldner, A. W. (1962). Anti-minotaur: The myth of a value-free sociology. *Social Problems, 9,* 199–213.

Green, B. F. (1987). Construct validity of computer-based tests. In H. Wainer & H. Braun (Eds.), *Test validity* (pp. 77–86). Hillsdale, NJ: Lawrence Erlbaum.

Green, B. F., Bock, D. R., Humphreys, L. G., Linn, R. L., & Reckase, M. D. (1984). Technical guidelines for assessing computerized adaptive tests. *Journal of Educational Measurement, 21,* 347–360.

Greeno, J. G. (1980). Some examples of cognitive task analysis with instructional implications. In R. E. Snow, P-A. Federico, & W. E. Montague (Eds.), *Aptitude, learning, and instruction: Vol. 2. Cognitive process analyses of learning and problem solving* (pp. 1–21). Hillsdale, NJ: Lawrence Erlbaum.

Gross, A. L., & Su, W. (1975). Defining a "fair" or "unbiased" selection model: A question of utilities. *Journal of Applied Psychology, 60,* 345–351.

Guba, E., & Lincoln, Y. (1981). *Effective evaluation.* San Francisco: Jossey-Bass.

Guilford, J. P. (1946). New standards for test evaluation. *Educational and Psychological Measurement, 6,* 427–439.

Guilford, J. P. (1967). *The nature of human intelligence.* New York: McGraw-Hill.

Guilford, J. P. (1982). Cognitive psychology's ambiguities: Some suggested remedies. *Psychological Review, 89,* 48–59.

Guion, R. M. (1965). *Personnel testing.* New York: McGraw-Hill.

Guion, R. M. (1966). Employment tests and discriminatory hiring. *Industrial Relations, 5,* 20–37.

Guion, R. M. (1974). Open a new window: Validities and values in psychological measurement. *American Psychologist, 29,* 287–296.

Guion, R. M. (1976). Recruiting, selection, and job placement. In M. D. Dunnette (Ed.), *Handbook of industrial and organizational psychology* (pp. 777–828). Chicago: Rand McNally.

Guion, R. M. (1977). Content validity: The source of my discontent. *Applied Psychological Measurement, 1,* 1–10.

Guion, R. M. (1978). Scoring of content domain samples: The problem of fairness. *Journal of Applied Psychology, 63,* 499–506.

Guion, R. M. (1980). On trinitarian doctrines of validity. *Professional Psychology, 11,* 385–398.

Guion, R. M., & Cranny, C. J. (1982). A note on concurrent and predictive validity designs: A critical reanalysis. *Journal of Applied Psychology, 67,* 239–244.

Gulliksen, H. (1950a). Intrinsic validity. *American Psychologist, 5,* 511–517.

Gulliksen, H. (1950b). *Theory of mental tests.* New York: John Wiley.

Gulliksen, H. (1976). *When high validity may indicate a faulty criterion* (RM-76-10). Princeton, NJ: Educational Testing Service.

Gulliksen, H. (1986). Perspectives on educational measurement. *Applied Psychological Measurement, 10,* 109–132.

Gutenberg, R. L., Arvey, R. D., Osburn, H. G., & Jeanneret, P. R. (1983). Moderating effects of decision-making/information-processing job dimensions on test validities. *Journal of Applied Psychology, 68,* 602–608.

Guttman, L. (1958). What lies ahead for factor analysis. *Educational and Psychological Measurement, 18,* 497–515.

Guttman, L. (1969). Integration of test design and analysis. *Proceedings of the 1969 Invitational Conference on Testing Problems* (pp. 53–65). Princeton, NJ: Educational Testing Service.

Haertel, E. (1985). Construct validity and criterion-referenced testing. *Review of Educational Research, 55,* 23–46.

Hakel, M. D. (1986). Personnel selection and placement. *Annual Review of Psychology, 37,* 351–380.

Hambleton, R. K. (1980). Test score validity and standard-setting methods. In R. A. Berk (Ed.), *Criterion-referenced measurement: The state of the art* (pp. 80–123). Baltimore: Johns Hopkins University Press.

Hambleton, R. K. (1984). Validating the test scores. In R. A. Berk (Ed.), *A guide to criterion-referenced test construction* (pp. 199–230). Baltimore: Johns Hopkins University Press.

Hambleton, R. K., & Swaminathan, H. (1985). *Item response theory: Principles and applications.* Hingham, MA: Kluwer Nijhoff.

Hammond, K. R., Hamm, R. M., & Grassia, J. (1986). Generalizing over conditions by combining the multitrait-multimethod matrix and the representative design of experiments. *Psychological Bulletin, 100,* 257–269.

Haney, W., & Madaus, G. (1988). The evolution of ethical and technical standards for testing. In R. K. Hambleton & J. Zaal (Eds.), *Handbook of testing.* Amsterdam: North Holland Press.

Hanson, N. R. (1958). *Patterns of discovery.* New York: Cambridge University Press.

Harman, H. H. (1976). *Modern factor analysis* (3rd ed.). Chicago: University of Chicago Press.

Harré, R. (1970). *The principles of scientific thinking.* Chicago: University of Chicago Press.

Harré, R. (1972). *The philosophies of science.* New York: Oxford University Press.

Heckman, J. J. (1979). Sample selection bias as specification error. *Econometrics, 47,* 153–161.

Hedberg, R., & Baxter, B. (1957). A second look at personality test validation. *Personnel Psychology, 10,* 157–160.

Hedges, L. V. (1988). The meta-analysis of test validity studies: Some new approaches. In H. Wainer & H. Braun (Eds.), *Test validity* (pp. 191–212). Hillsdale, NJ: Lawrence Erlbaum.

Hedges, L. V., & Olkin, I. (1985). *Statistical methods for meta-analysis.* New York: Academic Press.

Heller, K. A., Holtzman, W. H., & Messick, S. (Eds.). (1982). *Placing children in special education: A strategy for equity.* Washington, DC: National Academy Press.

Helmreich, R. L., Sawin, L. L., & Carsrud, A. L. (1986). The honeymoon effect in job performance: Temporal increases in the predictive power of achievement motivation. *Journal of Applied Psychology, 71,* 185–188.

Helmstadter, G. C. (1957). Procedures for obtaining separate set and content components of a test score. *Psychometrika, 22,* 381–393.

Hempel, C. G. (1952/1970). Fundamentals of concept formation in empirical science. In O. Neurath, R. Carnap, & C. Morris (Eds.), *Foundations of the unity of science: Toward an international encyclopedia of unified science* (Vol. 2, pp. 651–745). Chicago: University of Chicago Press.

Hempel, C. G. (1965). *Aspects of scientific explanation and other essays in the philosophy of science.* New York: Macmillan, Free Press.

Hills, J. R. (1971). Use of measurement in selection and placement. In R. L. Thorndike (Ed.), *Educational measurement* (pp. 680–732). Washington, DC: American Council on Education.

Hirsh, H. R., Schmidt, F. L., & Hunter, J. E. (1986). Estimation of employment validities by less experienced judges. *Personnel Psychology, 39,* 337–344.

Hively, W., Patterson, H. L., & Page, S. H. (1968). A "universe-defined" system of arithmetic achievement tests. *Journal of Educational Measurement, 5,* 275–290.

Howard, G. S. (1985). The role of values in the science of psychology. *American Psychologist, 40,* 255–265.

Howe, K. R. (1985). Two dogmas of educational research. *Educational Researcher, 14*(8), 10–18.

Huba, G. J., & Hamilton, D. L. (1976). On the generality of trait relationships: Some analyses based on Fiske's paper. *Psychological Bulletin, 83,* 868–876.

Hubbard, J. P. (1971). *Measuring medical education: The tests and procedures of the National Board of Medical Examiners.* Philadelphia: Lea & Febiger.

Hubert, L. J., & Baker, F. B. (1978). Analyzing the multitrait-multimethod matrix. *Multivariate Behavioral Research, 13,* 163–179.

Hulin, C. L., Drasgow, F., & Parsons, C. K. (1983). *Item response theory: Application to psychological measurement.* Homewood, IL: Dow Jones-Irwin.

Humphreys, L. G. (1962). The organization of human abilities. *American Psychologist, 17,* 475–483.

Hunt, E. (1978). The mechanics of verbal ability. *Psychological Review, 85,* 109–130.

Hunt, E. (1980a). The foundations of verbal comprehension. In R. E. Snow, P-A. Federico, & W. E. Montague (Eds.), *Aptitude, learning, and instruction: Vol. 1. Cognitive process analyses of aptitude* (pp. 87–104). Hillsdale, NJ: Lawrence Erlbaum.

Hunt, E. (1980b). Intelligence as an information-processing concept. *British Journal of Psychology, 71,* 449–474.

Hunt, E. B., Frost, N., & Lunneborg, C. E. (1973). Individual differences in cognition: A new approach to intelligence. In G. Bower (Ed.), *The psychology of learning and motivation: Advances in research and theory* (Vol. 7, pp. 87–122). New York: Academic Press.

Hunt, E., Lunneborg, C. E., & Lewis, J. (1975). What does it mean to be high verbal? *Cognitive Psychology, 7,* 194–227.

Hunt, J. McV. (1961). *Intelligence and experience.* New York: Ronald Press.

Hunter, J. E., & Hunter, R. F. (1984). Validity and utility of alternative predictors of job performance. *Psychological Bulletin, 96,* 72–98.

Hunter, J. E., & Schmidt, F. L. (1976). Critical analysis of the statistical and ethical implications of various definitions of test bias. *Psychological Bulletin, 83,* 1053–1071.

Hunter, J. E., Schmidt, F. L., & Hunter, R. (1979). Differential validity of employment tests by race: A comprehensive review and analysis. *Psychological Bulletin, 86,* 721–735.

Hunter, J. E., Schmidt, F. L., & Jackson, C. B. (1982). *Advanced meta-*

analysis: Quantitative methods of cumulating research findings across studies. San Francisco: Sage.

Jackson, D. N. (1967a). Acquiescence response styles: Problems of identification and control. In I. A. Berg (Ed.), *Response set in personality assessment* (pp. 71–144). Chicago: Aldine.

Jackson, D. N. (1967b). *Manual for the Personality Research Form.* Goshen, NY: Research Psychologists Press.

Jackson, D. N. (1969). Multimethod factor analysis in the evaluation of convergent and discriminant validity. *Psychological Bulletin, 72,* 30–49.

Jackson, D. N. (1971). The dynamics of structured personality tests: 1971. *Psychological Review, 78,* 229–248.

Jackson, D. N. (1975). The relative validity of scales prepared by naive item writers and those based on empirical methods of personality scale construction. *Educational and Psychological Measurement, 35,* 361–370.

Jackson, D. N. (1980). Construct validity and personality assessment. *Construct validity in psychological measurement. Proceedings of a colloquium on theory and application in education and employment* (pp. 79–90). Princeton, NJ: Educational Testing Service.

Jackson, D. N., Ahmed, S. A., & Heapy, N. A. (1976). Is achievement a unitary construct? *Journal of Research in Personality, 10,* 1–21.

Jackson, D. N., & Messick, S. (1958). Content and style in personality assessment. *Psychological Bulletin, 55,* 243–253.

Jackson, D. N., & Paunonen, S. V. (1980). Personality structure and assessment. *Annual Review of Psychology, 31,* 503–551.

James, L. R. (1973). Criterion models and construct validity for criteria. *Psychological Bulletin, 80,* 75–83.

James, L. R., Mulaik, S. A., & Brett, J. M. (1982). *Causal analysis: Assumptions, models and data.* Beverly Hills, CA: Sage.

Jensen, A. R. (1972). *Genetics and education.* New York: Harper & Row.

Jessor, R., & Hammond, K. R. (1957). Construct validity and the Taylor Anxiety Scale. *Psychological Bulletin, 54,* 161–170.

Jöreskog, K. G., & Sörbom, D. (1979). *Advances in factor analysis and structural equation models.* Cambridge, MA: Abt Books.

Kagan, J. (1971). *Change and continuity in infancy.* New York: John Wiley.

Kallenberg, A. L., & Kluegel, J. R. (1975). Analysis of the multitrait-multimethod matrix: Some limitations and an alternative. *Journal of Applied Psychology, 60,* 1–9.

Kane, M. T. (1982a). A sampling model for validity. *Applied Psychological Measurement, 6,* 125–160.

Kane, M. T. (1982b). The validity of licensure examinations. *American Psychologist, 37,* 911–918.

Kane, M. T. (1986). The future of testing for licensure and certification examinations. In J. V. Mitchell, Jr. (Ed.), *Buros-Nebraska symposium on measurement and testing: Vol. 2. B. S. Plake & J. C. Witt* (Eds.), *The future of testing* (pp. 145–181). Hillsdale, NJ: Lawrence Erlbaum.

Kaplan, A. (1964). *The conduct of inquiry: Methodology for behavioral science.* San Francisco: Chandler & Sharp.

Kavanagh, M. J., MacKinney, A. C., & Wolins, L. (1971). Issues in managerial performance: Multitrait-multimethod analyses of ratings. *Psychological Bulletin, 75,* 34–49.

Keating, D. P., & Bobbitt, B. L. (1978). Individual and developmental differences in cognitive-processing components of mental ability. *Child Development, 49,* 155–167.

Kelly, R. M. (1980). Ideology, effectiveness, and public sector productivity: With illustrations from the field of higher education. *Journal of Social Issues, 36,* 76–95.

Kenny, D. A. (1976). An empirical application of confirmatory factor analysis to the multitrait-multimethod matrix. *Journal of Experimental Social Psychology, 12,* 247–252.

Kirsch, I. S., & Guthrie, J. T. (1980). Construct validity of functional reading tests. *Journal of Educational Measurement, 17,* 81–93.

Kirsch, I. S., & Jungeblut, A. (1986). *Literacy: Profiles of America's young adults — Final Report* (NAEP Report No. 16-PL-01). Princeton, NJ: National Assessment of Educational Progress.

Kleiman, L. S., & Faley, R. H. (1985). The implications of professional and legal guidelines for court decisions involving criterion-related

validity: A review and analysis. *Personnel Psychology, 38,* 803–833.

Kornhauser, A. W., & Kingsbury, F. A. (1924). *Psychological tests in business.* Chicago: University of Chicago Press.

Kuhn, T. S. (1962). *The structure of scientific revolutions.* Chicago: University of Chicago Press.

Kuhn, T. S. (1977). Second thoughts on paradigms. In F. Suppe (Ed.), *The structure of scientific theories* (2nd ed., pp. 459–482). Urbana, IL: University of Illinois Press.

Lachman, R., Lachman, J. L., & Butterfield, E. C. (1979). *Cognitive psychology and information processing: An introduction.* Hillsdale, NJ: Lawrence Erlbaum.

Lakatos, I. (1970). Falsification and the methodology of scientific research programs. In I. Lakatos & A. Musgrave (Eds.), *Criticism and the growth of knowledge.* New York: Cambridge University Press. (Reprinted in J. Worral & G. Currie [Eds.]. [1978]. *The methodology of scientific research programs* (pp. 91–196). New York: Cambridge University Press).

Landy, F. J. (1986). Stamp collecting versus science: Validation as hypothesis testing. *American Psychologist, 41,* 1183–1192.

Lansman, M., Donaldson, G., Hunt, E., & Yantis, S. (1982). Ability factors and cognitive processes. *Intelligence, 6,* 347–386.

Lawler, E. E. (1967). The multitrait-multimethod approach to measuring managerial job performance. *Journal of Applied Psychology, 51,* 369–381.

Lawshe, C. H. (1952). Employee selection. *Personnel Psychology, 5,* 31–34.

Lawshe, C. H. (1975). A quantitative approach to content validity. *Personnel Psychology, 28,* 563–575.

Lawshe, C. H. (1985). Inferences from personnel tests and their validity. *Journal of Applied Psychology, 70,* 237–238.

Lawshe, C. H., & Balma, M. J. (1966). *Principles of personnel testing* (2nd ed.). New York: McGraw-Hill.

Leary, D. E. (1984). Philosophy, psychology, and reality. *American Psychologist, 39,* 917–919.

Lee, R., Miller, K. J., & Graham, W. K. (1982). Corrections for restriction of range and attenuation in criterion-related validation studies. *Journal of Applied Psychology, 67,* 637–639.

Lennon, R. T. (1956). Assumptions underlying the use of content validity. *Educational and Psychological Measurement, 16,* 294–304.

Lerner, B. (1980). Legal issues in construct validity. In *Construct validity in psychological measurement. Proceedings of a colloquium on theory and application in education and employment* (pp. 107–112). Princeton, NJ: Educational Testing Service.

Light, R. J., & Pillemer, D. B. (1984). *Summing up: The science of reviewing research.* Cambridge, MA: Harvard University Press.

Linn, R. L. (1968). Range restriction problems in the use of self-selected groups for test validation. *Psychological Bulletin, 69,* 69–73.

Linn, R. L. (1973). Fair test use in selection. *Review of Educational Research, 43,* 139–161.

Linn, R. L. (1976). In search of fair selection procedures. *Journal of Educational Measurement, 13,* 53–58.

Linn, R. L. (1980). Issues of validity for criterion-referenced measures. *Applied Psychological Measurement, 4,* 547–561.

Linn, R. L. (1982). Ability testing: Individual differences and differential prediction. In A. K. Wigdor & W. R. Garner (Eds.), *Ability testing: Uses, consequences, and controversies: Part II. Documentation section* (pp. 335–388). Washington, DC: National Academy Press.

Linn, R. L. (1983). Predictive bias as an artifact of selection procedures. In H. Wainer & S. Messick (Eds.), *Principals of modern psychological measurement: A Festschrift for Frederic M. Lord* (pp. 27–40). Hillsdale, NJ: Lawrence Erlbaum.

Linn, R. L. (1984). Selection bias: Multiple meanings. *Journal of Educational Measurement, 21,* 33–47.

Linn, R. L., & Dunbar, S. B. (1986). Validity generalization and predictive bias. In R. A. Berk (Ed.), *Performance assessment: The state of the art* (pp. 203–236). Baltimore: Johns Hopkins University Press.

Linn, R. L., Harnisch, D. L., & Dunbar, S. B. (1981a). "Corrections" for range restriction: An empirical investigation of conditions leading to conservative corrections. *Journal of Applied Psychology, 66,* 655–663.

Linn, R. L., Harnisch, D. L., & Dunbar, S. B. (1981b). Validity generalization and situational specificity: An analysis of the prediction of first-year grades in law school. *Applied Psychological Measurement, 5,* 281–289.

Linn, R. L., & Hastings, C. N. (1984). Group differentiated prediction. *Applied Psychological Measurement, 8,* 165–172.

Linn, R. L., & Werts, C. E. (1971). Considerations for studies of test bias. *Journal of Educational Measurement, 8,* 1–4.

Livingston, S. A., & Zieky, M. J. (1982). *Passing scores: A manual for setting standards of performance on educational and occupational tests.* Princeton, NJ: Educational Testing Service.

Loevinger, J. (1957). Objective tests as instruments of psychological theory. *Psychological Reports, 3,* 635–694 (Monograph Supp. 9).

Loevinger, J. (1965). Person and population as psychometric concepts. *Psychological Review, 72,* 143–155.

Lord, F. M. (1980). *Applications of item response theory to practical testing problems.* Hillsdale, NJ: Lawrence Erlbaum.

Lord, F. M., & Novick, M. R. (1968). *Statistical theories of mental test scores.* Reading, MA: Addison-Wesley.

MacCorquodale, K., & Meehl, P. E. (1948). On a distinction between hypothetical constructs and intervening variables. *Psychological Review, 55,* 95–107.

MacLeod, C. M., Hunt, E., & Mathews, N. N. (1978). Individual differences in the verification of sentence-picture relationships. *Journal of Verbal Learning and Verbal Behavior, 2,* 129–144.

Madaus, G. F. (1986). Measurement specialists: Testing the faith: A reply to Mehrens. *Educational Measurement: Issues and Practice, 5*(4), 11–14.

Manicas, P. T., & Secord, P. E. (1983). Implications for psychology of the new philosophy of science. *American Psychologist, 38,* 399–413.

Margenau, H. (1950). *The nature of physical reality.* New York: McGraw-Hill.

Margeneau, H. U. (1978). *Physics and philosophy: Selected essays.* Dordrecht, Holland: Reidel.

Mark, M. M. (1986). Validity typologies and the logic and practice of quasi-experimentation. In W. M. K. Trochim (Ed.), *Advances in quasi-experimental design and analysis* (pp. 47–66). San Francisco: Jossey-Bass.

Marsh, H. W., & Shavelson, R. J. (1985). Self-concept: Its multifaceted, hierarchical structure. *Educational Psychologist, 20,* 107–123.

McCloskey, M., Caramazza, A., & Green, B. (1980). Curvilinear motion in the absence of external forces: Naive beliefs about the motion of objects. *Science, 210,* 1139–1141.

McClung, M. S. (1978). Are competency testing programs fair? Legal? In the *Proceedings of the National Conference on Minimum Competency Testing.* Portland, OR: Clearinghouse for Applied Performance Testing.

McCormick, E. J. (1976). Job and task analysis. In M. D. Dunnette (Ed.), *Handbook of industrial and organizational psychology* (pp. 651–696). Chicago: Rand McNally.

McCormick, E. J., Denisi, A. S., & Shaw, J. B. (1979). Use of the Position Analysis Questionnaire for establishing the job-component validity of tests. *Journal of Applied Psychology, 64,* 51–56.

McCormick, E. J., Jeanneret, P. R., & Mecham, R. C. (1972). A study of job characteristics and job dimensions as based on the Position Analysis Questionnaire (PAQ). *Journal of Applied Psychology Monograph, 56,* 347–368.

McGrath, J. E. (1976). Stress and behavior in organizations. In M. D. Dunnette (Ed.), *Handbook of industrial and organizational psychology* (pp. 1351–1395). Chicago: Rand McNally.

McGrath, J. E., & Altman, I. (1966). *Small group research: A synthesis and critique of the field.* New York: Holt, Rinehart and Winston.

McGuire, C. H., & Babbott, D. (1967). Simulation technique in the measurement of problem-solving skills. *Journal of Educational Measurement, 4,* 1–10.

McGuire, C., Solomon, L., & Bashook, P. (1976). *Construction and use of written simulations.* New York: Psychological Corporation.

McGuire, W. J. (1960). A syllogistic analysis of cognitive relationships. In M. J. Rosenberg, C. I. Hovland, W. J. McGuire, R. P. Abelson, & J. W. Brehm, *Attitude organization and change: An analysis of con-*

sistency among attitude components (pp. 65–111). New Haven, CT: Yale University Press.

McNemar, Q. (1969). *Psychological statistics* (4th ed.). New York: John Wiley.

Meehl, P. E., & Golden, R. R. (1982). Taxometric methods. In P. C. Kendall & J. N. Butcher (Eds.), *Handbook of research methods in clinical psychology* (pp. 127–181). New York: John Wiley & Sons.

Meehl, P. E., & Rosen, A. (1955). Antecedent probability and the efficiency of psychometric signs, patterns, or cutting scores. *Psychological Bulletin, 52,* 194–216.

Messick, S. (1961). Separate set and content scores for personality and attitude scales. *Educational and Psychological Measurement, 21,* 915–923.

Messick, S. (1963). Computer models and personality theory. In S. S. Tomkins & S. Messick (Eds.), *Computer simulation of personality: Frontier of psychological theory* (pp. 305–325). New York: John Wiley.

Messick, S. (1964). Personality measurement and college performance. *Proceedings of the 1963 Invitational Conference on Testing Problems* (pp. 110–129). Princeton, NJ: Educational Testing Service. (Reprinted in A. Anastasi [Ed.]. [1966]. *Testing problems in perspective* [pp. 557–572]. Washington, DC: American Council on Education.)

Messick, S. (1967). The psychology of acquiescence: An interpretation of research evidence. In I. A. Berg (Ed.), *Response set in personality assessment* (pp. 115–145). Chicago: Aldine.

Messick, S. (1975). The standard problem: Meaning and values in measurement and evaluation. *American Psychologist, 30,* 955–966.

Messick, S. (1980). Test validity and the ethics of assessment. *American Psychologist, 35,* 1012–1027.

Messick, S. (1981a). Constructs and their vicissitudes in educational and psychological measurement. *Psychological Bulletin, 89,* 575–588.

Messick, S. (1981b). Evidence and ethics in the evaluation of tests. *Educational Researcher, 10,* 9–20.

Messick, S. (1982a). Issues of effectiveness and equity in the coaching controversy: Implications for educational and testing policy. *Educational Psychologist, 17,* 69–91.

Messick, S. (1982b). The values of ability testing: Implications of multiple perspectives about criteria and standards. *Educational Measurement: Issues and Practice, 1*(3), 9–12, 20, 26.

Messick, S. (1983). Assessment of children. In P. H. Mussen (Ed.), *Handbook of child psychology* (4th ed., 4 vols.): Vol. 1. W. Kessen (Ed.), *History, theories, and methods* (pp. 477–526). New York: John Wiley & Sons.

Messick, S. (1984a). Abilities and knowledge in educational achievement testing: The assessment of dynamic cognitive structures. In B. S. Plake (Ed.), *Social and technical issues in testing: Implications for test construction and usage* (pp. 155–172). Hillsdale, NJ: Lawrence Erlbaum.

Messick, S. (1984b). The nature of cognitive styles: Problems and promise in educational practice. *Educational Psychologist, 19,* 59–74.

Messick, S. (1984c). The psychology of educational measurement. *Journal of Educational Measurement, 21,* 215–237.

Messick S. (1987). Structural relationships across cognition, personality, and style. In R. E. Snow & M. J. Farr (Eds.), *Aptitude, learning, and instruction: Vol. 3. Conative and affective process analysis* (pp. 35–75). Hillsdale, NJ: Lawrence Erlbaum.

Messick, S. (1988). The once and future issues of validity: Assessing the meaning and consequences of measurement. In H. Wainer & H. Braun (Eds.), *Test validity* (pp. 33–45). Hillsdale, NJ: Lawrence Erlbaum.

Messick, S., & Barrows, T. S. (1972). Strategies for research and evaluation in early childhood education. In I. J. Gordon (Ed.), *Early childhood education: The seventy-first yearbook of the National Society for the Study of Education* (pp. 261–290). Chicago: University of Chicago Press.

Messick, S., & Jungeblut, A. (1981). Time and method in coaching for the SAT. *Psychological Bulletin, 89,* 191–216.

Messick, S., & Kogan, N. (1965). Category width and quantitative aptitude. *Perceptual and Motor Skills, 20,* 493–497.

Messick, S., & Ross, J. (1962). Psychological structure and measurement models in personality assessment. In S. Messick & J. Ross (Eds.), *Measurement in personality and cognition* (pp. 1–8). New York: John Wiley.

Messick, S., & Sigel, I. E. (1982). Conceptual and methodological issues in facilitating growth in intelligence. In D. K. Detterman & R. J. Sternberg (Eds.), *How and how much can intelligence be increased?* (pp. 187–195). Norwood, NJ: Ablex.

Millman, J. (1973). Passing scores and test lengths for domain-referenced measures. *Review of Educational Research, 43,* 205–216.

Millman, J., Bishop, C. H., & Ebel, R. (1965). An analysis of test-wiseness. *Educational and Psychological Measurement, 25,* 707–726.

Mitroff, I. (1974). *The subjective side of science: An inquiry into the psychology of the Apollo moon scientists.* Amsterdam: Elsevier.

Mitroff, I. I., & Sagasti, F. (1973). Epistemology as general systems theory: An approach to the design of complex decision-making experiments. *Philosophy of Social Sciences, 3,* 117–134.

Mosier, C. I. (1947). A critical examination of the concepts of face validity. *Educational and Psychological Measurement, 7,* 191–205.

Mossholder, K. W., & Arvey, R. D. (1984). Synthetic validity: A conceptual and comparative review. *Journal of Applied Psychology, 69,* 322–333.

Mulaik, S. A. (1972). *The foundations of factor analysis.* New York: McGraw-Hill.

Mulholland, T., Pellegrino, J. W., & Glaser, R. (1980). Components of geometric analogy solution. *Cognitive Psychology, 12,* 252–284.

Murnane, R. J., Newstead, S., & Olsen, R. J. (1985). Comparing public and private schools: The puzzling role of selectivity bias. *Journal of Business and Economic Statistics, 3,* 23–35.

Muthén, B., & Jöreskog, K. G. (1983). Selectivity problems in quasi-experimental studies. *Evaluation Review, 7,* 139–174.

Myrdal, G. (1944). *An American dilemma.* New York: Harper.

Newell, A., & Simon, H. (1972). *Human problem solving.* Englewood Cliffs, NJ: Prentice-Hall.

Norris, S. P. (1983). The inconsistencies at the foundation of construct validation theory. In E. R. House (Ed.), *New directions for program evaluation: No. 19. Philosophy of evaluation* (pp. 53–74). San Francisco: Jossey-Bass.

Novick, M. (1982). Ability testing: Federal guidelines and professional standards. In A. K. Wigdor & W. R. Garner (Eds.), *Ability testing: Uses, consequences, and controversies: Part II, Documentation section* (pp. 70–90). Washington, DC: National Academy Press.

Novick M. R., & Ellis, D. D. (1977). Equal opportunity in educational and employment selection. *American Psychologist, 32,* 306–320.

Novick, M. R., Jackson, P. H., Thayer, D. T., & Cole, N. S. (1972). Estimating multiple regressions in m-groups: A cross-validation study. *British Journal of Mathematical and Statistical Psychology, 25,* 33–50.

Nozick, R. (1974). *Anarchy, state, and utopia.* New York: Basic Books.

Nunnally, J. C. (1978). *Psychometric theory* (2nd ed.). New York: McGraw-Hill.

Okun, A. (1975). *Equality and efficiency: The big tradeoff.* Washington, DC: The Brookings Institute.

Osburn, H. G. (1968). Item sampling for achievement testing. *Educational and Psychological Measurement, 28,* 95–104.

Osburn, H. G., Callender, J. C., Greener, J. M., & Ashworth, S. (1982). Statistical power of tests of the situational specificity hypothesis in validity generalization studies: A cautionary note. *Journal of Applied Psychology, 68,* 115–122.

Pap, A. (1953). Reduction–sentences and open concepts. *Methodos, 5,* 3–30.

Pap, A. (1958). *Semantics and necessary truth.* New Haven, CT: Yale University Press.

Pask, G. (1976a). Conversational techniques in the study and practice of education. *British Journal of Educational Psychology, 45,* 12–25.

Pask, G. (1976b). Styles and strategies of learning. *British Journal of Educational Psychology, 46,* 128–148.

Paunonen, S. V. (1984). Optimizing the validity of personality assessments: The importance of aggregation and item content. *Journal of Research in Personality, 18,* 411–431.

Paunonen, S. V., & Jackson, D. N. (1985). The validity of formal and informal personality assessments. *Journal of Research in Personality, 19,* 331–342.

Peak, H. (1953). Problems of observation. In L. Festinger & D. Katz (Eds.), *Research methods in the behavioral sciences* (pp. 243–299). Hinsdale, IL: Dryden Press.

Pearlman, K., Schmidt, F. L., & Hunter, J. E. (1980). Validity generalization results for tests used to predict job proficiency and training success in clerical occupations. *Journal of Applied Psychology, 65,* 373–406.

Pellegrino, J. W., & Glaser, R. (1979). Cognitive correlates and components in the analysis of individual differences. *Intelligence, 3,* 187–214.

Petersen, N. S., & Novick, M. R. (1976). An evaluation of some models for culture-fair selection. *Journal of Educational Measurement, 13,* 3–29.

Phillips, D. C. (1983). After the wake: Postpositivistic educational thought. *Educational Researcher, 12*(5), 4–12.

Popham, W. J. (1978). *Criterion-referenced measurement.* Englewood Cliffs, NJ: Prentice-Hall.

Popper, K. (1956). Three views concerning human knowledge. In H. D. Lewis (Ed.), *Contemporary British philosophy: Personal statements.* New York: Macmillan. (Reprinted in K. Popper. [1965]. *Conjectures and refutations: The growth of scientific knowledge* [2nd ed.]. New York: Basic Books).

Popper, K. (1935/1959). *Logik der Forschung.* Vienna: J. Springer. (Reprinted *The logic of scientific discovery.* 1959. London: Hutchinson.)

Posner, M. I. (1978). *Chronometric exploration of mind.* New York: John Wiley.

Posner, M. I., & Rogers, M. G. K. (1978). Chronometric analysis of abstraction and recognition. In W. K. Estes (Ed.), *Handbook of learning and cognitive processes* (Vol. 5, pp. 143–188). Hillsdale, NJ: Lawrence Erlbaum.

Prien, E. P. (1966). Dynamic character of criteria: Organizational change. *Journal of Applied Psychology, 50,* 501–504.

Putnam, H. (1977). 'Scientific explanation.' In F. Suppe (Ed.), *The structure of scientific theories* (2nd. ed., pp. 424–436). Urbana, IL: Univserity of Illinois Press.

Quine, W. V. O. (1951). Two dogmas of empiricism. *Philosophical Review, 60,* 20–43.

Rapaport, D., Gill, M. M., & Schafer, R. (1945). *Diagnostic psychological testing.* Chicago: Year Book Medical.

Raudenbush, S. W., & Bryk, A. S. (1985). Empirical Bayes metaanalysis. *Journal of Educational Statistics, 10,* 75–98.

Rawls, J. A. (1971). *A theory of justice.* Cambridge, MA: Harvard University Press.

Reilly, R. R. (1973). A note on minority group bias studies. *Psychological Bulletin, 80,* 130–133.

Reilly, R. R., & Smither, J. W. (1985). An examination of two alternative techniques to estimate the standard deviation of job performance in dollars. *Journal of Applied Psychology, 70,* 651–661.

Robinson, D. N. (1984). The new philosophy of science: A reply to Manicas and Secord. *American Psychologist, 39,* 920–921.

Rock, D. A., & Werts, C. E. (1979). *Construct validity of the SAT across populations: An empirical study* (RDR 78-79, No. 5 and ETS RR 79-2). Princeton, NJ: Educational Testing Service.

Rock, D. A., Werts, C. E., & Grandy, J. (1982). *Construct validity of the GRE aptitude test across populations: An empirical confirmatory study* (GREB No. 78-1P and ETS RR 81-57). Princeton, NJ: Educational Testing Service.

Roid, G. H., & Haladyna, T. M. (1982). *A technology for test-item writing.* New York: Academic Press.

Rorer, L. G., Hoffman, P. J., & Hsieh, K. (1966). Utilities as base rate multipliers in the determination of optimum cutting scores for the discrimination of groups of unequal size and variance. *Journal of Applied Psychology, 50,* 364–368.

Rosenfeld, M., Thornton, R. F., & Skurnik, L. (1986). *Analysis of the professional functions of teachers: Relationships between job functions and the NTE Core Battery.* Princeton, NJ: Educational Testing Service.

Rosenthal, R. (1984). *Meta-analysis procedures for social research.* Beverly Hills, CA: Sage.

Rovinelli, R. J., & Hambleton, R. K. (1977). On the use of content specialists in the assessment of criterion-referenced test item validity. *Dutch Journal of Educational Research, 2,* 49–60.

Royce, J. R. (1963). Factors as theoretical constructs. *American Psychologist, 18,* 522–528.

Rubin, D. B. (1980). Using empirical Bayes techniques in the law school validity studies. *Journal of the American Statistical Association, 75,* 801–827.

Rudner, R. (1953). The scientist *qua* scientist makes value judgments. *Philosophy of Science, 20,* 1–6.

Rulon, P. J. (1946). On the validity of educational tests. *Harvard Educational Review, 16,* 290–296.

Russell, B. (1917). *Mysticism and logic.* London: G. Allen.

Sackett, P. R., & Wade, B. E. (1983). On the feasibility of criterion related validity: The effects of range restriction assumptions on needed sample size. *Journal of Applied Psychology, 68,* 374–381.

Sarnacki, R. E. (1979). An examination of test-wiseness in the cognitive test domain. *Review of Educational Research, 49,* 252–279.

Saunders, D. R. (1956). Moderator variables in prediction. *Educational and Psychological Measurement, 16,* 209–222.

Sawyer, R. L., Cole, N. S., & Cole, J. W. L. (1976). Utilities and the issue of fairness in a decision theoretic model for selection. *Journal of Educational Measurement, 13,* 59–76.

Schmidt, F. L. (1988). Validity generalization and the future of criterion-related validity. In H. Wainer & H. Braun (Eds.), *Test validity* (pp. 173–189). Hillsdale, NJ: Lawrence Erlbaum.

Schmidt, F. L., Gast-Rosenberg, I., & Hunter, J. E. (1980). Validity generalization results for computer programmers. *Journal of Applied Psychology, 65,* 643–661.

Schmidt, F. L., & Hunter, J. E. (1977). Development of a general solution to the problem of validity generalization. *Journal of Applied Psychology, 62,* 529–540.

Schmidt, F. L., & Hunter, J. E. (1978). Moderator research and the law of small numbers. *Personnel Psychology, 31,* 215–231.

Schmidt, F. L., & Hunter, J. E. (1981). Employment testing: Old theories and new research findings. *American Psychologist, 36,* 1128–1137.

Schmidt, F. L., & Hunter, J. E. (1983). Individual differences in productivity: An empirical test of estimates derived from studies of selection procedure utility. *Journal of Applied Psychology, 68,* 407–414.

Schmidt, F. L., Hunter, J. E., Croll, P. R., & McKenzie, R. C. (1983). Estimation of employment test validities by expert judgment. *Journal of Applied Psychology, 68,* 590–601.

Schmidt, F. L., Hunter, J. E., McKenzie, R., & Muldrow, T. (1979). The impact of valid selection procedures on workforce productivity. *Journal of Applied Psychology, 64,* 609–626.

Schmidt, F. L., Hunter, J. E., & Pearlman, K. (1981). Task differences and validity of aptitude tests in selection: A red herring. *Journal of Applied Psychology, 66,* 166–185.

Schmidt, F. L., Hunter, J. E., Pearlman, K. & Hirsh, H. R., with commentary by Sackett, P. R., Schmitt, N., Tenopyr, M. L., Keho, J., & Zedeck, S. (1985). Forty questions about validity generalization and meta-analysis. *Personnel Psychology, 38,* 697–798.

Schmidt, F. L., Hunter, J. E., Pearlman, K., & Shane, C. S. (1979). Further tests of the Schmidt–Hunter Bayesian validity generalization procedure. *Personnel Psychology, 32,* 257–281.

Schmidt, F. L., Hunter J. E., & Urry, V. W. (1976). Statistical power in criterion-related validation studies. *Journal of Applied Psychology, 61,* 473–485.

Schmidt, F. L., & Kaplan, L. B. (1971). Composite vs. multiple criteria: A review and resolution of the controversy. *Personnel Psychology, 24,* 419–434.

Schmidt, F. L., Mack, M. J., & Hunter, J. E. (1984). Selection utility in the occupation of U.S. park ranger for the three modes of test use. *Journal of Applied Psychology, 69,* 490–497.

Schmidt, F. L., Pearlman, K., & Hunter, J. E. (1980). The validity and fairness of employment and educational tests for Hispanic Americans: A review and analysis. *Personnel Psychology, 33,* 705–724.

Schmitt, N. (1978). Path analysis of multitrait-multimethod matrices. *Applied Psychological Measurement, 2,* 157–173.

Schmitt, N., Coyle, B. W., & Saari, B. B. (1977). A review and critique of analyses of multitrait-multimethod matrices. *Multivariate Behavioral Research, 12,* 447–478.

Schmitt, N., Gooding, R. Z., Noe, R. A., & Kirsch, M. (1984). Meta-analyses of validity studies published between 1964 and 1982 and the investigation of study characteristics. *Personnel Psychology, 37,* 407–422.

Secord, P. F. (1986). Explanation in the social sciences and in life situations. In D. W. Fiske & R. A. Shweder (Eds.), *Metatheory in social science* (pp. 197–221). Chicago: University of Chicago Press.

Seashore, S. E., & Yuchtman, E. (1967). Factorial analysis of organizational performance. *Administrative Science Quarterly, 12,* 377–395.

Shadish, W. R., Jr., Cook, T. D., & Houts, A. C. (1986). Quasi-experimentation in a critical multiplist mode. In W. M. K. Trochim (Ed.), *Advances in quasi-experimental design and analysis* (pp. 29–46). San Francisco: Jossey-Bass.

Shapere, D. (1977). Scientific theories and their domains. In F. Suppe (Ed.), *The structure of scientific theories* (2nd ed., pp. 518–589). Urbana, IL: University of Illinois Press.

Shavelson, R. J., Hubner, J. J., & Stanton, G. C. (1976). Self-concept: Validation of construct interpretations. *Review of Educational Research. 46,* 407–441.

Shavelson, R. J., & Webb, N. M. (1981). Generalizability theory: 1973–1980. *British Journal of Mathematical and Statistical Psychology, 34,* 133–166.

Sherman, S. W., & Robinson, N. M. (1982). *Ability testing of handicapped people: Dilemma for government, science, and the public.* Washington, DC: National Academy Press.

Shulman, L. S. (1970). Reconstruction of educational research. *Review of Educational Research, 40,* 371–396.

Shweder, R. A. (1986). Divergent rationalities. In D. W. Fiske & R. A. Schweder (Eds), *Metatheory in social science: Pluralisms and subjectivities.* Chicago: University of Chicago Press.

Sigel, I. E. (1974). When do we know what a child knows? *Human Development, 17,* 201–217.

Simon, H. A. (1976). Identifying basic abilities underlying intelligent performance of complex tasks. In L. B. Resnick (Ed.), *The nature of human intelligence* (pp. 65–98). Hillsdale, NJ: Lawrence Erlbaum.

Singer, E. A., Jr. (1959). *Experience and reflection.* (C. W. Churchman, Ed.). Philadelphia: University of Pennsylvania Press.

Skinner, B. F. (1971). *Beyond freedom and dignity.* New York: Knopf.

Smith, J. K. (1983a). Quantitative versus interpretive: The problem of conducting social inquiry. In E. R. House (Ed.), *Philosophy of evaluation* (pp. 27–51). San Francisco: Jossey-Bass.

Smith, J. K. (1983b). Quantitative versus qualitative research: An attempt to clarify the issue. *Educational Researcher, 12*(3), 6–13.

Smith, J. K. (1985). Social reality as mind-dependent versus mind-independent and the interpretation of test validity. *Journal of Research and Development in Education, 19*(1), 1–9.

Smith, J. K., & Heshusius, L. (1986). Closing down the conversation: The end of the quantitative-qualitative debate among educational inquirers. *Educational Researcher, 15*(1), 4–12.

Smith, P. C. (1976). Behaviors, results, and organizational effectiveness: The problem of criteria. In M. D. Dunnette (Ed.), *Handbook of industrial and organizational psychology* (pp. 745–775). Chicago: Rand McNally.

Snow, R. E. (1974). Representative and quasi-representative designs for research on teaching. *Review of Educational Research, 44,* 265–291.

Snow, R. E. (1980). Aptitude processes. In R. E. Snow, P-A. Federico, & W. E. Montague (Eds.), *Aptitude, learning, and instruction: Vol. 1. Cognitive process analyses of aptitude* (pp. 27–63). Hillsdale, NJ: Lawrence Erlbaum.

Snow, R. E. (1988). Aptitude complexes. In R. E. Snow & M. J. Farr (Eds.), *Aptitude, learning, and instruction: Vol. 3. Conative and affective process analyses* (pp. 11–34). Hillsdale, NJ: Lawrence Erlbaum.

Snow, R. E., Federico, P-A., & Montague, W. E. (Eds). (1980). *Aptitude, learning, and instruction* (Vols. 1 & 2). Hillsdale, NJ: Lawrence Erlbaum.

Snow, R. E., & Lohman, D. F. (1984). Toward a theory of cognitive aptitude for learning from instruction. *Journal of Educational Psychology, 76,* 347–376.

Snow, R. E., & Lohman, D. F. (1988). Implications of cognitive psychology for educational measurement. In R. L. Linn (Ed.), *Educational measurement* (3rd ed.). New York: Macmillan.

Stanley, J. C. (1961). Analysis of unreplicated three way classifications with applications to rater bias and trait independence. *Psychometrika, 26,* 205–219.

Stenner, A. J., Smith, M., III, & Burdick, D. S. (1983). Toward a theory of construct definition. *Journal of Educational Measurement, 20,* 305–316.

Stephenson, W. (1953). *The study of behavior: Q-technique and its methodology.* Chicago: University of Chicago Press.

Sternberg, R. J. (1977). *Intelligence, information processing, and analogical reasoning: The componential analysis of human abilities.* Hillsdale, NJ: Lawrence Erlbaum.

Sternberg, R. J. (1981). Testing and cognitive psychology. *American Psychologist, 36,* 1181–1189.

Sternberg, R. J. (1985a). *Beyond IQ: A triarchic theory of human intelligence.* New York: Cambridge University Press.

Sternberg, R. J. (1985b). Human intelligence: The model is the message. *Science, 230,* 1111–1118.

Sternberg, R. J., & Turner, M. E. (1981). Components of syllogistic reasoning. *Acta Psychologica, 47,* 245–265.

Sternberg, R. J., & Weil, E. M. (1980). An aptitude-strategy interaction in linear syllogistic reasoning. *Journal of Educational Psychology, 72,* 226–234.

Sternberg, S. (1969a). The discovery of processing stages: Extension of Donders' method. *Acta Psychologica, 30,* 276–315.

Sternberg, S. (1969b). Memory-scanning: Mental processes revealed by reaction-time experiments. *American Scientist, 4,* 421–457.

Stevens, A. L., & Collins, A. (1980). Complex learning processes. In R. E. Snow, P-A. Federico, & W. E. Montague (Eds.), *Aptitude, learning, and instruction: Vol. 2. Cognitive process analyses of learning and problem solving* (pp. 177–197). Hillsdale, NJ: Lawrence Erlbaum.

Strike, K. A., & Posner, G. J. (1977). Epistemological perspectives on conceptions of curriculum organization and learning. *Review of Research in Education, 4,* 106–141.

Suppe, F. (1977a). Alternatives to the received view and their critics. In F. Suppe (Ed.), *The structure of scientific theories* (2nd ed., pp. 119–232). Urbana, IL: University of Illinois Press.

Suppe, F. (1977b). Development of the received view. In F. Suppe (Ed.), *The structure of scientific theories* (2nd ed., pp. 16–56). Urbana, IL: University of Illinois Press.

Suppe, F. (1977c). Historical realism. In F. Suppe (Ed.), *The structure of scientific theories* (2nd ed., pp. 650–728). Urbana, IL: University of Illinois Press.

Suppe, F. (1977d). The waning of the Weltanschauungen. In F. Suppe (Ed.), *The structure of scientific theories* (2nd ed., pp 633–649). Urbana, IL: University of Illinois Press.

Taylor, H. C., & Russell, J. T. (1939). The relationship of validity coefficients to the practical effectiveness of tests in selection. *Journal of Applied Psychology, 23,* 565–578.

Tenopyr, M. L. (1986). Needed directions for measurement in work settings. In J. V. Mitchell, Jr. (Ed.), *Buros-Nebraska symposium on measurement & testing: Vol. 2. B. S. Plake & J. C. Witt (Eds.), The future of testing* (pp. 269–288). Hillsdale, NJ: Lawrence Erlbaum.

Thorndike, R. L. (1949). *Personnel selection.* New York: John Wiley.

Thorndike, R. L. (1971). Concepts of culture-fairness. *Journal of Educational Measurement, 8,* 63–70.

Thorndike, R. L., Hagen, E., & Sattler, J. M. (1986). *The Stanford-Binet Intelligence Scale (4th ed.): Guide for administering and scoring.* Chicago: Riverside.

Thurstone, L. L. (1938). Primary mental abilities. *Psychometric Monographs.* (Whole No. 1).

Thurstone, L. L. (1944). A factorial study of perception. *Psychometric monographs.* (Whole No. 4).

Thurstone, L. L. (1947). *Multiple-factor analysis: A development and expansion of the Vectors of the Mind.* Chicago: University of Chicago Press.

Thurstone, L. L. (1948). Psychological implications of factor analysis. *American Psychologist, 3,* 402–408.

Tittle, C. K. (1982). Use of judgmental methods in item bias studies. In R. A. Berk (Ed.), *Handbook of methods for detecting bias* (pp. 31–63). Baltimore: Johns Hopkins University Press.

Tomkins, S. S., & Messick, S. (Eds.). (1963). *Computer simulation of personality: Frontier of psychological theory.* New York: John Wiley.

Torgerson, W. S. (1958). *Theory and methods of scaling.* New York: John Wiley.

Toulmin, S. (1953). *The philosophy of science: An introduction.* London: Hutchinson.

Toulmin, S. (1972). *Human understanding* (Vol. 1). Princeton, NJ: Princeton University Press.

Toulmin, S. (1977). The structure of scientific theories. In F. Suppe (Ed.), *The structure of scientific theories* (2nd ed., pp. 600–614). Urbana, IL: University of Illinois Press.

Trott, D. M., & Jackson, D. N. (1967). An experimental analysis of acquiescence. *Journal of Experimental Research in Personality, 2,* 278–288.

Tryon, W. W. (1979). The test-trait fallacy. *American Psychologist, 34,* 402–406.

Tucker, L. R (1962). Factor analysis of relevance judgments: An approach to content validity. *Proceedings: 1961 Invitational Conference on Testing Problems* (pp. 29–38). Princeton, NJ: Educational Testing Service.

Tucker, L. R (1966). Some mathematical notes on three-mode factor analysis. *Psychometrika, 31,* 279–311.

Turner, M. B. (1967). *Philosophy and the science of behavior.* New York: Appleton-Century-Crofts.

Tyler, L. E. (1963). *Tests and measurements.* Englewood Cliffs, NJ: Prentice-Hall.

Tyler, R. W. (1960). What testing does to teachers and students. *Proceedings of the 1959 Invitational Conference on Testing Problems* (pp. 10–16). Princeton, NJ: Educational Testing Service. (Reprinted in A. Anastasi [Ed.]. [1966]. *Testing problems in perspective* [pp. 46–52]. Washington, DC: American Council on Education.)

van Fraassen, B. C. (1977). Discussion. In F. Suppe (Ed.), *The structure of scientific theories* (2nd ed., pp. 598–599). Urbana, IL: University of Illinois Press.

Vernon, P. E. (1962). The determinants of reading comprehension. *Educational and Psychological Measurement, 22,* 269–286.

Vickers, G. (1965). *The art of judgment.* New York: Basic Books.

Vickers, G. (1970). *Value systems and social process.* Harmondsworth, England: Penguin Books.

Voyce, C. D., & Jackson, D. N. (1977). An evaluation of a threshold theory for personality assessment. *Educational and Psychological Measurement, 37,* 383–408.

Wachtel, P. L. (1972). Field dependence and psychological differentiation: Reexamination. *Perceptual and Motor Skills, 35,* 179–189.

Wallace, S. R. (1965). Criteria for what? *American Psychologist, 20,* 411–417.

Ward, W. C., Frederiksen, N., & Carlson, S. B. (1980). Construct validity of free-response and machine-scorable forms of a test. *Journal of Educational Measurement, 17,* 11–29.

Webb, N. M., Shavelson, R. J., & Maddahian, E. (1983). Multivariate generalizability theory. In L. J. Fyans, Jr., (Ed.), *Generalizability theory: Inferences and practical applications* (pp. 67–81). San Francisco: Jossey-Bass.

Weber, M. (1949). *The methodology of the social sciences.* Glencoe, IL: Free Press.

Wechsler, D. (1958). *The measurement of adult intelligence* (4th ed.). Baltimore: Williams & Wilkins.

Weimer, W. B. (1973). Psycholinguistics and Plato's paradoxes of the *Meno. American Psychologist, 28,* 15–23.

Weitz, J. (1961). Criteria for criteria. *American Psychologist, 16,* 228–231.

Wernimont, P. F., & Campbell, J. P. (1968). Signs, samples, and criteria. *Journal of Applied Psychology, 52,* 372–376.

Werts, C. E., Jöreskog, K. G., & Linn, R. L. (1972). A multitrait-multimethod model for studying growth. *Educational and Psychological Measurement, 32,* 655–678.

Werts, C. E., Jöreskog, K. G., & Linn, R. L. (1973). Identification and estimation in path analysis with unmeasured variables. *American Journal of Sociology, 78,* 1469–1484.

Werts, C. E., & Linn, R. L. (1970). Path analysis: Psychological examples. *Psychological Bulletin, 74,* 193–212.

Wesman, A. G. (1953). Better than chance. *Test Service Bulletin, 45,* 1–5.

Whitehead, A., & Russell, B. (1910–1913). *Principia mathematica* (3 vols.). Cambridge: Cambridge University Press.

Whitely, S. E. (1980a). Modeling aptitude test validity from cognitive components. *Journal of Educational Psychology, 72,* 750–769.

Whitely, S. E. (1980b). Multicomponent latent trait models for ability tests. *Psychometrika, 45,* 479–494.

Whitely, S. E. (1981). Measuring aptitude processes with multicomponent latent trait models. *Journal of Educational Measurement, 18,* 67–84.

Whitely, S. E., & Schneider, L. M. (1981). Information structure for geometric analogies: A test theory approach. *Applied Psychological Measurement, 5,* 383–397.

Wigdor, A. K., & Garner, W. R. (Eds.). (1982). *Ability testing: Uses consequences, and controversies: Part I. Report of the committee.* Washington, DC: National Academy Press.

Wiggins, J. S. (1973). *Personality and prediction: Principles of personality assessment.* Reading, MA: Addison-Wesley.

Willingham, W. W. (1974). *College placement and exemption.* New York: College Entrance Examination Board.

Willingham, W. W. (1985). *Success in college.* New York: College Entrance Examination Board.

Willingham, W. W., & Breland, H. M. (1982). *Personal qualities and college admissions.* New York: College Entrance Examination Board.

Willingham, W. W., Ragosta, M., Bennett, R. E., Braun, H., Rock, D. A., & Powers, D. E. (1987). *Testing handicapped people.* Newton, MA: Allyn & Bacon.

Witkin, H. A., & Goodenough, D. R. (1981). *Cognitive styles: Essence and origins—field dependence and field independence.* New York: International Universities Press.

Wittenborn, J. R. (1955). The study of alternative responses by means of the correlation coefficient. *Psychological Review, 62,* 451–460.

Yalow, E. S., & Popham, W. J. (1983). Content validity at the crossroads. *Educational Researcher, 12*(8), 10–14.

Zedeck, S. (1971). Problems with the use of "moderator" variables. *Psychological Bulletin, 76,* 295–310.

Zuroff, D. C. (1986). Was Gordon Allport a trait theorist? *Journal of Personality and Social Psychology, 51,* 993–1000.

3

Reliability

Leonard S. Feldt

The University of Iowa

and

Robert L. Brennan

The American College Testing Program

Anyone who regularly plays a game with objective scoring, such as golf or bridge, is acutely aware of the variability in human performance. No one operates at his or her personal best on all occasions, be the domain one of physical activity or mental activity. This inconsistency stems from a variety of factors, depending on the nature of the measurement. Among the important factors are subtle variations in physical and mental efficiency of the test taker, uncontrollable fluctuations in external conditions, variations in the specific tasks required of individual examinees, and inconsistencies on the part of those who evaluate examinee performance. Quantification of the consistency and inconsistency in examinee performance constitutes the essence of reliability analysis.

The combined effect of these factors on an examinee's score is referred to as *error of measurement.* In everyday conversation the term *error* suggests an avoidable or correctable mistake on someone's part. In the measurement context, this is not the case. The bowler who scores far higher than her or his lifetime average and the history student who makes a far higher test score than anyone would expect on the basis of his or her "true" knowledge have both benefited from positive errors of measurement.

Except for isolated, exceptional cases, all measurements must be presumed to contain error. Some of this error might be systematic, as in the case of the anxious student who tends to perform more poorly when being formally evaluated than when being surreptitiously observed. Another portion of the error is essentially random, unpredictable as to size or direction. The term *measurement error,* when used in discussions of reliability, almost always refers to the random component of error. In many situations, there can be little opportunity and only crude methodology to document the potential seriousness of error. But lack of knowledge *about* measurement error does not remove it from any set of scores.

Preliminary Considerations

Historically, the reliability of a measuring instrument or process has been quantified via two indexes: the standard error of measurement and the reliability coefficient. Each statistic has virtues and limitations. The standard error summarizes potential within-person inconsistency in score-scale units: in IQ units for tests that provide IQs, in grade-equivalent units for tests that yield GEs, in raw score units for instruments that are scored by counting the number of correctly answered exercises. As the term suggests, the standard error represents the standard deviation of a hypothetical set of repeated measurements on a single individual. Because such repeated assessments are presumed to vary only because of measurement error, the standard deviation reflects the potency of random error sources.

The reliability coefficient quantifies reliability by summarizing the consistency (or inconsistency) among several error-prone measurements. To the extent that error is present and behaves randomly, it will produce distortions in the ranking of individuals within a group and obscure the true score differences among examinees. Thus, error depresses the correlation coefficient between two experimentally independent measurements on each of N persons. The correlation coefficient therefore constitutes indirect evidence of the presence of random measurement error.

As measurement theory has evolved, ingenious methods have been derived to substitute for direct estimation of this product-moment coefficient. These alternative approaches yield coefficients superficially similar to product-moment correlations, but their computational formulas and statistical properties differ from those of correlations.

Over the years, alternatives to the standard error of measurement and the reliability coefficient have been suggested. The only index that currently enjoys wide use is the square of the standard error—the variance of errors of measurement. From the perspective of the user of educational measurements, the variance represents no conceptual improvement over the standard error. In fact, the change to average *squared* error renders its units incompatible with examinee score units, a distinct limitation. But from a theoretical perspective, error variance has a mathematical advantage over error standard deviation. When independent error sources operate, and this may always be assumed to be the case, their separate variances cumulate. The total error variance equals the sum of the constituent error variances. Were this cumulative property mathematically characteristic of standard deviations, it is doubtful the variance would be regarded so favorably by theoreticians.

There is a second reason why the error variance is often useful. Classical treatments of measurement theory define the concept of the reliability coefficient in terms of a ratio of variances, not in terms of a correlation coefficient. The process of estimating reliability often takes the form of estimating the relevant variances and determining their ratio. For this purpose, the variance of errors constitutes a more convenient and natural statistic.

No effort will be made here to present a thorough analysis of the uses and limitations of the standard error and the reliability coefficient. Briefly stated, the primary advantage of the standard error is that it provides a useful yardstick of error in score-oriented units. When its value is assimilated by test users and by the examinees themselves, it provides a counteractive force to overinterpretation and overtrust of test data. In addition, the error variance, when analyzed by techniques to be described later, can be partitioned into components associated with various error sources. Thus, in many instances, it suggests to the researcher how the testing procedure can be improved. Because the standard error is scale specific, however, it cannot be compared from one instrument to another or from one scoring procedure to another. For such comparisons, the "unitless" reliability coefficient is clearly more useful. Also, over many decades, test users have become accustomed to viewing coefficients as indexes indicative of the "need for caution." It is generally believed that certain minimal levels are required for certain types of test use: assessment of individual weaknesses and strengths, diagnosis of group weaknesses and strengths, and evaluation of growth of individuals or groups. For example, although all such standards are arbitrary, most users believe, with considerable support from textbook authors, that instruments with coefficients lower than .70 are not well suited to individual student evaluations. Although one may quarrel with any standard of this sort, many knowledge-

able test users adjust their level of confidence in measurement data as a hazy function of the magnitude of the reliability coefficient.

The coefficient approach is often criticized because of its sensitivity to the character of the group on which it is computed. In this respect, reliability coefficients are similar to other correlational indexes. Critics argue that many consumers of test information fail to appreciate this sensitivity and are led to trust or distrust the accuracy of scores excessively. The standard error, on the other hand, exhibits considerably greater stability from group to group.

There are additional arguments for and against both indexes. Happily, the use of one index for one purpose does not preclude the use of the other for another purpose. Both provide helpful insights. It seems unlikely that either index will be rejected or replaced in the foreseeable future.

Regardless of how reliability is defined and quantified, it is somewhat unfortunate that this word was adopted originally for the phenomenon under consideration. In everyday conversation, *reliability* refers to a concept much closer to the measurement concept of *validity*. Weather reports, for example, are thought to be unreliable if they are frequently contradicted by prevailing conditions a day or two later. Medical tests are said to be unreliable if they often give false cues about the condition of a patient. In both of these contexts, the information might be highly reliable in the measurement sense. Meteorologists might have no reason to doubt the accuracy of the temperature, air pressure, and wind velocity measurements used in determining the forecast. Several experts, each using this information independently, might arrive at precisely the same forecast day in and day out. Similarly, the medical test might yield consistent, but often erroneous, conclusions about patients, if repeated several times on each individual. In measurement nomenclature these measures would be said to be highly reliable because they are self-consistent. But they would have questionable validity. The distinction is often lost on laypeople and many educators, however, and is a potential source of confusion when the results of testing are summarized.

The Concept of True Score

It is almost impossible to deal with issues of definition, quantification, and estimation of reliability without addressing the concept of true score. By conventional practice, the true score of an individual is regarded as a personal parameter that remains constant over the time required to take at least several measurements, though in some settings a person might be deemed to have a true score subject to change almost moment to moment. The true score is often thought of as the limit approached by the average of observed scores as the number of these observed scores increases. This definition is incomplete in several respects and leaves many observers uncomfortable. *First,* it ignores the fact that the measurement process itself, if repeatedly applied, is likely to change the examinee. In the physical sciences, this is rarely so. Estimation of a parameter such as the speed of light should not, in theory, alter the speed of light. However, measurement of an individual often alters the individual. Thus, in the behavioral sciences the notion of a constant true score is frequently inconsistent with the manner in which measurement procedures are carried out.

Second, the definition fails to specify what requirements must be met by the instruments that yield this multitude of observed scores. Each observed score is presumably derived from a repetition of the measurement process. For a test of physical fitness, the notion of repetition can probably be made sufficiently clear. For a test of reading comprehension, there is room for significant ambiguity. It is necessary to define what is meant by interchangeable test forms without using the concept of true score, lest the definition be circular. But complete avoidance of the notion of true score in a discussion of parallel forms is not easy.

Third, the *limit-of-an-average* concept is silent regarding what conditions can legitimately vary from score to score. If a score results from the application of a rating scale by an observer, do the many scores result from one application by many observers? Many applications by one observer? Many applications by many observers? Are the observational circumstances permitted to vary randomly along one or several dimensions? As these questions suggest, a case can be made for defining true score in a variety of ways. Flexible, alternative definitions of true score redefine error variance, of course, because the true score is the parameter around which observed scores vary. This, in turn, implies that any measuring instrument can have many reliabilities, even for a clearly identified population of examinees.

This point of view is implicitly recognized by all modern test theorists. It is made most explicit by those who study reliability via the methods of analysis of variance. This approach, called *generalizability theory* by Cronbach, Gleser, Nanda, and Rajaratnam (1972), is discussed in some detail in a later section of this chapter. Definition of parallel forms, avoiding as much as possible any reliance on an undefined and unobservable true score, will be presented in the major section devoted to classical theory.

Sources of Measurement Error

Some sources of intraindividual variation can be clearly categorized as error sources, almost without regard to the purposes of measurement. Others are less clearly classified. If the test score is viewed one way, a source might be reasonably perceived to contribute to error. From another perspective it might be regarded as a component of the true scores of individuals. Suppose, for example, an instructor in a political science course regards effectiveness in writing as a legitimate element in grading students. Other things being equal, good writers would receive higher grades than poor writers in the universe of grades arising from this instructor. Writing ability is a component of true score.

Consider, however, a large population of instructors, some rewarding effectiveness in writing, others rewarding effectiveness in oral presentation, and still others rewarding a variety of other abilities. If one conceives of the grade Jennifer might receive from instructor 1, from instructor 2, and so on, these grades would vary, in part, as a consequence of interinstructor differences in philosophy. If Jennifer's "true" grade is viewed as the average from an infinity of instructors, grade variation attributable to philosophical differences would be a part of total error variance.

It is impossible, then, to categorize factors unequivocally into one group that contributes to true score and a second group that contributes to error. Thorndike (1951) has provided an excellent organizational framework for both groups, and Stanley (1971) has further illustrated the categories that might be construed as error sources. These discussions will not be paraphrased here. A shorter exposition, based upon a fairly comprehensive definition of error, will suffice.

From almost any score perspective, error variance can be said to result in part from random variation within each individual in health, motivation, mental efficiency, concentration, forgetfulness, carelessness, subjectivity or impulsiveness in response, and luck in random guessing. The inherent variation in human performance on most tasks is included here. Some of this cyclical variation manifests itself minute to minute; other effects vary over longer periods only. If repeated measures are to reflect those that operate over longer time cycles, the several scores must naturally be separated by days, or even weeks. Data gathered in an hour's time will not reveal these effects, though they are present and add to interindividual differences.

A second category of potential sources of error includes situational factors: the working environment of examinees. Both psychological and physical factors are involved here. Examinees might be well or poorly prepared psychologically for the activities of measurement; a testing location might be conducive or destructive to best performance. In school testing situations, these effects can be significant.

A third factor includes evaluator idiosyncrasies and subjectivity. With objective tests, this category is unimportant. But with projective devices, free-response examinations, holistic evaluations of a product, and observational data, these often constitute a major source of error. Components included in this category are often classified as error under a broad definition of true score and as true score components under a narrowly focused definition of true score.

The final category might be termed instrumental variables. In some measurement procedures, electronic or mechanical equipment constitutes an important element. Such machinery sometimes behaves erratically from one occasion to another and inconsistently from one copy to another. This introduces error in the measurement process. The reference here is broader than this, however. When a measure consists of a series of exercises, the tasks and problems almost always represent a sample from a larger domain. The specific sample contained in any test form might unintentionally touch disproportionately on the knowledge of examinee A and on the misinformation of examinee B. When ongoing behavior is observed and evaluated, observers might chance to see one individual at her or his best and another at her or his worst. In all likelihood, only rarely does a set of exercises or a sample of ongoing behavior produce a precisely accurate representation of the total domain for any individual. Instrumental variables, therefore, constitute a major source of error.

In principle, one should gather reliability data in a manner that allows acknowledged error sources to reflect their effects in intraindividual variation and permits true-score components to remain constant. In practice, this is not easy to arrange.

Administrative constraints often compress data gathering into shorter time intervals than the researcher would desire. Opportunities for observation and for trained individuals to carry out the observation are often restricted. Reliability statistics, as a consequence, frequently present a biased picture. In general, reported reliability coefficients tend to overestimate the trustworthiness of educational measures, and standard errors underestimate within-person variability.

Notation

In the following sections, various approaches to test theory will be summarized, together with important results relevant to reliability. A symbolic system is needed to pursue this purpose. The conventional Greek symbols will be used for the population parameters: σ^2 for variance, μ for mean, and ρ for correlation, with suitable subscripts to identify the variables involved. The symbol σ_{XY} will be used for the covariance between scores X and Y. For estimators of these quantities, either English letters will be used or a caret ($\hat{}$) will be inserted over the Greek symbol. Often derived results will be left in terms of the parameter symbols. The obvious sample estimates must be substituted for these parameters in practical applications.

The observed score of examinee p on test form f will be represented by X_{pf} or Y_{pf}. In the case of tests composed of dichotomously scored items, X and Y will refer to the number of correct answers on the total test, unless an alternative meaning is specified. T will be used to represent true scores, and E_{pf} will signify the net error of measurement from all sources for examinee p on form f. In rigorous expositions of test theory, any particular value of X_{pf} or E_{pf} would be represented by a lowercase letter. However, for the purposes of this chapter, this convention seems unnecessary, with one exception: τ_p will be used to refer to the true score of person p.

Occasionally, it is necessary to refer to the mean or variance of scores for a select subgroup, that is, the parameters of a *conditional* population. For this purpose the symbol $\mu_{X.T}$ or $\sigma^2_{X.T}$ will be used. The intended reference is to the mean or variance of X for individuals who have a specific value of T, though the numerical value of T might not be specified. In almost all contexts the variance alluded to by σ^2_X applies to a collection of scores from many persons, with one score per person. When it is crucial to identify the form or portion of a test that gives rise to the data, an additional subscript will be added, as in $\sigma^2_{X_f}$. When no such additional subscript is added, it is to be understood that all the data arose from the administration of a single test form.

Reliability in Classical Test Theory

There are many references in textbooks and measurement journals to *classical theory*. The implication is that this body of assumptions and derived results is distinct from, and perhaps in some respects contradictory to, those of other theories. There is some truth to this inference. Other theories of more recent origin have been developed that conceptualize and portray the measurement process somewhat differently than does classical theory. Not surprisingly, these theories occasionally yield different results. Were this not the case, the alternative theories would probably attract little interest. In many respects, however, the several theories yield similar and consistent results, despite their differences in formulation. Thus, it is difficult to define classical theory in terms of the derivations uniquely associated with it. For present purposes, classical theory is loosely defined as that theory which assumes the following:

1. An observed score on a test or measurement is the sum of a true score component and a measurement error component. Symbolically, for person p and form f,

$$X_{pf} = \tau_p + E_{pf}. \tag{1}$$

2. Parallel forms $f, g, h, \ldots$ are measures constructed to the same specifications, give rise to identical distributions of observed scores for any very large (infinite) population of examinees, covary equally with each other, and covary equally with any measure (Z) that is not one of the parallel forms. Symbolically,

$$F(X_f) = F(X_g) = F(X_h) = \ldots$$
$$\sigma_{X_f X_g} = \sigma_{X_f X_h} = \sigma_{X_g X_h} = \ldots \tag{2}$$
$$\sigma_{X_f Z} = \sigma_{X_g Z} = \sigma_{X_h Z} = \ldots$$

3. If it were possible for individual p to be measured many times, using a different parallel form on each occasion, the average of the resultant errors of measurement ($E_{p1}, E_{p2}, \ldots$) would approach 0 as the number of measurements increased. For an infinite number of test forms, the symbolic statement is

$$\mathscr{E}_f E_{pf} = 0, \tag{3}$$

where "$\mathscr{E}_f$" represents the expected value (mean) taken over forms.

4. If any infinite population of examinees were tested via any given form of a test, the average of the resultant errors ($E_{1f}, E_{2f}, \ldots$) would equal 0, provided the examinees were not chosen on the basis of the magnitude of X_f. Symbolically,

$$\mathscr{E}_p E_{pf} = 0, \tag{4}$$

where "$\mathscr{E}_p$" represents the expected value over persons.

5. Consistent with the foregoing assumptions, the true score of an individual is perceived as a personal constant that does not change from form to form. For convenience, the true score is regarded as the average score the individual would obtain if tested on an infinite number of parallel forms.

Strictly speaking, the assumption of identical distributions of observed scores is stronger than necessary. For almost all of the derived results under classical theory, it is sufficient to assume only equal means and equal variances. However, the broader assumption is needed to justify some of the interpretive statements often ascribed to classical theory. For this reason, the more comprehensive assumption is made here.

A consequence of these assumptions is that the error scores arising from form f are linearly independent of the true scores embedded within X_f and independent of the error scores arising from any other form. They are also linearly independent of the observed, true, and error scores associated with any other measure, Z. The independence of E_f and T (on test X) leads to a fundamental variance relationship within classical theory:

$$\sigma^2_{X_f} = \sigma^2_T + \sigma^2_{E_f}. \tag{5}$$

For a population of examinees who took form f, the observed score variance, the only variance that may be estimated directly, equals the sum of true-score variance and measurement-error variance.

One might hold that classical theory conceptualizes the observed, true, and error scores as continuous, unbounded values. Certainly such fictions are convenient, and they could well be necessary if conditions 1 through 5 are to be met. The tacit assumption of continuity, in contrast with the obviously discrete character of most observed score distributions, is a major distinction between classical theory and some of the alternatives.

Two additional characteristics of scores are often imputed to classical theory: normality of form for the distributions of observed, true, and error scores and homogeneity of the error variance from one true-score level to another. Certainly these additional assumptions permit the derivation of additional useful results within classical theory if, indeed, real test scores come reasonably close to meeting these requirements. However, a substantial body of results can be derived without them. Moreover, there is ample evidence that substantial departures from normality and homoscedasticity are common in educational measurement.

The variance of many scores for a given person, obtained (hypothetically) through administration of an infinite number of parallel forms, is the error variance for that person. If this variance, symbolized $\sigma^2_{E.\tau_p}$, varies from person to person as a function of true score, the variance (and its square root) becomes a variable in the examinee population. It is a variable in the same sense that τ_p is a variable: it is a constant for the person but a variable when one visualizes a population of persons. In such a case the *error variance for the test* is the average or expected value of the individual error variances. Symbolically,

$$\sigma^2_E = \mathscr{E}_p \sigma^2_{E.\tau_p}. \tag{6}$$

Whether the error variance is constant for all persons or varies from person to person, the variance statement of Equation 5 still holds.

In practice, test forms do not exist in unlimited numbers. Even if they did, it would be impossible to administer very many before the examinee was permanently changed by the experience. Thus, measurement concepts such as true score and error variance are conceptual notions only. We might wish to regard the one or two existing forms as samples from an infinity of forms, but clearly this infinity is only a useful fiction.

Classical theory had its origins in the early years of the 20th century. The literature relating to it is voluminous, and the theory has been explicated by a number of writers. The interested reader may wish to consult the references cited by Stanley (1971) and the expositions of Zimmerman (1975, 1976) and Cliff (1979).

Definition of the Reliability Coefficient and the Error Variance for a Test

Under the early formulations of classical theory, the reliability coefficient was defined as the correlation between scores on parallel forms within a defined population of examinees. As more relaxed and realistic definitions of parallel forms evolved, this definition of the reliability coefficient lost its appeal. The problem under these relaxed definitions is that one pair of forms might yield a different value for the correlation than another pair. If $\rho_{X_f X_g} \neq \rho_{X_f X_h}$, what is the parameter value of the coefficient for form f? To avoid this awkward state of affairs, the reliability coefficient is now defined as $\rho^2_{TX_f}$ or $\sigma^2_T / \sigma^2_{X_f}$. These definitions have the advantage that they involve parameters of form f only. Under the classical model $\rho_{X_f X_g} = \rho^2_{TX_f} = \sigma^2_T / \sigma^2_{X_f}$, since $\sigma_{X_f} = \sigma_{X_g}$ and the covariance between forms f and g, $\sigma_{X_f X_g}$, equals σ^2_T. Hence, these definitions are interchangeable. However, it has been found convenient to adopt either $\rho^2_{TX_f}$ or $\sigma^2_T / \sigma^2_{X_f}$ as the basic definition, even for the classical model.

It seems odd to some students that reliability is defined as the *square* of the correlation between X_f and T. After all, if criterion-related validity is defined as the first power of the correlation between X_f and criterion scores, shouldn't reliability be defined as the correlation between the observed score and the personal parameter it estimates? There would be a logic to this consistency. However, in the classical model it is $\rho^2_{TX_f}$, not ρ_{TX_f}, that equals $\rho_{X_f X_g}$. With the decades of tradition behind $\rho_{X_f X_g}$ as a definition of the reliability coefficient, it is too late to use $\rho_{TX_f} = \sqrt{\rho_{X_f X_g}}$ as a substitute.

Whether error variance changes from person to person or is constant, the average for the population of examinees is

$$\mathscr{E}_p \sigma^2_{E.\tau_p} = \sigma^2_{E_f} = \sigma^2_{X_f}(1 - \rho_{XX'}).$$

(The symbol $\rho_{XX'}$ is used here and throughout this chapter as a generic symbol for the reliability coefficient.) There is good reason to suppose that, for number-right scores, $\sigma^2_{E.\tau}$ is *not* the same for all persons. The variance associated with the lowest and highest true scores tends to be smaller than that associated with scores in the middle of the range. Conversion to some form of derived score could reduce or enlarge this heterogeneity and could significantly alter the trends. Even within the classical test theory model, there is need for greater recognition, particularly in applied work, of the inapplicability of σ^2_E to all levels of examinees. Estimation of σ^2_E for specific score points will be considered in a later section.

Parallel Forms and Test–Retest Approaches to Estimation

It is an acknowledged principle in reliability estimation that the best estimate of the coefficient and the standard error is one that reflects the impact of all sources of measurement error. One such source is represented by the day-to-day, week-to-week variations in the efficiency of human minds and muscles. If this source is to be reflected in reliability data, one or more days must elapse between the several measurements or observations of each individual. To accomplish this, the evaluator must have available at least two interchangeable test forms or must readminister the form previously used. The use of alternate forms on different days is generally referred to as the *parallel-forms approach,* though the instruments might not strictly satisfy the definition of classical parallel forms. Readministration of the same instrument is usually called the *test–retest approach.*

Although the parallel-forms approach is highly regarded for paper-and-pencil tests, it is often incompatible with administrative realities. Publishers of standardized tests have difficulty persuading representative samples of schools to administer parallel tests. School authorities often balk at retesting pupils. Similarly, routine instructional use of tests rarely permits administration of a second form, even when one exists. Thus the parallel-forms approach is not often used, though its virtues are widely recognized.

A second administration of the same tasks or stimuli is a natural and appropriate procedure when two conditions are met: (a) no significant change in examinee proficiency or character is to be expected within the period of measurement, and (b) memory of the tasks or stimuli will not influence responses on subsequent presentations. Many of the tests used in physical education and other performance-oriented fields satisfy these conditions. With paper-and-pencil instruments, however, the second condition will almost certainly not be met. A second exposure to the same stimuli might elicit responses that are spuriously consistent with previous responses, even when the original responses are based on nothing more consequential than a guess or an impulse. More than a few examinees, when exposed to questions or stimuli that they have seen before, conclude that their consistency is being assessed. They might make a concerted attempt to respond as they did before. Because of false consistency, test–retest reliabilities are often viewed with skepticism. But many instruments exist in only one form and cannot be divided into even two parallel, separately scorable parts. Thus the test–retest approach might be the only method available that reflects day-to-day error factors.

Estimation of Reliability from a Single Administration of a Test

For more than three quarters of a century, measurement theoreticians have been concerned with reliability estimation in the absence of parallel forms. Spearman (1910) and Brown (1910) posed the problem; their solution is incorporated in the well-known formula bearing their names. In the ensuing decades a voluminous literature has accumulated on this topic.

The problem is an intensely practical one. For many tests, only one form is produced, because a second form would rarely be needed. If the trait under study is rapidly changing in each examinee, estimation of an instrument's reliability at a particular moment might be preferable to estimation of examinee consistency over a longer interval. Even when parallel forms exist and the trait or skill is not undergoing rapid change, practical considerations might rule out the administration of more than one form.

The fact that much thought and creative energy have been invested in this problem should not be interpreted as lack of awareness of the limitations of the proposed solutions by test developers and users. Such awareness is almost universal. When behavioral observations are gathered in an hour or less,

certain sources of error "stand still" for each examinee. Their effects obscure the true differences among persons but are not reflected in the estimate of test error variance. Artful manipulation of the data from a single testing occasion cannot alter this basic fact.

DEGREES OF PART-TEST SIMILARITY

Though reliability estimates derived from a single administration might share a common limitation, they are not interchangeable. They are based on different conceptions of the notion of parallel measurements. These varying conceptions of *parallel* constitute a basis for categorizing methods of estimation.

The most demanding and restrictive concept of repeated measurement is represented by the classical model. As previously set forth, this model dictates that examinee p has the same true score, τ_p, for every form. The parameters μ_X, σ_X^2, and σ_E^2 must be identical for every form. Clearly, this array of requirements is unrealistic for paper-and-pencil tests and exceedingly unlikely in contexts in which raters or observers constitute the forms. Given that a test includes only a finite number of exercises, each exercise differing from the others in mean score to at least a small degree, the total test mean and variance cannot be expected to remain constant across forms. Human judges cannot be expected to be exactly equal in their harshness. For carefully constructed forms, it might take many hundreds of examinees to demonstrate these inequalities convincingly. But there is little doubt that a sufficiently large sample, several thousand, perhaps, would document that no two forms are perfectly parallel. Thus, the statistical test of parallelism derived by Votaw (1948) seems certain to bear on a false null hypothesis.

Varying degrees of accommodation to the reality of nonparallel forms are incorporated into alternative models. *Tau-equivalent* forms (Lord & Novick, 1968, p. 50) allow for differences in error variances and, hence, in the observed score variances of the forms. Because σ_E^2 is an average over persons, tau-equivalence implies that individuals at any specified true-score level vary more in their form f observed scores than in their form g observed scores. The true score of person p does not vary from form to form, and error scores have expectations of 0. Thus, μ_X does *not* vary across forms.

Essentially tau-equivalent forms exhibit mean differences, in addition to variance differences. For person p, $\tau_{pf} = \tau_{pg} + C_{fg}$. The constant C_{fg} depends on the pair of forms but not on the individual. Thus, if $C_{fg} = +1.5$, every examinee will have a true score on form f that is 1.5 points higher than on form g. Any examinee population will have a mean on form f that is 1.5 points higher than the mean on form g.

Congeneric forms relax the notion of parallelism still further. True scores for forms f and g are perfectly correlated, in a linear sense, but differ more radically than under essential tau-equivalence. For individual p, $\tau_{pf} = (b_{fg})\tau_{pg} + C_{fg}$. The constants b_{fg} and C_{fg} depend on the forms but not on the individual. Error variances can vary across forms. The effect of b_{fg} may be likened to that of a lengthening or shortening factor. Form f may function as a test 1.2 times longer than form g. That its observed score mean does not equal 1.2 times that of form g is "explained" by the nonzero constant C_{fg}. Unlike essentially tau-equivalent forms, the observed score variances of forms f and g differ in part because of heterogeneity of true-score variances, not solely as a result of heterogeneity of error-score variances.

A final degree of dissimilarity is represented by *multi-factor congeneric* forms. The observed scores on two such forms, f and g, may be represented as follows (the person subscript p has been omitted for convenience):

$$X_f = a_{f1}T_1 + \ldots + a_{fk}T_k + C_f + E_f$$
$$X_g = a_{g1}T_1 + \ldots + a_{gk}T_k + C_g + E_g$$

For each form, the true score of person p equals a weighted sum of systematic components T_1 through T_k. The weighting of these components is not identical for the forms, however: that is, a_{f1} might not precisely equal a_{g1}, a_{f2} might not equal a_{g2}, and so on. In addition, the measurement error variances might be unequal for the two instruments and the means might differ. This latter possibility is allowed for by the constants C_f and C_g. Thus, in this model, the true scores of forms f and g represent a composite of the same factors, but not exactly the same combination of these factors. Therefore, true scores for forms f and g do not correlate perfectly, though one might expect them to correlate very highly.

The foregoing discussion has alluded to test forms as if the prime concern were full-length instruments. However, in the context of reliability estimation from a single test administration, the focus is upon units of test material shorter than the full test. All single-administration approaches are based on a partition of the instrument or measurement procedure into separately scorable portions: blocks of trials, sets of exercises, groups of observations, individual raters, etc. The similarity of these parts—classically parallel, essentially tau-equivalent, or congeneric—is the basis on which various coefficients may be categorized.

COEFFICIENTS BASED UPON TWO PARTS

By far the oldest, and probably the most widely used, two-part approach to reliability estimation is based on the Spearman–Brown formula. If the full-test score, X, is represented as the sum of two part-test scores, X_1 and X_2,

$$_{SB}\rho_{XX'} = \frac{2\rho_{X_1X_2}}{1 + \rho_{X_1X_2}}. \tag{7}$$

This formula assumes the part tests are parallel in the classical sense.

If the parts can be assumed to meet only the more flexible conditions of essential tau-equivalence, the assumption of $\sigma_{X_1}^2 = \sigma_{X_2}^2$ cannot be made. However, it remains true that the covariance between parts equals the variance of true scores on either part. Because $\sigma_T^2 = \sigma_{(2T_1)}^2 = 4\sigma_{T_1}^2 = 4\sigma_{X_1X_2}$,

$$_{F}\rho_{XX'} = \frac{4\sigma_{X_1X_2}}{\sigma_X^2}. \tag{8}$$

This formula (attributed to Flanagan, in Rulon, 1939) may be expressed in several algebraically equivalent versions (Guttman, 1945; Rulon, 1939):

$$_{GR}\rho_{XX'} = 2\left(1 - \frac{[\sigma_{X_1}^2 + \sigma_{X_2}^2]}{\sigma_X^2}\right) = 1 - \frac{\sigma_{(X_1-X_2)}^2}{\sigma_X^2}. \tag{9}$$

It can be easily shown that the tau-equivalent Estimators 8 and 9 always yield a lower coefficient than the Spearman–Brown estimator. It is also true that the estimator that assumes tau-equivalence rather than classical parallelism is almost always more defensible. Fortunately, given the popularity of the Spearman–Brown formula, the difference is rarely of practical significance. For example, with $\sigma_{X_1}^2 = 5.0$, $\sigma_{X_2}^2 = 6.0$, and $\rho_{X_1X_2} = .6$, the two full-test coefficients are .750 and .748.

If the researcher doesn't trust reflective judgment as a basis for assigning test units to parts, the matter can be handled empirically. Callender and Osburn (1977a, 1977b, 1979) have developed a computerized algorithm to assign units, maximizing the value of the Flanagan coefficient. However, there is danger of overestimation with such an approach.

In some circumstances, it might be impossible to divide an instrument into two essentially tau-equivalent parts. A reading test, for example, might include an odd number of selections. If the items on a given passage are to be treated as an intact unit of material in the test partition, as authorities advise, the lengths of the two parts might differ substantially. In such a case, it is unrealistic to presume essential tau-equivalence; the parts will be congeneric. Observed score variance will reflect inequalities in both σ_T^2 and σ_E^2. Formulas derived by Horst (1951), Angoff (1953), Raju (1970), Kristof (1971), and Feldt (1975) deal with this situation.

The Raju approach assumes that the lengths of the parts are known. Most often this information is conveyed by the number of items in each part. If k_1 and k_2 represent these lengths in an appropriate metric, $\lambda_1 = k_1/(k_1 + k_2)$ and $\lambda_2 = k_2/(k_1 + k_2)$. Then the part-test observed scores may be represented

$$X_1 = \lambda_1 T + C_1 + E_1 \quad \text{and} \quad X_2 = \lambda_2 T + C_2 + E_2.$$

Here, T is the true score on the total test, C_1 and C_2 are constants that allow for differences in part-test means, and E_1 and E_2 are measurement errors. The covariance between parts equals $\sigma_{X_1X_2} = \lambda_1\lambda_2\sigma_T^2$ and

$$\sigma_T^2 = \frac{\sigma_{X_1X_2}}{\lambda_1\lambda_2}.$$

Reliability of the total test equals

$$_{R}\rho_{XX'} = \frac{\sigma_{X_1X_2}}{\lambda_1\lambda_2\sigma_X^2}. \tag{10}$$

If $\lambda_1 = \lambda_2 = \frac{1}{2}$, Estimator 10 reduces to the Flanagan coefficient for tau-equivalent parts.

The Angoff (1953), Kristof (1971), and Feldt (1975) derivations deal with a less common situation: The lengths of the parts are not directly deducible from a countable characteristic, such as number of items, or the countable characteristic is not a trustworthy indicator of *functional* or *effective* length. Two raters, for example, might operate in this manner. There is no unique solution for this situation if the parts are congeneric and have unequal and unknown lengths. This is the case because there are four unknowns: σ_T^2, $\sigma_{E_1}^2$, $\sigma_{E_2}^2$, and λ_1 (note that $\lambda_2 = 1 - \lambda_1$). But there are only three estimable parameters that relate them: $\sigma_{X_1}^2$, $\sigma_{X_2}^2$, and $\sigma_{X_1 X_2}$. However, the problem becomes manageable if one assumes that the error variances differ according to the dictates of classical theory. If that assumption is well founded, then

$$\frac{\sigma_{E_1}^2}{\sigma_{E_2}^2} = \frac{\lambda_1}{\lambda_2} = \frac{\lambda_1}{1 - \lambda_1},$$

$$\sigma_{E_2}^2 = \frac{(1 - \lambda_1)}{\lambda_1} \sigma_{E_1}^2,$$

and the number of unknowns is reduced to three. Under the Angoff and Feldt approaches, this ultimately leads to the solution

$$_{AF}\rho_{XX'} = \frac{4\sigma_{X_1 X_2}}{\sigma_X^2 - \left(\dfrac{\sigma_{X_1}^2 - \sigma_{X_2}^2}{\sigma_X}\right)^2}. \tag{11}$$

This coefficient equals $_R\rho_{XX'}$ with $\lambda_1 = (\sigma_{X_1}^2 + \sigma_{X_1 X_2})/\sigma_X^2$ and $\lambda_2 = 1 - \lambda_1$.

With the data of the previous example, Estimator 11 yields $\rho_{XX'} = .7505$, certainly not a meaningful departure from .750 or .748. Larger differences between part-test variances would make for larger variation among the three coefficients. The Kristof (1971) approach to this problem is more elegant, but computationally more difficult. It appears to yield results highly consistent with Estimator 11.

How can one decide which model holds? Unfortunately, a two-part breakdown of the test does not yield sufficient data to identify the model precisely. Clear-cut heterogeneity of half-test variances will rule out the classical model and the use of the Spearman–Brown formula. But differences in variance are recognized by, and consistent with, the other models. In the unlikely event that the covariance exceeds one of the part-test variances, the tau-equivalent model may be rejected. No set of variances and covariances can distinguish between the congeneric model and the classical, unequal-length model of Angoff, Kristof, and Feldt. Moderate heterogeneity, with both variances greater than the covariance, implies that the tau-equivalent model is also compatible with the data.

THE DEFINITION OF PART TESTS

When an instrument consists of more than two separately scored items, trials, raters, or observers, the researcher has some flexibility in apportioning these units to the two parts. In general, content balance is a primary consideration. Unless this is achieved, none of the foregoing models applies, and a negative bias will be introduced into the reliability estimation process. Time factors are also crucial. When a significant proportion of the examinees fail to finish the tests, a spurious elevation of the coefficient usually occurs. Speeded tests require separately timed sections to adequately estimate reliability.

An informal survey of current practices suggests that most investigators assign items or other units of test material to parts in one of three ways: entirely at random, on an alternation basis (odd-numbered versus even-numbered units), or a combination of content coupled with alternation. Under the last of these, consecutive items within each content classification are assigned to different parts. This method is recommended over the others.

When items are clustered within a test, as in reading tests that contain a series of questions on each of several passages, it is usually advised that the clusters be kept intact. However, there are arguments for and against this practice. A reading test, to use this example to clarify the issues, often includes passages of several different types. There might be a poem, a short essay, an excerpt from a novel, some dialogue from a play, a newspaper article, and so on. Typically, there is only one passage of each type in the test. A parallel form also includes one passage of each type. In this setting, one may postulate four components of an observed score: (a) a component associated with general reading ability, (b) a component associated with materials of a given type, (c) a component associated with a specific example of a given type, and (d) a residual component encompassing other sources of variance including errors of measurement. If the assignment of exercises to halves is carried out on a passage basis, the second and third components are grouped with the fourth as sources of error. But parallel forms would be equalized with respect to the second component, an argument against classifying it as error and against assignment of items to halves on a passage basis. But, if exercises relating to a specific passage are split between the two halves, the third component is about equally divided between the halves. It adds to the consistency between half-test scores. In essence, it becomes a contributor to true-score variance. Parallel forms would categorize this third component as an error component, however, and quite rightly so.

Thus, treating passages as intact units tends to bias the resultant coefficient negatively. Splitting items within passages tends to bias the coefficient positively. Which of these is the more attractive, or the less unattractive, is a matter of opinion. It appears that conventional wisdom favors the procedure that leads to a more conservative estimate.

COEFFICIENTS BASED ON MORE THAN TWO TAU-EQUIVALENT PARTS

When an instrument includes more than two separately scored units that are parallel in content, the investigator has a choice: combine units and thereby reduce the number of parts to two or maintain the integrity of the n parts. One might well raise the question why maintaining the identity of many smaller parts is desirable. After all, almost all tests are constructed to adhere to a multi-category table of specifications. Part tests used in reliability estimation should, in shortened versions, duplicate the design of the full test. One might expect that reflection of full-test specifications would be more easily achieved with two longer parts than with many shorter parts. In addition, equalizing parts on statistical characteristics such as estimated mean-item difficulty and discrimination would become more difficult as the number of parts increases. Thus, it might appear disadvantageous to preserve the identity of the smallest scorable units of the measurement when estimating its reliability. To do so would very probably entail some compromise in the content and statistical comparability of the units.

There is justification for the retention of score information on smaller units, despite the validity of the foregoing argument. The rationale is based on considerations of sampling error. If the units in a test are perceived as a sample from a hypothetical population of such units, with parallel forms representing a collection of independent samples, sampling errors in the estimation of $\rho_{XX'}$ are reduced as the number of units is increased (Kristof, 1963). Therefore, it behooves the investigator to constitute the maximum number of parts consistent with the dictates of the reliability model.

Probably the most frequently used multi-part coefficient is Cronbach's coefficient alpha (1951). It is based on the assumption that the part scores are essentially tau-equivalent (Novick & Lewis, 1967). Violation of this assumption tends to depress the estimate. It should be noted, however, that alpha ignores day-to-day fluctuations in human performance, a major source of error in many instances. Thus, alpha is sensitive to opposing biases, either of which might prevail. The formula for coefficient alpha is

$$_\alpha\rho_{XX'} = \left(\frac{n}{n-1}\right)\left(\frac{\sigma_X^2 - \Sigma\sigma_{X_f}^2}{\sigma_X^2}\right). \tag{12}$$

Split-halves Estimators 8 and 9 may be seen as a special case with $n = 2$. If the n parts are defined by the n items in a test and the items are scored dichotomously (0 or 1), then $\sigma_{X_f}^2 = \phi_f(1 - \phi_f)$, where ϕ_f is the proportion of scores of 1. Coefficient alpha then reduces to Kuder–Richardson formula 20 (1937):

$$_{20}\rho_{XX'} = \left(\frac{n}{n-1}\right)\left(1 - \frac{\Sigma\phi_f(1 - \phi_f)}{\sigma_X^2}\right). \tag{13}$$

The use of dichotomous item scoring inevitably leads to violation of the requirement of essential tau-equivalence. Items with variances of .25 and .15 could hardly be expected to include the same variance of true scores. Despite this failure of dichotomously scored items to deliver tau-equivalent scores, Kuder–Richardson formula 20 has not been found to seriously underestimate split-halves coefficients when the test is reasonably homogeneous in content.

If $\Sigma\phi_f(1 - \phi_f)$ is estimated by $n\bar{\phi}(1 - \bar{\phi})$, where $\bar{\phi}$ is the average proportion correct for the n items, Kuder–Richardson formula 20 reduces to formula 21:

$$_{21}\rho_{XX'} = \left(\frac{n}{n-1}\right)\left(1 - \frac{\mu_X(n - \mu_X)}{n\sigma_X^2}\right). \tag{14}$$

For paper-and-pencil tests, this approximation always results in an underestimate of $_{20}\rho_{XX'}$, as is shown by the following equality, first presented by Tucker (1949):

$$_{20}\rho_{XX'} - _{21}\rho_{XX'} = \frac{n\Sigma(\phi_f - \bar{\phi})^2}{(n-1)\sigma_X^2} = \frac{n^2\sigma_{\phi_f}^2}{(n-1)\sigma_X^2}.$$

Variation among the n values of ϕ_f results in a negative bias for $_{21}\rho_{XX'}$.

In contexts other than paper-and-pencil tests, the assumption $\phi_f = \phi_g$ might be reasonable. In the area of physical education, for example, skills tests often consist of repeated trials of a task scored dichotomously. If the skill under study does not improve (or decline) in the examinee population during the course of testing, the proportion of successes does not change

from trial to trial. Then, $_{21}\rho_{XX'}$ adequately defines the reliability of the test.

Another multi-part approach is that proposed by Guttman (1945). The derivation of his coefficient λ_2 is based on the ingenious use of inequalities involving variances and covariances. The resultant estimator is

$$_G\rho_{XX'} = \frac{\Sigma\Sigma\sigma_{X_fX_g} + \sqrt{\dfrac{n}{n-1}\Sigma\Sigma\sigma_{X_fX_g}^2}}{\sigma_X^2}. \tag{15}$$

Ten Berge and Zegers (1978) refined this estimator, adding higher order roots, but the additional terms appear to make little numerical difference in the coefficient. If essential tau-equivalence holds for the parts, the parameter $_G\rho_{XX'}$ then equals $_\alpha\rho_{XX'}$. However, sample values of alpha and the Guttman coefficient will not generally be equal. The circumstances in which the one coefficient might be superior to the other, either as an estimate of reliability or as a lower bound, are not clear.

A third possible approach applicable to essentially tau-equivalent parts employs analysis of variance methods (Cronbach, Rajaratnam, & Gleser, 1963; Cronbach et al., 1972; Hoyt, 1941; Lindquist, 1953, chap. 16). For the case considered here, however, the ANOVA coefficient based on the mean squares for persons, $MS(p)$, and persons-by-items interaction, $MS(pi)$, is algebraically identical to coefficient alpha, an equality shown in a later section. Thus, the ANOVA coefficient contributes no new information to this situation. It does open new possibilities for more complex configurations of data, however, as discussed later.

COEFFICIENTS BASED ON MORE THAN TWO CONGENERIC PARTS

If one abides by the principle that clustered items should be kept together in the assignment of items to parts, an item cluster may then become a part. Such parts will quite possibly include unequal numbers of items, rendering them congeneric. Raju (1977) derived a generalization of his two-part coefficient (1970) that accommodates to this complication. Let the lengths of the parts, in terms of numbers of items, be k_1, k_2, . . . , k_n and let $\lambda_f = k_f/(\Sigma k_f)$. Then Raju's coefficient is

$$_R\rho_{XX'} = \frac{\sigma_X^2 - \Sigma\sigma_{X_f}^2}{(1 - \Sigma\lambda_f^2)\sigma_X^2}. \tag{16}$$

If the parts include equal numbers of items, all λ_f equal $1/n$, and Raju's coefficient equals coefficient alpha. Otherwise, it will exceed the value of coefficient alpha computed from the same part-test data. Of course, the use of coefficient alpha would entail the erroneous assumption that the n parts are tau-equivalent.

Kristof (1974) considered the interesting problem of estimating the reliability of a test composed of congeneric parts of *unknown* length. At first blush, this might appear to be an artificial, unrealistic problem. Doesn't an investigator always know how long test parts are? When parts are composed of discrete exercises, determination of lengths generally presents no difficulty. However, consider an essay test containing questions scored on a 10-point scale. The variances of scores on the several questions might well differ considerably, reflecting heterogeneity in both true-score variances and error-score variances. The investigator would have to depend on the observed data to estimate the "length" of each question.

Kristof considered a test with three such parts, which, it turns out, is a very convenient number. The model for part scores in a three-part test may be expressed in the manner of congeneric parts: $X_f = \lambda_f T + C_f + E_f$. This is identical to the model postulated for the Raju coefficient, but the present situation now requires estimation of the λ_f.

To obtain such estimates, we first note that $\sigma_{X_f X_g} = \lambda_f \lambda_g \sigma_T^2$ and $\Sigma \lambda_f = 1.0$ ($f,g = 1,2,3$). The ratios of selected pairs of covariances, taken with the fact that $\Sigma \lambda_f = 1$, lead to

$$\lambda_f = \left[\frac{\sigma_{X_g X_h}}{\sigma_{X_f X_g}} + \frac{\sigma_{X_g X_h}}{\sigma_{X_f X_h}} + 1 \right]^{-1}$$

These solutions for λ_1, λ_2, λ_3 may be substituted into Raju's coefficient (20). The end result, in simplified form, is Kristof's coefficient:

$$\kappa \rho_{XX'} = \frac{(\sigma_{X_1 X_2} \sigma_{X_1 X_3} + \sigma_{X_1 X_2} \sigma_{X_2 X_3} + \sigma_{X_1 X_3} \sigma_{X_2 X_3})^2}{\sigma_{X_1 X_2} \sigma_{X_1 X_3} \sigma_{X_2 X_3} \sigma_X^2}. \quad (17)$$

It can be seen at this point why Kristof focused on a three-part test. The three covariances and $\Sigma \lambda_f = 1$ constitute four relationships that lead to a unique solution for the four unknowns (λ_1, λ_2, λ_3, σ_T^2). Four or more parts give rise to a greater number of covariance relationships than unknowns, and, with empirical data, this almost certainly leads to an inconsistent set of equations. Various subsets of equations lead to nonidentical estimates of each λ. With even a moderate number of parts, say six or seven, the number of solutions for each λ would be quite large.

To resolve the problems arising from redundancy, the investigator may combine parts (with careful attention to balancing content) and reduce their number to three. Parts of relatively equal length are advantageous (Sedere & Feldt, 1977). An alternative solution that preserves the integrity of the parts and is manageable with hand-held calculators has been proposed by Gilmer and Feldt (1983). Another possibility is to use maximum likelihood estimates. This approach is made feasible through the LISREL computer program of Jöreskog and Sörbom (1985) and the EQS program of Bentler (1983, 1985). These programs may also be used to obtain reliability estimates based on the multi-factor congeneric model. They have the added virtue of making possible tests of the tenability of the various models (Werts, Linn, & Jöreskog, 1973, 1974; Werts, Rock, Linn, & Jöreskog, 1978; Linn & Werts, 1979). Still another multi-factor technique is one proposed by Conger and Lipshitz (1973). It also establishes dimensionality empirically, permits suitable significance tests, and delivers part-test weights that maximize the total test-reliability coefficient.

In some instances it might be reasonable to assume that the k test parts, although heterogeneous in length, function in the manner prescribed by classical test theory. This implies that the true-score variance and error variance of part f equal $\lambda_f^2 \sigma_T^2$ and $\lambda_f \sigma_E^2$, respectively. For congeneric parts, as this term has been defined, the error variance of part f could be less or greater than $\lambda_f \sigma_E^2$. If the parts function according to the dictates of classical theory, then it can be shown that $\lambda_f = \Sigma_{j=1}^{k} \sigma_{X_j X_f}/\sigma_X^2$. Thus, λ_f could be simply approximated by the sum of the elements in row f of the variance–covariance matrix divided by the variance of the total test scores. These estimates of λ_f ($f = 1, \ldots, k$) may be substituted in Equation 16 to estimate $\rho_{XX'}$. For convenience, this coefficient will be referred to as the *classical congeneric coefficient*. The Angoff–Feldt reliability estimate presented earlier is a special case, with k equal to 2.

Table 3.1 summarizes the coefficients presented in the foregoing discussion. The formulas are expressed in terms of sample statistics for user convenience. The model assumed for the part-test scores is indicated at the right.

A Numerical Example

A numerical illustration could be helpful at this point. A four-question essay test gave rise to the variance–covariance matrix presented at the left in the following list. To reduce the test to three parts, questions 3 and 4 were combined, producing the matrix in the center. To reduce the test to two parts, questions 1 and 2 were combined and questions 3 and 4 were combined. The resultant matrix is at the right.

$$\begin{pmatrix} 7.2 & 5.6 & 3.5 & 5.8 \\ 5.6 & 6.4 & 3.1 & 4.1 \\ 3.5 & 3.1 & 2.4 & 3.3 \\ 5.8 & 4.1 & 3.3 & 6.2 \end{pmatrix} \begin{pmatrix} 7.2 & 5.6 & 9.3 \\ 5.6 & 6.4 & 7.2 \\ 9.3 & 7.2 & 15.2 \end{pmatrix} \begin{pmatrix} 24.8 & 16.5 \\ 16.5 & 15.2 \end{pmatrix}$$

For the two-part breakdown of the total test, the difference between part-test variances seems quite pronounced. This would, if statistically significant, lead to rejection of the classical model. The difference also appears rather large to attribute solely to a difference in error variances. This fact, and the fact that the covariances exceed the smaller variance, also constitutes a challenge to the assumption of tau-equivalence. Whether the parts may be construed as differential in length, but classical in their variance relationships, cannot be determined from this matrix alone.

Despite questions about the tenability of the various models, all of the two-part estimates can be computed. The unique formulas (Flanagan, Rulon, and Guttman estimates are identical) yield the following results:

Spearman–Brown:	$\hat{\rho}_{XX'} = .9188$
Flanagan:	$\hat{\rho}_{XX'} = .9041$
Angoff–Feldt:	$\hat{\rho}_{XX'} = .9200$

It is obvious from the formulas that, when the variances differ, the last of these three values must be greater than the second. It is also true that the first must be greater than the second in such a case.

Application of Kristof's estimation technique to the three-part matrix delivers a coefficient of .9277. It can be expected to exceed coefficient alpha for the same matrix because it attributes a part of the inequality in the $\sigma_{X_f}^2$ to σ_T^2 and a part to σ_E^2. The essential tau-equivalent model attributes all of the differences to error variance. Coefficient alpha for this three-part matrix equals .9082.

TABLE 3.1 Summary of Internal Consistency Coefficients

	Formula	*Model*
A. Two Part Subdivision ($X = X_1 + X_2$)		
1. Spearman-Brown	$\dfrac{2r_{X_1 X_2}}{1 + r_{X_1 X_2}}$	Classical halves
2. Angoff-Feldt	$\dfrac{4S_{X_1 X_2}}{S_X^2 - \left(\dfrac{S_{X_1}^2 - S_{X_2}^2}{S_X}\right)^2}$	Classical (Unknown lengths)
3. Flanagan	$\dfrac{4S_{X_1 X_2}}{S_X^2}$	Essentially tau-equivalent
4. Callender and Osburn	Computer Implemented (Maximized value of $_F r_{XX'}$)	Essentially tau-equivalent
B. Three-Part Subdivision ($X = X_1 + X_2 + X_3$)		
1. Kristof	$\dfrac{(S_{X_1 X_2} S_{X_1 X_3} + S_{X_1 X_2} S_{X_2 X_3} + S_{X_1 X_3} S_{X_2 X_3})^2}{S_{X_1 X_2} S_{X_1 X_3} S_{X_2 X_3} S_X^2}$	Congeneric (Unknown lengths)
C. Multi-Part Subdivision ($X = X_1 + X_2 + \ldots + X_n$)		
1. Cronbach alpha	$\dfrac{n}{n-1}\left(\dfrac{S_X^2 - \Sigma S_{X_f}^2}{S_X^2}\right)$	Essentially tau-equivalent
2. Hoyt ANOVA	$\dfrac{MS(p) - MS(pi)}{MS(p)}$	Essentially tau-equivalent
3. Guttman λ_2	$\dfrac{S_X^2 - \Sigma S_{X_f}^2 + \sqrt{\dfrac{n}{n-1} \sum_{f \neq g}\sum S_{X_f X_g}^2}}{S_X^2}$	Essentially tau-equivalent
4. Raju	$\left(\dfrac{1}{1 - \Sigma \lambda_f^2}\right)\left(\dfrac{S_X^2 - \Sigma S_{X_f}^2}{S_X^2}\right)$	Congeneric (Known lengths)
5. Feldt-Gilmer ($n \geq 3$) Kristof ($n = 3$)	$\left(\dfrac{(\Sigma D_f)^2}{(\Sigma D_f)^2 - \Sigma D_f^2}\right)\left(\dfrac{S_X^2 - \Sigma S_{X_f}^2}{S_X^2}\right)$	Congeneric (Unknown lengths)
	$D_f = \dfrac{\displaystyle\sum_g S_{X_f X_g} - S_{X_f X_l} - S_{X_f}^2}{\displaystyle\sum_g S_{X_l X_g} - S_{X_f X_l} - S_{X_l}^2}$	
	Row l is the row of the matrix with the largest sum of interpart covariances. When $f = l$, $D_f = 1.0$.	
6. Feldt	$\dfrac{S_X^2(S_X^2 - \Sigma S_{X_f}^2)}{S_X^4 - \displaystyle\sum_f S_{X_f X}^2}$	Classical congeneric (Unknown lengths)
7. Jöreskog Bentler Conger-Lipshitz	Computer Implemented	Single- and Multi-Factor Congeneric (Unknown lengths)

(Formulas C.1 and C.2 are bracketed as "Algebraically Identical")

For the four-part matrix the following values are obtained:

Cronbach's alpha: $\hat{\rho}_{XX'} = .9279$
Guttman's λ_2: $\hat{\rho}_{XX'} = .9353$
Feldt–Gilmer: $\hat{\rho}_{XX'} = .9401$
Classical Congeneric: $\hat{\rho}_{XX'} = .9402$
LISREL: $\hat{\rho}_{XX'} = .9483$

Because the last three coefficients, like Kristof's coefficient, attribute some of the variance heterogeneity to true-score variance, they can be expected to exceed the others. In effect, the congeneric model is more "permissive" than the essential tau-equivalence model.

Reliability of Composite Scores

In many settings, test users deal with combinations of scores rather than with single scores. For example, the composite score for an achievement or aptitude battery is often defined as the mean of the separate subtest scores. The difference between verbal and performance intelligence quotients, a value often regarded as significant by school psychologists, is essentially a two-score combination. A predicted grade point average derived by multiple-regression methods is a combination of weighted predictor scores. Measures of under- or overachievement, usually defined by the difference between observed and expected achievement scores of some kind, are another weighted combination of scores.

In all of these instances one may view the score as an algebraic sum of weighted scores. The weights might be negative or positive and might be less than, equal to, or greater than 1.0, depending on the nature and uses of the resultant value. In essence, a linear composite for a person, Z_p, may be represented as

$$Z_p = w_o + w_1 X_{p1} + w_2 X_{p2} + \ldots + w_k X_{pk}, \quad (18)$$

where the w_j are the weights used to combine the k constituent values.

It is a tenet of sound test development and use that every score, or combination of scores, proposed for individual or group interpretation should be documented with regard to its reliability. Thus, the techniques for investigating the reliability of composites take on considerable importance.

A BASIC APPROACH TO LINEAR COMPOSITES

Because so many composites are algebraic sums of weighted scores, it is useful to consider three simple statistical theorems about such sums:

1. $\sigma^2_{wX} = w^2\sigma^2_X = w^2\sigma^2_T + w^2\sigma^2_E.$ (19)

2. $\sigma_{(w_1 X_1)(w_2 X_2)} = w_1 w_2 \sigma_{X_1 X_2}.$ (20)

3. $\sigma^2_Z = \Sigma w_i^2 \sigma^2_{X_i} + \Sigma\Sigma w_i w_j \sigma_{X_i X_j}.$ (21)

A final relationship used repeatedly in the ensuing derivations is

$$\rho_{ZZ'} = 1 - \frac{\sigma^2_{Ez}}{\sigma^2_Z}. \quad (22)$$

This is, of course, an expression for the reliability coefficient that follows directly from the variance relationship $\sigma^2_Z = \sigma^2_T + \sigma^2_E$ and the variance-ratio definition of reliability. This form is preferred in this setting for several simple, but compelling, reasons. The first is this: When one deals with linear composites, the error variances aggregate as a simple sum of weighted constituent error variances; that is,

$$\sigma^2_{E_{(w_1 x_1 + w_2 x_2 + \ldots)}} = \Sigma w_i^2 \sigma^2_{E_i}, \quad (23)$$

on the usual assumption of linear independence among the constituent errors. True-score variance for a composite, on the other hand, inevitably involves both the variances and covariances of the constituent true scores, complicating the derivations considerably.

The second reason is that this approach focuses attention on the error variance per se, as well as on the reliability coefficient. In the interpretation of scores of individual examinees, quantification of unreliability in terms of the standard error of measurement is highly desirable.

In the following sections, the foregoing approach will be used with a number of commonly encountered linear composites. Following each derivation are comments on the applicability and limitations of the resultant formulas.

GENERALIZED SPEARMAN–BROWN FORMULA

If the composite score Z is defined as

$$Z = X_1 + X_2 + \ldots + X_n,$$

where the test units are parallel in a classical sense, then

$$\begin{aligned}\sigma^2_{Ez} &= n\sigma^2_{E_1} = n\sigma^2_{X_1}(1 - \rho_{X_1 X_1'}), \\ \sigma^2_Z &= n\sigma^2_{X_1} + n(n-1)\rho_{X_1 X_1'}\sigma^2_{X_1},\end{aligned} \quad (24)$$

and

$$\rho_{ZZ'} = 1 - \frac{\sigma^2_{Ez}}{\sigma^2_Z} = \frac{n\rho_{X_1 X_1'}}{1 + (n-1)\rho_{X_1 X_1'}}. \quad (25)$$

This is the well-known Spearman–Brown formula for forecasting the reliability of a lengthened test. If Equation 25 is solved for $\rho_{X_1 X_1'}$ in terms of $\rho_{ZZ'}$, one obtains

$$\rho_{X_1 X_1'} = \frac{\frac{1}{n}\rho_{ZZ'}}{1 + \left(\frac{1}{n} - 1\right)\rho_{ZZ'}}. \quad (26)$$

Thus, it follows that the Spearman–Brown formula also serves to predict the reliability of a shortened test, that is, a test $1/n$ times as long as the instrument in hand. In essence, n, in the original version of Equation 25, may take on values less than 1 or greater than 1.

The Spearman–Brown formula is most often used in the early, experimental stages of instrument development. At this time the length of the final instrument could still be under consideration. A variety of item types can also be under consideration, with preliminary estimates of their reliabilities being based on pilot tests of arbitrary lengths. The Spearman–Brown formula permits the test developer to modify the available reliability data to compensate for inequities in the length of the experimental tests.

In the definition of comparable-length tests, it should be recognized that time requirement, not number of items, is the crucial dimension for most educational tests. Thus, if test V contained 25 items and test W contained 40 items, but both required 30 minutes for 85% of examinees to finish, these instruments would be comparable in length. It is presumed, of course, that both meet the test specifications in terms of content and skills.

The Spearman–Brown formula implicitly assumes that, if test length is changed, the rate and quality of examinee performance will not be affected. If these change, the formula will yield misleading results. Reading-rate measurements provide an example of this. In some tests, rate is measured by a count of words read in the first 2 minutes devoted to a relatively long selection. One might expect that the number of words read in the first 5 minutes would be a more reliable measure. It has been found, however, that the 2-minute and 5-minute reliabilities are not related as predicted by the Spearman–Brown formula with $n = 2.5$. The reason is that many readers do not maintain a constant reading rate from the first few seconds until time is called after k minutes. Whenever fatigue, boredom, or distractibility increases as examinees progress through a test, the Spearman–Brown formula may overestimate the reliability of a lengthened instrument.

RELIABILITY OF BATTERY COMPOSITES

Achievement and scholastic-aptitude batteries often use the mean subtest score to define the battery composite. Thus, for a battery of k tests,

$$Z_p = \frac{1}{k}(X_{p1} + X_{p2} + \ldots + X_{pk})$$

$$= \left(\frac{1}{k}\right)X_{p1} + \ldots + \left(\frac{1}{k}\right)X_{pk}.$$

The weights in this case all equal $1/k$. Thus,

$$\sigma_{E_Z}^2 = \frac{1}{k^2}\Sigma\sigma_{E_i}^2 = \frac{1}{k^2}\Sigma\sigma_{X_i}^2(1 - \rho_{X_i X_i'})$$

and

$$\rho_{ZZ'} = 1 - \frac{\Sigma\sigma_{X_i}^2(1 - \rho_{X_i X_i'})}{k^2\sigma_Z^2}. \tag{27}$$

If the subtests are scaled to have identical standard deviations, some simplification can be made in this formula. In this special case,

$$\rho_{ZZ'} = \frac{\left(\frac{1}{k-1}\right)\bar{\rho}_{X_i X_i'} + \bar{\rho}_{X_i X_j}}{\frac{1}{k-1} + \bar{\rho}_{X_i X_j}} \quad (i \neq j)$$

where $\bar{\rho}_{X_i X_i'}$ is the average reliability of the subtests and $\bar{\rho}_{X_i X_j}$ is the average intertest correlation. In this form, one can easily see that the reliability of the battery composite is a function of the subtest reliabilities and intercorrelations. For the limiting case of subtests that are classically parallel to each other, the composite-score reliability equals the Spearman–Brown projection (with $n = k$) applied to the reliability of any one subtest.

Formula 27 is most often used when a second administra-

tion of a battery, at least in its entirety, is impractical. Typically, the $\rho_{X_i X_i'}$ are estimated via one of the internal consistency coefficients discussed previously. The variances of subtests and the variance of the composite score can be directly estimated from distributions of these scores.

Clearly, there is opportunity for bias in an estimate of $\rho_{ZZ'}$ that employs estimates of the $\rho_{X_i X_i'}$ based on a single administration of each subtest. Day-to-day factors inflate σ_Z^2, because examinees are caught at different points in their personal diurnal cycles. But these same factors are not reflected in single-session estimates of $\rho_{X_i X_i'}$ nor in the $\sigma_{E_i}^2$.

Sometimes this bias can be avoided if authorities can arrange for samples of examinees to take a parallel form of at least one subtest in a second testing session. With k random or stratified samples of examinees, each taking a second form of one subtest, test developers can avoid the inconsistencies in the error sources reflected in $\sigma_{E_i}^2$ and σ_Z^2. An even better plan is to employ $2k$ samples. One group of k samples is assigned form A of the complete battery and each sample a single subtest from form B. The second group of k samples is assigned form B of the complete battery and a single subtest from form A. The reliabilities of form A and form B of subtest i are then defined as

$$\rho_{X_{iA} X_{iA}'} = \frac{\sigma_{(X_{iA})(X_{iB})}}{\sigma_{X_{iA}}^2} \quad \text{and} \quad \rho_{X_{iB} X_{iB}'} = \frac{\sigma_{(X_{iA})(X_{iB})}}{\sigma_{X_{iB}}^2}.$$

Reliability of the composite for form A (Formula 27) is computed by using the error variances for form A subtests and $\sigma_{Z_A}^2$. For the form B composite score, reliability is based on form B variances. The primary assumption in this approach is that form A and form B of subtest i are essentially tau-equivalent. For forms with this degree of similarity the interform covariance of observed scores equals the true score variance for any given subtest.

Stratified Coefficient Alpha

Only rarely do educational tests consist of exercises so homogeneous that the table of specifications lists no subcategories of content. By far, the more typical instrument is assembled from items drawn from five or more major content categories. If the design of the test specifies both content and skill dimensions, 15 or 20 categories are not uncommon. In such a case, the presumption of item tau-equivalence is difficult to maintain on content and statistical grounds. After all, to insist on a prescribed distribution of items over several content categories is to presume that at least a small, but important, degree of unique variance is associated with the categories. The basic assumption of coefficient alpha, then, is open to question when a test consists of several "strata" of exercises.

The reliability of stratified tests is easily handled by viewing the total test score as a linear composite. The total score is simply represented as a sum of k stratum scores: $X = X_1 + X_2 + \ldots + X_k$. For reliability estimation purposes (and quite possibly only for such purposes), each examinee's performance is scored as if each item category were a subtest. The observed score variance and coefficient alpha are then obtained for each category score. Finally, the error variance is estimated for each category score, the error variances are summed, and the total is substituted into the formula

$$\text{strat }_\alpha\rho_{XX'} = 1 - \frac{\Sigma\sigma^2_{X_j}(1 - {}_\alpha\rho_{X_jX_j})}{\sigma^2_X}. \qquad (28)$$

Will the foregoing expression for stratified coefficient alpha differ materially from the nonstratified version applied to the same data? The answer to this question depends on the nature of the categories and the degree of uniqueness associated with them. In general, stratification on estimates of item difficulty results in little difference between Estimators 12 and 28. Stratification on content can result in significantly greater impact (see Cronbach, Schönemann, & McKie, 1965).

Reliability of Difference Scores

The difference between two observed scores for the same individual takes on considerable importance in two settings: when an examinee's scores are compared within a profile of achievement, aptitude, interest, or attitude measures and when pupil growth is assessed over a learning period. For many experimenters, a simple change score has strong appeal as a dependent variable. For school authorities, the growth of a pupil over the preceding year is often of greater concern than current status, especially in conferences with parents.

Simple differences and the more elaborate measures discussed in the following section have both defenders and detractors. There are probably more of the latter than the former. Angoff (1971), Cronbach and Furby (1970), Harris (1963), Horst, Tallmadge, and Wood (1975), Knapp (1980), Linn and Slinde (1977), Lord (1956, 1958, 1963), Marks and Martin (1973), and McNemar (1958), to name only a partial list, marshal a variety of arguments against difference scores. Richards (1975), Rogosa, Brandt, and Zimowski (1982), Rogosa and Willett (1983), Webster and Bereiter (1963), and Zimmerman and Williams (1982a, 1982b) remain favorably disposed, at least under certain conditions.

The facts about the reliability of difference scores are simple to derive, because a difference is nothing more than a two-score weighted composite with weights of $+1$ and -1. For $D = X_2 - X_1$,

$$\rho_{DD'} = 1 - \frac{\sigma^2_{X_2}(1 - \rho_{X_2X_2}) + \sigma^2_{X_1}(1 - \rho_{X_1X_1})}{\sigma^2_{(X_2-X_1)}}. \qquad (29)$$

This formula is about as simple as any, for computational purposes. It presumes that a difference has been computed for each examinee, and, hence, the variance of differences can be directly estimated from the distribution of differences.

For expository purposes, it is useful to consider the special case of $\sigma_{X_1} = \sigma_{X_2}$. This case is more realistic in the profile setting than in the growth setting. In the former, scores are rarely plotted on a profile unless they have been scaled to a common mean and standard deviation. In the growth context, however, variability typically changes. When tests have ample "ceiling," effective instruction tends to increase the variability within a student group. On the other hand, if the test has a low ceiling or instruction achieves something close to mastery by many learners, scores might concentrate near the top of the score scale and variability might decline. Thus, the presumption of equal standard deviations is often contradicted by the empiri-

cal data. If variability does remain constant,

$$\rho_{DD'} = \frac{\bar{\rho}_{X_jX_j} - \rho_{X_1X_2}}{1 - \rho_{X_1X_2}}, \qquad (30)$$

where $\bar{\rho}_{X_jX_j}$ is the average of the reliabilities of X_1 and X_2.

Substitution of reasonable, representative values for the reliabilities and intercorrelation in Estimator 30 quickly establishes the relatively low reliability of the typical difference score. For example, with reliabilities of .85 and an intercorrelation of .70, the reliability of the difference (if $\sigma_{X_1} = \sigma_{X_2}$) is .50. In many applications where Equation 29 or Equation 30 yields higher coefficients, the evaluation is based on within-session reliabilities and between-session correlations. The resultant inconsistency in the definition of measurement error for the several statistics biases the estimate of $\rho_{DD'}$ upward.

The importance of the assumption of independence of the measurement errors must be reemphasized at this point. If independence does not hold, the foregoing formulas might yield erroneous and misleading reliability estimates. This possibility is well documented by the theoretical formulas of Zimmerman, Brotohusodo, and Williams (1981), which recognize the possibility of correlated error.

In profile interpretation, it is not uncommon to plot an interval based on σ_E around each observed score (such intervals are discussed in a later section). The rule-of-thumb is then adopted that a "trustworthy" difference is one for which the two score intervals do not overlap. Such a procedure has simplicity in its favor but several drawbacks. It presumes that σ_E estimated for any given test can be safely applied to each individual, often a dubious assumption. Also it tends to result in the labeling of some differences as *dependable* and others as *undependable,* ignoring the fact that a continuum of dependability is involved (see Feldt, 1967).

The argument against the use of $X_2 - X_1$ as the dependent variable in multi-group experiments merits at least brief attention. The conventional wisdom goes as follows: When the initial and final measures are highly correlated, reliability of differences is low. Low dependent-variable reliability is detrimental to the power of F tests bearing on mean differences among groups. Therefore, difference scores should be avoided when comparing experimental groups.

There is a flaw in this logic that should be noted, though the general conclusion might well be sound on other grounds. To state that a difference score has low reliability for some or all groups involved in an experiment is to declare that the ranking of individuals from highest to lowest growth is undependable *within each group.* This indictment could be quite accurate for the growth scores arising within each group. But this says nothing about the comparative values of the group means for the growth measure. The means could be identical, moderately different, or dramatically different. Not all commentators on this issue seem to be sensitive to this fact.

One might argue, of course, that good instruction rarely raises the mean of a group by affecting all subjects equally. Rather, some individuals progress faster than others. If there is marked average growth, this argument holds, there is likely to be variation in true growth. If one concedes this fact, then one implicitly concedes at least a certain degree of reliability to difference scores. Moreover, one might argue that, if a dependent variable has a sufficiently high ceiling, the treatments that produce higher mean true growth also produce greater variation among subjects in true growth.

These are speculative conjectures, of course. When one looks at the reported data for standardized achievement tests, as in reading, it is not uncommon to find reliabilities of status scores in grades 5 and 6 of about .88 and year-to-year correlations of .82. Thus, growth measures often have reliabilities in the neighborhood of .33 or lower. Yet no one would deny that the typical fifth-grade student makes considerable progress in a year's time. Such data suggest that important instances occur in which good instruction adds a constant to student scores and individual variations, the time-by-subject interaction, are minimal. In such circumstances, within-group reliability might be low, but the mean difference between groups that are well or poorly taught might be high. The one fact does not preclude the other. Therefore, low within-groups reliability does not inevitably dictate low experimental power in detecting between-groups differences in means.

Reliability of Modified Difference Scores

Some critics who find $D = X_2 - X_1$ unacceptable are less strongly opposed to, or even favor, modification of the simple difference. The most commonly proposed modifications are

$$Z_1 = X_2 - [b_X(X_1) + a_X], \tag{31}$$

$$Z_2 = w_1 X_1 + w_2 X_2 + C, \tag{32}$$

$$Z_3 = \rho_{DD'}(X_2 - X_1) + (1 - \rho_{DD'})\mu_D. \tag{33}$$

The first of these, usually called a *residual score,* is the difference between X_2 and a linear regression estimate of X_2 based on X_1. It is often used as a measure of over- or underachievement; X_1 might or might not be in the same metric as X_2. The general interpretation of $b_X(X_1) + a_X$ is that it represents an "expected" X_2 score, or an estimate of the average X_2 score made by previous individuals with any given value of X_1.

In the second modified score, Z_2, scores X_1 and X_2 are treated as independent variables to be optimally combined via multiple-regression methods to estimate $T_2 - T_1$. At first blush, it might seem impossible to derive the regression weights and constant in Equation 32, because the values of $T_2 - T_1$ are never known for an experimental sample. However, the correlations involved in determining these weights ($\rho_{X_1 T_1}$, $\rho_{X_1 T_2}$, etc.) can be expressed in terms of observed score correlations corrected for attenuation (see Lord, 1956, 1958; McNemar, 1958).

The third of the modified scores is the Kelley observed-score–true-score regression line estimate of $T_2 - T_1$ given $X_2 - X_1$. It treats the simple difference as an observed score entity to be regressed toward the group or population mean difference. This regressed score is generally viewed as a simplified form of the more accurate estimator, Z_2.

To derive an expression for the reliability of residual scores one must decide how the true score is to be defined. This has generated greater controversy than might have been expected. Some would define the true difference score as $T_2 - (b_T T_1 + a_T)$ (see O'Connor, 1972; Traub, 1967). Others prefer $T_2 - (b_X T_1 + a_X)$ (see Glass, 1968; Linn & Slinde, 1977; Stanley, 1971). The difference involves the regression constants; should they be based on true score parameters or observed

score parameters? The distinction affects the expression for the reliability coefficient.

The second definition is adopted here. There are advantages to such a definition, though the typical practitioner might find the subtleties of the arguments for one or the other difficult to follow. On this basis,

$$\rho_{Z_1 Z_1'} = 1 - \frac{\sigma_{X_2}^2(1 - \rho_{X_2 X_2'}) + b_X^2 \sigma_{X_1}^2(1 - \rho_{X_1 X_1'})}{\sigma_{Z_1}^2}. \tag{34}$$

For the original group on which b_X was determined,

$$\rho_{Z_1 Z_1'} = \frac{\rho_{X_2 X_2'} - \rho_{X_1 X_2}^2(2 - \rho_{X_1 X_1'})}{1 - \rho_{X_1 X_2}^2}. \tag{35}$$

For later individuals, b_X is an arbitrary constant and $\sigma_{Z_1}^2$ is estimated directly.

The Lord–McNemar score, Z_2, has a reliability

$$\rho_{Z_2 Z_2'} = 1 - \frac{w_1^2 \sigma_{X_1}^2(1 - \rho_{X_1 X_1'}) + w_2^2 \sigma_{X_2}^2(1 - \rho_{X_2 X_2'})}{\sigma_{Z_2}^2}. \tag{36}$$

For the group on which the regression weights are derived,

$$w_1 = \frac{1}{1 - \rho_{X_1 X_2}^2} \left[\frac{\rho_{X_1 X_2} \sigma_{X_2}}{\sigma_{X_1}} (1 - \rho_{X_2 X_2'}) - \rho_{X_1 X_1'} + \rho_{X_1 X_2}^2 \right]$$

$$w_2 = \frac{1}{1 - \rho_{X_1 X_2}^2} \left[\frac{\rho_{X_1 X_2} \sigma_{X_1}}{\sigma_{X_2}} (\rho_{X_1 X_1'} - 1) + \rho_{X_2 X_2'} - \rho_{X_1 X_2}^2 \right]. \tag{37}$$

For subsequent individuals, w_1 and w_2 become arbitrary constants. Like any other regression equation, Z_2 can potentially be improved by adding additional relevant variables (Cronbach & Furby, 1970).

The third modified score represents a linear transformation of $X_2 - X_1$. As with all linearly transformed scores, the reliability coefficient is unaffected by the transformation and, hence, equals $\rho_{DD'}$.

To illustrate these formulas, take $\rho_{X_1 X_1'} = \rho_{X_2 X_2'} = .9$, $\rho_{X_1 X_2} = .7$, $\sigma_{X_1} = 10$, and $\sigma_{X_2} = 12$. Then, $b_X = \rho_{X_1 X_2} \sigma_{X_2} / \sigma_{X_1} = .84$ and $\rho_{Z_1 Z_1'} = .7078$. To four places, the weights in the Lord–McNemar score are $w_1 = -.6392$ and $w_2 = +.6895$. Thus, $\sigma_{Z_2}^2 = w_1^2 \sigma_{X_1}^2 + w_2^2 \sigma_{X_2}^2 + 2 w_1 w_2 \rho_{X_1 X_2} \sigma_{X_1} \sigma_{X_2} = 35.2784$ and $\rho_{Z_2 Z_2'} = .6901$. In comparison, $\rho_{DD'} = .6667$.

Reliability of Predicted Scores and Factor Scores

When several scores ($X_1, \ldots, X_k$) are linearly combined to provide predicted values for criterion Y, the weights in Equation 18 are called regression weights and are typically symbolized b_j. The fact that these weights are determined via multiple-regression techniques does not introduce any new complications to reliability estimation. The error variance for each weighted score in the composite, here symbolized $\hat{Y}$, is

$$\sigma_{E_j}^2 = b_j^2 \sigma_{E_j}^2 = b_j^2 \sigma_{X_j}^2(1 - \rho_{X_j X_j'}). \tag{38}$$

The reliability of $\hat{Y}$ is then determined

$$\rho_{\hat{Y} \hat{Y}'} = 1 - \frac{\Sigma b_j^2 \sigma_{X_j}^2(1 - \rho_{X_j X_j'})}{\sigma_{\hat{Y}}^2}. \tag{39}$$

One would not ordinarily need to compute $\hat{Y}$ for every person in the original subject group from which the b_j are determined, because, for these individuals, the actual Y_p are known. It is an advantage, then, to know that $\hat{\sigma}_{\hat{Y}}^2$ equals $R^2\hat{\sigma}_Y^2$, where R^2 is the squared multiple correlation coefficient. When the b_j from the original sample are applied to a new sample, $\hat{\sigma}_{\hat{Y}}^2$ and $\hat{\sigma}_{X_j}^2$ must be estimated from the distributions for that new sample.

In a narrow sense, the factor scores of individuals determined from exploratory and confirmatory factor analyses may also be viewed as linear composites of observed scores. However, determination of weights and definition of factor scores constitute more controversial issues than determination of multiple-regression weights and predicted scores (see Harman, 1976; Schönemann & Wang, 1972). Thus, estimation of factorscore reliability is a complex issue. Gorsuch (1980), Kaiser and Michael (1977), and Tucker and Lewis (1973) provide useful formulas and discussion.

INTERRELATIONSHIPS AMONG AVERAGE PART-TEST RELIABILITY, THE SPEARMAN–BROWN PROJECTION, AND COEFFICIENT ALPHA

For a test of n parts, an interesting relationship, though not one of great utility for test users, holds among three reliabilities: the average or "pooled" single-part reliability, the Spearman–Brown projection based on this average, and coefficient alpha. This relationship was first noted by Stanley (1957).

The pooled single-part reliability may be defined as the ratio of the average covariance between parts to the average single-part variance:

$$\bar{\rho}_{X_f X_f} = \frac{\sum\sum_{f \neq g} \sigma_{X_f X_g}/n(n-1)}{\sum_f \sigma_{X_f}^2/n} = \frac{\sum\sum_{f \neq g} \sigma_{X_f X_g}}{(n-1)(\Sigma\sigma_{X_f}^2)}.$$

When the generalized Spearman–Brown formula, with a lengthening factor of n, is applied to this average, one obtains the following result:

$$\frac{n\,\bar{\rho}_{X_g X_g'}}{1+(n-1)\bar{\rho}_{X_g X_g'}} = \left(\frac{n}{n-1}\right)\left(\frac{\sigma_X^2 - \Sigma\sigma_{X_f}^2}{\sigma_X^2}\right) = {}_\alpha\rho_{XX'}. \quad (40)$$

Thus, coefficient alpha equals the projected reliability of an n-unit test when the extrapolation is based on the average of the single-unit reliabilities. This is an algebraic relationship, and it holds even when the n parts are individual test items. It was previously noted that the parameter value of coefficient alpha is negatively biased by the use of parts that are not essentially tau-equivalent. The present result is logically consistent with that earlier conclusion. In the absence of essential tau-equivalence, the average interpart covariance underestimates the average true-score variance of the parts. It is be expected that an extrapolation from an underestimate would result in an underestimate.

Another widely cited relationship involving coefficient alpha was first noted by Cronbach (1951) in the original explication of that coefficient. He demonstrated that alpha equals the average of all possible split-halves coefficients. It should be noted that the split-halves coefficients alluded to here are those defined by the Flanagan definition (Equation 9), not by the Spearman–Brown definition (Equation 8). For a test of $2n$ items, it turns out, after many algebraic steps, that

$${}_F\bar{\rho}_{XX'} = \frac{\left(\dfrac{2n}{2n-1}\right)\sum\limits_{f \neq g}^{2n}\sum \sigma_{X_f X_g}}{\sigma_X^2} \qquad (41)$$

$$= \frac{2n}{2n-1}\left(\frac{\sigma_X^2 - \Sigma\sigma_{X_f}^2}{\sigma_X^2}\right) = {}_\alpha\rho_{XX'}.$$

This algebraic equality holds regardless of the length of a part. Each part could, in fact, be a single item. Thus Kuder–Richardson formula 20 equals the mean of all split-halves of the Flanagan type. The equality also holds for parts of unequal length, provided Estimator 11 is used (Raju, 1977). Furthermore, it generalizes beyond split halves. Coefficient alpha equals the average of all possible "lower order" alpha coefficients based on three-part splits of the total test, the average of all coefficients based on four-part splits, and so on.

This property of coefficient alpha could be viewed as a virtue or a flaw, depending on the nature of the test. If one were willing to accept the partitioning of the items on a random or mechanical basis, as in odd-numbered versus even-numbered items, one should be even more willing to accept the average of all such coefficients. This mean is, after all, a unique value for the full test and avoids the potential sampling error in choosing one coefficient out of many equally acceptable coefficients. On the other hand, some item splits might well be regarded as unacceptable. Some splits, for example, place all items bearing on a particular aspect of content in the same part. Some splits place all the hardest items in one part and all the easiest items in another. Some splits place all of the early items in one part and all later items in another. If these represent unattractive possibilities, placing essential tau-equivalence in jeopardy, then an average that includes the resultant coefficients would also seem unattractive. In essence, the issue centers on item homogeneity. If one can make a case for meaningful uniqueness associated with categories of items, the stratified alpha coefficient should be used. Alternatively, parts should be defined that reflect, in miniature, the heterogeneity of the full test. No greater number of parts should be employed than can maintain this reproduction of all salient features of the full test.

Special Issues in Reliability

When a measure is not perfectly reliable, almost all individuals do not get the score they "truly deserve." Is X_p a biased estimate of τ_p? If so, does the value of the observed score have implications for its bias? Can facts abstracted for a given group of examinees contribute useful information about potential biases and be used to obtain a better estimate of a given individual's true score? Questions of this sort stimulate consideration of true-score–observed-score relationships.

POINT ESTIMATION OF TRUE SCORES

The relationship between τ_p and X_p can be viewed from two perspectives: wholly within a given individual or within the bivariate framework of one true score and one observed score for each of an infinity of individuals. Procedures for estimating τ_p depend upon which perspective is adopted.

If one concentrates upon a single individual, p, there is a single parameter, τ_p, of concern to us. Distributed around that parameter, there is (hypothetically) an infinity of observed scores arising from repetition of the measurement procedure. The process of measurement has delivered one value from this distribution. In the absence of any detailed knowledge about the state of the individual's health, motivation, alertness; the circumstances of test administration; and other temporary conditions, the single score in hand may be regarded as a randomly drawn observation from person p's distribution. So construed, the score may be viewed as an unbiased estimate of τ_p. Indeed, τ_p is defined as the expected value of X_p taken over an infinity of repeated measurements. Hence, X_p is by definition an unbiased estimator of τ_p.

If one changes the perspective to the bivariate framework, one envisions a pair of values, (τ_p, X_p), for each of many individuals measured via form f of an instrument. This bivariate distribution, the marginal distribution of T and X, and one conditional distribution of T given $X = x_o$ are crudely pictured in Figure 3.1. One may ask What is the expected value of T for all individuals who earned an observed score equal to x_o? The question concerns the mean of the conditional distribution at $X = x_o$, and it seems reasonable to employ regression techniques to arrive at an answer.

If one may assume that the conditional means over the full range of X fall on a straight line, that is, that the regression of T on X is linear, the straight line can be expressed as $\mu_{T \cdot X} = \beta_{TX}(X) + \alpha_{TX}$. In this equation $\beta_{TX} = \rho_{TX}\sigma_T/\sigma_X$ and $\alpha_{TX} = \mu_T - \beta_{TX}\mu_X$. Relationships derived for the classical model are of use here. It has been shown that $\mu_T = \mu_X$; $\rho_{TX} = \sigma_T/\sigma_X = \sqrt{\rho_{XX'}}$; $\sigma_T = (\sqrt{\rho_{XX'}})(\sigma_X)$. Substituting these values into the regression equation gives

$$\mu_{T \cdot X} = \rho_{XX'}(X) + (1 - \rho_{XX'})\mu_X = \rho_{XX'}(X - \mu_X) + \mu_X. \quad (42)$$

The conditional mean $\mu_{T \cdot X}$ is referred to as the *estimated true score* ($\hat{T}$) of individuals with observed score X.

What does this say about the potential bias in raw scores? For individuals with observed scores greater than μ_X, it says that, on the average, they are not as good as they seem. These people truly deviate from μ_X by a smaller amount than $(X - \mu_X)$ because $\rho_{XX'} < 1$. On the other hand, individuals with scores below μ_X are not, on the average, as poor as they seem. These statements clearly contrast with the conclusion reached from the within-person perspective.

It cannot be said that one of these perspectives is correct and the other incorrect. They simply differ. And the differences carry over to *interval estimates* for true scores, as will be seen in the following section. However, one can prefer the logic underlying one or the other perspective, and, for many researchers, the bivariate approach is more appealing. Counselors often interpret scores to students and parents by using statements like this: "Students who make scores like yours tend to have difficulty in handling the course work in nursing." The relationship of an observed score to estimated true score is analogous. The estimated true score is what "tends to be true" of all individuals who earn a given observed score.

If this logic is so appealing, why aren't raw scores routinely transformed to estimated true scores? Primarily, the reason is that raw scores rarely have meaning apart from normative information. If all scores for a norms group were transformed

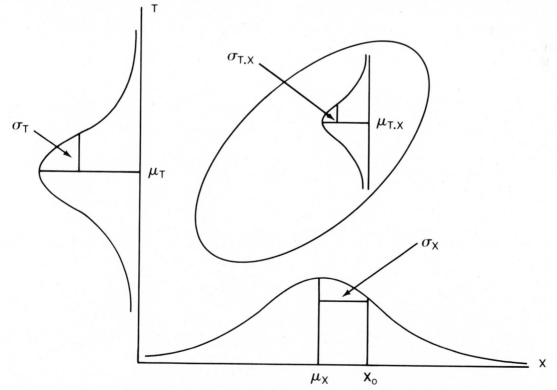

FIGURE 3.1 Bivariate Distribution, Marginal Distribution, and Conditional Distribution of True and Observed Scores.

to $\hat{T}$, and all interpretation was geared to $\hat{T}$, Janet's rank via $\hat{T}$ would be identical to her rank via X. Also, the reliabilities of $\hat{T}$ and X are the same. Thus, in most settings, nothing would be gained from the transformation. Only when scores are given criterion-referenced interpretations or when they are used to match experimental groups drawn from dissimilar pools of subjects does $\hat{T}$ have a clear advantage over X.

The derivation of the function relating $\hat{T}$ to X assumed linear regression. There is reason to question this assumption, particularly near the extremes of the distribution. For example, with multiple-choice tests, the means of the conditional distributions corresponding to $X = 0$, $X = 1$, and so on up to the chance score probably do not change as rapidly as later means. Changes in slope can also occur at the top of the score scale. However, over most of the score range, the assumption of linearity does not seem unreasonable.

In principle, there is no reason why T must be "predicted" solely from the observed score that includes T. In a battery of tests, one might estimate each true score from a linear composite of all observed scores or use curvilinear-regression methods. But, in practice, routine use of estimated true scores is too infrequent to warrant elaborate prediction techniques.

If the model for the conditional distribution of measurement errors, given τ, and the distribution of T belong to certain families, alternative estimates of $\mu_{T.X}$ become possible. Prominent among the models that have been considered is the combination of binomially distributed error coupled with a beta distribution for true scores (Keats & Lord, 1962; Lord, 1965). Another involves an angular transformation of the raw-proportion-correct scores, a transformation that has a normalizing effect on error-score distributions and is presumed to have a normalizing effect on the distribution of true scores (see Hambleton, Swaminathan, Algina, & Coulson, 1978). Still another adopts a compound-binomial model for error scores (Lord, 1965, 1969; Wilcox, 1978). Lord and Stocking (1976) derived a procedure, assuming the binomial-error model, which provides confidence intervals for $\mu_{T.X}$ at all values of X. These models avoid the potentially troublesome assumption of linearity, but they are more difficult to implement than the bivariate normal model except via computer.

INTERVAL ESTIMATION FOR TRUE SCORES

Interval estimation of true scores, like point estimation, can be viewed from the perspective of an isolated individual or in terms of the bivariate distribution of T and X. The first represents the traditional confidence-interval approach to estimation of a parameter. An interval is said to have a probability (γ) associated with it in a specific sense. One must conceptualize infinite repetitions of the process of interval estimation, each repetition tied to a randomly selected observed score. Some of these intervals would include the parameter, and some would not. The proportion that includes the parameter defines γ.

The second approach considers all examinees simultaneously. Of particular concern is the conditional distribution of T for a specific value of X (see Figure 3.1). An individual with a score of 30 is not viewed as an isolated examinee but as one of many who made this score. This subgroup, itself quite large, includes individuals with a range of true scores. The interval estimation process is viewed as one of determining two score values that "enclose" 100γ percent of the true scores in this conditional distribution. In the statistical literature this notion is often referred to as a tolerance interval.

Testing practice over the years has tended to favor the confidence-interval approach, though estimated true scores, when the need for them arose, have almost always been based on estimates of conditional distribution means. To determine γ, confidence intervals must be based on some knowledge of, or assumption about, the distribution of measurement errors. Customarily, the distribution has been assumed to be normal, with a mean of 0 and the same variance for all examinees. Thus, the traditional interval suggested to test users is $X \pm z\sigma_E$, with z determined from the unit normal distribution and $\sigma_E = \sigma_X\sqrt{1 - \rho_{XX'}}$. For example, for $\gamma = .50$, z is .6745. The reliability coefficient based on parallel forms has always received the strongest endorsement, but internal consistency coefficients have frequently been used as a practical necessity. The use of this interval has not been discouraged by tacit recognition that homogeneity of σ_E could be in doubt, and that even approximate normality might not hold.

The tolerance interval approach (see Stanley, 1971) has been less often used. When adopted, it has also typically used the assumption of normality for the conditional distributions. The interval has been centered about the estimate of $\mu_{T.X}$ under the linearity assumption. The variance of the conditional distribution has been estimated using the following theoretical relationship: $\sigma_{T.X}^2 = \sigma_T^2(1 - \rho_{XT}^2)$. Under the classical model, $\sigma_T^2 = \rho_{XX'}\sigma_X^2$ and $\rho_{XT}^2 = \rho_{XX'}$. Hence, $\sigma_{T.X}^2 = \rho_{XX'}\sigma_E^2$, and, under the assumption of normality, the interval based on observed score X is

$$[\rho_{XX'}(X - \mu_X) + \mu_X] \pm z\sigma_E\sqrt{\rho_{XX'}}. \qquad (43)$$

Stanley (1971) proposes that the multiplier for $\sigma_E\sqrt{\rho_{XX'}}$ be determined from the t distribution rather than the normal distribution, though it is not clear that this adequately allows for the finite sample size used to estimate the various parameters in Equation 43. Under the best of practical circumstances, the probability (γ) associated with this interval is approximate.

Jarjoura (1985) made extensive comparisons of normality-based confidence and tolerance intervals and intervals arising from alternative models. Among the latter were the beta-binomial model, angular transformation models, and a compound-binomial model. In general, the intervals arising under these latter models tended to agree rather closely. Those based on the normality assumption tended to be inconsistent with the others, especially at extreme score values. This was to be expected, because all normality-based intervals employed a single estimate of σ_E derived from the entire examinee group. Had σ_E been separately estimated for each score point, the intervals for extreme scores might have been more consistent with the others.

In general, Jarjoura favors the beta-binomial model on which to base tolerance intervals and the binomial-error model for confidence intervals. The formulas for the lower and upper bounds of the 100γ percent tolerance interval involve solution for two points in the cumulative distribution function, $I_X(\alpha, \beta)$, of the beta distribution. The parameters for this beta are $\alpha = a + X$ and $\beta = b + n - X$. The estimators of a and b are as follows, with n equal to the number of items:

$$\hat{a} = (\hat{\mu}_X)\left(\frac{1}{_{21}\hat{\rho}_{XX'}} - 1\right)$$

$$\hat{b} = (n - \hat{\mu}_X)\left(\frac{1}{_{21}\hat{\rho}_{XX'}} - 1\right). \tag{44}$$

The limits, L and U, are the values for which

$$I_L(\hat{a} + X, \hat{b} + n - X) = (1 - \gamma)/2$$

$$I_U(\hat{a} + X, \hat{b} + n - X) = (1 + \gamma)/2. \tag{45}$$

L and U are stated in terms of proportion of items correct (X/n) rather than number correct. Conversion to the scale of X is accomplished by multiplication by n.

A confidence interval for the true score of examinee p is obtained by solving the following binomial equations for L and U, respectively,

$$\sum_{j=X_p}^{n} \binom{n}{j} L^j (1 - L)^{n-j} = (1 - \gamma)/2$$

$$\sum_{j=0}^{X_p} \binom{n}{j} U^j (1 - U)^{n-j} = (1 + \gamma)/2. \tag{46}$$

In these formulas $\binom{n}{j}$ is the usual combinatorial coefficient. Some compromise in γ is necessary in view of the discrete nature of the binomial distribution. Again, L and U may be converted to the scale of X by multiplication by n.

The beta-binomial model implies a specific distribution form for observed scores: the negative hypergeometric. Keats and Lord (1962) and Wilcox (1981) report substantial evidence supporting its goodness-of-fit to standardized test data, though Brandenburg and Forsyth (1974) found other models that duplicated observed-score distributions even more accurately. In general, it seems safe to say that the negative hypergeometric fits observed data more accurately than does the normal distribution.

ESTIMATION OF ERROR VARIANCE AT SPECIFIC SCORE LEVELS

In the *Standards for Educational and Psychological Testing* (American Psychological Association [APA], 1985) it is recommended that conditional standard errors be reported. Such information is clearly valuable to all users of measurement data. It is especially helpful to those who wish to construct normality-based tolerance and confidence intervals.

A number of techniques are available for this purpose. The Thorndike approach (1951) employs stratified-parallel, tau-equivalent half-tests or full-length tau-equivalent forms. The theory is relatively simple. For half-tests 1 and 2, the model for observed scores is $X_i = (\frac{1}{2})T + C_i + E_i$ $(i = 1,2)$. T is the total test true score, and C_i are constants that account for any difference in observed-score means. The variance of E_1 is not necessarily equal to that of E_2. For the total test, $\sigma_E^2 = \sigma_{E_1}^2 + \sigma_{E_2}^2$. For half-test differences,

$$\sigma_{(X_1-X_2)}^2 = \sigma_{(E_1-E_2+C_1-C_2)}^2 = \sigma_{E_1}^2 + \sigma_{E_2}^2.$$

Thus, the variance of differences equals the error variance for the total test. By grouping individuals in a series of relatively short intervals on $X = X_1 + X_2$ and estimating $\sigma_{(X_1-X_2)}^2$, the investigator can approximate the error variance for each interval.

For full-length forms f and g, homogeneous groups are organized on the basis of $(X_f + X_g)/2$. Then, $\sigma_{(X_f-X_g)}^2 = \sigma_{E_f}^2 + \sigma_{E_g}^2$. There is insufficient information to partition this total into separate estimates for the two forms. Therefore, the error variance for each interval is approximated by $(\frac{1}{2})\sigma_{(X_f-X_g)}^2$. If this approach is employed, it is prudent to include both orders of administration and to pool the estimates of error variance arising from each order.

A weakness in the Thorndike method is that the numbers of individuals in the extreme intervals are likely to be quite small. The resultant variances might show erratic shifts from interval to interval, especially at some distance from the mode. As part of a longer study, Mollenkopf (1949) proposed a regression technique to smooth out these variations. For essentially tau-equivalent half-tests X_1 and X_2, consider the following quantity for person p:

$$Y_p = ([X_1 - X_2]_p - [\overline{X}_1 - \overline{X}_2])^2.$$

The mean of this quantity for any group of examinees estimates the variance of the half-test differences, which estimates σ_E^2 for the group. Let Y_p be construed as a dependent variable to be "predicted," via a polynomial regression model, from $X = X_1 + X_2$. How high a degree polynomial? This question can be answered essentially on an empirical basis: whatever degree seems to be required in terms of fit to the data. For achievement tests, a polynomial in the third or fourth degree has been found to be quite adequate. Substitution of successive values of X into the polynomial regression equation yields smoothed estimates of $\mu_{Y.X}$ or $\sigma_{E.X}^2$.

A third approach to estimation of conditional error variances draws upon the binomial theory of measurement error (Lord & Novick, 1968). Each test form is regarded as a random sample of n independent, dichotomously scored items from a defined domain. Each examinee is presumed to have a proportion-correct true score, $\phi_p = \tau_p/n$, for the domain. Errors of measurement, under this conceptualization, are represented by the difference $X_p - (n)(\phi_p)$. The variance of such differences for examinee p, over repeated independent samples of n items (that is, test forms) is

$$\sigma_{E.\tau_p}^2 = n(\phi_p)(1 - \phi_p).$$

With ϕ_p estimated by X_p/n and with the correction for the statistical bias in the sample variance, the estimate of error variance becomes

$$\hat{\sigma}_{E.X_p}^2 = \frac{(n - X_p)(X_p)}{n - 1}. \tag{47}$$

This model has been criticized because it fails to recognize the enforced similarities among test forms, particularly in their means. These similarities should reduce variation in X_p, and, hence, Formula 47 is generally regarded to overestimate $\sigma_{E.X}^2$. This is "confirmed" by the fact that the average value of Formula 47 equals $\sigma_{X_f}^2(1 - _{21}\rho_{XX'})$ for any examinee group. Keats (1957) proposed a simple correction, which appears to work quite well. He suggested that the values yielded by Formula 47 be multiplied by a constant that will force them to have a mean equal to $\sigma^2_{X_f}(1 - \rho_{XX'})$. The value of $\rho_{XX'}$ might be estimated through the use of parallel forms or, if necessary, by coefficient alpha. The constant that achieves this average is $(1 - \rho_{XX'})/(1 - _{21}\rho_{XX'})$. The third approach, then, uses the estimation formula

$$\hat{\sigma}^2_{E.X_p} = \frac{(n - X_p)(X_p)(1 - \hat{\rho}_{XX'})}{(n - 1)(1 - _{21}\hat{\rho}_{XX'})}. \quad (48)$$

A fourth approach (Feldt, 1984; Lord, 1965) modifies the binomial-error variance in a different way. It presumes that parallel forms constitute *stratified* random samples of items. The strata are defined by the item categories in the test specifications, usually content and skill classifications and intervals based on item difficulty and discrimination. The total test score is seen as a composite equal to the sum of the strata scores, though the strata scores are not typically obtained for interpretive purposes.

Let the numbers of items in the several strata be represented by $n_1, n_2, \ldots, n_k$ and strata scores by $X_{p1}, X_{p2}, \ldots, X_{pk}$. Presumably, the items in any given category can be regarded as a random sample from the corresponding portion of the overall domain. On this assumption, Estimator 47 should apply to the strata scores. On the additional assumption of independence of strata errors, the total test error variance can be estimated by the sum of strata estimates:

$$\hat{\sigma}^2_{E.X_p} = \sum_{i=1}^{k} \frac{(n_i - X_{pi})(X_{pi})}{n_i - 1}. \quad (49)$$

One difficulty with this approach is that the n_i might be quite small and give rise to untrustworthy estimates of personal σ^2_E. To offset this difficulty, individuals can be grouped into intervals on the basis of total score and the mean value of $\hat{\sigma}^2_{E.X_p}$ obtained for all persons in the interval. Thus, if there were N_1 individuals in the first interval, the average would equal

$$\begin{aligned} \hat{\sigma}^2_{E.X} &= \frac{1}{N_1} \sum_{p}^{N_1} \sum_{i}^{k} \frac{(n_i - X_{pi})(X_{pi})}{n_i - 1} \\ &= \sum_{i}^{k} \frac{(n_i - \bar{X}_i)(\bar{X}_i) - S^2_{X_i}}{n_i - 1}, \end{aligned} \quad (50)$$

where the k values of $\bar{X}_i$ and k values of $S^2_{X_i}$ are calculated from the scores of the N_1 examinees in this interval. Analogous computations would be carried out for other intervals. Note that, with this approach, individuals with the same total score might have different values for their $\hat{\sigma}^2_{E.X_p}$.

A fifth approach draws on analysis of variance methodology. For a test of n essentially tau-equivalent parts, one may organize the n part-test scores of N examinees into an $N \times n$ matrix. The score of person p on part i may be represented $X_{pi} = \mu + \pi_p + \alpha_i + e_{pi}$. The quantity α_i, with expectation of zero over parts, accounts for differences among the part-test means. The quantity π_p, with the expectation of zero over persons, allows for individual differences among persons. (The traditional true part score of person p equals $\mu + \pi_p$.) The quantity e_{pi} represents measurement error for person p on part i. If parts and persons are viewed as samples from their respective domains, the mean square (MS) for interaction approximates the average measurement-error variance for the parts. On the assumption of independence of part-test errors, the total-test-error variance is $\hat{\sigma}^2_E = [n][MS(pi)]$. If individuals are grouped into short intervals on X, this estimator may be applied to the matrix of data for each interval to estimate $\sigma^2_{E.X}$.

The ANOVA approach is closely related to the Thorndike technique. Suppose $\hat{\sigma}^2_{(X_1 - X_2)}$ were obtained for all possible pairs of parts and these $n(n-1)/2$ variance estimates were averaged. This mean would approximate the error variance for a two-part test, as noted in the discussion of the Thorndike method. A test of n parts, assuming error independence, could therefore be estimated to have an error variance of $n/2$ times this average. It can be shown that this latter quantity exactly equals n times the mean square for interaction. This is true for the total group of examinees and for any subgroup defined in terms of X. Thus, the ANOVA method shares the strengths of the Thorndike method—weak distributional assumptions—and also its weakness, susceptibility to sampling fluctuations associated with small interval subgroups.

The last method to be described here draws on item response curve theory (see chapter 4). That theory addresses the problem of estimating the parameters of the item function $P_i(\theta)$. This function indicates the probability that individual p with ability score θ_p will answer item i correctly. If these n functions are well approximated, error variance (in raw-score terms) may be estimated for subject p by a two-step process: (a) obtaining an estimator of the examinee's true ability score, $\hat{\theta}_p$, and (b) evaluating

$$\hat{\sigma}^2_{E.\hat{\theta}_p} = \sum_{i=1}^{n} [\hat{P}_i(\hat{\theta}_p)][1 - \hat{P}_i(\hat{\theta}_p)]. \quad (51)$$

This estimate may then be averaged for all persons in any interval of X.

Empirical investigation of these methods (Blixt & Shama, 1986; Feldt, Steffen, & Gupta, 1985; Lord, 1984) suggests that they agree quite closely when applied to standardized achievement tests. In view of this agreement, perhaps the Keats approach can be recommended. It requires the least computational effort, relying as it does only on the values of KR21 and the most defensible, practical estimate of $\rho_{XX'}$.

In general, these methods strongly support the conclusion that $\sigma^2_{E.X}$ varies as a curvilinear function of X and T. The binomial theory of error leads immediately to this conclusion, of course, because $n(\theta)(1 - \theta)$ is a quadratic function in $\theta = T/n$. Although other approaches do not mandate such a function, the empirical estimates they yield conform closely to values deduced from the Keats modification of the binomial estimate. Thus, it seems clear that raw-score-error variance is greatest near $T = n/2$ and declines rapidly at the extremes of the score scale. It should be emphasized that this conclusion concerns *raw-score* error. When raw scores undergo nonlinear transformations to various types of derived or norm-based scores, the trends might be markedly altered. Grade equivalent scores and deviation IQs, for example, can exhibit quite different trends from those that characterize raw scores.

CORRECTING RELIABILITY COEFFICIENTS FOR RESTRICTION IN RANGE

In some situations, test users are forced to estimate an instrument's reliability coefficient for population A from data gathered on population B. If one may assume homogeneity of error variance as a function of T, a tenuous assumption in many cases, the extrapolation from one population to another is simple. From population B

$$\sigma_E^2 = \sigma_{X_B}^2(1 - \rho_{XX_B}).$$

From the variance-ratio definition of reliability, it follows that

$$\rho_{XX_A} = 1 - \frac{\sigma_E^2}{\sigma_{X_A}^2} = 1 - \frac{\sigma_{X_B}^2(1 - \rho_{XX_B})}{\sigma_{X_A}^2}$$
$$= 1 - (\sigma_{X_A}/\sigma_{X_B})^2(1 - \rho_{XX_B}). \tag{52}$$

The potential inaccuracy in Equation 52 arises from its assumption of homogeneity. As noted in the previous section, there is evidence that this assumption frequently does not hold. The binomial model implies that it *never* holds. If population A includes a greater proportion of individuals than population B of those with larger error variances, Equation 52 will overestimate ρ_{XX_A}. If population A includes a heavy weighting of extreme scores, where σ_E^2 tends to be comparatively small, Equation 52 will underestimate ρ_{XX_A}.

Modification of Equation 52 demands detailed knowledge of the manner in which σ_E^2 varies as a function of X. If one accepts the binomial-error model, as modified by Keats (see Equation 48), it is possible to modify Formula 52 to take variation in $\sigma_{E.X}^2$ into account. The average error variance for population A may be estimated as follows:

$$\hat{\sigma}_{E_A}^2 = \frac{(1 - \hat{\rho}_{XX_B})}{(1 - {}_{21}\hat{\rho}_{XX_B})} \left[\frac{1}{N_A} \frac{\Sigma(n - X_p)(X_p)}{(n - 1)} \right].$$

However, as Lord (1955) has shown, the bracketed term equals the error variance estimated from KR21—in this case, for population A. Thus,

$$\hat{\sigma}_{E_A}^2 = \frac{(1 - \hat{\rho}_{XX_B})\sigma_{X_A}^2(1 - {}_{21}\hat{\rho}_{XX_A})}{(1 - {}_{21}\hat{\rho}_{XX_B})}. \tag{53}$$

Therefore, the estimated reliability coefficient for population A would be

$$\hat{\rho}_{XX_A} = 1 - \frac{(1 - \hat{\rho}_{XX_B})(1 - {}_{21}\hat{\rho}_{XX_A})}{(1 - {}_{21}\hat{\rho}_{XX_B})}. \tag{54}$$

How much difference does this modification of Estimator 52 make? Consider a 40-item test with observed scores ranging from 9 to 39. For population B, the test has a mean of 24.0, SD of 7.10, parallel-forms reliability of .86, and KR21 of .83. Suppose population A includes only those with scores above 20, eliminating about the lowest third of population B. The mean and SD of population A are 28.0 and 4.85, respectively. (These values approximate the parameters of the upper two-thirds of a normal distribution with $\mu = 24.0$ and $\sigma = 7.10$.) KR21 for population A equals .66. Estimators 52 and 54 yield the values .70 and .72, respectively.

Clearly, this difference is not important. However, had population A consisted of the upper half of population B, the values would have differed to a greater degree: .61 by Estimator 52 and .67 by Estimator 54. Thus, Estimator 54 could have an advantage when populations differ markedly.

COEFFICIENT ALPHA AND ANALYSIS OF VARIANCE

As noted in a previous section, the score of person p on part i, one of n essentially tau-equivalent parts of a test, may be represented $X_{pi} = \mu + \pi_p + \alpha_i + e_{pi}$. If the parts constitute a sample from a population of such parts, the expected value of the mean square for interaction equals the expected value of σ_E^2 for a single part. The expected value of the mean square within parts, $MS(w)$, equals the average value of $\sigma_{X_i}^2$ over the population of parts. The average reliability of a single part, then, may be estimated by $1 - MS(pi)/MS(w)$. Because the sum of squares within parts equals the sum of squares for persons plus the sum of squares for interaction, the following relationships hold:

$$MS(w) = \frac{SS(w)}{n(N-1)} = \frac{SS(p) + SS(pi)}{n(N-1)}$$
$$= \frac{MS(p) + (n-1)[MS(pi)]}{n}.$$

Therefore, the average single-part reliability is

$$\bar{\hat{\rho}}_{XX'} = \frac{MS(p) - MS(pi)}{MS(p) + (n-1)[MS(pi)]}. \tag{55}$$

Suppose this coefficient, often referred to as the *intraclass* coefficient, is extrapolated via the generalized Spearman–Brown formula to estimate the reliability of a test of n units. The resultant coefficient, applicable to the score $Y = X_1 + \ldots + X_n$, is

$$\hat{\rho}_{YY'} = \frac{MS(p) - MS(pi)}{MS(p)}. \tag{56}$$

The foregoing algebraic relationship places no restrictions on the score range for individual parts. The parts might, in fact, be individual items. However, it is exceedingly unlikely that dichotomously scored items would be essentially tau-equivalent. Hence, dichotomous scoring of items exerts a negative bias on Estimator 56.

The equivalence of Estimator 56 to Kuder–Richardson formula 20 was first noted by Hoyt (1941). Proof of the equality is not restricted to dichotomously scored items, and, hence, the equality holds more generally with coefficient alpha. Thus,

$$_\alpha\hat{\rho}_{XX'} = \frac{MS(p) - MS(pi)}{MS(p)}. \tag{57}$$

The use of Formulas 55 and 56 to estimate the reliability of ratings and other measurements with extended score scales was first proposed by Ebel (1951). Huck (1978), Lu (1971), and Maxwell (1968) proposed modifications of the formulas, designed to partition interaction into "pure" error variance and a nonerror component. Such modifications are accomplished more effectively by considering the total test score as a composite or by employing the multi-factor congeneric approach of Werts et al. (1978).

As discussed later, the extension of analysis of variance methodology to more complex measurement situations has been addressed by Brennan (1983), Cronbach et al., (1972), Lindquist (1953), and others.

THE RELATIONSHIP BETWEEN RELIABILITY AND POWER OF STATISTICAL TESTS

Improving the reliability of the dependent variable in an experiment enhances the power of the test of mean differences, if the null hypothesis is false (Cleary & Linn, 1969; Hopkins & Hopkins, 1979). How much the power increases depends on two factors: the initial level of reliability and the degree of falsity in the null hypothesis at the initial reliability.

The relationship can be derived from classical measurement theory. If the dependent variable is made more reliable, the effect is analogous to lengthening the instrument by a factor of n. To keep the dependent variable in the original metric, the more reliable score may be represented as the mean, Z, on n parallel units: $Z = (Y_1 + Y_2 + \ldots + Y_n)/n$.

The noncentrality parameter of the F test of H_o: $\mu_1 = \ldots = \mu_a$, where μ_j is the mean of treatment population j, is

$$\phi = \sqrt{\frac{\Sigma N_j(\mu_j - \mu)^2}{a(\sigma^2)}}.$$

In this expression, N_j is the size of treatment sample j, μ is the weighted mean of the μ_j, and σ^2 is the homogeneous within-treatments variance of the dependent variable. For measure Z, $\sigma_Z^2 = \sigma_Y^2(1 + [n-1]\rho_{YY'})/n$. The noncentrality parameter for Z may be expressed as follows in terms of $\rho_{YY'}$, $\rho_{ZZ'}$, n, and ϕ_Y, the noncentrality parameter for one Y unit:

$$\phi_Z = \sqrt{\frac{\Sigma N_j(\mu_j - \mu)^2}{a(\sigma_Z^2)}} = \sqrt{\frac{n}{1 + (n-1)\rho_{YY'}}}\,\phi_Y = \sqrt{\frac{\rho_{ZZ'}}{\rho_{YY'}}}\,\phi_Y.$$

It is also possible to incorporate in the expression for ϕ_Z a factor that reflects the effect of changes in treatment group size:

$$\phi_Z = \sqrt{\frac{\rho_{ZZ'}}{\rho_{YY'}}}\,\sqrt{\frac{\text{new } N_j}{\text{old } N_j}}\,\phi_Y. \tag{58}$$

It is clear that augmentation of sample size and enhancement of reliability operate in the same way. Whether raising reliability is more cost-effective than increasing sample size, only the experimenter can determine. Because $\rho_{ZZ'} < 1.0$, the benefit of an increase in sample size is potentially greater than that of an increase in reliability. The limit to the increase in ϕ through reliability improvement is $\sqrt{1/\rho_{YY'}}$.

There is a second way of viewing the relationship between reliability and power. Suppose the N subjects in an experiment are so chosen that their scores on a relevant control measure, X, lie within a narrow interval. This restricted sampling will tend to reduce σ_Y^2 and, as previously noted, lower the within-groups reliability coefficient. But the restricted sampling will have little or no impact on $\Sigma N_j(\mu_j - \mu)^2$ in many situations. The net result, then, will be an increase in ϕ_Y in the presence of a reduction in $\rho_{YY'}$.

This might seem, at first, to contradict the initial conclusion that an increase in the reliability of Y enhances power. Actually, the conclusions are not contradictory. The first analysis presumes a change in the criterion instrument and random sampling from the population of interest. The second analysis presumes a change in the target population (through restriction on X) but no change in the measuring instrument. For the first

change, one conclusion holds; for the second, the opposite conclusion holds (see Sutcliffe, 1980, for further discussion).

SAMPLING ERROR THEORY FOR RELIABILITY COEFFICIENTS

Situations that demand rigorous comparison of reliability coefficients are not uncommon. Modifications of testing procedures and the efficacy of various scoring formulas are generally judged, in part, by their effect on reliability. The impact of training programs for test scorers, observers, or raters is often considered in terms of reliability enhancement. Experimentation in the areas of item format and item-selection techniques often leads to the assessment of differences among coefficients. Comparisons among competing instruments and among distinct examinee populations raise the same issue.

If full-fledged parallel forms exist and the circumstances permit their administration, independent coefficients may be compared via the standard techniques employed with product-moment correlations. Fisher's transformation can be applied to each coefficient and the chi-square test used to test the null hypothesis (Hays, 1981, p. 467). A confidence interval for population reliability can also be obtained through the use of Fisher's transformation.

These same approaches may be employed with uncorrected split-halves coefficients based on independent groups. However, they are *not* appropriately applied to corrected (Spearman–Brown) coefficients (Lord, 1974). The statistical significance of differences must be demonstrated for the half-test correlations. If a confidence interval is desired for the full-test reliability, one must first obtain the interval for the half-test correlation. The Spearman–Brown formula can then be applied to the interval end points. Normality of the test-score distributions is an issue here, but probably a minor one. Although half-test and full-test score distributions invariably deviate from normality, the departures are not usually great enough to invalidate the approach.

When parallel forms or split-halves coefficients are based on the *same* sample, the testing of differences becomes more complex. With two coefficients, either parallel forms or half-test correlations, one may use the tests proposed by Olkin (1967) or an analogous test based on Fisher's transformation (Yu & Dunn, 1982). With more than two dependent coefficients of these types, repeated significance tests involving all pairs of coefficients can be carried out with a Bonferroni modification of critical values. Such a series of tests will have a true significance level numerically less than the nominal level.

When test reliability is estimated via coefficient alpha, the sampling theory is not the same as that which applies to product-moment coefficients. Feldt (1965) and Kristof (1963) independently developed the foundations of this theory. Bay (1973), Kristof (1970), and Pandey and Hubert (1975) have added useful refinements. Though based on the assumptions of normality and error independence, it has been shown to apply reasonably well with dichotomously scored items and, hence, to Kuder–Richardson formula 20.

Tests of the equality of independent alpha coefficients have been developed by Feldt (1969) and Hakstian and Whalen

(1976). The Feldt test, which is limited to two coefficients, employs the test statistic

$$W = \frac{(1 - \hat{\alpha}_2)}{(1 - \hat{\alpha}_1)},$$

where the $\hat{\alpha}_j$ are the sample alpha coefficients. The statistic is distributed approximately as an F with $N_1 - 1$ and $N_2 - 1$ degrees of freedom when the null hypothesis is true. The Hakstian–Whalen test permits comparison of K coefficients. With n_j parts (or items) in test j and N_j examinees, the test statistic is

$$M = \sum_j^K A_j - \frac{\left[\sum_j A_j(1 - \hat{\alpha}_j)^{-1/3}\right]^2}{\sum_j A_j(1 - \hat{\alpha}_j)^{-2/3}},$$

where $\quad A_j = \frac{(n_j - 1)(9N_j - 11)^2}{18(n_j)(N_j - 1)}.$

M is distributed approximately as chi-square with $K - 1$ degrees of freedom when equality holds.

Tests of the equality of two *dependent* coefficients have been developed by Kristof (1964) and Feldt (1980). The latter's test uses the ratio

$$t = \sqrt{\frac{(N - 2)(\hat{\alpha}_1 - \hat{\alpha}_2)^2}{4(1 - \hat{\alpha}_1)(1 - \hat{\alpha}_2)(1 - \hat{\rho}_{X_1 X_2}^2)}}, \tag{59}$$

that is distributed as t with $N - 2$ degrees of freedom. This is a two-ended test, and, therefore, its critical value is $t_{\alpha/2}$. The test assumes that Nn_j exceeds 1000. The Kristof test is based on half-test data. It is more complex computationally than the Feldt test, but it is applicable to smaller samples.

The general case involving K dependent coefficients was considered by Woodruff and Feldt (1986). Using a cube root transformation of $(1 - \hat{\alpha}_j)$, they developed a test statistic that is distributed approximately as chi-square. This test is essentially an extension of that by Hakstian and Whalen (1976) to the dependent case.

A final aspect of sampling theory concerns the tenability of various part-test models. As noted earlier, proper estimation of reliability coefficients requires a sound assumption about the structural relationships among the part-tests. Are they classically parallel, essentially tau-equivalent, single-factor congeneric, or multi-factor congeneric? Rigorous examination of this issue is greatly facilitated by the LISREL computer programs (Jöreskog & Sörbom, 1978). These programs enable the conscientious investigator to determine which models represent a significantly better fit than others to the observed variances and covariances and to implement the preferred model in estimating reliability.

Reliability of Group Means

In school achievement testing programs, interpretation of test results focuses on groups as well as individuals. At the administrative level, department heads, curriculum directors, principals, and superintendents are typically concerned with class averages. These summary statistics constitute critical evidence bearing on the strengths and weaknesses of instructional programs, and conscientious test publishers and state evaluation offices furnish norms for class averages. The reliability of means is therefore a relevant issue.

It is important to note that traditional measurement error is not the sole source, or even the most potent source, of unreliability affecting inferences drawn from class means. The test results for any given year reflect not only the character of the instructional program but also the character of students enrolled at that specific moment. These individuals must be regarded as a sample, in a longitudinal sense, from the population that flows through the district schools over a period of years. A curricular judgment can be in error if a particular year's class happens to be unusually strong or weak. Thus, even if authorities were privileged to know the true scores of current students, there could be substantial sampling error in using the results of one class to infer something about the impact of a program. An estimate of the reliability of class means must take this into account.

An estimate of the reliability of averages in this broad longitudinal sense can be obtained from the variance of the pupil-norms distribution, $\hat{\sigma}_X^2$, and the variance of the distribution of class means, $\hat{\sigma}_{\bar{X}}^2$. With G groups and a total of N examinees, the estimator is

$$\hat{\rho}_{\bar{X}\bar{X}'} = \left(\frac{N - 1}{N - G}\right)\left(1 - \frac{\hat{\sigma}_X^2}{\tilde{n}\,\hat{\sigma}_{\bar{X}}^2}\right). \tag{60}$$

There is no differential weighting of group means in the distribution of averages; each mean constitutes a single entry in the distribution, regardless of group size. The quantity $\tilde{n}$ is an average of the group sizes:

$$\tilde{n} = \frac{1}{G - 1}\left(N - \frac{\sum n_j^2}{N}\right).$$

When G and N are reasonably large, the value of $\tilde{n}$ can be estimated by the mean group size. Therefore, Estimator 60 can be based on $\bar{n}$ rather than $\tilde{n}$.

To illustrate this formula, data are taken from the Iowa High School Testing Program, in which the *Iowa Tests of Educational Development* is the evaluation instrument. In a recent year, 413 schools participated in the program, and 43,190 high school juniors were tested. For the Quantitative Thinking Test, the variance of school means equaled 2.86; the normative distribution for individual scores had a variance of 43.43. The mean class size was 104.6 and $\tilde{n}$ equaled 104.5. Estimator 60 yields

$$\hat{\rho}_{\bar{X}\bar{X}'} = \frac{43189}{42777}\left(1 - \frac{43.43/104.5}{2.86}\right) = .863.$$

This formula has a small positive bias. It counts a small fraction of the schools-by-items interaction variance as true-score variance, whereas this component, analogous to the pupils-by-items interaction variance, is more appropriately classified as error variance. In the Iowa program, the bias has not been found to be of practical consequence.

Reliability in Generalizability Theory

Generalizability theory can be viewed as an extension and liberalization of classical theory that is achieved primarily through the application of analysis of variance procedures to measurement data. In classical theory, measurement error is viewed as a unitary, global entity, though it is acknowledged to arise from a combination of sources. In contrast, the models and methods of generalizability theory are concerned with the errors from these multiple sources as *separate* entities. It is principally in this sense that generalizability theory "liberalizes" classical theory.

The basic theoretical foundations for generalizability theory can be found in papers by Cronbach et al., (1963) and Gleser, Cronbach, and Rajaratnam (1965). These papers were followed by an extensive explication of the theory in a monograph by Cronbach et al. (1972). Brennan (1983) provides a monograph on generalizability theory that is less comprehensive than the Cronbach et al. (1972) monograph but still detailed enough to convey many of the conceptual and statistical issues. Brief introductions are provided by Brennan and Kane (1979), Gillmore (1983), and van der Kamp (1976). Shavelson and Webb (1981) review the literature on generalizability theory for the decade following the seminal work of Cronbach et al. (1972), and Kane (1982) treats many validity issues from the perspective of generalizability theory.

Although generalizability theory makes extensive use of analysis of variance procedures, application of these procedures to measurement theory and issues began long before the work of Cronbach and his colleagues. Over 40 years ago, Burt (1936), Hoyt (1941), and Jackson and Ferguson (1941) discussed analysis of variance approaches to reliability. Subsequently, important contributions were made by Ebel (1951) and Burt (1955). Also, Lindquist (1953) discussed in considerable detail the use of analysis of variance procedures in reliability studies. Publications by Burt and Lindquist, in particular, appear to have anticipated the development of generalizability theory.

It should be noted, however, that the application of analysis of variance methods in generalizability theory differs considerably in emphasis and scope from the use of these methods in the analysis of experimental data. Generalizability theory emphasizes the estimation of specific components of score variance rather than tests of statistical significance. Furthermore, even though generalizability theory can be viewed as a liberalization of classical theory, there are clear differences between the two theories. For example, in generalizability theory, measurement procedures (e.g., tests) are parallel if they consist of an equal number of conditions (e.g., items) randomly sampled from the same universe. This notion of randomly parallel tests is a less restrictive concept than classically parallel tests.

Conceptual Framework

Also, generalizability theory employs concepts that are not an integral part of classical theory. Among these are *universes of admissible observations, universes of generalization, G (generalizability) study designs,* and *D (decision) study designs.* These concepts are central to generalizability theory but difficult to define in the abstract. The hypothetical scenario that follows provides a setting in which these concepts can be more readily understood.

G STUDY AND UNIVERSE OF ADMISSIBLE OBSERVATIONS

Suppose Mary Smith wants to develop one or more measurement procedures for evaluating writing proficiency. She might proceed by specifying a set of essay items that *could* be used to evaluate writing proficiency and a set of *potential* raters to evaluate responses to the items. Let us assume that the number of potential items and potential raters is essentially infinite. These specifications characterize the facets of measurement that Smith wants to consider. A *facet* is simply a set of similar *conditions of measurement.* In effect, she maintains that any one of the items constitutes an admissible condition of measurement for her item facet, and any one of the raters constitutes an admissible condition of measurement for her rater facet. Thus, Smith's *universe of admissible observations* contains an item facet and a rater facet, both of which are infinite.

Furthermore, it is likely that she would accept a pairing of any rater, r, with any item, i. If so, her universe of admissible observations would be described as *crossed* and denoted $i \times r$, where the "$\times$" is read "crossed with." Note that no explicit reference has been made to persons who might respond to the essay items. In generalizability theory the word *universe* is reserved for conditions of measurement, and the word *population* is used for the *objects of measurement* (usually persons).

To design a useful and efficient measurement procedure for some specific purpose, Smith needs to collect and analyze data to empirically characterize her universe of admissible observations. To do this, she conducts a study in which a sample of n_r raters evaluates each of the responses by a sample of n_p persons to a sample of n_i essay items. This is called a *G(generalizability) study.* The design of this particular study is denoted $p \times i \times r$, the symbolism implying that persons, items, and raters are all crossed. For this G study design, there are seven sources of variance that can be independently estimated from the G-study data. These sources of variance are called G-study *variance components.* When the conditions of both facets and the objects of measurement are infinite, the estimated variance components pertain to the random-effects model of analysis of variance.

D STUDIES AND UNIVERSES OF GENERALIZATION

Estimates of G-study variance components are important principally because they can be used to estimate results for one or more measurement procedures that might be used to make decisions about objects of measurement. A study that uses a measurement procedure to collect data about objects of measurement is called a *D (decision) study.*

Perhaps the most important consideration in designing a D study is the specification of a *universe of generalization.* This is the universe to which a decision maker wants to generalize in a D study with a particular measurement procedure. A universe of generalization may contain all of the conditions in the universe of admissible observations, or it may contain only a subset of the conditions. Indeed, a broadly defined universe of admissible observations provides a basis for considering many possible universes of generalization.

Suppose, for example, that the results of Smith's G study lead Sean Brown to employ a measurement procedure using $n'_r = 2$ raters and $n'_i = 4$ essay items. Also, suppose that, as Brown views the situation, a second randomly parallel measurement (if such were needed) would involve the same two raters but a different random sample of four items from the infinite set of items. This means that Brown's universe of generalization is restricted to two particular raters. The D-study design has items nested within raters, and the model is said to be mixed, with raters fixed in the universe of generalization. Given these specifications, Brown can estimate *D-study variance components, universe score variance* (the analogue of true-score variance), various types of error variance, and a *generalizability coefficient* (the analogue of a reliability coefficient).

This scenario is both idealized and incomplete, but it does introduce important concepts, terminology, and statistics employed in generalizability theory. The following subsections expand upon these issues through a consideration of single-facet universes and designs, multifacet universes and designs, and multivariate generalizability theory.

Single-Facet Universes and Designs

Assume that (a) the universe of admissible observations involves conditions from a single facet that will be called, for the sake of specificity, the *items facet;* (b) a population of persons is crossed with items, in the sense that an observation for any person, p, on any item, i, is admissible; and (c) both the population of persons and the universe of items can be considered infinite.

MEAN SCORES, LINEAR MODEL, AND VARIANCE COMPONENTS

Let X_{pi} denote the observed score for any person in the population on any item in the universe of admissible observations. The expected value of a person's observed score over the universe of items is

$$\mu_p \equiv \mathscr{E}_i X_{pi}. \tag{61}$$

Similarly, the population mean for item i is

$$\mu_i \equiv \mathscr{E}_p X_{pi}, \tag{62}$$

and the mean over both the population and the universe is

$$\mu \equiv \mathscr{E}_p \mathscr{E}_i X_{pi}. \tag{63}$$

Although these mean scores are not themselves observable, any observable score for person p on item i can be expressed in terms of them, using the following linear model:

$$
\begin{aligned}
X_{pi} = \mu & \qquad \text{(grand mean)} \\
+ \mu_p - \mu & \qquad \text{(person effect} = \pi_p) \\
+ \mu_i - \mu & \qquad \text{(item effect} = \alpha_i) \\
+ X_{pi} - \mu_p - \mu_i + \mu & \qquad \text{(residual effect} = \pi\alpha_{pi}).
\end{aligned} \tag{64}
$$

In abbreviated form,

$$X_{pi} = \mu + \pi_p + \alpha_i + \pi\alpha_{pi}. \tag{65}$$

Equations 64 and 65 represent the same tautology. In each equation, the observed score, X_{pi}, is decomposed into score effects or components. The only difference between the two equations is that, in Equation 64, each effect is explicitly represented as a deviation score, whereas, in Equation 65, different Greek symbols, or products of them, are used to represent effects. In Equation 65, note that the residual effect is denoted as an interaction effect, $\pi\alpha_{pi}$. Technically, with a single observed score for each person–item combination, the effect $\pi\alpha_{pi}$ is completely confounded with other sources of error (denoted e in a previous section). Cronbach et al. (1972) explicitly represented such confounding in their notational system. Here, as in Brennan (1983), it is to be understood that the highest order interaction effect is always completely confounded with e, and neither of these effects is assumed to be 0.

Without any additional assumptions, the manner in which the effects in Equation 65 have been defined implies that

$$\mathscr{E}_p \pi_p = \mathscr{E}_i \alpha_i = \mathscr{E}_p \pi\alpha_{pi} = \mathscr{E}_i \pi\alpha_{pi} = 0,$$

and the expected value of most products of score effects is 0, that is most pairs of effects are necessarily uncorrelated. When these definitions do not constitute a sufficient basis for some pair of effects to be uncorrelated, the additional assumption of uncorrelated effects is usually made for purposes of estimation. For example, the derivations of the estimators of some of the parameters discussed next require the assumption that $\mathscr{E}(\pi_p, \pi\alpha_{pi}) = 0$. Unless otherwise noted, however, none of the results discussed next require the common analysis of variance assumption of normality.

For each component in Equation 65, there is an associated variance, which is called a *variance component.* The variance components for persons, items, and their interaction are, respectively:

$$\sigma^2(p) = \mathscr{E}_p(\mu_p - \mu)^2 = \mathscr{E}_p \pi_p^2, \tag{66}$$

$$\sigma^2(i) = \mathscr{E}_i(\mu_i - \mu)^2 = \mathscr{E}_i \alpha_i^2, \tag{67}$$

$$\sigma^2(pi) = \mathscr{E}_p \mathscr{E}_i(X_{pi} - \mu_p - \mu_i + \mu)^2 = \mathscr{E}_p \mathscr{E}_i \pi\alpha_{pi}^2. \tag{68}$$

G STUDY $p \times i$ DESIGN

The previous development does not require specification of the manner in which observed data are collected in a particular G study. Let us now assume that G-study data are collected in the following manner: (a) a random sample of n_p persons is selected from the population, (b) an independent random sample of n_i items is selected from the universe, and (c) each of the n_p persons responds to each of the n_i items and the responses, X_{pi}, are obtained. Technically, this is a description of a G-study *random effects,* single-facet crossed design, denoted $p \times i$. The linear model for this design is given by Equation 65.

The principal purpose of such a G study is to estimate the variance components given in Equations 66–68. These estimates are usually obtained by employing the expected mean square (EMS) equations for the $p \times i$ design:

$$\text{EMS}(p) = \sigma^2(pi) + n_i\sigma^2(p)$$

$$\text{EMS}(i) = \sigma^2(pi) + n_p\sigma^2(i)$$

$$\text{EMS}(pi) = \sigma^2(pi).$$

Solving these equations for the variance components, and using mean squares in place of their expected values, we obtain the following estimators:

$$\hat{\sigma}^2(p) = [\text{MS}(p) - \text{MS}(pi)]/n_i \qquad (69)$$

$$\hat{\sigma}^2(i) = [\text{MS}(i) - \text{MS}(pi)]/n_p \qquad (70)$$

$$\hat{\sigma}^2(pi) = \text{MS}(pi). \qquad (71)$$

D STUDY $p \times I$ DESIGN

The G-study variance components discussed earlier are for one individual's score on a single item (X_{pi}) in the universe of admissible observations. Suppose, however, that a person takes a random sample of n_i' items (where n_i' need not equal n_i), and decisions will be based on his or her score over the n_i' items, not on a single item. From the perspective of generalizability theory, another parallel measurement of the person would consist of his or her score on a different random sample of n_i' items from the same universe. Such samples of items, or tests, are said to be *randomly parallel,* and the universe of randomly parallel tests is called the *universe of generalization.*

In generalizability theory *mean* scores over a sample of conditions of measurement (e.g., items) are usually indicated by uppercase letters. Thus, the single-facet, crossed D-study design is denoted $p \times I$. For this design, the linear model for the decomposition of a person's average score over n_i' items is

$$X_{pI} = \mu + \pi_p + \alpha_I + \pi\alpha_{pI}. \qquad (72)$$

Given this model, replacement of i by I in Equations 61–63 gives the mean scores for the population and universe of generalizability. For example,

$$\mu_p \equiv \mathscr{E}_I X_{pI},$$

which means that μ_p is defined as the expected value of X_{pI} over randomly parallel tests in the universe of generalization. This is a technical definition of what is meant by a person's *universe score.*

D-study variance components. Just as there are G-study variance components associated with each of the random effects in Equation 65, there are D-study variance components associated with the random effects in Equation 72. Definitions of these variance components are obtained by replacing i with I in Equations 66–68. It is evident that $\sigma^2(p)$ is unchanged by this replacement process, and it is called the *universe score variance.* The other two variance components are

$$\sigma^2(I) = \mathscr{E}_I(\mu_I - \mu)^2 = \mathscr{E}_I\alpha_I^2 \qquad (73)$$

$$\sigma^2(pI) = \mathscr{E}_p\mathscr{E}_I(X_{pI} - \mu_p - \mu_I + \mu)^2 = \mathscr{E}_p\mathscr{E}_I\pi\alpha_{pI}^2. \qquad (74)$$

These two variance components are for distributions of *mean* scores. Because the variance of a distribution of mean scores is the variance of the individual elements divided by the sample size,

$$\sigma^2(I) = \sigma^2(i)/n_i' \quad \text{and} \quad \sigma^2(pI) = \sigma^2(pi)/n_i'.$$

In generalizability theory, variance components are almost always expressed in the metric of *mean* scores over conditions of facets, rather than the total score metric usually employed in classical theory. If desired, the variance components for mean

scores can be multiplied by the square of n_i' to convert them to the total score metric.

Error variance $\sigma^2(\delta)$. Sometimes an investigator's interest focuses on the relative ordering of persons with respect to their test performance. In such cases, a person's score is typically interpreted relative to the mean score for the group with which the person is associated. In generalizability theory, the error for such interpretations is

$$\delta_{pI} \equiv (X_{pI} - \mathscr{E}_p X_{pI}) - (\mu_p - \mathscr{E}_p\mu_p)$$
$$= (X_{pI} - \mu_I) - (\mu_p - \mu). \qquad (75)$$

In Equation 75 the population test mean, μ_I, is the reference point for a person's observed mean score, X_{pI}, and the population and universe mean score, μ, is the reference point for a person's universe score, μ_p. In other words, for relative interpretations, a person's observed deviation score, $X_{pI} - \mu_I$, is interpreted as an estimate of the person's universe deviation score, $\mu_p - \mu$.

Substitution of $\mu_I = \mu + \alpha_I$ and $\mu_p = \mu + \pi_p$ into Equation 75 gives

$$\delta_{pI} = \pi\alpha_{pI}, \qquad (76)$$

which has an expectation of 0 and a variance of

$$\sigma^2(\delta) = \mathscr{E}_I\mathscr{E}_p\pi\alpha_{pI}^2 = \sigma^2(pI) = \sigma^2(pi)/n_i'. \qquad (77)$$

It can be shown that $\sigma^2(\delta)$ corresponds to the error variance in classical theory when $n_i' = n_i$.

Generalizability coefficient $\mathscr{E}\rho^2$. Cronbach et al. (1972) define an index called a *generalizability coefficient,* which is analogous to a reliability coefficient in classical theory. A generalizability coefficient is denoted $\mathscr{E}\rho^2$ and defined as the ratio of universe score variance to *expected* observed score variance. For the $p \times I$ design, expected observed score variance is

$$\mathscr{E}\sigma^2(X) \equiv \mathscr{E}_I\mathscr{E}_p(X_{pI} - \mu_I)^2 = \sigma^2(p) + \sigma^2(\delta). \qquad (78)$$

It follows that a generalizability coefficient is

$$\mathscr{E}\rho^2 \equiv \frac{\sigma^2(p)}{\sigma^2(p) + \sigma^2(\delta)}, \qquad (79)$$

which is an intraclass correlation coefficient that is approximately equal to the expected value of the squared correlation between observed and universe scores. $\mathscr{E}\rho^2$ may be interpreted also as an approximation to the correlation between the scores from two randomly parallel tests of length n_i'.

Given the estimators of the variance components in Equations 69–71, and, because $\hat{\sigma}^2(\delta) = \hat{\sigma}^2(pi)/n_i'$ for a $p \times I$ design, it follows that

$$\mathscr{E}\hat{\rho}^2 = \frac{\hat{\sigma}^2(p)}{\hat{\sigma}^2(p) + \hat{\sigma}^2(pi)/n_i'}. \qquad (80)$$

In terms of mean squares, this estimator can be expressed as

$$\mathscr{E}\hat{\rho}^2 = \frac{\text{MS}(p) - \text{MS}(pi)}{\text{MS}(p) + \left(\dfrac{n_i - n_i'}{n_i'}\right)\text{MS}(pi)}. \qquad (81)$$

Equations 80 and 81 are consistent, although not unbiased, estimators of $\mathscr{E}\rho^2$. When $n_i' = n_i$, $\mathscr{E}\hat{\rho}^2$ is identical to Cronbach's alpha in Equation 57. Furthermore, when $n_i' \neq n_i$, $\mathscr{E}\hat{\rho}^2$ yields a result identical to the Spearman–Brown extrapolation of Cronbach's alpha, the lengthening factor being equal to n_i'/n_i. In other words, a generalizability coefficient is defined in such a way that it directly incorporates a correction for any difference between the number of conditions sampled to estimate G-study variance components (n_i) and the number of conditions actually used to make decisions (n_i').

Error variance $\sigma^2(\Delta)$. Often an investigator's interest focuses on absolute, rather than relative, interpretations of scores. For such interpretations, the error is

$$\Delta_{pI} \equiv X_{pI} - \mu_p = \alpha_I + \pi\alpha_{pI}, \qquad (82)$$

which has an expectation of zero and a variance of

$$\sigma^2(\Delta) = \mathscr{E}_I\mathscr{E}_p(\alpha_I + \pi\alpha_{pI})^2 = \sigma^2(i)/n_i' + \sigma^2(pi)/n_i'. \quad (83)$$

A comparison of Equations 77 and 83 reveals that $\sigma^2(\Delta)$ is larger than $\sigma^2(\delta)$ by an additive factor of $\sigma^2(I) = \sigma^2(i)/n_i'$. The classical assumption of parallel tests means that μ_I is the same for all tests. Therefore, $\sigma^2(I)$ is 0 by definition in classical theory, and classical theory cannot formally distinguish between $\sigma^2(\delta)$ and $\sigma^2(\Delta)$. In contrast, generalizability theory allows for the possibility that tests might have different means, and $\sigma^2(I)$ is not assumed to equal zero. In other words, from the perspective of generalizability theory, any test might consist of a relatively easy or a difficult set of items, compared with the entire universe of items. Consequently, when X_{pI} is interpreted as an estimate of μ_p, variability in μ_I *does* contribute to the error in a person's observed score.

When X_{pi} is a dichotomous variable and the design is $p \times I$ with $n_i' = n_i$, Brennan and Kane (1977b) show that

$$\hat{\sigma}^2(\Delta) = \frac{1}{n_p} \sum_p \left[\frac{\bar{X}_p(1 - \bar{X}_p)}{n_i - 1} \right],$$

where $\bar{X}_p$ is an abbreviation for X_{pI}. The square root of the quantity in brackets is Lord's (1955) standard error of measurement for a person with an observed mean score of $\bar{X}_p$.

SINGLE-FACET NESTED DESIGNS

Suppose, as before, that the researcher is concerned with a single-facet, infinite universe of admissible observations that is crossed with an infinite population of persons. However, suppose that each person takes a *different* set of n_i items in a G study. This is called a *single-facet nested design.* It is denoted $i : p$, where the colon is read "nested within."

Nesting in both G and D studies. The linear model for the G-study $i : p$ design is

$$X_{pi} = \mu + (\mu_p - \mu) + (X_{pi} - \mu_p),$$

which can be expressed more succinctly as

$$X_{pi} = \mu + \pi_p + \alpha_{i:p}. \qquad (84)$$

Note that Equation 84 differs from Equation 72 for the $p \times i$ design in that the linear model for the $i : p$ design does *not* have a distinct term for the item effect. Also, the residual effects for the two models are different. These differences result from the fact that $\alpha_{i:p}$ in the $i : p$ design involves the confounding of the α_i effect and the $\pi\alpha_{pi}$ effect of the $p \times i$ design. Specifically,

$\alpha_{i:p} = \alpha_i + \pi\alpha_{pi}$. Because each person takes a different sample of items when the design is $i : p$, effects attributable solely to items are indistinguishable from interaction and other residual effects.

For the G-study $i : p$ design, the expected values of the mean squares are

$$\text{EMS}(p) = \sigma^2(i : p) + n_i\sigma^2(p) \quad \text{and} \quad \text{EMS}(i : p) = \sigma^2(i : p),$$

and the usual estimators of the variance components are

$$\hat{\sigma}^2(p) = [\text{MS}(p) - \text{MS}(i : p)]/n_i \quad \text{and} \quad \hat{\sigma}^2(i : p) = \text{MS}(i : p).$$

When the D-study design also involves nesting, the linear model is simply

$$X_{pI} = \mu + \pi_p + \alpha_{I:p}. \qquad (85)$$

The variance component associated with the π_p effect is the universe score variance, $\sigma^2(p)$, and the variance component associated with the $\alpha_{I:p}$ effect is

$$\sigma^2(I : p) = \sigma^2(i : p)/n_i'.$$

For any single-facet design (crossed or nested),

$$\Delta = X_{pI} - \mu_p \quad \text{and} \quad \delta_{pI} = (X_{pI} - \mathscr{E}_p X_{pI}) - (\mu_p - \mu).$$

For the $p \times I$ design, $\mathscr{E}_p X_{pI} = \mu_I$ (see Equation 75), but, for the $I : p$ design,

$$\mathscr{E}_p X_{pI} = \mu + \mathscr{E}_p \pi_p + \mathscr{E}_p \alpha_{I:p} = \mu.$$

In words, because each person takes a different randomly parallel test, taking the expectation of observed scores over persons involves taking the expectation over all randomly parallel tests. Consequently, for the $I : p$ design,

$$\delta = \Delta = X_{pI} - \mu_p = \alpha_{I:p} \quad \text{and} \qquad (86)$$

$$\sigma^2(\delta) = \sigma^2(\Delta) = \sigma^2(I : p) = \sigma^2(i : p)/n_i'. \qquad (87)$$

Thus, $\sigma^2(\delta)$ and $\sigma^2(\Delta)$ are indistinguishable in the $I : p$ design.

Equations 78 and 79 for $\mathscr{E}\sigma^2(X)$ and $\mathscr{E}\rho^2$, respectively, are general equations that are applicable to any design that has persons as the objects of measurement, including the $I : p$ design.

Crossed G study with nested D study. In a G-study $i : p$ design, the item and residual effects from a G-study $p \times i$ design are combined into one effect, $\alpha_{i:p}$. In terms of variance components, this means that

$$\sigma^2(i : p) = \sigma^2(i) + \sigma^2(pi), \qquad (88)$$

where the variance components to the right of the equality are independently estimable using a $p \times i$ design. Therefore, from a G-study $p \times i$ design, D-study variance components can be estimated for an $I : p$ design. One simply replaces $\hat{\sigma}^2(i : p)$ with $\hat{\sigma}^2(i) + \hat{\sigma}^2(pi)$, wherever $\hat{\sigma}^2(i : p)$ appears. For example, based on Equation 87, $\hat{\sigma}^2(\delta) = \hat{\sigma}^2(\Delta) = [\hat{\sigma}^2(i) + \hat{\sigma}^2(pi)]/n_i'$.

Multifacet, Infinite Universes and Random Models

Here we assume that all facets in both the universe of admissible observations and the universe of generalization are of infinite size, and the population of objects of measurement (usually persons) is infinite. Under these circumstances, the procedures discussed next are applicable for any complete, balanced design. A design is complete when no interactions are assumed to be 0. A design is balanced when there are no missing data and, if nesting is involved, an *equal* number of conditions of one facet are nested within every condition of the other facet.

For purposes of illustration, suppose that (a) the universe of admissible observations has two crossed facets, indexed by i and j; (b) both facets are crossed with persons, indexed by p; and (c) a G study involves random samples of n_i and n_j conditions from the i and j facets, respectively, and a random sample of n_p persons from the population.

G-STUDY CONSIDERATIONS

For such a universe of admissible observations, there are many possible G-study designs, two of which are depicted by Venn diagrams in Figure 3.2. The first design is the completely crossed $p \times i \times j$ design, which has the same structure as the universe of admissible observations. In the second design, $p \times (i : j)$, a different sample of n_i conditions from the i facet is nested within each condition of the j facet.

For G-study purposes, only the $p \times i \times j$ design provides estimates of every one of the variance components in the universe of admissible observations. However, the $p \times (i : j)$ de-

sign might be a practical necessity. For example, if i represents essay items and j represents raters, time constraints might preclude having every rater evaluate the response of every person to every item (the $p \times i \times j$ design). However, it might be possible to have the responses to each item evaluated by a different set of two or more raters [the $p \times (i : j)$ design].

Whichever G-study design is employed, the purpose of a G study is to obtain estimates of the variance components in the universe of admissible observations. These estimates can be used subsequently to estimate results for a universe of generalization and a specific D-study design. The most common procedure currently employed in generalizability theory for estimating variance components is called the *ANOVA procedure*. It involves using observed mean squares as estimates of their expected values. The linear models and random effects EMS equations for the illustrative two-facet designs are provided in Figure 3.2. Several approaches to implementing the ANOVA procedure have been discussed in the literature on generalizability theory.

Cronbach et al. (1972) suggest solving the EMS equations by starting with the least complex expressions and working toward the most complex expressions. Consider, for example, the EMS equations for the $p \times (i : j)$ design in Figure 3.2. First, we solve for an estimator of $\sigma^2(pi : j)$. This is simply MS$(pi : j)$. Then, to solve for an estimator of $\sigma^2(pj)$, note that

$$\text{MS}(pj) = \hat{\sigma}^2(pi : j) + n_i \hat{\sigma}^2(pj) = \text{MS}(pi : j) + n_i \hat{\sigma}^2(pj).$$

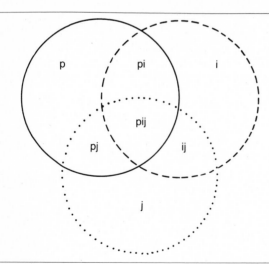

Completely Crossed $p \times i \times j$ Design

Model: $X_{pij} = \mu + \pi_p + \alpha_i + \beta_j + \pi\alpha_{pi} + \pi\beta_{pj} + \alpha\beta_{ij} + \pi\alpha\beta_{pij}$

$$\text{EMS}(p) = \sigma^2(pij) + n_i\sigma^2(pj) + n_j\sigma^2(pi) + n_in_j\sigma^2(p)$$

$$\text{EMS}(i) = \sigma^2(pij) + n_p\sigma^2(ij) + n_j\sigma^2(pi) + n_pn_j\sigma^2(i)$$

$$\text{EMS}(j) = \sigma^2(pij) + n_p\sigma^2(ij) + n_i\sigma^2(pj) + n_pn_i\sigma^2(j)$$

$$\text{EMS}(pi) = \sigma^2(pij) + n_j\sigma^2(pi)$$

$$\text{EMS}(pj) = \sigma^2(pij) + n_i\sigma^2(pj)$$

$$\text{EMS}(ij) = \sigma^2(pij) + n_p\sigma^2(ij)$$

$$\text{EMS}(pij) = \sigma^2(pij)$$

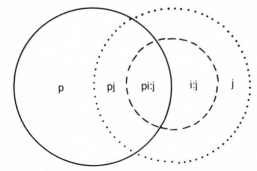

Partly Nested $p \times (i : j)$ Design

Model: $X_{pij} = \mu + \pi_p + \beta_j + \alpha_{i:j} + \pi\beta_{pj} + \pi\alpha_{pi:j}$

$$\text{EMS}(p) = \sigma^2(pi:j) + n_i\sigma^2(pj) + n_in_j\sigma^2(p)$$

$$\text{EMS}(j) = \sigma^2(pi:j) + n_i\sigma^2(pj) + n_p\sigma^2(i:j) + n_pn_i\sigma^2(j)$$

$$\text{EMS}(i:j) = \sigma^2(pi:j) + n_p\sigma^2(i:j)$$

$$\text{EMS}(pj) = \sigma^2(pi:j) + n_i\sigma^2(pj)$$

$$\text{EMS}(pi:j) = \sigma^2(pi:j)$$

FIGURE 3.2 The p × i × j and p × (i:j) designs.

Consequently, $\hat{\sigma}^2(pj) = [\text{MS}(pj) - \text{MS}(pi:j)]/n_i$. This approach is straightforward, provided none of the estimates is negative. If any estimate is negative, Cronbach et al. (1972) suggest setting it to 0 *everywhere* it occurs in the set of EMS equations.

Another approach involves a matrix solution discussed by Searle (1971, pp. 405–406), among others. The matrix solution always gives results identical to those obtained using an algorithm developed by Brennan (1983, p. 41).

All these approaches give the same estimates of variance components, if none of the estimates is negative. When one or more of the estimates is negative, however, the Cronbach et al. (1972) approach usually gives results that are *slightly* different from the matrix solution and Brennan's algorithm.

D-Study Considerations

For any random-effects, multifacet universe and design, equations can be derived for expressing universe score variance, error variances, and generalizability coefficients in terms of variance components. However, the derivations are tedious and a simpler procedure is to use certain rules provided by Brennan (1983, pp. 56–63).

Let $\hat{\sigma}^2(a)$ designate any one of the variance components estimated from a G study, and let τ designate the objects-of-measurement index. Usually $\tau = p$, where p stands for persons (Cardinet, Tourneur, & Allal, 1976, discuss contexts in which some facet other than a person facet plays the role of objects of measurement).

Given these notational conventions, the variance components for a D study employing the same design as the G study, except for possibly different sample sizes, are

$$\sigma^2(\bar{a}) = \sigma^2(a)/d(\bar{a}|\tau) \qquad (89)$$

where $d(\bar{a}|\tau) = \begin{cases} 1 \text{ if } \bar{a} = \tau \text{ and, otherwise, the product} \\ \text{of the D-study samples sizes } (n') \\ \text{for all indexes in } \bar{a} \text{ except } \tau. \end{cases} \quad (90)$

For example, given the variance components for a G-study $p \times i \times j$ design, the first column of Table 3.2 provides the $\sigma^2(\bar{a})$ for a D-study $p \times I \times J$ design. Similarly, the first column of Table 3.3 provides the $\sigma^2(\bar{a})$ for a D-study $p \times (I:J)$ design, in terms of the $\sigma^2(a)$ from a G-study $p \times (i:j)$ design.

Now, given the $\sigma^2(\bar{a})$, universe score variance is simply $\sigma^2(\tau)$,

Rule: $\sigma^2(\Delta)$ is the sum of all $\sigma^2(\bar{a})$ except $\sigma^2(\tau)$,
Rule: $\sigma^2(\delta)$ is the sum of all $\sigma^2(\bar{a})$ such that $\bar{a}$ includes τ and at least one other index.

The application of these rules to the $p \times I \times J$ and $p \times (I:J)$ designs with persons, p, as the objects of measurement is illustrated by the second columns of Tables 3.2 and 3.3.

Given these results, expected observed score variance is

$$\mathscr{E}\sigma^2(X) = \sigma^2(\tau) + \sigma^2(\delta), \qquad (91)$$

and a generalizability coefficient is

$$\mathscr{E}\rho^2 = \sigma^2(\tau)/[\sigma^2(\tau) + \sigma^2(\delta)]. \qquad (92)$$

These rules and equations apply for any random-effects, multifacet design, no matter how many facets are involved, *provided* the G and D studies employ the same type of design. If the G and D studies employ different design structures, an additional step is required. Suppose, for example, that estimated variance components are available for the $p \times i \times j$ design, but the D study will employ the $p \times (I:J)$ design. In this case, it is necessary to obtain the variance components for the partially nested $p \times (i:j)$ design from those for the crossed $p \times i \times j$ design. Variance components for the $p \times (i:j)$ design are $\sigma^2(p)$, $\sigma^2(j)$, $\sigma^2(pj)$, $\sigma^2(i:j)$, and $\sigma^2(pi:j)$. The first three of these variance components are directly available from the $p \times i \times j$ design. The last two are indirectly available, using the following equations:

$$\sigma^2(i:j) = \sigma^2(i) + \sigma^2(ij) \qquad (93)$$

$$\sigma^2(pi:j) = \sigma^2(pi) + \sigma^2(pij). \qquad (94)$$

The variance components to the left of the equal sign in Equations 93 and 94 are for the $p \times (i:j)$ design, and those to the right are for the $p \times i \times j$ design.

Equations 93 and 94 illustrate that a nested effect always involves confounded effects. For any nested effect, the effects that are confounded are represented by all sets of indexes from the nested effect that include the index or indexes before the (first) colon. For example, the effect $i:j$ involves the confounding of the i and ij effects, because these two effects include i, the index before the colon in $i:j$.

Because generalizability theory emphasizes the importance of considering multiple sources of random error, multifacet random designs are a central concern in the theory. Also, from a practical point of view, the differences between generalizability theory and classical theory are perhaps most evident when

TABLE 3.2 Variance Components for the $p \times I \times J$ Design

RANDOM EFFECTS VARIANCE COMPONENTS	VARIANCE COMPONENTS THAT ENTER $\sigma^2(\tau)$, $\sigma^2(\delta)$, AND $\sigma^2(\Delta)^a$		
	I,J RANDOM	J FIXED	I FIXED
$\sigma^2(p)$	τ	τ	τ
$\sigma^2(I) = \sigma^2(i)/n_i'$	Δ	Δ	
$\sigma^2(J) = \sigma^2(j)/n_j'$	Δ		Δ
$\sigma^2(pI) = \sigma^2(i)/n_i'$	Δ,δ	Δ,δ	τ
$\sigma^2(pJ) = \sigma^2(pj)/n_j'$	Δ,δ	τ	Δ,δ
$\sigma^2(IJ) = \sigma^2(ij)/n_i'n_j'$	Δ	Δ	Δ
$\sigma^2(pIJ) = \sigma^2(pij)/n_i'n_j'$	Δ,δ	Δ,δ	Δ,δ

^{a} τ designates universe score.

TABLE 3.3 Variance Components for the $P \times (I:J)$ Design

RANDOM EFFECTS VARIANCE COMPONENTS	VARIANCE COMPONENTS THAT ENTER $\sigma^2(\tau)$, $\sigma^2(\delta)$, AND $\sigma^2(\delta)^a$	
	I,J RANDOM	J FIXED
$\sigma^2(p)$	τ	τ
$\sigma^2(J) = \sigma^2(j)/n_j'$	Δ	
$\sigma^2(I:J) = \sigma^2(i:j)/n_i'n_j'$	Δ	Δ
$\sigma^2(pJ) = \sigma^2(pj)/n_j'$	Δ,δ	τ
$\sigma^2(pI:J) = \sigma^2(pi:j)/n_i'n_j'$	Δ,δ	Δ,δ

^{a} τ designates universe score.

one considers such designs. Two examples of these differences are discussed next.

EXAMPLES

It was noted previously that the Spearman–Brown formula applies in generalizability theory for single-facet random designs. The Spearman–Brown formula does not apply, however, when a design involves *more than one* random facet. Consider, for example, the generalizability coefficient for the random effects $p \times I \times J$ design, with I representing periods of observation and J representing observers who evaluate some aspect of children's behavior during play. The generalizability coefficient for this situation is

$$\mathscr{E}\rho^2 = \frac{\sigma^2(p)}{\sigma^2(p) + \left[\dfrac{\sigma^2(pi)}{n_i'} + \dfrac{\sigma^2(pj)}{n_j'} + \dfrac{\sigma^2(pij)}{n_i'n_j'}\right]}, \quad (95)$$

where the error variance $\sigma^2(\delta)$ is in square brackets. The generalizability coefficient for an observational scheme based on twice the number of periods may be estimated easily by replacing n_i' with $2n_i'$. This does not affect the variance component $\sigma^2(pj)/n_j'$ in the denominator of Equation 95, because this component does not involve sampling periods. In contrast, if one applies the Spearman–Brown formula for a double-length "test" to $\mathscr{E}\rho^2$ [i.e., $2\mathscr{E}\rho^2/(1 + \mathscr{E}\rho^2)$], *all* variance components in $\sigma^2(\delta)$ are halved. Generalizability theory permits the researcher to assess the effect of nonidentical changes in the number of conditions sampled from the several facets. The Spearman–Brown formula does not permit this flexibility.

In classical theory, increasing test length always leads to an increase in reliability. Usually this is true in generalizability theory, too, but not always. Consider the $p \times (I:J)$ random-effects design, where I represents n_i' observational periods nested within each of n_j' raters. A total of $n_i'n_j'$ measures are taken in this design. Under these circumstances,

$$\mathscr{E}\rho^2 = \frac{\sigma^2(p)}{\sigma^2(p) + \left[\dfrac{\sigma^2(pj)}{n_j'} + \dfrac{\sigma^2(pi:j)}{n_i'n_j'}\right]}. \quad (96)$$

Now, suppose that $\hat{\sigma}^2(p) = 1.0$, $\hat{\sigma}^2(pj) = .5$, and $\hat{\sigma}^2(pi:j) = 2.4$. Using these values with $n_j' = 5$ raters and $n_i' = 2$ periods in Equation 96 gives $\mathscr{E}\hat{\rho}^2 = .75$, and with $n_j' = 2$ raters and $n_i' = 6$ periods, $\mathscr{E}\rho^2 = .69$. Thus, with $5 \cdot 2 = 10$ measurements the generalizability coefficient is .75, but with

$2 \cdot 6 = 12$ measurements the generalizability coefficient is .69. Here, then, an increase in the total number of ratings is associated with a *decrease* in generalizability. This decrease occurs principally because $\sigma^2(pj)/n_j'$ increases as n_j' decreases, no matter what changes occur in the total number of measurements taken ($n_i'n_j'$).

Restricted Universes of Generalization and Mixed Models

In the previous section it was assumed that all facets in the universe of generalization were of infinite size. Frequently, however, an investigator wants to consider a restricted universe of generalization—that is, a universe of generalization that is more narrowly defined than the universe of admissible observations. In such a case, the investigator can employ the simplified procedures discussed below or the more general procedures discussed subsequently.

SIMPLIFIED PROCEDURES

Suppose that (a) the G-study variance components have been estimated for a random effects model, and (b) the D-study involves a mixed model in the usual ANOVA sense; that is, at least one facet in the universe of generalization is random, and at least one facet is restricted to the specific, finite set of conditions in the D study. Under these circumstances, Brennan (1983, pp. 20–21) provides a simple set of rules and equations for estimating universe score variance, error variances, generalizability coefficients, and so on.

First, Equation 89 is used to estimate the $\sigma^2(\bar{a})$. (Note that the resulting $\hat{\sigma}^2(\bar{a})$ are *not* estimates of the variance components for the *restricted* universe of generalization. Rather, given the assumptions of this section, the $\hat{\sigma}^2(\bar{a})$ are simply intermediate statistics employed in estimating universe score variance, error variances, etc. *Second,* let S be the set of facets in the universe of generalization that are assumed to have an *infinite* number of conditions. Then,

Rule: $\hat{\sigma}^2(\tau)$ is the sum of all $\hat{\sigma}^2(\bar{a})$ such that $\bar{a}$ includes τ and does *not* include any index in S; (97)

Rule: $\hat{\sigma}^2(\Delta)$ is the sum of all $\hat{\sigma}^2(\bar{a})$ such that $\bar{a}$ includes at least one of the indices in S; (98)

Rule: $\hat{\sigma}^2(\delta)$ is the sum of all $\hat{\sigma}^2(\bar{a})$ such that $\bar{a}$ includes τ and at least one of the indices in S. (99)

Finally, given these rules, Equations 91 and 92 (with parameters replaced by estimates) still apply for estimating $\mathscr{E}\sigma^2(X)$ and $\mathscr{E}\rho^2$, respectively. It is easy to verify that these three rules and equations give identical estimates to those discussed in the section on random models, when S contains all facets in the universe of generalization.

The results of applying these rules with the $p \times I \times J$ and $p \times (I:J)$ designs are provided in Tables 3.2 and 3.3, along with the results for the random model. It is evident from the rules themselves and these illustrations that fixing a facet results in a decrease in error variances and an increase in both universe score variance and generalizability coefficients. However, expected observed score variance is unchanged. What changes is the manner in which expected observed score variance is decomposed into universe score variance and $\sigma^2(\delta)$.

TRADITIONAL ESTIMATES OF RELIABILITY

To illustrate some of the differences between random and mixed-model D studies for different designs, some traditional estimates of reliability are now considered from the perspective of generalizability theory. In classical theory, a coefficient of stability is obtained by correlating scores for a group of persons on two administrations of the same test. In the terminology of generalizability theory this means that (a) data are collected using the $p \times i \times j$ design with $n_j = 2$ occasions, (b) items are a fixed facet, and (c) the generalizability coefficient corresponding to a coefficient of stability for $n_i' = n_i$ items is

$$\mathscr{E}\rho^2 = \frac{\sigma^2(p) + \dfrac{\sigma^2(pi)}{n_i}}{\sigma^2(p) + \dfrac{\sigma^2(pi)}{n_i} + \left[\sigma^2(pj) + \dfrac{\sigma^2(pij)}{n_i}\right]}. \quad (100)$$

Note that $\mathscr{E}\rho^2$ in Equation 100 is for $n_j' = 1$ occasion, even though a coefficient of stability involves collecting data over two occasions. This might seem inconsistent, but it is not. A coefficient of stability is an estimate of reliability for a test having n_i items that is administered on any single occasion. When the variance components in Equation 100 are replaced with estimates, there might be a difference between the resulting estimate of $\mathscr{E}\rho^2$ and the traditional product-moment coefficient of stability. This is attributable to the fact that the denominator for a coefficient of stability is the geometric mean of the observed variances for the two administrations of the n_i-item test, whereas the denominator for $\mathscr{E}\rho^2$ in Equation 100 is the expected observed score variance for scores on the n_i-item test administered on a single, random occasion.

Another traditional estimate of reliability is a coefficient of stability and equivalence. This is obtained by correlating scores for a group of persons on two different test forms, with each form administered on a different occasion. In the terminology of generalizability theory this means that (a) data are collected using the $p \times (i:j)$ design with $n_j = 2$ occasions, (b) both items and occasions are random facets, and (c) the generalizability coefficient corresponding to a coefficient of stability and equivalence for $n_i' = n_i$ items is

$$\mathscr{E}\rho^2 = \frac{\sigma^2(p)}{\sigma^2(p) + \left[\sigma^2(pj) + \dfrac{\sigma^2(pi:j)}{n_i}\right]}. \quad (101)$$

Equations 100 and 101 differ in two respects. *First,* items are fixed in Equation 100, whereas items are random in Equation 101. *Second,* the design is $p \times I \times J$ for Equation 100, whereas the design is $p \times (I:J)$ for Equation 101. The net effect of these two differences is that $\mathscr{E}\rho^2$ in Equation 100 is larger than $\mathscr{E}\rho^2$ in Equation 101. This corresponds to a well-known result in classical theory, namely, that a coefficient of stability can be expected to be larger than a coefficient of stability and equivalence.

Probably the most common estimates of reliability are coefficients of internal consistency such as Cronbach's alpha. As noted previously, alpha corresponds to a generalizability coefficient for a $p \times I$ design. Cronbach's alpha *can* be viewed as positively biased in the sense that it does not take into account variation in persons' scores over time. That is, Cronbach's alpha tends to overestimate reliability if the intended universe of generalization consists of both occasions and randomly parallel tests. From this perspective, occasion of administration is a (hidden) fixed facet when one estimates $\mathscr{E}\rho^2$ using the $p \times I$ design. Thus, Cronbach's alpha can be viewed as a generalizability coefficient for the $p \times I \times J$ design with $n_j' = 1$ *fixed* occasion and $n_i' = n_i$ randomly selected items:

$$\mathscr{E}\rho^2 = \frac{\sigma^2(p) + \sigma^2(pj)}{\sigma^2(p) + \sigma^2(pj) + \left[\dfrac{\sigma^2(pi)}{n_i} + \dfrac{\sigma^2(pij)}{n_i}\right]}. \quad (102)$$

If an investigator wants an estimate of generalizability for a D study using the $p \times I$ design, but she or he wants to generalize over occasions, then the appropriate generalizability coefficient is

$$\mathscr{E}\rho^2 = \frac{\sigma^2(p)}{\sigma^2(p) + \left[\sigma^2(pj) + \dfrac{\sigma^2(pi)}{n_i} + \dfrac{\sigma^2(pij)}{n_i}\right]}. \quad (103)$$

This coefficient is smaller than $\mathscr{E}\rho^2$ in Equation 102. Also, $\mathscr{E}\rho^2$ in Equation 103 equals $\mathscr{E}\rho^2$ in Equation 101. This equality occurs because items and occasions are random for both coefficients, and, with $n_j' = 1$, there is no substantive difference between the $p \times I \times J$ and the $p \times (I:J)$ designs.

RELIABILITY OF GROUP MEANS

Equation 60 provides an estimator of reliability for group means that can be obtained from a formal generalizability analysis. As a simple example, consider the *balanced* $(p:g) \times i$ design in which the number of persons within each group is a constant. This design is formally identical with the $p \times (i:j)$ design, in the sense that p, g, and i in the $(p:g) \times i$ design play the role of i, j, and p, respectively, in the $p \times (i:j)$ design.

Now, consider the D-study $(P:g) \times I$ design with groups, g, as the objects of measurement and assume that (a) $n_p' = n_p$ and persons are a random facet in the universe of generalization, and (b) $n_i' = n_i$ and items are a *fixed* facet in the universe of generalization. Given these assumptions,

$$\mathscr{E}\rho^2 = \frac{\sigma^2(g) + \dfrac{\sigma^2(gi)}{n_i}}{\sigma^2(g) + \dfrac{\sigma^2(gi)}{n_i} + \left[\dfrac{\sigma^2(p:g)}{n_p} + \dfrac{\sigma^2(pi:g)}{n_p n_i}\right]}. \quad (104)$$

When the variance components in this equation are replaced by their mean square estimators, we obtain

$$\mathscr{E}\hat{\rho}^2 = \frac{\text{MS}(g) - \text{MS}(p:g)}{\text{MS}(g)},$$

which can be shown to be identical with Equation 60 for the balanced situation. In short, with an equal number of persons in each group, Equation 60 gives $\mathcal{E}\hat{\rho}^2$ for a $(P{:}g) \times I$ design with items fixed and persons random.

If an investigator wants *both* persons and items as random facets, then, as discussed by Kane and Brennan (1977), the "reliability" of group means is

$$\mathcal{E}\rho^2 = \frac{\sigma^2(g)}{\sigma^2(g) + \left[\dfrac{\sigma^2(gi)}{n_i} + \dfrac{\sigma^2(p{:}g)}{n_p} + \dfrac{\sigma^2(pi{:}g)}{n_p n_i}\right]}$$

for the balanced case. In terms of mean square estimators,

$$\mathcal{E}\hat{\rho}^2 = \frac{MS(g) - MS(p{:}g) - MS(gi) + MS(pi{:}g)}{MS(g)}.$$

This result cannot be expressed solely in terms of the statistics and sample sizes in Equation 60.

GENERAL PROCEDURES

The procedures just discussed for mixed models are very powerful and relatively easy to use. However, they suffer from at least two limitations. *First,* they presume that the G-study variance components are estimated for a random model. Sometimes, however, a universe of admissible observations contains one or more facets that are clearly fixed in a G study. *Second,* these procedures do not always provide estimates of the variance components for the restricted universe of generalization. For example, with items fixed, the variance component for group means in the universe of generalization is the entire numerator of Equation 104, not simply $\sigma^2(g)$. In a sense, therefore, these procedures for mixed models are susceptible to misunderstanding. Brennan (1983, pp. 48–51, 79–81) and Cardinet, Tourneur, and Allal (1981) provide general (although slightly different) procedures for mixed models that avoid these limitations (see also Cardinet & Allal, 1983). These procedures are rather complex, however, and will not be described in detail here. Rather, results from the Brennan procedures are briefly discussed for a specific example.

Suppose that items, i, are nested within a finite number of content categories, j, in a universe of admissible observations. Suppose further that the G study incorporates all content categories, with an equal number of items nested within each cate-

gory. This means that the G-study design is $p \times (i{:}j)$, and the model is mixed, with j fixed. Under these circumstances, Table 3.4 provides definitions of the variance components and the EMS equations that can be used to estimate them. Note that the variance components for this mixed model are denoted $\sigma^2(a|J)$, to distinguish them from the $\sigma^2(a)$ for the random model. The EMS equations in Table 3.4 are those that would be obtained using the well-known Cornfield and Tukey (1956) procedures. Justification for these procedures in the context of generalizability theory is considered in some detail by Brennan (1983, 1984b).

Now, suppose that the universe of generalization includes all the n_j categories and that the D-study design is $p \times (I{:}J)$, with n_i' items nested within each of the n_j categories. Under these circumstances, universe-score variance is $\sigma^2(\tau) = \sigma^2(p|J)$, and the usual error variances are

$$\sigma^2(\delta) = \sigma^2(pi{:}j|J)/n_j n_i' \text{ and} \tag{105}$$

$$\sigma^2(\Delta) = [\sigma^2(i{:}j|J) + \sigma^2(pi{:}j|J)]/n_j n_i'. \tag{106}$$

Using Equation 92 to estimate $\mathcal{E}\rho^2$, we obtain

$$\mathcal{E}\hat{\rho}^2 = \frac{\hat{\sigma}^2(p|J)}{\hat{\sigma}^2(p|J) + \hat{\sigma}^2(pi{:}j|J)/n_j n_i'}. \tag{107}$$

For the same universe of generalization, design, and sample sizes, the simplified procedures discussed previously give

$$\mathcal{E}\hat{\rho}^2 = \frac{\hat{\sigma}^2(p) + \dfrac{\hat{\sigma}^2(pj)}{n_j}}{\hat{\sigma}^2(p) + \dfrac{\hat{\sigma}^2(pj)}{n_j} + \dfrac{\sigma^2(pi{:}j)}{n_j n_i'}}. \tag{108}$$

This estimator is identical to that given by Equation 107, because

$$\hat{\sigma}^2(p|J) = \hat{\sigma}^2(p) + \hat{\sigma}^2(pj)/n_j = [MS(p) - MS(pi{:}j)]/n_i n_j$$

and

$$\hat{\sigma}^2(pi{:}j|J) = \hat{\sigma}^2(pi{:}j) = MS(pi{:}j).$$

Although both estimates give the same result, only Equation 107 is expressed in terms of estimated variance components for the intended, restricted universe of generalization.

TABLE 3.4 Variance Components for the $p \times (i{:}j)$ Design Under the Mixed Model with j Fixed

EFFECT	DEFINITION OF $\sigma^2(a|J)$	EMS EQUATIONS
$p|J$	$\mathcal{E}\pi_p^2$	$\sigma^2(pi{:}j|J) + n_i n_j \sigma^2(p|J)$
$j|J$	$\sum_j \beta_j^2/(n_j - 1)$	$\sigma^2(pi{:}j|J) + n_i \sigma^2(pj|J) + n_p \sigma^2(i{:}j|J) + n_p n_i \sigma^2(j|J)$
$i{:}j|J$	$\sum_j (\mathcal{E}\alpha_{i{:}j}^2)/n_j$	$\sigma^2(pi{:}j|J) + n_p \sigma^2(i{:}j|J)$
$pj|J$	$\sum_j (\mathcal{E}\pi\beta_{pj}^2)/(n_j - 1)$	$\sigma^2(pi{:}j|J) + n_i \sigma^2(pj|J)$
$pi{:}j|J$	$\sum_j (\mathcal{E}\pi\alpha_{pi{:}j}^2)/n_j$	$\sigma^2(pi{:}j|J)$

Multivariate Generalizability Theory

The procedures discussed for mixed models are quite general, but they too have limitations. One is that the error variances in Equations 105 and 106 are *average* error variances over the n_j levels of the j facet. As such, these two equations do not reveal how variable $\sigma^2(\delta)$ and $\sigma^2(\Delta)$ can be for the different levels of the fixed j facet. A second limitation is that neither the simplified nor the general procedures for mixed models are applicable for unbalanced designs in which unequal numbers of levels of a random facet are nested within levels of a fixed facet. Both of these limitations can be precluded by employing multivariate generalizability theory.

In all of the procedures discussed earlier, for each object of measurement there has been a *single* universe score defined over all levels of all facets in a prespecified universe of generalization. In contrast, in multivariate generalizability theory, each object of measurement has as many universe scores as there are levels of a fixed facet (or combinations of levels of two or more fixed facets). Multivariate generalizability theory is succinctly discussed by Cronbach et al. (1972, chaps. 9, 10). Shavelson and Webb (1981) and Webb, Shavelson, and Maddahian (1983) review potential applications and provide illustrative analyses.

Next is an illustration of some aspects of multivariate generalizability theory based upon the $p \times (i:j)$ and $p \times (I:J)$ designs with $n_j = n_j'$ fixed levels of the j facet. The issues discussed are treated more fully by Brennan (1983) and by Jarjoura and Brennan (1981, 1982, 1983) in the context of items nested within categories in a table of test specifications.

With j fixed, the model for the $p \times (i:j)$ design can be viewed as a set of simultaneous linear models for n_j separate $p \times i$ designs. These designs may employ possibly unequal numbers of items, $n_{i:j}$, which are nested within each of the n_j categories. Any one of these n_j equations can be represented as

$$X_{pij} = \mu_j + (\mu_{pj} - \mu_j) + (\mu_{i:j} - \mu_j) + (X_{pij} - \mu_{pj} - \mu_{i:j} + \mu_j). \tag{109}$$

In Equation 109, μ_j is the population and universe mean for level j, $\mu_{i:j}$ is the population mean for item i in category j, and μ_{pj} is the mean score for person p over the universe of items in category j. In terms of score effects, this model equation is

$$X_{pij} = \mu_j + \pi_{pj} + \alpha_{i:j} + \pi\alpha_{pi:j}. \tag{110}$$

The corresponding equations for mean scores over samples of $n_{i:j}'$ items are obtained by replacing i by I everywhere in Equations 109 and 110.

VARIANCE AND COVARIANCE COMPONENTS

When the scores μ_{pj} are based on the expectation over random samples of $n_{i:j}'$ items, they are properly referred to as the universe scores for person p. For each person there are n_j universe scores and, consequently, there are n_j universe score variances and $n_j(n_j - 1)/2$ distinct universe-score covariances. These variances and covariances can be represented as the elements of an $n_j \times n_j$ symmetric matrix Σ_p with a general element of

$$\sigma_{jj'} = \mathscr{E}_p(\mu_{pj} - \mu_j)(\mu_{pj'} - \mu_{j'}) = \mathscr{E}_p \pi_{pj}\pi_{pj'}. \tag{111}$$

When $j = j'$, σ_{jj} is the universe-score variance for category j. When $j \neq j'$, $\sigma_{jj'}$ is the covariance between universe scores for categories j and j'.

There are also n_j variances for the item effects $\alpha_{i:j}$ and n_j variances for the interaction (plus residual) effects $\pi\alpha_{pi:j}$. These variances are

$$\sigma_{i:j}^2 = \mathscr{E}_i \, \alpha_{i:j}^2 \quad \text{and} \quad \sigma_{pi:j}^2 = \mathscr{E}_p\mathscr{E}_i \, \pi\alpha_{pi:j}^2.$$

Note that $\sigma_{i:j}^2$ and $\sigma_{pi:j}^2$ are to be distinguished from $\sigma^2(i:j|J)$ and $\sigma^2(pi:j|J)$. In the former notation, the indexes are used as subscripts to indicate that the variance components are for a particular level of j. In the latter notation the indexes are in parentheses to indicate that the variance components are for averages over the n_j levels of j (see the definitions in Table 3.4). Because different items are associated with each content category, the $\sigma_{i:j}^2$ can be represented as the diagonal elements in an $n_j \times n_j$ diagonal matrix Σ_i. Similarly, the $\sigma_{pi:j}^2$ can be represented as the diagonal elements of an $n_j \times n_j$ diagonal matrix Σ_{pi}.

An unbiased estimator of the j-th diagonal element of Σ_p, Σ_i, or Σ_{pi} is simply $\hat{\sigma}^2(p)$, $\hat{\sigma}^2(i)$, or $\hat{\sigma}^2(pi)$, respectively, for the $p \times i$ design associated with category j. Unbiased estimators of the universe-score covariances $\sigma_{jj'}$ (off-diagonal elements of Σ_p) are simply the covariances between persons' observed mean scores for all pairs of categories.

COMPOSITE UNIVERSE-SCORE VARIANCE AND ERROR VARIANCES

In some applications of multivariate generalizability theory, an investigator is interested in not only the elements of the matrices Σ_p, Σ_i, and Σ_{pi} but also some function(s) of these elements. For example, if the levels of j represent categories in a table of specifications or tests in a battery, then frequently interest focuses on composite universe scores:

$$\mu_{pJ} = \sum_j w_j \mu_{pj}, \tag{112}$$

where the w_j are some set of proportional weights such that $w_j \geq 0$ for all j and $\Sigma w_j = 1$. It is assumed here that these weights are specified a priori by an investigator, based on a judgment about the relative importance of the various levels of j for some type of decision. The variance of these composite universe scores is

$$\sigma^2(p|J) = \sum_j \sum_{j'} w_j w_{j'} \sigma_{jj'}, \tag{113}$$

where both j amd j' range from 1 to n_j. This is simply a weighted sum of the elements in Σ_p.

A simple unbiased estimator of μ_{pJ} is

$$\hat{\mu}_{pJ} = \sum_j w_j X_{pIj} = \sum_j \frac{w_j}{n_{i:j}'} \sum_i X_{pij}. \tag{114}$$

Given this estimator, the variance for $\Delta \equiv \hat{\mu}_{pJ} - \mu_{pJ}$ is

$$\sigma^2(\Delta) = \sum_j \frac{w_j^2}{n_{i:j}'} (\sigma_{i:j}^2 + \sigma_{pi:j}^2), \tag{115}$$

and the variance for δ is

$$\sigma^2(\delta) = \sum_j \frac{w_j^2}{n_{i:j}'} \sigma_{pi:j}^2. \tag{116}$$

MULTIVARIATE GENERALIZABILITY COEFFICIENTS

A multivariate analogue of a generalizability coefficient can be defined as the ratio of composite universe-score variance to the expected variance of composite observed scores. Applying this definition to the multivariate design considered here gives

$$\mathscr{E}\rho^2 = \frac{\sum_j \sum_{j'} w_j w_{j'} \sigma_{jj'}}{\sum_j \sum_{j'} w_j w_{j'} \sigma_{jj'} + \sum_j w_j^2 \sigma_{pi:j}^2/n_{i:j}'}, \tag{117}$$

where the numerator is $\sigma^2(p|J)$ in Equation 113 and the second term in the denominator is $\sigma^2(\delta)$ in Equation 116. For a balanced design ($n_{i:j}'$ the same value for each category) with equal weighting of categories ($w_j = 1/n_j$ for all j), the estimate of $\mathscr{E}\rho^2$ using Equation 117 is identical with that provided by Equation 107.

Some of the coefficients discussed in the context of classical theory can be viewed as special cases of Equation 117. For example, when $n_{i:j}' = n_{i:j}$ and $w_j = n_{i:j}/\Sigma n_{i:j}$ for all j, Equation 117 gives stratified coefficient alpha in Equation 28. One reason that Equation 28 can be viewed as a special case of Equation 117 is that the universe of generalization for Equation 117 has only one random facet. For multivariate designs with two or more random facets, a multivariate generalizability coefficient would not correspond with a classical reliability coefficient.

OTHER WEIGHTING SCHEMES

Note that $\mathscr{E}\rho^2$ in Equation 117 is defined in terms of weights, w_i, that are defined a priori by an investigator. For example, the w_i weights might be based on an a priori judgment about the relative importance of each category. In contrast, Joe and Woodward (1976) discussed a procedure for choosing weights that maximize the value of an estimated generalizability coefficient. In effect, the Joe and Woodward approach provides a set of a posteriori weights based on statistical characteristics of a particular set of data. Such weights might have little bearing on the relative importance of the categories from a judgmental perspective.

The w_j weights used previously are essentially *nominal* as opposed to *effective* weights (see Wang & Stanley, 1970). An effective weight is the covariance between a weighted variable and a composite. For the illustration considered earlier, the effective weight for category j is

$$v_j = \sigma(w_j\mu_{pj}, \sum_{j'} w_{j'}\mu_{pj'}) = w_j \sum_{j'} w_{j'}\sigma_{jj'}.$$

Because $\Sigma v_j = \sigma^2(p|J)$, v_j can be viewed as the contribution of category j to composite universe-score variance.

A COMMENT

In their review of generalizability theory, Shavelson and Webb (1981) suggested that generalizability theory can be (and

perhaps should be) viewed as an essentially random-effects theory. From some perspectives, such a statement might seem a gross exaggeration. After all, Cronbach et al. (1972), Brennan (1983), and other writers in the field have devoted considerable attention to mixed models with one or more fixed facets. However, as illustrated above, a univariate analysis with a mixed model can be formulated as a multivariate analysis in which a random model is assumed for each level of one or more fixed facets. The univariate analysis can be viewed as a special case of the multivariate approach. From this perspective, it is meaningful to say that generalizability theory is essentially a random-effects theory. This perspective on mixed models is not unique to generalizability theory. It corresponds closely, for example, to Scheffé's (1959) treatment of mixed models in the context of design and analysis of experiments.

Other Issues

Generalizability theory is sometimes viewed as simply a liberalization of classical reliability theory. However, generalizability theory also blurs many of the distinctions between reliability and validity. For example, Kane (1982) systematically treats a number of validity issues while staying within the framework of generalizability theory.

From a more general perspective, Cronbach states that generalizability theory, or G theory,

> has a protean quality. The procedures and even the issues take a new form in every context. G theory enables you to ask your questions better; what is most significant for you cannot be supplied from the outside. (1976, p. 199)

This protean quality of generalizability theory is largely attributable to its capability of treating multifaceted universes of generalization, different error variances, and multiple universe scores. The power of generalizability theory is purchased, however, at the price of certain computational and statistical complexities (see Brennan 1984b).

One complexity is that many computer programs for analysis of variance are of little help in generalizability analyses. Such programs frequently have core storage requirements that are dependent on the number of cells in the design. In generalizability analyses, this number is often prohibitively large. Also, very few analysis of variance programs provide estimated variance components. However, for univariate generalizability analyses with balanced designs, BMDP8V (Dixon & Brown, 1979) and GENOVA (Crick & Brennan, 1983) are quite useful. GENOVA was developed specifically for generalizability analyses and provides estimates of virtually all the parameters discussed in this chapter.

Also, although variance components are positive by definition, the ANOVA procedure for estimating them can lead to one or more negative estimates. Such estimates are usually replaced by 0. In general, the occurrence of a negative estimate is attributable to a problem with model fit or sampling error. Either problem should alert the investigator to exercise caution in interpreting results. In principle, one can preclude the possibility of obtaining negative estimates by using Bayesian procedures (e.g., Box & Tiao, 1973), but they are quite complicated and require additional assumptions.

VARIABILITY OF ESTIMATED VARIANCE COMPONENTS

Because the estimation and interpretation of variance components are critical to generalizability theory, the sampling error in these estimates is an important issue. Procedures for examining the variability of estimated variance components have been surveyed by Cronbach et al. (1972, pp. 49–57). More recently, Smith (1978, 1982) and Brennan (1983) have addressed this issue.

The estimated variance components from the ANOVA procedure are linear combinations of independent mean squares. In this case, Searle (1971, pp. 415–417) shows that, under the assumptions that score effects have a multivariate normal distribution, an estimator of the standard error of an estimated variance component is

$$\hat{\sigma}[\hat{\sigma}^2(a|M)] = \sqrt{\sum_j \frac{2(f_j \text{MS}_j)^2}{df_j + 2}}. \qquad (118)$$

Here, M designates the specific model under consideration, j indexes the mean squares that enter $\hat{\sigma}^2(a|M)$, and f_j is the coefficient of MS_j in the linear combination of the MS_j that gives $\hat{\sigma}^2(a|M)$. The square of $\hat{\sigma}[\hat{\sigma}^2(a|M)]$ is an unbiased estimator of the variance of $\hat{\sigma}^2(a|M)$. (These standard errors are provided by GENOVA but not by BMDP8V.)

The form of Equation 118 indicates that the standard error of $\hat{\sigma}^2(a|M)$ usually decreases as the degrees of freedom for the component a increase. Also, for estimated variance components involving several mean squares, the estimated standard errors are likely to be larger than for estimated variance components involving fewer mean squares.

With few exceptions (see Searle, 1971, p. 414), formulas for exact confidence intervals for variance components are unavailable. However, under the assumption of multivariate normality, one procedure for obtaining *approximate* confidence intervals was developed by Satterthwaite (1941, 1946), examined by Boardman (1974), and summarized by Graybill (1976, pp. 642–643). Brennan (1983, p.137) demonstrates that Satterthwaite's procedure can be employed using the ratio of an estimated variance component to its estimated standard error:

$$r = \hat{\sigma}^2(a|M)/\hat{\sigma}[\hat{\sigma}^2(a|M)]. \qquad (119)$$

Specifically, given r, Brennan (1983, pp. 138–140) provides a simple table lookup procedure for obtaining 66.67%, 75%, 80%, 90%, and 95% confidence intervals for variance components. Technically, when this procedure is used, the quantity $df_j + 2$ in Equation 118 should be replaced by df_j in computing the estimated standard error in the denominator of r in Equation 119. However, this change usually makes very little difference in the resulting confidence interval, unless degrees of freedom are very small.

POINT ESTIMATES OF UNIVERSE SCORES

The most frequently employed point estimate of a person's universe score is the observed mean score. However, Cronbach et al. (1972) discuss extensions of Kelley's (1947) regressed score estimates to generalizability theory. Also, Jarjoura (1983) has applied the work of Searle (1974) on "best" linear prediction functions to generalizability theory.

For any design, the regression equation for estimating universe scores can be represented as

$$\hat{\mu}_p = \mu + \rho^2(\overline{X}_p - \mathscr{E}_p \overline{X}_p), \qquad (120)$$

where ρ^2 is the squared correlation between observed and universe scores for the population.

For example, for the $p \times I$ design, $\mathscr{E}_p \overline{X}_p = \mu_I$, the regression equation is

$$\hat{\mu}_p = \mu + \rho^2(\overline{X}_p - \mu_I), \qquad (121)$$

and use of Equation 121 requires estimates of μ, μ_I, and ρ^2. Cronbach et al. (1972) suggest that μ can be estimated from the G study, the D study, or both. Ideally, they want both μ_I and ρ^2 to be estimated for the fixed set of items in a particular D study. In practice, however, use of Equation 121 often requires making one or more of the classical test theory assumptions of equal means, equal variances, and equal correlations of observed and universe scores. When all of these assumptions are made, there is no substantive difference between using Equation 121 or its classical counterpart (see Equation 42). When the classical assumptions are relaxed, however, regressed score estimates have properties that are difficult to ascertain (see Cronbach et al., 1972, pp. 138 ff.).

The prediction functions suggested by Jarjoura (1983) have some similarities with regressed score estimates. However, neither the derivation nor the estimation of his prediction functions necessitates the assumption of classically parallel tests.

For the $p \times I$ design, the best linear prediction function is

$$\hat{\mu}_p = \mu + A(\overline{X} - \mu) + B(\overline{X}_p - \overline{X}). \qquad (122)$$

Here, $\overline{X}_p$ and $\overline{X}$ are for a *particular* test form,

$$A = \frac{\sigma^2(p)/n'_p}{\sigma^2(p)/n'_p + \sigma^2(i)/n'_i + \sigma^2(pi)/n'_p n'_i}, \quad \text{and}$$

$$B = \frac{\sigma^2(p)}{\sigma^2(p) + \sigma^2(pi)/n'_i}.$$

Note that the regression equation 121 has no term corresponding to the second term in the prediction function 122. Furthermore, Cronbach et al. (1972) want ρ^2 in the regression equation to be dependent upon the particular form of a test used in a D study. In contrast, the parameters A and B in the best linear prediction function are for all randomly parallel forms of a test with a constant number of items, n'_i. In practice, to use the prediction function, one must estimate μ and the variance components $\sigma^2(p)$, $\sigma^2(i)$, and $\sigma^2(pi)$. Jarjoura (1983) suggested that estimates of these parameters be based on multiple test forms.

For simplicity, this discussion of regressed score estimates and best linear prediction functions has been restricted to the $p \times I$ design. However, these approaches to obtaining point estimates of universe scores have been extended by Cronbach et al. (1972) and Jarjoura (1983), respectively, to more complicated univariate and multivariate designs. Indeed, the conjunction of multivariate generalizability theory and regressed score estimates of universe scores (i.e., the estimation of universe score profiles) is viewed by Cronbach (1976) as "The most original feature of generalizability theory" (see also Bock, 1972).

UNBALANCED DESIGNS

One statistical issue that can involve considerable complexity in generalizability theory is the intended or unintended occurrence of an unbalanced design. Searle (1971) provides a review of statistical literature treating the estimation of variance components with unbalanced designs. Brennan (1984b) examines some aspects of this issue specifically from the perspective of generalizability theory.

If unbalancing is with respect to nesting only, estimation problems are not necessarily severe. For example, when unbalancing occurs in a completely nested random-effects design, analysis of variance procedures for estimating variance components are relatively straightforward (see Searle, 1971, chap. 11). Also, for at least some other unbalanced random-effects designs with a single observation per cell, there exists a straightforward decomposition of the total sums of squares. This leads to relatively simple, unbiased estimators of variance components. Jarjoura and Brennan (1981) illustrate this for the unbalanced $p \times (i{:}h)$ design. Finally, when a design is unbalanced with respect to nesting that occurs within levels of a *fixed* facet, multivariate generalizability theory can be employed without encountering the estimation problems or ambiguities that often arise with unbalanced designs.

Reliability for Criterion-Referenced Interpretations

Glaser (1963) introduced distinctions between what he called *criterion-referenced* and *norm-referenced* measurements. According to Glaser, criterion-referenced measurements "depend on an absolute standard of quality" whereas norm-referenced measurements "depend on a relative standard." It is generally recognized now that the terms criterion-referenced and norm-referenced, as applied to instruments, are somewhat misleading. It is the *interpretation* given to scores, not the instruments themselves, that are criterion-referenced or norm-referenced. Often, in fact, scores can be given both criterion-referenced and norm-referenced interpretations. Also, although distinctions are sometimes drawn among criterion-referenced, domain-referenced, and mastery interpretations of scores, there is no compelling need to make such distinctions here.

A few years after Glaser (1963) drew his distinctions between criterion-referenced and norm-referenced tests, Popham and Husek (1969) argued that classical indexes of reliability are not appropriate for criterion-referenced interpretations. They pointed out that the magnitude of a classical reliability coefficient depends, in part, on variability in persons' true scores. However, suppose all persons have the same true score, a value well above a prespecified cutting score. Might not their observed scores be highly trustworthy (i.e., reliable) indicators of their pass–fail status? Such arguments motivated a considerable amount of research into the development of reliability coefficients for criterion-referenced interpretations.

Some of these coefficients are essentially indexes of reliability for pass–fail status on single items (see, for example, Harris, Pearlman, & Wilcox, 1977). The most frequently discussed coefficients, however, are for "full-length" tests. Several of these are discussed next. Because these coefficients involve a consideration of pass–fail status, they could be viewed as reliability coefficients for dichotomous decisions.

Indexes Based on Squared-Error Loss

Two principal approaches have been pursued in developing such coefficients, one based on *squared-error loss* and the other based on *threshold loss*. The threshold-loss coefficients take into account whether or not persons are consistently classified as being above or below a prespecified cutting score. The squared-error-loss coefficients take into account the squared distance between each person's score and the cutting score. In a sense, therefore, the squared-error-loss coefficients involve both measurement-error variance and the errors of classification taken into account in threshold-loss coefficients.

LIVINGSTON'S COEFFICIENT

The first coefficient that received considerable attention was developed by Livingston (1972). Livingston drew upon the assumptions of classical theory, replacing the concept of variance (expected squared deviation from the mean) with the concept of expected squared deviation from the cutting score. He defined his coefficient as

$$k^2 \equiv \frac{\mathscr{E}_p(T_p - \lambda_+)^2}{\mathscr{E}_p(X_p - \lambda_+)^2} = \frac{\sigma_T^2 + (\mu_+ - \lambda_+)^2}{\sigma_T^2 + (\mu_+ - \lambda_+)^2 + \sigma_E^2}, \quad (123)$$

where μ_+ and λ_+ are the mean and cutting score, respectively, in terms of *number* of items correct. Clearly, k^2 can be positive and high even if σ_T^2 is 0. When $\lambda_+ = \mu_+$, k^2 equals the classical norm-referenced reliability coefficient. Livingston (1972) also showed that the Spearman–Brown formula applies to k^2.

In accordance with the usual convention in classical theory, the parameters in Livingston's coefficient are expressed in the metric of *total* number of items correct. Livingston provides an estimator of k^2 in the same metric. An equivalent estimator of k^2 expressed in the metric of *proportion* of items correct is

$$\hat{k}^2 = 1 - \frac{1}{n_i - 1} \left[\frac{\Sigma \bar{X}_i(1 - \bar{X}_i)/n_i - S^2(\bar{X}_p)}{(\bar{X} - \lambda)^2 + S^2(\bar{X}_p)} \right]. \quad (124)$$

Here, λ is the cutting score in terms of proportion of items correct, $\bar{X}_p$ is a person's mean score over n_i items, $\bar{X}$ is the sample mean over both persons and items, and $S^2(\bar{X}_p) = \Sigma(\bar{X}_p - \bar{X})^2/n_p$. When $\lambda = \bar{X}$, this estimator is identical to KR20.

BRENNAN AND KANE INDEXES OF DEPENDABILITY

Using the assumptions of generalizability theory, Brennan and Kane (1977a,b) derived two coefficients for criterion-referenced interpretations, which they called *indexes of dependability*. These indexes are discussed extensively by Brennan (1984a).

The index $\Phi(\lambda)$. The definition of one of the Brennan and Kane indexes, $\Phi(\lambda)$, is analogous to the definition of Livingston's k^2 coefficient in Equation 123. Specifically, for the $p \times I$ design,

$$\Phi(\lambda) \equiv \frac{\mathscr{E}_p(\mu_p - \lambda)^2}{\mathscr{E}_I \mathscr{E}_p(X_{pI} - \lambda)^2} = \frac{\sigma^2(p) + (\mu - \lambda)^2}{\sigma^2(p) + (\mu - \lambda)^2 + \sigma^2(\Delta)}. \quad (125)$$

The parameters in Equation 125 are for proportion of items correct. Otherwise, however, the principal difference between k^2 and $\Phi(\lambda)$ is in the error variances incorporated in each. For k^2, the error variance is σ_E^2, which is analogous to $\sigma^2(\delta)$ in generalizability theory. For $\Phi(\lambda)$, the error variance is $\sigma^2(\Delta)$. Because $\sigma^2(\delta) \leq \sigma^2(\Delta)$, it follows that $k^2 \geq \Phi(\lambda)$.

Estimation of $\Phi(\lambda)$ involves replacing variance components with their estimates. However, an unbiased estimator of $(\mu - \lambda)^2$ is *not* obtained by simply replacing μ with $\bar{X}$, the sample mean over persons and items. Rather, an unbiased estimator of $(\mu - \lambda)^2$ is $(\bar{X} - \lambda)^2 - \hat{\sigma}^2(\bar{X})$, where $\hat{\sigma}^2(\bar{X})$ is the estimated variability involved in using $\bar{X}$ as an estimator of μ. For the $p \times I$ design,

$$\hat{\sigma}^2(\bar{X}) = \hat{\sigma}^2(p)/n'_p + \hat{\sigma}^2(i)/n'_i + \hat{\sigma}^2(pi)/n'_p n'_i.$$

When items are scored dichotomously, the design is $p \times I$, and the G- and D-study sample sizes for items are equal, it can be shown that

$$\hat{\Phi}(\lambda) = 1 - \frac{1}{n_i - 1}\left[\frac{\bar{X}(1 - \bar{X}) - S^2(\bar{X}_p)}{(\bar{X} - \lambda)^2 + S^2(\bar{X}_p)}\right]. \quad (126)$$

The form of Equation 126 is like that of the estimator of Livingston's k^2 coefficient in Equation 124. The only difference between Estimators 124 and 126 is that $\Sigma \bar{X}_i(1 - \bar{X}_i)/n_i$ in Estimator 124 is replaced by $\bar{X}(1 - \bar{X})$ in Estimator 126. Recall that the estimator of k^2 in Equation 124 equals KR20 when $\lambda = \bar{X}$. Analogously, when $\lambda = \bar{X}$, Estimator 126 equals KR21. In other words, for dichotomously scored items, KR20 and KR21 can be viewed as lower limits *of the estimators* of k^2 and $\Phi(\lambda)$, respectively.

The index Φ. From Equation 125 it is clear that $\Phi(\lambda)$ achieves its lower limit when λ equals μ. That is, the lower limit of $\Phi(\lambda)$ is simply

$$\Phi = \frac{\sigma^2(p)}{\sigma^2(p) + \sigma^2(\Delta)}. \quad (127)$$

Because $\sigma^2(\Delta)$ is always at least as large as $\sigma^2(\delta)$, the index Φ must be less than or equal to the generalizability coefficient $\mathscr{E}\rho^2$ in Equation 79. Intuitively, this is a reasonable characteristic of Φ, because criterion-referenced interpretations of "absolute" scores are more stringent than norm-referenced interpretations of "relative" scores. The index Φ was suggested by Brennan and Kane (1977b) as a general-purpose index of dependability for criterion-referenced interpretations. As discussed next, Φ can also be interpreted as a chance-corrected index of dependability for criterion-referenced interpretations with squared-error loss.

Interpretations in Terms of Agreement Coefficients. Kane and Brennan (1980) provided a framework for interpreting $\Phi(\lambda)$ and Φ and for considering similarities and differences between these indexes and the threshold-loss indexes discussed later. This framework involves two general agreement coefficients, one of which incorporates a correction for chance agreement:

$$\theta \equiv A/A_m \quad \text{and} \quad (128)$$

$$\theta_c \equiv (A - A_c)/(A_m - A_c), \quad (129)$$

where A is expected agreement, A_m is maximum agreement, and A_c is chance agreement.

The specific definitions of A, A_m, and A_c are

$$A \equiv \mathscr{E}_I \mathscr{E}_J \mathscr{E}_p a(X_{pI}, X_{pJ}),$$
$$A_m \equiv \mathscr{E}_I \mathscr{E}_p a(X_{pI}, X_{pI}), \quad \text{and}$$
$$A_c \equiv \mathscr{E}_I \mathscr{E}_J \mathscr{E}_p \mathscr{E}_q a(X_{pI}, X_{qJ}),$$

where $a(X_{pI}, X_{qJ})$ is some agreement function for the scores of persons p and q on randomly parallel tests I and J. For criterion-referenced interpretations with squared-error loss

$$a(X_{pI}, X_{qJ}) = (X_{pI} - \lambda)(X_{qJ} - \lambda). \quad (130)$$

When this agreement function is used in the previous definitions, Kane and Brennan show that $\theta = \Phi(\lambda)$ and $\theta_c = \Phi$.

It follows that $\Phi(\lambda)$ indicates how closely scores of the form $X_{pI} - \lambda$ can be expected to agree on randomly parallel instances of a testing procedure. In contrast, Φ indicates how closely such scores can be expected to agree when the contribution of chance agreement is removed. The index $\Phi(\lambda)$, therefore, characterizes the dependability of decisions based on the testing procedure, whereas the index Φ characterizes the *contribution* of the testing procedure to the dependability of such decisions.

Indexes Based on Threshold Loss

Two general threshold-loss indexes have been proposed in the literature. The first is

$$p \equiv \begin{cases} \text{proportion of persons consistently} \\ \text{classified as masters or nonmasters} \\ \text{on two "equivalent" forms of a test.} \end{cases} \quad (131)$$

The second is Cohen's (1960) coefficient κ (kappa):

$$\kappa \equiv \frac{p - p_c}{1 - p_c}, \quad (132)$$

where p_c is the proportion of consistent classifications that would be expected by chance.

These indexes are referred to as threshold-loss indexes because all misclassifications or, equivalently, all inconsistent classifications are assumed to be equally serious. For example, consider two persons with the following differences between their scores and the cutting score:

Person a: 1 on the first form and -1 on the second form
Person b: 5 on the first form and -3 on the second form

The inconsistent classifications for person b might appear to be more serious, but both cases exert the same influence on lowering the values of p and κ.

Kane and Brennan (1980) show that θ and θ_c in Equations 128 and 129 are identical to p and κ, respectively, for randomly (or classically) parallel tests, when the agreement function is

$$a(X_{pI}, X_{qJ}) = \begin{cases} 1 & \text{if } X_{pI} - \lambda \geq 0 \text{ and } X_{qJ} - \lambda \geq 0, \\ & \text{or } X_{pI} - \lambda < 0 \text{ and } X_{qJ} - \lambda < 0; \\ 0 & \text{otherwise.} \end{cases} \quad (133)$$

Hence, the interpretation of p and κ parallels that of $\Phi(\lambda)$ and Φ, respectively. The difference between the two pairs of indexes is attributable to the difference between the agreement functions in Equations 130 and 133.

Hambleton and Novick (1973) and Swaminathan, Hambleton, and Algina (1974) were the first to propose using p and κ. Assuming the availability of two forms, their estimation procedures are direct applications of the definitions in Equations 131 and 132. Suppose that two forms of a test, X and Y, are administered to a group of persons and, based on some prespecified cutting score, each person is classified as a master or nonmaster on each form. Let p_{00} and p_{11} be the proportions of persons consistently classified on the two forms as nonmasters and masters, respectively. Also, let $p_{0\cdot}$ and $p_{1\cdot}$ be the marginal proportions of failing and passing persons, respectively, on form X. Similarly, $p_{\cdot0}$ and $p_{\cdot1}$ are the marginal proportions on form Y. Given these proportions, $p = p_{00} + p_{11}$, $p_c = p_{0\cdot}.p_{\cdot0} + p_{1\cdot}.p_{\cdot1}$, and κ is obtained using Equation 132.

One problem with this approach to estimating p and κ is that data must be available on *two* forms of a test. Consequently, much of the literature on threshold-loss indexes has focused on estimating p and κ from a single administration of a single form. Subkoviak (1984) provides an extensive review of such estimators. Here we provide only an overview.

HUYNH'S METHOD

Huynh (1976) proposed estimating p and κ using beta-binomial model assumptions (Keats & Lord, 1962) for an available form and a hypothetical second form. Specifically, Huynh's method assumes that each person's observed scores are distributed binomially, the true scores for a population of persons are distributed according to the beta distribution, and persons' observed scores on a form are distributed according to the beta-binomial (negative hypergeometric) distribution (see also Gross & Shulman, 1980).

Let $f(X, Y)$ be the bivariate distribution of *total* scores on two tests X and Y of length n_i. For the sake of specificity, we can think of X as the test for which scores are actually available and of Y as the hypothetical test. Given the beta-binomial model assumptions used by Huynh, this density is symmetric in the sense that $f(X, Y) = f(Y, X)$. Consequently, the marginal proportions are symmetric, that is $p_{1\cdot} = p_{\cdot1} = p_1$ and $p_{0\cdot} = p_{\cdot0} = p_0$. Under these circumstances, it can be shown that

$$p = 1 + 2(p_{00} - p_0) \quad \text{and} \quad \kappa = (p_{00} - p_0^2)/(p_0 - p_0^2).$$

Thus, to estimate p and κ for a cutting score of λ_+ items correct, one needs estimates of

$$p_{00} = \sum_{X,\,Y=0}^{\lambda_+ - 1} f(X, Y) \quad \text{and} \quad p_0 = \sum_{X=0}^{\lambda_+ - 1} \sum_{Y=0}^{n_i} f(X, Y).$$

The crux of the matter is to estimate $f(X, Y)$ for $X, Y = 0, \ldots, n_i$. Huynh provides a set of recursive equations for doing so.

These recursive equations are tedious to use, however, even when a test is relatively short. Consequently, Huynh (1976) proposed an approximation that employs an arcsine transformation of the proportion of items correct, X/n_i, and assumes that the joint distribution of scores on the two forms is approximately bivariate normal. Peng and Subkoviak (1980) suggest, however, that the added complexity of using the arcsine transformation seldom improves the resulting estimates of p and κ.

Let the normal deviate corresponding to the cutting score λ_+ be $z = [(\lambda_+ - .5) - \bar{X}_+]/S(X_p)$, where $\bar{X}_+$ and $S(X_p)$ are the mean and standard deviation, respectively, for persons' observed total scores. For the Peng–Subkoviak approximation, $\hat{p}_0$ is taken as the probability that a standard normal variable is less than z, and $\hat{p}_{00}$ is taken as the probability that two standard normal variables with a correlation equal to KR21 are both less than z. This latter probability can be obtained by using rather extensive tables provided by Brennan (1981, pp. 92–94) and Gupta (1963), or abbreviated tables provided by Huynh (1976) and Subkoviak (1984).

SUBKOVIAK'S METHOD

An estimation procedure developed by Subkoviak (1976) assumes that a person's observed scores are independent and distributed binomially with parameters n_i and ζ, where ζ is the person's proportion-correct true score. Under these assumptions, the probability that a person will be declared a master, $P_X = \text{Prob}(X \geq \lambda_+)$, can be estimated by using tables for the binomial probability distribution, provided one has an estimate of ζ. Subkoviak discusses several estimators of ζ, but he emphasizes the regressed score estimator $\hat{\zeta} = \hat{\rho}_{XX}(X/n_i) + (1 - \hat{\rho}_{XX})\bar{X}$, where $\bar{X}$ is the observed grand mean over both persons and items. Initially, Subkoviak (1976) used $\hat{\rho}_{XX} = \text{KR21}$ in this estimator, but subsequently he has suggested using $\hat{\rho}_{XX} = \text{KR20}$ (see Subkoviak, 1984).

In Subkoviak's method, P_X is the probability that a person with a score of X will be classified as a master on a single testing. Therefore, P_X^2 is the probability that the person will be classified as a master on two independent testings, $(1 - P_X)^2$ is the probability that the person will be declared a nonmaster on two independent testings, and $P_X^2 + (1 - P_X)^2 = 1 - 2(P_X - P_X^2)$ is the probability of a consistent classification for the person.

Letting $f(X)$ be the density of X, this development leads to the following estimators of p and p_c:

$$\hat{p} = \sum_{X=0}^{n_i} f(X)[1 - 2(\hat{P}_X - \hat{P}_X^2)] = 1 - 2\Sigma f(X)[\hat{P}_X - \hat{P}_X^2].$$

and

$$\hat{p}_c = 1 - 2\{\Sigma f(X)\hat{P}_X - [\Sigma f(X)\hat{P}_X]^2\}.$$

These estimators can be used to estimate kappa in Equation 132.

Other Issues

Virtually all of the coefficients or indexes that have been proposed for criterion-referenced interpretations employ either threshold-loss or squared-error loss. Arguments can be made in defense of both loss functions, but Brennan (1984a), Livingston and Wingersky (1979), and Novick and Lindley (1978), all noted that other loss or utility functions might be more realistic in some circumstances. Unfortunately, however, use of other loss functions involves considerable complexity.

If squared-error loss is judged appropriate, the indexes $\Phi(\lambda)$ and Φ are applicable to *any* design that might be employed in generalizability theory. They are not restricted to the simple persons-crossed-with-items design. Also, Raju (1982) has extended $\Phi(\lambda)$ to composites whose parts have different cutting scores. Furthermore, Brennan and Lockwood (1980) and Kane and Wilson (1984) have extended $\Phi(\lambda)$ to incorporate error variance attributable to the procedure used in establishing a cutting score.

One criticism sometimes voiced about all of the indexes discussed is that they are based on test performance for a *group* of persons (see, for example, Divgi, 1980). Strictly speaking, of course, a criterion-referenced interpretation for a person should be independent of the scores for any other person. However, there is no inherent contradiction in considering one or more group-based coefficients and some estimate of error variance or probability of misclassification for an individual or a group of persons with a particular observed score. Such error variances have been considered in a former section of this chapter, and several researchers have reported procedures for estimating probabilities of misclassification (e.g., Brennan, 1981; Wilcox, 1977).

Concluding Comments

More than one critic has observed that test theorists and researchers seem to devote an inordinate amount of attention to the reliability of measures, as compared with validity. A superficial survey of measurement journals and test manuals might support this criticism. Certainly the publication space accorded to reliability fails to reflect the widely accepted principle that the validity of a measure is a more crucial and comprehensive characteristic.

If there is some basis for the complaint, there is also an explanation. As this chapter clearly illustrates, the basic issues of reliability lend themselves to mathematical representation and treatment. Reasonable assumptions and deductions about error can be stated in mathematical terms. In any field where mathematical tools can be applied to the essential ideas, a large number of players with mathematical ingenuity will probably be attracted to the game. Its "purity," rigor, and richness are appealing, and the published literature reflects this.

A second part of the explanation lies in the fact that investigation of reliability is possible on the basis of test data alone. No data external to the measure itself are essential. This is rarely the case with research on validity. Though reliability might be of secondary importance in test research, there are fewer administrative problems related to its study.

A final consideration is the greater importance of subjective judgment in the study of validity. As the chapter on *validity* convincingly shows, there is no escaping the strong dependence on judgment when validity is assessed. Questions about the adequacy of criteria, the defensibility of definitions of human traits, the appropriateness of test content, the clarity of the boundaries of behavioral domains, and the implications of data for all of these matters inevitably involve the exercise of judgment. A game played by subjective, rather than mathe-

matical, rules may be harder to play well, more prone to professional controversy, and attract fewer players.

It is hoped that the length and concentrated focus of this chapter do not contribute to the impression of exaggerated concern for reliability. The authors readily acknowledge the primacy of validity in the evaluation of the adequacy of an educational measure. No body of reliability data, regardless of the elegance of the methods used to analyze it, is worth very much if the measure to which it applies is irrelevant or redundant.

REFERENCES

American Educational Research Association, American Psychological Association, & National Council on Measurement in Education. (1985). *Standards for educational and psychological testing.* Washington, DC: American Psychological Association.

Angoff, W. H. (1953). Test reliability and effective test length. *Psychometrika, 18,* 1–14.

Angoff, W. H. (1971). Scales, norms, and equivalent scores. In R. L. Thorndike (Ed.), *Educational Measurement* (2nd ed., pp. 508–600), Washington, DC: American Council on Education.

Bay, K. S. (1973). The effect of non-normality on the sampling distribution and standard error of reliability coefficient estimates under an analysis of variance model. *British Journal of Mathematical and Statistical Psychology, 26,* 45–47.

Bentler, P. M. (1983). Some contributions to efficient statistics in structural models: Specification and estimation of moment structures. *Psychometrika, 48,* 493–517.

Bentler, P. M. (1985). Theory and implementation of EQS: A structural equations program. Los Angeles: BMDP Statistical Software.

Blixt, S. L., & Shama, D. B. (1986). An empirical investigation of the standard error of measurement at different ability levels. *Educational and Psychological Measurement, 46,* 545–550.

Boardman, T. J. (1974). Confidence intervals for variance components: A comparative Monte Carlo study. *Biometrics, 30,* 251–262.

Bock, R. D. (1972). [Review of *The dependability of behavioral measurements*]. *Science, 178,* 1275–1275A.

Box, G. E. P., & Tiao, G. C. (1973). *Bayesian inference in statistical analysis.* Reading, MA: Addison-Wesley.

Brandenburg, D. C., & Forsyth, R. A. (1974). Approximating standardized achievement test norms with a theoretical model. *Educational and Psychological Measurement, 34,* 3–9.

Brennan, R. L. (1981). *Some statistical procedures for domain-referenced testing: A handbook for practitioners* (ACT Technical Bulletin No. 38). Iowa City, IA: American College Testing Program.

Brennan, R. L. (1983). *Elements of generalizability theory.* Iowa City, IA: American College Testing Program.

Brennan, R. L. (1984a). Estimating the dependability of the scores. In R. A. Berk (Ed.), *A guide to criterion-referenced test construction* (pp. 292–334). Baltimore: Johns Hopkins University Press.

Brennan, R. L. (1984b). *Some statistical issues in generalizability theory* (ACT Technical Bulletin No. 46). Iowa City, IA: American College Testing Program.

Brennan, R. L., & Kane, M. T. (1977a). An index of dependability for mastery tests. *Journal of Educational Measurement, 14,* 277–289.

Brennan, R. L., & Kane, M. T. (1977b). Signal/noise ratios for domain-referenced tests. *Psychometrika, 42,* 609–625.

Brennan, R. L., & Kane, M. T. (1979). Generalizability theory: A review. In R. E. Traub (Ed.), *New directions for testing and measurement: Methodological developments* (No. 4, pp. 33–51). San Francisco: Jossey-Bass.

Brennan, R. L., & Lockwood, R. E. (1980). A comparison of the Nedelsky and Angoff cutting score procedures using generalizability theory. *Applied Psychological Measurement, 4,* 219–240.

Brown, W. (1910). Some experimental results in the correlation of mental abilities. *British Journal of Psychology, 3,* 296–322.

Burt, C. (1936). The analysis of examination marks. In P. Hartog & E. C. Rhodes (Eds.), *The marks of examiners* (pp. 245–314). London: Macmillan.

Burt, C. (1955). Test reliability estimated by analysis of variance. *British Journal of Statistical Psychology, 8*, 103–118.

Callender, J. C., & Osburn, H. G. (1977a). A computer program for maximizing and cross-validating split-half reliability coefficients. *Educational and Psychological Measurement, 37*, 787–789.

Callender, J. C., & Osburn, H. G. (1977b). A method for maximizing split-half reliability coefficients. *Educational and Psychological Measurement, 37*, 819–825.

Callender, J. C., & Osburn, H. G. (1979). An empirical comparison of coefficient alpha, Guttman's lambda-2, and MSPLIT maximized split-half reliability estimates. *Journal of Educational Measurement, 16*, 89–99.

Cardinet, J., & Allal, L. (1983). Estimation of generalizability parameters. In L. J. Fyans (Ed.), *Generalizability theory: Inferences and practical applications* (pp. 17–48). San Francisco: Jossey-Bass.

Cardinet, J., Tourneur, Y., & Allal, L. (1976). The symmetry of generalizability theory: Applications to educational measurement. *Journal of Educational Measurement, 13*, 119–135.

Cardinet, J., Tourneur, Y., & Allal, L. (1981). Extension of generalizability theory and its applications in educational measurement. *Journal of Educational Measurement, 18*, 183–204. Errata, *Journal of Educational Measurement, 1982, 19*, 331–332.

Cleary, T. A., & Linn, R. L. (1969). Error of measurement and the power of a statistical test. *British Journal of Mathematical and Statistical Psychology, 22*, 49–55.

Cliff, N. (1979). Test theory without true scores? *Psychometrika, 44*, 373–393.

Cohen, J. (1960). A coefficient of agreement for nominal scales. *Educational and Psychological Measurement, 20*, 37–46.

Conger, A. J., & Lipshitz, R. (1973). Measures of reliability for profiles and test batteries. *Psychometrika, 38*, 411–427.

Cornfield, J., & Tukey, J. W. (1956). Average values of mean squares in factorials. *Annals of Mathematical Statistics, 27*, 907–949.

Crick, J. E., & Brennan, R. L. (1983). *Manual for GENOVA: A GENeralized analysis Of VAriance system* (ACT Technical Bulletin No. 43). Iowa City, IA: American College Testing Program.

Cronbach, L. J. (1951). Coefficient alpha and the internal structure of tests. *Psychometrika, 16*, 297–334.

Cronbach, L. J. (1976). On the design of educational measures. In D. N. M. de Gruijter & L. J. T. van der Kamp (Eds.), *Advances in psychological and educational measurement* (pp. 199–208). New York: John Wiley & Sons.

Cronbach, L. J., & Furby, L. (1970). How we should measure "change"—Or should we? *Psychological Bulletin, 74*, 68–80. Errata, *Psychological Bulletin, 1970, 74*, 218.

Cronbach, L. J., Gleser, G. C., Nanda, H., & Rajaratnam, N. (1972). *The dependability of behavioral measurements: Theory of generalizability for scores and profiles.* New York: John Wiley & Sons.

Cronbach, L. J., Rajaratnam, N., & Gleser, G. C. (1963). Theory of generalizability: A liberalization of reliability theory. *British Journal of Statistical Psychology, 16*, 137–163.

Cronbach, L. J., Schönemann, P., & McKie, D. (1965). Alpha coefficients for stratified-parallel tests. *Educational and Psychological Measurement, 25*, 291–312.

Divgi, D. R. (1980). Group dependence of some reliability indices for mastery tests. *Applied Psychological Measurement, 4*, 213–218.

Dixon, W. J., & Brown, M. B. (Eds.) (1979). *BMDP-79 biomedical computer programs, P series.* Los Angeles: University of California Press.

Ebel, R. L. (1951). Estimation of the reliability of ratings. *Psychometrika, 16*, 407–424.

Feldt, L. S. (1965). The approximate sampling distribution of Kuder–Richardson reliability coefficient twenty. *Psychometrika, 30*, 357–370.

Feldt, L. S. (1967). A note on the use of confidence bands to evaluate the reliability of a difference between two scores. *American Educational Research Journal, 4*, 139–145.

Feldt, L. S. (1969). A test of the hypothesis that Cronbach's alpha or Kuder–Richardson coefficient twenty is the same for two tests. *Psychometrika, 34*, 363–373.

Feldt, L. S. (1975). Estimation of the reliability of a test divided into two parts of unequal length. *Psychometrika, 40*, 557–561.

Feldt, L. S. (1980). A test of the hypothesis that Cronbach's alpha reliability coefficient is the same for two tests administered to the same sample. *Psychometrika, 45*, 99–105.

Feldt, L. S. (1984). Some relationships between the binomial error model and classical test theory. *Educational and Psychological Measurement, 44*, 883–891.

Feldt, L. S., Steffen, M., & Gupta, N. C. (1985). A comparison of five methods for estimating the standard error of measurement at specific score levels. *Applied Psychological Measurement, 9*, 351–361.

Gillmore, G. M. (1983). Generalizability theory: Applications to program evaluation. In L. J. Fyans (Ed.), *Generalizability theory: Inferences and practical applications* (pp. 3–16). San Francisco: Jossey-Bass.

Gilmer, J. S., & Feldt, L. S. (1983). Reliability estimation for a test with parts of unknown lengths. *Psychometrika, 48*, 99–111.

Glaser, R. (1963). Instructional technology and the measurement of learning outcomes: Some questions. *American Psychologist, 18*, 519–521.

Glass, G. V. (1968). Response to Traub's "Note on the reliability of residual change scores." *Journal of Educational Measurement, 5*, 265–267.

Gleser, G. C., Cronbach, L. J., & Rajaratnam, N. (1965). Generalizability of scores influenced by multiple sources of variance. *Psychometrika, 30*, 395–418.

Gorsuch, R. L. (1980). Factor score reliabilities and domain validities. *Educational and Psychological Measurement, 40*, 895–897.

Graybill, F. A. (1976). *Theory and application of the linear model.* North Scituate, MA: Duxbury Press.

Gross, A. L., & Shulman, V. (1980). The applicability of the beta binomial model for criterion-referenced testing. *Journal of Educational Measurement, 17*, 195–200.

Gupta, S. S. (1963). Probability integrals of multivariate normal and multivariate. *Annals of Mathematical Statistics, 34*, 792–828.

Guttman, L. A. (1945). A basis for analyzing test-retest reliability. *Psychometrika, 10*, 255–282.

Hakstian, A. R., & Whalen, T. E. (1976). A *k*-sample significance test for independent alpha coefficients. *Psychometrika, 41*, 219–231.

Hambleton, R. K., & Novick, M. R. (1973). Toward an integration of theory and method for criterion-referenced tests. *Journal of Educational Measurement, 10*, 159–170.

Hambleton, R. K., Swaminathan, H., Algina, J., & Coulson, D. B. (1978). Criterion-referenced testing and measurement: A review of technical issues and developments. *Review of Educational Research, 48*, 1–47.

Harman, H. H. (1976). *Modern factor analysis* (3rd ed. rev.). Chicago: University of Chicago Press.

Harris, C. W. (Ed.). (1963). *Problems in measuring change.* Madison, WI: University of Wisconsin Press.

Harris, C. W., Pearlman, A. P., & Wilcox, R. R. (1977). Achievement test items: Methods of study. *CSE Monograph Series in Evaluation, 6.* Los Angeles: Center for the Study of Evaluation.

Hays, W. L. (1981). *Statistics* (3rd ed.). New York: Holt, Rinehart, and Winston.

Hopkins, K. D., & Hopkins, B. R. (1979). The effect of the reliability of the dependent variable on power. *Journal of Special Education, 13*, 463–466.

Horst, P. (1951). Estimating total test reliability from parts of unequal length. *Educational and Psychological Measurement, 11*, 368–371.

Horst, D. P., Tallmadge, G. K., & Wood, C. T. (1975). A practical guide to measuring project impact on student achievement. Washington, DC: U. S. Government Printing Office.

Hoyt, C. (1941). Test reliability obtained by analysis of variance. *Psychometrika, 6*, 153–160.

Huck, S. W. (1978). A modification of Hoyt's analysis of variance reliability estimation procedure. *Educational and Psychological Measurement, 38*, 725–736.

Huynh, H. (1976). On the reliability of decisions in domain-referenced testing. *Journal of Educational Measurement, 13*, 253–264.

Jackson, R. W. B., & Ferguson, G. A. (1941). "Studies on the reliability of tests." Bulletin No. 12, Department of Educational Research, Ontario College of Education. Toronto: University of Toronto Press.

Jarjoura, D. (1983). Best linear prediction of composite universe scores. *Psychometrika, 48,* 525–539.

Jarjoura, D. (1985). Tolerance intervals for true scores. *Journal of Educational Statistics, 10,* 1–17.

Jarjoura, D., & Brennan, R. L. (1981). *Three variance components models for some measurement procedures in which unequal numbers of items fall into discrete categories* (ACT Technical Bulletin No. 37). Iowa City, IA: American College Testing Program.

Jarjoura, D., & Brennan, R. L. (1982). A variance components model for measurement procedures associated with a table of specifications. *Applied Psychological Measurement, 6,* 161–171.

Jarjoura, D., & Brennan, R. L. (1983). Multivariate generalizability models for tests developed from tables of specifications. In L. J. Fyans (Ed.), *Generalizability theory: Inferences and practical applications* (pp. 83–101). San Francisco: Jossey-Bass.

Joe, G. W., & Woodward, J. A. (1976). Some developments in multivariate generalizability. *Psychometrika, 41,* 205–217.

Jöreskog, K. G. (1971). Statistical analysis of sets of congeneric tests. *Psychometrika, 36,* 109–133.

Jöreskog, K. G., & Sörbom, D. (1985). *LISREL VI: Analysis of linear structural relationships by the method of maximum likelihood. User's guide.* Uppsala, Sweden: University of Uppsala.

Kaiser, H. F., & Michael, W. B. (1977). Little jiffy factor scores and domain validities. *Educational and Psychological Measurement, 37,* 363–365.

Kane, M. T. (1982). A sampling model for validity. *Applied Psychological Measurement, 6,* 125–160.

Kane, M. T., & Brennan, R. L. (1977). The generalizability of class means. *Review of Educational Research, 47,* 267–292.

Kane, M. T., & Brennan, R. L. (1980). Agreement coefficients as indices of dependability for domain-referenced tests. *Applied Psychological Measurement, 4,* 105–126.

Kane, M. T., & Wilson, J. (1984). Errors of measurement and standard setting in mastery testing. *Applied Psychological Measurement, 8,* 107–115.

Keats, J. A. (1957). Estimation of error variances of test scores. *Psychometrika, 22,* 29–41.

Keats, J. A., & Lord, F. M. (1962). A theoretical distribution for mental test scores. *Psychometrika, 27,* 59–72.

Kelley, T. L. (1947). *Fundamentals of statistics.* Cambridge, MA: Harvard University Press.

Knapp, T. R. (1980). The (un)reliability of change scores in counseling research. *Measurement and Evaluation in Guidance, 13,* 149–157.

Kristof, W. (1963). The statistical theory of stepped-up reliability coefficients when a test has been divided into several equivalent parts. *Psychometrika, 28,* 221–238.

Kristof, W. (1964). Testing differences between reliability coefficients. *British Journal of Mathematical and Statistical Psychology, 17,* 105–111.

Kristof, W. (1970). On the sampling theory of reliability estimation. *Journal of Mathematical Psychology, 7,* 371–377.

Kristof, W. (1971). On the theory of a set of tests which differ only in length. *Psychometrika, 36,* 207–225.

Kristof, W. (1974). Estimation of reliability and true score variance from a split of a test into three arbitrary parts. *Psychometrika, 39,* 491–499.

Kuder, G. F., & Richardson, M. W. (1937). The theory of the estimation of test reliability. *Psychometrika, 2,* 151–160.

Lindquist, E. F. (1953). *Design and analysis of experiments in psychology and education.* Boston: Houghton Mifflin.

Linn, R. L., & Slinde, J. A. (1977). The determination of the significance of change between pre- and posttesting periods. *Review of Educational Research, 47,* 121–150.

Linn, R. L., & Werts, C. E. (1979). Covariance structures and their analysis. In R. E. Traub (Ed.), *New directions for testing and measurement: Methodological developments* (No. 4, pp. 53–73). San Francisco: Jossey-Bass.

Livingston, S. A. (1972). Criterion-referenced applications of classical test theory. *Journal of Educational Measurement, 9,* 13–26.

Livingston, S. A., & Wingersky, M. S. (1979). Assessing the reliability of tests used to make pass/fail decisions. *Journal of Educational Measurement, 16,* 247–260.

Lord, F. M. (1955). Estimating test reliability. *Educational and Psychological Measurement, 15,* 325–336.

Lord, F. M. (1956). The measurement of growth. *Educational and Psychological Measurement, 16,* 421–437.

Lord, F. M. (1958). Further problems in the measurement of growth. *Educational and Psychological Measurement, 18,* 437–451.

Lord, F. M. (1963). Elementary models for measuring change. In C. W. Harris (Ed.), *Problems in measuring change* (pp. 21–38). Madison, WI: University of Wisconsin Press.

Lord, F. M. (1965). A strong true score theory, with applications. *Psychometrika, 30,* 239–270.

Lord, F. M. (1969). Estimating true-score distributions in psychological testing (an empirical Bayes estimation problem). *Psychometrika, 34,* 259–299.

Lord, F. M. (1974). Variance stabilizing transformation of the stepped-up reliability coefficient. *Journal of Educational Measurement, 11,* 55–57.

Lord, F. M. (1984). Standard errors of measurement at different score levels. *Journal of Educational Measurement, 21,* 239–243.

Lord, F. M., & Novick, M. R. (1968). *Statistical theories of mental test scores.* Reading, MA: Addison-Wesley.

Lord, F. M., & Stocking, M. (1976). An interval estimate for making statistical inferences about true score. *Psychometrika, 41,* 79–87.

Lu, K. H. (1971). Statistical control of "impurity" in the estimation of test reliability. *Educational and Psychological Measurement, 31,* 641–655.

Marks, E., & Martin, C. G. (1973). Further comments relating to the measurement of change. *American Educational Research Journal, 10,* 179–191.

Maxwell, A. E. (1968). The effect of correlated errors on estimates of reliability coefficients. *Educational and Psychological Measurement, 28,* 803–811.

McNemar, Q. (1958). On growth measurement. *Educational and Psychological Measurement, 18,* 47–55.

Mollenkopf, W. G. (1949). Variation of the standard error of measurement. *Psychometrika, 14,* 189–229.

Novick, M. R., & Lewis, C. (1967). Coefficient alpha and the reliability of composite measurements. *Psychometrika, 32,* 1–13.

Novick, M. R., & Lindley, D. V. (1978). The use of more realistic utility functions in educational aplications. *Journal of Educational Measurement, 15,* 181–189.

O'Connor, E. F. (1972). Extending classical test theory to the measurement of change. *Review of Educational Research, 42,* 73–97.

Olkin, I. (1967). Correlations revisited. In J. C. Stanley (Ed.), *Improving experimental design and statistical analysis* (pp. 102–128). New York: Rand McNally.

Pandey, T. N., & Hubert, L. (1975). An empirical comparison of several interval estimation procedures for coefficient alpha. *Psychometrika, 40,* 169–181.

Peng, C-Y. J., & Subkoviak, M. J. (1980). A note on Huynh's normal approximation procedure for estimating criterion-referenced reliability. *Journal of Educational Measurement, 17,* 359–368.

Popham, W. J., & Husek, T. R. (1969). Implications of criterion-referenced measurement. *Journal of Educational Measurement, 6,* 1–9.

Raju, N. S. (1970). New formula for estimating total test reliability from parts of unequal length. In *Proceedings of the 78th Annual Convention of the American Psychological Association, 5,* 143–144.

Raju, N. S. (1977). A generalization of coefficient alpha. *Psychometrika, 42,* 549–565.

Raju, N. S. (1982). The reliability of a criterion-referenced composite with the parts of the composite having different cutting scores. *Educational and Psychological Measurement, 42,* 113–129.

Richards, J. M., Jr. (1975). A simulation study of the use of change measures to compare educational programs. *American Educational Research Journal, 12,* 299–311.

Rogosa, D., Brandt, D., & Zimowski, M. (1982). A growth curve approach to the measurement of change. *Psychological Bulletin, 92,* 726–748.

Rogosa, D. R., & Willett, J. B. (1983). Demonstrating the reliability of the difference score in the measurement of change. *Journal of Educational Measurement, 20,* 335–343.

Rulon, P. J. (1939). A simplified procedure for determining the reliability of a test by split-halves. *Harvard Educational Review, 9,* 99–103.

Satterthwaite, F. E. (1941). Synthesis of variance. *Psychometrika, 6,* 309–316.

Satterthwaite, F. E. (1946). An approximate distribution of estimates of variance components. *Biometrics Bulletin, 2,* 110–114.

Scheffé, H. (1959). *The analysis of variance.* New York: John Wiley.

Schönemann, P. H., & Wang, M-M. (1972). Some new results on factor indeterminancy. *Psychometrika, 37,* 61–91.

Searle, S. R. (1971). *Linear models.* New York: John Wiley.

Searle, S. R. (1974). Prediction, mixed models, and variance components. In F. Proschan & R. J. Sterfling (Eds.), *Reliability and biometry* (pp. 85–107). Philadelphia: SIAM.

Sedere, M. U., & Feldt, L. S. (1977). The sampling distributions of the Kristof reliability coefficient, the Feldt coefficient, and Guttman's lambda-2. *Journal of Educational Measurement, 14,* 53–62.

Shavelson, R., & Webb, N. (1981). Generalizability theory: 1973–1980. *British Journal of Mathematical and Statistical Psychology, 34,* 133–166.

Smith, P. L. (1978). Sampling errors of variance components in small sample multifacet generalizability studies. *Journal of Educational Statistics, 3,* 319–346.

Smith, P. L. (1982). A confidence interval approach for variance component estimates in the context of generalizability theory. *Educational and Psychological Measurement, 42,* 459–466.

Spearman, C. (1910). Correlation calculated from faulty data. *British Journal of Psychology, 3,* 271–295.

Stanley, J. C. (1957). KR-20 as the stepped-up mean item correlation. In *14th Yearbook of the National Council on Measurement in Education* (pp. 78–92). Washington, DC: National Council on Measurement in Education.

Stanley, J. C. (1971). Reliability. In R. L. Thorndike (Ed.), *Educational measurement* (2nd ed., pp. 356–442). Washington, DC: American Council on Education.

Subkoviak, M. J. (1976). Estimating reliability from a single administration of a criterion-referenced test. *Journal of Educational Measurement, 13,* 265–276.

Subkoviak, M. J. (1984). Estimating the reliability of mastery-nonmastery classifications. In R. A. Berk (Ed.), *A guide to criterion-referenced test construction* (pp. 267–291). Baltimore: Johns Hopkins University Press.

Sutcliffe, J. P. (1980). On the relationship of reliability to statistical power. *Psychological Bulletin, 88,* 509–515.

Swaminathan, H., Hambleton, R. K., & Algina, J. (1974). Reliability of criterion-referenced tests: A decision theoretic formulation. *Journal of Educational Measurement, 11,* 263–267.

ten Berge, J. M. F., & Zegers, F. E. (1978). A series of lower bounds to the reliability of a test. *Psychometrika, 43,* 575–579.

Thorndike, R. L. (1951). Reliability. In E. F. Lindquist (Ed.), *Educational measurement* (pp. 560–620). Washington, DC: American Council on Education.

Traub, R. E. (1967). A note on the reliability of residual change scores. *Journal of Educational Measurement, 4,* 253–256.

Tucker, L. R. (1949). A note on the estimation of test reliability by the Kuder–Richardson formula (20). *Psychometrika, 14,* 117–119.

Tucker, L. R., & Lewis, C. (1973). A reliability coefficient for maximum likelihood factor analysis. *Psychometrika, 38,* 1–10.

van der Kamp, L. J. T. (1976). Generalizability and educational measurement. In D. N. M. de Gruijter, & L. J. T. van der Kamp (Eds.), *Advances in psychological and educational measurement* (pp. 173–184). New York: John Wiley & Sons.

Votaw, D. F., Jr. (1948). Testing compound symmetry in a normal multivariate distribution. *Annuals of Mathematical Statistics, 19,* 447–473.

Wang, M. C., & Stanley, J. C. (1970). Differential weighting: A review of methods and empirical studies. *Review of Educational Research, 40,* 663–705.

Webb, N. M., Shavelson, R. J., & Maddahian, E. (1983). Multivariate generalizability theory. In L. J. Fyans (Ed.), *Generalizability theory: Inferences and practical applications* (pp. 67–81). San Francisco: Jossey-Bass.

Webster, H., & Bereiter, C. (1963). The reliability of changes measured by mental test scores. In C. W. Harris (Ed.), *Problems in measuring change* (pp. 39–59). Madison, WI: University of Wisconsin Press.

Werts, C. E., Linn, R. L., & Jöreskog, K. G. (1973). A congeneric model for platonic true scores. *Educational and Psychological Measurement, 33,* 311–318.

Werts, C. E., Linn, R. L., & Jöreskog, K. G. (1974). Intraclass reliability estimates: Testing structural assumptions. *Educational and Psychological Measurement, 34,* 25–33.

Werts, C. E., Rock, D. R., Linn, R. L., and Jöreskog, K. G. (1978). A general method of estimating the reliability of a composite. *Educational and Psychological Measurement, 38,* 933–938.

Wilcox, R. R. (1977). Estimating the likelihood of false-positive and false-negative decisions in mastery testing: An empirical Bayes approach. *Journal of Educational Statistics, 2,* 289–307.

Wilcox, R. R. (1978). Estimating true score in the compound binomial error model. *Psychometrika, 43,* 245–258.

Wilcox, R. R. (1981). A review of the beta-binomial model and its extensions. *Journal of Educational Statistics, 6,* 3–32.

Woodruff, D. J., & Feldt, L. S. (1986). Tests for equality of several alpha coefficients when their sample estimates are dependent. *Psychometrika, 51,* 393–413.

Yu, M. C., & Dunn, O. J. (1982). Robust tests for the equality of two correlation coefficients: A Monte Carlo study. *Educational and Psychological Measurement, 42,* 987–1004.

Zimmerman, D. W. (1975). Probability spaces, Hilbert spaces, and the axioms of test theory. *Psychometrika, 40,* 395–412.

Zimmerman, D. W. (1976). Test theory with minimal assumptions. *Educational and Psychological Measurement, 36,* 85–96.

Zimmerman, D. W., Brotohusodo, T. L., & Williams, R. H. (1981). The reliability of sums and differences of test scores: Some new results and anomalies. *Journal of Experimental Education, 49,* 177–186.

Zimmerman, D. W., & Williams, R. H. (1982a). Gain scores in research can be highly reliable. *Journal of Educational Measurement, 19,* 149–154.

Zimmerman, D. W., & Williams, R. H. (1982b). The relative error magnitude in three measures of change. *Psychometrika, 47,* 141–147.

4

Principles and Selected Applications of Item Response Theory

Ronald K. Hambleton

University of Massachusetts at Amherst

The classical test-model and associated methods for constructing tests and interpreting scores have served measurement specialists well for a long time (see, for example, Gulliksen, 1950; Lord & Novick, 1968; de Gruijter & van der Kamp, 1984). The model itself is easy to understand and can be usefully applied to examinee achievement and aptitude test performance. Well-known and important formulas such as the Spearman-Brown formula, the standard error of measurement formula, the Kuder-Richardson formula-20, and the attenuation formulas are only a few of the many useful results emanating from, or closely associated with, the classical test model.

Unfortunately, there are a number of shortcomings with the classical model and associated test methods. For one, the well-known classical item difficulty (i.e., proportion of examinees passing the item) and item discrimination (i.e., item-total test biserial or point biserial), are group-dependent. The values of these statistics depend on the examinee group in which they are obtained. For example, item difficulty indices will be higher when examinee samples are of above average ability than when the examinee samples are of below average ability. Also, discrimination indices (as well as reliability estimates) tend to be higher in heterogeneous examinee samples than in homogeneous examinee samples. This result is obtained because of the effect of group heterogeneity on correlation coefficients (Lord & Novick, 1968).

If the examinee sample does not closely reflect the population for whom the test is intended, the item statistics and reliability estimates obtained in the sample are limited in their usefulness. Such a situation arises in pilot-test studies when the characteristics of the examinee sample cannot be closely matched to the population for whom the test is intended. Dependence on the examinee group reduces the usefulness of these item statistics in test development work and other applications.

Another shortcoming of classical test models is that the observed and true scores in the number-correct (or proportion-correct) metric are test-dependent. Observed and true test scores rise and fall with changes in test difficulty. The importance of this shortcoming becomes clear when it is recognized that examinees being compared often take different forms of a test, or even different sections within a test. For example, the American Board of Family Practice requires candidates seeking recertification to take a "core section" and three of six additional sections from the examination. Examinees are compared using scores based on an examination consisting of the core and three optional sections. Because the sections are not equally difficult, and there are 20 different combinations of three sections for a candidate to choose from, the desired comparisons of candidates cannot be done fairly using total number-correct examination scores. Adjustments must first be made to correct for the unequally difficult examinations administered to candidates (see Peterson, Kolen, & Hoover, this volume).

An application in which such information is essential is

NOTE: The author is grateful to Ross Traub and Wendy Yen for providing careful reviews and constructive suggestions for improving the technical quality and readability of the chapter and to Jane Rogers for editorial assistance.

147

computerized adaptive testing (Lord, 1980b; Weiss, 1983). Here examinees are administered test items that are matched to their ability levels. (Precisely how this is done will be described in a later section of the chapter.) High-ability examinees are administered substantially more difficult tests than average- or low-ability examinees. In fact, the goal is to administer items where the expected test performance for an examinee is 50% when guessing is assumed to be minimal and somewhat higher than 50% when it is not. For this goal to be accomplished, able students must receive harder tests than less able students. Such "optimal" tests lead to estimates of ability with smaller standard errors of measurement than estimates of ability obtained from "nonoptimal" tests such as a common test given to all examinees. Clearly, number-right scores from such optimal tests would not be useful for comparing examinees where the tests administered differ substantially in difficulty. The concept of adaptive testing is attractive, but to implement it, alternatives to conventional scoring are needed, as well as a basis for choosing test items matched to ability. The classical test model does not provide information about the likely outcome of administering a particular test item to an examinee with a known ability estimate.

Two other shortcomings of the classical test model having to do with the assumption of equal errors of measurement for *all* examinees and the definition of parallel tests have been described by Hambleton and Swaminathan (1985) and Hambleton and van der Linden (1982). Concerning the first of these, it may be sufficient to note that the classical model assumption of equal errors of measurement for all examinees that is made in the best-known and most commonly used form of the classical test model (Gulliksen, 1950) seems implausible (see, for example, Lord, 1984). Certainly, errors of measurement of scale scores on a difficult test are greater for low-ability examinees than for average- and high-ability examinees (see Yen, 1983a). Violations of the equal error variance assumption are the rule and, although the violations might not be threatening to the overall usefulness of the classical model, sometimes referred to as the *weak true-score model,* models where the assumption is not made are preferable. *Strong-true score models* (Feldt, 1984; Lord & Novick, 1968) represent one solution within the classical test theory framework, but such a solution does not address the other shortcomings of the classical model.

With respect to the other shortcoming just listed, satisfying the definition of strictly parallel tests is difficult to accomplish in practice, and violations undermine results based on the classical test models. The assumption that two tests are strictly parallel serves as the basis of the classical-model definition of test reliability. However, it is rare that strictly parallel tests are available, and, in fact, the construction of a parallel test is often not even attempted. Nonparallel tests, assumed to be parallel, result in inaccurate estimates of test reliability, of the standard errors of measurement, and of the test length needed to reach a desired reliability.

It is obviously desirable to have (a) item statistics that are *not* group dependent, (b) scores describing examinee proficiency that are *not* dependent on test difficulty, (c) test models that provide a basis for matching test items to ability levels, (d) test models that are *not* based upon implausible assumptions, and (e) test models that do *not* require strictly parallel tests for

assessing reliability. There is now substantial evidence to suggest that these five desirable properties, and others, can be obtained within the framework of another measurement theory, known as *item response theory* (Hambleton & Swaminathan, 1985; Hulin, Drasgow, & Parsons, 1983; Lord, 1980a; Wright & Stone, 1979). In its most common and popular form, item response theory postulates that (a) underlying examinee performance on a test is a single ability or trait, and (b) the relationship between examinee performance on each item and the ability measured by the test can be described by a monotonically increasing function. The function is called an *item-characteristic function* (or an item response function), and it provides the probabilities of examinees at various ability levels answering the item correctly. Examinees with more ability have higher probabilities for giving correct answers to items than lower ability examinees. Item-characteristic functions, or item-characteristic curves (ICC), as they are commonly called in unidimensional test models, are typically described by one-, two-, or three-item parameters, though other variations are becoming popular (see, for example, Andrich, 1978a, 1978b, 1978c; Embretson, 1984, 1985; Masters & Wright, 1984).

When the assumptions of item response theory can be met, at least to a reasonable degree, in a given data set, the estimates obtained have the following desirable properties: (a) Examinee ability estimates are defined in relation to the pool of items from which the test items are drawn but do not depend upon the particular sample of items selected for the test (an examinee has the same ability across the various samples of test items, though the estimates vary because of measurement errors and some estimates are better than others because of the use of more or less suitable test items), and, therefore, examinees can be compared even though they might *not* have taken identical sets of test questions; (b) item descriptors or statistics do not depend upon the particular sample of examinees used to estimate them. And, as will become clear later in the chapter, because items and ability scores are defined on the same scale, items can be selected to provide optimal measurement (minimum errors) at ability levels of interest. These two properties give rise to what are called *item-free ability estimates* and *sample-free or person-free item parameter estimates,* respectively. Finally, the concept of parallel test forms, which is central to the most popular and commonly used form of the classical test model, is replaced by a statistical method that permits estimation of different standard errors of measurement for examinees at different ability levels.

Presently, item response theory, particularly as manifested in the one-, two-, and three-parameter models, is receiving increasing use from test developers in test design and test-item selection, in addressing item bias, in computer-administered adaptive testing, and in equating and reporting test scores. Cognitive psychologists are exploring the uses of other types of IRT models in test development and analysis. Referred to as *multicomponent,* or cognitive-component, models, these models attempt to describe item difficulty in terms of fundamental cognitive processes that are needed to answer test items successfully. Measurement specialists are also exploring the uses of item response theory in preparing computerized banks of test questions and in conducting large-scale assessments. Useful sources of descriptions of many promising IRT applications are *Test Design* (Embretson, 1985); *Applications of Item Response Theory* (Hambleton, 1983); and *New Horizons in Testing* (1983) and related publications by Weiss (1978, 1980). In the past 10 years, IRT has been used widely. It is reasonable to predict, therefore, that item response theory will have a growing and substantial influence on the development and evaluation of educational and psychological tests and testing practices.

Considerable progress has been made since the seminal papers by Lord (1952, 1953a, 1953b) and Rasch (1960) in applying IRT to achievement and aptitude tests. Today, item response theory is being used by many test publishers (Cook & Eignor, 1983, in press; Woodcock, 1978; Yen, 1983b), state departments of education (Bock & Mislevy, 1981; Pandey & Carlson, 1983), school districts (Hathaway, 1980), and industries (Guion & Ironson, 1983) to construct both norm-referenced and criterion-referenced tests, to investigate item bias, to equate tests, and to report test score information. In fact, the various applications have been so successful that discussions of item response theory have shifted in recent years from a consideration of their advantages and disadvantages in relation to classical test models to consideration of such matters as model selection, parameter estimation, determination of model–data fit, and specific steps for a variety of important applications. There are several computer programs available to carry out item response model analyses (see, for example, Baker, 1985; Mislevy & Bock, 1982; Wingersky, 1983; and Wright & Stone, 1979). It would seem that item response model technology is more than adequate at this time to serve a variety of uses (see, for example, Lord, 1980a). Nevertheless, issues and technology associated with item response theory are neither fully developed nor without controversy. These topics will be addressed throughout the chapter.

The overall goal of this chapter is to provide an introduction to the field of item response theory and to describe several promising applications of the theory. In the remainder of the chapter, several aspects of item response theory will be presented: assumptions, models, and model advantages; ability scores; item and test information and efficiency; estimation of item and ability parameters; assessment of model–data fit; promising applications to test development, item bias, and adaptive testing; and issues, controversies, and possible future directions. Several other IRT applications, notably scaling and equating, are described elsewhere in the volume. Readers may wish to read Baker (1985), Hambleton (1979), and Hambleton and Cook (1977) for brief nontechnical introductions to item response models and applications. Traub and Lam (1985) and Traub and Wolfe (1981) have provided current reviews of many IRT developments.

Assumptions, Models, and Model Advantages

Any theory of test-item responses supposes that examinee performance can be predicted (or explained) by defining examinee characteristics, referred to as *traits* or *abilities*. Scores for examinees are estimated on these traits, referred to as *ability scores* in IRT; and used to predict or explain item and test performance (Lord & Novick, 1968). Because these traits are

not directly measurable, they are referred to as *latent traits* or *abilities*. The notion of an underlying latent ability, attribute, factor, or dimension is a recurring one in the psychometric literature; hence, the term *latent-trait theory* in the IRT literature (Lord, 1952). But, although appropriate, this term does not adequately convey the distinctions that exist among members of the family of procedures, which include factor analysis, multidimensional scaling, and latent-structure analysis, and the procedure for studying characteristics of test items in relation to an ability scale. The terms *item-characteristic curve theory* and *item response theory* seem more appropriate, and the latter term is now receiving wide use.

An item response model specifies a relationship between the *observable* examinee item performance (correct or incorrect responses) and the *unobservable* traits or abilities assumed to underlie performance on the test. This relationship is called an *item-characteristic curve*. Within the broad framework of item response theory, many models can be operationalized, because there are many choices possible for the mathematical form of the ICCs. A substantial body of IRT literature exists on this point alone. It should be noted that item response theory cannot be shown to be correct because it is simply a general framework for characterizing persons, items, and relationships between them. The situation changes as soon as a model within the IRT framework is specified. The appropriateness of particular IRT models with any set of test data can be established by conducting a suitable goodness-of-fit investigation.

The relationship between the *observable* quantities (item scores) and the *unobservable* quantities (examinee abilities) is described by a *mathematical function*. For this reason, item response models are called *mathematical models*. Mathematical models are based on specific assumptions about the test data. Different item response models are formed through specifying different sets of assumptions about the test data set under investigation. The more plausible a model's assumptions, the more useful it is likely to be in addressing practical testing problems.

McDonald (1982) provided a general framework, not only for organizing existing IRT models, but also for generating many new models. His framework includes a consideration of (a) unidimensional and multidimensional models, (b) linear and nonlinear models, and (c) dichotomous and polychotomous response models. To date, most attention has been directed toward unidimensional ($k = 1$), nonlinear, dichotomous response models.

Assumptions

Any mathematical model includes a set of assumptions about the data to which the model applies, and specifies relationships among the observable and unobservable variables described in the model. One problem pointed out by Traub (1983), a problem that is endemic to social science research, should be recognized at this juncture. There is no statistical basis for ever concluding that the assumptions of a model are met by a data set. In fact, the contrary situation applies. All of our statistical principles and methods of determining the viability of a set of assumptions are designed for rejecting the null hypotheses about the appropriateness of assumptions for a data set. The implication is that a logical basis does not exist for accepting the viability of the assumptions underlying any IRT model. However, evidence can be collected that addresses the viability of a set of assumptions, the consequences of violating model assumptions with particular applications can be studied, and judgments can be made about the usefulness of the model under the circumstances. Three common assumptions of item response models will be introduced next.

DIMENSIONALITY

In a general theory of latent traits, a set of k traits is assumed to underlie test performance. The k latent traits define a k-dimensional latent space, with each examinee's location in the latent space being determined by the examinee's position on each latent trait. An examinee's position or ability level on the ith trait is often denoted θ_i. The examinee's position in a k-dimensional latent space is represented by a vector of ability scores, denoted $(\theta_1, \theta_2, \ldots, \theta_k)$. The latent space is referred to as *complete* if all latent traits influencing the test scores of a population of examinees have been specified.

In most IRT applications, the assumption is made that one ability or trait is sufficient to "explain," or account for, examinee test performance and the interrelationships between pairs of test items. Item response models that assume a single latent ability are referred to as *unidimensional*. The assumption of a unidimensional latent space is a common one for test constructors to make because they usually want to construct unidimensional tests, in order to enhance the interpretability of a set of test scores. Also, test users frequently demand single scores (e.g., total battery scores) regardless of their interpretability. Of course, this unidimensionality assumption cannot be strictly met because there are always other cognitive, personality, and test-taking factors that effect test performance, at least to some extent. These factors include test motivation, test anxiety, speed of performance, test sophistication, and other cognitive skills. Reading proficiency, for example, often serves as a second, and irrelevant, factor in test performance. What is required for the assumption of unidimensionality to be met to a satisfactory extent by a set of test data is a *dominant* component or factor. The dominant component or factor is referred to as the ability measured by the test. This ability, however, should not be assumed to be innate or unchangeable. The ability is broadly defined to reflect whatever the test measures: a cognitive ability, a measure of achievement, a basic competency or skill, or a personality variable. What the ability is must be established in the same way that the construct measured by any test is identified: through a construct validation investigation.

Models assuming that more than a single ability is necessary to account for examinee test performance are referred to as *multidimensional*. The reader is referred to the work of Bock and Aitkin (1981), Mulaik (1972), Reckase (1985), and Samejima (1974) for discussions of multidimensional item response models. These models will be discussed only briefly in this chapter because technical developments have been limited to date.

LOCAL INDEPENDENCE

This assumption is that an examinee's responses to the items in a test are statistically independent *if the examinee's ability level is taken into account.* For this assumption to be true, an examinee's performance on one item must not affect, for better or for worse, his or her responses to any other items on the test. For example, no item should provide clues to the answers of other items. What the assumption specifies, then, is that only the examinee's ability and the characteristics of the test item influence (are factors in) performance. When the assumption of local independence is satisfied, the probability that any particular sequence of item scores occurs (e.g., 100110) for any examinee is simply the product of individual item probabilities. Each of the item probabilities depends on the statistics for the item and the examinee's ability. Alternately, the assumption of local independence is satisfied when the probability of any response pattern for an examinee is equal to the product of the probabilities associated with the examinee's responses to the items.

Suppose U_i is a random variable that designates the response of a randomly chosen examinee to item i ($i = 1, 2, \ldots, n$), such that $U_i = 1$ if the examinee answers the item correctly and $U_i = 0$ if the examinee answers the item incorrectly. Suppose also the symbols P_i and Q_i ($Q_i = 1 - P_i$) are used to denote the probability that the examinee answers the item correctly and incorrectly, respectively. The probabilities P_i and Q_i depend directly on an examinee's ability and should be designated as $P_i(\theta)$ and $Q_i(\theta)$, respectively; however, for reasons of convenience, the θ will be dropped from the notation at this point. The assumption of local independence can be stated in mathematical terms in the following way:

$$\text{Prob } (U_1 = u_1, U_2 = u_2, \ldots, U_n = u_n | \theta)$$
$$= (P_1^{u_1} Q_1^{1-u_1})(P_2^{u_2} Q_2^{1-u_2}) \cdots (P_n^{u_n} Q_n^{1-u_n})$$
$$= \prod_{i=1}^{n} P_i^{u_i} Q_i^{1-u_i}.$$

The probabilities are dependent on ability, which, in general, is multidimensional. The assumption of local independence in a unidimensional item response model requires that the probability of an examinee's complete response pattern be equal to the product of probabilities associated with the individual examinee's item scores. For example, consider a three-item test. For examinees at ability level θ_a, suppose $P_1(\theta_a) = .8$, $P_2(\theta_a) = .5$, and $P_3(\theta_a) = .4$. If the assumption of local independence is satisfied, the probabilities of observing each of the $2^3 = 8$ possible response patterns in the sample of examinees at ability level θ_a are given in Table 4.1. Similar calculations involving the item probabilities at different ability levels represented in Table 4.1 would need to be made to check that the local independence assumption is met for a sample of examinees from the population of examinees for whom the test is intended.

The assumption of local independence is a characteristic of all popular IRT models. In practice, for specific ability levels, probabilities of various response patterns based upon the assumption of local independence can be computed and com-

**Table 4.1 Probability of Occurrence of the
8 Response Patterns**

Response Pattern	Probability
0 0 0	$Q_1 Q_2 Q_3 = .2 \times .5 \times .6 = .06$
1 0 0	$P_1 Q_2 Q_3 = .8 \times .5 \times .6 = .24$
0 1 0	$Q_1 P_2 Q_3 = .2 \times .5 \times .6 = .06$
0 0 1	$Q_1 Q_2 P_3 = .2 \times .5 \times .4 = .04$
1 1 0	$P_1 P_2 Q_3 = .8 \times .5 \times .6 = .24$
1 0 1	$P_1 Q_2 P_3 = .8 \times .5 \times .4 = .16$
0 1 1	$Q_1 P_2 P_3 = .2 \times .5 \times .4 = .04$
1 1 1	$P_1 P_2 P_3 = .8 \times .5 \times .4 = .16$

pared to the occurrence rates of these same response patterns in a sample of examinees at the same ability levels.

It should be noted that the assumption of local independence in a case in which ability is unidimensional and the assumption of a unidimensional latent space are equivalent. *First,* suppose a set of test items measures only one common ability. Then, for examinees at a fixed level of this ability, item responses are statistically independent. If item responses were not statistically independent, with ability held fixed, the implication would be that some examinees at this ability level would have higher expected test scores than other examinees at the same ability level. Consequently, information about examinees' standing on more than one ability would be needed to account for their test performances. This would be in clear violation of the assumption that the items were unidimensional. *Second,* the assumption of local independence implies that item responses are statistically independent for examinees at a fixed ability level. Therefore, only one ability is necessary to account for the relationship among a set of test items.

It is important to note that the assumption of local independence does *not* imply that test items are uncorrelated over the total group of examinees (Lord & Novick, 1968, p. 361). Positive correlations between pairs of items result whenever there is variation among the examinees on the ability measured by the test items. But item scores are uncorrelated for examinees of a given ability level.

In concluding this section, it is useful to draw attention to some fairly recent work by McDonald (1981, 1982) on definitions of test dimensionality and the equivalence of assumptions concerning test-dimensionality and local independence. In McDonald's judgment (and we concur), a meaningful definition of dimensionality should be *based* on the principle (or assumption) of local independence. McDonald defined a set of test items as *k-dimensional* if, for examinees with the identical profile of ability scores in a *k*-dimensional space, the covariation between items in the set is 0. The dimensionality of a set of test items is defined as the number of traits needed to satisfy the principle of local independence. Because the covariation between items is typically nonlinear, McDonald recommended the use of nonlinear factor analysis (see McDonald, 1967) for IRT. Readers are referred to an extensive review by Hattie (1985) of the literature on definitions of unidimensionality and approaches for assessing it. In this review, McDonald's formulation of the test dimensionality question in terms of the princi-

ple of local independence is recommended. In sum, this formulation is that the dimensionality of a set of test items is defined as the number of latent abilities needed to represent ability to insure that the assumption of local independence is satisfied.

MATHEMATICAL FORMS OF ITEM-CHARACTERISTIC CURVES

An ICC is a mathematical function that relates the probability of success on an item to the ability measured by the item set or the test that contains the item. In simple terms, it is the nonlinear function for the regression of item score on the trait or ability measured by the test. The main difference to be found among currently popular item response models is in the mathematical form of the ICCs. It is up to the test developer or IRT user to choose one of the many mathematical functions to serve as the form of the ICCs. The appropriateness of the assumption can be addressed, in part, by how well the chosen IRT model accounts for the test results. If the model accounts for the data, the appropriateness of all of the model assumptions is justified. When model fit is unsatisfactory, one or more of the assumptions is untenable.

If both item and ability scores for a population of examinees were known, the form of an ICC could be discovered from a consideration of the distributions of item scores at fixed levels of ability. The mean of each distribution could be computed. The curve connecting the means of these conditional distributions would be the regression of item score on ability. In practice, however, item and ability scores are not known, and so other methods of determining ICCs must be found.

Because the probability that an individual examinee provides a correct answer to an item depends only on the form of the item-characteristic curve, this probability is *independent* of the distribution of examinee ability in the population of examinees of interest. Thus, the probability of a correct item response by an examinee will not depend on the number of examinees in the population who possess the same level of ability. This invariance property of item-characteristic curves in the population of examinees for whom the items were calibrated is one of the desirable features of item response models. The invariance of item response model parameters has important implications for adaptive testing, item banking, and other applications of item response theory. Principally, it means that, within limits, the variation in the distribution of abilities in the examinee sample used to calibrate the items will have no practical effect on the estimates of item parameters.

The feature of item-parameter invariance can be observed in Figure 4.1. Item-characteristic curves for two test items are shown in the upper part of the figure; ability distributions for two groups of examinees are shown in the lower part. When the IRT model fits the data set, approximately the same ICCs will be obtained for the test items, regardless of the distribution of ability in the sample of examinees used to estimate the item parameters. An ICC designates the probability that examinees at a given ability level will answer the item correctly, but this probability does *not* depend on the number of examinees located at the ability level.

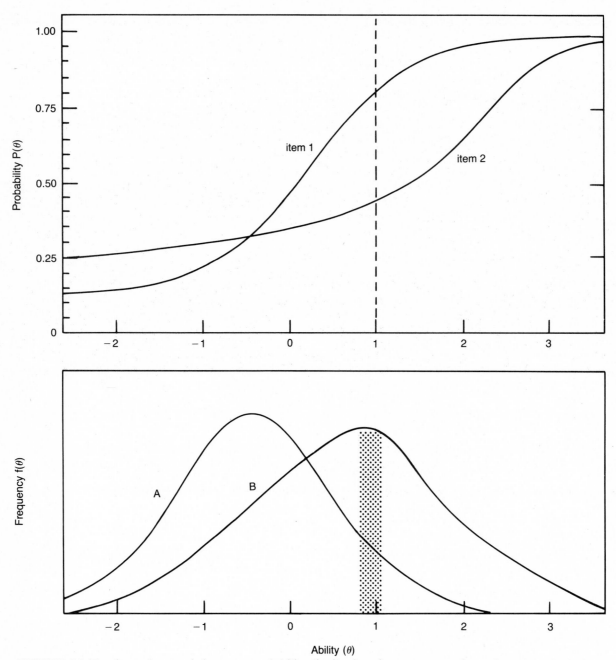

FIGURE 4.1 Two item-characteristic curves, and ability distributions for two groups of examinees (e.g., Canadians and Americans).

Consider the ability distributions at $\theta = 1.0$. Suppose there are 100 examinees from distribution B and 40 examinees from distribution A at this ability level. Though the numbers of examinees in the groups differ, the probability of success on Item 1 (or Item 2) is the same, .80 (or .45 for Item 2). Clearly, the shapes of the item-characteristic curves need not be influenced by the distributions of ability in groups of examinees for whom the test is intended.

Of course, suitable item-parameter estimation requires a heterogeneous distribution of examinees on the ability measured by the test. It would not be possible to properly estimate an ICC defined for the population of examinees of interest without data distributed along the ability continuum (Ree, 1979; Wingersky & Lord, 1984). For example, the lower asymptote of an ICC (i.e., the probability that an examinee of very low ability will answer the item correctly) cannot be estimated correctly if the number of examinees near the lower asymptote for the item is small.

Although item invariance might seem surprising to some researchers, this property also underlies several other well-known statistical procedures. For example, consider the linear relationship (as reflected in a regression line) between two variables, X and Y. The hypothesis is made that a straight line can be used to connect the average Y scores, conditional on the X

scores. When the hypothesis of a linear relationship is satisfied, the same regression line is expected, regardless of the distribution of X scores in the sample drawn. This follows because the regression line passes through the mean of Y values for given X values that does not depend on the sampling of X values. Of course, proper estimation of the line does require a suitably heterogeneous group of examinees.

It is common to interpret the value of the characteristic function for item i at ability level θ, denoted $P_i(\theta)$, as the probability that a *particular* examinee at that level will answer item i correctly. But such an interpretation is incorrect because any particular examinee answers the item either correctly or incorrectly. For example, consider an examinee of middle ability who knows the answer to an item of medium difficulty. The model would suggest that $P_i(\theta)$ for that examinee is close to .50, but, for this examinee, across independent administrations of the test item, the actual probability would be close to 1.0. Lord (1974a, 1980a) demonstrated that this interpretation of $P_i(\theta)$ leads to an awkward situation. Consider two examinees, A and B, and two items, i and j. Suppose Examinee A knows the answer to item i and does not know the answer to item j. Consider the situation to be reversed for Examinee B. Then, $P_i(\theta_A) = 1$, $P_j(\theta_A) = 0$, $P_i(\theta_B) = 0$, $P_j(\theta_B) = 1$. The first two equations suggest that item i is easier than item j. The other two equations suggest the reverse conclusion. Herein lies a dilemma that can be solved by each of several different interpretations of $P_i(\theta)$ and $P_j(\theta)$. One interpretation is that items i and j measure different abilities for the two examinees. An alternative solution is to interpret $P_i(\theta)$ as the probability of an examinee's giving a correct response to a randomly chosen item from the population of test items all possessed of identical item parameters. Another interpretation of $P_i(\theta)$ is that a randomly selected number of the population of examinees, all with ability θ, answers item i correctly. A third interpretation is probably the most useful: $P_i(\theta)$ can be viewed as the probability associated with a randomly selected examinee at ability level θ, answering item i correctly.

Each item-characteristic curve for a particular item response model is a member of a family of curves of the same general form. The number of parameters required to describe an item-characteristic curve depends on the particular item response model. It is common, though, for the number of parameters to be one, two, or three. For example, the item-characteristic curve of the latent linear model shown as illustration (a) in Figure 4.2 has the general form $P_i(\theta) = b_i + a_i\,\theta$, where $P_i(\theta)$ designates the probability of a correct response to item i by a randomly chosen examinee with ability level θ. The latent linear model was developed in some detail by Lazarsfeld and Henry (1968). The function is described by two item parameters, denoted b_i and a_i, respectively. Any item-characteristic curves of the latent linear model will vary in their intercepts (b_i) and their slopes (a_i) to reflect the fact that the test items vary in "difficulty" and "discriminating power." As the b parameter varies, item difficulty is affected (decreasing for high values; increasing for low values). As the a parameter increases, item discrimination is increased, because the difference between the item performance of high- and low-ability examinees is increased. Item difficulty and item discrimination have similarities to item statistics with the same names in classical

measurement. More information about these statistics will be provided later.

A major problem with linear ICCs is that they cannot be too steep, or they will result in probability estimates that are not meaningful. Only values between 0 and 1 are meaningful; values outside this range are not. For this reason, nonlinear ICCs have proven to be more useful.

Item-characteristic curves for Guttman's *perfect scale model* are shown in illustration (b) in Figure 4.2. These curves take the shape of step functions: Probabilities of correct responses are either 0 or 1. The critical ability level θ^* is the point on the ability scale where probabilities change from 0 to 1. Different items lead to different values of θ^*. When θ^* is high, the item is difficult. Easy items correspond to low values of θ^*. This model could be thought of as the limiting case of the latent linear model when item-discrimination indexes approach very large values. A variation on Guttman's perfect scale model occurs when item-characteristic curves take the shape of step functions, but the probabilities of incorrect and correct responses, in general, differ from 0 and 1. This model, known as the *latent distance model,* has been used by social psychologists in the measurement of attitudes (Lazarsfeld & Henry, 1968).

Illustrations (c), (d), and (e) in Figure 4.2 show "S"-shaped ICCs that are associated with the one-, two-, and three-parameter logistic models, respectively. With the *one-parameter logistic model* (4.2c), the item characteristic curves do not intersect, and they differ only by a translation along the ability scale. Items with such characteristic curves have different difficulty parameters. With the *two-parameter logistic model* (4.2d) item-characteristic curves vary in both slope (some curves rise more rapidly than others as ability increases, i.e., the corresponding test items are more discriminating than others) and location along the ability scale (some items are more difficult than others). Finally, with the *three-parameter model* (4.2e), ICCs can differ in slope, difficulty, *and* lower asymptote. With the one- and two-parameter ICCs, the probabilities of correct responses range from 0 to 1. In the three-parameter model, the lower asymptote can be greater than 0. When guessing is a factor in test performance and examinees with low abilities can get difficult items correct, inclusion of a third parameter in the ICC can improve the "fit" between the test data and the model.

In other models, such as the *nominal response model* and the *graded-response model,* there are *item option characteristic curves* (Bock, 1972). A curve depicting the probability that a response option is selected as a function of ability is produced for *each* option of the test item. An example of one such item with four options is depicted in illustration (f) in Figure 4.2. Such models can also handle polychotomous responses arising from ratings data (e.g., 5-point Likert scales).

Common Item Response Models

The purpose of this section is to introduce several item response models that are being used currently in the design and analysis of educational and psychological tests. The principal difference among the models is in the mathematical form of the item-characteristic curves. Another important difference is in the way item responses are scored.

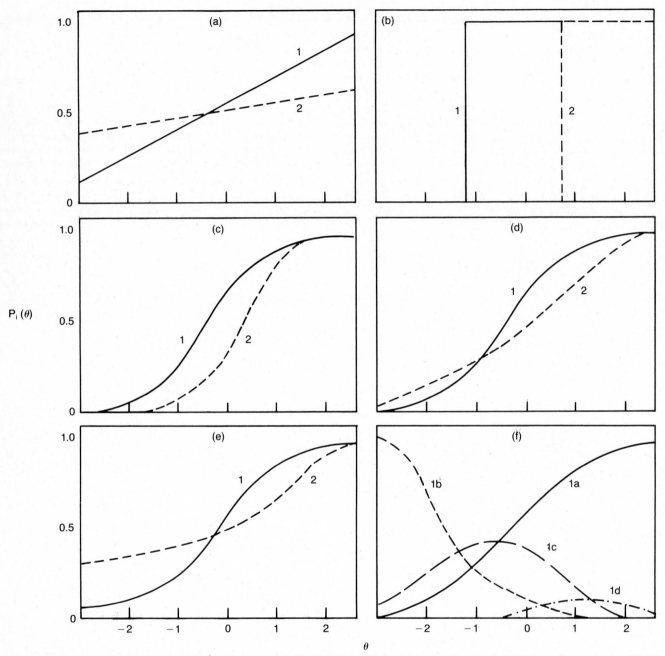

FIGURE 4.2 Examples of item-characteristic curves for six IRT models. (a) latent linear model (b) perfect scale model (c) one-parameter model (d) two-parameter model (e) three-parameter model (f) nominal response model

It should be noted at the outset that, on some occasions, a psychological justification can be offered for the choice of a mathematical form for the ICCs. For example, with difficult multiple-choice tests, a researcher might anticipate considerable guessing on the part of examinees. Needed, therefore, would be a model that could handle this situation. But, in general, the best support for a model comes from empirical evidence. Quite simply, does the model fit the data?

TWO-PARAMETER LOGISTIC MODEL

Birnbaum (1957, 1958a, 1958b, 1968) proposed an item response model in which item-characteristic curves take the

form of two-parameter logistic distribution functions:

$$P_i(\theta) = \frac{e^{Da_i(\theta - b_i)}}{1 + e^{Da_i(\theta - b_i)}} \quad (i = 1, 2, \ldots, n). \quad (1)$$

$P_i(\theta)$ is the probability that a randomly selected examinee with ability θ will answer item i correctly, and b_i and a_i are parameters characterizing item i. The variable n is used to define the number of items in the test. The result is a monotonically increasing function of ability. The parameter b_i is usually referred to as the index of *item difficulty* and represents the point on the ability scale at which an examinee has a 50% probability of answering item i correctly. The parameter a_i, called *item discrimination,* is proportional to the slope of $P_i(\theta)$ at the point $\theta = b_i$. D is a scaling factor introduced by Lord, Birnbaum, and others to bring the interpretation of the parameters of the logistic model in line with those of the two-parameter normal ogive model that was popular at one time in IRT research (see, for example, Lord, 1952; Lord & Novick, 1968).

When the abilities of a group are transformed so that their mean is 0 and the standard deviation is 1, the values of b vary (typically) from about -2.0 to $+2.0$. Values of b near -2.0 correspond with items that are very easy, and values of b near 2.0 correspond with items that are very difficult for the group of examinees.

The item-discrimination parameter, a_i, is defined, theoretically, on the scale $(-\infty, +\infty)$. However, negatively discriminating items are discarded from ability tests because there is something wrong with an item (such as miskeying) if the probability of answering it correctly decreases as ability increases. Also, it is unusual to obtain a_i values larger than 2. Hence, the usual range for item-discrimination parameters is (0, 2). High values of a_i result in item-characteristic curves that are very "steep," and low values of a_i lead to item-characteristic curves that increase gradually as a function of ability. Readers interested in experimenting with changing values of item parameters to determine their effects on ICCs are referred to some computer software for the IBM PC and Apple by Baker (1985).

Items with steep slopes are more useful for separating examinees into different ability groups than items with gradual slopes. In fact, the usefulness of an item for discriminating between examinees at an ability level θ_0 (separating examinees with abilities $\leq \theta_0$ from examinees with abilities $> \theta_0$) is proportional to the slope of the ICC at θ_0.

There is an alternative way to write $P_i(\theta)$ for the two-parameter logistic model. If the numerator and denominator of Equation 1 are divided by $e^{Da_i(\theta-b_i)}$, then $P_i(\theta)$ becomes

$$P_i(\theta) = \frac{1}{1 + e^{-Da_i(\theta-b_i)}}, \quad (2)$$

which also can be written as

$$P_i(\theta) = [1 + e^{-Da_i(\theta-b_i)}]^{-1}. \quad (3)$$

A third alternative is to write

$$P_i(\theta) = \{1 + \exp[-Da_i(\theta - b_i)]\}^{-1},$$

where $exp(x)$ is used to denote e raised to the power x.

Birnbaum substituted the two-parameter logistic cumulative distribution function for the two-parameter normal ogive function used by Lord (1952) as the form of the item-characteristic curve. Logistic curves have the important advantage of being more convenient to work with than normal ogive curves. Statisticians would say that the logistic model is more "mathematically tractable" than the normal ogive model because the latter involves integration, whereas the former is an explicit function of item and ability parameters. It has been shown that when $D = 1.7$, values of $P_i(\theta)$ for the two-parameter normal ogive and the two-parameter logistic models differ in absolute value by less than .01 for all values of θ (Haley, 1952).

An inspection of the two-parameter logistic test model reveals an implicit assumption: Examinees with low abilities cannot get items correct through lucky guessing. This must be so because, for all items with $a_i > 0$ (that is, items for which there is a positive relationship between performance on the test item and the ability measured by the test), the probability of a correct response to the item decreases to 0 as ability decreases.

THREE-PARAMETER LOGISTIC MODEL

The three-parameter logistic model is obtained from the two-parameter model by adding a third parameter, denoted c_i. The mathematical form of the three-parameter logistic curve is written

$$P_i(\theta) = c_i + (1 - c_i)\frac{e^{Da_i(\theta-b_i)}}{1 + e^{Da_i(\theta-b_i)}}(i = 1, 2, \ldots n). \quad (4)$$

where $P_i(\theta)$, b_i, a_i, and D have the same interpretations as in the two-parameter model, with one modification. At b_i on the ability scale, the probability of a correct response is $(1 + c_i)/2$ rather than .50.

The c parameter in the model is the lower asymptote of the item-characteristic curve and represents the probability that examinees with low ability correctly answer the item. The parameter c_i is included in the model to account for item response data from low-ability examinees on multiple-choice tests, where, among other things, guessing is a factor in test performance. It is now common to refer to the parameter c_i as the *pseudochance level* or pseudoguessing parameter. Typically, c_i takes on a value that is smaller than the value that would result if examinees of low ability were to randomly guess the item. Lord (1974a) noted that this phenomenon could probably be attributed to the ingenuity of item writers who develop "attractive" but incorrect answer choices. Low-ability examinees are attracted to these incorrect answer choices. They would actually score higher by randomly guessing the correct answers! For this reason, avoidance of the label *guessing parameter* to describe the parameter c_i seems desirable. Without this parameter in the model, low-ability examinee performance would typically exceed predicted item performance from the best fitting one- and two-parameter models (Hambleton & Murray, 1983).

Figure 4.3 (from Hambleton & Swaminathan, 1985, p. 39) provides an example of a typical item-characteristic curve for the three-parameter logistic model. The b value for the test item is located on the ability scale at the point where the slope of the ICC is a maximum. This point also corresponds to a probability of a correct answer of $(1 + c_i)/2$ (.50 when $c_i = .00$). The slope of the ICC at b_i equals $.425a_i(1 - c_i)$, where a_i is the discriminating power of the item. This result can be obtained by differentiating the mathematical expression for the ICC with respect to θ and then setting $\theta = b$.

The two-parameter logistic model is obtained from the three-parameter logistic model by assuming that the pseudochance level parameters have 0 values. This assumption is most plausible with free response items, but it can often be met approximately when a test is not too difficult for the examinees. The latter circumstance might arise, for example, with basic skills tests administered after effective instruction (Hambleton, Murray, & Williams, 1983). When large examinee samples are not available for item-parameter estimation,

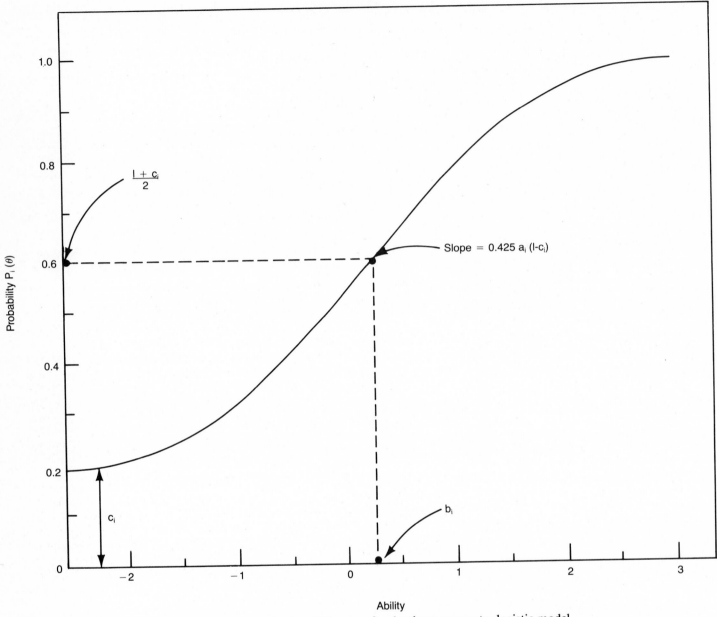

FIGURE 4.3 Item-characteristic curve for the three-parameter logistic model.

sometimes a modified three-parameter model is used which fixes the c parameter at a reasonable value (e.g., .20, or, preferably, a little lower for multiple-choice items with five options).

ONE-PARAMETER LOGISTIC MODEL (RASCH MODEL)

Many researchers have become aware since the early 1960s of the work in the area of item response models by Georg Rasch, a Danish mathematician, through both his own publications (Rasch, 1960, 1966) and those of proponents of his model. Benjamin Wright's presentation, "Sample-free Test Calibration and Person Measurement," delivered at the 1967 ETS Invitational Conference on Testing Problems (Wright, 1968), stimulated interest among test developers in Rasch's

model, which is a one-parameter logistic model. Since 1967, Professor Wright and his colleagues have given numerous training sessions, described the strengths and possible applications of the model (e.g., Wright, 1977a, 1977b; Wright & Panchapakesan, 1969; Wright & Stone, 1979), and developed fast and easy-to-use computer programs for its application. Because of these activities, the Rasch model is currently receiving considerable attention and use from practitioners.

The Rasch model, though it can be viewed as a special case of the three-parameter logistic model, was developed independently of other item response models and along quite different lines. Wright (1968) introduced the Rasch model in the following way: He began his model building by specifying the odds for success by examinee a on an item i as the product of an examinee's ability (denoted θ_a^*) and the easiness of the item (denoted $1/b_i^*$, where b_i^* is the item's difficulty). Therefore, the odds for success of Examinee a on item i are given by the expression θ_a^*/b_i^*, and θ_a^* and b_i^* are defined on the scale $[0, \infty]$. Clearly, the odds for success are high for bright examinees on easy items; they are very low for low-ability examinees on difficult items. The odds for an event occurring are defined as the ratio of $P/(1 - P)$ where P is the probability of the event's occurring. In the context of an examinee confronting a test item, the odds for success take the form of a ratio of $P_i(\theta_a)$ to $1 - P_i(\theta_a)$, where $P_i(\theta_a)$ is the probability of Examinee a's answering the ith item correctly. Therefore,

$$\frac{\theta_a^*}{b_i^*} = \frac{P_i(\theta_a)}{1 - P_i(\theta_a)}$$

and it is easily shown that

$$P_i(\theta_a) = \frac{\theta_a^*}{\theta_a^* + b_i^*}.$$

This form of the ICC is sometimes used in Rasch model applications. By setting $\theta_a^* = e^{D\bar{a}\theta_a}$ and $b_i^* = e^{D\bar{a}b_i}$, in the previous equation, $P_i(\theta_a)$ becomes

$$P_i(\theta_a) = \frac{e^{D\bar{a}\theta_a}}{e^{D\bar{a}\theta_a} + e^{D\bar{a}b_i}}$$

and can easily be shown to be equivalent to

$$P_i(\theta_a) = \frac{e^{D\bar{a}(\theta_a - b_i)}}{1 + e^{D\bar{a}(\theta_a - b_i)}} \quad (i = 1, 2, \ldots, n). \qquad (5)$$

Equation 5 is the form of the Rasch model when it is obtained as a special case of the three-parameter logistic model by assuming in Equation 4 that the pseudochance level parameters have values of 0 and all test items are equally discriminating. The factor $D\bar{a}$ in Equation 5, with $\bar{a}$ being the common item-discrimination value, can be eliminated through the transformations $\theta_a' = D\bar{a}\theta_a$ and $b_i' = D\bar{a}b_i$.

It is clear from Equation 5 that the model described by Rasch and Wright can be viewed as an item response model in which the choice of item-characteristic curve is a one-parameter logistic function. In this sense, then, Rasch's model is a special case of Birnbaum's three-parameter logistic model. The two additional assumptions of equal item discrimination and no correct guessing among low ability examinees are strong and, in practice, are not likely to be met by multiple-choice test data (see, for example, Divgi, 1986; Hambleton & Murray, 1983; Hills, Beard, Yotinprasert, Roca, & Subhiya, 1985; Traub, 1983). There is evidence, however, that for some applications the model is reasonably robust in the presence of moderate violations of model assumptions. Even when the model fails to fit the test data, some advocates of the Rasch model are not discouraged. A popular position of some proponents of the Rasch model is that, if the model fails to fit examinee responses to a set of test items, these misfitting items should be discarded sooner than the model.

Although it may be viewed as a special case of the two- and three-parameter logistic test models, the Rasch model does have some special properties that make it attractive to users. *First,* because the model involves fewer item parameters, it is easier to work with. *Second,* there are far fewer parameter esti-

mation problems with the Rasch model than with the more general models. *Finally,* the property of *specific objectivity* is obtained, which permits the complete separation of item and ability estimation (Rasch, 1960, 1966). This means that ability parameters can be estimated without bias and independently of the items chosen from those items that fit the model. Also, item parameters can be estimated without bias and independently from the distribution of abilities in the sample of examinees drawn from the population for whom the model fits. But to say that specific objectivity is obtained with the Rasch model is to distort Rasch's original intentions. It was to obtain the property of specific objectivity in his measurements that Rasch developed the model as he did. The property came about through design on his part rather than as a by-product of other goals he had in mind when he did his pioneering psychometric research in the late 1950s. On the other hand, it is harder to find items that fit the one-parameter model, and if the model does not fit, specific objectivity, as well as the other desirable properties to users, are not obtained.

FOUR-PARAMETER LOGISTIC MODEL

High-ability examinees do not always answer test items correctly, even easy ones. These examinees might be careless, or they might have information beyond that assumed by the test item writer, and, so, they choose answers not "keyed" as correct (see, for example, Wainer, Wadkins, & Rogers, 1984). To handle this problem, McDonald (1967) and, more recently, Barton and Lord (1981) described a four-parameter logistic model:

$$P_i(\theta) = c_i + (\gamma_i - c_i) \frac{e^{Da_i(\theta - b_i)}}{1 + e^{Da_i(\theta - b_i)}}$$

$$(i = 1, 2, \ldots, n). \qquad (6)$$

This model differs from the three-parameter model in that the presence of γ_i, which may assume a value slightly below 1, means that the ICC may have an upper asymptote less than 1. This model might be of theoretical interest only because Barton and Lord (1981) were unable to find any practical gains that accrued from the model's use.

ADDITIONAL MODELS

There is no limit to the number of models that can be generated within the IRT framework. Four unidimensional logistic models have been described, models that can be applied to dichotomous achievement and aptitude-item responses. Corresponding to each of these models is a normal-ogive alternative. In addition, there are (a) unidimensional logistic models that can handle polychotomous responses (unordered, ordered, or continuous); (b) extensions of the one-parameter model to incorporate cognitive components of item difficulty; (c) multidimensional logistic models; and (d) models in which groups of examinees rather than individual examinees (e.g., classes of students in a school) are treated as the units of analysis. These new models have permitted the application of IRT to a wide range of interesting and important problems such as differential weighting of response alternatives, processing of attitudinal data, and analysis of group data that arises in state and national assessments. Brief descriptions of several of these models follow.

In some of the earliest IRT work, Lord (1952) proposed a two-parameter IRT model in which ICCs took the form of the normal ogive:

$$P_i(\theta) = \int_{-\infty}^{a_i(\theta - b_i)} \frac{1}{\sqrt{2\pi}} e^{\frac{-t^2}{2}} dt$$

$$(i = 1, 2, \ldots, n) \qquad (7)$$

The integral in Equation 7 is the cumulative normal distribution, sometimes called a *normal ogive*. The mean of this distribution (which is *not* the distribution of ability in the population of examinees) is b_i, and the standard deviation is a_i^{-1}. The modifications that would have to be made to Equation 7 to obtain one-, three-, and four-parameter normal-ogive models are obvious. Computationally, Equation 7 is awkward to work with because it requires numerical integration to determine the probabilities. Today, the normal-ogive model is mainly of historical interest.

Bock (1972) was one of the first psychometricians to develop an IRT model that could handle polychotomous response data. The purpose of his *nominal response model,* as he called it, was to maximize the precision of ability estimates by using the information contained in each item response. Bock achieved this purpose by introducing a characteristic curve for *each* item response (answer choice), subject to the constraint that the sum of probabilities across the possible responses at a given ability must equal 1. Even the "omit" response was represented by a curve. For the correct response, the curve is monotonically increasing as a function of ability. For the incorrect options (or other response categories), the shapes of the curves depend on how the options are perceived by examinees at different ability levels. These curves can be monotonically decreasing, monotonically increasing, or unimodal distributions with varying levels of kurtosis.

Thissen (1976) showed the merits of using Bock's model, which assigns scoring weights to the responses to reflect their degree of correctness, using data from the Raven's Progressive Matrices Test: The precision of ability estimates was improved considerably for examinees in the low- and middle-ability ranges.

Bock (1972) assumed the probability that a randomly chosen examinee with ability level θ will select a particular item option k (from m available options per item) on item i, given by

$$P_{ik}(\theta) = \frac{e^{b_{ik}^* + a_{ik}^* \theta}}{\sum_{h=1}^{m} e^{b_{ih}^* + a_{ih}^* \theta}}$$

$$(i = 1, 2, \ldots, n; k = 1, 2, \ldots, m). \qquad (8)$$

The sum of probabilities at θ for selecting each of the m-item options is equal to 1. The quantities b_{ik}^* and a_{ik}^* are item parameters, item difficulty and item discrimination respectively, related to the kth item option. When $m = 2$, the items are dichotomously scored, and the two-parameter logistic model and the nominal-response model are identical, though the item and ability parameters are scaled differently in the two models.

A variation on the nominal-response model is the graded-response model of Samejima (1969). This model can be ap-plied to ratings obtained from scales with ordered categories, such as Likert and semantic differential rating scales. A characteristic curve is produced for *each* response category. In one version of Samejima's general graded-response model, a two-parameter logistic curve is produced for *each* possible category to represent the probability that examinees select that category or categories higher on the scale. Sometimes Samejima's models are referred to as *difference models* because the probability of an examinee's choosing the kth-ordered category is the difference in the probabilities of the category characteristic curves associated with the kth and the $(k - 1)^{\text{th}}$ categories (Thissen & Steinberg, 1986).

One important consequence of using the graded-response model instead of one of the dichotomous response models is that shifting from dichotomous to graded scoring increases the amount of information (and lowers the standard error) provided by the test. This result is nearly always observed with IRT models for polychotomous data.

A promising application of Samejima's graded-response model was described by Koch (1983), who was able to show, using Likert scale data, that the graded-response model and the traditional method of Likert scaling led to highly correlated item and person statistics. This finding supports the appropriateness of the graded-response model for attitude measurement. A comparison of the two approaches to modelling and data analysis also showed that use of the IRT model results in substantially more measurement precision for all points along the attitude scale continuum.

In a logical extension of the graded-response model, Samejima (1973) allowed the number of categories to become very large. The resulting model can be fitted to continuous response data such as that generated through use of a graphical rating scale.

In other developments of IRT models to handle polychotomous data, Andrich (1978b, 1978c, 1982) modified the one-parameter logistic model in a number of ways for application to attitudinal data. He referred to his models as the *binomial trials model* and the *rating scale model.* Masters (1982) developed another variation on the one-parameter logistic model, which he referred to as the *partial credit model.* More recently, Masters and Wright (1984) were able to show that a number of recent variations on the one-parameter logistic (or Rasch) model could be organized into a single "fundamental measurement model" that possessed some of the characteristics of the Rasch model: separable examinee and item parameters and sufficient statistics to estimate model parameters.

The mathematical form of the ICC for the Masters and Wright model is

$$P_{ix}(\theta^*) = \frac{e^{\theta^* - b_{ix}^*}}{1 + e^{\theta^* - b_{ix}^*}}, x = 1, 2, \ldots, m_i, \qquad (9)$$

which gives the probability of a person scoring x rather than $(x - 1)$ on item i as a function of the person parameter θ^* and an item parameter b_{ix}^*. Thus, for each item, there are a series of m_i logistic curves (where m_i is the number of score points for item i) that differ in terms of their difficulty values (b_{i1}^*, $b_{i2}^*, \ldots, b_{im_i}^*$). The difference in the logistic curves for two consecutive categories, $(k - 1)$ and k, is the probability of the examinee's choosing the kth category. The dichotomous, partial credit, rating scale, and binomial trials models are all special cases of Equation 9. The models differ only in how b_{ix}^* is structured. For example, in the dichotomous case, $b_{ix_i}^* = b_i^*$. For more details on the general model, and special cases of it, readers are referred to Masters and Wright (1984). These models by Andrich, Masters, Samejima, Wright, and others extend the applicability of IRT to polychotomous data (ordered ratings) such as might be obtained from rating scales.

Two other extensions of the one-parameter model are currently attracting the attention of cognitive psychologists and psychometricians. One of the extensions is found in the work of Fischer (see, for example, Fischer & Formann, 1982) on the *linear logistic latent trait model;* the other is in the work of Embretson (formerly Whitely) on the *multicomponent latent trait model* (Whitely, 1980; Embretson, 1984). Fischer and Embretson both incorporate parameters in their models for the underlying cognitive components that are presumed to influence examinee test-item performance.

To be more specific, Fischer and his colleagues in Europe extended the Rasch model by representing the item-difficulty parameter in the model as a linear combination of factors that influence item difficulty. This generalized Rasch model, referred to as the *linear logistic model,* is presently being used successfully by psychologists (see, for example, Embretson, 1984) to understand the cognitive processes that influence item difficulty, among other applications. The item-difficulty parameter b_i in the one-parameter logistic model is represented in the following way:

$$b_i = \sum_{j=1}^{m} w_{ij} n_j + \lambda,$$

where n_j, $j = 1, 2, \ldots, m$ account for the difficulty of a cognitive operation or component of the item presumed to influence item performance, and w_{ij}, $j = 1, 2, \ldots, m$ is the weight that reflects the importance of each operation or component with item i. The value λ is a scaling factor.

Although Fischer's work represents a unidimensional extension of the Rasch model, Embretson, on the other hand, introduced a model to explain item (task) performance in terms of not one but several underlying examinee cognitive skills or components. Each cognitive skill was important for completing one of the subtasks necessary to answer the item (or task) correctly. She introduced a two-parameter logistic model to link subtask performance to the underlying cognitive skill that was needed to perform the subtask. The probability of correct performance on the item (or task) was assumed by Embretson to be the product of probabilities associated with success on the subtasks associated with the item. Because a different ability (cognitive skill) is presumed to be tapped by each subtask, the model can be viewed as a multi-dimensional extension of the Rasch model. In Embretson's model,

$$P(x_{ij} = 1) = \prod_{k=1}^{m} P(x_{ijk} = 1) \qquad (10)$$

and

$$P(x_{ijk}) = \frac{e^{\theta_{jk} - b_{ik}}}{1 + e^{\theta_{jk} - b_{ik}}}, \qquad (11)$$

where $P(x_{ij} = 1)$ is the probability that person j answers item

(task) i correctly, $P(x_{ijk} = 1)$ is the probability of the same person j answering subtask k correctly, and b_{ik}, $k = 1, 2, \ldots, m$ and θ_{jk}, $k = 1, 2, \ldots, m$ are the subtask difficulties for item i and the abilities for person j, respectively, on the m subtasks. One implication of her model is that researchers must collect performance data on the subtasks in addition to the test item itself.

More recently, Embretson (1984) extended her model in Equations 10 and 11 such that the new model included her earlier work and the work of Fischer and his colleagues as special cases. How useful her general model will be remains to be determined, but Embretson's research does highlight, among other things, the scope of IRT model building. Also, Embretson's and Fischer's work is helping to bring cognitive psychology and psychometrics together (see, for example, Sternberg, 1984). One possible implication of this work is a new basis for the design of aptitude tests (Carroll, 1986; Snow & Lohman, this volume). Specifically, it could be that tests can be systematically produced to reflect precisely the cognitive skills of interest. New methods of test analysis are also possible with these IRT models by Fischer, Embretson, and their colleagues. Though limited test development has been done to date, the general line of model building and test development appears promising.

Another direction in which IRT model building has been taken by Fischer (1976) is in measuring change. This kind of measurement is difficult to do well within the classical measurement framework, because, in part, of problems associated with a measurement scale that is bounded by 0 and n (where n is the number of items in the test). The boundedness of the scale makes the measurement of growth problematic, especially when the same test (or a parallel form) must be used before and after the treatment or intervention. When the treatment has been effective, a negatively skewed distribution of posttreatment scores is often the result, and growth scores are restricted. A positively skewed set of pretreatment scores, when it arises, is also a problem because of the "bottom effect" where low performers as well as very low performers receive nearly the same scores. Within an IRT framework, however, the before and after treatment tests need not be identical to permit the comparison of pre- and posttreatment scores. Ability scores are invariant over different samples of test items. One test can be constructed to provide suitable measurements before the treatment; and the other test, after the treatment. The differences in examinee ability scores over the two test administrations provide estimates of growth that are not affected (to any extent) by a bounded scale. The appropriateness of this application depends on the construction of the pre- and posttreatment tests. In general, each test should not be too easy or too hard for the group of examinees it is administered to. Both tests, however, must be constructed from the same well-defined domain of content.

Interest in multidimensional IRT models has increased recently (see, for example, Reckase, 1985). The basic form of the model is

$$P_i(\theta_j) = \frac{e^{\sum_{l=1}^{k} a_{il}(\theta_{jl} - b_{il})}}{1 + e^{\sum_{l=1}^{k} a_{il}(\theta_{jl} - b_{il})}} \qquad (i = 1, 2, \ldots, n) \quad (12)$$

where θ_j is a vector of ability scores for examinee j, θ_{jl}, $1 = 1$, $2, \ldots, k$ is a set of abilities for examinee j on the k abilities assumed to underlie test performance, and b_{il} and a_{il}, $1 = 1$, $2, \ldots, k$, are the item difficulty and item discrimination parameters, respectively, on the k dimensions or traits. Of course, the multidimensional two-parameter logistic model can be revised in several ways. One variation would include the addition of a pseudochance level parameter. Probably the best application to date has been to develop a multidimensional definition of item difficulty (Reckase, 1985). Impeding progress with these models, however, is the shortage of readily available computer programs, which in turn cannot be developed until proper model parameter estimation methods are available.

Another direction for IRT-based model building appears in the work of Lord (1970a) and Mokken and Lewis (1982). These researchers obtained ICC's without making strong assumptions about their mathematical forms. IRT models based on weaker assumptions appear to be one promising direction for further research.

Finally, Bock and his colleagues (Bock & Mislevy, 1981; Bock, Mislevy, & Woodson, 1982; and Pandey & Carlson, 1983) have developed and applied an IRT model that appears useful in the context of large-scale assessments where the unit of analysis is the class, school, district, or other subgroup of examinees, rather than the individual. The basic data for analysis are the item proportion-correct scores for the subgroups of interest. An ability estimate for each subgroup replaces the ability estimate for each examinee in the IRT model.

Reporting ability estimates rather than proportion-correct scores (p values) is preferable in large-scale assessments because of problems associated with p statistics. The p-value scale is *not* equal-interval, and, therefore, valid comparisons of groups are problematic and the assessment of growth or change over time is more difficult. Other advantages of this group-centered IRT model are described by Bock et al. (1982).

Model Advantages

Once the assumptions of the chosen IRT model are satisfied, the advantages associated with the model can be gained. There are three primary advantages of item response models.

1. An examinee's estimated ability is not dependent on the particular sample of test items chosen from the calibrated pool of items. (However, the precision of the estimate is.)
2. The statistical descriptors of a test item (for example, item difficulty and discrimination indexes) are independent of the particular sample of examinees drawn from the population of examinees for whom the test is intended.
3. A statistic indicating the precision of the estimated ability is provided for each examinee. This statistic is dependent on examinee ability and the number and the statistical properties of the items in the test.

Advantages one and two are not present in any form of classical test theory. The third advantage is *not* present in weak true-score theory, but it is present in strong true-score theory. The extent to which the three advantages are gained in any

application of an item response model depends on the closeness of the "fit" between a set of test data and the model. If the fit is poor, these three desirable features will not be obtained or will be only roughly approximated. An additional desirable feature is that the concept of parallel-forms reliability in classical test theory is replaced by the concept of statistical estimation and associated standard errors. Finally, IRT models provide a common scale for describing persons and items. This feature of IRT models opens up new possibilities for test development, test score reporting, and test score interpretations.

Regardless of the number of items administered to an examinee (so long as the number is not too small) or the statistical characteristics of the items, the ability estimate for each examinee will be an asymptotically unbiased estimate of her or his true ability, provided the item response model fits the data set. Any variation in examinee ability estimates across repeated test administrations with different sets of test items is due to measurement errors only (assuming minimal learning between test administrations). From a classical test theoretic framework, we would say that the tests administered are tau-equivalent. This means that each examinee has the same expected ability score across item samples, although measurement errors from one test to the next are not necessarily equal (see Lord & Novick, 1968; Yen, 1983a). Ability estimation independent of the particular choice (and number) of items represents one of the major advantages of item response models. Hence, item response models provide a way of comparing examinees, even though they might have taken different sets of test items from a calibrated bank of items measuring the ability or trait of interest.

Ability Scores

The purpose of item response theory, as with any test theory, is to provide a basis for making predictions, estimates, or inferences about abilities or traits measured by a test. These abilities or traits can be broadly or narrowly defined achievement, aptitude, or personality variables; they are influenced by instruction or time; and what the scores actually measure must be established empirically with a construct validity investigation. Several aspects of ability scores will be considered next: appropriate scale transformations, relationship between true scores and ability scores, and validity of ability score interpretations.

The researcher usually begins with a set of item responses from a group of examinees. An IRT model is then chosen and fitted to the response data. With some applications, such as adaptive testing or test construction using a bank of test items, IRT statistics are already available (or *calibrated*) for the items, and, so, only ability estimates are needed. With other applications, both ability estimates and item-parameter estimates are needed. Model parameter estimates are assigned so that there is maximum agreement between the chosen model and the data. The ability scale is determined, to maximize the agreement between the IRT model and the test data. It is the scale on which the ICCs have the desired mathematical form. Once the ability and item-parameter estimates are obtained, the fit of the model to the data can be examined. In later sections of this chapter, both parameter estimation and goodness-of-fit will be addressed in detail.

Appropriate Scale Transformations

The scale on which ability is reported is arbitrary. Because of the arbitrariness of the θ (and b) scale, a common way of establishing the scale is to standardize either the ability scores or the item difficulties and adjust the other model parameter values accordingly. Alternately, a particular subset of examinees or items is used to anchor the scale (for example, a core set of test items or a group of examinees of special interest). Scale transformations that preserve the probabilities specified under the model are acceptable. Thus $\theta^* = f(\theta)$ is an acceptable transformation, so long as $P_i(\theta^*) = P_i(\theta)$.

It is easy to show that linear transformations of θ, say $\theta^* = x\theta + y$, are acceptable, provided the corresponding linear adjustments are made to the item parameters in the model:

$$b_i^* = xb_i + y, \quad \text{and}$$
$$a_i^* = \frac{1}{x} a_i,$$

No transformation of the c parameter is required

$$(\text{i.e., } c_i^* = c_i).$$

For example, given the three-parameter logistic model and the foregoing transformations,

$$
\begin{aligned}
P_i(\theta^*) &= c_i^* + (1 - c_i^*)[1 + e^{-Da_i^*(\theta^* - b_i^*)}]^{-1} \\
&= c_i + (1 - c_i)[1 + e^{-Da_i/x_i(x\theta + y - xb_i - y)}]^{-1} \\
&= c_i + (1 - c_i)[1 + e^{-Da_i(\theta - b_i)}]^{-1} \\
&= P_i(\theta).
\end{aligned}
$$

Linear transformations of ability scores are often made to provide new scales that are more convenient for users (see, for example, Bashaw, 1982; Pandey & Carlson, 1983; Rentz & Bashaw, 1977, and Peterson, Kolen, & Hoover, this volume). For example, test users rarely like to work with negative scores or scores with decimals.

Because linear transformations of the scale are permissible, equal-interval scale properties are ascribed to the ability scores. Other factors to consider when choosing a scale are described in some detail by Yen (1986), such as internal consistency, relationships to external variables, and statistical properties.

Several techniques can be used to enhance the meaning of the ability scale. For one, selected percentile scores for clearly described samples of examinees can be marked on the scale. Also, the location of various test items (probably using the item b values) or groups of items can be marked along the scale. Meaning is given to the scale because users then have knowledge about the types of items along the scale that examinees can be expected to answer correctly with known probabilities. Readers are referred to Bock and Mislevy (1986) and Pandey and Carlson (1983) for specific examples of reporting scores using IRT models.

Relation Between True Scores and Ability Scores

If two tests measuring the same ability were administered to the same group of examinees and the tests were not strictly parallel, two different test score distributions would result. The extent of the differences between the two distributions would depend, among other things, on the difference between the difficulties of the two tests. Because there is no basis for preferring one test score distribution over the other, the test score distributions do not provide information about the distribution of ability scores. This situation occurs because the raw-score units from each test are unequal and different. On the other hand, examinees will have the same score on the ability scale for nonparallel tests that measure a common ability. Thus, even though an examinee's true scores (in the number-correct scale) vary across nonparallel forms of a test, the ability score, θ, for the examinee will be the same on each form.

The concept of true score (or relative true score) is of primary importance in classical test theory. It can be defined as the expected test score (over a set of test items) for an examinee. If the test score, denoted X, is defined as the number of correct answers on an n-item test, then

$$X = \sum_{i=1}^{n} u_i$$

where u_i, the response to item i, is either 1 or 0. An examinee's true score, T, is defined as

$$T = E(X) = \sum_{i=1}^{n} E(u_i). \tag{13}$$

For an examinee with ability θ, this expression is conditional on θ and should be so expressed. Thus,

$$T = \sum_{i=1}^{n} E(u_i|\theta), \quad \text{and} \tag{14}$$

$$T = \sum_{i=1}^{n} P_i(\theta). \tag{15}$$

Equation 15 follows from 14 because

$$
\begin{aligned}
E(u_i|\theta) &= 1 \times P_i(u_i = 1|\theta) + 0 \times P_i(u_i = 0|\theta) \\
&= P_i(u_i = 1|\theta) \\
&= P_i(\theta).
\end{aligned}
$$

The expression in Equation 15 is called the *test characteristic curve* (TCC). It reflects the monotonic relationship between true scores (expected number-correct scores) and ability scores for a particular set of test items.

The two concepts, θ and T, are the same, except for the scale of measurement used to describe each. That the scales differ is clear from the fact that the true score is defined on the interval $[0, n]$, whereas ability scores are defined in the interval $(-\infty, +\infty)$. The most important difference is that, whereas the scale for ability is independent of the items, the scale for true scores is dependent on the items in the test.

Ability estimates have the definite advantage over true-score estimates of being *item-free*. However, ability scores are measured on a scale that is less familiar to test users than the true-score scale. True-score estimates are defined on the interval $[0, n]$ and provide information about, for example, examinee levels of performance in relation to the content measured by a test. True-score estimates (in IRT usually $\sum_{i=1}^{n} P_i(\hat{\theta})$ is used) are reported in the test-score metric. Therefore they are in a scale that is familiar to many users.

TCCs have many uses. For one, they can be used to predict examinee test scores on a particular set of items of interest when ability scores are available, possibly estimated from a different set of items measuring the same ability. "Customized" tests draw heavily on TCCs to predict performance on one set of items (sometimes a nationally normed achievement test) from another set of test items (sometimes basically the same norm-referenced test but with at least a few different items to satisfy local needs). TCCs also play an important role in test-score equating. The TCCs for the two tests to be equated are obtained on a common ability scale. Estimated true scores obtained using the TCCs at each ability level are assumed to be equivalent (interchangeable) test scores. TCCs have also been used to predict true- and test-score distributions (see, for example, Hambleton & Traub, 1973; Lord, 1974a; Lord & Novick, 1968). Such predictions are often helpful in the design of tests to accomplish particular purposes (see, for example, Lord, 1977b). A fourth use is to transform ability estimates onto the test-score metric (or scale). Lord (1980a) prefers to compute test statistics on the bounded test score scale $[0, n]$ to minimize the influence of very large ability estimates that often arise in practice.

Validity of Ability-score Interpretations

The fact that a set of test items can be fitted by a unidimensional item response model provides evidence that the items measure one trait in common. Construct validity studies are still needed, however, to describe the characteristic or trait measured by the test (see Messick, this volume). In this respect, the problem of validating ability-score interpretations is no different from the problem of validating the interpretations of any other set of test scores. Some researchers have offered model fit statistics as validity evidence. Such information does, for example, help in judging the plausibility of the unidimensionality assumption but does not help show what the test actually measures. To illustrate, Wood (1978) found that he could fit an item response model to random data (item scores derived from tosses of a coin). In this instance, the underlying trait is an invalid measure of any trait of interest, and the scores have zero reliability too!

Evidence must be accumulated to help judge whether or not the ability scores serve their intended purpose. For example, when a test is constructed to measure reading comprehension, a series of studies might have to be conducted to ascertain if the ability scores are reliable, if they correlate with other indications of reading comprehension ability (convergent validity evidence), if they are uncorrelated with measures of ability unrelated in theory to reading comprehension (divergent validity evidence), and if they are influenced by instruction. When the results of such studies are consistent with expectations, that is, when the ability scores function as if the test actually measured the trait it was designed to measure, the test developers and test-score users can have confidence in the validity of their ability-score interpretations. When the results are inconsistent, the following possibilities must be entertained: (a) The ability scores do not measure the trait of interest; (b) parts of the theory, the hypotheses, or both, generated for the validity investigation, are incorrect; (c) the data analysis is faulty; or (d) some combination of these possibilities pertains.

A final point bearing on validity considerations involves the treatment of misfitting test items. It is not unusual for test developers using item response models to define a domain of content; write, edit, and pilot their test items; and, finally, discard test items that fail to fit the selected model. This last action might create a problem. In the deletion of test items, the characteristics of the item domain might be changed in subtle or unknown ways. The types of items (content and format) being discarded must be carefully scrutinized, because it might be necessary to redefine the domain to which ability scores are referenced or use a less restrictive model to expand the number of items that can be fitted by the IRT model of choice.

Item and Test Information and Efficiency

Item response models provide a powerful method of describing items and tests, selecting test items, and comparing tests (see, for example, Birnbaum, 1968; Hambleton & de Gruijter, 1983; Lord, 1977b; Samejima, 1977). The method involves the use of *item-information functions,* denoted $I_i(\theta)$, where

$$I_i(\theta) = \frac{[P_i'(\theta)]^2}{P_i(\theta)Q_i(\theta)} \qquad (i = 1, 2, \ldots, n). \qquad (16)$$

or, in the case of the three-parameter logistic model

$$I_i(\theta) = \frac{2.89\, a_i^2\, (1 - c_i)}{[c_i + e^{1.7a_i(\theta - b_i)}][1 + e^{-1.7a_i(\theta - b_i)}]^2} \quad (i = 1, 2, \ldots, n).$$

$I_i(\theta)$ is the information provided by item i at θ, $P_i'(\theta)$ is the first derivative of $P_i(\theta)$ with respect to θ, and $P_i(\theta)$ and $Q_i(\theta)$ were defined earlier.

The derivation of Equation 16 given by Birnbaum (1968, chap. 17) is not especially important here; however, the result is. Item-information functions can play an important role in test development and item evaluation in that they display the contribution items can make to ability estimation at any point along the ability continuum. This contribution depends to a great extent on an item's discriminating power (the higher it is, the steeper the slope of P_i), and the location at which this contribution will be realized is dependent on the item's difficulty. Birnbaum (1968) showed that an item provides maximum information at θ_m, where

$$\theta_m = b_i + \frac{1}{Da_i}\, log_e\, .5\, (1 + \sqrt{1 + 8c_i}). \qquad (17)$$

If guessing is minimal, that is, $c_i = 0$, then $\theta_m = b_i$. In general, an item provides its maximum information at an ability level slightly higher than its difficulty. Considerable emphasis is placed on the importance of model-data fit in this chapter. However, even when the fit is good, an item may have limited value in all tests (if the a parameter is low), and its usefulness in other tests will depend on the specific needs of the test developer.

Figure 4.4 shows ICCs and corresponding item-information functions for four test items. The figure highlights several important features:

1. An item provides less information when guessing is a

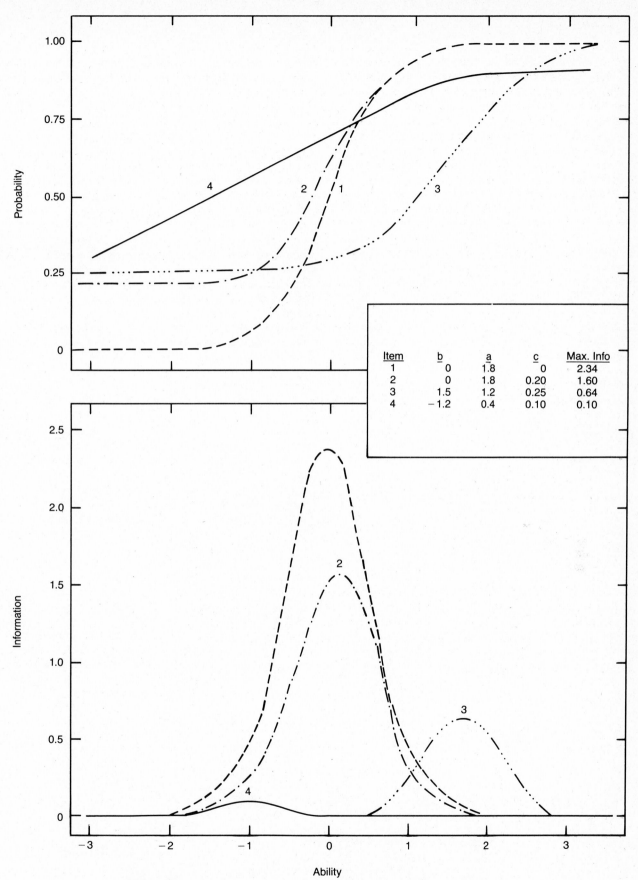

Item	b	a	c	Max. Info
1	0	1.8	0	2.34
2	0	1.8	0.20	1.60
3	1.5	1.2	0.25	0.64
4	−1.2	0.4	0.10	0.10

FIGURE 4.4 Four ICCs and corresponding item-information function.

factor in test performance. This can be observed by comparing the information functions for items 1 and 2.

2. When guessing occurs, an item provides its maximum information at a point on the ability continuum that is slightly above the point corresponding to its difficulty level. Again, this point can be observed by comparing the item-information functions for items 1 and 2.
3. An item with a low discriminating power is almost useless for ability estimation (see item 4).
4. Even the most discriminating item provides limited information for significant portions of the ability continuum. This point can be seen by studying the information functions for items 1 and 3. Item 3 is considerably more useful than item 1 with high-ability examinees, though the discriminating power for item 1 is 50% higher and its pseudochance level parameter is 0, which makes it generally more informative.

Because item-information functions are lower, generally, when $c > 0$ than when $c = 0$, researchers might be tempted to consider fitting only one- and two-parameter models to their test data. Information functions will be higher; however, the one- and two-parameter item-information functions will only be useful when the ICCs from which they are derived fit the test data. The use of improperly fitting ICCs and corresponding item-information functions is far from optimal and can give misleading results (see, for example, de Gruijter, 1986).

The information function for a test, denoted $I(\theta)$, and derived by Birnbaum (1968, chap. 17), is given by

$$I(\theta) = \sum_{i=1}^{n} \frac{[P_i'(\theta)]^2}{P_i(\theta)Q_i(\theta)}, \quad \text{or} \quad I(\theta) = \sum_{i=1}^{n} I_i(\theta). \quad (18)$$

The information provided by a test at θ is simply the sum of the item-information functions at θ. From Equation 18, it is clear that items contribute independently to the test-information function. Thus, the contribution of individual test items can be determined without knowledge of the other items in the test. The advantage of this feature will be highlighted later in the chapter. In passing, we note that this is not a feature of the classical test model and associated item and test statistics. The contribution of test items to such statistics as test reliability and item discrimination indexes (e.g., point biserial correlations) cannot be determined independently of the characteristics of the remaining items in the test. This is true because the test score, which is used in these calculations, is dependent on the particular selection of test items. When even one item is changed, test scores are changed and, so, too, are all of the classical item and test statistics. Also, it must be noted that the result above is only true when the $\hat{\theta}$ is based on maximum likelihood estimation using the vector of item responses. It is not true if, for example, maximum likelihood estimation is used to get $\hat{\theta}$ from other data, such as the number correct score (see Yen, 1984a or Lord, 1980a).

Information functions can be used to provide an IRT definition of parallel tests (Samejima, 1977). Tests are said to be *weak parallel forms* when they measure the same ability and have equal information functions. *Strong parallel forms* must satisfy one additional condition: Corresponding items in the forms must have identical item parameters.

The amount of information provided by a test at θ is inversely related to the precision with which ability is estimated at that point:

$$SE(\theta_o) = \frac{1}{\sqrt{I(\theta_o)}}, \quad (19)$$

where $SE(\theta_o)$ is called the *standard error of estimation*. This result holds whenever maximum likelihood estimates of θ (to be considered in the next section) are computed. With knowledge of the test information at θ_o, a confidence band can be found for use in interpreting the estimate of ability. In the framework of IRT, $SE(\theta)$ serves the same role as the standard error of measurement in classical measurement theory. One notes, however, that the value of $SE(\theta)$ depends on ability level, whereas the classical standard error of measurement does not. The classical standard error of measurement is a group statistic that is applied in the same way to all examinees in the sample.

$SE(\theta_o)$ is the standard deviation of the (approximately) normal distribution associated with the estimates of ability for members of the subpopulation having ability θ_o. The approximation is best when the amount of information is not too small. Even with information as low as (about) 7.0, Samejima (1977) found that the normal approximation was satisfactory for most purposes. The size of this standard error depends, in general, on (a) the number of test items (smaller standard errors are associated with longer tests); (b) the quality of test items (in general, smaller standard errors are associated with highly discriminating items for which the correct answer cannot be obtained by guessing); and (c) the match between item difficulty and examinee ability (smaller standard errors are associated with tests composed of items with difficulty parameters approximately equal to the ability parameter of the examinee, as opposed to tests that are relatively easy or relatively difficult). Figure 4.5 provides an indication of the relationship between standard errors and test information. It is clear from the figure that the size of the standard error quickly stabilizes, so that increasing information beyond a value of, say, 25 has only a small effect on the size of errors in ability estimation.

On occasion, there might be interest in comparing the information functions for two or more tests that measure the same ability. For example, a test selection committee might want to compare the information functions for several standardized tests to identify the one that seems to provide the most information in the region or regions on the ability scale in which the committee has the most interest. Comparing information functions for two or more tests can serve as a new aid in test evaluations and selections (see, for example, Lord, 1974b).

The comparison of information functions is done by computing the relative efficiency of one test, as compared with the other, as an estimator of ability at $\theta = \theta_o$:

$$RE(\theta) = \frac{I_A(\theta)}{I_B(\theta)}, \quad (20)$$

where $RE(\theta)$ denotes relative efficiency and $I_A(\theta)$ and $I_B(\theta)$ are the information functions for tests A and B, respectively, defined over a common ability scale, θ. If, for example, $I_A(\theta_o) = 10.0$ and $I_B(\theta_o) = 8.0$, then $RE(\theta_o) = 1.25$, and it is said that at θ_o, Test A is functioning as if it were 25% longer than Test B.

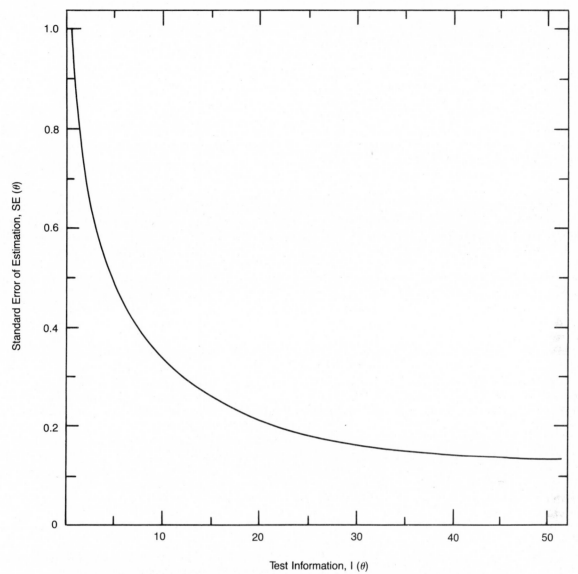

Test Information, I (θ)

FIGURE 4.5 Relationship between the standard error of estimation and test information.

Then, Test B would need to be lengthened by 25% to yield the same accuracy of measurement as Test A at $\theta = \theta_o$. Alternatively, Test A could be shortened by 20% and still produce estimates of ability at $\theta = \theta_o$ possessing the same accuracy as estimates produced by Test B. These conclusions concerning the lengthening and shortening of tests are based on the assumption that items added or deleted are comparable in statistical quality to other items in the test.

Relative efficiency has been used as a way of comparing standardized achievement tests (Lord, 1980a) and assessing the consequences of changing some of the items of a test. Lord (1977b, 1980a), for example, asked what would be the implications for the SAT of

1. Shortening the test by removing randomly equivalent parts;
2. Adding five items similar to the five easiest items in the original test;

3. Removing five items of medium difficulty;
4. Replacing five medium-difficulty items by five very easy items;
5. Replacing all reading items with a typical set of nonreading items;
6. Removing the easier half of the items;
7. Removing the harder half of the items;
8. Replacing all items with items of medium difficulty.

Lord answered the eight questions by computing the *relative efficiency* of the two tests of interest: the original test and the revised test. The answers are as follows:

1. If the test is shortened to n_B from n_A items by removing a random selection of items, the relative efficiency of the shortened test relative to the original test is n_B/n_A.
2. Adding five very easy items increases the relative effi-

ciency across the scale slightly, but the influence at the lower end of the ability scale is substantial.

3. Deleting five items of medium difficulty lowers the relative efficiency of the revised test across most of the scale, especially near the middle of the scale.

4. Deleting five items of medium difficulty and adding five very easy items results in a new test that provides more information at the lower end of the ability scale and less information in the middle of the ability scale.

5. As Lord noted, the results of this revision are not generalizable to other tests, but the question does describe a type of question that can be addressed through relative efficiency.

6. Deleting the easiest items dramatically affects the measurement precision of the revised test at the lower end of the ability scale. There is even some loss (about 10%) in measurement precision at the upper end of the ability scale.

7. Removing the hardest items has the predicted effect: Measurement precision is lost at the high end of the ability scale. But there are also surprise results. Because the most difficult items are removed, low-ability examinees do less guessing, and the revised test, therefore, actually functions substantially better at the lower end of the ability scale, even though the revised test is only half as long as the original test.

8. Loading the test with items of medium difficulty results in a revised test with substantially more measurement precision in the middle of the scale and less measurement precision at the ends of the ability scale.

Lord has demonstrated very nicely how the consequences of test revisions can be studied with the aid of relative efficiency. A variety of new test designs can be proposed, relative efficiency curves can be computed, and then the best of the designs can be selected and implemented. However, these test-design activities do require a set of test items for which item-parameter estimates are available. In the next section, item-parameter estimation will be considered in detail.

All the foregoing results are based on the assumption that test scoring is done using item scoring weights that are appropriate for the IRT model being used. Those weights are described in a subsequent section of this chapter. When the less than optimal weights are used, test information falls short of the result given by Equation 18. Birnbaum (1968) derived the *information function* of a given scoring formula:

$$I_y(\theta) = \frac{\left(\sum_{i=1}^{n} w_i P_i'\right)^2}{\sum_{i=1}^{n} w_i^2 P_i Q_i}. \tag{21}$$

Here, $I_y(\theta)$ is the amount of information at ability level θ provided by the scoring formula y, where

$$y = \sum_{i=1}^{n} w_i u_i, \tag{22}$$

u_i is the binary score for item i, and w_i is the scoring weight. Birnbaum (1968) derived Equation 21 from the notion that the information function for a scoring formula should be inversely proportional to the square of the length of the asymptotic confidence interval for estimating ability from the scoring formula.

Birnbaum (1968) also showed that the maximum value of $I_y(\theta)$ is given by Equation 18. The information function given by Equation 21 is maximized when the scoring weights are

$$w_i = \frac{P_i'}{P_i Q_i}. \tag{23}$$

This equation implies that optimal scoring weights for the one-, two-, and three-parameter logistic test models should be chosen to be 1, Da_i, and $\dfrac{Da_i(P_i - c_i)}{(1 - c_i)P_i}$, respectively (Lord, 1980a). Test information functions for the best scoring weights for several other item response models are given by Samejima (1969; 1972). Use of the weights given by Equation 23 makes it possible to construct the smallest possible confidence bands for the estimates of ability obtained using the same scoring weights.

If nonoptimal scoring weights are used with a particular logistic test model, the information function given by Equation 21 will be lower, at all ability levels, than the one that would result from the use of optimal weights given by Equation 23. Again, relative efficiency can be used to assess the information loss due to the use of less than optimal scoring weights. Hambleton and Traub (1971) found that, when there was no guessing (i.e., $c_i = 0$), the efficiency of unit scoring weights was relatively high (over 85%) for typical levels of variation in the item-discrimination parameters (.20 to 1.00, which roughly translates into a range of item-test biserial correlations from .20 to .70). When guessing was introduced, the situation changed substantially. For low-ability examinees, the efficiency of unit scoring weights dropped to the 60%–70% range. It is clear that, when a test is being used with examinees who vary widely in ability and when guessing is a factor in test performance, the scoring system of the three-parameter logistic model is to be preferred to simple number-correct scores. The latter, which implies use of scoring weights equal to 1, leads to efficient estimates of ability when there is little or no guessing and when there is relatively little variation in the discrimination parameters.

Lord (1968) investigated the efficiency of unit scoring weights on the verbal section of the SAT. Under the assumption that the three-parameter model was the best model for the data, he found that the efficiency of unit scoring weights varied from 55% at the lowest level of ability to a maximum of 90% at the highest level of ability. Using unit scoring weights was equivalent to discarding about 45% of the test items for the low-ability examinees.

Estimation of Item and Ability Parameters

The IRT literature abounds with parameter-estimation methods. In this section, several of the well-known estimation methods will be considered: conditional maximum likelihood, joint maximum likelihood, marginal maximum likelihood, Bayesian, and heuristic.

Two main estimation situations arise in practice:

1. Estimation of ability with item parameters known.
2. Estimation of item and ability parameters.

These two situations will be considered separately, followed by some guidelines concerning test lengths and examinee sample sizes and descriptions of several parameter-estimation computer programs.

Estimation of Ability with Item Parameters Known

When the item parameters are assumed to be known, as they are in applications of IRT models to adaptive testing and test development, ability estimation is straightforward. Several methods will be considered next. Assuming the item parameters are known simply means that the item-parameter estimates obtained from an earlier analysis are treated as the true values.

CONDITIONAL MAXIMUM LIKELIHOOD ESTIMATION

The probability that an examinee with ability θ will obtain a response U_i ($U_i = 1$ for a correct response, and $U_i = 0$ for an incorrect response) can be represented as $P(U_i|\theta)$. Because U_i is a Bernoulli variable,

$$P(U_i|\theta) = P(U_i = 1|\theta)^{U_i} P(U_i = 0|\theta)^{1 - U_i}, \quad (24)$$

which can be represented as

$$P(U_i|\theta) = P_i^{U_i}(1 - P_i)^{1 - U_i}$$

or

$$= P_i^{U_i} Q_i^{1 - U_i} \quad (25)$$

with $Q_i = 1 - P_i$.

If an examinee with ability θ responds to n items, the joint probability of the outcomes, $U_i \ldots, U_2, \ldots, U_n$ can be represented as $P(U_1, U_2, U_n|\theta)$. If the assumption of local independence applies, then

$$P(U_1, U_2, \ldots, U_n|\theta) = P(U_1|\theta)P(U_2|\theta) \ldots P(U_n|\theta)$$

$$= \prod_{i=1}^{n} P(U_i|\theta)$$

$$= \prod_{i=1}^{n} P_i^{U_i} Q_i^{1 - U_i}. \quad (26)$$

Equation 26 is an expression of the joint probability of responses to the n items. In practice, the random variables U_1, $U_2, \ldots, U_n$ are replaced with the actual item scores for the examinee, denoted $u_1, u_2, \ldots, u_n$, in which case Q_i drops out of Equation 26 when $u_i = 1$, and P_i drops out when $u_i = 0$. With the item scores for the examinee substituted in Equation 26, the resulting expression is no longer a probability statement. Instead, it is called a *likelihood function* and is denoted

$$L(u_1, u_2, \ldots, u_n|\theta) = \prod_{i=1}^{n} P_i^{u_i} Q_i^{1 - u_i}. \quad (27)$$

If, for example, $u_1 = 1$, $u_2 = 1$, $u_3 = 0$, $u_4 = 0$, and $u_5 = 1$,

$$L(1, 1, 0, 0, 1|\theta) = P_1 P_2 Q_3 Q_4 P_5.$$

In other words, the likelihood of the 11001 pattern of item scores is given by the product of the values of P_1, P_2, Q_3, Q_4, and P_5. With item parameters and item scores known, the value of the likelihood function depends on the single unknown variable, θ. The value of the ability parameter that maximizes the likelihood function L is called the *maximum likelihood estimate of ability*. Maximum likelihood estimation involves choosing a value (or values) for the parameter (or parameters) that makes the data appear *most likely*. That is, parameter values are chosen that maximize the probability, given by Equation 27, of the item responses that were actually made.

There are several ways that Equation 27 can be solved for θ: trial and error, systematic search, graphing the likelihood function, and using numerical methods (see Hambleton & Swaminathan, 1985, chaps. 5, 7; Lord, 1980a, chap. 4). The latter method is the most popular in current computer programs because it works well with large samples of examinees. The other methods are slow and sometimes inconvenient with large samples.

In applying numerical methods, it is usually most convenient to find parameter estimates that maximize the natural logarithm of the likelihood function (denoted $ln\,L$) rather than L. After the taking of the natural logarithm of the likelihood function, the product on the right side of Equation 27 is replaced by a sum, as follows:

$$ln\,L(u_1, u_2, \ldots, u_n|\theta)$$

$$= \sum_{i=1}^{n} [u_i ln\,P_i + (1 - u_i) ln\,Q_i]. \quad (28)$$

The maximum of $ln\,L$ is attained at the value θ where the slope of $ln\,L$ as a function of θ is 0, that is, where

$$\frac{d}{d\theta} ln\,L(u_1, u_2, \ldots, u_n|\theta) = 0. \quad (29)$$

For the common logistic item response models, Equation 29 can be expressed as follows:

$$\frac{dln\,L(u_1, u_2, \ldots, u_n|\theta)}{d\theta} = \sum_{i=1}^{n} k_i u_i - \sum_{i=1}^{n} k_i P_i = 0. \quad (30)$$

The values of k_i for the one-, two-, and three-parameter models are

$k_i = D$	(one-parameter model), and
$k_i = Da_i$	(two-parameter model), and
$k_i = Da_i(P_i - c_i)/P_i(1 - c_i)$	(three-parameter model).

The value of k_i is always positive because $a_i \geq 0$ and $P_i \geq c_i$. Analogous expressions for Equation 30 can easily be derived for other IRT models.

A problem in finding a practical solution to Equation 30 arises when all u_i are 0s or 1s. The ability estimates are easy: $\hat{\theta} = \pm\infty$. It is the practical application of this solution which is problematic. In this case, several alternative solutions can be tried (see Hambleton & Swaminathan, 1985).

It is easy to generalize Equation 30 to the case of N examinees. Because the responses of different examinees are independent, the joint likelihood function for the responses of N examinees is given by

$$L(u_1, u_2, \ldots, u_a, \ldots, u_N|\theta) = \prod_{a=1}^{N} L(u_a|\theta_a)$$

$$= \prod_{a=1}^{N} \prod_{i=1}^{n} L(u_{ia}|\theta_a)$$

$$= \prod_{a=1}^{N} \prod_{i=1}^{n} P_{ia}^{u_{ia}} Q_{ia}^{1-u_{ia}}. \tag{31}$$

This result follows, like Equation 26, from the assumption of local independence. In Equation 31,

$$P_{ia} = P_i(\theta_a), \quad \text{and}$$

$$u_a = (u_{1a}, u_{2a}, \ldots, u_{na}), \quad \text{and}$$

$u_{ia} = 1$ for a correct response of examinee a on item i, and $u_{ia} = 0$, otherwise.

The abilities θ_a, $a = 1, 2, \ldots, N$ that maximize the likelihood function in Equation 31 are called *maximum likelihood estimators*. Again, the likelihood function can be differentiated with respect to each θ_a. Each differential equation (there are N in total) can be set equal to 0 and solved for the one unknown, θ_a. This equation is identical to Equation 30. The resulting estimates of θ_a are said to be *conditional maximum likelihood estimates*. They are conditional in the sense that they depend on the known item parameters. Presently, conditional maximum likelihood is the most frequently used estimation method when the item parameters are known.

BAYESIAN ESTIMATION

Bayesian estimation methods involve specifying distributions to represent prior beliefs about the unknown model parameters. For example, a narrow prior distribution could be used if the researcher had considerable information about the parameter values. A more diffuse or heterogeneous prior distribution might be specified if less information about the parameter were available. The prior information could come from knowledge of how similar groups of examinees performed on the test or how these same examinees performed on similar but different tests. The prior distribution is combined with the test data to produce a distribution of revised belief (called *posterior distribution*) about the unknown parameters. Usually the mode or mean of the posterior distribution for the ability parameter is taken as the ability parameter estimate. When the test is short, the sample size is small, or many examinees obtain near 0 or near perfect scores, Bayesian estimation methods are especially helpful (see, for example, Swaminathan & Gifford, 1982, 1985, 1986).

Bayesian estimation methods are based upon applications of Bayes's theorem, which relates the conditional and marginal probabilities associated with two events, say, A and B, as follows:

$$P(B|A) = P(A|B)P(B)/P(A). \tag{32}$$

It follows that

$$P(\theta|u_1, u_2, \ldots, u_n)$$
$$= P(u_1, u_2, \ldots, u_n|\theta)P(\theta)/P(u_1, u_2, \ldots, u_n), \tag{33}$$

where the ability parameter is substituted for B and the item scores for the examinee are substituted for A. $P(u_1, u_2, \ldots, u_n)$ is a constant for all examinees, whereas $P(u_1, u_2, \ldots, u_n|\theta)$ is the likelihood function and $P(\theta)$ is the distribution representing the prior belief about θ. It is common to state Equation 33 as follows:

$$\text{posterior} \propto \text{likelihood} \times \text{prior}.$$

This means that the posterior distribution for the model parameter of interest is proportional to the product of the likelihood expression and the prior distribution for the parameter. The likelihood function for the IRT model of interest is given by Equation 27. The prior is a distribution representing the parameter of interest. The most common situation is for a researcher to choose a mathematical distribution, for example, the normal curve, to reflect his or her prior knowledge. Then different values of the parameters of the distribution can be chosen to produce a wide range of prior distributions. For example, with priors shaped like normal curves, the mean can be chosen to center the distribution anywhere on the ability continuum. The standard deviation can be chosen to reflect the availability of relatively precise prior information (small SD) or of almost no information (large SD). Additional details are provided by Birnbaum (1969), Owen (1975), and Swaminathan and Gifford (1986).

Estimation of Item and Ability Parameters

Estimation of both item and ability parameters is far more complicated than estimation of either item or ability parameters alone. One problem involves indeterminacy of the parameter estimates. Transformations of the form $\theta^* = x\theta + y$, $b^* = xb + y$, and $a^* = a/x$ to the logistic model parameter estimates leave the ICCs invariant. This indeterminacy is usually removed by scaling either the θ or b parameters to a desired mean and standard deviation (see, for example, Stocking & Lord, 1983).

A second problem is that numerical procedures are not guaranteed to yield true solutions of likelihood equations. When the likelihood function is nonlinear, it can have several local maxima, with only one being the absolute maximum. The solution that is found might correspond to one of the "local" maxima and not the absolute maximum. The value of a parameter at a local maximum cannot be taken as the maximum likelihood estimate of the parameter.

A third problem is that, as a consequence of the numerical procedures employed, the parameter estimates might fall outside the accepted range of values. Reasonable bounds must be imposed on the estimates, a practice that does cause objections to be raised (Wright, 1977b).

JOINT MAXIMUM LIKELIHOOD ESTIMATION

The function appropriate for joint maximum likelihood estimation (see Lord, 1974a; 1980a) is given by Equation 31. The procedure outlined earlier for ability estimation easily generalizes to ability and item-parameter estimation. This time, however, there are many more parameters. With N examinees, n items, and the three-parameter logistic model, there are $N + 3n$ model parameters to be estimated. For the two-parameter logistic model, there are $N + 2n$ model parameters; for the one-parameter logistic model, there are $N + n$ model parameters.

Once the mathematical form of $P_i(\theta)$ in Equation 31 is specified, the joint maximum likelihood parameter estimates can be obtained by seeking the values of θ_a, $a = 1, 2, \ldots, N$; and $b_i, a_i, c_i, i = 1, 2, \ldots, n$ that maximize $L(u_1, u_2, \ldots, u_n | \theta_1, \theta_2, \ldots, \theta_N, b_1, a_1, c_1, b_2, a_2, c_2, \ldots, b_n, a_n, c_n)$ or its natural logarithm. The latter is given as

$$\sum_{a=1}^{N} \sum_{i=1}^{n} [u_{ia} \ln P_{ia} + (1 - u_{ia}) \ln Q_{ia}]. \tag{34}$$

To obtain joint maximum likelihood parameter estimates for the three-parameter logistic model, the following sets of nonlinear equations must be solved:

$$\frac{\partial Ln\,L}{\partial \theta_a} = 0, a = 1, 2, \ldots, N$$

$$\frac{\partial Ln\,L}{\partial b_i} = 0, \frac{\partial Ln\,L}{\partial a_i} = 0, \frac{\partial Ln\,L}{\partial c_i} = 0, i = 1, 2, \ldots, n.$$

With the one- and two-parameter logistic models, there are fewer equations to solve. Moreover, the equations are correspondingly simplified. Consider the equations in greater detail. For the three-parameter logistic model, those for the examinees,

$$\frac{\partial Ln\,L}{\partial \theta_a} = 0, a = 1, 2, \ldots, N$$

can be written as

$$D \sum_{i=1}^{n} \frac{a_i(P_{ia} - c_i)}{1 - c_i} \frac{(u_{ia} - P_{ia})}{P_{ia}} = 0,$$

$$a = 1, 2, \ldots, N. \tag{35}$$

There is one equation for each examinee; and with known item scores and item-parameter estimates, this equation can be solved to obtain θ_a. The equations for the ith item are

$$\frac{\partial Ln\,L}{\partial b_i} = 0,$$

which becomes

$$\frac{-Da_i}{(1 - c_i)} \sum_{a=1}^{N} \frac{(P_{ia} - c_i)}{P_{ia}} (u_{ia} - P_{ia}) = 0; \tag{36}$$

$$\frac{\partial Ln\,L}{\partial a_i} = 0,$$

which becomes

$$\frac{D}{(1 - c_i)} \sum_{a=1}^{N} \frac{(\theta_a - b_i)(P_{ia} - c_i)(u_{ia} - P_{ia})}{P_{ia}} = 0; \tag{37}$$

and

$$\frac{\partial Ln\,L}{\partial c_i} = 0,$$

which becomes

$$\frac{1}{(1 - c_i)} \sum_{a=1}^{N} \frac{(u_{ia} - P_{ia})}{P_{ia}} = 0. \tag{38}$$

Given the known ability estimates and known scores on the ith item for the N examinees, the three equations for item i involve only three unknowns, b_i, a_i, c_i. The three equations can be solved by numerical methods to obtain maximum likelihood estimates of the item parameters. There is a set of three such equations to be solved for each item. Joint maximum likelihood estimation for the Rasch model is further described by Wright and Douglas (1977a, 1977b).

As the foregoing description of the joint maximum likelihood procedure implies, either initial-item- or initial-ability-parameter estimates are needed to start the simultaneous estimation process. Ability estimates could be normal deviates derived from the distribution of number-correct test scores for the examinees or maximum likelihood estimates based on number-correct scores (Yen, 1984a). Alternatively, initial-item-parameter estimates could be derived from conventional item-parameter estimates of difficulty (proportion correct) and discrimination (biserial correlation). Equations for such initial item-parameter estimates are given later in this section.

Suppose the initial item-parameter estimates are obtained first. Ability estimates can then be obtained using Equation 35. There are N equations, each with only one unknown, θ_a. The resulting N ability estimates can be scaled and treated as known while solving equations 36, 37, and 38 for the item parameters b_i, a_i, and $c_i, i = 1, 2, \ldots, n$. Using these revised item-parameter estimates, Equation 35 can be solved again to obtain revised ability estimates. One cycle of the process of solving for new estimates of ability, given the most recent estimates of the item parameters, and then solving for new estimates of the item parameters, given the most recent estimates of ability, is called a *stage*. This process can be continued until the item and ability estimates do not change from one stage to the next by more than some small user-specified amount.

In practice, the foregoing steps are implemented somewhat differently to speed the rate of convergence. Also, bounds are placed on the values of parameters when they exceed desirable limits. Wingersky (1983) provides details on the process of model parameter estimation used in LOGIST, a program for joint maximum likelihood estimation. Lord (1974a) and Wingersky (1983) note that it is possible and desirable to revise the likelihood function in Equation 31 to distinguish omitted and not-reached test items from correct and incorrect responses and also to distinguish omitted items from items that were not reached.

Standard errors for ability estimates were given in the last section on information functions. Standard errors for item-parameter estimates are given in Lord (1980a) and Wingersky and Lord (1984). In the latter, the authors provided empirical evidence to support their estimates of standard errors when all model parameters are unknown. In earlier work, standard errors of ability estimates were derived by assuming the item parameters to be known. Standard errors of item parameters were derived by assuming the abilities to be known.

The estimation of the c parameter in the three-parameter model has proven to be a problem in some data sets (Thissen &

Wainer, 1982). The problem is undoubtedly due to the small numbers of examinees positioned at the lower ends of the ICCs. The resulting estimation problem highlights the importance of drawing a heterogeneous sample of examinees in item calibration (possible oversampled for low-ability examinees), and of being especially careful in interpreting the c parameter estimates when they are obtained with small samples. Lord (1975b) recommended that the c parameter for an item only be estimated when certain conditions are present: (a) The item must be difficult enough that there are examinees along the portion of the ability scale corresponding to the lower asymptote of the ICC (easy items are often located on the ability scale in regions where there are limited numbers of examinees); and (b) the item must be sufficiently discriminating (steep) that the ICC approaches its lower asymptote in a region of the ability scale where, again, there are examinees (with flatter ICCs, often there are very few examinees in the region of an item's asymptote). Lord (1975b) offered the following rule to use in deciding whether or not to estimate an item's c parameter:

$$\text{Estimate } c_i \text{ if } b_i - 2/a_i > -3.$$

(When sample sizes are very large, -4 can be substituted for -3 in the rule.) If the condition is not met, Lord recommends that the c parameter be fixed at a suitable value (e.g., somewhat lower than .25 with 4-choice items and .20 with 5-choice items). In a small study, Thissen and Wainer (1985) report support for Lord's rule. In another contribution addressing the problem, de Gruijter (1984) is able to show that a prior distribution on the c parameter may be better than fixing the parameter when it cannot be estimated. Formal Bayesian estimation algorithms for obtaining the c parameter are also given by Swaminathan and Gifford (1986).

CONDITIONAL MAXIMUM LIKELIHOOD ESTIMATION

It is well known that the maximum likelihood estimators described in the last section are not consistent because the bias in the estimators does not disappear when examinee sample sizes are increased (Andersen, 1972). One solution is to use a conditional procedure, but this requires the availability of sufficient statistics for the ability parameters (Swaminathan, 1983). Fortunately, at least for the Rasch model, the number-right score (R) is a sufficient statistic for ability estimation, and, so, it is possible to replace the likelihood function $L(u_1, u_2, \ldots, u_n | \theta_a, b)$ with $L(u_1, u_2, \ldots, u_n | R, b)$. In this way, the item-difficulty parameters can be estimated without any influence from the ability parameters (Andersen, 1972). The result is item-parameter estimates that are *consistent;* that is, these estimates approach their true values for large examinee samples. The algorithms for obtaining the estimates are complicated, and currently computations are only effective for up to 40 items (Wainer, Morgan, & Gustafsson, 1980), though programs are available to handle up to 100 items (Gustafsson, 1980a).

MARGINAL MAXIMUM LIKELIHOOD ESTIMATION

Computational problems aside, the conditional maximum likelihood procedure is a desirable one because consistent esti-

mators can be obtained. Unfortunately, the likelihood function must be conditioned on sufficient statistics to obtain the desired results, and sufficient statistics are only available for the Rasch model. Bock and Aitkin (1981), Bock and Lieberman (1970), and Thissen (1982) have proposed alternative estimation procedures in which ability estimates are removed from the estimation of item parameters by integrating them out of the likelihood function. The resulting likelihood function, referred to as the *marginal likelihood function,* is then used to find item-parameter values that maximize the marginal likelihood function. The general marginal maximum likelihood of item parameters is given as

$$L(a, b, c) = \prod_{a=1}^{N} \int_{-\infty}^{\infty} g(\theta_a) L(\theta_a; a, b, c) \, d\theta_a. \quad (39)$$

Values for item parameters are found to maximize $L(a, b, c)$ where a, b, and c are vectors of item parameters $(a_1, a_2, \ldots, a_n), (b_1, b_2, \ldots, b_n)$, and $(c_1, c_2, \ldots, c_n)$, respectively. The estimators are found by differentiating $\ln L(a, b, c)$ with respect to the parameters a, b, and c and solving the resulting likelihood equations.

According to Lord (1986), marginal maximum likelihood estimation is a useful improvement over joint maximum likelihood estimation because it can estimate item parameters without having to estimate ability parameters. The biggest improvement is with short tests (10 to 15 items). Joint maximum likelihood estimates of ability are biased, which in turn causes the item parameters to be misestimated, even for large sample sizes.

BAYESIAN PARAMETER ESTIMATION

The principle of Bayesian parameter estimation remains the same when both abilities and item parameters are estimated. However, the equations used in parameter estimation are considerably more complex because of the increase in the number of model parameters. For complete descriptions of the equations and details for specifying the priors, readers are referred to Swaminathan and Gifford (1982, 1985, 1986). Perhaps the major advantage of the Bayesian estimation over maximum likelihood estimation is that constraints do not need to be imposed on the parameter solution to minimize parameter drift to unacceptable values (e.g., a values less than 0, or c values over .35). However, because Bayesian estimates are biased, Lord (1986) has suggested that, for some applications, their main value might only be in estimating the a and c parameters in the three-parameter model. The bias in these parameters has less implication than in the b and θ parameters. Swaminathan and Gifford (1986) show that the use of informative priors on the a and c parameters and noninformative, or diffuse, priors on the b and θ parameters is effective. That is, the complexity of the estimation is reduced considerably and so is the regression effect (bias) on the ability estimates. This reduction is important when examinees are being compared who might have taken different forms of the test (e.g., adaptive tests) or the same form at different times. Yen (1987) contains detailed comparisons of maximum likelihood, marginal maximum likelihood, and Bayesian.

HEURISTIC ESTIMATION

Heuristic estimation methods, or intuitive methods, as they are sometimes called, use direct relationships that can be established between model parameters and conventional item statistics. Urry (1974, 1977) has been the strongest advocate of these methods. For example, under the assumptions that (a) the ability measured by the test is normally distributed with 0 mean and unit variance and (b) the form of the ICCs is a two-parameter normal ogive, Lord and Novick (1968, pp. 377–378) show that the biserial correlation ρ_i between scores (0 or 1) on item i and the ability measured by the test is given by

$$\rho_i = \frac{a_i}{1 + a_i^2}, \qquad i = 1, 2, \ldots, n.$$

By simple algebra, it follows that

$$a_i = \frac{\rho_i}{\sqrt{1 - \rho_i^2}} \qquad i = 1, 2, \ldots, n. \qquad (40)$$

If an estimate of ρ_i (for example, item score – total score correlation) is substituted in Equation 40, an estimate of a_i can be obtained. Lord and Novick also showed that

$$b_i = -\phi^{-1}(\pi_i)/\rho_i \qquad i = 1, 2, \ldots, n, \qquad (41)$$

where $\phi^{-1}(\pi_i)$ is the normal deviate that corresponds to an area of π_i under the normal curve. (For $\pi_i > .50$, the value of b_i is negative.) Estimates for π_i and ρ_i are substituted in Equation 41 to obtain item-difficulty-parameter estimates.

Heuristic estimation methods are usually easy to implement and require a minimum amount of computer time, but there are problems. One is that the parameter estimates supplied by these methods do not have known sampling distributions. This means, for example, that the standard errors associated with the estimates are unknown. Another problem is that the relationships between model parameters and conventional item statistics are based on highly restrictive assumptions (e.g., that θ is normally distributed). The usefulness of the parameter estimates is considerably reduced if the assumptions made in deriving a relationship are not satisfied by real data (see, for example, Ree, 1979; Swaminathan & Gifford, 1983).

Jensema (1976), Schmidt (1977), and Urry (1974, 1977) have refined the heuristic estimation method outlined by Lord and Novick and produced improved computational formulas. Various researchers (see, for example, Ree, 1979, 1981) have concluded, not surprisingly, that, when the normality assumption about ability is satisfied, the heuristic estimates of Lord and Novick (1968) and others such as Urry (1974, 1977) are quite acceptable.

Suitable Test Lengths and Sample Sizes

Questions about the length of tests and the size of examinee samples needed for proper parameter estimation are difficult to answer. The reason is that answers depend upon many factors: (a) the choice of IRT model (in general, the more model parameters, the larger the examinee samples need to be); (b) the choice of parameter estimation method and way of applying the method (in general, Bayesian methods perform better than maximum likelihood methods with shorter tests and smaller sample sizes); (c) the distribution of ability in the examinee sample (in general, homogeneous samples are far less satisfactory than heterogeneous samples); (d) the fact of whether it is item parameter or ability parameters or both that are being estimated (in general, longer tests and larger examinee samples are needed when *both* item and ability parameters are estimated); and (e) the importance of the intended IRT application (acceptable errors with important applications are smaller and longer tests and larger samples are therefore needed).

A number of researchers have suggested guidelines for the test lengths and sample sizes needed to obtain satisfactory maximum likelihood estimates. Wright and Stone (1979) recommend minimum test lengths of 20 items and sample sizes of 200 examinees for the one-parameter model. Hulin, Lissak, and Drasgow (1982) recommend the following minimum test lengths and sample sizes: 30 and 500 for the two-parameter logistic model, 60 and 1,000 for the three-parameter logistic model. Swaminathan and Gifford (1983) find that tests as short as 20 items, and with 1,000 examinees, lead to satisfactory model parameter estimates using LOGIST. All model parameter estimates were excellent with 80 items. The a and θ parameters were especially helped by increasing test lengths. Poor estimates of the a parameter resulted when the tests were short ($n < 15$ items).

Computer Programs

Several computer programs are now available for estimating ability and item parameters. Some information follows about eight programs: LOGIST, BILOG, MULTILOG, BICAL, MicroCAT, NOHARM, ANCILLES, and OGIVA.

LOGIST (Wingersky, 1983; Wingersky, Barton, & Lord, 1982) can be used to obtain estimates of examinee abilities and the item parameters of the one-, two-, and three-parameter logistic models. A joint maximum likelihood method is used (Lord, 1974a). The item and ability parameters are estimated simultaneously. To ensure that estimates of the parameters converge, various restrictions are placed on the estimates. Ability estimates can be scaled to a desired mean and standard deviation. Estimates of the standard errors of model parameter estimates are provided.

BILOG (Mislevy & Bock, 1982) can also be used to fit the one-, two-, and three-parameter logistic models to binary data. BILOG provides output similar to that of LOGIST; supplies plots of ICCs and test information curves, item fit statistics, overall fit statistics, and conventional-item statistics; and has the capability to link items into a scale with common anchor items. BILOG differs from LOGIST in several important ways. Marginal maximum likelihood is used as the method of estimation and Bayesian priors can be placed on any item parameters that are difficult to measure (e.g., test items that are very easy or very hard for the calibration sample of examinees). Recently, Scientific Software, Inc. published a PC version of BILOG that runs on an IBM PC, XT or AT with a math coprocessor. MULTILOG (Thissen, 1983) is an extension of the BILOG program that handles polychotomous item response models.

BICAL (Wright & Stone, 1979) is a program for analyzing test data to estimate the ability and item-difficulty parameters in the one-parameter logistic (Rasch) model. Joint maximum likelihood is the method of estimation that is used (Wright & Panchapakesan, 1969). The program provides, in addition to model parameter estimates, statistical tests of model fit at the item level, residuals, the test characteristic curve, conventional item statistics, and other useful information.

MicroCAT (Assessment Systems Corporation, 1984) is a complete microcomputer-based system for computer-assisted and computerized adaptive testing for the IBM PC, XT, and AT computers. Included among the features are test administration, scoring, and interpretation capabilities. Both maximum likelihood and Bayesian estimation methods are used in parameter estimation.

NOHARM (Fraser, 1981) is a Fortran program for fitting unidimensional and multidimensional normal-ogive IRT models. The program can be used for models that include one-, two-, and three-item parameters. A special feature is the ability to print the residual item covariances after the model has been fit. The pattern of residuals can be used for assessing overall model fit and for locating subgroups of items that are not fit by the model (see, for example, McDonald, 1981, 1982).

ANCILLES and OGIVA (Urry, 1977) were prepared to provide heuristic parameter estimates. Both Ree (1979) and Swaminathan and Gifford (1983) determined that these programs provide excellent estimates when the strong normality assumption about ability is met.

Comparisons of various computer programs will not be attempted because the findings would almost certainly be quickly out of date. Nearly all of the IRT computer programs described here are being updated on a regular basis. Program weaknesses are constantly being addressed in the updates, and new features are being added to speed up processing time, to improve or extend the types of output, to simplify user requests for desired analyses, and so on.

Summary

It should be clear from the material in this section that a considerable number of advances in the area of model parameter estimation has been made. Unfortunately, only a small number of the contributions could be described here, and those that were were described without much elaboration. For additional developments and details, readers are referred to review papers by Baker (1977, 1987), Swaminathan (1983) and Traub and Lam (1985); books by Hambleton and Swaminathan (1985)), Lord (1980a), and Wright and Stone (1979); and the original contributions.

Assessment of Model – Data Fit

The potential of item response theory for solving many problems in testing and measurement is high; however, the success of particular IRT applications is not assured simply by processing test results through one of the available computer programs. The advantages claimed for item response models can be realized only when the fit between the model and the

test data set of interest is satisfactory. A poorly fitting model cannot yield invariant item- and ability-parameter estimates.

In many IRT applications reported to date, the researchers have failed to investigate model fit and the consequences of misfit to the extent required. As a result, less is known about the appropriateness of particular IRT models for various applications than might be assumed from the voluminous IRT literature. In some cases, goodness-of-fit studies have been carried out using what now appear to be less than suitable statistics (see, for example, Divgi, 1986; Rogers & Hattie, 1987). Errors in judgment about model appropriateness have resulted.

A second shortcoming of many IRT applications to date is that researchers have overrelied on statistical tests of model fit. These tests have a serious flaw: their sensitivity to examinee sample size. Almost any departure in the data from the model under consideration (even the condition where the practical significance of a departure is minimal) leads to rejection of the null hypothesis of model–data fit if sample size is sufficiently large. But if sample size is small, even large model–data discrepancies might not be detected, due to the low statistical power. Note, too, that, although the null hypothesis cannot often be rejected with small samples, uses of model parameter estimates are limited because of large estimation errors. In addition, the sampling distributions of some IRT goodness-of-fit statistics are not what they have been claimed to be, so errors can be made when these statistics are interpreted in light of tabled values of known statistics (see, for example, Divgi, 1986; Rogers & Hattie, 1987; van den Wollenberg, 1982a, 1982b).

The problem associated with significance tests and examinee sample sizes is highlighted in Table 4.2. A computer program, DATAGEN (Hambleton & Rovinelli, 1973), was used to simulate the item responses of 2,400 examinees on a 50-item test. The items were described by three-parameter logistic ICCs, and examinee ability was simulated to be normally distributed (0,1). Choice of item parameters was consistent with values commonly found in practice (b, -2 to 2; a, $+.40$ to 2.00; c, .00 to .25). BICAL (Wright & Stone, 1979) was then used to obtain item- and ability-parameter estimates for five samples of examinees: the first 150, the first 300, the first 600, the first 1,200, and the total sample of 2,400 examinees. Then, with each of the five data sets, the "t statistic" calculated by the BICAL program was used to determine the number of misfitting test items at the .05 and .01 levels of significance. There is a technical problem with this statistic (van den Wollenberg, 1980), but, for our present purposes, interest is centered on the effect of sample size on power. It is sufficient to note that the

TABLE 4.2 Misfitting Test Items for Several Examinee Sample Sizes

SAMPLE SIZE	NUMBER OF MISFITTING ITEMS	
	$p < .05$	$p < .01$
150	20	5
300	25	17
600	30	18
1,200	38	28
2,400	42	38

number of test items associated with "significant" t statistics increased as examinee sample size increased. The results in Table 4.2 show this effect. In a recent paper, Hambleton and Rogers (in press) conclude that

> statistical tests of model fit do appear to have some value. Because they are sensitive to sample size and because they are not uniformly powerful, the use of any of these statistics as the sole indicator of model fit is clearly inadvisable. But two situations can be identified in which these tests may lead to relatively clear interpretations. When sample sizes are small and the statistics indicate model misfit, or when sample sizes are large and model fit is obtained, the researcher may have reasonable confidence that, in the first case, the model does misfit the data, and in the second, that the model fits the data. These possibilities make it worthwhile to employ statistical tests of fit despite their problems and despite the alternate possibility of equivocal results.

The principal purpose of the remaining parts of this section of the chapter is to describe a set of promising methods for assessing model fit. This material is an update and expansion of earlier work by Hambleton and Murray (1983) and Hambleton and Swaminathan (1985).

Overview

Hambleton and Swaminathan (1985) recommend that judgments about the suitability of models for solving particular measurement problems be based on three kinds of evidence:

1. Appropriateness of model assumptions for the test data
2. Extent to which advantages expected from the use of a model (i.e., invariant item and ability estimates) are obtained
3. Accuracy of model predictions using real and, where appropriate, simulated test data

Evidence bearing on model assumptions (first kind) can often be helpful in selecting IRT models for use in investigating areas two and three. Evidence of the second kind, the extent of the invariance of model parameter estimates, is relevant when the model parameter estimates are going to be used in test development, test score equating, and other applications. The third kind of evidence assesses the appropriateness of models for accounting for, or explaining, the actual test results and helps us understand the nature of model–data discrepancies and their consequences. Fitting more than one model to the test data and comparing the results or comparing the results to simulation results that were generated to fit the model of interest are especially helpful activities in determining the appropriateness of models for fitting data and in choosing a model.

Hambleton and Swaminathan (1985) prepared a list of promising empirical methods for determining the usefulness of IRT models. Table 4.3 is an update of this list. It includes brief descriptions of the methods.

Checking Model Assumptions

Item response models are based on *strong* assumptions that will not be completely met by any set of test data (Lord & Novick, 1968; Lord, 1980a). There is some evidence that the models are robust to moderate departures from the assumptions, but the extent of "model robustness" has not been fully established (Hambleton, Swaminathan, Cook, Eignor, & Gifford, 1978), and it probably cannot be fully established. This follows because there are a myriad of ways in which model assumptions can be violated, and the seriousness of the violations depends on the nature of the examinee sample and the intended application.

Model robustness concerns the extent to which a model leads to useful results, though the test data violate one or more of the model assumptions. Model-robustness studies of real and simulated data are prevalent in the literature. The use of simulated data is especially common because the researcher can control the nature and extent of model violations and study the consequences. For example, van de Vijver (1986) showed that the Rasch model was robust to reasonable violations of the equal item discrimination assumption when the objective was to estimate examinee ability. The model was less robust to the assumption that the probability of a correct response approaches zero as θ decreases.

Given doubts about model robustness, researchers might be tempted to simply fit the most general IRT model available, because it will be based on the least restrictive assumptions. The less restrictive the assumptions, the more likely a model fits the data to which it is applied. Unfortunately, the most general models are complex multi-dimensional ones that are not ready for wide-scale use. Alternatively, the most general of the unidimensional models in common use, the three-parameter logistic model, could be adopted. This model should result in a better fit than either the one- or two-parameter models. But, three problems are encountered in following this course of action: (a) More computer time is required to conduct the analyses, (b) larger samples of examinees and items are often required to obtain satisfactory model parameter estimates, and (c) the additional item parameters (item discrimination and pseudochance levels) complicate the use of the model for practitioners (see also Baker, 1986).

Model selection can be aided by an investigation of four principal assumptions underlying the popular unidimensional item response models: (a) unidimensionality, (b) equal discrimination indexes, (c) minimal guessing, and (d) nonspeeded test administrations. Several methods of studying these assumptions are summarized in Table 4.3.

Regarding the assumption of unidimensionality, Hattie (1984) provides a comprehensive review of 88 indexes for assessing unidimensionality. Suffice it to report that he found many of the methods in the older literature unsatisfactory, whereas methods based upon nonlinear factor analysis and the analysis of residuals were the most successful. The six methods described in Table 4.3 for assessing unidimensionality appear to be among the most promising at this time. However, considerable research remains to be carried out on the topic. Fortunately, the subject is currently being actively studied, with several new methods being developed and several comparison-of-methods studies in progress (see, for example, Tucker, Humphreys, & Roznowski, 1986; Zwick, 1987).

Evidence bearing on the robustness of IRT models to violations of the unidimensionality assumption is mixed. In addi-

TABLE 4.3 Approaches for Assessing Goodness of Fit

POSSIBLE METHODS

Checking Model Assumptions

1. Unidimensionality (applies to nearly all of the popular IRT models).

   • Eigenvalue plot (from largest to smallest) of the interitem correlation matrix (tetrachoric correlations are preferable to phi correlations). The plot is studied to determine if a dominant first factor is present (Reckase, 1979).

   • Comparison of the plots of eigenvalues from the interitem correlation matrix, using the real data, and an interitem correlation matrix of random data (the random data consist of random normal deviates in a data set with the same sample size and with the same number of variables as the real data). The two eigenvalue plots are compared. If the unidimensionality assumption is met in the real data, the two plots should be similar except for the first eigenvalue of the plot of eignevalues for the real data. It should be substantially larger than its counterpart in the random data plot (Horn, 1965). Recent modifications and examples of this method can be found in the work of Montanelli and Humphreys (1976) and Drasgow and Lissak (1983).

   • Investigation of the assumption of local independence by checking the variance-covariance or correlation matrix for examinees at different intervals on the ability or test score scale (McDonald, 1981; Tucker, Humphreys, & Roznowski, 1986). The entries in the off-diagonal elements of the matrices will be small and close to zero when the unidimensionality assumption is (approximately) met.

   • Fitting a nonlinear one-factor analysis model to the interitem correlation matrix and studying the residuals (McDonald, 1981; Hattie, 1985). McDonald was probably the first researcher to propose the use of a factor analysis method to study unidimensionality that could handle nonlinear relationships between pairs of items, and items and the underlying abilities (defined in a multidimensional space). Promising results for this approach were recently obtained by Hambleton & Rovinelli (1986).

   • Using a method of factor analysis based directly on IRT (Bock, Gibbons, & Maraki, 1985): A multidimensional version of the three-parameter normal ogive is assumed to account for the vector of item responses. Estimation of model parameters is time-consuming and complicated but results can be obtained, and the results to date have been promising. Of interest is the suitability of a one-dimensional solution.

   • Items that appear most likely to violate the assumption are checked to see if they actually function differently. The b-values for these items are calibrated separately as a test and then again in the context of the remaining items in the test. Context of item calibrations is unimportant if model assumptions are met. If the plot of b-values calibrated in the two contexts is linear, the unidimensionality assumption is viable (Bejar, 1980).

2. Equal Discrimination Indices (Applies to the one-parameter model).

   • The distribution of item-score correlations (biserial or point biserial correlations) from a standard item analysis can be reviewed. When the distribution is reasonably homogeneous, the assumption is met.

3. Minimal Guessing (applies to the one- and two-parameter models).

   • The performance of low-ability students on the most difficult items can be reviewed. If performance levels are close to zero, the assumption is viable.

   • Plots of item-test score regressions will be helpful (Baker, 1964, 1965). Near-zero test performance for low-ability examinees would lend support for the viability of the assumption.

   • The test difficulty, time limits, and item format should be reviewed to assess the role of guessing in test performance.

4. Nonspeeded (Power) Test Administration (applies to nearly all of the popular IRT models).

   • The variance of number of omitted questions should be compared to the variance of number of items answered incorrectly (Gulliksen, 1950). The assumption is met when the ratio is close to zero.

   • The test scores of examinees under the specified time limit and without a time limit are compared. High overlap in performance is evidence for the viability of the assumption.

   • The percent of examinees completing the test, percent of examinees completing 75% of the test, and the number of items completed by 80% of the examinees are reviewed. (These simple checks are routinely carried out by ETS in their test evaluation work.) When nearly all examinees complete nearly all of the items, speed is not a serious factor in test performance.

Checking Expected Model Features

1. Invariance of Ability Parameter Estimates (applies to all IRT models).

   • Ability estimates are compared for different samples of test items (for example, hard and easy items; or tests reflecting different content categories within the item pool of interest). Invariance is established when the estimates do not differ, in excess of the measurement errors associated with the estimates (Whitely & Dawis, 1974; Wright, 1968).

2. Invariance of Item Parameter Estimates (applies to all IRT models).

   • Comparisons of model item parameter estimates (e.g., b-values, a-values, and/or c-values) obtained in two or more subgroups of the population for whom the test is intended (for example, males and females; blacks, whites, and Hispanics; instructional groups; high- and low-test performers; examinees in different geographic regions). When the estimates are invariant, the plot should be linear with the amount of scatter reflecting errors due to the sample size only. Often the comparisons can be done with bivariate plots. Baseline plots can be obtained by using randomly equivalent samples (Hambleton & Rogers, 1986; Shepard, Camilli, & Williams, 1984).

Checking Model Predictions of Actual and Simulated Test Results

   • Investigation of residuals and standardized residuals of model fit to a data set. Both the fit of the model to individual items at various points along the ability continuum and to persons are of value. The determination of the nature of model misfits to items and/or persons can be of great value in choosing a satisfactory IRT model (see Hambleton & Swaminathan, 1985; Hulin et al., 1983; Ludlow, 1985, 1986; Wright & Stone, 1979).

TABLE 4.3 *(Continued)*

Possible Methods

- Comparisons of observed and predicted test score distributions obtained from assuming all model parameter estimates are correct. Chi-square statistics (or other equivalent statistics) or graphical methods can be used to report the results (Hambleton & Traub, 1973).
- Investigations of the effects of item placement (Kingston & Dorans, 1984; Yen, 1980), practice effects, test speededness (Levine & Rubin, 1979), cheating (Levine & Drasgow, 1982), boredom (Wright & Stone, 1979), curriculum (Phillips & Mehrens, 1987), poor choice of model (Wainer & Thissen, 1987), recency of instruction (Cook, Eignor, & Taft, 1988), cognitive processing variables (Tatsuoka, 1987), and other threats to the validity of IRT results can be carried out and used to provide evidence appropriate for addressing particular IRT model uses.
- Scatterplot of ability estimates and corresponding test scores. The relationship should be high with scatter around the test characteristic curve reflecting measurement error only when the fit is acceptable (Lord, 1974a).
- Comparisons of ICCs estimated in two or more substantially different ways. For example, ICCs obtained without specifying their mathematical form can be compared to ICCs obtained when the form is specified (Lord, 1970a). The similarity of the ICCs will be high when the choice of mathematical form for the ICCs is correct.
- Applying a myriad of statistical tests to determine overall model fit, item fit, and person fit (see, for example, Andersen, 1973; Gustafsson, 1980b; Hambleton & Rogers, in press; Hambleton, Swaminathan, Cook, Eignor, & Gifford, 1978; Ludlow, 1985, 1986; Traub & Wolfe, 1981; Wright and Stone, 1979; Yen, 1981, 1984b).
- Comparisons of true and estimated item and ability parameters (Hambleton & Cook, 1983). These studies are carried out with computer simulation methods.
- Investigations of model robustness using computer simulation methods. For example, the implications of fitting one-dimensional IRT models to multidimensional data can be studied (Ansley & Forsyth, 1985; Drasgow & Parsons, 1983).

tion to the findings of van de Vijver (1986) mentioned above, Drasgow and Parsons (1983) show that IRT model parameters could be properly estimated in the presence of test data that were not strictly unidimensional. On the other hand, Ansley and Forsyth (1985) arrived at the opposite conclusion by using what they believed to be more realistic test data. In the presence of this kind of uncertainty, researchers are well advised to be concerned about the viability of the unidimensionality assumption.

Tests of other model assumptions are more straightforward. The methods in Table 4.3 use descriptive evidence provided by the statistics, but they can be informative. For example, in an analysis of NAEP mathematics items (Hambleton & Swaminathan, 1985), it was learned that the item biserial correlations ranged from .02 to .97! This information indicated that a one-parameter model could not possibly fit the data.

Checking Model Features

In practice, because the extent of robustness of the response models to violations of underlying assumptions is unknown, researchers should be encouraged to proceed to check model features regardless of the evidence obtained in studies of assumption violations. Insights gained from the latter studies, however, will point to models for further study and provide a frame of reference for interpreting the evidence collected in checking model features and predictions.

The invariance of model parameters can be assessed by means of several straightforward methods. The invariance of ability parameters can be studied, for example, by administering examinees two (or more) sets of items where the items in each set vary widely in difficulty. The item sets are constructed from the pool of test items over which ability is defined (Wright, 1968). It is most common to conduct this type of study by administering both sets of test items to examinees within the same test. Assume there are two sets of items. Then the ability estimates are obtained for each examinee, one from

each set of items. The pair of ability estimates for each examinee is plotted on a graph. This plot should define a straight line, because the expected ability score for each examinee does not depend upon the choice of test items, provided the item response model under investigation fits the test data. Some scatter of points about a best fitting line is to be expected, however, because of measurement error. When a linear relationship is not obtained, or the scatter exceeds that which is expected from knowledge of the standard errors of measurement associated with the ability estimates, one or more of the assumptions underlying the item response model might be violated by the test data set.

One weakness of the foregoing method is that there is no readily available basis for interpreting the plot though observed and predicted standard error curves can be compared and some rational judgment made about this similarity. How is one to know whether the amount of scatter is acceptable, assuming model–data fit? An alternative is to perform a statistical test of the differences between abilities as estimated from two or more subtests. The question about statistical power and sample size must always be kept in mind.

Divgi (1986); Forsyth, Saisangjan, and Gilmer (1981); Whitely and Dawis (1974); Wright (1968); and others have suggested that researchers consider the distribution of ability differences obtained in two subsets of test items. When the differences are divided by their standard errors, the distribution has an expected mean of 0 and a standard deviation of 1, assuming the invariance of the ability estimates. A substantial departure from the expected distribution is used as evidence of model–data misfit.

One method of checking the invariance property of item-parameter estimates was suggested by Hambleton and Rogers (1986). These researchers generated a plot of b values for randomly equivalent groups and then compared the plot to the plot of b values for two subgroups that might be expected to respond differently to some of the items (e.g., males versus females, blacks versus whites). The first plot provides a baseline for interpreting the second plot. If the plots are similar, then it is reasonable to assume that the subgroups of interest (e.g., male and female) are no more different in their response processes than the randomly equivalent groups. Sex can then be ruled out as a factor in item parameter estimation, and the hypothesis of parameter invariance over male and female samples cannot be rejected. If, on the other hand, the plots are very different, the feature of item-parameter invariance is not obtained, and attention shifts to identifying those test items that performed consistently differently in the subgroups of interest or to methodological problems that might have arisen in the item-parameter estimation process.

Figures 4.6 and 4.7 illustrate applications of the method. The data came from one form of the NAEP mathematics assessment administered to about 2,500 examinees in 1977. The item invariance property would be viable if plots (a), (b), (c), and (d) in Figure 4.6 were highly similar. When they are not, and they are not in the figure, items that account for the differences can be identified from plot (f). On the other hand, when plots (a), (b), (c), and (d) are similar, plot (f) will show the same circular pattern of points as baseline plot (e). Items showing consistently large differences between the two subgroups are of special interest. These items will be located in the top right and the bottom left corners of plot (f).

Figure 4.7, on the other hand, clearly shows the invariance of item difficulty parameters in high- and low-scoring ability groups. Studies like those undertaken to obtain Figures 4.6 and 4.7 should become standard for IRT researchers. Subgroups can be identified to determine the most stringent test of the invariance property possible for the relevant populations of items and examinees. For example, if there is a reason to suspect that a different ability is operating when males and females answer a particular set of items, the invariance of the item-parameter estimates should be checked. It can be checked for as many groups as necessary, to insure that the calibrated bank of test items will be applicable to all subgroups of examinees in the population for whom tests from the bank will be constructed.

Bergan and Stone (1987) provide a demonstration of an investigation of item-parameter invariance using a statistical test. Noteworthy was the age of the examinees (3 to 6 years), the ethnic groups involved (black, Hispanic, Caucasian, Indian, and Asian), and the timing of the item calibration (i.e., before and after instruction). Bergan and Stone used a statistical test of the hypothesis of equal item parameter estimates across groups and over time against the alternate hypothesis of unequal item parameter estimates across groups, over time, or both. Their results supported the null hypothesis of item parameter estimate stability.

Checking Model Predictions

Several methods of checking model predictions are described in Table 4.3. One of the most promising of these methods involves the analysis of item residuals. In this method, an item response model is chosen, item and ability parameters are estimated, and predictions about the performance of various ability groups are made, assuming the validity of the chosen model. Predicted results are then compared with actual results (see, for example, Kingston & Dorans, 1985; Hambleton & Swaminathan, 1985).

A residual (sometimes called a raw residual) is the difference between actual item performance for a subgroup of examinees and the subgroup's expected item performance:

$$r_{ij} = p_{ij} - E(p_{ij}),$$

where i denotes the item, j denotes the subgroup, r_{ij} is the residual, p_{ij} is the proportion of correct responses on item i in the jth subgroup, and $E(p_{ij})$ is the expected proportion of correct responses. In practice, the ability continuum is usually divided into equally spaced intervals (10 to 15) for the purpose of computing residuals. The intervals should be wide enough that the number of examinees in each interval is not too small. The use of small samples can lead to unstable statistics. On the other hand, the intervals should not be so wide that it becomes unreasonable to consider the examinees within each interval as similar to one another. The expected item performance for a subgroup is determined by averaging the probabilities associated with correct responses for examinees within the subgroup. To obtain these probabilities, the ICC and examinee ability scores are used. Alternatively, sometimes the probability associated with the middle ability in the category is used to approximate the value of $E(p_{ij})$.

Figure 4.8 provides item-performance data, best-fitting one-parameter ICCs, and corresponding residuals for four items. Possible explanations for the patterns of results are provided in the figure.

Standardized residuals are also used to assess model fit at the item level. The formula for a standardized residual is

$$SR_{ij} = \frac{p_{ij} - E(p_{ij})}{\sqrt{\dfrac{p_{ij}(1 - p_{ij})}{N_j}}}, \qquad \begin{array}{l} i = 1, 2, \ldots, n \\ j = 1, 2, \ldots, m \end{array}$$

where m is the number of categories used to group examinees on the ability scale, and N_j, the only other undefined term, is the number of examinees in the jth subgroup. A standardized residual is a raw residual divided by the estimated standard error of the p statistic. Standardized residuals have one desirable feature that raw residuals do not share: They take into consideration the sampling distribution of the p statistics. Large differences are given less weight when sample sizes are small or when they arise with p_{ij} values near the middle of the p-value scale [0,1].

In the choice of an IRT model, a study of residuals, standardized residuals, or both obtained for several models can provide valuable information. Figure 4.9 shows the pattern of standardized residuals for the one- and three-parameter logistic models with three items from the 1977 NAEP mathematics assessment for 13-year-olds. In (a) the one-parameter ICC is more discriminating than is necessary to account for the observed p values, in (b) the reverse situation is observed, and in (c) the fits of the ICCs are excellent; the standardized residuals are small and randomly distributed about 0. When there is a pattern to the residuals such as in (a) and (b) with the one-parameter model, usually the fit can be improved by choosing a more general model. For all three items, the three-parameter logistic model provided good fits to the actual item-performance data in the 12 subgroups.

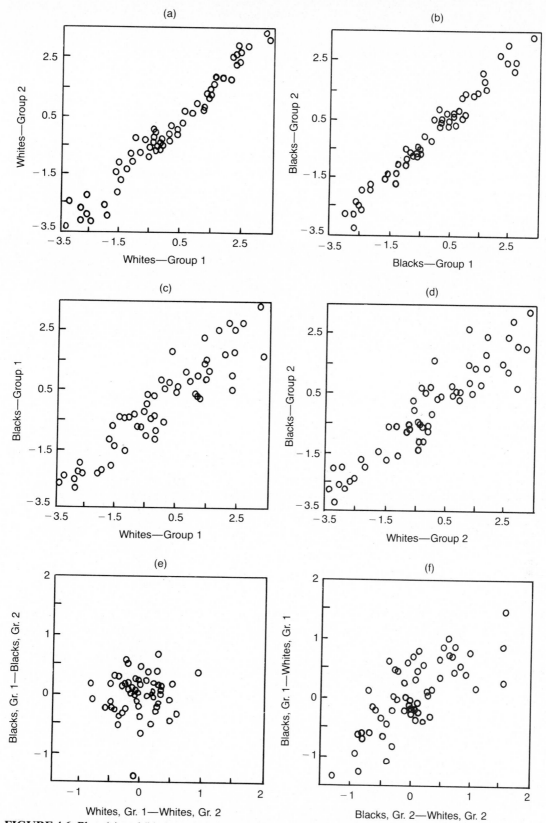

FIGURE 4.6 Plots (a) and (b) show the consistency in b-values across randomly equivalent groups. Plot (c) shows the consistency in b-values across different groups. Plot (d) is a replication of plot (c) with different samples. Finally, plot (e) shows the consistency between b-value differences in the randomly equivalent groups and plot (f) shows the consistency of b-value differences in different groups across independent samples. Items associated with consistently large differences (positive or negative) should be carefully studied.

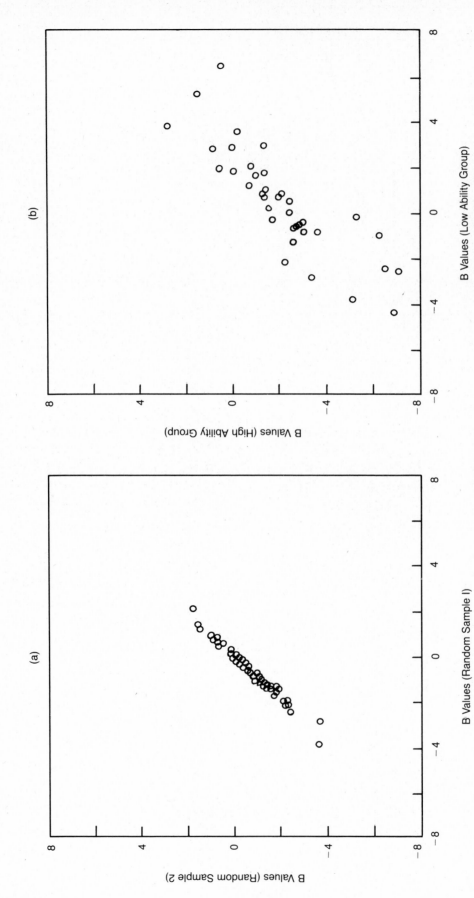

FIGURE 4.7 Invariance study of item difficulty parameters. Plot (a) shows the similarity of b-values in two randomly equivalent groups; plot (b) shows the similarity of b-values in high- and low-ability groups.

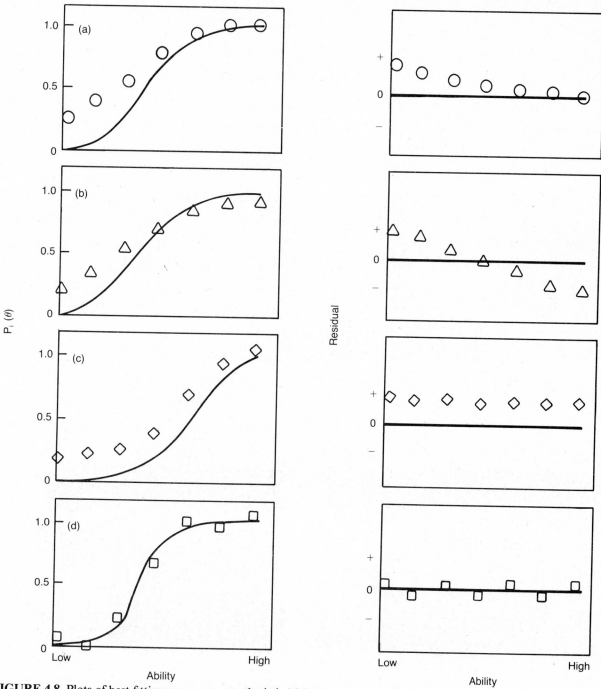

FIGURE 4.8 Plots of best fitting one-parameter logistic ICCs and corresponding item-performance data at various levels of ability. Possible explanations for the patterns of results are as follows:

(a) low-ability examinees answer the item by guessing;
(b) the item is less discriminating than the remainder of the items in the test—the common level of item discriminating power used in the ICCs with the one-parameter model is inappropriate;
(c) the item systematically underestimates the item-performance data—this pattern of residuals sometimes arises in item-bias studies; and
(d) the ICC fits the test data well—residuals are both small and random.

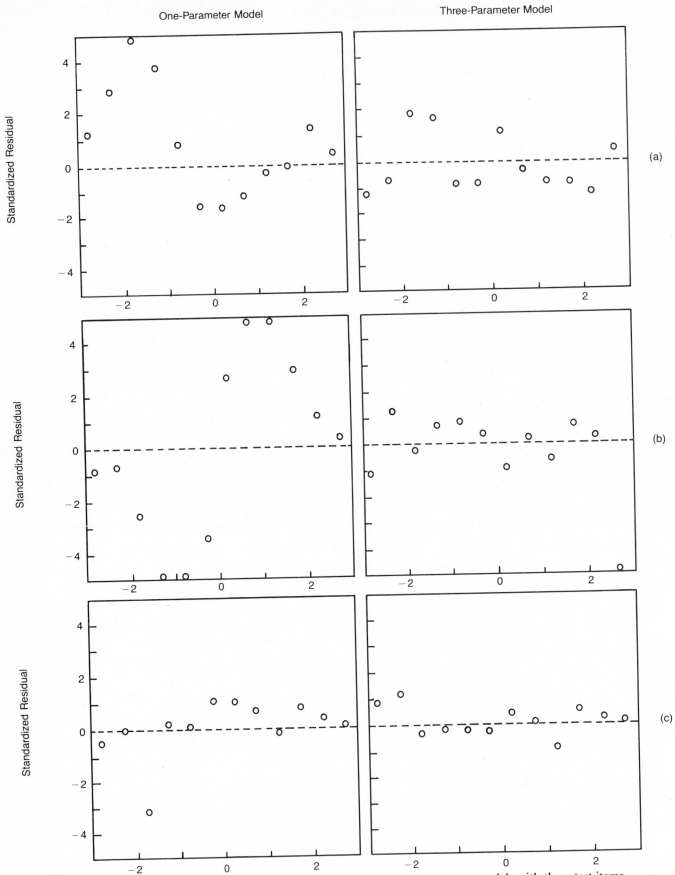

One-Parameter Model   Three-Parameter Model

FIGURE 4.9 Plots of standardized residuals for the one- and three-parameter models with three test items.

180

Table 4.4 provides the results of another type of analysis of standardized residuals (SRs) for 75 items from the 1982 Maryland Functional Reading Test. The one-, two-, and three-parameter models were fitted to a sample of 2,662 examinees who took the test. The distributions of the standardized residuals obtained with the two- and three-parameter logistic models suggest that these models fit the test data considerably better than the one-parameter logistic model. These results were surprising because some preference was given in test development to items that fit the one-parameter model. With the one-parameter model, about 30% of the SRs exceeded an absolute value of 2.0, whereas only about 10% and 7% exceeded an absolute value of 2.0 with the two- and three-parameter models, respectively. Analyses like the one in Table 4.4 are very helpful in model–data fit investigations.

Ludlow (1986) described a second and complementary way for interpreting residuals. He recommended that test data be simulated to fit the model of interest, and then the distribution of resulting residuals can be used to provide a baseline for interpreting residuals obtained from fitting the model of interest to the actual test data. He provided numerous examples, along with some new ways of reporting the residual information, based on the work of Tukey (1977) and others. Rogers and Hambleton (in press) also used simulated data to help in interpreting IRT item bias statistics.

Figures 4.10 and 4.11 were produced in an attempt to understand residual patterns like those portrayed in Figure 4.9. Figure 4.10 shows that the largest absolute-valued standardized residuals for the one-parameter model were obtained for those items that were very low or very high in discrimination. This is not a surprising finding because, in the one-parameter model, it is assumed that the discriminating power of items is equal. Figure 4.11 shows clearly that the standardized residuals for the three-parameter ICCs were considerably smaller. Moreover, the curvilinear pattern seen in Figure 4.10 is not present in Figure 4.11. As with Figure 4.8, an analysis of Figures 4.10 and 4.11 provides strong evidence for choosing one model over the other with the particular data set.

The analyses of item misfit statistics and residuals are becoming standard methods of investigation for IRT researchers. Misfit statistics for examinees are less common, but their use is also becoming more frequent in practice (Ludlow, 1985; Wright & Stone, 1979). Essentially, a misfit statistic is obtained for an examinee by comparing her or his pattern of actual item scores to the expected scores obtained from the fitted IRT model. Large misfit statistics for examinees identify them as individuals for whom the chosen IRT model has not provided valid scores. When patterns are observed among the residuals

(for example, an examinee fails items measuring particular objectives), diagnostic information is available. The use of the more general models minimizes the confounding of meaningful diagnostic information with model misfit to the test data.

Inappropriateness measurement is the term used by Drasgow (1982), Drasgow, Levine, and McLaughlin (1987), Levine and Drasgow (1982), and Levine and Rubin (1979) to describe a whole array of formulas and methods for analyzing the mismatch between an examinee's item responses and the underlying IRT model that is assumed to account for the data. Among the problems addressed with the methods are the detection of cheaters on tests, alignment errors on answer sheets, and unusual interpretations of easy questions.

In addition to residual analyses for items and examinees, it is possible and desirable to generate testable questions about model–data fit. Examples of such questions are as follows: Is there a pattern between item misfit statistics and item content? (Linn & Harnisch, 1981). What effect does the context in which an item is pilot tested have on the associated item-parameter estimates? (Yen, 1980). Is there a relationship between item-misfit statistics and item format or item difficulty? (Hambleton & Murray, 1983). Answers to these and other questions like them should influence judgment concerning the merits of a model for a particular data set and application.

Researchers should also be encouraged to consider, whenever possible, the consequences of model–data misfit. Hambleton and Cook (1983), for example, considered the effect of using the wrong model to obtain ability estimates for ranking examinees. They also looked at the effect of test length and sample size on the errors in item-parameter estimates and the effect of these same errors on the resulting accuracy of test-information functions. Other researchers have studied the effects of parameter-estimation errors on equating and adaptive testing (e.g., Divgi, 1986; Kingston & Dorans, 1984). To judge the practical consequences of using some items in a test that were not equal in two subgroups of interest, Drasgow and Guertler (1987) compared the TCC obtained in each subgroup. A comparison of the estimated test scores for examinees at the same ability level provides an excellent basis for judging the practical significance of including items in a test that are operating differently in two subgroups.

Other examples of analysis of misfit studies include investigations of (a) the consequences of fitting unidimensional models to multidimensional data (Drasgow & Parsons, 1983; Ansley & Forsyth, 1985), (b) test score distribution predictions (Lord, 1974a), and (c) the effects of violations of the unidimensionality assumption on IRT applications such as equating (Dorans & Kingston, 1985).

Statistical tests, usually chi-square tests, are also applied to determine model fit. An extensive review is provided by Hambleton and Rogers (in press), Traub and Lam (1985), and Traub and Wolfe (1981). The chi-square statistic of Yen (1981, 1984b), referred to by her as Q_1, is typical of the chi-square statistics proposed by researchers for addressing model fit. The statistic is given as

$$\text{Yen Statistic} = \sum_{j=1}^{m} \frac{N_j(O_{ij} - E_{ij})^2}{E_{ij}(1 - E_{ij})}$$

TABLE 4.4 Analysis of the Absolute-Valued Standardized Residuals[1] with Three Logistic Test Models for the MFRT

| LOGISTIC MODEL | PERCENT OF ABSOLUTE-VALUED STANDARDIZED RESIDUALS | | | |
	|0 TO 1|	|1 TO 2|	|2 TO 3|	|OVER 3|
1	42.6	27.8	15.0	14.6
2	60.6	29.7	7.3	2.4
3	63.3	29.6	6.0	1.1

[1] Total number of residuals is 825.

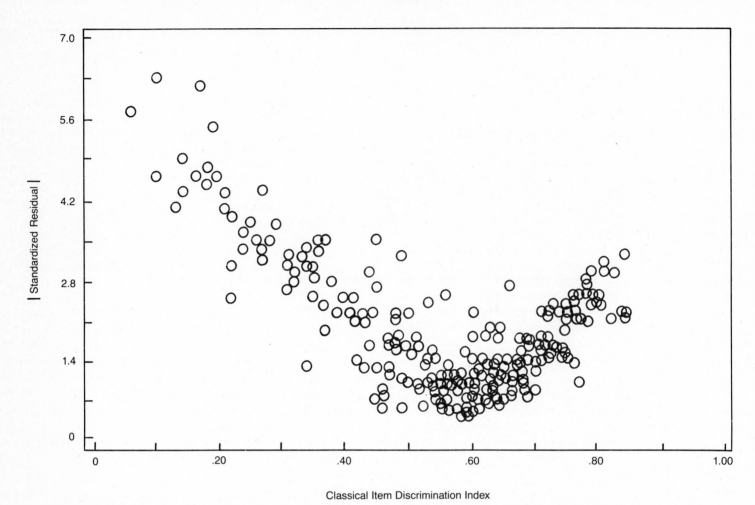

FIGURE 4.10 Scatterplot of absolute-valued standardized residuals obtained after fitting the one-parameter logistic model, and corresponding item biserial correlations.

where examinees are divided into m categories on the basis of their ability estimates, O_{ij} is the proportion of correct answers to item i in category j, E_{ij} is the predicted proportion of correct answers to item i in category j, and N_j is the number of examinees in the jth category. Yen (1981) set the value of m to be 10. Other researchers have chosen different values (see, for example, Bock, 1972). The Yen statistic is distributed approximately as a chi-square statistic with 10-k degrees of freedom where k is the number of model parameters. McKinley and Mills (1985) found that the statistic worked well for sample sizes between 500 and 1,000. It works for some things (e.g., evaluating the appropriateness of the 1-p model) but not others (e.g., detecting multi-dimensionality). Other statistics are available for the latter case.

Summary

In assessing model fit, the best approach involves (a) designing and conducting a variety of analyses that are designed to detect expected types of misfit, (b) considering the full set of results carefully, and (c) making a judgment about the suitability of the model for the intended application. Analyses should include investigations of model assumptions, of the extent to

which desired model features are obtained, and of the differences between model predictions and actual data. Statistical tests can be carried out, but care must be shown in interpreting the statistical information. There is almost no limit to the number of investigations that can be carried out. The amount of effort and money expended in collecting, analyzing, and interpreting results should be related to the importance and nature of the intended application. For example, small school districts using the one-parameter model in item banking and test development for classroom tests will not need to expend as many resources on goodness-of-fit studies, as, say, the Educational Testing Service when equating multiple forms of a nationally standardized aptitude test. Hills, Beard, Yotinprasert, Roca, and Subhiya (1985) provide an excellent example of the types of analyses recommended here in assessing the viability of the three-parameter model with the Florida Statewide Assessment Tests.

Selected Promising Applications of IRT Models

The psychometric literature contains descriptions of numerous applications of IRT models. In this section, three of the most successful applications to test development, item bias,

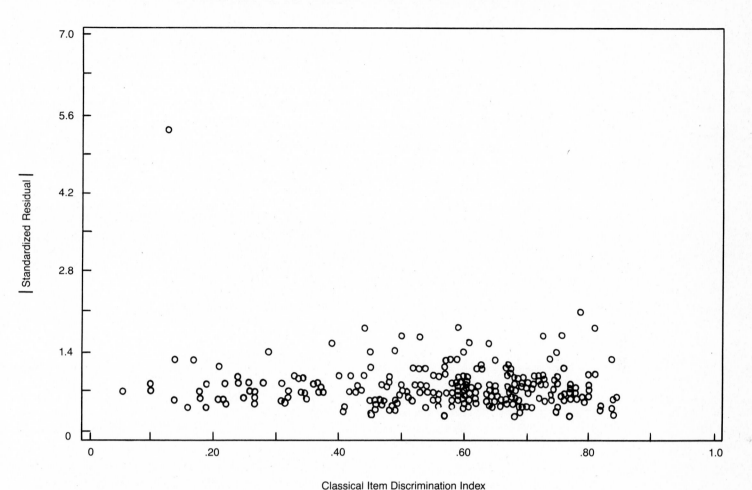

Standardized Residual

Classical Item Discrimination Index

FIGURE 4.11 Scatterplot of absolute-valued standardized residuals obtained after fitting the three-parameter logistic model, and corresponding item biserial correlations.

and adaptive testing will be briefly considered. Test score equating, which is one of the most popular and important IRT applications, is addressed in another chapter (Peterson, Kolen, & Hoover, this volume). For other reviews of IRT equating, readers are referred to Cook and Eignor (1983, in press) and Skaggs and Lissitz (1986). Hulin et al. (1983) provide an excellent review of IRT model applications to the detection of aberrant responses. Numerous other applications not considered in this section are contained in Hambleton (1983).

Test Development

The test development process consists of nine main steps:

1. Preparation of test specifications
2. Preparation of the item pool
3. Field testing the items (data collection and analysis)
4. Selection of test items
5. Final test production
6. Compilation of norms (for norm-referenced tests) (data collection and analysis including scaling)
7. Specification of cutoff scores (for criterion-referenced tests)

8. Reliability studies
9. Validity studies

The important differences between developing tests using standard methods and those using item response models occur at Steps 3, 4, 6, and 8. The discussion in this section will center on Steps 3 and 4. Peterson, Kolen, & Hoover (this volume) have provided a discussion of the scaling problems and methods that arise at Step 6. Samejima (1977) has provided a thorough discussion of Step 8.

FIELD TESTING

Standard item analysis techniques involve an assessment of item difficulty and discrimination indexes and the item distractors. The major problem with the standard approach is that the item statistics are not sample invariant. But one advantage of the standard approach to item analysis is that estimation of item parameters (difficulty and discrimination) is straightforward and requires only a moderate sample size for obtaining stable parameter estimates.

Detection of faulty or less useful items (for norm-referenced tests at least) using standard procedures is basically a matter of studying item statistics. Items need to be identified that are too easy, too difficult, or nondiscriminating (i.e., have a low item–total score correlation) in the population of examinees for whom the test is designed.

The process is quite different when item response models are employed to execute the item analysis. The major advantage of item response model methods and procedures is that they lead to item parameters that are sample invariant. Difficulties that have been cited are the necessity for large sample sizes, in order to obtain stable item-parameter estimates, and the mathematical complexity of the techniques used to obtain these estimates.

The detection of faulty items is not as straightforward as when standard techniques are employed. Items are generally evaluated in terms of their goodness-of-fit to a model using a statistical test or an analysis of residuals. Faulty items can be identified by a consideration of their discrimination indexes (the value of a_i will be negative or low positive) and their difficulty indexes (items should not be too easy or too difficult for the group of examinees to be assessed). Another reason for an item's being judged as faulty occurs when the chosen model does not fit the item response data. Item statistics are of limited value when the fit is poor. The situation can often be improved substantially by fitting a more general model to the data.

In summary, the item analysis process, when employing standard test development techniques, consists of the following steps: (a) determining sample-specific item parameters employing simple mathematical techniques and moderate sample sizes, and (b) deleting items based on statistical criteria. In contrast, item analysis using item response models involves (a) determining sample-invariant item parameters using relatively complex mathematical techniques and large sample sizes, and (b) utilizing goodness-of-fit criteria to detect items that do not fit the specified item response model. Both approaches can also benefit from an analysis of item distractors, to determine their effectiveness.

When IRT parameter estimates for items are obtained at different times, are taken from different samples, or both, steps must be taken to insure that the values are reported on a common scale. This can be accomplished in several ways (see, for example, Cook & Eignor, 1983, in press). Perhaps the most common approach involves an "anchor test" design, in which a few items (usually between 5 and 20) are common to the various test administrations. A plot of the b values for anchor test items obtained in two samples provides a basis for determining a linear transformation for mapping item statistics obtained in one sample to values obtained in another (Lord, 1975a; Stocking & Lord, 1983).

ITEM SELECTION

In the application of standard test-development techniques to the construction of norm-referenced tests, in addition to concerns for content validity, items are selected on the basis of two statistical characteristics: item difficulty and item discrimination. An attempt is always made to choose items with the highest discrimination parameters though even high discriminating items need to be scrutinized to be sure they are discriminating on the variable of interest and not on an undesirable

variable (e.g., speededness) (Masters, 1988). The choice of level of item difficulty is usually governed by the purpose of the test and the anticipated ability distribution of the group the test is intended for. The important point is that, because standard item parameters are not sample invariant, the success of the techniques depends directly on how closely the sample used to determine the item parameters employed in the item-selection process matches the population for which the test is intended. Matching samples is straightforward in school achievement testing but time consuming, whereas in the credentialing examination area, matching of samples is sometimes impossible and almost always very difficult.

Item response theory offers the test developer a more powerful method of item selection. Of course, item selection is, as are standard methods, based on the intended purpose of the test. However, the selection of items depends on the amount of information they contribute to the total amount of information supplied by the test. As can be seen in Figure 4.4, items with the highest a values might not always be the most useful to the test developer. Figure 4.12 provides an example of the information function for the general science subtest of the Armed Services Vocational Aptitude Battery (Ree, Mullins, Mathews, & Massey, 1982).

Lord (1977b) outlines a procedure for the use of item-information curves to build tests to meet any desired set of specifications. The procedure employs an item bank with item statistics available for the IRT model of choice, with accompanying information curves. The procedure outlined by Lord consists of the following steps:

1. Decide on the shape of the desired test-information curve. [Lord (1977b) called this the *target information curve*.]
2. Select items from the item bank with item-information curves that will fill up the hard-to-fill areas under the target-information curve.
3. After each item is added to the test, calculate the test-information curve for the selected test items.
4. Continue selecting test items until the test-information curve approximates the target-information curve to a satisfactory degree.

For a criterion-referenced test with a cut-off score to separate "masters" and "nonmasters," the desired target information curve would be highly peaked near the cut-off score on the ability scale. On the other hand, for a broad-range ability test, the target information curve could be fairly flat, highlighting the desire to produce a test with equal precision of ability estimates over the ability scale.

Yen (1983b) provides an example of how the steps were applied in one large test-development project. The use of item-information functions in the manner described earlier should allow the test developer to produce a test that will very precisely fulfill any set of desired test specifications, assuming, of course, that the item bank is sufficiently large with items of high quality.

Using Lord's procedure with a pool of items known to fit a particular item response model, it is possible to construct a test that "discriminates" well at one particular region or another

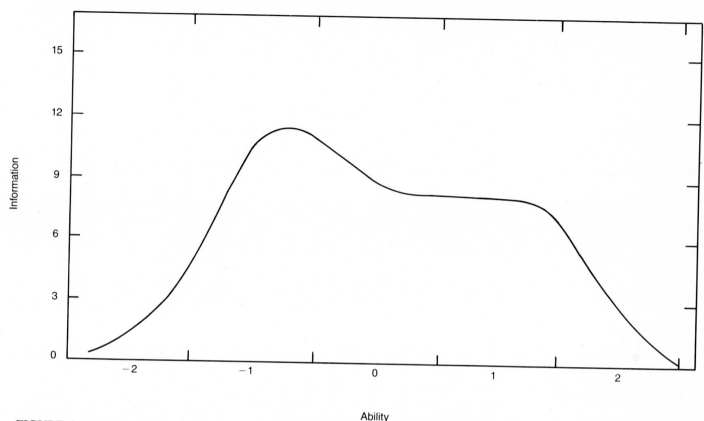

FIGURE 4.12 Test information curve for the general science subtest of the ASVAB. (From Ree, Mullins, Mathews, & Massey, 1982.)

on the ability continuum. That is to say, if we have a good idea of the ability of a group of examinees, test items can be selected to maximize test information in the region of ability spanned by the examinees being tested. This optimum selection of test items will contribute substantially to the precision with which ability scores are estimated. To be more concrete, with criterion-referenced tests it is common to observe lower test performance on a pretest than on a posttest. Given this knowledge, the test constructor might select easier items for the pretest and more difficult items for the posttest. Then, on each testing occasion, precision of measurement will have been maximized in the region of ability where the examinees would most likely be located. Moreover, because the items on both tests measure the same ability and ability estimates do *not* depend on the particular choice of items, growth can be measured by subtracting the pretest ability estimate from the posttest ability estimate.

De Gruijter and Hambleton (1983) and Hambleton and de Gruijter (1983) conducted investigations of the effects of optimal item selection on the decision-making accuracy of a test when the intended cutoff score for the test is known in advance of the test development. To provide a baseline for interpreting the results, tests were also constructed by selecting test items on a random basis. Figure 4.13 shows a comparison of decision accuracy with two (similar) optimally constructed criterion-referenced tests and a randomly constructed test, for tests consisting of 8 to 20 items. Error rates (probabilities of misclas-

sification) were nearly double with the randomly constructed test. In passing, it should be noted that the use of random item-selection procedures to date has been common in criterion-referenced test construction. Optimal item selection is made possible within an IRT framework because items, persons, and cut-off scores are reported on the same scale.

Another way to highlight the advantage of optimal item selection is in terms of how long the test constructed using random item selection would need to be to produce similar results to those results obtained through optimal item selection. With an acceptable error rate of, say, .20, the optimal item-selection method produced this result with 8 items or so. The random item-selection method needed somewhere between 15 and 20 items (or about twice as many).

Figure 4.14 provides an example of test-information functions corresponding to tests constructed with four different item-selection methods. "Random" and "Classical" were based on standard procedures: random involved the random selection of items from the bank, and classical involved the selection of items with moderate p values (.40 to .90) and as high biserials as possible. "Optimal" and "Content-optimal" methods involved the use of item-information functions. With optimal item selection, items were drawn to provide maximum information at a particular cutoff score. Three cutoff scores on the test-score scale were studied: 65%, 70%, and 75%. Corresponding cutoff scores on the ability scale (θ_o) were obtained from the TCC

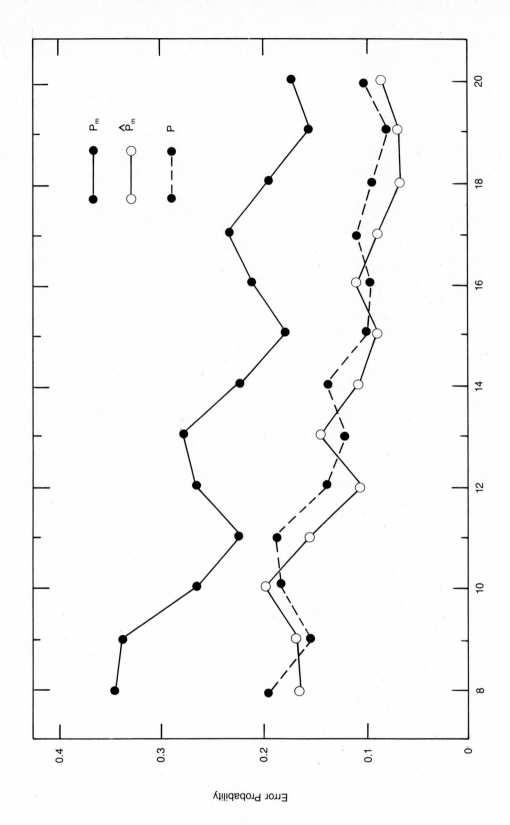

FIGURE 4.13 Error probabilities as a function of test length (n). (Adapted from de Gruijter & Hambleton, 1983).

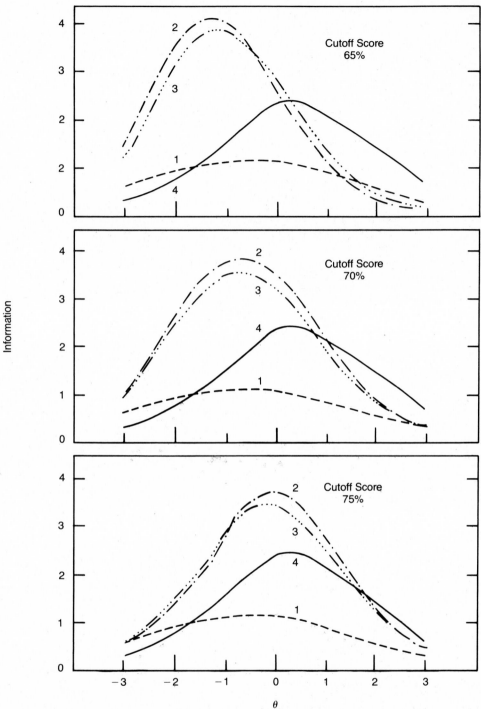

FIGURE 4.14 Test information functions for the 20-item tests. (From Hambleton, Arrasmith, & Smith, 1987.)

$$\pi_o = \frac{1}{t} \sum_{i=1}^{t} P_i(\theta_o)$$

defined for the total item bank (t = the number of items) and the cutoff score of interest π_0 set on the test-score scale. The content-optimal method involved optimal item selection, with the restriction that the final test should match a set of content specifications (such a restriction should be common practice). The results in Figure 4.14 highlight clearly the advantage of optimal and content-optimal item-selection methods. These tests provided nearly twice as much information in the region of interest near the cutoff score. Figure 4.15 compares one of the optimally constructed tests with the TCC for the full bank. The steepness of the 20-item TCC around θ_o highlights its usefulness near θ_o for making pass–fail decisions.

Kingston and Stocking (1986) provide an expanded discussion of the process of setting target curves and selecting items. Several problems, however, remain. Ways must be found to

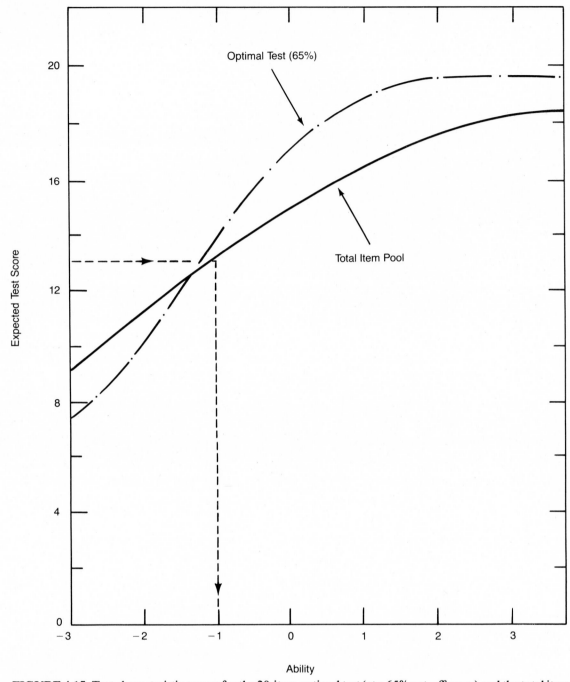

FIGURE 4.15 Test characteristic curves for the 20-item optimal test (at a 65% cut-off score) and the total item pool (about 250 items).

interface content with statistical criteria in item selection and to train test developers in IRT test-development methods. Also, because high a values are likely to be overestimated, actual tests are likely to be somewhat different from what was intended by the test developers. Possibly, inclusion of a couple of extra items is a way to address the problem. Also, the quality of test items must not be forgotten in any IRT applications to test development. There can be a tendency to get involved in the statistical data and minimize the important roles that item content and item quality play in the development of any test.

Poor quality items might mean that tests must be lengthened to achieve desired levels of precision. Failure to attend to content considerations might result in a charge that the test lacks content validity.

Item Bias

The fact that some items in a test might be unfair to one subgroup or another has become a matter of great concern to test developers and test users. Applications of standard item-bias techniques have not been very successful, in part because of definitional problems (see Cole, this volume). The most extreme definition of item and test bias is that a test is biased to the extent that the means of two groups of interest are different. The obvious problem with this definition is that other variables besides item bias contribute to these differences (see Hunter, 1975). By this definition, a measuring stick is biased because it shows that females are, on the average, shorter than males.

A second definition of item bias that can be advanced is that an item is unbiased if the item-difficulty index (or p value) for one group is the same as that for the second group of interest. This definition raises the same difficulty as the previous one. Angoff (1982) has indicated that the disparity that can be found between the p value for the two groups might be the result of social and educational bias.

A definition of item bias in terms of item–group interaction has also been suggested (Cleary & Hilton, 1968). In this method, a comparison is made between groups of interest in their performance on the test item and the total test. When the patterns are different, items are suspected of being biased. However, Hunter (1975) clearly pointed out that a perfectly unbiased test could show item–group interaction if the items are of varying item difficulty.

By considering the item difficulties for the two groups and taking into account the variation among the item difficulties within each group, the objection raised with the Cleary–Hilton definition of item bias can be overcome. The import of these observations leads to a further refined definition of item bias. When a set of items is unbiased, it is reasonable to expect the rank ordering of the p values to be the same for two groups (as long as the discriminating powers of the items are similar). A more stringent expectation is that the correlation between the p values is 1. When this happens, all the p values lie on a straight line. In this case, it could be said that the items are unbiased (or equally biased). Thus, items that do not fall on the best fitting line of the scatterplot of item-difficulty values may be taken as biased items. A major shortcoming, however, is that the plots of item difficulties will *not* be linear so long as there are group differences in ability (Lord, 1980a).

One definition of item bias that shows more promise is:

> A test item can be considered to be unbiased if all individuals having the same underlying ability level have an equal probability of correctly answering the item, regardless of their subgroup membership (Pine, 1977, p. 38).

This definition has obvious implications in terms of item response theory. However, non-item-response theoretic procedures based on this definition have been given by Scheuneman (1979) and Shepard, Camilli, & Averill (1981). With these procedures, an item is defined as biased if individuals from different groups, who have the same total score on the test, have different probabilities of responding correctly to that item. Clearly this approach is an approximation of the item response theoretic approach, in that the total score is used, rather than the ability.

The definition of item bias in terms of the probability of correct response can be restated easily in terms of item response theory. When it is restated, a large number of possibilities for measuring bias can be generated.

Because the probability of a correct response is given by the item-characteristic curve, this definition follows:

> A test item is unbiased if the item characteristic curves across different groups are identical.

This means that item-characteristic curves, which provide the probabilities of correct responses, must be identical, apart from sampling error, across different groups of interest. Figure 4.16 shows three patterns of results reflecting bias. In (a), the pattern of bias is reversed at a point on the ability continuum; in (b), the bias is substantial, but only at the high end of the ability continuum; and in (c), the pattern of bias is consistent over the full ability continuum. These results were found for three items in an item-bias study of a pilot version of a reading competency test.

Shepard et al. (1981) and Ironson (1983) provide reviews of procedures based on item response theory for assessing the bias of an item. The major acceptable procedures fall into two categories: comparison of item-characteristic curves and comparison of the vectors of item parameters. In the first, there are many ways in which ICCs can be compared. Figure 4.17 illustrates the *total-area method,* in which the area between two ICCs along a region of interest on the ability continuum is calculated. When the area between two ICCs is large, the item is described as *potentially biased.* Variations on this method involve substituting squared differences for the area (Linn, Levine, Hastings, & Wardrop, 1981), keeping track of the area that represents bias against each group, and weighting either the area or squared differences by the ability distributions of the two groups. Other variations and important comparisons among the statistics are offered by Shepard, Camilli, and Williams (1984, 1985). Linn and Harnisch (1981) offered a special method for handling the case when one of the groups is very small and it is inadvisable to estimate ICCs separately by group.

With respect to the second category, Lord (1977c, 1980a) has offered two contributions. If an item is unbiased, its item parameters should be the same in the two groups of interest. Lord set up a chi-square test of the hypothesis that the item-parameter values in the two groups are *not* equal. There is evidence in the literature that his method probably overidentifies the number of potentially biased items (McLaughlin & Drasgow, 1987). There is one other drawback. Hulin, Lissak, and Drasgow (1982) showed that different configurations of item parameters can produce very similar item characteristic curves. Clearly then, users of Lord's method will need to look at plots of the ICCs, too.

In one variation, Hambleton and Rogers (1986) substituted the concept of replicability for the concept of statistical significance. They describe a procedure in which item-difficulty differences between the groups of interest are calculated and then compared with the differences obtained in second samples from each group. Items showing consistently large differences are identified for further study. Figure 4.6 highlights the steps in this method.

One shortcoming of several of the currently popular IRT item-bias statistics is that they tend to be unstable over random samples (Hoover & Kolen, 1984). Also, these statistics have

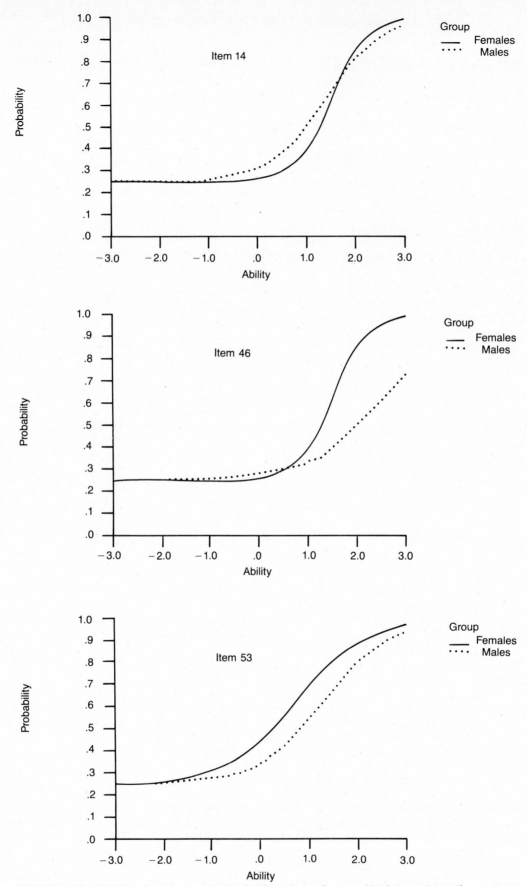

FIGURE 4.16 ICCs for Females and Males for three items from a 1985 9th grade competency test.

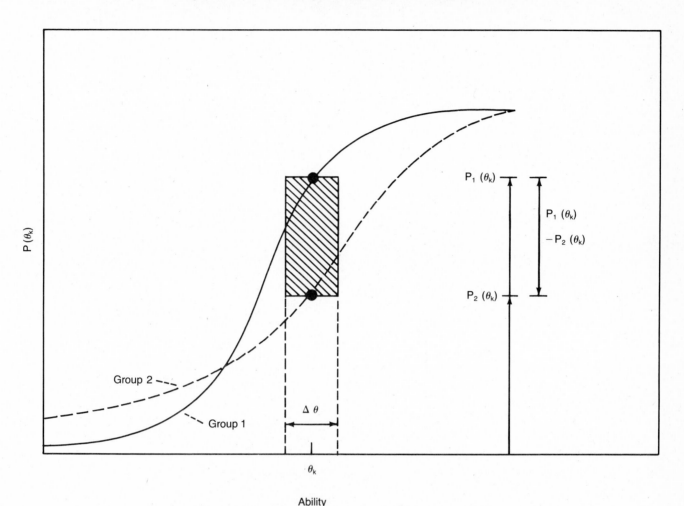

FIGURE 4.17 Area method for assessing item bias in two groups.

not been found to relate, to the extent that might be expected, to judgmentally based item-bias indicators. Clearly, more research is needed to identify the most useful IRT item-bias statistics and to develop ways of using the information provided by the statistics in operational test-development work.

Adaptive Testing

Numerous changes in testing are taking place at present because of the availability of new computer capabilities (see, for example, Brzezinski & Hiscox, 1984; Weiss, 1983, 1985; Bunderson, Inouye, & Olsen, this volume). There is wide recognition of the immense power of the computer for storing test information (e.g., test items) and for producing, administering, and scoring tests. Many testing agencies already store their item pools in computer memory. These test items can be recalled on an as-needed basis. Computer software is also available for completely constructing tests to fit a set of psychometric specifications. Especially attractive is the ability to prepare tests for printing without any additional typing or typesetting of test items. Many errors can be reduced because of this capability.

Presently, computers are also being used in some testing

programs to tailor or adapt the particular items an examinee is administered. Tests that are too easy or too hard for examinees are not administered. In this way, tests can be shortened without any loss of measurement precision. After each response to a test item presented at a computer terminal, a revised ability estimate for the examinee is obtained. Then the examinee is branched to the next item in the item bank that will contribute the most information to the estimation of his or her ability. Details of how test items are selected, and ability estimates obtained, are given by Lord (1980a, 1980b). The administration of items to the examinee continues until some specified number of items is administered or a desired level of measurement precision is obtained. Figure 4.18 provides the information functions for an adaptively administered version of the Preliminary Scholastic Aptitude Test with three conventionally constructed and administered forms of the same test (adjusted to a length of 25 items). It is clear that, for all ability levels, the adaptive version of the test was working (about) twice as well as the other versions of the test (Lord, 1977a). This finding is fairly typical of research studies involving adaptive tests. With adaptive tests, only about 50% of the items in a conventional test are needed to produce a test of the same basic quality (Lord, 1970b).

The earliest work on *adaptive testing,* or *tailored testing,* as

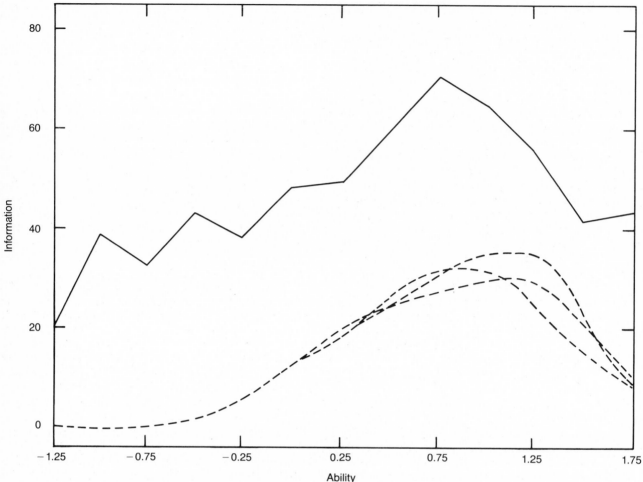

FIGURE 4.18 Information function for the 25-item tailored test, and for three forms of the Preliminary Scholastic Aptitude Test (dotted lines) adjusted to a test length of 25 items. (Adapted from Lord, 1977c.)

it was originally called, can be traced to the psychometric research of Fred Lord at ETS in the late 1960s (for a summary, see Lord, 1980b). Since the late 1960s, a tremendous amount of research has been supported by the U. S. Armed Services and other federal agencies, special conferences have been held, and the number of published papers has reached into the hundreds (see, for example, Weiss, 1983).

Almost all standard testing to date has been done in settings in which a group of examinees take the same test (or parallel forms). Typically, these examinees vary in the ability being measured by the test. It can be shown that a test would maximally measure the ability of each examinee in the group if test items were presented to each examinee such that the probability of answering each item correctly is halfway between the c value and 1.0, or .50 when $c = 0$. This, of course, is not possible using a single test; consequently, there is a need for adaptive testing. Item response models are particularly important in adaptive testing because it is possible to derive ability estimates that are independent of the particular choice of test items administered. Thus, examinees can be compared, even though they have taken sets of test items of varying difficulty.

In adaptive testing, an attempt is made to match the difficulties of the test items to the ability of the examinee being

measured. To match test items to ability levels requires a large pool of items whose statistical characteristics are known, so that suitable items can be drawn. Because the item-selection procedure does not lend itself easily to paper-and-pencil tests, the adaptive testing process is typically done by computer. According to Lord (1980a), a computer must be programmed to accomplish the following in order to tailor a test to an examinee:

1. Predict from the examinee's previous responses how the examinee would respond to various test items not yet administered
2. Make effective use of this knowledge to select the test item to be administered next
3. Assign, at the end of testing, a numerical score that represents the ability of the examinee tested

Research has been done on a variety of adaptive testing strategies built on the following decision rule: If an examinee answers an item correctly, the next item should be more difficult; if an examinee answers incorrectly, the next item should be easier. These strategies can be broken down into two-stage strategies and multistage strategies. The multistage strategies are of either the fixed branching variety or the variable branching variety.

In the *two-stage procedure* all examinees take a routing test and, based upon this test, are directed to one of a number of tests constructed to provide maximum information at certain points along the ability continuum. Ability estimates are then derived from a combination of scores from the routing test and the optimum test. This procedure was also incorporated into Bock and Mislevy's (1986) *duplex design* for large-scale assessments.

Multistage strategies involve a branching decision after an examinee responds to an item. If the same item structure is used for all examinees, but each examinee can move through the structure in a unique way, then it is called a *fixed-branching model.*

For these multistage fixed-branching models, all examinees start at an item of medium difficulty and, based upon a correct or an incorrect response, pass through a set of items that have been arranged in order of item difficulty. After completion of a fixed set of items, either of two scores is used to obtain an estimate of ability: the difficulty of the (hypothetical) item that would have been administered after the nth (last) item or the average of the item difficulties, excluding the first item and including the hypothetical $n + 1$st item. IRT models are not required in item selection or ability estimation.

Multistage strategies are also available with variable branching structures. At each stage in testing, an item in the established item bank is selected for an examinee in a fashion such that the item, if administered, will maximally reduce the uncertainty of the examinee's ability estimate. This is where item-information functions are useful, because they provide the needed data for item selection. After administration of the item, the ability estimate is recalculated, using maximum likelihood procedures (Lord, 1980a) or Bayesian procedures.

There have been numerous applications of computer-adaptive tests (see, for example, Weiss, 1982; Weiss & Kingsbury, 1984). The armed services, for example, are planning to administer the Armed Services Vocational Aptitude Battery (ASVAB) using computer-adaptive testing procedures, and one testing company currently has adaptive testing projects in over 180 school districts. In addition, most of the major testing firms are researching possible uses of computer-adaptive testing. The next few years should see many applications, along with evaluative data concerning the success of these applications.

Two main questions about computer-adaptive testing that arise concern (a) the relationship between scores and associated decisions with conventionally administered and computer-administered tests, and (b) the viability of IRT models for providing a technically adequate measurement system. In the spirit of insuring that computer-administered tests based upon IRT models and methods perform as well as paper-and-pencil tests for the ASVAB, Green, Bock, Humphreys, Linn, and Reckase (1984) provided a set of guidelines for evaluating computer-adaptive tests. These guidelines, however, are generally applicable to all forms of computer-adaptive tests. The authors divided the guidelines into nine main categories: content considerations, dimensionality, reliability, validity, item-parameter estimation, linking of item parameters, item-pool characteristics, item selection and test scoring, and human factors. A selected list of the guidelines, organized by category from Green et al. (1982), is contained in Table 4.5.

Recently, both Green (1988) and Wainer and Kiely (1987) have highlighted a number of difficult problems to overcome in CAT systems. Green was especially concerned with problems in the areas of equating and item selection. The equating problem arises because, while two tests—a paper-and-pencil test and an adaptive test—can be equated or calibrated on the same scale using an IRT model, in general the two tests will not provide the same degree of measurement precision at points along the ability continuum (i.e., the information functions for the two tests will, in general, differ). Therefore, the students being assessed will not (or should not) be indifferent as to which test they prefer. Good students should prefer the test leading to the most accurate scores; poor students should not. The implication of this nonequivalence of the measurement properties of a paper-and-pencil test and an adaptive test remains a problem in practice.

The problem in item selection arises because of a concern that the context in which an item appears (e.g., item position) and its content may influence item performance. If, for example, item performance is influenced by items that may have been administered previously, then valid comparisons of examinees when examinees are not administered the same items—and, in general, they will not be in adaptive testing—are problematic. The influences of item context and content represent threats to the validity of IRT models and, specifically, to the invariance of both item and ability parameter estimates. Wainer and Kiely (1987) also documented the context effect of (1) item parameter estimates due to an item's location in a test; and (2) ability estimates due to the sequence and emphasis (or de-emphasis) of specific test content.

Wainer and Kiely (1987) proposed that "testlets," rather than items, become the building blocks for CAT based on multistage fixed branching. Here, a testlet is

> a group of items related to a single content area that is developed as a unit and contains a fixed number of predetermined paths that an examinee may follow. In this way, each item is embedded in a predeveloped testlet, in effect carrying its own context with it. The paths through a testlet may follow a hierarchical branching scheme that routes examinees to successive items of greater or lesser difficulty depending on their previous responses and culminates in a series of ordered score categories. Or the testlet may contain only a single linear path of a number of items that are administered to all examinees. The form chosen depends critically on the application for which it is intended.
>
> Just as branching schemes may vary within testlets, the testlets themselves may also be combined to form a complete test by linking them hierarchically or in a linear fashion, or some combination of the two, again depending on the intended purpose of the test. This arrangement allows for the construction of a wide variety of tests for specific purposes by combining hierarchical and linear branching both between and within testlets in any desired combination. (Wainer and Kiely, 1987, pp. 190–191)

Clearly, considerably more research is needed both to document the strengths and shortcomings of IRT-based CAT models and to pursue alternate CAT models such as testlets within an IRT framework.

TABLE 4.5 Guidelines for Evaluating Computer-Adaptive Testing (CAT)[1]

CATEGORY	NUMBER	GUIDELINES
Content Considerations	C1	Specifications for item content should be the same for CAT and paper-and-pencil tests.
	C2	The content of items selected for the item pool should match the content specifications.
	C3	Test items must be designed to match the computer equipment available.
Dimensionality	D1	The fit of the IRT model should be checked.
	D2	Highly discriminating items should be selected.
	D3	A factor analysis of the interitem tetrachoric correlations should be performed.
	D4	Local independence assumption should be examined.
	D5	Subtests should be formed when tests are not unidimensional.
Reliability	E1	The standard error of measurement of each test score should be reported as a function of the test score, in the metric of the reported score.
	E2	The standard error of measurement of each test should also be reported in the ability metric.
Validity	V1	The similarity of variance-covariance matrices for CAT and paper-and-pencil tests should be assessed.
	V2	The covariance structures of the two versions should be compared.
	V3	The CAT and paper-and-pencil versions of a test should be validated against the same external criteria.
	V4	The extent of prediction bias should be assessed for important subpopulations.
Item Parameters—Estimation	IE1	The sample for item calibration should be of adequate size, currently at least 1,000 cases.
	IE2	The calibration sample should be selected so that a sufficient number of examinees are available in the range of ability needed to estimate the lower asymptote and the point of inflection of the item-characteristic curve.
	IE3	The procedure for estimating item parameters should be shown to be "empirically consistent" (large sample should lead to good estimates).
	IE4	The procedure for estimating item parameters should be shown to be unbiased, or the extent and nature of the bias should be specific.
	IE5	The item-characteristic curves should fit the observed data.
	IE6	The difficulty of items administered in the CAT and paper-and-pencil versions should be compared.
Item Parameters—Linking	IL2	The linking procedure for placing items on a common scale should be fully described.
	IL4	When using an equivalent groups procedure for linking, the equivalence of groups should be demonstrated.
Item Pool Characteristics	IP1/2/3	The distribution of the b- and c-parameter estimates and descriptive statistics for the estimates should be presented.
	IP4	The information for the total item pool should be presented.
Item Selection and Test Scoring	IS1	The procedure for item selection and ability estimation must be documented explicitly and in detail.
	IS2	The procedure should include a method of varying the items selected, to avoid using a few items exclusively.
	IS4	The computer algorithm must be capable of administering designated items, and recording the responses separately, without interfering with the adaptive process.
	IS5	The computer must be able to base the choice of a first item on prior information.
Human Factors	HF1	The environment of the testing terminal should be quiet and comfortable, and free of distractions.
	HF2	The display screen should be placed so that it is free of glare.
	HF3	The legibility of the display should be assessed empirically.
	HF6	The display must be able to include diagrams that have fine detail.

[1] A selection of the guidelines from Green, Bock, Humphreys, Linn, & Reckase (1982) is contained in this table to highlight the analyses that they believe should be required to support the use of a CAT system.

Issues, Controversies, and Possible Future Directions

The goal of this chapter has been to review many IRT developments, to demonstrate the applicability of IRT models to specific measurement problems, and finally, to point to advantages of the IRT approach over the standard approach for the solution of many mental measurement problems. As pointed out, IRT models have several advantages over standard test models. Despite the advantages, there are several unresolved issues that need further investigation. Because IRT models require strong assumptions, the question that naturally arises is that of the robustness of IRT models. The studies reported to date have often produced different conclusions. A related issue is that of determining the fit of the model to data. It is obvious that the assumptions of any IRT model will never be completely satisfied by a data set. Hence, the important questions are whether IRT analyses provide useful summaries of the test data, lead to better test score interpretations, and predict appropriately chosen criteria. The issues of robustness and fit of the model are not completely resolved as of yet, and further work is needed.

Another issue that remains to be finally solved is that of estimation of parameters in IRT models. As pointed out earlier, the simultaneous estimation of item and ability parameters in IRT models could lead to difficulties. In addition, the estimates of the item parameters, especially that of the c parameter, will not be stable unless examinees with a wide range of abilities are used. Furthermore, current estimation procedures require a large number of examinees and items before stable estimates can be obtained. Further research is clearly needed in these areas. Although it might not be possible to show that the maximum likelihood estimates of item- and ability-parameters possess optimal properties, these estimates might approximate the ideal estimates in some situations. For instance, the comparison of the unconditional estimates and the conditional estimates of the item parameters in the Rasch model (Wright & Douglas, 1977a, 1977b) has provided a meaningful insight into the nature of the estimates. These comparisons can be carried out for the two- and three-parameter logistic models. The feasibility of Bayesian procedures should be investigated more fully, too. Incorporation of prior information in the estimation procedure will provide improved estimates of the parameters and also permit estimation of parameters with a small sample size and a small number of items. However, poor specification of priors could adversely affect the estimates, and, hence, a careful study of appropriate priors is necessary.

A good example of a current controversy concerns model selection. The Rasch model and the three-parameter model developed by Birnbaum and Lord have many similarities, but they are conceptually different. Proponents of the two- and three-parameter models typically begin their work with large quantities of item response data that they wish to understand and explain. Their goal is to find a model that fits the data.

In contrast, George Rasch's goal was to develop a model, not on the basis of actual test data, but rather on the basis of axioms, to produce a measurement system with desirable properties. For Rasch and his followers, test items must "fit" the model if they are to be useful for measurement. Nonfitting items are discarded.

Sometimes, the distinctions between these two approaches have been lost. Advocates of the general IRT models criticize the Rasch model because it doesn't fit data very well. Advocates of Rasch criticize the parameter-estimation methods for the two- and three-parameter models and the failure to obtain specific objectivity. Although the criticisms are, for the most part, correct, it seems important for each group to recognize the premises on which the other group is operating. Each approach has something substantial to offer measurement practice.

For those researchers who prefer to choose their psychometric models on an empirical basis, basically, sound methods are now available. Many of the methods were outlined in an earlier section of the chapter. Other factors are also important to consider in choosing a model: the availability of a suitably large and appropriate sample of examinees to facilitate parameter estimation, the availability of computer software and funds to analyze the data, and the choice of a parameter estimation method.

Another current IRT controversy concerns the development of scales for measuring achievement and ability (Hoover, 1984; Yen, 1985, 1986). Hoover (1984) criticized the IRT-derived CTBS achievement scales because they showed less score variability at the higher grades than the lower school grades. This finding runs counter to commonly held views about patterns of school achievement. Yen (1986) responded by providing a set of possible criteria for judging the appropriateness of measuring scales: internal consistency, relationships to external variables including an idealized trait, statistical properties, common sense, and intended use of the scale. Within Yen's broad framework for developing and reviewing scales, she felt scales like those criticized by Hoover could be defended. The controversy surrounding the development of scales is far from over, but both Hoover and Yen have advanced our knowledge considerably about an underexplored topic that will surely receive more attention from IRT researchers in the near future.

Currently, the IRT field appears to be moving in many promising directions while, at the same time, consolidating and refining the plethora of research findings in the psychometric literature. With respect to new directions, two topics should be singled out: (1) multidimensional models; and (2) polychotomous response models. Neither direction is completely new; after all, Lord and Novick (1968), McDonald (1967), and Samejima (1969, 1972, 1974) wrote about these topics more than 20 years ago. But now the research is being aggressively pursued by many researchers in several countries, and the findings are providing a theoretical and practical basis for test development, test analysis, and additional research. Polychotomous item response models seem especially useful presently, because of the current testing movement away from dichotomously scored multiple-choice items and toward new item formats utilizing polychotomous scoring. In fact, a merger of these two topics—polychotomously scored, multidimensional item response models—is currently providing a foundation for new types of tests developed from a cognitive perspective (see, for example, Embretson, 1984, 1985; McDonald, in press).

As for other new applications, three seem especially promising: criterion-referenced testing, customized testing, and state and national assessments. Hambleton and Rogers (in press) have provided a review of the multiple uses of IRT models for solving measurement problems that arise with criterion-referenced tests: selecting optimal test items, determining test lengths, assessing reliability, making mastery decisions, and reporting scores.

Customized testing is currently one of the IRT applications that is receiving attention from test publishers and school districts (see, for example, Yen, Green, & Burket, 1987). School districts are given the flexibility of substituting some number of items in a commercially available norm-referenced test with items of their own choice (usually items written to measure important school objectives that are not assessed in the norm-referenced test). IRT models are then used to equate the two tests, so that student performance on the customized test can be used to predict performance on the norm-referenced test.

Some school districts like the application because customized tests seem fairer to their students, and customized tests are more widely accepted in the school district. On the other hand, when schools teach to the content covered by the customized test, overpredictions of performance on the norm-referenced test may result and lead to improper interpretations of school performance in relation to national norms. The usefulness of this IRT application is currently being actively researched, in particular, the invariance of item-parameter estimates of students receiving instruction using different methods, and the extent to which tests can be customized without adversely affecting the validity of the test score norms.

Finally, Bock and Mislevy (1986) have highlighted the utility of IRT models in large-scale assessments. Using matrix sampling, a two-stage adaptive testing scheme, and both individual and group-based three-parameter IRT models, Bock and Mislevy were able to provide a comprehensive array of individual and group test results for individual assessments as well as program evaluation. This initial demonstration work will undoubtedly be followed up by additional IRT applications as state and national test results become more important in educational policy discussions and analyses. This type of application is *not* without controversy (see, for example, Goldstein, 1980); however, with the success of IRT models in providing meaningful reporting scales for the National Assessment of Educational Progress, there is every indication that both state and national assessments will be carried out in the future within an IRT framework.

In conclusion, we note that IRT offers the promise of solving many problems that arise in mental measurement. The advantages of the IRT approach over the standard approach are obvious. It appears that the major factors that have hindered widespread use of these methods are the lack of familiarity on the part of practitioners and the lack of user-oriented computer programs. These problems have been overcome in recent years, and, hence, we can expect IRT methods to emerge as methods of the future for the measurement of mental abilities.

REFERENCES

Andersen, E. B. (1972). The numerical solution of a set of conditional estimation equations. *Journal of the Royal Statistical Society, Series B, 34,* 42–54.

Andersen, E. B. (1973). A goodness of fit test for the Rasch model. *Psychometrika, 38,* 128–140.

Andrich, D. (1978a). Applications of a psychometric rating model to ordered categories which are scored with successive integers. *Applied Psychological Measurement, 2,* 581–594.

Andrich, D. (1978b). A binomial latent trait model for the study of Likert-style attitude questionnaires. *British Journal of Mathematical and Statistical Psychology, 31,* 84–98.

Andrich, D. (1978c). A rating formulation for ordered response categories. *Psychometrika, 43,* 561–573.

Andrich, D, (1982). An extension of the Rasch model for ratings providing both location and dispersion parameters. *Psychometrika, 47,* 105–113.

Angoff, W. H. (1982). Use of difficulty and discrimination indices for detecting item bias. In R. A. Berk (Ed.), *Handbook of methods for detecting test bias.* Baltimore: The Johns Hopkins University Press.

Ansley, T. N., & Forsyth, R. A. (1985). An examination of the characteristics of unidimensional IRT parameter estimates derived from two-dimensional data. *Applied Psychological Measurement, 9,* 37–48.

Assessment Systems Corporation. (1984). *User's manual for the MicroCAT testing system.* St. Paul, MN: Author.

Baker, F. B. (1964). An intersection of test score interpretation and item analysis. *Journal of Educational Measurement, 1,* 23–28.

Baker, F. B. (1965). Origins of the item parameters X_{50} and β as a modern item analysis technique. *Journal of Educational Measurement, 2,* 167–180.

Baker, F. B. (1977). Advances in item analysis. *Review of Educational Research, 47,* 151–178.

Baker, F. B. (1985). *The basics of item response theory.* Portsmouth, NH: Heinemann.

Baker, F. B. (1986, April). *Two parameter: The forgotten model.* Paper presented at the annual meeting of the American Educational Research Association, San Francisco, CA.

Baker, F. B. (1987). Methodology review: Item parameter estimation under the one-, two-, and three-parameter logistic models. *Applied Psychological Measurement, 11,* 111–142.

Barton, M. A., & Lord, F. M. (1981). *An upper asymptote for the three-parameter logistic item-response model* (Research Bulletin 81–20). Princeton, NJ: Educational Testing Service.

Bashaw, W. L. (1982). Educational testing applications of the Rasch model. In C. R. Reynolds & T. Gutkin (Eds.), *Handbook of school psychology.* New York: John Wiley & Sons.

Bejar, I. I. (1980). A procedure for investigating the unidimensionality of achievement tests based on item parameter estimates. *Journal of Educational Measurement, 17,* 283–296.

Bergan, J. R., & Stone, C. A. (1987, April). *Item parameter stability in IRT models for developmental assessment.* Paper presented at the annual meeting of the American Educational Research Association, Washington, DC.

Birnbaum, A. (1957). *Efficient design and use of tests of a mental ability for various decision-making problems* (Series Report No. 58–16. Project No. 7755-23). Randolph Air Force Base, TX: USAF School of Aviation Medicine.

Birnbaum, A. (1958a). *Further considerations of efficiency in tests of a mental ability* (Technical Report No. 17. Project No. 7755-23). Randolph Air Force Base, TX: USAF School of Aviation Medicine.

Birnbaum, A. (1958b). *On the estimation of mental ability* (Series Report No. 15. Project No. 7755-23). Randolph Air Force Base, TX: USAF School of Aviation Medicine.

Birnbaum, A. (1968). Some latent trait models and their use in inferring an examinee's ability. In F. M. Lord & M. R. Novick, *Statistical theories of mental test scores.* Reading, MA: Addison-Wesley.

Birnbaum, A. (1969). Statistical theory for logistic mental test models with a prior distribution of ability. *Journal of Mathematical Psychology, 6,* 258–276.

Bock, R. D. (1972). Estimating item parameters and latent ability when responses are scored in two or more nominal categories. *Psychometrika, 37,* 29–51.

Bock, R. D., & Aitkin, M. (1981). Marginal maximum likelihood estimation of item parameters: An application of an EM algorithm. *Psychometrika, 46,* 443–459.

Bock, R. D., Gibbons, R., & Muraki, E. (1985). *Full-information item factor analysis* (MRC Report No. 85-1). Chicago: National Opinion Research Center, University of Chicago.

Bock, R. D., & Lieberman, M. (1970). Fitting a response model for n dichotomously scored items. *Psychometrika, 35,* 179–197.

Bock, R. D., & Mislevy, R. J. (1981). An item response curve model for matrix-sampling data: The California Grade-Three Assessment. In D. Carlson (Ed.), *New directions for testing and measurement: Testing in the states: Beyond accountability* (pp. 65–90). San Francisco: Jossey-Bass.

Bock, R. D., & Mislevy, R. (1986). *Comprehensive educational assessment for the states: The duplex design* (CSE Report No. 262). Los Angeles: Center for the Study of Evaluation, UCLA.

Bock, R. D., Mislevy, R., & Woodson, C. (1982). The next stage in educational assessment. *Educational Researcher, 11,* 4–11.

Brzezinski, E., & Hiscox, M. (Eds.) (1984). Microcomputers in educational measurement. *Educational Measurement: Issues and Practice, 3,* 3–50 (special issue).

Carroll, J. B. (1986). A review of Embretson's *Test Design: Develop-*

ments in Psychology and Psychometrics. Journal of Educational Measurement, 23, 274–278.

Cleary, T. A., & Hilton, T. L. (1968). An investigation of item bias. *Educational and Psychological Measurement, 28,* 61–75.

Cook, L. L., & Eignor, D. R. (1983). Practical considerations regarding the use of item response theory to equate tests. In R. K. Hambleton (Ed.), *Applications of item response theory* (pp. 175–195). Vancouver, BC: Educational Research Institute of British Columbia.

Cook, L. L., & Eignor, D. R. (in press). Using item response theory in test score equating. *International Journal of Educational Research.*

Cook, L. L., & Eignor, D. R., & Taft, H. L. (1988). A comparative study of the effects of recency of instruction on the stability of IRT and conventional item parameter estimates. *Journal of Educational Measurement, 25,* 31–45.

de Gruijter, D. N. M. (1984). A comment on "some standard errors in item response theory." *Psychometrika, 49,* 269–272.

de Gruijter, D. N. M. (1986). Small N does not always justify the Rasch model. *Applied Psychological Measurement, 10,* 187–194.

de Gruijter, D. N. M., & Hambleton, R. K. (1983). Using item response models in criterion-referenced test item selection. In R. K. Hambleton (Ed.), *Applications of item response theory* (pp. 142–154). Vancouver, BC: Educational Research Institute of British Columbia.

de Gruijter, D. N. M., & van der Kamp, L. J. Th. (1984). *Statistical models in psychological and educational testing.* Lisse, The Netherlands: Swets & Zeitlinger.

Divgi, D. R. (1986). Does the Rasch model really work for multiple choice items? Not if you look closely. *Journal of Educational Measurement, 23,* 283–298.

Dorans, N. J., & Kingston, N. M. (1985). The effects of violations of unidimensionality on the estimation of item and ability parameters and on item response theory equating of the GRE verbal scale. *Journal of Educational Measurement, 22,* 249–262.

Drasgow, F. (1982). Choice of test model for appropriateness measurement. *Applied Psychological Measurement, 6,* 297–308.

Drasgow, F., & Guertler, E. (1987). Study of the measurement bias of two standardized psychological tests. *Journal of Applied Psychology, 72,* 19–29.

Drasgow, F., Levine, M. V., & McLaughlin, M. E. (1987). Detecting inappropriate test scores with optimal and practical appropriateness indices. *Applied Psychological Measurement, 11,* 59–79.

Drasgow, F., & Lissak, R. I. (1983). Modified parallel analysis: A procedure for examining the latent dimensionality of dichotomously scored item responses. *Journal of Applied Psychology, 68,* 363–373.

Drasgow, F., & Parsons, C. K. (1983). Application of unidimensional item response theory models to multidimensional data. *Applied Psychological Measurement, 7,* 189–199.

Embretson, S. E. (1984). A general latent trait model for response processes. *Psychometrika, 49,* 175–186.

Embretson, S. E. (Ed.) (1985). *Test design: Developments in psychology and psychometrics.* New York: Academic Press.

Feldt, L. S. (1984). Some relationships between the binomial error model and classical test theory. *Educational and Psychological Measurement, 44,* 883–891.

Fischer, G. H. (1976). Some probabilistic models for measuring change. In D. N. M. de Gruijter & L. J. T. van der Kamp (Eds.), *Advances in psychological and educational measurement* (pp. 97–110). New York: John Wiley & Sons.

Fischer, G. H., & Formann, A. K. (1982). Some applications of logistic latent trait models with linear constraints on the parameters. *Applied Psychological Measurement, 6,* 397–416.

Forsyth, R., Saisangjan, U., & Gilmer, J. (1981). Some empirical results related to the robustness of the Rasch model. *Applied Psychological Measurement, 5,* 175–186.

Fraser, C. (1981). *NOHARM: A Fortran program for non-linear analysis by a robust method for estimating the parameters of 1-, 2-, and 3-parameter latent trait models.* Armidale, Australia: University of New England, Centre for Behavioral Studies in Education.

Goldstein, H. (1980). Dimensionality, bias, independence, and measurement scale problems in latent trait test score models. *British Journal of Mathematical and Statistical Psychology, 33,* 234–246.

Green, B. F. (1988). Critical problems in computer-based psychological measurement. *Measurement in Education, 1,* 223–231.

Green, B. F., Bock, R. D., Humphreys, L. G., Linn, R. B., & Reckase, M. D. (1982). *Evaluation plan for the computerized Adaptive Vocational Aptitude Battery.* Baltimore, MD: Johns Hopkins University, Department of Psychology.

Green, B. F., Bock, R. D., Humphreys, L. G., Linn, R. L., & Reckase, M. D. (1984). Technical guidelines for assessing computerized adaptive tests. *Journal of Educational Measurement, 21,* 347–360.

Guion, R. M., & Ironson, G. H. (1983). Latent trait theory for organizational research. *Organizational Behavioral and Human Performance, 31,* 54–87.

Gulliksen, H. (1950). *Theory of mental tests.* New York: John Wiley & Sons.

Gustafsson, J. E. (1980a). A solution of the conditional estimation problem for long tests in the Rasch model for dichotomous items. *Educational and Psychological Measurement, 40,* 377–385.

Gustafsson, J. E. (1980b). Testing and obtaining fit of data to the Rasch model. *British Journal of Mathematical and Statistical Psychology, 33,* 205–233.

Haley, D. C. (1952). *Estimation of the dosage mortality relationship when the dose is subject to error* (Technical Report No. 15). Stanford, CA: Stanford University, Applied Mathematics and Statistics Laboratory.

Hambleton, R. K. (1979). Latent trait models and their applications. In R. Traub (Ed.), *Methodological developments: New directions for testing and measurement (No. 4)* (pp. 13–32). San Francisco: Jossey-Bass.

Hambleton, R. K. (Ed.) (1983). *Applications of item response theory.* Vancouver, BC: Educational Research Institute of British Columbia.

Hambleton, R. K., Arrasmith, D., & Smith, I. L. (1987, April). *Optimal item selection with credentialing examinations.* Paper presented at the annual meeting of the American Educational Research Association, Washington, DC.

Hambleton, R. K., & Cook. L. L. (1977). Latent trait models and their use in the analysis of educational test data. *Journal of Educational Measurement, 14,* 75–96.

Hambleton, R. K., & Cook, L. L. (1983). The robustness of item response models and effects of test length and sample size on the precision of ability estimates. In D. Weiss (Ed.), *New horizons in testing* (pp. 31–49). New York: Academic Press.

Hambleton, R. K., & de Gruijter, D. N. M. (1983). Application of item response models to criterion-referenced test item selection. *Journal of Educational Measurement, 20,* 355–367.

Hambleton, R. K., & Murray, L. N. (1983). Some goodness of fit investigations for item response models. In R. K. Hambleton (Ed.), *Applications of item response theory* (pp. 71–94). Vancouver, BC: Educational Research Institute of British Columbia.

Hambleton, R. K., Murray, L. N., & Williams, P. (1983). *Fitting item response models to the Maryland Functional Reading Tests* (Laboratory of Psychometric and Evaluative Research Report No. 139). Amherst, MA: University of Massachusetts, School of Education. (ERIC Document Reproduction Service No.: ED 230 624)

Hambleton, R. K., & Rogers, H. J. (1986). Evaluation of the plot method for identifying potentially biased test items. In S. H. Irvine, S. Newstead, & P. Dann (Eds.), *Computer-based human assessment.* Boston, MA: Kluwer Academic Publishers.

Hambleton, R. K., & Rogers, H. J. (in press, a). Promising directions for assessing item response model fit to test data. *Applied Psychological Measurement.*

Hambleton, R. K., & Rogers, H. J. (in press, b). Solving criterion-referenced measurement problems with item response models. *International Journal of Educational Research.*

Hambleton, R. K., & Rovinelli, R. J. (1973). A Fortran IV program for generating examinee response data from logistic test models. *Behavioral Science, 17,* 73–74.

Hambleton, R. K., & Rovinelli, R. J. (1986). Assessing the dimensionality of a set of test items. *Applied Psychological Measurement, 10,* 287–302.

Hambleton, R. K., & Swaminathan, H. (1985). *Item response theory:*

Principles and applications. Boston, MA: Kluwer Academic Publishers.

Hambleton, R. K., Swaminathan, H., Cook, L. L., Eignor, D. R., & Gifford, J. A. (1978). Developments in latent trait theory: Models, technical issues, and applications. *Review of Educational Research, 48,* 467–510.

Hambleton, R. K., & Traub, R. E. (1971). Information curves and efficiency of three logistic test models. *British Journal of Mathematical and Statistical Psychology, 24,* 273–281.

Hambleton, R. K., & Traub, R. E. (1973). Analysis of empirical data using two logistic latent trait models. *British Journal of Mathematical and Statistical Psychology, 26,* 195–211.

Hambleton, R. K., & van der Linden, W. J. (1982). Advances in item response theory and applications: An introduction. *Applied Psychological Measurement, 6,* 373–378.

Hathaway, W. E. (1980). A school-district-developed, Rasch-based approach to minimum competency achievement testing. In R. M. Jaeger & C. K. Tittle (Eds.), *Minimum competency achievement testing: Motives, models, measures, and consequences* (pp. 345–357). Berkeley, CA: McCutchan.

Hattie, J. A. (1984). An empirical study of various indices for determining unidimensionality. *Multivariate Behavioral Research, 19,* 49–78.

Hattie, J. A. (1985). Methodological review: Assessing unidimensionality of tests and items. *Applied Psychological Measurement, 9,* 139–164.

Hills, J. R., Beard, J. G., Yotinprasert, S., Roca, N. R., & Subhiya, R. G. (1985). *An investigation of the feasibility of using the three-parameter model for Florida's State Wide Assessment Tests.* Tallahassee, FL: Florida State University, College of Education.

Hoover, H. D. (1984). The most appropriate scores for measuring educational development in the elementary schools: GE's. *Educational Measurement: Issues and Practices, 3,* 8–14.

Hoover, H. D., & Kolen, M. J. (1984). The reliability of six item bias indices. *Applied Psychological Measurement, 8,* 173–181.

Horn, J. L. (1965). A rationale and test for the number of factors in factor analysis. *Psychometrika, 30,* 179–185.

Hulin, C. L., Drasgow, F., & Parsons, C. K. (1983). *Item response theory: Application to psychological measurement.* Homewood, IL: Dow Jones-Irwin.

Hulin, C. L., Lissak, R. I., & Drasgow, F. (1982). Recovery of two- and three-parameter logistic item characteristic curves: A Monte Carlo study. *Applied Psychological Measurement, 6,* 249–260.

Hunter, J. E. (1975, December). *A critical analysis of the use of item means and item-test correlations to determine the presence or absence of content bias in achievement test items.* Paper presented at Education Conference on Test Bias, Annapolis, MD.

Ironson, G. H. (1983). Using item response theory to measure bias. In R. K. Hambleton (Ed.), *Applications of item response theory* (pp. 155–174). Vancouver, BC: Educational Research Institute of British Columbia.

Jensema, C. J. (1976). A simple technique for estimating latent trait mental test parameters. *Educational and Psychological Measurement, 36,* 705–715.

Kingston, N. M., & Dorans, N. J. (1984). Item location effects and their implications for IRT equating and adaptive testing. *Applied Psychological Measurement, 8,* 147–154.

Kingston, N. M., & Dorans, N. J. (1985). The analysis of item-ability regressions: An exploratory IRT model fit tool. *Applied Psychological Measurement, 9,* 281–288.

Kingston, N. M., & Stocking, M. L. (1986, August). *Psychometric issues in IRT-based test construction.* Paper presented at the annual meeting of the American Psychological Association, Washington, DC.

Koch, W. R. (1983). Likert scaling using the graded response latent trait model. *Applied Psychological Measurement, 7,* 15–32.

Lazarsfeld, P. F., & Henry, N. W. (1968). *Latent structure analysis.* Boston: Houghton Mifflin.

Levine, M. V., & Drasgow, F. (1982). Appropriateness measurement: Review, critique and validating studies. *British Journal of Mathematical and Statistical Psychology, 35,* 42–56.

Levine, M. V., & Rubin, D. B. (1979). Measuring the appropriateness of multiple-choice test scores. *Journal of Educational Statistics, 4,* 269–290.

Linn, R. L., & Harnisch, D. L. (1981). Interactions between item content and group membership on achievement test items. *Journal of Educational Measurement, 18,* 109–118.

Linn, R. L., Levine, M. V., Hastings, C. N., & Wardrop, J. L. (1981). An investigation of item bias in a test of reading comprehension. *Applied Psychological Measurement, 5,* 159–173.

Lord, F. M. (1952). A theory of test scores (*Psychometric Monograph* No. 7). Psychometric Society.

Lord, F. M. (1953a). An application of confidence intervals and of maximum likelihood to the estimation of an examinee's ability. *Psychometrika, 18,* 57–75.

Lord, F. M. (1953b). The relation of test score to the trait underlying the test. *Educational and Psychological Measurement, 13,* 517–548.

Lord, F. M. (1968). An analysis of the Verbal Scholastic Aptitude Test using Birnbaum's three-parameter logistic model. *Educational and Psychological Measurement, 28,* 989–1020.

Lord, F. M. (1970a). Estimating item characteristic curves without knowledge of their mathematical form. *Psychometrika, 35,* 43–50.

Lord, F. M. (1970b). Some test theory for tailored testing. In W. H. Holtzman (Ed.), *Computer-assisted instruction, testing and guidance* (pp. 139–183). New York: Harper & Row.

Lord, F. M. (1974a). Estimation of latent ability and item parameters when there are omitted responses. *Psychometrika, 39,* 247–264.

Lord, F. M. (1974b). Quick estimates of the relative efficiency of two tests as a function of ability level. *Journal of Educational Measurement, 11,* 247–254.

Lord, F. M. (1975a). The "ability" scale in item characteristic curve theory. *Psychometrika, 40,* 205–217.

Lord, F. M. (1975b). *Evaluation with artificial data of a procedure for estimating ability and item characteristic curve parameters* (Research Bulletin 75–33). Princeton, NJ: Educational Testing Service.

Lord, F. M. (1977a). A broad range tailored test of verbal ability. *Applied Psychological Measurement, 1,* 95–100.

Lord, F. M. (1977b). Practical applications of item characteristic curve theory. *Journal of Educational Measurement, 14,* 117–138.

Lord, F. M. (1977c). A study of item bias, using item characteristic curve theory. In Y. H. Poortinga (Ed.), *Basic problems in cross-cultural psychology* (pp. 19–29). Amsterdam: Swets & Zeitlinger.

Lord, F. M. (1980a). *Applications of item response theory to practical testing problems.* Hillsdale, NJ: Lawrence Erlbaum.

Lord, F. M. (1980b). Some how and which for practical tailored testing. In L. J. Th. van der Kamp, W. F. Langerak, & D. N. M. de Gruijter (Eds.), *Psychometrics for Educational Debates* (pp. 189–205). New York: John Wiley & Sons.

Lord, F. M. (1984). Standard errors of measurement at different ability levels. *Journal of Educational Measurement, 21,* 239–243.

Lord, F. M. (1986). Maximum likelihood and Bayesian parameter estimation in item response theory. *Journal of Educational Measurement, 23,* 157–162.

Lord, F. M., & Novick, M. R. (1968). *Statistical theories of mental test scores.* Reading, MA: Addison-Wesley.

Ludlow, L. H. (1985). A strategy for the graphical representation of Rasch model residuals. *Educational and Psychological Measurement, 45,* 851–859.

Ludlow, L. H. (1986). On the graphical analysis of item response theory residuals. *Applied Psychological Measurement, 10,* 217–229.

Masters, G. N. (1982). A Rasch model for partial credit scoring. *Psychometrika, 47,* 149–174.

Masters, G. N., & Wright, B. D. (1984). The essential process in a family of measurement models. *Psychometrika, 49,* 269–272.

McDonald, R. P. (1967). Non-linear factor analysis (*Psychometric Monograph* No. 15). Psychometric Society.

McDonald, R. P. (1981). The dimensionality of tests and items. *British Journal of Mathematical and Statistical Psychology, 34,* 100–117.

McDonald, R. P. (1982). Linear versus non-linear models in item response theory. *Applied Psychological Measurement, 6,* 379–396.

McDonald, R. P. (in press). Future directions for item response theory. *International Journal of Educational Research.*

McKinley, R. L., & Mills, C. N. (1985). A comparison of several goodness-of-fit statistics. *Applied Psychological Measurement, 9,* 49–57.

McLaughlin, M. E., & Drasgow, F. (1987). Lord's chi-square test of item bias with estimated and with known person parameters. *Applied Psychological Measurement, 11,* 161–173.

Mislevy, R., & Bock, R. D. (1982). *BILOG: Maximum likelihood item analysis and test scoring with logistic models.* Mooresville, IN: Scientific Software.

Mokken, R. J., & Lewis, C. (1982). A nonparametric approach to the analysis of dichotomous item responses. *Applied Psychological Measurement, 6,* 417–430.

Montanelli, R. G., & Humphreys, L. G. (1976). Latent roots of random data correlation matrices with squared multiple correlations on the diagonal: A Monte Carlo study. *Psychometrika, 41,* 341–348.

Mulaik, S. A. (1972). *The foundations of factor analysis.* New York: McGraw-Hill.

Owen, R. (1975). A Bayesian sequential procedure for quantal response in the context of mental testing. *Journal of the American Statistical Association, 70,* 351–356.

Pandey, T. N., & Carlson, D. (1983). Application of item response models to reporting assessment data. In R. K. Hambleton (Ed.), *Applications of item response theory* (pp. 212–229). Vancouver, BC: Educational Research Institute of British Columbia.

Phillips, S. E., & Mehrens, W. A. (1987). Curricular differences and unidimensionality of achievement test data: An exploratory analysis. *Journal of Educational Measurement, 24,* 1–16.

Pine, S. M. (1977). Applications of item response theory to the problem of test bias. In D. J. Weiss (Ed.), *Applications of computerized adaptive testing* (Research Report 77-1). Minneapolis: University of Minnesota, Psychometric Methods Program, Department of Psychology.

Rasch, G. (1960). *Probabilistic models for some intelligence and attainment tests.* Copenhagen: Danish Institute for Educational Research.

Rasch, G. (1966). An item analysis which takes individual differences into account. *British Journal of Mathematical and Statistical Psychology, 19,* 49–57.

Reckase, M. D. (1979). Unifactor latent trait models applied to multifactor tests: Results and implications. *Journal of Educational Statistics, 4,* 207–230.

Reckase, M. D. (1985). The difficulty of test items that measure more than one ability. *Applied Psychological Measurement, 9,* 401–412.

Ree, M. J. (1979). Estimating item characteristic curves. *Applied Psychological Measurement, 3,* 371–385.

Ree, M. J. (1981). The effects of item calibration sample size on adaptive testing. *Applied Psychological Measurement, 5,* 11–19.

Ree, M. J., Mullins, C. J., Mathews, J. J., & Massey, R. H. (1982). *Armed Services Vocational Aptitude Battery: Item and factor analyses of forms 8, 9, and 10* (AFHRL-TR-81-55). Brooks Air Force Base, TX: Air Force Human Resources Laboratory.

Rentz, R. R., & Bashaw, W. L. (1977). The national reference scale of reading: An application of the Rasch model. *Journal of Educational Measurement, 14,* 161–180.

Rogers, H. J., & Hambleton, R. K. (in press). Evaluation of computer simulated baseline statistics for use in item bias studies. *Educational and Psychological Measurement.*

Rogers, H. J., & Hattie, J. A. (1987). A Monte Carlo investigation of several person and item fit statistics for item response models. *Applied Psychological Measurement, 11,* 47–58.

Rosenbaum, P. R. (1984). Testing the conditional independence and monotonicity assumptions of item response theory. *Psychometrika, 49,* 425–435.

Samejima, R. (1969). Estimation of latent ability using a response pattern of graded scores (*Psychometric Monograph* No. 17). Psychometric Society.

Samejima, R. (1972). A general model for free response data (*Psychometric Monograph* No. 18). Psychometric Society.

Samejima, F. (1973). Homogeneous case of the continuous response model. *Psychometrika, 38,* 203–219.

Samejima, F. (1974). Normal ogive model on the continuous response level in the multidimensional latent space. *Psychometrika, 39,* 111–121.

Samejima, F. (1977). A use of the information function in tailored testing. *Applied Psychological Measurement, 1,* 233–247.

Scheuneman, J. (1979). A method of assessing bias in test items. *Journal of Educational Measurement, 16,* 143–152.

Schmidt, F. L. (1977). The Urry method of approximating the item parameters of latent trait theory. *Educational and Psychological Measurement, 37,* 613–620.

Shepard, L. A., Camilli, G., & Averill, M. (1981). Comparison of procedures for detecting test-item bias with both internal and external ability criteria. *Journal of Educational Statistics, 6,* 317–375.

Shepard, L. A., Camilli, G., & Williams, D. M. (1984). Accounting for statistical artifacts in item bias research. *Journal of Educational Statistics, 9,* 83–138.

Shepard, L. A., Camilli, G., & Williams, D. M. (1985). Validity of approximation techniques for detecting item bias. *Journal of Educational Measurement, 22,* 77–105.

Skaggs, G., & Lissitz, R. W. (1986). IRT test equating: Relevant issues and a review of recent research. *Review of Educational Research, 56,* 495–529.

Sternberg, R. J. (1984). What cognitive psychology can and cannot do for test development. In B. S. Plake (Ed.), *Social and technical issues in testing: Implications for test construction and usage* (pp. 39–60). Hillsdale, NJ: Lawrence Erlbaum.

Stocking, M. L., & Lord, F. M. (1983). Developing a common metric in item response theory. *Applied Psychological Measurement, 7,* 201–210.

Swaminathan, H. (1983). Parameter estimation in item-response models. In R. K. Hambleton (Ed.), *Applications of item response theory* (pp. 24–44). Vancouver, BC: Educational Research Institute of British Columbia.

Swaminathan, H., & Gifford, J. A. (1982). Bayesian estimation in the Rasch model. *Journal of Educational Statistics, 7,* 175–192.

Swaminathan, H., & Gifford, J. A. (1983). Estimation of parameters in the three-parameter latent trait model. In D. Weiss (Ed.), *New horizons in testing* (pp. 9–30). New York: Academic Press.

Swaminathan, H., & Gifford, J. A. (1985). Bayesian estimation in the two-parameter logistic model. *Psychometrika, 50,* 349–364.

Swaminathan, H., & Gifford, J. A. (1986). Bayesian estimation in the three-parameter logistic model. *Psychometrika, 51,* 589–601.

Tatsuoka, K. K. (1987). Validation of cognitive sensitivity for item response curves. *Journal of Educational Measurement, 24,* 233–245.

Thissen, D. M. (1976). Information in wrong responses to Raven's Progressive Matrices. *Journal of Educational Measurement, 13,* 201–214.

Thissen, D. M. (1982). Marginal maximum likelihood estimation for the one-parameter logistic model. *Psychometrika, 47,* 175–186.

Thissen, D. M. (1983). *MULTILOG: Item analysis and scoring with multiple category response models.* Chicago: International Educational Services.

Thissen, D. M., & Steinberg, L. (1986). A taxonomy of item response models. *Psychometrika, 51,* 567–577.

Thissen, D. M., & Wainer, H. (1982). Some standard errors in item response theory. *Psychometrika, 47,* 397–412.

Thissen, D. M., & Wainer, H. (1985). *Some supporting evidence for Lord's guideline for estimating 'c'* (Technical Report No. 85–57). Princeton, NJ: Educational Testing Service.

Traub, R. E. (1983). A priori considerations in choosing an item response model. In R. K. Hambleton (Ed.), *Applications of item response theory* (pp. 57–70). Vancouver, BC: Educational Research Institute of British Columbia.

Traub, R. E., & Lam, R. (1985). Latent structure and item sampling models for testing. *Annual Review of Psychology, 36,* 19–48.

Traub, R. E., & Wolfe, R. G. (1981). Latent trait theories and the assessment of educational achievement. In D. C. Berliner (Ed.), *Review of research in education* (*Vol. 9,* pp. 377–435). Washington, DC: American Educational Research Association.

Tucker, L. R., Humphreys, L. G., & Roznowski, M. A. (1986). *Comparative accuracy of five indices of dimensionality of binary items.*

Champaign-Urbana, IL: University of Illinois, Department of Psychology.

Tukey, J. W. (1977). *Exploratory data analysis.* Reading MA: Addison-Wesley.

Urry, V. W. (1974). Approximations to item parameters of mental test models and their uses. *Educational and Psychological Measurement, 34,* 253–269.

Urry, V. W. (1977). Tailored testing: A successful application of latent trait theory. *Journal of Educational Measurement, 14,* 181–196.

van de Vijver, F. J. R. (1986). The robustness of Rasch estimates. *Applied Psychological Measurement, 10,* 45–57.

van den Wollenberg, A. L. (1980). *On the Wright–Panchapakesan goodness of fit test for the Rasch model* (Internal Report 80-MA-02). Nijmegen, The Netherlands: Katholieke Universiteit Nijmegen, Vakgroep Mathematische, Psychologisch Laboratorium.

van den Wollenberg, A. L. (1982a). A simple and effective method to test the dimensionality axiom of the Rasch model. *Applied Psychological Measurement, 6,* 83–91.

van den Wollenberg, A. L. (1982b). Two new test statistics for the Rasch model. *Psychometrika, 47,* 123–140.

Wainer, H., & Kiely, G. L. (1987). Item clusters and computerized adaptive testing: A case for testlets. *Journal of Educational Measurement, 24,* 195–201.

Wainer, H., Morgan, A., & Gustafsson, J. E. (1980). A review of estimation procedures for the Rasch model with an eye toward longish tests. *Journal of Educational Statistics, 5,* 35–64.

Wainer, H., & Thissen, D. (1987). Estimating ability with the wrong model. *Journal of Educational Statistics, 12,* 339–368.

Wainer, H., Wadkins, J. R. J., & Rogers, A. (1984). Was there one distractor too many? *Journal of Educational Statistics, 9,* 5–24.

Weiss, D. J. (Ed.) (1978). *Proceedings of the 1977 Computerized Adaptive Testing Conference.* Minneapolis: University of Minnesota.

Weiss, D. J. (Ed.) (1980). *Proceedings of the 1979 Computerized Adaptive Testing Conference.* Minneapolis: University of Minnesota.

Weiss, D. J. (1982). Improving measurement quality and efficiency with adaptive testing. *Applied Psychological Measurement, 6,* 473–492.

Weiss, D. J. (Ed.) (1983). *New horizons in testing.* New York: Academic Press.

Weiss, D. J. (1985). Adaptive testing by computer. *Journal of Consulting and Clinical Psychology, 53,* 774–789.

Weiss, D. J., & Kingsbury, G. G. (1984). Application of computerized adaptive testing to educational problems. *Journal of Educational Measurement, 21,* 361–375.

Whitely, S. E. (1980). Multicomponent latent trait models for ability tests. *Psychometrika, 45,* 479–494.

Whitely, S. E., & Dawis, R. V. (1974). The nature of objectivity with the Rasch model. *Journal of Educational Measurement, 11,* 163–178.

Wingersky, M. S. (1983). LOGIST: A program for computing maximum likelihood procedures for logistic test models. In R. K. Hambleton (Ed.), *Applications of item response theory* (pp. 45–56). Vancouver, BC: Educational Research Institute of British Columbia.

Wingersky, M. S., Barton, M. A., & Lord, F. M. (1982). *LOGIST user's guide.* Princeton, NJ: Educational Testing Service.

Wingersky, M. W., & Lord, F. M. (1984). An investigation of methods for reducing sampling error in certain IRT procedures. *Applied Psychological Measurement, 8,* 347–364.

Wood, R. (1978). Fitting the Rasch model: A heady tale. *British Journal of Mathematical and Statistical Psychology, 31,* 27–32.

Woodcock, R. W. (1978). *Development and standardization of the Woodcock–Johnson Psycho-Educational Battery.* Hingham, MA: Teaching Resources Corporation.

Wright, B. D. (1968). Sample-free test calibration and person measurement. *Proceedings of the 1967 Invitational Conference on Testing Problems.* Princeton, NJ: Educational Testing Service.

Wright, B. D. (1977a). Misunderstanding of the Rasch model. *Journal of Educational Measurement, 14,* 219–226.

Wright, B. D. (1977b). Solving measurement problems with the Rasch model. *Journal of Educational Measurement, 14,* 97–116.

Wright, B. D., & Douglas, G. A. (1977a). Best procedures for sample-free item analysis. *Applied Psychological Measurement, 1,* 281–295.

Wright, B. D., & Douglas, G. A. (1977b). Conditional versus unconditional procedures for sample-free analysis. *Educational and Psychological Measurement, 37,* 573–586.

Wright, B. D., & Panchapakesan, N. (1969). A procedure for sample-free item analysis. *Educational and Psychological Measurement, 29,* 23–48.

Wright, B. D., & Stone, M. H. (1979). *Best test design.* Chicago: MESA Press.

Yen, W. M. (1980). The extent, causes and importance of context effects on item parameters for two latent trait models. *Journal of Educational Measurement, 17,* 297–311.

Yen, W. M. (1981). Using simulation results to choose a latent trait model. *Applied Psychological Measurement, 5,* 245–262.

Yen, W. M. (1983a). Tau equivalence and equipercentile equating. *Psychometrika, 48,* 353–369.

Yen, W. M. (1983b). Use of the three-parameter model in the development of a standardized achievement test. In R. K. Hambleton (Ed.), *Applications of item response theory* (pp. 123–141). Vancouver, BC: Educational Research Institute of British Columbia.

Yen, W. M. (1984a). Obtaining maximum likelihood trait estimates from number-correct scores for the three-parameter logistic model. *Journal of Educational Measurement, 21,* 93–111.

Yen, W. M. (1984b). Effects of local dependence on the fit and equating performance of the three-parameter logistic model. *Applied Psychological Measurement, 8,* 125–145.

Yen, W. M. (1985). Increasing item complexity: A possible cause of scale shrinkage for unidimensional item response theory. *Psychometrika, 50,* 399–410.

Yen, W. M. (1986). The choice of scale for educational measurement: an IRT perspective. *Journal of Educational Measurement, 23,* 299–325.

Yen, W. M. (1987). A comparison of the efficiency and accuracy of BILOG and LOGIST. *Psychometrika, 52,* 275–291.

Yen, W. M., Green, D. R., & Burket, G. R. (1987). Valid normative information from customized achievement tests. *Educational measurement: Issues and practices, 6,* 7–13.

Zwick, R. (1987). Assessing the dimensionality of NAEP reading data. *Journal of Educational Measurement, 24,* 293–308.

5

Bias in Test Use

Nancy S. Cole
University of Illinois at Urbana-Champaign

Pamela A. Moss
University of Pittsburgh

Test bias has been a dominant theme in educational measurement since the mid-1960s and was a recurring, though less dominant, concern before that time. Its dominance as a testing issue began during the civil rights movement of the 1960s and gained fuel from the women's rights movement that followed. Many of the situations coming under scrutiny by those concerned with fairness and equal rights for certain groups (such as employment opportunities, admission to higher education, completion of a high school diploma, or assignment to a special educational environment) involved tests as sources of information used in decision making. As a consequence, the possibility of bias in test use has received wide attention from the public and the measurement profession. Test critics, the courts, legislators, journalists, measurement scholars, and other groups interested in the testing process have joined in the public debate.

The wide diversity of views of the many parties concerned with test bias has added considerable complexity to attempts to resolve the issues. The difficulties can be illustrated by an example. Suppose one group of high school students, Group A, scored higher on a high school achievement test than another group, Group B. Such an event might lead to a headline in the local newspaper, "Group B Students Score Lower." Callers on a local radio talk show might say "I always knew those Group B students were dumber," or "The schools are not doing a good job with those Group B students." A letter to the editor in the local newspaper might argue that "the test score results do not mean anything because those tests are biased."

The task of attempting to judge whether bias in the test is a reasonable explanation for the test-score differences is made especially difficult because of the implicit and emotional assumptions people make that lead them to view the same information in different ways. For example, if Group A were simply students with an A average in high school and Group B were students with a B average, few reactions would be generated. Most observers would accept the results as an accurate reflection of differences between A students and B students—as valid results, not an indication of bias.

However, suppose Group A were white students and Group B were black students, with Group A scoring higher on the test and making better grades in high school. In this case, different observers bring different values, prior assumptions, and standards of evidence to the question of whether the test score difference is a valid, or correct, reflection of differences in school performance shown by the grade differential or the result of bias in the tests. To some, the test score and grade differentials would be an indication of bias in both the test and the high school grades; to others, the grade differential would be evidence of lack of bias in the test scores. Among those who rejected the notion of bias, some would explain the differences in high school grades by differences in opportunities and experiences of the students; others, by racially linked capacities. In fact, the racial differences on the test scores and on the grades raise a host of issues about the test and about the school that deserve close scrutiny and careful explanation.

An additional complicating factor concerns the different beliefs about the value of the interpretations, decisions, or actions being based on test scores, whether biased or not. For

NOTE: The authors are indebted to Lloyd Bond, Catherine Cornbleth, Paul LeMahieu, and Lorrie Shepard for helpful comments on an earlier draft and to Robert Linn for suggestions on several versions of the chapter. We hope we have done justice to their excellent suggestions.

example, the high school achievement test scores might be used as a part of college admission decisions or to assign students to college preparatory high school courses. When the identification of capable students for college is seen as desirable and appropriate, such decisions and the tests used in them are easily accepted. When such actions are seen as limiting the opportunity of deserving students, then the same decisions and the tests are viewed negatively. As another example, the way people interpret and explain test score differences can range from an assumption that there are genetic differences between the races to one that the schools are not doing a good enough job educating black children. Obviously, these different explanations create very different reactions to the explanation itself and to the test connected with it.

Given this diversity of values and beliefs, it is not surprising that consensus conclusions about bias and the merits of test use in debated situations have been rare. Because the issues are so complex, it is important to give a clear and defensible technical meaning to the term *bias* that will help those with a stake in the testing process reach conclusions about the presence or absence of bias in particular situations. However, the nature of the public debates about bias and test use also require an understanding of the broader concerns of social justice and the appropriateness of test use for groups affected by testing. In this chapter, the technical meaning of bias is addressed first in connection with the concept of validity to which it is closely tied. The second section describes methods of studying, identifying, and eliminating bias in this technical sense. The final section of the chapter discusses the broader issue of evaluting the appropriateness of a test's use, which includes concerns beyond the technical validity domain, called *extra-validity concerns*. This section offers an approach that might help to expose for consideration implicit values and assumptions deeply embedded in issues of bias in test use.

Validation Theory and the Meaning of Bias

The response to a test question is a sample of behavior. Consider the following example of an arithmetic word problem that might appear on a fourth-grade test:

If Mary has 8 apples and John brings her 5 more, then how many apples will Mary have?

a. 3   c. 15
b. 13   d. 40

A student's answer to this question is a sample of behavior. A test score is a summary of several such answers. The issue is, What do these behavior samples tell us?

If all the questions ask for simple addition like this one, and the student answers few correctly, achieving a low test score, then the obvious conclusion is that the student cannot add well and needs practice on addition facts. But this is not the only possibility. Perhaps the student knows what $8 + 5$ is but does not recognize that this is the operation called for in the word problem. Then a different type of practice with addition in real-world situations could be in order. Perhaps the student cannot read the question, in which case the low score might tell us instead about the student's reading difficulty. Perhaps the student selected answers at random and never even read the

question. Then the low score might just indicate lack of motivation on the test or inattentiveness.

We can never be certain which of various possible reasons for a test score is the correct one for an individual student. However, we can try to learn what a test score indicates about most of the students who take that test. Validation is the name we give the process of gathering evidence about what a test score indicates, about what inferences we can generally make correctly from the scores.

As described in the 1985 *Standards for Educational and Psychological Testing,* validity

refers to the appropriateness, meaningfulness, and usefulness of the specific inferences made from test scores. Test validation is the process of accumulating evidence to support such inferences. A variety of inferences may be made from scores produced by a given test, and there are many ways of accumulating evidence to support any particular inference. Validity, however, is a unitary concept. Although evidence may be accumulated in many ways, validity always refers to the degree to which that evidence supports the inferences that are made from the scores. The inferences regarding specific uses of a test are validated, not the test itself. (American Educational Research Association [AERA] et al., 1985, p. 9)

This conception of test validation as a "unitary" concept, a *process* of accumulating evidence in support of *specific inferences from or uses of test scores* (which summarize samples of *observed behavior*), enjoys wide acceptance by measurement theorists (e.g., Cronbach, 1971, 1980; Guion, 1977; R. L. Linn, 1979; Messick, 1975, 1980, 1981; Tenopyr, 1977). However, there are some fundamental issues about the explication and application of this concept of validity over which there is less agreement in theory and in practice (see Messick, this volume, for a more complete description of controversial areas). Here, we review four of these critical issues that have considerable impact on how bias is addressed and present our own positions with respect to them. These issues are (a) the need to integrate various types of evidence into a unitary view of validity, (b) the way in which the validation process should be tied to the context in which a test is used, (c) how the generation of rival hypotheses about what the test measures should drive the validation process, and (d) the relationship between values and validity in test evaluation.

An Integrated Concept of Validity

Traditionally, validation activities have been divided into three broad categories: content validation, criterion validation, and construct validation. *Content validation* has typically been used to label (primarily judgmental) activities that investigate the adequacy with which the test content samples the defined domain about which inferences are to be made. If we wish to infer that a test measures the ability to spell third-grade-level words, we examine the range of content of the test questions. If most of the words are more appropriate for first and second graders, we should not conclude that high-scoring students can spell third-grade words.

Criterion validation has typically been associated with activities that investigate the empirical relationship between performance on a test (a predictor) and performance on a different variable (a criterion). The criterion might grow out of the situation, as when a test is used to predict subsequent performance. For example, for a test used in medical school admissions, a criterion could be eventual medical school grades. A criterion can also be a "real-life" measure of the attribute the test is intended to measure (Guion, 1977). One might wish to use a 10-minute typing test to judge speed and accuracy when hiring typists. More thorough information about typing skill could be gathered over many weeks in actual office situations, although such information would be too expensive to obtain for all applicants for typist jobs. A criterion study could be done on a small group of typists to determine how well the short test approximates the more thorough information, here called the *criterion.*

Construct validation refers to the process of collecting evidence to support or refute a given interpretation or explanation of test behavior. The proposed interpretation is the construct, and a variety of logical and empirical information may be used to consider the appropriateness of interpreting the test score as a reflection of that construct. Construct validation has typically been invoked when the desired interpretation is about a hypothetical attribute like intelligence or aptitude (Cronbach, 1971; Cronbach & Meehl, 1955). Construct validation has been viewed as necessary whenever "no criterion or universe of content is accepted as entirely adequate to define the quality being measured" (Cronbach & Meehl, 1955, p. 282).

The tendency to view these three categories as separate and independently sufficient considerations of validity has come under fire from a number of measurement theorists (e.g., Cronbach, 1980; Fitzpatrick, 1983; Guion, 1977; Messick, 1975, 1980, 1981; Tenopyr, 1977). These and other writers argue for the integration of the validity concept. Cronbach (1980) and Messick (1975, 1980) have argued, in essence, that no criterion or universe of content is *ever* entirely adequate to define the quality being measured, that a variety of types of logical and empirical evidence is necessary to support a given interpretation, and that all test score interpretations should be construct referenced. The recent Standards (AERA et al., 1985) moves towards this position by emphasizing the unity of the validity concept and by using the three traditional labels to distinguish types of evidence about validity, as opposed to types of validity. However, it stops short of identifying construct validation as the unifying concept underlying all test validations, as Cronbach and Messick do.

We agree with Cronbach and Messick (and others) that all test-score interpretations should be examined within a broad construct validation type of framework. Taken alone, neither content- nor criterion-related evidence of validity is sufficient to rule out plausible counterexplanations for test results (Messick, this volume). Even a test of a seemingly straightforward domain, such as the arithmetic word problem described earlier, lends itself to alternative interpretations. Poor scores might indicate difficulty with addition facts, with understanding word problems, with reading, with motivation, or with attention span. Content-related evidence alone cannot eliminate all plausible explanations. Neither can criterion-related evidence alone eliminate rival explanations, because the validity of the criterion must also be investigated. In the typing test example, the criterion, though based on a longer sample of work in an office situation, requires someone's judgments

about the way in which typing skill will be measured. The nature of the criterion construct will be influenced by factors like the kind of typing to be done, the nature of the drafts from which the typist is working, the extent of time pressure involved, and so on. Thus, an integrated conception of validation, in which multiple types of evidence are considered, is essential to judging the appropriateness of a test-score interpretation. This is especially important in relation to issues of bias.

Context-based Construct Validation

A possible limitation, or inadequacy, we see in the construct validation approach involves its traditional focus on the construct as independent from, and possibly of greater importance than, the purpose for which the test is being used. In contrast, the practical concern in most educational measurement is the appropriateness of a test for some particular purpose. The construct is of practical interest primarily as a way of understanding the score and its appropriateness for the use. Although many measurement theorists have emphasized the importance of investigating the appropriateness of a use, they have not examined the way the use influences the meaning constructed for the test score. We wish to emphasize the importance of the context of test use in influencing the meaning given the score and, thus, the need for context-based construct validation.

It is our sense that the meaning given a test score should not (perhaps even cannot) be evaluated fully apart from the context in which the scores are to be used (Moss, 1985). In educational measurement, we test particular types of persons in a particular setting for a particular purpose. Tests are used to provide summative information about students in the form of grades, to provide diagnostic information about students for the teacher to use in remediation, to help educators make important decisions about placement of students into particular programs, to determine whether students should be promoted or given a diploma, to evaluate teachers or principals, to provide information about where a school or district stands with respect to other schools or districts, to focus curriculum, and so on. Even in basic measurement, if the goal is simply the extension of understanding of a construct, certain test properties or qualities are suggested. The purpose and context of an intended use clearly influence the kind of test we construct or choose, the kind of interpretive meaning we look for in a score, the kind of information we collect to evaluate the test, as well as what is considered bias.

To emphasize the importance of considering constructs in relation to the context in which the test is to be used, we will refer to *context-based construct validation.* We conceptualize the context of test use broadly as test content administered to examinees to produce a score that is used for a decision that has an intended outcome. The meaning attributed to the test score (the nature of the construct) derives from all aspects of this broadly conceived context. Without looking to that context, we have no way of choosing among the myriad possible validity questions. The context influences all stages of the testing process, from the definition of the construct, through the construction of the test, to the collection and evaluation of the validation evidence. Although separate questions may be asked about constructs and test use and the two may be distinguished conceptually, we will treat them in tandem as context-based construct validation, so that questions about meaning always include considerations of the context of use.

Investigating Rival Hypotheses

Implicit in the notion of construct validity is the idea that the particular construct under consideration is hypothesized as a possible explanation of scores on a test. There are always other plausible hypotheses about the meaning of the test score besides the intended one. In the addition-test example given earlier the hypothesized construct was arithmetic skill; plausible rival hypotheses included reading skill and motivation. The application of validation theory in common practice often focuses almost exclusively on the particular construct hypothesis and the evidence to support its plausibility. Such a focus overlooks the powerful information that can be gained from considering rival hypotheses and the evidence that supports or refutes them.

Under this conception, validation should be guided by the generation of rival hypotheses or possible explanations for test scores, in addition to the construct hypothesis. Such hypotheses guide the search for evidence and also lead to the need for logical and empirical evidence of both a convergent and a discriminant type. It is the exploration of *rival* hypotheses that provides evidence about bias.

LOGICAL AND EMPIRICAL EVIDENCE

Validity evidence may be classified according to the extent to which it is logical or empirical. Purely logical evidence is based upon rational arguments concerning the fit among the test task(s), scoring procedures, and the domain or construct of interest. As such, it encompasses much of what has been labeled *content-related evidence,* but logical evidence applies to more than just content concerns. Logical analysis can also be used to examine the fit among observed test responses, the construct or domain of interest, and the context of the use. More broadly still, logical analysis generates the hypotheses or constructs that can then be tested empirically. It is also required to relate the results of empirical studies to the construct theory. In contrast, empirical evidence is based upon the relationships among test responses and between test responses and observations on other relevant variables. These categories are not strictly separate, however; they overlap in many ways, and both types of evidence are necessary in test validation. The integration of rational argument with observation is fundamental to the conduct of all scientific investigations, and it is essential that both logical and empirical evidence be a part of the validation process.

CONVERGENT AND DISCRIMINANT EVIDENCE

Validity evidence can also be classified according to the extent to which it is convergent or discriminant. Cronbach (1971) has described the need to collect data in support of the convergence of indicators, as well as data to test counter hypotheses. Messick (1980) describes the two major requirements of construct validity as convergent evidence, which demonstrates that a test is related to other variables that it should relate to on theoretical grounds, and discriminant evidence, which shows that the test is not unduly related to indicators of other distinct constructs. These categories are also not dichotomous because the theory or network surrounding the construct could lead one to predict patterns of stronger or weaker relationships among relevant variables. However, whether as discrete categories of evidence or as a continuum of evidence, both convergent and discriminant evidence are especially important in bias considerations.

Values and Validity

Any investigation is guided by a variety of implicit values, and the validation process is no less subject to investigator values than any other investigation. Values guide the type of questions asked, the type of information collected, and the weight given various types of evidence. In this sense, values are an important implicit part of the conception of validity.

There are a host of other types of values held by those with an interest in testing situations. These are values about different types of outcomes from testing: instructional goals, equal opportunity, selection based on qualifications, diverse representation in instructional groups, labels attached to test scores. Messick (1980, 1981) includes such values and evidence about the consequences of testing in his broadly defined validation concept. Others (e.g., Cronbach, 1976) have noted the importance of such values to considerations of test use. We share these writers' and others' sense of the tremendous importance and legitimacy of considering values in the evaluation of a particular use of a test. However, we have limited the concept of validity to only a portion of all the information relevant to the decision to use a test, namely, evidence about the appropriateness of the scores to accomplish the immediate purpose of test use. One's values about those immediate purposes are relevant and important to the decision of test use, but they are outside our technical concept of validity. Also important but also excluded from the validity domain here are values and evidence about purposes or unintended outcomes further removed from the testing itself. These elements are critical to the general evaluation of a test use but not part of the validity of a particular test for that use. We reserve these value issues to the extra-validity domain addressed in the third section of this chapter. We choose to make this distinction because we feel it will help eliminate confusion inherent in the different ways the term *bias* has been used. Public use of the term most frequently involves social justice concerns. A test use might be unbiased in a technical sense, that is, the same score interpretation might be appropriate for different groups of concern, but be labeled *biased* by some because of values associated with the consequences of testing. Meaningful debate requires that these different issues be discussed clearly and explicitly.

The Technical Meaning of Bias

We approach the issue of what bias is from the technical perspective of validation theory. However, even within this context, the term has been used in a variety of different ways. Questions have been raised about whether bias is inherent in a test, in the way in which a test is used, in the people taking the test, or in some combination of these sources (Bond, 1981; Flaugher, 1978; Scheuneman, 1984; Shepard, 1982). Although many definitions of bias have been closely tied to validity theory (e.g., Reynolds, 1982a; Shepard, 1981, 1982), they have frequently been limited to particular kinds of tests, test uses, test features, or investigation methods. In this section we let the critical features described in validation theory guide the meaning of and the investigation of bias.

An inference from a test score is considered sufficiently valid when a variety of types of evidence support its plausibility and eliminate primary counterinferences. An inference is biased when it is not equally valid for different groups. Bias is present when a test score has meanings or implications for a relevant, definable subgroup of test takers that are different from the meanings or implications for the remainder of the test takers. Thus, *bias is differential validity of a given interpretation of a test score for any definable, relevant subgroup of test takers.*

As an example, suppose a variety of types of evidence indicate that the word problem arithmetic addition test referred to earlier generally measures fourth-grade students' addition skills. Suppose, however, it is used to identify children with arithmetic difficulties in a group of primarily Spanish-speaking fourth graders. With these children, low scores might indicate that they have difficulty reading the questions in English rather than difficulty with addition. If so, we would say the use of the test to identify children with arithmetic difficulties is biased with respect to such Spanish-speaking fourth graders. In contrast, had a test of reading comprehension in English been used to identify children with reading problems for additional instruction, the inability of children for whom Spanish was the dominant language to do well on the test would not necessarily indicate bias for this use. On the other hand, if the same reading test were used as a measure of intelligence or learning potential, it would likely be biased with respect to the Spanish-speaking group for that use. So, the desired interpretation in the context of use determines what is, or is not, evidence of bias.

It should be noted that group definition is central to this notion of bias. Concerns with bias originally centered around major racial–ethnic or sex groups that were the particular focus of civil rights efforts and legislation. Concern with age groups followed. Many other group identifications have been proposed, and many others are possible. Issues of bias could logically extend to any identifiable class of test takers, including high-scoring groups and low-scoring groups. For example, suppose a reading test involved passages quite familiar to some group, resulting in high scores that overestimated the ability to read unfamiliar material. The test would be biased for estimating reading skill for such a group. Whenever we can identify classes of individuals for whom the meaning of test scores is different, bias methodology can be applied. In this chapter, we will refer to *group of concern* to designate any identifiable special group in relation to the broad class of test takers in general.

Implications for Investigating Bias

Because bias is differential validity, validation theory provides the conceptual basis for investigating bias. The major features of validation theory that guide the analysis of bias may be summarized as follows:

1. The appropriate unifying concept of test validation is construct validation.
2. Evidence traditionally associated with the terms *content validity* and *criterion validity* should be considered within the construct validity notion.
3. Construct validation should be context based; it should be guided by information about test content, the nature of the examinees, and the purposes the test is intended to serve.
4. Validity evidence should include logical and empirical evidence, divergent and convergent evidence collected within a hypothesis-generating orientation that requires the examination of plausible rival hypotheses.

Although the definition of bias as differential validity is rather simply stated, the determination of bias, like the determination of validity, is a complex process. For every validation question, there is a related bias question concerning differences in interpretation for different groups of concern. It is the interpretation of a test score that is possibly biased, not the test per se, so several interpretations might need to be considered for each test. Just as the validation process requires the integration of a variety of types of evidence in the judgment of the appropriateness of an inference from a test score, the bias investigation process requires similar integration of evidence for each group of concern. Like validity considerations, considerations of bias involve explorations of plausible rival hypotheses using logical and empirical data and divergent and convergent evidence. This complex validation process does not necessarily yield results that are clear and unambiguous. It often yields equivocal results that must be carefully interpreted, weighed, and judged (Messick, 1981). The same is clearly true for the process of examining bias.

Some guide for working through this complex validation and bias-investigation process is needed. Although many approaches to validation (and bias) are possible, the simplest and perhaps most helpful derives directly from the testing process. The educational-testing process typically begins with specification of a proposed use and definition of one or more constructs relevant to that use. A test is then developed with some particular content and with questions and answers in some particular format. That test must be administered and scored. How test takers respond to that test is reflected in the internal structure of items or parts of the test and in external relations of scores to other variables. We propose here that it is useful to consider as categories of potential evidence about the appropriateness of an interpretation or use (and differential appropriateness for different groups) the following five aspects of the testing process:

1. Constructs in context
2. Content and format
3. Test administration and scoring
4. Internal test structure
5. External test relationships

Within each category, one should be guided by hypotheses about what the test measures and consider logical and empirical evidence and convergent and discriminant evidence. The categories do not represent separate validities; consideration of all five categories is part of the unitary process of construct validation. Similarly, considerations of bias involve all five categories. The categories are seen, not as different types of bias, but as different areas in which evidence about bias can be examined.

Methods of Investigating Bias

In this section we use the five categories as a framework for present methods of studying, identifying, or eliminating bias. With construct validation as the conceptual basis and the testing process as the organizing framework, the existing literature on bias can be recast to (a) provide a conceptual unity the concept of bias has lacked; (b) illustrate that the existing literature fills some sections of the framework, but others have as yet not been considered in relation to bias; and (c) provide methodological suggestions from other areas of the technical literature that have not previously been related to bias.

Constructs in Context

Investigations of validity and bias begin with consideration of the proposed use(s) for a test and the explication of one or more constructs that may fit that use. The proposed use influences the very nature of the construct selected. For example, if the intended use is to provide diagnostic information to be used in planning mathematics instruction, the proposed test might comprise a series of narrowly defined constructs (such as the ability to add mixed numbers), with items designed in such a way as to provide specific information on the cause of errors (such as failure to find a common denominator). If, on the other hand, the purpose is to select students for a scholars' mathematics class, the construct might be much more broadly defined (mathematics skills) and the information sufficient only to rank students or to make a yes–no decision. Of course, the same construct might serve multiple uses, but it does not usually serve them all equally well.

This specification of construct in the planned context of use should be done at a level of detail from which hypothetical implications can be derived. The goal of this stage is to provide the basis for deriving the test characteristics that the use and construct require and the broad hypotheses that will guide both construct validation and investigation of bias.

Consideration of context raises the issue of an intended population of test takers. At this stage, one should begin to specify the relevant groups for which hypotheses about bias need to be tested. One can also begin to evaluate the importance of concerns about bias in light of finite resources for validation activities. The key questions of validity can then be asked for each group of concern.

When proposed uses could result in decisions that have significant consequences for individuals or systems (classes, teachers, schools, etc.), issues of bias become particularly sa-

lient. In many instances, groups are chosen on the basis of a priori concerns of social justice. Might the proposed interpretation be less valid for certain ethnic or sex groups, for handicapped persons, for nonnative English speakers, for others? In other instances, groups of concern might emerge from an investigation of the degree of fit between the test characteristics implied by the construct specification and the intended purpose. Does the construct specification imply some skills or knowledges that are irrelevant to the intended interpretation and use, suggesting that the test is less valid for students not possessing those abilities? For example, a test of analogical reasoning that requires students to know certain facts to answer the questions could be less valid for students who lack the necessary knowledge. Is the construct specification appropriate for all relevant age groups? To what degree do instruction and preparation influence performance on the test? Is a college admissions decision differentially valid for students who have been coached? Is the evaluation of a school's instructional program via an externally imposed test differentially valid for schools using curricula that do not overlap closely with the construct as defined? Other groups of concern might emerge as the construct becomes operationalized into the actual test document and the validation activities proceed.

Content and Format

Although the content and format are influenced by the construct and the context in which they are to be used, there is often some latitude in the specifics of content and format. The validity question here is Are the content and format appropriate for the intended construct and use? The subquestion concerning bias adds "for each group of concern" to that general question.

There are a variety of judgmental and empirical methods for examining the appropriateness of content and format for various groups of concern. Shepard (1982) considers judgmental analyses about the appropriateness of content for the intended construct integral to the construct validity process. Tittle (1982) notes the need for judgments, often from representatives of the groups of concern, throughout the test-development process, including review of test specifications, of the guidelines for test-item writers, and of test items. These judgments typically concern issues of stereotyping, representation of groups in content, and familiarity of groups with content and format. Tittle (1982) describes a variety of checklists for such judgments, and many major test developers include such judgmental reviews in the test-development process. However, reviewers often do not agree in their judgments (Reynolds, 1982b; Shepard, 1982).

Judges might identify bothersome content that might or might not be bothersome to test takers. Reactions of test takers have not generally been directly studied. Even if test takers react negatively, such reactions might or might not affect how they perform on the test. Several authors have tried to address experimentally such effects on test performance. For example, Schmeiser (1982) examined the effect of positive representation of minority groups in test content on the test scores of minority group members. Sherman (1976) studied the effects of different test formats on subgroup test performances. Scheuneman (1985) constructed tests with format and content changes thought to possibly produce bias, to check the effects on scores. The entire area of study of item bias, discussed later, is intended to address these same issues of irrelevant effects on test scores.

An issue that has arisen repeatedly is whether aspects of content and format that are troublesome to some group, prompting criticism of the test and public claims of bias but *not* affecting test scores, should be considered bias (Cole & Nitko, 1981; Shepard, 1982; Tittle, 1975). Cole and Nitko label these concerns *facial bias* and note that

> Facial bias would occur when particular words, [art work,] or item formats appear to disfavor some group whether or not they, in fact, have that effect. Thus, an instrument using the male pronoun "he" throughout or involving only male figures in the items would be facially biased whether or not such uses affected the scores of women. (1981, p. 50)

Tittle (1975, 1982) links such content issues with the test takers' and the minority groups' self-respect and argues that, to be fair, "test content should include balanced representation of the least advantaged groups" (Tittle, 1975, p. 89).

This issue of facial bias is outside the traditional validity arena and, hence, not bias in the sense used in this chapter. Even though not associated with validity, it represents an important and legitimate concern that should be addressed. In this chapter we include concerns such as facial bias under the extra-validity issues and argue that test makers should respond to them because of values held, regardless of evidence of impact on test scores.

Administration and Scoring

The way in which a test is administered can affect its validity for groups of concern (its appropriateness for particular uses and constructs) and must, therefore, be examined with respect to bias. In theory, test-administration procedures should be designed to elicit maximal performance of all groups. This requires suitable physical conditions (a comfortable place to write, good lighting, a comfortable temperature), clear directions on how to take the test, proper motivation to do well from a test administrator, and adequate time to complete the test (if speed itself is not being tested). Standardization of testing conditions leads to a thoroughly specified test-administration process for standardized tests. However, any of the test-administration conditions that affect groups differently can produce bias. Examples of test-administration conditions that have been examined include the race or sex of the test administrator, the extent to which the directions motivate different groups, the effects of speededness on group performance, and the interpretation of directions about how to take the test.

Issues of possible bias produced in scoring tests must be considered whenever scoring procedures are not completely objective. The greater the latitude permitted examinees in *constructing* responses, the more susceptible the scoring to irrelevant influences and the greater the possibility of bias. That the

scoring of constructed response tests can lead to problems in agreement among different raters has been repeatedly demonstrated (see, for example, Diederich, French, & Carlton, 1961; see Coffman, 1971 for a review). Concerns with interrater reliability become bias concerns whenever raters are influenced by group-related characteristics of an examinee (or the examinee's response) that are irrelevant to the construct and purposes of the test.

In some testing situations, raters might either know an examinee personally or be able to infer group membership on the basis of the examinee's name, course or school designation, or cues in the response such as handwriting or characteristic surface errors. Here, the danger exists that the assigned score might be influenced by the raters' conscious or unconscious expectations about an examinee's probable ability, based upon sex, ethnic origin, ability level, social class, and so forth (Jacobs, Zingraf, Wormuth, Harftel, & Hughey, 1981). For example, Rosner (in Diederich, 1974), after randomly and artificially labeling pairs of identical essays as from "regular" or "honors" students, found that scores given by experienced teachers to the "honors" essays were significantly higher than those given to the identical regular essays and concluded that teachers' "knowledge" of the writers influenced the scores. Of course, the best way to combat this potential bias problem is to eliminate, to the extent possible, information that might lead to rater inferences about group membership.

A different kind of bias arises when examinees' responses reflect skills, knowledge, or values irrelevant to the construct(s) of interest. Features such as handwriting, mechanics and usage errors, content knowledge (when a test is intended to measure writing skill) or, conversely, writing skill (when a test is intended to measure content knowledge) are all potentially irrelevant influences on scores that have been investigated through correlational and experimental studies (e.g., Breland & Jones, 1982; Freedman, 1979; Rafoth & Rubin, 1984). In these cases, the groups of concern could be examinees with poor handwriting, inadequate knowledge of an arbitrary topic, limited facility with standard written English, or even flawless command of standard written English.

Carlson, Bridgeman, Camp, and Waanders (1983) have suggested that subjective judgments can be particularly difficult whenever the examinees and the raters do not share a common cultural heritage and, hence, common values about what constitutes competent performance. For instance, investigations by Kaplan (1966) and by Takala, Purves, and Buckmaster (1982) have found consistent differences in such features as logic, organization, and style when comparing composition of writers from different nations. Bernstein (1975) and Heath (1982) described differences in the oral rhetorical patterns of working-class children and middle-class children. M. D. Linn (1975) found similar differences between speakers of black English vernacular and of standard English. Although careful training and monitoring of raters can help minimize threats of bias resulting from the potential influence of irrelevant factors, where culturally bound value differences between raters and examinees are present, it becomes especially important to consider the purpose of the testing in specifying the scoring criteria. For example, if foreign applicants to American colleges are given a writing test to determine whether they should be placed in a remedial writing course, evidence of rhetorical patterns not valued in standard American academic writing are relevant to the test use. If, on the other hand, the same writing test is used for admission decisions, the test use could be considered biased for students from nations where different rhetorical patterns are valued.

Internal Test Structure

The planned uses and interpretations of test scores imply particular interrelations among parts of the test. Those parts could be individual items or subsets of items. In either case, scores on the parts can be computed (zero–one for incorrect–correct for items; various numerical scales, usually from summing item scores for subsets). Interrelations can then be considered by examining the relationship of part scores to the total test score or the relationship among different part scores.

The examination of internal test structure has, of course, long been a part of test construction and test analysis. Item-analysis procedures to assess item difficulty and item discrimination are traditional item-level procedures. Correlations between items within subscales versus items not on subscales are commonly used in subscale construction. Similarly, factor-analytic procedures on subset scores for multiscore tests or batteries of tests have been common. All such procedures were designed to insure a test's validity (either directly through construct considerations or indirectly through reliability considerations).

To examine the possibility of differences in validity for different groups, these internal test-analysis procedures have been extended to multiple groups of concern. Two basic types of indexes are available from internal test analyses: means (or levels of performance) and relations. Constructs typically have implications for expected relations (among items, between items and part or total scores, among part scores) but often do not carry particular expectations for means. For example, a mathematics achievement construct might carry the expectation that a mathematical computation subscore would be more highly related to a mathematical concepts subscore than either subscore to a reading score without expectations concerning the absolute size of the means of these scores. In fact, for measurement purposes, tests are often constructed to have means slightly above one-half the number of items for the group of intended test takers, in order to optimize the test's measurement properties. Thus, such means are not meaningful in an absolute sense.

Similarly, constructs typically do not imply an a priori expectation of group mean similarities or differences. Although we might be interested to know of group differences on some score, the nature of the construct does not typically require that groups have either the same or different means. (Exceptions do occur, for example, when the groups are age or grade-in-school groups on some developmental variable expected to increase with age or grade.) In early considerations of bias, especially outside the technical literature, mean differences between groups were often interpreted as evidence of bias. However, item mean differences or mean differences on subscores or total scores are not necessarily indications of bias within the

validity framework; the groups might, in fact, differ on the construct, in which case such differences would be valid.

In contrast, one would typically expect the same interrelations of items or part scores for different groups of concern. If mathematics achievement is expected to be an applicable construct for children attending U. S. schools, for example, then the interrelation of mathematics items or test parts would be expected to be similar for various groups of concern attending those schools. If the interrelation is not similar, it would imply that the construct is not equally applicable to all groups or that there is differential validity of the construct in different groups. The examinations of internal test structure for different groups are all based on this logic, with differences in internal test structure indicating possible differential validity.

It should be noted that analyses based solely on relations among items or scores without any external criterion (as analyses of internal test structure are) cannot detect influences that pervade all items or scores. Thus, if a pervasive form of bias exists on an entire test, these internal test-analysis procedures cannot identify it. They can only detect differences in the relationships among items or scores across groups, items or scores that are anomalous in some group in relation to other items or scores. In addition, such approaches can only identify the ways items or scores differ across groups in these relations; they cannot directly imply bias. The items so identified must still be interpreted in terms of the intended meaning for the scores before conclusions of bias can be reached. These limitations illustrate the importance of viewing bias as an integrated issue involving various types of evidence rather than relying on one form of evidence alone such as internal test analysis.

In this section, several different types of methods for examining differences in internal test structure for different groups will be reviewed. We begin with the factor-analytic approaches applied to subscores and then turn to the more varied techniques applied to item-level studies.

FACTOR-ANALYTIC APPROACHES

Factor-analytic procedures have been the primary methods used to examine subscore relationships in different groups of concern. Most of the empirical studies of factor structure of ability and achievement tests in different groups have reported similar factor structures across groups (e.g., Gutkin & Reynolds, 1981; Humphreys & Taber, 1973; Jensen, 1977, 1980; Miele, 1979; Reynolds & Paget, 1981). Recent studies using maximum-likelihood factor-analytic techniques and structural equation models carry the study of structure from subscores to the item level, essentially merging part-score analyses with item-level analyses (Mayberry, 1984; Muthen & Lehman, 1985).

A major problem in factor-analytic studies has been the comparison of factor structures found in different groups so as to judge how similar or how different they are. A variety of ad hoc procedures have been proposed and used (e.g., Reynolds, 1982a). The much more complicated structural-equation procedures have stronger theoretical bases for such comparisons (e.g., Jöreskog, 1969, 1971; Muthen & Christoffersson, 1981), but they are not widely used because of the complexity of the theory and the required computer programs.

We know little about the sensitivity of any of the factor-analytic procedures to levels of bias that might be expected in practice. However, for tests of many school subjects present factor-analytical evidence suggests that the global structure imposed by instruction outweighs possible group differences. More differences, but ones less easy to interpret, might appear as procedures move from global-score relationships to finer parts of the tests.

COMPARISON OF ITEM DIFFICULTIES

There have been numerous approaches to the study of item interrelationships in different groups. The early efforts involved considering the relative ordering of item difficulties (proportion correct on an item or p value) in different groups. The goal was to identify item-by-group interactions, that is, items that behaved differently in relation to other items on the test in some group. Several related procedures have been used to detect such item-by-group interactions, including analysis of variance and graphic methods.

This approach reached its fullest development in the work of Angoff (Angoff, 1972; Angoff & Ford, 1973; Angoff & Sharon, 1974). Item difficulty in terms of p values was normalized to z scores corresponding to the $(1-p)$th percentile, to remove the curvilinearity in the relationship between two sets of item values. These z scores were then transformed to deltas, with a mean of 13 and a standard deviation of 4 to eliminate negative values. The paired deltas were plotted for two groups, yielding a scatter plot around a diagonal line describing the typical difference in items for the two groups, as shown in Figure 5.1. Computations for the line (a principal axis line) and the perpendicular item deviations from it are given in Angoff and Ford (1973). Items that deviate noticeably from the line are those that are relatively more difficult for one group than other items in the set.

Although appealing in its conceptual simplicity and ease of implementation, the Angoff method can give an inappropriate

picture of bias because it fails to take into account item-discrimination properties that can produce the appearance of bias (Angoff, 1982; Hunter, 1975; Lord, 1977; Shepard, 1981). Figure 5.2 illustrates the problem. The left-hand portion of the figure shows plots of proportion correct for two items for two groups differing markedly in achievement. If differences in p values on the test were typically of the order of magnitude illustrated by item 2, the Angoff procedure would identify the item-1 difference as unusual and possibly biased.

However, if we superimpose hypothetical item-characteristic curves relating the proportion correct to achievement levels, as shown on the right-hand portion of the figure, we find that item 1 is no more or less biased than item 2, only more discriminating, as shown by the steeper slope of the curve, that is, the item better distinguishes high-achieving test takers from lower achieving ones, regardless of group membership.

As Camilli and Shepard (1987) demonstrate, the problem with these item-by-group interaction procedures based on item difficulty is greater than just the identification of false positives as illustrated. The procedures can also miss the presence of real bias. These problems are especially disturbing because many existing empirical item-bias studies have relied on these procedures.

COMPARISON OF ITEM-CHARACTERISTIC CURVES

Once we consider curves relating proportion correct to achievement level throughout the achievement-level values (not just for group means), the appeal of such characterizations is obvious. Rather than asking whether p values are similarly ordered across groups, regardless of group achievement differences or whether item discriminations are comparable, the issue becomes one of whether the curve relating achievement to proportion correct is the same in all groups of concern. We characterize the major determiner of item performance as a hypothetical achievement or ability parameter. The issue then is whether group membership relates to performance beyond the influence of this achievement or ability parameter. If group membership is such an influence, then the item-characteristic curves would differ by group. If not, one curve would relate item performance to achievement, regardless of group.

Item-characteristic curves like those illustrated in Figure 5.2 are defined by three parameters corresponding to the item's difficulty, b (roughly, the level of ability required to achieve a proportion correct of 0.5); discrimination, a (the slope at the point of inflection of the curve; and the probability of getting the item correct with zero knowledge, c (the so-called guessing parameter). The shape of the item-characteristic curve may be assumed to be a normal ogive or, more typically, a logistic ogive. Methods of estimating item-characteristic curves are developed in item response theory (the achievement dimension in Figure 5.2 represents the latent trait) and have been described and developed by Lord (1968, Lord & Novick, 1968, 1977, 1980) and others. The computations require complex computer programs with LOGIST (Wood, Wingersky, & Lord, 1976) among the most widely used. These ICC procedures also require very large sample sizes to reach stable parameter estimates (as many as 1000 or more per group) and

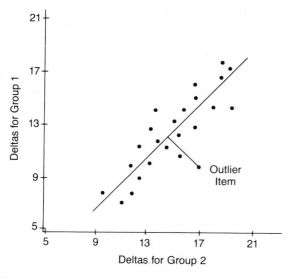

FIGURE 5.1 Angoff's delta-plot method showing outlier item relatively more difficult for Group 2.

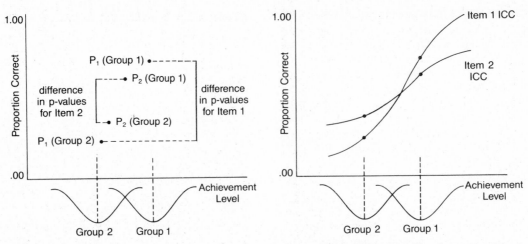

FIGURE 5.2 Possible interpretation of differences between item difficulties for two groups due to item discrimination (slope of ICC curves) adapted from Shepard, 1981.

consequently pose practical problems of number as well as complexity. See Hambleton, this volume, for a discussion of item response theory procedures, uses, and problems.

Although clearly the preferable approach to item analysis of groups on logical and empirical grounds (see Ironson & Subkoviak, 1979; Rudner, Getson, & Knight, 1980; Shepard, Camilli, & Averill, 1981; Shepard, Camilli, & Williams, 1984, 1985; Subkoviak, Mack, Ironson, & Craig, 1984) when adequate sample sizes are available, the lack of required numbers in many practical instances, plus the complexity of the computational procedures, leaves room for simpler approximate procedures.

APPROXIMATIONS TO ICC COMPARISONS

The one-parameter latent-trait method (the Rasch model) provides greater simplicity, with some of the properties of the three-parameter model but "is not recommended for bias detection because it will confound other sources of model misfit (particularly differences in item discrimination) with item 'bias'" (Shepard et al., 1984, p. 95).

Another approximation procedure was proposed by Scheuneman (1979), with extensions and corrections by Baker (1981), Ironson (1982), and others. In this method the ability

or achievement dimension is approximated by the total test score divided into intervals. For each item within each interval (usually five), the frequency of correct and incorrect responses for each group is tabulated. For example, if two groups are compared for three test-score intervals, the three 2×2 tables shown in Figure 5.3 would be constructed. The conventional 2×2 Chi-square statistics would be computed for each table and summed across the three total score regions. This sum is distributed approximately as X^2 with three degrees of freedom (the number of ability-score intervals). Within any one score level, one is testing the independence of correctness of response and group, paralleling the notion of the same ICC curve for both groups. However, the score level groupings, when the groups differ overall in mean test score, lead to regression effects that can appear as bias. In spite of this difficulty, this approximation procedure has fared reasonably well among approximate methods in comparisons of item-bias procedures (Shepard et al., 1984, 1985).

Mellenbergh (1982) proposed a log-linear or logit model variant of the Chi-square procedure, and Van der Flier, Mellenbergh, Ader, and Wijn (1984) applied an iterative extension of this method with reestimation after eliminating potentially biased items. In a study with experimentally induced bias, this iterative logit procedure was found to identify biased items well

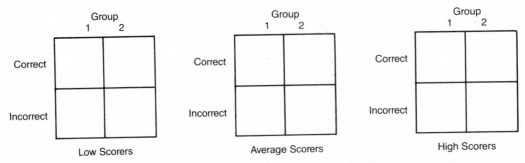

FIGURE 5.3 Frequency tables of item response-by-group for three levels of test scores (low, average, high).

(Kok, Mellenbergh, & Van der Flier, 1985). The suggestion of using iterative procedure to "purify" the criterion is an important one that could have applications for a number of item-bias approaches.

Yet another variant of the log-linear approaches is the use of the Mantel and Haenszel (1959) statistic. This statistic has had wide use in medical research studies examining dichotomous outcomes in differentiated groups with a blocking variable and is being applied as an indicator of differential item performance in one large testing organization (Holland & Thayer, 1986). It has desirable statistical properties, and there is considerable practical experience with its operation in other settings. Some preliminary and reasonably promising explorations have begun on educational admissions testing data (McPeek & Wild, 1986), and a variant for descriptive, rather than hypothesis-testing, purposes has been explored (Dorans & Kulick, 1986).

The major distinguishing feature of the Mantel–Haenszel procedure is that, instead of testing against a general alternative hypothesis of any difference in correct response rates between groups, this statistic tests against a particular alternative of a common odds-ratio of correct response across all blocking (matching) categories. Practical implications of the different alternative hypotheses in test item studies are not yet known. Even so, the procedure appears to be among the most promising of the Chi-square variants.

R. L. Linn and Harnisch (1981) proposed an IRT approximation that estimates three-parameter IRT curves for the groups combined and then divides the IRT achievement or ability scale into intervals. For each interval, the difference between expected probability of correct response (based on the estimated ICC) and observed proportion correct is computed for the special group of concern. After standardization of the difference within each interval, the standardized differences are summed across intervals to produce an overall index of bias for each item. Shepard et al. (1985) referred to this approximation as a pseudo-IRT method and found it had desirable properties for cases in which the sample size was too small in one group for the full IRT analysis.

INTERPRETATION PROBLEMS OF ITEM-BIAS INDEXES

A critical difficulty in interpreting item-bias studies is that the conclusion of bias does not directly follow the statistical results. One must still judge whether the basis of the differences on items is irrelevant to the construct and, hence, bias or whether it is relevant to the construct and, therefore, not an issue of bias (Shepard, 1982). Consider a geometry item on a mathematics survey test on which female students score considerably lower than male students, although the total test score difference is fairly small. Suppose the use of that test score is to identify high-achieving mathematics students for placement in an honors mathematics class, and students who are ready for the advanced material are being sought. If that honors class requires prior knowledge of geometry, the results on the geometry item might be relevant to whether the student is adequately prepared for the honors class, regardless of the group difference on it. If, however, a student who had not

learned geometry would be minimally affected in the particular honors class, the geometry item could be said to introduce an irrelevant effect and could be labeled as biased.

There is yet another set of possibly interrelated problems of item-bias studies. First, such studies involve large numbers of comparisons or, when distribution theory of bias indexes is available, of tests of hypothesis (at least one for each item). Such multiple comparisons invite problems of inflated Type 1 error rates and, when the distribution theory is approximate at best, control of that error rate becomes an additional problem. Further, the IRT procedures (though optimal on logical and theoretical grounds) are complex to implement, involving judgmental choices that can affect results. One particularly difficult step is that of placing parameters estimated separately for two groups on the same scale. Errors in these procedures can further confound bias studies. Further, as noted, other bias procedures (e.g., Angoff's Delta Plot and the Rasch approach) are known to be subject to influences other than bias.

When these difficulties are considered along with the fact that, in most item-bias studies, the authors were not able to interpret or explain the results for items identified by the statistical procedures, one is left to wonder if there are not substantial artifactual interferences in typical bias studies. Several writers have been concerned about this problem. Lord (1980) proposed that independent sets of samples be used in bias studies to provide a replication or reliability check and that baseline studies of same-group comparisons be done to check the procedures in conditions of no bias. Ironson and Subkoviak (1979) used white–white comparison groups as a baseline to assess several bias indexes.

Angoff (1982) suggested that the most appropriate baseline studies for interpreting bias indexes would be white–white groups differing in mean scores comparable to mean differences between groups of concern, a strategy similar to that used by Jensen (1974). Shepard et al. (1984) implemented both types of baseline comparisons (randomly equivalent and pseudo-ethnic) in a comprehensive study of statistical artifacts in IRT bias indexes using large samples. Under these conditions, considerable stability of the IRT procedures was found. These results support the small level of artifactual interference in IRT procedures with large samples. In a later study (Shepard et al., 1985), these authors studied IRT approximation procedures for more moderate samples (majority group 1,000, minority group 300) and found the pseudo-IRT procedure of R. L. Linn, Levine, Hastings, and Wardrop (1981) and the Chi-square procedure to be reasonably good procedures for samples of moderate size. These studies do not answer the issue, however, for other procedures or the more frequently occurring small sample cases where artifacts remain a problem for interpretation. It would certainly seem desirable for any application of item-bias methods in moderate to small samples to include replication or baseline procedures if the analyses are to lead to decisions such as eliminating items from a future test.

It has been proposed that, not only should performance on correct responses be compared for different groups, but also performance on incorrect responses or distractors (e.g., Donlon, 1984; Eells, Davis, Havighurst, Herrick, & Tyler, 1956; Jensen, 1980; Thissen, 1979; Veale and Foreman, 1976). Essentially any of the methods applied to studying bias in correct answers that have been discussed here can be applied to wrong answers. In addition, all the problems and difficulties also apply, only they are multiplied by the number of distractors.

A final difficulty in interpreting item-bias studies concerns the direction of the possible bias. With Angoff's method, an item found to be more difficult for a group than other items in the set is said to be biased against that group. When, however, two item-characteristic curves are to be compared, such a straightforward interpretation of bias cannot be made. Suppose the item-characteristic curves shown in Figure 5.2 apply to two groups, rather than to two items. Then test takers in Group 1 with high achievement levels are favored over their counterparts in Group 2, but those in Group 1 with low achievement levels are disadvantaged relative to Group 2 members of similar ability. Shepard et al. (1985) considered seven different indexes for ICC comparisons, ranging from the absolute value of the area between the two curves (retain no information on direction of bias) to comparisons of differences in the a and b parameters to indexes of signed area, so that, in the example, the two areas favoring different groups would largely cancel each other out. It might be important to a judgment of the practical effect of any of these indexes to weight the areas of difference by the number of individuals affected. The issue of signed or unsigned differences also applies to the Chi-square and pseudo-IRT approaches. Shepard et al. (1984, 1985) found the more interpretable signed indexes to also produce closer agreement with crossvalidated IRT results and, in particular, favored a sum of squares index for ICC comparisons. Often, however, there is no known distribution for the signed indexes, so that some baseline procedure to identify discrepant values is crucial.

External Test Relationships

The interpretation given a test score implies numerous forms of relationship between the score and other variables external to the test. The concern of bias is that those relationships might differ for various groups, implying differences in meaning or differential validity for different groups.

STRUCTURE OF EXTERNAL RELATIONSHIPS

The relationships of test scores to external variables has traditionally been a central concern of construct validity, and several methods of study have been proposed. Convergent and discriminant validity address the fact that test scores should strongly relate to some conceptually similar external variables and relate less strongly to other conceptually different variables. The multitrait–multimethod matrices proposed by Campbell and Fiske (1959) are an instance of this distinction, with the multitrait dimension representing various external measures of supposedly different traits and the multimethod dimension representing different measurement approaches to the same trait. The multiple methods of measuring the same trait should converge (show strong relationships), whereas the multiple traits should diverge (show weak relationships).

These conceptions are also relevant to experimental approaches and other comparisons. It is often useful to consider test-score differences between groups known to be different on some external variable. For example, different age or grade groups might be expected to differ on tests thought to measure a developing or instructed characteristic. If one of two randomly assigned groups is given instruction in the content of a test designed to measure short-term school achievement, that group would be expected to perform better on the test after instruction than the control group. If, however, a test is supposed to measure a very stable construct (one thought to be not readily altered by short-term instruction) such as some conceptions of ability or aptitude, differences between instructed and noninstructed groups should not occur or should be small. Tests of such aptitude constructs should not be coachable.

Whether the multitrait–multimethod matrices are comparable across groups can be approached in a similar manner to the factor-analytic approaches to internal structure. The relationship implied by the construct may be examined variable by variable, or the structure of the entire matrix may be examined as a whole.

PREDICTION STUDIES

In some instances a particular external variable takes on special significance within the class of relevant external variables. This occurs when an external variable is thought to be another measure of the intended construct. The issue then is whether the test score can be used as an adequate substitute for, or predictor of, this criterion variable in practical cases where the criterion is not available. The study of predictor–criterion relationships across groups has been the focus of a large body of literature on tests used for selection. From this perspective, the test score is used as a predictor of subsequent success in college, for example. The goal of selecting persons for admission to college is characterized as the achievement of a group of students likely to do well in college. The standard predictive validity issue for such a use is how well the test score serves as a prediction of the desired eventual successful performance (the criterion). In college admissions, the criterion has most often been freshman college grades, although longer term criteria have sometimes been studied. A critical part of the study of predictive validity concerns both the adequacy of the predictor and the adequacy of the criterion.

The bias in selection literature addresses the possibility of differences in the predictor–criterion relationship for different groups. A number of different aspects of that relationship have been considered. R. L. Linn (1982) divided the topic into studies of differences in the predictor–criterion correlation (the traditional concern of predictive validity) and differences in the prediction systems (particularly the linear regression equations from which predictions are derived). Most studies of either type have dealt with two major comparisons: male–female and black–white. A smaller number of studies compare Chicano and Anglo samples.

In a survey of results based on comparing predictor–criterion correlations across groups, R. L. Linn (1982) reported somewhat different results for different settings. In both undergraduate education and law schools, the test–criterion correlations were higher for women than for men. A trend for higher correlations for whites than for blacks was indicated at the undergraduate level but not in the law schools. In a number of studies of employment settings, no consistent black–white difference in correlations was found, but in air force training schools there was a consistent tendency for final training criteria to be better predicted for whites than blacks.

Even if predictor–criterion correlations are identical, the prediction systems can differ in standard errors of estimate, in regression line slope, and in regression line intercepts. In a review of studies of group differences in prediction systems, R. L. Linn (1982) found consistent underprediction of freshmen grades for women with respect to men, for whites with respect to blacks (but not Chicanos), and for older students with respect to younger ones. This underprediction for women largely disappeared at the law school level, but overprediction for black and Chicano students was found at this level. A similar tendency was found in the employment literature (for blacks and Chicanos) and in the air force training setting (where only black–white comparisons were made) for overprediction of minority performance using test scores. Thus, there have been consistent though puzzling suggestions that, rather than underestimating performance, as many intuitively expected, test scores might actually overpredict such performance for men, blacks, and sometimes Chicanos. In the narrow prediction sense, test scores do not appear to be a hindrance to minority selection, as many supposed, a result that led Cleary, Humphreys, Kendrick, and Wesman (1975) to conclude that differential validity evidence negative to minority groups had not been found.

This counterintuitive finding appropriately raised the need for careful consideration, and more careful analyses of these prediction results raised several warning flags. R. L. Linn and Werts (1971) warned of the misleading effects of unreliability and missing predictors. R. L. Linn (1983) illustrated the problems in comparing group regressions after selection had been operating. Novick (1982) reviewed some of the complexities and paradoxes in comparing subpopulations. Birenbaum (1979, 1981) used path-analytical arguments to demonstrate the effects of the fallibility of both the predictor and the criterion on conclusions with respect to observed regression system differences.

R. L. Linn used Birenbaum's argument to demonstrate that in certain cases "the condition of no bias . . . implies that the within-group regressions should be unequal" (1984, p. 40). With reasonable assumptions, again in the condition of no bias, Linn further showed "that the intercept of the regression for the higher scoring group will be above the one for the lower scoring group" (p. 40), the common empirical finding noted above. Thus, as Linn concludes,

What the above formulation shows is that the common overprediction result is not necessarily an indication of bias in favor of the minority group. Rather it may simply be a consequence of imperfect measurement (p. 40).

Thus, it appears that considerable caution should be used in interpreting prediction system findings as representing true forms of relationships in unselected groups with perfectly reliable measures. The boundary condition methods suggested by R. L. Linn (1984) give a more reasonable basis for interpretations but suggest that findings of differences of the size reported to date often do not suggest actual underlying group differences in intercept.

In addition to the empirical results about correlations and prediction systems, the technical literature has included extensive discussion of so-called models of selection fairness (e.g., Cole, 1973; Darlington, 1971; Petersen & Novick, 1976; Thorndike, 1971). These models go beyond examination of possible differences in the prediction systems to the specification of the characteristics of the system or of the selection outcomes that were required to be equal between groups to accomplish selection fairness. Cole (1981) noted that these models arose in the context, not of what inferences can correctly be made (the validity question), but of what outcomes should be accomplished (the social policy issue). For these reasons we consider these selection models part of the extra-validity concerns that test users should consider in the decision to use a test, concerns addressed in the following section.

The Extra-Validity Domain

Although validity has been a central focus of technical measurement efforts, it has long been recognized that the decision to use a particular test for a particular purpose involves a variety of considerations in addition to validity considerations. For example, introductory textbooks on measurement often include checklists of the various items that are important to consider in selecting a test, such as the appropriateness of the test materials for the groups to be tested, the time required, and the cost of testing, along with technical validity evidence (Anastasi, 1976).

We argue, too, that a broader evaluation of test use is needed than that provided by technical validity evidence alone. Such an evaluation should critically examine the purposes for which a test is used, the extent to which those purposes are accomplished by the actions taken, the various side effects or unintended consequences, and possible alternatives to the test that might serve the same purpose.

Many of the prominent public concerns with bias raise important issues that belong largely in this extra-validity category. As Messick (this volume) makes clear, such concerns with consequences of use require value judgments about the importance of the consequences and the collection of relevant evidence. It is with such considerations that we begin to bridge the gap between the technical validity-related issues of bias and the important social policy concerns for fairness for different groups.

We propose here a framework for both validity and extra-validity concerns relevant to the decision to use a particular test in a particular situation for a particular purpose. We address issues of evidence, values, and consequences in ways similar to, but not isomorphic with, those discussed by Messick (1975, 1980, 1987).

Outcomes: Purposes and Side Effects

The outcomes of testing are, of course, critically important to the decision to do the testing. Outcomes may be not only intended (in which case we think of them as purposes) but may also be unintended (in which case, they are side effects of testing). Outcomes may also be considered at several levels ranging from outcomes very close to the testing and the construct intended to be measured to those far removed from the test and the construct with implications only indirectly connected to the particular test, if at all.

LEVEL ONE PURPOSES

A Level One intended outcome may be described as the identification of persons with certain characteristics or an immediate action taken on the basis of those characteristics. If the outcome is intended, we say the purpose of the testing is to identify persons with certain characteristics. These "certain characteristics" represent the construct being measured, and Level One purposes (or Level One intended outcomes) are viewed as synonymous with constructs in context described earlier. For example, if one were using a test to assign students for possible remedial instruction in math, a Level One purpose would be to identify who was weak in mathematics for assignment to a remedial section. In using a test as the basis for a college admissions decision, a Level One purpose is to identify and admit students who will be successful in college. A Level One purpose essentially describes a meaning intended to be given to the test scores and, as such, is not differentiated from the construct in context. Thus, when we speak of validating a construct we are addressing a Level One intended outcome.

LEVEL TWO PURPOSES

One can probe purposes (or outcomes) beyond Level One by asking further about what the user hopes to accomplish with respect to persons with the identified characteristics. In many educational settings, test use involves an intervention (such as instruction) on the basis of the identified characteristics. An arithmetic achievement test might be used to identify students for assignment to a remedial section. In these cases, a Level Two purpose can be identified: to accomplish some goals with the intervention. At Level Two, we will be concerned about the success of the intervention (an extra-validity concern) well beyond consideration of the appropriateness of the meaning given the test score (a validity concern).

Level Two purposes do not necessarily involve interventions. They include any purpose that moves beyond the type of desired outcome associated directly with the test-score meaning. Consider, for example, the college admissions use noted. Level One purposes, not differentiated from context-based constructs, might be to admit students who are academically well prepared for college or who have a good chance of academic success in college. To move to Level Two, we might ask Why does the user prefer students to have good preparation, or a good chance of success, or both? A variety of answers (purposes) might follow: (a) because professors can teach better if the students are all similarly prepared, (b) because it will help the financial health of the college if students are able to stay enrolled, (c) because it is bad for students to experience failure in college, or (d) because it gives the college prestige to have good students. Each of these Level Two purposes involves aspects about which evidence could be obtained, but such evidence would have no bearing on the meaning given the test score. For example, evidence about whether the professors teach homogeneous groups better could be obtained to check

whether the Level Two purpose was being accomplished. If that were the purpose for selective admissions, we would want to know if the purpose was being accomplished as an extra-validity concern.

LEVEL THREE PURPOSES

Beyond Level Two purposes and outcomes are a variety of more far-reaching, ultimate purposes and outcomes, referred to here as Level Three purposes. For example, when a Level Two purpose is increasing student learning by intervention, a Level Three purpose would address why we want to increase student learning—perhaps to better prepare students for jobs or future citizenship. When our Level Two goal for selective admissions is to have better teaching by professors, a Level Three goal might be that a high level of knowledge be achieved at graduation by all students or that the reputation of the institution be enhanced as a place where excellent teaching occurs. Whether the intermediate purposes have, in fact, the desired connection to ultimate purposes is almost never addressed directly with formal evidence, whether in relation to test use, education, business decisions, or personal actions. However, it is useful to recognize such ultimate goals that are implicit to much of education and educational test use and for which we could, at least in theory, collect evidence to examine.

SIDE EFFECTS AT DIFFERENT LEVELS

The purpose, or intended outcome, of a test's use is not necessarily the only consequence, or outcome, of that use. There can also be various side effects. Consider, for example, identifying students for a special educational intervention. The purpose is to help the students learn; however, the identification process could have negative side effects such as (a) making the child feel unusual, not normal, or dumb; (b) having other children call the child names; (c) leading some teachers to view the child as able to learn little and therefore worthy of little effort; or (d) producing separate classes largely segregated in terms of sex, racial and ethnic group, or socioeconomic status. There can also be positive side effects such as alerting parents to problems and increasing parental involvement in the student's education. Similarly, in the college admissions example, side effects might include having entering classes that are predominantly from certain schools, regions, or racial or ethnic backgrounds. Any of the Level Two purposes noted, if unintended, could be side effects. The labels given tests can be particularly important in the types of side effects that occur. A test labeled an "achievement" test might produce very different side effects from the same test labeled an "intelligence" test. Side effects at any level are an appropriate consideration in the decision to use a test.

Evidence and Values

Validity has to do with evidence about the appropriateness of inferences from test scores. Although values enter the evidence-gathering process in various ways, the purpose of the validation is the evidence gained. However, values, in their own right, are an important part of the decision to test in a particular situation. Although, in considering validity, we concentrated on evidence, in the broader context of information relevant to the decision to test, values about outcomes and evidence about outcomes are both critical.

Messick (1975) proposes two questions that should be asked about any test use: "First, is the test any good as a measure of the characteristic it is interpreted to assess? . . . Should the test be used for the proposed purpose?" (p. 962). Messick's broad second question is for us an extra-validity question that implies an important third question: Should the purpose be served? Or, put another way, Is the purpose worthy? The importance or worthwhileness of the purpose is basically a matter of value judgments about which not all persons will necessarily agree.

To further complicate the picture, Level Two and Level Three purposes, and the implicit value judgments about them, are often unarticulated. People have such purposes and value them, but they might never state them explicitly in a debate about test use. When interested parties in a testing situation have different purposes and these remain unarticulated, debates might never reveal the fundamental reasons for differences of opinion. It is the failure to articulate underlying purposes and values that has led to many inconclusive debates about bias in testing.

Values and evidence enter the consideration of side effects and purposes. One might appropriately choose *not* to use a test for an extremely worthy purpose if the side effects are strongly negative. Similarly, a negative side effect that is unlikely to occur (an evidential issue) would carry less weight than a similarly negative one likely to occur.

Alternatives to a Particular Test

There are various alternatives to a particular test that can be considered in a decision about test use. There are the options of other tests, of nontest alternatives, and of doing nothing. Some options might produce scores closer to the intended meaning (with greater validity) but produce more negative side effects. Others might be less valid but produce less negative side effects. Validity evidence about how well each alternative accomplishes the Level One purpose is not sufficient alone to choose among options (Cole, 1976). Reasonable judgments in choosing among options require, in addition to validity evidence, consideration of evidence and values about interpretations, purposes, and side effects for each option.

Definition of the Extra-Validity Domain

With outcomes of various levels including purposes and side effects, evidence and values, and alternative procedures, we can begin to partition the types of information about test use associated with technical validation and the other important types that are extra-validity concerns. Validity of a particular test for a particular use most centrally involves evidence about Level One purposes (about constructs in context). Level One side effects can occur in the form of other inferences made from the test scores. Evidence about the appropriateness of such alternative interpretations could also be obtained. Such evidence would be validation evidence with respect to the alternative interpretation but would be extra-validity evidence

for the particular test for the particular use, except when such interpretations are rival hypotheses. Then evidence about them actually intrudes into the validity domain to the extent that it is evidence relevant to the use of the particular test for a particular purpose. Alternatives to the test in question should also be validated if being considered for possible use. This is clearly relevant information to the decision to choose one test over an alternative. Yet this evidence, too, is extra-validity evidence for the test in question for the purpose being considered (although validity evidence for the alternative procedure).

Although validity concerns very valuable and important information, it is not adequate to address Messick's second question (Should the test be used?). Evidence of lack of validity can support a test's *not* being used, but additional information is required to judge that a test should be used. The additional extra-validity information needed includes evidence about Level Two and Level Three outcomes (both purposes and side effects), along with articulation of the values associated with outcomes at all levels.

Figure 5.4 illustrates the total domain of information relevant to the decision to use Test A for a Level One purpose. It shows the relatively small part of the domain that actually involves validity evidence. The nonshaded areas represent extra-validity information.

This broad and complex domain is important to any consideration of test use, but it is especially critical to discussions and debates about bias in test use. Technical considerations of bias have been limited almost exclusively to the validity part in the domain and even within that part focused primarily on Level One purposes, not side effects or alternatives. Yet public discussions make clear the dominance of concern with values and side effects, especially as they relate to special groups, as well as the desire to seek alternatives with less negatively valued side effects for those groups. The technical and the public discussions address different parts of the domain of information, with the public debate centering on Level Two and Level Three outcomes, values, and evidence. We argue that both the validity and extra-validity discussions are relevant to decisions about test use and see the described domain as a way to integrate the apparently different issues and debates.

Domain Applications

Next we examine three specific cases in which the existing technical professional literature has overflowed the validity portion of the domain into the extra-validity areas. Although these instances are traditionally included within the technical bias and validity literature, there has not been agreement about how they relate to bias. Examining these cases in relation to the proposed domain assists, we believe, in understanding how they are different from validity-based bias concerns yet important to the consideration of test use. The first case considered is the issue identified earlier in this chapter as facial bias of items.

FACIAL BIAS OF ITEMS

In considering the content of test items with respect to possible bias, two types of content issues have arisen (Cole & Nitko, 1981). First is the issue of whether the content intro-

		Test A		Alternatives to Test A	
		Evidence	*Values*	*Evidence*	*Values*
Intended Outcomes	Level One Purpose	Validity			
	Level Two Purposes				
	Level Three Purposes				
Unintended Outcomes	Level One Side Effects				
	Level Two Side Effects				
	Level Three Side Effects				

FIGURE 5.4 The domain of information relevant to the use of Test A for a Level One purpose with the shaded area indicating the portion of the domain concerned with the validity of Test A for that Level One purpose.

duces difficulties irrelevant to the meaning that differentially affect performance on the test. Such content (or format) would be said to be biased in the standard validity-based meaning. The test scores would, as a result of that content, have different meanings for different groups. Both empirical and judgmental methods have been proposed to try to identify such possibly bias-producing content or format.

It has been a common occurrence, however, for judges of item content to raise concerns about aspects of content for which no effect on scores can be found. Such concerns typically involve inadequate or stereotypical representation of some group or certain types of language usage (such as the generic *he* or language with emotional overtones for some group). These judges are concerned that such occurrences perpetuate stereotypes and might affect self-image or self-respect of students. These are possible side effects. In this case they are side effects that are very negatively valued by some people. One could also reasonably examine whether they occur. In doing so, one would collect evidence about stereotypes held by students and about students' self-image or self-respect. If these issues also affect test scores, then there are also validity concerns. However, even if they do not affect test scores and the side effect is the only result (e.g., lowering of self-respect), these concerns are appropriate. Test makers might reasonably conclude that some potential side effects are sufficiently negative to avoid such test content even in the absence of evidence about whether the side effects actually occur and in the absence of actual effects on test performance.

SELECTION BIAS MODELS

As noted earlier, a number of models of fairness in selection have been proposed. The basic starting point was the model of no regression differences (Cleary, 1968), which follows the validity approach closely. However, there soon followed Thorn-

dike's (1971) proposal that the ratio of proportion selected to proportion successful should be the same in all groups. Darlington (1971) examined several potential definitions of regression system equivalence that might be considered fair by some. Cole (1973) argued that many persons' values involved the opportunity for selection of those applicants who could succeed. From this perspective, a model of fairness was proposed that required the conditional probability of selection given success to be the same in all groups of concern.

Petersen and Novick (1976), following Gross and Su (1975), formalized a decision-theoretic approach to selection requiring the explicit determination of utilities associated with outcomes of success or failure for various groups. In each of the previous models, the values were implicit in the characteristic chosen to be equated across groups. The decision-theoretic model made the values explicit as utilities. Cronbach (1976) considered a variety of values implicit to various selection models (e.g., values for group outcomes, values for different definitions of merit) and Sawyer, Cole, and Cole (1976) argued for a broader decision model in which broader values for selection could be accommodated.

In all these instances, it is clear that models of selection fairness moved beyond the validity arena to direct consideration of values as well. However, they might be distinguished even further in terms of the proposed domain. The individual success–failure outcomes considered in the Petersen–Novick decision model are outcomes of the Level One purpose variety, outcomes directly related to the meaning given the test score. Thus, because Level One purposes are considered part of the meaning issue, this model might be classified in part in the traditional validity domain. In contrast, the other models involve outcomes of groups, not individuals, and seem to move beyond the Level One purpose associated with the meaning to a Level Two purpose. Thus, we would classify Thorndike's, Darlington's, Cole's models, plus the variants considered by

Cronbach, as part of the extra-validity domain. Even when the issues raised by these models are not part of the purpose of a use, they enter as side effects, either positive or negative, depending on values. With the domain as a guide we can perhaps better understand the issues these models have raised and the types of information (values and evidence) they require in a decision to use a test for selection with different groups.

EFFECTIVENESS OF INTERVENTIONS

We have noted that one Level Two purpose of testing might be to provide a particular educational intervention (often some form of remediation) for students identified by tests as weak in some area of study. There has been an increasing awareness in recent years of the need to examine the effectiveness of the intervention, as well as the validity of the test, in justifying the total testing–intervention system. A different group of concern might be differentially affected by an intervention. We, too, reaffirm the great importance of this type of information in justifying test use for this purpose. In our conception such information is primarily extra-validity information in the decision to use a test and provide remediation. We call it extra-validity information because the failure of the remediation to increase learning might occur as a result of ineffective remediation, not failure of the test to identify students with difficulties in the subject. However, success of the remediation could be indirect validity evidence that the test was properly identifying students. In previous discussions of such information, its importance was clearly recognized, but its relation to validity was unclear. Elaboration of the extra-validity domain provides better understanding, we believe, of the important role of this type of information.

Concluding Remarks

If one is convinced, as we are, that more explicit formal attention needs to be given to the full range of information relevant to a testing decision, then the issue becomes one of assigning responsibility for seeing that this full range is examined. Who is responsible for such a difficult task? Clearly, responses to technical questions about whether a test *can* be used for a particular purpose, whether there is sufficient evidence to support the validity of a desired interpretation, fall within the purview of test developers, test users, and measurement scholars. Responses to questions of whether a test *should* be used for a particular purpose and whether that purpose should be served, our extra-validity questions, are the right and responsibility of all persons affected by test use. This includes test takers and others to whom the consequences of testing are of concern, as well as the measurement profession. Within the extra-validity arena, measurement specialists can aid the public debate by clarifying the validity and extra-validity issues; pointing out potential or actual consequences (outcomes and side effects); collecting evidence about those consequences, where possible; and suggesting values that might be implied in accepting or rejecting a test use. In essence, it is the responsibility of the measurement profession to raise and clarify issues for others who have a concern in the testing debate. We agree with Cronbach's statement that, "Our task is not to judge for non-

professionals but to clarify, so that in their judgements they can use their power perceptively" (Cronbach, 1980, p. 100).

The complexity and extent of validity and extra-validity information needed to evaluate the decision to use a particular test place extreme demands on the decision process. How can a formal analysis of all purposes, all possible side effects, and all alternative options possibly be accomplished? The answer is, of course, that they cannot. All possible purposes and side effects cannot be discovered; all possible options cannot be thoroughly evaluated. However, many aspects of this domain are already considered in practice informally and without the guide of such a domain. Some test makers have explicitly warned against potential misuses or misinterpretations (side effects). Test users often defend their purposes in terms of their importance (values) and their accomplishment (evidence). Sometimes alternative options are formally considered and evaluated, at least in terms of validity. We believe, in the context of bias, it is especially important that consideration of these extra-validity questions continue and expand. It seems useful to have a framework guiding such considerations even when we omit numerous parts. At a minimum we are aware of the omissions. At best, critical omissions can be eliminated.

REFERENCES

American Educational Research Association, American Psychological Association, & National Council on Measurement in Education. (1985). *Standards for educational and psychological testing.* Washington, DC: APA.

Anastasi, A. (1976). *Psychological testing* (4th ed.). New York: Macmillan.

Angoff, W. H. (1972, September). *A technique for the investigation of cultural differences.* Paper presented at the meeting of the American Psychological Association, Honolulu.

Angoff, W. H. (1982). Use of difficulty and discrimination indices for detecting item bias. In R. A. Berk (Ed.), *Handbook of methods for detecting test bias* (pp. 96–116). Baltimore: Johns Hopkins University Press.

Angoff, W. H., & Ford, S. F. (1973). Item-race interaction on a test of scholastic aptitude. *Journal of Educational Measurement, 10,* 95–106.

Angoff, W. H., & Sharon, A. L. (1974). The evaluation of differences in test performance of two or more groups. *Educational and Psychological Measurement, 34,* 807–816.

Baker, F. B. (1981). A criticism of Scheuneman's item bias technique. *Journal of Educational Measurement, 18,* 59–62.

Bernstein, B. (1975). *Class, codes, and control: Vol. 1.* New York: Holt, Rinehart & Winston.

Birenbaum, M. H. (1979). Procedures for detection and correction of salary in equity. In T. R. Pezzullo & B. F. Birtingham (Eds.), *Salary equity* (pp. 121–144). Lexington, MA: Lexington Books.

Birenbaum, M. H. (1981). Reply to McLaughlin: Proper path models for theoretical partialling. *American Psychologist, 36,* 1193–1195.

Bond, L. (1981). Bias in mental tests. In B. F. Green (Ed.), *New directions for testing and measurement: Issues in testing — coaching, disclosure and ethnic bias,* no. 11 (pp. 55–77). San Francisco: Jossey-Bass.

Breland, B., & Jones, R. J. (1982). *Perceptions of writing skill* (RR-82-47). Princeton, NJ: Educational Testing Service.

Camilli, G., & Shepard, L. A. (1987). The inadequacy of ANOVA for detecting test bias. *Journal of Educational Statistics, 12,* 87–99.

Campbell, D. F., & Fiske, D. W. (1959). Convergent and discriminant validation by the multitrait-multimethod matrix. *Psychological Bulletin, 56,* 81–105.

Carlson, S. B., Bridgeman, B., Camp, R., & Waanders, J. (1983). *Relationship of admission test scores to writing performance of native and nonnative speakers of English* (RR-85-21). Princeton, NJ: Educational Testing Service.

Cleary, T. A. (1968). Test bias: Prediction of grades of Negro and White students in integrated colleges. *Journal of Educational Measurement, 5,* 115–124.

Cleary, T. A., Humphreys, L. G., Kendrick, S. A., & Wesman, A. (1975). Educational uses of tests with disadvantaged students. *American Psychologist, 30,* 15–41.

Coffman, W. E. (1971). Essay examinations. In R. L. Thorndike (Ed.), *Educational measurement* (2nd ed., pp. 271–302). Washington, DC: American Council on Education.

Cole, N. S. (1973). Bias in selection. *Journal of Educational Measurement, 10,* 237–255.

Cole, N. S. (1976). Evaluating standardized tests and the alternatives. In A. J. Nitko (Ed.), *Exploring alternatives to current standardized tests.* [Summary]. Proceedings of the 1976 National Testing Conferences. Pittsburgh, PA: University of Pittsburgh.

Cole, N. S. (1981). Bias in testing. *American Psychologist, 36*(10), 1067–1077.

Cole, N. S., & Nitko, A. J. (1981). Measuring program effects, In R. A. Berk (Ed.), *Educational evaluation methodology: The state of the art.* Baltimore: Johns Hopkins University Press.

Cronbach, L. J. (1971). Test validation. In R. L. Thorndike (Ed.), *Educational measurement* (2nd ed.). Washington, DC: American Council on Education.

Cronbach, L. J. (1976). Equity in selection: Where psychometrics and political philosophy meet. *Journal of Educational Measurement, 13,* 31–41.

Cronbach, L. J. (1980). Validity on parole: How can we go straight? *New directions for testing and measurement: Measuring achievement, progress over a decade,* no. 5 (pp. 99–108). San Francisco: Jossey-Bass.

Cronbach, L. J., & Meehl, P. E. (1955). Construct validity in psychological tests. *Psychological Bulletin, 52,* 281–302.

Darlington, R. B. (1971). Another look at "culture fairness." *Journal of Educational Measurement, 8,* 71–82.

Diederich, P. B. (1974). *Measuring growth in English.* Urbana, IL: National Council of Teachers of English.

Diederich, P. B., French, J. W., & Carlton, S. T. (1961). Factors in judgments of writing ability (RB-61-15). Princeton, NJ: Educational Testing Service.

Donlon, T. F. (1984, April). *Distractor analysis as evidence of test fairness in the Scholastic Aptitude Test.* Paper presented at the meeting of the National Council on Measurement in Education, New Orleans.

Dorans, N. J., & Kulick, E. M. (1986). Demonstrating the utility of the standardization approach to assessing unexpected differential item performance on the Scholastic Aptitude Test. *Journal of Educational Measurement, 23,* 4, 355–368.

Eells, K., Davis, A., Havighurst, R. J., Herrick V. E., & Tyler, R. W. (1951). *Intelligence and cultural differences.* Chicago: University of Chicago Press.

Fitzpatrick, A. R. (1983). The meaning of content validity. *Applied Psychological Measurement, 7*(1), 3–13.

Flaugher, R. L. (1978). The many definitions of test bias. *American Psychologist, 33*(7), 671–679.

Freedman, S. W. (1979). How characteristics of students' essays influence evaluators. *Journal of Educational Psychology, 71,* 328–338.

Gross, A. L., & Su, W. (1975). Defining a "fair" or "unbiased" selection model: A question of utilities. *Journal of Applied Psychology, 60,* 345–351.

Guion, R. M. (1977). Content validity: The source of my discontent. *Applied Psychological Measurement, 1*(1), 1–10.

Gutkin, T. B., & Reynolds, C. R. (1981). Factorial similarity of the WICS-R for white and black children from the standardization sample. *Journal of Educational Psychology, 73,* 227–231.

Heath, S. B. (1982). *Language in society.* London: Cambridge University Press.

Holland, P. W., & Thayer, D. T. (1986, April). Differential item performance and the Mantel–Haenszel procedure. Paper presented at the meeting of the American Educational Research Association, San Francisco.

Humphreys, L. G., & Taber, T. (1973). Ability factors as a function of

advantaged and disadvantaged groups. *Journal of Educational Measurement, 10,* 107–115.

Hunter, J. E. (1975, December). *A critical analysis of the use of item means and item-test correlations to determine the presence or absence of content bias in achievement test items.* Paper presented at the National Institute of Education Conference on Test Bias, Annapolis, MD.

Ironson, G. H. (1982). Use of chi square and latent trait approaches for detecting item bias. In R. A. Berk (Ed.), *Handbook of methods for detecting test bias* (pp. 117–160). Baltimore: Johns Hopkins University Press.

Ironson, G. H., & Subkoviak, M. J. (1979). A comparison of several methods of assessing item bias. *Journal of Educational Measurement, 16,* 209–225.

Jacobs, H. L., Zingraf, S. A., Wormuth, D. R., Harftel, V. F., & Hughey, J. B. (1981). *Testing ESL composition: A practical approach.* Rowley, MA: Newbury House.

Jensen, A. R. (1974). How biased are culture-loaded tests? *Genetic Psychology Monographs, 90,* 185–244.

Jensen, A. R. (1977). An examination of cultural bias in the Wonderlic Personnel Test. *Intelligence, 1,* 51–64.

Jensen, A. R. (1980). *Bias in mental testing.* New York: Free Press.

Jöreskog, K. G. (1969). A general approach to confirmatory maximum likelihood factor analysis. *Psychometrika, 34,* 183–202.

Jöreskog, K. G. (1971). Simultaneous factor analysis in several populations. *Psychometrika, 36,* 409–426.

Kaplan, R. B. (1966). Cultural thought patterns in inter-cultural education. *Language Learning, 16,* 1–20.

Kok, F. G., Mellenbergh, G. J., & Van der Flier, H. (1985). Detecting experimentally induced item bias using the iterative logit method. *Journal of Educational Measurement, 22*(4), 295–303.

Linn, M. D. (1975). Black rhetorical patterns and the teaching of composition. *College Composition and Communication, 26,* 149–153.

Linn, R. L. (1979). Issues of validity in measurement for competency-based programs. In M. A. Bunda & J. R. Sanders (Eds.), *Practice and problems in competency based measurement* (pp. 108–123). Washington, DC: National Council on Measurement in Education.

Linn, R. L. (1982). Ability testing: Individual differences, prediction, and differential prediction. In A. K. Wigdor & W. R. Garner (Eds.), *Ability testing: Uses, consequences, and controversies: Part II* (pp. 335–388). Washington, DC: National Academy Press.

Linn, R. L. (1983). Pearson selection formulas: Implications for studies of predictive bias and estimates of educational effects in selected samples. *Journal of Educational Measurement, 20,* 1–16.

Linn, R. L. (1984). Selection bias: Multiple meanings. *Journal of Educational Measurement, 21*(1), 33–47.

Linn, R. L., & Harnisch, D. L. (1981). Interactions between item content and group membership on achievement test items. *Journal of Educational Measurement, 18,* 109–118.

Linn, R. L., Levine, M. V., Hastings, C. N., & Wardrop, J. L. (1981). Item bias in a test of reading comprehension. *Applied Psychological Measurement, 5,* 159–173.

Linn, R. L., & Werts, C. E. (1971). Considerations in studies of test bias. *Journal of Educational Measurement, 8*(1), 1–4.

Lord, F. M. (1968). An analysis of the Verbal Scholastic Aptitude Test using Birnbaum's three-parameter logistic model. *Educational and Psychological Measurement, 28,* 989–1020.

Lord, F. M. (1977). A study of item bias, using item characteristic curve theory. In Y. H. Poortinga (Ed.), *Basic problems in cross-cultural psychology* (pp. 19–29). Amsterdam: Swets and Zeitlinger.

Lord, F. M. (1980). *Applications of item response theory to practical testing problems.* Hillsdale, NJ: Lawrence Erlbaum.

Lord, F. M., & Novick, M. R. (1968). *Statistical theories of mental test scores.* Reading, MA: Addison-Wesley.

Mantel, N., & Haenszel, W. (1959). Statistical aspects of the analysis of data from retrospective studies of disease. *Journal of the National Cancer Institute, 22,* 719–748.

Mayberry, P. W. (1984, April). *A study of item bias for attitudinal measurement using maximum likelihood factor analysis.* Paper presented at the meeting of the National Council on Measurement in Education, New Orleans.

McPeek, W. M., & Wild, C. L. (1986, April). *Performance of the Mantel–Haenszel statistic in a variety of situations.* Paper presented at the meeting of the American Educational Research Association, San Francisco.

Mellenbergh, G. J. (1982). Contingency table models for assessing item bias. *Journal of Educational Statistics, 7,* 105–118.

Messick, S. (1975). The standard problem: Meaning and values in measurement and evaluation. *American Psychologist, 30,* 955–966.

Messick, S. (1980). Test validity and the ethics of assessment. *American Psychologist, 35,* 1012–1027.

Messick, S. (1981). Constructs and their vicissitudes in educational and psychological measurement. *Psychological Bulletin, 89,* 575–588.

Miele, F. (1979). Cultural bias in the WISC. *Intelligence, 3,* 149–164.

Moss, P. A. (1985). *Assessing the validity of a test of critical thinking. Unpublished manuscript,* University of Pittsburgh.

Muthen, B., & Christoffersson, A. (1981). Simultaneous factor analysis of dichotamous variables in several groups. *Psychometrika, 46,* 407–419.

Muthen, B., & Lehman, J. (1985). Multiple group IRT modeling: Applications to item bias analysis. *Journal of Educational Statistics, 10*(2), 133–142.

Novick, M. R. (1982). Educational testing: Inferences in relevant subpopulations. *Educational Researcher, 11,* 8, 4–10.

Petersen, N. S., & Novick, M. R. (1976). An evaluation of some models for culture-fair selection. *Journal of Educational Measurement, 13,* 3–29.

Rafoth, B. A., & Rubin, D. L. (1984). The impact of content and mechanics of judgments of writing quality. *Written Communication, 1*(4), 446–458.

Reynolds, C. R. (1982a). Methods for detecting construct and predictive bias. In R. A. Berk (Ed.), *Handbook of methods for detecting test bias* (pp. 199–227). Baltimore: Johns Hopkins University Press.

Reynolds, C. R. (1982b). The problem of bias in psychological assessment. In C. R. Reynolds & T. B. Gutkin (Eds.), *The handbook of school psychology* (pp. 178–208). New York: John Wiley & Sons.

Reynolds, C. R., & Paget, K. D. (1981). Factor structure of the revised Children's Manifest Anxiety Scale for blacks, whites, males, and females with a national normative sample. *Journal of Consulting and Clinical Psychology, 49,* 352–359.

Rudner, L. M., Getson, P. R., & Knight, D. L. (1980). Biased item detection techniques. *Journal of Educational Statistics, 5,* 213–233.

Sawyer, R. L., Cole, N. S., & Cole, J. W. L. (1976). Utilities and the issue of fairness in a decision theoretic model for selection. *Journal of Educational Measurement, 13,* 59–76.

Scheuneman, J. (1979). A method of assessing bias in test items. *Journal of Educational Measurement, 16,* 143–152.

Scheuneman, J. D. (1984). A theoretical framework for the exploration of causes and effects of bias in testing. *Educational Psychologist, 19,* 219–225.

Scheuneman, J. (1985). Exploration of causes of biased items (GRE Board Report GREB No. 81-21 P). Princeton, NJ: Educational Testing Service.

Schmeiser, C. B. (1982). Use of experimental design in statistical item bias studies. In R. A. Berk (Ed.) *Handbook of methods for detecting test bias* (pp. 64–95). Johns Hopkins University Press.

Shepard, L. A. (1981). Identifying bias in test items. In B. F. Green (Ed.), *New directions for testing and measurement: Issues in testing —coaching, disclosure and ethnic bias,* no. 11 (pp. 79–104) San Francisco: Jossey-Bass.

Shepard, L. A. (1982). Definitions of bias. In R. A. Berk (Ed.), *Handbook of methods for detecting test bias* (pp. 9–30). Baltimore: Johns Hopkins University Press.

Shepard, L., Camilli, G., & Averill, M. (1981). Comparison of procedures for detecting test-item bias with both internal and external ability criteria. *Journal of Educational Statistics, 6*(4), 317–375.

Shepard, L., Camilli, G., & Williams, D. (1984). Accounting for statistical artifacts in item bias research. *Journal of Educational Statistics, 9*(2), 93–128.

Shepard, L., Camilli, G., & Williams, D. (1985). Validity of approximation techniques for detecting item bias. *Journal of Educational Measurement, 22,* 77–105.

Sherman, S. W. (1976, April). *Multiple choice test bias uncovered by use of an "I don't know" alternative.* Paper presented at the meeting of the American Educational Research Association, San Francisco.

Subkoviak, M. J., Mack, J. S., Ironson, G. H., & Craig, R. D. (1984). Empirical comparison of selected item bias detection procedures with bias manipulation. *Journal of Educational Measurement, 21*(1), 49–58.

Takala, S., Purves, A. C., & Buckmaster, A. (1982). On the interrelationships between language, perception, thought, and culture and their relevance to the assessment of written composition. In A. C. Purves & S. Takala (Eds.), *Evaluation in education: An international review series. An international perspective on the evaluation of written composition.* Elmsford, NY: Pergamon Press.

Tenopyr, M. L. (1977). Content-construct confusion. *Personnel Psychology, 30,* 47–54.

Thissen, D. M. (1979). Information in wrong responses to the Raven Progressive Matrices. *Journal of Educational Measurement, 13,* 201–214.

Thorndike, R. L. (1971). Concepts of culture fairness. *Journal of Educational Measurement, 8,* 63–70.

Tittle, C. K. (1975). Fairness in educational achievement testing. *Education and Urban Society, 8,* 86–103.

Tittle, C. K. (1982). Use of judgmental methods in item bias studies. In R. A. Berk (Ed.), *Handbook of methods for detecting test bias* (pp. 31–63). Baltimore: Johns Hopkins University Press.

Van der Flier, H., Mellenbergh, G. J., Ader, H. J., & Wijn, M. (1984). An iterative item bias detection method. *Journal of Educational Measurement, 21*(2), 131–145.

Veale, J. R., & Foreman, D. I. (1976, April). *Cultural variation in criterion-referenced tests: A "global" item analysis.* Paper presented at the meeting of the American Educational Research Association, San Francisco.

Wood, R. L., Wingersky, M. S., & Lord, F. M. (1976). *LOGIST: A computer program for estimating examinee ability and item characteristic curve parameters* (Research Memorandum 76-6). Princeton, NJ: Educational Testing Service.

6

Scaling, Norming, and Equating

Nancy S. Petersen

Educational Testing Service

Michael J. Kolen

The American College Testing Program

H. D. Hoover

The University of Iowa

Score reports based on the administration of an educational achievement or aptitude test often contain a variety of scores. This multiplicity of scores is often necessary because of the many uses to which test results may be put. Some of the reported scores might reflect an examinee's standing relative to different reference groups, others might be intended for special purposes, and still others might reflect performance on subparts of the test. The goal of providing all of these scores is to supply more useful information.

The process of associating numbers with the performance of examinees is referred to as *scaling,* and this process results in a *score scale.* A reference group of examinees is often used in establishing a score scale. The process of collecting data on such a reference group and describing the performance numerically is referred to as *norming.* Multiple forms of a test are often necessary when a test is administered more than one time. The process of *equating* is used to ensure that scores resulting from the administration of the multiple forms can be used interchangeably.

In this chapter, we will describe the processes of scaling, norming, and equating. We suggest supplementing this chapter with the work by Angoff that originally appeared in the second edition of *Educational Measurement* in 1971. Angoff's chapter was reprinted by the Educational Testing Service in 1984 as a separate monograph.

Scaling

A score scale refers to numbers, assigned to individuals on the basis of test performance, that are intended to reflect increasing levels of achievement or ability. For many educational achievement and aptitude tests, one score scale is used as the *primary score scale* for reporting scores. Scores on alternate test forms are typically reported on the primary score scale, and a system of equating is used to insure that primary scale scores have the same meaning regardless of the test form an examinee takes. *Auxiliary score scales* are used to enhance the meaning of primary scale scores. Percentile ranks are probably the most widely used auxiliary score scales. Other types include normal curve equivalents, stanines, and percentage correct in subareas. The focus of this section is on tests that have the following three basic components: a primary score scale, a system of equating alternate forms, and, potentially, a variety of auxiliary score scales.

NOTE: The authors thank William H. Angoff, Robert L. Brennan, Richard M. Jaeger, Deborah J. Harris, and William Rice for reviewing earlier outlines and drafts of this chapter.

The usefulness of a primary score scale depends on its fulfilling two goals: facilitating meaningful interpretations and minimizing misinterpretations and unwarranted inferences. Meaningful interpretations can be enhanced by incorporating information on content, norm groups, or score precision into a primary score scale at the time the scale is established. Misinterpretation can be minimized by avoiding the use of scales that suggest unwarranted meanings or that can be confused with other scales, as well as by developing interpretive materials that educate test users in the proper uses of test scores.

The primary score scale can facilitate score interpretation in a variety of ways. A primary score scale used in conjunction with an equating process aids the comparison of examinee performance on different forms of a test. Because this process leads to scores on alternate forms being on the same scale, individual examinee growth and trends in the performance of groups over time can be evaluated. A primary score scale can enhance the comparison of examinee performance on levels of a test that differ in difficulty. Also, with the consistent establishment of score scales for all of the tests in a battery, primary score scales can facilitate the comparison of an examinee's performance across different tests. For a battery, primary score scales can also enhance the formation of composites. In addition, a primary score scale aids the presentation of auxiliary score scales by providing a common reference scale. In summary, primary score scales can facilitate each of the following functions of testing: (a) the interpretation of an examinee's performance on a single test, (b) the comparison of performance of examinees on different forms of a test, (c) the assessment of an examinee's growth, (d) the tracking of trends in group performance over time, (e) the reporting of auxiliary score scales, (f) the comparison of the performance of examinees on different difficulty levels of a test, (g) the formation of composites, and (h) the comparison of an examinee's performance on different tests in a battery.

Auxiliary score scales are used because, in many situations, it is desirable to convey more information about test performance than can be incorporated into a single primary score scale. Auxiliary score scales are used to convey additional normative information, test-content information, and information that is jointly normative and content based. For many test uses, an auxiliary scale conveys information that is more crucial than the information conveyed by the primary score scale. In such instances, the auxiliary scale is the one that is focused on, and the primary scale can be viewed more as a vehicle for maintaining interpretability over time.

In this section, the term *scale score* is used to refer to scores reported on the primary score scale. It is assumed that an initial test form is used in establishing the primary score scale. Equating is used so that scores on alternate test forms can be interpreted with regard to the primary score scale that was established with the initial test form.

The methods of establishing primary score scales considered here are all potentially applicable to educational achievement tests. According to Lindquist (1953),

A good educational achievement test must itself define the objective measured. This means that the method of scaling an educational achievement test should not be permitted to determine the content of the test or to alter the definition of objectives implied in the test. From the point of view of the tester, the definition of the objective is sacrosanct; he has no business monkeying with that definition. The objective is handed down to him by those agents of society who are responsible for decisions concerning educational objectives, and what the test constructor must do is to attempt to incorporate that definition as clearly and as exactly as possible in the examination that he builds. (p. 35)

Scaling methods that, for example, involve removing items from a test that do not fit a particular statistical model will not be considered here.

This section takes the perspective that the main purpose of scaling is to aid users in interpreting test results. In this vein, we stress the importance of incorporating useful meaning into score scales as a primary means of enhancing score interpretability.

A variety of perspectives on scaling and measurement exist. Jones (1971), Stevens (1951), and Suppes and Zinnes (1963), for example, presented general discussions of measurement and scaling. Michell (1986) contrasted approaches to measurement and scaling using some examples in the area of mental measurement. Yen (1986) considered many of the problems and issues involved when applying some of these perspectives to educational achievement tests.

Scales for a Single Test

The usefulness of a primary score scale depends on how well it helps to convey meaning and prevent erroneous interpretations. Score scales that are linearly related to raw scores and score scales that are nonlinearly related to raw scores are described next. Procedures for incorporating meaning into score scales and issues involved in maintaining score scales over time are discussed later.

RAW SCORES

The number, proportion, or percentage of items an examinee answers correctly should seldom be used as the primary score scale, because raw scores are rarely directly comparable across alternate test forms. However, the raw-score scale on an initial form of a test can be used as a primary score scale, and scores on subsequent test forms can be equated to the scale of the initial form. For example, in some professional certification and licensure examinations, a standard setting study is conducted on the initial form of a test, and the resulting passing score is expressed in raw-score units on this initial form. As new forms are developed and administered, scores on these forms are equated to the scores on the initial form. In this way, the raw-score scale of the initial form is used as the primary score scale.

A raw score scaling system is problematic in that it can lead to confusion between raw scores and scale (equated) scores on subsequent forms, because these two types of scores are so similar. For example, an examinee with a number-correct score of 35 on a 50-item test might receive a scale score of 38 if the test form the examinee was administered was more difficult than the initial form. The examinee might then misinterpret the scale score of 38 as 38 correct on the form taken.

Score conversions for three forms of a 50-item hypothetical

professional certification test are shown in Table 6.1, to further illustrate problems in using raw scores as the primary score scale. Assume that a passing score study was conducted on Form 1, a raw score of 30 was judged to be the lowest passing score, and the raw score scale of Form 1 was used as the primary score scale. Thus, raw scores on Forms 2 and 3 are equated to the raw-score scale of Form 1. Then a raw score of 28 on Form 2 is considered to be passing, because it converts to a scale score of 30.

An examinee with a raw score of 28 on Form 2 would pass the test with a scale score of 30. However, an examinee with a raw score of 31 on Form 3 would fail the examination with a scale score of 29. This later examinee might argue that two points were erroneously being subtracted from her or his raw score. A primary score scale other than the Form 1 raw score should be chosen to prevent this sort of misinterpretation.

Despite the problems inherent in using number correct, proportion correct, and percentage correct as primary scale scores, they can be useful as auxiliary scale scores, especially for achievement tests that are curriculum based. For test forms that are built by random sampling of items from a well-defined domain (Ebel, 1962; Nitko, 1984), these scores provide an estimate of the proportion of the items in the domain that the examinee can answer correctly. These types of scores can be used advantageously as indicators of students' strengths and weaknesses in subareas of achievement. For example, on Level 12 of the Iowa Tests of Basic Skills (ITBS) Language Usage and Expression Test (Hieronymus & Hoover, 1986), which is typically administered to sixth graders, percentages correct on the subareas of "use of verbs," "use of pronouns," "use of modifiers," and "use of context" are often reported as auxiliary scores. The meaning of the scores in these subareas is enhanced by also reporting the average percentage correct for the student's classroom and for a national norm group. Often the scores on subareas are of low reliability, so it is necessary to encourage test users to interpret subarea scores with caution. In general, the usefulness of these types of raw scores as auxiliary scores depends on how easily they can be related to the test-content domain and to relevant norm groups.

Raw scores that are based on some function of the number of items an examinee answers correctly, answers incorrectly,

TABLE 6.1 Number-Correct to Scale Score Conversions for Three Forms of a Hypothetical Professional Certification Test

NUMBER CORRECT SCORE	SCALE SCORE EQUIVALENT		
	FORM 1	FORM 2	FORM 3
⋮	⋮	⋮	⋮
33	33	35	31
32	32	34	30*
31	31	33	29
30	30*	32	28
29	29	31	27
28	28	30*	26
27	27	29	25
⋮	⋮	⋮	⋮

* Minimum passing score.

and omits are sometimes used (e.g., number right minus number wrong, divided by the number of answer choices minus one). Examinees who know nothing about an item typically are instructed that pure guessing will not be helpful, on the average. Formula raw scores are as problematic for use as primary scale scores as are other types of raw scores previously described. In addition, formula scores are less useful as auxiliary score scales than number-correct scores, because formula scores do not reflect the proportion of items in a domain that an examinee can answer correctly.

LINEAR AND NONLINEAR TRANSFORMATIONS

Primary score scales are often established by transforming raw scores on an initial test form so that the resulting scale scores have certain desirable properties. These properties are defined by the constructor of the scale. The transformation can be linear or nonlinear. Linear transformations of raw score (x) to scale score (s) follow the form

$$s = Ax + B, \tag{1}$$

where A is the slope and B the intercept of the line.

The location of the scale scores can be defined by specifying that a particular raw score x_1 is equivalent to a particular scale score s_1. Spread of the scale scores can be established by specifying a second raw-to-scale score equivalence; say that x_2 is equivalent to s_2. For Equation 1, this leads to

$$A = (s_2 - s_1)/(x_2 - x_1) = (s_1 - s_2)/(x_1 - x_2) \text{ and}$$
$$B = s_2 - Ax_2 = s_1 - Ax_1. \tag{2}$$

For example, on a hypothetical 50-item test, 10 items correct could be specified to correspond to a scale score of 70; and 50 items correct, to a scale score of 90. Then, from Equations 2,

$$A = (90 - 70)/(50 - 10) = 0.5,$$

and

$$B = 90 - 0.5(50) = 65.$$

From Equation 1, raw scores of 0, 20, and 40, for example, would correspond, respectively, to scale scores of 65, 75, and 85.

Alternatively, the slope and intercept of Equation 1 can be established by specifying one equivalence between scores, say, between s_1 and x_1, and the desired variability of the raw and scale scores for a particular population of examinees. For this situation,

$$A = \sigma_s/\sigma_x$$

and

$$B = s_1 - Ax_1, \tag{3}$$

where, σ_s is the desired scale score standard deviation and σ_x the raw score standard deviation for a particular population of examinees. Other indexes of variability, such as the mean absolute deviation or semi-interquartile range, could be used in place of the standard deviations. For example, suppose that, for a reference group of examinees, the scale score mean is specified to be 100 and the standard deviation, 10. If the mean of the raw scores is 60 and the standard deviation is 8 for this group, then from Equations 3, $A = 10/8 = 1.25$, and $B = 100 - (1.25)(60) = 25$. These values of A and B are entered into Equation 1.

The equivalences needed for applying Equations 2 and 3 can be based on test content or on designated characteristics of the distribution of the scale scores (e.g., means or percentiles) for a particular group of examinees. Issues of basing equivalences on test content and characteristics of score distributions are discussed later in this chapter.

For tests and scales considered here, nonlinear conversions of raw score to scale score can take on almost any monotonically nondecreasing form, that is, the scale score corresponding to a particular raw score is greater than or equal to the scale score corresponding to a lower raw score. Nonlinear conversions might be needed when more than two equivalences between raw and scale scores are specified. Nonlinear conversions result in the shape of the scale score distribution being different from the shape of the raw score distribution.

One of the least complicated curvilinear conversions involves truncating a linear conversion. This process is illustrated in Figure 6.1. A linear function of the form $s = Ax + B$ is used for the middle raw scores. A horizontal line is used to convert raw scores above the upper truncation point and below the lower truncation point. In practice, truncation may be used in situations where meaningful distinctions cannot easily be made beyond a certain point. Sometimes the scale is truncated at a point that corresponds to chance-level performance. For example, consider a hypothetical 50-item test reported on a

scale with $A = 1$ and $B = 20$, which results in a scale that extends from 20 to 70. If it were also specified that scale scores not go below 30, then the linear function would be truncated; all raw scores at or below 10, which would have been assigned a scale score at or below 30 with no truncation, would be assigned a scale score of 30.

A variety of other nonlinear transformations can be applied to raw scores. Many are so complicated that they are communicated most easily by using a conversion table that gives the scale score equivalent of each raw score. Nonlinear transformations sometimes involve establishing raw-to-scale score equivalences for content or normative reasons. Also, they can involve transforming scores to a particular distributional shape, such as the normal distribution, for a particular group of examinees. These types of nonlinear transformations are described more fully later in this chapter.

In practice, linear and nonlinear methods of establishing a primary score scale differ principally in complexity and in the amount of flexibility provided. One advantage of using a linear transformation is simplicity; the transformation to scale score is expressed as a slope, an intercept, and a rounding rule.

Nonlinear methods of establishing score scales are sometimes preferable for reasons of flexibility. Whereas, for linear transformations, the shape of the scale score distribution for any group of examinees is necessarily the same as the shape of the raw-score distribution, for nonlinear transformations, raw scores can be transformed to almost any prespecified distributional shape for a particular group of examinees. Major poten-

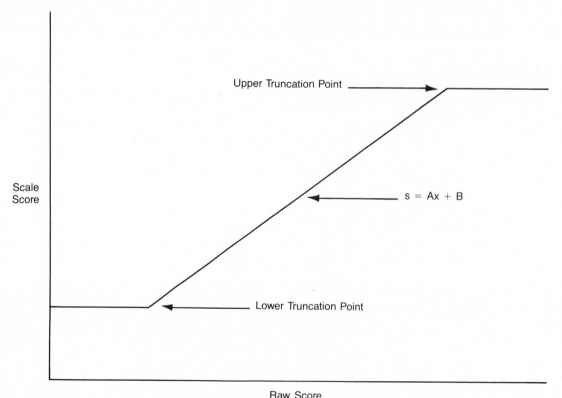

FIGURE 6.1 Linear conversion truncated at upper and lower ends.

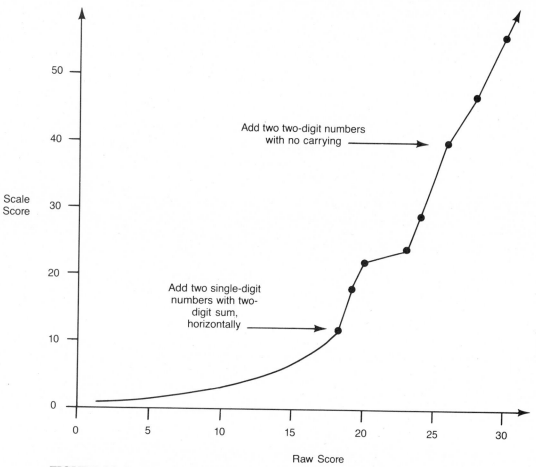

FIGURE 6.2 Raw score to scale score conversion for a hypothetical arithmetic test.

tial drawbacks of nonlinear methods of establishing score scales are that they are more complicated to implement and describe than linear methods, and they might require larger samples of examinees than linear methods.

INCORPORATING CONTENT MEANING

Test-score interpretation can be facilitated by using mechanisms that relate test score to test content (Ebel, 1962). Nitko (1980, 1984) suggested defining scale scores for tests measuring well-defined ordered-item domains with reference to specific levels of achievement. The advantage of this approach is that particular scale scores can be chosen to represent achievement bench marks, which can aid in the interpretation of examinees' scores in relation to instruction. Nitko presented an example of a hypothetical test that covers the domain of elementary addition defined by Cox and Graham (1966). In this example, a raw score of 18 is specified to be equivalent to a scale score of 12, which is considered to be indicative of the ability to add two single-digit numbers with a two-digit sum, horizontally. A raw score of 28 is specified to be equivalent to a scale score of 40, which is considered to be indicative of the ability to add two two-digit numbers with no carrying. These specified equivalences could be entered into Equations 2 to obtain the slope and intercept for Equation 1.

If more than two raw-to-scale score equivalences are stated, a nonlinear conversion might be needed. In a full hypothetical example, Nitko (1980, 1984) specified eight equivalences. Unspecified equivalences can be arrived at in a variety of ways including drawing straight lines between the points; drawing, by hand, a smooth curve that passes through the points; and using an analytic interpolation technique such as cubic interpolating splines (Ahlberg, Nilson, & Walsh 1967; de Boor, 1978). Figure 6.2 illustrates the use of analytic interpolation for Nitko's hypothetical example. The eight specified equivalences, each of which is considered an achievement bench mark, are indicated by dots, and cubic spline interpolation is used to arrive at a smooth curve that passes through the eight points.

One way to specify the raw scores indicative of particular levels of achievement would be to use judgmental standard-setting techniques (Livingston & Zieky, 1982; Shepard, 1984; Jaeger, this volume). For example, using a method described by Angoff (1984, p. 10), knowledgeable judges could rate each item on the test. Their ratings would be estimates of the proportion of examinees, among those who just barely mastered a particular skill, who would correctly answer the question. The raw score needed to indicate achievement of that skill could be based on a sum of the ratings over items for each judge, averaged over judges. Of course, this method would require judges to make a large number of ratings. Another method would be to choose the raw scores at which a certain proportion of examinees correctly answers the items measuring an objective. For example, the raw score indicative of the ability to add two single-digit numbers with a two-digit sum, horizontally, could be defined as that raw score at which examinees, on average, correctly answered 90% of the items covering that ability.

The arithmetic example just described comes from an area with a content domain that is well ordered by complexity (Nitko, 1980, 1984). Often there is no such natural ordering to the content, but there still is a desire to have certain scale scores represent achievement bench marks. Professional licensure and certification examinations typically are built from domains that are not well ordered. In these examinations, the focus is on differentiating between two groups of examinees: those who do and those who do not possess the minimum knowledge and skills to perform acceptably at a beginning level (Burns, 1985). Judgmental standard-setting techniques (Livingston & Zieky, 1982; Shepard, 1984; Jaeger, this volume) can be used to establish the raw passing score indicative of minimum acceptable test performance on one test form. This raw passing score is specified to be equal to a particular scale score that has been chosen for ease of interpretation. After a second point is specified, Equations 1 and 2 can be used to establish the initial linear transformation of raw scores to scale scores. Because the focus is on the passing score, nonlinear transformations usually are not required; when nonlinear transformations are used, they are typically of the truncation variety.

INCORPORATING NORMATIVE MEANING

Incorporating normative meaning into scale scores is another way of enhancing their interpretability. Several authors have advocated the incorporation of normative information when establishing score scales (e.g., Flanagan, 1951; Gardner, 1962, 1966; Hoover, 1984a; Lindquist, 1953). The process of incorporating meaning into scale scores requires that test-score data be collected on a relevant group of examinees. The particular norm group selected has a strong influence on the meaningfulness of the resulting scale scores. For example, the norm group used to establish a score scale for elementary school achievement test batteries is typically selected to be representative of elementary students in the nation. Score scales established in this manner usually carry clearer meaning than those established from a group of examinees that happens to take a test on a particular test date or during a particular time.

Specification of two raw-to-scale score equivalents based on normative data can be used in the establishment of a linear score scale that incorporates normative meaning. The following example is based on one described by Angoff (1984, pp. 8–9). Suppose that it is decided that the bottom 35% of the examinees from a reference group will fail a 150-item test and that the 35th percentile is a raw score of 89. Also, the top 10% will earn honors, and the 90th percentile is a raw score of 129. To arrive at scale scores where a 70 is passing and a 95 represents honors, from Equations 2, $A = (95 - 70)/(129 - 89) = .625$ and $B = 95 - (.625)(129) = 14.375$. These A and B values are entered into Equation 1 to produce the linear equa-

tion that relates raw scores to scale scores. If more than two points are specified, then the relationship, in general, will be nonlinear.

Normative data on a series of intact examinee groups are sometimes used to establish the transformation to scale score. If two points are specified, the transformation is linear. If more than two points are specified, it is likely to be nonlinear. For a nonlinear example, consider an achievement test that is developed to be appropriate for third through eighth graders. The test could be administered to representative samples of third, fourth, fifth, sixth, seventh, and eighth graders. The raw score corresponding to the third graders' mean could be assigned a scale score of 30, the raw score corresponding to the fourth graders mean could be assigned a scale score of 40, and so on. Between the specified raw-to-scale score equivalents, the conversion could be arrived at in the ways that were previously suggested for scales specified in relation to content: linear interpolation, curvilinear interpolation by hand, or cubic smoothing splines. This sort of procedure is used in the establishment of developmental score scales, which will be described in more detail in a later section. In general, the degree of useful meaning incorporated by use of intact groups depends on how important these groups are for score interpretation.

A nonlinear transformation is required in establishing the score scale if the shape of the raw-score distribution for the reference group is to be altered. One such nonlinear conversion is to percentile ranks. However, percentile ranks are rarely used as primary score scales, because they are easily confused with percentage-correct scores; they are easily confused with percentile ranks for other examinee groups; and the distribution of percentile ranks is necessarily rectangular, although it is commonly believed that educational aptitude and achievement variables are not rectangularly distributed.

On the other hand, percentile ranks might be the most often used auxiliary score scales. They facilitate comparisons of the scores of an examinee with scores of examinees in a wide variety of groups. For example, with college entrance examinations, percentile ranks are often reported that refer the scores of an examinee to a national group of college-bound examinees, as well as to groups of examinees enrolled in the various colleges that an examinee is considering attending. All of this information could not possibly be incorporated into a single primary score scale.

The conversion of raw scores to scale scores that are normally distributed for a particular reference group of examinees is a nonlinear transformation that is often used. The process, rationale, and history behind normalizing scores were described in detail by Angoff (1984, pp. 10–16). In this process, raw scores are transformed to percentile ranks, which are then transformed to normally distributed scores, using an inverse normal transformation. Smoothing procedures can be used to insure that the relationship between raw and scale scores appears smooth. The mean and standard deviation of the scale scores can be set by the developer of the scale. For example, normalized scores with a mean of 50 and a standard deviation of 10 for the reference group are referred to as T scores (McCall, 1939). Usually there is no good theoretical reason for normalizing scores. Observed scores are not usually normally distributed (Lord, 1955b), and there is often reason to expect test-score distributions to be nonsymmetric (Hoover, 1984a). The advantage of normalized scores is that they can be interpreted by using facts about the normal distribution. For example, a scale score that is one standard deviation above the mean has a percentile rank of approximately 84 in the reference group for normalized scores. Thus, from a practical viewpoint, normalizing can aid in the interpretability of scores.

Intelligence test scores (IQ scores) are one type of frequently used normalized score. Typically, IQ scores are normalized scale scores with a mean of 100 and a standard deviation of 15 or 16 within age group. Angoff (1984, pp. 26–27) presents a historical discussion of IQ scores.

Stanines (Flanagan, 1951, p. 727) are another type of frequently used normalized scores. They are integer scores ranging from 1 to 9, with a mean of 5 and a standard deviation of approximately 2 for the reference group. The advantage of stanines is that the single-digit scale appears to be simple and to reduce the likelihood of overemphasizing the importance of small differences among examinees. However, Flanagan (1951, p. 747) points out that stanines are so coarse that they can lead to loss of information; in some cases the range of raw scores that corresponds to a single stanine exceeds the standard error of measurement.

Normal curve equivalents are still another type of normalized score and are used in Chapter I evaluations of federally funded educational programs. Normal curve equivalents are normalized scale scores with a mean of 50 and a standard deviation of 21.06 for a representative national reference group. Reported scores are rounded to integers over the range 1 to 99. Normal curve equivalents can be thought of roughly as stanines calculated to one decimal place and multiplied by 10. The major drawback of normal curve equivalents is that they can be easily confused with percentile ranks and proportion-correct scores. In addition, they do not discriminate particularly well among examinees for whom their use was primarily intended: low scoring ones. A fairly large proportion of Chapter I students obtain percentile ranks of 1. Because a normal curve equivalent of 1 and a percentile rank of 1 are equal, Chapter I students exhibiting a wide range of achievement levels are grouped together.

INCORPORATING SCORE PRECISION INFORMATION

The interpretability of primary scale scores is affected by the number and range of distinct points on the primary score scale. As was already mentioned in connection with stanines, the use of too few distinct score points leads to loss of information. Too many score points leads test users to inappropriately attach significance to score differences that are small in comparison with the standard error of measurement. This problem is especially evident when score scales have substantially more values than there are raw scores in a test. As suggested by Flanagan (1951, p. 746), these problems might be addressed by incorporating score precision information when the score scale is established.

The score scale for the Iowa Tests of Educational Development (ITED, 1980a, 1980b) and the cognitive tests of the ACT Assessment is one example of a scale that was constructed by incorporating score precision information. This scale was originally designed in 1942, using integer scores with the property that an approximate 50% confidence interval could be constructed by adding and subtracting one point to an examinee's scale score (American College Testing Program [ACT], 1960; ITED, 1958). In a similar vein, Truman L. Kelley suggested that scale scores be constructed with the property that an approximate 68% confidence interval can be constructed by adding and subtracting three points from an examinee's scale score (W. H. Angoff, personal communication, February 17, 1987). These properties are designed to lead to score scales that do not encourage finer distinctions than can be supported by the reliability of the test.

The incorporation of score precision information in the establishment of a score scale involves taking errors of measurement into account. The following scheme is based on a description by Kolen (1986, 1988). Assume that there is interest in developing a score scale possessing the property that $s \pm h$ is an approximate $100\gamma\%$ confidence interval, where the developer of the scale chooses h and γ. If these methods are applied with $h = 1$ and $\gamma = .50$, for example, an approximate 50% confidence interval can be formed by adding and subtracting one point from any examinee's scale score. If $h = 3$ and $\gamma = .68$, an approximate 68% confidence interval can be formed by adding and subtracting 3 points from any examinee's scale score.

To establish a score scale that is linearly related to raw score and defined in relation to measurement error, assume that errors are constant in variability along the raw score scale, approximately normally distributed, and independent. Designate the standard error of measurement for raw scores as $\sigma_{x''}$, where $\sigma_{x''}$ could be based on alternate form, test–retest, or single administration methods of assessing measurement error (Lord & Novick, 1968; Feldt & Brennan, this volume). Also, designate z_y as a unit-normal deviate that establishes a $100\gamma\%$ two-sided confidence interval. For example, $z_y \doteq .6745$ establishes a 50% confidence interval. Then $s \pm h$ is an approximate $100\gamma\%$ confidence interval, where

$$
\begin{aligned}
A &= h/(z_y\sigma_{x''}), \\
B &= s_1 - Ax_1,
\end{aligned}
\tag{4}
$$

and these A and B values are used in Equation 1 ($s = Ax + B$).

For example, suppose it were desired that primary scale scores be established with the property that an approximate 50% confidence interval could be formed by adding and subtracting one score point from an examinee's scale score, as was done in developing the ITED score scale. In this case, for Equations 4, $h = 1$, $z_y \doteq .6745$, and $A \doteq 1/(.6745)\sigma_{x''}$. In practice, the scale scores would typically be rounded to integers. On the basis of results presented by Kolen (1986, 1988), this process of rounding scale scores to integers results in a minimal (less than 5%) increase in measurement error when $h = 1$ and $\gamma = .50$ or when $h = 3$ and $\gamma = .68$.

The method associated with Equations 4 assumes that measurement error variance is constant across score points. However, there is a great deal of evidence indicating that this assumption does not hold in practice (see, for example, Feldt, Steffen, & Gupta, 1985). Typically, raw scores have larger error variances near the middle of the score range and smaller error variances at the extremes. Kolen (1986, 1988) presents methods of incorporating score precision information that are designed to accommodate unequal error variances on the raw-score scale. These methods are based on Freeman and Tukey's (1950) arcsine transformation of raw scores and on the binomial and compound binomial error models (Feldt, 1984; Jarjoura, 1985; Lord, 1965; Lord & Novick, 1968; Wilcox, 1978, 1981), and these methods result in scale scores that have more nearly constant error variance at all score points. Refer to Kolen (1986, 1988) for a detailed description of these methods.

Table 6.2 illustrates the raw-to-scale score conversions resulting from application of the constant error variance method associated with Equations 4 and a method based on the compound binomial error model that allows error variance of raw scores to vary across score points. These results are based on the 100-item test presented in Kolen (1986, 1988), with $h = 1$, $\gamma = .50$, $\sigma_{x''} \doteq 3.96$, a scale score of 100 set equal to a raw score of 50, and scale scores rounded to integers. As can be seen, the two methods produce similar conversions over most of the score range. The differences that do occur are the result of the arcsine transformation, used to equalize error variance, condensing the score scale in the middle and stretching it at the ends. The differences between the methods found in Table 6.2 are typical of the differences found in Kolen (1986, 1988), and they led him to conclude that the constant error method associated with Equations 4 might be acceptable in many of the situations in which a linear relationship is preferable for practical reasons.

UNIDIMENSIONAL IRT ABILITY SCALES

Unidimensional item response theory (IRT) postulates a model for the relationship between examinee ability θ and the probability of correctly answering a test item (Hambleton, this volume; Hambleton & Swaminathan, 1985; Lord, 1980; Lord & Novick, 1968). The present discussion focuses on the use of the ability scale in IRT as a primary score scale for tests that have been found to adequately fit an IRT model.

Use of the IRT θ scale of ability (or a linear transformation of it) for score reporting poses a variety of practical problems. One problem is that ability estimates for high- or low-ability examinees are subject to relatively great amounts of measure-

ment error. For the three-parameter logistic model, measurement error variance for examinees of extreme ability could easily be 10 or even 100 times that for more typical examinees. Lord presented an example that illustrates this problem (1980, p. 183). In practice, adequate interpretation of θ-ability estimates for individual examinees requires, at a minimum, that the error in estimating θ be taken into account. Also, as suggested by Lord (1980, p. 183), the great amount of variability in measurement error associated with estimates of θ can create problems in interpreting summary statistics such as means and correlations. Another problem in using the θ scale for score reporting is that estimates of θ can be costly to obtain.

For many tests that are developed using IRT, these problems are avoided by establishing the primary score scale as a transformation of raw scores on an initial test form. Content or normative information can be incorporated by using methods described previously. The IRT equating methods to be described in a subsequent section of this chapter can be used to equate alternate forms to the primary score scale. These equating methods are followed with the Scholastic Aptitude Test (Donlon, 1984, pp. 15–20).

For some testing programs, θ is estimated for all examinees as a matter of course. In these programs, estimates of θ can be nonlinearly transformed, to obtain the estimated true scores suggested by Lord (1980, p. 183), and they can be used to establish the primary scale. For the initial test form, the estimated true score is $\Sigma P_i(\hat{\theta})$, where $\hat{\theta}$ is estimated ability, P_i is an item-characteristic function, and the summation is over items on the initial form. The estimated true score can be transformed through methods described earlier to incorporate content or normative information. The IRT equating methods to be described later in this chapter can be used in the process of converting scores on new forms to the primary score scales.

Adaptive testing using IRT, where examinees are administered items tailored to their ability, is one situation in which the use of estimated true scores has the potential to improve score reporting over the use of $\hat{\theta}$. A "standard" test, one that is representative of the domain of items, can be assembled. Instead of reporting $\hat{\theta}$ on the basis of the items an examinee took, an estimated true score (or a transformation of it that incorporates content or normative information) on the standard test can be used as the primary score scale. Stocking (1984) described the process and rationale for using estimated true scores in adaptive testing situations.

MAINTAINING SCORE SCALES

As was discussed earlier, the interpretation of test scores can be facilitated by incorporating content, normative, and score precision information into the score scale at the time it is established. Over time, however, the meaning that was initially incorporated might become less relevant for score interpretation. The norm group that was central to score interpretation when the scale was established might not be the norm group that is most appropriate for test-score interpretation 5 or 10 years later.

In addition, test content often changes as a testing program evolves. These changes can be small and subtle from one test form to the next, but over time the cumulative effect can be so

TABLE 6.2 Raw-to-Scale Score Conversions for a 100-Item Test

RAW SCORE	SCALE SCORE	
	CONSTANT ERROR	VARIABLE ERROR
100	119	123
90	115	114
80	111	110
70	107	106
60	104	103
50	100	100
40	96	97
30	93	94
20	89	90
10	85	86
0	81	77

large that a form constructed in a given year can differ markedly from one constructed, say, 5 to 10 years earlier. Even if the score scale is maintained through equating, due to content considerations, it would be impossible to argue convincingly that scores on the forms have the same meaning or that the forms could be used interchangeably at a given time.

Professional certification and licensure examinations are especially affected by these types of problems. Often a passing score is set on an initial test form, and this score is maintained by the process of equating. However, over time it becomes more difficult to claim that a new form and the initial form could be used interchangeably. Professions change in their emphases, knowledge bases, and legal contexts. Test items administered in one year can become irrelevant in future years. Sometimes even the key for a given item must be changed as a result of changes in the law or changes in the knowledge base of a profession.

Changes in norm groups and test content can lead to misinterpretations of scores. For example, solely because the mean of the verbal Scholastic Aptitude Test (SAT) was 500 for the initial reference group in 1941, a test user might conclude erroneously that a student with a 500 in 1986 is average. Angoff (1962, 1984) argued that, because the potential for score misinterpretation exists, interpretive information should not be incorporated into score scales. Angoff (1962) preferred scales with "nonmeaningful units of measurement," which are scales developed to have no inherent or built-in meaning. For these scales, score interpretation is facilitated by other accompanying information (e.g., percentile ranks for meaningful subgroups) and through the familiarity gained by using the score scale over time, rather than through information built into the scale at the time it was established.

In some situations, scales with nonmeaningful units can help avoid score misinterpretation. However, even when it is stressed that scores have no inherent meaning, test users often attempt to attach meaning to them. For example, even though the College Board maintains that the units on the SAT score scale are not meaningful, a common misconception is that a score of 500 represents the mean of all test takers "in some recent year" (Donlon, 1984, p. 15).

Other authors have stressed the importance of including normative or content information at the time a score scale is established (Ebel, 1962; Flanagan, 1951; Gardner, 1962, 1966; Hoover, 1984a; Lindquist, 1953). The incorporation of information is encouraged as a way of enhancing the meaningfulness of scores reported to examinees. Potential misinterpretations are minimized by educating test users to the proper use of scale scores. When a score scale is established it is unfamiliar to test users, and information that is incorporated into the score scale can be an aid to score interpretation at that time. As the test and norm groups change, the information that was initially built into the score scale can be deemphasized in score interpretation, so that the familiarity that test users gain by using the scale supplants the information that was used for score interpretation initially. This evolution of proper score interpretation can be conveyed to test users through changes in the interpretative documentation for a test.

Another way to minimize score misinterpretation is to periodically rescale tests. For example, each new edition of the ITBS is rescaled. That is, the grade-equivalent scale is based on scores for examinees in the national norm group at the time the normative study is conducted, so that the reported scores are always scaled with reference to a recent norm group. For professional licensure and certification tests, score scales or passing scores sometimes are reestablished when it is judged that the profession or the test content has changed substantially.

One problem with periodic rescaling is that scores from forms given before and after the rescaling are not directly comparable. Thus, examinee scores cannot be compared directly, and trends in performance cannot be assessed directly. To handle this problem, it is sometimes possible to use a transformation that facilitates these sorts of comparisons, at least approximately.

Incorporating normative or content information when a score scale is established can enhance the interpretability of scale scores, at least initially. However, this initial advantage needs to be weighed against the potential disadvantage of misinterpretation of the scores in terms of a current reference population rather than the one on which the scale was actually established. Because of the potential for misuse or misinterpretation of scores in the future, test users need to be educated about the proper use of these scale scores.

Scales for Test Batteries and Composites

In many testing programs, examinees are administered a *test battery* consisting of tests in a variety of areas, and separate scores are provided in each area. In addition, *composite scores* that reflect performance over two or more tests in a battery are often reported to examinees. For example, on the ITBS battery, a mathematics total score is reported that is based on performance on the mathematics concepts, mathematics problem solving, and mathematics computation tests.

TESTS IN A BATTERY

The use of test batteries facilitates the comparison of examinee performance on different tests when the processes of test construction, scaling, and norming are handled in a similar manner for each of the tests in a battery. For scales that are established by incorporating content information, the use of similar procedures for incorporating this information into the scales of the different tests in the battery can lead to comparability in score interpretation across tests. For example, based on judgmental standard-setting techniques, a score of 100 could be used to indicate satisfactory performance on each test in the battery.

The comparison of examinee scores on different tests in a battery can also be enhanced by incorporating normative information into the score scale of each test at the time that the score scales are established. This normative information typically is based on an administration of the whole battery to a particular group of examinees. One way to incorporate normative information is to establish nonlinear raw-to-scale score transformations that result in scale scores on each test in the battery having identical frequency distributions for the reference group. When this is done, scale scores on different tests can be compared without reference to separate norms tables.

Sometimes only the location and spread of the scale scores are set equal for each test in a battery through linear transformations of raw scores to scale scores. When the shapes of score distributions differ, a particular scale score on one test in the battery has a different percentile rank from the same scale score on another test.

For example, a reference group of examinees at the end of the 10th and the beginning of the 11th grades in 1942 was used to establish the score scales for the ITED (1980a, 1980b), using nonlinear transformations. To establish scale scores, the scores on each test were normalized, the mean was set equal to 15, and the standard deviation was set equal to 5 for the reference group. Consider a student in 1942 who earned, say, scale scores of 20 on quantitative thinking and 25 on vocabulary. Because of the way the scores were scaled, we can conclude that, relative to the reference group, this student ranked lower in quantitative thinking than in vocabulary. Because the scores were normalized, facts about the normal curve can be used to conclude that, relative to the reference group, this student was at approximately the 84th percentile in quantitative thinking and the 98th percentile in vocabulary. If normative information had not been incorporated into the score scale, separate norms tables would have been required to make these sorts of comparisons.

To the extent that the reference group is important for score interpretation, the use of a common reference group scale score distribution for all tests in a battery can facilitate score interpretation. For comparing scores on different tests with reference to other groups, auxiliary score scales, such as percentile ranks in these other groups, are needed.

COMPOSITES

Test-score composites are used to summarize examinee performance over two or more tests from a battery. The formation of a composite involves deciding on the desired "contribution" of each test to the composite and the distributional properties of the composite scores if scaling is based on a reference group of examinees. Typically, composite scores are based on linear, rather than nonlinear, combinations of either raw scores or scale scores, and, for this reason, only linear combinations will be considered in this section.

One conception of composites is based solely on test content. As an example, assume that the domain for mathematics achievement is defined as consisting of 50% mathematics computation items and 50% mathematics problem-solving items. Because these problem-solving items take twice as long to administer as computation items and the time limits must be equal, assume there are 40 items on the computation test and only 20 on the problem-solving test. To form a composite that would accurately reflect the mathematics achievement domain, it is necessary to weight the scores on the problem-solving items twice as much as the scores on the computation items. Thus, the contribution of each test to the composite can be defined in terms of proportional representation in the domain of content.

Other definitions of the contribution of a test to a composite require the collection of data on a group of examinees. These definitions take into account moments of the joint distributions of scores on the tests and, often, the reliability of the tests. Wang and Stanley (1970) distinguish between *nominal weights* and *effective weights.* A nominal weight is the weight that is applied to a test score in forming a composite. An effective weight is an index of the contribution of the test to a particular composite. They define the effective weight as the covariance between a test score and the score on a composite. This effective weight (ϵ_i) for test i is defined as

$$\epsilon_i = w_i^2 \sigma_i^2 + w_i \sum_{j \neq i} w_j \sigma_{ij}, \qquad (5)$$

where σ_i^2 is the variance of scale scores on test i, σ_{ij} is the covariance between scale scores on tests i and j, w_i is the nominal weight for test i, and the summation is over all of the tests used to form the composite, except test i. Test scores with larger effective weights are considered to contribute more to the composite than those with smaller effective weights. The proportional effective contribution of a test to the composite can be arrived at by taking $\epsilon_i / \Sigma_i \epsilon_i$.

Because of its complexity, it is difficult to intuitively understand Equation 5. The following simplification might aid in this understanding. Assume that, prior to forming the composite, scores on each test are standardized to have unit variance (e.g., use a z-score transformation). Also assume that all weights associated with these standardized scores in forming the composite are one. Then it can be shown (see Wang & Stanley, 1970) that,

$$\epsilon_i = 1 + \sum_{j \neq i} \rho_{ij}, \qquad (6)$$

where ρ_{ij} is the correlation between tests i and j. In this simplified case, ϵ_i is equal to 1 plus the sum of the correlations between score i and scores on the other variables. Thus, the more related a score is to the other scores, the greater its effective weight.

As a further simplification, consider a case where there are only two tests that form the composite. Then $\epsilon_1 = 1 + \rho_{12}$ and $\epsilon_2 = 1 + \rho_{12}$, so that the effective weights are equal. This implies that equally weighted composites of two standardized test scores with equal variances have equal effective weights. For composites of more than two such scores, the effective weights are equal only when the correlations among test scores are equal. In practice, if the intercorrelations are not too disparate, standardizing and then weighting each standardized score equally might lead to effective weights that are close enough to being equal for practical purposes.

The issue of effective weights can become very complicated. For example, if true scores are considered, then effective weights also involve test reliabilities (Jarjoura & Brennan, 1982, 1983; Feldt & Brennan, this volume).

For many of the unweighted composites formed from tests in a battery, the nominal and effective weights are close to being proportionally equal. Often, tests in a battery are built to be similar in reliability, the scores are scaled to have equal variances, and the scale scores are summed (unweighted) to arrive at the composite. In such cases, so long as the intercorrelations among the tests are not too disparate, the nominal and effective weights will be reasonably similar. However, the difference between nominal and effective weights (in terms of proportional contribution) can be considerable in situations in which tests have very different standard deviations, intercorrelations, or reliability. For example, nominal and effective weights might be quite different for composites formed from multiple-choice and essay examinations. It is important to recognize that effective weights for a particular composite are specific to the group of examinees used in their specification.

In addition to deciding on the contribution of each test to the composite, it is necessary to decide how to scale the composite scores. Composite scores are sometimes formed (e.g., on the ACT tests) by summing the scale scores and dividing by the number of tests in the composite. The variability and distributional shape of composite scores formed in this manner typically differ in variability and distributional shape from the scores on the tests making up the composite. Alternatively, in those situations in which all tests in a battery have been scaled to have the same distributional properties, composite scores are sometimes scaled to have the same distributional properties as scores on each test in the battery. This allows for the relative comparison of performance of examinees on different tests and composites.

Maintaining Scales for Batteries and Composites

When the tests that form a battery are scaled to have the same distributional characteristics, scores on the different tests can be compared without reference to a norms table. However, as test content and the most relevant population of examinees change over time, scale scores on the different tests in a battery usually become less comparable. When, for example, the Scholastic Aptitude Test was scaled in 1942, a score of 500 on the Mathematical test indicated a comparable level of ability, relative to the reference group, as a score of 500 on the Verbal test. However, as measured by the SAT, student performance on Verbal and Mathematical tests has not changed in parallel fashion; the Verbal test would have a different mean in a recent norm group from the Mathematical test. So, over time, the information that is built into a score scale that originally allows scale scores to be compared across tests becomes less useful. Unless periodic rescaling is conducted, it becomes necessary to caution test users against directly comparing scale scores across tests. Instead, interpretative material should stress that the comparison of examinee scores across tests needs to be based on interpretive information such as percentile ranks in relevant norm groups.

The interpretability of composite scores can be problematic when new test forms are introduced. Typically, each test on the new form is equated to its corresponding test on an old (previously equated) form, and this process results in raw-to-scale score conversions for each test in the new form. Sometimes composite scores on the new form are then calculated using the same weights that were used to form the composite with the initial form. If the tests are not parallel and the interrelationships among the tests differ for the two forms, this process leads to composite scores on the new form that, in general, are not comparable to composite scores on the old form. As a simplified situation, consider that the tests on the old and new forms have the same variances, but their covariances differ. On the basis of fundamental results about variances of linear combi-

nations, the variance of linearly derived composite scores on the new form would differ from the variance of these composite scores on the old form. In situations where the longitudinal comparability of composite scores is important, these problems can be avoided by equating composite scores on the new form to composite scores on the old form.

Developmental Score Scales

Elementary school achievement test batteries measure student achievement throughout the elementary grades. Each test in the battery is designed to cover a wide range of content, much of which might not be taught to students until the later grades. The tests are usually administered in levels, to increase the efficiency of the measurement process. For example, the Multilevel Battery of the ITBS has levels intended for the typical student in each of the grades 3 through 8. The levels contain substantial item overlap. For example, on the 6th-grade level of the ITBS Mathematics Problem Solving test, there are items that also appear on the 4th-, 5th-, 7th-, and 8th-grade levels. Given appropriate reading and computational levels, it would not seem unreasonable to expect a superior Grade 4 student to be able to solve many, if not most, of the same story problems as the typical Grade 7 student. However, in an area such as mathematics computation, where even the best Grade 4 student might not have been introduced to any of the fraction or decimal computational algorithms, such performance would seem highly unlikely. Consequently, on the ITBS Mathematics Computation test, item overlap occurs only at adjacent grade levels.

The content represented in all levels of a test from an elementary achievement test battery can be viewed as defining a *developmental continuum* for a particular area of achievement. A *developmental score scale* is used to indicate examinee performance on the continuum for each of the levels of a test. Developmental score scales, in which tests designed for use at different grade levels are calibrated against one another to span several grades, facilitate the estimation of an individual's growth. These score scales also allow for individualized test administration, in which each student in a classroom is administered the test level that corresponds most closely to his or her level of development.

The term *vertical equating* is sometimes associated with the process of forming a developmental score scale, including grade-equivalent scales. However, we strongly prefer that the term *equating* be restricted to situations in which scale scores on multiple forms of a test can be used interchangeably. Because it is unlikely that scale scores from different levels of a test can be used interchangeably, terminology other than *equating* is more appropriate. We prefer the use of the terms *scaling* or *scaling to achieve comparability* to describe the process of forming a developmental scale. The scores resulting from this process should be referred to as *scale scores or comparable scores.*

Introduction to Grade Equivalents

Because the grade framework is so familiar to elementary schoolteachers and parents, the *grade-equivalent* score scale is probably the most popular type of developmental score scale. A grade equivalent is defined with reference to the performance of the typical student in a particular grade. For example, a 6.3 (or, for some tests, 63) would be indicative of the performance of the typical student after the third month of sixth grade.

The construction of grade equivalents can be viewed as involving three possibly interwoven stages. The first stage is to provide a mechanism for rank ordering examinees from a wide range of grade levels on a single developmental continuum. Different procedures for accomplishing rank ordering have been found to produce score scales with very different properties (Cole, 1982; Hoover, 1984a; Mittman, 1958). The outcome of this stage is typically a rank ordering of students on an *interim-score scale* that is used to place examinees on the developmental continuum. In the second stage, the interim-score scale is rescaled by stretching and compressing it at different points to arrive at a scale with the grade-equivalent properties mentioned earlier. The third stage involves providing a mechanism for converting scores earned on each level of the test to the grade-equivalent scale.

The construction of the interim-score scale for ordering examinees requires consideration of the developmental continuum. Content of achievement tests is chosen to be a valid representation of the achievement domain. This content is selected by educators who are most able to specify precisely what the test should measure throughout all of the grade levels of interest. Thus, the most direct way to rank order examinees on the developmental continuum would seem, on the surface, to involve administering all levels of the test battery to examinees in each grade. For example, administration of the test normally taken by seventh graders to a Grade 4 student would indicate directly whether this student has the computational ability of the typical Grade 7 student. However, the collection of these data is beset by practical problems. Even if it were feasible to administer such a long test, much of the content would be inappropriate for students in early grades, which could lead to frustration and lack of motivation on their part. Motivation might also be a problem at the upper grades because of the necessity of responding to many very easy questions. For these reasons, other procedures have been used to construct the interim-score scale.

Any of the potential alternative procedures for constructing the interim scale involve some compromises. One alternative that illustrates some of the issues is the use of raw scores on a single test level as an interim-score scale, where the single level is administered to examinees from all grades of interest. Assume, for example, that the raw-score scale for the fourth-grade level is chosen as the interim-score scale and that the fourth-grade level is administered to students in all grades. Consider a fourth grader and a seventh grader who earn identical raw scores on the fourth-grade level. With the use of the fourth-grade raw-score scale as the interim-score scale, these two examinees are of equal achievement. However, what would happen if these same two examinees were administered the seventh-grade level of the test? It is likely that the seventh grader would perform better than the fourth grader because there is material on the seventh-grade level that the fourth grader would not have been exposed to. Thus, the choice of test level to use in forming the interim-score scale could have a

profound effect on the resulting grade equivalents. For this reason, a single level is rarely used as an interim-score scale. Mittman (1958) illustrated the problems with the methodology in a study involving the fourth- and seventh-grade levels of two ITBS tests.

So far, we have described grade equivalents and illustrated some of the complexities involved in their construction. To provide an example of the process used to construct grade equivalents in one testing program, the construction of the ITBS grade-equivalent scale is described in some detail. The ITBS process is then compared to processes used to construct other grade-equivalent scales. Finally, grade-equivalent scales are compared to other developmental score scales, and issues in interpreting resulting scores are discussed.

The ITBS scaling procedures described in the following section were developed by Professor A. N. Hieronymus at The University of Iowa. They were first applied to Forms 1 and 2 of the ITBS in the 1950s. The entire process would be most appropriately referenced as Hieronymus scaling.

THE ITBS GRADE-EQUIVALENT SCALE

A scaling test was used to define the interim-score scale in the construction of the ITBS grade-equivalent score scale. A scaling test is composed of test items that represent the domain of content over all levels of the test; items are drawn from each level, and the scaling test is designed to be short enough to be administered in a single sitting. Thus, a scaling test is a single set of items chosen to represent the total test and administered in all grades. If the scaling test is truly representative of the total test, it could be expected to measure the same developmental continuum and to rank examinees in approximately the same order as the total test. In the administration of the scaling test for the ITBS, students in lower grades were told that many of the items would be extremely difficult and that they were not expected to be able to answer all of the questions. If they did not know the answer they were instructed to skip the items and explicitly told *not* to guess. Students in upper grades were given similar directions, except they were told that some of the earlier test items might be very easy for them and that they should still do their best.

The scaling test was constructed to be representative of content from low third- through superior eighth-grade levels. This test was then administered to representative samples of examinees from each grade from three through eight. The result of this administration was a distribution of raw scores of examinees for each of these grades on the developmental continuum. To arrive at distributions of true scores for each grade, the true-score distributions for each grade were assumed to have the same shape and mean as the raw-score distributions, but the true-score distributions were assumed to have a variance of $\rho_{xx}\sigma_x^2$ (as would be expected under classical test theory; see Feldt & Brennan, this volume), where ρ_{xx} is the test reliability of the scaling test at a particular grade, estimated using split-half methods. The resulting estimated true-score distributions were used in the scaling process.

Information about the grade-to-grade overlap of score distributions on the developmental continuum is imbedded in the within-grade distributions on the scaling test. For example, the

TABLE 6.3 Score Median for ITBS Language Usage Scaling Test

Grade	Median on Scaling Test	Grade Equivalent
8	23.8	8.5
7	22.0	7.5
6	20.8	6.5
5	18.0	5.5
4	15.6	4.5
3	12.1	3.5

percentage of fifth graders scoring above the sixth-grade median is an indicator of grade-to-grade overlap of the fifth- and sixth-grade score distributions. The following example for the ITBS Language Usage test, adapted from Hieronymus and Lindquist (1974), might help clarify this notion.

The medians of scaling test-score distributions for the ITBS Language Usage test are shown in Table 6.3. In this table the sixth-grade median is a scaling test score of 20.8. Because the scaling test was administered at midyear, the grade equivalent corresponding to a scaling test score of 20.8 is 6.5. This table provides grade equivalents corresponding to scaling test scores of 23.8, 22.0, 20.8, 18.0, 15.6, and 12.1.

Grade-to-grade overlap can be assessed in detail by using the scaling test data. For example, from the data collected for the Language Usage Test on the ITBS, the percentages of students scoring below the sixth-grade median of 20.8 on the scaling test were as follows: 24.4% of the eighth graders, 35.6% of the seventh graders, 50% of the sixth graders (by definition), 68.1% of the fifth graders, 87.0% of the fourth graders, and 98.7% of the third graders. Similar data for all grades are shown in Table 6.4. The column with the heading 6.5 contains the percentages for the sixth-grade median just described. Extrapolation procedures were then used above 8.5 and below 3.5. These extrapolations were performed according to one basic principle: average growth from grade to grade should increase with the level of pupil ability. Not only is such growth indicated by the empirical data between 8.5 and 3.5, but it also makes intuitive sense. It seems likely that students who have learned more rapidly in the past will be more likely to learn more rapidly in the future. In addition, that individual differences increase over time has long been a generally held belief in differential psychology (see Anastasi, 1958, p. 195).

The percentages across a given row of Table 6.4 represent the within-grade percentile ranks on the grade-equivalent scale of each of the grade medians. These values are presented graphically in Figure 6.3 for each grade level given in the first column

of Table 6.4. Smooth curves have been fitted through the plotted values to establish percentile ranks at points in the grade-equivalent scale other than the grade medians (i.e., points other than 3.5, 4.5, . . . , 8.5). This figure presents the grade-to-grade overlap for the Language Usage test and can be conceptualized as a *growth model* illustrating the relationship between grade equivalents and within-grade percentile ranks at midyear. Interpolation between the curves could be used to arrive at curves for students tested other than at midyear. Or, once raw-score-to-grade-equivalent values are obtained for individual test levels as described later, the test levels may be administered at a time other than midyear and grade-equivalent-to-percentile ranks empirically established.

An examination of Figure 6.3 illustrates some of the properties of grade-equivalent scales. Note that, at the 50th percentile, the adjacent curves are 1.0 grade-equivalent unit apart. This occurs because, by definition, growth at the median is 1.0 grade-equivalent unit per year. The other points on the curves depend on the grade-to-grade overlap that results from administering the scaling test. Refer to the 10th percentile on Figure 6.3. Growth at the 10th percentile appears to be approximately 0.7 grade-equivalent units per year. At the 90th percentile, growth is approximately 1.2 grade-equivalent units per year.

Refer again to Figure 6.3. In this figure there is substantial overlap between adjacent grade levels but relatively little overlap between third and eighth grades. For example, the 10th percentile of the eighth-grade distribution is nearly the same as the 90th percentile of the third-grade distribution. In general, tests with content that is more curriculum dependent will show less grade-to-grade overlap. That is, they have steeper curves than those shown in Figure 6.3.

To establish raw-score-to-grade-equivalent conversion tables, a nationally representative sample of students was administered the test level intended for students at their grade level. Percentile ranks of raw scores were then tabulated separately for students at each grade level. For a particular grade level, a raw score was assigned the grade-equivalent value with the same percentile rank as that of the grade equivalent established in the scaling study and illustrated in Figure 6.3. In this manner, raw scores on each test level were converted to grade equivalents. Raw scores on different test levels assigned the same grade equivalent can be thought of as comparable.

Other Designs for Constructing Grade-equivalent Scales

As indicated earlier, the manner in which the interim score scale is formed can have a profound effect on the resulting

TABLE 6.4 Midyear Percentile Ranks of Grade Medians for Each Grade for the Language Usage Test of the ITBS

Grade	Extrapolated 1.5	2.5	Determined from Scaling Study 3.5	4.5	5.5	6.5	7.5	8.5	Extrapolated 9.5	10.5	11.5	12.5
8		0.1	0.9	5.5	13.5	24.4	37.4	50.0	63.9	78.5	91.6	99.1
7		0.4	1.9	10.9	22.7	35.6	50.0	64.6	80.0	92.8	99.3	
6	0.1	0.9	6.6	19.4	34.4	50.0	66.0	81.4	94.5	99.4		
5	0.3	2.6	15.3	31.1	50.0	68.1	85.0	96.5	99.6			
4	0.9	10.5	29.2	50.0	69.6	87.0	98.3	99.8				
3	4.2	24.6	50.0	70.2	88.4	98.7	99.9					

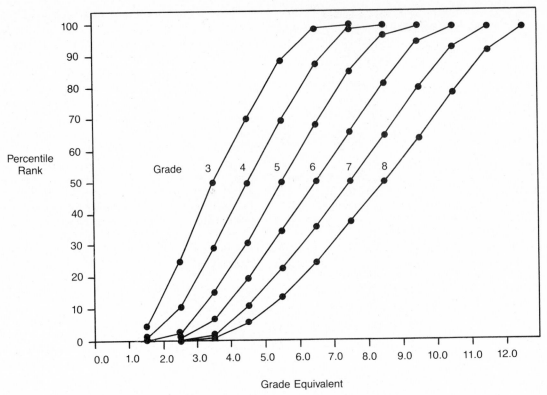

FIGURE 6.3 Midyear growth model: ITBS Language Usage Test.

grade-equivalent score scale. One alternative method is to use an *anchor-test design* instead of the scaling test design. In an anchor-test design, representative groups of examinees are administered the level that is most appropriate for their grade. Anchor-test equating methods discussed later in this chapter are then used to "equate" scores on adjacent levels. These methods require that adjacent levels have at least some items in common or that an anchor test be used to link adjacent levels. By use of the "equating" relationships, scores on each of the levels are converted to an interim score scale. Grade equivalents are then formed in a manner similar to that described earlier. The use of the anchor-test design with common items in adjacent levels of the test has the practical advantage that tests can be scaled without constructing a special scaling test and without a special scaling test administration.

Another design for obtaining grade equivalents (sometimes called the *equivalent-groups design*) is described by Angoff (1984, pp. 123–125). In this design, samples of examinees from adjacent grade levels are combined into a single group. These examinees are then randomly divided into two groups. One group takes the level of the test typically administered at the upper grade level; the other, the level intended for use at the lower grade level. Comparable scores on the adjacent levels are then established, using one of the equating methods described later. An anchor test consisting of representative items from both levels may also be administered to both groups and used in this process.

The scales that result from use of the various data collection designs generally differ. Mittman (1958) conducted an empirical study in which he found that the common-items–anchor-

test design results in grade-equivalent scales that possess greater grade-to-grade overlap than scales constructed by using the scaling test design. As a possible explanation for this greater overlap, consider that items common to the two levels represent the more advanced items on the lower level and the less advanced items on the higher level. Examinees from the lower grade are likely to have been exposed more to the material on the higher level that is covered by the common items than to the higher level material not covered by the common items. Examinees from the upper grade probably would have been exposed to all of the material on both levels. This would result in the size of the difference between the two groups on the developmental continuum being underestimated by their performance on the common items. This, in turn, would lead to the anchor test design producing more grade-to-grade overlap than the scaling test design.

The grade-to-grade overlap produced by the equivalent-groups design is likely less than that for the common-items–anchor-test design, but still more than for the scaling test design. In an equivalent-groups design, examinees at adjacent grade levels are administered not only the items common to the two test levels but also those in either level. However, items on levels of the test intended for grade levels above those being equated are *not* represented. It is still likely that differences in performance between the two grade groups on the entire developmental continuum would be underestimated.

The overestimation of grade-to-grade overlap on the developmental continuum has implications for interpretation. One of the most often repeated criticisms of grade-equivalent scales is that when, for example, a fourth-grade student receives a grade equivalent of 8.2, it is noted that the student did not take the Grade 8 test. However, in the case of a scale constructed by using the scaling test method, a fourth grader obtains such a grade-equivalent value only if some fourth graders scored above the median score for eighth graders on the scaling test, a test containing eighth-grade content. This inclusion of content spanning the developmental continuum is the substantive difference between the scaling test and the anchor test and Angoff designs. As noted earlier, it would seem unlikely that a fourth grader could perform as well as the typical seventh grader on a mathematics computation test containing fractions and decimals. A grade-equivalent value of 7.5 in mathematics computation is well above the 99th percentile for fourth graders on the ITBS. Such a value is not at all unusual on tests scaled by using other data collection designs (Cole 1982).

It needs to be made explicit that the differences between the grade-equivalent scales of test publishers lie mainly in the method of data collection, (e.g., scaling test versus anchor test), *not* in the statistical method used to link the test levels. For example, Hoover (1982) obtained similar scales when applying both equipercentile and item response theory methods to data gathered across six grade levels on language usage and mathematics concepts scaling tests.

OTHER TECHNICAL ISSUES

In addition to questions about which design to use for the construction of grade equivalents, a variety of other issues in the construction of grade equivalents have not been completely resolved. Although we will not address these in depth, we will mention some of them.

Should grade-to-grade overlap be defined on the true-score scale, as with the ITBS, or on the observed-score scale? If the true-score scale is used, how should the true-score distribution be estimated? Keats and Lord (1962) and Lord (1965, 1969) presented alternative methods for estimating true-score distributions that might be beneficial in the construction of developmental score scales. Should guessing be discouraged on the scaling test? If so, how? What are the best interpolation, extrapolation, and smoothing techniques to use?

If the scaling-test design is used, what is the best technique for converting scores on each level to grade equivalents? Phillips (1986) found that Rasch-based methods produced different results than equipercentile-based methods. If an anchor-test design is used, what is the best way to achieve score comparability across levels? Studies by Loyd and Hoover (1980), Petersen, Marco, and Stewart (1982), and Slinde and Linn (1979a, 1979b) address this question.

Are there other sensible ways of defining grade equivalents? Cole (1982) proposed grade development score scales that are similar to grade equivalents in many respects. One major difference is that the score that a student earns depends on her or his grade level. For example, a second and third grader earning the same raw score on the same level of the test would earn different grade development scores. The 3Rs test (Cole, Trent, & Waddell, 1982) was developed by using a grade development score scale, and it was found to produce less grade-to-grade overlap than most grade-equivalent scales.

Typically, constant rate of growth during the school year is assumed when constructing grade equivalents. Does the degree to which this assumption is violated (Beggs & Hieronymus, 1968) result in substantial interpretational problems? What is the maximum value that should be used for grade equivalents? For example, a grade equivalent of 17.0 makes little sense, because the grade levels end at grade 12. For this reason, plus the fact that the curriculum does not change as a function of high school grade, grade equivalents are rarely used for high school level tests.

SOME LIMITATIONS OF GRADE EQUIVALENTS

Grade equivalents have an apparent simplicity of meaning that might lead some practitioners to misinterpret them. The potential for misinterpretation has led to a variety of criticisms of them. There are some limitations that need to be considered.

A grade equivalent should be regarded as an estimate of a student's achievement on a developmental continuum. It does not indicate where he or she should be placed in the graded organization of school. Suppose, for example, that a fifth-grade student earns a grade equivalent of 7.4, which ranks at the 90th percentile of fifth graders in the fall. This grade equivalent indicates that the student scored as well on the developmental continuum as the typical seventh-grade student, and it indicates that the student scored above the average fifth grader. The grade equivalent of 7.4 does not necessarily indicate readiness for the seventh-grade curriculum or that the student should skip fifth and sixth grades. The student's performance in other achievement areas, the student's maturity, school policies, and a variety of other issues would need to be considered before any reasonable decisions about the student's future education could be made.

A second possible misinterpretation occurs when examinee performance is compared in different achievement areas. A score in reading that is 2 years below grade level could be associated with a very different percentile rank than a score in mathematics computation that is 2 years below grade level, because the grade-to-grade overlap is different for these two areas. If a student's performance in one achievement area is to be compared with his or her performance in another achievement area, based on how he or she ranks with other students, then percentile ranks are more appropriate than grade equivalents.

Grade equivalents resulting from a scaling procedure necessarily depend on the group of examinees used in the procedure and on their educational experiences. Even if a nationally representative group of examinees is used to construct grade equivalents, the appropriateness of the grade-equivalent scale for examinee subgroups can be questioned. Characteristics of the local situation could influence grade-to-grade overlap. An example of such influences is a local course of study that deviates from general practice in the longitudinal placement of skills in the curriculum. Hieronymus and Lindquist (1974) suggest, however, that, in many cases, the amount of grade-to-grade overlap is very similar for different types of schools. As an example, they provide data showing such similarity for large city schools, compared with the national norm group. Still, the issue of placement of skills in the local curriculum needs to be considered when interpreting the results from elementary achievement test batteries.

As indicated earlier, the grade-equivalent scales of different publishers for the same content area are far from comparable. However, the apparent similarity of these scales invites comparison.

OTHER DEVELOPMENTAL SCALES

Grade-oriented score scales might not be very useful for schools that employ other types of organization, such as non-graded and continuous progress, or for schools making major adjustments in age grouping or employing flexible grouping. Age-equivalent score scales might be more appropriate in such situations. Age-equivalent scales are continuous developmental scales that are referenced to age groups rather than to grade groups. The construction of such scales is similar to that of grade equivalents. Grade equivalents are used more often than age equivalents because most schools are grade oriented.

In addition to reporting scores on a grade-equivalent scale, most elementary level achievement batteries also report scores on a *developmental standard score scale.* Such scales are constructed by using a psychometric model that is intended to produce an "equal interval" scale.

Developmental standard scores have traditionally been constructed by using Thurstone scaling procedures. In Thurstone scaling, an interim-score scale is formed, just as in the construction of grade equivalents. The within-grade distributions are then normalized. These normalized distributions are placed on the same developmental standard score scale by taking into account the mean and standard deviation of each within-grade distribution. Flanagan (1951, pp. 732–738) described this process in detail and Angoff (1984, pp. 17–19) commented on the process.

Thurstone scaling is based on the assumption that within-grade achievement is normally (symmetrically) distributed. This assumption of within-grade normality seems to be unwarranted in most areas of achievement. For example, in a subject matter area such as reading, the achievement of children beginning school is apt to be markedly skewed to the right, because most children cannot read at all, whereas a few can read very well. Noting the unrealistic nature of the normality assumption, Gardner (1966) suggested using a Pearson Type III distribution, which allows for positive and negative skewness, rather than a normal distribution, as a basis for fitting within-grade distributions.

Item response theory methods have also been used to construct developmental standard score scales. CTB/McGraw-Hill (1986) employed a three-parameter IRT model to develop the score scales used with the *Comprehensive Tests of Basic Skills* and the *California Achievement Tests.* For the *Stanford Achievement Tests* and the *Metropolitan Achievement Tests,* the Psychological Corporation (1985) used the Rasch model. Data are typically gathered in one of the ways described in the development of a grade-equivalent scale. The parameters of the IRT model are estimated and the resulting θ-scale or a linear transformation of θ is used as the basis for score reporting. Hoover (1984a, 1984b) pointed out some limitations of

scores from an achievement battery reported on a θ-scale. IRT scaling is based on the assumption that achievement is unidimensional. Yen (1985) discussed some of the problems that might occur when this assumption is violated. Even if the IRT model were to hold, there is no reason to believe that the θ-scale is the optimal "equal interval" scale from an educational point of view. A monotonic transformation of the θ-scale might be more appropriate educationally. For example, Lord (1975) describes a situation in which the IRT model held but a monotonic transformation of θ was preferable to θ for interpretational reasons.

In summary, to be useful, developmental standard scores require the assumptions that a particular scaling model holds and that the scale produced by the model is educationally relevant. It is questionable that these models hold for elementary achievement test batteries. Developmental standard scores have been found to produce patterns of growth that some consider to be educationally unreasonable (Hoover, 1984a), and they express growth in units that do not have a direct relationship to norm groups the way that grade equivalents do. Although there could be some technical or theoretical reasons for using developmental standard scores (Burket, 1984), in the elementary grades they seem to be much less useful educationally than grade equivalents.

Norming

Normative data are crucial to many score interpretations. Norms provide a basis for comparing the achievement of an individual examinee with that of a relevant group of examinees. For test batteries, norms allow for the analysis of a student's relative strengths and weaknesses through a comparison of the student's performance on each test in the battery with every other test in the battery. Norms are a description of achievement; they are not a standard or an indicator of satisfactory achievement. What constitutes satisfactory achievement depends on a variety of concerns that could include, for example, objectives of instruction and the decisions to be made. To be useful, *a particular set of norms needs to be relevant to the desired interpretation of examinee performance.* The group of examinees used in the construction of norms needs to be representative of the population with which comparisons are to be made, and the size of the sample needs to be sufficient for producing accurate estimation.

Norms provide a statistical description of test performance for a group. Summary statistics such as means, standard deviations, and percentile ranks are used to convey norms. Some norms describe a group of examinees, whereas others describe the average performance of aggregates of examinees such as schools or school districts. Many issues relevant to norms as they relate to score scales were already addressed in the preceding sections of this chapter. In this section we consider issues central to the collection and interpretation of normative data, and we focus on the use of percentile ranks for the presentation of normative data. Angoff's (1984) discussion of norms should be consulted as supplementary material. In addition, many educational measurement texts provide good introductions to norms (e.g., Mehrens & Lehmann, 1984).

Norms and Norm Groups

The usefulness of norms in a particular situation depends on the relevance of the norm group to the interpretation that is to be made. For some purposes, norms based on a nationally representative group of examinees are most relevant. For other purposes, norms based on a local group are most appropriate. In any case, norms based on one group can be quite different from norms based on another group.

For example, consider a student who scores at the 80th percentile nationally among college-bound students on a college entrance examination. This student is well above average among college-bound students and would seem to have a reasonably good chance for success at many colleges. Suppose, however, that this student is interested in attending a highly selective college where the score that was at the 80th percentile nationally is only at the 10th percentile at the highly selective college. Based on this information, the test score suggests that the student's chances for success at (and possibly admittance to) the highly selective college are not very high.

The preceding example indicates that different norms can be relevant for different purposes and that an individual can rank quite differently in different norm groups. The national norms can suggest whether a student should consider attending college. The norms for the highly selective college are more relevant to the question of whether or not the student should consider attending this particular college. This example also illustrates the profound effect that the norm group can have on the percentile ranks reported.

Normative data often make possible the evaluation of a student's relative strengths and weaknesses on the tests in a test battery. Without normative information, questions such as "Is a student more able in mathematics or language skills?" might seem nonsensical. However, normative data allow for this sort of comparison, albeit only with reference to a particular norm group. A student who scores at the 90th percentile in mathematics and at the 60th percentile in language skills can be said to rank higher in mathematics than in language skills, with reference to the group of examinees used to establish the norms. Of course, comparisons such as these need to take into account the reliability of difference scores (see Feldt and Brennan, this volume).

Consider the data shown in Table 6.5 for the Grade 8 language tests of the ITBS. These data illustrate that profile comparisons can be greatly influenced by the norm group used. In Table 6.5, Iowa percentile ranks of 50 and 10 are shown in the left-hand column, and national percentile ranks corresponding to the same score are shown in the body of the table. For instance, the same score that yields an Iowa percentile rank of 50 in spelling yields a national percentile rank of 62. This

information indicates that eighth graders in Iowa perform better on the ITBS language tests than the national group. More importantly, the data in the table indicate that these differences are not uniform across the tests, which has an effect on individual student profile comparisons. A student at the 50th percentile on the Iowa norms in both spelling and punctuation would be considered equal in these two areas with respect to the Iowa norms. However, with respect to the national norms, this same student would be considered much better in punctuation than in spelling. For achievement tests, differences such as those found in Table 6.5 can often be traced to curriculum differences. It seems likely that capitalization and punctuation receive relatively greater curricular emphasis in the seventh and eighth grades in Iowa than in the rest of the nation.

A description of the group of examinees used in the construction of test norms is one basis for distinguishing among different types of norms. The type of score, such as subtest score, item score, or difference score, is another way to distinguish among types of norms. In addition, the sampling unit of interest is an important consideration. For example, norms for school averages typically are quite different from norms for individual students.

NATIONAL NORMS

Norms based on a nationally representative sample of the nation's individuals at the age or educational level for which the test is designed are referred to as *national norms*. For instance, national eighth-grade norms for an educational achievement test are designed to reference a student's test performance to that of a representative national sample of eighth graders. National norms have the advantage of being relevant to all students in the nation. National norms provide a basis for comparing any examinee's score on an individual test and any examinee's profile of scores on a battery with norms that represent estimates of performance for a relevant national population.

NATIONAL SUBGROUP NORMS

National normative data are sometimes provided for separate subgroups of examinees. These subgroups might be identified by gender, ethnic group, school type (e.g. public and private), large city, or ability level on a different test. These *national subgroup norms* allow for the comparison of the performance of an individual from a particular subgroup with that of a nationally representative sample from that subgroup. In addition to aiding in the interpretation of the performance of individual examinees, subgroup norms facilitate the comparison of examinee subgroups with one another.

TABLE 6.5 National Percentile Ranks Corresponding to Iowa Percentile Ranks for Grade 8 on the ITBS Language Tests

IOWA PERCENTILE RANK	NATIONAL PERCENTILE RANK OF SAME SCALE SCORE			
	SPELLING	CAPITALIZATION	PUNCTUATION	USAGE
50	62	74	80	65
10	16	25	31	20

NORMS BY AGE AND GRADE

The construction of age and grade equivalents, which are normative score scales, was already discussed. For elementary achievement test batteries, percentile ranks within age or grade groups are often reported in addition to age or grade equivalents. As indicated earlier, percentile ranks present a very different indication of growth from year to year than does the grade-equivalent scale. A student who remains at the 10th percentile over the elementary school years usually falls further and further behind in terms of the grade-equivalent scale. Together, percentile ranks and grade-equivalent scores provide more information than either of the two score types alone.

LOCAL NORMS

Norms based on examinees from a particular educational or geographical unit are referred to as *local norms.* Local norms can often be collected in a way that allows for their use in making specific educational decisions. For example, for individualizing instruction, it is often important to know how a student ranks in relation to his or her classmates. For placement decisions, the relationships of test scores to performance in specific courses at an institution are often of primary importance. In these instances, local norms can be more useful than national norms. In addition to being based on the group involved in decision making, local norms are based on the group with which the test user has direct experience.

USER NORMS

Norms based on those examinees who happen to have taken a test during a given time period are referred to as *user norms.* In many testing programs, user norms are the only norms available.

The college-bound norms on the ACT Assessment tests and the SAT that are based on the examinees who are administered these tests over a given time period are widely used user norms. These user norms cannot be viewed as nationally representative. For instance, the SAT is administered proportionally more on the east and west coasts, and the ACT is used more in the middle of the country. The usefulness of user norms for interpreting individuals' scores is limited because the examinees are necessarily self-selected and do not reflect any educationally or demographically definable population.

The lack of a nationally representative and well-defined norm group creates some problems in comparing group performance on the ACT or SAT tests. Changes in the makeup of the candidate pool are confounded with the test performance of groups of examinees. For example, just on the basis of ACT and SAT norms, it is difficult to identify the sources of the test-score decline that took place in the 1970s. Because the composition of the user groups changed during that period, it is possible that the score declines were related to changes in demographic characteristics of test takers. These issues are considered in depth in the reports of the Congressional Budget Office (1986, 1987) and the College Board (1977).

User norms for the ACT and SAT can facilitate score interpretation, despite their lack of national representativeness and its associated problems just described. The ACT and SAT

groups are fairly stable, at least over short periods of time (say 3 – 5 years). This stability is sufficient to allow the norms to be used for meaningful profile comparisons and to allow an examinee to assess, reasonably accurately, where she or he stands in relation to a group of college-bound students. In addition, these college-bound norms are usually supplemented by norms based on students from a particular college. As indicated earlier, these local college norms are often more relevant for decision making than the college-bound norms.

In some cases, the group of examinees who take a test can be viewed as the *population of interest* for a given decision or set of decisions. This is often the case in licensure and certification testing programs, where all of the individuals attempting to be certified or licensed during a particular time period are tested and included in the norms; in such cases, user norms can be quite valuable. However, even in these cases, it is important to consider whether or not examinee data should be pooled over test dates. In programs in which there are two or more test dates per year, norms based on pooling examinee data from the two or more test dates (provided the test scores are equated) might make the most sense, especially when there are large differences in mean scores between the test dates. In programs in which many examinees take the test more than once, it is often desirable to base the norms on first-time test takers.

CONVENIENCE NORMS

Sometimes norms are based on a group of examinees that happens to be available at the time the test was constructed. For example, a test developer might be able to administer only a reading test to a local group of students to develop norms, even though the test is intended for nationwide use. Or, when a new test is initially developed, it might only be possible to report norms for the group of examinees that happens to take the test on the first test date. In either of these cases, the convenience norms that are developed have very limited usefulness, and it is the responsibility of the test developer to point this out to potential test users.

NORMS FOR SCHOOL AVERAGES

Norms for school averages are used to compare the average test results from one school with the average test results from a national sample of schools. Norms for school averages are constructed by sampling schools from a population of schools, administering the test to students in the schools, tabulating the average score for each school, and forming percentile ranks for the school averages. In this process, the school is considered the unit of analysis.

Norms for school averages can differ markedly from norms for student scores. Consider that the mean score of the highest scoring school will be lower than the score of the highest scoring student in that school. Also, the mean score of the lowest scoring school will be higher than the score of the lowest scoring student in that school. Therefore, school averages are less variable than student scores, and the percentile rank of a particular score will be more extreme in the norms for school averages than in the norms for student averages.

Even though school norms and student norms are different, both can be useful for interpreting the average performance in a school. The national percentile rank in *student norms* of the school average can be interpreted as the percentile rank of the *average student* in the school *among students* in the nation. The national percentile rank in *school norms* of the school average indicates where the *school* ranks *among schools.*

As an example of this distinction, suppose that the mean score for School A is at the 90th percentile in the school norms and at the 75th percentile in the student norms. On the basis of school norms, School A is among the top 10% of the schools in the nation. On the basis of student norms, the average student in School A is at the 75th percentile among students nationwide.

The distinction between student and school norms is often a source of confusion, and, if it is misinterpreted, misleading conclusions can result. It has been recommended that student norms not be reported for school averages (American Psychological Association [APA], 1974). However, it is not uncommon for this interpretation to be made when school norms are used. Reporting of both requires that a distinction be made between the two. The explanation of school norms to test users should be detailed and clear on this point, to avoid confusion.

As noted earlier, normative data make it possible to evaluate the profile of relative strengths and weaknesses on a test battery. However, it is extremely difficult to obtain norms for other than school (building) averages; for example, classrooms, school systems, or states. For either the superintendent of a large district or a classroom teacher, the percentile rank of the average student should facilitate profile comparisons.

In situations in which the sole purpose of a test is to compare groups of examinees rather than individuals, methodology for constructing norms has been developed that is intended to minimize testing time by administering any examinee very few items over an area. Even though the number of items administered to an examinee is too small to precisely estimate the achievement of individual examinees, the methodology is intended to allow for precise estimation of group averages and of norms for group averages.

This type of methodology involves item sampling. Examinees are administered a sample of items considered to be drawn from a population of items. The different methods can be distinguished by the way items are administered to examinees and by the statistical methods used to estimate norms. Lord and Novick (1968) describe one set of schemes that they referred to as *matrix sampling.* Bock and Mislevy (1981) and Mislevy and Bock (1983) describe a method based on an item response theory model for group data and an application of the model to data from the California Assessment. Messick, Beaton, and Lord (1983) describe an intended application of item sampling methods with an item response theory model used to generate norms for the National Assessment of Educational Progress.

ITEM AND SKILL NORMS

For elementary-level achievement test batteries, norms based on performance on specific items or sets of items are sometimes provided. These item and skill norms may be used to aid in assessing specific strengths and weaknesses of individual students. Item norms are typically presented as the percentage of students in the norm group that correctly answer an item. For items that cover a particular skill, skill norms represent the average percentage of items correctly answered by examinees in the norm group. Item and skill norms can provide useful information. However, for individuals, only tentative decisions should be made on the basis of item- or skill-level data. Test scores of individuals at this level are apt to be unreliable, due to the small number of items on which these scores are based.

Item and skill norms are also useful for comparing group performance with that of a national group in specific content areas. Through the use of item and skill norms, the performance of a classroom or school system on specific items and skills can be compared with the performance of a national sample.

Technical Issues in Norm Development

National norming studies are designed to estimate test-score characteristics for a national population of examinees. These test-score characteristics normally include population means, standard deviations, and percentile ranks. Norming involves drawing a representative sample of examinees from the population and administering these examinees the test to be normed. Norming requires that the population of examinees and the design used for drawing the sample from the population be specified.

Many of the concerns that arise in developing national norms are in the domain of the design of sample surveys. Cochran (1977), Kish (1965), and Yates (1981) are among the authors who have treated the general area of sample survey design. Jaeger (1984) specifically addressed sampling issues in educational applications. Angoff (1984) and Lord (1959) discussed some of the sampling issues as they specifically pertain to test norms. Refer to these sources for a more in-depth discussion of sampling than can be provided in this chapter.

The focus of the present discussion is on the development of norms for the whole national population of examinees. Similar issues are of concern in the development of national subgroup and national school norms.

SOME SAMPLING CONCEPTS

Norms are defined for a population of examinees, referred to as the *population of interest.* For example, in a national norming study of a tenth-grade achievement test, the population of interest could be defined as all tenth-grade students enrolled in the United States. The characteristic or characteristics to be estimated (e.g., means, percentile ranks) are also specified. For the purposes of discussion, assume that π is the *population characteristic* or *population parameter* to be estimated.

A process for sampling examinees from the population is specified, and it is referred to as a *sampling design.* A sample is drawn, the test is administered, and the population parameter is estimated. Refer to $\hat{\pi}$ as this sample estimate of π. Conceive of sampling and estimating the population parameter a large number of times. Define E as the expectation operator over this large number of replications. Then $E(\hat{\pi})$ is the expected value of $\hat{\pi}$ over repeated applications of the sampling process.

Define *bias* as $E(\hat{\pi}) - \pi$. That is, bias is the difference between the expected value of the estimated population parameter and the population parameter. In norming studies, bias typically results from practical problems that cause the sample to be nonrepresentative. For example, many schools or school districts that are asked to participate in norming studies decline, and this nonresponse can lead to bias.

Define *sampling error variance* as $E[\hat{\pi} - E(\hat{\pi})]^2$ and *mean-squared error* as $E(\hat{\pi} - \pi)^2$. It can be shown that mean-squared error is equal to the sum of squared bias and sampling error variance.

The design of the norming study is intended to result in a practically acceptable level of mean-squared error by controlling error variance and bias. The sampling design and its associated sample size are the primary means of controlling sampling error variance. The primary means of controlling bias is ensuring that the sample is representative of the population of interest.

CONTROLLING SAMPLING ERROR VARIANCE

There are a variety of sampling designs, and norming studies usually use a combination of these designs. In *simple random sampling,* each examinee in the population has an equal and independent probability of being included in the sample. *Stratified random sampling* is sometimes used to decrease error variance. In stratified random sampling, the population of interest is divided into strata on the basis of an examinee characteristic. For example, the United States could be divided into geographical regions (e.g., Northeast, Southeast), with each region defining a stratum. In stratified random sampling, a sample of fixed size is drawn from each stratum, and the sample sizes might differ across strata. The estimates from the different strata are often weighted differentially to estimate the population parameter. Stratification can potentially decrease error variance to the extent that the strata differ on the measured variable.

In *systematic sampling,* every Cth examinee is chosen from the population after the first examinee is randomly chosen from among the first C examinees in the population. As an example, assume that a sample of 20 is to be drawn from a population size of 100. A random number is drawn from among the first five integers. The systematic sample then is the examinee indexed by the random number and every fifth examinee after that. If the random integer chosen was three, then the systematic sample would consist of examinees 3, 8, 13, . . . 98.

If the examinees are ordered randomly, then systematic sampling is the same as simple random sampling. If the examinees are ordered on a variable related to the measured variable, then systematic sampling could result in substantially lower sampling error variance than simple random sampling.

In the development of norms, it is usually impractical to use simple random, stratified random, or systematic sampling to sample individual students. In general, it is more practical to sample schools or school districts first and then use all or a subset of all of the students in the school or in the school district. This process of sampling schools or districts, where the interest is in norms for individuals, is referred to as *cluster sampling.* In cluster sampling for norms, it is usually necessary to weight each school by some function of school size in arriving at the estimate.

Cluster sampling typically requires testing many more students than would be required with simple random sampling to achieve the same sampling error variance. Angoff (1984) suggested that, in some cases, 25 times as many examinees would need to be tested in cluster sampling, as compared with the number needed to achieve equivalent sampling error variance with simple random sampling of examinees. In the development of norms, sampling error variance for cluster sampling is larger to the extent that schools differ on the measured variable.

Cluster sampling is often combined with other methods in the test norming process. In one combination, the population of schools or school districts is stratified, and the schools or school districts are selected within strata, using cluster sampling. School size, geographic region, school type (e.g., public and private), and community socioeconomic status are often-used stratification variables. Systematic sampling is sometimes used by itself or in combination with stratification methods in the process of sampling schools. Stratified and systematic sampling methods can lead to substantial decreases in sampling error variance when used in combination with cluster sampling.

Two-stage sampling is sometimes used along with cluster sampling to decrease error variance in relation to the number of students given a test. In a norming study using two-stage sampling, schools might be selected in the first stage using cluster sampling, and students might be sampled from within schools as a second stage.

As an example of two-stage sampling, consider that a norming study of tenth-grade English and mathematics tests with equal time limits is being conducted. First, a cluster sample of schools is drawn. Assume that the test booklets are packaged so that an English booklet is followed by a mathematics booklet, and so on. If the books are distributed within the schools in the packaged order, then every other student would receive a mathematics book. This distribution process leads to a systematic sample of students taking English and a systematic sample taking mathematics within each classroom. Thus, in this example, the first stage is a cluster sample of schools and the second stage for either mathematics or English is a systematic sample of students within school.

In designing a norming study, a maximum acceptable amount of sampling error variance for estimating the population characteristics is usually stated. Within the practical constraints that are operating, a sampling design and sample size are selected that will lead to no greater than the maximum stated acceptable sampling error variance.

CONTROLLING SAMPLING BIAS

The process of developing national norms requires that the population of interest be specified clearly. Decisions need to be made about whether or not to include special schools and students (e.g., students requiring special administration conditions).

Once this population is identified, it is necessary to obtain a list of sampling units. In norming studies, these sampling units are normally schools or school districts. The lists of schools or school districts need to be complete and up to date, or sampling bias could result.

Schools or school districts are invited to voluntarily participate in national norming studies. Baglin (1981) points out that a substantial proportion of invited schools or school districts typically do not agree to participate, and this nonparticipation can lead to serious sampling bias. Various means can be used to attempt to increase participation. Free score reports and acknowledgment of the participating school or school districts in the technical report are often-used incentives. Participation might also be increased by contacting schools far enough in advance of the study and with enough flexibility in the dates of test administration that there is sufficient time to incorporate the test administration into school schedules. Also, it might be possible to increase participation by shortening administration time. Administration time sometimes can be shortened by having each student take only a subset of the tests to be administered.

Regardless of the methods used to encourage schools to participate in norming studies, there always seems to be a substantial nonparticipation rate. There are some methods that can be used to reduce sampling bias due to nonparticipation, however.

If nonparticipation were random, or at least unrelated to test score, then it would be easy to handle. We would just invite additional schools to participate, and there would be no additional sampling bias due to nonparticipation. However, it seems much more likely that there is a relationship between participation and test scores. Thus, just adding more schools would probably lead to substantial sampling bias.

One means of addressing this nonparticipation problem is to draw a secondary sample in addition to the primary sample. Each school or school district in the secondary sample is matched with a school or school district in the primary sample on such characteristics as size, geographical region, and school type. If a primary sample school or school district declines to participate, then its matched secondary school or school district is contacted. A third and fourth sample might also be used.

This process of using multiple samples could possibly reduce sampling bias. At a minimum, through the use of this process, the school or school districts being administered the test will appear to be representative, because the proportional representation on the matched characteristics in the schools or school districts tested will be similar to their proportional representation in the primary sample. Thus, for example, the proportion of schools from the Northeast in the sample tested would be similar to their proportion in the primary sample.

Student nonparticipation is another potentially serious source of sampling bias. In conducting a norming study, it is important to stress in the instructions that all students to be included in the study need to be tested. If, for example, schools decide to test only their highest achieving students, then sampling bias would certainly occur. Even if schools attempt to test all students, some students will be absent on the day the norming study is conducted. If these students are not representative of the student body, then sampling bias will probably result. Sometimes the problem of student nonparticipation can be lessened by encouraging schools to have a makeup period for students who were absent when the test was administered.

Sampling bias is potentially a very serious problem that is difficult to control. It is important in the design and execution of the study to minimize sampling bias by attempting to increase school and student participation rates. It is often better to have a smaller, more representative sample than to have a larger, less representative sample.

The participation rates of schools and students and the characteristics of the students tested need to be documented so that test users can judge the adequacy of the sampling process for themselves. The technical documentation of the norming study *should indicate the composition* of the group of students tested on such characteristics as geographical region, socioeconomic status, ethnic group, and gender and compare these characteristics with the corresponding characteristics of the national population.

Where weighting has been used to improve the estimation of a population parameter, the composition of the weighted sample on which norms are actually based, as well as the composition of the population of interest, should be indicated.

Special Issues

One technical problem that sometimes arises in developing norms is how to construct norms on a full-length test when only a portion of the test is administered to examinees. Lord (1965, 1969, 1980) describes some methods based on strong true-score theory that address this problem for number-correct multiple-choice tests, when the portion of the test that is administered is constructed to be representative of the full-length test. Angoff (1984, pp. 81–83) described some other methods of accomplishing this purpose.

When percentile ranks are the norms of interest, methods of smoothing the observed-score distributions could potentially improve the estimation by reducing sampling error variance. Angoff (1984, p. 12) describes a method he attributes to Cureton and Tukey (1951), in which the distribution is smoothed by using weighted averages of frequencies. Lord's (1965, 1969, 1980) strong true-score models may also be used to smooth frequency distributions. Silverman (1986) describes a variety of methods for smoothing distributions that also seem promising for norming applications.

Equating

Many testing programs use multiple forms of the same test. In situations such as college admission, where decisions are made about people who might have taken the test at different administrations during a year or in different years, the primary reason for having multiple forms of a test is to maintain security and fairness. If the same questions were used at each administration, they would gradually become known, and people taking the test at a later administration would have an obvious advantage over those who had taken it earlier. In situations such as program evaluation, where it is necessary to retest people, the primary reason for having different forms of a test is to insure that a person's score is a measure of his or her current level of competence and not a measure of ability to recall questions asked on the form initially administered.

Although different forms for a given test are built to be very similar in content, format, and types and ranges of difficulty of the questions asked, the actual questions used might all be different in each form. Thus, two forms of a test cannot be expected to be precisely equivalent in level and range of difficulty. As a consequence, any comparison of raw scores on the two forms of the test would be unfair to the people who happened to take the more difficult form.

Whenever scores on different test forms are to be compared, it is necessary that they be equivalent in some sense. Statistical procedures, referred to as *equating methods,* have been developed to deal with this problem. Equating methods are empirical procedures for establishing a relationship between raw scores on two test forms that can then be used to express the scores on one form in terms of the scores on the other form. When equating is successful, it becomes possible to measure examinees' growth, to chart trends in the variable measured, and to compare or merge data, even when the separate pieces of data derive from different forms of a test with somewhat different item characteristics.

Conditions for Equated Scores

The purpose of equating is to establish, as nearly as possible, an effective equivalence between raw scores on two test forms. Because equating is an empirical procedure, it requires a design for data collection and a rule for transforming scores on one test form to scores on another. Viewed simply as an empirical procedure, an equating method imposes no restrictions on the properties of the scores to be equated or on the method used to determine the transformation. It is only when we contemplate the purpose of equating and try to define what is meant by an effective equivalence between scores on two test forms that it becomes necessary to impose restrictions.

Many practioners would agree with Lord (1980) that scores on test X and test Y are equated if the following four conditions are met:

1. Same Ability—the two tests must both be measures of the same characteristic (latent trait, ability, or skill).
2. Equity—for every group of examinees of identical ability, the conditional frequency distribution of scores on test Y, after transformation, is the same as the conditional frequency distribution of scores on test X.
3. Population Invariance—the transformation is the same regardless of the group from which it is derived.
4. Symmetry—the transformation is invertible, that is, the mapping of scores from form X to form Y is the same as the mapping of scores from form Y to form X.

The equity condition stems from Lord's (1980) argument that, if an equating of scores on tests X and Y is to be equitable, it must be a matter of indifference to each examinee which test she or he takes. If two tests were not both measures of the same characteristic, in the sense that inches and centimeters are both measures of length, for example, it would not be a matter of indifference to most examinees which test they took, because most people are not equally competent in all areas. However, for the indifference condition to be fully satisfied, it is not sufficient that the tests both be measures of the same characteristic. It must also be a matter of indifference to examinees at every ability level which form of the test they take. For example, if the two forms were not equally reliable, the more competent examinee would probably prefer to take the form with the smaller error variance so that his or her competence would be sure to be identified, and the less competent examinee would probably prefer to take the less reliable form in the hope of benefiting from a score with a large error variance. Taken to its extreme, the equity condition requires that the standard error of measurement and the higher order moments for any group of individuals of identical ability be the same for both tests when the scores are expressed on a common scale. To fully satisfy this requirement, scores on the two tests to be equated must be either perfectly reliable or strictly parallel after conversion (i.e., a given examinee will have the same true score and error variance on each test), in which case equating is not necessary (Lord, 1980).

In reality, equating is necessary because of our recognition that it is impossible to construct multiple forms of a test that are strictly parallel. Equating is used to fine-tune the test-construction process. This does not necessarily mean that the equity condition should be deleted from the definition of equated scores. Inclusion of the equity condition might help us to better understand the goal of equating.

The population invariance and symmetry conditions follow from the purpose of equating: to produce an effective equivalence between scores. If scores on two forms of a test are equivalent, then there is a one-to-one correspondence between the two sets of scores. This implies that the conversion must be unique, that is, the transformation must be the same regardless of the groups of individuals used to derive the conversion. And, it further requires that the equating transformation be invertible. That is, if score y_o on test Y is equated to score x_o on test X, then x_o must equate to y_o. Therefore, the equating problem is not simply a regression problem, because, in general, the regression of x on y does not coincide with the regression of y on x. Thus, all regression methods are excluded as potential equating procedures.

The same-ability and population-invariance constraints imposed on the concept of equated scores go hand in hand. For, if the two tests were measures of different abilities, then the conversions would certainly differ for different groups. A conversion table relating scores on a mathematics test to scores on a verbal test developed from data on men, for example, would be noticeably and predictably different from a similar conversion table developed from data on women because, in our society, women tend to do less well than men on mathematics tests. This is not to say that conversions between scores on tests measuring different characteristics are not useful or appropriate in some situations, but they do not satisfy the purpose of equating, which is to establish an effective equivalence between scores (Angoff, 1963).

Unfortunately, in practice, the four conditions of same-ability, equity, population-invariance, and symmetry can never be fully satisfied. Consequently, there is some disagreement among practitioners as to what equating is and what methods can be used. There seems to be general agreement among practitioners that equated scores should satisfy the population-invariance and symmetry conditions. The disagreements revolve primarily around the equity condition and, to a lesser extent, around the same-ability condition.

Although all practitioners would probably agree that scores on two tests to be equated must be measures of the same characteristic, there is some disagreement as to whether that same characteristic must be unidimensional. Strictly speaking, if scores on two multidimensional tests satisfied the equity, the population-invariance, and the symmetry conditions, it would be a matter of indifference to each examinee which form of the test she or he took. The disagreement stems from the fact that, on a multidimensional test, two people could receive the same score for different reasons. For example, if questions on a test were a measure of both verbal and mathematical abilities, one person might obtain a given score because of verbal skill, and another person might obtain that same score because of mathematical skill. No attempt will be made here to answer the question of whether or not a definition of equated scores should require like scores on the same test to have the same meaning. However, when two tests measure a combination of skills, even the exact same combination of skills, it is unlikely that the population-invariance condition will be satisfied, because not all subpopulations will have the same distribution of ability on each skill measured.

The equity condition is unlikely to be precisely satisfied in practice. Although it might be possible to build two forms of a test that measured the same characteristic and were equally reliable generally, it is highly unlikely that one could ever build two forms that were equally reliable at every ability level, let alone that produced the same conditional frequency distributions. Because of the impossibility of meeting this "strong" equity condition, some practitioners have suggested that it be removed altogether from the list of conditions for equated scores; others have suggested that it be replaced by the "weak" equity condition that, for every group of examinees of identical ability, the conditional mean score on test Y, after transformation, must be the same as the conditional mean score on test X (Morris, 1982). If, in the definition of equated scores, the strong equity condition were to be replaced by the weak equity condition, it would be possible to equate scores on two forms of a test that differ in difficulty or reliability. This weak definition of equated scores does not fully satisfy the indifference condition, a high-ability examinee might still prefer to take the more reliable test. However, it would insure equity in the sense that an examinee's expected score would be the same on both tests. Moreover, it would provide a more realistic goal, as it might be possible to build two forms of the same test that differ only in difficulty or reliability.

Unfortunately, even if we could build two tests that measured the same characteristic(s) and satisfied the weak equity requirement, we would still stumble over the requirement that the equating be population invariant. Unlike the measurement of physical characteristics, such as the measurement of length, the characteristics measured by a test might differ somewhat from one group of individuals to another. This is especially true of achievement or subject matter tests. For example, biology test scores that are equated for the subgroup of all high school students who have just completed a biology course might not be equated for that subgroup who completed the course a year ago (Cook & Petersen, 1987). Also, even if the characteristics measured by the two tests were the same for all subgroups of the population of interest, the properties of the two tests might appear to differ somewhat from one group of examinees to another (Lord & Wingersky, 1984). To take an extreme example, suppose that two test forms were alike in all important respects except that one was more difficult than the other. Suppose that the equating was carried out on groups of examinees who guessed at random on most of the items. Then, the difference in difficulty between the two forms would not manifest itself, and the transformation derived would be essentially an identity function. However, if a more competent group of examinees were used, the difference in difficulty between forms would manifest itself, and scores on the more difficult form would be adjusted accordingly in relation to scores on the easier form. Thus, in practice, it is desirable to use relatively heterogeneous groups for equating.

Although it is improbable that an equating based on observed scores will be population invariant even if the same-ability, the equity, and the symmetry conditions are satisfied, from a practical point of view, the equating might be quite satisfactory for many subgroups. It is unlikely, however, that it will be satisfactory for any subpopulation having a mean and variance of ability that is sharply different from that of the population used to derive the equating transformation. Therefore, *in practice, whenever one refers to scores on two tests as being equated, it is important to add a qualifying phrase describing the population for which the equating is likely to hold* (Braun & Holland, 1982).

On the surface, it would seem that one way to surmount the problems surrounding observed-score equating would be to equate true scores instead. For unidimensional tests, an equating of true scores on two forms of the same test would satisfy both the equity and the population-invariance conditions. The problem, though, is how to use this true-score equating, because, in practice, we never have true scores.

In practice, then, there is probably no equating method that will produce truly equivalent scores on two forms of the same test. Approximations to this ideal can often be achieved, however. Given that test scores are frequently used in making certification, selection, and placement decisions that can have important consequences for the examinee, an approximate equating of scores on two forms of a test will generally be more equitable to the examinee than no equating at all, particularly if the test forms differ in difficulty. Thus, when scores on different test forms are used interchangeably, it is important that the score user take into account the fact that an examinee might earn somewhat different scores on different forms. Also, because the seriousness of the consequences of an incorrect decision or score misinterpretation can vary with the manner in which scores are to be used, it is important that the practitioner fully understand the strengths and weaknesses of the various equating studies that might be conducted and that he or she select an equating that will be sufficiently accurate for the intended score use. Some practical issues in equating are discussed by Angoff (1987), Brennan and Kolen (1987a, 1987b), Cook and Petersen (1987), and Dorans (1986).

Data Collection Designs

Not all data collection designs can be used to equate scores of examinees on several test forms. For instance, data collected from the administration of two different forms to two different groups cannot be used for equating. In general, for a data collection design to be suitable for equating, it must call for a common group (or equivalent groups) of examinees to take each test form or it must call for items to be common to both test forms. Seven basic data collection designs that permit score equating are illustrated in Table 6.6 and described next (Angoff, 1984; Holland & Wightman, 1982; Lord, 1950, 1980; Marco, 1981).

SINGLE-GROUP DESIGN

The single-group design is the simplest of the data collection designs to be described. In the single-group design, the two forms of the test to be equated are administered to the same group of examinees (see Table 6.6a). The forms are administered one after the other, preferably on the same day, so that intervening experiences do not affect performance. Because the same group of examinees takes both forms, this design has the advantage that differences in the difficulty levels of the forms are not confounded with differences in the ability levels of the groups taking each form. In using this design, however, it is necessary to assume that an examinee's score on the second

TABLE 6.6 Schematic Representation of Data Collection Designs*

a. SINGLE-GROUP DESIGN

	TEST	
SAMPLE	X	Y
P_1	✓	✓

b. COUNTERBALANCED RANDOM-GROUPS DESIGN

	TEST			
	X		Y	
SAMPLE	1ST	2ND	1ST	2ND
P_1	✓			✓
P_2		✓	✓	

c. EQUIVALENT-GROUPS DESIGN

	TEST	
SAMPLE	X	Y
P_1	✓	
P_2		✓

d. ANCHOR-TEST–RANDOM-GROUPS DESIGN

	TEST		
SAMPLE	X	Y	V
P_1	✓		✓
P_2		✓	✓

e. ANCHOR-TEST–NONEQUIVALENT-GROUPS DESIGN

	TEST		
SAMPLE	X	Y	V
P_1	✓		✓
Q_1		✓	✓

f. SECTION PRE-EQUATING DESIGN WITH ONE VARIABLE SECTION

	SECTION					
SAMPLE	X_1	X_2	X_3	Y_1	Y_2	Y_3
P_1	✓	✓	✓	✓		
P_2	✓	✓	✓		✓	
P_3	✓	✓	✓			✓

TABLE 6.6 (*Continued*)

g. SECTION PRE-EQUATING DESIGN WITH TWO VARIABLE SECTIONS

	SECTION							
SAMPLE	X_1	X_2	X_3	X_4	Y_1	Y_2	Y_3	Y_4
P_1	✓	✓	✓	✓	✓	✓		
P_2	✓	✓	✓	✓	✓		✓	
P_3	✓	✓	✓	✓	✓			✓
P_4	✓	✓	✓	✓		✓	✓	
P_5	✓	✓	✓	✓		✓		✓
P_6	✓	✓	✓	✓			✓	✓

h. ITEM PRE-EQUATING DESIGN

	SECTION								
SAMPLE	V_1	W_1	W_2	X_1	X_2	Y_1	Y_2	Z_1	Z_2
P_1	✓	✓	✓						
P_2		✓	✓			✓			
P_3		✓	✓						✓
Q_1	✓			✓	✓				
Q_2				✓	✓		✓		
Q_3				✓	✓			✓	

* P_1 are random samples from population P and Q_1 are random samples from population Q. ✓ = data are collected; otherwise data are not collected.

form of the test is unaffected by the fact that she or he has previously taken the first form. In other words, the design depends on the strong, and often untenable, assumption that factors such as learning, fatigue, and practice have no effect on the scores on the second form of the test.

COUNTERBALANCED RANDOM-GROUPS DESIGN

In practice, it is probably unreasonable to assume that the order in which two tests are administered to an examinee has no effect on his or her scores. Consequently, a modification of the single-group design, the counterbalanced random-groups design, is more frequently used in practice. In this design, the single group is divided into two random half-groups and both half-groups take both test forms in counterbalanced order, that is, one group takes the old form first, and the other takes the new form first (see Table 6.6b). Provided the time limit is the same for both forms, the group is usually divided into two half-groups by spiraling the test booklets. That is, the booklets are packaged sequentially so that every other booklet is a new form. Then, when the test booklets are distributed, every other examinee takes a new form first. The half-groups resulting from this procedure are essentially random, if enough examinees are used and if the examinees are not seated in an alternating sequence, such as by gender, that might be correlated with test score. The intent of counterbalancing is to ensure that scores on both forms are equally affected by such factors as learning, fatigue, and practice.

EQUIVALENT-GROUPS DESIGN

In practice, it is often impossible to arrange for enough testing time for every examinee to take more than one test form. The equivalent-groups design is a simple alternative to the single-group and the counterbalanced random-groups de-

signs that does not require every examinee to take every test form. In the equivalent-groups design, the two forms of the test to be equated are administered to two random groups, one form to each group (see Table 6.6c). If the time limit is the same for each test form, the spiraling method described under the counterbalanced design can be used to create the groups. In using the equivalent-groups design, it is important that the groups be as similar as possible with respect to the ability being measured; otherwise, an unknown degree of bias will be introduced in the equating process. It is impossible to adjust for random differences between groups because there are no data common to the groups. The primary way in which random differences can be minimized is by using large sample sizes. However, this design does have the advantage of avoiding learning, fatigue, and practice effects.

ANCHOR-TEST–RANDOM-GROUPS DESIGN

Use of the anchor-test–random-groups design, in place of the equivalent-groups design, makes it possible to adjust for random differences between groups. In the anchor-test–random-groups design, one form of a text (X) is administered to one group of examinees, a second form (Y) is given to a second group of examinees, and a common test (V) is administered to both groups (see Table 6.6e). The common test is referred to as the *anchor test*. The anchor test should be administered in the same order to both groups, so that scores on the anchor test or on the old and new forms are affected in the same way by learning, fatigue, and practice effects.

The anchor test can be either internal or external to the tests to be equated. An internal anchor test is a subset of items contained in both tests to be equated. Scores on this set of common items are used in computing scores on the total tests. Use of an internal anchor test requires no more testing time than does the equivalent-groups design. An external anchor test is a separately timed test that each examinee takes in addition to taking one or the other of the test forms to be equated. Scores on the external anchor test are not used in computing scores on the total tests. Use of an external anchor test requires more testing time than does the equivalent-groups design, but, if the anchor test is short, this design need not require as much testing time as the single-group or the counterbalanced random-groups designs.

Scores on the anchor test can be used to estimate the performance of the combined group of examinees on both the old and new forms of the test, thus simulating, by statistical methods, the situation in which the same group of examinees takes both forms of the test. Ideally, the anchor test would be composed of questions like those in the two forms to be equated. The higher the correlation between scores on the anchor test and scores on the new and old forms, the more useful the anchor test data. However, when the groups are random groups, even anchor tests that are not measures of the same ability as the new and old forms can provide useful information and reduce the variance error of equating, compared with that of the equivalent-groups design (Lord, 1950).

ANCHOR-TEST–NONEQUIVALENT-GROUPS DESIGN

In many testing programs, it is not feasible to give more than one form of a test at the same administration because of security or disclosure considerations. The anchor-test–nonequivalent-groups design is the most commonly used data collection design in this situation. The data are collected in the same manner as with the anchor-test–random-groups design except that nonequivalent or naturally occurring groups are used (see Table 6.6e). For example, one test form and the anchor test are administered to examinees who take the test in the fall, and another test form and the anchor test are administered to examinees who take the test in the spring. Groups that take the test at different administrations are generally self-selected and, thus, might differ in systematic ways.

In this design, it is important that the anchor test be as similar as possible in content and difficulty to the tests to be equated (Klein & Jarjoura, 1985). Scores on the anchor test are used to reduce equating bias resulting from differences in ability between the two groups. The anchor test scores provide common reference points for equating tests administered to naturally occurring groups. No statistical procedure can provide completely appropriate adjustments when nonequivalent or naturally occurring groups are used, but adjustments based on an anchor test that is as similar as possible to the tests to be equated are much more satisfactory than those based on non-parallel tests.

SECTION PRE-EQUATING DESIGN

The five data collection designs described so far require the administration of intact tests to sample(s) of examinees from some population(s). Section pre-equating, on the other hand, is a design for collecting data to be used to equate form Y to form X before form Y is given as an intact test.

In many testing programs, the test booklets consist of a series of separately timed sections. Some of the sections are referred to as operational and others, as variable. The operational sections are the same in every test booklet, and scores on the operational sections count toward the reported score on the total test. The content of the variable sections can vary from one test booklet to the next, and scores on the variable sections do not count toward the reported score on the total test.

The format and content of each variable section are usually made to mirror that of an operational section, so that examinees cannot readily distinguish between the two types of sections and, thus, are equally motivated to do well on all sections. The variable sections can be used for a variety of purposes. For instance, they can be used for pretesting of new items or for experimenting with new item types. They can contain anchor tests for use in an external anchor test data collection design or, alternatively, they can contain new test sections for use in a section pre-equating design.

In general, in a section pre-equating design, the old form X and the new form Y each consist of m sections $X_1, \ldots, X_m$ and $Y_1, \ldots, Y_m$. Sections X_i and Y_i are assumed to be parallel in content and format; and, it is assumed that the total raw score on each test form is obtained by summing the section raw scores, that is,

$$X = \sum_{i=1}^{m} X_i \quad \text{and} \quad Y = \sum_{i=1}^{m} Y_i.$$

Each version of the test booklet for form X for a given administration would contain a total of m + v (where v is a fixed value from 1 to m − 1) sections, that is, the m operational sections for form X plus v variable sections from form Y. Thus, use of a section pre-equating data collection design usually requires more testing time than an anchor test design, particularly if more than one variable section is used; however, it still requires less testing time than a single-group or counterbalanced random-groups design (see Tables 6.6f and 6.6g).

For concreteness, suppose that the old test form X and the new test form Y each contains four sections. Further, suppose that each test booklet for form X contains six sections, the four X sections and two variable sections V_1 and V_2. The order of these sections in each test booklet might be $X_1, X_2, V_1, X_3, X_4, V_2$, although the two variable sections could be placed in any of the six positions. The variable sections V_1 and V_2 could be used to collect data for equating Y to X via a section pre-equating design, as follows. Six distinct versions of the test booklet (one for every possible combination of variable sections) would be made containing the following test sections:

Booklet 1: $X_1, X_2, Y_1, X_3, X_4, Y_2$
Booklet 2: $X_1, X_2, Y_1, X_3, X_4, Y_3$
Booklet 3: $X_1, X_2, Y_1, X_3, X_4, Y_4$
Booklet 4: $X_1, X_2, Y_2, X_3, X_4, Y_3$
Booklet 5: $X_1, X_2, Y_2, X_3, X_4, Y_4$
Booklet 6: $X_1, X_2, Y_3, X_3, X_4, Y_4$

The test booklets should be distributed in such a way that random samples are tested with each of the six booklets (see Table 6.6g). The resulting combination of complete data on X and incomplete data on Y would then be used to estimate the mean and standard deviation on each test form that would have been obtained if every examinee had taken both forms (Holland & Wightman, 1982). These estimates would then be used to estimate the parameters of the desired equating function.

In a section pre-equating data collection design, examinees' old form and new form section scores might be affected by context, learning, fatigue, and practice effects stemming from the order in which the sections are administered. These factors can influence the score examinees earn on the operational test. For instance, in the example, suppose two examinees, A and B, are of equal ability. A is administered Booklet 1, and B is administered Booklet 6. Examinee A takes section Y_1, followed by X_3. Examinee B takes section Y_3, followed by X_3. If practice is helpful, then B will score higher on X_3 than A, because B had an opportunity to practice on section-3 type items before taking the operational section 3. Thus, the design could lead to examinees' being advantaged (or disadvantaged) by the particular variable sections they happen to be administered. Order effects could also influence the equating relationship, thus introducing equating error. In the example, suppose sections X_1 and Y_1, are equal in difficulty. Section Y_1 always comes after section X_1. If practice is helpful, then section Y_1 will appear to be easier than X_1, and the equating relationship will be biased.

ITEM PRE-EQUATING DESIGN

An item pre-equating data collection design provides a means of obtaining data needed to generate a large pool of calibrated items, that is, items with estimated item response theory (IRT) parameters on a common scale (see, for example, Hambleton, this volume) from which future test forms can be built and subsequently equated. Many variants of the item pre-equating design can be developed (for an example, see Lord, 1980). In planning such a design, the only requirements are that, in every calibration analysis (procedure for simultaneously estimating the IRT parameters for one or more sets of items), each group of examinees needs to have taken some items in common with at least one other group and at least one set of items must be precalibrated (have IRT item parameters estimated from another calibration analysis).

An item pre-equating design, unlike the other data collection designs, can be used to equate scores on two tests that have not yet been administered as intact tests nor been administered in variable sections along with the same intact test. For example, suppose that test forms V, W, X, Y, and Z each consist of two sections that are parallel in content and format, the total raw score on each form is the sum of the raw section scores, and each test booklet contains two operational sections and one variable section. Further suppose that W is given at one administration, along with sections V_1, Y_1, and Z_2, and that X is given at another administration, along with sections V_1, Y_2, and Z_1 (see Table 6.6h). After each administration, data from that administration can be calibrated in a single analysis. This will result in item-parameter estimates for V_1, W, Y_1, and Z_2 on one scale and item parameter estimates for V_1, X, Y_2, and Z_1 on another scale. The two sets of parameters for V_1 can then be related to each other, and this relationship can be used to place the item-parameter estimates for V, W, X, Y, and Z on a common scale. IRT methods can then be used to equate scores on forms Y and Z to each other and to X and W, even though Y and Z have not been administered as intact tests (see section on IRT and equating, this chapter, and Hambleton, this volume.) Taken to its extreme, it is possible to devise an item pre-equating data collection design such that each item to be included in the new form was previously administered in different pretest sections to different groups of examinees.

In an item pre-equating design, examinees' responses to an item might be affected by context, that is, by differences in item placement (e.g., first versus last) and by statistical and content differences in the surrounding items between the two administrations. These factors might make the item appear easier (or harder) and more (or less) discriminating in the pretest administration than in an operational administration. Such effects would distort the item-parameter estimates and, hence, the equating relationship, thus introducing bias into the equating.

Equipercentile Equating

In equipercentile equating, a transformation is chosen such that raw scores on two tests are considered to be equated if they correspond to the same percentile rank in some group of examinees (Angoff, 1984). Equipercentile equating is based on the definition that the score scales for two tests are comparable with respect to a certain group if the score distributions for the two tests are identical in shape for that group (Braun & Holland, 1982; Lord, 1950). When the score distributions for two tests are identical in shape for some group, a table of pairs of raw scores with identical percentile ranks can be constructed. However, the pairs of raw scores will not in general be numerically equal. To produce equivalent or equated scores, it is necessary to transform one set of scores into the other set or to convert both sets to a different set.

Equipercentile equating possesses the desirable property that, if score x_o on test X is the equipercentile equivalent of score y_o on test Y and scores x_o and y_o are used as cutting scores on tests X and Y, respectively, then, for groups similar to those used to derive the transformation, the proportion of examinees selected on the basis of test X will be the same as the proportion selected on the basis of test Y (Lord & Wingersky, 1984). It should be noted, however, that as a mathematical model, equipercentile equating makes no assumptions about the tests to be equated. Application of equipercentile equating simply compresses and stretches the score units on one test so that its raw-score distribution coincides with that on the other test. Only common sense and the desired condition of population invariance keep one from applying the method to scores on tests measuring different characteristics.

Illustration of the Equipercentile Equating Process

Equipercentile equating can be thought of as a two-stage process (Kolen, 1984). *First,* the relative cumulative frequency (i.e., percentage of cases below a score interval) distributions are tabulated or plotted for the two forms to be equated. *Second,* equated scores (e.g., scores with identical relative cumulative frequencies) on the two forms are obtained from these relative cumulative frequency distributions. In practice, this latter stage is not as simple as it sounds, because a raw score on form X with exactly the same percentile rank as a given raw score on form Y will seldom be found. Thus, to make equipercentile equating possible, it is necessary to make the distributions continuous. Consequently, some subjective elements, such as choice of interpolation method, must be introduced into the equating process.

A graphical method for doing equipercentile equating is illustrated in Figure 6.4. First, the relative cumulative frequency distributions, each based on 471 examinees, for two forms (designated X and Y) of a 60-item number-right-scored test were plotted. The crosses (and stars) represent the relative cumulative frequency (i.e., percent below) at the lower real limit of each integer score interval (e.g., at $i - .5$ for $i = 1$, $2, \ldots, n$, where n is the number of items). Next, the crosses (stars) were connected with straight line segments. Graphs constructed in this manner are referred to as *linearly interpolated relative cumulative frequency distributions*. The line seg-

ments connecting the crosses (stars) need not be linear. Methods of curvilinear interpolation, such as the use of cubic splines, could also be employed.

Let the form-X equipercentile equivalent of y_i be denoted $e_x(y_i)$. The calculation of the form X equipercentile equivalent $e_x(18)$ of a number-right score of 18 on form Y is illustrated in Figure 6.4. The left-hand vertical arrow indicates that the relative cumulative frequency for a score of 18 on form Y is 50. The short horizontal arrow shows the point on the curve for form X with the same relative cumulative frequency (50). The right-hand vertical arrow indicates that a score of 30 on form X is associated with this relative cumulative frequency. Thus, a score of 30 on form X is considered to be equivalent to a score of 18 on form Y. A plot of the score conversion (equivalents) is given in Figure 6.5.

Examination of Figure 6.5 reveals a difficulty encountered frequently in equipercentile equating: the conversion fails to cover the entire raw-score range on both test forms. In equipercentile equating, the maximum observed scores and the minimum observed scores on each form automatically converge

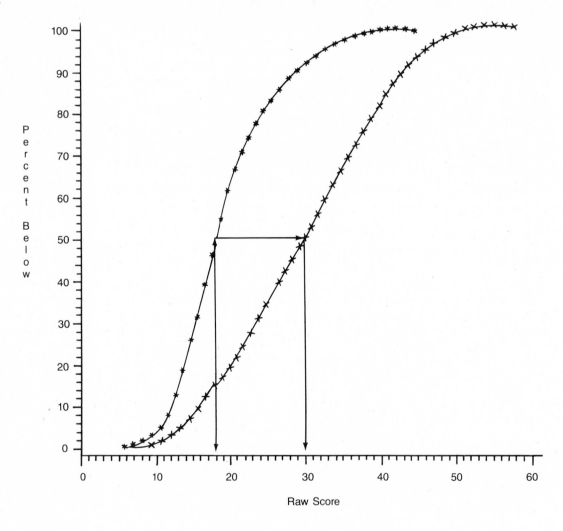

FIGURE 6.4 Illustration of equipercentile equating process.

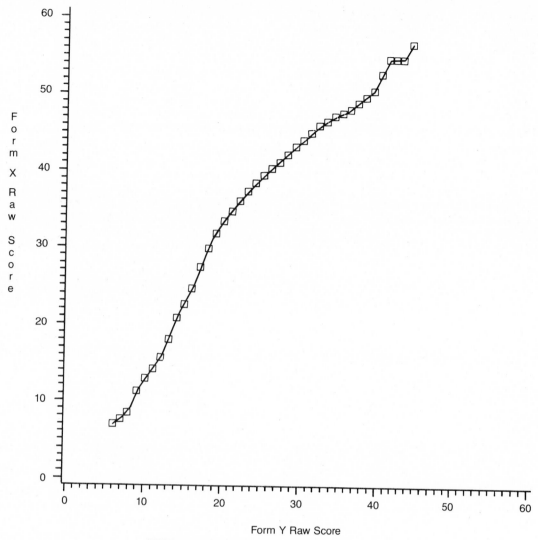

FIGURE 6.5 An equipercentile conversion.

because they have the same percentile rank. Thus, the conversion will fail to cover the possible raw-score range whenever the observed scores fail to cover the possible raw-score range. When this happens, it becomes necessary to extrapolate the conversion without the benefit of supporting data. Obviously, such a procedure can lead to large errors. For this reason, it is important that relatively parallel tests and relatively heterogeneous groups be used for equating.

The equipercentile transformation between scores on two forms, X and Y, of a test will usually be curvilinear. If form X is more difficult than form Y, the conversion will tend to be concave upward when plotted with X on the vertical axis and Y on the horizontal axis. If form X is easier than form Y, the conversion line will tend to be concave downward. If the distribution of scores on form X is flatter, more platykurtic, than that on form Y, the conversion will tend to be S-shaped. If the shapes of the score distributions on the two forms are the same (i.e., have the same moments except for the first two), the conversion line will be linear.

Use of Smoothing Techniques

The plots in Figures 6.4 and 6.5 are somewhat irregular, particularly at the extremes of the observed score range, where there is little data. The irregularities are due primarily to the effects of random error in sampling examinees from the population of interest. To mitigate these effects, smoothing techniques can be used in the equating process prior to stage one or after stage two or both. Unlike with interpolation, with smoothing, the resulting function need not pass through the observed data points. Smoothing can be done by hand or analytically; however, the results of hand smoothing vary across practitioners.

A wide variety of analytic techniques for smoothing frequency distributions has been described in the literature. The rolling weighted average of frequencies method described by Angoff (1984) and attributed to Cureton and Tukey (1951); the nonparametric probability density estimation procedures, such as kernel estimators, described by Tapia and Thompson

(1978); and the techniques for smoothing empirical distributions, such as moving medians, described by Tukey (1977), are methods applicable to a wide range of distributional forms requiring minimal statistical assumptions. Regression-based polynomial functions, smoothing cubic spline functions (Reinsch, 1967), and theoretical distributions can be fitted to empirical distributions. Keats and Lord (1962) have suggested use of the negative hypergeometric distribution, and Brandenburg and Forsyth (1974) have suggested use of the Pearson Type I (general beta) function. A procedure for estimating the population observed-score distribution, based on item response theory, has been described by Lord (1980).

Most of these procedures should not be used to smooth the conversion line; either they are applicable only to empirical distributions or they are regression based and, thus, will destroy the symmetry of the conversion. However, Kolen (1984) has suggested a procedure using cubic spline functions for smoothing the conversion line. To make the procedure symmetric, splines are fitted in both directions, and the average is used.

Fairbank (1987) investigated a variety of analytical techniques for smoothing empirical distributions (presmoothers) and conversion lines (postsmoothers) to determine whether statistical smoothing could increase the accuracy of equipercentile equating. The presmoothing techniques used in his study were moving medians, rolling weighted averages, and the negative hypergeometric distribution. Postsmoothing techniques used were the logistic ogive, cubic splines, rolling weighted averages, and linear, quadratic, cubic, and orthogonal regression. For the tests used in the study, the most effective technique was the negative hypergeometric, and the most effective postsmoother was cubic smoothing splines. It was also found that combining presmoothers and postsmoothers did not result in an improvement beyond that obtained with the more effective of the combined pair used alone.

Lord (1982) indicated that, although smoothing has the potential to reduce sampling error, it might introduce bias that does not disappear even in large samples. The studies by Fairbank (1987), Kolen (1984), and Kolen and Jarjoura (1987) attempt to separately analyze sampling error and bias in the context of smoothing.

APPLICATION OF EQUIPERCENTILE–EQUATING DATA COLLECTION DESIGNS

Equipercentile equating can be carried out using the procedure described earlier in this chapter for the single-group and the equivalent-groups data collection designs (see Tables 6.6a and 6.6c). Application of this procedure to the single-group design assumes that factors such as learning, fatigue, and practice have no effect on the scores on the second test taken. Application of this procedure to the equivalent-groups design assumes that sampling differences between the two groups can be ignored.

This procedure can also be applied to the counterbalanced random-groups design (see Table 6.6b), but, first, it is necessary to combine the data for the two groups on each test form, X and Y. This procedure assumes that sampling differences between the two groups can be ignored. Pooling of the data for the two groups for each test form will cancel out the effects due to learning, fatigue, and practice, provided the effect is proportional to the standard error on each form (Lord, 1950).

Equipercentile equating can be carried out for the anchor-test–random-groups design (see Table 6.6d) in the same manner as for the equivalent-groups design, in which case the data on test V (the anchor test) are ignored and not used. Equipercentile equating can also be carried out for the anchor-test–random-groups design in the following manner:

1. Using the data for the group taking tests X and V, for each raw score on test V, determine the score on test X with the same percentile rank.
2. Using the data for the group taking tests Y and V, for each raw score on test V, determine the score on test Y with the same percentile rank.
3. Tabulate pairs of scores on tests X and Y that correspond to the same raw score on test V.
4. Using data from step 3, for each raw score on test Y, interpolate to determine the equivalent score on test X.

The last procedure uses the data on test V to adjust for differences in ability between the two groups. This procedure really involves two equatings, instead of just one, and therefore doubles the variance of equating error. Thus, if the correlations between scores on the anchor test and the total tests are relatively small, it would be advisable to ignore the anchor test data, to reduce the equating error (Lord, 1950). This procedure can also be used with the anchor-test–nonequivalent-groups design (see Table 6.6e); however, Braun and Holland pointed out theoretical problems with this application (1982, pp. 39–42).

The frequency estimation procedure described by Angoff (1982) can also be used with either anchor-test–data-collection design. This procedure simulates the situation in which the same group takes both tests. That is, the data for both groups on test V are combined and used to estimate the frequency distributions for forms X and Y that would have been obtained if the combined group had taken each test form. The equipercentile-equating procedure used for the single-group and equivalent groups data collection designs is then applied to the estimated frequency distributions for forms X and Y. Jarjoura and Kolen (1985) studied the frequency estimation procedure and found it to be viable from the perspective of equating error.

Strictly speaking, equipercentile equating procedures cannot be applied to the data obtained from either the section pre-equating or the item pre-equating designs (see Tables 6.6f–6.6h). Frequency distributions do not exist for both test forms, because at least one of the two forms to be equated is not administered as an intact test. However, using either data collection design, it might be possible to estimate the frequency distribution of raw scores on each form that would have been obtained if each examinee had taken both tests. The equipercentile-equating procedure described earlier for the single-group and equivalent groups data collection designs could then be applied to the estimated frequency distributions for the two test forms. Methods of estimating the frequency distributions are described later in this chapter.

STANDARD ERRORS OF EQUIPERCENTILE EQUATING

Equating, like all statistical procedures, is subject to random error. Standard errors of equating provide a means of expressing the amount of error in test form equating that is due to the sampling of examinees. For a given score on one form of a test, the error in estimating its equated score on another form is often indexed by a standard error. These standard errors generally differ by score level. Standard errors of equating are used as a means of expressing equating error when scores are reported, in the estimation of the sample size required to achieve a given level of equating precision, and as a basis for comparing equating methods and designs.

In the case of equipercentile equating, the random error is due to sampling fluctuations in the relative cumulative frequency distributions of scores on forms X and Y. The equating error is the standard deviation of the transformed scores $e_x(y_o)$ on the scale of X for a fixed value y_o of Y, where each $e_x(y_o)$ is computed following resampling from the population of interest.

Lord (1982) derived asymptotic standard errors of equipercentile equating for four situations: test score continuous, one group; test score discrete, one group; test score continuous, two groups; and test score discrete, two groups. The one-group procedures are appropriate for the equipercentile-equating method used with data collected via a single-group design or a counterbalanced random-groups design with the data for the two groups combined. The two-group procedures are appropriate for the equipercentile equating method used with data collected in either an equivalent-groups design or an anchor-test–random-groups design with the anchor test data ignored. Jarjoura and Kolen (1985) derived asymptotic standard errors of equipercentile equating for the frequency estimation procedure that may be employed with data collected using either anchor test design.

The following is an adaptation of Lord's (1982) results for the two-group case and continuous data. Let p be the proportion of scores below y_o and $q = 1 - p$. Let N_x and σ_x^2 be the sample size and variance, respectively, for form X, and let N_y be the sample size for form Y. Also, let ϕ be the ordinate of the standard normal density at the unit-normal score below which p of the cases fall. Then, if test scores on form X are normally distributed, the standard error of equipercentile equating under an equivalent-groups design is

$$SE[e_x(y_o)] = \{\sigma_x^2 (pq/\phi^2)[(1/N_x) + (1/N_y)]\}^{1/2}.$$

Even though the normality assumption is not likely to be met in practice, this expression might produce reasonably accurate results for many practical purposes, such as estimating sample sizes needed for a desired degree of precision. The standard errors presented by Lord (1982) for the other three cases are more complicated and, for this reason, are not presented here.

Another procedure that may be used to estimate the standard error of an equipercentile equating is the bootstrap method (Efron, 1982). In general, to compute a bootstrap standard error, a random sample is drawn with replacement from the sample data at hand; the statistic of interest is computed, in this case $e_x(y_o)$, and the process is repeated a large number of times. The bootstrap standard error is the standard deviation of the computed values of $e_x(y_o)$. This procedure can be costly, as it requires extensive resampling. However, one advantage of the bootstrap procedure is that it can be applied to any of the equipercentile-equating methods described in the preceding section.

Linear Equating

In linear equating, a transformation is chosen such that scores on two tests are considered to be equated if they correspond to the same number of standard deviations above (or below) the mean in some group of examinees (Angoff, 1984). Linear equating methods all produce an equating transformation of the form

$$\ell_x(y) = Ay + B, \tag{7}$$

where ℓ_x is the equating transformation, y is the test score to which it is applied, and A and B are parameters estimated from the data.

Some of the authors who have developed linear equating methods (e.g., Potthoff, 1966) have estimated the parameters of the equating transformation directly from the observed data. Others (e.g., Levine, 1955; Lord, 1955a) have estimated them by means of an equation that expresses the idea of equating in standard-score terms. For observed-score equating, this latter approach begins with the relationship

$$(x - \mu_x)/\sigma_x = (y - \mu_y)/\sigma_y, \tag{8}$$

where x and y refer to scores on the test forms to be equated and μ and σ refer to the means and standard deviations, respectively, of x and y in some population of examinees.

Rearrangement of terms in Equation 8 yields

$$x \equiv \ell_x(y) = (\sigma_x/\sigma_y)y + (\mu_x - \mu_y\sigma_x/\sigma_y), \tag{9}$$

which is in the form of Equation 7, with $A = \sigma_x/\sigma_y$ and $B = \mu_x - A\mu_y$. It is important not to confuse this equation with an ordinary regression equation, where the correlation between x and y is 1.00. Although the equations look the same, they are derived from different assumptions. This equation is not concerned with the prediction of an examinee's score on test x from her or his score on test y. And because, in practice, data from two tests will never be perfectly correlated, the linear equation derived for equating will not be the same as that derived for prediction.

Suppose forms X and Y differ in reliability. Application of Equation 9, or any other linear transformation, will not produce transformed y scores (form Y scores converted to the form X scale) that have the same reliability as the x scores. Rather than attempting to do the impossible and linearly equate unequally reliable observed scores, true scores x' and y' could be equated using the relationship

$$(x' - \mu_{x'})/\sigma_{x'} = (y' - \mu_{y'})/\sigma_{y'}.$$

Solving for x' we have

$$x' = (\sigma_{x'}/\sigma_{y'})y' + (\mu_x - \mu_y\sigma_{x'}/\sigma_{y'}), \tag{10}$$

because it is assumed that $\mu_{x'} = \mu_x$ and $\mu_{y'} = \mu_y$. In practice, the conversion table resulting from the definition of linear equating for unequally reliable tests is usually applied to raw scores. Because raw scores have different properties than true scores, this is done as a practical procedure.

ILLUSTRATION OF THE LINEAR EQUATING PROCESS

Linear equating, like equipercentile equating, can be thought of as a two-stage process. *First,* compute the sample means (m) and sample standard deviations (s) of scores on the two forms to be equated. *Second,* obtain equated scores on the two forms by substituting these values into Equation 9. For example, suppose the raw-score means and standard deviations for two forms, X and Y, of a 60-item number-right-scored test administered to a single group of 471 examinees are

$$m_x = 29.5860 \qquad m_y = 19.1805$$

$$s_x = 10.0464 \qquad s_y = 6.4879.$$

Substitution of these values into Equation 9 yields

$$x = 1.5485y - 0.1147.$$

Then, for instance, the form X linear equivalent of a number-right score of 18 on form Y is 27.8 (i.e., $1.5485 * 18 - 0.1147$).

LINEAR VERSUS EQUIPERCENTILE EQUATING

Estimation of the equipercentile-equating transformation between scores on two forms of a test for a given population requires, first, estimation of the frequency distribution for each form. Usually, one then proceeds nonparametrically from these estimates, to obtain equipercentile-equivalent scores. This process requires the estimation of a large number of parameters, one per score. Estimation is most accurate when the number of parameters is small relative to the sample size. When the sample sizes are small, it could be better to fit a particular theoretical frequency distribution to the data, to reduce the total error of estimation, even though this could introduce some bias into the estimation.

Different versions of the same test are constructed to be as similar as possible in all important respects. Thus, it could be reasonable to assume, for a given population, that the shape of the raw-score distribution will be very similar for each test form. If the distributions were identical in shape, equipercentile equating could be accomplished simply by using a linear transformation; that is, by adjusting only the first two moments, the mean and the standard deviation, of either distribution (Braun & Holland, 1982). Often, use of a linear model produces a very reasonable solution.

Because the linear and equipercentile procedures yield the same equating transformation when the shapes of the score distributions are identical, linear equating can be thought of as a special case of equipercentile equating. However, unlike equipercentile equating, linear equating is entirely analytical and free from any errors of smoothing that can produce serious errors in the score ranges where data are scant or erratic. Thus, if one is willing to assume that differences in the shapes of the raw-score distributions are trivial, say, due to sampling error, and may be disregarded, linear equating is to be preferred to equipercentile equating.

Neither linear nor equipercentile transformations will produce an exact equating unless the equity condition is satisfied. Observed scores on two tests will have the same distribution for a group of examinees if the tests are strictly parallel. When scores on the two forms are not equally reliable, the score distributions will not be identical, and the two procedures will yield somewhat different results. When the shapes of the raw-score distributions differ, choice between the two methods might depend on how the scores are to be used (e.g., will cut scores be applied?) and the extent to which it is important to preserve the characteristics of the test (e.g., is it important to discriminate as much as possible among the more able students?).

If the two forms differ greatly in difficulty, equipercentile equating could compress and stretch the score scale of form Y such that the raw-score difference on form Y corresponding to a given raw-score difference in one part of the score range on form X might be two or three times that in another part of the score range. Linear equating, on the other hand, does not change the shape of the score distribution. The raw-score difference on form Y corresponding to a given raw-score difference on form X will be the same throughout the score range.

As noted earlier, equipercentile equating suffers from floor and ceiling effects. Before smoothing, the maximum observed score on one form must converge by definition to the maximum observed score on the other form. This is not so with linear equating. For example, if the new form is harder and more discriminating among the more able students than the old form, use of equipercentile equating compresses the scores of the more able students on the new form so that they all receive similar scores. Use of linear equating, however, preserves these discriminations, and scores on the new form could convert to scores on the old form that were beyond the possible score range. For instance, suppose we have two forms, X and Y, of a 60-item test. Further, suppose that, for a given group of students, the top 5% received scores above 55 on form X and above 50 on form Y, at least one student received a score of 60 on each form, the mean was 35 on form X and 30 on form Y, and the standard deviation was 10 on both forms. Then, if scores on form Y were equated using equipercentile methods to scores on form X, scores of 50 and 60 on form Y would be equivalent to scores of 55 and 60 on form X. Ignoring the problems due to the discreteness of the score scale, after conversion, the distribution of scores on form Y would be the same as that on form X. Use of linear equating, on the other hand, would not change the shape of the score distribution for form Y; a score of 50 on form Y would be equivalent to a score of 55 on form X and a score of 60 would be equivalent to a score of 65 on form X, a score that could not be achieved by examinees who took form X.

APPLICATION OF LINEAR EQUATING TO DATA COLLECTION DESIGNS

Linear equating can be carried out by using the procedure described earlier in this chapter for the single-group and the equivalent-groups data collection designs (see Tables 6.6a and 6.6c). As with equipercentile equating, linear equating applied to the single-group design assumes that factors such as learning, fatigue, and practice have no effect on the scores on the second test taken; and linear equating applied to the equivalent-groups design assumes that sampling differences between the two groups can be ignored.

This procedure can also be applied to the counterbalanced random-groups design (see Table 6.6b), but, first, it is necessary to combine the data for the two groups on each test. Treating the data as though they were collected using a single-group design, one assumes that sampling differences between the two groups can be ignored and the effects due to learning, fatigue, and practice will cancel out. Alternatively, one can treat the data as though there were four potential scores for each examinee:

$x - X$ score unpracticed
$x* - X$ score practiced
$y - Y$ score unpracticed
$y* - Y$ score practiced

In Table 6.6b then $(x, y*)$ is observed for group P_1 and $(x*, y)$ is observed for group P_2. To relate the parameters of $(x*, y*)$ to (x, y), Lord (1950) proposed the following model:

$$\mu_{x*} = \mu_x + k\sigma_x \qquad \mu_{y*} = \mu_y + k\sigma_y$$

$$\sigma_{x*} = \sigma_x \qquad \sigma_{y*} = \sigma_y,$$

where k is a constant. If the number of examinees is the same in both groups, combining the practiced and unpracticed sample data for both groups yields the following estimates:

$$\hat{\mu}_x = (m_x + m_{x*} - ks_x)/2$$

$$\hat{\sigma}_x^2 = (s_x^2 + s_{x*}^2)/2$$

$$\hat{\mu}_y = (m_y + m_{y*} - ks_y)/2 \qquad (11)$$

$$\hat{\sigma}_y^2 = (s_y^2 + s_{y*}^2)/2.$$

Substitution of the estimates from Equations 11 into Equation 9 gives a linear equation of the form $x = Ay + B$ with

$$A = [(s_x^2 + s_{x*}^2)/(s_y^2 + s_{y*}^2)]^{1/2}$$

and

$$B = (m_x + m_{x*})/2 - A(m_y + m_{y*})/2.$$

Linear equating can be carried out for the anchor-test–random-groups design (see Table 6.6d) in the same manner as for the equivalent-groups design, in which case, the data on anchor test V are ignored. However, even when the groups are chosen at random, it is inevitable that there will be some differences between them, which, if ignored, will lead to bias in the conversion line. The data on test V can be used to adjust for differences between the groups by means of the maximum-likelihood approach (Lord, 1955a). Maximum-likelihood estimates of the population means and standard deviations on forms X and Y are as follows:

$$\hat{\mu}_x = m_{x\xi} + s_{xv\xi}(m_{v\tau} - m_{v\xi})/s_{v\xi}^2$$

$$\hat{\sigma}_x^2 = s_{x\xi}^2 + s_{xv\xi}^2(s_{v\tau}^2 - s_{v\xi}^2)/s_{v\xi}^4$$

$$\hat{\mu}_y = m_{y\delta} + s_{yv\delta}(m_{v\tau} - m_{v\delta})/s_{v\delta}^2 \qquad (12)$$

$$\hat{\sigma}_y^2 = s_{y\delta}^2 + s_{yv\delta}^2(s_{v\tau}^2 - s_{v\delta}^2)/s_{v\delta}^4,$$

where the symbols subscripted ξ and δ are the usual sample means, standard deviations, and covariances for the groups P_1 and P_2 taking tests X and Y, respectively, and τ represents the combined group $\xi + \delta$. Substitution of the estimates from Equations 12 into Equation 9 yields a linear equation of the form $x = Ay + B$ with $A = \hat{\sigma}_x/\hat{\sigma}_y$ and $B = \hat{\mu}_x - A\hat{\mu}_y$.

A variety of linear equating models applicable to an anchor-test–nonequivalent-groups design (see Table 6.6e) is described by Angoff (1984) and Petersen et al. (1982). Only the three most commonly used models (Tucker, Levine Equally Reliable, and Levine Unequally Reliable), each derived for a different situation, will be described here. Although these models differ in the array of explicit assumptions they make about the data, they all use statistical methods to simulate the single-group design. That is, the scores on the anchor test V are used to estimate the means and standard deviations for test forms X and Y that would have been obtained if each examinee had taken both forms.

The Tucker model (Angoff, 1984) was derived for an anchor-test–nonequivalent-groups design in which the test forms are similar in reliability and the groups are similar in ability. The derivation rests on three assumptions related to the constancy of regression:

1. The regression coefficient of X (or Y) on V is the same for groups τ ($\tau = \xi + \delta$) and ξ (or δ):

$$\beta_{xv\tau} = \beta_{xv\xi} \qquad \text{and} \qquad \beta_{yv\tau} = \beta_{yv\delta}. \qquad (13)$$

2. The intercept of X (or Y) on V is the same for groups τ and ξ (or δ):

$$\mu_{x\tau} - \beta_{xv\tau}\mu_{v\tau} = \mu_{x\xi} - \beta_{xv\xi}\mu_{v\xi}$$

and $\qquad (14)$

$$\mu_{y\tau} - \beta_{yv\tau}\mu_{v\tau} = \mu_{y\delta} - \beta_{yv\delta}\mu_{v\delta}.$$

3. The variance of the errors of estimate of X (or Y) on V is the same for groups τ and ξ (or δ):

$$\sigma_{x\tau}^2(1 - \rho_{xv\tau}^2) = \sigma_{x\xi}^2(1 - \rho_{xv\xi}^2)$$

and $\qquad (15)$

$$\sigma_{y\tau}^2(1 - \rho_{yv\tau}^2) = \sigma_{y\delta}^2(1 - \rho_{yv\delta}^2).$$

Because $\beta_{xv} = \sigma_{xv}/\sigma_v$ and $\rho_{xv}\sigma_x = \beta_{xv}\sigma_v$ (and similarly for Y), substituting Equation 13 in Equations 14 and 15, simplifying, and rearranging terms, yields estimates, for the Tucker model, for the means and standard deviations on forms X and Y in the combined population. These estimates are the same as the maximum-likelihood estimates given in Equations 12, even though the derivations differ. A more general form of the Tucker model that does not assume that the conditional expectations are linear and the conditional variances are constants, is given by Braun and Holland (1982, pp. 23–24).

The Levine Equally Reliable model (Angoff, 1984; Levine, 1955) was derived for an anchor-test–nonequivalent-groups design in which the test forms are similar in reliability and the groups differ in ability. The derivation rests on four assumptions related to (a) the parallelism of each test form and the anchor test and (b) the constancy of regression:

1. True scores on X (or Y) and V are perfectly related:

$$\rho_{x'v'} = 1 \quad \text{and} \quad \rho_{y'v'} = 1. \qquad (16)$$

2. The slope of the line relating true scores on X (or Y) to true scores on V is the same for groups τ ($\tau = \xi + \delta$) and ξ (or δ):

$$\sigma_{x'\tau}/\sigma_{v'\tau} = \sigma_{x'\xi}/\sigma_{v'\xi}$$

and $\qquad (17)$

$$\sigma_{y'\tau}/\sigma_{v'\tau} = \sigma_{y'\delta}/\sigma_{v'\delta},$$

3. The intercept of the line relating true scores on X (or Y) to true scores on V is the same for groups τ and ξ (or δ):

$$\mu_{x\tau} - \sigma_{x'\tau}\mu_{v\tau}/\sigma_{v'\tau} = \mu_{x\xi} - \sigma_{x'\xi}\mu_{v\xi}/\sigma_{v'\xi}$$

and $\qquad (18)$

$$\mu_{y\tau} - \sigma_{y'\tau}\mu_{v\tau}/\sigma_{v'\tau} = \mu_{y\delta} - \sigma_{y'\delta}\mu_{v\delta}/\sigma_{v'\delta}.$$

4. The standard error of measurement for X (or Y) and for V is the same for groups τ and ξ (or δ):

$$\sigma_{x''\tau} = \sigma_{x''\xi}$$

and $\qquad \sigma_{y''\tau} = \sigma_{y''\delta} \qquad (19)$

$$\sigma_{v''\tau} = \sigma_{v''\xi}(= \sigma_{v''\delta}).$$

Because $\sigma_x^2 = \sigma_{x'}^2 + \sigma_{x''}^2$ (and similarly for Y and V), substituting Equation 17 in Equations 18 and 19, simplifying, and rearranging terms yields the following estimates for the means and standard deviations on forms X and Y in the combined population:

$$\hat{\mu}_x = m_{x\xi} + (m_{v\tau} - m_{v\xi})[(s_{x\xi}^2 - s_{x''\xi}^2)/(s_{v\xi}^2 - s_{v''\xi}^2)]^{1/2}$$
$$\hat{\sigma}_x^2 = s_{x\xi}^2 + (s_{v\tau}^2 - s_{v\xi}^2)(s_{x\xi}^2 - s_{x''\xi}^2)/(s_{v\xi}^2 - s_{v''\xi}^2)$$
$$\hat{\mu}_y = m_{y\delta} + (m_{v\tau} - m_{v\delta})[(s_{y\delta}^2 - s_{y''\delta}^2)/(s_{v\delta}^2 - s_{v''\delta}^2)]^{1/2} \qquad (20)$$
$$\hat{\sigma}_y^2 = s_{y\delta}^2 + (s_{v\tau}^2 - s_{v\delta}^2)(s_{y\delta}^2 - s_{y''\delta}^2)/(s_{v\delta}^2 - s_{v''\delta}^2).$$

Substitution of the estimates from Equations 20 into Equation 9 yields a linear equation of the form $x = Ay + B$ with $A = \hat{\sigma}_x/\hat{\sigma}_y$ and $B = \hat{\mu}_x + A\hat{\mu}_y$.

The Levine Unequally Reliable model (Angoff, 1984; Levine, 1955) was derived for an anchor-test–nonequivalent-groups design in which the test forms differ in reliability and the groups differ in ability. When scores on two forms are unequally reliable, there is no way to make them truly equivalent. Nevertheless, situations arise in practice that call for such an "equating."

The Levine Unequally Reliable model is derived from the first three assumptions used for the Levine Equally Reliable model, namely, Equations 16–18. Reexpressing Equation 17 in terms of the relationship $\sigma_x^2 = \sigma_{x'}^2 + \sigma_{x''}^2$ (and similarly for Y and V) and substituting Equation 17 in Equation 18 yields the following estimates of the means and true-score standard deviations on forms X and Y for the combined population:

$$\hat{\mu}_x = m_{x\xi} - (m_{v\tau} - m_{v\xi})[(s_{x\xi}^2 - s_{x''\xi}^2)/(s_{v\xi}^2 - s_{v''\xi}^2)]^{1/2}$$
$$\hat{\sigma}_{x'}^2 = (s_{x\xi}^2 - s_{x''\xi}^2)(s_{v\tau}^2 - s_{v''\tau}^2)/(s_{v\xi}^2 - s_{v''\xi}^2)$$
$$\hat{\mu}_y = m_{y\delta} - (m_{v\tau} - m_{v\delta})[(s_{y\delta}^2 - s_{y''\delta}^2)/(s_{v\delta}^2 - s_{v''\delta}^2)]^{1/2} \qquad (21)$$
$$\hat{\sigma}_{y'}^2 = (s_{y\delta}^2 - s_{y''\delta}^2)(s_{v\tau}^2 - s_{v''\tau}^2)/(s_{v\delta}^2 - s_{v''\delta}^2).$$

The estimates from Equations 21 are then substituted into Equation 10 to yield a linear equation of the form $x' = Ay' + B$ with $A = \hat{\sigma}_{x'}/\hat{\sigma}_{y'}$ and $B = \hat{\mu}_x - A\hat{\mu}_y$. In practice, the resulting A and B parameters are applied to observed scores.

The derivations for the Tucker and the Levine estimates, just presented, actually assume that the summary statistics for groups ξ and δ are weighted proportionally to sample size in computing the summary statistics for the combined group τ, that is, $\tau = \lambda_x\xi + \lambda_y\delta$ where $\lambda_x = N_x/(N_x + N_y)$, $\lambda_y = N_y/(N_x + N_y)$, and N_x and N_y are the sample sizes of examinees taking forms X and Y, respectively. More generally, group τ may be defined as $\tau = \lambda_x\xi + \lambda_y\delta$, where $(\lambda_x + \lambda_y) = 1$ and λ_x, $\lambda_y \geq 0$. Issues in weighting groups ξ and δ to form group τ are discussed by Angoff (1987), Brennan and Kolen (1987b) and Kolen and Brennan (1987).

The Levine models, unlike the Tucker model, require error variance estimates. A variety of different methods of estimating error variances may be used, and these methods involve still more assumptions. For example, Angoff's method (1953, 1982) assumes that the tests to be equated and the anchor test are parallel except for length (i.e., the tests are congeneric and the ratio of error variances of the two tests is the square root of the ratio of their true-score variances). Feldt's method (1975) assumes that the tests to be equated and the anchor test can each be divided into two parts that are parallel except for length. Coefficient alpha assumes that all items within a test are congeneric with equal true-score variances.

Angoff's method is the most commonly used method of estimating error variances in the context of linear equating, and it is of particular interest because several of the different linear equating methods described by Petersen, et al. (1982) become mutually equivalent when Angoff's error variance estimates are used. When the anchor test is a part of the total test (internal anchor), Angoff's error variance estimates for the total test X (or Y) and the anchor test V in group ξ (or δ) are

$$s_{x''\xi}^2 = s_{x\xi}^2(s_{x\xi}^2 s_{v\xi}^2 - s_{xv\xi}^2)/s_{xv\xi}(s_{x\xi}^2 - s_{xv\xi})$$

and $\qquad (22)$

$$s_{v''\xi}^2 = (s_{x\xi}^2 s_{v\xi}^2 - s_{xv\xi}^2)/(s_{x\xi}^2 - s_{xv\xi}).$$

And when the anchor test is not included in the total test (external anchor), Angoff's error variance estimates for the total test X (or Y) and the anchor test V in group ξ (or δ) are

$$s_{x''\xi}^2 = (s_{x\xi}^2 s_{v\xi}^2 - s_{xv\xi}^2)/(s_{v\xi}^2 + s_{xv\xi})$$

and $\qquad (23)$

$$s_{v''\xi}^2 = (s_{x\xi}^2 s_{v\xi}^2 - s_{xv\xi}^2)/(s_{x\xi}^2 + s_{xv\xi}).$$

As with equipercentile equating, linear equating procedures cannot be directly applied to the data obtained from either a section pre-equating design or an item pre-equating design (see Tables 6.6f–6.6h). Means and standard deviations do not exist for both tests, because at least one of the two tests to be equated is not administered as an intact test. However, using either procedure, it might be possible to estimate the mean and standard deviation of raw scores on each form that would have been obtained if each examinee had taken both tests. The linear equating procedure described earlier for the single-group and equivalent-groups data collection designs can then be applied to the estimated parameters for the two test forms. Methods of estimating the summary statistics are described later in this chapter.

STANDARD ERRORS OF LINEAR EQUATING

Standard errors of equating provide a means of expressing the amount of error in test form equating that is due to examinee sampling. In the case of linear equating, the random error is due to sampling fluctuations in the means and standard deviations of scores on forms X and Y. The equating error is the standard deviation of the transformed scores $\ell_x(y_o)$ on the scale of X for a fixed value y_o of Y, where each $\ell_x(y_o)$ is computed following resampling from the population of interest.

The bootstrap procedure (Efron, 1982) described earlier can be used to estimate the standard errors of linear equating. Alternatively, large sample estimates of standard errors can also be used. Large sample standard errors of observed-score linear equating, assuming normality and equal sample sizes, were given by Lord (1950) and Angoff (1984) for a single-group design, a counterbalanced random-groups design, an equivalent-groups design, and an anchor-test–random-groups design.

Braun and Holland (1982) put forth a more general formula than that given by Lord or Angoff for the standard error of linear equating under an equivalent-groups design. Their derivation, which takes skewness and kurtosis into account, suggests that standard errors of equating based on the normality assumption might produce misleading results when score distributions are skewed or more peaked than a normal distribution. If test scores are normally distributed, Braun and Holland's general formula for the standard error of linear equating under an equivalent groups design reduces to

$$\mathrm{SE}[\ell_x(y_o)] = \{(\sigma_x^2/2)[2 + (y_o - \mu_y)^2/\sigma_y^2][(1/N_x) + (1/N_y)]\}^{1/2}.$$

Even though the normality assumption is not likely to be met in practice, this expression could produce reasonably accurate results for many practical purposes such as estimating sample sizes needed for a desired degree of precision.

Kolen (1985) derived large sample standard errors, with and without the normality assumption, for the Tucker model under the anchor test nonrandom-groups design. The results of his computer simulation study suggest that the standard errors derived without the normality assumption are more accurate than those derived with the normality assumption for sample sizes of 250 or more examinees per test form. The results also indicate that standard errors derived with the normality assumption might be acceptable when test score distributions are nearly symmetric, but these standard errors appear to be inadequate, producing underestimates of the equating error in the crucial score range, for nonsymmetric distributions.

IRT and Equating

Item response theories suppose that the performance of an examinee on a test can be explained by examinee characteristics, referred to as latent traits, abilities, or skills that cannot be directly measured; that scores on these traits can be estimated for examinees; and that these scores can be used to predict item or test performance (Lord & Novick, 1968). Item response theory models specify a relationship between observable examinee test-item performances and underlying unobservable abilities. Because the actual relationship cannot be observed, for the abilities are unobservable, item response theories describe the relationship between performance on an item and ability by using a mathematical function based on specific assumptions about the test data. Although any theory of item responses cannot be shown to be either correct or incorrect, the utility of a given model for a set of test data can be investigated (Hambleton & Swaminathan, 1985; Lord & Novick, 1968).

IRT MODELS

Item response theory assumes that there is a mathematical function that relates the probability of a correct response on an item to an examinee's ability (see Hambleton, this volume). Many different mathematical models of this functional relationship are possible. A common assumption is that this probability can be represented by the three-parameter logistic function. In this model, where θ represents an examinee's ability, the probability of a correct response to item i, $P_i(\theta)$, is

$$P_i(\theta) = c_i + (1 - c_i)L[a_i(\theta - b_i)],$$

where $L(x) = (1 + e^{-1.7x})^{-1}$ is the logistic function and a_i, b_i, and c_i are three parameters describing the item. These parameters have specific interpretations: b_i is the point on the θ metric at the inflection point of $P_i(\theta)$ (i.e., the ability level for which the probability of a correct answer is halfway between c_i and 1.0) and is interpreted as the item difficulty; a_i is proportional to the slope of $P_i(\theta)$ at the point of inflection and represents the item discrimination; and c_i is the lower asymptote of $P_i(\theta)$ and represents a pseudoguessing parameter. When there is no guessing, $c_i = 0$. Hambleton (this volume) provides illustrations of item response functions and more detailed explanations of the item parameters for this model and for several alternative models.

If performance on a set of items can be fully explained by an IRT model, the item parameter estimates are invariant across populations. The advantage of IRT models over classical test models is that, once a set of items has been fitted to an IRT model, it is possible to estimate, on the same scale, the ability of examinees who have taken different subsets of those items. For a more detailed discussion of IRT and a description of procedures for estimating IRT item and ability parameters see Hambleton and Swaminathan (1985), Lord (1980), Lord and Novick (1968), and Wright and Stone (1979). For a thorough review of issues and recent research related to IRT equating see Skaggs and Lissitz (1986).

INDETERMINACY OF PARAMETER SCALE

The logistic and normal ogive models for $P_i(\theta)$ are functions of the quantity $a_i(\theta - b_i)$. If the same constant is added to every θ and b_i, the quantity $a_i(\theta - b_i)$ is unchanged and so is the item response function $P_i(\theta)$. Also, if every θ and b_i is multiplied by the same constant and every a_i is divided by that same constant, the quantities $a_i(\theta - b_i)$ and $P_i(\theta)$ are unchanged. Thus, the origin and unit of measurement of the ability scale are arbitrary; we can choose any scale for θ so long as we choose the same scale for b_i.

This indeterminancy of the parameter scale means that, if we independently estimated the b_is and a_is for a set of items using two different groups (denoted ξ and δ) of examinees, the resulting two sets of parameters would not be identical. However, the two sets of θs and b_is should have a linear relationship to each other (i.e., $b_\xi = \alpha b_\delta + \beta$ and $\theta_\xi = \alpha \theta_\delta + \beta$, except for sampling variability). Similarly, the two sets of a_is should be identical apart from the unit of measurement (i.e., $a_\xi = a_\delta / \alpha$, except for sampling variability). The two sets of c_is should be identical as the c_is are not affected by changes in the origin and unit of measurement.

The most common procedure for setting the parameter scale for a single set of items is to set the mean and standard deviation of θ (and b_i) to 0 and 1, respectively, for the group taking those items. To put parameters for two forms of a test on the same scale, it is necessary to have either a set of items common to both tests or a subgroup of examinees who take both tests. Four commonly used procedures for putting the item parameters for two tests on the same scale are (a) concurrent calibration, (b) the fixed bs method, (c) the equated bs method, and (d) the characteristic curve transformation method.

In concurrent calibration, parameters for the two tests are estimated simultaneously. A group of common examinees or a set of common items serves to tie the data for the two tests together and results automatically in all ability- and item-parameter estimates being on a common scale.

In the fixed bs method, the parameters for each test are estimated sequentially (Petersen, Cook, & Stocking, 1983). After parameters have been estimated for one test, the bs for the common items are used as input for the estimation of parameters for the second test and are not reestimated. This results in the ability and item parameters for the second test being on the same scale as those for the first test.

In the equated bs method, parameters for each test are estimated separately. Then, for the set of common items, the means and standard deviations of the two sets of bs are set equal. This linear transformation is then applied to the ability parameters and the a and b parameters for all items in the second test. A variation on the equated bs method, which gives low weights to poorly estimated parameters and outliers, is described by Stocking and Lord (1983).

For the characteristic curve method, parameters for each test are estimated separately. To place all parameters on the same scale, a sequential transformation process developed by Stocking and Lord (1983) is employed. This procedure, which uses the two sets of parameter estimates for the common items, is based on the principle that, if estimates were error free, the proper choice of linear parameters would cause the true scores on the common items derived from the two sets of estimates to coincide. Application of the characteristic curve transformation procedure yields a linear transformation obtained from minimizing the difference between the true scores on the common items that is then applied to the ability and the a and b parameters for all items in the second test. In theory, this procedure should be an improvement over the fixed bs and the equated bs methods, because it uses information on both the bs and the as in computing the constants α and β of the linear transformation.

CALIBRATION PROCEDURES FOR DATA COLLECTION DESIGNS

The simplest procedure for calibrating the data obtained from either a single-group design (see Table 6.6a) or a counterbalanced random-groups design (see Table 6.6b) is to estimate the parameters for the two tests simultaneously (concurrent calibration). Because each examinee takes both tests, the group of common examinees will link the data for the two tests and thereby place all ability- and item-parameter estimates on the same scale. Alternatively, the data for each test could be calibrated separately, with the metric for the ability parameters fixed to be the same for each calibration run. The resulting two sets of parameters will be on the same scale because each examinee took both tests, and, thus, the ability distribution is the same for each test. Application of either calibration procedure to the single-group design assumes that factors such as learning, fatigue, and practice have no effect on scores on the second test taken. In calibrating data obtained from a counterbalanced random-groups design, the order in which each examinee took each test is ignored. Application of either calibration procedure assumes that sampling differences between the two groups can be ignored and that effects due to learning, fatigue, and practice will cancel out.

In the equivalent-groups design (see Table 6.6c), neither a common group nor a set of common items exists to tie together the data for the two tests. The data are calibrated separately for each test, with the metric for the ability parameters fixed to be the same for each calibration run. One then treats the two resulting sets of ability and item parameters as though they were on the same scale. This procedure assumes that the distribution of ability is the same for each group of examinees.

Three different procedures can be used to calibrate the data obtained from an anchor-test–random-groups design (see Table 6.6d). *One,* the data can be calibrated in the same manner as for the equivalent-groups design, in which case, the data on the common anchor test V are ignored. *Two,* the data for the two groups can be calibrated simultaneously. Because each examinee takes test V, pooling of data on the items in V will tie together the data for the two groups and the two tests and thereby place the ability- and item-parameter estimates on the same scale. *Third,* the data for each group can be calibrated separately and all parameter estimates placed on the same scale by using the fixed bs, the equated bs, or the characteristic curve transformation procedure with the item-parameter estimates for test V. These last two procedures can also be used to calibrate the data obtained from an anchor-test–nonrandom-groups design (see Table 6.6e). For either design, the last two calibration procedures use the data on anchor test V to adjust for differences in ability between groups.

The data obtained from a section pre-equating design can be calibrated simultaneously, separately for each group, or separately for subsets of the groups. For example, in Table 6.6g, the data for all six samples could be calibrated together in a single run, the data for each of the six samples could be calibrated separately, or, say, the data for samples $P_1–P_3$ and the data for samples $P_4–P_6$ could be calibrated in two separate runs. If more than one calibration run is used, then the fixed bs, the equated bs, or the characteristic curve transformation procedure can be used to put the parameter estimates on a common scale. Because each examinee takes test X, the items in test X are used to link the data, regardless of the number of calibration runs.

As with a section pre-equating design, the data obtained from an item pre-equating design can be calibrated in one or more analyses. However, unlike a section pre-equating design, an item pre-equating design does not have a set of items common to every sample. Thus, not all subsets of samples can be calibrated together. For instance, in Table 6.6h, samples P_3 and Q_2 have no items in common and, thus, cannot be calibrated together in a single run. Furthermore, not all calibration runs can be directly linked together. For example, in Table 6.6h, suppose the data were calibrated in three separate runs: one for samples P_1 and Q_1, one for samples P_2 and P_3, and one for samples Q_2 and Q_3. None of the methods of putting item-parameter estimates from separate calibrations on the same scale can be used to link the last two analyses, because they have no items in common. However, the second analysis (P_2 and P_3) can be linked to the first (P_1 and Q_1) using the items in test W. After the parameters for all four samples contained in these two analyses have been put on a common scale, they can be linked to the third analysis (Q_2 and Q_3) by using the items in test X.

Ability-score Equating

Suppose tests X and Y are both measures of the same ability θ. If item and ability parameters for both tests are estimated simultaneously, then the parameters for both tests will be on the same scale and $\theta_x = \theta_y$. Thus, when several tests are calibrated concurrently, the need for equating of ability scores on the tests does not arise.

If item and ability parameters are estimated separately for each test, the parameter scales for the two tests will be linearly related and $\theta_x = \alpha\theta_y + \beta$. Once the constants α and β are determined, the equating of ability scores on the two tests is accomplished.

Consequently, in the framework of item response theory, there is no need to equate raw test scores if scores can be reported on the ability scale (or on a derived scale that is a simple linear transformation of the ability scale). However, estimated ability scores are seldom used for reporting purposes because they are costly to obtain. (One exception is California Test Bureau's 1986 use with the Comprehensive Test of Basic Skills and the California Achievement Tests.) It is much harder to provide users with an understandable interpretation of an ability score of, say, $\theta = 1.5$ than a number-right score of, say, 45 on a 60-item test. And it is hard to explain to users or examinees why two examinees with the same raw score, but different sets of item responses, usually have different ability scores.

True-score Equating

Because the expected score of examinee g on item i is $P_i(\theta_g)$, the examinee's expected number of right answers on an n-item test is $\Sigma_{i=1}^n P_i(\theta_g)$. In classical test theory, this expectation is called the number-right true score. If the test is formula scored (i.e., formula score $= \Sigma_{i=1}^n I(i)$ where $I(i) = 1$ if answer is cor-

rect; $I(i) = -1/k_i$, where ($k_i + 1$) is number of item options, if answer is incorrect; and $I(i) = 0$ if answer is omitted), the examinee's expected formula true score is

$$\sum_{i=1}^n \{[(k_i + 1)/k_i]P_i(\theta_g) - 1/k_i\}.$$

Suppose tests X and Y are both measures of the same ability θ and that item parameters for both tests have been placed on a common scale so that $\theta_x = \theta_y = \theta$. Then, the number-right (or formula) true scores ζ and η on tests X and Y, respectively, are related to θ by their test-characteristic functions (the sum of the item response functions for those items included in the test), that is,

$$\zeta = \sum_{i=1}^n P_i(\theta)$$

and

$$\eta = \sum_{j=1}^m P_j(\theta). \tag{24}$$

The variables ζ, η, and θ are all measures of the same characteristic (latent trait, ability, or skill). They differ only in the numerical scale on which the measurements are expressed. The measurement scales for ζ and η depend on the number of items in each test, whereas the measurement scale for θ is independent of the number of items in the test. Thus, pairs of true scores (ζ_o, η_o) corresponding to a given θ_o represent identical levels of ability and are equated.

In practice, the true-score equating relationship is estimated by first using estimated item parameters to approximate the test characteristic functions given in Equations 24. Paired values of ζ and η are then computed for a series of arbitrary values of θ. The resulting paired values constitute an equating of these true scores.

Like equipercentile equating, IRT true-score equating suffers from floor and ceiling effects. True scores less than $\Sigma_{i=1}^n c_i$ cannot be estimated, and the true scores corresponding to the maximum observed scores on each form automatically converge. Thus, the conversion might fail to cover the possible score range.

Estimated true scores are seldom used for reporting purposes because, like ability scores, they usually do not have a one-to-one correspondence with raw scores, and they are costly to compute. However, unlike ability scores, true scores are expressed on the same scale as raw scores. In practice, then, the true-score conversion table is usually applied to raw scores. Because raw scores have different properties than true scores, this last step is done simply as a practical procedure, to be justified only by whatever usefulness and reasonableness can be empirically demonstrated for the results.

Observed-score Equating

The relationship between true scores and raw scores on two tests is not necessarily the same. For example, the minimum true score cannot be less than $\Sigma_{i=1}^n c_i$ whereas, on a number-right scored test, the minimum raw score can be 0. Thus, true-score equating cannot provide an equating for examinees with raw scores below the chance level.

Item response theory does provide a means of predicting

the theoretical raw-score distribution for a test. The basic problem is to construct the frequency distribution $f(x|\theta)$ of raw scores x on test X for a person of ability level θ. If the response functions for each of the n items in test X were identical, that is, $P_i(\theta) = P(\theta)$, the relative frequency of number-right score x for person g would be given by the binominal distribution

$$f(x|\theta_g) = \binom{n}{x} P^x Q^{n-x},$$

where $P = P(\theta_g)$ and $Q = 1 - P$. The terms of $f(x|\theta_g)$ for successive values of $x = 0, 1, \ldots, n$ are given by the generating function

$$(Q + P)^n = \sum_{i=1}^{n} \binom{n}{x} P^x Q^{n-x}.$$

For example, if $n = 3$, the scores $x = 0, 1, 2, 3$ occur with relative frequencies $Q^3, 3PQ^2, 3P^2Q, P^3$, respectively. Usually, the response functions vary from item to item. In this case, the frequency distribution $f(x|\theta_g)$ is a generalized binomial with generating function

$$\prod_{i=1}^{n} (Q_i + P_i).$$

Then, if $n = 3$, the scores $x = 0, 1, 2, 3$ occur with relative frequencies $Q_1Q_2Q_3$, $(P_1Q_2Q_3 + Q_1P_2Q_3 + Q_1Q_2P_3)$, $(P_1P_2Q_3 + P_1Q_2P_3 + Q_1P_2P_3)$, $P_1P_2P_3$, respectively. In either case, the marginal frequency distribution of number-right scores x for a group of N examinees can be found by

$$f(x) = \sum_{g=1}^{N} f(x|\theta_g), \tag{25}$$

once ability- and item-parameter estimates are obtained.

Item response theory can be used to equate raw scores on tests X and Y in the following manner:

1. Put ability and item parameters for all groups and tests on a common scale.
2. Using Equation 25, generate the marginal frequency distribution of scores on test X, using item-parameter estimates for the items in test X and ability-parameter estimates for all groups of examinees used in Step 1.
3. Repeat Step 2 for test Y.
4. Perform an equipercentile equating between raw scores on tests X and Y, using the estimated marginal frequency distributions generated in Steps 2 and 3.

It is unclear whether an equipercentile equating of estimated raw scores is better than applying a true-score equating to raw scores. In a cross-validation study by Kolen (1981), results of the two procedures varied across equating situations. In a study by Lord and Wingersky (1984), the two procedures gave very similar results. At least the equipercentile equating of estimated raw scores covers the observed raw-score range. However, unlike true-score equating, this procedure is group dependent.

Equating Using a Section Pre-Equating Data Collection Design

In a section pre-equating data collection design (see Tables 6.6f–6.6g), each test form, say, X and Y, consists of m sections, and the total raw score on the test is the sum of the section raw scores, that is,

$$X = \sum_{i=1}^{m} X_i$$

and

$$Y = \sum_{i=1}^{m} Y_i. \tag{26}$$

The sections X_i and Y_i are assumed to be parallel in content and format; however, the sections (X_i, X_j) and (Y_i, Y_j) need not be measures of the same ability. This means that the sections of the test can cover diverse material but that different forms of the test, viewed as a whole, must measure the same combination of abilities. However, if an IRT model is to be applied to the data, all sections of both tests must be measures of the same ability. If the sections cover diverse material, it is important to specify the population for whom the equating is expected to hold, because, in general, equated scores on the two tests are unlikely to satisfy the population-invariance condition.

In a section pre-equating data collection design, each version of the test booklet for form X contains the m sections of X plus v $(1 \leq v \leq m - 1)$ sections of form Y. A minimum of $m!/v!(m - v)!$ versions of the test booklet is needed. This minimum assumes that the order of the variable and operational sections is the same in every version of the test booklet and that each possible combination of variable sections is given only once, in a single order. The test booklets should be distributed in such a way that random groups are created if a linear or equipercentile transformation is to be used. The groups may be random or nonrandom if an IRT equating transformation is to be used.

The data for each examinee can be envisioned as a vector containing the $2m$ elements

$$(X_1, \ldots, X_m, Y_1, \ldots, Y_m). \tag{27}$$

The actual data obtained consist of partial information on this vector. The available data are then used to estimate for the $2m$-dimensional vector in Equation 27, the mean vector

$$\underset{\sim}{\mu} = (\mu_{x_1}, \ldots, \mu_{x_m}, \mu_{y_1}, \ldots, \mu_{y_m}), \tag{7.3}$$

where μ_{x_i} and μ_{y_i} are the section means, and the covariance matrix

$$\underset{\sim}{\Sigma} = \left[\begin{array}{cccc|cccc} \sigma^2_{x_1} & \rho_{x_ix_j}\sigma_{x_i}\sigma_{x_j} & & & & & & \\ & \cdot & & & & \rho_{x_iy_j}\sigma_{x_i}\sigma_{y_j} & & \\ & & \cdot & & & & & \\ \text{---} & & & \sigma^2_{x_m} & & & & \\ \hline & & & & \sigma^2_{y_1} & \rho_{y_iy_j}\sigma_{y_i}\sigma_{y_j} & & \\ & & & & & \cdot & & \\ \text{---} & & & & & & \cdot & \\ & & & & & & & \sigma^2_{y_m} \end{array} \right], \tag{29}$$

where $\sigma_{x_i}^2$ and $\sigma_{y_i}^2$ are the section variances, and $\rho_{x_ix_j}$, $\rho_{y_iy_j}$, and $\rho_{x_iy_j}$ are the section intercorrelations. The estimates of μ and Σ can then be used to estimate the parameters of either a linear or an equipercentile equating function for equating scores on form Y to scores on form X. (IRT methods for equating Y to X using data obtained from a section pre-equating data collection design are described earlier in the chapter.)

ESTIMATION OF MEAN VECTOR AND COVARIANCE MATRIX

It is easier to estimate μ (Equation 28) and Σ (Equation 29) for a two-variable section pre-equating data collection design than for a one-variable section design. In a two-variable section design, every possible pair of Y sections (Y_i, Y_j) is administered to at least one group, so some information is available for every element in μ and Σ (see Table 6.6g). In a one-variable section design, no information is directly observed on the intercorrelations $\rho_{y_iy_j}$ among the sections in form Y (see Table 6.6f).

For a two-variable section pre-equating data collection design, the simplest procedure for estimating μ and Σ is to use the observed sample estimates. *First,* combine all samples who were tested with X (e.g., P_1–P_6 in Table 6.6g), and then use the resulting section means, standard deviations, and intercorrelations as estimates of μ_{x_i}, σ_{x_i}, and $\rho_{x_ix_j}$, respectively. *Second,* combine all samples who were tested with Y_i (e.g., P_1, P_4, and P_5 for Y_2 in Table 6.6g) and use the resulting section mean, standard deviation, and cross products as estimates of μ_{y_i}, σ_{y_i} and the population cross moments $E(X_iY_j)$. The estimated cross moments can then be combined with the estimates $\hat{\mu}_{x_i}$, $\hat{\sigma}_{x_i}$, $\hat{\mu}_{y_i}$, and $\hat{\sigma}_{y_i}$ obtained in Steps 1 and 2, to estimate $\rho_{x_iy_j}$. *Third,* to estimate $\rho_{y_iy_j}$, use data from the sample, taking the pair of sections (Y_i, Y_j) (e.g., P_2 for (Y_1, Y_3) in Table 6.6g) to estimate the population cross moment $E(Y_iY_j)$. Combine this estimate with the estimates $\hat{\mu}_{y_i}$, $\hat{\sigma}_{y_i}$, $\hat{\mu}_{y_j}$, and $\hat{\sigma}_{y_j}$ obtained in Step 2 to estimate $\rho_{y_iy_j}$.

Holland and Wightman (1982) referred to this simple method of estimating μ and Σ as the "pairwise present" method. Unfortunately, it can only be used with section pre-equating designs that have at least two variable sections.

For a one-variable section design, Steps 1 and 2 of the pairwise present method can be used to obtain estimates of μ_{x_i}, σ_{x_i}, μ_{y_i}, σ_{y_i}, $\rho_{x_ix_j}$, and $\rho_{x_iy_j}$. But this procedure cannot be used to estimate $\rho_{y_iy_j}$ because no examinee takes both Y_i and Y_j. If X_i and Y_i are parallel in content and format, one solution to this problem is to assume that $\rho_{x_ix_j} = \rho_{y_iy_j}$ and then to use the intercorrelations among the X sections as estimates of the corresponding intercorrelations among the Y sections (Holland & Wightman, 1982).

Holland and Wightman (1982) pointed out that, for a one-variable section design, it is not strictly true that no information exists about $\rho_{y_iy_j}$. Rather, it is the partial correlation between Y_i and Y_j, after partialing out X_i, . . . , X_m, that cannot be estimated. If this partial correlation were known, then it would be possible to compute a unique maximum-likelihood estimate of $\rho_{y_iy_j}$ (Rubin & Thayer, 1978). Thus, another possible solution to the problem of estimating $\rho_{y_iy_j}$ for a one-variable section design is to impute the unknown partial corre-

lations and then combine the resulting estimated correlations with the estimates of the estimable parameters in Σ (Holland & Wightman, 1982).

Another approach to the problem of estimating μ and Σ for either the one- or two-variable section pre-equating design, is to derive maximum-likelihood estimates of μ and Σ, assuming that the 2m-dimensional vector in Equation 27 is multivariate normal for the population. This approach requires iterative procedures to maximize the likelihood. The EM algorithm (Dempster, Laird, & Rubin, 1977) can be used to obtain maximum-likelihood estimates for μ and Σ (Holland & Wightman, 1982).

All of these estimation procedures assume that the order in which an examinee takes the sections has no effect on his or her scores. For example, suppose, for examinees in sample P_6 in Table 6.6g, the test sections were administered in the order X_1, X_2, Y_3, X_3, X_4, Y_4. Then, for those examinees, the previous estimation procedures would assume that examinees' scores on X_3 are unaffected by their having taken Y_3 first, and examinees' scores on Y_4 are unaffected by their having taken X_4 first. Holland and Thayer (1984) described a maximum-likelihood estimation procedure that uses the EM algorithm and allows for the effects of practice on both old and new test form sections.

LINEAR EQUATING

The linear equating function given in Equation 9 requires estimates of μ_x, σ_x, μ_y, and σ_y. Making use of the relationship given in Equation 26 and the usual rules for computing the mean and standard deviation of a sum,

$$\mu_x = \sum_{i=1}^m \mu_{x_i}$$

$$\mu_y = \sum_{i=1}^m \mu_{y_i}$$

$$\sigma_x^2 = \sum_{i=1}^m \sigma_{x_i}^2 + 2\sum_{i<j} \rho_{x_ix_j}\sigma_{x_i}\sigma_{x_j} \qquad (30)$$

$$\sigma_y^2 = \sum_{i=1}^m \sigma_{y_i}^2 + 2\sum_{i<j} \rho_{y_iy_j}\sigma_{y_i}\sigma_{y_j}.$$

Now all the information needed to compute the estimates in Equations 30 is contained in the mean vector (Equations 28) and the covariance matrix (Equation 29). Once μ and Σ are estimated, these estimates can be used in Equations 30 to estimate μ_x, σ_x, μ_y, and σ_y. Substitution of these estimates into Equation 9 then yields the linear function for equating scores on Y to scores on X.

EQUIPERCENTILE EQUATING

Equipercentile equating requires an estimate of the population frequency distribution for each test. Because every examinee takes X, all samples can be combined, and the resulting observed frequency distribution for X can be used as the estimate of the population frequency distribution. But, because no examinee takes Y as an intact test, no simple sample estimate of the population frequency distribution for Y exists.

Keats and Lord (1962) and Lord (1962) have suggested that the negative hypergeometric probability model might provide an adequate fit to many test-score distributions. If the binomial error model is assumed and if the regression of true score on observed score is linear, the observed number-right score has the negative hypergeometric distribution (Lord & Novick, 1968). The negative hypergeometric probability distribution is a function of three parameters: the mean, the standard deviation, and the number of items. Lord and Novick (1968) gave an example of how the negative hypergeometric distribution can be used to estimate the relative frequency distribution for a number-right scored test.

Once estimates of μ_y and σ_y are obtained for a section pre-equating design, these estimates, plus the number of items in Y, can be used to generate, via the negative hypergeometric probability model, an estimated frequency distribution of scores on Y. This estimated frequency distribution for Y can then be used along with the observed frequency distribution for X to equate scores on Y to scores on X via the equipercentile procedures described earlier for a single-group design.

REFERENCES

Ahlberg, J., Nilson, E., & Walsh, J. (1967). *The theory of splines and their applications.* New York: Academic Press.

The American College Testing Program. (1960). *The American College Testing Program technical report, 1960–61 ed.* Chicago: Author.

Anastasi, A. (1958). *Differential psychology* (3rd. ed.). New York: Macmillan.

Angoff, W. H. (1953). Test reliability and effective test length. *Psychometrika, 18,* 1–14.

Angoff, W. H. (1962). Scales with nonmeaningful origins and units of measurement. *Educational and Psychological Measurement, 22,* 27–34.

Angoff, W. H. (1963). Can useful general purpose equivalency tables be prepared for different college admissions tests? *Proceedings of the 1962 Inventional Conference of Testing Problems.* Princeton, NJ: Educational Testing Service.

Angoff, W. H. (1962). Summary and derivation of equating methods used at ETS. In P. W. Holland & D. B. Rubin (Eds.), *Test equating.* New York: Academic Press.

Angoff, W. H. (1984). *Scales, norms, and equivalent scores.* Princeton, NJ: Educational Testing Service. (Reprint of chapter in R. L. Thorndike (Ed.), *Educational measurement* (2nd ed.). Washington, DC: American Council on Education, 1971.)

Angoff, W. H. (1987). Technical and practical issues in equating: A discussion of four papers. *Applied Psychological Measurement, 11,* 291–300.

APA, American Psychological Association. (1974). *Standards for educational and psychological tests.* Washington, DC: Author.

Baglin, R. F. (1981). Does "nationally" normed really mean nationally? *Journal of Educational Measurement, 18,* 97–107.

Beggs, D. L., & Hieronymus, A. N. (1968). Uniformity in growth in basic skills throughout the school year and during the summer. *Journal of Educational Measurement, 5,* 91–97.

Bock, R. D., & Mislevy, R. J. (1981). An item response theory model for matrix-sampling data: The California grade-three assessment. *New Directions for Testing and Measurement, 10,* 65–90.

Brandenburg, D. C., & Forsyth, R. A. (1974). Approximating standardized achievement test norms with a theoretical model. *Educational and Psychological Measurement, 34,* 3–9.

Braun, H. I., & Holland, P. W. (1982). Observed score test equating: A mathematical analysis of some ETS equating procedures. In P. W. Holland & D. B. Rubin (Eds.), *Test equating.* New York: Academic Press.

Brennan, R. L., & Kolen, M. J. (1987a). Some practical issues in equating, *Applied Psychological Measurement, 11,* 279–290.

Brennan, R. L., & Kolen, M. J. (1987b). A reply to Angoff, *Applied Psychological Measurement, 11,* 301–306.

Burket, G. R. (1984). Response to Hoover. *Educational Measurement: Issues and Practices, 3,* 15–16.

Burns, R. L. (1985). Guidelines for developing and using licensure tests. In Jim C. Fortune and Associates (Ed.), *Understanding testing in occupational licensing. Establishing links between principles of measurement and practices of licensing.* San Francisco: Jossey-Bass.

Cochran, W. G. (1977). *Sampling techniques.* New York: John Wiley & Sons.

Cole, N. S. (1982 March). *Grade equivalent scores: To GE or not to GE.* AERA Division D Vice Presidential Address at the meeting of the American Educational Research Association, New York.

Cole, N. S., Trent, E. R., & Wadell, D. C. (1982). *The 3R's Test. Achievement Edition (Grade Examination K–12).* Chicago: Riverside.

College Entrance Board. (1977). *On further examination.* New York: Author.

Congressional Budget Office (1986). *Trends in educational achievement.* Washington, DC: U. S. Government Printing Office.

Congressional Budget Office (1987). *Educational Achievement: Explanations and Implications of Recent Trends.* Washington, DC: U. S. Government Printing Office.

Cook, L. L., & Petersen, N. S. (1987). Problems related to the use of conventional and item response theory equating methods in less than optimal circumstances. *Applied Psychological Measurement, 11,* 225–244.

Cox, R. C., & Graham, T. T. (1966). The development of a sequentially scaled achievement test. *Journal of Educational Measurement, 3,* 147–150.

CTB/McGraw Hill. (1986). *California Achievement Tests, Forms E and F, Technical Bulletin 2.* Monterey, CA: Author.

Cureton, E. E., & Tukey, J. W. (1951). Smoothing frequency distributions, equating tests and preparing norms (Abstract). *American Psychologist, 6,* 404.

de Boor, C. (1978). *A practical guide to splines.* New York: Springer-Verlag.

Dempster, A. P., Laird, N. M., & Rubin, D. B. (1977). Maximum likelihood from incomplete data via the EM algorithm. *Journal of the Royal Statistical Society, B, 39,* 1–38.

Donlon, T. F. (Ed.) (1984). *The College Board technical handbook for the Scholastic Aptitude Test and achievement tests.* New York: College Entrance Examination Board.

Dorans, N. J. (1986). The impact of item deletion on equating conversions and reported score distributions. *Journal of Educational Measurement, 23,* 245–264.

Ebel, R. L. (1962). Content standard scores. *Educational and Psychological Measurement, 22,* 15–25.

Efron, B. (1982). *The jackknife, the bootstrap, and other resampling plans.* Philadelphia, PA: Society for Industrial and Applied Mathematics.

Fairbank, B. A. (1987). The use of presmoothing and postsmoothing to increase the precision of equipercentile equating. *Applied Psychological Measurement, 11,* 245–262.

Feldt, L. S. (1975). Estimation of the reliability of a test divided into two parts of unequal length. *Psychometrika, 40,* 557–561.

Feldt, L. S. (1984). Some relationships between the binomial error model and classical test theory. *Educational and Psychological Measurement, 44,* 883–891.

Feldt, L. S., Steffen, M., & Gupta, N. C. (1985). A comparison of five methods for estimating the standard error of measurement at specific score levels. *Applied Psychological Measurement, 9,* 351–361.

Flanagan, J. C. (1951). Units, scores, and norms. In E. F. Lindquist (Ed.), *Educational measurement.* Washington, DC: American Council on Education.

Freeman, M. F., & Tukey, J. W. (1950). Transformations related to the angular and square root. *Annals of Mathematical Statistics, 21,* 607–611.

Gardner, E. F. (1962). Normative standard scores. *Educational and Psychological Measurement, 22,* 7–14.

Gardner, E. F. (1966). The importance of reference groups in scaling procedures. In A. Anastasi (Ed.), *Testing problems in perspective.* Washington, DC: American Council on Education.

Hambleton, R. H., & Swaminathan, H. (1985). *Item response theory: Principles and applications.* Hingham, MA: Kluwer, Nijhoff.

Hieronymus, A. N., & Hoover, H. D. (1986). *Iowa Tests of Basic Skills manual for school administrators.* Chicago: Riverside.

Hieronymus, A. N., & Lindquist, E. F. (1974). *Manual for administrators, supervisors, and counselors. Levels edition. Forms 5 & 6. Iowa Tests of Basic Skills.* Boston: Houghton Mifflin.

Holland, P. W., & Thayer, D. T. (1984). *Section pre-equating in the presence of practice effects* (Program Statistics Research Technical Report No. 84–44). Princeton, NJ: Educational Testing Service.

Holland, P. W., & Wightman, L. E. (1982). Section pre-equating: A preliminary investigation. In P. W. Holland & D. B. Rubin (Eds.), *Test equating.* New York: Academic Press.

Hoover, H. D. (1982). *Some comments on vertical equating using item response theory.* Paper presented at the meeting of the American Educational Research Association, New York City.

Hoover, H. D. (1984a). The most appropriate scores for measuring educational development in the elementary schools: GE's *Educational Measurement: Issues and Practices, 3,* 8–14.

Hoover, H. D. (1984b). Rejoinder to Burket. *Educational Measurement: Issues and Practices, 3,* 16–18.

Iowa Tests of Educational Development. (1958). *Manual for school administrators, 1958 revision.* Iowa City, IA.: State University of Iowa.

Iowa Tests of Educational Development. (1980a). *Manual for administrators and testing directors. Forms X-7 and Y-7.* Iowa City, IA.: Iowa Testing Programs.

Iowa Tests of Educational Development. (1980b). *Manual for teachers, counselors, and examiners. Forms X-7 and Y-7.* Iowa City, IA.: Iowa Testing Programs.

Jaeger, R. M. (1984). *Sampling in education and the social sciences.* New York: Longman.

Jarjoura, D. (1985). Tolerance intervals for true scores. *Journal of Educational Statistics, 10,* 1–17.

Jarjoura, D., & Kolen, M. J. (1985). Standard errors of equipercentile equating for the common item nonequivalent populations design. *Journal of Educational Statistics, 10,* 143–160.

Jarjoura, D., & Brennan, R. L. (1982). A variance components model for measurement procedures associated with a table of specifications. *Applied Psychological Measureement, 6,* 161–171.

Jarjoura, D., & Brennan, R. L. (1983). Multivariate generalizability models for tests developed from tables of specifications. In L. J. Fyans, Jr., (Ed.), *Generalizability theory: Inferences and practical applications.* (New directions for testing and measurement, No. 18). San Francisco: Jossey-Bass.

Jones, L. V. (1971). The nature of measurement. In R. L. Thorndike (Ed.), *Educational Measurement* (2nd Ed.), Washington, DC: American Council on Education.

Keats, J. A., & Lord, F. M. (1962). A theoretical distribution for mental test scores. *Psychometrika, 27,* 59–72.

Kish, L. (1965). *Survey Sampling.* New York: John Wiley & Sons.

Klein, L. W. & Jarjoura, D. (1985). The importance of content representation for common-item equating with nonrandom groups. *Journal of Educational Measurement, 22,* 197–206.

Kolen, M. J. (1981). Comparison of traditional and item response theory methods for equating tests. *Journal of Educational Measurement, 18,* 1–11.

Kolen, M. J. (1984). Effectiveness of analytic smoothing in equipercentile equating. *Journal of Educational Statistics, 9,* 25–44.

Kolen, M. J. (1985). Standard errors of Tucker equating. *Applied Psychological Measurement, 9,* 209–223.

Kolen, M. J. (1986). *Defining score scales in relation to measurement error.* (ACT Technical Bulletin No. 50). Iowa City, IA.: American College Testing Program.

Kolen, M. J. (1988). Defining score scales in relation to measurement error. *Journal of Educational Measurement, 25,* 97–110.

Kolen, M. J., & Brennan, R. L. (1987). Linear equating models for the common item nonequivalent populations design. *Applied Psychological Measureement, 11,* 263–277.

Kolen, M. J., & Jarjoura, D. (1987). Analytic smoothing for equipercentile equating under the common item nonequivalent populations design. *Psychometrika, 52,* 43–59.

Levine, R. (1955). *Equating the score scales of alternate forms administered to samples of different ability* (RB-55-23). Princeton, NJ: Educational Testing Service.

Lindquist, E. F. (1953). Selecting appropriate score scales for tests. In *Proceedings of the 1952 Invitational Conference on Testing Problems.* Princeton, NJ: Educational Testing Service.

Livingston, S. A., & Zieky, M. J. (1982). *Passing scores. A manual for setting standards of performance on educational and occupational tests.* Princeton, NJ: Educational Testing Service.

Lord, F. M. (1950). *Notes on comparable scales for test scores (RB-50-48).* Princeton, NJ: Educational Testing Service.

Lord, F. M. (1955a). Equating test scores: A maximum likelihood solution. *Psychometrika, 20,* 193–200.

Lord F. M. (1955b). A survey of observed test-score distributions with respect to skewness and kurtosis. *Educational and Psychological Measurement, 15,* 383–389.

Lord, F. M. (1959). Test norms and sampling theory. *Journal of Experimental Education, 27,* 247–263.

Lord, F. M. (1962). Estimating norms by item-sampling. *Educational and Psychological Measurement, 22,* 259–267.

Lord, F. M. (1965). A strong true score theory with applications. *Psychometrika, 30,* 59–72.

Lord, F. M. (1969). Estimating true-score distributions in psychological testing (an empirical Bayes estimation problem). *Psychometrika, 34,* 259–299.

Lord, F. M. (1975). The "ability" scale in item characteristic curve theory. *Psychometrika, 40,* 205–217.

Lord, F. M. (1980). *Applications of item response theory to practical testing problems.* Hillsdale, NJ: Lawrence Erlbaum.

Lord, F. M. (1982). The standard error of equipercentile equating. *Journal of Educational Statistics, 7,* 165–174.

Lord, F. M., & Novick, M. R. (1968). *Statistical theories of mental test scores.* Reading, MA: Addison-Wesley.

Lord, F. M., & Wingersky, M. S. (1984). Comparison of IRT observed-score and true-score 'equatings.' *Applied Psychological Measurement, 8,* 453–461.

Loyd, B. H., & Hoover, H. D. (1980). Vertical equating using the Rasch model. *Journal of Educational Measurement, 17,* 179–193.

Marco, G. L. (1981). Equating tests in an era of test disclosure. In B. F. Green (Ed.), *Issues in testing: Coaching, disclosure, and ethnic bias.* San Francisco: Jossey-Bass.

McCall, W. A. (1939). *Measurement.* New York: Macmillan.

Mehrens, W. A., & Lehmann, I. J. (1984). *Measurement and evaluation in education and psychology* (3rd ed.). New York: CBS College Publishing.

Messick, S., Beaton, A., & Lord, F. (1983). *National Assessment of Educational Progress reconsidered: A new design for a new era.* Princeton, NJ: Educational Testing Service.

Michell, J. (1986). Measurement scales and statistics: A clash of paradigms. *Psychological Bulletin, 3,* 398–407.

Mislevy, R. J., & Bock, R. D. (1983). Item response models for grouped data. *Journal of Educational Statistics, 8,* 271–288.

Mittman, A. (1958). *An empirical study of methods of scaling achievement tests at the elementary grade level.* Unpublished doctoral dissertation, The University of Iowa, Iowa City.

Morris, C. N. (1982). On the foundations of test equating. In P. W. Holland & D. B. Rubin (Eds.), *Test equating.* New York: Academic Press.

Nitko, A. J. (1980). Distinguishing the many varieties of criterion-referenced tests. *Review of Educational Research, 28,* 95–104.

Nitko, A. J. (1984). Defining "criterion-referenced test." In R. A. Berk (Ed.), *A guide to criterion-referenced test construction.* Baltimore: Johns Hopkins University Press.

Petersen, N. S., Cook, L. L., & Stocking, M. L. (1983). IRT versus conventional equating methods: A comparative study of scale stability. *Journal of Educational Statistics, 8,* 137–156.

Petersen, N. S., Marco, G. L., & Stewart, E. E. (1982). A test of the adequacy of linear score equating models. In P. W. Holland & D. B. Rubin (Eds.), *Test equating.* New York: Academic Press.

Phillips, S. E. (1986). The effects of the deletion of misfitting persons on vertical equating via the Rasch model. *Journal of Educational Measurement, 23,* 107–118.

Potthoff, R. F. (1966). Equating of grades or scores on the basis of a common battery of measurements. In P. R. Krishnaiah (Ed.), *Multivariate anglysis.* New York: Academic Press.

The Psychological Corporation, Harcourt Brace Jovanovich. (1985). *Stanford Achievement Test Series, Technical Data Report.* San Antonio: Author.

Reinsch, C. H. (1967). Smoothing by spline functions. *Numerische Mathematik, 10,* 177–183.

Rubin, D. B., & Thayer, D. T. (1978). Relating tests given to different samples. *Psychometrika, 43,* 3–10.

Shepard, L. A. (1984). Setting performance standards. In R. A. Berk (Ed.), *A guide to criterion-referenced test construction.* Baltimore: Johns Hopkins University Press.

Silverman, B. W. (1986). *Density estimation for statistics and data analysis.* London: Chapman and Hall.

Skaggs, G., & Lissitz, R. W. (1986). IRT test equating: Relevant issues and a review of recent research. *Review of Educational Research, 56,* 495–529.

Slinde, J. A., & Linn, R. L. (1979a). The Rasch model, objective measurement, equating, and robustness. *Applied Psychological Measurement, 3,* 437–452.

Slinde, J. A., & Linn, R. L. (1979b). Vertical equating via the Rasch model for groups of quite different ability and tests of quite different difficulty. *Journal of Educational Measurement, 16,* 159–165.

Stevens, S. S. (1951). Mathematics, measurement, and psychophysics. In S. S. Stevens (Ed.), *Handbook of experimental psychology.* New York: John Wiley.

Stocking, M. L. (1984). *Two simulated feasibility studies in computerized adaptive testing.* (Research Report No. 84–15). Princeton, NJ.: Educational Testing Service.

Stocking, M. L., & Lord, F. M. (1983). Developing a common metric in item response theory. *Applied Psychological Measurement, 7,* 201–210.

Suppes, P., & Zinnes, J. L. (1963). Basic measurement theory. In R. D. Luce, R. R. Bush, & E. Galanter (Eds.), *Handbook of Mathematical Psychology:* Vol. I. New York: John Wiley.

Tapia, R. A., & Thompson, J. R. (1978). *Non-parametric probability density estimation.* Baltimore: Johns Hopkins University Press.

Tukey, J. W. (1977). *Exploratory data analysis,* Reading, MA: Addison-Wesley.

Wang, M. W., & Stanley, J. C. (1970). Differential weighting: A review of methods and empirical studies. *Review of Educational Research, 4,* 663–705.

Wilcox, R. R. (1978). Estimating true score in the compound binomial model and its extensions. *Psychometrika, 43,* 245–258.

Wilcox, R. R. (1981). A review of the beta-binomial model and its extensions. *Journal of Educational Statistics, 6,* 3–32.

Wright, B. D., & Stone, M. H. (1979). *Best test design.* Chicago: MESA.

Yates, F. (1981). *Sampling methods for measures and surveys.* New York: Macmillan.

Yen, W. M. (1985). Increasing item complexity: A possible cause of scale shrinkage for unidimensional item response theory. *Psychometrika, 50,* 399–410.

Yen, W. M. (1986). The choice of scale for educational measurement: An IRT perspective. *Journal of Educational Measurement, 23,* 299–325.

7

Implications of Cognitive Psychology for Educational Measurement

Richard E. Snow

Stanford University

David F. Lohman

University of Iowa

Introduction and Overview

This chapter examines the rapid advance of cognitive psychology over the past few decades, in an attempt to identify implications for research in educational measurement over the next few decades. Unlike most other chapters in a volume of this sort, this chapter aims more at what might be than at what is. Cognitive psychology, as a body of theory, evidence, and research technique, has its strengths and weaknesses today. So does the field of educational measurement. Where there are complementary strengths and weaknesses, opportunities exist for useful integration between the two fields. We here emphasize what cognitive psychology seems to offer to improve educational measurement. One can also imagine a parallel chapter on the implications of educational and psychological measurement for cognitive psychology, but only a few points in this direction are included here in passing.

Educational measurement has advanced significantly in recent decades. Through item response models, matrix sampling, new equating and bias detection procedures, confirmatory factor analysis, and a host of other techniques, educational and psychological measurements have been made more useful

today than ever before, for individuals, institutions, and society at large. The advent of computerized adaptive testing, and the growing recognition of the intimate relationship between testing and teaching, opens an exciting vista for future research and development. At the same time, a new view of substantive psychology in education has been launched. Experimental psychology has finally attacked the problem of mind, not only in the laboratory but also, increasingly, in the medium of real-world tasks including school learning tasks. If differential psychologists could claim to be the cognitive theorists of the first half of this century, experimental psychologists can claim to be the cognitive theorists of the second half.

In this chapter, we review key developments in recent experimental cognitive psychology. Our function is partly instructional, because we think that measurement experts now need to know much more of cognitive psychology than they were taught or are likely to learn without a précis. We first touch briefly on history and then contrast the measurement models that underlie both fields. We then build up conceptions of theory and research technique from modern basics, particu-

NOTE: The authors acknowledge with much thanks constructive criticisms of an earlier draft from Robert Calfee, John Carroll, Lee Cronbach, Robert Glaser, and the editor, Robert Linn. Responsibility for the final product, of course, remains with the authors.

larly to identify advances in cognitive analysis relevant to measurement. There follows a summary of what cognitive psychological research implies for new theories of aptitude and achievement and new methods by which to understand educational measurements. This chapter is but a start toward what is needed in educational measurement. We hope at least it provides impetus for experts and novices alike to learn further.

An Outline of Modern Cognitive Psychology

HISTORICAL NOTES

Systematic cognitive psychology began in Europe in the last century, and its ties there with early developments in educational and psychological assessment were close. The works of Binet (see Wolf, 1973), Ebbinghaus (1913/1985), Galton (1883), Selz (see Frijda & DeGroot, 1981), Spearman (1927), Vygotsky (1978), and Wundt (1911) all display aspects of the connection. So does Piagetian theory, which began with the study of error patterns on test items in the Binet–Simon laboratory (Flavell, 1963). In early U.S. work, the interplay between experimental and correlational psychology was similarly strong. As psychologists sought to establish their science, however, and as behaviorism gained the central ground, the two disciplines went their separate ways (Cronbach, 1957).

The cognitive revolution that has taken place since the late 1950s has roots in the psychologies that preceded it. As in most revolutions, however, the extent to which the new perspectives differ from the old, replace them, and also solve adjacent problems is often overstated. Much of the new derives, at least in part, from older theories and methods. As Greeno and Simon (in press) note, for example, the condition-action production rule of modern cognitive theory is a generalization of the stimulus-response bond of Thorndike and Hull. Simon (1981) also credits Selz and DeGroot with early versions of several concepts now basic to current theories. Other modern concepts were foreshadowed by Hall (1883) and James (1890) or were studied directly in the functionalist psychology of this century's first third (see, e.g., Woodworth, 1938; also Tolman, 1932).

To acknowledge that modern cognitive psychology is in part a return to earlier bases is not to devalue it; there have also been substantial advances built on those bases and remarkable new initiatives. Rather, the point is that, in the earlier bases, the aims of cognitive psychology and educational measurement were closely allied; there are thus old grounds for expecting a renewed alliance to be productive. This expectation is increasingly shared by modern researchers representing both camps (see e.g., Bejar, 1985; Carroll, 1976, 1980b; Dillon, 1986; Embretson, 1985a; Glaser, 1981, 1985; Hunt, 1982, 1985a; Hunt & Pellegrino, 1985; Ippel, 1986; Messick, 1984; R. J. Sternberg, 1977, 1981, 1984c; Ward, 1985).

There is no space here for historical details, nor for a comprehensive delineation of the rich store of empirical results, methods, and theoretical concepts developed in cognitive psychology in the modern era. Thousands of references exist, with hundreds more added each month. Because we believe that cognitive psychology will play an increasingly important role in educational measurement, we urge measurement specialists

and those responsible for training them to gain a solid grounding now. For a history, critique, and sampling of current contents, the interested reader should at least review Gardner (1986), Neisser (1967, 1976), Simon (1979), and one or another of the better general textbooks (e.g., J. R. Anderson, 1985; M. Eysenck, 1984; Glass & Holyoak, 1986; Lachman, & Butterfield, 1979; Mayer, 1983). Educational researchers might also be particularly interested in three chapters in the *Review of Research in Education* consisting of a discussion of cognitive psychology in relation to educational practice, treatment of the assessment of intellectual performance, and a philosophical critique of the cognitive model for education (see Calfee, 1981; Curtis & Glaser, 1981; Floden, 1981). Increasingly, cognitive psychology in education is the topic of journal articles and special issues (see e.g., N. Frederiksen, 1984a; Glaser & Takanishi, 1986; Levin & Pressley, 1986). Edited volumes focused on cognitive psychology in testing have now begun to appear (see Glover, in press).

CURRENT GOALS AND APPROACHES

Cognitive Psychology does not label a unified science but rather a spectrum of researchers and theorists who use a variety of methods to study an equally diverse array of problems. And there are many controversies. The common ground is the view that the cognitive processes and contents involved in attention, perception and memory, thinking, reasoning and problem solving, and the acquisition, organization, and use of knowledge are the central subjects of inquiry for psychological science. Cognitive tasks, including school learning tasks and educational and psychological tests, that appear to reflect these phenomena can be analyzed to reach deeper understanding of the mental processes and content knowledge that comprise complex performance. Indeed, school learning tasks are of increasing interest to cognitive psychologists precisely because they represent a class of tasks chosen and shaped over the years to require and promote the cognitive functions of most importance to society and, thus, to theory (Greeno, 1980a). Exactly the same argument motivates cognitive psychology's new interest in mental tests.

In one part of the cognitive research spectrum, investigators analyze relatively fast information processing in relatively simple kinds of performances such as those required in common laboratory tasks and in some mental tests, but also in reading and elementary mathematics. Response latency and error measures presumed to reflect the action of constituent stages or component functions in task processing provide the principal data in this work. Of use also in some studies are behavioral records, such as verbal reports or eye-fixation sequences during performance, and neurophysiological indicators obtained from electroencephalograms. Most investigators search for general mechanisms that might underlie human cognition and intelligence as broadly defined and perhaps be useful as models for the development of artificial intelligence as well; others focus on the individual differences typically observed in such human performances, though their goal is also general theory.

In another part of the spectrum, the aim is to understand the relatively slower and more complex kinds of cognitive performances, where the use of organized prior knowledge plays a large role. The focus here is often on the tasks involved in learning and doing science and mathematics, in medical diagnosis, in the construction and control of complex physical systems, in text or discourse processing generally, and in complex games such as chess. The data medium is likely to be the verbal and behavioral records left by the performer in action or in retrospective interviews aimed at detailed diagnosis. The goal might be a computer-based model of knowledge structure. But empirical experiments also play a key role here. Again, most researchers concentrate on general theory; some examine individual differences, such as those between expert and novice performers, to test individual and general hypotheses.

Along the spectrum, there are many combinations of these techniques. There are also categories of research dominated by a particular kind of laboratory task. These are called *paradigmatic tasks* because they have been explicitly designed to display a theoretical distinction. Such measures are often included in research focused elsewhere on the spectrum. In recent years, however, there has been less emphasis on these tasks and more on analyses of tasks derived from natural human environments.

Almost all of these kinds of work rely on an information-processing approach. Cognitive psychology has advanced because, as J. R. Anderson and Bower (1973) put it, the information-processing model suggested both a way to theorize about the cognitive machinery connecting stimulus and response and a way to experiment on the connections (see also Estes, 1975). The computer, then, has become a metaphor for theory and a medium for the realization and evaluation of it. In education, the computer has also become the host for intelligent adaptive tutors and adaptive tests, wherein distinctions between theory, instruction, and assessment begin to blur. The lines between research on human and artificial intelligence have also become fuzzy in many areas.

Cognitive science is the term now used to label the confluence of psychological, computer, linguistic, and neurophysiological sciences. But the psychologists in this confluence continue to emphasize the understanding, assessment, and improvement of human cognition as primary. For them, the computer is a valuable source of analogies for theory and of computational power to allow the formation and testing of sophisticated simulations of complex human cognition. For us, it is one important medium within which to integrate cognitive theory and educational measurement. Aside from noting this possibility, however, we limit our focus to the human psychology in cognitive science. We leave out computer science and linguistics, and also the more molecular, neuropsychological theories based on information-processing approaches, even though these might also ultimately have implications for educational measurement. On the other hand, we include some developments in European cognitive psychology, stemming from Gestalt and phenomenological traditions, though they are not strictly information-processing approaches.

A PROVISIONAL TAXONOMY

The textbook view of cognitive psychology typically lays out sections pertaining to each of the presumably basic or general functions of human information processing. There are usually chapters on pattern recognition, perception and attention, learning, memory, reasoning, problem solving, thinking, language comprehension and production, and knowledge representation, among others. But it is also possible to organize the contents of cognitive psychology according to ecologically important activities of modern life and of education, distinguishing, for example, reading, writing, mathematics, problem solving in various specified subject matter domains, skillful motor performance in various everyday tasks, and discoursing in various contexts. The result is a rectangular matrix with rows for the familiar general functions and columns for the important educational activities. One can then focus on a particular row's function as it is manifested across the columns of educational activities. But one can also focus on the nature and organization of all the cognitive functions involved in a particular column of educational activity.

Elshout (1985) described such a matrix especially to emphasize that problem solving appears as both a row and a column; it is regarded in cognitive psychology as both one of the several basic functions and one of the several educational activities of importance. Elshout's implication is that problem solving, as a function, is involved in all educational activities, and, as an activity, it involves all of the basic cognitive functions. Problem solving is thus not a special domain of cognitive psychology but rather an aspect of central concern in all of its domains.

Two further implications set the stage for the present chapter. *First*, the cognitive psychology of problem solving is a central concern for educational measurement because all mental tests are, in some sense, problem-solving tasks. Hence, existing or proposed test designs ought to be evaluated as such. The methods of cognitive psychology seem particularly well suited to this purpose. *Second*, the two most general purposes of educational measurement, the assessment of student aptitudes and achievements, would appear to cut across the matrix of cognitive psychology in different ways. Tests designed to serve primarily as indicants of aptitude (i.e., for the purposes of prediction, or classification, or readiness diagnosis) have traditionally been structured to represent, or distinguish, the rows of Elshout's matrix. Obvious examples are the differential aptitude batteries or the ability-factor distinctions available from Cattell (1971), Ekstrom, French, and Harman (1976), and Guilford (1967). On the other hand, tests designed primarily to assess achievement (i.e., for the purposes of student or program evaluation or remedial diagnosis) have traditionally been focused on one or more of the columns, because these are more clearly related to stated educational goals. Thus, different slices across the field of cognitive psychology might be needed to inform test design and evaluation for the two different purposes. One criticism of conventional tests of cognitive aptitude could be that the assessment of separate functions (such as verbal, spatial, and reasoning ability; memory; and perceptual speed) that are presumably important across all educational contents and activities, even if done well, fails to recognize the unique cognitive content and organization of these functions in different educational achievement domains. One criticism of conventional achievement tests might be that the emphasis on particular educational content domains and activities fails to assess all of the cognitive functions required, and their unique organization, in that domain or activity.

AVENUES OF CONTRIBUTION

Cognitive psychology can contribute to educational measurement in several related ways. Both its theories and its methods offer new avenues through which to improve the design and evaluation of educational measures for different purposes. Three broad avenues of contribution are addressed in this chapter.

First, cognitive analyses of existing measures can help improve understanding of the construct(s) represented by them. The correlational networks typically used to interpret test performance might thus be augmented by information-processing models of test performance. Sources of item difficulty might be understood and manipulated in new ways. The processing skill and knowledge components of test performance that do and do not produce individual differences in scores could be clarified. And aspects of test performance that were not intended to be included in the construct might also be identified. Cognitive psychology thus offers a new source of evidence for construct validation.

Second, cognitive study of the target aptitudes, achievements, and content domains for which educational measures are to be built or used might suggest alternative measurement strategies and refinements of existing instruments. Given a clearer, more detailed view of the goals and of the instructional treatments usually used to achieve them, educational tests might be made more diagnostic of malfunctions in learning and more informative for instructional adaptation. Both content and format of tests might thus be made to conform more fully or more representatively to the cognitive character of the intended target.

Third, new and improved theories of aptitude, learning, and achievement in education might be derived from cognitive psychological research. New perspectives on the cognitive performance goals, requirements, demands, and conditions of educational environments could be developed. These could indicate entirely new directions, needs, and forms for educational measurement.

How one uses cognitive psychology in these ways of course depends on the intended purposes, uses, and interpretations of measurement. We can note here some important distinctions of purpose to be kept in mind, without belaboring all of their subtleties. Tests designed to serve as indicants of aptitude, or readiness to profit from subsequent instruction, differ from tests designed to assess achievement following instruction. Tests aimed at norm-referenced interpretation differ from tests aimed at criterion- or domain-referenced interpretation. Some tests are intended to support diagnoses of learning abilities or disabilities or the presence or absence of specified knowledge. Speed is purposely an important aspect of some tests, but not others. These test purposes and characteristics map onto the matrix of cognitive psychology in different ways, as noted earlier. In some instances, advances in cognitive psychology might apply directly to one type of test or test use. But existing theory or evidence from cognitive psychology might be only superficially relevant in other cases. The buyer must beware of many subtleties.

Overarching these various measurement purposes are two dimensions of test type that closely parallel two important dimensions of cognitive psychology. One is the distinction between declarative and procedural knowledge, or more simply, content knowledge and process knowledge (J. R. Anderson, 1976, 1983; Greeno, 1978; Ryle, 1949). The other distinguishes controlled and automatic processing (Ackerman, 1986, 1987; Schneider, Dumais, & Shiffrin, 1984; Schneider & Shiffrin, 1977). Although many other useful theoretical distinctions derive from cognitive psychology, these two seem most basic for educational measurement; they thus recur throughout this chapter. We introduce these distinctions here and discuss them further in later sections. Other distinctions are taken up as they apply in particular sections.

Declarative knowledge is factual knowledge about the meaning or perceptual characteristics of things, from anecdotal memories about daily events to the highly organized conceptual knowledge of some subject matter. A novice's knowledge of a newly learned theorem of geometry, for example, is declarative knowledge. *Procedural knowledge* is knowledge of how to do something, from pronouncing a word or driving a car, to transforming and rehearsing information in working memory, to assembling new methods of solving problems and monitoring the effectiveness with which these methods are implemented. Organizing geometry theorems into a sequence to reach a certain proof, for example, requires procedural knowledge.

All cognitive tasks require both declarative and procedural knowledge, and, in the abstract, the two can be seen as one (Greeno, 1978; Winograd, 1972, 1975). Procedural knowledge can often be stated declaratively, and declarative knowledge can become proceduralized with practice. Nevertheless, educational tasks differ in the demands they place on one or the other type of knowledge. For example, achievement tests that sample factual knowledge in a domain place heavy demands on the examinee's store of declarative knowledge, its organization, and its retrievability. On the other hand, tests of inductive reasoning or spatial-visualization ability place heavier demands on the examinee's execution of certain cognitive procedures or skills. Some tasks require complex mixtures of factual knowledge and cognitive skill (e.g., mathematical reasoning tests). Note also that instructional presentations may emphasize declarative knowledge, leaving required procedural knowledge implicit or unpracticed (see, e.g., Greeno, 1978, 1980b); therefore, educational measures may need to be made sensitive to both types of knowledge, the kind excluded and the kind included in instruction, to provide useful assessments.

The controlled-versus-automatic-processing distinction refers to the degree to which a knowledgeable or skillful performance requires conscious attentional resources for successful operation. Automatization occurs when cognitive tasks are consistent in their information-processing demands such that a transition from controlled to automatic processing can occur with practice. Using arithmetic facts is a controlled process for a child. For the practiced adolescent, their use has become automatic. Automatization is thought to free memory space for other controlled processing. Tasks with inconsistent information-processing requirements remain consciously controlled; automatization is not possible. Tests of ability and achievement can emphasize either type of processing, or some mixture, and a given test could vary on this continuum as a function of where on a learning curve it is administered (Ackerman, 1986). A perceptual speed test, such as Number Comparison reflects automatic processing for most adults, but it might reflect controlled processing for children. A test composed of algebra word problems will likely require both kinds of processing.

Cognitive psychology contributes to the measurement of procedural knowledge through its methods of developing and testing information-processing models of skilled performance; it studies how and how well individuals process information in controlled and automatic modes and shift between them. It contributes to the assessment of declarative knowledge through its methods of devising and testing models of knowledge acquisition, representation, organization, and use. Ultimately, it aims to show how declarative and procedural knowledge and controlled and automatic processing are integrated in competent performance.

Contrasting Models of Cognitive Performance: Overview and Critique

All measurement presumes some model of the property measured. But there are several different kinds of models of interest here. Psychometric models have served the development of educational measurement to date. Cognitive information-processing models now emanate from cognitive psychology in two basic forms: models based on experimental task manipulations and models built as computer programs. However, one form can sometimes also be realized in the other form, and there are emergent forms based on qualitative distinctions that might or might not eventually be defined by experimental variables or computer programs. To complicate matters further, cognitive psychology now recognizes an important distinction between all of the models that represent *investigators'* conceptualizations of subjects' mental functioning, and the mental models that *subjects* use to guide their own functioning in the world as they experience it (see Rouse & Morris, 1986; also Marton, 1981). To reduce confusion, we usually refer to these latter sorts of models as *schemata*.

EDUCATIONAL AND PSYCHOMETRIC MEASUREMENT MODELS

From classical test theory (Feldt & Brennan, this volume) through the Rasch (1960) model to item response theory (Lord, 1980), psychometric research has produced a variety of powerful models for educational and psychological measurement. There are also variations aimed at criterion-referenced or domain-referenced, rather than norm-referenced, interpretations (Glaser & Nitko, 1971). Despite varying assumptions from one to another, all these models are aimed at estimating a person's location on an underlying latent variable. This location is typically interpreted as an "amount" on the latent scale, which can be dichotomous or continuous. For simplicity, we refer to this whole family as educational psychometric measurement (EPM) models. We need not review their many variants and details here (see Hambleton; this volume).

By way of initial criticism from the point of view of cognitive psychology, there are three important and related points to note about EPM models. *First*, they might have no substantive psychological justification at the level of item performance. *Second*, they make particular, and often simplistic, assumptions about the psychology of the items. *Third*, the psychology of the test as a whole is left implicit or omitted from the model; validation of the test's meaning is considered largely a matter external to the EPM model itself. Lord addressed the first issue directly: "The reader may ask for some a priori justification of . . . [the three-parameter logistic model]. No convincing a priori justification exists. . . . The model must be justified on the basis of the results obtained, not on a priori grounds" (1980, p. 14). Thus, the model is justified by how well it describes a certain type of empirical data, not by its psychological reasonableness.

Regarding the second issue, both classical test theory (Lord & Novick, 1968) and generalizability theory (Cronbach, Gleser, Nanda, & Rajaratnam, 1972) assume that errors are uncorrelated. Yet, just as with any sequenced cognitive task, we know that examinees often learn during test performance, react to successes or failures on previous items, reallocate remaining time accordingly, and probably also act in other ways to violate the independence assumption (e.g., Rocklin & O'Donnell, in press). Items are also sometimes designed in groups, as in reading comprehension tests, where several questions pertain to the same passage. Thus, there are many potential sources of context effects on particular items. Such effects also challenge the assumption of local independence in item response theory. Lord's (1980) three-parameter logistic model assumes that the probability of success on an item for a person of a given ability level depends only on the three item parameters for that item. In other words, if the three-parameter logistic model is correct, then the person's ability is the only parameter needed to predict success on a given item, because item parameters are the same for all persons. Knowledge of the person's level on other abilities or performance on other items adds nothing. Items are assumed to form a unidimensional scale, and this same scale is assumed to apply to all persons. As Lord put it, "Unidimensionality is a property of the items; it does not cease to exist just because we have changed the distribution of ability in the group tested" (1980, p. 20).

Yet much of the cognitive research on the nature and development of ability suggests that learner experience is an important determiner of what attributes are measured by any test, and how many different attributes are measured. For example, a test might be unidimensional for novices because all problems are relatively novel for them and, thus, require the same general problem-solving skills, whereas experts might show different patterns of skill development on different types of problems. Ferguson (1954, 1956) years ago advanced similar hypotheses from a factor-analytic perspective, namely, that abilities tend to differentiate with practice (see Anastasi, 1970, for a supporting review). Aside from practice, it has also long been known that persons differ in the strategies they pursue on different tests (French, 1965). And this is also now clearly true for items within a test (Snow, 1978; R. J. Sternberg & Weil, 1980). If persons' performances differ qualitatively within a test, it is unlikely that a set of test items can somehow give the same psychological scale for all subjects, regardless of ability level or strategy type. As a substantive focus for cognitive psychology then, "ability," the latent trait Θ in EPM models, is not considered univocal, except as a convenient summary of amount correct regardless of how obtained. Rather, a score reflects a complex combination of processing skills, strategies, and knowledge components, both procedural and declarative and both controlled and automatic, some of which are variant and some invariant across persons, or tasks, or stages of practice, in any given sample of persons or tasks. In other samples of persons or situations, different combinations and different variants and invariants might come into play. Cognitive psychology's contribution is to analyze these complexes. Robustness of EPM models with respect to violations of such assumptions is now being examined (see e.g., Ansley & Forsyth, 1985). Proposals to allow for planned dependencies have been advanced but, so far, only within the EPM perspective (see, e.g., Andrich, 1985; Ward, 1985; Weiss, 1982). Also, new EPM models are being devised to address the problems of multicomponent processes and strategies in test scores (see e.g., Embretson, 1985b; Mislevy & Verhelst, 1987). Time and trial will tell how well these work.

Another way to characterize this issue is to argue that item difficulty cannot be unidimensional, even in the simplest task, except as a gross summary. Cognitive psychology predicts that there will be many sources of item difficulty. A prime objective of experimental analysis is to determine just what these sources are, so that they can be systematically manipulated to investigate the cognitive processes influenced by each. Typically, test-item writers are not prepared to identify or manipulate these psychological facets of the test. Item writers are more likely to be content specialists working from test specifications that bear no relation to the specifications of relevant psychological theory (see Embretson, 1985b). In the view of cognitive psychology, then, item difficulty emerges from the item-writing process as a complex combination of various item attributes that the item writer has wittingly or unwittingly employed. The mix of attributes of any item influences the mix of cognitive processing required for successful performance. In other words, person and item parameters are both summary statistics; they might have important uses, but they do not reflect homogeneous psychological functions.

The third point brings in the overarching construct validity issue most directly. Traditional EPM models treat item and test scores as black boxes; they do not explicitly include substantively meaningful explanations of the performances they model. Although the necessity for valid explanation of test scores has been an accepted standard for educational and psychological measurement since the early 1950s, the practice of test validation has typically sought mainly external corroboration of test interpretation for various test uses; it has rarely penetrated to the test model itself. Yet central discussions in the field have long been clear on the need to do so.

In the previous edition of this volume, Cronbach put the general point this way:

> Validation examines the soundness of *all* the interpretations of a test—descriptive and explanatory interpretations as well as situation-bound predictions.
>
> To explain a test score, one must bring to bear some sort of theory about the causes of the test performance and about its impli-

cations. Validation of test interpretations is similar, therefore, to the evaluation of any scientific theory. . . . Since each experiment checking upon a theory is an opportunity to modify or extend the theory, validation is more than corroboration; it is a process for developing sounder interpretations of observations. Construction of a test itself starts from a theory about behavior or mental organization, derived from prior research, that suggests the ground plan for the test. Studies of the new test show how to improve it and sometimes lead to a change in the very conception of the variable to be measured. (1971, p. 443)

Although both the theory and the practice of test validation have evolved in the ensuing years, the core argument for construct explanation has not changed. Cronbach (1984) and Messick (1984, and this volume) have consistently argued that it is the confluence of evidence about the meaning of test scores that constitutes construct validity. This meaning includes interpretation of the mental organizations and processes that underlie obtained test scores. But even a longtime critic of the concept of construct validity made a closely parallel point. Ebel noted that

> The quantitative sophistication of many specialists in educational measurement is displayed, not in the precision and elegance of their procedures for obtaining initial measurements, but rather in the statistical transformations and elaborations, and analyses they are prepared to perform on almost any raw data given them. The term "raw" may be particularly appropriate when applied to the original data yielded by many educational tests. What we often overlook is the limited power of statistical transformations to refine these raw data and make them more precisely meaningful. If more systematic and standardized processes of test production could be developed and used, our educational measurements should become not only more consistently reproducible, but what is perhaps even more important, they should become more meaningful. (1962, p. 22)

In short, cognitive psychology's first challenge is the same as the challenge put to testing by various measurement experts over the years and by the evolving theory of validation as codified for the profession over the several editions of *Standards for Educational and Psychological Testing* (American Educational Research Association, American Psychological Association, and National Council on Measurement in Education, 1985). The challenge is to experiment upon the internal character of tests, to test the assumptions of EPM models, to make them explain the nature of test performance in substantive psychological terms, and to state explicitly the theories upon which the tests are constructed, scored, and interpreted. As Carroll (1976) has argued and demonstrated, cognitive tests are cognitive tasks, not different in kind from the tasks that cognitive psychology has set itself up to analyze and understand. The experimental and theoretical analysis of cognitive tasks has led to the development of methods and has distinguished substantive psychological processes that might, in turn, be useful in analyzing educational and psychological tests. Furthermore, to understand test performance in more fundamental and substantive ways could be to take a significant step toward understanding the educational performances the tests are designed to predict or reflect.

Cognitive psychology's second, and broader, challenge is to develop improved substantive theories of the aptitudes and achievements that are the goals of education and that educational measurements should be designed to assess and promote. Expanded and revised theories of the nature of educational performance could show conventional tests and the EPM models on which they are based to be limited and unrepresentative. It could appear, for example, that key aspects of competent performance or key distinctions within it are omitted or ignored. So far, research on new technologies in educational measurement, such as adaptive testing, seem aimed only at increasing the efficiency of testing within the standard EPM perspective. When both ability and item difficulty are seen as complexes, however, it is clear that the most efficient test design or subset of items might well provide only a restricted and perhaps distorted sampling of the domain to be represented. EPM models and test designs ought not to be driven primarily by the criterion of efficiency (see N. Frederiksen, 1984b, on this point).

We would add a complementary point. Educational and psychological tests deserve special status as objects of new cognitive experimental research precisely because they display so many real-world correlates. Through more fundamental understanding of their functioning, and experimental redesign to improve it, tests might be made to serve as vehicles connecting laboratory and field research; tests that embody theoretical distinctions from the laboratory transport them to enrich the understanding of field phenomena with which they correlate, while, at the same time, their empirical relations with field phenomena bring back implications for the improvement of theory (Snow & Peterson, 1985). There is a two-way street; better designed and understood educational measurements can play a unique role moving in both directions.

COGNITIVE INFORMATION-PROCESSING MODELS

Some of the models of mathematical learning theory (see Greeno, 1980a) and some still used in cognitive psychology (e.g., the power law of skill learning in Newell, 1980) bear formal similarities to EPM models. But the models toward which cognitive psychology strives serve primarily the development and testing of substantive psychological theory. That is, they are attempts to explain the internal workings of the human cognitive system, the mental events and processes that connect stimulus and response in an item, test, or task performance, and thus to penetrate the black box of EPM models. The level of abstraction sought for such explanations is more molecular than theories concerned only with observable terminal response and more molar than theories concerned only with neurophysiological functioning, while still being consistent with both behavioral and neurophysiological evidence. We refer to all such models as cognitive information-processing (CIP) models, though there are many variants.

All CIP models posit one or more sequences of processing steps or stages in which cognitive operations are performed on incoming or stored information. Indeed, a principal aim of much experimental task development and analysis has been to examine these stage distinctions. Some CIP models are simple mathematical constructions with only one or two parameters to reflect the functioning of different processing stages in performance on paradigmatic laboratory tasks. Others are mathematical models designed as analyses of more complex tasks

that appear important in their own right outside the laboratory. Some take the form of computer programs (J. R. Anderson, 1983; Newell & Simon, 1972) for complex tasks that reach a level of detail far more explicit than most mathematical models; here quantitative fits to data are often impossible to compute (as in most protocol analyses, e.g., Newell & Simon, 1972) and difficult to interpret even when computed (as in some attempts to model item data by multiple-regression methods, e.g., R. J. Sternberg, 1977). In any event, CIP models tend to be richer, if more complicated, than EPM models. Because the two types make different assumptions, each can yield results that test the adequacy of the assumptions of the other. Each can thus contribute differently to understanding the attributes being measured.

A detailed CIP model is the single most important outcome of a cognitive-task analysis or an attempt at computer simulation. In the best methods for reaching this goal, the investigator specifies the details of each component process or stage and how these component processes combine, then finds ways to operationalize the model, then evaluates it by comparing its fit to data with that of rival models, then revises and reevaluates accordingly. The style is functionalist: close cyclical interplay between theory development and data analysis. Alternative assumptions are checked all along the way. This is an important departure from methods in which an investigator attempts to infer a full model from one or two statistically significant effects (see Greeno, 1980a, for further discussion). It is also a significant departure from the way EPM models are typically used; the experimentalist continually compares rival models with data.

There are also further steps, laid out long ago as principles in psychometric research, that experimentalists are now beginning to take. These include the use of multiple tasks to estimate reliability and to attempt to generalize the provisional CIP model to account for performance on other tasks to which the target task is related. A model for one test or task, then, is considered insufficient until it is generalized to account for performance on other tests or tasks purported to represent the same psychological constructs. If the best-fitting task models differ for two highly correlated reasoning tests, for example, either the models or the construct must be adjusted. Thus, the inner workings of a CIP model are examined across tasks to check adequacy of construct representation. EPM models, on the other hand, are often applied across tasks with little regard to constructs. Correlation, or the lack of it, between resulting total scores for two tests will bear on the construct interpretation but not back on the EPM model(s) chosen to produce the scores. In this sense, the test designer's choice of, say, one or another item response model, is often construct insensitive.

In the more comprehensive models developed as computer programs to simulate human thinking, learning, or problem solving, other forms of evaluation come into play. Such programs are considered good models only if they incorporate what is already known about human performance. In the context of solving specific problems, the programs should make mistakes similar to those that humans make. The rank order of problem difficulty (as indexed by the number of central processing unit cycles or solution failures) should also be similar to the rank order of problem difficulty observed when the same problems are administered to humans. In this way, the computer is used as a tool for evaluating any CIP model of thinking that can be represented in a programming language. Early attempts at modeling of this sort focused on developing programs for particular types of tasks, such as spelling, algebra word problems, and chess (see, e.g., Simon, 1979). Increasingly, problem-solving programs have been designed for broader applicability (Newell & Simon, 1972). Large syntheses have been attempted, notably in the research programs of J. R. Anderson (1976, 1983; see also J. R. Anderson & Bower, 1973) and Schank and Abelson (1977). Such models have had an enormous impact on psychological theory, in spite of the well-recognized limitations of conventional digital processors for modeling analog and parallel processes. Now, even these limits are being removed (J. R. Anderson, 1984; Rumelhart, McClelland, & the PDP Research Group, 1986; McClelland, Rumelhart, & the PDP Research Group, 1986), though not without controversy (see Dreyfus & Dreyfus, 1986). By providing a way of representing detailed hypotheses about the internal nature of human cognition that would otherwise be difficult or impossible to evaluate, these models have changed the evidentiary base of psychology to include something other than human behavioral data.

The evidentiary base of theory has also changed in subtler ways since the 1960s, shifting progressively from measures that assess terminal performance to those that allow inferences about process. The aim is to increase the density of observations (Ericcson & Simon, 1984). Thus, trials-to-criterion and simple counts of items answered correctly (or incorrectly) have been replaced by response latencies for parts of tasks, eye fixations during performance or retrospections thereafter, and fine-grained error analyses.

Further, all such measures are gathered in ways that facilitate model building and testing. This is probably the most significant difference between cognitive psychology today and the cognitive psychology that flourished before behaviorism. Eye fixations, latencies, error analyses, and protocol analyses were well known by the turn of the century. The early investigators used such measures to isolate particular processes or response styles, but they did not build and test full models of all the putative cognitive processes occurring between stimulus onset and response.

Beyond the drive to increase the density of observations, and to reach general process models of cognition based on such observations, there has also been a marked increase in research on individual differences in information processing. This is considered a historic move, not only because it brings in individual difference data to test the adequacy of general theories (Underwood, 1975), but also because it advances toward the unification of experimental and correlational disciplines in psychology in a new way. The literature of cognitive differential psychology is thus also now blossoming in journals and book compendia (see, e.g., Dillon, 1985; Dillon & Schmeck, 1983; Embretson, 1985; Snow & Farr, 1987; Snow, Federico, & Montague, 1980a, 1980b; R. J. Sternberg, 1982a, 1982b, 1984a, 1985a, 1986). The research has generated a range of methodological approaches that augment the general modeling techniques discussed to this point. These include the analysis of correlations between laboratory task parameters and mental tests, the direct experimental analysis of tests to identify component processes, diagnoses of knowledge content and organization, direct training studies, specialized aptitude-treatment interaction analyses, and the comparison of cognitive status groups such as high and low achievers, different age groups, or experts and novices in some field. All these methods, in various combinations, are exemplified later in this chapter.

But modern cognitive psychology also has its critics, and some of their criticisms are just, in our view. The field has been fragmented and, in some respects, noncumulative. Research attention has flitted, until recently, from interesting task to interesting task without much attention to intertask relations. Its experimental side has paid little attention to ecological validity and still tends to specify its research questions as simple dichotomies for laboratory analysis only. Its computer side argues that "cognitive theory should be like a computer program . . . a precise specification of the behavior, but . . . sufficiently abstract to provide a conceptually tractable framework for understanding the phenomenon" (J. R. Anderson, 1985, p. 10). Yet conceptually tractable, computerized theories often seem to be abstracted too far from data to judge whether they are empirically tractable. Some basic questions regarding the nature of mental representations, the need for higher order executive and control processes, and the integration of serial and parallel processing have not yet been sufficiently considered or satisfactorily answered. And some presumably central aspects of cognitive functioning, such as emotion, motivation, and volition, have been ignored almost completely (see Snow & Farr, 1987).

Furthermore, as cognitive psychology turned toward investigating individual differences in information processing, simplistic assumptions borne of earlier experiments that had ignored individual differences were automatically extended. First it was assumed that a general process model would fit all persons on average and that individual differences could be adequately expressed merely as parameter variations within the general model. This is an assumption that dates at least from Hull (1945; see also Glaser, 1967). When it became clear that different persons might perform the same task in qualitatively different ways, it was still assumed that, within a person, the same model should fit performance on all items. Learning and strategy shifting within the task were ignored by CIP models, just as they were by EPM models, until recently. There was also a tendency to assume that response latency and error measures should tell the same story. This led to the practice of purifying response latency data by excluding error-prone items or persons from the analysis and, thereby, distorting the range of ability and item difficulty included. Univariate analyses of either errors or latencies can be misleading, in part because speed and accuracy often reflect fundamentally different aspects of cognition, but also because the meaning of either variable depends on the form of the functional relationship between them. Furthermore, parameters of this function can vary systematically with ability (Lohman, 1986a). It was further assumed in some early work that the results of within-person experiments could identify independent elementary information processes, whereas the results of factor analysis could not. It is now clear, however, that either method might or might not and that, in any case, terms such as *independent* and *elementary* are relative, not absolute.

We need not belabor these issues here, however. Lachman

et al. (1979) provided a chapter-sized summary and references on some of the criticisms. Others have been discussed in some detail by Carroll (1980a, 1980b, 1981), Snow (1978, 1981), and R. J. Sternberg (1977, 1980). The criticisms, for the most part, apply to any science in its youth. Also for the most part, they are irrelevant to our purpose here. Cognitive psychology's functionalist style is self-corrective with respect to some of these problems, at least; current research is moving rapidly to remove them. Moreover, its methods of task analysis and process modeling can provide innovative suggestions for research in educational measurement, even if the substantive theories derived from them are faulty. The substantive theories at least identify *possible* cognitive mechanisms and phenomena that *might* exist outside the laboratory even if they have not yet been demonstrated there. In both method and substance, cognitive psychology can be richly suggestive in many ways for educational measurement, despite the shortcomings.

POSSIBILITIES FOR COMBINED MODELS

Some recent efforts have sought to combine the strengths of EPM and CIP models. This could be the most important wave of the future.

Carroll, Meade, and Johnson (in press), for example, have demonstrated the use of the person characteristic function, based on the three-parameter latent-trait model, to investigate the unidimensionality of a test in the face of multiple sources of item difficulty. The method can establish construct meanings for the latent-trait scale based on an analysis of the item and task attributes that produce difficulty.

Embretson (1983, 1985b) has developed several multicomponent latent-trait models that combine CIP models of skill and knowledge components involved in item processing with the latent-trait EPM model. Her approach seeks first to explicate the cognitive components involved in solving psychometric items and to obtain a CIP model of these components based on responses to subtasks designed to reflect the components. Probability of correct item response is assumed to be a multiplicative combination of the probabilities of correct subtask response. In turn, the Rasch model is applied, to give the probability of each person's passing each component subtask. It is assumed that the list of component subtasks is exhaustive and that all components must be performed correctly for a correct response to the item. Alternative CIP models can be compared, to obtain the best-fitting construct representation for each test. Two tests that purport to represent the same construct and involve the same performance components could, nonetheless, differ in the weighted combination of components that best predicts item scores. The two tests are then said to have different nomothetic spans, because they show different degrees and patterns of correlation with external variables. The relationship of construct representation and nomothetic span for each test is evaluated by using structural regression methods.

Mislevy and Verhelst (1987) have applied item response theory to items on which respondents differ in the processing strategies they employ. Their model makes it possible to estimate item parameters associated with each strategy, the number of respondents employing each, and the distribution of person parameters within each strategy group. The probability

that each person used a given strategy is also estimated. The method does assume, however, that a given person applies the same strategy to all items.

Both Haertel (1984a, 1984b, in press) and Rindskopf (1987) have studied latent-class models as alternatives to latent-trait models. It appears, in some cases, that the former analyses fit the supposed character of cognitive functioning in tests better than do analyses based on continuous variables. The latent-class models avoid assumptions about dimensionality and can distinguish between skills or skill levels reflecting item difficulty and item difficulty arising from incidental item features. Haertel's applications have been to hypotheses about levels of skill mastery. Rindskopf's have been to developmental-level hypotheses. But both are clearly relevant to analyses of CIP models for tests more generally.

The value of these and related methods of combining CIP and EPM considerations depends, however, on the adequacy of the cognitive analyses of each test. Thus, we turn next to this topic and return to the possibilities of combined models in a later section.

Advances in Cognitive Analysis Relevant to Measurement

Under this major heading, we present a selection of empirical, methodological, and theoretical developments across the various categories of cognitive psychology, following an order that approximates a path down the main diagonal of the taxonomic matrix previously described. We have rearranged and relabeled the columns of the matrix, however, to bring out more clearly the categories of aptitude and achievement that educational measurement specialists typically use to structure their work. Figure 7.1 provides the resulting provisional taxonomy, with the major divisions of this section mapped into it.

We do not here review comprehensively the contemporary theories in these categories or try to resolve the many continuing controversies over alternative CIP models and hypotheses. The aim, rather, is to provide a flavor for styles of thinking and research, through a sampling of studies addressing different cognitive functions and activities or using different methods. The examples are chosen to suggest possibilities for research, particularly on existing forms and goals of educational measurement. But some of the findings noted also bear on the last major section of this chapter, where we address the possibilities for new cognitive theories of aptitude and achievement and improved methods of measurement research and evaluation.

Perception, Memory, Attention, and Special Abilities

Incoming visual and auditory stimuli must be received and held long enough in a sensory system, segmented or synthesized somehow, and recognized, encoded, or otherwise represented in a memory system so that attention can be directed and further cognitive work can be done. The further work might be as simple as identifying or comparing perceived patterns or as complex as using accumulating information to build a novel train of thought. But an important hypothesis has been that the characteristics of the initial perception-memory-

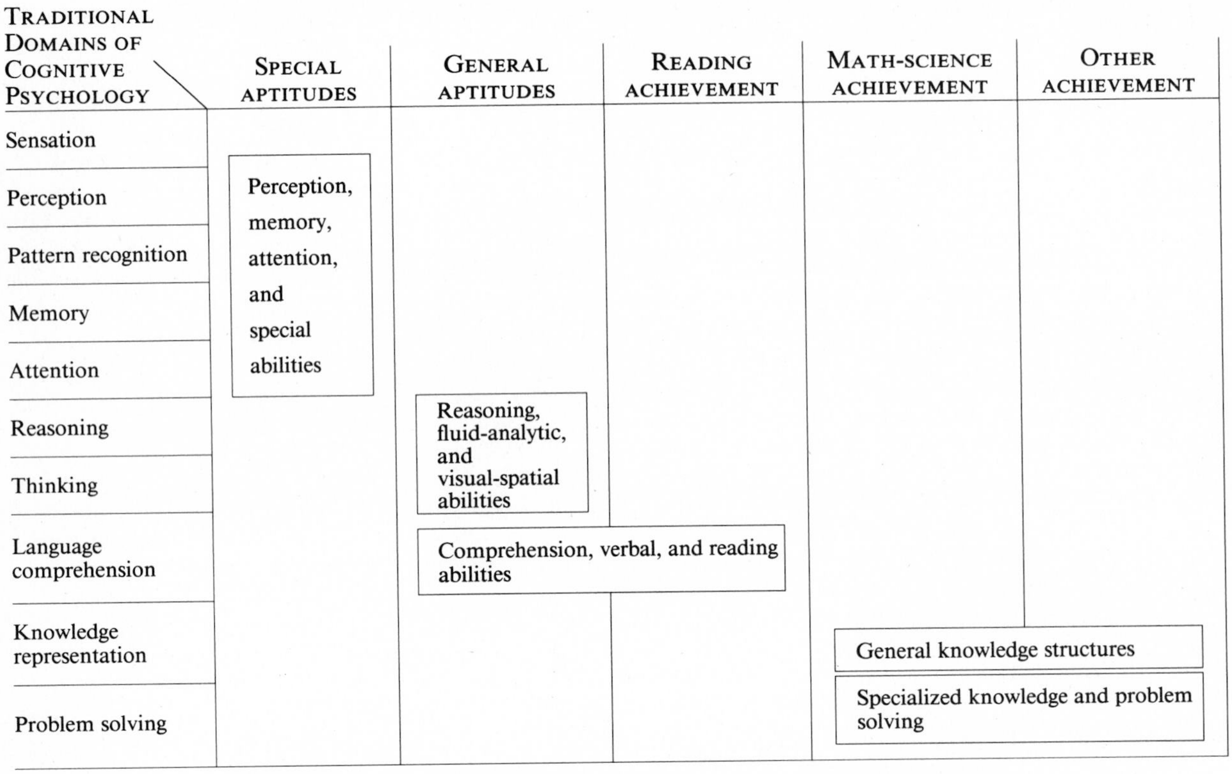

TRADITIONAL DOMAINS OF COGNITIVE PSYCHOLOGY	SPECIAL APTITUDES	GENERAL APTITUDES	READING ACHIEVEMENT	MATH-SCIENCE ACHIEVEMENT	OTHER ACHIEVEMENT
Sensation					
Perception	Perception, memory, attention, and special abilities				
Pattern recognition					
Memory					
Attention					
Reasoning		Reasoning, fluid-analytic, and visual-spatial abilities			
Thinking					
Language comprehension		Comprehension, verbal, and reading abilities			
Knowledge representation				General knowledge structures	
Problem solving				Specialized knowledge and problem solving	

FIGURE 7.1 Traditional Domains of Cognitive Educational Measurement

attention system, and the skills involved in working it, are fundamentally important in conditioning the success of further cognitive processing. This topic, therefore, comes first in the taxonomy, and came first in the modern development of cognitive psychology. The implications for educational measurement are many, because the perception-memory-attention system could be the seat of many specific learning abilities and disabilities; skills based here might also underlie the development of complex problem solving and specialized expertise.

VISUAL MASKING

The initial visual (or auditory) processing system appears to be staged in such a way that stimuli are first registered in an iconic (or echoic) memory store, so that information can be selected from it before it decays or is replaced. An early suggestion of such staged processing came from studies by Sperling (1960) and Averbach and Coriell (1961) on what they called "backward visual masking" effects. Their tasks were designed to measure the capacity (in amount and duration) of information storage in the initial iconic register or sensory memory store, before the information was transferred to working memory. They found that stimuli presented tachistoscopically to individuals could appearently be "erased" from this iconic register if a subsequently presented masking stimulus or marker arrived at the same retinal location within about 100 msec. By manipulation of the character of the marker and the delay interval between initial stimulus and marker, subjects' accuracy of verbal report (e.g., of letters seen) could be made high or low. Short delay intervals (less than 50 msec) between a random array of letters and a circle marker on one letter seemed to allow subjects to perceive a superimposition of letter and circle marker, producing high letter recognition scores. Long delay intervals (more than 200 msec.) seemed to permit two distinct percepts and also high recognition scores. In the delay interval between these extremes (in the vicinity of 100 msec), the erasure or masking effect made letter recognition difficult or impossible. The interpretation posited two initial processing stages, iconic registration followed by encoding into working memory (plus response production), and suggested that erasure occurs if the mask catches the letter icon during transition to encoding. Clearly, there were capacity, and thus speed, limits in initial processing.

This interpretation persists, despite dispute (Lachman et al 1979). Nonetheless, a visual masking test developed by Seibert and Snow (1965) has given similar results in large samples and shown interesting correlations with more conventional ability tests, as shown in Figure 7.2 (see Snow, 1978, for details). Letter recognition accuracy at short delay intervals between letters and markers correlated substantially with an individual difference factor, based on motion picture tests, interpreted as a "perceptual integration" ability. At intermediate marker delays, correlations with a verbal ability factor were evident. With later marker delay, a perceptual speed factor seemed to enter. The implication is that at least three sources of systematic ability differences can be distinguished along the delay time line; these seem to correspond to three stages of visual

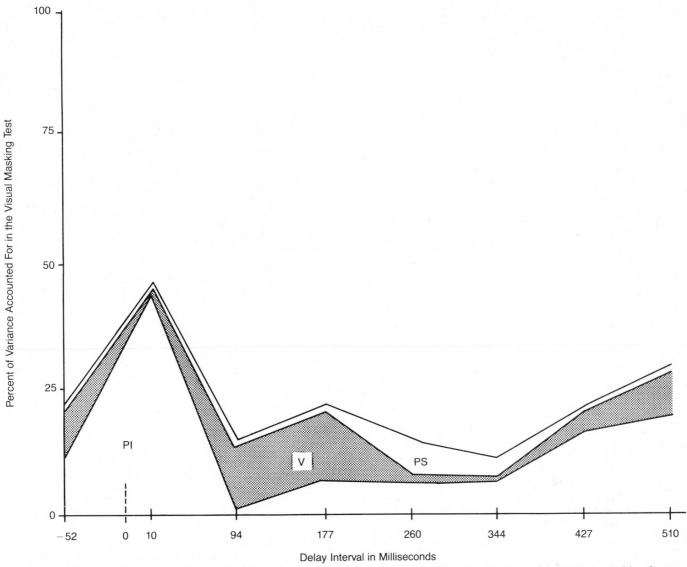

FIGURE 7.2 Percent of variance accounted for at each marker delay interval in the visual masking task by ability factors representing perceptual integration (PI), verbal comprehension (V), and perceptual speed (PS). (Adapted from Seibert & Snow, 1965; Snow, 1978.)

processing. In the iconic register, individual differences in icon decay, or in the perception of superimposition, connect to measurable differences in a hypothesized perceptual integration ability. Differences in speed or accuracy of verbal encoding into working memory are associated with conventional measures of verbal ability, and differences in speed or accuracy in comparing or matching distinct percepts in working memory are associated with conventional measures of perceptual speed. Furthermore, the masking technique could provide a new method of studying these and related abilities in more detail. There is also old and new evidence that perceptual performance under tachistoscopic conditions might reflect deeper seated cognitive and emotional processing (Allport, 1955; Bruner & Krech, 1950; C. Cooper & Kline, in press; Klein, 1970; Kragh & Smith, 1970).

PATTERN RECOGNITION

The perceptual-integration ability just proposed is based on measures that require recognition of common objects from degraded pictures, much like the partially blocked-out silhouettes used in Gestalt completion tests to measure the ability factor usually called *closure speed*. Unlike the paper-and-pencil versions, however, the motion picture tests used by Seibert and Snow (1965) sharply control item exposure time (and might also provide a kind of visual masking effect). Recognition is clearly the outcome of earlier perceptual processing, but it is not clear just how this initial processing is conducted, that is, we do not know what a perceptual-integration factor might represent. Introspective reports on both paper and film versions of such tests (and pilot work on eye movement analyses of them) suggest that at least two strategies exist; an indiscriminant gaze, followed by a report that the object "popped out," and a careful scrutinization of each displayed part, followed by construction of the object from these identified features. Most cognitive psychologists have tried not to hypothesize that different persons operate in different ways, so this observation has not been highly regarded.

Computer models, in particular, are usually built on the assumption that there is only one way to process information. Some computer models, for example, recognize stimulus patterns by extracting features and comparing these to lists of features held in memory. The letter A would be recognized by extracting such features as "cross-bar," "oblique-left," and "oblique-right" and comparing these with feature descriptions of each letter of the alphabet already in memory. Although this form of feature analysis and comparison might have its analogue in human perception, it is known that human pattern recognition also relies on knowledge of feature combinations and organizational properties, as well as on expectations and contextual cues. Thus, contemporary CIP models of the human perception-memory system posit both feature detectors and Gestalt organizers, or holistic descriptions of stimulus relations, operating in the process of comparing sensory and memory representations. They also posit the synthesis of analyzed input with information available from experiences and context. The resulting "analysis-by-synthesis" models work well in accounting for much evidence on both speech and visual perception including that involved in reading (see J. R. Anderson, 1985; Juola, 1979; Rumelhart, 1977). There is also an approach called *structural information theory* that avoids the distinction between feature and Gestalt processing, using an interpretive coding system that accommodates both aspects of the stimulus (Leeuwenberg & Buffart, n.d.; Restle, 1982). It appears that either type of model could suggest methods of coding visual material in tests or learning tasks as part of an analysis of sources of task difficulty, providing a kind of "readability" analysis for figural stimuli. Using the Leeuwenberg–Buffart system, for example, figures would be coded for each possible interpretation. The theory posits that the preferred interpretation will have the simplest code. By implication, item difficulty would be expected to increase as figures yielded no clearly simplest code. Common misinterpretations might have characteristic codes. So far as we know, such an approach has not been used in the design or evaluation of educational tests.

But the holistic-versus-analytic contrast is a persistent problem. This contrast, and a way to examine it further, is well demonstrated in L. A. Cooper's (1982) research. She has shown that at least some persons can be characterized reliably as using either one or the other of these forms of processing and has demonstrated several methods of exploring this individual difference further. The distinction is based on tasks that require subjects to compare a random shape held in memory with one available visually and to respond "same" or "different". The test shapes differ in various degrees from the shape in memory. Response latency data across differences in item difficulty show distinct patterns for the two groups of subjects: those apparently using holistic, parallel processing show no effects of variation in item difficulty, whereas those presumed

to be using analytic, feature processing show marked increase in response latency as test items become more similar to the memory item. Holistic processors seem to seek a match of whole shapes, responding "different" if no match is found; analytic processors seek features that distinguish test and memory shapes, responding "same" if no such feature is found. The groups are also distinguishable by various combinations of accuracy and latency scores.

Using systematic variations on this and similar tasks, L. A. Cooper has also tested the degree to which these two forms of processing are interchangeable as strategies. In one task variation, subjects had to locate dissimilar features. In another, the probability of same-versus-different pairs of shapes was manipulated. It was found that holistic processors could readily adopt an analytic strategy when task conditions made this strategy more efficient. It proved difficult to prompt all analytic processors to use a holistic strategy. Task directions can thus play a crucial role in what is measured. By varying the part structure of the stimuli, L. A. Cooper also provided evidence that the two groups of subjects use different visual memory representations. It is clear that the design of figural test items could prompt either type of processing.

Continuing research has only begun to examine the issue of correlation between other measures and this holistic–analytic distinction and the issue of whether typology or continuum offers the better representation (Agari, 1979). However, it is not hard to think of hypotheses tying this distinction into a variety of perceptual ability and cognitive style constructs or into performance on more complex spatial relations and visualization tests. For example, the distinction between whole and part processing might relate to similar contrasts observed by Goldner (1957) and Schorr, Bower, and Kiernan (1982) in Block Design performance. The difference in error patterns is also reminiscent of the old cognitive style construct of "leveling" versus "sharpening" (P. S. Holzman & Klein, 1954).

THE SUBTRACTIVE FACTORS METHOD

Another approach to processing stage analysis takes one step deeper into the working memory system: the subtractive factors method originally developed by Donders (1868/1969). The goal is to determine the duration of processing stages in a task. A series of two or more nested tasks is developed in which each successive task is presumed to require all of the processing stages required by previous tasks, plus an additional stage. Through use of a total latency measure for each task, the duration of each stage is estimated by subtraction between tasks. One typical example is a set of stimulus-comparison tasks developed by Posner and Mitchell (1967). In one task, subjects are required to compare letters of the alphabet, tachistoscopically presented, and to respond yes if the two letters are physically identical, as in *aa* or *AA* and no otherwise. A second task requires comparisons of the same sets of upper- and lowercase letters, but the correct response is yes if the two letters have the same name. In Task 1, then, the correct answer to the stimulus pair *Aa* would be no, whereas, in Task 2, the correct answer would be yes. An information-processing model for Task 1 would posit the following processing stages: register physical stimuli in iconic store; encode the physical features of the two stimuli into working memory; compare these representations; and respond. Presumably, Task 2 includes these same stages, plus an additional stage: retrieve the name codes associated with the two stimulus representations. Thus, the difference between time to respond in Task 2 and time to respond in Task 1 is an estimate of the duration of this retrieval stage. The resulting score is called the NIPI difference (for Name Identity minus Physical Identity) and has been widely studied as a measure of speed of lexical access (see Carroll, 1980a; L. A. Cooper & Regan, 1982; and Hunt, 1985b, for reviews).

Research by Hunt, in particular (see e.g., Hunt, Lunneborg, & Lewis, 1975), has used these and similar tasks to relate speed of lexical access to individual differences in verbal ability. Correlations with standard verbal tests are typically found to center around $r = -.3$. From the lowest to the highest levels of verbal ability among college students, the NIPI difference ranges from 100 msec to about 65 msec, respectively; mildly retarded individuals show NIPI differences of about 400 msec. It is possible, then, that speed of lexical access is one basic process in verbal comprehension and learning and one candidate for learning-disability assessment (see Hunt, 1985b, and our later section on verbal ability).

THE ADDITIVE-FACTORS METHOD

S. Sternberg (1969, 1975) proposed an additive-factors method to test the assumption of stage independence without assuming that a stage is completely deleted with impunity. In essence, the method prompts execution of a particular component process more than once by manipulating some experimental variable. Taylor (1976) has provided an extensive discussion of this method that shows how the simple models we discuss here can be modified to permit dependencies among processes (see Ippel, 1986; Pieters, 1983; and Taylor, 1976, for additional discussion). The basic model for the additive-factors method is

$$T = b_0 + b_1 X,$$

in which T is a vector of trial latencies, X is a vector indicating the number of times the stage must be executed or the amount of processing required on each trial, b_1 is the slope of the function, and b_0 is a constant representing time for all other processes. Note that this same equation could be used to model data collected by the subtractive method; however, X would then be a dummy vector of *1s* and *0s*, indicating presence or absence of the processing stage rather than variable amounts of processing, as in the additive-factors method. But there is another important difference: The dummy vector for the subtractive method assumes that the process can be reduced to 0, that is, there is a ratio scale for X. The model for the additive-factors method, however, assumes that the amount of processing increases linearly with increases in X, that is, an interval scale for X. S. Sternberg generalized the model to include more than one stage but kept strictly within the analysis of variance framework in which the X_i for different stages in the model were kept uncorrelated. Thus, for a two-stage model, the equation would be

$$T = b_0 + b_1 X_1 + b_2 X_2 + b_3 X_1 X_2,$$

with cov $(X_1, X_2) = 0$. The interaction term in the model tests for the independence of Stages 1 and 2.

The fact that independent variables are constrained to be orthogonal is at once an important strength and an important weakness. The model meshes easily with faceted test design and with generalizability theory. Estimates of model parameters are more stable and more easily interpreted than when model predictors covary. However, complex conceptions of cognitive functioning often do not fit neatly into an orthogonal mold. If the goal is to estimate an overall model fit rather than individual beta weights, a weaker model that allows for correlations among predictors is usually more appropriate.

Calfee (1976) has produced a substantial extension of this approach, suggesting how six different sources of dependency among stages might be examined. He suggested an analysis of variance framework for examining these sources and demonstrated how this might be done (see also Calfee & Hedges, 1980). Ward (1973) also contributed an empirical example of how stage independence might be tested in this paradigm and also in a related visual search task, using a multitrait–multimethod design.

Ippel (1986) argued that both the additive-factors method and the subtraction method provide *observation designs* (i.e., a method for collecting information in a systematic and controlled way) and a *logic of inference* to relate observations to theoretical constructs. However, they do not provide *measurement designs* (rules to assign values of variables to objects of measurement). Ippel (1986) showed how the observation design of the additive-factor method can be transformed into various measurement designs.

The empirical example chosen for presentation here, however, is that of Chiang and Atkinson (1976). Although their study is based on a small sample of college students, they included both the memory search and the visual search tasks that differed systematically in the process models represented, and they also estimated reliability for each processing parameter and correlations with an external reference test of ability (SAT). This allows us a demonstration of coordinated EPM and CIP thinking.

The memory search task is S. Sternberg's: Commit to memory a 2, 3, 4, or 5 letter or digit string, then decide whether a single letter or digit presented later is or is not in the memory set. The visual-search task reverses the procedure: A single letter or digit is stored, and the variable string is then presented, requiring that the subject indicate whether or not the stored symbol is in the presented string. Figure 7.3 shows the models and parameter measures for the two tasks. Each task yields a slope for reaction time as a function of string size and an intercept parameter, MSLOPE and MINT for memory search and VSLOPE and VINT for visual search. Note that, although the two tasks are assumed to involve the same sequence of four processing stages or components, the parameter estimates reflect variance from different combinations of stages. MSLOPE is the only pure measure of the comparison component; VSLOPE combines encoding and comparison. MINT includes encoding with decision and response production; VINT does not. The figure also includes correlations between parameters corrected for attenuation (see Snow, 1978, for details).

The results allow reasoning about process components in a

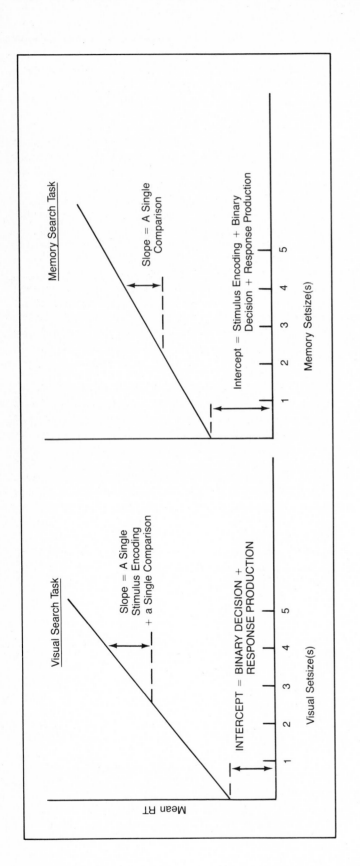

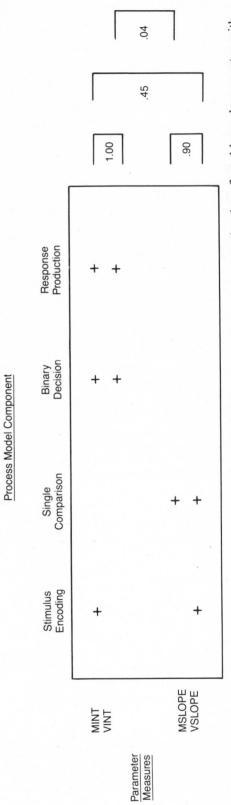

FIGURE 7.3 Process models for the visual search and memory search tasks showing components presumed to be reflected by each parameter, with theoretical correlations between them. (Adapted from Chaing & Atkinson, 1976, and Snow, 1978.)

new way. Note first that the two intercept parameters differ by one component, yet correlate perfectly. There are three possibilities: (a) Stimulus encoding might be a constant, indicating that there are no individual differences in this stage of processing; (b) individual differences in stimulus encoding might be perfectly coincident with individual differences in the decision and response components and, thus, deserve no status as a separate construct; (c) one or both models might be wrong in some way. If we start by assuming that the models are correct, then the three other correlations make sense. VINT and MSLOPE have no components in common and correlate near zero. MINT and VSLOPE have one component in common and show about 20% common variance; but the common component is stimulus encoding! If the correlation arises from individual differences in encoding, then the first possible explanation for perfect correlation between intercepts must be incorrect; encoding cannot be a constant. This also argues against the second possibility. We conclude then that one or both models must be changed in some way. The most parsimonious change consistent with the data is to assume that individual differences in encoding are also present in VINT. This explains the perfect correlation between VINT and MINT, and it preserves the reasoning associated with 0 correlation between VINT and MSLOPE. Note also that the estimate that 20% of the variance in MINT and VSLOPE is due to encoding is corroborated by the correlation between the slope parameters. This correlation indicates that 81% of the variance of these parameters is due to individual differences in the comparison stage, and, thus, 19% is due to the encoding stage. Jensen (1987) has corroborated these findings in a similar analysis using memory search, visual-search, and choice reaction time tasks.

In short, psychometric thinking might help clarify the structure of process models just as the process models might help analyze what is being measured by these or other tasks. Unfortunately, the Chiang–Atkinson data on SAT verbal and quantitative scores are not clear in this latter respect. Hunt and his coworkers (Hunt, Frost, & Lunneborg, 1973; Hunt & Lansman, 1975) had hypothesized that MSLOPE, the memory comparison time, should be negatively correlated with verbal ability. Here, however, all correlations with SAT scores were nonsignificant, and an inexplicable interaction with sex complicated the picture; it appears to have been due to outliers. Hunt's hypothesis was strongly supported for males, for both verbal and quantitative ability scores, but the opposite relations were obtained for females.

Sentence Verifications

Clark and Chase (1972) provided an early demonstration that regression analysis with correlated predictors could be used to test process models based on response latency data. Their interest was in sentence comprehension processes. Independent variables were entered into the regression equation in the presumed order in which corresponding processes were executed. Because Clark and Chase were not concerned with individual differences, data were averaged over subjects. The sentence verification task they developed, however, has been used by others to represent the processes involved in encoding and analyzing propositions in working memory during reading, listening, and other complex verbal performances.

In the sentence verification paradigm, each item presents a sentence, followed by a simple picture that is or is not described by the sentence. The task is to judge whether the sentence is true or false, given the picture. Reaction time to verify or reject each such sentence is the dependent measure. As expected, the syntactic complexity of the sentence influences difficulty and, hence, verification time. For example, it takes less time to verify "the plus is above the star" than to verify "the plus is not below the star." The process model for such tasks would typically posit that the subject must first encode the sentence into working memory and then compare it, or some transform or analysis of it, with the presented picture.

Individuals differ substantially in speed of sentence verification, and these differences show noteworthy correlations with verbal and reading ability measures (see, e.g., Hunt et al., 1975; Lansman, Donaldson, Hunt, & Yantis, 1982). Hunt in a summary of research on component processes in verbal ability (1985b), suggested that 20% to 30% of verbal comprehension variance might be accounted for by sentence verification time; furthermore, this time and the lexical access time measured by the NIPI difference previously discussed might identify independent components of verbal processing.

The analysis of sentences in working memory takes not only time but also "space"; the typical CIP model of working memory assumes that memory span or capacity is limited. This was clearly shown by S. Sternberg (1969, 1975) in the additive-factors experiments previously noted (see also Baddeley, 1976). If the sentence verification task is performed while the subject also must hold other information in memory, verification takes longer. These and other measures of ability to hold information in memory while analyzing sentences also correlate substantially with verbal ability (see Hunt, 1985b; also Daneman & Carpenter, 1980). The implication is that individual differences in the sort of semantic processing required for understanding school discourse, and reflected in verbal ability tests, might involve simultaneous lexical access and sentence analysis, while the results of previous analysis are held in memory.

Attention Allocation

The experiments just noted, that require two different performances to share working memory in the same time interval, are special cases of the dual-task paradigm used to study attention allocation more generally. In this method, two concurrent tasks must be performed and attention is assumed to be a finite resource divided according to some priority relationship between the tasks. Typically, there is a primary and a secondary task, each with different priorities.

The basic theory and method of attention research in dual tasks were reviewed by Kahneman (1973). But Hunt and Lansman (1982; see also Hunt, 1985b) have been foremost in applying attention theory to analyses of individual differences in cognitive performance. Their basic point is that human cognition will not be understood by relying solely on studies of its parts operating in isolation. Two tasks done concurrently will impose different demands than they would if done separately;

that is, task difficulty or complexity is a function of process interaction. By studying dual-task performance, we gain an understanding of these interactions. In particular, two mental tasks that require the same information-processing capacities will compete or interfere with one another and thus exhibit some of the limitations of the system, because attention resources are assumed to be limited. Also, with dual-tasks, some attention must be devoted to the higher order task of coordinating the two performances. On the other hand, if one task performance can be made automatic through learning, it will demand less attentional resource capacity, thereby freeing attentional resources for the other task and for coordination.

One kind of dual-task experiment used by Hunt and Lansman (1982) involves continuous paired-associates learning, where the paired associates change in subsequent blocks of trials (see Atkinson & Shiffrin, 1968). A periodic probe-reaction requirement is the secondary task. For example, asterisks might appear above an item during a paired-associate study trial, signaling the need to press a button. The parameters of the continuous paired-associates model are presumed to reflect processes such as the probability of entering terms into a short-term memory store and the rate of loss of information from an intermediate-term memory store. Hunt et al. (1973) reported significant relations between such parameters and scholastic aptitude test scores among college students.

It is easy to think of dual-task attention problems in education. Learning to coordinate declarative and procedural knowledge in formulating geometry proofs, learning to learn from a teacher's lecture while attending to cues that signal possible examination questions, learning to read music while operating a musical instrument are some examples. But dual attention is also an aspect of test performance. Some complex ability tests, such as Raven Matrices, appear to have multiple attentional demands. Paragraph comprehension tests with multiple questions per paragraph might be another example. And most ability and achievement tests call for item processing while attending to time.

Because we have used mainly ability-test examples to this point, the empirical example chosen here comes from research on test anxiety in achievement measurement. Schmitt and Crocker (1981) administered a multiple-choice course examination, dividing the students randomly between two item formats. One was conventional multiple-choice format, with stem and alternatives adjacent on each page. In the other, examinees read the item stem on one page and constructed their answers, then turned the page to see the alternatives on the next page, and only then selected a response. Marked interaction between students' test-anxiety scores and item format conditions was obtained. Performance on the achievement test was significantly higher in the constructed response condition than in the conventional condition among students low in test anxiety, but it was significantly lower with constructed response than with conventional format among high-anxiety students.

The interpretation is that anxious persons are self-conscious as well as task conscious; they worry, allowing self-doubts and other disruptive thoughts to draw attention away from task processing. The constructed response format promotes this disruptive self-consciousness in the interval between stem and alternatives, whereas the conventional format

better maintains attention to the task. In other words, test-anxious examinees might create a dual-attention task for themselves or a metacognitive coordination problem; their performance suffers because attentional resources are insufficient for this more complex task. Low-anxiety students have no dual attention or coordination problem; they benefit from constructed response, presumably because this format stimulates attention to deeper processing or more activation of stored knowledge structures (see Snow & Peterson, 1985, for further discussion).

EXTENSIONS AND IMPLICATIONS

The development of laboratory tasks to distinguish particular cognitive processes and stages of perception, memory, and attention has yielded, in turn, a body of correlations of these tasks with various educational measures. These prompt specialized and more general questions for further research.

One kind of special question, for example, concerns why it is that the NIPI difference correlates with certain measures of verbal ability or why, under some conditions, its correlation is higher with measures of perceptual speed ability than with verbal ability (see Lansman, et al., 1982). Other questions along this line might be: What are the psychometric properties of NI and PI and their difference score? Does the correlation arise particularly from the speed or the power aspect of verbal ability tests or from items with other identifiable characteristics such as use of high-frequency or concrete words? What changes in item format alter the correlations with verbal or perceptual measures? Parallel questions attach to each of the elementary laboratory tasks and their correlations with tests thus far studied. The laboratory tasks themselves suggest experimental techniques that might be used to analyze conventional tests and that might be incorporated into computer versions of new tests.

Research on tests representing special ability factors such as perceptual speed, closure speed, or memory span also ties in here. For example, the work of Royer (1971) on perceptual speed, Ippel and Bouma (1981) on closure speed, and Chase and Ericsson (1982) on memory span all contribute specifications of elementary processes that link to those purportedly measured by the laboratory tasks discussed previously. It is conceivable that learning abilities and disabilities measured by collections of these tasks would provide sharper diagnostic pictures than are available from conventional tests.

The attentional analysis reveals systematic individual differences in attentional capacity that might limit performance in single as well as dual tasks, depending on the degree to which single tasks are resource limited, that is, require controlled processing. According to Hunt and Lansman (1982), it also provides a kind of interpretation of intelligence that is not based on particular cognitive structures or processes alone. They think of Spearman's (1927) "mental energy" as attentional resources. The positive manifold of correlations among ability tests, and the resulting general factor, could thus derive from the resource-limited character of all ability-test performances. Then each test performance would be a function of special abilities and general attentional capacity.

Specialized research that analyzes iconic and working

memory, and the attentional and encoding processes that operate between them, could be important for another reason. These aspects of the cognitive system might be most closely associated with the biological substrate, because they are known to be selectively disrupted by brain injury. And they are one logical place to look for explanations of relationships between complex intelligence measures and apparently simple measures of choice reaction time, inspection speed, and cortical evoked potentials (see H. Eysenck, 1982; Jensen, 1982).

Beyond these detailed questions, however, are several more general questions for further research. One of these concerns the possibility that batteries of these elementary cognitive tasks might account for the variance–covariance matrices from typical batteries of conventional tests in a new way. Multitrait–multimethod analyses in such batteries could clarify the number and kind of elementary processes that deserve listing as separable constructs. Factor analyses or other multivariate studies could combine or differentiate constructs available from such task batteries and from conventional test batteries. And predictive validity studies could determine if these new elementary cognitive tasks or factors added to, or substituted for, prediction based on conventional measures.

These sorts of questions have been addressed by Rose (1974, 1980; see also Fernandes & Rose, 1978, and Rose & Fernandes, 1977); by Fairbank, Tirre, and Anderson (1984; see also Kyllonen, 1986); and by Carroll (1980a). The Rose–Fernandes work sought to produce a battery of paper-and-pencil tests of basic information-processing abilities for use in performance assessment. Each elementary task was chosen to represent one or more cognitive operations in a taxonomy. Care was taken to check that each test could be used to replicate the original group results obtained from the laboratory version of the task. Empirical correlations among the task variables were then compared with the theoretical distances among tasks, defined to reflect the number and kinds of operations each pair of tasks had in common. Regression analyses also examined goodness-of-model fit for each task. Results so far have been promising, although the provisional battery has not been fully evaluated, particularly against external ability measures and achievement criteria.

Carroll (1980a) undertook a far-reaching reanalysis of data on the Rose–Fernandes tasks and on many others obtained from recent experimental literature combined with cognitive-ability factors. He conducted factor analyses of existing correlation matrices and his own task analyses of many of these measures, to provide indications of as many as 25 to 30 factors of individual differences. Some of these factors display high reliability, some do not. Some are extremely narrow as dimensions, whereas some show substantial referent generality. Some suggest ways in which conventional tests might be modified, to distinguish speed and accuracy components, for example. And some suggest that they might provide important supplements to conventional measures. Carroll's work is exploratory, based on what data now exist in the literature. But it is a treasure trove of ideas and implications for the researcher who wishes to pursue either intensive analysis of particular tests and tasks or extensive analysis across ranges of tests and tasks.

Another general question would aim at organizing collections of elementary tasks to provide improved diagnoses of performance abilities and disabilities in educational domains such as learning to read or to do elementary mathematics. The potential advantage of elementary cognitive tasks in these pursuits, in addition to aiding process explanation, is their provision of absolute measurement scales based on stimulus and task characteristics to replace the norm-referenced scales of conventional measures. Current research has begun to address this question, but only in a few domains. One example is J. R. Frederiksen's (1980, 1982) battery of measures to assess component processes in reading, to be described in a later section. The beginnings of another such battery have taken shape in the assessment of learning disabilities (see A. L. Brown & Campione, 1986). The military has been using these bases in developing batteries for job classifications such as pilot selection and training and air traffic controller (Halff, Hollan, & Hutchins, 1986). Specialized batteries of component process measures could be investigated in many other domains.

Still a third general question concerns the degree to which processes examined in this section are critical factors in more complex problem solving. Pattern recognition, in particular, has been proposed as a key to all subsequent cognitive processing (Newell, 1980). And it appears to be centrally important in several kinds of specialized expertise. One must recognize something as wrong, or different, or new, in order to activate appropriate performance processes. It does appear that specialized pattern recognition is centrally important for chess masters, physicists, radiologists, and many other kinds of experts (see Glaser, in preparation).

A final general question concerns, not what component processes are involved in complex performance, but what processes are left out. By careful measurement of component processes, it might be possible to isolate superordinate executive, control, or coordinative processes indirectly. Some steps in this direction have been taken in the study of reasoning, our next topic.

Reasoning, Fluid-Analytic, and Visual-Spatial Abilities

Analysis of information processing in the perception-memory-attention system could be critical to understanding some of the abilities and disabilities important in education. But beyond (or above) this level, there are more complex abilities and achievements involving reasoning and comprehension in abstract, and often novel, instructional tasks. Understanding these functions is central to the most general problems of individual differences in education. This section addresses research on general reasoning and spatial problem solving. The next section takes up verbal and reading comprehension abilities. Thereafter we turn to content knowledge structures, in which these abilities also play a part.

COMPONENTIAL ANALYSIS

In the middle 1970s, R. J. Sternberg (1977) formulated a methodology called *componential analysis* to analyze individual performances on some of the more complex tasks found in general mental tests. He combined and capitalized upon the strengths of previous methods of process analysis to expand substantially the relevance of cognitive psychology to educational measurement.

Sternberg recognized that the type of regression model proposed by Clark and Chase (1972) could be performed on individual data and that model parameters could then be taken as estimates of the speed or accuracy with which individual subjects executed particular component processes. He also combined this approach with the subtractive method, to unconfound otherwise confounded component processes. For example, Sternberg proposed that analogy items of the form A:B::C:D required at least five component processes: encoding the various terms, inferring the relationship between A and B, mapping the relationship between A and C, applying the A–B relationship to the C–D terms, comparing the constructed answer with the alternative D answers provided, and responding. By the definition of analogy, however, the nature of the A to B transformation is the same as that of the C to D transformation. For example, in a test composed of geometric analogies, if A is related to B by a 90-degree rotation, C must be related to D by a 90-degree rotation. Thus, independent variables representing the type of inference or amount of transformation required in the inference stage would be perfectly correlated with corresponding independent variables for the application stage, so only one set of variables could be entered into the regression equation. This is a problem if one wants to test the assertion that two component processes are required or to estimate the speed or efficiency with which these separate component processes are executed for individual subjects. Perhaps some subjects quickly infer the correct relationship between A and B but have difficulty remembering the relationship and, thus, have difficulty applying it to C in order to generate an ideal answer D.

R. J. Sternberg (1985a) describes several experimental manipulations designed to unconfound these correlated variables. One method is called *precuing*. Here, the subject first examines a part of the problem for as long as necessary, then signals readiness to see the remainder of the item. Two latencies are obtained: time taken to view the precue, called a *cue latency* (which is sometimes discarded), and time taken to solve the remainder of the problem, called a *solution latency*. For example, given the analogy,

A:B::C:D   (true or false?),

one could precue with

A:B::   (measure T_1)

and then present

C:D   (true or false)   (measure T_2 and subject's response).

The precuing time (T_1) would include time for encoding A and B, and for inferring the relationship between A and B. The separate solution time (T_2) would include the time for encoding C and D and for the mapping, application, and comparison-response processes. Precuing only the first term (A:) or the first three terms (A:B::C:) would permit separation of other component processes.

Precuing has probably been less frequently used than experimental decomposing of a complex task into two or more consecutively presented steps. For example, Kyllonen, Loh-

man, and Woltz (1984) studied performance on a spatial task in which subjects were required to synthesize two or three geometric shapes, and, on some trials, to rotate the synthesized image 90 or 180 degrees. On some trials, four separate latencies were recorded: time to memorize the first stimulus, time to combine the memory of the first stimulus with a second stimulus, time to rotate the synthesized image, and time to accept or reject a probe stimulus. Pellegrino (1985b), Snow and Lohman (1984), and R. J. Sternberg (1985a, 1985b) summarize many other experiments in which tasks have been decomposed in this way.

Two empirical examples of R. J. Sternberg's work with componential analysis are depicted in Figure 7.4. These also serve as a more general example of the functionalist style of CIP modeling over time and experiments. In his original research (R. J. Sternberg, 1977, which remains the best source of details on the methodology), four alternative CIP models were fitted to response latency and accuracy data collected under various experimental and whole-item conditions, as previously described. Figure 7.4 shows flowcharts for the four alternative CIP models hypothesized. Component processes are identified inside the boxes; parameters reflecting the operation of each component are listed at the side of each box.

In Model I, the inference, mapping, and application components are all exhaustively applied, that is, all attributes of the terms of the analogy are compared. In Model II, the application component is self-terminating, that is, after D is encoded, attributes are tested one at a time until a correct attribute is found for response. In Model III, both mapping and application are self-terminating. In Model IV, inference also becomes self-terminating. Model III best fit the data in R. J. Sternberg's (1977) first experiments, accounting for 92% and 59% of the variance in the latency and accuracy data, respectively (low error rates limited the percentages in the latter case). The analysis, and ultimate choice among these models, exemplifies the internal validation step of Sternberg's approach. Correlations between the parameters of the best-fitting model and external reference measures for reasoning and perceptual speed abilities then provide the external validation step. In early experiments, R. J. Sternberg (1977) used tasks based on schematic picture, verbal, and geometric analogies, and he obtained rather variable and sometimes unexpected correlations between parameters and external ability factors. Revision of the component structure was needed, and components representing comparison and justification processes had to be added. In later experiments, latency parameters for reasoning, comparisons, and justification components displayed strong correlations with external reasoning factors but not with perceptual speed factors, as predicted (see R. J. Sternberg & Gardner, 1983).

Sternberg and his colleagues (see R. J. Sternberg, 1985a for a review) have now conducted componential analyses of a large number of reasoning tasks, and the method seems to serve well across tasks. It thus suggests one powerful approach to the decomposition of other kinds of tests, particularly those that are process intensive, in other words, those that do not require retrieval of complex declarative knowledge previously stored. It also provides an experimental method of evaluating item formats. Different formats can place demands on different component processes. There is evidence, for example, that

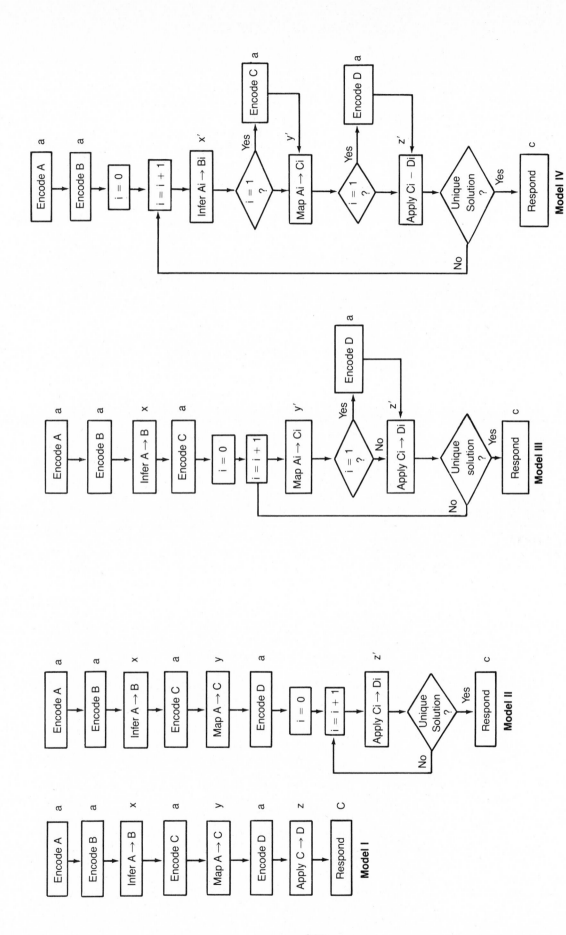

FIGURE 7.4 Schematic flow charts for four possible models of analogical reasoning. (After Sternberg, 1977.)

281

multiple-choice analogy items differ in processing demand as a function of whether true–false, two-alternative, or four-alternative response formats are used (see Bethell-Fox, Lohman, & Snow, 1984).

STRATEGIES AND STRATEGY SHIFTING

The first results from componential analyses were process models for several kinds of reasoning tasks. But the assumption that the same model should fit all subjects on a given task was quickly recognized as unwarranted. Persons appeared to differ in strategies, not only on reasoning tasks but also on simpler tasks. It was noted in the earlier discussion of pattern recognition that L. A. Cooper was able to distinguish qualitatively different strategies for performing spatial comparison tasks. She also demonstrated that some individuals could sometimes change their previously adopted strategies and take up others if induced to do so. Both R. J. Sternberg (1977) and Snow (1978) had predicted that strategic variations would be an important source of individual differences in complex information processing. Indeed, French (1965) had demonstrated the importance of strategy variations in mental tests much earlier. Different process models might thus be needed to fit the performance of different persons. Different models might even be needed to fit the same person's performance in different parts of a task if strategy shifting occurred during task processing (Snow, 1981). Other studies, in addition to L. A. Cooper's work, have now confirmed this.

MacLeod, Hunt, and Mathews (1978) demonstrated, in the sentence verification task, that some subjects' performances were well fit by a linguistic processing model, whereas others seemed to use a spatial strategy. In other words, a linguistic processor might read the presented sentence; encode it in memory linguistically; encode the picture similarly when it appeared; and then compare these linguistic descriptions. A spatial processor might use the sentence to visualize the expected picture and then compare this image to the picture when it appeared. The two groups were distinguishable by verbal and spatial ability test profiles. It was also clear that a subject could change from one strategy to the other if asked to do so. R. J. Sternberg and Weil (1980) also conducted a training experiment in which either linguistic or spatial strategies were developed for reasoning in linear syllogisms. Componential models were fitted to identify four different strategy groups, and correlations with reference ability tests showed strikingly different patterns across groups. Success with the linguistic strategy correlated with verbal, but not spatial, ability. The opposite pattern occurred with the spatial strategy, and a mixed strategy group showed correlation with both abilities. Those using a fourth strategy, a simplified algorithmic procedure, showed reduced correlation with ability.

Kyllonen, Lohman, and Woltz (1984) next showed how componential models can be generalized to account for cases in which subjects not only use different strategies but also shift between them during task performance. They identified three kinds of ability–strategy relationships: In a Case I relationship, ability limits strategy selection. In Case II, strategy choice is unrelated to ability, but the effectiveness of implementing a strategy depends on ability. In Case III, ability both limits strategy and predicts performance within strategy groups. Evidence for all three cases was found in componential analyses of a complex form board task that contained three steps. In the first step, subjects were required to memorize a geometric figure. In the second step, they were required to combine this first figure, which was no longer in view, with one or two new shapes displayed on a screen. In the third step, they were shown another figure and asked whether the two or three previously shown shapes would combine (in the order indicated) to form this final shape.

Models for each of the three steps (encoding, synthesis, and comparison) were constructed from retrospective reports of experimental subjects, introspections of the experimenters, and the literature on spatial cognition. Each was then tested by regressing latencies for each step on independent variables that estimated the amount or difficulty of each hypothesized process. Independent variables were formed by coding objective features of items or by obtaining ratings of the desired characteristic from subjects not included in the main study. Two types of models were tested: single-strategy models and strategy-shift models. Single-strategy models presume that the subject solves all items in basically the same way. R. J. Sternberg (1977) described this type of model in some detail, and it is the model underlying much of the cognitive analysis of ability tests to date. Strategy-shift models, however, presume that the subject uses different strategies to solve different types of items.

Suppose that two strategies are postulated for a given task. Strategy A is represented by independent variables a_1, a_2, and a_3; strategy B is represented by independent variables b_1, b_2, and b_3. Single-strategy models could be tested by regressing the dependent variable (Y) on variables a_1, a_2, and a_3, and then, in a separate analysis, by regressing Y on b_1, b_2, and b_3. A "mixed" model could be formed by regressing Y on all six independent variables, a_1, a_2, a_3, b_1, b_2, and b_3. A strategy-shift model would also regress Y on these six independent variables, but it would require that only three predictors (a_1, a_2, and a_3 or b_1, b_2, and b_3) have nonzero values for any one item; performance on some items would be predicted by strategy A, whereas performance on the other items would be predicted by strategy B. Further, one can hypothesize some variable that will predict strategy shifting (e.g., overall problem difficulty) and then specify a value of that variable (the "shift point") at which the subject is hypothesized to change strategies. For example, subject 1 might solve most items using strategy A and only a few items using strategy B, whereas subject 2 might show the reverse pattern. Thus, several types of information must be evaluated for each subject: the nature of the best-fitting model (single-strategy or strategy-shift), the goodness-of-fit of the model compared with other models and an absolute standard (i.e., even the "best" model for a subject might account for only trivial variation in the task), and the value of the shift variable (i.e., the ratio of items solved by each strategy).

The results of fitting these sorts of models to response latencies for each of the three task steps has shown two important effects. *First*, for each task step, different subjects solved different items in predictably different ways. *Second*, solution strategies were systematically related to the profile of scores on reference ability tests. For example, for the synthesis step, subjects who were best fitted by the most complex strategy-shifting model had the highest average ability profile. Subjects who followed more restricted strategies had more extreme profiles, either always synthesizing figures (high on spatial but low on verbal ability) or synthesizing only those figures presently in view (very low on spatial but average on verbal ability).

Follow-up studies have generally supported the utility of strategy-shift models and have also shown that seemingly minor variations in task demands can have a pronounced impact on how subjects solve items on spatial and figural reasoning tasks (see Lohman, 1988; Lohman & Kyllonen, 1983). Bethell-Fox et al. (1984) also demonstrated that strategy shifting within persons in geometric analogy tasks could account for differences between previous models offered by R. J. Sternberg (1977) and Mulholland, Pellegrino, and Glaser (1980). Furthermore, analyses of eye movements during performance of analogy items added evidence that subtle individual differences in strategy shifting, not previously incorporated in componential models of reasoning, had to be recognized in future research. Finally, Marquer and Pereira (1987) have reported that substantial strategy shifting occurs even on the sentence verification task used previously to contrast strategies that were assumed to be stable. More than two-thirds of the subjects in their study exhibited nonrandom shifts during performance. It is possible, then, that strategy shifting is a key aspect of individual differences in verbal and spatial and reasoning task performance (see, e.g., Spiro & Myers, 1984).

Strategy shifts can represent noise or substance, depending on the goal of test analysis. They contribute noise if the goal is to estimate a particular set of process parameters from a sample of items (e.g., rate of rotation). They represent substance important for theory if, at some point, a higher level of ability means having a more flexible approach to problem solving. In either case, in interpreting research on abilities, it is evidently incorrect to assume that all items or problems in a task are solved in the same way and that subjects differ only parametrically or, in other words, in the speed or power with which they execute a common set of processes. It is also incorrect to assume that subjects can be typed by strategy or even that they shift strategies all in the same way. At least, the general abilities with which educational measurement is most concerned such as verbal comprehension, reasoning, and spatial visualization appear to be more complex than this. Higher levels of performance in these ability domains seem to involve flexible strategy shifting to a substantial degree.

COMPUTER SIMULATION AND RECONSTRUCTION OF A REASONING TASK

Componential analyses and studies of strategies and strategy shifting in reasoning lead to computer-based models. But direct attempts at computer simulation of reasoning processes have also indicated a need for improvement of assessment techniques. The early attempts at computer models of reasoning have been reviewed in detail by R. J. Sternberg (1977), so we need not cover them here. For the most part, these models are limited anyway, because they are based on the assumption that all subjects process all items in the same way. The empirical evidence now refutes this assumption, as noted. One computer simulation does deserve attention here because it

addresses a reasoning task, Thurstone Letter Series, that is often used in psychometric research and because work on it has now been carried forward to address the problem of representativeness of item or domain sampling.

Kotovsky and Simon (1973) and Simon and Kotovsky (1963) produced a computer model for letter series that describes performance as being composed of two major steps: representation and continuation. In representation, subjects are hypothesized to use their knowledge of identities and forward–backward relations in the alphabet to assign the letters in a series item to strings or subseries. Then they calculate a period for a string and use that period to help assign other letters to strings. Then they form a rule that expresses how each string in memory is to be used to continue the series and, thus, solve the item. The purpose of the theory was to predict item difficulty. The Simon–Kotovsky work, and further studies by T. G. Holzman, Pellegrino, and Glaser (1982, 1983), showed that the model was partially successful but that there were also limitations (e.g., period length was found not related to solution accuracy, though the theory predicts a relation).

Butterfield, Nielsen, Tangen, and Richardson (1985) have now revised the model and elaborated on it, to account for item difficulty in all possible series items, not just the nonrepresentative samples of items that might happen to appear on some particular existing test. Their point is that a good theory of how people solve series problems, and of what makes such problems easy or difficult to solve, must apply to representative samples of items from a defined universe that includes all known item attributes. As some attributes are over- or underrepresented in the sample of items studied, the resulting theory of solution processes or item difficulty will be distorted and will vary unpredictably from study to study.

The revised theory discards period length as important in the representation stage, positing several levels of knowledge about what are called *moving strings* and predicting that item difficulty is determined by the string that is most difficult to represent. It also subdivides the memory load aspect of the continuation stage of performance. The theory accounts well for the data from the earlier work and from several new experiments. Furthermore, a notation and rule system is created that specifies the universe of items in terms of the item attributes that influence item difficulty. The computerization of series item generation and test administration for various kinds of tailored tests is also described. The result allows the coordination of cognitive theory-based and computer-based test design. For example, the item production and selection system can be used to insure that all, or a specified set, of the theoretical attributes influencing item difficulty are represented or systematically manipulated in the resulting test. Also, any existing test can be mapped onto the system to determine what item attributes that are important for theory have or have not been included.

FLUID-ANALYTIC REASONING ABILITIES

Componential analyses, computer simulations, and demonstrations of strategy shifts on particular reasoning tasks can now be brought together with factor-analytic research to yield enriched theories of "general reasoning ability," or "abstract, analytic intelligence," or what Cattell and Horn have called "fluid intelligence" (or *Gf*; see Cattell, 1971; Horn, 1976, 1978). Definitions of *Gf* typically refer to processes of perceiving relationships, educing correlates, maintaining awareness, and abstracting rules and concepts in complex tasks involving figural and nonword symbolic materials (Horn, 1976, 1978). We refer here to the constellation of fluid-analytic abilities and the symbol *Gf* without necessarily endorsing the details of the Cattell–Horn theory (see also Carroll, 1985a). Studies by Gustafsson (1984) suggest that *Gf* could be equivalent to the third-order general factor (*G*) typically obtained in large factor analyses of ability tests and also to Thurstone's primary induction factor (*I*); in other words, three hierarchical levels are connected through $G = Gf = I$.

Tests of inductive reasoning, such as series completions, analogies, Raven matrices, and classification problems, but also Wechsler performance scales such as Block Design and Object Assembly, are considered good measures of the *Gf* construct. But school learning tasks, particularly many used as exercises in science and mathematics problem solving, bear formal similarity to *Gf* tests. Greeno (1978) collectively refers to such tasks as problems of inducing structure. Snow (1980a) noted that the problem of inducing structure in instruction, as well as in such exercises, is probably why reasoning tests so often correlate with achievement tests. The problem for educational measurement, then, is one of predicting and detecting failures of induction in school learning and problem solving. The theoretical support for such measures should come from identifying the process and content structures common to *Gf* test and instructional-task performance.

Although analogical reasoning has been the most extensively studied, a large range of other inductive and deductive reasoning tasks has now been subjected to componential analysis, through the work of Embretson (1985b, 1986; see also Whitely, 1976), Pellegrino and Glaser (1980, 1982), R. J. Sternberg (1982c, 1985a) and many others. Reviews of much of this work are available from Goldman and Pellegrino (1984), and R. J. Sternberg (1985a), but see also Holland, Holyoak, Nisbett, and Thagard (1987) and Johnson-Laird (1983). Taken together, the findings to date suggest a provisional but much-elaborated, process-based theory, or perhaps set of theories, of *Gf*.

Figure 7.5, for example, shows schematic charts for the R. J. Sternberg and Gardner theory of analogies, series completions, and classifications (R. J. Sternberg & Gardner, 1983; see also R. J. Sternberg, 1985a). Analogy items here are of the form A:B::C: (D_1, D_2), that is A is to B as C is to one of two given D alternatives. Series completion items are of the form A B C ::D: (E_1, E_2), where the series A B C must be carried to D and then extended to one of two given E alternatives. Classification items are of the form A B, C D :E, where subjects decide whether E fits better with class A B or class C D. These three item formats are, of course, only special cases of the kinds of items used in conventional tests. Sternberg's point is that, at least for these three item types, a common CIP model can be shown to apply; it thus becomes an ability construct model, not just an ability task model.

The proposal is that solving such items requires seven different component processes: encoding, inference, mapping, application, comparison, justification, and response. *Encoding* refers to the process of activating information in long-term memory on the basis of information received through the senses. What is activated depends on the contents and organization of information in memory, as well as on the perceived demands of the task and on residual activation from previously encoded items. *Inference* refers to the process of discovering relationships between two concepts activated by encoding processes. For verbal analogies, this may be modeled as the attempt to discover whether two concepts are related in semantic memory and if they are, what the nature of that relationship might be. A weak knowledge base might support the inference that two concepts are somehow associated, but it might not contain information on the nature of that association. Some relationships seem to be prestored, whereas others must be determined by comparing attributes of the terms or by comparing their labeled relationships with other terms in memory. For example, the inference processes on difficult geometric analogies might involve the systematic testing of several hypotheses about the nature of the internal operation that would be used to transform the first term into the second term. The correctness of this inference would depend on the store of procedural knowledge (i.e., internalized transformation rules) and the ability of the examinee to execute such transformations (e.g., rotation of figures, deletion of figures). The inference step can also require the finding of relationships between relationships. For example, the pairs *up–down* and *black–white* are both opposites; so the relationship between the relationships is one of identity. Piaget (1963) argued that the ability to identify such "second-order" operations marked the transition from concrete-to formal-operational thought. *Mapping* and *application* are similar. Mapping refers to the process of inferring the relationship between the A and C terms. Application refers to the process of generating a term that is related to C in the same way that A was inferred to be related to B. *Comparison* or evaluation refers to the process of comparing the internally generated answer (D) to the D options provided, to determine which is most nearly correct. If none of the available options meets the individual's criterion for acceptability, the individual may recycle through some or all of the previous model steps. a process sometimes called *justification*. Of course, simple true–false analogies in which a single-answer option is presented do not require this step. *Response* is not estimated as a separate component but is assumed to be combined with preparatory and other unspecified sources of variance and reflected in the catchall intercept parameter.

Individual differences in the speed of some or all of these component processes in analogical reasoning tasks should show correlation with external, reference ability tests, especially reasoning tests. But early studies (R. J. Sternberg, 1977) found generally small and inconsistent relationships between component latencies and reference tests. The strong correlations with reasoning tests came from the preparation–response parameter, suggesting that executive strategies or other unspecified aspects of the performance were the critical factors in reasoning-test variance. This work, however, had relied on college undergraduates as subjects performing generally easy items. In later studies, in which more difficult items were attempted by more representative and better practiced

A

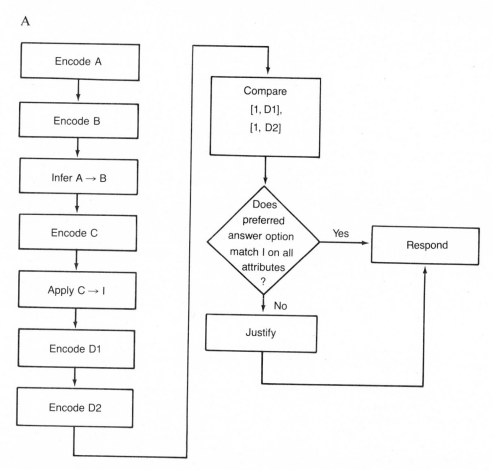

FIGURE 7.5 Flowcharts representing the sequence of information processing during solution of analogy (Panel A), series completion (Panel B), and classification (Panel C) problems. (After Sternberg & Gardner, 1983.)

subjects, latencies for the inference component showed significant correlations with reference ability measures, especially when error rate was controlled statistically (Bethell-Fox et al., 1984; R. J. Sternberg & Gardner, 1983). When accuracy was the dependent measure, scores for the encoding and comparison components showed the greatest ability differences (Pellegrino, 1985a; Whitely, 1980). Nevertheless, degree of correlation between component scores and reference tests is less important at this stage of research than is the identification of substantive differences in the way information is processed in such tasks (Lohman & Kyllonen, 1983).

For example, developmental changes in analogical reasoning have been studied by several investigators, with interesting results. In one study of pictorial analogies, 8-year-olds appeared not to use a mapping process (R. J. Sternberg & Rifkin, 1979). In another study using verbal analogies, preadolescents appeared to shift strategies as item complexity increased, changing from an analogical reasoning strategy to a strategy in which responses were chosen on the basis of their associative relatedness to the C term. Adolescents and adults continued to use analogical reasoning, even on the more difficult items. Heller (1979) reported similar ability-related differences among high school students, with low-verbal subjects more often using the associative strategy. Goldman, Pellegrino, Par-

seghian, and Sallis (1982) also found that older children (10-year-olds) were less likely to be distracted by foils that were associates of the C term than were younger children (8-year-olds). Retrospective reports suggested even more substantial differences in processing strategy. Older children were more likely to understand that the C to D relationship had to mirror the relationship between A and B. Pellegrino (1985a) argued that younger and less able students have particular difficulty remembering and comparing multiple relationships, possibly because they do not understand the rules of the game or because problem complexity exceeds mental resources.

Distractors also function differently for adults and children and for subjects of high and low ability. Bethell-Fox et al. (1984) found that four alternative items like those found in many mental tests were solved differently from otherwise similar two-alternative items. Other data (see Pellegrino, 1985a, p. 212) suggest that high-ability subjects are better able to recognize the correct answer on a forced-choice analogy test, even when they have processed the stem incorrectly. Snow (1980b) and Whitely and Barnes (1979) report similar evidence for subjects working backwards from the options provided. By combining analyses of eye fixation and componential models of latencies and errors, Bethell-Fox et al. (1984) also found evidence that lower ability adolescent subjects shifted strate-

B

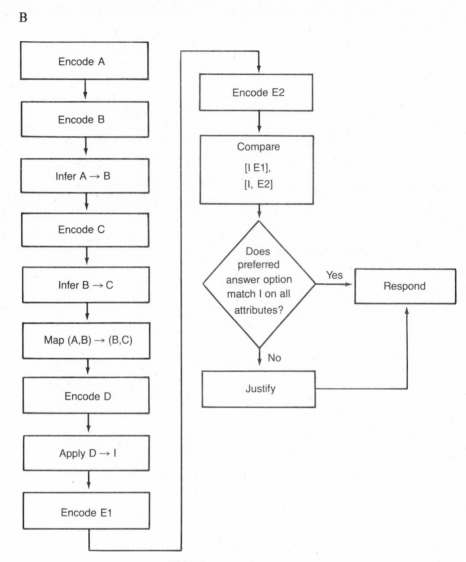

FIGURE 7.5 *(Continued)*

gies on difficult items, changing from one in which they constructed a response and compared it with the alternatives to
one in which they attempted to eliminate response alternatives. High-ability subjects, however, showed little evidence of
strategy shifting, probably because most items were relatively
easy for them.

Embretson, Schneider, and Roth (1986; see also Embretson, 1985b, 1986) report additional evidence of strategy shifting in a study of errors on difficult verbal analogies. Embretson
used multicomponent latent-trait models to test the hypothesis
that subjects attempted to solve items in more than one way.
She proposed that subjects first attempt to solve verbal analogy
items using a rule-oriented procedure much like Sternberg's
string of components; they infer a rule that relates the first and
second terms of the analogy, apply this rule to the third term to
generate an answer, then compare this answer with the response alternatives. However, subjects switch to a secondary
strategy if any part of the rule strategy fails. Three secondary
strategies were proposed, based on associations, partial rules,
and response elimination. In the association strategy, subjects

choose the alternative that is most highly associated with the
third term, which is sometimes also the keyed answer (Gentile,
Kessler, & Gentile, 1969). In the partial-rule strategy, subjects
infer only part of the rule that relates the first and second terms,
but this partial rule might be sufficient to eliminate all distractors. In the response elimination strategy, subjects again infer
only a partial rule, but this partial rule serves to eliminate only
some of the distractors, so other item features or guessing must
be used. Component scores for exact-rule construction, partial-rule construction, and response elimination were estimated by showing subjects the first two terms of each analogy
and asking them to write the rule that described the A to B
relationship. Exact rules stated the keyed relationships; partial
rules stated only some of the keyed relationships but served to
eliminate all foils; response elimination was scored if the partial rule eliminated only some foils. A rule-evaluation component was scored by providing subjects with the exact A-B rule
and asking them to select the correct alternative.

Different strategies were then formulated by combining
these five component probabilities (plus another variable for

C

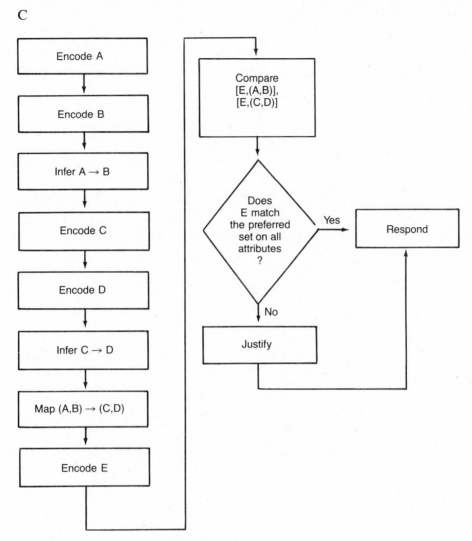

FIGURE 7.5 *(Continued)*

overall probability of strategy execution) in different ways. For example, the probability that person j solves the full (T) item i by the rule strategy is given by

$$P_{rule}(X_{ijT}) = P_a P_{ij1} P_{ik2},$$

where

P_{ij1} is the probability of correctly inferring the exact A-B rule,
P_{ik2} is the probability of correctly applying the exact A-B rule,
P_a is the probability in the sample of applying the rule strategy.

The multiplicative relationship among component probabilities indicates that component operations are seen as sequentially dependent: Failure on one component leads to failure of the strategy. Also note that P_a does not vary over persons or items in this model.

Multiple-strategy models were formed by summing the probabilities for individual strategies. For example, the probability of solving an item by first attempting, but failing with, the rule strategy and then selecting the correct response by choosing the alternative most highly associated with the C term is

$$P_{assoc + rule}(X_{ijT}) = P_{rule}(X_{ijT}) + P_{assoc}(X_{ijT}),$$

where

$$P_{assoc}(X_{ijT}) = P_c P_{ij3}(1 - P_{ij1}P_{ij2}),$$

and

P_{ij3} is the probability of choosing the correct answer by simple association,
$(1 - P_{ij1}P_{ij2})$ is the probability that the rule strategy failed,

and

P_c is the probability in the sample of applying the association strategy when available.

Adding probabilities for mutually exclusive strategies makes these models compensatory, like the strategy-shift models studied by Kyllonen, Lohman, and Woltz (1984) for response latencies. Such models differ from models tested in many studies (e.g., R. J. Sternberg & Weil, 1980) in which all components contribute to the solution of every item.

Analyses showed that Model III (rule or partial-rule strategy) and Model IV (rule strategy or response elimination) both predicted substantially more of the variation in estimated item difficulties than did Model I (rule strategy alone). However, all models were equally good predictors of subject differences. Thus, these models suggest that strategy shifts contributed significantly to item difficulty but not to individual differences in overall performance of the task. This might reflect the fact that the probability of executing each strategy (P_a, P_b, or P_c) could not be separately estimated for each subject. Kyllonen, Lohman, and Woltz (1984) and Lohman (1988) found that an analogous variable in their regression models of complex spatial synthesis, called the *shift point*, varied over subjects. The shift point was simply the place of estimated difficulty of a component process at which the subject changed strategies. This value was significantly related to reference ability measures. Furthermore, the regression models that Kyllonen, Lohman, and Woltz (1984) used allowed dependable evaluation of each model for each subject and showed that more able subjects were best fitted by different models than less able subjects. High *Gf* subjects showed the greatest flexibility of all subjects.

Ippel and Beem (1987) also found that the point at which subjects shifted strategies correlated with *Gf*. They administered problems in which subjects were required to determine if two stimuli could be rotated into congruence. If subjects can rotate stimuli in clockwise and counterclockwise directions with equal facility, then a clockwise rotation strategy should be most efficient when stimuli are separated by less than 180 degrees, whereas a counterclockwise strategy should be most efficient when stimuli are separated by more than 180 degrees. Ippel and Beem (1987) estimated the point at which each subject shifted between a clockwise and a counterclockwise strategy. They then determined the absolute discrepancy between this point and the rationally optimum shift point of 180 degrees. This difference score was uncorrelated with measures of spatial ability but showed significant negative correlations with measures of *Gf*.

These and other findings suggest that a theory of fluid-analytic reasoning ability must include alternative component processes, organized into multiple strategies, between which persons shift during performance. Individual differences arise from component execution, strategy choice, and flexibility of strategy shifting as a function of features of item difficulty. We consider this sort of theory further in a later section.

Several specific implications for reasoning item and test construction flow from these findings and should be acknowledged here. *First*, items could be constructed to distinguish use of different strategies such as association versus rule production in analytical reasoning (see, e.g., the test by Achenbach, 1970) or rule production versus response elimination, with separate scores being derived for each strategy. *Second*, tests could be designed to assess strategy shifting, using computer-adaptive procedures, perhaps, to locate the key difficulty thresholds where shifts occur for each person; shift flexibility scores might thus be fashioned. *Third*, early items in a test should not mislead examinees, particularly children and less able students, into believing that an association strategy is useful in solving all the items. *Fourth*, vocabulary should not be made a significant or uncontrolled source of item difficulty,

because the inclusion of difficult words is likely to cause a shift away from reasoning toward verbal associative processes, thus changing the construct measured, at least for some students. These implications might seem similar to older rules for item construction such as the rules against use of the word *always* or correct response alternatives of markedly different lengths than distractors. The old rules do seem to channel cognitive processing by reducing the usefulness of construct-irrelevant test-taking strategies. But the new suggestions go further, not only toward eliminating construct-irrelevant strategies but also toward identifying and contrasting alternative construct-relevant strategies.

VISUAL-SPATIAL ABILITIES

Spatial abilities hold a prominent place in theories of human cognition and in all models of human abilities. However, tests of spatial ability are not widely used, except as "performance" or "nonverbal" reasoning tests. Tests of more specific spatial abilities add little to the prediction of educatonal achievement, once general reasoning or general crystalized abilities have been entered into the regression (McNemar, 1964), except in specialized courses such as engineering drawing, architecture, and dentistry. Nor have spatial abilities shown consistent interactions with instructional treatments (Cronbach & Snow, 1977; Gustafsson, 1976). Nevertheless, spatial abilities have been much studied and hundreds of spatial tests have been devised (see Eliot & Smith, 1983, for examples of 392 spatial tests), particularly by the engineer Thurstone (e.g., Thurstone 1951) and by Guilford and his coworkers in the Army Air Force Aviation Psychology program (Guilford & Lacey, 1947) and his later Aptitude Research Project (e.g., Hoffman, Guilford, Hoepfner, & Doherty, 1968).

Reviews of factor-analytic studies of spatial abilities (G. V. Anderson, Fruchter, Manuel, & Worchel, 1954; Lohman, 1979b; McGee, 1979) show a broad array of spatial factors that can be organized hierarchically. However, this hierarchy is not neat; relations among tests are not consistently ordered in simplex patterns, as in the domains of reasoning or verbal measures (Lohman, 1979b; Snow, Kyllonen, & Marshalek, 1984). A complex visualization factor (*Vz*) appears at or near the top of this hierarchy (Carroll, 1985a; Horn, 1976), usually defined by complex spatial tests such as Paper Form Board, Paper Folding, and Surface Development (see Ekstrom et al., 1976). However, the *Vz* factor is often difficult to separate from a *Gf*, or reasoning, factor (Guilford & Lacey, 1947; Lohman, 1979b; Marshalek, Lohman, & Snow, 1983). Indeed, *Vz* tests appear to be primarily measures of *G* or *Gf*, secondarily measures of task-specific functions, and thirdly measures of something that covaries uniquely with other *Vz* tests. A Spatial Orientation (*SO*) factor can sometimes be distinguished from *Vz*. *SO* tests require subjects to imagine how an array would appear from a different perspective and then make a judgment from that imaged perspective. A Speeded Rotation (*SR*) factor emerges if two or more simple, highly speeded, rotation tasks are included in a test battery. Complex, three-dimensional, rotation tasks (such as the Vandenberg–Kruse [1978] adaptation of the Shepard–Metzler [1971] figures) generally split their variance between *SR* and *Vz* factors. Other distinguishable visual-spatial factors include Flexibility of Closure, Speed of Closure,

Perceptual Speed, Visual Memory, Serial Integration, and Kinesthetic (see Lohman, 1979b, 1988).

Along with the research on fluid-analytic reasoning, there has also been vigorous research on the nature of spatial abilities. This work provides another good example of what coordinated factor analyses and cognitive-task analyses can do in unpacking complex ability constructs. It also attacks an important problem in test construction, because figural reasoning and spatial ability tasks are often highly correlated; each kind of task could well be soluble by processes associated with the other construct. Research interest in spatial tasks has been fueled in part by the amenability of such tasks to information-processing analyses. But a more important motivation is the challenge posed to some proposition-based theories of cognition (e.g., J. R. Anderson & Bower, 1973) by the possible existence of analog processes that operate on nonpropositional mental representations.

There are now valuable summaries of research on spatial cognition. Pinker (1984) provides a good introduction. Shepard and Cooper (1982) summarize a decade of careful research on mental rotation, one of the earliest demonstrations of the analog possibility (see Shepard & Metzler, 1971). Kosslyn (1981) and Pylyshyn (1981) debate the interpretation of research on imagery, with Pylyshyn (1981) claiming that spatial knowledge is represented internally as abstract propositions and Kosslyn defending a functional role for quasi-pictorial images. J. R. Anderson (1978) concluded that it is probably impossible to resolve this debate experimentally, and so, unless some decisive physiological evidence emerges, rival theories must be evaluated by the criteria of parsimony and coherence. On these grounds, J. R. Anderson (1978) reversed his own long-standing commitment to a proposition-based theory of long-term memory and argued instead for multiple memory codes. One of these codes is said to preserve the configuration of elements in a stimulus array and is called the *image code* (J. R. Anderson, 1983, 1985). Several organizational schemes for spatial knowledge have also been advanced. Both J. R. Anderson (1983) and Palmer (1977) argue for a pseudo-hierarchical representation of spatial knowledge that contains both propositionally coded spatial knowledge (e.g., that squares have four sides of equal lengths) and image-coded spatial knowledge (e.g., an image-generating representation of a square in a prototypic orientation).

Research on individual differences in spatial cognition has used two approaches. In one, researchers have studied individual differences in experimental tasks, such as L. A. Cooper's (1982) careful studies of individual differences in visual comparison tasks. Although this research has sometimes shown striking patterns of individual differences, it is not at all clear what if any relationship exists between individual differences on these tasks and individual differences on other experimental tasks or conventional tests of spatial abilities (L. A. Cooper, 1982).

In the second approach, spatial tests commonly taken as indicants of particular factors are themselves subjected to experimental analysis. Although some attempts have been made to study tests taken as indicants of many different spatial factors, most process-guided research has focused on *Vz*- and *SR*-factor tests.

Experimental analyses have been performed on several *Vz* tests, such as paper folding (Kyllonen, 1984; Kyllonen, Lohman, & Snow, 1984), surface development (Alderton & Pellegrino, 1984; Shepard & Feng, 1972), and form board (Kyllonen, Lohman, & Woltz, 1984; Lohman, 1979a, 1988; Mumaw & Pellegrino, 1986). Analyses of form board tasks provide a good example of how correlational and componential analyses of a faceted task can clarify the nature of an ability construct.

Form board tasks have been used to measure intellectual competence since the early work of Itard in 1801 (cited in Spearman & Wynn-Jones, 1950), and they helped define a spatial factor in the early studies of El Koussy (1935), Kelley (1928), and Thurstone (1938b). The experimental analysis of such tasks could aim at modeling performance on items taken directly from an existing test such as the Minnesota Paper Form Board test (Likert & Quasha, 1970) or the Form Equations Test (El Koussy, 1935). However, sources of difficulty vary unsystematically across items, so investigators begin by constructing items that emulate test items but in which sources of difficulty are manipulated systematically and, if possible, independently. Figure 7.6 shows sample items from an experimental task modeled after El Koussy's Form Equations test. On the simplest items (column 1), the task is to remember an irregular polygon, to determine whether it matches a test stimulus, and to respond yes or no. On more difficult items, the first polygon must be rotated 90 or 180 degrees (columns 2–3), or it must be combined with one or two additional polygons (columns 4–7). The most difficult items require both synthesis and rotation (columns 8–9). Item difficulty thereby varies systematically with the numbers and types of cognitive operations required.

Different hypotheses about how subjects might perform each of the task steps were formulated and then tested by regressing latencies for the particular task step on independent variables hypothesized to influence the amount or difficulty of each process included in the model (see Kyllonen, Lohman, & Woltz, 1984, and Lohman, 1988, for details). Although total errors on the task were highly correlated with a reference Visualization factor ($r = .66$), componential analyses suggested that, on each of the task steps, most subjects used different strategies for different items. For example, on the first step, some subjects appeared to memorize the initial stimulus by representing the figure in memory as a set of basic features. Other subjects appeared to decompose the figure into more elementary units such as rectangles and triangles before representing the basic features of these elementary units in memory. Still other subjects appeared to label some of the figures and decompose others, shifting strategy according to the comparative difficulty of labeling or decomposing the figure.

For the synthesis step, some subjects consistently synthesized figures and stored the resulting product, whereas others consistently failed to synthesize figures and instead stored the three figures as separate units. However, most subjects appeared to shift back and forth between these two strategies or between one or both of these and a strategy of combining only two of the figures, depending on the complexity of the final image.

For the comparison step, the analyses suggested that some

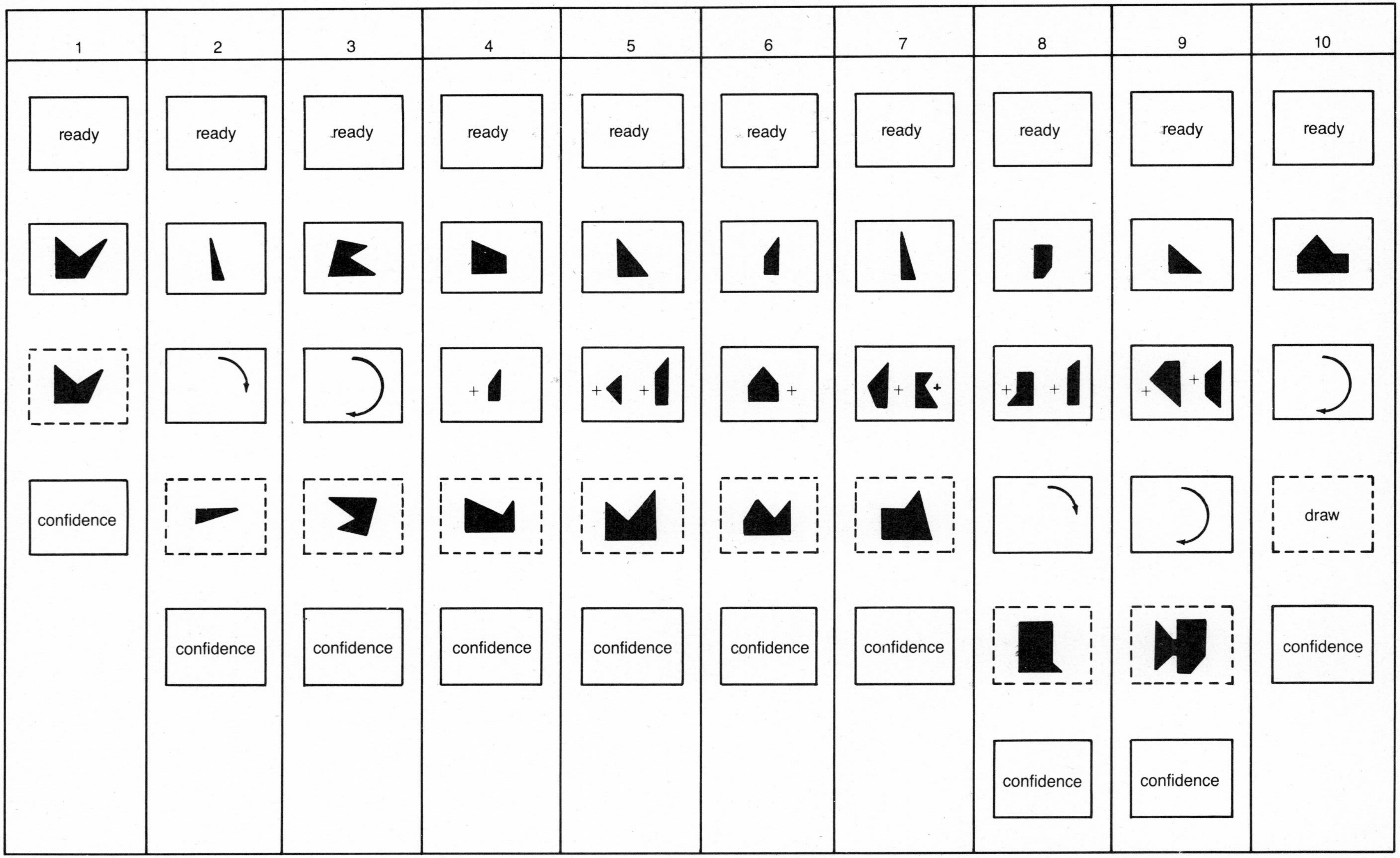

FIGURE 7.6 Examples of trial types in the faceted form-board task. Figures were black on white background. Probe slides (dashed border) had yellow backgrounds. From Lohman, 1979b, also reproduced in D. F. Lohman and P. C. Kyllonen, "Individual differences in solution strategy on spatial tasks," in R. F. Dillion & R. R. Schmeck (Eds.), *Individual differences in cognition*, Vol. 1, p. 124. Copyright © 1983 by Academic Press. Reproduced by permission.

subjects compared their mental image of the set of figures with the test probe one feature at a time; some subjects compared the two in larger units, one chunk at a time; and still others shifted back and forth between the feature- and unit-comparison strategies, depending on the relative difficulty of the two methods.

In two of the three task steps, some of the strategies appeared to be better than others, in that subjects who used them made fewer errors or performed the task step more quickly. For example, those who consistently decomposed the first stimulus made fewer errors and encoded faster than subjects in the other strategy groups. Further, strategies were systematically related to ability factors. For the encoding step, for example, those who selected the decomposition strategy tended to score higher on measures of Visualization and Closure Speed (*Cs*). For the synthesis step, the subjects who selected the most demanding shift strategy, which required constant synthesis and evaluation processes, tended to score well on all ability tests.

Analysis of subscores for this faceted task provided additional information. Here, the facet design helped demonstrate the fact that various spatial factors are arbitrary points in a continuous, but multidimensional, space. Correlations between subscores for different item types and reference ability factors varied systematically according to the information-processing requirements of the items. For example, subscores computed by averaging over selected facets of the task were correlated with these reference ability factors. Correlations between synthesis trials and the *Vz* factor increased systematically with number of synthesis operations required ($r = .21$, $.43$, and $.55$ for zero-, one-, and two-piece additions, respectively). Correlations with the *Vz* factor were highest for items requiring a single addition, followed by rotation ($r = .67$). As complexity was increased further by requiring the addition of two stimuli to the base and then a rotation (columns 8 and 9 in Figure 7.6), correlations with the *Vz* factor declined, whereas correlations with a Memory Span factor increased.

The coordinated correlational and information processing analyses of this form board task is but one example of many analyses of *Vz*-factor tests now in hand. Reviews of these studies (Lohman, 1988; Lohman, Pellegrino, Alderton, & Regian, 1987; Pellegrino & Kail, 1982) suggest new interpretations of old facts. One of the puzzles in the factor-analytic literature has been the difficulty of separating a *Vz* factor from a *Gf* factor (Guilford & Lacey, 1947; Marshalek et al., 1983; Spearman, 1927). Process analyses of tests that define both constructs reveal that, in spite of dissimilar surface structures and task demands, both types of tasks require flexible adaptation of solution strategies to changing item demands. Thus, most complex spatial tests are probably better characterized as figural reasoning tests with a spatial component than as measures of one or more uniquely spatial processes (Lohman et al., 1987).

Tests that define the *SR* factor have also been extensively investigated. The model Shepard and Metzler (1971) proposed for their mental rotation task provided a starting point for this research and for research on other spatial tasks requiring the mental rotation of stimuli. Subjects in Shepard and Metzler's study saw perspective drawings of pairs of three-dimensional shapes and were required to determine whether pairs were identical or mirror images. Time to make this decision was found to be a linear function of the difference in orientation between the two figures. Shepard and Metzler argued that the slope of this line estimated time to rotate images, whereas the intercept estimated time for encoding, comparison, and response processes.

Pellegrino and Kail (1982) summarize several studies in which they administered much simpler rotation tasks modeled after Thurstone's (1938b) Cards and Figures tests. Time to determine whether two figures could be rotated into congruence was regressed on the angular separation between figures. Slopes and intercepts were estimated for children, adolescents, and adults, then correlated with performance on the Primary Mental Abilities (PMA) Space test. Only intercepts predicted PMA scores for children, whereas both intercepts and slopes were significantly related to PMA scores for adolescents and adults. Following the Shepard–Metzler model previously described, this suggests that the primary source of individual differences in spatial ability among children is in speed of encoding and comparing stimuli; only older subjects showed evidence of involving the rotation rate. However, model fits were quite poor for approximately half of the children and adolescents in these studies, indicating that either performance was erratic or children were solving items in other ways. Thus, the finding that the intercepts show correlations with reference tests, whereas slopes do not, might merely reflect the fact that intercepts are a reasonably good estimate of average solution latency for all subjects, whereas slopes are meaningful and dependable only for subjects well-fitted by the model.

The CIP models for these simple rotation tasks have been modified in recent studies to improve their characterization of individual performance. For example, Kail, Carter, and Pellegrino (1979) proposed different models for trials on which stimuli could be rotated into congruence from those for trials in which stimuli could not be rotated into congruence. Other models have been proposed to account for the performance of subjects who appear not to rotate stimuli in such tasks or to rotate only the subset of stimuli not shown in an easily labeled position in space, that is, left, right, up, or down (see Lohman, 1988).

Other studies suggest that adolescents and young adults who perform poorly on spatial tests differ qualitatively from other subjects (Lohman & Nichols, 1985; Mumaw, Pellegrino, Kail, & Carter, 1984). In particular, such subjects seem to have great difficulty generating memories of geometric shapes that retain information about the exact configuration of elements in a figure. Differences among medium- and high-ability subjects seem better described by other variables such as the speed and accuracy with which subjects can perform certain operations, by their repertoire of solution methods, and by their store of spatial knowledge.

Work along these lines has substantially improved our understanding of spatial abilities. This research has important implications for the construct validity of existing spatial measures and for how these might be modified to improve the diagnosis and understanding of visual-spatial processing in educational performance. We now understand, however, that deciphering engineering line drawings is only one aspect of spatial ability. For example, the dynamic mental models that are generated while reading to integrate prose or while solving story problems in mathematics require not only spatial imagery but also the ability to coordinate images with other verbal and reasoning processes. New measures of spatial abilities should aim at assessing these abilities directly.

A comprehensive theory of spatial cognition is gradually taking shape that can guide the development of such theory-based measures of spatial abilities. Kosslyn's (1980) theory is the most ambitious effort in this direction. Kosslyn has also developed a computer simulation to test assumptions of the theory. In the simulation, a visual image corresponds to a quasi-pictorial two-dimensional spatial array in a visual memory store. Images are generated from two kinds of "deep representations" stored in long-term memory: literal encodings and propositional encodings. Literal encodings consist of lists of actual coordinates for the image, such as would presumably be needed to imagine a familiar face. Propositional encodings, on the other hand, contain only lists of abstract propositions and pointers to other literal or propositional encodings (e.g., imagine a blue square atop a red triangle). An image in the visual store is constructed from either or both of these encodings. This "surface representation," like the picture on a cathode-ray tube, has a limited extent (i.e., screen size) and limited resolution. Images displayed in this store are transient, starting to decay as soon as activated. Thus, the complexity of the image that can be displayed is limited because some parts of a complex image might decay before others can be generated.

Kyllonen's (1984) analysis of errors on a paper-folding task led him to conclude that individual differences in rate of decay (or, conversely, rate at which images can be refreshed) could account for many of the errors in his subjects' drawings. Kosslyn's model also includes image-inspection processes, image-transformation processes (e.g., rotating, scanning), and image-utilization processes. Different tests of spatial abilities appear to emphasize one or more of these processes, particularly transformation processes. Attempts to relate processes hypothesized in the Kosslyn model and performance on standard spatial tests suggest that different processes make independent contributions to individual differences on *Vz*-factor tests (Poltrock & Brown, 1984). However, many of the tasks used to estimate processes relied on self-report. This presents a problem because subjects might respond to the demand characteristics of the task (Pylyshyn, 1981) and because self-report might not be a dependable way to assess individual differences, especially for less able subjects (Lohman, 1988). Nevertheless, additional attempts to link constructs postulated in Kosslyn's theory with ability factors seem worthwhile, especially if dependable process measures can be devised and if a broad array of spatial factors can be represented.

EXTENSIONS AND IMPLICATIONS

Cognitive psychology, particularly the development of componential analytic methods, has already contributed substantially to our understanding of how subjects attempt to solve the kinds of novel and often figural tasks typically used as indicants of reasoning and spatial abilities. This work has also taken important steps toward distinguishing the two categories of ability in process terms. This is no small feat, because, in test correlational research, the two are often inextricably confounded.

The CIP models of performance on fluid reasoning tasks have begun to capture some of the adaptiveness and flexibility of thought that the term *fluid* might be taken to imply. It now appears that early CIP models of performance on these tasks were undercomplicated. Aimed at continuous measurement of individual differences at the parameter level, they relied on typological classification of individuals at the level of solution strategy. More recent work has shown that multiple strategies are available to most individuals and that they often shift among such strategies as items become difficult (Bethell-Fox et al., 1984; Embretson, 1986; Pellegrino, 1985a). However, strategy use does not imply conscious strategy selection; only a few studies have examined the more fundamental issues of who uses what strategy when and of the relationship between strategy use and ability. The handful of studies of this sort that have been conducted suggest that fluid ability involves being able to assemble and reassemble a workable strategy for complex, novel problems. But the issue is not by any means well understood at present.

Similarly, the cognitive analysis of visual-spatial abilities has uncovered a complexity of strategies and skills that have to be considered in developing, modeling, and interpreting spatial test scores. In so doing, it has confirmed the suspicions of Spearman, Thurstone, and others that such tasks often measure different abilities in different subjects. As with reasoning tasks, recent research has added the additional complication that subjects are not easily categorized according to solution strategy on many spatial tasks because they appear to shift strategy, particularly as items become more difficult. The unresolved questions are whether we can use this new understanding and the technologies at our disposal to develop better ways to measure these constructs. Therefore, one goal for future research would be to develop measures to identify the component skills of reasoning on problems that vary systematically in both novelty and the demand for spatial processing, the strategies that organize these skills, and the features of problems that cause shifts among these strategies. Parallel analyses of instructional tasks and conditions could support more detailed predictions of when and where each sort of strategic organization of skills would be instructionally relevant. A change in task demands (whether in a test or in instruction) that causes a change in the skill organization required is an example of aptitude–treatment interaction described at a process level (Cronbach & Snow, 1977; Snow & Peterson, 1985). Educational researchers have too often erroneously assumed that the ability demands of tests and instructional tasks were constant across such tests and tasks and could be judged by their surface features. Cognitive analysis now shows why this view is indeed superficial.

Several more immediate implications for measurement research are as follows: *First*, the measurement of fluid abilities requires that problems be relatively novel to the subject. But problem novelty cannot be determined from an objective analysis of the stimuli because it is defined by a discrepancy between subjects' prior experience and the new problem demands, that is, by the amount and type of transfer required.

Therefore, detailed studies of problem solving on novel tasks can lead not only to the enumeration of reasoning skills and their organization but also to explicit models of their transfer to new problems. Such models can guide efforts to assess amount and type of transfer for particular problems and persons. These steps might also help us understand how such skills are developed through experience and, thus, how to promote their development.

Second, the analysis and assessment of both fluid and spatial reasoning might be improved by requiring subjects to construct their answers. Constructed responses can provide much useful data for error analysis (e.g., Kyllonen, 1984), even though variables such as psychomotor abilities and time and care taken to construct a response influence performance. In spatial tests especially, drawn responses can be scored for correct proportions, a procedure long favored by British psychologists for increasing the spatial loading of a task (Smith, 1964). This hypothesis has been supported in several recent studies (Eliot & Smith, 1983; Lohman, 1979a).

Third, both kinds of tests could be devised using foils systematically designed to reflect major differences in solution strategy. Bialystok (1986) used this approach with some success in the design of a rotation task. Careful documentation of errors that subjects tend to make on constructed-response items would seem an important first step, as in Kyllonen's (1984) analysis of errors on a paper-folding test.

Fourth, with computer-controlled stimulus exposure, solution latencies can be recorded and studied. Of interest particularly is the time taken to accept or reject test probes. For example, in one experiment (Lohman, 1979a), the distribution of comparison latencies for each subject was determined. Then items on which a subject took an unusually long time to accept or reject the test probe were disallowed, under the hypothesis that long comparison latencies indicate items on which the subject had not completely synthesized or rotated the image. When scored this way, number correct showed higher correlations with reference spatial factors, and lower correlations with general reasoning and verbal factors, than when scored conventionally.

Fifth, assessment of spatial image production or processing might also be enhanced by verbally describing a problem to subjects rather than by requiring them to decipher line drawings. Analyses of verbal responses or choices among carefully designed test alternatives might allow strategy diagnosis and distinctions between logical–analytic and spatial–analog processes.

Sixth, although there have been a few forays into the domain of dynamic spatial and reasoning abilities (e.g., Gibson, 1947; Seibert & Snow, 1965), research guided by newer theories of cognition that capitalized on new technologies for presenting graphic displays and recording responses could be successful, particularly in isolating important spatial skills not measurable by paper-and-pencil tests. It seems clear that some such skills exist (Snow, Bethell-Fox, & Seibert, 1985) and that the frontiers of this domain have only begun to be explored (Hunt & Pellegrino, 1985).

Finally, the computer allows the specification of item universes and the systematic sampling of item attributes for a wide variety of fluid and spatial reasoning tasks, following the example of Butterfield et al. (1985) with letter series problems and Bejar (1986) with hidden-figures items. Existing tests can thus be characterized precisely as samples, and probably nonrepresentative samples, from these universes. Coupled with error analyses associated with each item attribute or combination of attributes, CIP models for existing tests can be understood as only part of a range of theoretical possibilities. Their intercorrelations and correlations with criteria can be more precisely controlled. And their value in diagnostic generalization can be understood.

Comprehension, Verbal, and Reading Abilities

Verbal Abilities

Verbal abilities have central importance for education, both as aptitudes for further school learning and as significant outcomes of that learning. A verbal factor was one of the first to be dependably separated from general ability (Spearman, 1927). Thurstone (1938a) soon identified two verbal abilities that he called "verbal relations" and "word fluency." Carroll (1941) then showed that at least eight verbal factors could be identified, including factors for associational fluency, oral fluency, speed of articulation, verbal knowledge, verbal reasoning, and speed of naming objects. Guilford (1967) posited even more verbal abilities in the semantic slice of his Structure of Intellect and perhaps another 30 related auditory-verbal abilities (Guilford, 1985). The main higher order factor distinction in the verbal domain is shown by Carroll (1985a) as Gc versus Gi, that is, crystallized intelligence versus general idea production.

A central problem in the definition of verbal abilities has been the overlap between reasoning abilities and performance on verbal tests, particularly tests of vocabulary and reading comprehension. The overlap is understandable for verbal reasoning tests, such as verbal analogies, but not for vocabulary tests; the latter appear, at face value, simply to estimate the examinees' stock of "conventional linguistic responses" (Carroll, 1941). Jensen summarized the paradox:

> The scores on the vocabulary subtests [of the Wechsler scales] are usually the most highly correlated with total IQ of any of the other subtests. This fact would seem to contradict Spearman's important generalization that intelligence is revealed most strongly by tasks calling for the eduction of relations and correlates. Does not the vocabulary test merely show what the subject has learned prior to taking the test? How does this involve reasoning or eduction. (1980, pp. 145–146)

Two sources of evidence help explain this apparent paradox: comparisons of verbal tests that do and do not correlate highly with reasoning and investigations of the process of word acquisition.

Verbal tasks that show relatively low correlations with reasoning measures have several distinguishing characteristics. Such tasks usually are simpler, thereby placing a greater premium on speed of response (e.g., Expressional Fluency and Word Fluency tests, in Carroll, 1941); or they emphasize specialized knowledge of linguistic conventions (e.g., grammar, understanding idioms, knowledge of infrequent words); or they demand phonological or articulatory processing instead of semantic processing; or they require the examinee to remember the exact order of letters or sounds (e.g., spelling, memory span). On the other hand, correlations with reasoning measures increase as the tasks demand increasing inference (as in analogies or when words must be defined, not merely recognized) require integration across sentences (as in comprehension tests) use relatively abstract words (as opposed to simply infrequent words) or require precise understanding of concepts (Cronbach, 1943; Marshalek, 1981). Marshalek (1981) also suggested that the relationship between verbal and reasoning abilities might be strongest for younger and less able persons, where abilities are presumably less differentiated or specialized.

Cognitive research has suggested some possible mechanisms underlying this contrast. One possible difference between tasks that show high correlations with reasoning and tasks that define more specific verbal abilities such as fluency or spelling could be the nature of the memory code on which performance is based. General reasoning measures might estimate facility in creating, retaining, and transforming information coded in a way that would preserve meaning (e.g. abstract propositions). More specific verbal (and spatial) measures might estimate both how well and how fast one can create, retain, and transform information coded in one of several perception-based codes. A string code would preserve order information for sounds, letters, words, and other stimuli. An image code would preserve configural information for spatial arrays. Specific phonological, articulatory, or other codes also seem highly likely but have not been studied much (see J. R. Anderson, 1983, 1985).

Werner and Kaplan (1952) (see also Johnson-Laird, 1983) claim that word meanings are learned in two ways: by explicit definition and through contextual inference, in other words, through the process of inferring the meaning of a word from its context. Daalen-Kapteijns and Elshout-Mohr (1981) studied the process of abstracting word meanings from contexts, based on extensive protocol analyses of verbal reports of medium- and high-verbal subjects as they read a series of sentences containing unfamiliar words. These investigators propose that subjects first generate a schema or hypothesis for the meaning of the word, based on their best interpretation of its meaning in the first sentence in which it occurs. The schema has slots that can then be either confirmed or contradicted by new evidence. This can lead to adjustment or complete reformation of the schema. Ideally, the initial schema would be sufficiently well articulated to permit an active search for information to confirm it. In their research, low-verbal subjects were less likely to use this strategy of schema-guided search, possibly because they did not have, or were not able to activate, the appropriate knowledge schema for the neologisms.

Rumelhart (1980) provided an almost identical model for the process of comprehending written prose. In a series of experiments, Rumelhart presented subjects with a series of somewhat ambiguous sentences describing an event. After each sentence, subjects were asked to tell what they thought the passage was about. For example, in one experiment, 10 subjects read the following sentences:

Business had been slow since the oil crisis.
Nobody seemed to want anything really elegant anymore.
Suddenly the door opened and a well-dressed man entered the showroom floor.
John put on his friendliest and most sincere expression and walked toward the man.

After reading only the first sentence, four subjects thought the passage was about a gas station, five were uncertain, and one correctly guessed the auto showroom scheme. Two additional hypotheses emerged after the second sentence (something about the nation or a luxury store). After reading the third sentence, however, all 10 subjects correctly identified the auto showroom scheme.

Although Rumelhart (1980) did not investigate individual differences in his experiments, J. R. Frederiksen (1981) has found that subjects differ in the extent to which they use contextual cues when reading; skilled readers prime a wider range of relevant concepts in memory, for a given set of contextual cues, than do less skilled readers.

R. J. Sternberg and Powell (1983) have also presented a process theory of verbal comprehension that is based on learning from context. Their theory has three parts: context cues, mediating variables, and processes of verbal learning. Context cues are hints about the meaning of the unknown word contained in the passage. Mediating variables (e.g., "variability of context") attempt to specify how contextual cues help or hinder the inference process in any particular situation. The theory also hypothesizes three verbal learning processes: selective encoding, selective combination, and selective comparison (see R. J. Sternberg & Powell, 1983, for details; also R. J. Sternberg, Powell, & Kaye, 1983). Selectivity in encoding, combination, and comparison in part reflects the contribution of well-structured knowledge. Experts in medical diagnosis, for example, selectively attend to certain symptoms because their thinking is guided by their declarative knowledge of diseases (see Lesgold, 1984). Nevertheless, declarative knowledge cannot be the only difference between high- and low-ability subjects, because one then could not explain how some individuals acquire more precise and useful knowledge in the first place. One possibility is that learners differ in their use of certain metacognitive or performance processes when learning, such as systematically testing alternative interpretations in unfamiliar situations, that then lead to a richer and more usefully organized knowledge base to guide new learning (see, e.g., Robinson & Hayes, 1978).

Parts of the Sternberg–Powell theory were tested in an experiment in which high school students were asked to read passages containing from one to four extremely low-frequency words presented with different frequencies and with different contextual cues. Students then defined words, and their definitions were rated for quality. These ratings were then regressed on independent variables coded to estimate variables hypothesized in the model. When averaged over four types of passages, the model variables accounted for 67% of the variance in the ratings. Rated quality of definition for individuals correlated approximately $r = .6$ with IQ, as well as vocabulary and reading comprehension tests. This is consistent with Marshalek's (1981) claim that the ability to infer word meanings from the contexts in which they occur is the cause of the high correlation typically observed between vocabulary and reasoning tests.

Thus, Marshalek (1981) and R. J. Sternberg and Powell (1983) have addressed the overlap between vocabulary and reasoning. Daalen-Kapteijns and Elshout-Mohr (1981), Rumelhart (1980), and others have addressed the overlap between word (or concept) acquisition and reading comprehension. In contrast, Hunt and his colleagues have attempted to isolate those elemental processes that might account for ability differences in a bottom-up fashion. The Hunt method follows a *cognitive-correlates* approach: task parameters are derived for each subject that reflect an information-processing model of a paradigmatic task performance, and they are then correlated with reference scores for verbal and other abilities.

For example, as noted earlier, the letter-matching task of Posner and Mitchell (1967) yields a parameter called the NIPI difference, thought to represent the time required to access certain aspects of lexical memory. This parameter typically correlates $r = -.30$ with verbal comprehension measures, suggesting that high-verbal subjects activate lexical information in long-term memory (LTM) more rapidly than do low-verbal subjects. However, this interpretation has been questioned by Carroll (1980a), who suggests that such results are more parsimoniously attributed to a general speed dimension. Indeed, Lansman et al. (1982) found the NIPI parameter to be more highly related to a perceptual speed factor than to a verbal ability factor. A study by Schwartz, Griffin, and Brown (1983) also supports Carroll's hypothesis.

In our view, however, such findings would be expected if one were assessing basic verbal processing skills, because factors such as perceptual speed, memory span, and word fluency better represent speed or efficiency of performing specific verbal processing than does performance on the general verbal comprehension factor. Additional support for this hypothesis comes from the finding that high-verbal subjects are better able than low-verbal subjects to preserve order information in short-term memory (Hunt et al., 1975). We previously suggested that the ability to create, retain, and transform information coded as strings might underlie some specific verbal abilities. Perceptual (or, better, clerical) speed tasks require rapid comparison of strings of letters or numbers. Span tests require short-term memory for the order of letters or numbers. Spelling tests require long-term memory for order information. Word fluency tasks require rapid access to words according to their spelling. Some auditory skills might have similar speed aspects, even though demanding different memory codes (as both Horn, 1985, and Guilford, 1985, suggested).

R. J. Sternberg and McNamara (1985) have now attempted to bring some of these strands together in a model of current functioning in verbal comprehension tests. Their model includes both the representation of word meaning and the nature and speed of word processing in verbal comparison tasks. They showed that overall latency scores on their tasks correlated significantly with a combination of rate and comprehension scores from conventional reading comprehension tests. The multiple correlation was not strikingly high ($R = .47$), but samples were small.

Their two-step componential analysis first compared alternative possibilities for word representation by contrasting defining attribute models and characteristic attribute models. In the former, word meaning depends on a stored list of semantic features that are both necessary and sufficient for a word to refer to an object or concept. In the latter, attributes are neither necessary nor sufficient but rather combine to characterize the referent, as in family-resemblance models of concepts (Rosch & Mervis, 1975). The best fit to data was obtained with a mixed model that assumed both defining attributes and a weighted sum of characteristic attributes specifying a word referent. Then various alternative models were compared to determine whether processing of word attributes, answer options, or both were best thought of as exhaustive or self-terminating. The implication was that subjects always process answer options exhaustively, that is, they search all answer options given and apparently also always use both defining and characteristic information about the stimulus words in doing so.

The results support a view of verbal ability that posits the acquisition of word meanings from contexts using contextual and other cues to guide selective encoding, combination, and comparison processes to produce schemata. These, in turn, drive further search and hypothesis-testing processes. Such schemata have slots for both defining and characteristic attributes of words, and they are used exhaustively in tasks requiring the demonstration of verbal comprehension.

Clearly, exhaustive search and comparison processes are particularly dependent on speed of lexical access and comparison of attributes in working memory. In other words, the alternative lines of research seem to converge on a coherent, if complex, picture of verbal comprehension ability. As Hunt concludes,

> Comprehension is a complex process, composed of many subprocesses. These range from the automatic, involuntary acts of lexical identification to the planned strategies people use to extract meaning from lengthy texts. There are individual differences in all of these subprocesses. They combine to produce "verbal intelligence."
>
> There is no disagreement between the psychometricians' observation that verbal comprehension behaves, statistically, as if it were a unitary ability and the experimental psychologists' and linguists' contention that verbal comprehension can be broken down into its component processes. The elementary behaviors build on each other. Sentence analysis cannot take place without lexical analysis. Text comprehension depends on sentence comprehension. There is a built-in correlation. . . . In fact, the value of the correlation between a simpler and a more complex task should rise as the complexity of the simpler task rises, because the two tasks will share more and more components . . . and people who acquire skill in one [component] are likely to acquire skill in another. (1985b, p. 55)

In short, cognitive psychology has now produced a provisional theory of verbal ability. The component processes and strategies identified, and the methods used to do this, suggest contrasts that can be built into psychometric measures. Indeed, a battery of closely articulated reasoning, spatial, and verbal measures can be envisioned; series of experimental contrasts derived from such a battery could provide a sharp picture of processing strengths and weaknesses relevant to learning.

These aptitude profiles should be much more useful for diagnostic purposes than the profiles from conventional ability tests have proven to be.

READING COMPREHENSION

Although verbal comprehension as a construct includes both reading and oral comprehension, models of oral comprehension tend to mimic models of reading comprehension. Further, individual differences in reading comprehension have been studied more extensively. Therefore, although recognizing important possible differences between the two, we discuss only reading comprehension here.

A model of reading comprehension proposed by Perfetti (1985, 1986) is consistent with, but expands, the previous discussion in several ways. First, it is important to note that much cognitive research on verbal processes and reading ability has been conducted on college students. At this level, the evidence to date suggests that reading ability depends closely on general verbal ability. The poor reader in college is likely to show deficits in verbal knowledge including syntax, vocabulary, spelling, and composition. In other words, college-level problems are only rarely unique to reading. Two separate cognitive processing factors seem to underlie these general deficits; less able college readers are slower to access symbolic representations in memory (as in the Hunt research), and they are less able to understand spoken language.

Among children (and possibly noncollege adults) however, a diverse array of cognitive and linguistic components seems to play a role in the differences in reading ability. Less able readers display, for example, less accurate and slower word identification, less knowledge of orthographic and phonological structure, less working memory capacity, smaller vocabulary size, less use of phonetic codes, slower semantic decisions, less spontaneous inferences, and low understanding of spoken language. The Perfetti model attempts to account for this vast array of findings by identifying three overlapping component processes: lexical access, proposition encoding, and text modeling. These overlap because they interact in the continuous process of reading from text, but also because they depend on the allocation of processing resources among them. Word meanings, represented as attributes, are activated through the process called *lexical access*. Eye movement and related studies suggest that most words in a text are fixated, although the reader's purpose and text familiarity must also be considered. Contrary to popular belief and the pronouncements of speedreading experts, it appears that only about two word units are processed at a time; the second of each pair is presumably activated automatically, which reduces its eventual access time, whereas the meaning of the first word is accessed in memory. Individual word meanings are then combined and retained in working memory in predicatelike structures called *propositions*. This information is combined with the reader's prior schematic knowledge to form a *text model* that is updated as reading continues. Kintsch (1986) argued that the text model must be tied to a *situation model* before true understanding can occur. For example, when the subject is attempting to assemble a toy from written directions, the text model captures the reader's representation of the written instructions, whereas the situation model might contain a mental image of the required step. Understanding requires a constant coordination and updating of both kinds of mental models (see Kintsch, 1986, for details).

Efficiency in all components makes for high reading ability. Inefficiency in one taxes attention, reducing the resources available for the other component processes. Perfetti's "verbal efficiency" theory suggests that poor readers are forced to allocate attention heavily to lexical access processes, making this component the central factor in individual differences in reading. But individual differences in proposition encoding, arising from the limits of working memory capacity, are also prevalent and appear to be reflected in the sorts of retrieval and comparison processes required by the sentence verification task. In text schemata, also, two kinds of individual differences are likely. Persons differ in prior content knowledge and, thus, are constrained in various ways to the schemata they can construct or retrieve. But persons are also likely to differ in the application of schemata they possess, and one can expect individual differences in both effortful search processes to find applicable schemata and effortless automatic schemata applications triggered by the developing text model.

Furthermore, there will be changes in the interaction of prior-knowledge-based and text-based processing as reading of a text continues. There is evidence that some individuals rely too heavily on one or the other and also use them maladaptively in further reading (Spiro & Myers, 1984). For example, inappropriate shifting from one prior-knowledge schema to another when the text disconfirms the first has been shown to occur among some students of low verbal ability; more able students shifted appropriately to more intensive text-based processing when the text disconfirmed prior schema. It is thus not true that prior-knowledge unavailability is the only topdown problem to be diagnosed in the study of text comprehension and reading achievement. To date, most cognitive psychological research on reading has aimed at understanding bottom-up processes such as those posited in the Perfetti theory. But the interaction of top-down prior knowledge and bottom-up text knowledge during reading is now receiving increased attention. There are many possible processing interdependencies such as those noted by J. R. Frederiksen (1982). New research is also suggesting the role of flexible adaptation of all the interdependent component skills of reading to the demands of particular situations. Wagner and Sternberg (1984) have suggested the crucial role of this sort of flexibility. It has long been considered a key aspect of scholastic aptitude (Snow, 1980a). Spiro and Myers (1984) discuss the many facets of adaptation to different reading tasks and contexts and note that the complexity of individual and contextual differences in this domain requires new kinds of measures for performance assessment. Calfee (1982) has also addressed the problem of context, noting, for example, the rather different processing demands put on the reader by narrative and expository forms of text. Calfee and Chambliss (1987) further demonstrate the structural varieties to be found in school textbooks. Conventional tests are designed on a single-correct-answer principle. But most comprehension problems in school and in the world involve multiple, alternative, or optional correct answers, depending on contextual circumstances. The development of adaptive flexibility in reading is not likely to be assessed directly by existing tests, though it might be partially reflected in total scores.

EXTENSIONS AND IMPLICATIONS

Cognitive theories of reading have been used to develop new measures of reading competence that promise greater diagnostic and instructional utility than existing tests of reading achievement (Calfee, 1977, 1982; Curtis & Glaser, 1983; J. R. Frederiksen, 1982; Johnston, 1983; Schwartz, 1984). J. R. Frederiksen's (1982) attempts to develop and validate a battery of experimental measures of component processes in reading can serve as the example here. The aim is to show how theory-based measures of reading processes can be used both to inform instruction and test and revise a theory of reading. The combined power of advanced correlational and experimental methods is also shown.

Frederiksen distinguishes three types of information-processing skills that are important for reading: *word analysis processes* (e.g., encoding single and multiletter units, translating graphemic units into phonological units, and activation of appropriate lexical categories); *discourse analysis processes* (e.g., retrieving and integrating word meanings, comprehending basic propositions underlying sentences, integrating processes across sentences, resolving problems of reference, and inferring nonexplicit but essential relations by elaborating from prior knowledge); and *integrative processes* (e.g., generating extrapolations from the text model, combining information from perceptual and contextual sources). These three types of component processes can interact by virtue of their usage of shared processing resources or their effects on a common data base. Components also differ importantly in the degree to which they have been automatized; skilled readers have automatized more components than have less skilled readers (see Figure 7.7).

The construction and validation of such a battery proceeds in several steps. *First,* tasks hypothesized to require particular

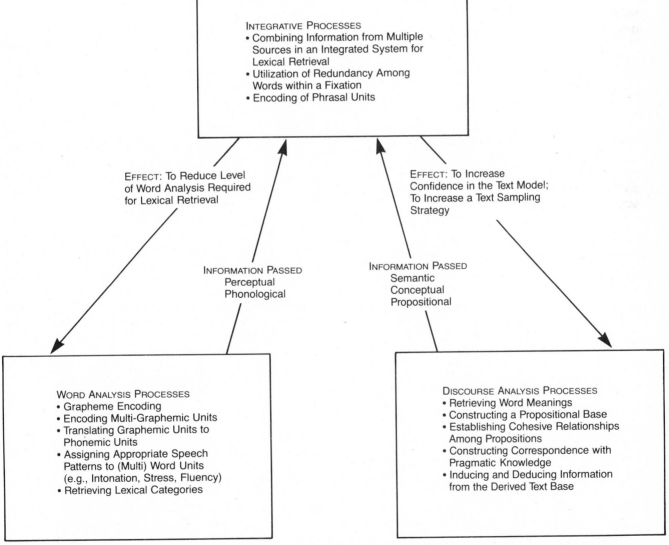

FIGURE 7.7 Categories of reading processes and their interactions. (After J. Frederiksen, 1982.)

components are selected. *Second*, stimulus variables are identified that can be manipulated to alter processing difficulty of the designated components. *Third*, contrasts among task conditions are computed for each subject that represent the extent to which performance is degraded as stimulus variables are manipulated. Predicted declines in performance constitute a first-level validation of the task and its process model. Convergent and discriminant validity of individual contrast scores constitutes the second level of validation. This is accomplished through the formation and testing of a set of structural equations.

J. R. Frederiksen (1982) summarized several studies in which he developed measures for eight component processes, then tested several models for interactions among these processes, and finally correlated components with a range of reference tests of cognitive abilities. His analysis also indicates that existing tests of reading speed, vocabulary, and comprehension do not include some important discourse processing skills.

With the initial battery assembled, J. R. Frederiksen, Warren, and Roseberg (1985a, 1985b) then selected for training three of the eight components identified in the earlier work. Selection was based on two criteria: Performance on the component should influence higher level components and automatic performance of the component should significantly reduce the drain on processing resources required by other components. Components thus selected were perception of multiletter units within words, decoding of orthographic patterns to phonological units of speech, and utilization in context. Computer games were then devised to train each skill. Extensive study of a few poor readers showed that training was effective for some subjects on some components. Frederiksen's work is ongoing and will be strengthened by larger validation and training studies. Nevertheless, it is a prime example of the sort of improvement to educational measurement that can be produced by combining sophisticated measurement models with good cognitive theory.

General Knowledge Structures

One of the most important contributions of cognitive theory to educational measurement might come from theories that describe the acquisition, organization, and use of knowledge in particular domains. Considerable progress has already been made toward this end in such fields as mathematics and physical science, for example (Carey, 1986). We start here with general issues, however, bringing in distinctions from cognitive psychology that seem at least heuristically useful in thinking about the assessment of knowledge and skill in many domains. We focus first on declarative and procedural knowledge. We then discuss generalized knowledge structures that combine aspects of both: schemata, mental models, and personal theories. We conclude with a brief discussion of Marton's (1981) phenomenological approach to investigating qualitative changes in the learner's understanding of concepts in a domain.

As noted in the introductory section, the distinction between declarative and procedural knowledge represents the difference between knowing that something is the case and being able to do something, often automatically and effortlessly; between facts and skills; and in the computer analogy, between the data and the program that operates on the data. It is the difference between knowledge that can be acquired in one presentation and knowledge that is automatized over many trials. For example, it is the difference between knowing why combining three and four yields seven and automatically responding "seven" when asked to add three plus four.

DECLARATIVE KNOWLEDGE AND ITS ORGANIZATION

Declarative knowledge is usually modeled as one or more semantic networks of labeled relations among knowledge units or packets (nodes). An example of a small portion of one such network is shown in Figure 7.8. These units are sometimes hypothesized to contain combinations of memory codes that preserve meaning (abstract propositions), or configuration of elements (images), or orders of elements in an array (string or linear ordering), or other perception-based memories (e.g., echoic, olfactory, kinesthetic). Knowledge thus stored is usable when particular nodes are activated (thus, in some theories, short-term, or working, memory is defined as knowledge in an active state). Activation rapidly spreads to associated nodes in the network but dissipates through the system unless particular nodes are constantly refreshed (J. R. Anderson, 1983; Collins & Loftus, 1975). There are also new classes of models that represent knowledge, not as addressable nodes and relations, but as patterns of connected activity distributed over many simpler neural units. This "new connectionism" offers a different view of the microstructure of knowledge organization and retrieval and, thus, of learning (see Rumelhart et al., 1986). It is not clear, however, that this newer approach has implications for educational measurement that are radically different from those of older, more abstractive, macrostructural models of knowledge processing.

Recall of information depends critically on how and how well information is organized in some such network. New knowledge units that are more elaborately connected with existing units and with each other can be activated and, thus, retrieved more readily than units not so elaborately connected (Reder, 1982). Some theorists also distinguish between knowledge that is elaborated to cues in the ongoing experience of the learner, called *episodic memories*, and knowledge that is elaborated in the meaning of concepts, called *semantic memories* (Tulving, 1972). Episodic memories are context bound, whereas semantic memories are context free. For example, the student who remembers "I studied it last Friday" or "it was on the right side of the page" is retrieving an episodically coded memory, because the new information was stored by elaborating to contextual cues. Such a learning strategy can be ineffective for learning and retrieval over the long haul, even though it might be momentarily effective: there are many Fridays and even more right sides of pages in a lifetime. On the other hand, elaborations that focus on the meaning or context-invariant characteristics of new information might be more difficult to construct, especially for unfamiliar material; yet the information becomes more easily retrieved when context cues have faded and, thus, more useful for further learning. Note

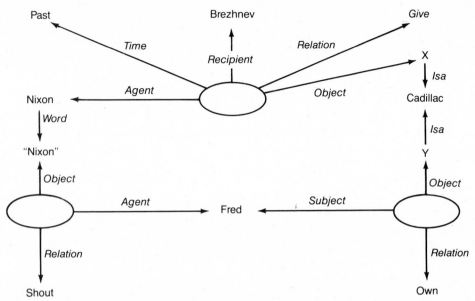

FIGURE 7.8 Examples of a propositional network for the three sentences "Nixon gave Brezhnev a Cadillac," "Fred owns a Cadillac," and "Fred shouted 'Nixon'." Circles represent modes, lines represent different types of labelled relationships. From *Cognitive Psychology* (2nd ed.) by J. R. Anderson, 1985, New York: W. H. Freeman and Company. Copyright 1985 by W. H. Freeman and Company. Reprinted by permission.

that the distinction here is not between rote learning and meaningful learning but between different forms of meaningful learning.

If organization of ideas in memory is important, then achievement tests might aim to estimate the amount and type of organization a student has achieved. Although some studies have attempted to assess through self-report the types of elaborative activities students use when learning (Schmeck, 1983; Weinstein, 1978), most researchers have focused on the effects of different elaborative strategies on the organization of knowledge achieved by the learner. This second type of investigation began with attempts to quantify the extent to which subjects in verbal learning experiments recalled words in a consistent order (subjective organization) or in an order that reflected predetermined categories defined by the experimenter (see Pellegrino & Hubert, 1982, for an introduction to these methods). More complex theories of knowledge led to the development of a broader array of methods. Introductions to this literature are provided by Gilbert and Watts (1983), Sutton (1980), and West and Pines (1985).

Studies of knowledge organization for learners with differing degrees of expertise have been conducted in several domains including psychology (Fenker, 1975), geology (Champagne, Klopfer, Desena, & Squires, 1981), mathematics (Geeslin & Shavelson, 1975), physics (Jong & Ferguson-Hessler, 1986), and computer science (Adelson, 1981), to name a few (see Gilbert & Watts, 1983, for references to specific topics in science).

Studies of knowledge organization have focused either on the within-domain organization of concepts, for example, how concepts in physics are related to one another, or on the influence of structured prior knowledge and belief systems on the acquisition of new knowledge, particularly when the two con-

flict. Both types of studies have been pursued most vigorously in science and mathematics, where the publicly affirmed structure of knowledge (as reflected in textbooks, for example) is relatively consistent across experts in the discipline (see Rorty, 1979, or Scarr, 1985, for implications of this constructivist view of knowledge). Several methods have been used to assess knowledge organization for individual learners, such as word association, free sorting of concept labels, and graph or map construction. Some investigators attempt to determine simply the extent to which concepts are associated with one another, for example, by counting the number or type of associations generated in a free-association task. More sophisticated analyses also attempt to determine the nature of the association (Preece, 1978); the overall amount of organization (Naveh-Benjamin, McKeachie, Lin, & Tucker, 1986); the type of organization such as network, hierarchy, or serial list (Cooke, Durso, & Schvaneveldt, 1986; Pellegrino & Hubert, 1982); the similarity among organizational structures for different individuals or the same individual at different times (Biggs & Collis, 1982; Carroll, 1972; Naveh-Benjamin et al., 1986; Pellegrino & Hubert, 1982) or under different frames of reference (R. C. Anderson & Freebody, 1979).

Such studies show that learners' knowledge organizations change with instruction, becoming more like that presented in the text (Geeslin & Shavelson, 1975; Shavelson, 1972). However, the degree of similarity between private and publicly endorsed structures of knowledge is sometimes related to the learner's ability to solve problems (Fenker, 1975; Thro, 1978), but sometimes it is not related to problem-solving skills in the domain (Geeslin & Shavelson, 1975). One study (Naveh-Benjamin et al., 1986) found small correlations on an index of similarity between student and instructor conceptual organization and performance on an examination ($r = .2$ to $.3$) but much higher correlation with the final course grade ($r = .5$). Thus, organization could be more important for long-term than for short-term learning. This same study found that amount of organization was related to examination scores only for students whose organizational structure was similar to that of the instructor. Other organizational schemes were either incorrect or judged to be so. A related finding by Majasan (1972; see Cronbach & Snow, 1977, for discussion) suggested that achievement declined as students' belief systems about the subject matter departed from that of their instructors. Still other studies (for example, Gray, 1983, discussed by Snow & Lohman, 1984) suggest, however, that more successful learners reorganize information in personally meaningful ways and recall larger amounts of newly learned information in a single chunk. The Gray study used a teach-back procedure to collect verbal protocols from students that could be scored for amount and kind of paraphrasing, degree of order change of concepts from initial presentation, and chunk size (using an interresponse latency measure to identify chunks, as developed by Chi, 1978).

Whatever the evidence regarding the relation of achievement to idiosyncrasy, as opposed to similarity of student knowledge structure relative to instructor or text, it is clear from this work that the assessment of such declarative knowledge structures, and the organizational skills and strategies used to produce them, are important targets for measurement research.

PROCEDURAL KNOWLEDGE AND ITS ACQUISITION

The organizational skills and strategies just referred to constitute instances of metacognitive or other complex systems of procedural knowledge used to structure new declarative knowledge. On the other hand, new procedural knowledge is thought of as prior declarative knowledge that has been tied to the conditions of its use. Thus, there could be some reciprocity. But theories that attempt to describe the acquisition of new procedural knowledge also emphasize discrimination and generalization, and, particularly, automatization.

J. R. Anderson (1983) proposed a three-stage model of the process of automatization of skills, building on the earlier work of Fitts (1964). In Stage I, knowledge is represented declaratively and must be processed consciously using general-purpose procedural knowledge. In this stage of learning, students understand what it is they are supposed to do, even though they cannot yet do it automatically. In Stage II, students begin to develop (or "compile") specific production rules through practice with feedback. Lesgold (1984) described proceduralization as the process of storing a memory of the conditions that prevailed when a successful action was executed. Only parts of a complex procedure can be proceduralized at one time, due to limitations of working memory. Because incorrect procedures are learned as readily as correct procedures, feedback is crucial at this stage. Either learners must be able to generate feedback for themselves (e.g., comparing their printed letter to a stimulus letter at the top of the page or to an internal standard), or feedback must be provided by an external monitor (tutor, teacher, or computer). Instruction that encourages students to develop internal standards for judging the adequacy of their own performances promotes skillful independent learning. Learners who do not have such internalized standards must rely on external feedback, which is not always immediately available, and are thus more likely to practice an incorrect procedure. With additional practice, separately learned procedures that are executed sequentially can be condensed into a single production, which further accelerates performance. For example, children carefully write each letter in their names; adults sign their names in a single motion. In Stage III, the range of application of the procedure is either generalized so that it applies under a broader range of conditions or, conversely, its range of application is specialized. These changes occur through extensive practice with feedback. Often, hundreds of trials are required, and performance might still be improving significantly after thousands of trials. For further discussion of this process, see J. R. Anderson (1983).

Many cognitive psychologists thus view learning and thinking as the process of developing and executing sequences of overlearned production rules. Some of these rules are specific (IF the goal is to add 3 and 2, THEN the answer is 5), whereas others are quite general (IF I am reading and IF the goal is to understand what I am reading and IF I do not understand, THEN I try rereading the offending sentence). Sequences of such conditional if–then rules are called *production systems*. With continued practice and experience, such systems can be generalized to cover more examples and specialized to particular domains of examples. In effect, the system is developed through generalization of rules across the series of examples faced. Such computer models need not posit executive controls over productions, because each system itself contains the if–then conditions needed to trigger other systems. An example of a compiled production system for elementary mathematics problems is given in Figure 7.9.

As Greeno (1978, 1980b) and J. R. Anderson (1983) have both emphasized, if humans develop procedural skills at all in the way such models do, effective instruction requires sequences of carefully juxtaposed examples. Observing instruction in geometry or algebra, for example, they noted that teachers often leave such juxtapositions implicit, fail to produce them in the first place, or destroy what planned juxtapositions might have been built into textbook exercises by assigning only every other problem for homework. On the other hand, it remains an open question whether procedural knowledge can be taught explicitly and still be effectively learned. Fairly specific skills can clearly be trained, with short-term benefit to those previously deficient in such skills. Training in learning strategies seems to have similar benefits. But some evidence also suggests that such training interferes with performance among more able learners (Snow & Lohman, 1984). Both positive and negative effects could be short lived, however. Measurement research could seek effective ways to distinguish the declarative and procedural aspects of such performances and to trace their development or training over the long haul.

As noted previously, it is useful to distinguish between the cognitive skills used to perform the encoding, storing, retrieval, and transformation of information and the higher order, or metacognitive, processes used to plan, activate, monitor, eval-

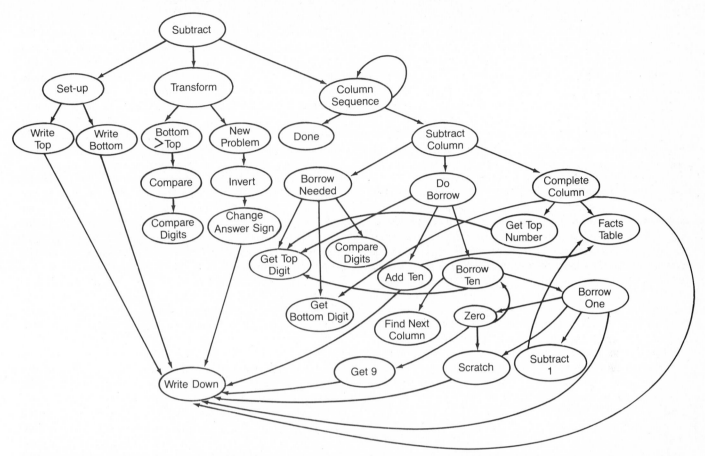

FIGURE 7.9 Examples of a system of production rules for subtraction. Each procedure can be formalized as an IF . . . THEN statement. Procedures higher in the figure are composed of procedures lower in the figure. For example, the SET-UP procedure consists of WRITE TOP (write the top number) and WRITE BOTTOM (write the bottom number). From "Diagnostic models for procedural bugs in basic mathematical skills" by J. S. Brown and R. Burton, 1978, *Cognitive Science, 2,* p. 180. Copyright 1978 by Ablex Publishing Corporation. Reprinted by permission.

uate, and modify these lower order performance processes. The terms used to distinguish between lower order and higher order thinking skills vary widely (see, e.g., A. L. Brown, 1978; Lawson, 1984; Wagner & Sternberg, 1984), but there is now some consensus that these metacognitive skills are among the most transferable mental competencies (Wagner & Sternberg, 1984).

Some of the metacognitive processes that have been found to distinguish older or more able from younger or less able students are comprehension monitoring (less able and younger students often fail to notice when they do not understand something); use of internal cues to evaluate one's performance (less able and younger students often have difficulty judging the adequacy of their performance without external feedback and often significantly overestimate the quality of their performance); planning (many complex activities require at least a modicum of planning, which involves much more than monitoring—poor problem solvers and younger children often proceed impulsively without taking time to consider options or to develop and test strategies); goal maintenance (complex thinking requires that the subject keep thoughts on target—less able and younger students often have difficulty ignoring internal and external distractions, a skill that Binet [in

Terman, 1916] called "the tendency to take and maintain a definite direction in one's thinking", p. 45); flexibility (detecting that a particular set of cognitive operations are not producing a desired output is of little value unless one can activate another approach to the problem—more able subjects often evidence a substantially greater flexibility in their thinking than do less able subjects). See Campione, Brown, & Ferrara, 1982; Snow & Lohman, 1984; Wagner & Sternberg, 1984.

Schemata, Personal Theories, and Mental Models

Procedural and declarative knowledge is stored, retrieved, and used in an organized way, and the organization is presumed to be provided by schemata. Although some theorists would list schemata as a form of organization of declarative knowledge, the typical conceptualizations of schemata contain elements of both declarative and procedural knowledge and, thus, might best be understood as higher order structures that combine properties of the simpler representational schemes previously discussed (see Rumelhart & Norman, 1985, for a discussion of different proposals). In Greeno's definition, schemata are data structures or procedures that are used to organize the components of specific experience and to expand the representation of an experience or message to include components that were not specifically contained in the experience, but that are needed to make the representation coherent and complete in some important sense. (1980a, pp. 718–719)

Procedural knowledge, as noted, is often modeled as a system of production rules compiled through exercise and feedback in performing a series of related tasks or solving problems that form a class. General-purpose procedural knowledge is also sometimes discussed as runnable mental programs or as scripts for various familiar situations. In the case of declarative knowledge, the dominant schemata are thought to be networks of interrelated facts and concepts. The individual builds such networks by associative processes and elaborates and reorganizes the structure as experience accumulates (J. R. Anderson & Bower, 1973; Norman, Rumelhart, & the LNR Research Group, 1975). R. C. Anderson and his colleagues (see R. C. Anderson & Pearson, 1984) have shown how different expectations about a text can activate radically different schemata for its interpretation and hence influence what is learned from it. Test items might be designed to detect appropriate schema use in reading comprehension or to discover flexibility in shifting among alternative appropriate schemata.

One important kind of general schemata are those labeled *personal, tacit,* or *naive* theories, to distinguish such belief systems from those that are publicly affirmed. Much recent research has examined the extent to which new knowledge becomes integrated into the learner's belief systems. Of particular interest are studies that examine conflicts between naive or personal theories of knowledge and publicly affirmed theories of knowledge. As was the case with studies of organization of concepts, most of this work has been conducted using science curriculum (e.g., Clement, 1982; McClosky, 1983), although belief systems operate powerfully in other domains (Lackoff & Johnson, 1980; Majasan, 1972).

A recurring theme in this research is the resistance of personal theories to change, especially when contradictory evidence comes from textbooks. Students maintain erroneous beliefs about basic concepts in physics even after extensive instruction (Champagne, Klopfer, & Anderson, 1980; Elshout, 1985). Conceptual change, when it does occur, might be better described as revolutionary than as evolutionary (Champagne, Gunstone, & Klopfer, 1985; Johansson, Marton, & Svensson, 1985). Methods used in this research vary widely, depending on the comprehensiveness of the personal theory investigated. Following Piaget (e.g., Inhelder & Piaget, 1958), several investigators have used clinical interviews of varying degrees of structure (Johansson et al., 1985; Pines, Novak, Posner, & VanKirk, 1978). Biggs and Collis (1982) proposed an extensively documented hierarchical scheme for scoring open-ended responses that was also initially grounded in Piagetian theory. Theories that apply to a narrower range of events have been inferred from patterns of responses to systematically structured tasks, as in Siegler's (1976) studies of children's increasing sophistication in solving balance beam problems.

A related possibility is a method that combines the emphases of European phenomenological psychology with a dedication to systematic description of concrete cases, an approach called *phenomenography* (Marton, 1981). The phenomenographic approach aims to discover students' conceptions and misconceptions in a knowledge domain and also student self-perceptions, or concepts of themselves, as learners. Substantial verbal protocols are collected through interviews before and after instruction. Typically, the reports reflect students' attempts to explain why certain natural or social phenomena operate as they do, in response to open-ended or "naked" questions. The protocols are analyzed to reconstruct the qualitative categories and concepts that seem to describe, and to operate in, the students' mental experiences. Learning is then represented as a transition among these qualitative categories. Marton, 1983 (see also Dahlgren, 1979; Johansson et al., 1985; Marton, Hounsell, & Entwistle, 1984), illustrates how this approach can be used in diagnoses of achievement. For example, interview questions for a course in mechanics might be "A car is driven at high constant speed straight forward on a highway. What forces act on the car?" and "A puck has left a hockey stick and glides straight forward on smooth ice. What happens?" For these two questions, students displayed any of eight different explanations, depending on their use of the concepts of equilibrium, velocity, movement, force, and energy. Different sorts of shifts among these categories were observed as a function of learning and course content. Two other examples are shown in Figure 7.10. In panel A, a question on optics yielded five kinds of explanations, as shown. Although 38% of the high school seniors in this study could answer questions on key concepts made explicit in the text, few said there was light in all sections of the figure, and only 11% reasoned in a manner suggesting response category E. In panel B, a question used following a college economics course is shown. Dahlgren (1979) found many students exhibiting type C explanations and some even shifting from D to C as a function of the course. There are also examples showing the presence of serious misconceptions, even among students who have successfully passed objective achievement tests. The suggestion is that theories of achievement and improved assessments require a level of cognitive analysis not available with conventional tests.

From a developmental perspective, the goal of such evaluation should be to determine what kind of foundation knowledge in a discipline contributes most, not just to immediate learning, but also to the strength and receptiveness of the knowledge structure that is assembled over a period of years. For example, although certain mnemonic activities might be beneficial in the short run and even over the course of a full semester's learning, the long-term effects could conceivably be quite negative (Snow & Lohman; 1984; Lohman, 1986b). The issue is not merely the building of a strong knowledge foundation, but also the building of a foundation that actually facilitates the addition of increasingly complex knowledge structures. We know little about such effects, but it seems likely that prescriptions for both teaching and testing that would derive from such understanding would differ significantly from those based on a more myopic analysis (Calfee, 1981; Norman, 1977).

The goal for all such research is to describe the types of personal theories learners construct to explain phenomena in their world, to describe the evaluation of such theories, and, finally, to design instructional interventions to assist students

A. *Physics Question*

On a clear, dark night, a car is parked on a straight, flat road. The car's headlights are on and dipped. A pedestrian standing on the road sees the car's lights. The situation is illustrated in the figure below, which is divided into four sections. In which of the sections is there light? Give reasons for your answer.

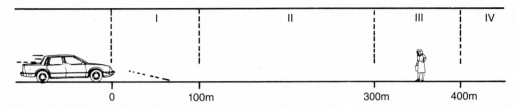

Response Categories
a. The link between eyes and object is taken for granted. There is no problem — we can simply see.
b. A picture goes from the objects to the eyes. When it reaches the eyes, we see.
c. Beams come out from the eyes. When they hit the object, we see.
d. Beams go back and fourth between the object and the eyes. The eyes send out beams which hit the object, return and tell the eyes about it.
e. The object reflects light. When it hits the eyes, we can see the object.

B. *Economics Question*

Why does a bun cost one Swedish crown?

Response Categories
a. Irrelevant answers (e.g., "I like buns").
b. Price is determined by properties of commodities such as taste, shape, size, etc.
c. Price is determined by the value of commodities or the accumulated value of their constituents.
d. Price is determined by the relationship between supply and demand for commodities.

FIGURE 7.10 Examples of interview questions in physics (Panel A) and economics (Panel B) and some categories of responding student conceptions. (After Marton, 1983, and Dahlgren, 1979, respectively.)

in progressing to more sophisticated theories. A goal for measurement is to devise ways to detect and describe these commonly held theories (Glaser, Lesgold, & Lajoie, in press), and also idiosyncratic variations on them.

Another type of higher order knowledge structure that combines elements of declarative and procedural knowledge is the so-called *mental model*. Human beings are assumed to understand their worlds by constructing working models of it in their minds (Johnson-Laird, 1983). These working models can then be used to control, explain, and predict events (Gentner & Stevens, 1983; Rouse & Morris, 1986). Although some would classify such models under the general rubric of schemata (e.g., Rumelhart & Norman, 1985), mental models seem sufficiently unique to warrant separate attention. One important difference between mental models and schemata that represent particular concepts or sequences of events is that schemata are directly tied to particular objects and events, whereas a mental model might or might not be; the choice of a model to represent a problem could be arbitrary. Thus, a "going-to-the-library" scheme will not be of much assistance in understanding a passage on eating at a restaurant. However, a variety of different mental models, such as images of groups of people or of more formal representations such as Euler's Circles, Venn Diagrams, or other symbolic constructions, might be useful if the goal is to solve a syllogism.

Mental models range from the arbitrary but explicit instan-

tiations readers generate as they attempt to comprehend text (R. C. Anderson, 1977), through executable analog models of spatial or temporal events (e.g., predicting the trajectory and point of impact of a flying object or an oncoming car), to abstract models people appear to generate when confronted with problems in syllogistic reasoning (Johnson-Laird, 1983). Skill in generating such models to integrate and summarize incoming information in a way that permits reasonable inferences and predictions appears to be an essential component of reading comprehension (R. C. Anderson, 1977; Bransford & Johnson, 1973), of solving word problems in mathematics (Kintsch, 1986; Kintsch & Greeno, 1985), and of working in many other domains (Johnson-Laird, 1983). Although such models can be quite abstract, they are often represented by specific visual images. Indeed, clinical reports suggest that patients who have lost the ability to generate or recognize concrete images (such as faces) also experience great difficulty coordinating ideas long enough for new learning or even for recovering a thought, once interrupted (Sacks, 1985). Similarly, some of the more successful attempts to develop comprehension skills (e.g., Palincsar & Brown, 1984) appear primarily to provide structured practice in the process of developing good mental models for events described in the text.

Research on the nature of mental models that are developed, held, and used by individuals in learning and performance is a relatively new emphasis and is quite diverse. Work is progressing in such widely separated fields as the study of problem solving in physics, the maintenance and control of devices, the design of engineering systems, and the use of human judgment and choice in decision making. For a review of general issues, see Rouse and Morris (1986). For our purposes, the key issue is how individual mental models operating in educational settings can be assessed, and this issue cannot be decided in the abstract. Some examples of the possibilities in the particular domains of science and mathematics are included in a later section.

EXTENSIONS AND IMPLICATIONS

Students build up vast structures of particularized knowledge, both declarative and procedural, over their educational years. These include networks of meaning for thousands of words, phrases, and concepts; cognitive maps of places and events; schematized knowledge of properties of the physical and social world; beliefs, values, goals, and plans regarding the self and others; and a host of skills and strategies for various kinds of reasoning and problem solving. Such knowledge is often partial, incomplete, or incorrect in idiosyncratic ways. It is also often tied to particular situations. And it can be brought into new learning in ways that distort the new learning, as well as in ways that allow new learning to complete or correct or supplant the old. The improvement of knowledge assessment would seem to depend generally on diagnosis, both of prior knowledge and of knowledge in the process of being acquired. Such assessment should include direct attempts to assess how concepts are organized, particularly at the level of belief systems and personal theories. For mental models, assessment might estimate the extent to which students spontaneously generate integrative models and their appropriateness to the problematic situation.

The general methods so far developed for assessing knowledge structure show some promise. But they vary widely, from methods based on relatively constrained response formats such as those used by Naveh-Benjamin et al (1986) and Shavelson (1972), through more open, relatively unconstrained methods such as the open-response scoring systems of Biggs and Collis (1982) and Gray's (1986) teach-back procedure, to the unstructured depth interviews used by Marton (1983) and his colleagues. Measurement research has not yet been undertaken to compare and evaluate these methods or to combine and improve upon them. It would seem that, to date, cognitive theories about knowledge structures have progressed far ahead of research on methods for their assessment that would be useful in education. This is therefore a major item for the measurement research agenda.

For assessment of procedural knowledge, speed of execution and automaticity are the keys. Declarative knowledge of how to do something does not imply proceduralization of a skill. Knowing the rule "invert and then multiply" is a useful first step in learning to divide fractions. But proceduralized knowledge here would be evidenced by automatically and rapidly performing the operation, without necessarily being aware of the rule.

Assessment of skilled performance could also make considerably better use of error analysis to detect typical overgenera-

lizations or incorrectly learned rules. Psychometrically sound distractors in test items could also be made diagnostically useful. Assessment of some specific cognitive skills might be conducted as follows, for example. First, the range of skills and subskills generally required by the tasks in question would be specified. These skills can be described as organized sets of if–then rules, such as the rules for capitalization, for long division, or for constructing orthogonal projections. Problems assumed to require these skills in isolation or in combination would then be constructed and presented to subjects. For any particular skill, assessment would then attempt to examine the following aspects or components:

1. *Conceptual foundation.* Mindless execution of a misunderstood skill is rarely useful, particularly when the learner must use the new skill in a meaningful way. A good conceptual understanding of the principles that underlie the skill must therefore be coordinated with practice aimed at automatization of skills (see Resnick, 1984).
2. *Correctness of output.* Given a certain set of inputs, or conditions, does the subject execute the correct action? If not, are there consistent errors or bugs?
3. *Automatization of skill.* Simply knowing what to do (e.g., "invert and then multiply") does not mean that knowledge is proceduralized. Proceduralized knowledge is executed rapidly and with minimal demands on attentional resources. Therefore, assessment must estimate speed of executing the skilled action and the degree to which the performance holds up when concurrent tasks or processing demands are placed on the subject.
4. *Degree of composition.* With continued practice, skilled performances that were once executed as a series of steps come to be executed in a smaller number of steps. For example, the many separate skills required for composing a well-organized paragraph or solving an algebraic equation might be executed as a unit. Smoothness of performance and continued increases in speed are two indications of composition.
5. *Generalization.* It is important to determine the range of performances to which a particular skill transfers. Specific skills might be inappropriately overgeneralized, and general skills might be inappropriately specific.
6. *Metacognition.* It is also important to determine the kinds of functional and dysfunctional metacognitive processes that operate during an individual's performance. Some of these might be quite general; some might be domain specific. Although much metacognitive processing is automatic and thus not available to introspection, experimental tasks can be designed to detect some of these processes. Where metacognition is conscious, it is at least potentially detectable in self-reports.

Finally, studies of knowledge acquisition suggest that we must attend more carefully to learning and knowledge organization over the long haul. A strong foundation might not be so important as one that not only allows, but also promotes, well-structured additions over the years. A strong, but impoverished, base promotes premature closure. Thus, assessment methodology for long-range knowledge acquisition is another important item for the measurement research agenda.

Specialized Knowledge and Problem Solving

Although the cognitive structures and processes investigated to date might be quite general, increasing research attention is being focused on particular domains of knowledge. The hypothesis is that much important cognitive activity is domain specific. At least it seems likely that even general problem-solving strategies are conditioned by or adapted to the particular characteristics of the knowledge domain in which they are used. Certainly, experts appear to be experts only in specialized domains. By far the most research attention has been paid to mathematics and physical science, so the bulk of this section concerns this work. But mathematics and physics instruction typically present well-structured problems, problems that have clear initial states, a defined set of permissible operations, and a clear goal state. Other curriculum domains might contain both well-structured problems and not-so-well-structured problems, the latter being problems without well-specified initial or end states or operations. Still other domains might be characterized by problems that are ill-structured or wholly unspecified in this sense. Cognitive research in these relatively unstructured domains has only recently begun. Yet the need for improved assessment in these domains is as essential, as a guide to curriculum evaluation and improvement, as it is in mathematics and science. Thus, we add at the end of this section a brief listing of the domains in which initial work has been done, to provide references on which further measurement research can build. We also note research in some domains of professional expertise such as medical diagnosis, for example, which has received substantial attention.

MATHEMATICAL ABILITIES

Mathematical abilities differ from verbal or spatial abilities in two important respects. First, even among adults, numerical abilities are not as strongly differentiated as are verbal or spatial abilites. Whereas several specific verbal and spatial abilities have been repeatedly demonstrated, only two numerical-ability factors appear with consistency; these are typically called *numerical facility* and *quantitative reasoning*. Numerical facility appears most clearly in samples of older children and adults, and it is defined by speed of performing simple arithmetic computations. Quantitative reasoning tests are more diverse, but they appear to depend heavily on the ability to assemble a plan for solving a problem, as in the Necessary Arithmetic Operations test (see Ekstrom et al., 1976). Tests of differing complexity often form a simplex array, with end points defined by simple addition tests at the periphery of the radex map and complex quantitative reasoning at the center (see Snow et al., 1984). This simplicial structure might reflect the inherently hierarchical structure of mathematics; or the fact that numerical skills are less well developed in this society, hence, less differentiated than verbal and spatial abilities; or the fact that fewer numerical (or perhaps symbolic) tests are usually included in test batteries. Perhaps, also, mathematics is

inherently more abstract and, thus, not tied to a particular perception-based memory code, as are verbal, visual-spatial, and auditory abilities.

This last possibility is supported by the second important difference between mathematical abilities and verbal and spatial abilities: It is usually difficult, and often impossible, to separate a first-order factor for quantitative reasoning and a second-order factor for G, or Gf (Gustafsson, 1984; Marshalek et al., 1983). This might also be a statistical constraint, because, in three-factor space, quantitative ability inevitably falls between verbal and spatial abilities. Or it could indicate that mathematical reasoning requires both verbal and spatial abilities. In any event, mathematical knowledge is necessarily abstract and, thus, depends for its development on the individual's ability to understand and manipulate increasingly abstract concepts.

Although less voluminous than research on reading, research on mathematical abilities has grown rapidly in recent years. Several themes are apparent. *First*, even seemingly simple operations such as counting depend on successful integration of a surprisingly complex set of general principles (Gelman & Meck, 1983) and specific procedural rules (Greeno, Riley, & Gelman, 1981). *Second*, the processes children use to perform computations change with experience, so even simple computation tests measure predictably different abilities in experienced and less experienced students. *Third*, children often invent new ways of solving problems, sometimes in circumventing instructed procedures and sometimes in unsuccessful efforts to repair incomplete or partial knowledge. *Fourth*, word problems are difficult because they require the coordination of several different types of mathematical, linguistic, and world knowledge with an accurate mental model of the situation (Kintsch, 1986). We review only a few examples of this research here, beginning with some of the studies of basic computation skills.

Research on computational skills in children has focused on developmental changes in the strategies children use to add and subtract numbers. Groen and Parkman (1972) hypothesized that children could add two numbers in five different ways, three of which we discuss here. Children using the first strategy (COUNT BOTH) count the number of units represented by the first addend and then increment this count by the number of units represented by the second addend. Children using the second strategy (COUNT FROM FIRST) set the counter to the value of the first addend and then increment the counter by the number of units represented in the second addend. Finally, children using the third strategy (COUNT FROM MAX) set the counter to the value of the larger addend and then increment the counter the number of times indicated by the smaller addend. According to the first model, time to add numbers a and b is a linear function of $a + b$; according to the second model, time is a linear function of b; and according to the third model, time is a linear function of a or b, whichever is smaller. Groen and Parkman (1972) found that only the last model described response latencies of first-grade children in their study (none of the models tested fit 32% of the learners). In another study, Houlihan and Ginsburg (1981) used retrospective reports and found that 31% of the first graders, but only 3% of the second graders, in their study used the first strategy of counting both numerals. Similarly Fuson (1982) found that most children follow a count-from-first model of addition prior to formal instruction.

As computational skills are overlearned, response becomes quite rapid. Groen and Parkman (1972) observed this pattern first for problems in which both addends were the same. Older children and adults for whom computation has become automatic respond rapidly to most types of computation problems. The acquisition of this computational competence can be well described by general theories of skill acquisition in which knowledge is first represented in a declarative form and then becomes proceduralized, composed, and tuned with practice (J. R. Anderson, 1983).

One implication of these theories is that assessment of computational skill might specify the degree to which particular procedures have been automatized, as indexed by speed of response and by resistance to interference from other tasks executed simultaneously. As computational skills become increasingly proceduralized, individual differences in speed of computation become less related to general reasoning abilities and define an increasingly specific numerical factor. But it is also noteworthy that, although children might be taught to add using a count-from-first strategy, they soon discover the count-from-max strategy for themselves. Resnick (1976) has shown that children invent strategies that often deviate substantially from what they have been taught. And this phenomenon might also be expected in later mathematics instruction. Gelman and Gallistel (1978) have also shown that children display generative knowledge; they use untaught implicit principles to adapt their counting behavior to constraints. Achievement measurement, however, rarely aims to assess invention or adaptation processes.

J. S. Brown and Burton (1978) and Ginsburg (1977) have examined computational skills from a different cognitive perspective. Their research stems from the tradition in which procedural knowledge is modeled as a system of production rules or if–then statements. Some of the errors children make on computation tasks are then seen to be predictable consequences of incorrect or "buggy" production rules. J. S. Brown and Burton (1978) first developed a rational model of the subtraction process using nested and cross-referenced production rules. They then developed a computer program that identified consistent errors in subtraction problems that could be predicted from their model. Although the program was able to identify hundreds of "bugs" in students' performance, the program could not identify bugs that would have produced 47% of the incorrect answers students gave. Thus, their model was incorrect in some important respects, possibly in its premise that bugs would function like incorrect statements in a computer program and produce consistent mistakes. Children's behavior in such situations appears more probabilistic or idiosyncratic than computer programs are usually made to be. Some have suggested that children are more afflicted by a general bugginess than by particular sets of bugs. Nevertheless, analysis of errors can be valuable for diagnostic testing purposes, particularly if response options are chosen to reflect systematic flaws in procedural knowledge. This seems a relatively easy, yet potentially quite useful, way to modify tests to reveal more about how students think (see, e.g., Tatsuoka & Baillie, 1982, for one attempt).

In summary, studies of computational abilities in children suggest that the processes children use to solve such problems change with practice, that some children invent more efficient strategies than those they are taught, that some of the errors they make on subtraction problems reveal systematic flaws in procedural knowledge, and that other errors reflect specialized and perhaps idiosyncratic processing. As with early information-processing models of reading, most work on arithmetic computation presumes serial processing of a given set of stages. However, it seems likely that good computational skills are better accounted for by models similar to those that have recently gained popularity in research on reading (e.g., McClelland & Rumelhart, 1981), in which multiple processes are executed simultaneously. Good computational skills require not only the rapid and accurate execution of a sophisticated system of procedural knowledge, but also the ability to ignore irrelevant information and inhibit incorrect procedures (Fischbein, Deri, Saindti, & Marino, 1985) and to reject implausible or impossible results (Ryes, Rybolt, Bestgen, & Wyatt, 1982).

Numerical competence is thus more than a mindless execution of procedural knowledge. As Resnick (1984) has argued, the incorrect or buggy procedures children invent to repair incomplete procedural knowledge are best characterized as *syntactic,* in that they represent attempts to modify the surface structure of subtraction procedures, while ignoring the underlying "semantics," or meaning, of the operations. This distinction between syntax and semantics, or between automatic procedural knowledge and meaningful declarative knowledge, has been reinforced by attempts to correct consistent error patterns or bugs. Direct instruction aimed at correcting buggy procedures has met with only moderate success. More successful instruction, on the other hand, would link conceptual understanding and the procedures that support it. Several studies suggest that, although students enter school with a conceptual approach to mathematics, by third or fourth grade they solve mathematical problems syntactically, that is, by applying memorized rules to the manipulation of symbols (Davis & McKnight, 1980; De Corte & Verschaffel, 1984; Resnick, 1982). This fixation on syntax and procedure continues as students learn decimal computations (Hiebert & Wearne, 1985) and even algebra (Rosnick & Clement, 1980). Nevertheless, improvements in mathematical problem solving have been repeatedly linked to advances in conceptual or semantic knowledge (Briars & Larkin, 1984; Riley, Greeno, & Heller, 1983). Therefore, one important goal for measurement would be to determine the discrepancy between semantic and syntactic knowledge of mathematical operations.

Mathematical Problem Solving

Two main approaches have been taken to the study of quantitative reasoning. One focuses on the process of solving problems; the other focuses on the influence of prior knowledge organization on problem solving.

Studies of problem solving commonly distinguish problem representation from problem solution (Hayes, 1981). *Problem representation* refers to the internal mental model the problem solver constructs. *Problem solution* refers to the process of applying mathematical operations to this representation, often iteratively, to achieve an answer. How (and if) a problem is solved depends fundamentally on how it is represented. A widely supported conclusion is that subject matter experts represent problems differently from subject matter novices. Novices are more likely to classify and remember problems according to their surface characteristics, whereas experts classify and recall problems according to general principles used to solve them (Chi, Feltovich, & Glaser, 1981; Novick, 1986/1987).

Mayer (1985) suggested that understanding story problems requires five different types of knowledge: (a) linguistic knowledge (how to parse sentences, what various words mean); (b) factual knowledge (general world knowledge such as units of measurement); (c) schema knowledge for problem types (such as distance-rate-time problems); (d) strategic knowledge of how to develop, monitor, and revise a solution plan; and (e) algorithmic knowledge of how to perform an operation such as multiplication.

Mayer hypothesized further that problem representation is composed of two parts: problem translation (understanding each statement in the problem) and problem integration (assembling a coherent representation from the story–problem propositions). Translation requires linguistic and factual knowledge, whereas integration requires schema knowledge. This distinction between translation and integration parallels Van Dijk and Kintsch's (1983) distinction between a textbase model and a situation model in reading. Studies of errors in the translation process indicate that students have greater difficulty encoding relations between two propositions than in concretizing or assigning a value to a particular proposition (Mayer, 1982; Riley et al., 1983). Thus, students are more likely to misinterpret or to forget "John is 10 years older than Jim" than "John is 10 years old." Further, students are far more likely to convert a relational proposition to an assignment proposition than the reverse, that is, to convert "John is 10 years older than Jim" to "John is 10 years old" rather than vice versa. On average, correct encoding of relational facts improves throughout the school years (Trabasso, 1977).

Schema knowledge assists students in integrating propositions in several ways. *First,* when a problem type is recognized (e.g., this is a motion problem), irrelevant information (such as color or temperature) can be ignored (Robinson & Hayes, 1978). *Second,* the problem schema defines slots for particular pieces of information and relations among these facts. This can greatly assist in correctly organizing propositions (Mayer, 1982). *Third,* the schema can guide the search for needed information (Hinsley, Hayes, & Simon, 1977). *Fourth,* problems that are exemplars of more frequently encountered problem schemata are easier to recall (Mayer, 1982).

Individual differences in schematic knowledge for problem types are in part attributable to exposure (Greeno, 1980b; Mayer, 1982; Riley et al., 1983). However, simply being exposed to multiple instances of a particular problem type is no guarantee the student will abstract a useful schema for such problems. Practice in interpreting and classifying problems and less emphasis on solving problems might assist some (see Gagné, 1985).

Subtle differences in problem phrasing can substantially alter children's ability to solve simple word problems (De Corte, Verschaffel, & DeWin, 1985). For example, Hudson (1983, p.) presented arithmetic problems structured as follows:

1. There are five birds and three worms. How many more birds are there than worms.
2. There are five birds and three worms. How many birds won't get a worm?

Problem 1 was solved by only 39% of the children in Hudson's study, whereas the arithmetically equivalent Problem 2 was solved by 79% of the children. Kintsch (1986) argued that questions such as Problem 2 are easier because they suggest a definite (and familiar) situation model (birds eating worms), whereas the abstract relational term "more than" in Problem 1 provides no such crutch.

Mayer (1982) divided problem solution into two phases: solution planning and solution execution. Problem solvers rely on both general strategic knowledge (heuristics) and specific strategic knowledge (e.g., term collecting). Further, solution strategy depends on how problems are represented, which in turn depends on whether the problem is expressed as an equation or is embedded in a story (Mayer, 1978). Although students appear to have a variety of solution methods at their disposal, studies have not examined the extent to which some students use a greater diversity of strategies than do others. Greeno (1978, 1980b) observed that strategic knowledge is often not explicitly taught and instead must be inferred from examples. Simon (1980) added that, even when students are taught how to execute a particular strategy, they are rarely taught when to use it. Indeed, it is this fact that might cause *Gf* to relate to learning outcome in such instruction. Those who can infer the procedure for themselves, do so; those who cannot, do not; and the difference is predictable from such tests as the Raven Progressive Matrices (Snow, 1982). Yet useful procedural knowledge must have clearly defined conditions that trigger its use. For subject matter experts in other domains, problem representation appears to be closely tied to solution strategy (Chi et al., 1981).

Solution strategy assumes increasing importance as problem complexity increases. For example, Greeno's (1980b) studies of theorem proving in geometry suggest that the successful theorem prover must devise a systematic plan, with goals and subgoals, perhaps tied together by repeated use of the general heuristic of "generate and test." But complex sequences of repeatedly executed processes are also gradually proceduralized with practice. J. R. Anderson (1983) describes this transition for one student who had just learned the Side-Angle-Side (SAS) postulate in geometry. The student's first attempts to apply the postulate were halting, repetitive, and piecemeal. However, after much practice on this and other postulates, the student seemed to recognize immediately that the SAS postulate might be useful and then confirmed that expectation by applying it. J. R. Anderson (1983) provides other examples of how practice with carefully juxtaposed examples can lead to procedural learning, if humans learn as his computerized theory learns.

Finally, solution execution depends on how well the problem solver has correctly automatized algorithms for solving equations, multiplying numbers, and the like. This is the most obvious, yet, in one sense, the least important step in the process. Poor problem solvers often rush to this step before they adequately understand the problem. Previously summarized research on computation is relevant here.

PHYSICAL SCIENCE PROBLEM SOLVING

Much of what has been learned through cognitive research on knowledge structures and mathematical problem solving also applies to the study of knowledge structures and problem solving in physical science. Indeed, many examples cited in previous sections come from research on physics problems. There are especially notable findings concerning the degree to which subject matter experts have more complex and complete knowledge schemata than do novices. Experts can concentrate on the fundamental principles relating different problems rather than on the superficial features attended to by novices (Chi et al., 1981), and they can generate rich problem representations as a guide to solution search and computation (Larkin, 1983). There has also been much research delineating solution strategies for searching the alternative paths in a problem space. These might well characterize important differences in students' achievement in scientific problem solving. One possible strategy is random search of the problem space. Another is exhaustive search, pursuing each possible path systematically to see if the goal can be reached. A more powerful strategy uses means–end analysis to characterize the difference between initial state and goal state in a problem, and then tests available means of reducing them. This heuristic might be used in either forward or backward searches. A related technique is to choose various subgoals toward which to work. Still another is to generate and test a variety of possible solutions. The development of more powerful problem-solving strategies is presumably a goal of instruction in science. Their distinction is thus an important target for assessment.

Developments in computer modeling of problem solving in science are also now reaching the design of expert systems and intelligent tutors for aspects of physics and engineering, as well as for mathematics. The work provides an increasingly detailed specification of reasoning processes and steps that are useful in teaching thinking and problem solving in science (see N. Frederiksen, 1984a; Nickerson, Perkins, & Smith, 1985). Most important for assessment purposes, this research is beginning to specify some of the chaotic and flexible reasoning observed in novices and experts respectively.

One example is a problem-solving system, called FERMI, that is not only expert in one domain but can also respond flexibly to novel situations from other domains (Larkin, Reif, Carbonell, & Gugliotta, 1985). Designed initially to solve problems in the physics of fluid statics, it appears able to transfer its expertise with minimal additions to solving problems in aspects of electronics and chemistry. It achieves its generality by encoding declarative and procedural knowledge separately in hierarchies that also distinguish domain-specific and general knowledge at different hierarchical levels. It might also thus simulate important features of the psychology of human experts and suggest how assessments might be designed to make these same separations (see also Larkin, McDermott, Simon, & Simon, 1980).

Another example is an intelligent tutor for thermodynamics that builds up a model of each learner as it proceeds through a sequence of problems (Elshout, Jansweijer, Wie-

linger, 1986; Jansweijer, Konst, Elshout, & Wielinga, 1982). One component of the program consists of a hierarchical network of procedural and declarative knowledge about the physics needed to solve problems in a way that models human subjects. Another program component is a system of production rules that supplies a think-aloud protocol representing the events generated by the first component. When this protocol does not agree with that generated by the human subject, a third component is called. It is equipped with rules about deviations from normal behavior, and it can identify difficulties and redirect the model's performance. The simulation so far accounts for intermediate student behavior; it is being extended now to account for extreme novices.

A third example comes from work by Mettes (1986; see also Mettes, Pilot, & Roossink, 1981), on the design of courses in thermodynamics, mechanics, and electromagnetism, among others, explicitly to teach scientific problem solving. The approach is based on Soviet learning theory (particularly that of Gal'Perin; see De Corte, 1977) but relies also on the sorts of analyses of think-aloud protocols typical of U.S. cognitive psychology. Instructional learning is seen as a process of planned progressive internalization of external actions. The stage-by-stage formation of new mental actions starts with an orienting stage in which the learner is given a complete demonstration of a perfect performance including the goal, the composition of all actions, and the conditions under which each action can and cannot be performed. The learner then performs the complete action in a materialized form, is observed and corrected, and then practices to mastery in progressively less materialized and more mental forms, to achieve clearly transferable, abbreviated, and automatic performance. Most of the actions learned concern use of particular algorithms and heuristics. There is also emphasis on the systematization in operational form of all declarative and procedural knowledge relevant to particular kinds of problem solving. A strength of the approach, for both instruction and assessment, lies in its explication of procedural strategies that are often left implicit in formal instruction.

All these programs provide prototypical tests, though they were not designed to produce tests. The first is a computer model of an expert that embodies exactly what distinctions corresponding tests should make, if human experts function at all like the model does. The second example is a diagnostic test in its present form, which diagnoses the present state of performance at an individual level, specifying how this performance deviates qualitatively and quantitatively from the instructional line presented. The third, similarly, provides a detailed template against which to compare individual student performance and diagnose deviations. All provide important new patterns that new educational measurement devices could emulate. In the computer programs coming from this work, furthermore, the distinctions between expert, instruction, and assessment fade; the instruction automatically produces its assessment by comparison of expert with novice.

SOCIAL SCIENCE PROBLEM SOLVING

Problems in the social sciences and social studies tend to be ill structured. Thus, it is important, as research pushes into these fields, to examine the degree to which problem-solving activities and strategies take on a cognitive character that differs from that observed in mathematics and physics. Voss and his associates have initiated the study of social science problem solving using expert–novice comparisons (see Voss, Greene, Post, & Penner, 1983, and Voss, Tyler, & Yengo, 1983; see also Voss, 1986). The problems studied have dealt with the politics and economics of agricultural problems or the sociology of crime rates. Experts were found to concern themselves initially with problem identification and representation to a greater extent than novices and, particularly, to include alternative general causes of problems in their initial representations. The experts used heuristic strategies not unlike those of expert physicists and mathematicians; they also clearly added information to the problem on the basis of their extensive background knowledge in the domain. Novices, on the other hand, related possible solutions specifically and directly to individual and relatively superficial causes, and they failed to take into account important and complex background factors. Another important finding suggested that novices showed little change in their approaches before and after a relevant course; although relevant knowledge had presumably been acquired in the course, it seemed not to be organized in ways that promoted more effective problem solving.

Some researchers have developed simulated social problems on computers, in order to study problem-solving styles and effectiveness. Dörner (n. d., 1984) created a hypothetical city with a city manager (the subject) who decides how the multivariate indicators of city health and well-being must be controlled periodically over several decades. Spada (n. d.; see Opwis & Spada, 1984) has similarly used ecological problems to study search and solution processes. Lüer and his colleagues (Hesse & Lüer, 1986; Lüer, Hubner, & Lass, 1984) have also examined problem solving in social and economic domains, with strategies measured with the recording of eye movements and ability tests.

As with the work of Marton (1983) previously described, Voss's research implies that conventional courses and tests do not address important features of knowledge organization and use in problem solving, features that appear critical in characterizing different levels of expertise in a domain. The computer modeling research further suggests that simulated problems might provide a medium through which some of these features could be distinguished and diagnosed.

OTHER CURRICULAR AND PROFESSIONAL DOMAINS

Ideas for the design of improved assessments useful in other curricular and professional domains come from a scattering of other innovative research programs. Representative sources are as follows, in alphabetical order by domain: in *art,* see Somerville and Hartley (1986) and also Arnheim (1974), Eisner (1976), and Gardner (1982), Perkins and Leondar (1977); *foreign language learning* is addressed by Carroll (1985b, 1986); for *medical diagnosis and problem solving* see Clancey and Shortliffe (1983), Elstein, Shulman, and Sprafka (1978), and Wijnen and Snow (1975), who address an example of longitudinal assessment of medical knowledge and skill acquisition; for *Music,* see Serafine (1986), and also Gabrielsson (1981) and Sloboda (1985); new work by Shulman and Sykes

(1986) has begun to identify the knowledge and skill domains that must be assessed in improved measures of *teacher professional competence;* technical expertise in electronics and related fields is addressed by Lesgold (1984). Finally, advances in the cognitive psychology of *writing* are comprehensively reviewed by Bereiter and Scardamalia, 1987, (see also Scardamalia & Bereiter, 1986). Beyond these domains, of course, there are also domains of everyday thinking, reasoning, and decision making that are receiving attention from cognitive analyses. Results from this work might reflect on our theories of school learning and on our plans for educational measurement (see, e.g., Cole, 1986: Greeno, 1986).

EXTENSIONS AND IMPLICATIONS

Research on mathematical and scientific problem solving, and also the beginnings of work in other domains, suggests several ways in which educational measurements could be improved. These suggestions would all have the effect of making assessment more diagnostic within a theory of knowledge in the domain of concern. Such theories are only now developing. Yet a beginning framework for what needs to be assessed in general and in each domain is in hand.

First, theory-guided assessment would seek to pinpoint the sources of a student's difficulties in solving each kind of problem faced. For word problems in mathematics, for example, separate consideration might have to be given to each of Mayer's (1985) phases of problem representation and solution. Slightly different phases might be needed in physical or social science problem solving. More extreme variations might be required in the theoretical framework that guides assessment in other domains. But a start toward a general framework was suggested by Heller and Greeno (1979), based on their review of work on word problems in both mathematics and physics. It is adapted here as Figure 7.11. The cognitive psychology of high and low skill is abstracted for each of four phases of problem solving; the phases are chosen to apply to a wide variety of problems, however. Note that the skill continua are anchored in Figure 7.11, but the gradations between extremes are not. There is thus much need for research to fill in these gaps; they might well be shown to be multivariate and to contain qualitative and quantitative shifts.

Second, assessment would seek to determine the degree to which the component skills in each phase have been automatized. Different component skills might well call for different kinds of assessment. However, speed of response is one useful index of automatization for many kinds of components including both numerical computation skills and verbal comprehension skills. And speed can easily be assessed in computerized tests.

Third, computerized simulation of problem domains offers an opportunity to integrate diagnostic teaching (or tutoring) and diagnostic testing. It further allows exploration of the many personal styles and conceptions that students bring to bear on ill-structured and well-structured problems. Such assessment devices would not only link directly to improved teaching but also substantially enrich the cognitive psychology of domain knowledge and problem solving.

Fourth, research that describes expertise and its development in particular domains can guide achievement testing in

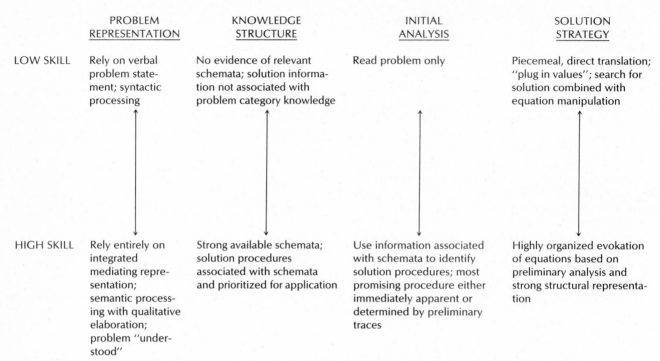

	PROBLEM REPRESENTATION	KNOWLEDGE STRUCTURE	INITIAL ANALYSIS	SOLUTION STRATEGY
LOW SKILL	Rely on verbal problem statement; syntactic processing	No evidence of relevant schemata; solution information not associated with problem category knowledge	Read problem only	Piecemeal, direct translation; "plug in values"; search for solution combined with equation manipulation
HIGH SKILL	Rely entirely on integrated mediating representation; semantic processing with qualitative elaboration; problem "understood"	Strong available schemata; solution procedures associated with schemata and prioritized for application	Use information associated with schemata to identify solution procedures; most promising procedure either immediately apparent or determined by preliminary traces	Highly organized evokation of equations based on preliminary analysis and strong structural representation

FIGURE 7.11 Continua of word problem solution variation. (After Heller & Greeno, 1979.)

those domains. The first step in developing an achievement test is to construct a blueprint for the test. This blueprint should contain "a theoretical outline, or prototype of what (the test constructor) considers to be a high achievement in the area being measured" (Tinkelman, 1971, p. 49). Research on the nature of expertise can contribute to this task and thereby enable the test constructor to insure that the summary of "the knowledge and skills of a well-educated person" contained in the test blueprint rest "upon as sound and defensible a basis as possible" (p. 50). It is difficult to imagine a more fundamental contribution that psychological research might make to the practice of educational measurement.

An example can now show how the implications of the research reviewed in previous sections might be integrated in diagnostic measures for adaptive instruction. Though partly hypothetical, the example is built largely from work by Lesgold, Bonar, and Ivill (1987), with ideas from Gentner and Gentner (1983) and Stevens and Collins (1980). It is designed to fill in some of the parts of an ideal system for adaptive instruction described by Snow (1982, 1983; see also Glaser, 1977).

Consider an instructional unit of electricity. Prior to instruction, aptitudes for learning are assessed with an adaptive test battery designed to assess, among other things (a) strength of certain abilities such as numerical computation skills, reasoning by analogy, and comprehension and production of abstract drawings; (b) declarative knowledge about electricity, for instance, the common and restricted meanings of such terms as *current, resistance, and parallel;* and (c) availability of certain prior schemata that might facilitate or impede learning of the schemata to be presented, for example, analogies between

electrical current and "water flowing in pipes" or "people racing on a track." The content of this battery is determined in part by an aptitude theory about relevant individual differences in learning and in part by a theory of field achievement for this domain. The latter is represented by networks of declarative and procedural knowledge to be acquired, as developed from studies of curriculum, of experts in the field, and of previous learners, successful and unsuccessful. These networks provide a curriculum goal structure that contains multiple hierarchies of subordinate nodes and arcs or relations between nodes. They are built around central concepts such as Ohm's and Kirchhoff's laws, procedures such as testing currents with voltage meters, and analogies such as to hydraulic systems or race tracks. The structure is not simply a linear hierarchy of subgoals, because expert performance and successful learning seem to depend on flexible use of multiple schemata. The strength of each node or arc can be tested by carefully chosen items. Imagine four possible levels of strength: strong, probable, weak, absent. Scores from the aptitude battery thus describe the starting state of each student for each part of the goal structure, as well as the relevant abilities. This is a model of a student.

Instruction might then begin with the use of rules from a theory of treatment design. One such rule might be "Work first on those fragments most closely associated with Ohm's Law that are in a probable state." Treatment design is also coupled with aptitude information, with rules such as "Use diagrammed circuits with simple computations for students strong in figural comprehension but weak in numerical skill," or "start with the hydraulic or racetrack analogies for students strong in analogical reasoning." As instruction proceeds, a diagnostic cycle sweeps through the student model, to identify the parts that should now be tested and to accumulate a list of constraints on item type or format. Rules here might be "If understanding of voltage meters and resistors is now strong, choose a problem that requires voltage computation with one resistor," or "If the racetrack analogy is understood for simple circuits, choose a problem that requires drawing a parallel circuit, given the racetrack analog." Figure 7.12 shows items that might be chosen or made to order based on these rules and the aptitude constraints previously noted. Other items might test for bugs resulting from some more general misconception such as persistent reliance on a hydraulic analog when a racetrack analog is more interpretable or vice versa. Because complex learning often calls for shifts among multiple models of analogs, some items might test such shifts.

Results of this testing update the student model and steer the next instructional cycle in directions indicated, again by treatment design rules. Cycles of instruction and testing continue until the goal structure is complete and generalization or transfer is also demonstrated. Adaptive diagnostic testing, in other words, is closely geared to the student cognitive model; items are formulated cyclically to track progress through the structure along many lines as it occurs, and each item result implies the next instructional step. But two kinds of diagnostic and instructional decisions are involved, and these might sometimes require different kinds of test items. One kind aims at readiness diagnosis, to allow next instructional steps to capitalize on a learner's strengths and circumvent the weaknesses apparent in the aptitude and prior achievement profile. Because instruction cannot work on the whole student model at once, it must always sidestep some weaknesses while removing others. The other kind aims at remedial diagnosis, to determine why the learner failed a step that should have been taken successfully, given the present state of the student model. Subsequent instruction must also be steered toward repairing whatever bugs still remain that the student model had not accounted for.

At some appropriate point, also, the instructional system must shift away from its primary focus on basic electricity to concentrate on building up weak but essential aptitudes di-

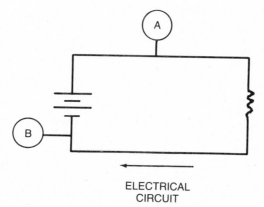

ELECTRICAL
CIRCUIT

If meter A reads 16, then what should meter B show?

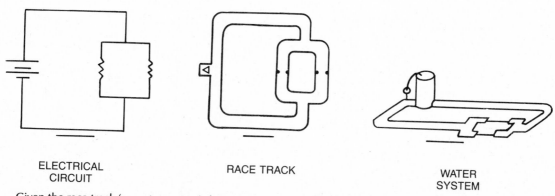

ELECTRICAL
CIRCUIT

RACE TRACK

WATER
SYSTEM

Given the race track (or water system) drawing, draw the analog electrical circuit and explain its operation.

FIGURE 7.12 Possible items designed to test voltage computation (Panel A) and electrical circuit analog comprehension (Panel B) as instructional subgoals in a unit on electricity. (After Lesgold, Bonar & Ivill, 1987, and Gentner & Gentner, 1983, respectively.)

rectly. In this case, these are at least the computational or figure diagramming skills needed for higher levels of learning in electronics. Here too, there will need to be a student model based on diagnostic analyses of the form just discussed and adaptive instruction geared to it.

To realize such systems, certainly much research remains to be done on instruction, diagnostic testing, and their coordination. But the student models even now derivable from the cognitive psychology of novice aptitude, expert field achievement, and curricular and instructional treatment design, go a long way beyond the blueprints for tests described by Tinkelman (1971) and a long way toward the goals for adaptive instruction envisioned by Glaser and Nitko (1971).

Toward Improved Theories and Methods for Measurement Research

The accumulation of new theory, evidence, and research techniques from the work here reviewed, and much other work, is gradually elaborating and reshaping our conceptions of aptitude and achievement and the approaches that can fruitfully contribute to their study in education. But this accumulation needs to be coordinated with the evidence and methods developed through traditional psychometric research in education. One kind of evidence can alter the interpretation of the other, but neither dismisses the other as evidence. Similarly, one methodology can throw new light on problems typically studied with another methodology, but the broadest advances are likely to come from combined approaches. In this final section, we seek to prepare educational and psychometric measurement theory for the incorporation of cognitive psychology and to suggest, at least provisionally, the kinds of integrated theory that might result. We also review briefly the methodological approaches of cognitive psychology, to suggest their advantages and limitations and coordinated application to measurement research. In the process, we identify some new kinds of test designs that deserve research attention and draw implications for the experimental evaluation of existing tests.

Measurement Design and Evaluation

As experimental psychology turned to the development of tasks that would display theoretically important characteristics of information processing, it sought also to model these processes at the level of the individual performer. With model parameters expressed as individual scores, it was not long before these came to be examined for correlation with ability-test scores available in the records of the student subjects. After all, if the model parameters reflect important aspects of verbal processing, for example, they should correlate with global measures of verbal ability. Much of the work cited previously on perception and memory displays this approach. As investigators sought interesting cognitive tasks to model directly, it was not long before they recognized that cognitive-ability tests were an important class of such tasks. Experiments could be used to separate and manipulate key features of such tasks and, thus, identify component processing skills. To provide a pro-

cessing theory of vocabulary, or analogy, or letter series, or spatial visualization items is to help explain why such tasks have important correlates in practice and ultimately to build a theory of human intelligence. The cited work on reasoning best exemplifies this approach. Similarly, achievement tests and the instructional tasks and learning performances they are designed to evaluate could be studied systematically to reach theories of achievement in particular domains. The cited work on declarative and procedural knowledge aims at this goal.

The first two approaches came to be distinguished as the *cognitive-correlates* and the *cognitive-components* methods (Pellegrino & Glaser, 1979). R. J. Sternberg (1984c) called the third the *cognitive-contents* approach. But these are relative emphases, not alternatives, for design and evaluation. The methods can be seen to blend together, and several other methodological devices such as coaching, training, and transfer conditions; various kinds of status group comparisons; and aptitude–treatment interaction (ATI) analyses can also be used in tandem with each.

COGNITIVE CORRELATES AND COMPONENTS

The aim of the cognitive-correlates approach is to understand complex cognitive performances and their measures by studying their correlations with theoretically more explicit performance measures based on paradigmatic laboratory tasks. In the best instance, the investigator first selects and administers a battery of such tasks and then estimates one or more information-processing parameters for each subject on each task. These parameters should be based on CIP models derived from previous investigations, and there should be at least two independent measures for each parameter, so that reliability can be estimated. Multitrait–multimethod design possibilities (Campbell & Fiske, 1959) apply here also, though they have rarely been considered. The cited work of Chiang and Atkinson (1976), and Rose (1980) exemplifies early steps in these directions. The parameters derived from the laboratory tasks are then correlated with the complex test, or with factor scores estimated from a battery. Alternatively, status groups such as differing age groups, gifted and retarded individuals, experts and novices in some field, or students with high or low scores on the target performance may be compared on average parameters. High correlations or average group differences suggest that the process represented by a particular parameter (e.g., speed of access to lexical memory) is instrumental in the complex performance (e.g., performance on a vocabulary test) or perhaps in the development of the ability represented by the test. Conversely, parameters not correlated with test performance are presumed not to reflect individual differences in processes instrumental to the complex. To the extent that one can identify a collection of clear and reliable process measures that fully account for the complex variance, one has an important set of constituents for a process theory of the complex ability. These account only for individual differences, of course, not for processes that are invariant across individuals, and they are only correlates. Important questions remain as to their necessity, sufficiency, and organization.

There are other important limits to cognitive-correlates research so far. Some CIP models emanate from research that assumed the same model for all persons. The models must be tested anew in each application, because seemingly minor variations in experimental procedure can sometimes effect substantial changes in how subjects process information (Glushko & Cooper, 1978; Lohman & Kyllonen, 1983; MacLeod et al., 1978). Further, experimenters often limit, wittingly or unwittingly, the range of individual differences in their samples, so models that are good descriptors of all subjects in some previous study might not be good descriptors of the performance of all subjects in a new experiment explicitly designed to study individual differences. Much of this research did not consider the range characteristics of the samples used and applied absolute labels such as *high* and *low* or *expert* and *novice* without regard to the relativity of their meanings.

Nonetheless, this correlational approach, whether based on correlations or on status group comparisons, has important uses in test analysis. The list of process correlates can focus further research attention on aspects of the test and construct that need to be amplified or eliminated by changes in test design. The laboratory task can itself be converted into a test suitable for individual or group administration. And the experimental technique used in the task can be separately used to evaluate alternative test designs and interpretations. Systematically limiting or varying item exposure time is perhaps the simplest example. Surprisingly, this technique has only rarely been used in test evaluation, even though it has long been suspected that item exposure time variations would have marked effects on test-taking strategies and thus on the constructs reflected by scores, in both visual ability tests such as Gestalt completion (see Thurstone, 1944) and verbal achievement tests (see Heckman, Tiffin, & Snow, 1967).

In the cognitive-components method, the experimenter attempts to devise and test models that describe how subjects solve items on a particular testlike task directly. The investigator first develops an experimental task that is based on an existing test. The experimental task may be almost identical to the source test in content. For example, items might be taken directly from the test and used with the same instructions. The format and context are usually changed in significant ways, however. Items are often presented one at a time to individual subjects in an apparatus where response latencies, eye fixations, or both are recorded. Sometimes the items in the experimental task bear only superficial resemblance to those in the source task. For example, to obtain unambiguous response latency data, items on a difficult reasoning test may be simplified so that errors are virtually eliminated, and hundreds of trials may be presented. Each item may also be decomposed experimentally into several steps that must be performed in a fixed order.

Regardless of the degree of similarity between source task and experimental task, the two tasks rarely require exactly the same mental processes. Even if items are merely adapted for individual presentation, this format prevents subjects from surveying the entire task initially or reallocating time as the time limit approaches or referring back to previous items to change an answer or to double-check. Some changes from the source test could improve measurement, of course. Controlling item exposures, for example, might reduce the number of items solved by strategies that circumvent the intended pur-

pose of the test. The point, however, is that one can never simply assume that an experimental task measures the same constituent processes as the source test. As in the cognitive-correlates approach, the investigator must correlate some index of overall performance on the experimental task (such as total errors) with external reference tests. Low correlations challenge the assumption that CIP models of performance on the experimental task contribute to the construct validity of the source tests. High correlations, on the other hand, are especially important if they can be attributed to particular components of the CIP model.

Nevertheless, the primary contribution of a cognitive-components analysis to the understanding of a task and, indirectly, the construct it is presumed to represent, comes from the CIP models that are formulated and tested on the data. The process of developing theoretically interesting alternative models, devising methods to estimate variables thought to influence different mental operations, and testing and revising models can be a sobering experience for those accustomed to broad traitlike interpretations of test scores.

A superficial contrast between the correlates method and the components method points to the choice of task to be modeled. The correlates method derives from research using the paradigmatic tasks of the experimental laboratory, whereas the components method derives from experimental analysis of the typical tests used in psychometric research. But this is not really basic. Historically, many ability tests were derived from the laboratory tasks of an earlier era. Thurstone's factor-analytic studies of perception (1938a, 1944) offer prime examples, but there are many others. Conversely, some of today's paradigmatic laboratory tasks are improvements on tasks that were originally developed as mental tests; spatial rotation and visualization tasks provide a notable example.

Choice of method depends more on the nature of the construct under investigation. CIP models of ability tests are most informative for process-intensive tasks such as measures of fluid-analytic reasoning or spatial visualization, where performance does not depend heavily on stored prior knowledge. CIP models from paradigmatic experimental tasks and learning studies are more informative when the ability reference tests are not process intensive in this sense. For example, a componential analysis of performance on a vocabulary test might have its uses, but it does not reveal much about the processing that led to the development of the verbal knowledge sampled by the vocabulary test, which is certainly one important aspect of verbal ability. On the other hand, componential models of the test are more likely to capture all of the processes, variant and invariant, that are actually involved in performance, whereas a correlates analysis might not. Componential analysis relies on external correlations as evidence of construct validity but not as evidence of constituent process involvement in the construct; and it can suggest directly which constituents contribute most to the overall correlation.

COGNITIVE CONTENTS

In contrast to the more purely process emphasis of cognitive correlates and components research, the cognitive-contents approach emphasizes the content knowledge acquisition, organization, and use involved in test or instructional task performance. Using experimental methods and status group comparisons, but also verbal reports and other behavioral records, the investigator constructs a model of how declarative and procedural knowledge might be structured and used in performance. The aim is a cognitive-task analysis or, rather, family of analyses, of the subject matter domain, the instructional goals, and the ways in which successful and not-so-successful students acquire it and operate within it. Often persons representing differing degrees of learning or expertise in a domain are studied. These expert–novice studies help to identify the kinds of knowledge structures and procedural skills possessed by experts and the kinds of misconceptions, missteps, partial procedures, and discontinuities that mark novice performance. The level of description reached is often far more detailed than that represented in typical descriptions of curricular or instructional goals or in conventional tests, even those developed to represent learning or performance samples or to allow branching as a function of previous responses. Such analyses should lead to specific tests and sequential testing ¡ strategies that offer substantially improved diagnoses of learning progress. They also offer a means of tying testing closely to decisions about instructional adaptation to individual performance.

A good example of the approach applied in the analysis of electronics troubleshooting is provided by Lesgold, Lajoie, Logan, and Eggan (1986), who also offer a more general guide to cognitive-task analysis. Lesgold et al. (1987) have also described how diagnostic testing proceeds in conjunction with computerized tutoring in basic electricity principles. We used this work in constructing our example in a previous section.

Much of the research in this direction uses introspective and retrospective reports by subjects about the cognitive processes and contents of their thinking while performing. A system of guidelines for the study of such verbal reports and think-aloud protocols has developed (Ericsson & Simon, 1984), and the application of this approach to the investigation of ability and achievement test performance has now begun. As noted in previous sections, some investigators use teach-back procedures to measure knowledge acquisition or organization (Gray, 1983). Others use interviews to detect student conceptions and misconceptions in a knowledge domain (see Gentner & Stevens, 1983; Marton, 1983). Still others have developed scoring procedures to apply to open-ended responses to questions (Biggs & Collis, 1982).

Of course, the complexities of coding verbal protocols from think-aloud or teach-back sessions or interviews makes this sort of research difficult and makes wide-scale testing with this medium impractical. But small-scale studies of this sort can help evaluate the construct validity of conventional achievement tests, and it is now possible to develop computer text processing systems for scoring verbal protocols, even voice input protocols, according to alternative hypothesized misconceptions, ways of organizing concepts, and the like. Content-referenced cognitive theories that are also test referenced would be the goal. New item construction for diagnostically useful achievement tests could be guided by such content-referenced theories of knowledge and its development, with special focus on understanding common misconceptions. This presumes an understanding of the types of commonly held misconceptions that facilitate or impede further cognitive development. It is possible that the sources of errors or bugs in some performance domains are highly idiosyncratic and also even variable within persons; parts of mathematics could have this character (Bricken, 1987). In science, however, research so far implies that misconceptions fall into relatively few common categories (Glaser et al., in press; McCloskey, Caramazza, & Green, 1980). In other words, it might not be necessary to catalog the nature of idiosyncratic understandings and misunderstandings in all areas. Rather, the goal would be to identify the main personal theories or mental models that guide students' thinking and problem solving across many problems. Further, it might be possible to order these belief systems on a developmental scale (e.g., the child's understanding of living systems is at level X, which is characterized by . . .). Indeed, learning appears to be increasingly conceived as a series of developmental transitions in performance (Glaser, 1980; Messick, 1984). Because learning is multivariate, however, there will be parallel series and an uneven transition profile.

How might developmentally diagnostic achievement tests be created? One method might rely on the construction of the sort of expert systems and intelligent tutors described in our section on science problem solving and in the example from Lesgold, et al. (1987). The computer would be geared to build up a model of the learner in relation to the knowledge domain as problem-solving performance progresses and deviations are noticed. A related possibility would make use of expert systems as they are now used in medical diagnosis (Clancey & Shortliffe, 1983) to pursue alternative hypotheses about a student's errors or intuitive theories. Computer-generated questions would probe understanding of the nodes and arcs of a chosen concept; foils would be chosen to appeal to students with different misconceptions. Subsequent items would then be selected to test the hypothesis indicated by the response to the first item (see e.g., Ward, 1986). Still another related possibility is faceted tests, in which facets are manipulated explicitly to identify common misconceptions or key features of knowledge organization.

FACETED TESTS

Faceted tests are suggested not only by the research on cognitive contents and achievements but also by the correlates and components approaches to ability analysis. This form of mental test is based on the principles of within-person or repeated-measures experimental design; a *facet* is an experimental variable consisting of two or more levels or categories to be contrasted. Systematic manipulations of item or test characteristics are used to permit experimental contrasts among parts of the test, that is, between cells of the experimental design. Such tests yield separate scores for each cell or orthogonal contrast scores for differences between cells. Although not really a new idea in measurement (see Foa, 1965; Guttman, 1954), the value of faceting in performance tests for the study of their construct validity and for diagnostic uses had not been seriously considered before the advent of cognitive experimental psychology. As Embretson (1985b) noted, the power of experimental and psychometric methods can now be applied jointly in test design, if tests are fully developed in this pattern.

It is important to recognize that both the paradigmatic laboratory tasks used in the cognitive-correlates approach and the subdivided ability tests used in the cognitive-components approach are within-person experiments of the same form. The NIPI difference in the Posner matching task, for example, is a contrast score reflecting the difference in the subject's performance under two experimental conditions, name matching and physical matching. Similarly, R. J. Sternberg's component parameters arise from the differences between different precuing conditions or different item types. One can imagine whole batteries of faceted ability tests, ranging across fluid-analytic and spatial abilities and verbal and mathematical abilities, designed in coordination to test hypotheses about common and unique processes operating in sets of tests. Many of the studies of Embretson (1985b), Lohman (1988), Pellegrino (1985b), and R. J. Sternberg (1985a), cited previously, provide examples of faceted fluid and spatial reasoning tests. The studies by Marshalek (1981) and R. J. Sternberg and Powell (1983) show faceted tests of verbal ability.

Good examples of faceted achievement tests have been available for some time. Calfee and Drum (1979) showed how reading tests could be faceted to contrast different oral and silent reading conditions, different questioning modes, and different aspects of vocabulary and topic difficulty, as an aid in diagnosis. Faceted tests have also been used to assess some of the qualitative and structural cognitive differences resulting from different kinds of instruction, as in the early work of Greeno and his colleagues (see Egan & Greeno, 1973; Greeno & Mayer, 1975; Mayer, Stiehl, & Greeno, 1975). In the Egan and Greeno work on mathematics learning, for example, a faceted posttest contrasted problem context (word problems versus problems with symbols) and problem type (familiar problems versus problems requiring some transformation before application of a known formula versus problems that would be unsolvable by direct application of a known formula). The 2 × 3 test design allowed qualitative descriptions of instructional effects, in addition to descriptions of different "amounts learned" under different instructional conditions. It was possible, for example, to characterize the internal-versus-external connectedness of the knowledge structures produced by the instruction and to predict the relative usefulness of each kind of structures in further learning and transfer.

Egan and Greeno (1973) also observed significant ATI effects connecting an external measure of scholastic ability with performance on different types of problems. In effect, such research posits aptitude × instructional treatment × achievement test facet interactions. This suggests the importance of a combined ATI and CIP framework for the study of faceted tests. A test facet is designed to manipulate the degree of involvement of some component process(es) in test performance. It should thus manipulate the relation between a contrast score reflecting that degree and an external reference test, if the external test also involves the same component processes. This prediction calls for ATI analysis in within-person experimental terms. The facet is a "treatment" variable. Differential regression of cell scores on the external score, or a significant correlation of cell contrast and external scores, indicates ATI. The statistical complexities of such studies will re-

quire careful study, particularly in their within-person form (see Cronbach & Snow, 1977; Snow & Peterson, 1985). But CIP models of tests and ATI analysis of faceted tests can be combined to provide a powerful new methodology for construct validation. Conceivably such research could lead to theories that explain aptitude and achievement in common process and content terms and account for the effects of specified instructional treatments on these cognitive commonalities (Snow, 1980a).

Many cognitive experiments, of both between-person and within-person designs, can be used to suggest important facets to be incorporated into educational tests. Each such facet would be chosen to bring out the effects of one or more component processes or content structures. Potentially, such contrasts could then be sharpened through continuing research with the test design to distinguish for diagnostic purposes particular information-processing skills, strategies, and knowledge structures that are now confounded in the total scores of conventionally designed tests.

Using faceted test design, furthermore, test developers might ultimately come to study and report analyses of sources of difficulty ("stimulus variance") as routinely as they report analyses of individual differences ("subject variance"). Results of both types of analyses depend on the characteristics of the sample that is tested (i.e., what is difficult for more able or older students might not be the same as what is difficult for younger or less able students). It would be most useful if such analyses tested well-formulated theories of aptitude or achievement in the domain, although even a simple listing of sources of difficulty would be useful, especially for detecting irrelevant difficulties.

LEARNING AND TRANSFER SAMPLES

As implied at several points earlier, cognitive psychology has also been moving rapidly into the study of how information-processing skills, strategies, and structures are learned, how they might be taught, and how they might be transferred to novel situations. This frontier also carries important implications for test design and analysis.

Vygotsky (1978) long ago proposed, in effect, that tests be readministered, with coaching, as many times as it took each individual to reach maximum performance. One implication was that the final trials in such a series would provide the most valid predictions. Another was that the "zone of proximal development" between initial, independent performance and final, coached performance was the most important target for assessment, because it represented the dynamic state of development most relevant for understanding the individual's performance in the immediate future. However, early psychometric research aimed at directly assessing learning and transfer was based on simplistic learning theory, ran into methodological problems, and was abandoned (see Cronbach & Snow, 1977; Glaser, 1967). Since then, conventional tests have rarely been constructed or analyzed in parts or blocks of items designed to assess learning or practice or transfer effects within the test. Nor have coaching or training conditions been systematically included in tests to benefit their use in diagnosis. But the new experiments, previously cited, that have included analyses of performance changes resulting from experience across items or blocks of items, or from inserted coaching or training, have shown marked effects on individual differences in information processing during the test (see Kyllonen, Lohman, & Snow, 1984; Kyllonen, Lohman, & Woltz, 1984; R. J. Sternberg & Weil, 1980). The implication is that new attempts to assess the more dynamic properties of task performance, understood in modern information-processing terms, might well pay off. From a cognitive psychological view, coaching, training, and transfer effects in tests are an important source of evidence for theories of aptitude and achievement, as well as for improved assessment.

There are important methodological problems to be addressed in the design of tests to measure gain or change across experimental conditions, just as there are in tests designed as faceted within-person experiments. And, given the evidence showing the dynamic properties of performance on so-called "static" mental tests, it is superficial to label some test designs *static* and some *dynamic*. But new research incorporating Vygotskian or other proposals (e.g., Feuerstein, 1979) for explicitly dynamic assessment is nonetheless a worthy effort.

The best example of a direct attack on Vygotskian, as well as modern, cognitive hypotheses in this realm is the research of A. L. Brown and Campione (1986) and their colleagues (see, e.g., A. L. Brown & Ferrara, 1985; Campione & Brown, 1984; Campione, Brown, Ferrara, Jones, & Steinberg, 1985). Their experimental procedure is to administer sets of problems (from ability tests such as Raven matrices or letter series or achievement tests in arithmetic, for example) and to provide hints where difficulties occur. The hint giving is designed to assess amount of instruction needed by each individual to solve a problem. The tasks are arranged to provide measures of learning gain but also transfer distance (i.e., how different a transfer problem could be and still be solved). Results to date show that learning and transfer measures are related to conventional ability tests, but they are better predictors of independently measured pre–post gains in achievement and provide diagnostic information not available from the conventional tests. It appears, furthermore, that measures of flexible or "far" transfer offer particularly useful prediction and diagnosis, and the work further implicates the importance of metacognitive thinking skills in learning and transfer.

A further study by Novick (1986/1987) deserves particular note because it demonstrates both positive and negative transfer in analogical reasoning on testlike mathematical word problems, and it also brings in an expert–novice, or aptitude, dimension. As with many new studies in cognitive psychology, it also emphasizes assessment of the procedures used by subjects, not just solution time or accuracy. Novick's experiments manipulate the order of problem presentation so that a preceding problem and a target problem might have an analogically related deep structure but unrelated surface structure or vice versa. Subjects are also prompted with suggested solution procedures. These are between-person experiments, but within-person tasks could be built on the same principles. Measures of the kinds of solution procedures actually used on target problems have demonstrated that experts transfer efficient procedures from previous problems, whereas novices do not, and that persons classed as intermediate in expertise perform like

experts when analogous problems are close in time to target problems and like novices when related problems are not close in time. Furthermore, both experts and novices show negative transfer when surface properties of different problems are closely similar, but this sort of negative transfer is much less prevalent for experts. The differences are attributable to the cognitive representations of deep and surface features of problems by persons differing in expertise and to their transfer of solution procedures based on these representations. The research leads to a performance model of analogical transfer (see also Holyoak, 1984) and also to a procedure for assessing such transfer. It is important to note that Novick defined levels of expertise in her college student subjects using SAT-Quantitative (SAT-Q) scores. Students at different levels also differed in the levels of mathematics courses they had previously studied. Inevitably, then, as in almost all expert–novice comparisons, ability and knowledge, or aptitude and achievement, are confounded, as they must be in any study conducted at one particular time. The important implication is that Novick's CIP model and assessment procedures, and her findings, constitute an important contribution to the construct validation of measures such as SAT-Q.

Interpretation of Aptitude and Achievement Constructs

The new emphases on learning, transfer, and development as complex cognitive representational, organizational, and procedural phenomena and on cognitive performance as flexible adaptation of an array of component processes suggest a picture of aptitude and achievement quite different from that implicit in much educational measurement research and practice over past decades.

As Snow put it elsewhere,

School achievement is no longer to be understood as simply the accretion of facts and content specific skills. Certainly, bits and amorphous masses of information are internalized, and specific habits of thought and action are acquired. But educational learning is not just cumulative in the old associationistic sense; a significant part of the learner's task is continually to assemble, reassemble, structure, and tune the cumulating body of knowledge into functional systems for use in thought, and in further learning. Thus, achievement is as much an organization function as it is an acquisition function. And new achievement depends as much on transfer of such organization as it does on transfer of specific prior skills and facts. . . .

As one emphasizes the representation and reorganization of knowledge, and use of new retrieval schemes and strategies, ability constructs reenter the interpretation of achievement . . . organization, generalization, facile adaptation and application of knowledge in new contexts; that is what . . . is meant by "verbal and quantitative ability" or "scholastic aptitude" or "crystallized intelligence.". . . (1980a, p. 43)

In short, tests used as indicants of either aptitude or achievement are samples from a larger universe, but one that consists of organizations of declarative and procedural knowledge, not merely bits of information. Both refer to psychological constructs with more general referents and deeper interpretations than is implied by the routine terminology of educational measurement. New theories of aptitude and achievement will strive for explanations of both kinds of constructs, or test uses, in common psychological process and content terms, and these will need to reflect the dynamic, developmental view of human mental life now emanating from cognitive psychology (Glaser, 1984).

SIGN VERSUS SAMPLING INTERPRETATIONS

Summary test scores, and factors based on them, have often been thought of as "signs" indicating the presence of underlying, latent traits. But nothing about cognitive tests, or their administration and scoring or their intercorrelations, demands a sign–trait interpretation. An alternative interpretation of test scores as samples of cognitive processes and contents, and of correlations as indicating the similarity or overlap of this sampling, is equally justifiable and could be theoretically more useful. The evidence from cognitive psychology suggests that test performances are comprised of complex assemblies of component information-processing actions that are adapted to task requirements during performance. The implication is that sign–trait interpretations of test scores and their intercorrelations are superficial summaries at best. At worst, they have misled scientists, and the public, into thinking of fundamental, fixed entities, measured as amounts. Whatever their practical value as summaries, for selection, classification, certification, or program evaluation, the cognitive psychological view is that such interpretations no longer suffice as scientific explanations of aptitude and achievement constructs.

The sampling view, in contrast, emphasizes the dynamic person–situation interaction. The task performance situation, whether it be an instructional learning task or a test, requires that a particular sample of the person's extant knowledge structure be assembled and controlled in performance. Even slight changes in task demands can change this sampling, however. Some ability tests can be reasonably interpreted as "tapping underlying traits." But many are better described as sampling some parts of the organization of mental content and process components, previously assembled by the cognitive-developmental and learning history of the person or assembled anew by the person from that history to meet the demands of novel task situations. Achievement tests have long been interpreted as samples from a content universe, but the new view emphasizes sampling of mental organizations, not just bits and pieces, as well as their dynamic assembly or reassembly to meet task demands. The sampling and assembly operations shift during tests and learning tasks, as a function of item variations.

ABILITY ORGANIZATION

We believe with Thurstone (1938b) that factor analysis, multidimensional scaling, hierarchical clustering, and any other method that sorts cognitive tasks into categories of closely related (i.e., similarly sampled) performances provides a map to guide further cognitive psychological analysis. In other words, such a map is a first step, not an end step, toward understanding individual differences in cognitive performances. It is so for two reasons: It identifies other tasks that a theory of any one task must sooner or later encompass, and, it shows a whole organization of correlational facts to be explained by any proposal that presumes to be a theory of intelligence.

Recent factor-analytic work by Gustafsson (1984) has confirmed the basic distinctions of Cattell (1971) between crystallized intelligence (*Gc*), fluid intelligence (*Gf*), and visual-spatial abilities (*Gv*). The Gustafsson model also suggests that *Gf* might be equivalent to *G*, making Vernon's (1950) conception roughly interchangeable with the Cattell–Horn formulation. Carroll (1985a) and Horn (1986) also showed the *Gf-Gc-Gv* distinction in their distillations of the factor analytic literature, with additional general categories for idea production (*Gi*), auditory perception (*Ga*), memory (*Gm*), and speed (*Gs*). Applying nonmetric multidimensional scaling to the *Gf-Gc-Gv* region (not including *Ga*, *Gm*, and *Gs*), Snow et al. (1984; see also Marshalek et al., 1983) found that the hierarchical factor model emanating from previous work and an inside-out version of Guttman's (1954, 1970) radex model of ability organization appeared to be conformable. The result is the recognition that ability-test intercorrelations regularly display a continuum of complexity from periphery to center of a new inverted radex structure. This inverted radex is shown in Figure 7.13 in a smoothed, schematic form. Though based on empirical analyses of learning task intercorrelations and several studies of ability tests, it remains an incomplete, hypothetical structure. It does provide, however, a provisional map of ability constructs that can be used in several ways to tie in existing evidence from cognitive psychology and to guide continuing cognitive task analyses.

First, information-processing analyses of tests that are highly correlated (that appear in the same cluster or region of the radex) should lead to CIP models that are similar. So, for example, the separate models for performance on geometric analogies, verbal analogies, letter series, and block design tests referred to in earlier sections must be integrated into a common theory if an understanding of the *Gf* construct is to be reached. The theory must also be generalized to account for performance on other tests in or close to the *Gf* region, such as Necessary Arithmetic Operations, and Surface Development, and performance on reasoning tasks studied in the laboratory but not typically administered with conventional *Gf* tests, such as the Towers of Hanoi problem or cryptarithmetic (see Simon, 1979). Further, the analysis of tests such as Necessary Arithmetic Operations or Surface Development allows the construction of linkages between models of tests and models of the knowledge structures involved in school learning tasks, such as arithmetic word problems or geometry proofs (see Greeno, 1986). The linkage between reasoning tests, vocabulary tests, and text comprehension problems might also be better explicated this way (see Marshalek, 1981; Perfetti, 1985). If reasoning is a central ability in the radex, as both correlational and experimental psychologists now think, an integrated CIP theory of all these tasks should be possible, perhaps with a model of Raven Matrices at its core, even if specific components are also required for an account of each included test or task. For a related discussion of the centrality and generality of a theory of reasoning, see Rips (1984). Failure to reach a common CIP theory for *Gf* tasks, however, would indicate the need for construct distinctions within this domain. It is, after all, theories of ability constructs, not individual tasks,

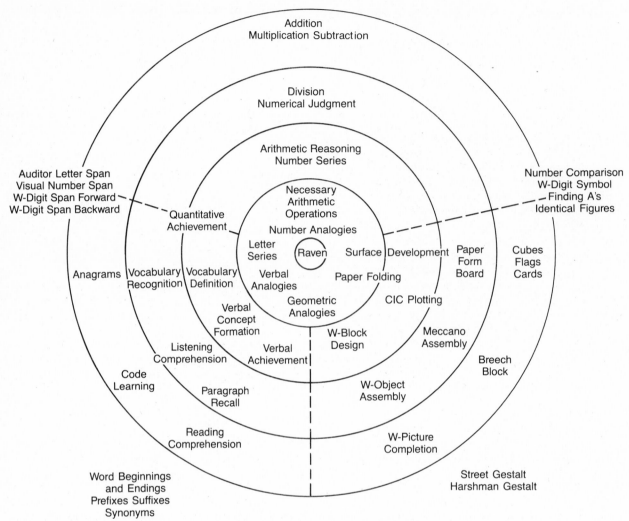

FIGURE 7.13 Hypothetical radex map showing suggested ability and learning simplexes and the content circumplex. "W" identifies subtests of the Wechsler Adult Intelligence Scale. (After Snow, Kyllonen, & Marshalek, 1984.)

that are the goal. The same points hold for *Gc*, *Gv*, and any other construct in the radex map.

Second, the arrays of tests and tasks from center to periphery give the map a topographic character. Coordinated task analyses along the arrays should help clarify the nature of changes in information-processing complexity as one moves from peripheral to central tests. Performances on peripheral tasks might call for fewer component processes, more algorithmic or automatic processing, or less adaptation from item to item. Performances on more central tasks might require more strategic adaptation to novelty from item to item, more component processes, more controlled used of key components, more metacognitive monitoring or self-regulation, or more attentional resources. Note that Hunt's (1985b) remark about correlations between simpler and more complex tasks (quoted on p. 295) is a hypothesis about the peripheral-to-central array in the verbal region of a radex structure of test intercorrelations. A few studies have begun to explore these possibilities. For example Pellegrino (1985b) conducted componential

analyses of an array of spatial tests that appeared to increase in processing complexity. His CIP models fit to each task suggested increases in both the number of component processes required and the amount of strategic variance involved in performance across the progression from more peripheral tasks to more central tasks. The fact that learning tasks also distribute along the arrays of the radex makes possible the tracking of ability and learning complexity together. Coordinated CIP analyses of ability and learning tasks should in turn lead to coordinated theories of aptitude and achievement.

Further, the radex topography might be shown to differ for arrays of tasks in different regions. There is evidence, for example, that verbal and numerical tasks can be more neatly and continuously organized in a hierarchy of increasing process complexity, whereas, for spatial tasks, the complexity gradient might be steep or ragged (see Snow et al., 1984; Snow & Lohman, 1984). These possibilities need to be kept in focus as the task analytic work continues.

DEVELOPMENT OF FLUID AND CRYSTALLIZED INTELLIGENCE

In Cattell's early formulation (1963), fluid intelligence (*Gf*) was hypothesized to reflect the physiological integrity of the organism for adapting to novel situations that, when invested in particular learning experiences, produced crystallized intelligence (*Gc*). The interpretation of the two constructs was parallel to Hebb's (1949) Intelligence A and B (see also H. J. Eysenck's, 1984, Intelligence A, B, and C). Others (e.g., Crano, 1974; Undheim, 1981a) have also argued for an investment theory of intellectual development, based largely on the fact that correlations between intelligence test scores taken at one time and achievement test scores taken at a later time tend to be higher than when such tests are administered in reverse order. The correlational methodology previously used for such studies must be rejected (see Rogosa, 1980). Yet, the hypothesis remains and can now be investigated at a more analytic level by tracing the development of different process and knowledge components and metacomponents of fluid and crystallized ability (see, e.g., A. L. Brown & Campione, 1986; Osherson, 1974; Siegler, 1986; R. J. Sternberg, 1984b).

Other modern theorists view both *Gf* and *Gc* as products of education and experience, and some also subscribe to an investment theory without presuming that fluid abilities are somehow more innate. Horn interpreted *Gf* simply as "facility in reasoning, particularly in figural or non-word symbolic materials" (1976, p. 445). Cronbach went further, arguing that "fluid ability is itself an achievement" that reflects the "residue of indirect learning from varied experience" (1977, p. 287; see also Undheim, 1981b, 1981c, 1981d). More recently, Horn echoed the same theme; "there are good reasons to believe that *Gf* is learned as much as *Gc*, and that *Gc* is inherited as much as *Gf*" (1985, p. 289). *Gc* reflects individual differences in "acculturation learning" whereas *Gf* reflects individual differences in "casual learning" and "independent thinking" (Horn, 1985, pp. 289–290). Proponents of this view point out that, if tests of fluid abilities were somehow better estimates of the physiological integrity of the organism and achievement tests were more a product of experience, scores on tests of fluid abilities should show relatively higher heritabilities, which they do not (Horn, 1985; Humphreys, 1981; Scarr & Carter-Saltzman, 1982; Willerman, Horn, & Loehlin, 1977). Again, the complexity of test performance, as shown by cognitive analysis, implies that the meaning and role of physiological integrity in past and present mental functioning must be traced at the level of information processing, particularly in the speed and accuracy of perceptual, attentional, and working memory processes, rather than at the level of *Gf* and *Gc* test scores. Work by H. J. Eysenck (1982) and Jensen (1982) exemplifies this pursuit.

If *Gf* performance results largely from indirect, casual learning through varied experiences in everyday life and *Gc* performance results from direct acculturation learning, as promoted especially in schools, then ability development should show the characteristic pattern that it does indeed show: *Gf* development preceding *Gc* development, with high correlation between them, and gradual differentiation and specialization of ability and achievement as a function of experience, particularly through education and occupation (see, e.g., Anastasi,

1970; Balke-Aurell, 1982; Horn, 1978). A learning and transfer interpretation of this correlational developmental evidence has long been in hand (Ferguson, 1954, 1956) and is quite consistent with new theory emerging from cognitive psychology. Adding a developmental expansion to the radex map provides further framework for continuing cognitive research.

Analyses of *Gf* measures suggest that these tests sample some of the same mental processes required in the learning of academic skills whose products are sampled by *Gc* measures. The overlap represents a common assembly of general inductive and metacognitive thinking skills or procedural knowledge. But success on tests of *Gf* typically also requires the flexible adaptation or reassembly of these skills to the demands of relatively unfamiliar, or novel, tasks, whereas success on tests of *Gc* depends more heavily on the retrieval of previously assembled declarative and procedural knowledge and its application to the demands of relatively familiar tasks. Relative to *Gf* tests, *Gc* tests sample from a much larger organization of general and domain-specific declarative and procedural knowledge (Lohman, 1986b; see also R. J. Sternberg, 1985a). Different kinds and degrees of transfer from previous learning to new performance are implied (Snow, 1980a, 1981, 1982). Attempts to develop *Gf* and *Gc* directly by planned educational experiences start from this point, and the dynamic training and assessment research of A. L. Brown and Campione (1986), Feuerstein (1979), and others previously cited applies.

SPECIALIZED ACHIEVEMENTS AND THE DEVELOPMENT OF EXPERTISE

As one moves from the consideration of generalized, standardized ability and achievement tests to the problem of assessment in specialized achievement domains, there is increasing need for substantive theories of domain-specific achievement and how it is developed (Glaser, 1984). Cognitive theory implies that acquisition must go through several stages, in which declarative knowledge is accumulated and organized, restructured and converted into sets of procedures, and then tuned and practiced so as to function autonomously. Thus, becoming an expert in some domain means in part that thinking that once required investment of general problem-solving skills, declarative knowledge, and attention comes to be executed automatically, or perhaps intuitively, thereby freeing attentional resources for other tasks. Experts do not reason better; rather they need to reason less, because their automatized abilities to recognize patterns reduce the possibilities to be considered. In chess, in reading, in physics, in operating a taxi cab, the evidence seems to be the same. Declarative knowledge becomes tied to the conditions of its use. Developing expertise also means, in part, a shift from the surface features to the deep structures of a field. Novices, like preoperational children, must work out the problems they confront using the only information available to them. Experts, in physics for example, can be shown to classify problems immediately according to the underlying principles that apply to them (Chi et al., 1981). Finally, becoming an expert requires enormous amounts of dedicated practice in a large variety of situations, even though at base it also requires certain prerequisite aptitudes.

Cognitive research has concentrated more on the differences between experts and novices in particular fields and less on the differences between higher and lower achieving novices in those fields. Nonetheless, there are other important implications to be drawn. It is clear, for example, that the preconceptions held by students prior to entering formal study of a domain are often not made to disappear with new learning. Misconceptions often result when new concepts are meshed with old ones. And the misconceptions can be subtle. Further, novice knowledge and problem solving can often be chaotic and disorganized, with new concepts and procedures existing side by side with old concepts and procedures, all loosely coupled to each other and to their use.

The design of specialized achievement measures must be predicated on a specification of what constitutes the desired achievement goals but also on an understanding of the alternative routes by which individuals accomplish these goals and the kinds of misunderstandings and mishaps that are likely to occur along these routes. Substantive achievement theories are needed if achievement measures are to be made diagnostic in these ways. In an earlier section, it was argued that important steps toward such theories have been taken by cognitive research in mathematics and physics. Advances have been realized in certain other fields as well, such as computer programming, electronics troubleshooting, and medical diagnosis. But it was also noted that the vast array of other domains important for educational measurement have yet to receive concerted research attention. The cognitive analysis of achievement in these domains is a crucial next step for cognitive psychologists and educational measurement specialists working in consort. Cognitive analysis of existing achievement tests in these domains would be an excellent place to start.

EXPERIMENTAL EVALUATION OF EXISTING TESTS

Most well-known and widely used tests are the products of sound educational and psychometric research and development. The conventions that guide this kind of work are well established in the *Standards for Educational and Psychological Testing* (AERA-APA-NCME, 1985). But cognitive psychology now challenges conventional work to extend itself, particularly with respect to construct validation. A range of cognitive theories and experiments suggests that test instructions and administration conditions, item order, response format, and difficulty, timing, and even examinee expectancies about these characteristics of testing can have significant effects on the psychology of the scores obtained. And the psychology of the test might have significant effects on the psychology of the instruction that precedes or follows it. Thus, the challenge is to create a combined experimental and correlational cognitive psychology of educational measurement design and evaluation.

Suppose research demonstrates that multiple-choice versus constructed-response format, or order of item difficulty, or instructions regarding test-taking strategies are experimental variables that manipulate the involvement of verbal-versus-spatial abilities, or test anxiety or the inclination to seek deep structure in accompanying instruction. Decisions about test design cannot then rest simply on conventional professional judgment or considerations of testing efficiency. If one achievement test design affords advantage to high spatial ability and disadvantage to high test anxiety, whereas another affords the opposite, the resulting achievement scores reflect different construct mixtures; such scores cannot be justified or interpreted on evidence of content validation alone. A similar pattern of results for an aptitude test would likewise suggest that evidence on predictive validity is insufficient for clear interpretation.

All possible design alternatives and all possible hypotheses about the psychology of the test cannot be experimentally evaluated. But a test-development program, even of moderate size, can distill from cognitive research to date a list of plausible hypotheses about psychological processes operating in the test that connect to test-design alternatives and can investigate the most important of these. The advances in cognitive analysis noted in previous sections can be incorporated into traditional research and development on measurement design and use with significant benefit to that enterprise and, in many cases, without significant cost. As a test is widely used, over extended periods, for decisions that have substantial impact on individuals or institutions, one can expect the experimental research program on the test to become considerable. Beyond improved test development and construct validation, such a research program would make a substantial contribution to psychological science.

Challenges for the Future

We cannot summarize this meander through cognitive psychology and what it means for educational measurement. This chapter has sought to review enough of cognitive psychology to prompt deeper reading and to whet appetites for new research. The main aim, it must be admitted now, has been to tempt psychologically oriented measurement researchers to consider new ways of investigating their measures, present or projected, and to entertain new aspects of the overall educational objectives they serve. We have, therefore, distributed hypotheses liberally throughout this text, and we invite the reader to conduct research on one or another of them.

It seems clear to us, at least today, that cognitive psychology has no ready answers for the educational measurement problems of yesterday, today, or tomorrow. But it also seems clear to us that cognitive psychology has opened a spectrum of questions about what educational measurements do and do not represent and an equally large spectrum of methods for investigating such questions. For the measurement specialist, cognitive psychology is an open supermarket of possibilities. We have merely provided a survey of some of the departments and some of the brands within each. It remains to be seen what use educational measurement makes of what is available, and what becomes available, from the research efforts of the coming years. This concluding section notes briefly three challenges to research in educational measurement that derive from the previous pages.

TESTS AS VEHICLES BETWEEN LABORATORY AND FIELD

Examination of the cognitive content and process demands involved in successful performance of conventional tests contributes not only to the elaboration of their construct meanings but also to the interpretation of their correlation with laboratory measures. When laboratory measures correlate with tests in the field, furthermore, a communicative link between laboratory and field is suggested that enriches interpretation of the laboratory measure. As both test and laboratory tasks are redesigned to sharpen important structural and process distinctions, they help to build common constructs applicable in both environments. The best contributions to theory and practice will derive from instruments that can be used in either environment, that can transport interpretive issues from laboratory to field and vice versa.

The laboratory is well controlled but artificial and simple. The field is poorly controlled but real and complex. Correlations of other variables with a theory-based instrument in the field imply theoretical, situational, and practical issues with which the laboratory research has not dealt. To convey these implications to laboratory research is to bring the test back from the field for further analytic experiments. Similarly, to understand performance on a faceted laboratory measure is to provide a distinction that might clarify at least part of the network of complex relations apparent in field research, if the laboratory instrument can be used there. Tests designed to serve well in both environments can provide principal vehicles connecting theory and practice. There are as yet only a few examples of such instruments, and these have not yet been much used as the sort of vehicles envisioned.

TESTS AS GOALS FOR EDUCATIONAL IMPROVEMENT

As cognitive analysis is brought to bear on educational goals, the psychological nature of those goals is better understood. The question is: What constitutes expertise in field X, and how does it develop? The answer, even if provisional, provides a theory for test design. Such tests will need to distinguish clearly between what was taught and what was not, or between what was taught well and what was not taught well. They will further need to distinguish between alternative routes and strategies in accomplishing the goal, and the abilities, the partial knowledge, and the misconceptions that students brought with them to instruction as aptitudes or inaptitudes.

As cognitive psychology proceeds to identify what constitutes expertise in mathematics or physical science, or history or literacy or art, it will also yield design suggestions for adaptive diagnostic assessment of achievement that educational measurement experts should be prepared to accept, study, and improve upon. Examples of especially important steps in this direction come from Lajoie (1986/1987) and Lesgold et al. (1987). Coupled with the strengths of CIP analysis of both aptitude and achievement phenomena, the strengths of EPM models carry educational assessment to a profoundly more useful level. Embretson's (1985b) combined CIP–EPM models, along with the Gustafsson (1984) and Carroll (1985a) factor-analytic results, the universe definition procedures of Butterfield et al. (1985), and the theory-based diagnostic battery demonstrated by J. R. Frederiksen (1982), provide an important collection of examples with which to start.

THE EDUCATION OF EDUCATIONAL MEASUREMENT EXPERTS

Measurement specialists will need to know as much in the future as they have in the past. But much more will be required. Part of the purpose of this chapter is thus educative: to provide brief descriptions, examples, and related references for all the principal categories of cognitive psychology, as an introduction, so that readers can probe deeper in the most relevant directions.

We believe the future holds no productive alternative other than the making of cognitive measurement experts who understand both fields as well as experts in each now know their own. Substantial revisions of research programs, and of doctoral training programs, are likely to be forthcoming. They must be, if the promise of this chapter, and this book, are to be realized. The objective for us is not less than it was for the originators of educational measurement: It is theory-based assessments that demonstrably do good, for students and educational institutions, individually and collectively.

REFERENCES

Achenbach, T. M. (1970). The children's associative responding test: A possible alternative to group IQ tests. *Journal of Educational Psychology, 61,* 340–348.

Ackerman, P. L. (1986). Individual differences in information processing: An investigation of intellectual abilities and task performance during practice. *Intelligence, 10,* 101–139.

Ackerman, P. L. (1987). Individual differences in skill learning: An integration of psychometric and information processing perspectives. *Psychological Bulletin, 102,* 3–27.

Adelson, B. (1981). Problem-solving and the development of abstract categories in programming languages. *Memory and Cognition, 9,* 422–433.

Agari, T. (1979). *Individual differences in visual processing of nonverbal shapes.* Unpublished master's thesis, University of Washington, Seattle.

Alderton, D. L., & Pellegrino, J. W. (1984). *Analysis of mental paperfolding.* Unpublished manuscript, University of California, Santa Barbara, CA.

Allport, F. H. (1955). *Theories of perception and the concept of structure.* New York: John Wiley.

American Education Research Association, American Psychological Association, National Council on Measurement in Education. (1985). *Standards for educational and psychological testing.* Washington, DC: Author.

Anastasi, A. (1970). On the formation of psychological traits. *American Psychologist, 25,* 899–910.

Anderson, G. V., Fruchter, B., Manuel, H. T., & Worchel, P. (1954). *Survey of research on spatial factors* (Research Bulletin AFPTRC-TR-54-84). San Antonio: Lackland AFB.

Anderson, J. R. (1976). *Language, memory, and thought.* Hillsdale, NJ: Lawrence Erlbaum Associates.

Anderson, J. R. (1978). Arguments concerning representations for mental imagery. *Psychological Review, 85,* 249–277.

Anderson, J. R. (1983). *The architecture of cognition.* Cambridge, MA: Harvard University Press.

Anderson, J. R. (1984). Cognitive psychology. *Artificial Intelligence, 23*, 1–11.

Anderson, J. R. (1985). *Cognitive psychology and its implications* (2nd ed.). San Francisco: W. H. Freeman.

Anderson, J. R., & Bower, G. H. (1973). *Human associative memory.* Washington, DC: V. H. Winston.

Anderson, R. C. (1977). The notion of schemata and the educational enterprise: General discussion of the conference. In R. C. Anderson, R. J. Spiro, & W. E. Montague (Eds.), *Schooling and the acquisition of knowledge* (pp. 415–431). Hillsdale, NJ: Lawrence Erlbaum Associates.

Anderson, R. C., & Freebody, P. (1979). *Vocabulary knowledge* (Tech. Rep. No. 136). Champaign, IL: University of Illinois.

Anderson, R. C., & Pearson, P. D. (1984). A schema-theoretic view of basic processes in reading. In P. D. Pearson, R. Barr, M. L. Kamil, & P. Mosenthal (Eds.), *Handbook of reading research* (pp. 255–292). New York: Longman.

Andrich, D. (1985). A latent trait model for items with response dependencies: Implications for test construction and analysis. In S. E. Embretson (Ed.), *Test design: Developments in psychology and psychometrics* (pp. 245–278). New York: Academic Press.

Ansley, T. N., & Forsyth, R. A. (1985). An examination of the characteristics of unidimensional IRT parameter estimates derived from two-dimensional data. *Applied Psychological Measurement, 9*, 37–48.

Arnheim, R. (1974). *Art and visual perception.* Berkeley, CA: University of California Press.

Atkinson, R. C., & Shiffrin, R. M. (1968). Human memory: A proposed system and its control process. In K. Spence & J. Spence (Eds.), *The psychology of learning and motivation: Vol. 2* (pp. 89–195). New York: Academic Press.

Averbach, E., & Coriell, A. S. (1961). Short-term memory in vision. *Bell System Technical Journal, 40*, 309–328.

Baddeley, A. D. (1976). *The psychology of memory.* New York: Basic Books.

Balke-Aurell, G. (1982). *Changes in ability as related to educational and occupational experience.* Göteborg, Sweden: Acta Universitatis Gothoburgensis.

Bejar, I. I. (1985). Speculations on the future of test design. In S. E. Embretson (Ed.), *Test design: Developments in psychology and psychometrics* (pp. 279–294). New York: Academic Press.

Bejar, I. I. (1986). *A generative approach to the development of hidden-figure items* (ETS RR-86-20-ONR). Princeton, NJ: Educational Testing Service.

Bereiter, C., & Scardamalia, M. (1987). *The psychology of written composition.* Hilsdale, NJ: Lawrence Erlbaum Associates.

Bethell-Fox, C. E., Lohman, D. F., & Snow, R. E. (1984). Adaptive reasoning: Componential and eye movement analysis of geometric analogy performance. *Intelligence, 8*, 205–238.

Bialystok, E. (1986, August). Implicit display structure as a frame of reference. In J. Eliot (Chair), *Different frames of reference in children's spatial representation.* Symposium conducted at the meeting of the American Psychological Association, Washington, DC.

Biggs, J. B., & Collis, K. F. (1982). *Evaluating the quality of learning: The SOLO Taxonomy.* New York: Academic Press.

Bransford, J. D., & Johnson, M. K. (1973). Considerations of some problems in comprehension. In W. G. Chase (Ed.), *Visual information processing* (pp. 383–438). New York: Academic Press.

Briars, D. J., & Larkin, J. G. (1984). An integrated model of skill in solving elementary word problems. *Cognition and Instruction, 1*, 245–296.

Bricken, W. M. (1987). Analyzing errors in elementary mathematics. Unpublished doctoral dissertation, Stanford University, Stanford, CA.

Brown, A. L. (1978). Knowing when, where, and how to remember: A problem of metacognition. In R. Glaser (Ed.), *Advances in instructional psychology: Vol. 1* (pp. 77–165). Hillsdale, NJ: Lawrence Erlbaum Associates.

Brown, A. L., & Campione, J. C. (1986). Psychological theory and the study of learning disabilities. *American Psychologist, 41*, 1059–1068.

Brown, A. L., & Ferrara, R. A. (1985). Diagnosing zones of proximal development. In J. Wertsch (Ed.), *Culture, communication and cognition: Vygotskian perspectives* (pp. 273–305). Cambridge: Cambridge University Press.

Brown, J. S., & Burton, R. R. (1978). Diagnostic models for procedural bugs in basic mathematical skills. *Cognitive Science, 2*, 155–192.

Bruner, J. S., & Krech, D. (1950). *Perception and personality: A symposium.* Durham, NC: Duke University Press.

Butterfield, E. C., Nielsen, D., Tangen, K. L., & Richardson, M. B. (1985). Theoretically based psychometric measures of inductive reasoning. In S. E. Embretson (Ed.), *Test design: Developments in psychology and psychometrics* (pp. 77–148). New York: Academic Press.

Calfee, R. C. (1976). Sources of dependency in cognitive processes. In D. Klahr (Ed.), *Cognition and instruction* (pp. 23–49). Hillsdale, NJ: Lawrence Erlbaum Associates.

Calfee, R. C. (1977). Assessment of independent reading skills: Basic research and practical applications. In A. S. Reber & D. L. Scarborough (Eds.), *Toward a psychology of reading* (pp. 289–323). Hillsdale, NJ: Lawrence Erlbaum Associates.

Calfee, R. C. (1981). Cognitive Psychology and educational practice. *Review of Research in Education, 9*, 3–74.

Calfee, R. C. (1982). Cognitive models of reading: Implications for assessment and treatment of reading disability. In R. N. Malatesha & P. G. Aaron (Eds.), *Reading disorders: Varieties and treatments* (pp. 151–176). New York: Academic Press.

Calfee, R. C., & Chambliss, M. J. (1987). The structural design features of large texts. *Educational Psychologist, 22*, 357–375.

Calfee, R. C., & Drum, P. A. (1979). How the researcher can help the reading teacher with classroom assessment. In L. B. Resnick & P. A. Weaver (Eds.), *Theory and practice of early reading: Vol. 2* (pp. 173–205). Hillsdale, NJ: Lawrence Erlbaum Associates.

Calfee, R. C., & Hedges, L. V. (1980). Independent process analyses of aptitude-treatment interactions. In R. E. Snow, P-A. Federico, & W. E. Montague (Eds.), *Aptitude, learning, and instruction: Vol. 1. Cognitive process analyses of aptitude* (pp. 293–314). Hillsdale, NJ: Lawrence Erlbaum Associates.

Campbell, D. T., & Fiske, D. W. (1959). Convergent and discriminant validation by the multitrait-multimethod matrix. *Psychological Bulletin, 56*, 81–105.

Campione, J. C., & Brown, A. L. (1984). Learning ability and transfer propensity as sources of individual differences in intelligence. In P. H. Brooks, C. McCauley, & R. Sperber (Eds.), *Learning and cognition in the mentally retarded.* Hillsdale, NJ: Lawrence Erlbaum Associates.

Campione, J. C., Brown, A. L., & Ferrara, R. A. (1982). Mental retardation and intelligence. In R. J. Sternberg (Ed.), *Handbook of human intelligence* (pp. 342–492). Cambridge: Cambridge University Press.

Campione, J. C., Brown, A. L., Ferrara, R. A., Jones, R. S., & Steinberg, E. (1985). Breakdown in flexible use of information: Intelligence-related differences in transfer following equivalent learning performance. *Intelligence, 9*, 297–315.

Carey, S. (1986). Cognitive science and science education. *American Psychologist, 41*, 1123–1130.

Carroll, J. B. (1941). A factor analysis of verbal abilities. *Psychometrika, 6*, 279–307.

Carroll, J. B. (1972). Individual differences and multidimensional scaling. In R. N. Shepard, A. K. Romney, & S. B. Nerlove (Eds.), *Multidimensional scaling: Theory and applications in the behavioral sciences: Vol. 1* (pp. 105–155). New York: Seminar Press.

Carroll, J. B. (1976). Psychometric tests as cognitive tasks: A new "structure of intellect." In L. B. Resnick (Ed.), *The nature of intelligence* (pp. 27–56). Hillsdale, NJ: Lawrence Erlbaum Associates.

Carroll, J. B. (1980a). *Individual differences in psychometric and experimental cognitive tasks* (NR 150-406 ONR Final Report). Chapel Hill, NC: University of North Carolina, L. L. Thurstone Psychometric Laboratory.

Carroll, J. B. (1980b). Remarks on Sternberg's "Factor theories of intelligence are all right almost." *Educational Researcher, 9*, 14–18.

Carroll, J. B. (1981). Ability and task difficulty in cognitive psychology. *Educational Researcher, 10*, 11–21.

Carroll, J. B. (1985a), May). *Domains of cognitive ability.* Paper presented at the meeting of the American Association for the Advancement of Science, Los Angeles.

Carroll, J. B. (1985b). Second language abilities. In R. J. Sternberg (Ed.), *Human Abilities: An information-processing approach* (pp. 83–102). San Francisco: W. H. Freeman.

Carroll, J. B. (1986). Second language. In R. F. Dillon, & R. J. Sternberg (Eds.), *Cognition and instruction* (pp. 83–125). New York: Academic Press.

Carroll, J. B., Meade, A., &Johnson, E. S. (in press). Test analysis with the person characteristic function: Implications for defining abilities. In R. E. Snow, & D. Wiley (Eds.), *Straight thinking in education, psychology, and social science.*

Cattell, R. B. (1963). Theory of fluid and crystallized intelligence: A critical experiment. *Journal of Educational Psychology, 54,* 1–22.

Cattell, R. B. (1971). *Abilities: Their structure, growth, and action.* Boston: Houghton Mifflin.

Champagne, A. B., Gunstone, R. F., & Klopfer, L. E. (1985). Instructional consequences of students' knowledge about physical phenomena. In L. H. T. West & A. L. Pines (Eds.), *Cognitive structure and conceptual change* (pp. 61–90). New York: Academic Press.

Champagne, A. B., Klopfer, L. E., & Anderson, J. H. (1980). Factors influencing the learning of classical mechanics. *American Journal of Physics, 48,* 1074–1079.

Champagne, A. B., Klopfer, L. E., Desena, A. T., & Squires, D. A. (1981). Structural representations of students' knowledge before and after science instruction. *Journal of Research in Science Teaching, 18,* 97–111.

Chase, W. G., & Ericsson, K. A. (1982). Skill and working memory. In G. H. Bower (Ed.), *The psychology of learning and motivation: Vol. 16* (pp. 1–58). New York: Academic Press.

Chi, M. (1978). Knowledge structures and memory development. In R. S. Siegler (Ed.), *Children's thinking: What develops?* (pp. 73–96). Hillsdale, NJ: Lawrence Erlbaum Associates.

Chi, M. T. H., Feltovich, P., & Glaser, R. (1981). Categorization and representation of physics problems by experts and novices. *Cognitive Science, 5,* 121–152.

Chiang, A., & Atkinson, R. C. (1976). Individual differences and interrelationships among a select set of cognitive skills. *Memory and Cognition, 4,* 661–672.

Clancey, W. J., & Shortliffe, E. H. (Eds.) (1983). *Readings in medical artificial intelligence: The first decade.* Reading, MA: Addison-Wesley.

Clark, H. H., & Chase, W. G. (1972). On the process of comparing sentences against pictures. *Cognitive Psychology, 3,* 472–517.

Clement, J. (1982). Students' preconceptions in introductory mechanics. *American Journal of Physics, 50,* 66–71.

Cole, N. S. (1986). Future directions for educational achievement and ability testing. In B. S. Plake & J. C. Witt (Eds.), *The future of testing* (pp. 73–88). Hillsdale, NJ: Lawrence Erlbaum Associates.

Collins, A. M., & Loftus, E. F. (1975). A spreading-activation theory of semantic processing. *Psychological Review, 82,* 407–428.

Cooke, N. M., Durso, F. T., & Schvaneveldt, R. W. (1986). Recall and measures of memory organization. *Journal of Experimental Psychology: Learning, Memory, and Cognition, 12,* 538–549.

Cooper, C., & Kline, P. (in press). *The validity of the Defense Mechanism Test.* Exeter, UK: University of Exeter, Department of Psychology.

Cooper, L. A. (1982). Strategies for visual comparison and representation: Individual differences. In R. J. Sternberg (Ed.), *Advances in the psychology of human intelligence; Vol. 1* (pp. 77–124). Hillsdale, NJ: Lawrence Erlbaum Associates.

Cooper, L. A., & Regan, D. T. (1982). Attention, perception, and intelligence. In R. J. Sternberg (Ed.), *Handbook of human intelligence* (pp. 123–169). Cambridge: Cambridge University Press.

Crano, W. D. (1974). Causal analyses of the effects of socioeconomic status and initial intellectual endowment on patterns of cognitive development and academic achievement. In D. R. Green (Ed.), *The aptitude-achievement distinction* (pp. 223–261). Monterey, CA: CTB/McGraw-Hill.

Cronbach, L. J. (1943). Measuring knowledge of precise word meaning. *Journal of Educational Research, 36,* 508–534.

Cronbach, L. J. (1957). The two disciplines of scientific psychology. *American Psychologist, 12,* 671–684.

Cronbach, L. J. (1971). Test validation. In R. L. Thorndike (Ed.), *Educational measurement* (pp. 443–507). Washington, DC: American Council on Education.

Cronbach, L. J. (1977). *Educational Psychology* (3rd ed.). New York: Harcourt Brace Jovanovich.

Cronbach, L. J. (1984). *Essentials of psychological testing* (4th ed.). New York: Harper & Row.

Cronbach, L. J., Gleser, G. C., Nanda, H., & Rajaratnam, N. (1972). *The dependability of behavioral measurements.* New York: John Wiley.

Cronbach, L. J., & Snow, R. E. (1977). *Aptitudes and instructional methods: A handbook for research on interactions.* New York: Irvington.

Curtis, M. E., & Glaser, R. (1981). Changing conceptions of intelligence. *Review of Research in Education: Vol. 9* (pp. 111–148). Washington, DC: American Educational Research Association.

Curtis, M. E., & Glaser, R. (1983). Reading theory and the assessment of reading achievement. *Journal of Educational Measurement, 20,* 133–147.

Dahlgren, D. O. (1979). *Understanding students' understanding: Some qualitative aspects of process and outcome of teaching and learning at university level* (Report from the Institute of Education, No. 80). Göteborg, Sweden: University of Göteborg.

Daneman, M., & Carpenter, P. A. (1980). Individual differences in working memory and reading. *Journal of Verbal Learning and Verbal Behavior, 19,* 450–466.

Davis, R. B., & McKnight, C. (1980). The influence of semantic content on algorithmic behavior. *Journal of Mathematical Behavior, 3,* 39–87.

De Corte, E. (1977). Some aspects of research on learning and cognitive development in Europe. *Educational Psychologist, 12,* 197–206.

De Corte, E., & Verschaffel, L. (1984). First graders' solution strategies of addition and subtraction word problems. In J. M. Moser (Ed.), *Proceedings of the Sixth Annual Meeting of the North American Chapter of the International Group for the Psychology of Mathematics Education* (pp. 15–20). Madison, WI: Wisconsin Center for Educational Research.

De Corte, E., Verschaffel, L., & DeWin, L. (1985). Influence of rewording verbal problems on children's problem representations and solutions. *Journal of Educational Psychology, 77,* 460–470.

Dillon, R. F. (Ed.) (1985). *Individual differences in cognition: Vol. 2.* New York: Academic Press.

Dillon, R. F. (Ed.) (1986). Information processing and testing. *Educational Psychologist, 21,* 163–174.

Dillon, R. F., & Schmeck, R. R. (Eds.). (1983). *Individual differences in cognition: Vol. 1.* New York: Academic Press.

Donders, F. C. (1969). On the speed of mental processes (W. G. Koster, Trans.). *Acta Psychologica, 30,* 412–431. (Original work published 1868).

Dörner, D. (n. d.). *Time regulation in problem solving.* Unpublished manuscript. University of Bamberg, Psychological Institute, Bamberg, Federal Republic of Germany.

Dörner, D. (1984). Thinking and the organization of action. In J. Kuhl, & J. Beckman (Eds.). *Action-control: From cognition to behavior.* Berlin: Springer-Verlag.

Dreyfus, H. L., & Dreyfus, S. E. (1986). *Mind over machine.* New York: Free Press.

Ebbinghaus, H. (1985). *Memory: A contribution to experimental psychology* (H. A. Ruger & C. E. Bussenues, Trans.). New York: Teachers College Press. (Original work published 1913).

Ebel, R. L. (1962). Content standard test scores. *Educational and Psychological Measurement, 22,* 15–25.

Egan, D. E., & Greeno, J. G. (1973). Acquiring cognitive structure by discovery and rote learning. *Journal of Education Psychology, 64,* 85–97.

Eisner, E. W. (Ed.). (1976). *The arts, human development, and education.* Berkeley, CA: McCutchan.

Ekstrom, R. B., French, J. W., & Harman, H. H. (1976). *Kit of factor-referenced cognitive tests.* Princeton, NJ: Educational Testing Service.

El Koussy, A. A. H. (1935). The visual perception of space [Monograph]. *British Journal of Psychology, 20,* pp. 1–89.

Eliot, J. C., & Smith, I. M. (1983). *An international directory of spatial tests.* Windsor, UK: NFER-Nelson.

Elshout, J. J. (1985, June). *Problem solving and education.* Paper presented at the meeting of the European Association for Research on Learning and Instruction, Leuven, Belgium.

Elshout, J., Jansweijer, W., & Wielinga, B. (1986, April). *Modeling the genuine beginner.* Paper presented at the meeting of the American Educational Research Association, San Francisco.

Elstein, A. S., Shulman, L. S., & Sprafka, S. A. (1978). *Medical problem solving: An analysis of clinical reasoning.* Cambridge, MA: Harvard University Press.

Embretson, S. E. (1983). Construct validity: Construct representation versus nomothetic span. *Psychological Bulletin, 93,* 179–197.

Embretson, S. E. (Ed.) (1985a) *Test design: Developments in psychology and psychometrics.* New York: Academic Press.

Embretson, S. E. (1985b). Multicomponent latent trait models for test design. In S. E. Embretson (Ed.), *Test design: Developments in psychology and psychometrics* (pp. 195–218). New York: Academic Press.

Embretson, S. E. (1986). Intelligence and its measurement: Extending contemporary theory to existing tests. In R. J. Sternberg (Ed.), *Advances in the psychology of human intelligence: Vol. 3* (pp. 335–368). Hillsdale, NJ: Lawrence Erlbaum Associates.

Embretson, S. E., Schneider, L., & Roth, D. (1986). Multiple processing strategies and the construct validity of verbal reasoning tests. *Journal of Educational Measurement, 23,* 13–32.

Ericsson, K. A., & Simon, H. A. (1984). *Protocol analysis: Verbal reports as data.* Cambridge, MA: MIT Press.

Estes, W. K. (1975). The state of the field: General problems and issues of theory and metatheory. In W. K. Estes (Ed.), *Handbook of learning and cognitive processes: Introduction to concepts and issues: Vol. 1* (pp. 1–24). Hillsdale, NJ: Lawrence Erlbaum Associates.

Eysenck, H. J. (1982). *A model for intelligence.* New York: Springer.

Eysenck, H. J. (1984). The theory of intelligence and the psychophysiology of cognition. In R. J. Sternberg (Ed.), *Advances in the psychology of human intelligence: Vol. 3* (pp. 1–34). Hillsdale, NJ: Lawrence Erlbaum Associates.

Eysenck, M. (1984). *A handbook of cognitive psychology.* Hillsdale, NJ: Lawrence Erlbaum Associates.

Fairbank, B., Tirre, W., & Anderson, N. A. (1984, December). *Selection, administration, and analysis of 30 cognitive tests of individual differences.* Paper presented at the meeting of the NATO Advanced Study Institute on cognition and motivation, Athens, Greece.

Fenker, R. M. (1975). The organization of conceptual materials: A methodology for measuring ideal and actual cognitive structures. *Instructional Science, 4,* 33–57.

Ferguson, G. A. (1954). On learning and human ability. *Canadian Journal of Psychology, 8,* 95–112.

Ferguson, G. A. (1956). On transfer and the abilities of man. *Canadian Journal of Psychology, 10,* 121–131.

Fernandes, K. & Rose, A. M. (1978). *An information processing approach to performance assessment: II. An investigation of encoding and retrieval processes in memory.* (Technical Report AIR 58500-11/78-TR). Washington, DC: American Institutes for Research.

Feuerstein, R. (1979). *The dynamic assessment of retarded performers: The learning potential assessment device, theory, instruments, and techniques.* Baltimore: University Park Press.

Fischbein, E., Deri, M., Sainati, N., & Marino, M. S. (1985). The role of implicit models in solving verbal problems in multiplication and division. *Journal for Research in Mathematics Education, 16,* 3–18.

Fitts, P. M. (1964). Perceptual-motor skill learning. In A. W. Melton (Ed.), *Categories of human learning* (pp. 243–285). New York: Academic Press.

Flavell, J. H. (1963). *The developmental psychology of Jean Piaget.* New York: Van Nostrand Reinhold.

Floden, R. E. (1981). The logic of information-processing psychology in education. In D. C. Berliner (Ed.), *Review of Research in Education: Vol. 9* (pp. 75–109). Washington, DC: American Educational Research Association.

Foa, U. G. (1965). New developments in facet design and analysis. *Psychological Review, 72,* 262–274.

Frederiksen, J. R. (1980). Component skills in reading: Measurement of individual differences through chronometric analysis. In R. E. Snow, P-A. Federico, & W. E. Montague (Eds.), *Aptitude, learning, and instruction: Vol. 1. Cognitive process analyses of aptitude* (pp. 105–138). Hillsdale, NJ: Lawrence Erlbaum Associates.

Frederiksen, J. R. (1981). Sources of process interaction in reading. In A. M. Lesgold & C. A. Perfetti (Eds.), *Interactive processes in reading* (pp. 361–386). Hillsdale, NJ: Lawrence Erlbaum Associates.

Frederiksen, J. R. (1982). A componential theory of reading skills and their interactions. In R. J. Sternberg (Ed.), *Advances in the psychology of human intelligence: Vol. 1* (pp. 125–180). Hillsdale, NJ: Lawrence Erlbaum Associates.

Frederiksen, J. R., Warren, B. M., & Roseberg, A. S. (1985a). A componential approach to training reading skills: Part I. Perceptual units training. *Cognition and Instruction, 2,* 91–130.

Frederiksen, J. R., Warren, B. M., & Roseberg, A. S. (1985b). A componential approach to training reading skills. Part 2. Decoding and use of context. *Cognition and Instruction, 2,* 271–338.

Frederiksen, N. (1984a). Implications of cognitive theory for instruction in problem solving. *Review of Educational Research, 54,* 363–408.

Frederiksen, N. (1984b). The real test bias: Influences of testing on teaching and learning. *American Psychologist, 39,* 193–202.

French, J. W. (1965). The relationship of problem-solving styles to the factor composition of tests. *Educational and Psychological Measurement, 25,* 9–28.

Frijda, N., & DeGroot, A. D. (Eds.). (1981). *Otto Selz: His contribution to psychology.* The Hague, The Netherlands: Mouton.

Fuson, K. C. (1982). An analysis of the counting-on solution procedure in addition. In T. P. Carpenter, J. M. Moser, & T. A. Romberg (Eds.), *Addition and subtraction: A cognitive perspective* (pp. 67–81). Hillsdale, NJ: Lawrence Erlbaum Associates.

Gabrielsson, A. (1981). Music psychology: A survey of problems and current research activities. In *Basic musical functions and musical ability* (pp. 7–80). Stockholm: Royal Swedish Academy of Music.

Gagné, E. D. (1985). *The cognitive psychology of school learning.* Boston: Little, Brown.

Galton, F. (1883). *Inquiries into human faculty and its development.* London: Macmillan.

Gardner, H. (1982). *Art, mind, and brain: A cognitive approach to creativity.* New York: Basic Books.

Gardner, H. (1986). *The mind's new science: A history of the cognitive revolution.* New York: Basic Books.

Geeslin, W. E., & Shavelson, R. J. (1975). An exploratory analysis of the representation of a mathematical structure in students' cognitive structures. *American Educational Research Journal, 12,* 21–39.

Gelman, R., & Gallistel, C. R. (1978). *The child's understanding of number.* Cambridge, MA: Harvard University Press.

Gelman, R., & Meck, E. (1983). Preschoolers' counting: Principles before skill. *Cognition, 13,* 343–359.

Gentile, J. R., Kessler, D. K., & Gentile, P. K. (1969). Process of solving analogy items. *Journal of Educational Psychology, 60,* 494–502.

Gentner, D., & Gentner, D. R. (1983). Flowing waters or teeming crowds: Mental models of electricity. In D. Gentner & A. L. Stevens (Eds.), *Mental models* (pp. 99–129). Hillsdale, NJ: Lawrence Erlbaum Associates.

Gentner, D., & Stevens, A. L. (Eds.). (1983). *Mental models.* Hillsdale, NJ: Lawrence Erlbaum Associates.

Gibson, J. J. (Ed.). (1947). Motion picture testing and research. *Army Air Forces aviation psychology program* (Report No. 7). Washington, DC: Government Printing Office.

Gilbert, J. K., & Watts, D. M. (1983). Concepts, misconceptions, and alternative conceptions: Changing perspectives in science education. *Studies in Science Education, 10,* 61–98.

Ginsburg, H. (1977). *Children's arithmetic.* New York: Van Nostrand Reinhold.

Glaser, R. (1967). Some implications of previous work on learning and individual differences. In R. M. Gagné (Ed.), *Learning and individual differences* (pp. 1–22). Columbus, OH: Charles E. Merrill.

Glaser, R. (1977). *Adaptive education: Individual diversity and learning.* New York: Holt, Rinehart and Winston.

Glaser, R. (1980). General discussion: Relationships between aptitude, learning, and instruction. In R. E. Snow, P-A. Federico, & W. E. Montague (Eds.), *Aptitude, learning, and instruction: Vol. 2. Cognitive process analyses of learning and problem solving* (pp. 309–326). Hillsdale, NJ: Lawrence Erlbaum Associates.

Glaser, R. (1981). The future of testing: A research agenda for cognitive psychology and psychometrics. *American Psychologist, 36,* 923–936.

Glaser, R. (1984). Education and thinking: The role of knowledge. *American Psychologist, 39,* 93–104.

Glaser, R. (1985). The integration of testing and instruction. In E. E. Freeman (Ed.), *The redesign of testing for the 21st Century.* (pp. 45–58) Princeton, NJ: Educational Testing Service.

Glaser, R. (Ed.). (in preparation) *The nature or expertise.*

Glaser, R., Lesgold, A., & Lajoie, S. (in press). Toward a cognitive theory for the measurement of achievement. In R. Ronning, J. Glover, J. C. Conoley, & J. Witt (Eds.), *The influence of cognitive psychology on testing and measurement: The Buros-Nebraska Symposium on measurement and testing* (Vol. 3). Hillsdale, NJ: Lawrence Erlbaum Associates.

Glaser, R., & Nitko, A. J. (1971). Measurement in learning and instruction. In R. L. Thorndike (Ed.), *Educational measurement* (2nd ed., pp. 625–670). Washington, DC: American Council on Education.

Glaser, R., & Takanishi, R. (Eds.). (1986). Special issue: Psychological science and education. *American Psychologist, 41,* 1025–1168.

Glass, A. L. & Holyoak, K. J. (1986). *Cognition* (2nd ed.). New York: Random House.

Glushko, R. J., & Cooper, L. A. (1978). Spatial comprehension and comparison processes in verification tasks. *Cognitive Psychology, 10,* 391–421.

Goldman, S. R., & Pellegrino, J. W. (1984). Deductions about induction: Analyses of developmental and individual differences. In R. J. Sternberg (Ed.), *Advances in the psychology of human intelligence: Vol. 2* (pp. 149–197). Hillsdale, NJ: Lawrence Erlbaum Associates.

Goldman, S. R., Pellegrino, J. W., Parseghian, P. E., & Sallis, R. (1982). Developmental and individual differences in verbal analogical reasoning by children. *Child Development, 53,* 550–559.

Goldner, R. H. (1957). Individual differences in whole-part approach and flexibility-rigidity in problem solving. *Psychological Monographs, 71,* No. 21.

Gray, L. E. (1983). *Aptitude constructs, learning processes, and achievement.* Unpublished report, Stanford University, Stanford, CA.

Greeno, J. G. (1978). A study of problem solving. In R. Glaser (Ed.), *Advances in instructional psychology: Vol. 1* (pp. 13–75). Hillsdale, NJ: Lawrence Erlbaum Associates.

Greeno, J. G. (1980a). Psychology of learning, 1960–1980: One participant's observations. *American Psychologist, 35,* 713–728.

Greeno, J. G. (1980b). Some examples of cognitive task analysis with instructional implications. In R. E. Snow, P-A. Federico, & W. E. Montague (Eds.), *Aptitude, learning, and instruction: Vol. 2. Cognitive process analyses of learning and problem solving* (pp. 1–21). Hillsdale, NJ: Lawrence Erlbaum Associates.

Greeno, J. G. (1986, April). *Mathematical cognition: Accomplishments and challenges in research.* Invited address to the American Educational Research Association, San Francisco.

Greeno, J. G., & Mayer, R. E. (1975). *Structural and quantitative interaction among aptitudes and instructional treatments.* Unpublished manuscript, University of Michigan, Ann Arbor, MI.

Greeno, J. G., Riley, M. W., & Gelman, R. (1981). *Young children's counting and understanding of principles.* Unpublished manuscript, University of Pittsburgh, Learning Research and Development Center, Pittsburgh.

Greeno, J. G., & Simon, H. A. (in press). Problem solving and reasoning. In R. C. Atkinson, R. Herrnstein, G. Lindzey, & R. D. Luce (Eds.), *Stevens' handbook of experimental psychology* (rev. ed.). New York: John Wiley & Sons.

Groen, G. J., & Parkman, J. M. (1972). A chronometric analysis of simple addition. *Psychological Review, 79,* 329–343.

Guilford, J. P. (1967). *The nature of human intelligence.* New York: McGraw-Hill.

Guilford, J. P. (1985). The structure-of-intellect model. In B. B. Wolman (Ed.), *Handbook of intelligence* (pp. 225–266). New York: John Wiley & Sons.

Guilford, J. P., & Lacey, J. I. (Eds.). (1947). Printed classification tests. *Army Air Forces aviation psychology research program* (Report No. 5). Washington, DC: Government Printing Office.

Gustafsson, J. E. (1976). Verbal and figural aptitudes in relation to instructional methods: Studies in aptitude–treatment interaction. *Göteborg Studies in Education Sciences,* No. 17. Göteborg, Sweden: University of Göteborg.

Gustafsson, J. E. (1984). A unifying model for the structure of intellectual abilities. *Intelligence, 8,* 179–203.

Guttman, L. (1954). A new approach to factor analysis. The radex. In P. F. Lazarfield (Ed.), *Mathematical thinking in the social sciences* (216–257). New York: Free Press.

Guttman, L. (1970). Integration of test design and analysis. *Proceedings of the 1969 Invitational Conference on Testing Problems* (pp. 53–65). Princeton, NJ: Educational Testing Service.

Haertel, E. (1984a). An application of latent class models to assessment data. *Applied Psychological Measurement, 8,* 333–346.

Haertel, E. (1984b). Detection of a skill dichotomy using standardized achievement test items. *Journal of Educational Measurement, 21,* 59–72.

Haertel, E. (in press). Using restricted latent class models to map the skill structure of achievement items. *Journal of Educational Measurement.*

Halff, H. M., Hollan, J. D., & Hutchins, E. L. (1986). Cognitive science and military training. *American Psychologist, 41,* 1131–1139.

Hall, G. S. (1883). The content of children's minds. *Princeton Review,* 249–272.

Hayes, J. R. (1981). *The complete problem solver.* Philadelphia: Franklin Institute Press.

Hebb, D. O. (1949). *The organization of behavior.* New York: John Wiley.

Heckman, R., Tiffin, J., & Snow, R. E. (1967). Effects of controlling item exposure in achievement testing. *Educational and Psychological Measurement, 27,* 113–125.

Heller, J. I. (1979). Cognitive processing in verbal analogy solution. (Doctoral dissertation, University of Pittsburgh), *Dissertation Abstracts International, 40,* 2553A.

Heller, J. I., & Greeno, J. G. (1979). Information processing analyses of mathematical problem solving. In R. W. Tyler & S. H. White (Eds.), *Testing, teaching and learning* (pp. 113–135). Washington, DC: National Institute of Education.

Hesse, F. W., & Lüer, G. (1986, April). *Acquiring knowledge to solve complex problems.* Paper presented at the meeting of the American Educational Research Association, San Francisco.

Hiebert, J., & Wearne, D. (1985). A model of students' decimal computation procedures. *Cognition and Instruction, 2,* 175–205.

Hinsley, D., Hayes, J. R., & Simon, H. A. (1977). From words to equations. In P. Carpenter & M. Just (Eds.), *Cognitive processes in comprehension* (pp. 89–108). Hillsdale, NJ: Lawrence Erlbaum Associates.

Hoffman, K. I., Guilford, J. P., Hoepfner, R., & Doherty, W. J. (1968). *A factor analysis of the figure-cognition and figural-evaluation abilities* (Report No. 40). Los Angeles: University of Southern California, Psychological Laboratory.

Holland, J. H., Holyoak, K. J., Nisbett, R. E., & Thagard, P. R. (1987). *Induction: Processes of inference, learning, and discovery.* Cambridge, MA: MIT Press.

Holyoak, K. J. (1984). Analogical thinking and human intelligence. In R. J. Sternberg (Ed.), *Advances in the psychology of human intelligence Vol. 2* (pp. 199–230). Hillsdale, NJ: Lawrence Erlbaum Associates.

Holzman, P. S., & Klein, G. S. (1954). Cognitive system principles of leveling and sharpening: Individual differences in visual time-error assimilation effects. *Journal of Psychology, 37,* 105–122.

Holzman, T. G., Pellegrino, J. W., & Glaser, R. (1982). Cognitive dimensions of numerical rule induction. *Journal of Educational Psychology, 74,* 360–373.

Holzman, T. G., Pellegrino, J. W., & Glaser,R. (1983). Cognitive variables in series completion. *Journal of Educational Psychology, 75,* 602–617.

Horn, J. L. (1976). Human abilities: A review of research and theory in the early 1970's. *Annual Review of Psychology, 27,* 437–485.

Horn, J. L. (1978). Human ability systems. In P. B. Baltes (Ed.), *Lifespan development and behavior: Vol. 1* (pp. 211–256). New York: Academic Press.

Horn, J. L. (1985). Remodeling old models of intelligence. In B. B. Wolman (Ed.), *Handbook of intelligence* (pp. 267–300). New York: John Wiley & Sons.

Horn, J. L.(1986). Intellectual ability concepts. In R. J. Sternberg (Ed.), *Advances in the psychology of human intelligence: Vol. 3* (pp. 35–77). Hillsdale, NJ: Lawrence Erlbaum Associates.

Houlihan, D. M., & Ginsburg, H. P. (1981). The addition methods of first- and second-grade children. *Journal for Research in Mathematics Education, 12,* 95–106.

Hudson, T. (1983). Correspondence and numerical differences between disjoint sets. *Child Development, 54,* 84–90.

Hull, C. L. (1945). The place of innate individual and species differences in a natural-science theory of behavior. *Psychological Review, 52,* 55–60.

Humphreys, L. G. (1981). The primary mental ability. In M. P. Friedman, J. P. Das, & N. O'Connor (Eds.), *Intelligence and learning* (pp. 87–102). New York: Plenum.

Hunt, E. (1980). The foundations of verbal comprehension. In R. E. Snow, P-A. Federico, & W. E. Montague (Eds.), *Aptitude, learning, and instruction: Vol. 1. Cognitive process analyses of aptitude* (pp. 87–104). Hillsdale, NJ: Lawrence Erlbaum Associates.

Hunt, E. (1982). Towards new ways of assessing intelligence. *Intelligence, 6,* 231–240.

Hunt, E. (1985a). Cognitive research and future test design. In E. E. Freeman (Ed.), *The redesign of testing for the 21st century* (pp. 9–24). Princeton, NJ: Educational Testing Service.

Hunt, E. (1985b). Verbal Ability. In R. J. Sternberg (Eds.), *Human abilities: An information-processing approach* (pp. 31–58). NY: W. H. Freeman.

Hunt, E. B., Frost, N., & Lunneborg, C. (1973). Individual differences in cognition: A new approach to intelligence. In G. Bower (Ed.), *The psychology of learning and motivation: Vol. 7* (pp. 87–122). New York: Academic Press.

Hunt, E., & Lansman, M. (1975). Cognitive theory applied to individual differences. In W. K. Estes (Ed.), *Handbook of learning and cognitive processes: Introduction to concepts and issues:* Vol. 1 (pp. 81–110). Hillsdale, NJ: Lawrence Erlbaum Associates.

Hunt, E., & Lansman, M. (1982). Individual differences in attention. In R. J. Sternberg (Ed.), *Advances in the psychology of human abilities: Vol. 1* (pp. 207–254). Hillsdale, NJ: Lawrence Erlbaum Associates.

Hunt, E. B., Lunneborg, C., & Lewis, J. (1975). What does it mean to be high verbal? *Cognitive Psychology, 7,* 194–227.

Hunt, E., & Pellegrino, J. (1985). Using interactive computing to expand intelligence testing: A critique and prospectus. *Intelligence, 9,* 207–236.

Inhelder, B., & Piaget, J. (1958). *The growth of logical thinking from childhood to adolescence.* New York: Basic Books.

Ippel, M. J. (1986). *Component-testing: A theory of cognitive aptitude measurement.* Amsterdam, The Netherlands: Free University Press.

Ippel, M. J., & Beem, A. L. (1987). A theory of antagonistic strategies. In E. De Corte, H. Lodewijks, R. Parmentier, & P. Span (Eds.), *Learning and instruction: European Research in an international context: Vol. 1* (pp. 111–121). Oxford: Leuven University Press and Pergamon Press.

Ippel, M. J., & Bouma, J. M. (1981). Determinanten van strategiekeuze op verborgen-figuren-tests [Determinants of strategy-selection on hidden-figure-tests]. *Nederlands Tijdschrift voor de Psychologie, 36,* 289–305.

James, W. (1890). *Principles of psychology: Vol. 1.* New York: H. Holt.

Jansweijer, W. H. N., Konst, L., Elshout, J. J., & Wielinga, B. J. (1982). PDP: A protocol diagnostic program for problem solving in physics. *Proceedings of the European Conference on Artificial Intelligence,* Paris.

Jensen, A. R. (1980). *Bias in mental testing.* New York: Free Press.

Jensen, A. R. (1982). The chronometry of intelligence. In R. J. Sternberg (Ed.), *Advances in the psychology of human intelligence: Vol. 1* (pp. 255–310). Hillsdale, NJ: Lawrence Erlbaum Associates.

Jensen, A. R. (1987). Process differences and individual differences in some cognitive tasks. *Intelligence, 11,* 107–136.

Johansson, B., Marton, F., & Svensson, L. (1985). An approach to describing learning as change between qualitatively different conceptions. In L. H. T. West, & A. L. Pines (Eds.), *Cognitive structure and conceptual change* (pp. 233–257). New York: Academic Press.

Johnson-Laird, P. N. (1983). *Mental models: Towards a cognitive science of language, inference, and consciousness.* Cambridge, MA: Harvard University Press.

Johnston, P. H. (1983). *Reading comprehension assessment: A cognitive basis.* Newark, DE: International Reading Association.

Jong, T. D, & Ferguson-Hessler, M. G. M. (1986). Cognitive structures of good and poor novice problem solvers in physics. *Journal of Educational Psychology, 78,* 279–288.

Juola, J. F. (1979). Pattern recognition. In R. Lachman, J. L. Lachman, & E. C. Butterfield, *Cognitive psychology and information processing: An introduction* (pp. 489–523). Hillsdale, NJ: Lawrence Erlbaum Associates.

Kahneman, D. (1973). *Attention and effort.* Englewood Cliffs, NJ: Prentice-Hall.

Kail, R., Carter, P., & Pellegrino, J. (1979). The locus of sex differences in spatial ability. *Perception and Psychophysics, 26,* 182–186.

Kelley, T. L. (1928). *Crossroads in the mind of man.* Stanford, CA: Stanford University Press.

Kintsch, W. (1986). Learning from text. *Cognition and Instruction, 3,* 87–108.

Kintsch, W., & Greeno, J. G., (1985). Understanding and solving word arithmetic problems. *Psychological Review, 92,* 109–129.

Klein, G. S. (1970). *Perception, motives, and personality.* New York: Alfred A. Knopf.

Kosslyn, S. M. (1980). *Image and mind.* Cambridge, MA: Harvard University Press.

Kosslyn, S. M. (1981). The medium and the message in mental imagery: A theory. *Psychological Review, 88,* 46–66.

Kotovsky, K., & Simon, H. A. (1973). Empirical tests of a theory of human acquisition of concepts for sequential events. *Cognitive Psychology, 4,* 399–424.

Kragh, U., & Smith, G. S. (1970). *Percept genetics.* Lund, Sweden: Gleerups.

Kyllonen, P. C. (1984). Information processing analysis of spatial ability (Doctoral dissertation, Stanford University). *Dissertation Abstracts International, 45,* 819A.

Kyllonen, P. C. (1986). *Theory-based cognitive assessment* (AFHRL-TP-85-30). Brooks AFB, TX: Air Force Human Resources Laboratory.

Kyllonen, P. C., Lohman, D. F., & Snow, R. E. (1984). Effects of aptitudes, strategy training, and task facets on spatial task performance. *Journal of Educational Psychology, 76,* 130–145.

Kyllonen, P. C., Lohman, D. F., & Woltz, D. J. (1984). Componential modeling of alternative strategies for performing spatial tasks. *Journal of Educational Psychology, 76,* 1325–1345.

Lachman, R., Lachman, J. L., & Butterfield, E. C. (1979). *Cognitive psychology and information processing: An introduction.* Hillsdale, NJ: Lawrence Erlbaum Associates.

Lajoie, S. P. (1987). Individual differences in spatial ability: A computerized tutor for orthographic projection tasks (Doctoral dissertation, Stanford University, 1986). *Dissertation Abstracts International, 47,* 3370A.

Lakoff, G., & Johnson, M. (1980). *Metaphors we live by.* Chicago: University of Chicago Press.

Lansman, M., Donaldson, G., Hunt, E., & Yantis, S. (1982). Ability factors and cognitive processes. *Intelligence, 6,* 347–386.

Larkin, J. H. (1983). Teaching problem solving in physics: The psychological laboratory and the practical classroom. In D. T. Tuma & F. Reif (Eds.), *Problem solving and education: Issues in teaching and research* (pp. 111–125). Hillsdale, NJ: Lawrence Erlbaum Associates.

Larkin, J., McDermott., J., Simon, D. P., & Simon, H. A. (1980).

Expert and novice performance in solving physics problems. *Science, 208,* 1335–1342.

Larkin, J., Reif, F., Carbonell, J., & Gugliotta, A. (1985). *FERMI: A flexible expert reasoner with multi-domain inferencing.* Unpublished report, Carnegie-Mellon University, Psychology Department, Pittsburgh.

Lawson, M. J. (1984). Being executive about metacognition. In J. R. Kirby (Ed.), *Cognitive strategies and educational performance* (pp. 89–110). New York: Academic Press.

Leeuwenberg, E. & Buffart, H. (n.d.). *An outline of coding theory* Unpublished Report. University of Nijmegen, Psychology Department, Nijmegen, The Netherlands.

Lesgold, A. M. (1984). Acquiring expertise. In J. R. Anderson & S. M. Kosslyn (Eds.), *Tutorials in learning and memory* (pp. 31–60). San Francisco: W. H. Freeman.

Lesgold, A., Bonar, J., & Ivill, J. (1987). *Toward intelligent systems for testing* (Tech. Rep. No. LSP-1). Pittsburgh: University of Pittsburgh, Learning Research and Development Center.

Lesgold, A., Lajoie, S., Logan, D., & Eggan, G. (1986). *Cognitive task analysis approaches to testing.* Unpublished manuscript, University of Pittsburgh, Learning Research and Development Center, Pittsburgh.

Levin, J. R., & Pressley, M. (1986). Special issue: Learning strategies. *Educational Psychologist, 21,* (1–2).

Likert, R., & Quasha, W. H. (1970). *Manual for the revised Minnesota Paper Form Board test.* New York: Psychological Corporation.

Lohman, D. F. (1979a). *Spatial ability: Individual differences in speed and level* (Tech. Rep. No. 9). Stanford, CA: Stanford University, Aptitude Research Project, School of Education. (NTIS No. AD-A075 973).

Lohman, D. F. (1979b). *Spatial ability: A review and reanalysis of the correlational literatures* (Tech. Rep. No. 8). Stanford, CA: Stanford University, Aptitude Research Project, School of Education. (NTIS No. AD-A075 972).

Lohman, D. F. (1986a). The effect of speed-accuracy tradeoff on sex differences in mental rotation. *Perception and Psychophysics, 39,* 427–436.

Lohman, D. F. (1986b). Predicting mathemathanic effects in the teaching of higher-order thinking skills. *Educational Psychologist, 21,* 191–208.

Lohman, D. F. (1988). Spatial abilities as traits, processes, and knowledge. In R. J. Sternberg (Ed.), *Advances in the psychology of human intelligence: vol. 4.* pp. 181–248. Hillsdale, NJ: Lawrence Erlbaum Associates.

Lohman, D. F., & Kyllonen, P. C. (1983). Individual differences in solution strategy on spatial tasks. In R. F. Dillon & R. R. Schmeck (Eds.), *Individual differences in cognition: vol. 1* (pp. 105–135). New York: Academic Press.

Lohman, D. F., & Nichols, P. D. (1985, April). *Spatial ability: The effects of encoding processes and representational quality on mental synthesis.* Paper presented at the meeting of the American Educational Research Association, San Francisco.

Lohman, D. F., Pellegrino, J. W., Alderton, D. L., & Regian, J. W. (1987). Dimensions and components of individual differences in spatial abilities. In S. H. Irvine & S. E. Newstead (Eds.), *Intelligence and cognition: Contemporary frames of references* (pp. 253–312). Dordrecht, The Netherlands: Martinus Nijhoff.

Lord, F. M. (1980). *Applications of item response theory to practical testing problems.* Hillsdale, NJ: Lawrence Erlbaum Associates.

Lord, F. M., & Novick, M. (1968). *Statistical theories of mental test scores.* Reading, MA: Addison-Wesley.

Lüer, G., Hubner, R., & Lass, U. (1984). *Studies in problem solving processes* (Report No. 8). Göttingen, Federal Republic of Germany: University of Göttingen, Institute for Psychology.

Macleod, C. M., Hunt, E. B., & Mathews, N. N. (1978). Individual differences in the verification of sentence-picture relationships. *Journal of Verbal Learning and Verbal Behavior, 17,* 493–508.

Majasan, J. K. (1972). College students' achievement as a function of the congruence between their beliefs and their instructor's beliefs. (Doctoral dissertation, Stanford University), *Dissertation Abstracts International, 33,* 4180A.

Marquer, J., & Pereira, M. (1987, April). *Individual differences in sentence-picture verification.* Paper presented at the meeting of the American Educational Research Association, New York.

Marshalek, B. (1981). *Trait and process aspects of vocabulary knowledge and verbal ability* (Tech. Rep. No. 15). Stanford, CA: Stanford University, Aptitude Research Project, School of Education. (NTIS No. AD-A102 757).

Marshalek, B., Lohman, D. F., & Snow, R. E. (1983). The complexity continuum in the radex and hierarchical models of intelligence. *Intelligence, 7,* 107–128.

Marton, F. (1981). Phenomenography: Describing conceptions of the world around us. *Instructional Science, 10,* 177–200.

Marton, F., (1983). Beyond individual differences. *Educational Psychology, 3,* pp. 291–305.

Marton, F., Hounsell, D., & Entwistle, N. (1984). *The experience of learning.* Edinburgh, Scotland: Scottish Academic Press.

Mayer, R. E. (1978). Qualitatively different encoding strategies for linear reasoning. Evidence for single association and distance theories. *Journal of Experimental Psychology: Human Learning and Memory, 4,* 5–18.

Mayer, R. E. (1982). Memory for algebra story problems. *Journal of Educational Psychology, 74,* 199–216.

Mayer, R. E. (1983). *Thinking, problem solving, and cognition.* San Francisco: W. H. Freeman.

Mayer, R. E. (1985). Mathematical ability. In R. J. Sternberg (Ed.), *Human abilities: An information processing approach* (pp. 127–150). San Francisco: Freeman.

Mayer, R. E., Stiehl, C. C., & Greeno, J. G. (1975). Acquisition of understanding and skill in relation to subjects' preparation and meaningfulness of instruction. *Journal of Educational Psychology, 67,* 331–350.

McClelland, J. L., & Rumelhart, D. E. (1981). An interactive model of context effects in letter perception: I. An account of basic findings. *Psychological Review, 88,* 375–407.

McClelland, J. L., Rumelhart, D. E., & the PDP Research Group. (1986). *Parallel distributed processing: Vol. 2. Psychological and biological models.* Cambridge, MA: MIT Press.

McCloskey, M. (1983). Naive theories of motion. In D. Gentner & A. L. Stevens (Eds.), *Mental Models* (pp. 299–324). Hillsdale, NJ: Lawrence Erlbaum Associates.

McCloskey, M., Caramazza, A., & Green, B. (1980). Curvilinear motion in the absence of external forces: Naive beliefs about the motion of objects. *Science, 210,* 1139–1141.

McGee, M. (1979). *Human spatial abilities: Sources of sex differences.* New York: Praeger.

McNemar, Q. (1964). Lost: Our intelligence? Why? *American Psychologist, 19,* 871–882.

Messick, S. (1984). The psychology of educational measurement. *Journal of Educational Measurement, 21,* 215–237.

Mettes, C. T. C. W. (1986). Factual and procedural knowledge: Learning to solve science problems. In E. DeCorte, H. Lodewijks, R. Parmentier, & P. Span (Eds.), *Learning and instruction: European research in an international context: Vol. 1* (pp. 285–296). Oxford: Leuven University Press and Pergamon Press.

Mettes, C. T. C. W., Pilot, A., & Roossink, H. J. (1981). Linking factual and procedural knowledge in solving science problems: A case study in a thermodynamics course. *Instructional Science, 10,* 333–361.

Mislevy, R. J., & Verhelst, N. (1987). *Modeling item responses when different subjects employ different solution strategies.* Technical Report RR-87-47-ONR, Educational Testing Service, Princeton, NJ.

Mulholland, T. M., Pellegrino, J. W., & Glaser, R. (1980). Components of geometric analogy solution. *Cognitive Psychology, 12,* 252–284.

Mumaw, R. J., & Pellegrino, W. J. (1986). Individual differences in complex spatial processing. *Journal of Educational Psychology, 76,* 920–939.

Mumaw, R. J., Pellegrino, J. W., Kail, R. V., & Carter, P. (1984). Different slopes for different folks: Process analysis of spatial aptitude. *Memory and Cognition, 12,* 515–521.

Naveh-Benjamin, M., McKeachie, W. J., Lin, Y-G., & Tucker, D. G. (1986). Inferring students' cognitive structures and their development using the "Ordered Tree Technique." *Journal of Educational Psychology, 78,* 130–140.

Neisser, U. (1967). *Cognitive psychology.* New York: Appleton-Century-Crofts.

Neisser, U. (1976). General, academic, and artificial intelligences. In L. B. Resnick (Ed.), *The nature of intelligence* (pp. 135–144). Hillsdale, NJ: Lawrence Erlbaum Associates.

Newell, A. (1980). Reasoning, problem-solving, and decision processes: The problem space as a fundamental category. In R. Nickerson (Ed.), *Attention and performance VIII* (pp. 693–718). Hillsdale, NJ: Lawrence Erlbaum Associates.

Newell, A., & Simon, H. A. (1972). *Human problem solving.* Englewood Cliffs, NJ: Prentice-Hall.

Nickerson, R., Perkins, D. N., & Smith, E. (1985). *The teaching of thinking.* Hillsdale, NJ: Lawrence Erlbaum Associates.

Norman, D. A. (1977). Notes toward a theory of complex learning. In A. M. Lesgold, J. W. Pellegrino, S. D. Fokkema, & R. Glaser (Eds.), *Cognitive psychology and instruction* (pp. 29–48). New York: Plenum.

Norman, D. A., Rumelhart, D. E., & the LNR Research Group. (1975). *Explorations in cognition.* San Francisco: W. H. Freeman.

Novick, L. R. (1987). Analogical transfer in expert and novice problem solvers. (Doctoral Dissertation, Stanford University, 1986). *Dissertation Abstracts International, 47,* 3991B.

Opwis, K., & Spada, H. (1984). *Prozessdaten und Prozessmodellierung in einem umweltpsychologischen konfliktspiel.* [Process data and process modeling in an ecological psychology conflict game.] Unpublished report, University of Freiburg, Psychological Institute, Freiburg, Federal Republic of Germany.

Osherson, D. N. (1974). *Logical abilities in children: Vol. 2. Logical inference: Underlying operations.* Hillsdale, NJ: Lawrence Erlbaum Associates.

Palincsar, A. S., & Brown, A. L. (1984). Reciprocal teaching of comprehension-fostering and comprehension monitoring activities. *Cognition and Instruction, 1,* 117–175.

Palmer, S. E. (1977). Hierarchical structure in perceptual representation. *Cognitive Psychology, 9,* 441–474.

Pellegrino, J. W. (1985a). Inductive reasoning ability. In R. J. Sternberg (Ed.), *Human abilities: An information-processing approach* (pp. 195–225). San Francisco: W. H. Freeman.

Pellegrino, J. W. (1985b, April). *Information processing and intellectual ability.* Paper presented at the meeting of the American Educational Research Association, New Orleans.

Pellegrino, J. W., & Glaser, R. (1979). Cognitive correlates and components in the analysis of individual differences. In R. J. Sternberg & D. K. Detterman (Eds.), *Human intelligence: Perspectives on its theory and measurement* (pp. 61–88). Norwood, NJ: Ablex.

Pellegrino, J. W., & Glaser, R. (1980). Components of inductive reasoning. In R. E. Snow, P-A. Federico, & W. E. Montague (Eds.), *Aptitude, learning, and instruction: Vol. 1. Cognitive process analyses of aptitude* (pp. 177–218). Hillsdale, NJ: Lawrence Erlbaum Associates.

Pellegrino, J. W., & Glaser, R. (1982). Analyzing aptitudes for learning: Inductive reasoning. In R. Glaser (Ed.), *Advances in instructional psychology: Vol. 2* (pp. 269–345). Hillsdale, NJ: Lawrence Erlbaum Associates.

Pellegrino, J. W., & Hubert, L. J. (1982). The analysis of organization and structure in free recall. In C. R. Puff (Ed.), *Handbook of research methods in human memory and cognition* (pp. 129–172). New York: Academic Press.

Pellegrino, J. W., & Kail, R. (1982). Process analyses of spatial aptitude. In R. J. Sternberg (Ed.), *Advances in the psychology of human intelligence: Vol. 1* (pp. 311–366). Hillsdale, NJ: Lawrence Erlbaum Associates.

Perfetti, C. A. (1985). Reading ability. In R. J. Sternberg (Ed.), *Human Abilities: An information-processing approach* (pp. 59–81). San Francisco: W. H. Freeman.

Perfetti, C. A. (1986). *Reading ability.* New York: Oxford University Press.

Perkins, D. & Leondar, D. (Eds.) (1977). *The arts and cognition.* Baltimore: Johns Hopkins University Press.

Piaget, J. (1963). *The psychology of intelligence.* New York: International Universities Press.

Pieters, J. P. M. (1983). Sternberg's additive factor method and under-

lying psychological processes: Some theoretical considerations. *Psychological Bulletin, 93,* 411–426.

Pines, A. L., Novak, J. D., Posner, G. J., & Van Kirk, J. (1978). *The clinical interview: A method for evaluating cognitive structure.* (Research Rep. No. 6). Ithaca, NY: Cornell University, Department of Education.

Pinker, S. (1984). Visual cognition: An introduction. *Cognition, 18,* 1–63.

Poltrock, S. E., & Brown, P. (1984). Individual differences in visual imagery and spatial ability. *Intelligence, 8,* 93–138.

Posner, M. I., & Mitchell, R. F. (1967). Chronometric analysis of classification. *Psychological Review, 74,* 392–409.

Preece, P. (1978). Exploration of semantic space: Review of research on the organization of scientific concepts in semantic memory: *Science Education, 63,* 547–562.

Pylyshyn, Z. W. (1981). The imagery debate: Analogue media versus tacit knowledge. *Psychological Review, 87,* 16–45.

Rasch, G. (1960). *Probabilistic models for some intelligence and attainment tests.* Copenhagen: Nielson & Lydiche.

Reder, L. M. (1982). Elaborations: When do they help and when do they hurt? *Text, 2,* 211–224.

Resnick, L. B. (1976). Task analysis in instructional design: Some cases from mathematics. In D. Klahr (Ed.), *Cognition and instruction* (pp. 51–80). Hillsdale, NJ: Lawrence Erlbaum Associates.

Resnick, L. B. (1982). Syntax and semantics in learning to subtract. In T. P. Carpenter, J. M. Moser, & T. A. Ronberg (Eds.), *Addition and subtraction: A cognitive perspective* (pp. 136–155). Hillsdale, NJ: Lawrence Erlbaum Associates.

Resnick, L. B. (1984). Beyond error analysis: The role of understanding in elementary school arithmetic. In H. N. Cheek (Ed.), *Diagnostic and prescriptive mathematics: Issues, ideas and insights* (1984 Research Monograph, pp. 2–14). Kent, OH: Research Council for Diagnosis and Prescriptive Mathematics Research.

Restle, F. (1982). Coding theory as in integration of Gestalt psychology and information processing theory. In J. Beck (Ed.), *Organization and representation in perception.* Hillsdale, NJ: Lawrence Erlbaum Associates.

Ronning, R., Glover, J., Conoley, J. C., & Witt, J. (Eds.). (in press). *The influence of cognitive psychology on testing and measurement: The Buros-Nebraska Symposium on measurement and testing* (Vol 3.) Hillsdale, NJ: Lawrence Erlbaum Associates.

Riley, M. S., Greeno, J. G., & Heller, J. I. (1983). Development of children's problem-solving ability in arithmetic. In H. P. Ginsburg (Ed.), *The development of mathematical thinking* (pp. 153–196). New York: Academic Press.

Rindskopf, D. (1987). Using latent class analysis to test developmental models. *Developmental Review, 7,* 66–85.

Rips, L. J. (1984). Reasoning as a central intellective ability. In R. J. Sternberg (Ed.), *Advances in the psychology of human intelligence: Vol. 2* (pp. 105–148). Hillsdale, NJ: Lawrence Erlbaum Associates.

Robinson, C. S., & Hayes, J. R. (1978). Making inferences about relevance in understanding problems. In R. Revlin & R. E. Mayer (Eds.). *Human reasoning* (pp. 195–206). Washington, DC: V. H. Winston.

Rocklin, T., & O'Donnell, A. M. (in press). Self-adaptive testing: A performance improving variant of computerized adaptive testing. *Journal of Educational Psychology.*

Rogosa, D. A. (1980). A critique of cross-lagged correlation. *Psychological Bulletin, 88,* 245–258.

Rorty, R. (1979). *Philosophy and the mirror of nature.* Princeton, NJ: Princeton University Press.

Rosch, E. R., & Mervis, C. B. (1975). Family resemblances: Studies in the internal structure of categories. *Cognitive Psychology, 7,* 573–605.

Rose, A. M. (1974). *Human information processing: An assessment and research battery* (Tech. Rep. No. 46). Ann Arbor, MI: University of Michigan, Human Performance Center.

Rose, A. M. (1980). Information-processing abilities. In R. E. Snow, P-A. Federico, & W. E. Montague (Eds.), *Aptitude, learning, and instruction: Vol 1. Cognitive process analyses of aptitude* (pp. 65–86). Hillsdale, NJ: Lawrence Erlbaum Associates.

Rose, A. M. & Fernandes, K. (1977, November). *An information pro-*

cessing approach to performance assessment: I. Experimental investigation of an information processing performance battery (Tech. Rep. No. AIR-58500-TR). Washington, DC: American Institutes for Research.

Rosnick, P., & Clement, J. (1980). Learning without understanding: The effect of tutoring strategies on algebra misconceptions. *Journal of Mathematical Behavior, 3,* 3–24.

Rouse, W. B., & Morris, N. M. (1986). On looking into the black box: Prospects and limits in the search for mental models. *Psychological Bulletin, 100,* 349–363.

Royer, F. L. (1971). Information processing of visual figures in the digit symbol substitution task. *Journal of Experimental Psychology, 87,* 335–342.

Rumelhart, D. E. (1977). *An introduction to human information processing.* New York: John Wiley & Sons.

Rumelhart, D. E. (1980). *Understanding understanding.* (Tech. Rep. 8101). San Diego: University of California, Center for Human Information Processing.

Rumelhart, D. E., McClelland, J. L., & the PDP Research Group. (1986). *Parallel distributed processing: Vol 1. Foundations.* Cambridge, MA: MIT Press.

Rumelhart, D. E., & Norman, D. A. (1985). Representation of knowledge. In A. M. Aitkenhead & J. M. Slack (Eds.), *Issues in cognitive modeling* (pp. 15–62). Hillsdale, NJ: Lawrence Erlbaum Associates.

Ryes, R. E., Rybolt, J. F., Bestgen, B. J., & Wyatt, J. W. (1982). Processes used by good computational estimators. *Journal for Research in Mathematics Education, 13,* 183–201.

Ryle, G. (1949). *The concept of mind.* London: Hutchinson's University Library.

Sacks, O. (1985). *The man who mistook his wife for a hat.* New York: Summit Books.

Scardamalia, M., & Bereiter, C. (1986). Research on written composition. In M. C. Wittrock (Ed.), *Handbook of research on teaching* (3rd ed., pp. 778–803). New York: Macmillan.

Scarr, S. (1985). Constructing psychology: Making facts and fables for our times. *American Psychologist, 40,* 499–512.

Scarr, S., & Carter-Saltzman, L. (1982). Genetics and intelligence. In R. J. Sternberg (Ed.), *Handbook of human intelligence* (pp. 792–896). Cambridge: Cambridge University Press.

Schank, R. C., & Abelson, R. P. (1977). *Scripts, plans, goals, and understanding.* Hillsdale, NJ: Lawrence Erlbaum Associates.

Schmeck, R. R. (1983). Learning styles of college students. In R. F. Dillon & R. R. Schmeck (Eds.), *Individual differences in cognition: Vol. 1* (pp. 233–280). New York: Academic Press.

Schmitt, A. P., & Crocker, L. (1981, April). *Improving examinee performance on multiple-choice tests.* Paper presented at the meeting of the American Educational Research Association, Los Angeles.

Schneider, W., Demais, S. T., & Shiffrin, R. M. (1984). Automatic and control processing and attention. In R. Parasuraman & D. R. Davis (Eds.), *Varieties of attention* (pp. 1–27). New York: Academic Press.

Schneider, W., & Shiffrin, R. M. (1977). Controlled and automatic human information processing: I. Detection, search, and attention. *Psychological Review, 84,* 1–66.

Schorr, D., Bower, G. N., & Kiernan, R. (1982). Stimulus variables in the block design task. *Journal of Clinical and Consulting Psychology, 50,* 479–488.

Schwartz, S. (1984). *Measuring reading competence: A theoretical-prescriptive approach.* New York: Plenum.

Schwartz, S., Griffin, T. M., & Brown, J. (1983). Power and speed components of individual differences in letter matching. *Intelligence, 7,* 369–378.

Seibert, W. F., & Snow, R. E. (1965). *Studies in cine-psychometry I: Preliminary factor analysis of visual cognition and memory.* Lafayette, IN: Purdue University, Audio Visual Center.

Serafine, M. L. (1986). Music. In R. F. Dillon & R. J. Sternberg (Eds.), *Cognition and instruction* (pp. 299–341). New York: Academic Press.

Shavelson, R. J. (1972). Some aspects of the correspondence between content structure and cognitive structure in physics instruction. *Journal of Educational Psychology, 63,* 225–234.

Shepard, R. N., & Cooper, L. A. (1982). *Mental images and their transformation.* Cambridge, MA: MIT Press.

Shepard, R. N., & Feng, C. (1972). A chronometric study of mental paper folding. *Cognitive Psychology, 3,* 228–243.

Shepard, R. N., & Metzler, J. (1971). Mental rotation of three-dimensional objects. *Science, 171,* 701–703.

Shulman, L. S., & Sykes, G. (1986). *A national board for teaching: In search of a bold standard.* Unpublished paper, Stanford University, School of Education, Stanford.

Siegler, R. S. (1976). Three aspects of cognitive development. *Cognitive Psychology, 8,* 481–520.

Siegler, R. S. (1986). *Children's thinking.* Englewood Cliffs, NJ: Prentice-Hall.

Simon, H. A. (1979). *Models of thought.* New Haven, CT: Yale University Press.

Simon, H. A. (1980). Problem solving and education. In D. T. Tuma & F. Reif (Eds.), *Problem solving and education: Issues in teaching and research* (pp. 81–96). Hillsdale, NJ: Lawrence Erlbaum.

Simon, H. A. (1981). Otto Selz and information processing psychology. In N. Frijda & A. D. DeGroot (Eds.), *Otto Selz: His contribution to psychology* (pp. 147–163). The Hague, The Netherlands: Mouton.

Simon, H. A. & Kotovsky, K. (1963). Human acquisition of concepts for sequential patterns. *Psychological Review, 70,* 534–546.

Sloboda, J. A. (1985, January). *An exceptional musical memory.* Paper presented at the meeting of the Experimental Psychology Society, London.

Smith, I. M. (1964). *Spatial ability.* San Diego: Knapp.

Snow, R. E. (1978). Theory and method for research on aptitude processes. *Intelligence, 2,* 225–278.

Snow, R. E. (1980a). Aptitude and achievement. *New Directions for Testing and Measurement, 5,* 39–59.

Snow, R. E. (1980b). Aptitude processes. In R. E. Snow, P-A. Federico, & W. E. Montague (Eds.), *Aptitude, learning, and instruction: Vol. 1. Cognitive process analyses of aptitude* (pp. 27–64). Hillsdale, NJ: Lawrence Erlbaum Associates.

Snow, R. E. (1981). Toward a theory of aptitude for learning: Fluid and crystallized abilities and their correlates. In M. P. Friedman, J. P. Das, & N. O'Connor (Eds.), *Intelligence and learning* (pp. 345–362), New York: Plenum.

Snow, R. E. (1982). Education and intelligence. In R. J. Sternberg (Ed.), *Handbook of human intelligence* (pp. 493–585). Cambridge: Cambridge University Press.

Snow, R. E. (1983). Aptitude Theory. Presidential address to Division 15, American Psychological Association, Washington, D.C.

Snow, R. E., Bethell-Fox, C. E., & Seibert, W. F. (1985). *Studies in cine-psychometry.* (Technical Report). Stanford, CA: Stanford University, Aptitude Research Project, School of Education.

Snow, R. E., & Farr, M. J. (Eds.). (1987). *Aptitude, learning, and instruction: Vol. 3. Conative and affective process analyses.* Hillsdale, NJ: Lawrence Erlbaum Associates.

Snow, R. E., Federico, P-A., & Montague, W. E. (Eds.). (1980a). *Aptitudes, learning, and instruction: Vol 1. Cognitive process analyses of aptitude.* Hillsdale, NJ: Lawrence Erlbaum Associates.

Snow, R. E., Federico, P-A., & Montague, W. E. (Eds.). (1980b). *Aptitude, learning, and instruction: Vol. 2. Cognitive process analyses of learning and problem-solving.* Hillsdale, NJ: Lawrence Erlbaum Associates.

Snow, R. E., Kyllonen, P. C., & Marshalek, B. (1984). The topography of ability and learning correlations. In R. J. Sternberg (Ed.), *Advances in the psychology of human intelligence: Vol. 2* (pp. 47–104). Hillsdale, NJ: Lawrence Erlbaum Associates.

Snow, R. E., & Lohman, D. F. (1984). Toward a theory of cognitive aptitude for learning from instruction. *Journal of Educational Psychology, 76,* 347–376.

Snow, R. E., & Peterson, P. (1985). Cognitive analyses of tests: Implications for redesign. In S. E. Embretson (Eds.), *Test design: Developments in psychology and psychometrics* (pp. 149–166). New York: Academic Press.

Somerville, S. C., & Hartley, J. L. (1986). Art. In R. F. Dillon & R. J. Sternberg (Eds.), *Cognition and instruction* (pp. 241–298) New York: Academic Press.

Spada, H. (n.d.). *Knowledge acquisition and knowledge application in solving ecological problems.* Unpublished report, University of Freiburg, Psychological Institute, Federal Republic of Germany.

Spearman, C. E. (1927). *The abilities of man.* London: Macmillan.

Spearman, C., & Wynn-Jones, L. L. (1950). *Human ability.* London: Macmillan.

Sperling, G. A. (1960). The information available in brief visual presentation. *Psychological Monographs, 74,* Whole No. 498.

Spiro, R. J., & Myers, A. (1984). Individual differences and underlying cognitive processes. In P. D. Pearson, R. Bar, M. L. Kamil, & P. Mosenthal (Eds.), *Handbook of reading research* (pp. 471–501). New York: Longman.

Sternberg, R. J. (1977). *Intelligence, information processing, and analogical reasoning: The componential analysis of human abilities.* Hillsdale, NJ: Lawrence Erlbaum Associates.

Sternberg, R. J. (1980). Sketch of a componential subtheory of human intelligence. *Behavioral and Brain Sciences, 3,* 573–614.

Sternberg, R. J. (1981). Testing and cognitive psychology. *American Psychologist, 36,* 1187–1189.

Sternberg, R. J. (Ed.). (1982a). *Advances in the psychology of human intelligence: Vol. 1.* Hillsdale, NJ: Lawrence Erlbaum Associates.

Sternberg, R. J. (Ed.). (1982b). *Handbook of human intelligence.* Cambridge: Cambridge University Press.

Sternberg, R. J. (1982c). Reasoning, problem solving, and intelligence. In R. J. Sternberg (Ed.), *Handbook of human intelligence.* Cambridge: Cambridge University Press.

Sternberg, R. J. (Ed.). (1984a). *Advances in the psychology of human intelligence: Vol. 2.* Hillsdale, NJ: Lawrence Erlbaum Associates.

Sternberg, R. J. (Ed.). (1984b). *Mechanisms of cognitive development.* San Francisco: W. H. Freeman.

Sternberg, R. J. (1984c). What cognitive psychology can (and cannot) do for test development. In B. S. Plake (Ed.), *Social and technical issues in testing: Implications for test construction and usage* (pp. 39–60). Hillsdale, NJ: Lawrence Erlbaum Associates.

Sternberg, R. J. (1985a). *Beyond IQ: A triarchic theory of human intelligence.* Cambridge: Cambridge University Press.

Sternberg, R. J. (1985b). Cognitive approaches to intelligence. In B. B. Wolman (Ed.), *Handbook of intelligence: Theories, measurements, and applications* (pp. 59–118). New York: John Wiley & Sons, Wiley-Interscience.

Sternberg, R. J. (Ed.). (1986). *Advances in the psychology of human intelligence: Vol. 3.* Hillsdale, NJ: Lawrence Erlbaum Associates.

Sternberg, R. J., & Gardner, M. K. (1983). Unities in inductive reasoning. *Journal of Experimental Psychology: General, 112,* 80–116.

Sternberg, R. J., & McNamara, T. P. (1985). The representation and processing of information in real-time verbal comprehension. In S. E. Embretson (Ed.), *Test design: Developments in psychology and psychometrics* (pp. 21–43). New York: Academic Press.

Sternberg, R. J., & Powell, J. S. (1983). Comprehending verbal comprehension. *American Psychologist, 38,* 878–893.

Sternberg, R. J., Powell, J. S., & Kaye, D. B. (1983). Teaching vocabulary-building skills: A contextual approach. In A. C. Wilkinson (Ed.), *Classroom computers and cognitive science* (pp. 121–143). New York: Academic Press.

Sternberg, R. J., & Rifkin, B. (1979). The development of analogical reasoning processes. *Journal of Experimental Child Psychology, 27,* 195–232.

Sternberg, R. J., & Weil, E. M. (1980). An aptitude-strategy interaction in linear syllogistic reasoning. *Journal of Educational Psychology, 72,* 226–234.

Sternberg, S. (1969). Memory-scanning: Mental processes revealed by reaction time experiments. *American Scientist, 57,* 421–457.

Sternberg, S. (1975). Memory-scanning: New findings and current controversies. *Quarterly Journal of Experimental Psychology, 27,* 1–32.

Stevens, A. L., & Collins, A. (1980). Multiple conceptual models of a complex system. In R. E. Snow, P-A. Federico, & W. E. Montague (Eds.). *Aptitude, learning, and instruction: Vol 2. Cognitive process analyses of learning and problem solving.* (pp. 177–197). Hillsdale, NJ: Lawrence Erlbaum Associates.

Sutton, C. R. (1980). The learner's prior knowledge: A critical review of techniques for probing its organization. *European Journal of Science Education, 2,* 107–120.

Tatsuoka, K. K., & Baillie, R. (1982). *Rule space, the product space of two score components in signed-number subtraction: An approach to dealing with inconsistent use of erroneous rules* (Research Report No. 82-3-ONR). Urbana, IL: University of Illinois, Computer-based Education Research Laboratory.

Taylor, D. A. (1976). Stage analysis of reaction time. *Psychological Bulletin, 83,* 161–191.

Terman, L. M. (1916). *The measurement of intelligence.* Boston: Houghton Mifflin.

Thro, M. P. (1978). Relationships between associative and content structure of physics concepts. *Journal of Educational Psychology, 70,* 971–978.

Thurstone, L. L. (1938a). The perceptual factor. *Psychometrika, 3,* 1–12.

Thurstone, L. L. (1938b). Primary mental abilities. *Psychometric Monographs, 1.*

Thurstone, L. L. (1944). *A factorial study of perception.* Chicago: University of Chicago Press.

Thurstone, L. L. (1951). *An analysis of mechanical aptitude* (Report No. 62). Chicago, IL: University of Chicago, Psychometric Laboratory.

Tinkelman, S. N. (1971). Planning the objective test. In R. L. Thorndike (Ed.), *Educational measurement* (2nd ed., pp. 46–80). Washington, DC: American Council on Education.

Tolman, E. C. (1932). *Purposive behavior in animals and men.* New York: Appleton-Century-Crofts.

Trabasso, T. (1977). The role of memory as a system in making transitive inference. In R. V. Kail & J. W. Hagen (Eds.), *Perspectives on the development of memory and cognition* (pp. 333–366). Hillsdale, NJ: Lawrence Erlbaum Associates.

Tulving, E. (1972). Episodic and semantic memory. In E. Tulving & W. Donaldson, (Eds.), *Organization of memory* (pp. 381–403). New York: Academic Press.

Underwood, B. J. (1975). Individual differences as a crucible in theory construction. *American Psychologist, 30,* 128–140.

Undheim, J. O. (1981a). On intelligence I: Broad ability factors in 15-year-old children and Cattell's theory of fluid and crystallized intelligence. *Scandinavian Journal of Psychology, 22,* 171–179.

Undheim, J. O. (1981b). On intelligence II: A neo-Spearman model to replace Cattell's theory of fluid and crystallized intelligence. *Scandinavian Journal of Psychology, 22,* 181–187.

Undheim, J. O. (1981c). On intelligence III: Examining developmental implications of Cattell's broad ability theory and of an alternative neo-Spearman model. *Scandinavian Journal of Psychology, 22,* 243-249.

Undheim, J. O. (1981d). On intelligence IV: Toward a restoration of general intelligence. *Scandinavian Journal of Psychology, 22,* 251–256.

Vandenberg, S. G., & Kruse, A. R. (1978). Mental rotations: Group test of three-dimensional spatial visualization. *Perceptual and Motor Skills, 47,* 599–604.

van Daalen-Kapteijns, M. M., & Elshout-Mohr, M. (1981). The acquisition of word meanings as a cognitive learning process. *Journal of Verbal Learning and Verbal Behavior, 20,* 386–399.

van Dijk, T. A., & Kintsch, W. (1983). *Strategies of discourse comprehension.* New York: Academic Press.

Vernon, P. E. (1950). *The structure of human abilities.* London: Methuen.

Voss, J. F. (1986). Social studies. In R. F. Dillon & R. J. Sternberg, (Eds.)., *Cognition and instruction* (pp. 205–298). New York: Academic Press.

Voss, J. F., Greene, T. R., Post, T. A., & Penner, B. C. (1983). Problem solving skills in the social sciences. In G. Bower (Ed.), *The psychology of learning and motivation: Advances in research and theory: Vol. 17* (pp. 165–213). New York: Academic Press.

Voss, J. F., Tyler, S., & Yengo, L. (1983). Individual differences in solving social science problems. In R. F. Dillon & R. R. Schmeck (Eds.), *Individual differences in cognition,* Vol. 1 (pp. 205–232). New York: Academic Press.

Vygotsky, L. S. (1978). *Mind in society: The development of higher psychological processes.* Cambridge, MA: Harvard University Press.

Wagner, R. K., & Sternberg, R. J. (1984). Alternative conceptions of intelligence and their implications for education. *Review of Educational Research, 54,* 179–224.

Ward, W. C. (1973). *Individual differences in information processing units* (Research Bulletin No 73-70). Princeton, NJ: Educational Testing Service.

Ward, W. C. (1986). Measurement research that will change test design for the future. In E. E. Freeman (Ed.), *The redesign of testing for the 21st century* (pp. 25–34). Princeton, NJ: Educational Testing Service.

Weinstein, C. E. (1978). Elaboration skills as a learning strategy. In H. F. O'Neil, Jr. (Ed.), *Learning strategies* (pp. 31–55). New York: Academic Press.

Weiss, D. (1982). *Robustness of adaptive testing to error in item parameter estimates and to multidimensionality.* Paper presented at the meeting of the Item Response Theory and Computerized Adaptive Testing Conference, Minneapolis.

Werner, H., & Kaplan, E. (1952). The acquisition of word meanings: A developmental study. *Monographs of the Society for Research in Child Development* (No. 51).

West, L. H. T., & Pines, A. L. (Eds.). (1985). *Cognitive structure and conceptual change.* New York: Academic Press.

Whitely, S. E. (1976). Solving verbal analogies: Some cognitive components of intelligence test items. *Journal of Educational Psychology, 68,* 234–242.

Whitely, S. E. (1980). Modeling aptitude test validity from cognitive components. *Journal of Educational Psychology, 72,* 750–769.

Whitely, S. E., & Barnes, G. M. (1979). The implication of processing event sequences for theories of analogical reasoning. *Memory & Cognition, 7*(4), 323–331.

Wijnen, W. H. S. W., & Snow, R. E. (1975). Implementation and evaluation of a system for medical education (Tech. Rep. No. 1). Maastricht, The Netherlands: Medical Faculty.

Willerman, L., Horn, J. M., & Loehlin, J. C. (1977). The aptitude-achievement test distinction: A study of unrelated children reared together. *Behavior Genetics, 7,* 465–470.

Winograd, T. (1972). Understanding natural language. *Cognitive Psychology, 3,* 1–191.

Winograd, T. (1975). Frames and the declarative-procedural controversy. In D. G. Bobrow & A. Collins (Eds.), *Representation and understanding: Studies in cognitive science* (pp. 185–210). New York: Academic Press.

Wolf, T. H. (1973). *Alfred Binet.* Chicago: University of Chicago Press.

Woodworth, R. S. (1938). *Experimental psychology.* New York: Henry Holt.

Wundt, W. (1911). *Grundzüge der physiologischen Psychologie* [Foundations of physiological psychology.] Leipzig: Verlag vom Wilhelm Engelmolmm.

2

Construction, Administration, and Scoring

8

The Specification and Development of Tests of Achievement and Ability

Jason Millman and Jennifer Greene

Cornell University

This chapter is about making tests. It is directed to the professional test constructor, not to the classroom teacher. Our goal is to emphasize options for specifying and developing tests, not to produce a procedural manual.

This single chapter has the primary responsibility for the topics found in seven chapters of the second edition of *Educational Measurement*.[1] Readers are encouraged to consult those chapters for details of the topics not fully presented here. In condensing the coverage of the earlier volume, we imposed a mysterious blend of criteria that included the importance of the topic, the degree to which the state of the art has changed, and the match to our interests and areas of competence.

Attention is limited to tests of achievement and aptitude having right (or better) answers and wrong (or worse) answers. For the most part, the discussion is confined to technical matters, although we appreciate the importance of such factors as the cost, the consequences of an incorrect decision or inference, and the political and organizational milieu in which test planning and development take place.

The sequence of topics is traditional. The discussion begins with the purposes of tests, because the way in which a test is built depends so much upon its use. Even the cost of the disposal of used test copy depends on test purpose, a point made again at the very end of this chapter.

Next, possible elements of a test plan are considered. Many of these topics are treated in more detail later in this and other chapters of this volume.

Attention is then drawn to the items themselves, to types of items and how they can be written. An *item* is viewed in the broadest sense, as any task or series of tasks presented to exa-

minees. Ways of thinking about types of items are suggested, rather than recounting and illustrating their varieties still one more time. Consequently, certain important methods of testing are given short shrift, and some methods are not mentioned at all (e.g., oral examinations and self-assessments). Item-writing approaches are discussed; some rules of thumb of item writing are summarized.

The evaluation and selection of items are examined next. Techniques and concerns that stemmed from the interest in criterion-referenced measurement and competency testing are stressed. Item response theory and methods are excluded, because they are treated elsewhere in the volume.

The chapter concludes with a brief section on putting the items together into a test.

Test Purposes

The first and most important step in educational test development is to delineate the purpose of the test or the nature of the inferences intended from test scores. A clear statement of purpose provides the test developer with an overall framework for test specification and for item development, tryout, and review. A clear statement of test purpose also contributes significantly to appropriate test use in practical contexts. According to the *Standards for Educational and Psychological Tests* (American Psychological Association [APA], American Educational Research Association & National Council on Measurement in Education, 1985), it is the test developers' responsibility "to anticipate how their tests will be used and

---

[1] Defining and assessing educational objectives; planning the objective test; writing the test item; gathering, analyzing, and using data on test items; reproducing the test; performance and product evaluation; and essay examinations.

misused . . . and to design tests and accompanying materials in ways that promote proper use" (p. 3–1). The *Standards* constitute an additional and important guide for proper test development and use.

Descriptive Classification of Test Purposes

The measurement literature is replete with breakdowns and classifications of the purposes of educational achievement and ability tests. These classifications typically emphasize differences among the various kinds of educational decisions in which test scores play a role. For example, Mehrens and Lehmann (1984) suggest that educational tests are used for (a) instructional decisions such as diagnosis and grading; (b) guidance decisions in occupational, educational, and personal domains; (c) administrative decisions such as selection, classification, and curriculum planning; and (d) research-related decisions. Gronlund (1981) offers four evaluative decision settings for educational tests: placement, formative, diagnostic, and summative. This is similar to Bloom, Hastings, and Madaus's (1971) distinctions among tests used for initial evaluation (diagnosis, placement), formative evaluation (prescription), and summative evaluation (attainment).

A widely accepted typology of testing purposes, however, remains elusive, largely because educational tests serve so many different functions in so many varied settings. In addition, achievement and ability tests, which comprise the two major classes of educational tests, are conceptually different but often not functionally so, in that both kinds of tests are commonly used for the same purpose. This functional overlap between achievement and ability tests also blurs the lines of classification systems. With this functional perspective, Table 8.1 presents a descriptive classification of test purposes. This description distinguishes among three major educational decision settings (the table columns), characterized in terms of the relevant domain to which test-score inferences will be made. Within each decision setting, desired inferences are further

differentiated as descriptive or mastery information for individual examinees or descriptive information for groups (the table rows).

The key distinction among the three major decision settings is the *source* of content definition for the domain to be tested and, thus, for the domain of inference as well. That is, curricular, cognitive, and criterion decision settings represent different sources of test content and different uses of test inferences, rather than different content per se. Testing in the curricular domain is directly linked to specific, identifiable curricula. In the cognitive domain, testing is linked to theories of mental abilities and functioning, and, in the criterion domain, it is linked to analyses of the requirements for successful criterion performance. Thus, a test of critical thinking skills would be classified dependent on its source of domain definition and inference. If this test were intended to assess examinees' performance vis-à-vis a specific critical thinking skills curriculum, it would be placed in the curricular decision setting. If intended to measure examinees' status with respect to a particular theoretical conceptualization of critical thinking skills, it would be placed in the cognitive-decision setting. And, if intended to measure the critical thinking skills judged or found to be important in another setting, it would be placed in the criterion decision setting. This distinction is expanded in the discussion that follows.

INFERENCES TO A CURRICULAR DOMAIN

In the first decision setting, tests are used to help make decisions about examinee performance with reference to an identified curricular domain. *Curricular domain* is defined here as the skills and knowledge intended or developed as a result of deliberate instruction on identifiable curricular content. These learnings can include the content taught, as well as transfer skills and curricular side effects. Within this definition, a curricular domain can range widely, from the target of a single unit of instruction (e.g., addition with carrying) to a broad component of a curriculum (e.g., basic computation

TABLE 8.1 Functional Description of Achievement and Ability Test Purposes

	DOMAIN TO WHICH INFERENCES WILL BE MADE				
	CURRICULAR DOMAIN				
TYPE OF INFERENCE DESIRED	BEFORE INSTRUCTION	DURING INSTRUCTION	AFTER INSTRUCTION	COGNITIVE DOMAIN	FUTURE CRITERION SETTING
Description of individual examinees' attainments	Placement	Diagnosis	Grading	Reporting (e.g., to parents)	Guidance and counseling
Mastery decision (above/below a cutoff for individual examinees)	Selection	Instructional guidance	Promotion	Certification Licensing	Selection Admission Licensing
Description of performance for a group or system	Pre-instruction status for research/ evaluation	Process and curriculum evaluation	Post-instruction status for research/evaluation Reporting (e.g., on effectiveness of instructional program)	Construct measurement for research/ evaluation Reporting (e.g., on educational achievement at state or national level)	Research

skills). A curricular domain is also likely to include both the acquisition of knowledge (achievement) and the development of cognitive processing skills (ability), as discussed more fully later. The key characteristic of a curricular domain is its direct link to instruction and curricula. Thus, all test inferences in this first decision setting concern the examinee's status with respect to the effectiveness of curricula and instruction.

Within this curricular decision setting, test purposes can be further differentiated by their timing with respect to instruction. Tests administered *before* instruction yield information on the degree to which examinees are already proficient in the relevant curricular domain prior to being taught. This information is useful instructionally for individual placement and selection decisions and for research and evaluation group "pretest" purposes. Tests administered *during* instruction yield information on examinee progress through the relevant curricular domain. This information is helpful for such instructional purposes as ongoing individual diagnosis and prescription and for such evaluation purposes as curricular and process evaluation. Tests administered *after* instruction yield information on examinee proficiency in the relevant curricular domain after being taught, information important for a variety of instructional and research and evaluation summative purposes.

INFERENCES TO A COGNITIVE DOMAIN

In the second decision setting, tests are used to generate inferences about examinee performance with reference to an identified cognitive domain. *Cognitive domain* is defined here as a circumscribed set of cognitive skills usually derived from theory, though also from practical contexts, but not from specific curricula or instruction. Like a curricular domain, a cognitive domain is likely to include both knowledge and skill or both achievement and ability components. Yet test-score inferences here pertain, not to examinee status with respect to an identified unit of instruction, but rather to areas of cognitive performance that are more indirectly or broadly related to learning. Test inferences in this domain emphasize examinee status vis-à-vis cognitive skills that *underlie or cut across* other domains, whereas inferences in the curricular domain emphasize examinee status vis-à-vis the cognitive skills that *define* a particular curricular unit.

For example, some tests of minimum-competency reference skills are considered essential for adult functioning, but they are not directly taught (the source of challenges to instructional validity of the results of such tests). That is, these skills are derived more from a theory or conceptualization of minimum adult competence than from identifiable curricula. As such, these tests are more appropriately considered within the cognitive than the curricular domain. Similarly, although inferences from certification tests can have instructional implications, these implications are often not curriculum specific but, rather, are linked to a cross-curriculum conceptualization of relevant skills and knowledge.

In short, cognitive domains come from theoretical conceptualizations of mental abilities and achievements rather than from the skills and knowledge defined by specific curricula. Probably most common in this cognitive domain setting is the use of general and specialized ability tests for research and evaluation purposes. For example, research on human factors specifically investigates interrelationships among examinee performance on batteries of ability tests. Another example is a test of spatial reasoning ability used as a covariate in an evaluation of videodisc learning. Also included in this decision setting are tests used for individual and group reporting purposes, including, again, some minimum competency and many large-scale assessment tests.

INFERENCES TO A FUTURE CRITERION SETTING

In the third and final decision setting, tests are used to help make decisions about expected individual examinee performance in a future criterion setting. *Criterion domain* is defined here as the knowledge, skills, and behaviors needed for successful performance in the criterion setting. The common purpose of criterion-related testing is to predict examinee performance in the future setting. Thus, inferences from criterion-related tests are predictive, and the instructional implications of these inferences are, at most, indirect. The most prevalent criterion settings for this kind of testing are educational, such as, expected performance in college or graduate school, and occupational, such as, expected performance in a given job. (Certification tests are placed in the second decision category because their purpose is more often to assess current examinee attainment of job-related competencies than to predict future on-the-job performance.)

Important Themes in This Test Purpose Classification

Several important themes characterize the classification of testing purposes offered in Table 8.1. *First,* this classification reflects a decision-oriented framework that emphasizes differences in the kinds of inferences to be made from test scores. This framework underscores the importance of the match between the intended purpose and the actual use of a test in generating accurate and credible inferences. *Second,* test purposes related to inferences about examinee performance in reference to a curricular domain comprise the most detailed category in this classification system. This suggests that the most prevalent uses of educational tests are to help make decisions about examinee status with respect to specific curricula, the effectiveness of deliberate instruction on such curricula, or both. *Third,* the relevant domain for all three categories of test-score inferences was defined to include both the acquisition of knowledge (achievement) and the development of cognitive processing skills (ability), highlighting the functional interrelatedness of achievement and ability in practical measurement contexts. Although a comprehensive discussion of the distinctions between these two constructs is beyond the scope of this chapter (see Cole, 1984; Gagné, 1984; Glaser, 1984; D. R. Green, 1974; Messick, 1984; Schrader, 1980; Snow & Lohman, 1984; Sternberg, 1984), brief conceptual definitions will help to clarify this overlap of function and, thus, of test purpose.

Within recent advances in cognitive theory, achievement is conceptualized as the amount and nature of knowledge an individual has acquired about a specific subject area, the way in which this knowledge is organized or structured, and the functional uses an individual can make of this knowledge structure, for example, to solve problems, to think creatively, to evaluate the merit of competing arguments, and to continue learning about this subject area (Messick, 1984). This conceptualization is clearly not process free, just as the operating conceptualization of ability is not content free. As suggested by Glaser (1984), the development of such cognitive processes as reasoning and problem solving interacts strongly with the development and utilization of organized bodies of conceptual and procedural knowledge (or knowledge structures). In Snow's emerging aptitude theory (Snow & Lohman, 1984), aptitude implies prediction in a particular environmental context (or educational treatment, including subject matter content); hence, describing that context is part of defining aptitude. Thus, in current cognitive theories, ability is conceptualized as a set of relatively stable, generic processes, developed over time through learning experiences, that an individual uses to identify, organize, plan, strategize, monitor, automate, and evaluate her or his learning performance in a given situation.

Paraphrasing from Cole (1984), the significant implications of these conceptualizations include the following: (a) The ultimate goals of education can be described as the development of both achievement and ability; (b) both constructs include high-level cognitive activities and build upon lower ones; (c) both arise through learning, often over a substantial period of time; (d) achievement and ability are intricately interrelated because the development of one is iteratively contingent upon the development of the other; (e) achievement and ability should be intertwined in educational practice, and they will be intermixed in educational measurement.

An Example of the Role of Test Purpose in Test Development

To reinforce the key role of intended test purpose in test development, the following illustration is offered. A test is needed by a large school district to evaluate the strengths and weaknesses of its instructional program in mathematics. Program level, rather than individual student performance information, is desired. Given this purpose, test content should cover not only the learning objectives represented by the district's curriculum, but also potential, and perhaps unanticipated, outcomes. Knowledge and skills should be measured not only by using question types employed during instruction, but also by other means. This requirement for a wide range of item content and format needs to be balanced against the requirement for in-depth measurement of specific program strengths and weaknesses. These substantive requirements further need to be balanced against such practical test-administration factors as the time the district is willing to allocate to this mathematics testing.

These needs can all be accommodated to some extent by administering different items to different students, a test-administration scheme made reasonable because of the intention to derive test scores for groups, not for individual students. Test booklets, representing different subsets of items, should also be randomly assigned, so that the different items will be administered to comparable students. Given the absence of individual student scores and the subsequent decision making based on them, the collection of items answered by any particular student need not be representative of the domain. Individual items should be included primarily for their content, and the total collection of items should appropriately sample the domain. Scoring in this example would be by learner objectives.

In short, decisions about item content and type, item selection, test administration and scoring, and other aspects of test development all depend on a test's purpose. Moreover, these test-development decisions are interdependent and rely on skillful balancing of diverse considerations. These considerations are addressed more fully in the next section.

Test Specification

With purpose(s) clarified, the next logical step in test construction is to specify important attributes of the test. The major function of this step is, quite simply, to enhance the ultimate validity of test-score inferences. Derived directly from the designated purpose of the test, the specification of test attributes provides a guide to subsequent item development, tryout, evaluation, selection, and assembly. This direct grounding of developmental activities in test purpose helps to insure the congruence between intended and actual test-score inferences and, thus, the validity of the latter.

Foremost among the attributes of a test requiring specification is its content. Other important attributes include item types and psychometric characteristics, scoring criteria and procedures, and number of items to be developed. Again, the interdependence of these test-development decisions should be emphasized, such as in the careful matching of item format to test content. Of comparable importance to these internal decisions about test attributes are the mitigating influences of external contextual factors related to conditions of test administration. In most test settings, the most important of these external factors are the practical or psychological constraints on available testing time. Other external factors include characteristics of the examinee population, individual versus group administration, and standardization. These internal and external factors are reflected in a list of test-development questions presented in Table 8.2.

The key to successful test planning and development is thus the skillful balancing of these diverse and often conflicting demands on test content and form. The proficient test developer must decide what is discretionary and what cannot be compromised, determinations made largely on the basis of intended test purpose.

In this section, external contextual factors related to conditions of test administration are briefly presented, followed by a discussion of internal test-attribute specification. The particular influences of the external factors on internal test-development decisions will also be noted, as appropriate. This section on test specification then concludes with the consideration of specificity in test planning, the need for external test-plan validation, and the role of iteration in test development.

TABLE 8.2 Some Questions to be Addressed in a Test Development Plan

External Contextual Factors

What is the purpose of the test?
Who will be taking the test?
How much testing time is available?
How shall the test be administered?

Internal Test Attributes

What will the test cover?

What sources of content will be used?
What is the desired dimensionality of the content?
How specific or broad will the domain of inferences be?
How will the items be distributed among content components?

What types of item formats will be used?
How many items will be produced?
What psychometric characteristics *of the items* are desired?
How will the items be evaluated and selected?
How will the test items be arranged, sequenced and reproduced?
How will the items/test be scored?
What psychometric properties *of the test* are desired?

Further Considerations

How specific will be the test development plan itself?
How shall the test development plan be validated?
Who shall carry out the test development steps, following what time schedule, and using what resources?

External Contextual Factors

Embedded in the delineation of test purpose is a determination of the test setting or the required conditions of test administration. These conditions generally represent contextual boundaries or constraints within which the final test must fit. Thus, they often imply compromises with the theoretically or psychometrically based "ideal" specification of internal test attributes. The most important of these contextual factors are noted next.

CHARACTERISTICS OF THE EXAMINEE POPULATION

In the realms of achievement and ability testing, the most important characteristics of the intended examinee population are obviously their cognitive skills and knowledge. For a given test purpose, conceptualization and operationalization of these characteristics are the essence of the process of specifying the internal attributes of the test. For a given test setting, however, this specification must take into account both noncognitive and cognitive examinee characteristics that fall outside the identified boundaries of test purpose and content but that could constrain or confound examinees' demonstrations of performance within these boundaries. Examples of these characteristics include level of cognitive development, attention span, handicapping conditions such as physical inability to write, native language and culture, and reading proficiency. The last two are of particular importance to tests that must be read but that are not intended to measure reading. As suggested, what is considered a constraining or confounding characteristic depends entirely on the test purpose.

Careful consideration of these "external" examinee characteristics can imply minor or, in some cases, wholesale modifications to internal test-attribute specification and subsequent item development. As an example of a minor modification, a test intended for examinees with short attention spans (e.g., very young or hyperactive children) might have to be reduced in length or segmented into several separate administrations. To illustrate a major modification, a test of mechanical reasoning intended for a population that includes non-English-speaking examinees might have to be limited to items and responses that do not require the use of English. As another example, by relying heavily on lengthy verbal descriptions of life situations that the examinee must first read and understand, some existing high school graduation tests thoroughly confound examinees' reading proficiency and ability to follow directions with their life skills or functional literacy.

TIME CONSTRAINTS

Limits on the time available for testing arise from both examinee characteristics, as noted, and, more commonly, practical characteristics of the test setting, such as permissible interruptions in the school day. Where speed of response is not part of the domain being tested, these time constraints often conflict directly with internal requirements for valid, reliable test results. This conflict is most acute in terms of the number of items needed versus the time available for testing. As articulated by Thorndike (1982), "[t]he pressure for brevity in testing is real. But the pressure for precision in test appraisals is equally real, and the test maker is in a perennial conflict between producing a test that is brief enough to be acceptable to users and creating one that provides accurate enough information to permit useful decisions" (1982, p. 15).

The sources of this pressure for precision, however, vary considerably with test purpose. For example, a relatively large number of items might be specified for a test intended to yield reliable results for each of several dimensions of a multifaceted domain. A similarly large number of items might be specified for a unidimensional test yielding just one score but also intended to precisely measure each examinee's ability. These different test purposes suggest different responses to external time constraints such as dropping one dimension or changing item formats in the first instance and administering the test adaptively in the second. Thus, although time constraints are a nearly universal problem in test development, responses to these constraints are purpose specific.

GROUP VERSUS INDIVIDUAL TEST ADMINISTRATION

For reasons of practicality and efficiency, most tests have to be administered to groups of examinees rather than to examinees individually. Group administration permits no interaction between examinee and examiner or use of extensive or elaborate hands-on equipment or stimuli, thus precluding items requiring such interaction or stimuli. Group administration also requires that the directions to examinees be clear and easy to follow, thereby limiting the number and nature of items and accompanying directions. The use of too many item types or of items with especially complicated directions can introduce unwanted sources of error into resulting test scores.

The major practical considerations in individual test administration are the training and expertise required of the examiner. It is especially advantageous to administer items individually when they require personal interaction, the manipulation of stimuli, or ongoing decisions about scoring and which items to present next. Such items, however, also require carefully trained examiners. Thus, for many individually administered tests, the test constructor is also responsible for developing appropriate test-administration training procedures and materials, and for developing proficiency criteria. In this context, technological advances in computerized testing are creating expanded opportunities for individualized and adaptive testing that substitute for the resource costs of highly trained examiners those associated with testing by computer.

STANDARDIZATION

A standardized test is one for which the conditions of administration and the scoring procedures are designed to be the same in all uses of the test. The conditions of administration include the physical test setting, the directions to examinees, the test materials, and the time factors. Scoring procedures include both derivation and transformation of raw scores. The psychometric value of standardization is the reduction of variations in, and thus error arising from, administration conditions and scoring practices. The practical value of standardization is its appeal to, and credibility among, many test users. Because of these values, standardization represents good measurement practice for all tests and test purposes and, thus, should be included as part of test specification and development. Again, computerized testing advances represent opportunities for improved standardization and a concomitant reduction of unwanted sources of error, though (like many innovations) they might introduce new error sources such as confounding with eye–hand coordination and with variations in hardware and software equipment.

Internal Test Attributes

It is within the external context of test administration conditions that specification of internal test attributes is conducted. Although all testing situations do not require decisions about each attribute, it behooves the careful test constructor to review all attributes and determine the relevance of each to a particular testing situation. This will help ensure that all important components of the test have been adequately considered.

TEST CONTENT

For many test situations, the stated purpose of the test provides broad identification of test content; for example, to measure junior high science achievement, to assess decoding ability in reading, to determine ability to succeed academically in college, to evaluate the achievement of participants in an experimental biology curriculum. For test development purposes, such broad identifications need considerable elaboration. What specific areas of subject matter should be included? Which uses of a knowledge structure should be assessed? Which cognitive planning, monitoring, and evaluative processes are relevant to this learning situation? Which subject areas, knowledge uses, and cognitive processes warrant greatest emphasis in the test and which are less important? Answers to these questions can be attained through careful consideration of the following five substantive characteristics of test content. Such specification of test content should provide clear delineation of the domain to be assessed within the boundaries outlined by test purpose and context.

Sources of test content. The specification of test content begins with determination of the appropriate source for this content. As noted previously, this determination depends wholly on test purpose, that is, on the decision setting or domain to which test-score inferences will be made.

For tests intended as aids in curricular decisions, the appropriate source of content is the specific educational curricula relevant to that testing situation. This content is commonly represented in statements of specific objectives, curricular outlines, textbooks, and other instructional materials. Within this curricular domain, the particular sources that should be consulted depend on additional elements of the test purpose, specifically its geographic scope and its timing with respect to instruction. *Geographic scope* refers to whether the test is intended for local, state, regional, or national use. The curricular sources consulted should adequately reflect and represent the designated geographic scope. The instructional timing factor is most relevant to tests intended to assess mastery of a previous curriculum as an aid in determining placement in a future curriculum. In specifying the content for such tests, both curricula should be consulted.

For example, the content specification of a world history test intended for national use should adequately represent the varying history curricula used throughout the country. A common procedure for achieving this representativeness is to base test content on a synthesis of the dozen or so most frequently used textbooks. For an individual state's high school proficiency examinations, the content of a world history test need only adequately represent that one state's history curricula. Further, if the test is intended to be used for placement or selection, such as for an upper level high school or introductory college history course series, the specification of test content should also include consideration of the knowledge and applications most relevant to future learning in history. In contrast, with a test whose purpose is solely summative, for example, to grade, only the content of the curriculum followed is relevant.

However, in deriving test content from specific curricula, particularly for local tests, the test developer should keep in mind the more general issues of scope and depth of coverage. Results from a test based solely on the content of a specific local curriculum require careful interpretation within the larger educational context. That is, one needs always to ask whether or not the content of a given curriculum is sufficiently representative of such curricula in general, in terms of coverage. If not, these limitations should be revealed, not masked, by the test.

For tests intended to generate inferences about examinee performance vis-à-vis an identified cognitive domain, the appropriate source of content is the specific educational or cognitive theory relevant to that testing situation. Explications of this theory, its component variables, their interrelationships, and supporting research are commonly found in the professional literature (e.g., the conceptualizations of spatial ability offered by Lohman, 1979, and Pelligrino, Alderton, & Shute, 1984). The test developer's task here is to use these sources to fully describe the cognitive domain being assessed. The mapping sentence (Guttman, 1969) represents one form for expressing this description.

If the test is intended to predict examinee performance in a future criterion setting, the appropriate source of test content is an analysis of the cognitive requirements of that setting. This analysis consists of three major steps. *First,* the specific cognitive requirements of the criterion setting are identified, through a job analysis for employment settings, through a task analysis for specific performance settings, or through independent research or research syntheses for broad future settings, such as academic performance in college or graduate school. *Second,* the content specification of the predictive test is developed, using (a) the identified criterion cognitive requirements directly; (b) a combination of these requirements and past performance or achievement, or, more commonly; (c) cognitive indicators known or hypothesized to be positively related to the criterion requirements. In this last procedure, for example, paper-and-pencil verbal questions about fire-fighting safety are considered proxies for actual safety performance in a real fire-fighting situation. In this same example, however, other performance components of fire fighting, such as appropriate and efficient use of equipment, may be tested directly via performance measures. *Third,* the relationship between performance on the predictive test and performance in the criterion setting must be established. A strong, positive, criterion-related validity estimate indicates that the test is fulfilling its intended purpose well. Derivation of this estimate, however, is a difficult task. In employment settings, where predictive validity estimates are typically precluded by lack of criterion performance information on the individuals not hired, use of the less satisfactory concurrent validity estimate is often the only alternative. In all settings, unreliability in the criterion measure, as well as lack of evidence of its validity, are also commonly problematic.

For all three test-purpose domains, the specification of test content can be aided by clear conceptualization of the meaning of high performance in the specific domain being tested. What are the nature, scope, and range of tasks an accomplished performer or proficient learner in this area can do successfully? What would be convincing evidence of these accomplishments? What can experts do that novices cannot? An intriguing line of related research is investigation into the reasoning and problem-solving approaches used by different kinds of experts and into the linkages between these approaches and the ways in which the experts' substantive knowledge is organized and structured (e.g., Chi, Glaser, & Rees, 1982; Larkin, McDermott, Simon, & Simon, 1980). A comprehensive understanding of these phenomena for a given domain of expertise would represent an exemplar of high performance and, thus, a standard for evaluating degrees of proficiency in that domain.

Dimensionality of test content. A second substantive consideration in specifying test content is the dimensionality of the domain being measured. Dimensionality refers, most impor-

tantly, to the conceptual or theoretical homogeneity or heterogeneity of the content of this domain, and it is typically reflected in the number of test scores to be derived. A unidimensional conceptualization implies a single test score derived from a relatively homogeneous set of items. A multidimensional conceptualization often implies multiple test scores, each derived from different sets of items, and the consequent need for relatively more items to obtain stable estimates of performance on each dimension. For either conceptualization, item homogeneity with a single dimension does not necessarily mean that the items are pure or uncomplicated, only that the complexities are uniform across items. The test developer should provide empirical support or justification for the identified dimensionality of a test's domain, via extant research or statistical evaluations of interitem relationships (e.g., correlational, factor, or scaling analyses).

There are also testing contexts in which a single composite score is desired to represent a multidimensional domain, for instance, many summative achievement tests and some tests of verbal ability. Of critical importance in these situations is the appropriate weighting of the several dimensions in deriving the composite score. This score should accurately reflect the relative importance of each dimension in the relevant conceptualization of the domain. As discussed later in this section, weighting can be accomplished by specifying differing numbers of items per dimension and by applying various scoring adjustments.

The dimensionality of a given domain should be addressed within the identified source of test content. For example, for Test A in writing achievement, the relevant curriculum could be conceptualized as multidimensional, consisting of such components as grammar, syntax, organization, and style, and implying a parallel componential scoring system, with or without an overall composite score. In contrast, a unidimensional conceptualization of writing could underlie the curriculum relevant to Test B in writing achievement. Although, in this case, item type might not differ from Test A to Test B, scoring procedures for the latter would involve a holistic system.

Domain- versus norm-referenced interpretation. Specification of test content is influenced by whether domain- or norm-referenced test-score inferences or both are desired. This measurement alternative is germane to all testing purposes and should be specified as part of the test purpose. Domain-referenced inferences represent information within a specific domain about the absolute level and particular strengths and weaknesses of examinees' performance. Norm-referenced inferences represent comparative information, usually within a general domain, about examinees' performance relative to one another or to an identified norm group.

A key concern here is the specificity versus breadth of the domain to which inferences will be made. Domain-referenced inferences are typically based on a profile of multiple indicators of examinee performance with respect to highly specific and differentiated elements of a circumscribed domain. Meaningful domain-referenced inferences thus require clear explication of each element. Norm-referenced inferences are commonly based on a single summary score representing examinee performance with respect to a more general domain. Meaningful norm-referenced inferences thus require a clear explication of the broader components that constitute this more general domain.

When both domain- and norm-referenced interpretations are desired, the specification of test content should clearly delineate the bases of both sets of inferences. This dual-inference test setting, however, requires careful balancing of several additional contrasting, if not competing, test-attribute considerations. *First,* the scope of the domain to be tested should be somewhere between the broad, multifaceted domains commonly associated with norm-referenced testing (e.g., 10th-grade American history) and the specific, circumscribed domains more often linked with domain-referenced testing (e.g., the role of economic factors in the Civil War). *Second,* criteria for item development and selection should address both the discriminatory power needed for normative inferences and the content validity of prime importance to domain-referenced inferences. *Third,* in the distribution of test content, each element of the desired domain-referenced interpretations must be allocated sufficient items for reliable measurement. At the same time the overall distribution of test content must appropriately match the specifications underlying the desired norm-referenced interpretations. Alternatively, the latter could be appropriately derived through scoring adjustments.

Bandwidth versus Fidelity. As just illustrated, a fourth consideration in specifying test content is the desired balance between the breadth of content coverage and the accuracy or reliability of scores representing each content component. As Cronbach (1984) states it, for any test of a given length, a balance must be achieved between its bandwidth and its fidelity. Underlying this balance are substantive content trade-offs to be considered within the external limitations on test length.

These trade-offs vary with test purpose, as reflected in other elements of test-content specification. Regarding content dimensionality, a unidimensional test usually has low bandwidth but high fidelity. Measurement is concentrated on a narrow range of content, but the resulting score for that range is highly accurate. In a multidimensional test, test bandwidth, or content coverage, is broader and more differentiated. When a single composite score for this kind of test is desired, external limitations on test length are not particularly problematic. These limitations will still typically allow for enough items that the single composite score reliably represents the multifaceted domain. However, when multiple scores are desired for a multidimensional test, the bandwidth–fidelity balance becomes paramount. External constraints might not allow sufficient items for accurate measurement of each dimension. In these cases, depending on test purpose, the test developer might want to consider deleting a dimension, deleting one or more of the desired scores, reconceptualizing and combining two or more dimensions, adopting an item format that minimizes response time, or utilizing a matrix sampling approach to test administration. Alternatively, in exploratory test contexts like preliminary theory development, "[p]ractitioners who remain mindful of these risks [in interpreting unreliable differences among subscores] can make use of tentative leads from short tests" (Cronbach, 1984, p. 175).

Regarding the type of test interpretation desired, precise measurement of a specific, circumscribed range of content is the aim of domain-referenced tests, whereas norm-referenced tests tend to focus on accurate assessment of a broader, more differentiated content range. Thus, domain-referenced tests commonly have greater fidelity than bandwidth, whereas the reverse usually characterizes norm-referenced tests. However, when several scales yielding domain-referenced interpretations are included in one longer test, the fidelity for any one scale can be quite low. This situation parallels that of multiple-scored, multidimensional tests described earlier. Developing a test with both broad bandwidth and high fidelity is as difficult a challenge as developing a test yielding valid domain- and norm-referenced interpretations simultaneously.

Content distribution. The fifth substantive consideration in test-content specification is the appropriate distribution of test items across the individual topics or components comprising the content domain. As a prerequisite to overall test validity, this distribution should match the relevant domain conceptualization. In practice, this match is accomplished by allocating test items among content components and by weighting schemes applied during test scoring. At this point, only the conceptual issues in content distribution will be discussed.

For tests intended as aids in curricular decisions, content distribution should be based on the relevant educational curricula, appropriately reflecting the relative instructional emphases given to different topics and applications. For example, in a prescriptive test in beginning reading achievement, relatively more weight should be given to letter recognition and other decoding skills than to word comprehension, if the relevant curricula are conceptualized and sequenced that way. With a different curriculum, based on a different conceptualization of beginning reading skills, the relative weights might be reversed. For national achievement tests, weighting is commonly based on the average amount of coverage allocated to different topics within the dozen or so most frequently used texts in that curricular area, thus defining importance as curricular or instructional time spent. In this context, a cautionary note is warranted, particularly for tests intended for summative purposes. In these situations, the relative importance of various components of the content domain might be better reflected in statements of terminal objectives or expected outcomes than in curricular coverage or enabling objectives. Curriculum content represents the building blocks of learning, and objectives represent the completed tower of achievement. In both substance and form, a tower is a very different entity from the individual blocks comprising it.

Similarly, for tests intended to generate inferences to a cognitive domain, the content distribution process should be based on the relevant educational or cognitive theory; and for predictive tests, distribution at this stage of planning should be based on the relative importance of the constituent cognitive elements of the criterion setting.

To summarize thus far, the specification of test content requires consideration of a number of substantive factors as they pertain to test purpose. This internal component of test planning is of critical importance, because it is in the specification of test content that the test developer translates a general test label, such as "math computation achievement" or "information sequencing ability," into a specific blueprint of actual test content. Grounded in test purpose, this blueprint provides a comprehensive framework for additional planning decisions about desired test attributes.

ITEM TYPES

Following the specification of test content, the next major planning decision involves the types of items to be developed. As discussed later in this chapter in the context of item development, the particular format of an item matters less than the skill with which it is used (Ebel, 1980). For the test planner, then, the important task at this point is to determine (a) what structural elements of test items are needed to elicit the cognitive skills and processes identified in the content specification, (b) what item types include these structural elements, and (c) which of these types, if any, might be preferred for reasons of economy, precision, and feasibility.

These decisions about item types should be based on conceptualization of the specific components of the relevant achievement or ability domain, as represented by the specification of test content. This specification overall might suggest one or more particular types of items. For example, for multidimensional content specification, several different types of items, each tapping different knowledge uses or cognitive processes, might be needed to represent fully the content domain. In contrast, a highly explicit content specification might indicate just one item type, consistent with the intent to obtain an accurate assessment of the delimited domain. The major issue is which item types will generate appropriate samples of the components specified in the content domain or, in other words, which item types are most valid in this particular testing context. As noted, this aspect of item validity, the matching of item form to test content, can conflict with such other desirable test characteristics as scoring ease and high reliability. In this regard, test developers are cautioned not to sacrifice validity for these other concerns.

PSYCHOMETRIC CHARACTERISTICS OF ITEMS

In addition to deciding about item types, the test developer should address the desired level and range of item difficulty and item discriminatory power and the desired pattern of item responses. Item difficulty is the proportion of examinees answering a dichotomously scored (right or wrong) item correctly. Item discrimination is (a) the correlation between the score on that item and some criterion variable or (b) the difference in performance on that item for examinees in different criterion groups. Item response patterns are noted in observed relationships among items, such as whether interitem correlations are higher within than between subtests. This information is needed by item writers and editors, data analysts, and test assemblers alike, and it is thus an important component of test planning. Once again, decisions about the desired values for these psychometric item characteristics are based directly on test purpose, particularly as reflected in test-content decisions about the type of interpretation desired (domain- or norm-referenced) and the structure and dimensionality of the domain being assessed.

To illustrate, the following typify the differing decisions about item difficulty or discrimination emanating from different test purposes. A normative test intended to measure a homogeneous content domain needs highly discriminating items of average levels of difficulty. A test intended to identify the few most or the few least competent examinees requires items that are quite difficult or quite easy, respectively, for the average test

taker, though only if the test is highly unidimensional. In contrast, prespecified item difficulty and discrimination values are not needed for items whose content is closely prescribed by very explicit item specifications, as can be the case for a domain-referenced test. Similarly, when assessing mastery of a clearly defined domain, item difficulty is more a description of examinee performance than a prespecified item characteristic.

To illustrate further, expected patterns of item responses are related most directly to the conceived dimensionality of the domain being measured. For a unidimensional test, an item can be expected to correlate highly with all other potential items. For a multidimensional test, with distinct subparts corresponding to different conceptual dimensions, an item can be expected to have relatively high correlations with items from the same subpart and low or moderate correlations with items from other subparts. This implies that item analyses for multidimensional tests should be conducted both within and across subparts of the test.

Further discussion on desired psychometric properties of items, as related to test purpose, is provided later in this chapter in the section on item evaluation.

SCORING CRITERIA AND PROCEDURES

By definition, items on achievement and ability tests have right and wrong answers. Scoring for these tests is thus commonly a matter of ascertaining whether the right answer was marked or supplied for each item and then totaling the number of right answers. Yet, for many test purposes and test content specifications, scoring criteria and procedures are either optionally or necessarily more complex. For example, in item response theory, test scores are derived from item-based calibrated estimates of examinees' ability rather than from right-wrong item scoring. These two scoring procedures can yield different scale score results (see chapter 4). So, because scoring concerns can have direct implications for item development, they are appropriately considered in the test-planning stage. The ensuing discussion highlights the most important of these concerns.

Giving partial credit for individual item responses. Partial credit is the allocation of points to an item response based on the degree of completeness of accuracy of that response. This scoring option is discussed here in the context of tests comprising a relatively large number of individual items, each intended to be an independent assessment of examinee proficiency. Scoring for tests with relatively fewer items, each eliciting multifaceted, interrelated responses, is discussed later in this section.

Partial credit is psychologically desirable in many testing situations because it matches the partial (rather than all-or-none) knowledge or skill proficiency of examinees. However, with right-wrong scoring for objective tests, even though individual items are scored dichotomously, total scores can still be interpreted as the degree of examinee knowledge or skill. Right-wrong scoring of objective test items also has the important advantage of scoring ease.

The principal *advantage* of an elaborated or modified scoring scheme, however, is that the reliability of tests of a given length can often be increased, a common need in test settings with time constraints. Two general strategies for this purpose are adaptive testing (Holtzman, 1970) and differential weighting of options of multiple-choice items (Guttman, 1941). Both strategies attempt to loosen the stranglehold of test length on the amount of measurement precision by obtaining more information from each item than is obtained under traditional test administration and scoring procedures. Adaptive testing is discussed in chapter 9. In differential weighting, each option is assigned a different scoring weight, based either on the inherent value of the options or on the results of an empirical item analysis. Haladyna (1985) reviews methods and a study of the effect of option weighting on decision reliability. Confidence weighting (see, e.g., Shuford, Albert, & Massengill, 1966) and answer-until-correct schemes (Pressey, 1926) are similar to option weighting in that each chosen option can enter differentially into the scoring for a given item.

With modifications that elicit additional data from examinees, objective items can be amenable to other partial-credit scoring alternatives. Clearly, these modifications also represent enhancements of, or changes in, what is being measured. A common modification of items assessing achievement in science or math or assessing a dimension of mathematical reasoning ability involves asking examinees to "show all of their work" in addition to selecting the right answer. Depending on test purpose, this allows for the awarding of points for computing accurately, using correct formulas and information, and following correct reasoning. With this scoring scheme, an examinee who selects the wrong answer only because of a computation error might receive nearly full credit for his or her response, assuming, of course, that computational skills are not part of the domain being measured. More generic modifications of objective items include asking examinees to tell why they selected the response they did, to identify the errors in each of the other response alternatives, and to state the limiting conditions under which the answer they selected is correct or true or the specific conditions under which this answer would become incorrect or false. Additional possibilities are limited only by the creativity of the test developers and item writers. In the context of test planning, decisions are thus required about whether to allow for partial credit in item response scoring and, if so, about the item formats needed and the criteria used to allocate points within a partial-credit scoring scheme.

The use of partial-credit scoring procedures could be particularly relevant to tests intended to yield information on specific examinee strengths and weakness. These include diagnostic, prescriptive, and evaluative tests intended as aids to decisions made during the course of instruction and guidance tests intended as aids to future-oriented decisions.

Scoring essay, performance, and simulation item responses. Though different on many counts, these items typically share the feature than an examinee response is complex and multifaceted, comprising multiple, interrelated parts. In fact, tests with such items frequently have just one "item," or at most a few, better described as stimulus conditions. Scoring such responses thus presents a special challenge that should be addressed in the test-planning stage, again primarily because of its possible implications for item development.

There are two major approaches to scoring these kinds of responses, each with many variations (see Quellmalz, 1984, and Quellmalz, Smith, Winters, & Baker, 1980, for more com-

prehensive discussions of scoring of writing assessments and Fitzpatrick & Morrison, 1971, for performance and product scoring). The first approach uses componential scoring procedures, in which (a) key components of the domain are distinguished, (b) operational criteria are developed for each component, (c) scores are assigned to each, and (d) total scores are often derived from some combination of the individual component scores. This approach is clearly appropriate for multidimensional content specifications, where the desired inferences are primarily at the level of the separate dimensions or components of the domain. A performance test assessing knowledge of health-fitness-equipment use, for example, might generate separate scores for the conceptually separate dimensions of mechanical operation, safety, muscle development, and aerobic development. This approach also has the relative advantage of greater operational specificity.

The second major approach to scoring these kinds of items is most appropriate for unidimensional content specifications. It employs holistic scoring procedures, in which a single set of scoring criteria is developed and a single score is assigned to represent the whole domain. Particularly for essay tests, these criteria are commonly developed as a series of five or six sample, or model, responses, each reflecting greater proficiency in the domain as a whole, ranging from "virtually none" to "near perfect." Variations in these sample responses thus represent variations in the gestalt of the domain, rather than increased proficiency in separate dimensions or components.

Germane to both scoring approaches are two additional considerations. *First,* the development of scoring criteria requires clear conceptualization of proficiency, competence, or mastery in the relevant domain. The delineation of proficiency in the form of exemplars of high performance included in a test-content specification could provide an excellent resource for this task. In some test contexts, however, consensus on exemplary performance could be difficult to achieve, due to competing perspectives or theories about the structure and elements of the domain being measured. A system of multiple scores, each representing a different perspective, might be needed in these situations. *Second,* implementation of the scoring procedures developed during test tryout, operational administration, or both requires careful selection and training of scorers, as well as interrater and rater-trainer reliability checks both at the end of training and throughout the scoring period. Persistent difficulties with both componential and holistic scoring procedures are scorer inconsistency and drift. Particularly for holistic approaches, these difficulties are compounded across different test administrations, making between-group comparisons (e.g., year-to-year comparisons in a statewide assessment program) highly problematic.

Weighting. As noted previously, a prerequisite to overall test validity, and thus an important part of test planning, is the appropriate distribution of the various components of the test-content specification across items of the test. This requirement should be met by (a) differentially allocating numbers of test items among content components, based on their conceptual importance; and (b) applying weights in scoring that adjust further for differences in item or subtest parameters or both.

The differential allocation of test items among content components provides an appropriate framework for valid content distribution. However, in many test settings deriving scores from this framework alone will not yield the intended relative emphases across content categories. All items do *not* provide the same amount of information; an individual item's contribution to a total score varies with such item parameters as discrimination value. More discriminating items provide more information. So, for unidimensional tests yielding one total score or for multidimensional tests yielding multiple scores, if these scores are derived simply by summing item scores, content categories containing the more discriminating items will actually be weighted more heavily in the scores. More content-valid test scores in these cases might thus require differential item weights derived from selected item parameters.

For multidimensional tests yielding a composite score, the variability of the different subtest or part scores must be considered in addition to individual item parameters. One common example of this test setting is the derivation of composite scores on standardized, norm-referenced, achievement batteries, composed of separate subtests in such areas as reading, language arts, mathematics, and work study skills. Another example is the calculation of composite scores in componential approaches to scoring essay, performance, and simulation items. In these kinds of settings, content-valid composite scores might also require differential subtest weights based on subtest variability.

Determining passing scores. A final scoring consideration in test planning is the point at which to set cut off scores, or indeed, whether to have such scores at all. Unless test scores produce differential actions (e.g., award or deny a graduation certificate), passing scores need not be established. When passing scores *are* needed, a series of important operational and procedural concerns should be addressed in the test-planning stage.

Operationally, for example, passing levels can be set to insure minimum performance in all areas (e.g., 70% of the items in each of the subtests must be answered correctly). Alternatively, passing levels can be set to allow stronger performance in some areas to compensate for weaker performance in others (e.g., 80% of all items on the test must be answered correctly, with no passing levels set for subtests). Combination schemes are also common. Further, in terms of item characteristics, the test developer must consider the extent to which items should be targeted to the competence level represented by the passing score or standard.

Setting passing scores is both psychologically and psychometrically difficult, and it is often further complicated by external political considerations. Under the rubric of *standard setting,* a relatively large body of literature addresses these difficulties, debates the issues, and offers a variety of procedures (see chapter 14).

NUMBER OF ITEMS

A final internal test attribute requiring a decision in the planning stage is the number of items to be developed. This decision involves three interrelated considerations. How many items are needed on the operational test for satisfactory reliability and content coverage? How can this internal test re-

quirement be most skillfully balanced against external constraints on test length? How many items should be written initially to insure that a sufficient number will survive pretesting and be available for use on the operational test?

The first consideration is a sampling decision about how best to represent the domain of interest, using as criteria subtest–test reliability and content validity. This decision should logically flow from previous specification of internal test attributes. The type and number of items to be drawn from the domain are determined by test purpose, as represented by the specification of test content, item types and characteristics, and scoring considerations. For example, multidimensional content specifications require enough items to yield reliable scores for each dimension, domain-referenced interpretations mandate full coverage of the content domain, and the need for a wide range of item difficulties would imply more items than a narrow range would require. Depending on these attributes, the number of items needed for reliability and validity purposes should be specified for the total test, for each content dimension or component (e.g., objective), and for each type of item.

Second, the number of test items needed must be reviewed within the constraints imposed by the external conditions of test administration. In most test settings, these constraints, particularly on testing time available, limit, and thus require, compromises in overall test length. However, these compromises are not made all at once, at the end of the test planning process. Rather, as noted throughout this discussion of internal test-attribute specification, these compromises are part of the planning decisions about each attribute. That is, the specification of each attribute involves trade-offs between conceptual and psychometric requirements and information about examinee characteristics, testing time available, and other fixed test-administration conditions. Examples of such trade-offs include deleting or combining one or more dimensions in a multidimensional content specification, adopting a more economical item format that requires less response time, and developing a partial-credit scoring scheme that generates more information per item.

Moreover, decisions about optimal trade-offs between internal and external demands on test-attribute specification are not made for each attribute in isolation. Rather, these decisions are interdependent and iterative, as, for example, in the case of external conditions precluding the use of more than one essay question, which has concomitant implications for content dimensionality and bandwidth–fidelity specifications. Determining the optimal balance among all internal and external demands on test specification for a given test purpose defies general prescriptions and is indeed the province of the master test developer.

Thus, from the interrelated, iterative process of test-attribute specification, the number of items desired on the final test is determined, again, for the total test, for each dimension, and for each item type, as appropriate. With this as a baseline, the test developer can then determine the total number of items to be written. Good measurement practice dictates the development of more items than needed. Even after several levels of scrutiny (e.g., for accuracy, content validity, appropriateness, lack of bias), some items will not "behave" as intended; their empirical properties will not conform to theoretical expectations. Planning for this inevitability, by writing and testing more items than needed, allows the test developer to select only the best items in the final test-assembly stage.

Factors influencing the number of items to be made available include item format; item-selection procedures and standards employed; tryout procedures, if any, to be conducted; and experience of the item writers. Additional parameters of the testing situation that can influence the number of items to be written include the desire to create equivalent forms of the test, to establish an item bank, and to assess the properties and interrelationships of experimental types of items.

Further Considerations in Test Specification

Several additional concerns are related to the process of test specification, concerns that pertain more to the nature and presentation of the overall test plan than to any particular component thereof.

SPECIFICITY OF TEST PLANS

One important concern is the degree of specificity needed in the overall test plan. That is, in what test contexts should all attributes be fully specified in the test plan, and in how much detail should decisions about test attributes be communicated to item writers, review committees, and test users? This planning consideration pertains to all test attributes, content conceptualizations and psychometric properties alike. For example, specification of test content can range from a listing of the major components of the domain of interest to detailed prescriptions of the item characteristics needed to elicit each domain component (later in this chapter, these alternative item-writing schemes are discussed and illustrated more fully).

In general, a high degree of specificity in a test plan represents good measurement practice. By aiming for a highly specified test plan, test developers are encouraged to consider very carefully the nature of each attribute of the test to be developed in light of the test purpose. Such careful consideration can help to ensure that the resulting test successfully fulfills its intended purpose. Highly specific test plans are useful and effective guides to items writers and review committees, as well as being important guides for potential test users (Hall, 1985). Specificity in test planning further encourages a process that is open and public.

However, in many test settings, this general guideline for specificity should be balanced against considerations of cost, importance, and feasibility. Because specificity can require additional resources (e.g., a test tryout with proven anchor items might be needed to estimate item psychometric properties), the importance of the information to be gained should be evaluated against the costs required. To illustrate, specificity of test content is especially important for domain-referenced tests, so that test results can be clearly and accurately interpreted as indicators of the specific knowledge and skills that have or have not been learned. For reasons of fairness and openness, overall specificity is also important for tests intended to help make decisions about individuals, rather than groups or systems.

Also relevant to this concern about specificity is the feasibility of having a high level of detail in various parts of the test plan. For example, compared with other test purposes, content specificity is often more possible for tests intended for curricular purposes, because of their direct links to existing, detailed, curricular materials. Similarly, content specificity is often more possible for achievement than for ability tests. In both theory and practice, representations of achievement domains are typically more elaborated and more detailed than those for ability domains. Further, some test purposes can mandate specific item psychometrics, and some content conceptualizations can mandate particular item forms. Other purposes and conceptualizations are less delimited.

EXPERT AND USER VALIDATION OF TEST PLANS

In addition to considerations of test-plan specificity are concerns related to their external validation. *First* is the importance of judgmental reviews by selected outside experts, where expert is defined by test purpose, such as curriculum specialists for a formative achievement test or clinical specialists for a diagnostic ability test. Any group of expert consultants should command user respect and represent a relevant diversity of skills and viewpoints. Appropriate tasks for these experts include reacting to a draft outline of test content, providing direct input to a distribution of content, and critiquing the complete set of specified test attributes.

Second, in some test settings, user validation of the test plan is a critical ingredient of the resulting test's face validity, credibility, and political acceptability. In these settings, the decision context, in which test results are intended to contribute, is known to be sensitive or politicized. Prime examples of such decision contexts are the evaluation of examinee minimum competency, the certification of high school graduation eligibility, and the selection of job applicants where affirmative action or other equity considerations are of recognized importance. Because of the predictable political sensitivity of test results in these decision contexts, the wise test developer attempts to garner support for the test while it is being developed. Respected representatives of key constituencies or key actors in the setting should be consulted regarding major test attributes. Suggested modifications to these attributes should then be made to the extent that they will enhance the political credibility of test results without compromising their technical integrity. The primacy of test quality should be maintained throughout all external reviews, lest all the different suggestions result in a test that meets only lowest-common-denominator criteria.

ITERATION IN TEST PLANNING

Finally, it should be reemphasized that the process of test planning is fundamentally an iterative one. Throughout the process of test-attribute specification, decisions about one attribute can imply revisions to another, and the balancing of these interrelated decisions can require repeated evaluations of alternative trade-offs and compromises. Perhaps more importantly, the process of operationalizing a test plan, specifically the writing of items, can also suggest needed revisions to the plan and its list of attributes. Often, it is not until item writers struggle with the challenging task of operationalization that ambiguities, inconsistencies, or gaps in the plan are revealed. The process of test planning and development can thus be characterized as one of repeated cycling among decisions about test attributes and between this set of decisions and its concrete manifestation in the form of specific items.

Item Development

For the most part, item writing still resembles Wesman's description in the second edition of *Educational Measurement*. As conceived by him, it is "essentially creative — it is an art" (1971, p. 81). But in many quarters, two major changes are altering what items look like and how they get produced. The availability of computers and related technology is encouraging the use of item formats that have often been neglected. The emphasis on criterion-referenced interpretations, and the behavioristic soil in which they have been nourished, is shifting more of the item development responsibility from the creative brain of the item writer to the analytical and inventive brain of the item specifier. Renewed attention to often neglected item formats is coming; the shift in responsibility for item writing has already occurred in many test-development programs.

Item Types

It is useful to distinguish between what is measured and how it is measured; between substance and form; between content and format. The two are not independent, for form affects substance, and, to some extent, substance dictates form. Nevertheless, the emphasis here is on form, on how items are presented. *First,* a set of attributes of item formats is offered that can serve to classify item types. *Second,* the importance of an item's format is discussed: its relationship to what is measured and its effect on item parameters.

FORMAT ATTRIBUTES

Categories of paper-and-pencil objective item types are well known. They include multiple-choice, alternate-choice, matching, and others. Within each category are subcategories. For example, alternate-choice items include true – false, yes – no, right – wrong, cluster, and correction forms (Wesman, 1971). Completion, short-answer, and essay questions are the most common "supply" types of items.

Performance assessment and simulation exercises are often contrasted with the paper-and-pencil item types. Varieties of such assessment devices and examples of their use are presented by Fitzpatrick and Morrison (1971) and Priestley (1982).

The recent widespread availability of computers and the likely increase of computer-administered testing can be expected to affect the kinds of items that are used in the future. Four capabilities of computers and their likely effects are

1. *Logical branching.* Because computers can adapt their presentations to the responses of examinees, it is reason-able to expect the use of a series of interrelated exercises that simulate problem-solving situations or diagnose learning difficulties.
2. *Delivery of instruction.* Because computers are used to provide instruction, one can expect a closer integration of instruction and testing. Items can be so embedded within the presentation that they do not even appear to the learner to be test items. They look more like part of the instruction.
3. *Graphic presentation.* Because it is becoming easier to display graphics via a computer terminal and even to present motion, test items will probably become increasingly pictorial and less verbal and, for many areas of application, closer approximations to the criterion tasks.
4. *Measurement of latency.* Because computers are able to measure response time easily, timed tasks are likely to become more frequent or latency to be added more often as a response measure.

These computer-testing capabilities and other considerations suggest three attributes for describing test exercises, two that describe the administration process and one that characterizes its content. The first attribute is obtrusiveness, the quality of being readily detectable as a test item and the corresponding change in mental set or interference with normal routine. Formal examination settings rate high on the obtrusiveness dimension. Test items embedded in instructional materials and ratings made when the examinee is unaware of being observed are unobtrusive measurements.

Unobtrusive items have the advantage of being nonreactive, that is, the performance is less likely to be affected by the testing process, and, presumably, the measurement is more valid. On the other hand, validity might not be enhanced, because an examinee's *maximum* performance might not occur when testing is unobtrusive. Further, ethical considerations argue against unobtrusive testing, especially when results are to be used to make decisions about examinees.

The second attribute of a test exercise is response contingency, the quality of having each stimulus that is presented conditioned upon the examinee's responses to previous stimuli in the same exercise. A response-contingent exercise must thus consist of two or more related tasks. An example is a case management problem, in which the examinee is presented with a description of a problem (e.g., a patient with medical symptoms) and asked what should be done first. Additional questions are posed to the examinee contingent upon the first set of responses. In an observational setting, the dimensions being rated might be contingent upon the behaviors displayed earlier by the examinee.

The primary advantage of response-contingent exercises is that they mirror criterion tasks. Skills are displayed as a flow of performances and not as isolated behaviors out of context. On the other hand, response-contingent items are more costly to produce and more difficult to administer. The fact that each examinee might take a different pathway through the component tasks challenges the comparability of exercises and complicates their scoring.

The third attribute of test items is the similarity of the item stimulus and the required item response to the criterion behavior. Items that are high on this attribute are those having realistic tasks and direct measurement. Items presented verbally and items requiring only a check mark are often low on this attribute. To illustrate, Figure 8.1 presents the classification of four sample items and several item types within this similarity attribute. This figure, however, is an oversimplification, because most item types can be close or far from the criterion task, depending on how they are used and the context in which they are employed.

In the first edition of this book, Lindquist argued forcefully for items that mirror the criterion. As he put it,

> it should always be the fundamental goal of the achievement test constructor to make the elements of his test series as nearly equivalent to, or as much like, the elements of the criterion series as considerations of efficiency, comparability, economy, and expediency will permit. . . . The aim of the test constructor is thus always to make his test as much of the identical elements type as he possibly can, and to resort to the use of the other types only when no other procedure is at all practical. . . . In such tests [critical thinking or of the ability to interpret and evaluate complex materials] the most important consideration is that the test questions require the examinee to do the *same* things, *however complex*, that he is required to do in the criterion situations. . . . (1951, pp. 152, 154)

FORMAT IMPORTANCE

Notwithstanding Lindquist's forceful statement, the importance of proximity to criterion tasks or other format considerations remains questionable. The answer hinges in part on what format variations are compared and what criteria are employed. Most often studied are the effects of different for-

mat variations on the item's difficulty index and its construct or predictive validity.

Item difficulty. Investigations of the effect of how questions are asked on item difficulty have taken place over a long time (see, e.g., K. Green, 1984; Washburne & Morphett, 1928). Factors studied include adherence to multiple-choice item-construction principles (e.g., Schrock & Mueller, 1982), complexity of language (e.g., Bolden & Stoddard, 1980), and information-processing components (e.g., Whitely, 1981). From this voluminous literature, it appears that item difficulty is very sensitive to changes in how questions are asked. The magnitude of the effect depends not only on the variations studied but also on the content of the item and the sophistication of the examinees with respect to both the content and the variations being compared. Much of the work, especially that performed by cognitive psychologists, views format factors, not as nuisance variables, but as guides to understanding what an item is measuring and to constructing new items.

Item validity. It is probably true that any format of item can measure almost any kind of thinking ability. Consider this multiple-choice item that measures recall, rather than recognition:

> The *fourth* letter of the last name of the editor of the *first* volume of *Educational Measurement* is:
> 1. d   2. n   3. o   4. r   5. z

Or consider this true–false item that measures more than simple recall:

> If the number of items in a test is doubled, the standard error of measurement is likely to be doubled also. (Ebel, 1980, p. 123)

Ebel summarizes his view of the relation between an item's format and what it can measure this way:

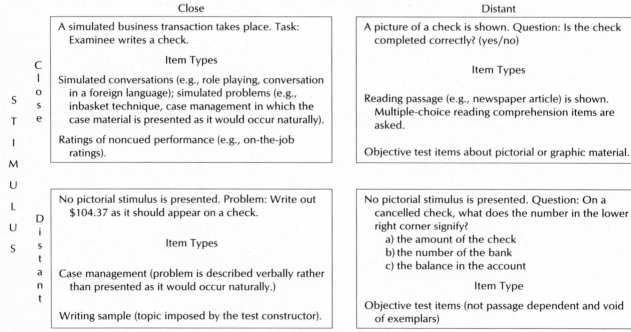

Figure 8.1 Classification of four illustrative items and of item types according to the relation between their stimulus and response components and the criterion behavior.

While each type [of item] has its own special values and limitations, they are largely interchangeable. The quality of an examination depends less on the particular form used than on the skill with which it is used. (p. 124)

Much empirical research (see Brown, 1970, for one review and Traub & Fisher, 1977, for a more recent study) supports the view that multiple-choice and open-ended items on the same content measure the same construct, or at least produce the same relative ordering of examinees. The correlations between tests of the different types, when corrected for attenuation, typically hover near unity. Frederiksen (1984), however, offers counterevidence for problem-solving items that are "ill-structured," that is, not neatly laid out or defined.

When format is viewed more broadly than traditional item types, some writers believe that "the form of the task can be as important as the substance" (Cronbach, 1984, p. 146). Cronbach presents evidence of the effect on predictive validity of changing the format from verbal to pictorial. The effect of such variables as speed on the factorial structure of items has been demonstrated (see, e.g., Davidson & Carroll, 1945). Perhaps the most important contribution arising from the attention of cognitive psychologists to measurement (see chapter 7) will be to sensitize test constructors to the importance of scrutinizing what their items are measuring and of including process variables as factors in their item and test specifications.

Item Writing

Item writing can be viewed along a continuum. At one end, the content of the test question emanates from the thoughtfulness and creativity (some would say, idiosyncrasy) of the item writer. As Wesman has said, "Every test item begins with an idea in the item writer. . . . There is no automatic process for the production of item ideas. They must be invented. . . ." (1971, p. 86). *A Technology for Test-item Writing* (Roid & Haladyna, 1982) is invoked as one moves toward the other end of the continuum, in which an item is not so much written as it is generated. It is produced by formulas, as soup is prepared from recipes, rather than by trial and taste of the creative worker. The continuum is one of increasing specificity and constraints on the item writer's inventiveness.

Proponents of creative item writing claim that higher level thinking processes can best be measured by tasks developed by knowledgeable and trained item writers who are free to invent novel or thought-provoking situations. Although conceding that items can be cranked out by mechanical algorithms, they consider such products to be limited in scope. Acknowledging the value of item-writing rules, they yet believe that applying these rules requires a skill that cannot easily be automated. "The inventiveness and imagination of professionals will contribute more to the improvement of test items than any technology applied unimaginatively" (Roid & Haladyna, 1982, p. 229).

Proponents of generating items from detailed item specifications claim that the veracity of criterion-referenced interpretations requires constraining specifications. In the absence of such specifications, how can one describe a learner's performance, these proponents ask, except by resorting to vague verbal terms. How can we assure that item writing remains public, replicable, efficient, and congruent with intended test content without abridging the creative freedom of the item writer. "If you cannot quell an item writer's zest for invention, send that individual scurrying to more congenial pursuits, such as sculpture, gymnastics, or erotic dance" (Popham, 1984, p. 32).

ITEM-WRITING SCHEMES

Listing of behaviors or tasks in the domain. The most informal scheme involves specifying only the construct to be measured. Instructions to produce 25 items on the American Civil War fit this scheme, which is rarely employed by professional test producers but is frequently used by teachers.

Among professional test developers, a more common item-writing scheme, still informal or at least not very restricting, is to provide item writers with a listing of the specific, observable behaviors and tasks on which examinees will be assessed. For curricular test purposes, this scheme might consist of a set of specific instructional objectives. The listing could be constructed from a detailed task analysis of the relevant curricular, cognitive, or criterion domain. Also commonly included are the number of items to be developed or the weight for each objective or behavioral task requirement. An example of this alternative is presented in Figure 8.2.

Thus, this item-writing scheme focuses on outlining the specific content of the test, without addressing item parameters. As such, the item writer has unbridled leeway in determining item types and forms, and different sets of items will be constructed by different item writers. For some test purposes, such item variety might represent an asset. The relative ease of developing a list of behaviors or tasks and the list's communicability to examinees are also advantages. However, this scheme is most effectively used when each behavior or task corresponds to a test item. More or less detailed listings of behaviors will be less useful as guides to item writers.

Content-by-process matrix. Also commonly used is another item-writing scheme that focuses on outlining test content. In this scheme, however, substantive, or subject matter, content is differentiated from process, or performance, content by means of a two-way content-by-process matrix, also called a table of specifications. More specifically, the subject matter content identified for the test is divided into meaningful chunks and listed along one axis of a two-way matrix. The identified cognitive processes, or performances, comprise the other axis. Entries in the cells of this matrix thus represent the particular intersections of content and process, including the allocated weights. A hybrid form of the first and second item-writing schemes is the presentation of detailed objectives in a content-by-process matrix.

One formulation of content and process categories and illustrative tasks is shown in Figure 8.3. An example of a content-by-process matrix for a standardized, norm-referenced elementary grade science achievement test is presented in Figure 8.4.

In its general form, this item-writing scheme is amenable to all test purposes, though it is most commonly recommended and used for testing within the curricular domain. Various extant learning taxonomies and hierarchies are particularly

FIGURE 8.2 Example of a content listing item-writing scheme for a certification test.

Test components	Desired weight (percent)	
Independent client care issues	22.5	
Assessment		5.0
Nursing diagnosis		2.5
Planning		4.5
Implementation		8.0
Evaluation		2.5
Interdependent client care issues	40.0	
Nurse-physician collaborative practice		31.0
Interdisciplinary collaborative practice		9.0
Professional and practice issues	12.5	
Advocacy		1.5
Legal/ethical issues		1.5
Research		0.5
Quality assurance		1.5
Teaching		3.0
Environment		1.5
Professional/collegial issues		1.0
Consultation		0.5
Referral		1.5
Clinical specialist in medical-surgical nursing	25.0	
Research: Investigation		1.5
Research: Utilization		1.5
Consultation		3.5
Professional activities		3.0
Client care issues		7.0
Quality assurance		2.5
Teaching/perceptor		6.0

Sample listing of specific knowledge areas
- Anatomical and physiological parameters
- Human responses
- Disease classification dimension
- Medical treatment regimens (e.g., drugs, equipment, tests, procedures)
- Physical examination
- Institutional protocols
- Policies and procedures
- Communication principles/techniques
- Conflict resolution
- Legal/ethical issues

Sample listing of specific knowledge areas
- Communication principles/techniques
- Institutional resources
- Professional roles and responsibilities of caregivers
- Assertiveness
- Peer review
- Self-evaluation
- Current scientific base of practice
- Networking
- Leadership skills
- Community resources
- Service and resource evaluation

Source: American Nurses' Association, Division of Medical-Surgical Nursing Practice, 1983.

applicable to the process component of a content-by-process matrix for many instructional tests (of course, these resources only apply to the degree that they match the relevant curricular domain).

At least since the time of Aristotle's *Categories,* philosophers, psychologists, educators, and others have sought to identify the basic processes of human thinking. For a quarter of a century, the six general levels of Bloom's (Bloom, Engelhart, Furst, Hill, & Krathwohl, 1956) taxonomy of the cognitive domain (knowledge, comprehension, application, analysis, synthesis, and evaluation) have productively guided many instructional test developers, especially by encouraging the inclusion of relatively complex cognitive processes, in addition to the simpler ones. Gagné (1977, 1984) provides a list of performances that an examinee can be asked to do: (a) tell something (verbal information); (b) demonstrate how to do something (intellectual skill); (c) execute a skilled movement sequence (motor skill); (d) choose a course of personal action (attitude); and (e) originate a solution to a novel problem and discover the higher order rule (cognitive strategy). Each performance is broken down into finer categories. Stahl and Murphy (1981) offer eight broad domains of cognition (preparation, reception, transformation, retention, transfersion, incorporation, organization, and generation), and Miller, Williams, & Haladyna (1978) offer five (recalling, summarizing, predicting, evaluating, and applying). Less recent taxono-

PROCESS (PERFORMANCE)

CONTENT	REMEMBER	USE	FIND
Fact	X		
Concept	State definition	Classify examples	Invent categories
Procedure	State steps	Demonstrate task	Derive steps
Principle	State relationship	Explain problem	Discover relationship

Source: Adapted from Merrill, 1983.

Figure 8.3 Illustrative tasks in a content-process matrix.

FIGURE 8.4 Example of a content-by-process item-writing scheme for a science achievement test.[a]

CONTENT	PROCESS[b]				
The student will demonstrate knowledge of the language, concepts, or methods used to communicate and inquire about . . .	RECALL	EXPLICIT INFORMATION SKILLS	INFERENTIAL REASONING	EVALUATION	CONTENT TOTALS
Botany	2	6			8
Zoology	3	2	3		8
Ecology	3		1	2	6
Physics	4		1	2	7
Chemistry	4	1	1	1	7
Land, sea, or space sciences	1	1	2		4
Process totals	17	10	8	5	40

[a] Numbers in the matrix refer to the weight of items designated for Form U, Level F. In number-correct scoring, each item receives equal weight.
[b] The levels of this process classification scheme are defined as follows.
   Recall: The item can only be answered by use of previous knowledge either asked for directly or asked to be applied.
   Explicit information skills: The item can be answered using only information explicitly supplied in the passage or item.
   Inferential reasoning: The item can be answered only by making predictions, making deductions, or drawing conclusions.
   Evaluation: The item requires the student to evaluate passage or item information in terms of explicit or implied objective criteria and to render a judgment.
Source: Adapted from the Comprehensive Test of Basic Skills Test Coordinator's Handbook, 1981.

mies of intellectual skills have been provided by Guilford (1959, 1967), Melton (1964), and Tiemann and Markle (1973), among others.

Taxonomies of process, or performance, in specific domains are also available. As examples, six formulations of critical thinking skills have been compiled by Kneedler (1985), and skill lists in reading comprehension have been given by Carroll (1972). As one attempts to teach these process skills, the distinction between the content and process dimensions of the matrix becomes blurred.

Matrix schemes for item writing need not be limited to the dimensions of content and process. For example, for developing professional licensing examinations, D'Costa (1985) advocates a three-factor matrix that contains assigned functions (things, data, people), problem or situation type (type of setting, type of client, type of intervention), and background or resources (educational content, supervision, experience, facility or resources).

The content-by-process or other matrix schemes for item writing still allow considerable freedom of movement for the item writer. As the matrix becomes multidimensional and restricts the item format, the item's reading level, the type of examples that can be included, the formation of distractors (for multiple-choice items), and so forth, the item writer's freedom becomes more constrained. This higher level of constraint is represented by item-writing schemes that address characteristics of the item, in addition to item content.

Specifications for items. Detailed definitions of the domain and specifications of the item have been advocated, especially for criterion- or domain-referenced tests (APA et al., 1985; Popham, 1978, 1984). Such detail is intended to permit knowledgeable judgments of the relations of items to the domains they represent and to permit explicit descriptions of what knowledge and skills the examinee possesses. Item-writing schemes that specify particular characteristics of the items to be developed are intended to provide instructions of suffi-

cient detail that different item writers, working independently, will generate psychometrically parallel sets of items. The actual psychometric comparability of such item sets, of course, would have to be tested empirically.

Item specifications generally represent detailed, prescriptive instructions for a particular kind of item identified for a particular component of the test's domain. For selected-response items, these instructions could include (a) a complete explication of permissible content; (b) rules for generating the item stimulus, including the specific nature of the problem posed and format, wording, length, and vocabulary; (c) rules for generating the correct response, including format and placement; (d) rules for generating each distractor, including number of distractors, use of such options as "all of the above" or "none of the above," and format; and (e) desired psychometric characteristics of the items such as difficulty, discrimination, and homogeneity.

Specifications for constructed-response, performance, and simulation items could include (a) a complete and detailed explication of the stimulus conditions, including, as appropriate, equipment required, physical arrangement of the test setting, and specific instructions to examinees; (b) a similar explication of response conditions, such as time limits and the nature and degree of interaction permitted; and (c) a complete explication of the scoring procedures and criteria to be used.

With respect to performance items, for many years Edwin Fleishman headed a project to describe and classify human performance tasks (see, e.g., Farina & Wheaton, 1971). Fleishman (1982) defines a task as the totality of the situation imposed on the subject or as specific performances required. He lists five bases for classifying tasks, one of which is task characteristics; namely, the conditions imposed on an individual that have an objective existence quite apart from the activities they might trigger, the processes they might call into play, or the abilities they might require. Five categories of task characteristics are task stimuli (e.g., type of display); instructions (e.g., degree of operator control); procedures (e.g., number of steps); response categories (e.g., amount of muscular effort involved); and goals (e.g., number of output units).

The item-specification approach yields test plans that contain an item specification for each type of item within each component of the test's domain. An example of specifications for producing items to measure the skill of identifying misleading advertisements is presented in Figure 8.5.

It is possible to make the specifications so exacting that an item writer is not needed at all. The item writing, if it can be called that, occurs in the formation of the algorithms executed to produce the items. The most common approach is to use one or more item forms, fixed syntactical structures for each item with one or more variable elements. The elements are selected from a set of possibilities called a *replacement set*. Each form, with its replacement sets, is capable of producing many

---

Performance Indicator (Objective)

Use criteria for determining particularly misleading ads to identify such ads.

Rationale

The realities of inflationary prices and the declining quality of many manufactured products mandate closer scrutiny of advertising by consumers in order to protect themselves and their investments. The ability to recognize advertising which misrepresents a product or service is crucial for the individual and for the general welfare of the country. Individuals who can identify misleading ads will be in a position to purchase better products, allowing them to save money over the long run.

General Description

The student will be presented with four or five product or service advertisements. Multiple-choice questions will be designed to determine if the student can use criteria for determining misleading ads to identify misleading information, poor advertising practices, and/or misrepresentation of the product or service advertised. The ads will be presented in their original form, as in actual ads, or be specifically written for the test.

Sample Item

[Presentation of four ads (not reproduced in this illustration)]

Which of these ads can be considered misleading because it uses excessive language to sell the product?

*A. the ad for body building
 B. the ad for astringent cleanser
 C. the ad for ice cream
 D. the ad for toothpaste

Stimulus Attributes

The general stimulus for this performance indicator should contain four or five sample ads, developed or selected and presented according to the following guidelines:

1. For each item (or set of items), four or five actual or simulated advertisements drawn from a variety of sources (newspapers, magazines, radio, television, etc.) should be presented.
2. One set of ads may be used for several items.
3. Ads should describe products or services designed for only males or for only females in addition to products or services designed for both sexes.
4. Ads should describe products or services designed for the general age level of the students being tested.
5. Ads may be of three types:
   a. written
   b. written with illustrations or pictures
   c. oral (presented on a tape recorder)

6. Ads should be no longer than one typewritten page or 300 words.
7. A minimum of four and a maximum of five ads should be presented for any one item or set of items.

Stem Attributes

1. Following the presentation of the ads, there should be either a single item or a set of items.
2. Item stems should ask students to identify which ad is misleading according to a specified criterion.
3. The criteria should come from the following list. An ad may be misleading if it:
   a. creates an impression that is different from the single statements or facts presented, even though every statement is correct.
   b. conceals important facts about the product or service (e.g., price, guarantees).
   c. diverts attention from the actual terms and conditions of the offer.
   d. makes false or misleading comparisons with other products or services.
   e. makes an offer that appears to be too good to be true, thus creating false expectations.
   f. appeals to ideas or sentiments that are loved, cherished, or respected by many people (e.g., the family or patriotism), otherwise known as "flag waving."
   g. appeals to scientific authority or documentation.
   h. appeals to one's desire to be part of the group, up with the times, in tune with the latest fad, otherwise known as the "bandwagon approach."
   i. employs "snob appeal" by using famous individuals or people from prestigious groups or occupations to advertise the product or service.
   j. uses many superlatives and other forms of excessive language (e.g., the best, the newest, the greatest) to try to sell the product or service, otherwise known as "glittering generalities."

   Only criteria listed above may be used.

4. The stem should be written in language not to exceed the seventh-grade reading level.

Response Attributes

1. The responses should follow a four-alternative multiple choice format.
2. The correct response should be the name or a brief description of the only ad that is misleading for the reason given.
3. Distractors should be the names or brief descriptions of the ads that are either not misleading or are misleading for reasons other than the one given.

Source: Adapted from the Rhode Island Statewide Assessment Program, 1980.

FIGURE 8.5 Example of an item specification item-writing scheme for a "life skills" test.

versions of the same class of items. Computers are usually relegated to the trivial task of picking the elements and producing the test questions.

A noteworthy, but short-lived, attempt to have the computer "think" like an item writer was carried out by Fremer and Anastasio (1969) and Anastasio, Marcotte, and Fremer (1969). They created computer designs for generating plausible distractors for spelling items and sentences for use in sentence-completion items. Wolfe (1976) provided another example of using the artifical intelligence of the computer in item writing. His procedures linguistically transformed sentences of text into test questions. Although the majority of questions made sense, many did not, and Wolfe has abandoned this line of item writing.

In the item forms approach, as described, every word that appears in the computer-generated item was first entered into the computer by the author. The computer merely fabricates permutations and combinations of author-supplied wordings. In the linguistic transformations of text and creations of distractors for spelling and sentence-completion items, the computer output is, in one sense, a fresh, artificially intelligent production. Use of any of these computer-aided approaches to item writing is likely to be most germane to situations requiring the production of large numbers of similar items.

An approach between the item form and artificial-intelligence schemes is possible. An interactive computer program in which the author will be prompted to provide substance that will be added to structures resident in the computer is currently being designed by Millman. Several reviews of item-writing schemes are now available (Millman, 1974; Popham, 1984; Roid, 1984; Roid & Haladyna, 1982).

ITEM-WRITING RULES

Advice on writing the most common paper-and-pencil item types is not in short supply and can be found in many textbooks on educational measurement. A list of frequently cited rules for preparing multiple-choice achievement items is presented in Table 8.3. Rules for test exercises that are not in paper-and-pencil format are not readily available, except for performing systematic observations (see chapter 10). Some of the suggestions for preparing paper-and-pencil items, however, also hold for other types of exercises.

Item-writing rules are based primarily on common sense and the conventional wisdom of test experts. Some rules, like the one specifying that the item writer should balance the key in multiple-choice items so that no one option position is correct an undue number of times, make sense regardless of the outcome of empirical studies on the effect of violating that rule. Haladyna and Downing (1985) report the results of 56 empirical studies on multiple-choice item-writing rules, including 6 studies on the rule cited earlier. Typically, results are inconclusive.

Attention needs to be devoted to writing item and test *directions,* as well as to writing the items themselves. Directions are part of the larger task of preparing the examinees (see chapter 11). The overriding purpose of test directions is to insure that the item measures whether the examinee has, or can quickly obtain, the skill being referenced by the item. Mislead-

ingly low performance can occur because the examinee did not understand the task, received inadequate practice, or followed a less than optimum test-taking strategy. To raise an examinee's performance to an appropriate maximum level, directions should include practice items that indicate why the keyed response is correct, suggestions for allocating one's time, honest advice about whether or not to guess, and disclosure of test-taking strategies unrelated to the construct being measured but known to help or to hinder test performance.

TABLE 8.3 Rules for Writing Multiple-Choice Test Items

Be Accurate and Valid

1. Construct each item with one and only one correct or best answer, unless the directions state otherwise.
2. Test for the intended knowledge and abilities, which *may* suggest:
   a. avoiding trivial questions and including questions about important facts and concepts, and
   b. including questions emphasizing higher-level thinking ability rather than rote recall.
3. More generally, construct items that conform to the assessment criteria shown in Table 8.2.
4. Avoid "none of the above" and "all of the above" as options when examinees are to choose the best answer rather than an answer that is precisely correct.

Communicate Well

1. Use either a direct question or an incomplete statement as the item stem, whichever seems more appropriate for efficient presentation of the item.
2. Write items in clear and simple language, with vocabulary kept as simple as possible.
3. State the central problem of the item clearly and completely in the stem; include most of the reading in the stem.
4. Base each item on a single central problem; construct options homogeneous in content.
5. Consistent with clarity, include in the stem any words that must otherwise be repeated in each option.
6. Emphasize negative words or words of exclusion (e.g., not, except); avoid such words in tests for young examines.
7. Place options at the end of the item stem; do not embed the options in the middle of the item stem.
8. Arrange the options in a logical order, if one exists.

Don't Give Away the Answer

1. Make all options plausible and attractive to examinees who lack the information or ability referenced by the item.
2. Avoid unintended associations between the stem and the options that may be based on:
   a. grammatical consistency or inconsistency between the stem and the options,
   b. repetition of keywords in the stem and the keyed option, or
   c. rote or other verbal associations between keywords in the stem and the keyed option.
3. Avoid extraneous clues within the option set that may be based on the:
   a. unusual length of the keyed option,
   b. degree of qualification stated in the keyed option or use of specific determiners, such as "never" and "always" in the distractors,
   c. lack of independence and mutual exclusivity of the options, or
   d. frequency with which the keyed option is placed in a given option position or pattern of the location of the keyed position.
4. Avoid allowing one item to cue another when that is not the intention.

Item Evaluation

The content of and responses to items may be scrutinized for many reasons. The goal of such scrutiny is most often to select the best items and, thereby, to construct a quality test. The item-evaluation methods described here can also provide useful information for instruction, for program improvement, for defining constructs and building theory, and for judging the value of the test as a whole. This section, however, is limited to a description of item-evaluation methods and indicators. Later in this chapter, suggestions are offered as to when the methods are most applicable.

Each method described here requires that items be evaluated individually. Each item's content or responses must be assessed, and, then, decisions must be made about whether to retain, revise, or discard the item. In contrast, procedures that lead to summary judgments about the quality of the entire test are discussed in chapters 2 and 3. Although the emphasis here is on assessing items, in fact, all aspects of the testing situation should be scrutinized, such as the test's directions and time limits. Discussion of some of these concerns can be found in chapter 11.

Item-evaluation methods can be divided into two categories: those in which the *item content, or format,* is judged against stated criteria and those in which the *examinee responses to the items* are evaluated. In the former category, the raw data are judgments about the item's content; in the latter category, the raw data are the examinees' item responses. Item-content methods require that the items have been written but not necessarily administered to examinees, whereas item-response methods require that the items have been answered by one or more groups of examinees.

The increased attention to item-content methods of item evaluation since the last edition of *Educational Measurement* parallels the increased attention to criterion-referenced test interpretations. It would be a mistake, however, to conclude that many of these methods were believed unimportant by testing experts in years past. It would also be a mistake to conclude that item-content methods are appropriate only for criterion-referenced tests or achievement tests and that item-response methods are appropriate only for norm-referenced tests or ability tests. Any test-development effort can profit from both approaches.

Item-Content Methods

All item-content methods require that one or more individuals evaluate one or more items against one or more assessment criteria. Test developers need to consider which criteria should be addressed, how many and what type of judges should be employed, and what specific techniques should be used to gather what information. Which assessment criteria are relevant depends upon the context in which the test will be used. In turn, the number and type of judges, the information to be asked of the judges, and how the information will be gathered all depend upon the assessment criteria.

Several criteria are listed in Table 8.4, together with a description of the relevant judges and judgments. No one type of judge is best suited for all assessment criteria. Further, more

judges are not necessarily better than fewer judges, especially when, to obtain more judges, the expertness of the selected judges to make the required evaluations is compromised. Also, some item flaws should be obvious to all, once they are pointed out. Consensus about the deficiency of an item is less likely when the judgments are made about an item's congruence with environments that vary across locations. When the goal is consensus, it is desirable to make provision for judges to interact with each other after the original judgments have been independently made.

Not all the criteria are relevant for all test uses, but several are apt to be appropriate for any one test development effort. Test purposes guide the choice of criteria, and a design for obtaining judgments effectively can be part of the test plan. Relationships between test purposes and criteria for item assessment are discussed in the section on item selection.

ITEM ACCURACY AND COMMUNICABILITY

Accuracy. Experts ought to agree on the keyed answer for each question that has one right answer. Notwithstanding the value of multiple perspectives arising from using multiple judges, relatively few experts are needed to establish the keyed answer for each item. The judges should be very knowledgeable about the content area being assessed by the item and should independently choose the right answer for items presented, without the proposed key. The important judgment is whether, given the way the question is worded, one defensible answer exists. This judgment is best obtained after all editorial revisions to the item have been made.

Establishing the accuracy of the keyed answer is not a voting matter. The goal is consensus, not a majority. If one judge differs from the others, an opportunity to present the discrepant view needs to be provided, and unanimity among these highly qualified judges is expected, if not essential.

Communicability. Presumably items will be edited for readability, correctness and clarity of expression, consistency of style, and other items in a list of item-writing principles and guides (see Table 8.4). No one editor, no matter how expert, can be expected to catch all flaws and lapses of clarity or to anticipate all possible misunderstandings. Experts in testing and others can be expected to make additional improvements to the format and wording of items.

Items can be administered to examinees, not only to obtain tryout data (see the treatment of item response methods later), but also to seek their reactions to the items and test directions. Some advantage can accrue from using examinees at a level of functioning somewhat different from that of the target population. Directions, including the time limits, can be tried out with less able examinees. Both less and more able examinees might be asked to (a) circle the words whose meaning they do not know, (b) explain why they answered a designated objective item as they did (different students can be given different items to comment upon), (c) note any item that seems to have either no right answer or two or more right answers and explain why that is the case, and (d) identify items that seem confusing and what is confusing about them. Fremer, Kastrinos, & Jones (1972) found it of value to ask college-level examinees to judge not only an item's communicability but also its suitability and conformity to instruction.

TABLE 8.4 Item-Content Methods of Item Evaluation

ASSESSMENT CRITERION	PRIMARY QUESTION ADDRESSED	WHO SHOULD JUDGE?	RELATIVE NUMBER OF JUDGES	SHOULD CONSENSUS BE EXPECTED?
Accuracy and Communicability				
Accuracy	Is the keyed answer correct?	Subject matter & testing experts	Fewer	Yes
Communicability	Does the form & wording meet item writing standards?	Subject matter & testing experts (examinees)	Fewer (more)	Maybe
Suitability				
Difficulty	Is the item of appropriate difficulty?	Teachers/supervisors	More	No
Importance	Is the knowledge or skill important?	Subject matter experts; teachers/supervisors	More	Maybe
Bias	Is the item offensive or relatively unfamiliar to specified groups?	Members of identified groups	More	Probably Not
Conformity to Specification	Does the item match its specification as given in the test plan?	Subject matter & testing experts	Fewer	Mabye
Relevant environment	Does the item measure the knowledge or skill found in the curricula, instructional materials, criterion tasks, or role delineations?	Subject matter experts; teachers/supervisors	Many more	No
Opportunity	Did the examinee have an adequate opportunity to acquire the knowledge or skill measured by the item?	Teachers/supervisors; possibly students	Many more	No

ITEM SUITABILITY

Difficulty. Even for very detailed item specifications, questions covering a range of difficulty are possible to construct. Especially for new test programs, in which experience with similar items is not available, it is reasonable to gather perceptions about whether the proposed item is of suitable difficulty. Accurate estimates of an item's difficulty are not easy to make, and no attempt to reach consensus among the judges is required.

Importance. Most often items are written to conform to some objective or task specified in the test plan, and the *statement* of the skill or knowledge, the objective, or the task is rated on importance. When the test plan is sufficiently general, it can be more appropriate to judge the importance of the knowledge or skill as measured by the item itself. Importance may be considered with respect to the knowledge and skills that are most central to the discipline or subject matter, most crucial for a minimally competent person to have, most needed for success in the next unit of instruction, and so forth. When items are rated on importance, it is adviseable to indicate the referent for importance and customary to permit discrimination among degrees of importance (e.g., essential, very important, somewhat important, not important). Further, especially in job-related situations, separate ratings may be made for how often the skill or ability is needed and for how important it is. Although a consensus judgment might be reached on whether an item should be in a test, consensus on an item's degree of importance is less likely. Some merit is seen in permitting raters who take notably different positions with respect to importance to present their cases before a final judgment is made.

Bias. No reputable test developer wants to administer items that are offensive to examinees, that include inappropriate stereotyping, or that are, because of reasons unrelated to the knowledge or skills being measured, particularly difficult for selected subgroups. Securing ratings from members of groups likely to be affected negatively by the items' content is one way to reduce the appearance of unfairness and bias. Biasing features of an item are usually subtle, so that using several reviewers increases the chances of spotting a troublesome item. The practice of retaining items that some high percentage (e.g., 80%) independently rate as unbiased without having the benefit of a discussion about the item is apt to lead to relatively few items being discarded. A more sensible procedure is to discuss the reasons given for suspecting an item to be biased. Even if only one judge initially considers an item biased, but can persuade others of that view, the item should not be kept unrevised. Consensus is a worthy goal but often unattainable. Further discussion of detecting item bias appears in chapter 5.

CONFORMITY

Specifications. Increasingly, a judgment is made about whether items are congruent with their specifications in the test plan. The specifications can range from a simple statement of an instructional objective to an elaborate description of format restrictions, stimuli attributes, distractor generation rules, and the like. Matching an item to its specifications is a technical task, which can be more straightforward for elaborate specifications and more subjective for specifications stated generally. In the latter situation, judges need to infer the cognitive or other skills that are truly required to answer the item correctly.

What an item measures depends in part on the instructional and other history of the examinee, adding to the difficulty of the matching task. Highly skilled judges are required.

Items may be rated one by one as to whether or not they match their specifications. Intermediate judgments expressing degree of match are sometimes allowed. Reasons for failure to match the specification should be solicited. A more stringent method requires judges to select from all the specifications (usually instructional objectives) the one that the item matches or to indicate no match. A third method, more time consuming and less practical, is to have judges rate each item with respect to each specification. An index of congruence has been provided by Rovinelli and Hambleton (1976) to be used with this third method. Further discussion of this and other measures of item-specification congruence can be found in Hambleton (1984) and Simon (1984).

Judgments should be made about whether the *collection* of items provides a representative or otherwise appropriate coverage of the test domain. The process of making these judgments has been called *content validation,* and it is discussed in chapter 2.

Relevant environment. Items can be judged according to whether they match a body of content or performance tasks "out there." *Curricular validity* occurs when the test items, as a collection, match the major objectives covered in textbooks, courses of study, and the like (see, e.g., Madaus, 1983). The match can also be with respect to elements of job-related tasks, competency expectations, functional responsibilities, or criterion behaviors. Procedures for conducting job analyses were referenced and evaluated by Levine, Ash, Hall, & Sistrunk (1983). D'Costa (1985) suggests procedures for identifying job-relevant tasks and functional responsibilities *(role delineation).*

The match of individual items to the elements of such criteria can be judged by using the previously described methods for evaluating item-specification congruence. Because conformity is with respect to criteria, such as job elements, that might be different from place to place, use of a large number of judges representing these varied settings is recommended.

Opportunity. The court decision in the *Debra P. vs. Turlington* (1981) case seems to have established the necessity that, at least for certification tests for high school graduation, the tested material must consist of content that is currently taught, that is, the student must have been provided adequate preparation and, thus, had a fair opportunity to learn the material. McClung (1978) calls this match between what is taught and what is tested *instructional validity.* Legally speaking, it is not clear whether the test user must show that all students had an opportunity to learn the knowledge and skills required to answer each item or whether it is sufficient to demonstrate that omission of any content area or exclusion of any student from an opportunity to learn was not capricious. The latter is a much more reasonable requirement.

Because opportunity is apt to vary across localities, judgments from many, if not all, of the affected sites seem called for. Instructional validity can be assessed, in part, by knowing what instructional materials (e.g., textbook chapters) were actually employed by the teacher. Teachers (and students) are obvious sources for establishing the instructional validity of the items. They might be asked what instructional materials were used and if they taught (or were taught) the knowledge and skills being measured. Note that the question is not whether the specific content in the item was discussed but whether or not the student had an opportunity to acquire the knowledge and skills needed to answer the item. Because students might not be able to make such judgments, their assessments should be directed to statements of the knowledge and skills rather than to the items themselves.

Item Response Methods: Tryout Procedures

Procedures for gathering the responses of examinees to the potential items for a test are discussed in this section. Analyses of the item response data will be of little value if the data themselves are inadequate. So, one should be as conscientious about gathering item response data as about choosing analytical procedures for processing the information.

PRELIMINARY TRYOUT

Whenever possible, draft items should be administered by the test developers to a small group of examinees, as a part of the item-writing and revision process. This administration can be informal; the items themselves need not be typeset. Not only can such a preliminary tryout provide potentially valuable feedback from the examinees about the items themselves, but it can also alert the developers to gross inadequacies in the wording of directions and items, in the expected time requirements, and in the difficulty of the items. Because the number of examinees participating in such a tryout is small and unrepresentative, summary statistical results must be interpreted cautiously.

ASSIGNMENT OF EXPERIMENTAL ITEMS TO TEST FORMS

In addition to this preliminary tryout, three major strategies for gathering item response data are suggested. Variations and combinations of these strategies are, of course, possible.

Experimental items as the operational test. The first strategy is to combine the major item tryout and the actual test administration. That is, the item tryout and the operational testing are performed simultaneously. The examinees' responses are first used to evaluate the items and then used to provide scores on the test. The answers to items having unsatisfactory statistical properties are not considered during scoring.

This strategy is popular in situations in which a separate tryout of potential items is not feasible, either because an appropriate tryout sample is hard to find (as in the case of some certification programs) or because the developers are operating under severe time or financial constraints. Because the tryout sample consists of examinees who are affected by the test results, the strategy has the unique advantage of producing item response information from the target population itself under targeted test administration and motivation conditions. Because the item tryout and operational testing are one, test-development time and cost are substantially reduced, in comparison with a strategy that requires separate tryout and operational test administrations.

The strategy of combining the tryout and operational testing is not without its drawbacks, however. Chief among them is that the total number of items tried out is restricted, because the time for administering the test is limited. Ideally, the test developer tries out many more items than will actually be retained, to insure a sufficient number of acceptable items corresponding to each aspect of the domain. With the strategy of combining tryout and operational testing, the test developer runs the risk of not having enough items of the appropriate type and content to insure precise measurement. Also, unless some of the test is devoted to items having known statistical properties (*anchor items,* as they are called), the test developer cannot satisfactorily relate scores on the test to those on other forms of the test. Further, the developer does not have the opportunity to make even minor changes to items. If the answers to the items are to count in the scoring, the items must stand as written. Not surprisingly, the strategy works best when the test developers have had experience writing items of the type on the test and when the items are relatively homogeneous in format and content.

Experimental items embedded within an operational test. A second strategy is to embed the experimental items among the proven items during the operational administration of the test. Only the proven items are counted in the scoring. To insure enough items for future tests, several operational forms of the test are constructed, each containing different sets of embedded experimental items.

This embedding strategy has the advantages of requiring only a single test administration and obtaining item statistics from the targeted population under targeted administration and motivation conditions. Because many more experimental items can be tried out, albeit each on a fewer number of examinees, the embedding strategy is far less risky than the first strategy described. Further, the proven items on the test can serve as a referent against which the experimental items can be compared.

Compared with the first strategy, however, the embedding strategy (a) necessitates that an operational form presently exist, (b) requires that the test booklets be secure, and (c) involves somewhat more effort and expense, because multiple forms of the test must be created and scored.

Experimental items evaluated in a separate tryout. In the third approach, the tryout of the items is separate from the operational testing. The items are distributed among several tryout forms. If the test is speeded, items should appear in more than one form in different locations, and the data for items at the end of the test should be discarded (see Henrysson, 1971, pp. 133–134 for allocation methods). After item analyses, the selected items are assembled into one or more operational forms of the test, which can then be published and distributed.

The strategy of separating the item tryout from the operational testing facilitates evaluating a large number of prospective items. This larger pool of prospective items increases the likelihood that items will be available with the desired content and statistical characteristics. If the item tryout is extensive enough, sufficient items for two or more statistically parallel test forms would be available before the tests are administered operationally.

The disadvantages of this separate tryout strategy mirror the advantages of one or both of the other strategies. Insuring comparability of the tryout and operational groups of exa-minees is usually difficult. Motivating examinees to take the tryout testing seriously can also be difficult. Further, the strategy is more costly and time consuming than the others. Provision for securing the tryout forms must be made.

SAMPLE OF EXAMINEES

Concern about the examinees used in the item tryout arises when the tryout is separate from the operational testing, the third strategy described. The tryout examinees should be as much like the target population as possible. Even the so called sample-free methods of item analysis are dependent to some extent on the instructional history, attitudes during testing, and other characteristics of the sample of examinees. If examinees are not representative of the target population, for example, if they are volunteers, it is especially important to include items with known statistical characteristics among the experimental items so the item statistics calculated on the data from the tryout group can be calibrated.

The appropriate number of examinees responding to each item depends upon at least three factors. The first consideration is how the examinees are chosen. More examinees are needed if they are not representative of the target population, a condition likely to occur if the examinees come from a relatively few sites. A second consideration is the amount of information and precision one wishes to obtain from the analysis. In general, the larger the sample, the greater the resultant information and precision. For example, if item bias measures will be run for racial or gender groups, or if norms are contemplated for several school grades, the total number of examinees needed for the tryouts must be greater than otherwise, to insure an adequate number in each subgroup. A third factor influencing sample size is the choice of item-analysis method. Statistics such as factor loadings, which are determined from patterns among correlations, and the lower asymptotes of three-parameter item characteristic curves require many more observations for stable estimation than do such statistics as a proportion or a biserial correlation. Specifically, with appropriately selected samples of 100 to 200 cases, it is possible to obtain reasonably reliable estimates of an item's difficulty level. On the other hand, samples in excess of 2,000 might be required for stable estimates of the lower asymptote of a three-parameter item characteristic curve.

NUMBER OF ITEMS

Because some items will have undesirable item statistics and should be discarded, the test developer needs to try out more items than will appear on the operational form of the test. As for the appropriate number, Thorndike wrote,

> There is no universal prescription for the percentage of surplus items to be prepared for a test-construction project. The surplus required depends on too many variables. A plausible minimum might be 50%. Conditions that would call for a larger surplus include the following:
>
> 1. The type of item is difficult to prepare, and past experience has shown that a good many items tend to be ambiguous or nondiscriminating.
> 2. The items are in subsets (such as a set of items on a reading

passage) and, accordingly, enough satisfactory items are required in *each* set if the set is to be usable.
3. The test must match a detailed content outline, so satisfactory
   items are needed for each of the content areas.
4. The test maker wishes to maintain precise control of item difficulty, to match the difficulty of an existing test, or to control the
   information provided at specified levels on the scale of the latent
   attribute. (1982, p. 53)

Item Response Methods: Statistical Indexes

Once item response data have been obtained from the examinees, they are usually summarized. In this section we discuss
specific indexes of item quality. A discussion of the use of these
indexes in selecting items for a test is presented later in the
chapter, in the section on item selection.

GENERAL APPROACHES TO ITEM ANALYSIS

Two approaches to evaluating items using item response
data are widely followed. The classical approach begins by
computing difficulty, discrimination, and other traditional
statistical indexes for the sample of examinees who responded
to the items. The second approach begins by computing the
parameters of an item characteristic curve, which estimate the
probability that an item will be answered correctly as a function of an examinee's status on the underlying construct being
measured by the test. This chapter is limited to the former
approach; item analysis techniques that use item characteristic
curve theory are described in chapter 4.

The classical approach has the advantages of greater simplicity and familiarity. Also, it might require data from somewhat fewer examinees than do the ICC approaches. Further,
the frequently used ICC approaches might not work well when
the test items do not uniformly measure a common set of traits.
Classical-approach analogues are available for most item parameters used with ICC techniques. It is true, however, that
ICC techniques do provide an elegant solution to the problems
of identifying items that discriminate poorly among examinees
within a given range of ability, that do not measure the same
construct as the other items do, and that are statistically biased.
ICC methods gain an edge over classical approaches when existing items are to be reconfigured into new test forms.

In this age of easy computations, test developers should
employ both approaches whenever feasible. Results are likely
to be mutually reinforcing, but even when they are not, such
discrepancies can be illuminating.

INDEXES OF ITEM DIFFICULTY

By far, the most frequently used measure of item difficulty
is the proportion of examinees in the sample answering a dichotomously scored item correctly. When graded scoring is
used, as with essay or other items with more than two score
categories, an item's mean score or some variant of it such as
the ratio of the mean score to the maximum score serves as an
index of difficulty (University of Iowa, 1984). Although the
attention here is on the proportion-correct index, the *p* value,
much of what is written applies to other difficulty indexes as
well.

The *p* value can be misleading if it is interpreted as anything
more than the proportion of examinees *in a particular sample*
who *answered the item correctly*. It is not an accurate estimate
of difficulty for some other sample. Neither is it a measure of
what proportion of examinees truly know the correct answer,
nor a direct measure of the ability of a group of examinees. The
p value depends on the sample of examinees responding to the
item, is influenced by the opportunity to guess the correct
answer, and is nonlinearly related to the trait being measured
by the item. These characteristics are discussed next.

P value and the sample of examinees. Randomly selected
samples of examinees from a common population yield different *p* values. Large samples minimize these *random* fluctuations among samples. Often, however, the sample providing
item statistics is not representative of the population that will
be given the operational test. Such differences between groups
produce *systematic* fluctuations in item statistics, fluctuations
that large samples do not eliminate. It is in this context of
systematic differences between samples that concerns about
the sample dependency of classical item statistics are often
aired. And perhaps no index is more sample dependent than
the *p* value.

A major advantage of ICC theory is that its estimates of
item parameters provide more accurate information about the
measurement quality of the item across a wide span of the
ability scale than do the *p* value and other classical item-analysis statistics described in this chapter. It is possible, however, to
use hand calculator methods for estimating the *p* value in one
group, when the item has been administered to a different
group (Thorndike, 1982, pp. 66–70). The method requires
that both groups have responded to a common set of items but
not necessarily to the item in question.

P value and guessing. If the item is a recognition, rather
than a supply, item, some examinees are likely to obtain the
correct answer by guessing. In such a case, the proportion of
examinees in the sample who answer the item correctly (the *p*
value) will be greater than the proportion of examinees in the
sample who know the correct answer. If one is willing to make
the dubious assumption that examinees who do not know the
correct answer guess randomly among the choices, the *p* value
corrected for guessing is

$$p_c = p - p_w/(a - 1),$$

where

p_c is the difficulty index corrected for random guessing,
p is the uncorrected *p* value,
p_w is the proportion of examinees who attempted the item
      and missed it, and
a is the number of alternatives in the item.

If all of the items have the same number of options, and if
all of the examinees attempt all of the items, the corrected and
uncorrected *p* values will be perfectly correlated. In that situation, the corrected *p* value might be a more accurate indicator
of the proportion of examinees who know the answer to the
question, yet, the relative difficulties of all the items being
considered will be the same, regardless of which measure is
computed. Adjustment of the *p* values is advocated in norm-

referenced applications in which the number of omitted answers varies widely from examinee to examinee, as can occur in speeded tests.

P value and ability. The *p* value of an item is not a linear measure of the ability (skill, trait, competence, attribute, etc.) measured by the item. This is so because the underlying ability is probably not distributed rectangularly in the population. Assume the distribution is normal, as shown in Figure 8.6. If an item requires an amount equal to θ_1 in ability to answer it correctly, the 96% (that is, 23% + 23% + 50%) of the examinees who exceed that ability will answer the item correctly (see Figure 8.6) and $p_1 = .96$. Similarly, the *p* values corresponding to θ_2 and θ_3 are $p_2 = .73$ and $p_3 = .50$. The important point of Figure 8.6 is that, although the *p* values drop in equal intervals from .96 to .73 to .50, the corresponding estimates of ability needed to answer the item correctly do not uniformly increase, as shown by their unequal spacing on the ability axis.

One method of converting the *p* value into an estimate of the underlying ability needed to answer the item correctly is to consult a table of areas under the unit normal curve that is available in most elementary statistics books. For *p* values of .96, .73, and .50, the corresponding ability estimates are −1.75, −.61, and 0. Another method is to use an arc sine transformation. Transformed values can be converted to convenient units such as Educational Testing Service's delta, which has a mean of 13 and a standard deviation of 4. The difficulty parameter in ICC theory locates an item directly on a scale of ability, not on a scale of item difficulty.

INDEXES OF ITEM DISCRIMINATION

For those who view the *raison d'être* of measurement as permitting one to differentiate among examinees, the key indicator of an item's value is its discrimination index. In ICC theory, that index is the steepness of the curve itself. In classical theory, the index is based either on a correlation between whether or not the item was answered correctly and some criterion or on the differences among difficulty indexes for examinees in different groups. The numerical value of the index for any given item depends on the sample of examinees for whom data are available, on the specific index used, and especially on what variable is taken to be the criterion.

Choice of criterion. Ideally, the criterion should be a perfectly valid indicator of the variable the test developer hopes to measure or predict. Such is almost never the case, because each criterion has its own set of contaminating factors that make it less than perfect for the purpose. For that reason, the test developer might be well advised to use several and to note the effectiveness of the item with respect to each.

Criteria are usually divided into two types, internal and external. An internal criterion is some function, usually the total score, of the performance on all items on the test or subtest. It is recommended that the performance on the item in question not be included in the total score that serves as the criterion for the item, so as not to inflate the value of the discrimination index. This caution is important primarily when the item set is small, as is the case with objectives-based tests. Often the use of an internal criterion for item analysis is a compromise dictated by the difficulty of obtaining an external criterion. The rationale for using an internal criterion is that the sum of all the items in the test is likely to be a good indicator of the ability being measured. ICC theory employs an internal criterion.

External criteria are all the measurements of the examinee other than performance on the test items themselves. They might be ratings by teachers or others, grades or other indicators of success, scores on other tests designed to measure the same ability, or other factors. The rationale for using an external criterion is that, in many instances, it is closer to the ideal.

Criteria can also be differentiated on the basis of whether they are treated as continuous or dichotomous. The discrimination indexes are different for the two types. Although, for convenience, the discussion of indexes that follows is organized according to whether the criteria are continuous or dichotomous, the more important issue is what underlying variables are chosen as the criteria.

Indexes for continuous criteria. The two most frequently used classical indexes of item discrimination are the point-biserial correlation, r_{pbi}, and the biserial correlation, r_{bis}. Both can be used with an internal or an external criterion. Their formulas are

$$r_{pbi} = \frac{\overline{Y}_p - \overline{Y}_t}{S_t} \sqrt{\frac{p}{(1-p)}} \quad \text{and} \quad r_{bis} = r_{pbi} \frac{\sqrt{p(1-p)}}{u},$$

where $\overline{Y}_p$ is the mean score on the criterion of examinees who passed the item; $\overline{Y}_t$ and S_t are the mean and standard deviation on the criterion of all the examinees; *p* is the proportion of examinees answering correctly; and *u* is the ordinate of the unit normal curve at the point that divides the distribution into the

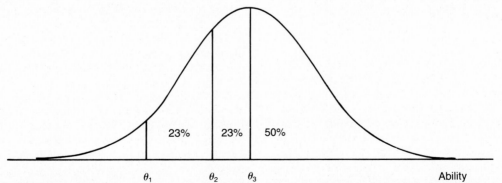

FIGURE 8.6 Distribution of examinees in the sample assuming the underlying attribute is normally distributed.

proportions p and $1 - p$. So long as r_{pbi} does not equal 0, r_{bis} will be at least 25% greater than r_{pbi} computed on the same data.

The point-biserial correlation is the product-moment correlation between the dichotomous item scores and the criterion measure; the biserial correlation is the product-moment correlation between a normally distributed latent variable underlying the right–wrong dichotomy and the criterion measure. Thus, the difference between the measures is whether item performance is treated as a dichotomy or as a normally distributed variable.

The advantage of the point-biserial correlation is that it provides a true reflection of the item's contribution to the functioning of the test. It measures how well actual item performance correlates with the criterion, not how well some abstract, underlying construct such as ability correlates with the criterion. It is the value of r_{pbi} that has the simpler, more direct relation to the test's statistics.

The point-biserial correlation can never have a value of 1.00, because only variables with distributions of the same shape can correlate perfectly, and a continuous variable (the criterion) and the dichotomously scored items do not have the same shape. The shape of the dichotomously scored item's distribution depends on the proportion of examinees answering the item correctly. In turn, the value of the point-biserial correlation depends heavily on this proportion. Thus, item discrimination as measured by r_{pbi} is confounded with item difficulty, and therein lies what many consider a major disadvantage of r_{pbi}. An item's discrimination, as measured by the point-biserial correlation, changes with the ability level of the sample of examinees. Like the p value, the r_{pbi} is highly sample dependent.

The biserial correlation tends to be more stable from sample to sample. It is a more accurate estimate of how well the item can be expected to discriminate at some different point in the ability scale. It is the value of r_{bis} that has the simpler, more direct relations to the ICC discrimination indicators.

The point-biserial and biserial correlations are intended for dichotomously scored items. If item responses are graded, the test developer can compute point-polyserial and polyserial correlations between item performance and the criterion. The point-polyserial and polyserial correlations are generalizations of the point-biserial and biserial correlations. The point-polyserial correlation can be computed by using the standard formula for the product-moment correlation, r. Procedures for estimating polyserial correlations are provided by Olsson, Drasgow, and Dorans (1982). It has been suggested by Glass and Stanley (1970, pp. 171–172) that the values of the polyserial correlations might not differ greatly from the biserial correlations computed after the scoring categories have been coalesced into two.

Indexes for dichotomous criteria. When each examinee is a member of one of only two criterion groups, it is possible to compute the product-moment correlation between item performance (correct, incorrect) and group membership. The phi coefficient and the tetrachoric coefficient are such correlations, and they are analogous to the point-biserial and biserial coefficients, respectively. They share the same advantages and limitations as their serial counterparts. Formulas for computing the phi and tetrachoric coefficients are available in many elementary statistics textbooks. For the correlations to be more easily interpretable, the two groups should contain all of the examinees, not just the ones with extreme scores.

When an *internal* criterion is used, a frequently mentioned item-discrimination index is the difficulty index (p value) for a group of examinees who scored well on the test minus the p value for a group of examinees who scored poorly. Most often the two groups are defined as those scoring in the top and bottom 27% of the distribution. These percentages are chosen because, regardless of sample size, they maximize the critical ratio of the difference between the mean scores of the groups if the standard errors of measurement in each group are equal and if the scores for the entire examinee population are normally distributed. (The former assumption is apt to be violated because low-scoring examinees are more likely to guess and, thus, to add random error. If the distribution of scores is rectangular instead of normal, having 33% in each group would maximize the critical ratio.) The availability of computers, however, has prompted test developers to forego the p-value difference index when an *internal* criterion is used. Instead, the scores are treated as a continuous variable, and biserial or point-biserial correlations are computed directly.

As a result of the high interest in criterion-referenced testing during the 1970s, several item-analysis procedures have been proposed that involved a dichotomous *external* criterion. Berk (1984) provides a comprehensive overview of these procedures. The comparisons most often mentioned are between groups of masters (competent examinees) and nonmasters (incompetent examinees) and between groups of instructed (treated) and noninstructed (nontreated) examinees. The procedures all provide an index of the item's ability to discriminate between the groups. The numerical value of the indexes is very sensitive to the composition of the examinee sample and to the definition of the criterion groups. The practical value of these or other indexes depends upon the relevance of the criterion-group definitions to the test purposes, as will be discussed again later in this chapter.

An item's discrimination value for these externally defined groups can also be defined as the difference between p values for the groups (see Cox & Vargas, 1966). A variation involves dividing this difference by 1 minus the lower scoring group's p value. The latter index provides a measure of the proportion of the maximum possible difference between the groups that was obtained. These two indexes can yield very different values. Suppose the p values for an uninstructed and an instructed group are .85 and .95. The two discrimination indexes are, respectively, $.95 - .85 = .10$ (a modest value) and $.10/(1 - .85) = .67$ (a high value). Because both indexes provide different, but complementary, information, computing both, rather than only one of them, is recommended.

Subkoviak and Harris (1984) proposed a simple index when the criterion categories are such that the test developer would ideally wish examinees in one category (e.g., masters) to answer the item correctly and examinees in the other category (e.g., nonmasters) to answer the item incorrectly. The index is the proportion of examinees who are "hit," that is, masters who answered correctly and nonmasters who answered incorrectly. This index is essentially a measure of the *information* (as the term is used in ICC theory) the item has for examinees who are at the boundary between the two criterion groups.

When examinees are tested twice (with intervening instruction or some other treatment), Roudabush (1973) suggests computing the proportion of examinees who answered the item incorrectly the first time and correctly the second time. This proportion can be adjusted by subtracting the proportion of examinees who answered the item incorrectly both times (Kosecoff & Klein, 1974). These indexes can also be adjusted for random guessing. Item analyses employing these and other treatment-sensitive indexes are typically more appropriate for treatment effectiveness evaluation than for item selection.

INDEXES BASED ON A PATTERN OF ITEM RESPONSES

It is possible to assess the value of an item by noting examinee responses to both that item and other items. To some degree, relating an item to the score on the rest of a test (internal criterion) does involve all the items. The methods mentioned here, however, emphasize the patterns of responses among all the items.

All the methods discussed here can also be methods of determining test validity. Whether the method is being applied as an item-analysis technique or as part of a test-validity process depends upon the focus of the investigator. In item analysis, attention is directed to each item individually, and the question is whether the item is performing as expected. A negative answer implies that the item should be discarded or revised. In test validity, attention is directed to the pattern of item responses, and the question is whether the collection of items displays the expected pattern. In practice, the test developer addresses both the item evaluation and the test validation concerns.

As will be indicated, item-analysis methods differ in their concept of expected pattern for an ideal item. Which expected pattern to use as a criterion depends upon what the test is designed to measure and what interpretations are to be made from its scores.

Methods based on patterns of difficulty indexes. Perhaps the simplest technique, although one having limited value, is to ask whether the targeted item has the same p value as the other items in the same test or subtest. Because the p value of an item is volatile, subject to change by modifications in wording and context, it is unlikely that any set of items will, a posteriori, be homogeneous in p value, unless the domain spanned by the items is narrowly defined.

Test developers typically study the pattern of change in grade- or age-group p values as a measure of growth. Growth is a major item-selection criterion for tests that provide grade or age norms (D. R. Green & Yen, 1984).

Test developers also study whether the *relative* difficulty of the item, compared to other items, remains the same for groups of examinees who differ in race, gender, or similar characteristics. This procedure is essentially that used by more formal internal tests of item bias. Items that are relatively easier for one group than another may be considered biased in favor of that group.

Methods based on patterns of item correlations. When a set of items is hypothesized to reference a single dimension, examinees who answer an item correctly should tend to answer the other items in the set correctly, and examinees who answer the item incorrectly should tend to answer the other items in the set incorrectly. Epstein (1977) proposed an index to measure such a tendency:

$$\overline{D}^2 = \sum_{n=1}^{N} (P_{n(i \neq j)} - x_{nj})^2/N,$$

where

$\overline{D}^2$ = the squared discrepancy for item j (Epstein's index)

$P_{n(i \neq j)}$ = the average score for person n (proportion correct) based on all items except item j,

x_{nj} = the score for person n on item j (0,1)

N = the total number of examinees.

The best value for the index is 0, reflecting perfect consistency in examinees' responses to a set of items. For a single examinee (D_i^2), the index's maximum, but undesirable, value of $+1$ occurs when item j is the only item in the set the examinee answers correctly (or incorrectly). The value of Epstein's index is related to the average of the correlations between the item and each of the other items in the set.

The correlations among the items are the basic input into factor- and cluster-analysis programs. If the targeted item is predicted to measure the same underlying dimension as the other items, it should load highly on a single general factor. (Tetrachorics, rather than phi coefficients, should be used in the factor analysis to avoid having the general factor merely represent item difficulty.) In ICC theory, item-fit statistics are the analogue to a high loading on a common factor.

When the items are hypothesized to reference several dimensions, such as different parts of a table of specifications, one can note whether the targeted item loads highly on the appropriate factor and as expected on the other factors. The VARCLUS program in the Statistical Analysis System is one way to study whether the item is placed in its appropriate cluster. Some test developers compute scores for each subset of items and note whether the targeted item correlates highest with the score in its own subtest and appropriately lower with other subtest scores. One problem with this approach is that that sizes of the correlations depend, to some extent, on the number of items in the subsets. A refinement of the approach overcomes this problem by comparing an item's correlations with a profile of expected correlations (Kolen & Jarjoura, 1984).

Items can also be hypothesized to have a hierarchical relationship among themselves. For example, the prediction might be that examinees must be able to answer Question 1 correctly before the targeted item can be answered correctly. This simple prediction implies that a 2×2 table (right–wrong on Item 1 versus right–wrong on the targeted item) would have a 0 frequency cell. Several investigators (see Nitko & Hsu, 1983, for a listing of references) have proposed techniques to study whether an item is correctly placed in an expected hierarchical order among the other items. Because items measure so many specific skills that examinees acquire in different sequences, insisting that items fit a hierarchical pattern is a very stringent requirement that is unlikely to be met.

ANALYSIS OF DISTRACTORS

When the items are multiple choice in format, test developers find it instructive to obtain a measure of discrimination for each option, as well as for the correct answer. They usually calculate the proportions of high- and low-scoring groups who choose each option. Biserial or point-biserial correlations between whether or not the option was picked and the criterion may also be computed.

For many testing purposes, items should meet several criteria during a distractor analysis: (a) Among high-scoring examinees, the keyed answer should be popular (some say the most popular). If it is not, the item might be miskeyed or ambiguous, or these high-scoring examinees might be guessing. The guessing hypothesis can be tested by using procedures described in Nitko and Hsu (1983). (b) All foils should be chosen by a sufficient percentage of the low-scoring examinees (for example, 5%) to warrant their use. (c) The discrimination value of the keyed answer should be positive (for some applications, it should be relatively large as well); the discrimination values for the foils should be lower and, preferably, negative. If only a few examinees choose a foil, its discrimination index might be poorly estimated, and allowance for sampling variability is suggested.

Analysis of distractors can be particularly helpful in revising an item. Instructive examples are provided by Ebel (1979, pp. 268–272).

Item Selection

Several methods of evaluating items were identified in the last section. The problem of deciding which items to use in a test is considered here.

Item-Selection Situations

Test constructors having potential items available might find themselves in one of two situations, which are described next in their extreme forms. In the first, a rather large pool of items is available, and the pool will be dipped into repeatedly to produce many tests. Item selection is random, or random within content categories, because items are considered to be interchangeable. Item selection is routine and automatic, save for a final review to catch unanticipated coincidences or oversights in the preparation of the item pool. Item evaluations are considered, not in the selection of items to use on a given test, but rather in governing admission into the pool. For large pools, quality controls unfortunately are unlikely and often depend heavily only on the editorial review of relatively few individuals. Item response data might accompany the items in the pool, but usually they serve neither a gatekeeping nor a selection role.

Many fewer items are available in the second situation. Here, the task is to pick the subset of items that will produce the best test possible. Item evaluations, especially those based on item response data, are considered in making comparisons among items. The psychometric properties of the proposed test are often estimated in advance (see Thorndike, 1982, and Nitko & Hsu, 1983, for formulas). This situation commonly characterizes the development of tests whose inferences are to cognitive domains and future criterion settings.

In sum, in the first situation, the question is whether the item is good enough to be left in the running for possible selection on a future test; in the second situation, the question is whether the item is better than others competing for a place on a developing test.

Item-Evaluation Criteria and Test Inferences

Slavish attention to a single procedure for item assessment and selection is not advocated; gaining insight about the worth of an item for a given test is. Practically any valid information can be helpful in item assessment and selection, although some procedures are more universally applicable than others. These procedures are noted first; then, assessment and selection criteria for different domains of test inferences are highlighted.

DESIRABLE ITEM-SELECTION PROCEDURES

Regardless of the item-selection situation and the test's purpose, quality items are desired. Consequently, item-review procedures designed to weed out flawed items are recommended. Editorial review procedures to assess an item's accuracy and communicability, as described earlier, are appropriate for all tests. Poorly written items should not be included on any test.

Other item-content evaluation procedures are widely applicable. Items should be consistent with the content descriptions for the pool of items to which they are to be added or with the test and item specifications found in the test plan. (Incongruence is more likely to be noted when descriptions and specifications are explicit.) Rare is the textbook on educational measurement that does not admonish its reader against ignoring item content and relying solely on item statistics when evaluating items and choosing them for a test.

When item response data are available, an item-discrimination index should be calculated and, for multiple-choice items, a distractor analysis performed. Negatively discriminating items should be flagged for likely elimination from the item pool or from consideration for use on a test.

CURRICULAR DOMAIN

When inferences are to be made to curricular domains, all of the assessment criteria found in Table 8.4 might be relevant. Their relative importance, however, depends in part on whether inferences are to be made about an individual or about groups of examinees. When inferences are about an individual and important decisions are to be based on the test score, items on the test should be consistent with published test specifications, should themselves be judged important, and should pass checks on bias and on opportunity (to acquire the knowledge or skills). Care should be exercised that content representation of the items is not adversely affected by efforts to obtain highly discriminating items.

If these curriculum-related tests are intended to provide a description of performance for a group or system, rather than to serve as the basis for placement, graduation, or other individual decisions, many of these selection criteria become less important. Formal bias studies are less crucial; opportunity checks are not needed; p values can, and probably should, be much more heterogeneous; and lower discrimination indexes can be tolerated. Comparisons between p values for instructed and noninstructed groups, called instructional sensitivity measures, might be employed, but caution is suggested.

> Schools already have too great a tendency to teach what is easy to learn instead of more worthwhile objectives. Reinforcing that tendency by using instructional sensitivity as a statistical criterion is likely to be very detrimental. (R. Schweiker, personal communication, 1984)

COGNITIVE DOMAIN

Item response data usually assume more importance in the selection of items for tests intended to measure a cognitive domain. When ICC methods have been applied and appear to be working well, items with satisfactory fit (to the model) statistics are entered into an item pool, and items with the maximum information at the desired ability levels are given prime consideration for inclusion in a test (see chapter 4). Optimum procedures are also well developed for selecting items when tests are to be administered adaptively (see chapter 9). In the next paragraphs, it is assumed that ICC methods will *not* be used and that a single test, to be given to all examinees, is to be built.

For the construction of unidimensional tests, item-discrimination values are often the paramount statistic in item selection. Normally, the higher the value, the better. Items with p values somewhat higher than half the difference between the chance level and 1.00 are also recommended (Lord, 1952). For equally discriminating items, a test with homogeneously difficult items will, in general, produce greater precision than one with items having a range of p values. Unless the test items have high discrimination values, that is, biserials over .50, the use of items that are very hard or easy will detract more from the test's precision at the intermediate range of ability than it will contribute to precision at the ends of the ability range. "[T]he usual price one pays for uniform precision is lower overall levels of precision" (Baker, 1982, p. 965).

Also, for a unidimensional test or scale, items with high internal consistency are desired; such consistency supports the test's construct validity. To maximize the reliability of the resulting test, an iterative procedure reported by Thorndike (1982, pp. 90–93) is recommended. *First,* a factor analysis is performed, and the three or four items with the largest loadings on the factor of interest are retained. *Second,* the alpha coefficient of reliability for the retained set is computed. *Third,* the retained item set is temporarily augmented by one of the potential new items, and the alpha coefficient is recomputed. *Fourth,* step three is repeated for each potential item, and the one that augments the reliability value the most is permanently included in the retained set. *Fifth,* steps 2 through 4 are repeated until a satisfactory level of reliability is reached, until the limit of the test length has been reached, or until no additional items are available, whichever comes first.

Other item-evaluation procedures come into play when the goal is not to build a unidimensional test. Indexes based on a *pattern* of item responses can serve as the item-selection criteria for such tests.

FUTURE CRITERION SETTING

Item-content methods of item evaluation assume importance in building item pools or tests to select examinees for schools or jobs. In addition to the ubiquitous selection criteria of accuracy and match with test specifications, three other assessment criteria seem particularly relevant. As indicated, items that find their way into tests that govern access to valued opportunities should be checked for possible group bias, should be judged to measure important or essential skills, and should be judged to reference knowledge, skills, or abilities needed for successful criterion performance. Even when the test is to be used for guidance or other less controlling purposes, these selection criteria are still germane.

Item response criteria are, of course, also relevant. Correlations between item performance and criterion behavior (item-validity indexes) are the most important data. However, the best set of items to include on a test might not be that with the highest item validities, because the predictability of the item set depends in part on the intercorrelations among the items. Although multiple regression would appear to be a promising way to choose items to maximize predictive validity, with many items and fewer than hundreds of examinees, the solutions are sufficiently unstable to cause concern that results would not do well on cross-validation (tryout of the prediction system on a sample of examinees different from those used to develop the system).

Approaches that promise to be more robust, yet make use of the intercorrelations among the items, have been proposed (Schaffner & Darlington, 1977; Thorndike, 1982, pp. 258–259). In applying these or other methods, it is recommended that the predictive validity be calculated for a cross-validation group.

It is not uncommon to find oneself in a situation in which one wishes to build a test to reference a future criterion setting in which performance data on the criterion are not available. Darlington (1970) proposed a set of procedures for maximizing validity with an "unobserved" criterion. Discussion of how these procedures are applicable to item selection can be found in Millman (1974, pp. 380–383).

Test Assembly

Once items have been selected, the next stage in test development is the physical production of the test itself. The four component steps are ordering the items, physically arranging the items, reproducing the test, and providing for the security of the test materials.

Item Sequence

For reasons of efficiency at least, items having common directions should be grouped. Within each group, common sense suggests that items on conventionally administered tests be ordered roughly from easy to hard or be placed in logical sequence. However, research indicates that, although order has little effect on *test* performance under unspeeded conditions (see e.g., Kleinke, 1980; Sirotnik & Wellington, 1974), the position of an item on a test can affect that item's parameters (Yen, 1981). For example, the p value of an item placed at the beginning of a test is typically higher than the p value of the same item placed at the end of a test. Such effects imply that balancing the position of an item across several forms during item tryout is desirable.

When tests are administered adaptively, not only are different items presented to different examinees, but also any one item may be presented early or late in the testing session. Strong position effects could reduce the accuracy and precision of the ability estimates.

Item Layout

When two or more items share a common stem or common reference material (e.g., reading passage or graph), conventional wisdom is that the items should be grouped on a single page or, if that is not possible, on facing pages of the test booklet. Other common practices are to limit the number of questions appearing on the pages of tests administered to young children and to order the test questions such that the examinee is to proceed from column to column rather than to go across rows. A vertical line separating columns helps prevent the answering of questions out of order.

When tests are administered by computer, only a single item is presented on the screen at one time. The question for layout in that case is, What else should be displayed on the screen? If tests are administered *non*adaptively, three other pieces of information are sometimes shown: a replica of the answer sheet, so examinees can note their progress through the test; the time remaining; and a summary of the instructions for recording an answer, for choosing the next item, for omitting an item, for ending the testing session, and the like.

Test Reproduction

Test constructors have a great deal more flexibility in printing their tests than was the case at the time of the previous edition of *Educational Measurement* (see Thorndike, 1971). Changes can be made more easily, tests can be printed more quickly, and graphic material can be incorporated more automatically. For example, pictorial material can be scanned and transformed into a digital representation, merged with textual material, and printed on paper (Baker, 1984).

High-speed printers and computer-administered testing mean that testing can be done on demand. That is, tests can be produced as needed or at the time examinees wish to be tested. Further, with item banking, each examinee can receive a different set of questions, in which case it would be more accurate to say that the tests are produced rather than reproduced.

Test Security

When tests are used in making important decisions about examinees, test security becomes a major concern. Tests can be compromised at many steps: in item development and test production, in test delivery, in test administration, in test re-

turn, and in test disposal. Limited access to storage rooms and computer banks, special arrangements for delivery, unique test identifications, and permanently bonded test seals are among the precautions most often taken. Ensuring security can be very costly; one test developer admitted that just to provide secure disposal of used test booklets costs about $20,000 a year.

NOTE. This chapter was written in 1985.

REFERENCES

American Nurses' Association, Division on Medical-Surgical Nursing Practice.(1983). *Clinical specialist in medical-surgical nursing, certification examination test specifications.* Author.

American Psychological Association, American Educational Research Association, & National Council on Measurement in Education.(1985). *Standards for Educational and Psychological Tests.* Washington, DC: American Psychological Association.

Anastasio, E. J., Marcotte, D. M., & Fremer, J. (1969). *Computer-assisted item writing: II (sentence completion items)* (TDM-69-1). Princeton, NJ: Educational Testing Service.

Baker, F. B. (1982). Item analysis. In H. E. Mitzel (Ed.), *Encyclopedia of educational research: Vol. 3* (pp. 959–967). New York: Free Press.

Baker, F. B. (1984). Technology and testing: State of the art and trends for the future. *Journal of Educational Measurement, 21,* 399–406.

Berk, R. A. (1984). Conducting the item analysis. In R. A. Berk (Ed.), *A guide to criterion-referenced test construction* (pp. 97–143). Baltimore: Johns Hopkins University Press.

Bloom, B. S., Engelhart, M. D., Furst, E. J., Hill, W. H., & Krathwohl, D. R. (1956). *Taxonomy of educational objectives: The classification of educational goals. Handbook I: Cognitive domain.* New York: David McKay.

Bloom, B. S., Hastings, J. T., & Madaus, G. F. (1971). *Handboook of formative and summative evaluation of student learning.* New York: McGraw-Hill.

Bolden, B. J., & Stoddard, A. (1980, April). *The effects of language on test performance of elementary school children.* Paper presented at the meeting of the American Educational Research Association, Boston.

Brown, F. L. (1970). *Statistical criteria for determining regression slope sign changes: Applications for determining the ability of individual tests to differentiate between excellence and near excellence.* Unpublished doctoral dissertation, Cornell University, Ithaca, NY.

Carroll, J. B. (1972). Defining language comprehension: Some speculations. In J. B. Carroll & R. Freedle (Eds.), *Language comprehension and the acquisition of knowledge* (pp. 1–29). New York: Halstead Press.

Chi, M. T. H., Glaser, R., & Rees, E. (1982). Expertise in problem solving. In R. J. Sternberg (Ed.), *Advances in the psychology of human intelligence: Vol. 1* (pp. 7–75). Hillsdale, NJ: Lawrence Erlbaum.

Cole, N. S. (1984). Testing the crisis in education. *Educational Measurement: Issues and Practice, 3*(3), 4–8.

Cox, R. C., & Vargas, J. (1966, February). *A comparison of item selection techniques for norm-referenced and criterion-referenced tests.* Paper presented at the meeting of the National Council on Measurement in Education, Chicago.

Cronbach, L. J. (1984). *Essentials of psychological testing* (4th ed.). New York: Harper & Row.

CTB/McGraw-Hill. (1981). *Comprehensive test of basic skills: Test coordinator's handbook, Forms U and V.* Monterey, CA: Author.

Darlington, R. B. (1970). Some techniques for maximizing a test's validity when the criterion variable is unobserved. *Journal of Educational Measurement, 7,* 1–14.

Davidson, W. M., & Carroll, J. B. (1945). Speed and level components in time-limit scores: A factor analysis. *Educational and Psychological Measurement, 5,* 411–427.

D'Costa, A. (1985, April). *Documenting the job-relevance of certification and licensure examinations using job analysis.* Paper presented at the meeting of the American Educational Research Association, Chicago.

Ebel, R. L. (1979). *Essentials of educational measurement* (3rd ed.). Englewood Cliffs, NJ: Prentice-Hall.

Ebel, R. L. (1980). *Practical problems in educational measurement.* Lexington, MA: D. C. Heath.

Epstein, K. I. (1977, April). *Predictive sample reuse and an application for criterion referenced test item analysis.* Paper presented at the meeting of the American Educational Research Association, New York.

Farina, A. J., & Wheaton, G. R. (1971). *Development of a taxonomy of human performance: The task characteristics approach to performance prediction* (Tech. Rep. No. 7). Washington, DC: American Psychological Association. (Psychological Documents No. 323)

Fitzpatrick, R., & Morrison, E. J. (1971). Performance and product evaluation. In R. L. Thorndike (Ed.), *Educational measurement* (2nd ed., pp. 237–270). Washington, DC: American Council on Education.

Fleishman, E. A. (1982). Systems for describing human tasks. *American Psychologist, 37,* 821–834.

Frederiksen, N. (1984). The real test bias: Influences of testing on teaching and learning. *American Psychologist, 39,* 193–202.

Fremer, J., & Anastasio, E. J. (1969). Computer-assisted item writing: I (spelling items). *Journal of Educational Measurement, 6,* 69–74.

Fremer, J., Kastrinos, W., & Jones, C. (1972). *Student involvement in test development* (TDR-72-3). Princeton, NJ: Educational Testing Service.

Gagné, R. M. (1977). *The conditions of learning* (3rd ed.). New York: Holt, Rinehart and Winston.

Gagné, R. M. (1984). Learning outcomes and their effects: Useful categories of human performance. *American Psychologist, 39,* 377–385.

Glaser, R. G. (1984). Education and thinking: The role of knowledge. *American Psychologist, 39,* 93–104.

Glass, G. V., & Stanley, J. C. (1970). *Statistical methods in education and psychology.* Englewood Cliffs, NJ: Prentice-Hall.

Green, D. R. (Ed.). (1974). *The aptitude-achievement distinction: Proceedings of the Second CTB/McGraw-Hill Conference on Issues in Educational Measurement.* Monterey, CA: CTB/McGraw-Hill.

Green, D. R., & Yen, W. M. (1984, April). *Content and construct validity of norm-referenced tests.* Paper presented at the meeting of the American Educational Research Association, New Orleans.

Green, K. (1984). Effects of item characteristics on multiple-choice item difficulty. *Educational and Psychological Measurement, 44,* 551–561.

Gronlund, N. E. (1981). *Measurement and evaluation in teaching* (4th ed.). New York: Macmillan.

Guilford, J. P. (1959). Three faces of intellect. *American Psychologist, 14,* 469–479.

Guilford, J. P. (1967). *The nature of human intelligence.* New York: McGraw-Hill.

Guttman, L. (1941). An outline of the statistical theory of prediction. In P. Horst (Ed.), *Prediction of personal adjustment. Social Science Research Bulletin, 48,* 253–364.

Guttman, L. (1969). Integration of test design and analysis. In *Proceedings of the 1969 ETS Invitational Conference* (pp. 53–65). Princeton: NJ: Educational Testing Service.

Haladyna, T. M. (1985, April). *A review of research on multiple-choice item option weighting.* Paper presented at the meeting of the National Council for Measurement in Education, Chicago.

Haladyna, T. M., & Downing, S. M. (1985, April). *A quantitative review of research on multiple-choice item writing.* Paper presented at the meeting of the American Educational Research Association, Chicago.

Hall, B. W. (1985). Survey of the technical characteristics of published educational achievement tests. *Educational Measurement: Issues and Practices, 4*(1), 6–14.

Hambleton, R. K. (1984). Validating the test scores. In R. A. Berk (Ed.), *A guide to criterion-referenced test construction* (pp. 199–230). Baltimore: Johns Hopkins University Press.

Henrysson, S. (1971). Gathering, analyzing, and using data on test items. In R. L. Thorndike (Ed.), *Educational measurement 6* (2nd ed., pp. 130–159). Washington, DC: American Council on Education.

Holtzman, W. H. (1970). *Computer assisted instruction, testing, and guidance.* New York: Harper & Row.

Kleinke, D. J. (1980). Item order, response location and examinee sex and handedness and performance on a multiple-choice test. *Journal of Educational Research, 73,* 225–229.

Kneedler, P. E. (1985). *Assessment of the critical thinking skills in history-social science.* Sacramento, CA: California State Department of Education, California Assessment Program.

Kolen, M. J., & Jarjoura, D. (1984). Item profile analysis for tests developed according to a table of specifications. *Applied Psychological Measurement, 8,* 321–331.

Kosecoff, J. B., & Klein, S. P. (1974). *Instructional sensitivity statistics appropriate for objectives-based test items* (Report No. 91). Los Angeles: University of California, Center for the Study of Evaluation.

Larkin, J., McDermott, J., Simon, D. P., & Simon, H. A. (1980). Expert and novice performance in solving physics problems. *Science, 208,* 1335–1342.

Levine, E. L., Ash, R. A., Hall, H., & Sistrunk, F. (1983). Evaluation of job analysis methods by experienced job analysts. *Academy of Management Journal, 26,* 339–348.

Lindquist, E. F. (1951). Preliminary considerations in objective test construction. In E. F. Lindquist (Ed.), *Educational measurement* (pp. 119–184). Washington, DC: American Council on Education.

Lohman, D. F. (1979). *Spatial ability: A review and reanalysis of the correlational literature* (Tech. Rep. No. 8). Stanford, CA: Stanford University, School of Education.

Lord, F. M. (1952). The relation of the reliability of multiple-choice tests to the distribution of item difficulties. *Psychometrika, 17,* 181–194.

Madaus, G. F. (1983). Minimum competency testing for certification: The evolution and evaluation of test validity. In G. F. Madaus (Ed.), *The courts, validity, and minimum competency testing* (pp. 21–61). Hingham, MA: Kluwer-Nijhoff.

McClung, M. S. (1978). Are competency testing programs fair? Legal? *Phi Delta Kappan, 59,* 397–400.

Mehrens, W. A., & Lehmann, I. J. (1984). *Measurement and evaluation in education and psychology* (3rd ed.). New York: Holt, Rinehart and Winston.

Melton, A. W. (1964) The taxonomy of human learning: Overview. In A. W. Melton (Ed.), *Categories of human learning* (pp. 325–339). New York: Academic Press.

Merrill, M. D. (1983). Component display theory. In C. M. Reigeluth (Ed.), *Instructional-design theories and models: An overview of their current status* (pp. 279–333). Hillsdale, NJ: Lawrence Erlbaum.

Messick, S. (1984). The psychology of educational measurement. *Journal of Educational Measurement, 21,* 215–237.

Miller, H. G., Williams, R. G., & Haladyna, T. M. (1978). *Beyond facts: Objective ways to measure thinking.* Englewood Cliffs, NJ: Educational Technology Publications.

Millman, J. (1974). Criterion-referenced measurement. In W. J. Popham (Ed.), *Evaluation in education: Current applications* (pp. 311–397). Berkeley, CA: McCutchan.

Nitko, A. J., & Hsu, T. (1983). *Item analysis appropriate for domain-referenced classroom testing* (Tech. Rep. No. 1). Pittsburgh: University of Pittsburgh.

Olsson, U., Drasgow, F., & Dorans, N. J. (1982). The polyserial correlation coefficient. *Psychometrika, 47,* 337–347.

Pellegrino, J. W., Alderton, D. L., & Shute, V. J. (1984). Understanding spatial ability. *Educational Psychologist, 19,* 239–253.

Popham, W. J. (1978). *Criterion-referenced measurement.* Englewood Cliffs, NJ: Prentice-Hall.

Popham, W. J. (1984). Specifying the domain of content or behaviors. In R. A. Berk (Ed.), *A guide to criterion-referenced test construction* (pp. 29–48). Baltimore: Johns Hopkins University Press.

Pressey, S. L. (1926). A simple apparatus which gives tests and scores and teaches. *School and Society, 23,* 373–376.

Priestley, M. (1982). *Performance assessment in education & training: Alternative techniques.* Englewood Cliffs, NJ: Educational Technology Publications.

Quellmalz, E. S. (1984). Designing writing assessments: Balancing fairness, utility, and cost. *Educational Evaluation and Policy Analysis, 6,* 63–72.

Quellmalz, E. S., Smith, L. S., Winters, L., & Baker, E. (1980). *Characterizations of student writing competence: An investigation of alternative scoring systems.* Los Angeles: University of California, Center for the Study of Evaluation.

Rhode Island Statewide Assessment Program. (1980). *Domain specifications for life skills testing component.* Providence: Rhode Island Department of Education.

Roid, G. H. (1984). Generating the test items. In R. A. Berk (Ed.), *A guide to criterion -referenced test construction* (pp. 49–77). Baltimore: Johns Hopkins University Press.

Roid, G. H., & Haladyna, T. M. (1982). *A technology for test-item writing.* New York: Academic Press.

Roudabush, G. E. (1973, February). *Item selection for criterion-referenced tests.* Paper presented at the meeting of the American Educational Research Association, New Orleans.

Rovinelli, R. J., & Hambleton, R. K. (1976, April). *On the use of content specialists in the assessment of criterion-referenced test item validity.* Paper presented at the meeting of the American Educational Research Association, San Francisco.

Schaffner, P. E., & Darlington, R. B. (1977, August). *A new technique for personality scale construction: Preliminary findings.* Paper presented at the meeting of the American Psychological Association, San Francisco.

Schrader, W. B. (Ed.). (1980). *Measuring achievement: Progress over a decade. New Directions for Testing and Measurement* (No. 5). San Francisco: Jossey-Bass.

Schrock, T. J., & Mueller, D. J. (1982). Effects of violating three multiple-choice item construction principles. *Journal of Educational Research, 75,* 314–318.

Shuford, E. H., Jr., Albert, A., & Massengill, H. E. (1966). Admissible probability measurement procedures. *Psychometrika, 31,* 125–145.

Simon, R. A. (1984). *Development and validation of a criterion-referenced placement examination for measuring technical aspects of nursing.* Unpublished doctoral thesis, University of Massachusetts, Amherst, MA.

Sirotnik, K., & Wellington, R. (1974). Scrambling content in achievement testing: An application of multiple matrix sampling in experimental design. *Journal of Educational Measurement, 11,* 179–188.

Snow, R. E., & Lohman, D. F. (1984). Toward a theory of cognitive aptitude for learning from instruction. *Journal of Educational Psychology, 76,* 347–376.

Stahl, R. J., & Murphy, G. T. (1981, April). *The domain of cognition: An alternative to Bloom's cognitive domain within the framework of an information processing model.* Paper presented at the meeting of the American Educational Research Association, Los Angeles.

Sternberg, R. J. (1984). What should intelligence tests test? Implications of a triarchic theory of intelligence for intelligence testing. *Educational Researcher, 13,* 5–15.

Subkoviak, M. J., & Harris, D. J. (1984, April). *A short-cut statistic for item analysis of mastery tests.* Paper presented at the meeting of the American Educational Research Association, New Orleans.

Thorndike, R. L. (1971). Reproducing the test. In R. L. Thorndike (Ed.), *Educational measurement* (2nd ed., pp. 160–187). Washington, DC: American Council on Education.

Thorndike, R. L. (1982). *Applied psychometrics.* Boston: Houghton Mifflin.

Tiemann, P. W., & Markle, S. M. (1973). Re-modeling a model: An elaborated hierarchy of types of learning. *Educational Psychologist, 10,* 147–158.

Traub, R. E., & Fisher, C. W. (1977). On the equivalence of constructed-response and multiple-choice tests. *Applied Psychological Measurement, 3,* 355–369.

University of Iowa, Evaluation and Examination Service. (1984). *Improving essay examinations III. Use of item analysis* (Tech. Bull. No. 11). Iowa City: Author.

Washburne, C., & Morphett, M. V. (1928). Unfamiliar situations as a difficulty in solving arithmetic problems. *Journal of Educational Research, 18,* 220–224.

Wesman, A. G. (1971). Writing the test item. In R. L. Thorndike (Ed.), *Educational measurement* (2nd ed., pp. 81–129). Washington, DC: American Council on Education.

Whitely, S. E. (1981). Measuring aptitude processes with multicomponent latent trait models. *Journal of Educational Measurement, 18,* 67–84.

Wolfe, J. H. (1976). Automatic question generation from text: An aid to independent study. *SIGCSE Bulletin, 8,* 104–108.

Yen, W. M. (1981). The extent, causes, and importance of context effects on item parameters for two latent trait models. *Journal of Educational Measurement, 17,* 297–311.

9

The Four Generations of Computerized Educational Measurement

C. Victor Bunderson
Educational Testing Service

Dillon K. Inouye
Brigham Young University

James B. Olsen
WICAT Systems, Inc.

Introduction

Educational measurement, the specification of position on educationally relevant scales, is undergoing a revolution, due to the rapid dissemination of information-processing technology. Because the process of measurement is labor intensive, it is not surprising that the exponential increase in our capacity to do work should revolutionize educational measurement, making it possible for both the psychometrician and the consumer of psychometric services to do routinely what was previously impossible.

One of the most notable aspects of the revolution is the rapidity with which it has come upon us. Although other major innovations in education, like writing and printing, took centuries and even millennia to become the common possession of every person, the distribution of computing resources has occurred within decades. A measure of the rapidity with which computers have been adopted by educational measurement is seen in the fact that the previous edition of *Educational Measurement,* published in 1971, did not include a chapter on the subject. This was true despite the fact that a number of promising early experiments had been conducted, that computers were widely used in test scoring, and that a book had been published that included the words "computer assisted testing" in the title (Holzman, 1970).

The computer revolution has been marked by the growth in power and sophistication of computing resources. The computing power of yesterday's mainframes is routinely surpassed by today's supermicros. Yesterday's ENIAC computer, which filled an entire room, was less powerful than the current gener-

NOTE: The authors acknowledge with gratitude the assistance of Robert Linn, the general editor; Bill Ward; Howard Wainer; George Powell; Garlie Forehand; and Randy Bennett of Educational Testing Service, who reviewed earlier versions of the manuscript and made suggestions of substance that led to significant improvements. Myrtle Rice and Jeanne Inouye provided excellent editorial assistance. Kevin Ho coordinated production details with the two authors in Utah. Bobbi Kearns, Alice Norby, and Joyce Thullen were excellent under pressure in manuscript production and revisions.

ation of microcomputers, which fit on a desktop. Even in those cases in which computers are not sophisticated or powerful enough for educational measurement, they can easily be connected to others that are.

The computer revolution has also been marked by the widespread dissemination of computers in daily life. Yesterday, computing power was the exclusive possession of a few; today it is available to everyone. Yesterday, only the cognoscenti knew about computers and their related arcana; today one is embarrassed not to be computer literate. The recent Commission on Excellence in Education (Gardner, 1983) formally acknowledged the ubiquity and importance of computers in our society by branding American students "illiterate" in their knowledge of computers. This unprecedented characterization conveys the expectation that everyone should be familiar with computers. It signals one of the largest general education (and reeducation) tasks in history.

Perhaps inevitably, these changes in the power and distribution of computing resources have wrought irreversible changes in educational measurement. No evidence of the revolutionary character of these changes is stronger than the announcement, in recent years, of large-scale computerized measurement projects. The armed forces are developing a computerized version of the Armed Services Vocational Aptitude Battery (Green, Bock, Humphreys, Linn, & Reckase, 1982). Educational Testing Service has announced a major commitment to new priorities that will include the use of computerized measurement systems to better serve individuals (Ward, 1986), and it has implemented operational systems. And the State of California is developing a computerized prototype of its future Comprehensive Assessment System (Olsen, Inouye, Hansen, Slawson, & Maynes, 1984).

The significance of these large bellwether projects is that they show the direction in which the field is moving. They are milestones marking the transition from the classical era in the field of educational measurement to the beginning of another era, a transition that will affect every psychometrician and consumer of psychometric services.

Purpose of This Chapter

In what follows, we shall attempt to summarize recent developments in computerized measurement by placing them in a four-generation framework (Inouye & Bunderson, 1986; Inouye & Sorenson, 1985). In this framework, each generation represents a genus of increasing sophistication and power. We suggest that the framework be used as temporary scaffolding, to be discarded when more useful and powerful representations are built. Despite the obvious pitfalls associated with proposing a framework in a developing field, we hope that our suggestion of a four-generation framework will provide an *ad interim* contribution to the field's universe of discourse, one that will facilitate communication about the rapidly developing issues. Our nominees for the four generations are

Generation 1. Computerized testing (CT): administering conventional tests by computer
Generation 2. Computerized adaptive testing (CAT): tailoring the difficulty or contents of the next piece presented or

an aspect of the timing of the next item on the basis of examinees' responses
Generation 3. Continuous measurement (CM): using calibrated measures embedded in a curriculum to continuously and unobtrusively estimate dynamic changes in the student's achievement trajectory and profile as a learner
Generation 4. Intelligent measurement (IM): producing intelligent scoring, interpretation of individual profiles, and advice to learners and teachers, by means of knowledge bases and inferencing procedures

In that which follows, we present defining attributes of computerized educational measurement and discuss the four generations, suggesting some advantages, challenges, and immediate opportunities for research.

Defining Dimensions of the Four Generations

Computerized educational measurement is a subfield of educational measurement that is formed by the intersection of educational measurement and the technology of computer delivery systems. Computerized educational measurement is therefore that area formed by bringing educational measurement and computing resources into relationship with each other.

EDUCATIONAL MEASUREMENT

Definition. Educational measurement is the process of specifying the position, or positions, for educational purposes, of persons, situations, or events on educationally relevant scales under stipulated conditions. This definition is given to provide a framework of six categories along which types of educational measurement can differ and which enable us to contrast the attributes and properties of the four generations.

Educational measurement as process. Educational measurement is a process composed of several subprocesses, some occurring in parallel, some in series. Major processes are (a) test development including development of test specifications and candidate items, pretesting, and combining of selected and revised items into tests; (b) test administration including obtaining responses, scoring them, reporting them, and interpreting them; and (c) test analysis and research including equating, linking, validating, and analyzing for differential item functioning and group differences.

Because of their ability to do work at electronic speeds, computers are now having a major impact on all three classes of educational measurement processes. However, this chapter will narrow its focus to the subject of test administration; it will discuss obtaining examinee responses, scoring them, recording them for later use, reporting and interpreting the results, and giving prescriptive advice.

Specification of position. Educational measurement specifies a position, or positions, along educationally relevant scales. Specification can be static, measuring the position of a person, situation, or event at one particular time, or dynamic, measuring changes in position over time. Precision, reliability, power, and efficiency are other dimensions along which specification can differ.

The essential difference between static and dynamic measurement can be seen by analogy to the physical sciences. Early physicists were limited to an understanding of statics, the properties of objects in their motionless states. In contrast, later physicists invented tools that helped them understand dynamics, the properties of objects in motion. When early physicists studied a weight suspended from a spring, they could only measure the distension of the spring when it had stopped moving. In contrast, later physicists could understand both spring and weight as parts of a dynamic system in oscillatory motion.

The distinction between static and dynamic measurement in the physical sciences is analogous to the distinction between outcome and process in the social sciences. The measurement of achievement in U.S. public schools is an example of static measurement, because the purpose of measurement is to specify the state of learners with respect to achievement variables at single moments in time, usually at the beginning or end of the year. On the other hand, the measurement of growth in individual achievement as a function of instruction is an example of dynamic measurement, because the purpose of measurement is to describe changes in the learner over time.

If static measurement is the specification of a point, or points, in an educationally relevant measurement space, dynamic measurement is the specification of a trajectory, or path of points, over time. If a point defines a position along a relevant scale, then a trajectory defines changes in position over time.

A given trajectory of a person can be essentially linear, specifying uniform translation of position over time, or it can be curvilinear, specifying not only change in position but also change in the rate of change. Linear translation is analogous to constant velocity; curvilinear motion over time is analogous to acceleration. The first and second generations of computerized measurement usually deal with static measurement, and the third and fourth generations usually deal with dynamic measurement.

Educational purposes. Traditionally, the principal purpose of educational measurement has been to assist educational decision making by providing information about the position of a group or an individual along educationally relevant scales. Measurement has typically served two constituencies, institutions and individuals.

Historically, educational measurement has been used primarily for institutional purposes. Institutions use measurement to improve their admissions and placement decisions, to assess the achievement of educational goals, to evaluate personnel and programs, to evaluate organizational entities, and to motivate students. The traditional uses of educational measurement to serve individuals have included guidance and counseling of people, based on achievement, ability, aptitude, or interest test scores; monitoring of individual progress; and assistance in instructional decision making.

In addition to those uses of measurement for individuals that imply more formal and standardized application, there are myriad informal uses of unstandardized educational measurement by teachers, learners, and administrators. It has not yet proved cost effective, however, to provide in these settings educational measurement conforming to the high standards of development, administration, analysis, and use established by professional organizations and applied in admissions testing, research, and major summative evaluation projects.

The field is therefore open for serving individual purposes with new kinds of excellent educational measurement. In addition to guidance and counseling of individuals, educational measurement can be used to monitor learner trajectories in well-defined educational measurement spaces. It can be used to diagnose problems in velocity and acceleration and provide information for timely instructional intervention. Good educational measurement can provide data for profiling the characteristics of individuals and their progress in an achievement space. It can also guide the interpretation of these profiles and lead to prescriptive advice for individuals based upon their learner profiles and achievement trajectories.

Monitoring, profiling, and interpreting are individual purposes of educational measurement that are closely linked to instruction. Other instructional activities that could be more closely linked to measurement include selecting appropriate scope and sequence, providing nontrivial instructional guidance within that scope and sequence (as would an excellent coach), and recommending practice on exercises at the appropriate level for each individual.

The shift in emphasis from institutional purposes to individual purposes characterizes the distinction between the first two and the last two generations of educational measurement. This distinction is closely related to the shift from static to dynamic measurement.

Persons, situations, and events. The objects of educational measurement are persons, situations, and events. It is commonplace in the social sciences to see behavioral events *(B)* arising as a function of the interaction between person *(P)* and situation *(S)* variables; in other words, $B = f(P,S)$. Educational events, like learning, may also be seen under a similar functional rubric; learning *(B)* = f(aptitude *(P)*, treatment *(S)*).

Although global situations can be measured (e.g. "educational climate"), the important subset of situations addressed in this chapter is specially designed and calibrated tasks used to specify position along educationally relevant scales. In these cases, according to the behavior formula cited, a task situation, *S* (the test item), is presented, and a behavioral event, *B* (the examinee's response), is observed and scored, in order to infer or measure an examinee's relative position on a scale *(P)*.

The standardized task situations in the first two generations are test items. Usually the observed behaviors are given a binary score, right or wrong, but responses to more complex tasks might be scored holistically with a graded numerical score. A series of items, or situational tasks, which can be shown empirically to vary along a single dimension, are calibrated, and their position is specified along an inferred scale of a latent (unobserved) trait. In the third generation, the situational tasks become more complex, consisting of multiple responses and more realistic, worldlike simulations. These situations can also be measured and calibrated.

Aggregated data on persons or tasks are often used to make inferences about educational programs or about constructs thought to explain group differences on the scales. The scales provide a model that focuses on some dimension of the knowledge or skill domain and the positions of groups on these dimensions.

A broad class of events can have educational significance. Some of these, like participation or nonparticipation in a particular activity, might merely be noted and become a part of an educational record. Other events are significant because of the time they require. The measurement of time intervals is enormously enhanced by computerized measurement.

For each class of persons, situations, or events, the advent of computerized measurement makes possible some measurements that were previously impossible. This is true in at least two ways. In the first, or practical, sense, some objects previously unmeasured because of lack of money, time, and expertise can now be measured. For instance, expensive individually administered intelligence and aptitude tests can now be administered more inexpensively to more individuals by computer under the supervision of paraprofessionals. Other examples include case studies and simulations, previously administered manually or not at all, and frequent measures to produce learning trajectories.

A second way in which the previously impossible becomes possible is due to changes in the operating capabilities of the measurement delivery system. An example of this is seen in mental chronometry. Here, the chronometric properties of certain mental events, like the relative speeds of mental rotation of geometric figures, can be measured and recorded, scored, and interpreted. Other examples are the automatic processing of types of responses, digitized vocal responses, and movements of a joystick or a mouse.

Educationally relevant scales. Educational measurement is defined here as the specification of position along educationally relevant scales or dimensions. The dimensions of measurement spaces are always constructs, conceptual inventions, that are imposed on the persons or tasks being measured. They do not inhere in the objects themselves. Even in the physical sciences, constructs like weight, mass, and energy had to be invented before measurement could occur.

The constructs of education and the social sciences differ from those of the physicochemical sciences in both their degree of theoretical interrelationship and their empirical grounding. For example, although in physics $1°$ C is theoretically related to mass and velocity through the formula $\frac{1}{2} mv^2$, in the social sciences, no such network of interrelationships has been uncovered between, say, IQ scale points and mathematics achievement. In education, the lack of ratio scales, the lack of agreement on constructs, and the complex dimensionality of that being measured are factors that have posed severe difficulties in finding theoretical linkages.

Stipulated conditions. The final item in the definition of educational measurement refers to the conditions under which measurements are taken. As Cassirer (1923) has argued, the value and usefulness of any measurement are dependent upon specification of the conditions under which the measurement was made. When conditions differ, the meaning of two or more measurements can differ. The degree to which measurement conditions can be specified is the degree of control. To the extent that measurement conditions can be controlled, we may say that they are standardized. The threat of extraneous sources of variation is then minimized, and the conditions are made replicable. The four generations of computerized measurement add important new contributions to the control and standardization of measurement conditions, making possible comparisons between measurements of objects and events previously thought to be incommensurable.

THE COMPUTERIZED DELIVERY SYSTEM

Delivery system, work, and information technologies. The second set of dimensions that define computerized educational measurement refers to variations in the work capacities of delivery systems. The process of specifying position in an educationally relevant space requires a combination of theory, methods, and work. Theory is necessary to invent the constructs that define a measurement space. Methods are necessary to improve the quality, that is, the reliability and validity, of measurement. Work is necessary to process the information needed for the specification of position. We now turn to computing resources that supply the work necessary for information processing.

Administering, scoring, recording, reporting, and interpreting are labor-intensive processes. The rapid deployment of computing resources ensures the widespread capability to do this work at electronic speeds for increasingly lower costs. In this chapter we shall refer to the computing resources provided by modern information technologies as the *delivery system* or, more simply, *the computer.* The delivery system includes the hardware, software, testware, and human expertise necessary to deliver the intended instruction or measurement. Technology is not limited to hardware; it refers, more generally, to the application of knowledge.

Hardware. The hardware components of a single workstation of a modern computerized measurement system typically include

1. A single computer, possibly joined to others through a local area network or a long-distance communication line. The workstation could also be a terminal for a multiuser computer.
2. Sufficient memory for the applications intended
3. Mass storage capacity such as floppy disks, fixed disks, or videodiscs
4. A response input device or devices
5. Display devices for text and graphics and, sometimes, audio
6. A printer
7. Data communications to a central site

There are a large number of permutations and combinations of these essential hardware elements, as well as many enhancements to this basic system.

Software. To the hardware must be added the following essential software components:

1. An operating system with device drivers and utilities to harness and coordinate the resources of the delivery system
2. Applications software (testware), for administering, scoring, recording, reporting, and, in some cases, interpreting the results.

Software is the intelligence that channels and directs the work of the delivery system. Computerized-testing software has advanced considerably, and new software has been implemented in a variety of delivery systems for computerized and computer-adaptive tests (CAT). For CAT, several new item calibration programs are also available.

Among the more significant developments in software are those associated with knowledge-based (artificially intelligent) computing. Methods of developing knowledge bases and procedures for querying these knowledge bases open the prospect for the fourth generation of computerized testing, intelligent measurement. The software needed for this generation combines advances in both computerized testing algorithms and knowledge-based computing.

Implementation policies and strategies. The bitter lesson of many attempts to promote technological revolution is that revolutions only partially depend upon advances in hardware and software. The rate of revolution depends on people. Unless those responsible for sponsoring and maintaining the delivery system learn how to become effective change agents, successful transition from a print-based culture to an electronic one will be improbable. Technology is the application of knowledge, and knowledge has an important personal component. Because people carry their knowledge in their bodies, the transfer of knowledge occurs one person at a time.

The implementation of a successful computerized testing operation, therefore, requires a thorough, tested set of policies and procedures for training over a sufficient period of time. These procedures can insure that the computerized testing system is implemented in such a way that it achieves benefits and maintains conditions for validity and equity in its use.

Current state of the art. Our discussion of the essential hardware, software, and implementation policies as essential components of the delivery system has prepared us for a discussion of the state of the art in each of the component areas. Because the components of modern delivery systems are changing so rapidly, any attempt to catalog the current state of the art will quickly be outdated. Today's state-of-the-art devices might become exhibits in tomorrow's museum of antiquities. We discuss five generic kinds of work done by the delivery system that will persist, even when hardware and software become obsolete. For each kind, we illustrate trends of development.

Five kinds of work. Discussed next are five dimensions of work along which delivery systems, or their components, can differ. Each dimension represents a different kind of work that has its analog in human performance. Along each of these dimensions, technology has exponentially increased the amount and kinds of work that an individual can do. The five dimensions are: sensing, remembering, deciding, acting and communicating. It is in the particular combination of these five kinds of work that delivery systems in the four generations differ.

Sensing. Input devices do the work of sensing. They pick up information from the examinee or the environment, encode it as symbols, and transmit it to the system for interpretation and response. Input devices are evolving rapidly from keyboards to window-type interfaces, pull down menus, icons,

and mouse. Also available are touch screens, joysticks, and trackballs. Input by means of keyboards gives an advantage to examinees who have had previous experience, such as touch-typists. The expanded use of voice recognition and other methods of input might equalize advantages.

Remembering. Memory devices do the work of remembering stored information. They allow the system to remember the step-by-step sequence of operations it is to perform and the instructions and data it is to use. As with humans, memory makes it possible for the machine to recognize signals, decode stored instructions, record data, adapt to records of past experience, and organize data into structures, so that it can process these higher order units.

The memory capacity of most modern delivery systems is evolving rapidly. Most microcomputer workstations now have from ½ to 2 megabytes of random access memory. Future workstations will use even larger amounts of random access memory. The early, expensive, mass-storage devices are being replaced by inexpensive, high-density, magnetic and opto-electronic devices. Hard-disk storage exceeding 100 megabytes per workstation is becoming more common. Compact disk read-only memories, Write Once Read Many optical discs, and videodiscs will soon allow gigabytes of storage per workstation.

Deciding. Microprocessors that do the work of deciding perform the calculations necessary to make the decisions. This includes processing inputs, computing, and making decisions based upon information in memory. In the system, the work of deciding is done by the central processing unit(s). It performs the mathematical and logical operations required to make a decision. It also controls the operation of the machine by activating the computer's other functional units at appropriate times.

Most delivery systems of the future will utilize microprocessors that handle at least 16 to 32 bits at a time at speeds of from 6 to 50 million cycles per second. The evolution is toward larger information-handling capacities at higher speeds. The current state of the art is represented by 32-bit microprocessors, which have a full 32-bit architecture, a full 32-bit implementation, and a 32-bit data path (bus) to memory. Some technology writers predict that microprocessor performance will eventually exceed that of all but a few of our current mainframes.

Acting. Output devices execute the decisions made by the system. This work includes activating output devices that send information, turn on motors, switch lights, display the next test item, and position and activate mechanical devices. The work of acting allows the computer to change the environment or to control devices external to the system. It also allows the computer to communicate with people and with other machines. The most important subcategory of acting for the purposes of computerized measurement involves controlling display devices for the text, images, and audio used in testing situations.

Output devices are also undergoing rapid evolution in performance, price, and variety. Visual displays have improved tremendously since the days of the teletype. Soft-copy displays have become more and more prevalent, most of them in the form of cathode-ray tube (CRT) displays. The CRT is still the display of choice for most testing applications, although its competitors, liquid crystal, electroluminescent, and plasma displays, have made impressive gains and are gaining greater currency.

Communicating. In addition to the types of work listed, which, in combination, make a given delivery system more or less powerful, the linking of computers can also increase the amount and sophistication of work performed. Here, too, the cost of work devices relative to performance is decreasing. Local area networks make possible the linking of multiple workstations for individualized testing applications. Long-haul networks make possible the distribution of upgraded norms and experimental items from central test-development sites and the collection of statistics from distributed sites. Later generations of computerized testing will require linked workstations, to make use of the additional capabilities afforded by these developments, such as group-interactive tests for assessing team performance.

Computerized measurement systems can replicate many kinds of work hitherto done by humans. Some examples from which large savings of time and energy have resulted include the scoring of tests, the searching of large files to retrieve records or test items, the computing of statistics, the processing of text, and the keeping of records. Devices that do such work can be widely disseminated to increase exponentially the work available for educational measurement.

Table 9.1 summarizes our discussion to this point. It shows differences among the four generations of computerized measurement, based on differences in computer sophistication and in the six defining attributes of educational measurement. The generations have many superficially similar elements, but, just as a Model T differs from a modern automobile, the generations differ from each other. These differences affect the efficiency, speed, convenience, accuracy, and power of educational measurement.

Summary of Computerized Delivery System Features

The computer capabilities of the four generations have much in common. All four permit computer-controlled administration, rapid scoring and reporting, new display and response types, mass storage for displays and item banks, and network communications. The first generation does not require a fast floating-point processor for the item-by-item calculations required by some adaptive algorithms in the second generation. The third generation has, in addition, those computer-controlled features of display, response entry, and processing needed in computerized instruction. In the continuous measurement generation, testing disappears into the fabric of instruction and measurement becomes unobtrusive. In the fourth generation there begin to appear aspects of artificial intelligence for drawing inferences from knowledge bases to provide more sophisticated scoring, interpretation, and advice.

The scientific foundations of measurement differ among the generations. The first generation is frequently characterized by use of classical test theory or by having no underlying psychometric theory. Individuals familiar with interactive

TABLE 9.1 Features of Four Generations of Computerized Educational Measurement

Generation	Computerized Testing (CT)	Computer-Adaptive Testing (CAT)	Continuous Measurement (CM)	Intelligent Measurement (IM)
Computerized delivery system features	Computer-controlled administration; rapid scoring and reporting; new display and response types; mass storage for displays and item banks, network communications	Same as CT Fast floating-point calculations for adaptive algorithms	All of CAT features Computer-aided education features	All of CM features Knowledge-based inferencing
Scientific foundations	Varied, but usually classical test theory	Item response theory & related advances	Extensions of IRT Valid construct specifications Learner profiles Implementation design	Models of expert knowledge—scoring expertise, profile interpretation, teaching expertise
Educational measurement functions:				
Processes	Administering, Scoring, Recording, Reporting		Same as CAT plus more interpretation	Same as CM plus sophisticated interpretation
Specification of position	Static (usually)	Static (usually)	Dynamic (static possible)	Same as CM
Educationally relevant purposes	Institutional (usually)	Institutional (usually)	Individual (institutional possible)	Same as CM
Scales	Varied (can be informal)	Unidimensional for IRT-based tests; evolving	Multidimensional composite	Same as CM when needed
Educational objects	Persons Situations Events	Persons Standardized tasks Events	Persons Reference tasks Events	Same as CM
Degree of control	High for display and responses	More adaptive control than CT	CAT plus control over instruction	Same as CM, but much control can be given to user

computing frequently implement tests in an *ad hoc* manner. They are either unaware of or unconcerned with measurement issues such as validity, reliability, and equating from paper-and-pencil or individually administered versions to the computer version. Face validity of a new simulationlike test is often seen as sufficient.

The scientific bases of the second and higher generations are more advanced and are the subject of much current research. The second generation has prominently featured adaptive algorithms based on item response theory (IRT), and it is, consequently, limited to situations in which the assumption of unidimensionality of the underlying scale can be demonstrated, although current work could change this. The third generation will not reach full flower until there are extensions of IRT or new psychometric theories to allow entities other than items to be calibrated.

New developments in psychometric theory are a necessary, but not sufficient, scientific basis for the continuous measurement generation. Valid construct specifications of underlying scales and cognitive components are necessary for the successful use of calibrated item clusters and tasks. Also necessary, but coming later during the evolution of CM, is the measurement of learner profiles representing different learning abilities, styles, and preferences. All of these advances will fail unless implementation design principles and techniques are developed. Careful and extensive in-service training for users is needed, because new roles and traditions will have to evolve to take advantage of continuous measurement. A research basis for implementation design is thus a critical task for applied science. The fourth generation will introduce new scientific foundations including models of expert knowledge to accompany computer applications. Promising application areas include those involving the knowledge to score complex tasks, the professional knowledge to interpret profiles, and the knowledge of teaching experts capable of using data from continuous measurement and from learner profiles to provide prescriptive advice to learners and teachers.

SUMMARY OF EDUCATIONAL MEASUREMENT FUNCTIONS

The generations do not differ extensively on test-administration processes. The main distinction among them is in the extent to which the computer system is programmed to provide interpretation to the user, a major function usually reserved for a counselor or a teacher acting as counselor. Some interpretation by computer is possible in the continuous measurement generation, but knowledge-based computing with the programmed expertise of the teaching expert is necessary before sophisticated interpretation, analogous to the human teacher or counselor, will be possible.

It is useful to point out that the first two generations usually deal with static measurement, whereas the last two emphasize dynamic measurement. This fact is closely related to their educational purposes. The first two generations primarily serve institutional functions, because the psychometrically sophisticated tests implemented on computers so far are usually variations of current tests used for institutional purposes. The third and fourth generations emphasize individual educational purposes.

The measurement scales among the generations vary in psychometric sophistication. In the first generation we might have varied measurement scales. They could be informal and ordinal, nominal, or interval scales. The second generation requires a unidimensional equal-interval scale for tests based on IRT. The third generation requires that we also deal with the multi-dimensionality inherent in learning any complex knowledge domain. It is necessary to develop composite scales to provide reports for the learners of overall progress on more than one underlying scale. For providing advances in scoring and interpretation in the process of learning, intelligent measurement requires all of the scale sophistication of the CM generation. Intelligent measurement can also be used to enhance the scoring of first- and second-generation tests, in which case it might revert to simpler scales.

Item response theory has provided the major scientific advancement for developing educationally relevant scales. It allows the obtaining of scale values for both persons and tasks on the underlying single dimension. Item response theory scaling is widely used in second-generation applications and is possible on the first generation with a nonadaptive IRT test. The calibration of tasks more complex than multiple-choice items is almost a defining attribute of the third generation. By extending calibration methods from items to the more complex tasks used in instruction, the ability to track individuals in an educationally interesting growth space becomes feasible.

The degree of control refers to the stipulated conditions under which measurement can be standardized. The first two generations permit great control over the display and sequencing of visual and auditory stimulus materials, the form of response, and the timing of responses. The third generation introduces additional control over instructional events and causes the distinction between the instructional and testing events to fade. The fourth generation potentially introduces another degree of control: control of the process of instruction by the learner. Intelligent measurement thus poses some problems in standardization, due to increased user control over instructional options.

This concludes our presentation of the defining context in which computerized educational measurement may be viewed. In the next sections, we consider in some detail the unique promise and problems of each generation.

The First Generation: Computerized Testing (CT)

In the first generation of the computerization of any human activity, users tend to automate familiar but manually time-consuming processes. Later, having become more familiar with the capabilities of the computer, they begin to see ways in which computer power can make previously impossible or even unimagined tasks possible. This pattern can be seen in the evolution of computerized measurement. In the first generation, computerized testing (CT), computers are used to automate familiar measurement activities. The CT generation began with the translation, or conversion, of familiar paper-and-pencil tests, usually group administered, to a computer-administered format. The CT generation also includes the development of new nonadaptive tests, similar to manually administered tests but more efficient in utilizing computer capabilities for administration. *Nonadaptive* means that the number of items, their sequence, content, and timing, do not depend on examinees' responses in any way.

Definition

The first, or CT, generation is defined as the translation of existing tests to computerized format, or the development of new, nonadaptive tests that are similar to manually administered tests but utilize computer capabilities for all or most test-administration processes. The CT generation tests usually report a static position on an ordinal scale, and the scores are used for institutional purposes far more frequently than for individual purposes.

First-generation tests now constitute the largest set of exemplars of computerized measurement, and they will continue to proliferate. They do not require complex algorithms and psychometric models or the more sophisticated computer requirements of the second and higher generations. They are generally used for familiar purposes that do not require dramatic role shifts on the part of users (such as in the new teaching and learning roles found in the third generation).

Advances in Test Administration in the CT Generation

Although it introduces some new problems, computerized testing advances many of the processes of test administration. In this section we will review the improvements and problems associated with these test-administration procedures: presenting item displays, obtaining and coding responses, scoring, reporting and interpreting results, and obtaining records at a central site.

PRESENTING ITEM DISPLAYS

Greater standardization. Computerized testing introduces into test administration the precise control of item displays possible with computer administration. The timing of the displays can be precise, as can the control over what the examinee is seeing or hearing.

Computer-administered testing permits test administration conditions, directions, and procedures to be completely standardized in ways not possible with manually administered tests. Computerized test directions are always the same, no matter how many times the test is administered and no matter how many different locations or test administrators are involved. Some instructions are precluded, and others can be enforced. Instructions like "Do not turn the page until I give the signal" are not needed. The computer can rule out peeking in other situations by controlling the displays.

Greater standardization might, however, imply greater difficulty in adjusting testing conditions to meet local needs. The computer can be programmed to be very resistant to alterations in test administration conditions, or it can be programmed to give the examiners flexibility to alter testing conditions in certain prescribed ways such as breaking a test

into two different time intervals, restarting at the appropriate point with a review of the instructions for the last subtest.

Improved test security. Computerized testing also provides for increased test security. There are no paper copies of the tests or answer keys to be stolen, copied, or otherwise misused. The computer-administered test can include multiple levels of password and security protection, to prevent unauthorized access to the testing materials, item banks, or answer keys. The test displays and the item keys can be encrypted to prevent unauthorized printing or copying. The test items and associated answer keys can also be randomly resequenced, if necessary, so that a student cannot follow the screen of another examinee.

Enriched Display Capability. A printed test has obvious display strengths and limitations. It can present text and line drawings with ease. At greater cost, photographic illustrations can be presented. A printed test cannot provide timing, variable sequencing of visual displays, animation, or motion. Audio devices can be used to present standardized audio presentations associated with a printed test, but a trained administrator must deliver the audio in a group-paced mode or to the examinees one by one.

In the CT generation, a visual display device replaces the printed page display. The quality of the display varies with the resolution, the graphics circuitry, the bandwidth, and the memory available for storing the display data. As an example of what can be accomplished with good display features, Druesne, Kershaw, and Toru (1986) have been able to implement the CLEP artistic judgment test, which uses photographic illustrations, on an IBM personal computer equipped with an advanced graphics board, a high-resolution color digital monitor, and sufficient storage to hold the digitized photographic images. Even more advanced displays are possible, which equal the resolution of a printed photograph. Video images can be stored on a videodisc, which permits random access to single video images or short motion sequences and can provide for the dynamic overlay of text or graphics on the video. For example, ETS has demonstrated an interactive video test (CT generation) using a computer-controlled videodisc with graphics overlay in the areas of medical certification (podiatry) and English as a Second Language (Bridgeman, Bennett, & Swinton, 1986).

In general, computerized displays sacrifice some image resolution for greater flexibility and control over the presentation of text, graphics, animation, motion, audio, and video. System costs go up with the addition of color, audio, graphics resolution, and videodisc. The user is thus faced with a cost–capability trade-off when choosing a lower or higher resolution display screen and the presence or absence of audio and video. This trade-off affects the problems introduced by CT, because the resolution of the display screen affects how much of an existing test item can be shown at one time without scrolling or paging and how accurately line graphics or photographs can be reproduced.

New item types. New item types can be developed using advanced display capabilities. Such items are part of the first generation so long as they are not presented adaptively, are not part of a continuous measurement system embedded into a curriculum, or do not utilize intelligent advice or scoring.

WICAT System's Learner Profile, a battery of 45 CT and CAT tests covering a variety of learning-oriented aptitude and preference dimensions, provides numerous examples. Among its item types are gestalt completion items, in which more and more image detail is unfolded until an examinee recognizes a picture; animated displays that test visual concepts and memory for spatial sequences; accelerating object displays to test perceptual speed; and individually administered audio presentations using earphones and computer-controlled digitized audio to test auditory digit span.

Equivalent scores with reduced testing time. For the majority of items provided in current standardized achievement and psychological tests, computer-administered versions offer the promise of significant reductions in test-administration time. In two different research studies using subtests and items from the California Assessment Program, Olsen, Maynes, Slawson, and Ho (1986) found that computer-administered and paper-and-pencil tests produced statistically the same test-score distributions (means, standard deviations, reliabilities, and standard errors of measurement), but the computer-administered test required less administration time. Like the majority of standardized achievement tests, the California Assessment Program uses a computer-scannable answer sheet and test booklet. The gridding of answers on a separate sheet appears to take more time than responding to a screen display by using a keyboard. Figure 9.1 shows that the computer-administered tests were completed by examinees in significantly less time than the paper-and-pencil tests. Other studies have shown similar patterns, but the issue is not simple. (Calvert & Waterfall, 1982; Watts, Badeley, & Williams 1982). The effect for younger children is shown in Figure 9.1 to be larger, implying that the use of answer sheets is less natural and, so, more prone to disadvantaging children who lack test-taking experience.

OBTAINING AND CODING RESPONSES

The increased speed of some computer-administered tests over similar manually administered tests is at least as much a function of improvements in obtaining and coding responses as in increased control over the presentation and pacing of displays. A mark-sense sheet commonly used in manual testing requires the examinee to code each response by associating it with the item number and then marking one of several bubbles. The visual matching of item numbers and alternative numbers or letters takes time and produces errors. By presenting only one item per screen, the computer automatically matches responses with the item number, makes alternatives visually immediate, and reveals the selections for immediate verification. Convenient features for changing answers can replace time-consuming erasing on printed answer sheets. Computers can also administer item formats other than limited-choice items. Constructed responses involving numbers or formulas entered on a keyboard are quite easy to interpret unambiguously. Short answers involving keywords require more sophistication, but, even without natural-language-processing techniques, highly accurate coding can be obtained. One method of achieving good results is to obtain and sort a large collection of pretest answers. With this data, keyword processing with misspelling tolerance can be used with a range of acceptable answers. These methods can, with high accuracy, produce item coding as correct, partially correct, or incorrect.

Computers also facilitate other response formats such as pointing out and marking words in text or parts of pictures or drawings. Such forms of response entry have been possible in computer-aided instruction and in personal computing for many years. These response forms, increasingly easy and fa-

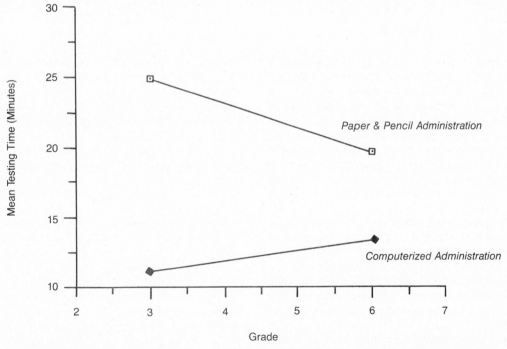

FIGURE 9.1 Mean Testing Times of Computerized Tests and Paper-and-Pencil Tests.

miliar to a population of examinees whose computer literacy grows yearly, can be standardized and automated and become an important part of the CT arsenal of item types. So long as both paper-and-pencil and CT versions of the same test are administered, studies are needed to compare computer-based response formats with their paper-and-pencil equivalents. Thus, coding of short answers, flexible pointing, and marking by computer should be compared experimentally with handwriting and human grading of the same item types done with paper and pencil. These studies should compare score distributions, error rate, cost, and testing time under each condition.

The new technology of voice recognition might be used in the future to accept vocalizations as responses to CT test items. This opens up new opportunities for testing vocal utterances in language or for examining preliterate or illiterate examinees, but will, in all likelihood, introduce measurement errors in identifying vocalized inputs.

Reduced measurement error. Computer-administered tests offer potentially significant reductions in several classes of measurement error. The elimination of answer sheets not only increases the speed of test taking but might also eliminate some traditional errors such as penciling in the answer to the wrong item number, failing to completely erase an answer, and inadvertently skipping an item in the test booklet but not on the answer sheet. A further reduction in measurement error occurs with computerized tests because examinees can focus on one item at a time without being distracted, confused, or intimidated by the numerous items per page for paper tests. Computerized tests might therefore provide more accurate measures of performance for students who have lower reading ability, lower attention span, and higher distractibility.

Computer-administered tests can also reduce measurement error associated with the testing process. As the computer accepts responses from a keyboard, keypad, mouse, or touch screen, these responses are already in digitized form. They do not require a separate optical scanning step to put them in a machine-readable format. This provides opportunities to code the digitized responses with great sophistication, reducing the requirement for manual coding of short constructed answers or marks on a drawing. It also makes changes and updates easier. With computerized testing, changes to answer keys, norm tables, and test-scoring algorithms can be more easily made than with paper-and-pencil scoring booklets, of which many copies must be updated or replaced. Computerized testing can eliminate the problems of lost or misplaced answer booklets and answer sheets, test scanning problems from use of pen and ink or pencil marks that are too light, test scanner registration and resolution problems, and use of the wrong answer keys for scoring.

Computerized testing might, however, introduce new classes of measurement error. The need for multiple computer screens to read lengthy comprehension items could introduce new measurement errors. Multiple screens might introduce a memory component into the construct being measured. The use of shorter paragraphs to reduce the need for multiple screens has been shown by Green (1988) to affect the construct being measured.

If the graphics resolution of the computer screen is not sufficient to produce quality equivalent to the graphics displays on paper-and-pencil tests, discrimination errors could interfere with measurement. Use of the response entry device, whether keyboard, touch screen, voice, or mouse, could also introduce new measurement errors. Additional research is needed to evaluate the effect of these new sources of measurement error. It might be that any new sources of measurement error attributable to CT will be dependent on item format, such as long reading passages, or will be quite subtle, by introducing changes in the cognitive processes and, thus, the construct being measured.

Ability to measure response latencies for items and components. The administration of tests by computer allows direct and precise measurement of response latencies. Latencies can be measured separately for specific item components (e.g. reading time for the item stem; analysis time for any complex drawing, graph, or table; reading time for each option; response selection time, or response speed). Dillon and Stevenson-Hicks (1981) and Sternberg (1982) note one consistent difference between good and poor problem solvers: the amount of time spent in mentally encoding reasoning problems. The good problem solvers spend more time reading and understanding the problem and the problem elements, whereas the poor problem solvers quickly begin trying out solutions. Response latencies to individual test items, subtests, and total tests can be easily measured and collected. Precise measurement of any of these latencies is virtually impossible with paper-and-pencil tests. New psychometric models are needed to deal with response latencies. Although investigators have collected latency data, standards for using it to make valid inferences are rare. A fairly recent book by Luce (1986) is an exception.

SCORING AND REPORTING

Benefits to scoring. The process of scoring requires not only an accurate coding of each response, described earlier, but also the combining of individual item scores into meaningful subscores. When applicable, scoring also involves the computation of composite scores. The time required and the errors associated with applying complex subscoring procedures can be eliminated entirely, because the computer can calculate subscores and composites in the blink of an eye. Because complex subscoring procedures such as those found in personality or biographical inventories introduce so many possibilities for error, it is hard to disseminate these traditionally administered instruments without careful training and certification of the examiners. Although computerized versions of these require examiner training to assure proper use and interpretation, the training associated with scoring can disappear.

Benefits to reporting and interpretation. Computerized testing provides for immediate reporting of scores and offers many aids to human interpretation of the scores. Within a few minutes after completing the test, the examinee or the test administrator can receive a score report and prescriptive profile. Most standardized paper-and-pencil tests currently used require a minimum of between 6 and 9 weeks for test scoring and reporting. Many standardized tests have been criticized as having little direct instructional value because of these lengthy delays.

A specific example of the benefit of immediate scoring and reporting is provided by a recent large-scale implementation of computer-administered testing by the Waterford Testing Center and at 39 schools in the Garland, Texas, school district (Slawson, 1986). The Waterford Testing Center developed a computer-administered version of the Garland PREDICTS test, a criterion-referenced and diagnostic test of reading, mathematics, and language arts at grades 3, 5, and 8. Using 34 WICAT 30-station supermicrocomputers, all third-, fifth-, and eighth-grade students in the district were tested within a 3-day period. Immediately following testing, score reports and diagnostic and prescriptive profiles were prepared at each school for each of the individual students, classes, grades, and schools. The prescriptions included specific computerized lessons and textbook pages for the students to study. The score reports and diagnostic prescriptions were provided to all teachers within 2 days of the completion of testing.

Although the test involved is part of the CT generation, the application goes a long way toward the use of measurement for individual purposes. If tests like PREDICTS were given frequently during the year in school districts, they would provide many of the benefits of third-generation testing. This example illustrates the power of the delivery system in advancing the generations of computerized testing. It would be unthinkable to invest the amount of money that the Garland district has for testing alone. The testing application came as a fringe benefit of the installation of a computer-aided education system with a substantial body of curricular materials.

OBTAINING RECORDS AT A CENTRAL SITE

Computerized testing produces a digitized version of the response vector, including latencies if desired, as a part of the act of receiving and encoding the responses. This digitized record precludes the need for physical transportation, processing, and storage of voluminous paper bundles. Digitized data can be transmitted with a very low error rate to a central site where the data can be processed for item statistics, further analysis for research or educational decision making, and archival purposes. Transmission can be accomplished over telecommunication networks or by mailing a magnetic disk or tape. The benefits of these processes over the collection, mailing, scanning, storing, and archiving of printed forms are obvious. Digital transmission and storage of records, however, complicates the administration of standards for fairness and, sometimes, state laws, which depend on access to printed documents with signatures to adjudicate disputes.

AUTOMATING INDIVIDUALLY ADMINISTERED TESTS

Individually administered tests such as the Wechsler Intelligence Tests, the Stanford-Binet Intelligence Test, the Kaufman Assessment Battery for Children, and the Luria/Nebraska Neuropsychological battery require standardized one-on-one administration by a trained examiner. Such tests will still require one-on-one administration by a trained person, but standardization and speed of administration could be improved, using test administrators who have been trained more narrowly. Interpretation and proper test use should continue to be under the direction of trained professionals.

To achieve these goals through CT, the computer may be programmed to interact primarily with the test administrator. It can prompt the administrator about which objects to arrange for performance tests, and it can provide easy response formats for entering the coded result for each item involving the interpretation of vocal responses or movements. In addition to the prompting of the human examiner for items requiring interpretive judgment, many of the items and item types in these tests may be presented on the computer display under the precise controls described earlier. In these cases, the examinee could respond by pointing, by pressing a key, or, in the case of older students, by typing a few words. Pointing is accomplished by use of a touch-sensitive screen, a mouse, or cursor arrow keys.

Creating Tests and Items By Computer

This chapter has deliberately been narrowed to focus on the processes of test administration, excluding computer applications to development and to analysis and research. It is impossible not to mention some implications for these other areas, however. Collection of data at a central site for such activities as the calibration and the computing of item statistics is closely related to test development.

COMPUTER-AIDED TEST ASSEMBLY

Closely associated with the first generation is the wider dissemination of computer aids to test assembly, using item banks and tools involving word, text, and graphics processing to aid in the process of creating items. Electronic publishing and fast laser printers make localized, or even individualized, paper test forms feasible in some applications. Products are now being introduced to permit users to create customized tests and items measuring individual goals and objectives of schools, districts, educational service agencies, and state departments. With such software for test creation, educational agencies are able to select the grades, subjects, and objectives of the tests to be created, review the domain specifications or expanded objectives, select the specific items to be included in the test, sequence the objectives and items, and create an operational test to be administered by computer. Paper-and-pencil tests can also be created with the software, then printed out on a laser printer. For computerized tests, the resulting software often includes all necessary modules for test registration, scheduling, management, administration, scoring, reporting, and providing specific curriculum prescriptions. These applications are discussed in Olsen et al. (1984) and Slawson, Maynes, Olsen and Foster (1986).

COMPUTER-CREATED TESTS

Instead of storing an item bank with fixed item contents and formats, the computer can also be used to create tests and items using a bank of item generation algorithms and item forms (see Millman, 1977, 1984a, 1984b; Baker, this volume). Such a bank would contain several hundred item skeleton structures or item forms. Through a series of interactive screen displays, developers can specify item-content elements, item formats, and scoring options that can be used by the computer to generate approximately equivalent items from the same content domain.

Research Issues for the CT Generation

The fundamental research question for the first generation is the equivalence of scores between a computerized version of a test and the original version. This is also an important issue for the second generation. For some time, testing organizations will wish to give users a choice between a paper-and-pencil or other conventionally administered version and a computerized version. The question of score equivalence will thus be fundamental for some years, as computerized tests become more widespread. Few of the underlying differences between CT and conventional tests are of lasting scientific interest, so as score-equivalence studies are completed, research on CT will shift to scientific issues dealing with matters like individual and group differences, how to use latency information, and what constructs are measured by advanced forms of computerized tests.

The American Psychological Association Committee on Professional Standards, together with the Committee on Psychological Tests and Assessment, developed a new set of APA *Guidelines for Computer Based Tests and Interpretations* (1986). They outline the conditions under which scores can be considered equivalent. The rank orders of scores of individuals tested in alternate modes must closely approximate each other. The means, dispersions, and shapes of the score distributions must be approximately the same, either directly or after rescaling the CT scores. The *Guidelines* hold test developers responsible for providing evidence of score equivalence. This might be an expensive proposition for test developers, requiring separate equating and norming studies for CT versions of tests, at least in those circumstances wherein the scores from the two modes of administration are to be used interchangeably. Costly equating and norming studies are a barrier to the introduction of computerized tests. Research that might show the circumstances and design features of computerized tests under which equivalence could be assumed would therefore be beneficial in advancing the field.

The research foundation in this area is currently quite shallow. The most recent review at the time of this writing, commissioned by the College Board and ETS, was conducted by Mazzeo and Harvey (1988). This review identified fewer than 40 studies comparing computerized with conventional tests. A number of the earlier studies did not consider computerized testing as we know it today. Today we assume a cathode-ray tube or some other kind of electronic display and a keyboard or pointing device for response entry, but several of the studies reviewed presented test items on projected colored slides and used a variety of response mechanisms including paper and pencil.

Table 9.2 summarizes the results of a representative set of the studies reviewed by Mazzeo and Harvey (1988). In general it was found more frequently that the mean scores were not equivalent than that they were equivalent; that is, the scores on tests administered on paper were more often higher than on computer-administered tests. The score differences were generally quite small and of little practical significance. A major exception to this was the Coding Skills Tests. These are speed tests in which the speed of responding on the computer keyboard greatly favors the computer group. A second notable exception was in certain computerized personality tests, where omit rates were quite significantly higher on computer-administered tests than on paper-and-pencil tests (indicating "cannot say" rather than "true" or "false" in response to a personality statement). Mazzeo and Harvey expressed concern that differential omit rates might also occur on other kinds of tests, affecting formula scoring on ability tests and personality scores. The personality subscores of the MMPI were reduced by the higher frequency of choosing "cannot say" and perhaps by other factors.

A third exception is the study by Hedl, O'Neil, and Hanson (1971). There was a large mean difference in favor of the paper-and-pencil group on the Slossen Intelligence Test. The computer scored the typed responses automatically and could have introduced scoring errors in this study. Small differences were found by Elwood (1972a, 1972b), who had the examinees type in the answers to questions on the Weschler Adult Intelligence Scale but scored the responses by hand.

Neither Mazzeo and Harvey (1988) nor the current authors are willing to make the generalization that computerized testing is more likely, in general, to lead to slightly lower scores. Indeed, as Table 9.2 shows, the reverse is often found. Another reason to doubt this generalization is that most of the studies reviewed suffered from several kinds of confounding difficulties. These we will discuss under the sections on engineering design issues and experimental design issues.

Engineering Design Issues

The field of computerized testing has not yet matured to the point where consistent specifications exist for the interface between testee and material for each item type. Consistent design standards are needed for administering the items, providing access to different parts of an item that requires more than one screen to display, and providing a means of correcting response entry errors immediately or changing an earlier item. The last process can be accomplished with paper-and-pencil tests by erasing the marks on the paper answer sheet. The lack of consistent interface engineering standards was suspected by Mazzeo and Harvey (1988) and, in many cases, by the original authors cited in Table 9.2, as being a causative factor in the score differences. For example, in the study by Lee et al. (1986), 585 naval recruits had previously taken a paper-and-pencil version of the ASVAB Arithmetical Reasoning Test between 2 and 6 months prior to taking a computerized version. Questions were presented one at a time on a computer terminal, but subjects could not refer to previous items or change answers. The mean number-right score in the paper-and-pencil condition was about one point higher (on a 30-item test) than in the CT condition. Unfortunately, the interface design did not per-

TABLE 9.2 Research Studies Contrasting Score Equivalence of Paper-and-Pencil and Computerized Tests

TYPE OF TEST	CT SCORES HIGHER THAN PAPER–ADMINISTERED	CT SCORES LOWER THAN PAPER–ADMINISTERED	NO SIGNIFICANT DIFFERENCES
Free-response tests		Elwood, 1972a; 1972b; Hedl, et al. 1971	
Computerized personality tests		Biskin & Kolotkin, 1977; Lushene, O'Neil, & Dunn, 1974; Scissons, 1976	Lukin, Dowd, Plake & Kraft, 1985; Parks, Mead & Johnson, 1985; White, Clements & Fowler, 1985
Aptitude tests	Johnson & Mihal, 1973 (for blacks)	Lee & Hopkins, 1985; Lee et al., 1986; Sachar & Fletcher, 1978 (timed test)	Johnson & Mihal, 1973 (for whites); McBride & Weiss, 1974
Achievement tests			Olsen et al., 1986; Wise, Boettcher, et al., 1987; Wise & Wise, 1986
Coding skills tests	Greaud & Green, 1986; Kiely, et al., 1986 (one item per screen)	Kiely et al., 1986 (numerical items)	
Graphics tests		Jacobs, Byrd & High 1985; Jonassen, 1986	Reckase, Carlson & Ackerman, 1986 (untimed); Kiely et al., 1986
Multiple page items		Kiely et al. 1986	Feurzeig & Jones, 1970

mit subjects to correct immediate key entry errors made in entering the responses or to review and change previous items. This was possible in the paper-and-pencil test. This is a trivial engineering design problem for which several good solutions exist.

Engineering and language-processing research are needed to improve the accuracy of identifying computerized free-response answers. Some possible variables are spelling tolerance algorithms, synonym dictionaries, and ignorable word lists. In the fourth generation, artificial-intelligence capabilities for processing natural language will become available. These capabilities might have a substantial impact on this issue.

Another engineering design problem exists in the area of providing simple and effective conventions for reviewing previous parts of a large textual item (e.g., a paragraph comprehension item) or a text-plus-graphic item. These standards are needed when the entire item cannot be displayed simultaneously on one screen. One good design solution is to make the question being asked visible in a foreground window while the previous material is paged or scrolled rapidly in a background window. Kiely, Zara, and Weiss (1986) recommend a variant of this solution in connection with a study of paragraph comprehension items. Each of three different CT conventions for reviewing parts of the paragraph, with and without the question visible, produced lower mean scores for the CT students than for students taking the same items with paper and pencil. Keeping the question visible simultaneously with the review of parts of the paragraph reduced the advantage of the paper-and-pencil group.

Paging among multi-screen items, whether text or graphics, is an engineering design problem that interacts with the resolution of the screen and with the windowing or scrolling conventions adopted. The trend in the field of user interfaces is more and more toward higher resolution screens, some equivalent to a page of text. The trend is also toward the scrolling and windowing conventions available on the Apple Macintosh computer and available on IBM and compatible equipment through the Microsoft Windows package. The speed and effectiveness with which a test taker can use these conventions interacts not only with the resolution of the display and the flexibility of the software, but also with the user's familiarity and facility with the conventions. Familiarity with conventions creates an experimental design issue, which was also discussed in the Mazzeo and Harvey review.

Experimental Design Issues

Mazzeo and Harvey (1988) found that the effects of practice were significantly different on tests taken in the two different modes. These practice effects in some cases confounded the results and in other cases produced puzzling interactions. In several studies they reported that the increase in scores on the automated test was more likely to be larger when that test was administered after the conventional test than when the two tests were administered in reverse order. They stated that such asymmetric practice effects argued against conducting equating studies based on single-group counterbalanced designs. These authors also expressed frustration in interpreting the results of a number of equating studies, which perfectly confounded alternate forms of the test with computer versus conventional administration or confounded the order of administration, intervening learning, and other factors.

User familiarity with a computerized testing interface is an important consideration in conducting equating studies between paper-and-pencil and computer administration. As the results in Figure 9.1 suggest, taking a test with a mark-sense answer sheet and a booklet is a learned skill. Third graders showed considerably less facility with it than sixth graders. Similarly, facility with a particular set of computer interface conventions for moving among pages of an item, changing answers, and reviewing parts of current and previous items is a learned skill. Most of the studies reported by Mazzeo and Harvey did not provide assurance through instruction and practice that the examinees were familiar with and had facility with the particular interface conventions. The study by Olsen et al. (1986) provides an important contrast. In this study the third and sixth graders had already had considerable time to familiarize themselves with the computer and its interface conventions. The 30-terminal computer system had been installed in their school long enough prior to the study that use of the computer for instruction and testlike items had become a familiar routine. In this study, score equivalence was found. Nevertheless, a considerable reduction in testing time was shown for computerized testing. The tests they studied were nonspeeded power tests.

The differential effects of computer administration versus conventional administration on the speed of test taking have now been demonstrated in several studies besides Olsen et al. (1986). Greaud and Green (1986) and Kiely et al. (1986) found it affected score differences on coding skills tests. Kiely et al. (1986) also found, however, a smaller effect in favor of paper and pencil in the numerical operations speeded test. Sachar and Fletcher (1978) found that the engineering design of a feature, or perhaps a particular computer's inherent speed in reviewing and correcting previous items, could have slowed the computer group down sufficiently that they completed fewer items in a speeded aptitude test, thus reducing the scores for the CT group. Speed effects are apt to differ between CT and conventional tests. When tests are speeded, there appears to be a three-way confounding of engineering design (including the speed of a particular computer in retrieving and displaying previous items), familiarity with the interface, and differential speed limits of human responding inherent to each medium. Anyone who has observed the response speed learning curve for a teenager on a complex computer game is well aware of the incredible levels of psychomotor speed that can be obtained through practice on a computer interface. It is doubtful that responding with a pencil on a mark-sense page has as high an upper limit for speed and simultaneously retains an acceptably low error rate.

The problem of equating computer and conventional speeded tests might not be an easy one to solve and could ultimately require separate norms. On the one hand, numerous studies show a speed advantage for CT. On the other hand, studies like that of Sachar and Fletcher (1978) indicate that a

likely cause of effects from mode of administration with the speeded power tests of aptitude they studied was the amount of time associated with the error correction and review features of the computer version. It is impossible to judge from these studies what the differential effects would be, given well-designed, well-practiced interface conventions. Some item types (e.g., paragraph comprehension with low-resolution screens) are likely to be fundamentally slower with the computer, some faster (e.g., coding speed items).

Scientific Issues

As the engineering design and experimental design issues become better stabilized and the methodologies for equating conventional and computerized testing become familiar and standardized, it is likely that the emphasis will shift toward scientific issues of greater import. Chief among these is the construct validity of new computerized measures. After all, mean differences disappear after equating; hence, they mean nothing so long as the two tests measure the same construct. Especially interesting subjects for construct validation are those measures that are difficult or impossible to obtain by conventional means. Items involving animation, motion, and audio presented by the computer need to be investigated. What constructs are being measured; new ones or familiar constructs previously measured by conventional methods? What, in particular, are the meanings of response latency, presentation time, and other aspects of temporal control in terms of the constructs being measured?

INDIVIDUAL AND GROUP DIFFERENCES

It could be that individual or group differences affect examinee performance on conventional tests versus CT. For example, research by Wise, Boettcher, Harvey, and Plake (1987) has shown nonsignificant effects of either computer anxiety or computer experience on conventional versus CT versions of the same test. D. F. Johnson and Mihal (1983), however, compared the performance of black and white examinees on the paper-and-pencil version, versus a CT version, of the Cooperative School and College Ability Test. The average total test score of the black students was 5.2 points higher (on the 100-item test) on CT than on conventional testing. The white students only scored .5 points better on total score when using CT. Johnson and Mihal's interpretation is that the black students were more motivated, due to the novelty of the CT environment. Furthermore, these authors state, their scores were less likely to be depressed by the negative expectations those blacks might have had toward intelligence and aptitude measurement.

Wide differences in well-practiced response speed might prove to be an important variable in individual differences. Response speed varies with age, and the sexes might be differently motivated to practice more or practice less. This individual difference in response speed could affect scores on CT tests involving pure speed and speeded power or when paging or keying facility is required.

Research is needed on using computers to aid paraprofessionals in administering and scoring individualized tests requiring the observation and judging of performance tasks and verbal productions. This is a frontier area. Little research has been reported on the adaptation of expensive individually administered tests to computerized format, to aid a human test administrator or observer who responds to the student when judging vocalizations and movements. This approach would broaden the opportunity for administering such tests. It would also provide a new alternative for testing preliterate, illiterate, or handicapped individuals who cannot read instructions from the screen or who are unable to respond by using conventional computer input devices.

The Second Generation: Computerized Adaptive Testing (CAT)

The primary difference between the CAT and the CT generations is that CAT tests are administered adaptively. This, of necessity, generally requires greater computer speed and computational capability and advances in psychometrics, including generally more sophisticated measurement scales. Adaptive tests provide even greater speed of administration than CT, because fewer items need to be administered for equal or greater precision.

Definition

The second, or CAT, generation of computerized educational measurement is defined as computer-administered tests in which the presentation of the next task, or the decision to stop, is adaptive. A task can be an item or a more complex standardized situation involving one or more responses. To be adaptive means that the presentation of the next task depends upon calculations based on the test taker's performance on previous tasks.

The calculations required to select the next task might require additional computer capabilities, such as floating-point arithmetic, and a faster processor than is required for minimal first-generation tests. Item response theory provides a psychometric foundation for one kind of CAT test, that which adapts primarily on the basis of the item-difficulty parameter. This type of test measures static position on an interval scale and has initially done so for primarily institutional purposes such as selection or placement. CAT tests may also be used for individual purposes.

Examples of Computerized Adaptive Tests

Three cases of adaptive tests will be described and an example given of each: *adapting item presentation,* based on item response theory parameters, particularly the difficulty parameter; *adapting item presentation times,* based on previous response times; and *adapting the content or composition of the item,* based on previous choices. In any of these cases a separate adaptive decision may be made: *adapting test length,* based on the consistency of previous performance.

Adapting item presentation on the basis of IRT parameters is the best understood among possible adaptive tests. It will be discussed in some detail later in this section. The other two types of adaptive tests will be discussed first.

ADAPTING ITEM PRESENTATION SPEED

A computer-administered test adaptive on item presentation speed was developed by the authors at the WICAT Education Institute in 1983 as part of the first experimental learner profile battery. The test was designed to assess a construct of perceptual speed. This construct involved processing that was presumed to require both cerebral hemispheres. Called the Word/Shape Matching test, it contained items involving both a word and a shape that either matched or did not match. An example stimulus would be the word *circle* with a square drawn above it. The examinee was instructed to strike one key for a match, another for a mismatch. If a choice was not made within a certain time, the item would time out, and another item would be presented. In this case, more time would be given for the next item. Correct responses within the current time interval would lead to a shorter interval the next time. Two scores were provided, percentage correct and the asymptotic time interval. It was hypothesized that the speed score would be a good predictor of success in other speeded tasks requiring processing of both pictorial and verbal stimuli; that the willingness to trade off speed for errors would be a useful indicator of cognitive style; and that low scores would be one indicator of potential learning disability. The confirming or disconfirming of these hypotheses required a long-term research program that we were not able to complete. The test was administered to groups of elementary school students, who had no difficulty with the operation of the test.

ADAPTING ITEM CONTENT

Simulation tasks are always adaptive, because the next piece of content to be presented depends on the responses of the user. Some simulations also adapt on the basis of endogenous events like the passage of a certain amount of time. Simulation items could be the most sophisticated contribution of computerized measurement to increased complexity and interest in testing. These often use a computer-controlled videodisc to present simulated displays adaptively. Examples are a patient having a medical examination, a piece of equipment needing repair, and images of fruit flies in a genetics breeding experiment. The student makes a series of decisions in the simulated environment, and scoring is accomplished by evaluating the outcome, the strategies, and the sophistication of the path followed. The National Board of Medical Examiners has investigated patient-management simulations extensively as a possible part of their medical certification examinations. They organized a short-lived company, Computer-based Testing and Learning, Inc., to develop and administer these new tests (National Board of Medical Examiners, 1987). The face validity and acceptance by users of such tests is high, but the industry is immature.

Simulations are not the only example of the adaptation of content on the basis of examinees' responses. A computer-administered test that adapted the next paired comparisons was developed by the authors in 1983, as part of the initial WICAT Learner Profile Battery. This test produced a preference profile on the two bipolar dimensions of analytical and logical thinking versus feeling and interpersonal preference and of intuitive, holistic processing versus controlled, sequential processes and preferences. Items were forced-choice, paired comparisons involving an illustration and a phrase such as "I like to hug," "I like to take things apart to see how they work," "I like to draw pictures of imaginary things," "I like to keep my desk neat and tidy." As in a tournament, winners were paired with winners and losers with losers, until a complete ranking of most preferred to most avoided statement was obtained.

Both of the Learner Profile tests described and most simulation tests should be considered experimental. Considerable work needs to be done to establish strong psychometric foundations for tests adaptive on presentation time, content presentation, or any other basis. With tournament-style ranking, for example, single elimination does not provide enough data to assess or to assure reliability of the ranking.

Adapting on the Basis of Item Parameters

Adapting item presentation order on the basis of IRT parameters is now founded on several decades of psychometric work. In the remainder of this section, the term *adaptive test* will refer to tests adaptive on IRT parameters.

In a conventional test administered by either paper and pencil or computer, the majority of items are too easy or too hard for a given examinee, because the examinee will likely answer all easy items correctly and miss the more difficult ones. The items that are too difficult or too easy will contribute little information for measurement of the person's true ability level.

Although the basic ideas and methods of adaptive testing have extensive historical roots in the work of Binet (1909), Birnbaum (1968), and Lord (1970), it was only with the development of digital computers that adaptive testing became feasible. The computer can quickly calculate ability and error estimates and check to see if the criterion for test termination has been met. With a computerized adaptive test, each examinee can be measured at the same level of accuracy or precision. In contrast, with conventional paper-and-pencil or CT tests, the scores near the mean are measured more accurately than those at the high or low end of the score scale.

A computerized adaptive test requires a large item bank that has been calibrated in advance to yield parameters fitting a theoretical item response curve. Each theoretical curve is a function relating probability of correct response to the underlying latent-trait dimension. The computerized adaptive test also requires that responses to items be locally independent (not influenced by responses to any other items). A further assumption is that the items in the bank for that subtest are measuring a single underlying unidimensional ability or latent trait. Psychometric research is under way to develop multidimensional models for use with computerized adaptive testing (Reckase, 1985; Hambleton, this volume).

Steps in Administering an Adaptive Test

There are four major steps in administering an adaptive test.

1. A preliminary estimate of ability is made for the examinee.
2. A test item is selected and administered that will provide maximum information at the estimated ability level. The information value of the item can be calculated on line or stored in a precomputed information matrix. Generally, if the examinee answers an item correctly, a more difficult item is presented; it the examinee misses the item, an easier item is administered. Of all the items available, the one selected is calculated to maximize new information about that examinee, subject to constraints due to content balance and limits placed to control excessive exposure of certain items.
3. The ability estimate is updated or revised after each item. A variety of methods have been proposed for ability estimate updating. Hambleton discusses these topics more fully in chapter 4 of this volume. The methods proposed include Bayesian Sequential Ability Estimation (Owen, 1969, 1975), Maximum Likelihood Ability Estimation (Birnbaum, 1968; Lord 1977, 1980; Samejima, 1977), Expected A Posterior Algorithm (Bock & Aitkin, 1981; Bock & Mislevy, 1982a) and biweighted Bayes estimates. The biweighted Bayes is a robustified ability estimator (Bock & Mislevy, 1982c; Jones, 1982; Wainer & Thissen, 1987; Wainer & Wright, 1980).
4. The testing process continues until a designated test termination criterion has been met. Typical termination criteria include a fixed number of test items, when the standard error reaches or is less than a specified value, and when the test information function reaches or exceeds a specified value.

Item Response Theory

Computerized adaptive testing is based on the psychometric theory called item response theory developed and explicated by Birnbaum (1968), Hambleton (this volume), Hambleton and Swaminathan (1984), Hulin, Drasgow, and Parsons (1984), Lord (1952, 1970, 1980), Lord and Novick (1968), Rasch (1960), and others. Item response theory postulates that examinees differ in their ability on a unidimensional continuum ranging from low to high ability. For each examinee, the probability of answering each item correctly is dependent on the current ability estimate of the examinee and the properties of the item response curve for the current item. Item response curves are usually specified by up to three parameters, the location of their most effective point (the difficulty), their slope at that point (the discrimination), and their y intercept (guessing parameter).

Calibrated Item Banks

CAT tests require the careful development and calibration of a relatively large pool of items. The usual minimum number of items in a pool is 100. These items are administered to a large number of examinees from the target population, and response vectors are obtained for each examinee. With the data from five hundred to one thousand response vectors, calibration programs are used to estimate the parameters of the chosen item response curve. Once calibrated, items can be added to the operational item banks and used in CAT systems. A program for continual updating of item banks through the obtaining of new response vectors for calibrating new experimental items is generally part of an operational CAT system. New experimental items are introduced into the item banks and administered on a planned schedule. These items are not part of the CAT scoring, but they are part of the process of developing a sufficient number of response vectors to calibrate the new items.

The study of the difficulty parameter, the discrimination parameter, and the guessing parameter represents a powerful form of item analysis and can be used to refine or discard experimental items. As an item analysis technique, a generalized form (Thissen & Steinberg, 1984) can even provide information on the attractiveness of distractors, but IRT item analyses have usually been considered deficient in this respect.

Several alternative item calibration programs have been developed. The most widely used are LOGIST (Wingersky, Lord, & Barton, 1982) and BILOG (Mislevy & Bock, 1982). More recent candidates include ASCAL (Vale & Gialluca, 1985), MICROSCALE (Linacre & Wright, 1984), M-SCALE (Wright, Rossner, & Congdon, 1984), and MULTILOG (Thissen, 1986).

Current Computerized Adaptive Testing Systems

With the emergence of microcomputers and low-cost multiprocessors, computerized adaptive testing has now become feasible for widespread operational research and implementation. Within the past few years, a variety of microcomputer-based computerized adaptive testing systems have been developed, demonstrated, and implemented. The military has sponsored the most far-reaching and complex development projects. The first of the military CAT system prototypes was developed for the Apple III computer by the Naval Personnel Research and Development Center (Quan, Park, Sandahl, & Wolfe, 1984). This prototype was developed to provide computerized adaptive administration of the subtests from the Armed Services Vocational Aptitude Battery (ASVAB). Following successful research on the validity and reliability of the computerized adaptive ASVAB, compared with the paper-and-pencil ASVAB, the Department of Defense contracted with three independent companies to design and develop operational CAT systems (WICAT Systems; Bolt, Beranek, and Newman; and McDonnell Douglas). The military elected not to complete the procurement process initiated with these contracts, but important lessons were learned for large-scale CAT development.

These system prototypes were developed for future administration of a computerized adaptive ASVAB in 69 military enlistment processing stations in larger cities and in up to 800 smaller mobile examining team sites. This required development of a large fixed-site configuration, a small portable configuration, and the communications to link them to one another and to a specified military base for central record keeping.

The components of an operational CAT system are numerous, involving hardware and software elements of some complexity. One of these prototype CAT systems included a portable supermicrocomputer system (the WICAT 150) with the powerful Motorola 68000 CPU chip. This processor had a multiprocessing operating system and the speed to handle up to eight portable graphics terminals simultaneously. The graphics resolution was sufficient to display effectively the line drawings found in ASVAB items, such as mechanical comprehension and automotive information items. The system developed by Bolt, Beranek, and Newman similarly supported eight graphics terminals from one central portable processor, but the McDonnell Douglas prototype used a separate CPU for each display.

The military procurement process is extremely thorough. It applies standards for the development of hardware, for software and applications programs, and for human factors that are not always considered by a civilian user who is contemplating system procurement for the transfer of widely distributed paper-and-pencil testing programs to computer. The military configuration is applicable to many civilian organizations that administer tests. These organizations frequently require fixed locations in major cities and portable systems that can administer tests on a less frequent basis to smaller groups of people in temporary locations. They often have one central site at which the test scores are finally archived and important personnel decisions are made. A number of professional or membership organizations who test for admission or certification of individuals for practice in a profession have such requirements. For these reasons, we will summarize some of the features such a large-scale user might look for.

SELECTION OF HARDWARE

An organization deploying a large testing configuration would profit from the use of standard hardware components including computers, buses, peripherals, and interface devices. Availability of a maintenance network and a strong record of reliability should be sought. Features to enhance maintainability include power-on testing, device initialization, failure logging, diagnostic monitors in read-only memory (ROM), and diagnostic downloading from a host computer to a remote computer.

Other maintenance considerations include modularity of parts, ease in connecting and disconnecting parts and cables, and uncomplicated cabling. The user should also be concerned with safety standards and electronic emission standards.

Human Factors. General operating factors such as table arrangements, good lighting, avoidance of glare from windows, and electrical requirements are important in all circumstances, but they must be considered each time for mobile operations in a temporary site. The portability, size, and weight of the equipment are of course the major factors in such operations. The attractiveness for possible pilfering of keypads and other small components must be considered in their design. They should not be easy to detach.

Legibility and visibility factors of the screen include the luminance, the contrast, the resolution, the display size, the effective viewing angle, and the viewing distance and glare, jitter, and drift of the screen. Proctor control of video adjustment controls is desirable. These are factors inherent in the hardware. Also important are what has earlier in this chapter been called the interface conventions. Good engineering design provides unambiguous screen formats including a standard format for each item type; a clear set of conventions for paging or scrolling on multi-page items; the visibility of the question in the foreground window on multi-page items; a rapid response to the examinees' inputs, so that response speed is not affected by computer delays; a legible type font; and clear and legible graphics.

The keyboard and keypad input factors include the ability to time responses and the ease with which the keyboard and its conventional uses with different item types can be learned and used. Also important is a compact size, an auditory click or sound to indicate engagement of a key, and the "feel" of the keys. If touch screens are to be used, parallax and the resolution of the active touch sites are important to consider. A joystick, a mouse, or curser-control arrows introduce differences in speed of response, in sources of error, and in the learning curve for fast and accurate responding.

A printer will always be associated with the computer at a larger fixed location, and a portable printer might be available in mobile applications. In this case, legibility, standard format and use, and speed of issuing the reports after testing are important factors.

In connection with the user friendliness of the system, not only must the user interface conventions be quick and easy to learn, but also enough familiarization should be provided at the beginning of the entire testing session and at the introduction of each new item format to assure that users are familiar with the conventions. Computer literacy and standard input and display conventions are rapidly becoming more widespread in our society. Any CAT system should use familiar and widely accepted conventions and should not introduce unfamiliar conventions that require the user to change established habits.

Selection of Software

Software subsystems can be grouped under three headings: software for the central development facility, software for the fixed site in major cities, and software for operations at both the fixed site and the portable systems.

Software at the Central Development Site. The authoring software should permit the simulation of a test for tryout by the developers, with full debugging tools. Item authoring programs should permit flexible screen editing of text and graphics. Being able to enter items in a batch mode from existing text files is a significant advantage that enhances productivity. Editing features should include access to files to update the test battery composition and composite score weights. Speeded (timed) test and item authoring might require a separate software module, as could familiarization sequence authoring.

Item calibration programs must be installed at the central development site, generally on larger computers. Programs to insert experimental items into test batteries and to schedule their introduction must be available. Encryption and decryption software must be available if items, item banks, and other secure information are to be transmitted to the fixed sites electronically or on a magnetic medium that might be intercepted. Communication software will be extensive at the central site, as it communicates with all fixed sites.

Software at the Fixed Locations. Item data collection and data consolidation programs are necessary at the cities to consolidate the data collected locally and at the satellite mobile sites reporting to a given fixed site. A test-score and student record archiving function must also be available. Communication software to transmit the archived scores to the central site where personnel records are kept is necessary, along with communication software to communicate with the portable computers at temporary sites. Finally, communications with the central test-development site are necessary. This site might be different from the central site for personnel records.

Software at the Temporary and Fixed Locations. Programs are needed to register the testees and obtain the necessary biographical information from examinees. For military enlistment this includes some medical information. Programs are necessary to assign each examinee to a particular workstation, to log the examinee in, and to provide computer familiarization. For the proctor or the operator with a portable computer, software should boot the computer, monitor the terminal ports from one proctor terminal, provide password security for the proctor versus the test taker, and permit control of the printer. Software to administer the test includes a program to provide the initial estimate of ability and instructional programs for familiarization with each subtest, including practice with the user interface conventions. Also needed are item-selection programs, programs to accept and code examinees' responses and response times, ability estimation routines, and programs to check the test-termination criterion. Software must record the subtest results, provide a subtest report and a consolidated report, and file the test results by each experimental item and by each examinee, so that response vectors can be obtained for calibration. The portable computer must have communication software and a modem to communicate with the fixed site. It must also have encryption and decryption software, if this degree of security is required.

Various software routines to assist the operator are necessary at the fixed site to check the integrity of files, to control the communications, to manage the disks, to provide maintenance functions, to configure and reconfigure the system for different numbers of terminals and different numbers of computers, and so on. Proctor functions are also needed at both the central and mobile sites. In addition to logging examinees and assigning them to a particular terminal, the proctor needs to be able to monitor the terminals and watch for signals of trouble at any one (a raised hand is sufficient at the mobile site). The proctor needs software to allow her or him to stop a test and restart it at another terminal, in the case of a breakdown midway through a test. Other programs are needed to delete old files and records, back up daily work onto disks or tapes, and restore records from magnetic medium.

The amount of storage required for this extensive software is surprisingly low for at least one of the prototype systems. The data for test items for nine ASVAB subtests consisted of less than 2 megabytes. Each of the nine subtests included about 200 items with 10 or 20 graphics and required 220 kilobytes. The examinee data for a fixed site might be maintained at about 2 megabytes. The CAT software only required about 800 kilobytes, and the file system overhead needed about 200 kilobytes. This amounted to 5 megabytes, which easily fit on a 10 megabyte hard disk. The procuring organization should consider much larger files. Hard-disk drives of much larger capacity are now available, and programs and data seem to obey a law that they always expand to fill the available space.

OTHER CAT SYSTEMS

Over the past few years several CAT systems have been developed by professional educational and psychological testing organizations. These systems are far less complicated than the military prototypes, except in the case of some test-development software subsystems. Current systems generally operate on personal computers. Educational Testing Service and the College Board have developed a CAT testing system for implementation on the IBM PC for measuring college level basic skills in English and mathematics (Abernathy, 1986; Ward et al., 1986). The Assessment Systems Corporation has developed a generalized microcomputer adaptive test-authoring and administration system (MicroCAT) implemented on an IBM PC (Assessment Systems, 1985). The MicroCAT system is being used by the Portland public schools and Montgomery County public schools for development of school-based adaptive testing. The Psychological Corporation has developed an adaptive version of the Differential Aptitude Test for administration on Apple II computers (Psychological Corporation, 1986). Psychological Corporation has also demonstrated a computerized adaptive Mathematics Locator test for administration on the Apple II computer (McBride & Moe, 1986). The Waterford Testing Center has developed a generalized CAT authoring, administration, and reporting system. This CAT system has been used to develop a school-based learner profile aptitude battery consisting of 45 different CT and CAT tests and a comprehensive school-based computerized testing system for grades 3–8 that measures achievement in reading, mathematics, and language arts (WICAT Systems, 1988). The Waterford Testing Center has also developed CAT tests of mathematics applications for the California Assessment Program (Olsen, Maynes, Ho, & Slawson, 1986). Unlike the personal computer implementations, these systems operate on the 30-terminal WICAT Computer-aided Education System for larger fixed sites primarily engaged in instruction, but they are also available on smaller configurations.

Advantages of Computerized Adaptive Tests

Because computerized adaptive tests are also administered by computer, all of the advantages over paper-based testing noted for the CT generation also apply to CAT. In summary these advantages are

1. Enhanced control in presenting item displays
2. Improved test security
3. Enriched display capability
4. Equivalent scores with reduced testing time
5. Improved obtaining and coding of responses
6. Reduced measurement error
7. Ability to measure response latencies for items and components
8. Improved scoring and reporting
9. Automation of individually administered tests
10. Obtaining of records at a central site
11. Ability to construct tests and create items by computer

Item response theory also provides many advantages in the score equating process, because each item has a calibrated position on an underlying latent-trait scale. Additional advantages of computerized adaptive tests are presented next (see also Green, 1983; Wainer, 1983, 1984; and Ward, 1986).

INCREASED MEASUREMENT PRECISION

Research has shown that conventional tests administered by computer or by paper have high measurement precision near the average test score, but they have low measurement precision for low- and high-ability levels. In contrast, a computerized adaptive test maintains high measurement precision, or accuracy, at all ability levels (low, average, high). Setting the CAT test-termination criterion at a specified value allows all examinees to be measured to the same level of precision.

EQUIVALENT ABILITY ESTIMATES WITH REDUCED TESTING TIME

With CAT each examinee is administered only the subset of items similar to his or her ability level. Items too difficult or too easy for a given examinee are not administered. Compared with conventional paper or computerized tests, a CAT test requires far fewer items. The strongest claims for fewer items have been in the area of school-based achievement tests (Olsen, Maynes, Ho, et al., 1986). These authors found that only 30% to 50% of the test items were needed to reach an equivalent level of precision, as compared with paper testing. Correspondingly less test administration time was needed. Ward (1984) notes that, with adaptive testing, "the length of a test battery can be cut by 50 to 60 percent and still maintain a measurement accuracy equivalent to that of the best standardized conventional test" (p. 17). The research on score comparability of paper-and-pencil, computer-administered, and computerized adaptive tests is quite complex. As noted in the last section, computerized tests do not always yield equal ability estimates and distributions. An example of when they do is given in the study by Olsen, Maynes, Ho et al. (1986). Figure 9.2 presents the key results. Equivalent ability estimates with reduced testing time have also been found by others (McKinley & Reckase, 1980, 1984a; Moreno, Wetzel, McBride, & Weiss, 1983).

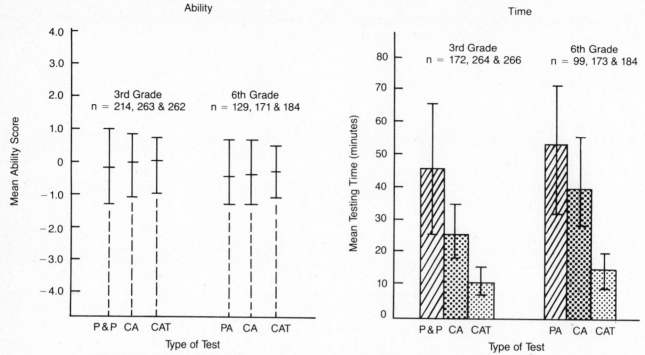

FIGURE 9.2 Mean ability score and mean testing time for test taken by computer.

FURTHER IMPROVEMENTS IN TEST SECURITY

Test security is enhanced with CAT beyond CT because each examinee receives an individually tailored test. It would be difficult to steal and memorize each of the hundred or so items for each of several such tests. Encryption can be used to protect item banks and examinee data. Randomization can be implemented to select one of a set of most informative items. With CAT there are no paper copies of the tests, answer booklets, or answer keys. Two examinees sitting next to one another are even less likely than with CT to see the same item at the same time.

Research Problems with Computerized Adaptive Testing

This section discusses several classes of research problems inviting investigation in current and future CAT systems. It is organized to respond to some research problems and needs identified by Wainer and Kiely (1987).

CONTEXT EFFECTS

Significant effects on item parameters and item performance have been shown to depend on the relationship with other items in the test (Eignor & Cook, 1983; Kingston & Dorans, 1984; Whitley & Dawis, 1976; Yen, 1980). In conventional testing, every examinee receives every item in the same order. Thus, the context effects are the same for all examinees. Because each examinee receives a tailored set of items in a tailored order in a CAT test, there is the possibility of differential context effects for different examinees. One potential solution to this problem is to conduct IRT calibration studies that coun-

terbalance the pairings and sequences among all the items in an item bank. The resulting parameter calibrations should average out the context effects. Research studies should also be conducted using repeated administrations that offer the same items in different sequences.

One kind of content effect is cross-information; that is, the correct or erroneous information that one item might provide concerning the answer to another item. To solve this problem, as in the conventional test-development situation, the item banks for computerized adaptive tests should be carefully checked by technical reviewers to remove any items that could provide cross-information to the examinee. Because it is virtually impossible to inspect all possible pairs in large item banks, technical review alone is unlikely to solve this problem, even at greatly increased cost for reviewing. Partial automation might help. New semantic search techniques by computer could be used to identify identical matches or synonym matches between any item stems or answers throughout the item bank.

UNBALANCED CONTEXT

This problem arises when there is repeated emphasis on a particular content area or skill throughout a test, rather than balanced emphasis across content and skills. Adaptive tests make it difficult to maintain constant specification, which requires a balanced sampling of different content areas. One potential solution to this problem is to administer a computerized adaptive test with some additional domain specification criteria. For example, the College Board and ETS computerized placement tests (Abernathy, 1986) call for a test specification template within which the computerized adaptive testing is conducted.

LACK OF ROBUSTNESS

This problem occurs because the shorter computerized tests lack the redundancy of longer tests. The impact of an incorrectly functioning item is much greater in a short CAT test than in a longer conventional paper-and-pencil or computerized test. One solution to this problem is to require a more stringent test-termination criterion in the computerized adaptive test (longer fixed test length, smaller standard error of estimate, or higher test-information values). Research has shown that computerized adaptive testing can reduce test length by 35%, perhaps by as much as 50% to 75% in some applications, while retaining the same precision. A partial solution is thus to administer more items, reducing the advantage in test length in favor of increased robustness.

ITEM DIFFICULTY ORDERING

In conventional test development, a test is typically designed to sequence items from less difficult to more difficult. This allows almost all examinees to warm up with some success on easy items. Although this feature might increase fairness and validity, it also favors strategies for guessing on the basis of presumed difficulty, which reduces validity and is inequitable in favor of those coached in test-taking strategies.

One standard approach to CAT is to administer an initial item of average difficulty. This is optimal for neither high-ability examinees nor low-ability examinees. A potential solution to this problem is to provide short locator tests consisting of 5 to 6 items, which span the spectrum of item difficulties in the item banks. The locator test approach can insure a more accurate initial estimate than single items of average difficulty. It also offers some easy items for low- and high-ability examinees.

A second solution to this problem is to initiate the computerized adaptive test at a lower difficulty value (for example, at the 30 or 35 percentile value, rather than at the 50 percentile value). On the average, this would require slightly longer computerized adaptive tests, but it would insure that the majority of examinees would experience some moderately easy items. In all cases, CAT reduces the effects of coaching in test strategies based on the information that test makers place easy items first and difficult items last.

Wainer and Kiely (1987) suggest the investigation of "testlets," groups of items that carry their own context. Testlets might reduce the effects of context, cross-information, and sequence that occur in CAT.

PARAGRAPH COMPREHENSION ITEMS

Wainer and Kiely (1987) note that most computerized adaptive testing systems have opted to develop and administer shorter paragraph comprehension items that present the text paragraph and multiple answers on a single screen. Research by Green (1988) shows that these short paragraph comprehension items are more similar to traditional word knowledge items than to previous paragraph comprehension tests, which changes the construct being measured. A potential solution to this problem is to develop longer computerized text paragraph comprehension items. This will require higher resolution screens or the development of easy paging and prompting techniques that will help examinees know which page of a multiple-page item they are reading, how many more pages are in the text selection, and how to move quickly to a given text page.

Research should also be conducted to identify the impact of calibrating multiple questions associated with a standard paragraph comprehension item. Andrich (1985) has done some promising work in the calibration of multiple questions associated with a single passage. If such sets of questions are administered intact, there appears to be no bias in ability estimation.

OTHER RESEARCH ISSUES

Research on multidimensional IRT models is needed, and some is under way (Mislevy, 1987; Reckase, 1985). Research is also needed to further clarify the strengths and weaknesses of alternative ability estimation approaches (Bayesian, maximum likelihood, expected a posteriori, etc.). New test-construction procedures such as the testlet approach (Wainer & Kiely, 1987) should be investigated.

Because examinees are tested at their level of ability, an adaptive test might be less boring for high-achieving examinees and less frustrating for low-achieving examinees. This claim has been made but not validated.

Additional research should be conducted with single and multiple test-termination criteria (fixed number of items, specified standard error, specified test information value, etc.).

The Third Generation: Continuous Measurement (CM)

Definition

The continuous measurement generation uses calibrated measures embedded in a curriculum to continuously and unobtrusively estimate dynamic changes in the student's proficiency. Tasks measured may be items, item clusters, exercises, unit tests, or independent work assignments. Changes may be observed in the amount learned, the proficiency on different tasks, changes in the trajectory through the domain, and the student's profile as a learner.

The differentiating characteristic of CM is the ability to specify dynamically a learner's position on the simple and complex scales that define a growth space. Continuous measurement produces a trajectory over time for the individual who is working to master a domain of knowledge and task proficiency. Measurement is accomplished by assessing the performance of each individual on tasks calibrated to serve as milestones of accomplishment. The milestones that make CM possible are embedded into a curriculum, so that measurement is unobtrusive.

The definition of the CM generation assumes a two-part definition of curriculum: (a) a course of experiences laid out to help the learner grow toward certain educational ends, that is, a path through a domain; (b) a set of course markers, or standards, that serve as milestones of accomplishment along the way, that is, beginning, intermediate, and terminal markers.

The continuous measurement generation will not spring full blown from either the curriculum side or the measurement side of its parentage. Rather it will grow slowly from its end points. Admissions testing, at the beginning, and certification, at the end of a course of study, have been well researched. As research and development progresses toward the center of a curriculum, rather than toward the end points, continuous measurement of progress can occur. Development of the CM generation will necessarily bring measurement scientists into the area of specifying or modeling more carefully the substantive *content domains* to be mastered. This will necessitate a major expansion of current practices in test specification (our current method of specifying domains) and augment these with methods of job, task, and cognitive analysis and knowledge-acquisition methods adapted from the field of expert systems. It will also bring measurement science more powerfully than ever before into issues of the construct validity of measures of cognitive and learning processes, and the measurement of change.

Associated with the definition of the CM generation are eight features, which follow generally the properties listed in the CM column of Table 9.1.

1. The computer requirements are those of a computer-aided education (CAE) system, with enough speed and capacity for CAT calculations. The CAE system is usually housed in a learning resource room where practice and assessment can take place. However, it is also possible to monitor responses in groups in regular classrooms using hand-held response devices.
2. Measurement occurs continuously, being embedded into the curriculum. Exercise modules themselves are calibrated in much the same manner as items are calibrated in the second generation.
3. Continuous measurement is unobtrusive. Because measurement occurs when students' responses are monitored as part of their ordinary learning activities, testing does not stand out as a separate activity. Achievement testing occurs automatically as students work through the curriculum exercises. The testing of learning strategies could occur automatically as students choose different methods of approaching or avoiding the curriculum exercises and these choices are monitored. Other measurements of learner profile variables, including preferences and abilities, can be accomplished unobtrusively by inserting items into the curriculum at appropriate intervals. It should be noted that unobtrusive does not mean measurement occurs without informed consent.
4. Continuous measurement differs from the first two generations in emphasizing dynamic, rather than static, measurement primarily for individual purposes, not institutional purposes.
5. Data from continuous measurement should be available to, and of value to, learners and teachers alike. A representation of the domain of knowledge and expertise to be mastered is available for reference by the students and teachers. The progress of individual students on this representation, which might be called a *mastery map,* is also available for continuous reference.
6. The scaling in CM is more complex than that in CAT. Instead of the unidimensional scales of the CAT genera-

tion, CM deals with multiple and often multidimensional scales but might summarize them into a single composite score or objective function, to track progress for each learner on a personalized mastery map.
7. Reference tasks are calibrated on interval scales of measurement in the CM generation. A reference task refers to, and might simulate, real-world or joblike performance requirements. Reference tasks generally are more complex than single items and require multiple responses. As learners encounter and experience these different tasks, a continuing estimate of changes in achievement (the learner's trajectory) can be estimated adaptively.
8. The CM generation will not be mature until research foundations have been established for the new psychometric procedures needed. This might involve extensions of IRT or new procedures entirely. Enhanced methods for construct specifications are needed to develop valid measures of learning outcomes at different stages of mastery. A useful set of learner profile measures is needed to characterize individual differences in learning while using such systems. Research is needed to establish implementation designs that will enable teachers and learners to become proficient over time in the new roles required for mixed forms of assessment and learning. Preservation of the conditions for validity and for the proper use of measurement depends on excellent implementation.

Examples of Partial CM Systems

No complete example of a CM generation system has been developed to date. However, several computerized educational systems have been developed that illustrate incomplete continuous measurement systems. These systems exemplify subsets of the eight properties that characterize CM. Two examples have been selected for discussion here. The first of them, the TICCIT system, was an ambitious CAE system of the early 1970s. It featured continuous and unobtrusive measurement, mastery maps, and a range of different reference tasks. TICCIT did not have calibrated reference tasks or scaling. The second example is a reading curriculum developed for the WICAT Computer-aided Education system. This reading curriculum illustrated most of the properties of a complete CM system, including calibrated exercises. A pilot study will be reported in which an attempt was made to scale the exercises. The CM concept has been developed further by researchers at ETS, under the designation *Mastery Assessment Systems.* The ETS concept is described herein.

THE TICCIT SYSTEM

TICCIT stands for Timeshared Interactive Computer-Controlled Information Television. The hardware for this system was designed by engineers at the Mitre Corporation in 1971 and 1972, and the instructional strategy, courseware, and instructional logic were designed by a group of instructional and computer scientists at the University of Texas and

Brigham Young University. TICCIT was one of two major National Science Foundation (NSF)-funded CAE systems developed in the early 1970s. The other was the PLATO system, developed at the University of Illinois.

The TICCIT hardware consisted of up to 100 color video monitors that could present mixed text and graphics in up to eight colors. Digitized audio was available, and videotapes could be switched to any terminal. Students responded with a typewriter keyboard when required to make a selection or to type a word or phrase. Most of their responses, however, were entered as single keystrokes on a special learner-control response pad at the right-hand side of the keyboard. This keypad had the keys MAP, OBJECTIVE, RULE, EXAMPLE, PRACTICE, EASY(er), HARD(er), HELP, and ADVICE.

TICCIT was initially designed with two courses in freshman and remedial mathematics and two courses in freshman English grammar and composition for community colleges. It was implemented at Phoenix College in Arizona and at Northern Virginia Community College in Alexandria. Educational Testing Service evaluated the project and found that TICCIT classes gained significantly more than control classes in both mathematics and English (Alderman, 1978).

Information about TICCIT can be found in Bunderson (1973) and Merrill, Schneider, and Fletcher (1980). An early history of CAE, including TICCIT and PLATO, can be found in Bunderson and Faust (1976). The TICCIT project assets were acquired by the Hazeltine Corporation after the NSF funding was completed, and the system was improved substantially during the subsequent 16 years. Its applications have primarily been in industrial and military training, rather than in education, in part because of the significant sociological and economic problems standing in the way of implementing computer-aided education in mainline college instruction. TICCIT has been acquired from Hazeltine by Ford Aerospace and continued at the time of this writing as a viable CAE alternative.

TICCIT exemplified CM, in that testing and measurement occurred unobtrusively whenever students were working at the terminal. Its psychometric theories were simple, and it did not have calibrated tasks or the particular research foundations discussed in point 8 of the definition of CM. However, TICCIT provides a continuing example of the first 5 properties of CM. It exemplifies particularly well the mastery map concept, including a means of tracking student progress through a knowledge domain.

The TICCIT map was represented as a series of "learning hierarchies" (see Gagné, 1968). At the top level was the course map. In the English course, for example, the course map defined a set of units for learning to structure and organize writing and another set for learning to edit written compositions for grammar, mechanics, and spelling. Each unit on the course map was represented in further detail by a unit map, which consisted of a series of lessons, also arranged in a learning hierarchy. Each lesson also had a map consisting of a hierarchically organized set of segments. Each segment constituted a single objective, usually a concept, a principle or rule, or a kind of problem to be solved. The objective and different versions of a definition or rule statement were available for each segment. The segments included many practice items, classified as easy, medium, and hard, each with help available.

The instructional prescriptions for each kind of objective were developed according to what has since come to be called *component display theory* (Merrill, 1983; Riegeluth, Merrill, & Bunderson, 1978). Component display theory was a substantial elaboration of Gagné's earlier concepts of a prescriptive instructional approach, first promulgated in his book *Conditions of Learning* (Gagné, 1965). TICCIT, therefore, had a type of construct validity based on a taxonomy of learning objectives and utilizing the associated conditions for teaching each type of objective.

TICCIT maps provided a continuous display of progress, always available to the students on their individual video screens. The data on these maps were summarized for the teachers on weekly printed reports. As a student progressed through a segment, the data for that segment box were updated, and the student was given feedback on her or his performance. When all the segments in a lesson had been mastered, the student could take a lesson test. Each lesson test used a simple kind of adaptive testing logic called the Wald Sequential Testing procedure, in which items were selected randomly or sequentially until a determination could be made to accept the student as having mastered or failed the lesson. Statistical calculations were made after each item. When the student was in an indeterminate state, further items were administered. Item administration stopped as soon as a determined state was reached.

TICCIT had the ability to track the progress of each student, even though students were moving at different rates through different sequences of lessons. Its lesson and unit maps with status information were a popular and successful feature. Menus, a currently popular interface convention, with the addition of continuously measured status information, would serve just as well.

Another continuous measurement feature of the TICCIT system was the advisor function. The complete advisor program as conceived was conceptually ahead of its time, because the artificial intelligence techniques needed to implement it properly were not available in 1972. The concept of the advisor was to employ measurements of the student's progress and use of different learning strategies and tactics to provide interpretive advice. The progress measurements would be used in connection with a set of prescriptive instructional rules to provide feedback to the learner when requested or when certain conditions were met, as calculated by the computer. Because of the complexity of programming such a system, by using decision tables instead of expert system and relational data base methods, the TICCIT advisor did not achieve its ambitious goals; indeed, it will be seen that such goals are the goals of the fourth generation of intelligent measurement applied in CM settings. Although the TICCIT advisor fell short of its goals, it did accomplish a major third-generation function. It provided each learner with a score indicating how well he or she was doing in the practice problems constituting a given segment. Students used this information frequently. There appeared to be a great thirst for dynamic information on how well an individual was doing.

The teachers' weekly reports of progress on the TICCIT lessons were also found to be an important part of the implementation plan. Computer activity became more and more closely integrated with teachers' classroom activities as they learned to use the reports. Success with continuous measurement in educational programs like TICCIT depends heavily on an excellent implementation plan in which teachers learn new roles and students learn new habits and practices.

Calibrating Computer-administered Learning Exercises

Research conducted by the authors of this chapter at the WICAT Education Institute in 1980 provides an example of some of the benefits of calibrating exercises embedded into a curriculum, in this case the WICAT Elementary Reading Curriculum.

The WICAT Elementary Reading Curriculum. First developed under an Office of Education grant, this computer curriculum was designed as a practice and feedback system to accompany classroom instruction in reading comprehension. it consisted of a series of stories especially written for different grade levels, spanning the range of difficulty from the third through about the seventh grade. The system was based on a learner control philosophy, not unlike TICCIT.

Learners were allowed to select stories to read, within their own grade level, from a graphic map that resembled the front page of a newspaper or magazine. At a higher level of generality, and somewhat equivalent to the TICCIT course map, was a list of different newspaper or magazine titles. The equivalent to the TICCIT unit map was the "front page" with printed titles, frequently accompanied by a graphic identifying each story inside the "magazine." No status information was provided by these maps, except a record of stories completed. They functioned as tables of contents more than as mastery maps with status information. The students would select a story to read and then enter into an exercise involving that story. Each exercise consisted of reading a screen or two of information, answering interspersed multiple-choice questions, underlining key words on the screen to explain why a particular answer was given, and typing short answers. The typed answers were not judged by the computer. Self-corrective feedback was given, so that the learner could judge her or his own free response. These types of questions were repeated several times until the story was finished. Ten to 20 scorable responses were available for each story. A grading standard for each exercise had been established by the curriculum authors, analogous to the scoring standards within the TICCIT segments.

Manager programs were available to keep track of responses at a detailed level, resulting in a rich set of data for use by researchers, teachers, and students. Systems like the WICAT System 300, a 30-terminal on-line computer system for schools, or networked systems that tie microcomputers together are needed for the centralized record keeping necessary in CM. The WICAT manager programs made research possible utilizing student response tapes from the children in the third through sixth grades at the Waterford School in Provo, Utah. As in the TICCIT system, the teachers had available to them weekly reports showing student progress through the various stories at the various grade levels. The students had access to less information than the TICCIT advisor provided, but

they were able to tell if they were doing well or poorly in each exercise. They had learner control that allowed them to respond to this information and move in and out of the exercises at will.

The WICAT reading curriculum also had an adaptive strategy for giving the students easier or more difficult reading exercises. When they passed a reading exercise at one grade level, the computer would move them to a harder grade level. The computer could also keep them at the same level or introduce them to easier exercises. The goal was to keep them at an optimally challenging level of difficulty. Thus, the WICAT reading curriculum involved continuous measurement, monitoring of progress, and some automatic adaptation of difficulty. Unfortunately, the teachers reported that the grade levels assigned by the computer in that early version of the courseware did not seem to work well. Students would advance into more difficult material too rapidly, creating problems with the quality of their work and with their motivation. The grade level parameters for each reading exercise had been established by the authoring team through the combination of Frye Reading Indexes and subjective judgments.

Cross-fertilization between instructional and measurement research occurred naturally at this time, because work in adaptive testing was going on simultaneously with the studies of the reading data. Two of the authors were at this time involved in the Armed Services Vocational Aptitude Battery Computerized Adaptive Testing that WICAT systems was conducting for the Department of Defense (Olsen, Bunderson, & Gilstrap, 1982). They had implemented CAT tests for ASVAB on a specially designed hardware system and were using the BILOG program (Mislevy & Bock, 1982) to calibrate items. It was thought that the curriculum exercises themselves could be calibrated as easily as single items and that the difficulty parameters obtained from the calibration would provide an excellent scaling for the reading exercises, potentially superior to the curriculum authors' judgments of reading difficulty and associated grade levels.

These considerations led to the design of a pilot study wherein the ratios of correct to attempted (using the first attempt in each reading exercise) would be used as a response vector to calibrate the exercises. This pilot study was seen as a demonstration of a concept: the potential benefit of equal-interval scaling of curriculum exercises. It was not seen as a finished methodology, because adherence to the assumptions of IRT could not be assured, nor were the samples as large as would be desired for each exercise. There was, nevertheless, reason to believe that the reading stories were sufficiently independent of one another that the assumption of local independence was not unreasonable. The assumption of unidimensionality is not unreasonable for reading items, but it was not checked. Because of learner choice, the stories were taken in a quasi-random order. The correct–attempted ratio of each student's performance within each reading exercise was more reliable than single-item responses.

The response vectors from the reading curriculum were accordingly calibrated using the BILOG program. As expected, the difficulty (theta) parameters showed that the grade level designations of each story in the curriculum were not supported by the empirical data on story difficulty.

Some grade level jumps rated large by the reading curriculum authors were in reality tiny steps in difficulty, whereas exercises presumably at the same grade level provided giant steps in empirically determined difficulty. The use of the calibrated difficulty parameter offered the curriculum developers an opportunity to make a substantial improvement in sequencing the on-line reading curriculum.

Table 9.3 compares the empirical difficulty parameters from the BILOG program for 48 argumentation stories, with the judged readability indexes for each story (WICAT, 1983). The correlation between these two difficulty estimates is very low ($r = -.07$). Clearly, tasks requiring learners to think and respond are different from the difficulty (readability) of a reading passage itself. Note that the two extreme stories (5 and 14)

TABLE 9.3 Comparison of IRT Difficulty Parameters with Judged Grade Level in a Set of Computerized Reading Exercises

STORY NO.	IRT DIFFICULTY PARAMETER	IRT RANK ORDER	JUDGED GRADE LEVEL (READABILITY)
5	1.98	1	7
34	1.86	2	5
35	1.82	3	5
12	1.79	4	7
32	1.65	5	5
26	1.31	6	4
1	1.28	7	7
29	1.23	8	4
27	1.21	9	4
3	1.11	10	7
7	1.11	11	7
2	1.10	12	7
28	1.08	13	4
44	1.02	14	6
13	1.01	15	7
4	.96	16	7
18	.92	17	6
16	.85	18	6
41	.81	19	4
43	.80	20	6
48	.77	21	4
42	.72	22	6
21	.71	23	4
39	.66	24	6
6	.61	25	7
31	.60	26	5
38	.60	27	6
45	.58	28	6
36	.58	29	6
47	.57	30	4
24	.55	31	4
33	.55	32	5
20	.53	33	6
37	.52	24	6
22	.40	35	4
19	.39	36	6
10	.36	37	7
23	.35	38	4
25	.34	39	4
46	.31	40	6
15	.26	41	7
17	.22	42	6
9	.20	43	7
11	.14	44	7
30	-.04	45	4
40	-.56	46	6
8	-.57	47	7
14	-.93	48	7

Rank Correlation = $-.07$

Note. It is possible for a calibrated set of curriculum-embedded exercises to serve as a standardized test of reading comprehension.

on the IRT scale both had a judged grade level of 7. Story 14 had a difficulty value of $-.9$, very easy, whereas story 5 had a difficulty value of 2.0. Notice also that the 6th and 45th ranked stories on the IRT scale both had a judged difficulty of 4, the easiest grade level for the argumentation exercises. (Only the argumentation exercises were calibrated. Other reading exercises were less difficult, and teachers reported fewer problems with the computer adaptive strategy.)

The scaling of exercise units has considerable promise, once the proper psychometric procedures can be developed for a wide class of exercise types (including hierarchial and cumulative curricula). It can provide valuable feedback to the curriculum developer, like helping to examine the details of exercises that prove to be much harder or easier than expected and to program an effective adaptive strategy for moving the students along. It can also provide a continuous measurement of achievement in reading comprehension for monitoring progress by using a mastery map. The standard scale values of the BILOG difficulty parameters can be converted to a grade-equivalent scale or normal curve equivalent scale. When there are multiple dimensions, a cumulative summary can be obtained by developing a function that summarizes progress toward the multiple objectives of the course of study.

The pilot research with the WICAT reading curriculum provided a more complete example of what a continuous measurement system might be like than had the TICCIT investigations. This example shows that measurement science has much to offer to education, both to the process of curriculum development and to the processes of administering the curriculum intelligently and adaptively. Continuous measurement holds the promise of providing unobtrusive, frequent, reliable, and valid data. The continuous and sequential nature of the tasks anchoring the measurement provides many opportunities for continually assessing and improving reliability and construct validity.

Preliminary Evidence of Construct Validity

Some evidence of construct validity was obtained by relating the IRT scores to standardized test scores. IRT estimates of students' ability were obtained from the individual response vectors of each Waterford student, coupled with the parameters of the exercises the students passed and failed. Reading comprehension scores on all of the students at the Waterford School were also available from the Iowa Test of Basic Skills. The individual ability levels estimated from the calibrated curriculum exercises were included in a factor analysis with scores from the Iowa Test reading comprehension subscores. The factor analysis showed that the continuous measurement scores loaded significantly on the factor represented by the four reading subscales of the Iowa Test of Basic Skills. The factor loadings of the Iowa subscales ranged between .79 and .86, whereas the continuous ability estimates from the computerized curriculum had significant, but smaller, loadings ranging between .24 and .45 on the same factors. The authors took these results as evidence that similar constructs were being measured by the paper-and-pencil reading exercises and the computer-administered reading exercises but that method-of-measurement variance was also present.

It is unlikely that factor analysis will prove to be the most useful tool for determining the construct validity of measures obtained through continuous measurement. Construct validity can and must be approached using a variety of correlational and experimental methods. Many new options exist for mixed correlational and experimental approaches to understanding the constructs that constitute a domain of knowledge, when the associated curriculum has an embedded continuous measurement system. Measurement science alone is not enough, however. An interdisciplinary synthesis is needed with the cognitive and instructional sciences. The emerging scientific foundations for construct validity and dynamic testing are discussed later in this chapter.

Differences in Utility between CM and School Achievement Tests

Turning from the topic of construct validity to the topic of utility is a strong move from basic to applied questions, from theory to pragmatics. The CM generation is intimately involved in pragmatics, as well as theory, because education and curricula are pragmatic subjects. Utility of measures deals with their practicality and ease of use in live educational settings. By becoming unobtrusive, CM takes a giant leap in utility.

The procedures for obtaining estimates of individual student proficiency on calibrated curriculum-embedded tasks are very different from those of a nationally standardized paper-and-pencil test. The contrasts between these procedures are useful for highlighting the benefits in utility of the third generation for learners and teachers.

In the case of the standardized test, "testing days" are an obtrusive intervention into the school week. For example, at the experimental Waterford School, where the pilot reading study took place, the headmistress would announce that testing would take place during a certain week in the spring, and the teachers would solemnly pass this information on to the students. Such testing had not been enjoyable in the past, and the news would be greeted with moans and groans from the students. Testing is a traumatic experience for most of them. On the testing day, test administrators entered the classroom, instead of the familiar teachers, and strove to create a highly standardized environment. They introduced careful timing of subtests, careful controls against cheating, and careful instructions on how to fill out the answer sheets or test booklets. The students knew that there would be a formal report and that it was very important for them to do well. Students had no choice about the testing date; some might have been ill or emotionally upset that day and others might have been at their best.

Administration of the computer curriculum with unobtrusive continuous measurement is strikingly different from group paper-and-pencil testing. At the beginning of the year, the teachers introduce the students to the computer room and establish ground rules. During the year, students go to the computer room happily, sometimes insisting that the teacher break off classroom activities so they won't miss any time. In the computer room, they settle down quickly to work at their own paces and at their own positions within the reading curriculum. Measurement takes place day after day, and the cumulative accuracy of the estimates of reading ability and its rate of change increases to higher and higher confidence levels. Given unidimensionality and an appropriate scale, the students' trajectories from easier to more difficult reading exercises can be tracked, plotted, and reported to teachers and researchers at frequent intervals.

Mastery Assessment Systems as Continuous Measurement

The concept of mastery assessment systems, a CM generation concept, was developed during 1986–1987 by ETS researchers. By mid-1987, several multiyear research projects had been initiated to develop mastery assessment systems. Mastery assessment systems were first described by Forehand and Bunderson (1987a, 1987b).

Two features of mastery assessment systems (abbreviated as MS from here on) can be noted at the outset. First, a mastery system has a role to play in curriculum planning but is not itself a curriculum. Second, the term *mastery* does not refer to minimum competence alone.

The developers of a mastery assessment system should go to some effort to map elements of the defined domain of knowledge and expertise into the goals of a variety of localized curricula. They should identify generally accepted milestones of learning in a particular domain, covering a particular level of learning and extending below and above it. They should calibrate these measures to make sure that they provide a smooth and continuous series and do not embody large jumps in difficulty or complexity that would trap many learners at a certain level. It is the task of local educational jurisdictions to develop or select curricula. As a part of this responsibility, they could select a subset of measurable milestones from the larger sets of the MS and embed them into their own curricula as a measurement framework.

When a measurement organization obtains group consensus on learning milestones in a particular subject area, that consensus usually converges on what might be called a minimum competence standard. The mastery that is assessed in a mastery system, on the other hand, looks forward to a time when, after long commitment and effort, the learner has obtained a lifelong capability.

Mastery signifies achievement of personal learning goals that go beyond minimum competence. Mastery is personal and unique and is achieved after long periods of persistence and commitment. The assessment of higher levels of mastery must involve unique productions (e.g., complex problem solving, oral presentations, written analyses, portfolios). Some of the precursors of mastery can be assessed at earlier levels of growth, by encouraging the learner to practice some element of mastery appropriate to his or her growth stage. At intermediate stages of learning, the student can thus experience what it means to persist and to expand upon what has been learned until able to do and know something really well.

Assessment includes the use of standardized measures of competence and guidance for judging the precursors of mastery at various levels. This guidance can include disciplined subjective scoring or, in the future, intelligent computerized scoring. Instructionally sensitive assessment will have new properties and paradigms not fully developed by a measurement science built to support certification, selection, and classification.

COMPONENTS OF A MASTERY SYSTEM

A mastery system would require a CAE system, as described. It need not be as elaborate initially as TICCIT or the WICAT system 300. Though the assessment systems could partly be implemented on paper, at least one computer for scoring and record keeping would be necessary. Major non-hardware components of a mastery system include the following:

1. Mastery map usable by learners and teachers to envision and communicate about learning goals
2. Reference tasks
3. Calibration of items and reference tasks
4. Instruction-oriented scoring system for each reference task
5. Professional development program for teachers

The first four of these components depend on measurement concepts; the fifth is an implementation concept. These components are intended to serve instruction; therefore, they could be linked to instructional components. Instructional components would include repeated practice in reference tasks, subscoring to guide the instructor in coaching, and report-generating systems for students and teachers. The term *coaching* is meant to be an analog to the instructional process that an excellent athletic coach uses. This might include modeling the desired performance, observing practice trials, prompting, encouraging, and fading the prompts as the performance becomes adequate.

The Mastery Map. In the development of a mastery system, responsible educational officials would work with measurement experts who are competent in CM to embody a selected subset of calibrated reference tasks as the markers, or milestones, needed within their own curricula. This plan would be visualized as a mastery map that would give the learners and teachers an overview of "the journey at a glance" at the beginning of learning. The mastery map would also permit communication about initial placement and about next steps in accumulating progress. The mastery map could be visualized on a large wall display for all, but individual maps with status information should be made available graphically on the computer, as exemplified by the TICCIT map displays.

Reference tasks. A reference task is generally more complex than a single item. It might be a testlet, as defined earlier; a curriculum-embedded exercise requiring multiple responses; or a simulation exercise. A reference task is contextualized. It refers to some real-world work that communicates to students, parents, and community the relevance of the things being practiced. A reference task might also refer to component process constructs important to the mastery of the task and useful in coaching. A record of an individual's accomplishment on reference tasks can build up the self-confidence of the learner. Table 9.4 contrasts test items and reference tasks.

Calibration. Reference tasks can be placed on scales to show the degree of growth they represent. Test items, perhaps grouped into clusters, or testlets, can also be placed on such scales. For example, the tasks listed below were used in the NAEP study of the literacy of young adults (Kirsch & Jungeblut, 1986). They assess literacy skills used in interpreting doc-

TABLE 9.4 Test Items versus Reference Tasks

Test Items	Reference Tasks
1. Usual administration is by paper and pencil.	1. Usual administration is by interactive computer.
2. Written objectives prescribe test items.	2. Flowcharts and interaction specifications prescribe reference tasks.
3. Each item requires a single response, usually multiple choice.	3. Each task requires multiple responses, which together provide for a quantitative assessment of degree of success.

4. Scoring is dichotomous
  a. Pass
  b. Fail
	4. Scoring is trichotomous
	  a. Pass (competence demonstrated)
	  b. Needs coaching and practice
	  c. Not ready for this task

5 A complete test with subtests can be used for diagnostic purposes.	5. Simultaneous subscores are taken to measure component processes and states, which provide data to guide coaching.
6. Items and entire tests are often decontextualized. Learners, parents, and community figures might not see the relevance of the question to valued capabilities in the real world.	6. Tasks refer to or simulate aspects of valued real-world activity, (e.g., in college or a job).
7. Items can be calibrated and placed on a measurement scale.	7. Reference tasks can either be calibrated into the same scale as items or positioned on a contrived growth-objective function, with different regions representing stages of mastery.
8. Except in CAT systems, administration of next item is fixed by its order on the page.	8. Next response request is determined dynamically.
9. Practice uses up test items after one attempt, making them of little value for repeated practice.	9. Some reference tasks require files of alternative stimuli for practice (e.g., paragraphs to read), but many of them, including a simulation or gamelike event, can be practiced repeatedly without using up material.
10. The objective and specification of how an examinee would succeed are neither suitable for learners to view nor now presented to learners.	10. A model of mastery can be made available to help learners see how it should be done. Contextual referencing makes modeling more realistic.

uments. The scale values are statistically determined measures of difficulty based on IRT. In the literacy study, they are also described and explained in terms of task features that account for variation in difficulty.

Sign your name on the line that reads "signature."
  Scale value: 110
Put an x on a map where two particular streets intersect.
  Scale value: 249
Fill in a check to pay a particular credit card bill.
  Scale value: 259
Use a bus schedule to answer: On Saturday morning, what time does the second bus arrive at the downtown terminal?
  Scale value: 334
Use a bus schedule to answer: On Saturday afternoon, if you miss the 2:35 bus leaving Hancock and Buena Ventura going to Flintridge and Academy, how long will you have to wait for the next bus?
  Scale value: 365

These examples illustrate the calibration of reference tasks in a mastery system. Calibrated values could reflect both the educator's or the expert's analysis and the empirical results. Once the reference tasks in a set are calibrated, the scale values are given meaning by demonstration of the constructs of knowledge and skills required to succeed at tasks with a given range of values. Each mastery system would have its own calibration. The scale and scale interpretation would be developed and validated for a particular content, level, and purpose.

Most instances of educational growth are not linear and additive. When experts are compared to novices on a wide variety of tasks, they are characterized not so much by quantitative increases in amount of knowledge as by differences in the perceptual and conceptual organization of knowledge. Experts, as contrasted with novices, organize knowledge hierarchically. They chunk information according to underlying principles, have easier access to the information they have stored, and use information more flexibly. Therefore, *calibration is a matter, not of adding up units of learning, but rather of determining indicators that mark progression along a continuum of growth from novice to expert.* Sharp increases in difficulty in a calibrated sequence are often a signal to perform a deeper cognitive analysis.

Educators use such terms as *novice, advanced beginner, competent, adept,* and *expert* to describe variations in growth. Calibration of reference tasks gives such descriptors meaning in terms of statistically determined scales and conceptual analysis of the properties of tasks at each scale position. It is expected that indicators and models of growth differ for psychomotor skills and for academic knowledge; for children's initial acquisition of academic skills and for professionals' acquisition of new knowledge; for learning science and for learning a foreign language. One of the challenges for research is to identify underlying principles that will permit a comparison of mastery systems across domains and to provide new guidance, and automated systems, to aid in developing such mastery systems. A challenge for developers of a new mastery system is to develop and justify useful and construct-valid calibrations for a given application.

Instruction-related scoring of reference tasks. Items are normally scored dichotomously, as correct and incorrect. It is possible to score reference tasks more finely, to connect performance with instructional strategy. Students might be placed in one of three categories: those whose performance demonstrates competence achieved, those who are in need of and ready for practice, and those who are not ready for practice on a given reference task. The development of scoring algorithms to make these classifications is based on a combination of expert judgment and systematic observation of the performance of students known to be proficient, as compared with those at a lower level. The scoring algorithms are based on the occurrence of correct responses and the nonoccurrence of particular responses that indicate misconceptions.

A professional development program for teachers. A mastery system is always accompanied by a professional development program for teachers, because it makes new professional roles possible in several ways. It frees some time for professional activities while learners are practicing on reference tasks. It provides a tracking system, so that teachers can make professional decisions about how to manage the progress of a class and its individual members. More advanced versions could provide information to guide the coaching of individuals and groups. Teachers learn new practices in relation to these particular technological tools involving a mastery system, so that they can be successful at using the system for placement, for the various aspects of tracking, for different aspects of classroom management, and, ultimately, for individual and small-group diagnosis and coaching.

A mastery system is designed to function within a community of learners and teachers, and users must learn to build and sustain such environments. A mastery system provides the opportunity to build and support a cooperative community of learners whose goal is to help and encourage one another, to teach one another, and to facilitate the maximum amount of learning for students and teachers. Professional development would include training in appropriate use and interpretation of measures and in methods to build and maintain appropriate climates.

How Mastery Systems Can Serve Individual Learners and Teachers

Mastery systems offer extended ways in which measurement can serve individual learners and teachers. Traditional test use has often emphasized such institutional purposes as admission, certification, job placement, grading, and classification. There have also been consistent efforts to serve individuals, such as through

Counseling and guidance
Advanced placement
Special recognition
Placement in a learning program
Diagnosis of learning problems
Self-assessment for personal knowledge and growth

Mastery systems multiply these opportunities by focusing measurement on growth in skill and knowledge. The goal of a mastery system is the advancement of students toward mastery. It provides data to help and ways to use the data. Table 9.5

TABLE 9.5 Possible Services to Individual Learners and Their Teachers Through a Mastery System

1. *Initial Placement* on the mastery map
2. *Tracking* within a well-defined map of competence and mastery to show current position, nearby options, achievement to date, and potential growth
3. *Repeated practice* on interesting and informative reference tasks
4. *Trichotomous scoring* systems for reference tasks to classify learners' current attempts as
   a. Fully demonstrating competence or mastery
   b. In need of coaching and more practice
   c. Not ready for the task
5. Presentation to learners of *informative models of mastery* (how successful students think and perform) relevant to particular reference tasks and mastery levels
6. *Simultaneous measurement* of component processes and states during reference task practice
7. *Data to guide coaching,* based on component processes and states
8. *Data to guide coaching,* based on metacognitive heuristics and strategies
9. Presentation to learners of information about their characteristic *learning profiles*
10. *Data to guide coaching,* based on learner profiles interacting with coaching needs
11. *Prediction of learning decay* to prescribe review
12. Analysis of group records to facilitate *classroom management*
    a. To adapt rate of progress and depth of instruction for the whole group
    b. To select subsets of learners for small-group coaching
    c. To identify individuals requiring special personal attention

lists 12 services that mastery systems offer to individual learners and their teachers. Early mastery systems are likely to address only a subset of these goals. Systems that succeed in meeting substantial subsets of these goals could provide successive new generations of services to learners and teachers.

The Role of Learner Profiles in the Continuous Measurement Generation

The use of a profile of scores descriptive of different learner styles, strengths, and weaknesses has long been a dream of educators and behavioral scientists. The WICAT learner profile is an attempt to achieve that goal. Initiated by the current authors at the WICAT Education Institute in 1983 and 1984, it consisted of a battery of computer-administered tests (CT and CAT generations) to profile the styles, abilities, and preferences of individual learners. The learner profile battery has been a source of illustrations for CT and CAT tests in this chapter, and batteries like it could become a major source of knowledge to the field of educational measurement, if their research potential can be realized. Learner profile batteries in a CAT system place a rich set of learner profile scores in the context of a substantial body of computerized curricula.

As with earlier attempts to introduce highly individualized levels of measurement into educational and training settings, there are many pragmatic obstacles to widespread use. Wide use makes it easy to obtain the data that can lead to advances in professional understanding of how to use such measures. Funding for the necessary research is always hard to obtain. Thus, the progress in practical and scientific matters possible with such potentially powerful new systems is elusive.

The introduction of a substantial battery of learner profile scores into a school brings with it a major problem of data interpretation for teachers and students. Instruction in how to use the scores to improve learning is seen as vital by potential users in schools, to achieve the goals of the schools. Finding out one's profile as a learner is very informative and interesting to individuals, and it could well help learners become more confident, self-accepting, and effective. It might also help teachers be more accepting and sensitive to differences, if they are taught how to avoid abuses. Unfortunately, a curriculum dealing with constructs about individual differences has no place in the school's schedule at present. Only if it can be shown to aid in achieving conventional academic goals can a learner profile presently be justified.

In common with the requirements for effective use of computer-aided education and mastery assessment systems, the proper use of a battery of learner profile scores in an educational setting would require a substantial professional development program for users, covering many months and years. Curricula for such a professional development program cannot be defined yet in a way likely to achieve wide acceptance, because there is no agreement among experts as to which variables are most important in a learner profile, let alone how to interpret and use prescriptively the variables that are better known. The field of education might have to wait until experience with learner profiles accumulates at user sites involved in CAE and CM before an expert knowledge base about effective use of such information can develop. Perhaps a prerequisite for development of such expert knowledge is the existence of CM systems described earlier. Until it is possible to measure individual learner growth trajectories, it will be difficult to evaluate alternate uses of learner profile data in improving the progress of learning in real educational or training settings.

NEW LEARNER PROFILE VARIABLES

It might prove to be the case that a new class of learner profile measures emerges from the continuous measurement generation. These new variables might be more readily understandable and usable by educators. An example is taken from the WICAT reading curriculum. In a study of the response protocols from that curriculum, it soon became apparent that there was a wide range of different strategies for approaching the learning exercises. Students were given much choice as to which reading selections to study and also the option of jumping in or out of the exercises before completing them. They had knowledge of the pass–fail scoring on the exercises and could judge how well they were doing. Two extremes of learner strategies were observed. At one extreme were those students who were not troubled by initial failure. They were aware that they could attempt the exercise over again and that initial failure would not become a part of their permanent record. These students used the strategy of quickly trying the exercise, often failing it, but in the process learning what was required. Then they would go back through it more carefully and pass it. This was more than memorization, because specific correct-answer feedback was not given. At the other extreme were those students who refused to allow any type of failure to blemish the record they assumed existed. These students would escape from the exercise and sometimes not reenter it if there were any indication that they might not pass it on the next attempt.

Various intermediate strategies were defined by the researchers, including fail–pass, escape–pass, fail and avoid, escape and avoid. Discussions with the teachers brought out the fact that some of these patterns seemed characteristic of the students' performance in classroom activities. At the most serious extreme (the escape and avoid extreme) were some students who were quite timid and unsure of themselves. other students at this extreme, however, were merely trying to avoid work. Such students appeared attentive while at the computer terminal (or in the classroom), but they were not actively engaged in the learning process. The ability of the computer system to define and quantify this new class of strategies, observable because approach and avoidance can be measured, can have important implications for helping a variety of students.

CONTINUOUS MEASUREMENT OF LEARNING PREFERENCES

With systems suitable for continuous measurement, the curriculum can have a variety of options, such as visual versus verbal, structured versus holistic, or sequential versus simultaneous approaches to the lessons. By choosing an option, students reveal their learning preferences. An ambitious attempt to provide learner control of different presentational formats was a feature of the TICCIT project. Students were given options to look at more visual, versus more verbal and teacher-like, explanations of the definitions or rules for each concept or principle. They could examine a selected range of examples. They could work more or fewer practice exercises. They were able to look at different versions of "Helps" as they worked the practice problems or examples.

The TICCIT concept of learner control of strategies and tactics was a good one, but it needed to be broadened into more kinds of learning components. Current and future CAE systems with color graphics and audio options could make more kinds of learning components possible. Continuous measurement based on voluntary choices among these components would provide teachers with knowledge of the preference profile of each individual, and also of the group as a whole. Teachers could then present different parts of their own lessons in different ways, appealing to different profiles in the process.

In addition to the measurement of learning preferences through voluntary choices of on-line options, standardized and calibrated preference questions can be introduced at strategic points in the curriculum. The use of preference data can become a viable and useful part of the teaching and learning process.

EMERGING SCIENTIFIC FOUNDATIONS FOR THE THIRD GENERATION

In a real sense, construct validity is the fundamental scientific position for all of measurement. The challenges of dynamic measurement demand that new solutions be found to the problems of construct validity of learning measures. Messick's chapter in this volume draws the inescapable conclusion that all validity concepts boil down to construct validity. There is, unfortunately, no simple and unitary set of procedures that can assure construct validity. The challenge of construct validity is to infer invisible constructs of human expertise from observable behaviors. The addition of certainty to this process is accomplished by testing as many inferences as possible, when the inferences are drawn from an understanding of the invisible constructs and their relationships to external behaviors. This might take researchers into such diverse realms as perception, learning, problem solving, and personality, and it will require cross-disciplinary cooperation.

For the third generation, the disciplines that appear most relevant at this time are the cognitive and instructional sciences. Embretson (1983) discusses the need to use models derived from cognitive science to represent the constructs involved in tests. She discusses how we need to link the construct representations to measures of individual difference that correlate with other measures of interest and value in applications. The ability constructs that have been the guides of psychometricians for many years are shown to be decomposable into functional components describable in terms of representations of cognitive constructs. A test item can function in different ways and can effectively measure different cognitive constructs, depending on the test takers' positions on the component cognitive constructs that comprise an ability.

Embretson (1985a) applies this view of the construct validity of tests to the problem of test design and shows how component latent-trait models can be used in the test-design process. She shows that test designers can use three levels of cognitive variables (stimulus features, components, and strategies) to predict the difficulty of items and to determine the meaning of a test score in terms of the cognitive components and strategies the test items call upon. To gain this control over stimulus features, components, and strategies, test designers need subtask data that will enable them to determine which strategies or components are significant in different tasks. Subtask data is also necessary to diagnose individual test takers in terms of their use of components or strategies. As Embretson points out,

> Computerized adaptive testing can estimate ability by administering fewer items to each person, thus giving time for other tasks. Furthermore, the interactive format of computerized testing makes subtasks quite feasible, thus component latent trait models may have wider applicability in future testing. (1985a, p. 217)

The analysis of cognitive components and strategies underlying tests of cognitive ability is now well advanced. Shephard and Metzler (1971) provide an important landmark in identifying the cognitive processes involved in the mental rotation of three-dimensional objects. Sternberg and his colleagues are building a systematic basis for componential analysis in measurement (see, e.g., Sternberg, 1977; Sternberg & MacNamara, 1985).

It is a different matter, however, to bring psychometrics and cognitive science together in the third generation than in the second, because dynamic measurement is required. Embretson (in press) summarizes some of the reasons for believing that significantly different new developments are needed in the field of psychometrics to accommodate the realities of correct cognitive processes, erroneous cognitive processes, and the dynamically changing nature of these processes during learning. In this article, Embretson reviews psychometric considerations for dynamic testing and shows that some views commonly held by psychometricians stand in the way of progress. Progress will require substantially different models and ways of thinking than have been sufficient for the static measurement of ability constructs.

Other researchers have dealt with the issues being forced upon the field of educational measurement by progress in cognitive and instructional science. Glaser (1986) summarizes several challenges that cognitive and learning theories have raised for psychometricians. He outlines objectives that measurement models should consider if they aspire to deal with the domains of learning and instruction. Tatsuoka (in press) has developed a promising psychometric model that integrates item response theory with cognitive diagnosis. Her contribution is based on a clear understanding of the implications of cognitive science for construct validity and the need for latent-trait models that will avoid certain philosophical and scientific problems inherent in the application of current models. Her resulting *Rule Space* model is applicable to the diagnosis of the status of learners on a set of correct and incorrect constructs of cognitive processing. This model treats the latent trait as a quantitative variable, not a categorical one. A test developed following Tatsuoka's procedures would yield diagnostic information about the probability of certain errors. Such information could lead to instructionally useful prescriptions.

The field of intelligent tutoring systems (Sleeman & Brown, 1982) offers a considerable challenge to psychometricians. Such systems provide models of underlying constructs that constitute expertise in a variety of subjects. Ideal, or expert, models are frequently accompanied by "buggy models" of incorrect procedures used by novices or students in the process of becoming more expert. These researchers are more interested in *what* is going on in the minds of learners than in *how much* of a quantity that might be scaled is being demonstrated. Therefore, there is a large gap to bridge between this work in artificial intelligence and cognitive science and the work of measurement scientists interested in dynamic measurement. Two recent efforts to create more dialogue are resulting in new books on the subject. The chapters in these books demonstrate clearly that the gap is far from closed (Freedle, in preparation; Frederiksen, Glaser, Lesgold, & Shafto, in preparation).

Research Issues in Continuous Measurement

Research issues in continuous measurement are too numerous to discuss in detail. The move from static to dynamic measurement and the move from controlled testing settings to a continuing and complex educational program produce research questions at many levels of measurement science, cognitive and instructional science, behavioral science, and computer and information science.

There are many psychometric issues. One is the issue of how to define the fungible unit of measurement. If it is no longer a test item, how do we define a testlet or a reference task? How do we scale and calibrate such entities? What about the assumptions of unidimensionality, local independence, and fixed, instead of moving and changing, proficiency? Another psychometric issue is the scaling and use of latency information.

As discussed, issues dealing with the cognitive and instructional sciences abound, and the continuous measurement environment provides a new instrument of vision for making visible to researchers the set of processes involved, within and across individual students, in performance on particular items or reference tasks. How these processes evolve over time as learners progress from one level of proficiency to another can become visible through continuous measurement. Another question deals with where, along a mastery map, might be ranges of proficiency extending from novice to expert? Sharp increases in the difficulty of calibrated tasks might signal places to look for interesting changes in underlying cognitive structures.

Continuous measurement introduces issues of human development, group organization, group management, interpersonal relationships, and individual differences in group functioning. It provides new dependent and independent variables to enrich these studies.

The processes of change in the introduction of new forms of education using new tools, the products of science and technology, constitute an important field of research. Without research-based design principles for introducing the change in bite-sized chunks and providing in-service training over long enough periods of time, continuous measurement systems will not achieve their promise. Implementation research is likely to involve a variety of social science disciplines including anthropology, sociology, economics, and organizational behavior.

The computer and information sciences are obviously fundamental to progress in the field of continuous measurement and computerized instruction. Advances in hardware and software can have a profound effect on the cost and capabilities of the subsystems involved in CAT systems, continuous measurement systems, and computerized education alternatives. In the next section we address another powerful contribution of the computer and information sciences: the impact of fifth-generation computing on educational measurement. The field of computer science has used a generational framework for many years that should not be confused with the generational definitions for educational measurement presented here.

In the remainder of this chapter we deal with knowledge-based expert systems and a touch of natural language processing, and do not deal with some other advances (e.g., computer vision, robotics, speech recognition) also attributed to the fifth generation of computing.

The Fourth Generation: Intelligent Measurement (IM)

Definition

Intelligent measurement is defined as the application of knowledge-based computing to any of the subprocesses of educational measurement. The term *knowledge-based computing* is used here rather than the more familiar term *artificial intelligence,* to draw attention to the notion that the knowledge and expertise of measurement professionals can be captured in a computer memory in a symbolic form called a *knowledge base.* This knowledge can then be used to replicate, at multiple sites through a computer, the expertise of humans, who are otherwise restricted to one site at any time. Thus, less expert humans, with the aid of the intelligent computing system, can perform measurement processes that require considerably more knowledge and experience than they presently have. Educational measurement is a knowledge-intensive discipline, and the knowledge is not commonly found among practitioners in education. Intelligent measurement introduces the ability to package knowledge, to replicate it in the form of a computer system that can interact with the user as an expert consultant or advisor, and to disseminate the expertise to many sites. It offers the field of educational measurement a powerful new way to bring the benefits of educational measurement to many educational practitioners who otherwise would have no opportunity to apply advanced methods knowledgeably.

The fourth, or IM, generation can be contrasted with the others in terms of the properties summarized in Table 9.1. It assumes the existence of a computer equipped with knowledge-based computing features, in either hardware or software. It also assumes that, through accumulated research and experience, it has been possible to capture symbolically expert knowledge and incorporate it into a computer as a knowledge base. For example, one type of knowledge base makes possible intelligent interpretations or prescriptive advice. Another type makes possible the automatic replication of complex scoring requiring human judgment. The first type of knowledge base models the expertise of counselors for applications in any generation involving interpretive comments about an individual's scores from a battery of measures. For CM generation applications, it models the knowledge of excellent teachers who are familiar with the subject, with the instructional system being used, with good pedagogical practices associated with the system, and with knowledge of how to relate instructional alternatives to different learner profiles and different trajectories. Another type of knowledge base (automatic holistic scoring) represents in the computer's memory the consensual knowledge of standards for mastery of certain reference tasks and the consensual scoring knowledge of experts in a subject domain.

As stressed in the discussion of CM, no computer-generated advice with important consequences for the individual should be used without scrutiny by the appropriate professional. The advice should come as a set of two or three alternative interpretations or prescriptions. The user, guided by a professional for critical issues, would select or modify one.

A major difference between the fourth and earlier generations in the automation of test-administration processes is in the capability for sophisticated interpretation of measures, both static measures and measures taken during a dynamic educational process. This capability is only partially available through the computer system in the third generation and available only through expert people in the earlier generations. Intelligent interpretations of a given profile of scores are now available in many application areas: however, validated expert knowledge does not yet exist for prescriptive advice in CM generation applications.

The definition of IM given at the beginning of this section is general. This packaged intelligence can be added to computer programs designed to augment the work of users involved in *any* of the processes of educational measurement. A computer application program would perform some function like developing certain complex items, scoring them, or analyzing them. In each case this application program could be accompanied by a knowledge base of expert decision rules and a data base of facts. This symbolically represented knowledge would be used by an "expert consultant" or advisor to guide the user in making informed decisions in the process of using the application program. Some examples are

Test Development Processes

Computer tools for job and task analysis, with advisor
Computer tools for developing test specifications, with advisor
Item and test development programs, with advisor

Test Administration Processes

Intelligent administration of individually administered tests, with advisor to guide the paraprofessional
Natural-language-understanding expertise for scoring constructed responses
Interpretation of profiles
Intelligent tutoring within a task when additional practice is needed

Analysis and Research Purposes

Statistical programs with an intelligent advisor
Intelligent scheduling and calibrating of experimental items
Intelligent data collection for studies in school settings

Our imaginations will produce many promising applications, far more than can be developed. The development of such programs is a time-consuming and costly process. Acquiring the knowledge bases alone, from human experts, is very time consuming and resource intensive. The state of the art in expert systems is not far enough advanced to assure success in each undertaking.

Despite the difficulties of the undertaking, certain applications will indeed be developed. This chapter has narrowed its focus to the automation of test-administration processes. Consistent with that focus, three of the more promising applications of IM are discussed.

Three Potential Contributions of IM to Test Administration

Of the three promising contributions of IM to test administration discussed in this section, the first two are more likely to be of practical use in the near future. The third is more complex, but it represents the natural progression beyond the third generation.

Intelligent measurement can use machine intelligence to (a) score complex constructed responses involved in items and in reference tasks, (b) generate interpretations based on individual profiles of scores, (c) provide prescriptive advice to learners and teachers, to optimize progress through a curriculum. These contributions will be discussed in order.

INTELLIGENT SCORING OF COMPLEX CONSTRUCTED RESPONSES

A knowledge base of scoring standards and rules can be used, along with automatic inferencing procedures, to provide the basis for automating complex scoring processes that now require costly human time. There is a natural pressure in educational measurement to move beyond decontextualized multiple-choice items toward other, more contextualized, item types. Two sorts of pressure always exist to broaden the types of items in the psychometric arsenal. The major form of pressure, from the scientific point of view, is for improved construct validity. The constructs involved in expertise relevant in real-world settings are what we seek: the roots of valued human performance relevant to social roles. We can do this best by modeling more accurately the critical aspects of work situations standardized for measurement, in which the constructs involved in expertise are required for success. Measurement organizations are criticized for reducing complex domains of human expertise to the knowledge aspects that can be tested with items requiring only a selection from alternatives. Multiple-choice items sample knowledge domains efficiently, but, as the cognitive scientists point out, declarative knowledge (knowing what) and procedural knowledge (knowing how) are two very different things. Without joining the argument of how much procedural knowledge can be assessed by limited-choice items, it can be stated that moving to reference tasks in the third generation offers considerable promise. These tasks refer to actual performances in valued human roles. They offer greater potential for requiring procedural knowledge, along with corresponding increases in construct validity. The use of reference tasks might also reduce the second kind of pressure, that from a concerned user public who sees greater face validity in joblike or lifelike reference tasks than in decontextualized knowledge items. The distinction between competence and mastery in the third generation is relevant to this discussion. Both measurement scientists and the user public want measurement to reflect behavior samples that possess greater face and construct validity, as related to valued human mastery. Minimum competence is not enough. Neither is the sampling of factual knowledge adequate. Complex constructed responses are closer to what masters do.

The problem for educational measurement in moving beyond limited-choice knowledge items to complex constructed response items is in finding the scoring models for each constructed response item or reference task. Such tasks have the stimulus standardized and loosen the standardization of the response. Each scoring model must assign values in a meaningful way to important variations in the complex response. The values must be assigned in a way that adequately models increments in expertise in the construct or constructs being measured by the task. It is also useful to keep additional information to help identify intermediate or erroneous cognitive structures evidenced by the examinee's performance. Such information can be used to guide prompting and coaching in CM applications or to guide interpretation and counseling.

The development of such complex scoring models is accomplished routinely by testing organizations, but it is not presently replicated in automated systems. Such organizations bring human experts together to spend many hours discussing how to score each of several constructed response items holistically and to assign incremental points. For example, in the College Board Advanced Placement programs and in some of the Graduate Record Examination (GRE) subject tests, ETS provides disciplined holistic scoring of constructed response items in the form of written essays or written protocols describing the solution of problems requiring mathematics. These problems partake of some of the attributes of mastery: individual and unique productions. The items in some of these examinations meet several parts of the definition of reference tasks given earlier. Such items and their scoring models are standardized. They become reliable through the application of established, disciplined, holistic scoring methods. Applied artificial intelligence, through the new tool of expert systems, might substantially reduce the labor associated with the reading of tens of thousands of items with constructed responses. (Note, however, that it does not reduce the intelligent labor of coming to an agreement on the scoring model.) In so doing, it might offer some of the benefits of mass scoring of multiple-choice items. Scoring could be used for both institutional and individual purposes, because the system could be programmed to provide feedback and repeated practice to learners on similar items and to produce a reliable and construct-valid score for institutional uses.

A project conducted by Bennett, Gong, Kershaw, and Rock (1988) examined this possibility in the context of the advanced placement program for computer science. Students currently deliver a program written in the Pascal language. They may submit it on a floppy disk, because a text file, rather than handwriting on a piece of paper, is the normal mode for editing such a program on a computer. Bennett, Gong, Kershaw, and Rock are working with Elliot Soloway of Yale University to examine the applicability of his artificially intelligent program called PROUST (Johnson & Soloway, 1985) for grading these questions automatically. The results indicate that such scoring can indeed occur automatically. It will be necessary to develop human quality-control procedures over the whole process and to develop a "manufacturing technology" to routinely capture the knowledge of experts and the variations in student behavior in standard Pascal programming situations.

As discussed in connection with the first generation, human observation and judgment in assigning the holistic score are necessary whenever vocalizations, skilled movements, unique written productions, or unique artistic productions are required. These responses inhere in much of what is valuable in the world, life, and work. Educational measurement, through utilizing expert systems to score such responses, can move beyond competence toward mastery for larger numbers of individuals in the future.

AUTOMATION OF INDIVIDUAL PROFILE INTERPRETATIONS

Human counselors and other professionals routinely examine profiles of scores and provide interpretive commentary for individuals. Career and vocational counseling, diagnosis of learning strengths and weaknesses, and placement decisions are some examples. Many of these experts have built up a base of experience and knowledge that can be captured through techniques of knowledge acquisition and programmed as an intelligent advice giver that mimics their expertise. The input would be the profile of scores, perhaps available in the same computer system that administered the tests through a CT and CAT battery. The output might include a series of questions for the counselor to ask to clarify ambiguous points. Then an interpretive commentary might be printed out as a small set of most likely pieces of advice. The professional could edit this initial draft if needed.

INTELLIGENT ADVICE DURING CONTINUOUS MEASUREMENT

Intelligent advice during learning is the most promising contribution of IM for learners and teachers. Its goal is the optimization of learning. It requires a curriculum administered in association with a continuous measurement delivery system. It requires that human expertise be acquired in a computerized knowledge base, analogous to that of the expert counselors who interpret individual profiles of static scores. The difference is that in CM the measurement is dynamic. This makes the knowledge more complex but the validation easier. The knowledge is complex because of the many variations of individual trajectories and individual learner profiles. The validation is easier because the measurement is continuous, and the results of decisions at one level are immediately known at the next level.

Intelligent advice during continuous measurement is the epitome of computerized educational measurement. The optimization of learning in a growth space of calibrated educational tasks represents a challenge for educational measurement scientists and practitioners that will require great effort over many years.

Intelligent Tutors: A Converging or Discontinuous Line of Development?

Intelligent tutoring is a current application of machine intelligence that does not fit into either a familiar educational framework or a measurement framework. Intelligent tutors are a relatively recent development that currently does not intersect with measurement thinking. The two fields have not been related to one another and have not benefited much from the work of one another. Sleeman and Brown (1982) and Kearsley (1987) provide a variety of examples of intelligent tutors applied in different subject matter areas. It is doubtful that the two fields will come together unless measurement scientists encompass cognitive components and strategies in their models, as Embretson, Tatsuoka, Sternberg, Glaser and his colleagues, and others have begun to do. Vaguely defined constructs inferred from aptitude factors have not proven useful to the developers of intelligent tutors. Even John Frederiksen, a person with strong psychometric credentials, has not yet found a psychometric approach to be of value in his work with intelligent tutors (Frederiksen & White, in press). Rather, the electronic troubleshooting tutor these authors have constructed tutors learners from module to module, motivating each module with the earlier ones and building the cognitive foundation for each new module in the process. No measurement scales are needed. Few developers of intelligent tutors, however, have come to grips with how to deal with individual differences in anything but a discrete and categorical way or with how to use measurement to more fully validate their constructs and their claims.

Intelligent tutors are currently contributing important insights, research vehicles, and models for both the third and the fourth generations. Some intelligent tutors of narrow scope are modules that could be treated as single lessons. These would be of interest in a continuous measurement system for dealing with the coaching, practice, and feedback inherent within a single reference task module. Working with these specific modules, measurement scientists and the developers of intelligent tutors could jointly define experimental and field-testing conditions for obtaining data relevant to the validation of the cognitive constructs in an intelligent tutoring model. The feedback, coaching, and repeated practice mechanisms in these models are examples of advanced tools for instruction. These tools could be used within the framework of a mastery map in a continuous measurement system, thus putting them in the framework of an entire course.

A few intelligent tutors have been implemented as entire courses. These systems are actually prototype continuous measurement systems with fourth-generation attributes. Unlike the examples of TICCIT and the WICAT Reading Curricula discussed earlier, they do not emphasize sequence control and status information made visible through the mastery map of the domain. They are less concerned with flexibility in sequencing through the domain. They simply establish a structured curriculum consisting of an ordered series of tasks that culminate in course mastery.

Two such courses have been in operation for over 10 years at the Institute of Mathematical Studies in the Social Sciences at Stanford University. The earliest of these is a computer-aided education course in axiomatic set theory (Suppes & Sheehan, 1981a). The next oldest, a CAE course in logic, is being used at other universities besides Stanford (Suppes & Sheehan, 1981b). Both of these intelligent tutoring courses use automatic theorem proving for checking the correctness of students' proofs in axiomatic set theory or symbolic logic. The feedback the computer gives in the course of checking students' proofs enables the computer–student dialogue to continue and the students to learn from their errors. Students also have access to graduate student proctors in the machine room. An ambitious new project to apply these methods to precollege calculus is currently under way under NSF funding (Suppes, et al., 1987).

Another multiyear effort that has resulted in entire courses using artificial intelligence and intelligent tutoring is being conducted under the direction of John Anderson at Carnegie-Mellon University. The LISP tutor (Anderson, in press) is an extremely interesting intelligent tutor based on Anderson's ACT* Theory of Cognition (Anderson, 1983). This theory makes claims about the organization and acquisition of complex cognitive skills. The LISP tutor currently teaches a full-semester, self-paced course. It embodies ACT* theory and is simultaneously a way of testing the claims of the ACT* theory, and of providing university students with automated instruction in LISP programming. It has been found that students working on problems with the LISP tutor get a letter grade higher on final exams than students not working with it. It is not claimed that students will do as well as they would with a human tutor.

The LISP tutor uses a mechanism called *model tracing*. A model is one of hundreds of ideal and buggy production rules. A production is an if–then statement: IF the goal is to x, THEN use the LISP function y and set the subgoal to z. Buggy rules have this same form. By tracing what the student is doing and matching it to one of these correct or buggy rules, the LISP tutor is able to generate helpful feedback messages. These feedback messages enable a student using a buggy rule to get back on the right track. Within both the same and subsequent lessons, the student might have many opportunities to practice on a given production. Data collected from the LISP tutor show an initial dramatic drop in learning a given production. This validates the ACT* Theory, which predicts that the knowledge is initially "compiled." Learning after the knowledge is compiled seems to fit the standard power law of practice.

In analyzing the data from the LISP tutor, Anderson (in press) attempted to trace the source of individual differences in learning productions. He found two major factors, one dealing with acquisition and the other dealing with retention.

The opportunities for measurement in these complete courses involving intelligent tutors are extensive, as they are in other computerized educational systems. It is a significant challenge, however, to analyze all of the data that can be generated. As researchers interested in psychometrically modeling the dynamic changes in learning become involved with such systems, we can hope for a convergence of the different scientific approaches, rather than a totally diverging line of development.

Complications of Artificial Intelligence: Future Generations

Artificial intelligence can deliver so much control and initiative into the hands of the user as to render the conditions for standardized measurement impossible to achieve. This challenge of artificial intelligence is inherent in the concept of an *intelligent curriculum.* It is possible to implement in a computer system another kind of expert knowledge base, that of the domain expert or experts, those who now write the textbooks and teach the classes constituting the curriculum. The term *intelligent curriculum* means that the curriculum must include such an expert knowledge base. Students will have access to an *inference engine* that can answer queries based on the expert knowledge in the domain. Students will be able to perform searches through and query the knowledge base, and the system will be able to answer these queries in a manner approximating that of human experts. Students will be able, at some point, to add the results of these queries back into the knowledge base and build a richer personalized system for answering a class of queries from a personal line of investigation. This scenario goes beyond the intelligent tutoring projects, which use carefully structured tasks, to a more substantial manipulation of entire textbooks and other sources of educational content.

This kind of creative, fluid behavior in investigating and manipulating knowledge in a new way has some of the properties of mastery defined earlier. Students in such a role will be manipulating and adding to knowledge in a personal way. This is an exciting prospect for education, but it will complicate the possible contributions of educational measurement. Scales of growing competence might be difficult or impossible to develop in an intelligent curriculum. There are no standardized items, testlets, or reference tasks. Where there is no standardization, there is no measurement. The tasks and abilities currently familiar to the educational measurement community might cease to be of much interest to the community at large, and the new tasks and abilities could be extremely hard to measure.

One avenue of approach is to let the work of searching, querying, and adding to the knowledge base itself be a very complex reference task. The construct to be measured would then be the new kinds of learning and problem-solving expertise required in the use of computerized knowledge bases of subject matter domains. Standardized tasks could be developed that require use of the knowledge base to produce different, personally constructed, productions. Disciplined subjective scoring protocols could then be developed for each standardized task. This approach might take us to the (perhaps more tractable) concepts of IM use for intelligent scoring of constructed responses.

Summary

This chapter was written at a time of dynamic change in the field of computer-administered measurement. It deals with some trends that are apparent and in prospect. So that this chapter will not become quickly dated, the strategy used was to describe four generations of computerized educational measurement, all based on rapidly emerging technological tools. The changes brought about by the wide availability and low cost of new technological delivery system alternatives are moving testing from its delivery through paper-and-pencil and printed booklets to delivery through on-line computer workstations. The key technologies making this possible include

1. Low cost and high computing and storage capabilities of newly available technologies.
2. Hardware and software to provide the communication between workstations or response stations and a single computer in which records can be kept for everyone in a group.
3. Availability of large-capacity optical memories such as videodiscs and CD-ROMS, which allow the distribution of curriculum and testing materials of great scope and extent at low cost. This development also permits the mediation of testing and teaching presentations by means of video, audio, computer graphics, and text.
4. Development of networking capabilities to distribute the testing displays and collect the responses in a central location.
5. Developments in psychometric procedures for calibrating tasks and estimating the position of individuals on scales (item response theory and its needed extensions).
6. Developments in knowledge-based computing and expert systems for building and querying interactive knowledge bases.

Together, these technologies expand and permit partial replication of the human capabilities of sensing, remembering, deciding, acting, and communicating. Before computer administration, these processes were implemented through mark-sense sheets and scanners, computer scoring and reporting of scanned test sheets, manual administration and scoring of individually administered tests, and disciplined holistic scoring of constructed responses. The four generations permit automation of these processes in new ways, with greater potential efficiency.

The first generation of computer-aided testing enables us to do better what we now do and do it faster, more accurately, and with much more interesting and realistic displays and responses. What we do now, in the main, is take static measurements for institutional purposes. Computerized Testing and CAT enhance these purposes and make possible some additional applications for individuals.

The second generation provides a new theory and adds considerable efficiency to the administration of computerized tests. The calibration of items makes possible the adaptive selection of items during test administration. Adaptive presentation, based on dynamic adjustment of the display or response time or adaptive arrangement of content, is also possible.

The third generation, continuous measurement, offers potential discontinuity from current methods in the practice of educational measurement, educational research, and teaching. The distinction between testing and the curriculum begins to dim. Measurement becomes unobtrusive. Development of education measurements will combine with curriculum development, and educational research will combine with educational practice. The CM generation offers learners and teachers continuous monitoring of progress on mastery maps of the domain to be mastered and the finer grained monitoring of progress within reference tasks, so that advice can be given to aid the teacher and the system in providing coaching to guide further practice. Individuals' trajectories through the domain represented in the mastery map will be available. Learner profiles will emerge made of both generic measures and new measures of approach, avoidance, and strategy within the system.

The third generation will not achieve its goals fully without the new tools provided by the knowledge bases and inference engines supplied by the fourth generation. Intelligent measurement will make possible adaptive and intelligent advice based on individual trajectories and learner profiles. Before this goal is achieved, machine intelligence will be used to score complex constructed responses automatically and to provide complex interpretations of individual profiles made of static measurements.

Future generations might include fully intelligent curricula: knowledge bases that can be queried and added to by users skilled in new learning and discovery strategies for using such symbolically represented expertise. In this case, the role of educational measurement will be reduced or will shift to the measurement of new forms of expertise in learning, problem solving, and production of individual reorganizations and contributions involving the knowledge domain.

Concluding Thoughts

Generational Enhancements in Powers of Observation

The technological developments of these four generations confer upon the educational community the possibility of increased powers of measurement and, thus, increased powers of observation. These increased powers make visible the previously invisible. This yields better information and specification, which, in turn, leads to expansion of the field of inquiry.

The significance of using the new technologies to enhance powers of observation can be seen by referring to two historical examples. The first is van Leeuwenhoek, the lens grinder, who invented the first microscope. When van Leeuwenhoek looked through his microscope at his sperm and his spit and saw "cavorting beasties" for the first time, his powers of observation were enhanced by the newly discovered technology of lens grinding. Whole new fields of science, technology, and human service have evolved from this technology and its refinement. To the biological classification of life into the plant and animal kingdoms, science had to add three more kingdoms, fungi, protista, and monera, partly because of the observations made possible by the new technology. As optical microscopes were improved and the electron microscope was developed, the fields of microbiology and genetics and new sciences of materials have evolved.

The second example of technology is the X ray. Here powers of observation of the interior of living organisms and other opaque objects were dramatically enhanced. A host of specialties within medical and dental science use diagnostic methods based on this enhanced observational power.

In both of these cases, technological innovation made visible the previously invisible. Powers of observation were enhanced and magnitudes of the newly observed phenomena were scaled and measured.

Will technological enhancements of powers of observation lead to similar breakthroughs in educational theory and practice? Our belief that they will is closely tied to a particular view of the ends of educational research and the role of measurement in fostering those ends: Educational research is the study of the trajectories of growth over time. Its major goal is the identification of key attributes that govern growth and improvement and prevent decay and deterioration. Measurement, on the other hand, is the quantitative specification of the position, direction, and velocity of an individual or group of individuals in an educationally relevant growth space. The goals of educational research are therefore dependent on the practice of measurement. The practice of measurement is significantly advanced by the introduction of computerized test administration, because, with the judicious application of hardware, software, and psychometric technologies, the specification of position and velocity in growth space can be accomplished.

REFERENCES

The topics discussed in this chapter are a part of a rapidly moving field. To have restricted the references to refereed journals or books would have narrowed the scope of the chapter to an unduly conservative position. Reports and other references not found in the public literature can be obtained in most cases from the authors.

Abernathy, L. J. (1986). *Computerized placement tests: A revolution in testing instruments.* New York: College Board.

Ager, T. A. (in press). From interactive instruction to interactive testing. In R. Freedle, (Ed.), *Artificial intelligence and the future of testing.* Hillsdale, NJ: Lawrence Erlbaum Associates.

Alderman, D. L. (1978). *Evaluation of the TICCIT computer-assisted instruction system in the community college.* Princeton, NJ; Educational Testing Service.

American Psychological Association Committee on Professional Standards (COPS) and Committee on Psychological Tests and Assessment (CPTA). (1986). *Guidelines for computer based tests and interpretations.* Washington, DC: Author.

Anderson, J. R. (1983). *The architecture of cognition.* Cambridge, MA: Harvard University Press.

Anderson, J. R. (in press). Analysis of student performance with the LISP tutor. In N. Frederiksen, R. Glaser, A. Lesgold, & M. Shafto, (Eds.), *Diagnostic monitoring of skill and knowledge acquisition.* Hillsdale, NJ: Lawrence Erlbaum Associates.

Andrich, D. (1985). A latent trait model for items with response dependencies: Implications for test construction and analysis. In S. E. Embretson (Ed.), *Test design: Developments in psychology and psychometrics.* New York; Academic Press.

Assessment Systems Corporation. (1987). *User's manual for the MicroCAT testing system.* St. Paul, MN; Author.

Baker, F. B. (1984). Technology and testing: State of the art and trends for the future. *Journal of Educational Measurement, 21,* 399–406.

Bennett, R.E., Gong, B., Kershaw, R.C., Rock, D.A., Soloway, E., & Macalalad, A. (1988). *Agreement between expert system and human ratings of constructed responses to computer science items.* Research Report (ETS RR 88-20). Princeton, NJ: Educational Testing Service.

Binet, A. (1909). *Les idées modernes sur les enfants* [Modern ideas about children]. Paris: Ernest Flammarion.

Birnbaum, A. (1968). Some latent trait models and their uses in inferring an examinee's ability. In F. M. Lord & M. R. Novick (Eds.), *Statistical theories of mental test scores.* Reading, MA: Addison-Wesley.

Biskin, B. H., & Kolotkin, R. L. (1977). Effects of computerized administration on scores on the Minnesota Multiphasic Personality Inventory. *Applied Psychological Measurement, 1*(4), 543–549.

Bock, R. D., & Aitkin, M. (1981). Marginal maximum likelihood estimation of item parameters: Application of an EM algorithm. *Psychometrika, 46,* 443–459.

Bock, R. D., & Mislevy, R. J. (1982a). Adaptive EAP estimation of ability in a micro computer environment. *Applied Psychological Measurement, 6*(4), 431–444.

Bock, R. D., & Mislevy, R. J. (1982b). *BILOG: Maximum likelihood item analysis and test scoring with logistic ogive models.* Mooresville, IN: Scientific Software.

Bock, R. D., & Mislevy, R. J. (1982c). Biweight estimates of latent ability. *Educational and Psychological Measurement, 42,* 725–737.

Bridgeman, B., Bennett R., & Swinton, S. (1986). *Design of an interactive assessment videodisc demonstration project.* Princeton, NJ: Educational Testing Service.

Bunderson, C. V. (1973). The TICCIT project: design strategy for educational innovation. In S. A. Harrison & L. M. Stolurow (Eds.). *Productivity in higher education.* Washington, DC: National Institutes of Education.

Bunderson, C. V., & Faust, G. W. (1976). Programmed and computer assisted instruction, Chapter III. In N. L. Gage (Ed.), Seventy-Fifth Yearbook, *The psychology of teaching methods* (pp. 44–90). Chicago, IL: National Society for the Study of Education.

Bunderson, C. V., & Inouye, D. K. (1987). Computer-aided educational delivery systems. In R. Gagné (Ed.), *Instructional technology.* Hillsdale, NJ: Lawrence Erlbaum Associates.

Calvert, E. J., & Waterfall, R. C. (1982). A comparison of conventional and automated administration of Raven's Standard Progressive Matrices. *International Journal of Man-Machine Studies, 17,* 305–310.

Cassirer, E. (1923). *Substance and function and Einstein's theory of relativity:* (W. C. Swabey & M. C. Swabey Trans.). New York: Dover.

Dillon, R. F., & Stevenson-Hicks, R. (1981). Effects of item difficulty and method of test administration on eye span patterns during analogical reasoning. (Technical Report No.1, Contract N66001-80-C0467). Carbondale, IL: Southern Illinois University.

Druesne, B., Kershaw, R., & Toru, O. (1986). *CLEP general examination: Humanities.* Princeton, NJ: Educational Testing Service.

Eignor, D. R., & Cook, L. L. (1983). *An investigation of the feasibility of using item response theory in the preequating of aptitude tests.* Paper presented at the meeting of the American Educational Research Association, Montreal.

Elwood, D. L. (1972a). Automated WAIS testing correlated with face-to-face testing: A validity study. *International Journal of Man-Machine Studies, 4,* 129–137.

Elwood, D. L. (1972b). Test retest reliability and cost analysis of automated and face-to-face intelligence testing. *International Journal of Man-Machine Studies, 4,* 1–22.

Embretson, S. (1983). *Psychometrics for theory based tests.* Paper presented at the meeting of the American Educational Research Association, Montreal.

Embretson, S. E. (1985a). Multicomponent models for test design. In S. E. Embretson (Ed.), *Test design: Developments in psychology and psychometrics.* New York: Academic Press.

Embretson, S. E. (1985b). (Ed.) *Test design: Developments in psychology and psychometrics.* New York: Academic Press.

Embretson, S. (in press). Diagnostic testing by measuring learning processes: Psychometric considerations for dynamic testing. In N. Fredericksen, R. Glaser, A. Lesgold, & M. Shafto (Eds.), *Diagnostic monitoring of skill and knowledge acquisition.* Hillsdale, NJ: Lawrence Erlbaum Associates.

Feurzeig, W., & Jones, G. (1970). *Reevaluating low achievers with computer-administered tests.* Unpublished manuscript, Bolt, Beranek, and Newman, Boston.

Forehand, G. A., & Bunderson, C. V. (1987a). *Basic concepts of mastery assessment systems.* Princeton, NJ: Educational Testing Service.

Forehand, G. A., & Bunderson, C. V. (1987b). *Mastery assessment systems and educational objectives.* Princeton, NJ: Educational Testing Service.

Freedle, R. (in press). (Ed.) *Artificial intelligence and the future of testing.* Hillsdale, NJ: Lawrence Erlbaum Associates.

Frederiksen, N., Glaser, R., Lesgold, A., & Shafto, M. (Eds.). (in press). *Diagnostic monitoring of skill and knowledge acquisition.,* Hillsdale, NJ: Lawrence Erlbaum.

Frederiksen, J., & White F. (in press). Intelligent tutors as intelligent testers. In N. Frederiksen, R. Glaser, A. Lesgold, and M. Shafto (Eds.), *Diagnostic monitoring of skill and knowledge acquisition.* Hillsdale, NJ: Lawrence Erlbaum Associates.

Gagné, R. M. (1965). *The conditions of learning* (1st ed.). New York: Holt, Rinehart and Winston.

Gagné, R. M. (1968). Learning Hierarchies. *Educational Psychologist, 6, 1–9.*

Gardner, D. P. (1983, April). *A nation at risk: The imperative for educational reform.* National Commission on Excellence in Education. Washington, DC:

Glaser, R. (1986). The integration of instruction and testing. *The Redesign of Testing for the 21st Century: Proceedings of the 1985 ETS Invitational Conference.* Princeton, NJ: Educational Testing Service.

Greaud, V. A., & Green, B. F. (1986). Equivalence of conventional and computer presentation of speed tests. *Applied Psychological Measurement, 10*(1), 23–24.

Green, B. F. (1983). The promise of tailored tests. In H. Wainer & S. Messick (Eds.), *Principles of modern psychological measurement.* Hillsdale, NJ: Lawrence Erlbaum Associates.

Green, B. F. (1988). Construct validity of computer-based tests. In H. Wainer & H. Braun (Eds.), *Test validity.* Hillsdale, NJ: Lawrence Erlbaum Associates.

Green, B. F., Bock, R. D., Humphreys, L. G., Linn, R. L., & Reckase, M. D. (1982). *Evaluation plan for the computerized adaptive vocational aptitude battery* (Research Report No. 82-1). Baltimore: Johns Hopkins University.

Green, B. F., Bock, R. D., Humphreys, L. G., Linn, R. L., & Reckase, M. D. (1984). Technical guidelines for assessing computerized adaptive tests. *Journal of Educational Measurement, 21,* 347–360.

Green, B. F., Bock, R. D., Linn, R. L., Lord, F. M., & Reckase, M. D. (1983). *A plan for scaling the computerized adaptive ASVAB.* Baltimore: Johns Hopkins University.

Hambleton, R. K., & Swaminathan, H. (1985). *Item response theory.* Boston, MA: Kluwer-Nijhoff Publishing.

Hedl, J. J., O'Neil, H. F., & Hansen, D. N. (1971, February). *Computer based intelligence testing.* Paper presented at the meeting of the American Educational Research Association, New York.

Heuston, D. (1985). *Some considerations affecting the use of computers in public education.* Provo, UT: WICAT Systems.

Hitti, F. J., Riffer, R. L., & Stuckless, E. R. (1971). *Computer-managed testing: A feasibility study with deaf students.* Rochester, NY: Rochester Institute of Technology, National Technical Institute for the Deaf.

Hoffman, K. I., & Lundberg, G. D. (1976). A comparison of computer-monitored group tests with paper-and-pencil tests. *Educational and Psychological Measurement, 36,* 791–809.

Holtzman, W. H. (Ed.). (1970). *Computer assisted instruction, testing and guidance.* New York: Harper & Row.

Hulin, C. L., Drasgow, F., & Parsons, C. K. (1983). *Item response theory: Application to psychological measurement.* Homewood, IL: Dow Jones-Irwin.

Hunt, E. (1986). Cognitive research and future test design. *The Redesign of Testing for the 21st Century: Proceedings of the 1985 ETS Invitational Conference.* Princeton, NJ: Educational Testing Service.

Inouye, D. K., & Bunderson, C. V. (1986). Four generations of computerized test administration. *Machine-Mediated Learning, 1,* 355–371.

Inouye, D. K., & Sorenson, M. R. (1985). Profiles of dyslexia: The computer as an instrument of vision. In D. B. Gray & J. F. Kavanagh (Eds.), *Biobehavioral measures of dyslexia.* Parkton, MD: York Press.

Jacobs, R. L., Byrd, D. M., & High, W. R. (1985). Computerized testing: The hidden figures test. *Journal of Educational Computing Research. 1*(2), 173–177.

Johnson, D. F., & Mihal, W. L. (1973). Performance of blacks and whites in computerized versus manual testing environments. *American Psychologist, 28,* 694–699.

Johnson, W. L., & Soloway, E. (1985). PROUST: An automatic debugger for Pascal programs. *Byte, 10*(4), 179–190.

Jonassen, D. H. (1986, January). *Effects of microcomputer display on a perceptual/cognitive task.* Paper presented at the meeting of the Association for Educational Communications and Technology, Las Vegas, NV.

Jones, D. H. (1982). *Redescending M-type estimators of latent ability* (Tech. Rep. No. 82-30). Princeton, NJ: Educational Testing Service.

Kearsley, G. P. (Ed.). (1987). *Artificial intelligence & instruction.* Reading, MA: Addison-Wesley.

Kiely, G. L., Zara, A. R., & Weiss, D. J. (1986). *Equivalence of computer and paper-and-pencil Armed Services Vocational Aptitude Battery Tests* (Research Report No. AFHRL-TP-86-13). Brooks Air Force Base, TX: Air Force Human Resources Laboratory.

Kingston, N. M., & Dorans, N. J. (1984). Item location effects and their implications for IRT equating and adaptive testing. *Applied Psychological Measurement, 146–154.*

Kirsch, I. S., & Jungeblut, A. (1986) *Literacy: Profiles of America's young adults—Final report* (NAEP Report No. 16-PL-01). Princeton, NJ: National Assessment of Educational Progress.

Knights, R. M., Richardson, D. H., & McNarry, L. R. (1973). Automated vs. clinical administration of the Peabody Picture Vocabulary Test and the Coloured Progressive Matrices. *American Journal of Mental Deficiency, 78*(2), 223–225.

Koch, W. R., & Reckase, M. D. (1978). *A live tailored testing comparison study of the one- and three-parameter logistic models.* (Research Report No. 78-1). Columbia, MO: University of Missouri, Tailored Testing Research Laboratory, Educational Psychology Department.

Koson, D., Kitchen, C., Kochen, M., & Stodolosky, D. (1970). Psychological testing by computer: Effect of response bias. *Educational and Psychological Measurement, 30,* 803–810.

Lee, J. A., & Hopkins L. (1985, April). *The effects of training on computerized aptitude test performance and anxiety.* Paper presented at the meeting of the Eastern Psychological Association, Boston.

Lee, J., Moreno, K. E., & Simpson, J. B. (1986). The effects of mode of test administration on test performance. *Educational and Psychological Measurement, 46,* 467–474.

Linacre, M., & Wright, B. D. (1984). *MICROSCALE.* Chicago: MESA Press.

Linn, R. L. (1986). Barriers to new test designs. *The redesign of testing for the 21st century: Proceedings of the 1985 ETS Invitational Conference.* Princeton, NJ: Educational Testing Service.

Lord, F. M. (1952). A theory of test scores. *Psychometric Monographs, No. 7.*

Lord, F. M. (1970). Some test theory for tailored testing. In W. H. Holtzman (Ed.), *Computer-assisted instruction, testing and guidance.* New York: Harper & Row.

Lord, F. M. (1977). Practical applications of item characteristic curve theory. *Journal of Educational Measurement, 14,* 117–138.

Lord, F. M. (1980). *Applications of item response theory to practical testing problems.* Hillsdale, NJ: Lawrence Erlbaum Associates.

Lord, F. M., & Novick, M. R. (1968). *Statistical theories of mental test scores.* Reading, MA: Addison-Wesley.

Luce, R. D. (1986). *Response times, their role in inferring elementary mental organization.* New York: Oxford University Press.

Lukin, M. E., Dowd, T., Plake, B. S., & Kraft, R. G. (1985). Comparing computerized versus traditional psychological assessment. *Computers in Human Behavior, 1,* 49–58.

Lushene, R., O'Neil, H., & Dunn, T. (1974). Equivalent validity of a completely computerized MMPI. *Journal of Personality Assessment, 13,* 407–412.

Mazzeo, J., & Harvey, A. L. (1988). *The equivalence of scores from automated & conventional versions of educational & psychological tests: A review of the literature* (Research Report No. CBR 87-8, ETS RR 88-21). Princeton, NJ: Educational Testing Service.

McBride, J. R., & Moe, K. C. (1986, April). *Computerized adaptive achievement testing.* Paper presented at the meeting of the National Council for Measurement in Education, San Francisco.

McBride, J. R., & Weiss, D. J. (1974). *A word knowledge item pool for adaptive ability measurement* (Research Report No. 74-2). Minneapolis: Minnesota University.

McKinley, R. L., & Reckase, M. D. (1980). Computer applications to ability testing. *Association for Educational Data Systems Journal, 13,* 193–203.

McKinley, R. L., & Reckase, M. D. (1984a, April). *Implementing an adaptive testing program in an instructional program environment.* Paper presented at the meeting of the American Educational Research Association, New Orleans.

McKinley, R. L., & Reckase, M. D. (1984b). *A latent trait model for use with sequentially arranged units of instruction.* (Research Report ONR 84-2). Iowa City, IA: American College Testing Program.

Merrill, M. D. (1983). Component display theory. In C. M. Reigeluth (Ed.), *Instructional design theories and models: An overview of their current status.* Hillsdale, NJ: Lawrence Erlbaum Associates.

Merrill, M. D., Schneider, E. W., & Fletcher, K. A. (1980). *TICCIT.* Englewood Cliffs, NJ: Educational Technology Publications.

Millman, J. (1977, April). *Creating domain referenced tests by computer.* Paper presented at the meeting of the American Educational Research Association, New York.

Millman, J. (1980). Computer-based item generation. In R. Berk (Ed.), *Criterion referenced measurement: The state of the art.* Baltimore: Johns Hopkins University Press.

Millman, J. (1984a, April). *Computer-assisted test construction.* Paper presented at the meeting of the American Educational Research Association, New Orleans.

Millman, J. (1984b). Individualizing test construction and administration by computer. In R. Berk (Ed.), *A guide to criterion-referenced test construction.* Baltimore: Johns Hopkins University Press.

Milson, R., Lewis, M., & Anderson, J. R. (in press). The teacher's apprentice project: Building an algebra tutor. In R. Freedle (Ed.), *Artificial intelligence and the future of testing.* Hillsdale, NJ: Lawrence Erlbaum Associates.

Mislevy, R. J., & Verhelst, N. (1987). *Modeling item responses when different subjects employ different solution strategies* (Research Report No. RR 87-47-ONR). Princeton, NJ: Educational Testing Service.

Mislevy, R. J., & Bock, R. D. (1982). *Maximum likelihood item analysis and test scoring with binary logistic models.* Mooresville, IN: Scientific Software.

Moreno, K., Wetzel, C. D., McBride, J. R., & Weiss, D. J. (1983). *Relationship between corresponding Armed Services Vocational Aptitude Battery (ASVAB) and computerized adaptive testing (CAT) subtests* (NPRDC TR 83-27). San Diego: Navy Personnel Research and Development Center.

National Board of Medical Examiners. (1987). Update on computer based testing. *National Board Examiner, 34,* 1–3.

Olsen, J. B., & Bunderson, C. V. (1980). *Toward the development of a learner profile battery: Theory and research.* Orem, UT: WICAT Systems.

Olsen, J. B., Bunderson, C. V., & Gilstrap, R. M. (1982). *Development of a preliminary design for a computerized adaptive testing service for the department of defense.* Orem, UT: WICAT Systems.

Olsen, J. B., Bunderson, C. V., & Gilstrap, R. M. (1983). *Prototype design and development of a computerized adaptive testing system.* Orem, UT: WICAT Systems.

Olsen, J. B., Inouye, D., Hansen, E. G., Slawson, D. A., & Maynes, D. M. (1984). *The development and pilot testing of a comprehensive assessment system.* Provo, UT: WICAT Education Institute.

Olsen, J. B., Maynes, D. M., Ho, K., & Slawson, D. A. (1986). *The development and pilot testing of a comprehensive assessment system, phase I.* Provo, UT: Waterford Testing Center.

Olsen, J. B., Maynes, D. M., Slawson, D. A., & Ho, K. (1986, April). *Comparison and equating of paper-administered, computer-admin-*

istered and computerized adaptive tests of achievement. Paper presented at the meeting of the American Educational Research Association, San Francisco.

Owen, R. J. (1969). *A Bayesian approach to tailored testing* (Research Bulletin No. 69–92). Princeton, NJ: Educational Testing Service.

Owen, R. J. (1975). A Bayesian sequential procedure for quantal response in the context of adaptive mental testing. *Journal of the American Statistical Association, 70,* 351–356.

Parks, B. T., Mead, D. E., & Johnson, B. L. (1985). Validation of a computer administered marital adjustment test. *Journal of Marital and Family Therapy, 11*(2), 207–210.

Patience, W. M., & Reckase, M. D. (1979). *Operational characteristics of a one-parameter tailored testing procedure* (Research Report No. 79-2). Columbia, MO: University of Missouri, Tailored Testing Research Laboratory, Educational Psychology Department.

Psychological Corporation. (1986). *Computerized Adaptive Differential Aptitude Test.* San Antonio, TX: Author.

Quan, B. L., Park, T. A., Sandahl, G., & Wolfe, J. H. (1984). *Microcomputer network for computerized adaptive testing research* (NPRDC TR 84-33). San Diego: Navy Personnel Research and Development Center.

Rasch, G. (1960). *Probabilistic models for some intelligence and attainment tests.* Copenhagen: Nielsen & Lydiche.

Reckase, M. D. (1985). *Models for multidimensional and hierarchically structured training materials* (Research Report No. ONR 85-1). Iowa City, IA: American College Testing Program.

Reckase, M. D., Carlson, J. E., & Ackerman, T. A. (1986, August). *The effect of computer presentation on the difficulty of test items.* Paper presented at the meeting of the American Psychological Association, Washington, DC.

Reigeluth, C. M., Merrill, M.D., & Bunderson, C. V. (1978). The structure of subject matter content and its instructional design implications. *Instructional Science, 7,* 107–126.

Robertson, J. R., Inouye, D. K., & Olsen, J. B. (1985). *Basic Skills Testing System.* Provo UT: Waterford Testing Center.

Rock, D., & Pollack, J. (1987). *Measuring gains: A new look at an old problem.* Princeton, NJ: Educational Testing Service.

Sachar, J. D., & Fletcher, J. D. (1978). Administering paper-and-pencil tests by computer, or the medium is not always the message. In D. J. Weiss (Ed.), *Proceedings of the 1977 Computerized Adaptive Testing Conference.* Wayzata, MN: University of Minnesota.

Samejima, F. (1977). A comment on Birnbaum's three-parameter logistic model in the latent trait theory. *Psychometrika, 38,* 221–233.

Scissons, E. H. (1976). Computer administration of the California Psychological Inventory. *Measurement and Evaluation in Guidance, 9*(1), 22–25.

Shephard, R. N., & Metzler, J. (1971). Mental rotation of three-dimensional objects. *Science* 171, 701–703.

Slawson, D. A. (1986). *District wide computerized assessment in Texas.* Provo, UT: Waterford Testing Center.

Slawson, D. A., Maynes, D. M., Olsen, J. B., & Foster, D. F. (1986). *Waterford test creation package.* Provo, UT: Waterford Testing Center.

Sleeman, D., & Brown, J. S. (1982). *Intelligent Tutoring Systems.* New York: Academic Press.

Sternberg, R. J. (1977). *Intelligence, information processing, and anological reasoning: The componential analysis of human abilities.* Hillsdale, NJ: Lawrence Erlbaum.

Sternberg, R. J. (1982). Reasoning, problem solving, and intelligence. In R. J. Sternberg (Ed.), *Handbook of human intelligence.* Cambridge: Cambridge University Press.

Sternberg, R. J., & McNamara, S. M. (1985). The representation and processing of information in real-time verbal comprehension. In S. E. Embretson (Ed.), *Test design: Developments in psychology and psychometrics.* New York: Academic Press.

Suppes, P., Ager, T., Berg, P., Chuaqui, R., Graham, W., Maas, R. E., & Takahashi, S. (1987). *Applications of computer technology to precollege calculus* (Technical Report No. 310). Psychology in Education Series. Stanford, CA: Stanford University, Institute for Mathematical Studies in the Social Sciences.

Suppes, P., & Sheehan, J. (1981a). CAI course in axiomatic set theory. In P. Suppes (Ed.), *University-level computer assisted instruction at*

Stanford: 1968–1980 (pp. 3–80). Stanford, CA: Stanford University, Institute for Mathematical Studies in the Social Sciences.

Suppes, P., & Sheehan, J. (1981b). CAI course in logic. In P. Suppes (Ed.), *University-level computer assisted instruction at Stanford: 1968–1980* (pp. 193–226). Stanford, CA: Stanford University, Institute for Mathematical Studies in the Social Sciences.

Tatsuoka, K. (in press). Toward an integration of item response theory and cognitive error diagnosis. In N. Fredericksen, R. Glaser, A. Lesgold, M. Shafto (Eds.), *Diagnostic monitoring of skill and knowledge acquisition.* Hillsdale, NJ: Lawrence Erlbaum Associates.

Thissen, D. (1986). MULTILOG [computer program] Mooresville, IN: Scientific Software.

Thissen, D., & Steinberg, L. (1984). A response model for multiple-choice item. *Psychometrika, 49,* 501–519.

Vale, C. D., & Gialluca, K. A. (1985). *ASCAL: A microcomputer program for estimating logistic IRT item parameters.* St. Paul: Assessment Systems Corporation.

Wainer, H. (1983). On item response theory and computerized adaptive tests. *Journal of College Admissions, 27,* 9–16.

Wainer, H. (1984). *The development of computerized adaptive testing system (D-CATS).* Unpublished manuscript, Princeton, NJ: Educational Testing Service.

Wainer, H., & Kiely, G. L. (1987). Item clusters and computerized adaptive testing: A case for testlets. *Journal of Educational Measurement, 24,*(3), 185–201.

Wainer, H., & Thissen, D. M. (1987). Estimating ability with the wrong model. *Journal of Educational Statistics.*

Wainer, H., & Wright, B. D. (1980). Robust estimation of ability in the Rasch model. *Psychometrika, 45,* 373–391.

Ward, W. C. (1984). Using microcomputers to administer tests. *Educational Measurement: Issues and Practice, 3,* 16–20.

Ward, W. C. (1986). Measurement research that will change test design for the future. *The Redesign of Testing for the 21st Century: Proceedings of the 1985 ETS Invitational Conference.* Princeton, NJ: Educational Testing Service.

Ward, W. C., Kline, R. G., & Flaugher, J. (1986). *College Board Computerized Placement Tests: Validation of an adaptive test of basic skills* (Report No. PR-86-29). Princeton, NJ: Educational Testing Service.

Watts, K., Baddeley, A., & Williams, M. (1982). Automated tailored testing using Raven's matrices and the Mill Hill vocabulary tests: A comparison with manual administration. *International Journal of Man-Machine Studies, 17,* 331–344.

Weiss, D. J. (1985). *Computerized adaptive measurement of achievement and ability* (Final report N00014-79-C-0172). Minneapolis, MN: University of Minnesota, Computerized Adaptive Testing Laboratory.

Weiss, D. J., & Kingsbury, G. G. (1984). Application of computerized adaptive testing to educational problems. *Journal of Educational Measurement, 21,* 361–375.

White, D. M., Clements, C. B., & Fowler, R. D. (1985). A comparison of computer administration with standard administration of the MMPI. *Computers in Human Behavior, 1,* 153–162.

Whitely, S. E., & Dawis, R. V. (1976). The influence of test context on item difficulty. *Educational and Psychological Measurement, 36,* 329–337.

WICAT Education Institute. (1983). *High technology and basic skills in reading.* Provo, UT: Author.

WICAT Systems (1988). *Learner profile and WICAT test of basic skills.* Orem, UT: Author.

Wise, S. L., Boettcher, L. L., Harvey, A. L., & Plake, B. S. (1987, April). *Computer-based testing versus paper-pencil testing: Effects of computer anxiety and computer experience.* Paper presented at the meeting of the American Educational Research Association, Washington, DC.

Wise, S. L., Plake, B. S., Boettcher, L. L., Eastman, L. A., & Lukin, M. E. (1987, April). *The effects of item feedback on test performance and anxiety in a computer-administered test.* Paper presented at the meeting of the American Educational Research Association, Washington, DC.

Wise, L. A., & Wise, S. L. (1986). *Comparison of computer-administered and paper-administered achievement tests with elementary school children.* Unpublished manuscript, University of Nebraska Lincoln, Department of Educational Psychology.

Wingersky, M. S., Barton, M. A., & Lord, F. M. (1982). *LOGIST User's Guide.* Princeton, NJ: Educational Testing Service.

Wright, B. D., Rossner, M., & Congdon, R. (1984). *M-SCALE.* Chicago: MESA Press.

Yen, W. M. (1980). The extent, causes, and importance of context effects on item parameters for two latent trait models. *Journal of Educational Measurement, 17,* 297–311.

Yen, W. M. (1981). Using simulation results to choose a latent trait model. *Applied Psychological Measurement, 5,* 245–262.

10

Computer Technology in Test Construction and Processing

Frank B. Baker

University of Wisconsin

Computer Technology and Testing

When the second edition of *Educational Measurement* (Thorndike, 1971) was published, the processing of test results was the primary use of computer technology in testing. High-capacity optical scanners were used to read answer sheets, to score the test, and to store the information in a computer-compatible medium. A computer was then used to analyze the information and produce a printed report for each student and for the group tested. As a result, the chapter dealing with computer technology in testing focused upon a systems approach to large-scale test scoring, analysis, and reporting. The capability of these high-capacity test-scoring systems, in terms of answer sheets processed per hour, has not changed very much since the late 1970s. However, the overall flexibility and ease of use of the scanner and computer system have been improved considerably. Through the use of time sharing techniques, these systems can now scan answer sheets, analyze test results, report results, and allow clerical personnel to edit questionable answer sheets simultaneously. Thus, the existing tasks associated with large-scale test processing are being done with greater ease and efficiency than they were in the past. Because this application of technology to testing is a mature one, the present chapter will not focus upon it. The interested reader is referred to the earlier chapter (Baker, 1971) for an in-depth discussion of this application.

Since the second edition of *Educational Measurement* was published, the microcomputer revolution has occurred and the computer age is upon us. Although the "computer on a chip" was developed around 1974, its impact in education was not felt until personal computers became widely available around 1978. These small computers possess a reasonably good mathematical computing capability, use a visual display similar to a television screen upon which both text and graphics can be shown, can generate sound, and provide considerable mass storage, excellent printers, and a typewriter-style keyboard. Microcomputer systems are relatively inexpensive, readily available, very reliable, and easily used by persons with little or no prior exposure to computer technology. Because of these characteristics, the microcomputer has had a major impact upon our society and has become truly ubiquitous. The nation's schools have embraced the microcomputer, and it is being used as an instructional vehicle in many subject matter areas. It is also widely used to promote "computer literacy" among the student body. We are rapidly approaching the time when there will be a microcomputer in every school building and, perhaps, every classroom. At the college level, the use of the microcomputer is particularly widespread, and a student without one is at a distinct disadvantage in many fields. Microcomputers and their associated technology have also been employed within the field of educational measurement. The present applications strongly suggest that the microcomputer is going to play an increasingly important role in the field of educational measurement in general and testing in particular. Consequently, the present chapter focuses upon the role of the microcomputer in testing.

A Systems Approach to Using Microcomputers in Testing

The capabilities of the microcomputer can be used in a broad range of testing-related activities. In particular, the microcomputer can be used in item writing, item banking, test construction, and test administration, as well as in the more traditional test scoring, analysis, and reporting phases of testing. As a result, the present chapter takes a systems approach to the overall process, rather than discussing only one element of the process. This has been done to emphasize the fact that there is an underlying continuity to the test construction and analysis process. In the past, this continuity was fractured by the necessity of employing technology in a piecemeal fashion. The microcomputer makes it possible to properly integrate the total process within the framework of a single hardware and software system. Figure 10.1 shows a typical microcomputer-based testing system that will serve as the basis of the present discussion.

The functional flow of the testing process is depicted in Figure 10.2. This functional flow assumes the existence of the definition of the variable of interest and the test and item specifications. The first step is item writing, during which the item author relies upon her or his knowledge of the subject matter areas, the intended examinees, and the item specifications to create an item. The microcomputer is used as an electronic typewriter to construct the items via the keyboard and its graphics capabilities used to create the item's figures. As each item is completed, its text and graphics are stored in the microcomputer's mass storage device, accompanied by descriptive information specifying the item content and its technical characteristics. The resultant collection of items is known as an *item pool* or *item bank*, and the process of storing the items by computer is known as *item banking* (see Lippey, 1974, and the chapter by Millman and Arter). The computer's mass storage could contain item pools for one or more subject matter areas or underlying variables. The second block in the functional flow represents the item-banking step.

With the test specifications in hand and an item pool available, one can construct a test using the microcomputer and its software. The test constructor uses the computer keyboard to enter specifications for the items to be selected from the item bank. The computer then searches the item bank for items matching the item specifications. When an item meeting the

specifications is located, the item is placed in the test. This process is repeated until the test specifications have been met, and then the desired test and its answer key are stored by the computer in its mass storage devices. Even though the computer plays a vital role, the test constructor uses his or her professional judgment throughout construction of the test and is in overall control of the process.

Once the test has been constructed, the use to which it will be put determines the next step. If the test is to be administered by the computer to the examinee, test-administration software is employed to test the examinee. Because chapter 9 deals with this topic in depth, it shall not be pursued further here. If the test is to be administered as a paper-and-pencil test, the computer must print the reproduction master copy of the test.

Given the test master, the necessary number of copies can be produced by a variety of available reproduction techniques. The test is then administered to the examinees. The results of the test administration are a set of answer sheets that can be scanned by an optical scanner connected to the microcomputer. As each sheet is scanned and the examinee's item responses are scored, a record containing the examinee's identification, test identification, item responses, and test score is stored in the computer's storage device. When the last examinee in the tested group has been processed, the analysis step is performed, using the data recorded during the answer sheet scanning process. The summary statistics of the test can be computed, item analysis can be performed, and the results can be stored in the item bank by individual item and by test. Upon completion of the analysis step, the computer-driven printer is used to print the desired reports. Because of the flexibility of the report-generating software, the results can be formatted in many different ways. For example, the test results could be reported by student, by instructional group, by administrative group, and by item.

Now that the overall test construction and analysis functional flow has been presented, the following sections examine each of the major steps from a technological point of view.

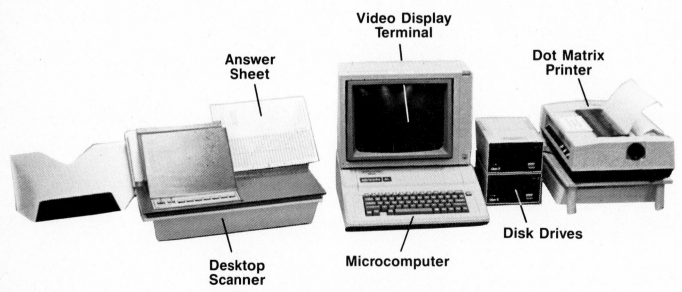

FIGURE 10.1 Typical microcomputer-based testing system.

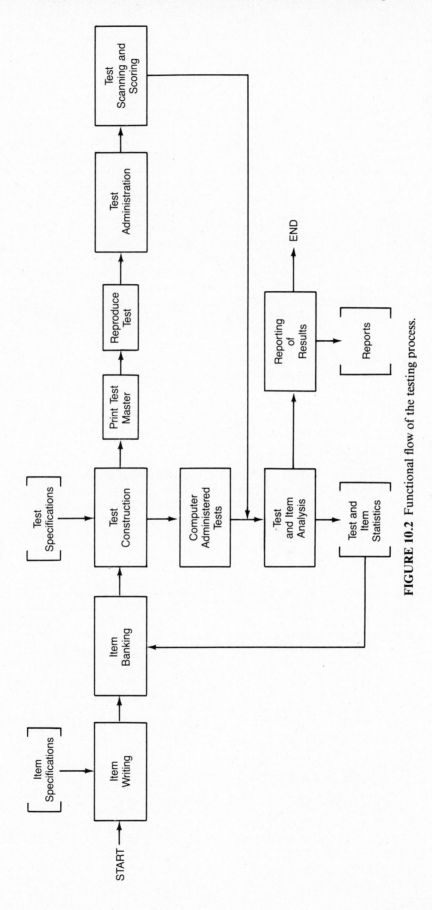

FIGURE 10.2 Functional flow of the testing process.

Technical Considerations

Item Writing

The task of item writing can be accomplished by using any of the available word-processing packages. These computer programs provide the capability to create text, to store it in mass storage, and to control the formatting of the printed page. However, these programs were intended for a different market. They have a wide range of features and capabilities designed for persons creating manuscripts, correspondence, and business-related communications. As a result, they are rather large programs. Item writing probably could be better supported by specially designed word-processing packages that have features unique to the task. A word processor for item writing could provide skeleton items for a number of widely used item types, such as multiple-choice, true–false, matching, and short-response questions that would be filled in by the user, thus relieving the item writer of much of the tedious layout work. Of course, the item writer would be free to modify the layout as he or she saw fit, to create a layout of his or her own design, and to edit the item content. Such specialized item-writing programs would be much smaller in terms of lines of code and would be easier to incorporate in a larger, integrated package of testing software.

A major advantage of item writing via a word-processing program is the ease with which the item can be modified. The item writer can visually inspect the item on the screen for common item-writing errors. When improprieties are found, the item can be easily corrected. Current word processing programs can also locate misspelled words and the item writer can select from a list of candidate words. It might even be possible to have a computer program that examines an item for the most common item-writing errors and informs the item writer of the problems. Thus, a considerable amount of quality control can be conducted at the time the item is written. The net result would be that better items would be created with a word-processing approach.

In the past, one of the major deterrents to using the computer for item writing has been the inclusion of figures, diagrams, and pictures in an item. Typically the graphics were prepared by artists or draftsmen as a separate document. When the master copy of the test was prepared, the graphics were pasted in the proper locations on the page. This was both a time consuming and expensive procedure and a potential bottleneck in the test development process. The microcomputer has the capability to display a wide range of graphics on its video display screen. Most microcomputers provide the ability to generate lines and plot points as part of their programming languages.

But this approach is tedious and lacks the flexibility needed by a test constructor. In recent years, three lines of development in computer graphics have occurred that have considerable importance for item writing. First there are a large number of graphics packages that allow one to create high-resolution graphics via a "sketch pad" approach. Programs such as Mac-Paint for the Apple Macintosh and Storyboard Plus for the IBM PC allow one to create graphics via icon selection and pull-down menus. Using such programs graphics can be cre-

ated quickly and easily. Second, the area known as "desk top publishing" has developed. This area had its origins in the APPLE Macintosh where the graphics software and word processing software were an integrated software package. This enables one to merge figures with text at the push of a button. The combined document can then be printed using the usual computer printer. Because of its utility in a wide range of settings, the state of the art in desk top publishing is advancing very rapidly. Third, inexpensive hardware/software for scanning pictures, diagrams, figures, etc and storing the results in graphics format in mass storage. This technology provides easy access to a wide range of graphical material that can be used in item writing.

The capability of merging high-resolution graphics and text is precisely what a test constructor needs, but from a testing point of view there is a serious deficiency in some of these developments. Many of the high-resolution graphics packages are designed only to create slide shows on the computer's visual display terminal. While the desk top publishing packages are intended to produce documents containing graphics, they are self-contained software packages. As a result of their design, neither approach makes the graphics or documents available to an external computer program such as a test construction system. Because of this, present test construction systems must provide their own medium-resolution graphics capabilities. Alternatively, they can use graphics packages like the Graphics Magician (Pelczarski, Lubar, Jochunson, 1983) for the APPLE II, which are compatible with a given programming language such as BASIC. With a bit of computer gymnastics it is possible to incorporate the graphics and text when the item is being displayed or printed even though they are not stored in a combined form. While this scheme works, it employs several different software packages and is a bit awkward. To be of greatest value, the graphics capabilities should be readily accessible from the item writing software and the resulting text and graphics be accessible to the testing system.

Third, many test items can use figures, diagrams, maps, pictures, etc from existing sources. Inexpensive technology has been developed to "digitize" this material. In the typical system, such as THUNDERSCAN (Thunderware, 1987), a small optical sensor is attached to the print head of a dot matrix printer. The figure to be scanned is positioned in the printer's paper feed mechanism. Then as the print head moves point by point across the paper, the optical device senses the light intensity in the figure. The reading at each point is converted to a grey scale and stored as a number in a disk file. Computer software is then used to translate this grey scale information into a figure on the computer's video display screen. At the present time, this technology can only reproduce "black and white" figures. Despite this limitation, it has considerable potential for handling the graphics part of item writing.

Item Banking

A common practice among those who construct tests is to maintain a file of test items. In the past, this was done by putting each item on a card. When a test was to be constructed, one went through the cards looking for items that could be used. Although such a scheme works well for small collections of items, it is clumsy and inefficient when larger sets of items are involved. Consequently, the computer has been used to store these collections of items. This allows easy access to each item, and large numbers of items can be stored. However, the item bank must be well designed if it is to facilitate the test-construction process (see Millman & Arter, 1984, and Wright & Bell, 1984, for a discussion of the issues involved in designing an item bank). Three different types of information should be stored for each item. *First*, the textual and graphical portions of the item must be entered. *Second*, information used to access the item from a number of different points of view should be stored. This information usually consists of keywords describing the item content, its curricular placement, its behavioral classification, and any salient features of interest. *Third*, psychometric data can be stored, such as the item's difficulty and discrimination indexes, the number of times the item has been used in a given period, the date of the last use of the item, and the identification of the last test the item appeared in.

It should be noted that the storage of item statistics represents a difficult measurement problem. Under classical test theory, item statistics are group dependent and, therefore, must be interpreted within the context of the group tested. Unless one is willing to make some assumptions about the groups of examinees being random samples from the same population and about the tests being random samples from the same item pool, it is not correct to store the running average of the item statistics in the item record (see Baker, 1974, for a discussion of the psychometric aspects of item banking). Consequently, only the item statistics from the most recent testing are usually stored in the item's records. However, the item bank can have an archival item file containing values of the item statistics from past testings. The records in this file would contain the item's statistics, the identification of the test it appeared in, the sample size, and the date of testing. This information would appear for a reasonable number of prior testings, say 5 to 10. Such a file enables one to examine the item's behavior in a variety of contexts and get an impression of the stability of the item statistics. It is also useful to include an archival test file in the system. This file contains the identification of the test, the date of testing; the identification of the group tested; the size, mean, and variance of the group; and the reliability of the test for each administration (see Baker, 1972, for the design of item bank files).

The several files contained within the item bank provide a wide range of information that is needed in the test-construction phase to make an informed selection of items from the item pool. They are also useful in controlling the quality of the items in the bank. With the use of the query capability of the item banking software, the history of an item can be studied. If an item historically exhibits poor distribution of distractors, low discrimination, and unusual difficulty, it can be a candidate for revision or deletion. In addition, the curricular content of an item must be evaluated, to insure that the item is in concert with what is being taught. The process of studying an item and modifying or deleting it is an important aspect of item banking and one that is facilitated by the use of a computer. If one does not perform these procedures consistently, the quality of the item bank can degrade as a function of time. Eventu-

ally the item bank becomes merely a collection of items and is of limited value.

The type of computer software used to implement the item-banking process is known generically as a *data base management (DBM) package*. This software provides the capability to define the files, the layout of records within the file, and the interrelationships among files. It also provides the means of entering data into the records and accessing these records from different perspectives. A number of general-purpose data base management packages exist for microcomputers. These can be used for item-banking purposes, but they usually occupy most of the computer's memory and, in many cases, do not allow other programs to access their capabilities. As a result, most item-banking software is custom programmed. This allows the designer to optimize the programs to the item-banking task and provide linkages that allow other modules, such as the test-construction routines, to access the capabilities of the data base management package. The resultant data base programs are usually much smaller than the general-purpose ones, as they only include features actually needed for testing purposes.

The mass storage devices employed by microcomputers are of two basic types, the floppy disk and the hard disk. The former is a $5\frac{1}{4}$ in. disk of mylar, coated with a recording medium and enclosed in a paper jacket. The floppy disk is inserted into the disk drive when it is needed and is removed as necessary. The capacity of the floppy disk varies, but, currently, a standard double-sided disk stores about 360,000 characters (bytes). In computer jargon, that is 360K bytes of storage. If one allocates 500 characters of memory space (about 7 lines of text) to an item, the disk can hold about 720 items. Thus, large-item pools can involve the use of multiple floppy disks. The problem then is that the user must continually be removing and replacing the disks as the computer works with different items, and the process can become time-consuming, error prone, and difficult for the user. The primary advantage of the floppy disk is low cost and flexibility of use.

The hard disk is a storage device similar in principle to the floppy disk, but the actual disk is rigid and generally cannot be removed from the unit containing it. The major advantages of the hard disk are that its storage capacity is measured in millions of characters, rather than in thousands, and that the time required to find data is much less than that of a floppy disk. The disadvantage is that the hard disk units cost roughly 3 to 5 times as much as a disk unit for a floppy disk. Hard disks can be obtained with capacities ranging from 10 to 40 million bytes. Thus, large numbers of items, on the order of 20,000 items of 500 bytes each, can be stored on a 40 megabyte hard disk. A technical problem associated with the use of hard-disk storage is backup. If there should be a problem with the disk or its mechanics, the stored data can be lost. For this reason, it is necessary to periodically transfer the contents of the hard disk to floppy disks or magnetic tape. This can be a rather time-consuming task, but it is a crucial one if the item pool is to be properly maintained. It should be noted that the technology of mass storage is changing very rapidly, and the storage cost per byte is decreasing as a function of time. Thus, in the 1990s, the mass storage needed to store large item pools will be relatively inexpensive and readily available.

When floppy-disk storage is used, there is a severe conflict between the amount of storage needed to bank an item and the amount of storage available. The usual multiple-choice item can easily use several hundred bytes to store the item stem and the distractors. Considerable memory can be used for the curricular descriptors and the psychometric data. In addition, graphical material is particularly demanding of storage, and including it within an item record dramatically increases the storage required by an item to many thousands of bytes. Thus, a trade-off exists between the size of the item's record and the storage available for the item pool. To a large extent, the trade-off depends upon the intended use of the item bank. Usually the designer of the item-banking software makes a decision as to what the user's range of needs are and designs the item record accordingly. However, it is feasible to allow the user to tailor the amount of information contained in an item record to his or her unique needs. Some test constructors might need a wide variety of information to construct a test, others might be interested only in the linkage of the item content to the curriculum.

Because an item bank alone has little intrinsic value, the item-banking software is usually contained within a program for interactive test construction. In an interesting development, a few publishers are now offering a floppy disk containing test-construction software, accompanied by item pools for specific curricula. For an exemplar, see the Microcomputer Test Administration System offered by Science Research Associates. This practice has a number of advantages. The teacher has access to well written tests and items measuring topics deemed important by the developers of the curricular materials. Through use of the test-construction software, the teacher has the flexibility to construct from these items tests that meet local needs. In addition, in a well-designed system, the teacher should be able to add locally constructed items to the publisher's item pool, to meet unique requirements or cover supplemental curricular topics. It would appear that the linkage of textbooks to item pools and test-construction software is an important trend.

Test Construction

The construction of tests and other measuring instruments has always been in iterative procedure involving considerable professional judgment on the part of the test constructor. This process is facilitated by the use of a microcomputer. Given a set of test and item specifications, the test constructor uses keywords to specify content and curricular placement of the desired item and the values of item statistics to specify the desired psychometric characteristics. Given these item specifications, the computer searches the item pool until an item meeting the specifications is found, and then it is shown on the visual display screen. Even though the item's curricular descriptors match the retrieval specifications, it does not insure that the item's content is appropriate. Thus, the test constructor must evaluate the item and make a decision as to whether or not to use it. If the item is acceptable, it can be included in the test by storage of its identification number in a test-construction file. If not, the next item found can be examined and the process repeated until a satisfactory item is obtained.

Typically, a test has several different subsets of item specifications, and the selection process is repeated for each subset. When the item-selection process has been completed, the resultant test can be reviewed. Each item can be shown on the visual display screen, and the test constructor can easily move from one item to another. This allows him or her to study the quality of the selected items, and look for repeated items, items that answer other items, and items whose statistics do not fit well within the overall test. One can also modify the order in which the items appear in the test. Depending upon the topic, it might be useful to have the items appear in some logical order or perhaps in order of increasing difficulty. This can easily be accomplished by relocating the item's identification number in the test-construction file. When an acceptable version of the test is completed, the computer can compute estimated summary statistics for the test on the basis of current item statistics, to obtain a rough idea of how the test will perform. Such estimates are only suggestive, as they are typically based upon item summary data from different test administrations.

The test-construction process can also be fully automated. The test constructor can enter the test and item specifications into the computer. The computer then searches for an item meeting the specifications. When the item is found, other criteria, such as the frequency of use and the date of last use, can be applied to further limit the item selected. If the item meets all the specifications, it is automatically included in the test. This process is repeated until the desired number of items have been included in the test. At this point the test constructor is able to review the test. If the test constructor does not like certain items, replacement items can be found by using the item-selection procedures just described. Thus, the initial item selection is automated, but the final test is the result of an iterative process involving the test constructor and the computer.

Test Printing

Once the test has been constructed and the identification numbers of the items have been put into a test-construction file, the test-production process can be initiated. The initial task is to create a master copy of the test from which multiple copies of the test can be reproduced. The standard printer used with a microcomputer is known as a dot matrix printer. These machines print letters and symbols using a 7 row by 5 column matrix of dots. Each dot in a vertical column corresponds to a small plunger pin on the print head that causes a dot to be printed. The use of this technology also enables the computer to print graphical materials such as figures, drawings, and even pictures. The horizontal resolution is, typically, 60 dots per inch, and it is adequate for most testing purposes. These printers are also inexpensive, about $400 in 1988. More expensive printers, based upon laser photo copying technology, can produce high-quality print. Even though the laser printer has very high resolution, the quality of the graphics is limited by the resolution of the video display terminal used to create and display the graphics. Again, considerable improvement in the resolution of the graphics created with microcomputers will occur as a function of time. The test printed via the inexpensive dot matrix printer is of sufficient quality for most classroom purposes, and the printed page photocopies quite well, so that one does not have to use the relatively slow printer to make multiple copies of a test.

Phototypesetting is another technology that can be accessed via the microcomputer to create a reproduction master copy of the test. A file containing test items is transferred on a computer-to-computer basis to the phototypesetting equipment, where the layout, type font, and other features of the test format can be specified. This equipment then produces the reproduction master, and the resulting output is of very high quality. At present, most phototypesetting equipment can only print textual material. However, the technology to incorporate graphical material is being developed. Once a master copy of the test is available, multiple copies can be produced with office equipment normally available in the schools. Given a good test master, most reproduction equipment can produce high-quality copies at a very reasonable cost. Therefore, the printing of tests does not represent a problem, and many opportunities exist for their innovative reproduction.

Test Scanning and Scoring

Once the test has been administered to the examinees, the next step is to read and score the item responses. The automation of this process depends upon the use of multiple-choice items and answer sheets marked by the examinees. Baker (1971) predicted the development of small optical-mark readers, which he designated *desktop scanners*. In the mid-1970s the first of these scanners, the DATUM (SCANTRON) 5098, appeared on the market. These scanners are about the size of a small microwave oven and are connected directly to the microcomputer with an electronic cable. The answer sheets are inserted manually one at a time, and the examinees' item responses are detected via optical means (see Baker, 1971, for a description of the technology employed). The item responses are encoded and transmitted to the microcomputer. These desktop scanners can process an answer sheet in about 5 seconds. The computer programming necessary to employ the desktop scanner is very simple and readily implemented in BASIC or other programming languages.

A number of different types of desktop scanners are in production, the simple ones being similar to that described and usually capable of scanning an array of 64 by 12 marking positions. More capable scanners, such as the SCANTRON 2100 or the NCS-3000 offer automatic sheet feeding, full sheet scanning, and considerable internal sophistication. Scanners of this class often incorporate a microprocessor to control the scanning process and perform sophisticated analyses of the detected marks to separate actual responses from erasures and other contamination of the answer sheets. These scanners can also score the answer sheet as it is scanned and use an internal print mechanism to put the score on the answer sheet. However, this feature is not of much interest when the scanner is connected to a microcomputer. It does, however, allow the scanner to be used as a stand-alone test-scoring device. Card readers employing optical-mark reading have also been used to put item responses in a microcomputer. These require the use of punched card stock, which is quite expensive, and therefore not practical in most testing situations. In addition, the use of punched cards is a thing of the past and technology based upon them is obsolete.

When the microcomputer receives the examinee's vector of item responses, the scoring can be done. There are two ways to obtain the answer key for the test. *First*, the test-construction procedures can store it in the data base and the test scoring program can retrieve it from the disk. *Second*, the answer key can be marked manually on an answer sheet and read in as the first sheet. The computer then stores the scanned responses as the answer key. The actual scoring consists of comparing the examinee's response vector with the answer key vector. Several pieces of information are created during this process. The examinee's item response is transformed into a binary vector, with a 1 indicating a correct response and 0 indicating an incorrect response. Vectors are also created of the number of examinees responding to each item and correctly answering each item. The total test score for each examinee is also stored. These vectors are updated as each examinee's answer sheet it scanned. Given these data vectors, it is a simple matter to compute item and test statistics. Surprisingly, the amount of computer programming needed to perform the scanning, scoring, and analysis tasks is quite small. Programs that perform these functions only require several hundred lines of code and can be written easily in BASIC, PASCAL, C, or other high-level languages available on microcomputers.

When the scoring and analysis steps have been completed, the item and test statistics files of the item bank are updated. This process is completely automated and requires no participation on the part of the user of the microcomputer other than to authorize the updating of the files. The list of item identifications stored in the test-construction file during the test construction phase is used to locate the items in the item bank, and the data base management program is used to enter the new values of the statistics. The test files are updated in a similar manner. Before updating, the existing values are transferred into the archival files.

Reporting of Results

Because it is quite difficult to mark the examinees' names on mark-sense answer sheets used with desktop scanners, only their identification numbers enter the microcomputer via the scanning process. Thus, to report the results, the data base needs to have a student roster file, so that an examinee's name and identification number can be matched. However, answer sheets used with more capable scanners, such as the NCS 3000, can contain the student's name. A typical report shows the student's name and test scores, as in Figure 10.3. Test results can also be reported by instructional or administration groupings, and Figure 10.4 shows a typical class report. The test results can be reported from a normative or a criterion-referenced point of view. In some cases, test results can be reported in narrative form, rather than as numbers. The issues involved in reporting test results in narrative form will be discussed in a later section.

STUDENT Allen Carter   TEACHER Olivia Brown   DISTRICT Johnson County   DATE 2/83

SCHOOL Newton Elementary   GRADE 4   LEVEL 13

TEST SECTIONS	raw	SS	GE	NP	10	20	30	40	50	60	70	80	90
Reading total score	49	317	6.1	85									
Reading vocabulary	24	305	5.2	74									
Reading comprehension	25	356	8.5	97									
Mathematics total score	37	220	3.3	27			X						
Math concepts	20	247	3.3	29			X						
Math computation	17	240	3.4	28			X						
Language arts total	50	240	3.1	27			X						
Language mechanics	19	229	3.1	30			X						
Language expression	15	259	2.7	27			X						
Language spelling	16	259	3.1	29			X						
Reference Skills	46	258	3.7	41				X					

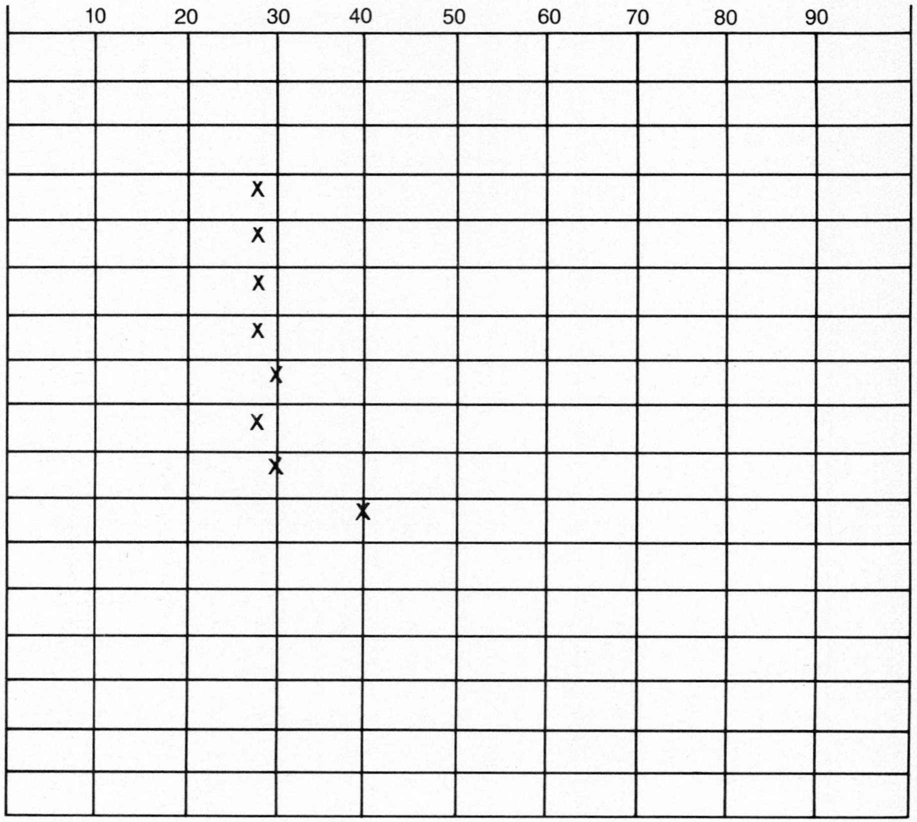

	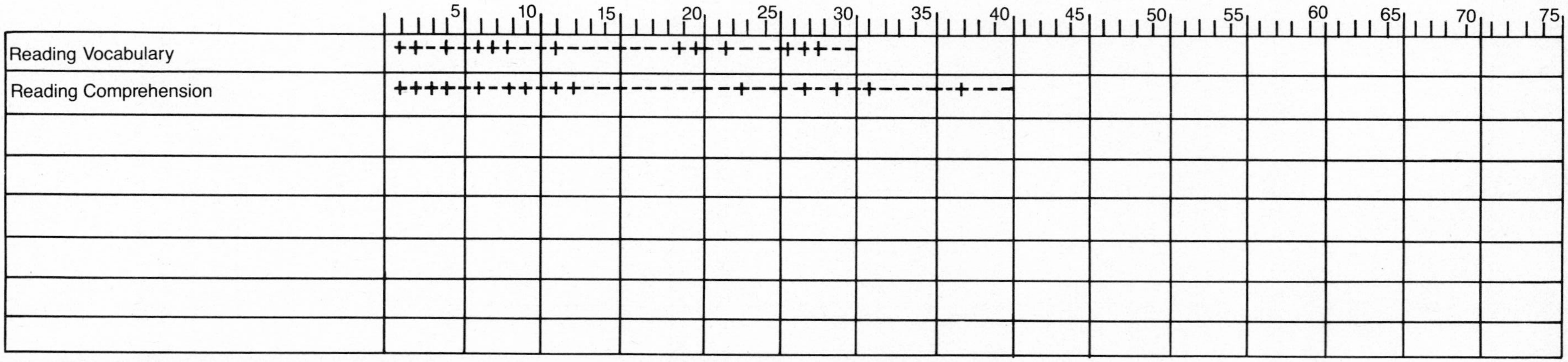 5	10	15	20	25	30	35	40	45	50	55	60	65	70	75
Reading Vocabulary															
Reading Comprehension															

FIGURE 10.3 A student's report.

416

FIGURE 10.4 A class report.

STUDENT NAME	AGE YRS. MOS.	SCORE	READ	VOC	CMP	MATH	MCON	MCMP	LART	LSPL	LUSG	LMCH	RSKL
ALLEN Carter	10-2	raw	49	24	25	37	20	17	50	19	15	16	46
		SS	317	305	356	220	247	240	240	229	259	259	258
		GE	6.1	5.2	8.5	3.3	3.3	3.4	3.1	3.1	2.7	3.1	3.7
		NP	85	74	97	27	29	28	27	30	27	29	41
BURNHAM Jeremy	10-4	raw	45	22	23	45	28	17	80	30	25	25	55
		SS	289	291	322	247	283	240	339	357	312	304	289
		GE	5.0	4.6	6.5	3.7	4.9	3.4	7.3	11.8	6.5	5.5	4.7
		NP	69	61	82	45	64	25	91	98	76	74	62
DOEBLER Lee	9-6	raw	45	22	23	45	28	17	80	30	25	25	55
		SS	289	291	322	247	283	240	339	357	312	304	289
		GE	5.0	4.6	6.5	3.7	4.9	3.4	7.3	11.8	6.5	5.5	4.7
		NP	69	61	82	45	64	25	91	98	76	74	62
EDGEMON Al	10-7	raw	43	20	23	50	20	30	70	15	29	26	54
		SS	278	277	322	265	247	297	294	205	359	311	285
		GE	4.6	4.0	6.5	4.4	3.3	5.1	4.9	2.4	10.3	6.0	4.6
		NP	61	47	82	57	29	83	68	15	98	81	60
KING Mary	9-11	raw	13	9	4	48	26	22	25	10	8	7	28
		SS	127	212	175	258	273	260	169	171	220	208	197
		GE	1.2	2.0	0.1	4.2	4.4	3.7	0.1	0.2	0.3	0.4	2.6
		NP	2	8	1	52	54	44	3	6	7	4	11
LONG Harriet	10-3	raw	21	12	9	50	25	25	37	10	16	21	36
		SS	192	232	225	265	269	273	213	171	263	281	226
		GE	1.9	2.5	2.0	4.4	4.1	4.3	2.4	0.2	3.0	4.1	3.2
		NP	11	16	12	57	50	59	14	6	30	50	22
LONGFELLOW Farquar	9-11	raw	31	19	12	59	35	24	48	15	1	12	46
		SS	235	271	244	297	354	268	236	205	286	243	258
		GE	3.0	3.7	2.6	5.4	8.1	4.2	3.0	2.4	4.3	2.6	3.7
		NP	30	42	22	78	99	53	24	15	53	17	41
SUDER Fred	10-3	raw	37	16	21	62	32	30	22	8	12	2	42
		SS	253	253	300	310	310	297	151	151	247	158	245
		GE	3.6	3.2	5.4	5.8	6.2	5.1	0.1	0.1	2.1	0.1	3.5
		NP	42	28	65	85	87	83	2	3	18	1	33
THOMAS Wayne	9-9	raw	56	30	26	47	25	22	75	30	21	24	59
		SS	398	393	383	254	269	260	313	357	286	298	312
		GE	10.7	9.6	10.6	4.1	4.1	3.7	6.1	11.8	4.3	5.0	5.4
		NP	99	99	98	50	50	44	80	98	53	68	75

Most test-scoring systems also report test and item statistics. Usually the test mean, the standard deviation, the range, and the internal consistency reliability coefficient are reported. A histogram of the test scores for the group of examinees is often produced. Reporting of item statistics is not done in a consistent manner. Some systems do not report them, some report only item difficulty and discrimination for the correct answer, and others provide extensive item data for all response choices. This variety seems to be a function of the intended uses of the system. Those designed for classroom teachers tend to report only a limited amount of item information.

State of the Art

At the time this chapter was written many computer programs performed only one or two of the steps in the overall testing process (See Hsu & Nitko, 1983, for a listing of the available software). Deck and Estes (1984) surveyed the item-banking and test-construction programs available as of the spring of 1984. The programs ranged in capability from rather limited to reasonably sophisticated. The majority were designed for use with the APPLE II computer and for storage of the items on floppy disks. As a result, the size of the item record was limited, as was the total number of items stored. The PRISM program (Psychological Corporation) constructs tests from an existing item bank by randomly selecting items meeting item specifications and then prints the test master. However, the test constructor cannot modify the resultant test. The Test Bank (Advanced Technology Applications) enables one to generate items using a word-processing approach; store them in an item pool of up to 700 items, along with keywords and other descriptors; construct a test; edit the test; and print a test master. However, it has no capability to process test results. The Microcomputer Scoring System (TESCOR, Inc.) does only test scoring, analysis, and reporting, using a desktop optical scanner connected to a microcomputer.

Even though some hardware and software systems support the major steps in the overall testing process, each of the existing systems involves trade-offs that were made to implement the system on a microcomputer. With a few exceptions, several different computer programs are necessary to perform all the major steps in the overall testing process, and these computer programs are not necessarily compatible with each other. For example, the analysis results from a given test-scoring program cannot be used to automatically update the item statistics in an item pool maintained by an item banking program.

A single software package that supports the total test construction, scoring, analysis, and reporting process would be of greater utility. A good approximation of such a package is the Micro Test Administration System (MTAS) ([SRA], 1982) that enables the user to construct a test by entering items on a line-by-line basis and to store them in a test file. The resultant test file can be edited, and a master copy of the test can then be printed with the dot matrix printer. A desktop scanner connected to the microcomputer is used to scan the examinees' item responses, and the microcomputer scores the test. It then uses a class roster file to print test results ordered alphabetically by examinee name and rank ordered by test score or by curricular objectives. In addition, student rosters from several classes can be merged to produce single lists of students and test scores. Although the MTAS supports the overall testing process, it has several limitations. The test files produced by this system are limited to a maximum of 100 items. It does not contain what would ordinarily be considered an item bank. Items are stored by test, and it is not possible to select an item from an item pool on the basis of its descriptive information. However, items can be selected from more than one test file to be included in a given test. The item-writing section does not use a word-processing approach, and items can be entered or edited only on a line-at-a-time basis.

Because of the limitations of the hardware, implementation of a total testing system on a small microcomputer such as the APPLE II series is difficult, and numerous trade-offs are normally made in the design stage. Typically, the designer trades off the size of the item record against the number of items in the item bank. This trade-off is further constrained by the relatively low storage capacity of the usual floppy disk. Many existing systems have traded off the flexibility of a word processing capability for a smaller, simpler, item-writing component. Another major trade-off involves the number of files in the data base and, consequently, the richness of both test construction and the reporting of results. If one is to maintain a

wealth of item and test-descriptive information, the number of files needed is large, as is the size of the individual records within each file, and considerable mass storage is required. Computer program size is also a limiting factor with most microcomputers. Once the computer program is too big to fit in memory, overlays and program chaining must be used to execute segments of the program. The transferring of program segments from disk to memory can slow the processing dramatically. Thus, it should be clear that the implementation of a full-capability test-processing system on a microcomputer is not a trivial task. It involves many design decisions that must take into account what one would like to do and what is feasible, given the limitations of the hardware.

Despite the many trade-offs involved and the limitations of the microcomputer, it is possible to develop a hardware and software system to support the total testing process. Two such state-of-the-art systems are the Pitt Educational Testing Aids (PETA) (Nitko and Hsu, 1984a,b) and MICROCAT (Assessment Systems Corporation, 1984). The PETA system was designed for use by classroom teachers. It was implemented on the APPLE II series of computers that are widely available in the classroom. The MICROCAT system was designed for use by persons knowledgeable in psychometrics and encompasses a range of rather sophisticated test construction, administration, and analysis procedures. As a result, the potential users of this system would tend to be college and university faculty as well as organizations such as a university testing service or a school district testing department. It was implemented on the IBM PC series of computers that are readily available to this audience. Since these two software packages represent quite different approaches to microcomputer based testing systems, each will be described below in some detail.

PETA

Basically the PETA system was designed for use in a single subject matter area by one teacher with up to 10 classes of up to 50 students each. Because of the intended audience, considerable care was taken to make the system "user friendly" in both terms of computer usage and its use of measurement techniques. In addition, it includes a number of capabilities that would ordinarily be considered part of a computer-managed instruction system (see Baker, 1978, for an in-depth presentation of computer-managed instruction). The system was implemented on an APPLE® II computer having 48k bytes of memory and two disk drives and was written in the APPLE-SOFT BASIC programming language. The system has three main components: (a) an item-banking and test-construction component, (b) a test-scoring, analysis, item-evaluation, and reporting component; (c) a student data base component with associated information retrieval and computational programs. The computer software for each component is contained on a separate floppy disk. At the bottom of these three components is a rather powerful data base management capability that provides considerable flexibility in the accessing of information and in the utilization of the same information in a number of contexts. Both the data base management programs and the files employed have been optimized to support the overall testing process. The capabilities of the system are accessed through a series of hierarchically nested menus.

The first component employs a simplified editing program, to allow the teacher to enter and edit items. The items can be characterized by curricular properties and by technical characteristics such as item difficulty and discrimination. The use of the DBM capability allows the teacher to store items in the item bank and to access existing items that can then be edited or deleted. The system does not permit the inclusion of graphical materials in the items. The maximum length of an item is 1,404 characters, which means that only 93 such items can be stored on a single 140k byte floppy disk. Assuming an average item consisted of 300 characters, about 420 items could be stored on a single disk. Several different item types, such as multiple-choice, matching, true-false, correct-answer, and essay can be used, but the majority of the software is designed for dichotomously scored multiple-choice items. The test-construction procedures allow the teacher to use the DMB capabilities to search for items on the basis of their characteristics and to select items for inclusion in a test. Once a test has been decided upon, this component also is used to print a copy of the test with a dot matrix printer for use as a reproduction master.

The second component focuses upon the processing of test results. The answer key and the examinee's item responses are entered manually via the keyboard. Once entered, the computer will score the test, yielding a total score and scores on specific curricular objectives and other instructionally relevant categories. These scores are then stored in the examinee's record. The item statistics in the item bank can also be updated using the results from the current testing. The teacher can also request standard reports such as class roster with scores to be shown on the video display screen or printed by the dot matrix printer. The teacher can ask for specific information to be retrieved and displayed or printed. The analysis portion of this component was designed to aid the teacher in making instructionally relevant decisions and in evaluating the items in a test. In addition to standard item and test statistics, the program derives the hierarchical ordering of the items in the test and identifies items with unusual patterns of response. It is important to note that the program presents tables of the numerical values of statistics only upon request. It usually presents the teacher with statistical results in interpreted form, based upon rules built into the computer programs.

The third component was designed to meet the needs of a single teacher for recording information about a given class of students in a single subject matter area. The data base consists of two interrelated sets of files on multiple floppy disks. One set consists of the item bank containing the actual items. A collection of coordinated computer programs facilitate's the use of this file for item-banking and test-construction purposes. The second set consists of 10 files that are classified into two major subsets: files for class (group) variables and files for individual student variables. The first subset contains variables describing class characteristics, specifications of tests, their summary statistics, curricular (skill) descriptors, and descriptive information about each item, but not the actual item. The second subset of files contains variables describing the students and their test results, such as names and ID numbers; test and activity scores; skill scores; item scores; and vectors of item

responses. The files are related to each other in a hierarchical manner: items within skills, skills within test and activities, test and activities within class, and classes of a single teacher. This structure, combined with the fact that each file is relatively small, facilitates rapid and flexible access to the information when needed. This second set of 10 files supports many of the functions normally associated with computer-managed instruction, in addition to those of the testing process. This is a natural combination, as most of the management functions of computer-managed instruction are based upon test results. Because of the scope of capabilities provided and the number of files, multiple floppy disks are employed. Thus, specific functions are on particular disks, and the use of multiple capabilities requires considerable disk switching. Due to the integrated nature of the software, all programs function within a consistent frame of reference.

The microcomputer system developed by Nitko and Hsu (1984a, 1984b) has a number of important characteristics. It provides the classroom teacher with computer support for all phases of the testing process. It employs an integrated suite of computer programs based upon a data base design that is optimized on two dimensions, one of which is test construction and the other instructional decision making based upon the results of the teacher-made tests. Perhaps the most important characteristic is that it costs only $99.

MICROCAT

The basic design of the MICROCAT system is oriented towards computerized adaptive testing with item response theory being the underlying psychometric model. It does, however, support all four combinations of IRT and classical test theory with adaptive and conventional testing. The system consists of five subsystems: Development, Examination, Assessment, Management, and Conventional Testing. Each subsystem can be purchased separately, however, a minimal system would require the Development and Conventional Testing subsystems. The capabilities of the system are accessed via a series of hierarchial menus with the five subsystems appearing on the main menu.

The Development subsystem enables one to create items, specify a test and its testing strategy. The Graphics Item Banker routine provides the capability for constructing items and editing existing items in the item bank. The first step in constructing an item is to provide an item identifier and some procedural information. Next the item graphics are created using a scheme based upon a set of primitive graphics commands which generate a box, circle, ellipse, line and similar elementary forms. Three letter abbreviations for these primitives are arranged around the perimeter of the VDT screen. A graphics cursor can be positioned on the screen and a primitive selected to generate the appropriate geometric form. The overall figure or diagram is created by using a series of these graphics primitives. A capability for adding text, such as labels, to the figure is also provided. The figure elements can be done in color and regions within the figure filled with a selected color. The complete series of commands can be stored and retrieved later for use in another item. The graphics routine employs a screen having a 200 rows by 320 columns grid so that the quality of the figures is limited by this medium resolution screen. The use of higher resolution graphics is to be included in future versions of MICROCAT. An interesting feature of the graphics item banker routine is the capability for letting the user define special symbols or alphabets. An eight by eight grid is provided and the user can mark the cells to define the symbol or letter. Once defined, these can be used in the same manner as the standard symbols and alphabet. Once the item and its graphics are completed, they can be stored in the item bank. The Development subsystem uses a special purpose language, the Minnesota Computerized Adaptive Testing Language (MCATL) to define both conventional and adaptive tests. Under the create option, the test constructor selects a prestored template (shell) for a given testing strategy. The computer then asks questions of the test constructor to obtain the information needed to complete the detailed test specification. The language also can be used directly to specify the items in the test, the scoring scheme and the logic of the conventional or adaptive testing strategy. In either case, the resulting test specification is stored in the item bank and it can be retrieved and edited. The completed test specification is then translated into a form used by the examination subsystem via a compile command on the menu.

The Examination subsystem assumes that the test is to be administered via an IBM PC microcomputer to an examinee seated at the console. It can administer the test to a single student or to a sequential series of students. An initial screen display provides procedural instructions to the examinee. As the test is administered, the examinee's item responses can be logged to a file so that an interrupted test can be restarted if so desired. Upon completion of the test, the results are printed and the relevant item sequence information and examinee item responses stored by examinee.

The Assessment subsystem allows the tester to investigate the measurement properties of the tests and test items. It consists of six components: collect, analyze, estimate, restimate, evaluate, and validate. The collect component aggregates the results for all the examines that have taken the same test into a file and stores it under a group identifier. Once the data have been aggregated, either a classical or item theory based analysis can be performed. The analyze component uses the ITEMAN routine to produce the usual classical test theory results. The test statistics are calculated for the whole test and its subscales. The item statistics are reported for all item response alternatives by item. Tables of the resulting statistics are then printed.

The estimate component employs the ASCAL routine to perform an IRT calibration of a test administered to a group of examines. The program uses a combined maximum likelihood and modal Bayesian estimation procedure. An examinee's ability is estimated using Bayesian modal estimation with a unit normal prior distribution of ability. Once the abilities are estimated, the examines are grouped into up to 20 fractiles and the item parameters estimated via a Bayesian adaptation of the maximum likelihood equations that places a normal prior on item difficulty and beta distributions as priors on item discrimination and guessing. An iterative procedure is used until some overall convergence criterion is met. The MICROCAT manual reports that the IRT calibration of 30 items for 1000 exam-

ines requires about two hours computer time using an IBM PC/XT microcomputer with an 8087 floating point coprocessor chip. A separate routine, called RASCAL and accessed via the restimate option, performs the standard maximum likelihood analysis under the one parameter logistic (RASCH) model.

The evaluate component uses the item parameters yielded by the ASCAL program to predict certain characteristics of a test before it is administered. The item parameters can be used to calculate the test characteristic curve and the test information function. This can be done for conventional tests or adaptive tests specified and compiled via the development subsystem.

The validate component provides the capability for evaluating the criterion-related validity of the tests constructed and analyzed via the other subsystems. It produces descriptive statistics for each of the test scores and external variables and performs a multiple regression analysis using one of the external variables as the dependent variable.

The Management subsystem is designed to allow one to administer and proctor tests administered when a number of IBM PC microcomputers are connected via a local area network (LAN). It is assumed that the network is a 3COM Ethershare® network. In addition, the server computer at the head of the network must have a hard disk for data storage. The Proctor command allows the examiner to assign tests to computers and to determine which students are at which computer i.e. testing station. Features are also provided for performing a number of administrative functions to assist the proctoring as well as for bringing the network into operation and shutting it down. A master file printing routine provides for retrieving data from the master files and creating new subfiles from the data and also printing data. The examinee files created at each testing station and stored in the master files serve as input to the collect component of the assessment subsystem.

The conventional testing subsystem consist of four components: build, print test, score, and pen plotting. The build component provides the capability for building conventional tests. Given the name of the item bank and the number of items, the routine will automatically create a test specification for a simple conventional test. The test is constructed by selecting items at random from the specified item bank. The test file can be reorganized and edited to meet the test constructors needs. The resultant test can be administered by the computer via the examination subsystem or printed. The latter is accomplished via the print test component. The item bank and test specification are identified and the type of printer, dot matrix or laser specified. In addition, the layout of the items on the page can be defined. Once the specification process is completed, the test is printed on the appropriate printer. The score component is designed to produce ability estimates for the examinees when the input data was obtained from a pencil and paper administration of the test. Parameter estimates for the items are obtained from other analyses and are simply read in from a file. The routine yields the number of items attempted, answered correctly, a corrected for guessing formula score, a Bayes modal estimate and a maximum likelihood estimate for each examinee. The pen plotting routine provides the capability for printing items and their graphics in color using a Hewlett-Packard pen plotter.

MICROCAT is a comprehensive test construction, administration, and analysis system. The overall design is oriented toward computerized administration of a test to one student at a time. As a result, the test administration aspects would appear to be best suited to other than classroom testing. However, one component does support the usual testing procedures. From a test constructors point of view, the outstanding feature of MICROCAT is the ability to create, store, edit, and administer items containing both graphics and text. It is also the only comprehensive testing system to implement IRT based procedures. The drawback to MICROCAT is its cost. The full system sells for $2,730 and a minimal system (Development and Conventional Testing) system costs $1,250 (circa 1987). This is a bit expensive for an individual to purchase. However, given the level of capabilities provided, the underlying developmental costs, and the limited market, the price is reasonable and could be afforded by a testing organization.

While the PETA and MICROCAT represent the current state of the Art (circa 1987) in testing systems, they are what may be called first-generation systems. In both cases, system integration has been accomplished through the development of custom computer programming and customized program interfaces. In the past few years, there has been a major change in the way that microcomputer manufacturers design their computers, the associated software and in their marketing approach. This change has been driven primarily by the needs of the business community, in which the bulk of potential customers are not technologically sophisticated, a characteristic shared by the educational community. The second generation of microcomputers is based upon very powerful computer chips and they have internal memories in the several megabyte range. Microcomputers of this type were designed to employ integrated sets of computer programs aimed at a particular application. For example, the APPLE MACINTOSH computer can be purchased with an integrated package consisting of a word processor, a graphics package, a data base management program, and a set of protocols for communicating with mainframe and other computers. The manner in which these capabilities are accessed and controlled represents a significant change in the computer-user interface. The video screen contains a number of graphical symbols, called *icons*, that represent the functions to be performed. A small device placed upon one's desk is used to control the position of a cursor on the screen. As this device, called a *mouse*, is moved over the desktop, the cursor also moves. When the cursor is over a desired icon, one presses a button on the mouse which activates the function. In some cases, a menu is "pulled down" and a function selected from the menu via the mouse. In other cases, the icon selection results in a specific function being implemented. The computer keyboard is then used to enter information into the computer, such as the text of a letter. The mouse can also be used to create graphics by selecting the capabilities of the graphics component and then drawing the graphs, diagrams, and figures, which can then be stored. The most important feature of this type of system is the ability to move information from one function of the system to another, under the control of the mouse. For example, a graph created with the business graphics capability can be inserted into the text of a letter by selecting the appropriate icons. In addition, these second-generation microcomputer systems can make displays associated with multiple tasks appear on the video display simultaneously. For example, the text of a letter could appear on the screen, and a diagram being considered for inclusion in the letter could also appear. The displays are known as *windows*, and the technique is called *using windows*.

The application of this second generation hardware and software to the testing process could result in some very powerful, yet easy-to-use systems. For example, the word-processing capability could be used to create items; the graphics routines, to create diagrams and figures for items; and the file-management capability, to implement the item bank. The mouse could be used to insert a figure in a test item before it is printed. The windowing feature could be used to simultaneously display the predicted test-score statistics and an item being considered for inclusion in a test. If the item is accepted, the predicted test-score statistics could be modified to reflect the inclusion of the item. Thus, the test constructor could dynamically observe the effects of editing a test under construction. The dash of cold water in all of this is that software implementing these second-generation features was not designed to be readily accessible to the ordinary user of the microcomputer. The manufacturers view these second-generation microcomputers as "applications machines" rather than general-use computers. Although some manufacturers, APPLE in particular, provide access to second-generation features, the sophistication and complexity of this software essentially limits such access to professional software developers. It should be noted that the MICROCAT program has many of the features of a second-generation system such as the use of a mouse and the ability to create graphics via primitives and include them within the item, and manage testing over a network of microcomputers. None-the-less it is a between generations system. The graphics are limited by the use of a medium resolution screen, the graphics editor has a small repertoire of primitives and it does not use pull down menus or the windows technique or display of items and data. Future versions of MICROCAT will provide for capturing high resolution screens created via second generation graphics editors and store the screen pixels in a disk file. Once captured on disk, the graphics can be used as part of an item and displayed via MICROCAT software on the high resolution screen. A true second-generation system would employ the integrated software provided by the computer system to achieve most of the functional integration needed in the item writing process. The data base management package of the computer system would be used for item banking and other information storage purposes. However, even such second generation systems would need to have customized software to administer and score the tests as well as perform the analyses unique to testing. To develop a comprehensive, integrated testing system similar to PETA or MICROCAT on a second generation microcomputer using system related software is technically feasible but economically questionable. As Hiscox (1984) points out, the potential market for such a system is on the order of a few thousand, as compared with millions for an integrated set of business applications, and the developmental costs are not likely to be recouped.

Some Issues

The majority of the microcomputer-based testing systems available as of 1988 had been designed for use by classroom teachers at the elementary and secondary school level. This probably reflects the level of availability of microcomputers to teachers and the desire to find a useful computer application. Without a desktop scanner, the entry of students' item responses via the keyboard is a slow, tedious process, likely to be done only for very small tests and small groups. Once such data are entered into the computer, the rest of the capabilities are readily available and clearly worth the teacher's time to employ. Thus, the key to such testing systems is the optical desktop scanner. With the exception of some obsolete mechanical mark-sense card readers, desktop scanners are expensive relative to the cost of the microcomputer. As a result, a school is not likely to place one in every teacher's classroom. However, one scanner per school is feasible, as testing is rarely a high-frequency activity. Either the scanner can be physically shared or one of the microcomputers in the school can be configured as a test processor. The availability of a truly low-cost desktop scanner would greatly facilitate the wide usage of classroom-level testing systems. It would not seem that a sheet-at-a-time optical scanner would be any more difficult to produce than a dot matrix printer. Again, the limited market probably works against the development of such a device and its achieving the economy of scale reached by printers. However, such scanners are widely used in commercial and industrial applications for data collection, proving that the market is larger than that of test-scoring alone.

Another feature of many existing testing systems is that they tend to be designed for the nonmeasurement specialist. As a result, they do not readily support the test-development process as performed by a person trained in measurement. The underlying rationale for this is probably that classroom teachers are rarely well versed in measurement theory. However, there are many testing environments at the college level and within school districts in which the flexibility and ease of use of a microcomputer-based system would be attractive to those well versed in measurement theory. MICROCAT is an excellent system for such persons. Most of the testing strategies currently in vogue, such as conventional testing, mastery testing as well as stradaptive and Bayesian adaptive testing are supported. It also provides analysis of test results based upon both classical and item response theory.

A characteristic of the microcomputer marketplace is the high rate of change in the available hardware. In the span of a few years, the capability of the microcomputer has increased dramatically. We are rapidly approaching the point where we can have the power of a large-scale computer on our desks. Such rapid change also brings with it a certain amount of instability, particularly in the area of software. To maximize the capability of a given software package, such as those for testing, advantage is often taken of features unique to a given computer. Transferring such software to another, often more capable, microcomputer can be an expensive proposition. As a result, there is both a tendency to retain older systems for a longer period and a reluctance to invest the resources needed to implement the testing of software on newer equipment. Again, the small market tends to inhibit the economic incentive to continually develop testing systems for new microcomputers.

The variety of item-banking and test-construction software also exposes another problem area. There is a clear and laudable trend for textbook publishers to provide prepared item banks on floppy disks to accompany their texts and curricula. However, these item banks can be used only with the test-construction software offered by their publishers. Typically, the layout of the records and their contents are unique to a specific software package and are often dependent upon a given computer. As a result, the item bank created through the use of one publisher's system cannot be used by another. From a competitive point of view, they probably do not want to have their copyrighted item banks used by other test-construction systems. However, there is a large community of persons who would like to be able to share locally developed item banks across various testing systems. This is particularly true at the college level (see Lippey, 1974). To do this, standards would need to be established for the exchange of items among item-banking systems implemented on a variety of microcomputers. Establishing any type of standard is a time-consuming task but the long-term advantages are worth the effort. It would seem to be reasonable for the National Council on Measurement in Education to assume responsibility for establishing standards in this area.

Whenever item banks are maintained, security becomes a concern. The storage of items on floppy disks opens the possibility of the item bank's being readily copied. Although computer programs can be protected against unauthorized copying, protecting data files is much more difficult. Encrypting schemes are available (see Demming & Demming, 1979), but whether they are worth the time and trouble in most testing situations is questionable. Ease of access of the teacher or test constructor and flexibility of use probably outweigh any advantages gained by encrypting the items. In most local testing situations, item-bank security can be maintained by the physical control of the floppy disks themselves and the use of passwords. Internal safeguards can be put into any software accessed by students, such as computer administered tests, so as to preclude use of the computer to copy the items.

Interpretive Scoring of Tests

There are many situations in which the ultimate users of test results are not fully conversant with a particular test and all the nuances of its proper interpretation. This is particularly true of complex clinical instruments such as the MMPI. As a result, one of the early applications of computers was the generation of verbal or narrative interpretive reports of test results. These early clinical systems provided a list of sentences that matched various scores and patterns of scores on the MMPI. The Mayo Clinic system (Rome, 1962) was intended to provide physicians with a quick psychological profile of a patient. Since that time, the level of sophistication of interpretive reports has increased considerably (see Herman & Samuels, 1985). Computer-generated reports, such as that shown in Figure 10.5, are virtually indistinguishable from the interpretation of test results prepared by a psychologist or a psychiatrist. This approach has also been employed to report the results of achievement tests. A dissertation by Mathews (1971) investigated the utility of computer generation of interpretive reports for achievement test results. This work appears to be one of the earliest examples of the use of such reports.

The algorithms used in the computer programs that produce interpretive test reports range from simple to very complex. The simplest procedure is one in which a given score or range of scores is linked to a set of short equivalent paragraphs interpreting the score in norm-referenced, criterion-referenced, or clinical terms and a paragraph is selected at random from the set of equivalent paragraphs. The computer then prints the report, accompanied by the examinee's name and other information relevant to the testing context. Such an approach is representative of reports generated for achievement tests and diagnostic instruments having a simple interpretation of subscale scores. In the case of instruments having a more complex score interpretation, a set of decision rules must be programmed. These can involve extensive networks of if-then decision rules that lead to a given interpretive statement from a particular pattern of subscale scores. These decision networks must be established by a skilled interpreter of the particular test. Once implemented in the form of a computer program, the computer will always produce the same result, given the same data. An interesting development in this area was a microcomputer-based system that could administer a number of different psychological inventories to a subject via the computer, score the inventory, and print an interpretative test report for each inventory. This hardware and software system was designed for use in settings where considerable human assessment work is performed, such as in industrial employment screening, counseling centers, psychological clinics, and medical settings. However, as of 1987, the company selling it was no longer in business.

A very disturbing development has been the sale of self-assessment software to the general public (Neimark, 1984). Such software implements the computer administration of a psychological assessment instrument to the user of the computer. The results are then reported in interpretive form by the computer. The intent is that a person evaluate his or her own psychological status. The article by Neimark appropriately referred to these programs as "psych-out" software. Due to copyright protection, few if any of the well-established and widely used instruments can be employed in this manner. However, this results in new and inadequately developed instruments being used. In addition, there is no interaction between the examinee and a professional to properly explain the results; consequently, the potential for harm clearly exists.

One of the weaknesses of interpretive test reports is that the reader must often read too much material to obtain the essential information on the test results. In addition, the use of algorithms and decision trees leads to the generation of the same verbal results for the same data. Unless some scheme, like random selection of equivalent prose, is used, the reports take on mechanistic flavor when cross-compared. It then becomes rather boring to read several reports, say, for a class, at one sitting.

Perhaps the area of greatest concern with respect to computer-generated interpretive reports is the linkage between the test scores and the prose. At the present, test-scoring companies generally do not make the linkage algorithms and decision networks available to the consumer of test results. In some cases, the linkage is obvious, and there is no problem. However, the more complex the interpretive process, the more at risk is the test consumer. With no knowledge of the underlying procedures, the interpretation provided must be taken on faith. Clinical experience with a large number of interpretive test reports accompanied by the actual test scores would enable the user to develop a level of confidence in any given company's procedures for a specific test. However, such confidence would have to be developed for each test.

The need for standards for computer generated interpretive test reports has been recognized. Standard 5.11 (APA, 1985) states: "Organizations offering automated test interpretation should make available information on the rationale of the test and a summary of the evidence supporting the interpretation given. This information should include the validity of the cut scores or configural rules used and a description of the samples from which they were derived." While this is a much needed standard, there is a conflict between it and the proprietary interests of the testing company. Such a company may have invested considerable resources in developing the interpretive algorithms. A company with a well-recognized procedure that engenders considerable acceptance and confidence in their reports has a competitive advantage. The company would be reluctant to put its procedures in the public domain. This issue was recognized by the standards committee, and in the comments on standard 5.11 it stated: "When proprietary interests result in withholding of such algorithms, arrangements might be made for an external review of these algorithms under professional auspices." If computer-generated interpretive test reports become widespread, such professional reviews will play an important role in maintaining the quality of such reports. Whether such reviews can be implemented remains in the hands of the testing companies.

Artificial Intelligence and Testing

In the 1930s and 1940s extensive use was made of diagnostic tests in subject matter areas, but since World War II such diagnostic tests have been somewhat out of vogue. However, recent work in the area of artificial intelligence (AI) and intelligent tutoring systems (Wegner, 1987), in particular, has renewed interest in subject matter diagnostic procedures. This has come about because a major function in computer-based intelligent tutoring systems is one of determining why a student is not learning. As a result, a considerable portion of the tutoring system must be devoted to diagnostic procedures. This in turn has led to research in the area of using artificial intelligence techniques to perform educational diagnosis. The pioneering work in this regard was due to Brown and Burton (1978) in the area of diagnosing errors in subtraction. They broke down the process of doing subtraction into a detailed network of procedures. Then a very large number of incorrect variants or applications of these procedures, called bugs, were

THIS GUIDANCE REPORT ASSUMES THAT THE MAPI ANSWER FORM WAS COMPLETED
BY A YOUNG PERSON AT THE LATER JUNIOR HIGH SCHOOL, SENIOR HIGH SCHOOL OR BEGIN-
NING COLLEGE LEVEL. IT SHOULD BE NOTED THAT THIS REPORT HAS BEEN WRITTEN WITHIN
THE FRAMEWORK OF SCHOOL COUNSELING OR GUIDANCE SERVICES. IT IS DESIGNED AS AN
AID IN IDENTIFYING, UNDERSTANDING AND PREDICTING STYLES OF SELF-EXPRESSION AND
SCHOLASTIC BEHAVIOR CHARACTERISTIC OF ADOLESCENTS, AS WELL AS PROBLEM AREAS THAT
TYPIFY THIS AGE GROUP. THE SPECIFIC DESCRIPTIONS THAT COMPRISE THIS INDIVIDUAL
REPORT DERIVE FROM BOTH RESEARCH AND THEORY. AS SUCH, THEY ARE PROBABILITY
INFERENCES RATHER THAN DEFINITIVE STATEMENTS, AND SHOULD BE EVALUATED WITHIN THE
CONTEXT OF THE DEVELOPMENTAL, SOCIAL AND ACADEMIC BACKGROUND OF THE STUDENT.
MOREOVER, THESE INFERENCES SHOULD BE REEVALUATED PERIODICALLY IN LIGHT OF THE
PATTERN OF ATTITUDE CHANGE AND EMOTIONAL GROWTH THAT TYPIFIES THE ADOLESCENT
PERIOD. THE FACT THAT THE REPORT IS OF A PERSONAL NATURE REQUIRES THAT IT BE
HANDLED WITH THE HIGHEST LEVEL OF DISCRETION AND CONFIDENTIALITY THAT CAN BE
GIVEN ASPECTS OF THE COUNSELING RELATIONSHIP.

      THIS YOUNGSTER SHOWED NO UNUSUAL CHARACTEROLOGICAL OR TEST-TAKING
ATTITUDES THAT MAY HAVE DISTORTED THE MAPI RESULTS.

                         PERSONALITY PATTERNS

      THE FOLLOWING PERTAINS TO THE MORE ENDURING AND PERVASIVE TRAITS THAT
CHARACTERIZE HOW THIS YOUNGSTER IS SEEN BY AND RELATES TO OTHERS. RATHER THAN
FOCUS ON SPECIFIC AREAS OF CONCERN, TO BE DISCUSSED IN LATER PARAGRAPHS, THIS
SECTION CONCENTRATES ON THE BROAD AND HABITUAL WAYS OF BEHAVING AND FEELING.

      THIS YOUNG WOMAN IS QUITE DIRECT AND OUTSPOKEN, EXPRESSING HER FEELINGS
AND THOUGHTS WITH MINIMAL RESTRAINT OR REFLECTION. STRUGGLING BETWEEN HER
DEPENDENCY NEEDS AND HER DESIRE TO REBEL AND ASSERT HERSELF, SHE IS LIKELY
TO EXHIBIT A WIDE RANGE OF DIFFERENT MOODS AND EMOTIONS. NOT DISPOSED TO
TOLERATE FRUSTRATIONS EASILY, NOR INCLINED TO INHIBIT HER IMPULSES, SHE IS
LIKELY TO BE RESTLESS AND CONTRARY, READILY OFFENDED BY THE MILDEST OF
RESTRICTIONS AND CRITICISM. HENCE, SHE MAY FEEL MISUNDERSTOOD AND UNAPPRECI-
ATED, BECOME MOODY AND WITHDRAWN, OR CONTENTIOUS AND DIFFICULT. VACILLATING
BETWEEN WANTING RESPECT AND ATTENTION, AND REJECTING OVERTURES OF KINDNESS
AND CONSIDERATION, SHE MAY GET INTO FREQUENT WRANGLES WITH OTHERS.
      HER RELATIONSHIPS WITH PEERS ARE LIKELY TO BE VARIABLE AND ERRATIC, SOME
GOING WELL FOR A WHILE, BUT MOST BECOMING PROBLEMATIC AND SHORT-LIVED. SHE
IS NOT LIKELY TO COMFORTABLY ASSUME A LEADERSHIP ROLE, NOR IS SHE SELECTED
FOR SUCH PURPOSES BY OTHERS. EXTRACURRICULAR ACTIVITIES ARE ALSO LIKELY TO
BE MINIMAL. HER CLASSROOM BEHAVIOR AND ACTIVITIES MAY BE TROUBLESOME,
ESPECIALLY IF SHE IS NOT A GOOD ACADEMIC STUDENT. ACTING OUT IS A DISTINCT
POSSIBILITY, THOUGH NOT A HIGH PROBABILITY. SHOULD HER BEHAVIOR BRING HER INTO
A COUNSELING OR GUIDANCE SITUATION, SHE IS NOT LIKELY TO BE ESPECIALLY COOPER-
ATIVE OR COMFORTABLE EXPLORING HER MORE TROUBLESOME ACTIONS.

                         EXPRESSED CONCERNS

      THE SCALES COMPRISING THIS SECTION PERTAIN TO THE PERSONAL PERCEPTION
OF THIS YOUNGSTER CONCERNING SEVERAL ISSUES OF PSYCHOLOGICAL DEVELOPMENT,
ACTUALIZATION AND CONCERN. BECAUSE EXPERIENCES DURING THIS AGE PERIOD
ARE NOTABLY SUBJECTIVE, IT IS IMPORTANT TO RECORD HOW THIS TEENAGER SEES
EVENTS AND REPORTS FEELINGS, AND NOT ONLY HOW OTHERS MAY OBJECTIVELY
REPORT THEM TO BE. FOR COMPARATIVE PURPOSES, THESE SELF-ATTITUDES REGARDING
A WIDE RANGE OF PERSONAL, SOCIAL, FAMILIAL AND SCHOLASTIC MATTERS ARE
CONTRASTED WITH THOSE EXPRESSED BY A BROAD CROSS-SECTION OF TEENAGERS
OF THE SAME SEX AND AGE.

FIGURE 10.5 Sample of computer-generated report. Page 2 of the Millon Adolescent Personality Inventory. Reprinted by permission.

identified in actual student solutions of subtraction problem. Then a computer program, called BUGGY, was written that would analyze student responses to a pencil and paper subtraction test. The computer program would then identify the underlying procedural errors made by the student and report them. The diagnoses are made to a much greater psychological depth than those typically reported for a diagnostic achievement test as they deal with processes rather than observed behavior. Due to the complexity of these diagnostic procedures, they can only be implemented via computer software. While this work has been done within the context of computer-based instruction, it has many implications for testing (see Wenger, 1987, for other exemplars). However, this approach to diagnosing test results can be quite expensive to conceptualize and implement. It should be noted that the application of artificial intelligence to diagnosis is but one manifestation of the impact cognitive science is having upon the field of testing. The reader is referred to Ronning, Glover, and Conoly (1987) for a general overview of this impact.

A major thrust in the area of computer science known as artificial intelligence is that of "knowledge based expert systems" (see Hayes-Roth, Waterman, & Lenat, 1983). Under this approach, both the knowledge base and the problem solving heuristics of an expert in a given area are implemented in computer software. The advantage of such systems is that they allow one to incorporate the "clinical hunches," odd bits of information and recognition of unusual data patterns into the interpretation process. Such systems have been developed for medical diagnosis, geophysics, and several other areas where the interpretation of raw data must be done within the context of the interpreter's own experience. Because of the kinds of problems to which expert systems are applied, they place heavy reliance upon heuristic approaches rather than algorithms. It would appear that the development of interpretive test reporting is already based to some extent upon this approach and will benefit from advances in the field of artificial intelligence. It is also possible to employ the expert system approach in the construction of achievement and/or ability tests. The procedures used by a skilled test constructor could be implemented in the form of a computer program. However, such a program of necessity involves a specific item pool and perhaps an arbitrary test specification. Due to the large investment in developing such a system, it would be feasible only for a widely used measure. A word of caution is in order. It is a difficult, time-consuming task to translate what an expert does into a computer program. In addition, the computer programs implementing these "expert systems" can be very large and costly to develop.

Item Response Theory and Test Processing

The decade of the 1980s saw the basis of measurement practice begin to make the transition from classical test theory to item response theory (IRT). The reader is referred to chapter 4 for a discussion of IRT. The present section examines the overall testing process from an item response theory point of view, with emphasis upon the role of the computer.

Item writing under IRT is basically the same as it is under classical test theory. Thus, the same word-processing style of software would be used to create and edit items. In most applications of IRT it is assumed that a single underlying variable, generically denoted ability, is being measured. Because of the sensitivity of IRT test results to items not measuring the ability, the item writer needs to pay considerable attention to the conceptual linkage between the items and the ability being measured. It is important to make sure that the items are consistent with the construct of interest. In practice, this is accomplished primarily through the use of well-defined test and item specifications.

There are major differences between the two theories in the area of item banking. The assumption of a single underlying variable of IRT requires that all items in the same item pool measure the same variable. In addition, it is necessary that the parameters of all the items in the item pool be measured in the same metric. When this holds, the items in the item pool are what is known as *precalibrated*. To accomplish this, it is necessary to use a given set of items administered to a specific group of examinees as the basal test calibration. Such a test would be administered to the group, and the item responses would be analyzed by using one of the IRT computer programs such as LOGIST (Wingersky, Barton, & Lord, 1982) or BILOG, (Mislevy & Bock, 1984). The metric yielded by this analysis becomes the basal metric. As new items are created, they are included in tests that also contain linkage items taken from the basal test. This new test is administered to another group drawn from the same population as was the basal group of examinees. Again, the item responses are analyzed via an IRT computer program. This analysis yields item-parameter values that are in a metric unique to this combination of test and examinees. The task then is to express the item-parameters of the new items in the metric of the item-pool. This is accomplished by using the obtained values of the item parameters and the item-pool values of the linkage items to equate the metric of the new items to that of the item pool (see Baker, 1984; Lord, 1980; Loyd & Hoover, 1980; Marco, 1977; Stocking & Lord, 1984; Wright & Stone, 1979, for the technical details of this equating process). It is also important that the items in the test follow the item-characteristic curve model being used. Thus, the goodness-of-fit of the model to the item response data is used to eliminate nonconforming items before they become included in the item pool (see Yen, 1984, for a discussion of fit indexes). This item writing, testing, editing, and equating process can be carried on until the item pool is of the desired size. At this point, the item parameters of all the items in the pool are in the same metric (see Haksar, 1983, for an example of developing an item pool under IRT). Given a precalibrated item pool, it is possible to construct many different tests that measure the underlying variable. The general test-construction procedures would be similar to those already described.

The use of a precalibrated item pool also allows the test constructor to obtain considerable information on how a constructed test might perform when administered. Under IRT, the test constructor can specify a target information function for a test. Theunissen (1985) has developed procedures based upon linear programming for the selection of items from the item pool such that the test information curve is matched or exceeded. Yen (1983) reported the prior use of this approach in the construction of actual tests. Once the items have been automatically selected, the test characteristic curve can also be computed and both curves displayed on the VDT screen or printed.

Inspection of these two curves provides the test constructor with an excellent picture of how the test is likely to behave when administered to a group of interest. If these two curves do not satisfy the test constructor, the test construction system can be used to replace items with other items from the precalibrated item pool, until the desired characteristics can be obtained. Thus, test construction under item response theory gives the test constructor considerable control over the characteristics of the resultant test. This control is obtained at the expense of the equating procedures necessary to build and maintain a precalibrated item pool.

Test scoring and analysis under IRT are generally based upon the maximum-likelihood procedures devised by Birnbaum (1968). These procedures simultaneously estimate the parameters of the items in the test and the ability parameters of the examinees. The paradigm is a two-stage iterative procedure involving considerable computing. As a result, the major computer programs for performing IRT tests analysis have run on large-scale computers where advantage can be taken of the computational speed and accuracy of such systems. Several of these programs should be mentioned. The LOGIST program (Wingersky et al., 1982) was developed by Fredrick M. Lord and his coworkers at the Educational Testing Service. It can analyze test results under a one-, two-, or three-parameter item-characteristics curve model, with emphasis upon the three-parameter model. The LOGIST program, initially developed in 1972, was designed primarily as a research vehicle and, as a result, it is somewhat difficult to learn to use. Also, the computer prints considerable information that is of interest from a mathematical point of view but of limited interest to a practitioner. The LOGIST program is widely used by measurement specialists involved in test development and psychometric research.

The BICAL computer program (Wright, Mead, & Bell, 1980) was developed by Dr. Benjamin D. Wright and his students, with the first version appearing in 1969. This program uses the Birnbaum paradigm to analyze tests under the Rasch (one parameter) logistic model. The program was designed for the practitioner and is relatively easy to use. In addition, the program is well documented from the point of view of both underlying theory and its use for tests analysis (see Wright & Stone, 1979). For many years, Professor Wright has conducted AERA training sessions on the use of BICAL. As a result, many practitioners are familiar with the program, and it is widely used by them.

The BILOG program is a recent development due to Mislevy and Bock (1984). This program also estimates item and ability parameters, but it does not employ the Birnbaum paradigm. BILOG is based upon marginal maximum likelihood estimation and uses a form of the EM algorithm (see Bock & Atkin, 1981; Dempster, Laird, & Rubin, 1977). The item parameters and ability parameters are estimated in separate stages and there is no alternating between the stages as in the LOGIST or BICAL programs. This program can use the one-, two-, and three-parameter item-characteristic curve model. In addition, the ability parameters can be estimated using Bayesian estimation. In the LOGIST program, estimation of the so

called guessing parameter of the three parameter model is fraught with many difficulties. Considerable code within LOGIST is devoted to overcoming mathematical difficulties arising from the estimation of the guessing parameter. Also, to obtain acceptable item-parameter estimates, relatively large groups of examinees must be used (see Hulin, Lissak, & Drasgow, 1982; Wainer & Thissen, 1982). Because of the complexity of the maximum-likelihood estimation procedures employed and the difficulties inherent in the three-parameter model, analysis of long tests given to large groups can be rather expensive.

Due to its use of the one-parameter model for the item-characteristic curve, the computational demands of the BICAL program are less than that of LOGIST, and it is less expensive to use. The BICAL program can also be used with tests having only a few items and with small groups of examinees yet yield reasonable parameter estimates (Lord, 1979). Because the BILOG program is relatively new (circa 1984), comparative studies of the results produced by it with other IRT computer programs are limited. The results due to Yen (1987), show that the parameter estimates obtained are comparable to those yielded by LOGIST.

All three of the IRT programs described were implemented on large-scale computers. The BICAL program has been implemented as the MICROSCALE program (Mediax, 1984), on the IBM PC microcomputer. This program implements the item and ability estimation procedures under the Rasch model for both dichotomously scored items and items scored on an ordered scale. The program is unusual in that it uses a spreadsheet program to input the examinees' item responses and to edit the data. Extensive use is made of the graphical capabilities of the computer to present the results. An interesting feature is the use of graphics to keep the user informed during the iterative parameter-estimation procedure. At this stage, the computer is involved in extensive computations and there is little for the user to do but wait. The graphics give the user something to watch. BILOG has also been implemented on the IBM-PC microcomputer. The MICROSCALE and the BILOG programs are indicative of the future direction of the development of IRT software. As microcomputers become more capable from a computational point of view, especially those that incorporate a separate arithmetic coprocessor chip, they will be able to perform more of the complex estimation procedures of IRT for larger data sets in less time. In addition, approximations to existing techniques and new estimation approaches might be developed that are not as computationally intensive as the existing procedures. These will increase the potential of the microcomputer as a vehicle for performing test analyses under IRT.

Summary

The salient feature of the use of computer technology in testing that has been reported in this chapter is the reorientation due to the microcomputer. Prior to 1980, the major use of technology was in support of large-scale testing programs. The primary emphasis was upon scanning, scoring, and reporting. Software was available on large-scale computers for item banking and test construction but rarely for item writing. This orientation was reflected in the corresponding chapter in the second edition of *Educational Measurement.*

The microcomputer has had a number of effects upon the application of technology to testing. It has made such technology, in the form of microcomputers and desktop scanners, available at the classroom level at a cost that is within reach of most levels of the educational system. It has also allowed the procedures associated with the overall testing process to be integrated into a single hardware and software package, such as MICROCAT. As a result, one can use a single system to perform all the tasks from item writing to reporting of test results. Although the capabilities of microcomputers, as of 1988, place some restrictions upon the scope of each of the processes, these restrictions will rapidly disappear as more capable computers become readily available. In particular, the second generation of microcomputers offers some interesting prospects in the area of computer-user interaction. The integration of the overall testing process should also facilitate improvement in the quality of tests. Such systems provide the test constructor with a wide range of information and considerable flexibility in employing system capabilities. One would hope that these will enable the user to write better items, construct more powerful tests, and use the results more effectively. A rather unheralded vehicle for the improvement of classroom testing is the development of item pools by textbook publishers, which are coordinated with the curriculum. If the item pools contain well-written high-quality items, they can improve testing practice in two ways. *First,* teachers can create good tests from the item pools with test-construction software. *Second,* the items can serve as a model for items constructed locally. The widespread availability of microcomputers at the classroom level makes item pools produced by publishers potentially significant factor's in educational measurement.

As microcomputers become more capable, possibilities exist for more sophisticated diagnostic analysis of item responses and interpretive reporting of test results. However, these two areas depend more upon the state of the art in education, psychology and artificial intelligence than they do upon technology. But improved technology will make it easier to implement more sophisticated techniques. Perhaps the most important contribution of the microcomputer has been to increase the awareness and participation of a wider community of educators in the testing process. Because of this the 1990s should see significant advances in the state of the art of testing.

REFERENCES

American Psychology Association. (1985). *Standards for educational and psychological testing.* American Educational Research Association, National Council on Measurement in Education. Washington, DC.

Baker, F. B. (1971). Automation of test scoring, reporting, and analysis. In R. L. Thorndike (Ed.), *Educational Measurement.* Washington, DC: American Council on Education.

Baker, F. B. (1972). A conversational item banking and test construction system. *Proceedings of the Fall Joint Computer Conference, 41,* 61–667.

Baker, F. B. (1974). The roles of statistics. In G. Lippey (Ed.), *Computer-Assisted Test Construction Systems.* Englewood Cliffs, NJ: Educational Technology Publications.

Baker, F. B. (1978). *Computer-Managed Instruction: Theory and Practice.* Englewood Cliffs, NJ: Educational Technology Publications.

Baker, F. B. (1984). Ability metric transformations involved in vertical equating under item response theory. *Applied Psychological Measurement, 8,* 261–271.

Birnbaum, A. (1968). Some latent trait models and their use in inferring an examinee's ability. In F. M. Lord & M. R. Novick, *Statistical theories of mental test scores (pp. 397–472).* Reading, MA: Addison-Wesley.

Bock, R. D., & Atkin, M. (1981). Marginal maximum likelihood estimation of item parameters: application of an EM algorithm. *Psychometrika, 46,* 443–469.

Brown, J., & Burton R. R. (1978). Diagnostic models for procedural bugs in mathematical skills. *Cognition Science, 2,* 155–191.

Deck, D., & Estes, G. (1984, April). *Microcomputer software support for item banking.* Paper presented at the annual meeting of the American Educational Research Association, New Orleans.

Demming, D. E., & Demming P. J. (1979). Data Security. *Computing Surveys, 1979, 11,* 227–249.

Dempster, A. P., Laird, N. M., & Rubin, D. B. (1977). Maximum likelihood from incomplete data via the EM algorithm. *Journal of the Royal Statistical Society, Series B, 39,* 1–38.

Haksar, L. (1983). Design and usage of an item bank. *Programmed Learning and Educational Technology, 20,* 253–262.

Hays-Roth, R., Waterman, D. A., & Lenat, D. B. (1983). *Building Expert Systems.* Reading, MA: Addison Wesley.

Herman, K., & Samuels, R. (1985). *Computers: an extension of the clinicians's mind-a source book.* Norwood, NJ: ABLEX.

Hiscox, M. D. (1984). A planning guide for microcomputers in educational measurement. *Educational Measurement: Issues and Practice, 3,* 28–34.

Hsu, T., & Nitko, A. J. (1983). Microcomputer testing software teachers can use. *Educational Measurement: Issues and Practice, 2,* 15–31.

Hulin, C. L., Lissak, R. I., & Drasgow, F. (1982). Recovery of two and three parameter logistic item characteristic curves: a Monte Carlo study. *Applied Psychological Measurement, 16,* 249–260.

Lippey, G., (Ed). (1974). *Computer-Assisted Test Construction.* Englewood Cliffs, NJ: Educational Technology Publications.

Lord, F. M. (1979). *Small numbers of items and Rasch model.* Paper presented at the biennial conference on adaptive testing. Minneapolis.

Lord, F. M. (1980). *Application of Item Response Theory to Practical Testing Problems.* Hillsdale, NJ: Lawrence Erlbaum.

Loyd, B. H., & Hoover, H. D. Vertical equating using the Rasch *model. Journal of Educational Measurement, 17,* 179–193.

Marco, G. L. Item characteristic curve solutions to three intractable testing problems. *Journal of Educational Measurement, 14,* 129–160.

Mathews, W. (1971). *The design, development and evaluation of computer-generated verbal testing reports for standardized achievement tests.* Unpublished doctoral dissertation, University of Wisconsin, Madison.

Millman, J., & Arter, J. A. (1984). Issues in item banking. *Journal of Educational Measurement, 21,* 315–330.

Mislevy, R. J., & Bock, R. D. (1984). *BILOG maximum likelihood item analysis and test scoring: Logistic model.* Chicago: International Educational Services.

Niemark, J. (1984). Psycho-Out Software. *Datamation, 30,* 32–40.

Nitko, A. J., & Hsu, T. (1984a). A comprehensive microcomputer system for classroom testing. *Journal of Educational Measurement, 21,* 377–390.

Nitko, A. J., & Hsu, T. (1984b). *Pitt Educational Testing Aids: Users Manual.* Pittsburgh: University of Pittsburgh, School of Education.

Pelczarski, M., Lubar, D., & Jochumson, C. (1982). *The Graphics Magician.* Geneve, IL: Penguin Software.

Rome, H. P. (1962). Automatic techniques in personality assessment. *Journal of the American Medical Association, 182,* 1069–1072.

Ronning, R. R., Glover, J. A., & Conoley, J. C. (1987). *The influence of Cognitive Psychology on Psychological testing.* Hillsdale, NJ: Lawrence Erlbaum.

Stocking, M. L., & Lord, F. M. (1983). Developing a common metric

in item response theory. *Applied Psychological Measurement, 7,*
201–220.

Theunissen, T. J. J. M. (1985). Binary programing and test design.
Psychometrika, 50, 411–420.

Thorndike, R. L. (1971). *Educational Measurement.* (pp. 768). Washington, D.C.: The American Council on Education.

Wainer, H., & Thissen, D. (1982). Some standard errors in item response theory. *Psychometrika, 47,* 397–412.

Wenger, E. (1987). *Artificial Intelligence and Tutoring Systems.* (pp. 486) Los Altos: Kaufmann.

Wingersky, M. S., Barton, M. A., & Lord, F. M. (1982). *Logist Users Guide: LOGIST 5, Version 1.* Princeton: Educational Testing Service.

Wright, B. D., & Bell, S. R. Item banks: What, why, how. *Journal of Educational Measurement, 21,* 331–345.

Wright, B. D., Mead, R. J., & Bell, S. R. (1980). *BICAL: calibrating items with the Rasch model.* Research Memorandum 23C. Chicago: University of Chicago, Department of Education.

Yen, W. (1987). A comparison of the efficiency and accuracy of BILOG and LOGIST. *Psychometrika, 52,* 275–292.

Yen, W. (1983). Use of a three-parameter model in the development of a standardized test. In R. K. Hambleton, (Ed.), *Applications of Item Response Theory.* Vancouver: Educational Research Institute of British Columbia.

Yen, W. (1984). Effects of local item dependence on the fit and equating performance of the three parameter logistic model. *Applied Psychological Measurement, 8,* 125–145.

COMPUTER SOFTWARE REFERENCES

MICROCAT
Assessment Systems Corporation
2233 University Avenue, Suite 440
St. Paul, MN 55114

Microcomputer Scoring System TESCOR, INC.
401 Carlisle Drive
Herndon, VA 22020

Microcomputer Test Administration System. Science Research Associates
155 North Wacker Drive
Chicago, IL 60606

MICROSCALE Mediax Interactive Technologies, Inc.
21 Charles Street
Westport, CT 06880-5899

THE TEST BANK Advanced Technology Applications
3019 Governor Drive
San Diego, CA 92122

PETA
Institute for Practice and
Research in Education, School of Education
University at Pittsburgh
SR02 Forbes Quadrangle
Pittsburgh, PA 15260

PRISM The Psychological Corporation
757 Third Avenue
New York, NY 10017

Optical Scanners

National Computer Systems
11000 Prairie Lakes Drive
P.O. Box 9365
Minneapolis, MN 55440

SCAN-TRON Corporation
3398E 70th Street
Long Beach, CA 90805

THUNDERWARE
21 Orinda Way
Orinda, CA 94563

11

The Effects of Special Preparation on Measures of Scholastic Ability

Lloyd Bond

University of North Carolina, Greensboro

Introduction

With the possible exception of the IQ controversy, the controversy surrounding the "coachability" of standardized measures of academic aptitude such as the Scholastic Aptitude Test and the Graduate Record Examination is perhaps the leading measurement dispute of our time. The coaching debate goes to the heart of several fundamental psychometric questions. What is the nature of the abilities measured by scholastic aptitude tests? To what extent do score improvements that result from coaching contribute to or detract from test validity? Are failures to substantially increase scores through coaching the result of failure in pedagogical technology or of the inherent difficulty of teaching thinking and reasoning skills?

This chapter examines these and related questions surrounding the instructability of verbal and mathematical skills measured by standardized multiple-choice tests, especially tests that purport to measure scholastic aptitude, as distinct from subject matter achievement. It will also discuss research on the coachability of traditional intelligence tests.

There is disagreement both over the nature of abilities measured by scholastic aptitude tests, and what constitutes "coaching" as an instructional experience. It will therefore be necessary to review extant definitions of and distinctions between aptitude tests and achievement tests, on the one hand, and forms of coaching on the other.

Aptitude, Ability, and Achievement

The distinctions among the terms *aptitude, ability,* and *achievement* are a favorite and long-lasting source of disagree-

ment in measurement circles (Anastasi, 1984; Cooley & Lohnes, 1976; Cronbach, 1984). Cooley and Lohnes have in fact claimed that the distinction is a purely *functional* one. If a test is used as an indication of past instruction and experience, it is an achievement test. If it is used as a measure of current competence, it is an ability test. If it is used to predict or forecast future performance, it is an aptitude test. Yesterday's achievement is today's ability and tomorrow's aptitude. Cooley and Lohnes make a persuasive case that test developers have certainly added to the confusion surrounding the distinctions among these three terms. These authors comingle items from the Otis–Lennon *Mental Ability* Test and the Stanford *Achievement* Test and challenge the reader to distinguish which are which. Their point is well taken. It is virtually impossible to do so.

The functional distinction is true as far as it goes, but one suspects that it does not go far enough. There is more to it than that. A test of one's factual knowledge of U.S. history or of French can and should be distinguished from the kinds of verbal reasoning abilities measured by, say, the SAT-Verbal. Similarly, the quantitative reasoning abilities measured by the SAT-Math are distinguishable from a test that assesses knowledge of algebraic rules or the manipulation of fractions.

In fact, whether we agree on the proper designation or not, the SAT and similar tests that explicitly attempt to measure verbal and mathematical reasoning and thinking differ from ordinary subject matter achievement tests in at least three ways. First, tests of reasoning ability, especially mathematical reasoning, require a relatively small declarative knowledge

NOTE: Preparation of this chapter was supported by the Learning Research and Development Center, University of Pittsburgh, funded in part by the National Institute of Education. I should like to thank Anne Anastasi and Don Powers for helpful comments on earlier drafts of this manuscript and Peg Emmerling and Deborah Saltrick for invaluable help in preparing and proofreading the manuscript.

base. The sheer amount of mathematical knowledge required by the typical SAT is rarely beyond that taught in a first-year high school algebra course and an introductory semester of geometry. Why, then, do so many students, many of whom have performed reasonably well in even advanced secondary courses such as trigonometry and analytic geometry, find the SAT so difficult? One answer lies in the SAT's demands on what cognitive psychologists call *procedural knowledge* or, more precisely, the procedural use of declarative knowledge.

This kind of skill, it turns out, is difficult to teach and is the principal reason why word problems continue to strike fear into the hearts of novice mathematics students. Beginning with early computer simulations of a word problem solver (Bobrow, 1968), heroic attempts to teach the ability to solve word problems systematically have been tried, but none has been very successful. This failure is one of the main reasons for the popular belief that targeted instruction for the SAT is unproductive.

A second way in which reasoning tests differ from subject matter tests is in the quite deliberate way they were constructed to not depend upon specific subject matter content. The verbal reasoning skills measured by the SAT-V, for example, have no specific secondary school course sequence to which they can be referred.

A final way in which verbal and mathematical reasoning tests differ from at least some achievement tests is in degree of problem solving and reasoning, as distinct from simple memory. Tests in subject matters such as geography, foreign languages, and history make primary demands on memory but minimal demands on problem-solving skills and reasoning.

The Pike Score Decomposition

In the context of the coaching controversy, Pike (1978) proposes a useful and highly informative decomposition of a given observed test score into four component domains: a true score component (e.g., actual verbal and mathematical reasoning ability), a primary test-specific component (e.g., test-wiseness abilities such as optimum pacing and optimum guessing strategies), a secondary test-specific component, and the traditional random error. According to Pike, the true-score components are as follows:

1. The composite of underlying knowledge (e.g., vocabulary, elementary algebra) and reasoning ability, developed over a long period of time (characterized by both long-term acquisition and long-term retention).
2. A state of being well reviewed, so that the individual's underlying developed competence is accurately reflected in the performance to be demonstrated (short-term acquisition, short or medium-term retention).
3. Integrative learning, overlearning, and consolidation (short-term acquisition, long-term retention).
4. The learning of criterion-relevant, analytic skills, such as the ability to identify the main idea in a passage or to simplify complex algebraic terms before comparing their value (short-term acquisition, long-term retention).

To distinguish components 1–4 from those that follow, the former will be referred to as *alpha* components of observed test scores.

Primary test-specific components, along with secondary test-specific components, reflect largely trait-irrelevant aspects of the test itself, and similarly, trait-irrelevant abilities of the test taker. These are referred to as *beta* components and include

5. The match between the domain of developed ability, including 1–4, and test content. (According to Pike, mismatches can occur in such areas as skill in locating information in reading passages and ability to work with the algebra of inequalities. In general, mistakes for any given individual are dependent above the vagaries of items sampling from the domain of interest.)
6. General test wiseness—test familiarity, pacing, general strategies for guessing, and so on.
7. Specific test wiseness—components similar to step 6 but referring to characteristics of specific item formats such as verbal analogies, quantitative comparisons, and number series.

Secondary components influencing performance include

8. Overall level of confidence for a given test.
9. Level of efficiency—the ability to access and use available knowledge quickly, with relatively few errors resulting from working rapidly.

and finally,

10. A random error component.

Pike's conceptualization will be modified here to reflect a model the author believes to be more consistent with traditional concepts from classical test theory. Specifically, an individual's true score is conceived to be a function of components 1–4 and components 5–9. The classical definition (Lord & Novick, 1968) of an individual's true score is the mean score the individual would obtain on a hypothetically infinite number of equivalent forms of a test, assuming no change in the individual. Thus, all of the score components except 10 contribute systematically and cumulatively to a person's true score *on a specific test*. True score, in the sense that Pike uses it, refers to an individual's hypothetical standing on the real ability or trait of interest. However, such a concept is unknowable and inestimable without a specific test to measure it. Inasmuch as any test is probably never completely free of beta components that give test-sophisticated subjects a slight advantage, true score can only be defined in terms of both alpha and beta abilities.

Several points can be made about this simple score model. First, although components 1–4 and components 5–9 can covary in practice, in theory, at least, they are independent of each other. It is probably the case that any empirical covariation can be largely removed through instruction, practice, and, possibly, test design.

The second point to note is that the last of the beta score components (i.e., level of efficiency) could arguably be considered the kind of ability that we are here considering trait-relevant, alpha abilities. This is especially the case with speeded, as distinct from power, tests. In fact, in a pure power test, this particular component would be largely irrelevant.

Finally, the implications of this score decomposition for test design should be briefly mentioned. Ideally, test developers should seek to maximize that part of the true-score variance due to alpha components and to minimize the contribution of beta components. Professionally constructed tests can, in fact, be judged by the extent to which they depend on the underlying domain-relevant abilities that they purport to reflect, on the one hand, and on the extent to which they depend on beta components, on the other. Pyrczak (1972, 1974), for example, employed a procedure for reading comprehension tests that closely approximated a "pure" measure of the extent to which a test is dependent upon beta components. Subjects were asked to attempt to answer reading comprehension items without having read the passage. Clearly, if people can score significantly above chance responding, the test is poorly constructed from a psychometric point of view. Pyrczak identifies two strategies used by persons who scored better than chance, one making use of interrelationships among the items accompanying a given passage, the other involving the tendency to select alternatives that state general principles rather than specific facts. (Prior knowledge and general verbal ability are also importantly related to this skill.) This study and others to be discussed elsewhere point up the care item writers must exercise in their attempts to minimize the contribution of beta components to test-score variance.

The Nature of Coaching

Coaching embraces a wide range of instructional content, from instruction in test wiseness, through highly specific instruction on the types of knowledge and skill required of a specific test, to instruction in the broad domain of secondary school mathematics, general vocabulary building, and other general verbal skills such as composition and criticism (Anastasi, 1981; Powers, 1982).

Beta Abilities: Test Wiseness and Test Sophistication

Because tests differ widely in mode of administration, timing, item format, and so forth, it is difficult to give a general description of what constitutes test sophistication. For the moderately speeded, objective paper-and-pencil test, it would include such things as not spending too much time on any one item, becoming familiar with separate answer sheets, checking *all* alternatives before deciding upon one's answer, carefully reading instructions before beginning the test, and (where random guessing is penalized) guessing only if at least one alternative can be eliminated. Test wiseness also involves reduced anxiety and increased confidence in he test situation.

Millman, Bishop, and Ebel (1965) define test wiseness as "a subject's capacity to utilize the characteristics and formats of the test and the test-taking situation to receive a high score" (p. 707). They also note the logical (though not necessarily empirical) independence of beta and alpha abilities and divide beta abilities into two broad categories:

1. General test wiseness—elements independent of any particular test or testing purpose and hence applicable to virtually all testing situations (such as, time use, guessing)
2. Test-specific test wiseness—elements dependent upon specific flaws and clues in a particular test

These two categories correspond to components 6 and 7 in the Pike decomposition.

Although particular instances of extremely inefficient, ineffective test taking or extreme test anxiety can be found, it is generally conceded, even by proponents of commercial coaching schools, that instruction that concentrates solely on beta components does not significantly affect performance. The reason for this is fairly obvious. No amount of training in test taking will affect one's performance on either aptitude or subject matter achievement tests if one has no knowledge in the area tested. One's vocabulary is not increased in any appreciable way by practicing guessing strategies or reading instructions carefully. The only situation in which extensive instruction in test-taking skill per se can yield a substantial payoff in terms of increased test performance is when the test is poorly constructed or administered or when clues to correct answers are contained in the items themselves or implied by the test administrator.

Studies of test wiseness have been reviewed by Ardiff (1965); Cole (1982); Downey (1977); Gibb (1964); Langer, Wark, & Johnson (1973); Oakland (1973); Slakter (1967, 1968a, 1968b, 1969); Slakter, Crehan, & Koehler (1975); Swineford & Miller (1953); White & Zammarelli (1981); and Woodley (1973) among others, and several generalizations emerged from this growing literature. Test wiseness has been shown to have low to modest correlations with several cognitive abilities such as verbal ability (Diamond & Evans, 1972; Rowley, 1974) and intelligence test scores (Ardiff, 1965; Diamond & Evans, 1972). It has been claimed that test wiseness increases steadily up through the late elementary school years but levels off in the high school years (Crehan, Koehler, & Slakter, 1974).

In a recent, highly controversial, polemical book by David Owen (1985) entitled *None of the Above,* the author challenges this finding, claiming that substantial increases in both general and specific beta components are possible in the high school years. In addition to teaching content directly related to the SAT, instructors at the "Princeton Review" expend considerable effort on test-wiseness techniques. For example, a computer analysis of the Quantitative Comparison (QC) items on recently released forms of the SAT uncovered a technical flaw in these items that might explain why they have been suspected of being more coachable than other item types. The QC item type requires the student to decide, on the basis of the information given, whether two quantities are equal, whether one is larger than the other, or whether insufficient information is given to decide. It turns out that, when the problem is relatively complex and involves extensive calculations, it is highly likely that the two quantities are equal. This is a natural by-product of the item analysis. Complex comparisons involving unequal quantities can be correctly answered by low-scoring students, who might make many errors during computation but who might still come up on the "correct" side of the inequality. The net result is that correlations of such items with the total test are reduced and they may well be discarded from the final test form.

Owen also claims to be able to teach students to recognize the "experimental" section of the SAT (i.e., the unscored section that is used for item tryout of future tests) and to simply rest during this period. To the extent that either of these strategies is effective, coached students would have a significant time advantage over uncoached students, an advantage that is traceable almost exclusively to trait-irrelevant elements of the test.

In general, the components of both general and specific beta abilities seem quite teachable. Some elements of test wiseness are little more than a set of rules that any individual can, with minimal practice, apply.

Test-Specific Instruction

Test specific instruction, the most popular form of coaching for both intelligence tests and paper-and-pencil aptitude tests, usually involves intensive instruction, with immediate feedback, on a sample of items like those found on the actual test. The effect of such instruction on test performance over and above what would be expected from normal school instruction is a major focus of this chapter.

Instruction in Broad Academic and Intellectual Skills

Recently, interest has centered on a form of special preparation that is relatively content free and attempts, literally, to "train intelligence." The work summarized by Nickerson, Perkins, and Smith (1985) and Whimbey (1975) constitutes examples of this approach. Perhaps the most well known attempt to teach broad reasoning skills that are relatively content free is the "dynamic assessment" program of Feuerstein (1979), discussed later.

Studies of Coaching and Special Preparation

The accumulating literature on the effects of specific instruction and other forms of special preparation on measures of verbal and mathematical aptitude (especially the SAT) is a mixed bag. At one extreme is the very loosely controlled survey study involving estimation of the effects upon performance of reading test-preparation materials such as *Taking the SAT*, a test familiarization bulletin provided by ETS to potential SAT candidates. In addition to the lack of control over such variables as demographics of respondents and nonrespondents to the survey, there is the very real problem of having to depend exclusively on self-reported information about the extent to which *Taking the SAT* was skimmed, read, or thoroughly examined. At the other extreme is the ideal experiment involving randomized assignment to treatment and control conditions and explicit descriptions of the actual experience of students in the experimental groups.

Effects of Practice and Growth

The baseline against which the effects of special instruction and coaching should be evaluated is the normal gains that occur upon retaking the SAT after some appropriate interval (Levine & Angoff, 1958). These gains are generally attributed to increased familiarity with the test, that is, to practice, and to normal growth and achievement in school. Cole (1982), combining data from several sources (including samples ranging from 96,000 in 1962 to 193,000 in 1966 of volunteer students who took the SAT in May of their junior year and December of their senior year), estimates the combined practice and 6-month growth effects to be 26 for the SAT-V and 21 for the SAT-M.

Messick (1980), using national samples of repeat test takers from the April–November candidate pools of 1975 and 1976, estimates the effects of practice and growth to be 12 (1975 sample) and 17 (1976 sample) for the SAT-V. The comparable figures for the SAT-M are exactly 17 for both years. Levine and Angoff (1958) and Pike (1978) report similar growth and practice effects.

The Cole estimate of a 26-point gain from practice and growth on the SAT-V is approximately 12 points higher than the 14.5 point gain reported by Messick, Pike, and others. Although this difference might not seem important on the 200–800 SAT scale, it nevertheless reinforces an important pattern of differential growth first elucidated by Messick (1980). Briefly, in his reanalysis of The Federal Trade Commission study of coaching (discussed later), he noted that initial status on the SAT-V and later growth tended to interact. Specifically, initially high-scoring students on the SAT-V tend to have larger practice and growth gains than do initially low-scoring individuals. This pattern of differential growth does not appear to obtain in mathematics.

Because of the widely discussed decline in SAT scores that began in the mid-1960s and continued through the late 1970s, Messick's estimate of verbal gains from practice and growth was based upon a sample of students that was less able than the Cole samples (the SAT-V difference averaged about 60 points).

Based upon the available evidence, one can expect an approximately 15 to 20 point increase in SAT-M scores over 6-month intervals during the high school years. This increase is purely a function of practice and typical high school achievement and does not appear to vary significantly with initial status.

The effects of practice and growth on the verbal reasoning skills measured by the SAT, however, appear to depend upon the initial abilities of the students involved. For students in the 450 range, the gains from practice and growth average around 15 points; for individuals with initial scores between 500 and

600, the gains from practice and growth average approximately 25 points. A systematic investigation of the effects of practice and growth throughout the SAT score range that takes into account regression and sampling artifacts would be a useful contribution to the coaching literature.

Effects of Test Disclosure and Test Familiarization Materials

No systematic study of the potential benefits of studying commercial test-preparation materials is available. Powers and Alderman (1983) found negligible effects of self-reported use of *Taking the SAT* (which contains a complete sample SAT test) on rate of work or extent of guessing. When SAT-V and SAT-M scores were regressed on the preliminary SAT-V and -M scores, high school rank, and a dichotomous variable indicating whether the examinee had reported using *Taking the SAT,* an insignificant effect (3.1 points) was obtained for the SAT-V, and a small (7.30 points) significant effect was obtained for the SAT-M.

Regarding test disclosure, the anticipated gains that were the basis of many public arguments in favor of legislated disclosures appear to have been too optimistic. Stricker (1982) found, for example, that test disclosure had no discernible affect on either SAT-M or SAT-V.

Studies with No Control Groups

To date, three studies have been conducted that lacked a specified control group for evaluating the effects of coaching programs (those by Coffman & Parry, 1967; Marron, 1965; Pallone, 1961).

Pallone's study consisted of both a short-term (6-week) summer program with approximately 20 students that met for 1 1/2 hr daily and a longer term program involving some 80 students and covering the 6-7 month period from September 1959 to March 1960, with daily meetings of 50 min each. The subjects in this study were all male students in their final year of precollege work at a private school for boys or high school graduates completing a year of post high school study in preparation for application to military academies. In addition to the specific coaching program, which included such special skills as practice with verbal analogies, the program included instruction designed to go beyond the routine coaching that had regularly been found to be ineffective. It focused, instead, on critical reading, skimming, vocabulary, and logical reasoning, abilities that the SAT-V is assumed to measure.

The raw gains after both the short-term and long-term programs were dramatic. Pallone reported a mean gain of 98 points from the March 1959 to August 1959 administration (after the short-term treatment). A mean score increase of 109 points was reported for the 80 students completing the long-term course. The mean increase in SAT-V scores for those students who underwent both the short- and long-term instruction was 122 points, 24 points above the increase reported after the summer course.

Marron (1965) studied the effects of special preparation on the performance of a select group of students, all male, at 10 well-known preparatory schools whose graduates typically went on to military academies and selective colleges. A special administration of the SAT (both V and M) and the College Board achievement tests in English Composition and Intermediate and Advanced Math served as the pretest. The posttest was the regular College Board administration of March 1963. According to Marron, the instructional treatment consisted of "six months of full-time exposure to course content that is directly related to the verbal and mathematics College Board tests" (p. 1). Because the schools differed significantly in both pre- and posttests (the posttest difference remained even after covariance adjustments), Marron reported the results on the basis of groups of schools that did not differ significantly among themselves. Score gains by group were as follows:

SAT-VERBAL

Group 1 (2 schools, $N = 83$)	77
Group 2 (6 schools, $N = 600$)	56
Group 3 (1 school, $N = 5$)	35
Group 4 (1 school, $N = 26$)	58
Weighted Mean Gain	58

SAT-MATH

Group 1 (4 schools, $N = 232$)	83
Group 2 (3 schools, $N = 405$)	78
Group 3 (3 schools, $N = 78$)	72
Weighted Mean Gain	79

In critiquing the Pallone and Marron studies, Messick (1980) noted three potentially confounding factors: the absence of an adequate control group, the special quality of the samples themselves, and the fact that the coaching programs closely approximated full-time instruction, as distinct from short-term coaching.

The last criticism is the source of some controversy (College Entrance Examination Board, 1968; Jackson, 1980; Slack & Porter, 1980a, 1980b). Is the distinction between coaching and regular instruction a distinction between the sheer amount of time devoted to the enterprise, or does the distinction turn on the *purpose* of the instruction, regardless of its duration? Given that there can be no sharp distinction between short-term and long-term instruction, it would appear that coaching embraces both and that the distinguishing feature of coaching is its purpose, rather than its length. If the purpose of the instruction is specifically to increase scores on a specified examination, and only incidentally to increase the general academic skills that the test purports to predict, then it is properly labeled *coaching.* Perhaps a more meaningful distinction is possible if the actual content of the instruction serves as the focus of substantive distinctions between coaching and full-time instruction. Sustained instruction in broad academic skills (Anastasia, 1981) of the type generally encountered in high school English and mathematics courses is full-time instruction and only incidentally affects performance on standardized admission tests.

Coffman and Parry (1967), in an attempt to explore further the effects of developmental reading instruction on the SAT-V score found by Pallone, studied three groups of college fresh-man who took the SAT-V before and after completing a course in accelerated reading. The authors describe the course as stressing speed and accuracy. Pre- and posttest scores were reported for 25 students who took a 3-hr-per-week course for 15 weeks. Scores were also available for two smaller groups of 10 and 9 students who took an 8-week course that met 6 hr per week. Surprisingly, a 29-point mean loss was reported for the 25 students taking the longer, 15 week, course. Modest score increases of 3.5 and 10 were observed for the two smaller groups.

Several plausible explanations for these results have been advanced. First, because of practical constraints, a shorter version of the SAT-V was administered to the 15-week group, calling into question the adequacy of the score equating. Additionally, the motivational level of college freshmen volunteers for what was essentially a research project is suspect. Finally, unlike the longer study by Pallone, this study did not include instruction in analogies, vocabulary, and other content relevant to the SAT-V.

Although the studies by Coffman and Parry, Marron, and Pallone are methodically weak, the sheer size of the presumed instructional effects in Marron's and Pallone's are such that the studies bear close scrutiny. Control-group adjustments of varying adequacy have been suggested. Pallone suggested 35 points on the SAT-V as a normal gain during the final year of secondary school and 15 points as the expected gain during the 5-month interval of his short-term study. Marron suggested 24 and 26 points, respectively, for Verbal and Math as typical 6-month gains for high school seniors. Slack and Porter averaged score increases from national samples of junior and senior repeat test takers who had the same initial scores as the Marron and Pallone samples. Pike (1978) averaged gains of control students in selective schools from other studies of commercial and proprietary coaching programs, and Messick (1980) averaged gains of control students in other studies who had mean

initial score levels comparable to students in the Marron and Pallone studies. Messick (1980) calculated the weighted average of all four adjustments and obtained a 38-point increase in the SAT-V and a 54-point increase in the SAT-M for the combined three studies. Table 11.1 summarizes these studies, along with estimated mean coaching gains after adjustments.

Studies with Nonrandom Assignment

In this group of studies, persons volunteering for participation in a coaching program were matched with persons who might or might not have been volunteers but who were approximately equivalent to the treatment groups. In the first three studies (Dear, 1958; Dyer, 1953; French, 1955a, 1955b), control groups were drawn from different schools than those from which experimental students were drawn, thus confounding treatment and school effects. In the second group of studies (Federal Trade Commission, 1978; Frankel, 1960; Johnson, Asbury, Wallace, Robinson, & Vaughn, 1985; Lass, 1958; and Whitla, 1962), attempts were made to match treatment and control students within the same schools on available variables that plausibly affect test performance. In one instance (Johnson et al., 1985), random assignment was attempted at three different sites but was successfully carried out in only one.

In the Dyer (1953) study, subjects were 225 senior students at a selective private school for boys. Control subjects were 193 seniors at a comparable private school. The students were matched on SAT scores, year in school, and number and level of foreign language and mathematics courses taken, all of which served as covariates in the analysis of program effects. The special preparation entailed 12 verbal practice exercises in sessions of 30- to 60-min each and 5 mathematics practice exercises in 60- to 90-min sessions. Score increases due to coaching were estimated to be 4.6 and 12.9 points, respectively, for SAT-V and SAT-M.

TABLE 11.1   Adjusted mean score gains in studies of SAT instructional interventions having no control groups

STUDY	SCHOOL	LEVEL	SEX	SAT-VERBAL ADJUSTED AVERAGE SCORE INCREASE[1]		N	SAT-MATH ADJUSTED AVERAGE SCORE INCREASED[1]		N
Pallone (1961)	Private	H.S. Seniors & Graduates	M		81	20+	–		–
Pallone (1961)	Private	H.S. Seniors & Graduates	M		68	80−	–		–
Marron (1965)	Private	H.S. Seniors & Graduates	M	Group 1 54	} 35	83	Group 1' 59		232
				Group 2 33		600	Group 2' 53		405
				Group 3 24		5	Group 3' 46		78
				Group 4 12					
Coffman & Parry (1967)[2]	Public	College Freshmen	M + F		4[3]	19			
Weighted Average					38		54		

[1] To estimate instructional effects, average score increases in the Pallone (1961) and Marron (1965) studies were adjusted by the average of the four adjustments discussed in the text.

[2] The 15-week program in Coffman and Parry (1967) was not included because the 29-point mean decrease in scores was considered atypical and possibly indicative of motivational and test administration problems.

[3] The two 8-week programs in Coffman and Parry (1967) were combined, but adjustments were made only by the Slack and Porter (1980) procedure, which attenuated by only a few points an already tenuous effect. None of the suggested comparison groups of SAT takers appeared to provide even remotely reasonable yardsticks for gauging score gains of students already enrolled in a college not requiring the SAT.

Adapted from Messick (1980).

Dyer also analyzed the results by separating students into those who were taking mathematics courses in their senior year and those who were not. Coached no-math students gained almost 30 points more on the SAT-M than their counterparts who were not coached. In contrast, coached boys who were taking mathematics gained only 3.3 points over their non-coached controls.

French (1955b) studied the effects of special preparation for the SAT at three schools, with one (School A, $N = 158$) serving as a control group for both Math and Verbal, a second (School B, $N = 110$) serving as a control group for Math and a treatment group for Verbal, and a third (School C, $N = 161$) serving as a treatment group for both Math and Verbal. Instruction at schools B and C differed in that the former emphasized primarily vocabulary, whereas the latter also covered 10 verbal exercises that included antonyms and verbal analogies. The vocabulary-only instruction involved five sessions of approximately 50 min each. Only total length of instruction (16.6 hr) at School C is available, and a reasonable assumption, following Messick (1982), is that half of the time was devoted to Verbal and half to Math. All students took the SAT in September 1953 and again in March 1954. The pretest served as a covariate in the analysis.

In schools A (no instruction), B (vocabulary instruction), and C (verbal and mathematics instruction), total unadjusted SAT-V gains were 28, 33, and 46, respectively. After adjustments for pretest score and practice, verbal gain attributed to vocabulary instruction alone was 5 points, and gains attributed to general verbal instruction were 18 points. A similar 18-point gain, after covariance and practice adjustments, was reported for the SAT-M. Significantly, the same pattern regarding students taking mathematics versus those not taking it that was observed in the Dyer study was obtained here, but this pattern varied, depending upon the sex of the student. Boys not currently taking mathematics gained 29 points, compared with one control group, and 9, compared with the other; those taking mathematics gained 19 points and 5 points. Girls not taking mathematics gained 5 points and 1 point for the same comparisons, whereas those taking mathematics showed a coaching effect of 30 points and 20 points.

Pike (1978) has suggested a possible explanation for these results: Boys currently taking mathematics exhibited a ceiling effect on the benefits of review and practice, but those not taking mathematics were able to obtain maximum benefit. For girls, those not taking mathematics were victims of "math anxiety" and simply could not benefit from the possibly intimidating review that the relatively brief instruction entailed. It should be noted, however, that such an explanation is highly speculative and, in fact, goes far beyond the data.

In 1958, Dear, in a study reported by French and Dear (1959), examined the effects of special preparation when classes are very small (two students each) and the pace of instruction is more leisurely (two class periods a week for 6 weeks and for 12 weeks, with one additional hour of homework). Ten high schools (four private and six public) were selected at random from a list of schools that had at least 15 students taking the May 1956 SAT. An experimental group was randomly selected at each school from among students who volunteered for the project. Nine schools from the same area (metropolitan New York City, New Jersey, and metropolitan Philadelphia) were randomly chosen as controls. Level of motivation was partially controlled by using only students for both the treatment and control groups who had previously indicated an interest in being coached. Ninety students (3 from each school) comprised the experimental group, and 81 students served as controls. The majority of the students took three different SATs: one in May 1956, one midway through the coaching session in January 1957, and a final one in March 1957.

The gains attributable to coaching for the January administration were estimated to be 22 points in Math, and a slight loss (-2.5) in Verbal. A 24-point coaching gain for Math was reported for the final posttest in March. (Verbal results were not reported because of a significant difference in regression slopes for the coached and uncoached groups.)

Of the five studies that have attempted to match controls within schools, three have involved evaluation of commercial coaching schools. Of these, the study by the Federal Trade Commission (FTC) is by far the most ambitious. This study is in fact two studies of the same set of data, one conducted by the Boston Regional office of the FTC (1978) and a second by the national office of the FTC (1979). This set of studies represents the first large-scale systematic attempt to evaluate the effects of commercial coaching programs on SAT scores. In addition to these two analyses, critical reanalyses and reevaluations have been done by Alderman (1980), Powers (1980), Rock (1980), and Stroud (1980). A complete summary of these analyses, plus additional ones, is reported in Messick (1980). Space does not allow a thorough review of the original study and the six critical reanalyses.

Briefly, the nonexperimental nature of these data and the use of archival records for control purposes render unambiguous interpretation of any coaching effects extremely difficult. In the original study by the Boston Regional Office, the coached groups (six subsamples of New York City area juniors and seniors during the period 1974–1977) differed in systematic ways from the uncoached group. The entire coached group was, for example, higher than the uncoached group in class rank, parental income, most recent English and mathematics grades, and number of mathematics courses taken. When these and other available demographic variables were controlled in the FTC reanalysis, all gains were reduced, some quite substantially. For example, in one of the highest scoring schools, an average SAT-V gain of 55 was reduced to 30, and a mean SAT-M gain of 40 was reduced to 19.

A second confounding circumstance involved the possibility of systematic negative errors of measurement on the part of students seeking coaching. Because all students, both those in commercial coaching schools and those selected as controls, had taken the SAT at least once, a plausible hypothesis is that those seeking coaching had already scored lower than expected. If this hypothesis were true, then coaching effects might be confounded with regression effects. The second FTC report considered this possibility but dismissed it because the coached students had obtained similarly low scores on the preliminary SAT. Thus, it was concluded that these were consistently poor test takers who might simply be especially responsive to coaching.

In the various reanalyses of the two FTC studies, other

background differences (e.g., motivation, self-selection) have been suggested as rival hypotheses to the presumed coaching effects, and none of these can be categorically discounted. For these reasons, the evidentiary status of this attempt to evaluate commercial coaching is dubious. A true experimental investigation of commercial coaching is of course possible, but unlikely, and, until such a study is undertaken, it is perhaps wisest to reserve judgment on the effectiveness of these programs.

Frankel (1960) studied the effects of 30 hours of instruction at a commercial coaching school on the SAT scores of 45 high school students at the prestigious Bronx High School of Science. When compared with a sample of 45 Bronx students matched on sex and prior SAT-V and SAT-M scores, control subjects gained 66 points between May 1958 and December 1958 or January 1959 SAT-M, compared with 57 points for the coached subjects, a 9-point advantage for the *uncoached* group. The SAT-V results were just the reverse. Coached students gained 47 points, whereas uncoached students gained 38 SAT-V points. This investigation and the following one by Whitla (1962) suffer from some of the same problems that plagued the FTC study and, indeed, plague all quasi-experimental studies. Nevertheless, the results of the study deserve special attention because they suggest an interaction between level of preparation and responsiveness to coaching noted elsewhere. The negligible differences in overall SAT scores between the coached and uncoached students, combined with the large raw gains for both groups, the highly select nature of the sample itself, and the well-known quality of instruction at the Bronx school, all suggest that, for some schools and students, there is little need for additional preparation over the above that obtained from normal schooling.

Like Frankel, Whitla (1962) examined the effects of commercially provided coaching at a proprietary school in Boston for 52 students who were matched on the spring and fall 1959 SATs with 52 uncoached students from the same area. The 10-hour course was designed to improve study habits, reading skills, and basic mathematics concepts. The control and coached students were within one point of each other on the average Verbal and Math pretest in the spring of their junior year (March–May 1959), and they were within two points of each other on a second pretest (Fall, 1959). When compared to the fall 1959 pretest, the January 1960 posttest revealed an 11-point advantage for the coached group on the SAT-V and a 5-point advantage for the *uncoached* group on the SAT-M. Comparable figures for the spring 1959 pretest were a 10-point advantage for coached students on Verbal and a 7-point advantage for uncoached students on Math.

Pike (1978) reports a study by Lass conducted in 1958 that compared students who received no coaching, outside coaching, and a school-provided orientation program. The last type of instruction provided students with SAT testing materials and procedures and familiarized them with test content, but it did not involve the kind of extensive drill on multiple-choice tests typically associated with coaching. SAT-M score gains for the three groups over the 6-month junior-to-senior-year interval were 53, 64, and 52 points, respectively. Corresponding gains on the SAT-V were 41, 44, and 53 points. Note that the verbal gains for the orientation group were higher than those for the coaching group, calling into question the initial comparability of the three groups.

A final nonequivalent control-group study is that of Johnson et al. (1985). The study is in fact three different studies (in Atlanta, New York City, and San Francisco), all sponsored by the National Association for the Advancement of Colored People. The studies represent an organized effort to raise the SAT scores of a group of volunteer disadvantaged black youth through two series of biweekly instructional sessions of 2 1/2 to 3 hr each, for 6 weeks, or a total of about 30 hours of instructional time. The 12 sessions were equally divided between mathematics and verbal instruction. Instructional materials were developed by the National Association of Secondary School Principals for preparing students for nationally standardized college admission tests and included instruction and practice in vocabulary, verbal analogies, reading comprehension, and basic algebraic and geometric concepts. In all three sites, random assignment to experimental and control groups was attempted, but, because of administrative difficulties, it was successful only at the San Francisco site (analysis of the San Francisco study is discussed in the next section). In all three sites, girls outnumbered boys by approximately two to one. Four parallel forms of the SAT were developed by halving existing tests after omitting the Test in Standard Written English, which was not a focus of the instructional program. Full-scale scores were estimated from ETS tables using standard linear equating procedures.

At the Atlanta site ($N = 18$), SAT-V score increases over the 12-week interval from pretest to final posttest averaged 12 points, whereas SAT-M gains were 19 points. For students at the New York site ($N = 66$), Verbal gains averaged 13 points and Math gains averaged 28 points. It should be noted that these are unadjusted gains. (Gains adjusted for practice and growth were reported only for the San Francisco sample and will be discussed later). It is nevertheless of some interest that an analysis of the results by initial pretest level directly contradicts the earlier findings of Roberts and Oppenheim (1966), to be discussed later. Briefly, these investigators found no practice, growth, or coaching effects for low-scoring volunteer black students. In the present investigation, the greatest gains across all sites were registered by the lowest scoring (below 300) groups. These gains remained highly significantly and nontrivial, even after regression adjustments. Across all sites (including San Francisco), the following gains were registered:

	Pretest Level	n	Mean Gain
Verbal	Less than 300	37	40.52
	300–400	48	30.00
	Greater than 400	32	−5.00
Math	Less than 300	33	74.85
	300–400	47	19.36
	Greater than 400	36	22.75

The results of the studies by Johnson et al. (1985) and Roberts and Oppenheim, when considered along with Messick's analysis of the FTC data by race, present a confusing picture indeed. Messick (1980) identified a subsample of 13 black students whose verbal coaching and self-selection effect was 46.7 points above that for white students at the same school, a highly significant difference ($p < .0001$) despite the small sample size. Messick also undertook an analysis of scores from 8 black students in the Alderman and Powers (1979) study, which revealed only minor differences in differential effectiveness for black students over whites at the same school. Unfortunately, these analyses involved small sample sizes. But the results of the study by Johnson et al., vis-à-vis that of Roberts and Oppenheim, and the Messick analyses of the FTC and Alderman and Powers results point up the need for systematic research on the differential effectiveness of coaching for black and white students, particularly low-scoring black students. Table 11.2 summarizes these 13 studies.

Studies with Randomized Control Groups

The most technically and experimentally adequate coaching studies are those in which participants are randomly assigned to control and experimental groups. Four such studies have been undertaken to date. Roberts and Oppenheim (1966) carried out their study on 18 predominantly black, low-achieving secondary schools in rural and urban Tennessee. The Preliminary Scholastic Aptitude Test (PSAT) was employed as both pre- and posttest. Students in 8 of the 18 schools received

TABLE 11.2 Average difference between experimental and control groups in studies of SAT interventions.

	Sample Characteristics						
Study/Design	School	Level	Sex	SAT-Verbal Difference[1]	N Exp./Control	SAT-Math Difference[1]	N Exp./Control
Dyer (1953) Control, different school	Private	H.S. Seniors	M	4.6	225/193	12.9	225/193
French (1955) Control, different school	Public	H.S. Seniors	M + F	18.3	161/158	6.2	161/158
French (1955) Control, different school	Public	H.S. Seniors	M + F	5.0	110/158	18.0	161/110
Dear (1958) Control, same and different schools	Public	H.S. Seniors	M + F	−2.5	60/526	21.5	60/526
Dear (1958) Control, same and different schools	Public & Private	H.S. Seniors	M + F	[2]	–	23.6	71/116
Frankel (1960) Control, same school statistically matched	Public	H.S. Seniors	M + F	8.4	45/45	9.4	45/45
Whitla (1962) Control, statistically matched	Public	H.S. Seniors	M + F	11.0	52/52	−5.3	50/50
Roberts & Oppenheim (1966) Randomized	Public	H.S. Juniors	M + F	14.4[3]	154/111	8.1[3]	188/122
Evans & Pike (1973) Randomized	Public	H.S. Juniors	M + F	No coaching for SAT-V	–	16.5	288/129
Alderman & Powers (1979) Randomized	Public & Private	H.S. Juniors	M + F	8.4	239/320	No coaching for SAT-M	
Johnson et al. (1985) Control, same and different schools	Public	H.S. Juniors and Seniors	M + F	[4]	84/83	[4]	84/83
Johnson et al. (1985) Randomized	Public	H.S. Juniors and Seniors	M + F	121[5]	23/12	57[5]	23/12
Average weighted by size of experimental sample				9.1		13.0	

[1] The coaching effects are intercept differences between regression lines for experimental and control groups or (for Frankel, Whitla, Roberts, & Oppenheim; Pike & Evans; and Johnson et al.) average score increases of experimental over control groups, both weighted in the case of multiple experimental or control groups by their respective sample sizes.

[2] Not calculated; variance and regression slopes differed significantly for experimental and control groups.

[3] This study employed the PSAT as both pre- and posttest; the averages shown have been converted to the SAT score-scale ranging from 200 to 800 points.

[4] Control and treatment differences were not reported.

[5] These unusually large gains were based upon a comparison of mean scores on a shortened version of the SAT. They represent "gains" in the following sense: Scores on the pretest for both control and experimental students were not reported. The figures represent the difference between control and treatment groups on the posttest. An unreported number of attritions in the treatment group may have resulted in the two groups being of unequal motivation.

special instruction in mathematics, students in 6 schools received special instruction in verbal material, and students in 4 schools received no special instruction. In addition, students within the 14 treatment schools were randomly assigned to coached and uncoached groups. The treatment consisted of 15 one-half-hour sessions over a 4- to 6-week period. A total of 154 students constituted the experimental group for verbal coaching, and 111 students served as controls. The corresponding figures for mathematics instruction were 188 and 122, respectively. Students coached in mathematics showed a .81 PSAT point increase over their noncoached counterparts. For students instructed in the verbal material, the relative gain was 1.44 points. These increases correspond to 8 points on the SAT-M and 14 points on the SAT-V.

Pike and Evans (1972) and Evans and Pike (1973) investigated the effects on test performance of specific instruction and practice on three item types: Regular Math (RM), Data Sufficiency (DS), and Quantitative Comparison (QC). A total of 509 students in 12 schools participated in the study. In each school, three groups of students were randomly assigned to QC, RM, or DS instruction or to a control group. Experimental groups received 21 hours of instruction and 21 hours of homework over a 7-week period. All students took a special administration of the SAT in October 1970 (pretest), a second special administration in December 1970 (posttest), and a regular administration in April 1971, which served as a delayed posttest. Students in the experimental group were given instruction between the pretest and the posttest; control group students were given the identical instruction between the posttest and the delayed posttest.

Although the program emphasized instruction in the particular item types under scrutiny, the authors also included systematic content review, basic geometric principles, inequalities, and various aspects of test wiseness. According to the authors, the instruction was highly systematic, with control of instruction provided through student workbooks and teachers' lesson plans.

It should be noted that this study was specifically designed to investigate the effects of special instruction on three particular item types, so that estimation of gains on the total SAT-M is problematic. The authors' best estimate of score increases due to coaching for all four groups over the entire period from October to April is 25 points. Pike (1978) estimates that "a judicious combination of RM and DS instruction, still keeping within the 21 hours of instruction, would be expected to yield . . . about 33 points" (p. 16).

Alderman and Powers (1979) investigated the effectiveness of secondary school programs that were specifically designed to improve performance on the SAT-V. Students from eight schools for whom PSAT scores were available were randomly assigned to special preparation and control groups. As in the Evans and Pike and Johnson et al. studies, delayed access to special preparation was provided to the control group. Preliminary SAT scores served as the pretest, and a special administration of a retired SAT served as the posttest. Across all eight schools, coaching effects averaged 8 points (the actual range was from −3 to 28 points). Significant score *decreases* at three schools suggest that problems in motivation were possible, given that the test was not an operational one.

The final study using random assignment to experimental and control conditions was that of Johnson and her colleagues (1985) discussed earlier. Briefly, unadjusted gains were 57 points for the SAT-V ($N = 33$) and 44 points for the SAT-M ($N = 34$). The authors compared pretest scores of the Session II (delayed, $N = 12$) control students with posttest scores of the Session I experimental students ($N = 23$). The SAT-V difference was an extraordinary 121 points, and the SAT-M difference was 57, both of which are significant at the .05 level, despite the small sample sizes. It should be noted that there was some attrition in the experimental group, which might explain some of these unusually large differences. The authors note, in this regard, that the students who did not complete the program were not significantly different on pretest scores from the controls, but differences in the motivation of those completing the program are probable.

Before considering some cumulative implications of these studies, we will briefly consider research that has been conducted on special preparation for other cognitive measures including objective tests of English composition, verbal analogies, standardized achievement measures, and traditional measures of intelligence.

Coaching and Other Measures of Cognitive Ability

Because the SAT is used for college admissions, the literature on special preparation for this test is more widely known and more controversial by far than any other test.

Special preparation for the GRE, a test very similar to the SAT, has been investigated by Powers (1985), Powers and Swinton (1984) and Swinton and Powers (1983). These investigations have concentrated on the Analytical section of the GRE in particular and have found that section to be more susceptible to specific instruction than the traditional Verbal and Math sections. For example, Swinton and Powers (1983) estimated the gains from a brief program of special preparation on the Analytical section of the GRE to be 66 points on the 200–800 score scale. This effect is substantially larger than the 10–20 points typically found in well-designed studies of the SAT. The gains appeared to stem from improved performance on two of the three analytical item types (analysis of explanations and logical diagrams) that were part of the test from 1977 to 1981. Unlike the authors reporting many other coaching studies, these authors provide explicit descriptions of techniques used in the program.

There is also a growing literature on special preparation for measures of English composition, verbal analogies, and others. Marron's (1965) study, cited earlier, included the effects of coaching on the College Board English Composition Test (ECT), as did a study by Jacobs (1966). The ECT is an objective, multiple-choice test with three distinct item formats (Sentence Correction, Construction Shift, and Paragraph Organization). Like the SAT, its score scale ranges from 200 to 800. The Marron study showed a general and highly significant mean increase across all schools (83 points). The Jacob study, however, highlighted substantial between-school differences after six 3-hour sessions, with about half of the time spent on directly relevant alpha components (components 1, 2, and 4 in the Pike decomposition) and half of the time spent on primary test-specific components (component 7). His results suggest that, with respect ot English composition, instructor differences, even for short-term courses, could be quite substantial.

Specific instruction in understanding verbal analogies is, of course, a part of many SAT-V coaching programs. Verbal analogical reasoning has also been investigated in its own right, both in the laboratory (Glaser & Pellegrino, 1982) and as a dependent measure after coaching (Moore, 1971; Whitely & Dawis, 1974). Whitely and Dawis' results suggest that practice with verbal analogies, even if accompanied by corrective feedback, has little effect unless it is coupled with instructional materials carefully designed to elucidate categories of relationships such as "class membership," "opposites," and so forth.

Coaching and Achievement Tests

Coaching and *special preparation* normally carry no negative connotations when applied to efforts to increase students' *achievement* scores in reading, arithmetic, and other traditional school subjects. This, after all, is what instruction should be about. Bangert-Drowns, Kulik, and Kulik (1983) recently subjected to a metanalysis 30 studies of special instruction for various teacher-made tests and popular standardized tests of reading and mathematics such as the Metropolitan Achievement Test, the Stanford Achievement Test, and the California Achievement Test. Consistent with the nebulous distinction between standardized measures of achievement and aptitude noted earlier, these authors found little to choose from between measures of aptitude and achievement. The sizes of the effects of coaching on performance were roughly comparable, and the regression of coaching effects on student contact time was logarithmic for both kinds of tests.

Coaching and Traditional IQ Tests

Studies of special preparation for traditional IQ tests and other measures of intelligence have been undertaken with varying degrees of success. During the early 1950s, the debate over the effectiveness of coaching and practice was especially intense in England, where much of the early research on the instructability of intelligence was being conducted. As with the current controversy in the United States over the coachability of the SAT, the debate in England was both political and scientific. In fact, many of the same fears that educators now express over the deleterious effects of coaching on the curriculum and on matters of equity were evident during the English debate.

Reviews of the IQ literature have been conducted by James (1953), Jensen (1980), Vernon (1954), Whimbey (1975), Wiseman & Wrigley (1953), and Yates (1953), among others. The Jensen and Vernon reviews separate the results of these studies into three categories: unassisted practice effects, coaching (without practice) effects, and combined coaching and practice effects. With respect to practice effects alone, the results can be summarized as follows:

1. Practice effects are largest for "naive" subjects (subjects with no test-taking experience), and such effects are greatest on group paper-and-pencil tests, as distinct from individually administered tests, and on heterogeneous, as distinct from homogeneous, tests.
2. More able subjects (as measured by a pretest) tend to benefit more from practice than less able subjects.
3. As with the SAT, the curve of gains from unassisted practice is negatively accelerated, with initial gains being substantially greater than gains from extended practice.
4. Practice effects are greater for speeded than for untimed tests.
5. Practice effects tend to be greater for nonverbal and performance tests than for verbal tests such as vocabulary and verbal reasoning tests.
6. The transfer of training from practice gains tends, in general, to be relatively small. Largest gains logically result from retaking the identical test after practice, with gains falling off increasingly for parallel tests, similar or comparable tests, different tests in the same general domain (such as vocabulary and verbal analogies), and completely different tests. Jensen (1980) estimates that practice gains from forms L to M of the Stanford–Binet average about 2 or 3 points; gains from parallel forms of group tests average about 3 or 4 points after one practice session and 5 or 6 points after several practice sessions.
7. Practice effects are not ephemeral; rather, they are enduring, with fully half of the gain remaining after 1 year.

In contrast, the effects of coaching without concomitant practice appear singularly ineffective. In this type of coaching, examinees are formally instructed in efficient test-taking strategies, including optimum guessing strategies, time allocation, and analysis of sample questions and solutions with immediate feedback. The essential point here is that the coaching is *not* accompanied by actual practice by the subjects in taking actual tests. Rather, the "instruction" consists primarily of listening and, perhaps, taking notes. Jensen (1980) and Vernon (1954) summarized the effects of this type of coaching as follows:

1. The coaching effect (over and above the gain due solely to the practice effect of taking a similar test once or twice previously) is about 4 or 5 points.
2. The typical *combined* coaching and practice gain is approximately 9 IQ points (Jensen, p. 591), so the *initial* coaching and practice effects are about equal. However, considerably faster decay in Stanford–Binet coaching gains have been reported by Greene (1928).
3. As with practice effects, IQ score increases are greater for non-verbal, performance, and numerical reasoning items than for verbal items.
4. Again, similar to practice effects, coaching gains are greatest for naive subjects, and greater still for the more able naive subject.
5. The coaching effect for IQ tests appears to be specific, with as yet little demonstrated transfer to other types of tests.

Intelligence is an elusive construct. It is not entirely clear what attribute is being coached in these studies. Presumably, verbal ability, which is largely what the Stanford–Binet measures, is less subject to decay than numerical ability and other kinds of skills such as piano playing and typing. It thus seems logical that both dramatic short-term decreases *and* increases in verbal ability are unlikely. Yet Greene, in point 2, reported mean 3-7 week increases in the Stanford–Binet after coaching of over 29 points, or almost two standard deviations. These gains fell to 17.5 points after 3 months, to 12.6 points after 1 year, and to only 4.3 points after 3 years. Anastasi (1982) has reported similar changes. Conceivably, some individuals or groups of individuals do not engage in the kinds of verbal interchange or reading that facilitate retention of short-term verbal instruction. Systematic, longitudinal case studies may be the only way to provide useful information on this topic.

Cognitive Modifiability: The Work of Feuerstein

The conventional, norm-referenced tests of intelligence and aptitude we have considered so far measure intellectual achievements at the time of testing. In this sense, they are static reflections of the individual's current scholastic aptitude. In using such measures to predict future performance in a variety of endeavors, an underlying presumption, implicit in many investigations but quite explicit in others, is that scholastic intelligence is a faculty that develops naturally, with minimal and incidental influence from experience. Feuerstein (1979) and his colleagues in the United States and Israel have extensively studied the extent to which intelligence and abstract reasoning can be taught. In this research, they employ an instrument (actually a procedure) called the Learning Potential Assessment Device, which is composed of progressive matrices similar to those found on Raven's Progressive Matrices, as well as other figural and verbal problems. Instead of the traditional psychometric assumption that the future will reflect the past, Feuerstein focuses on the processes of intellectual functioning, with a view to discerning ways they can be improved.

Feuerstein's shift in emphasis from the products of intellectual effort to the processes of mental problem solving and from existing abilities to "cognitive modifiability" implies fundamental changes in examiner–examinee interactions. The neutral examiner is replaced by an examiner or teacher who constantly intervenes, makes remarks, requires and gives explanations, anticipates mistakes and difficulties, and warns the examinee about them. Additionally, the occasional insightful remark by retarded performers is immediately seized upon in Feuerstein's assessment approach as a point of departure for remediation and education, not as a random, deviant response representing errors.

Feuerstein relates in his book, *The Dynamic Assessment of Retarded Performers* (1979) a long series of remarkable successes in getting children in the 50–75 IQ range to perform surprisingly high-level abstract thinking. The author personally witnessed an approximately 2-hour session where a 12-year-old boy with a measured Stanford–Binet IQ of 57 was, at the end of the session, solving fairly complex progressive matri-ces and explaining haltingly, but correctly, his reasoning. Despite notable failures by others, Feuerstein has at least documented that abstract thinking, as measured by such items as progressive matrices, is not only coachable but is coachable with subjects long thought to be incapable of such deductive reasoning.

Left unanswered in much of this work, however, is the extent to which the effects of such dynamic assessment transfer laterally to other cognitive tasks and vertically to even more difficult problem solving. Feuerstein responds to this observation by noting that such transfer, although an empirical question, is currently not a major part of his research agenda. Rather, he has demonstrated with a variety of cognitive tasks that persons labeled *retarded* and incapable of abstract reasoning are in fact quite capable of performing such tasks. With this line of argument, Feuerstein maintains, no "external" validity is required, at least not as an integral part of his program of research.

Coaching and Test Validity

A continuing concern on the part of testing specialists, admissions officers, and others is that coaching, if highly effective, could adversely affect predictive validity and could, in fact, call into question the very concept of *aptitude*. Both concerns would appear to be fundamentally unfounded.

With respect to the possible adverse effects on predictive validity, three outcomes of coaching are possible. First, coaching might result in improving both the abilities presumably measured by the tests and the scholastic abilities involved in doing well in college. For the borderline student, coaching in this case would have the wholly laudatory effect of moving the student from the "valid rejection" category to the "valid acceptance" category. No one could reasonably argue against such an outcome.

A second possible effect concerns the student who, because of extreme anxiety or grossly inefficient test-taking strategies (Allison, 1970), obtains a score that is not indicative of her or his true scholastic ability. Coaching in the fundamentals of test taking, such as efficient time allocation and guessing, might conceivably cause the student to be more relaxed and efficient and, thus, improve his or her performance. The test will then be a more veridical reflection of his or her ability. This second case might result in a student moving from the false rejection category to the valid acceptance category, and, again, this is an unarguably positive outcome.

A third possible result of coaching is not so clearly salutary. The result involves an effect that moves the student from the valid rejection category to the false acceptance category. That is, the coached student increases her or his facility with, say, verbal analogies, an item type rarely, if ever, encountered in actual college work, but there is no corresponding increase in the student's ability to get good grades. Case three is an example of what McClelland (1973) calls "faking high aptitude."

The one study devoted specifically to the issue of coaching and test validity is that of Powers (1985), who found that special preparation for the Analytical section of the GRE had no discernible affect upon the test's convergent validity and negligible effects upon the GRE's discriminant validity. Because graduate school grades were unavailable at the time this study was conducted, Powers correlated hours of analytical test preparation with *undergraduate* grade point average ("postdictive" validities). This correlation (.70) is higher than those typically found between scholastic aptitude measures and school performance, suggesting that the criterion-related validity of the GRE Analytical section might have increased as a result of special preparation.

In the absence of more studies devoted specifically to this issue, it is impossible to determine the extent to which each of these outcomes occurs. Clearly, if the first two results dominate, that simply adds to the validity of the test. The author believes the third possibility to be highly unlikely. But, if it turns out to be widespread, then it implies not so much flaws in our understanding of aptitude as serious deficiencies in tests designed to tap that aptitude. In any event, what is needed is serious research on precisely such issues, not continued debate over whether "teaching to the test" is somehow vaguely disreputable. Finally, it is worth pointing out that one of the most efficient and informative ways of understanding a phenomenon is to attempt to change it. It is in this way that we come to understand the nature of expert performance, the optimum conditions under which it progresses, and the instructional environments that foster its development.

Cumulating Results Across Studies: Some General Conclusions

Several investigations of the coaching literature have employed analytical reviews similar to the metanalytic procedures recommended by Glass, McGaw, and Smith (1982), Hedges (1981), Hunter, Schmidt, and Jackson (1982), and DerSimonian and Laird (1983). The review of special preparation for achievement tests by Bangert-Drowns, et al. (1983) has already been mentioned. For the SAT, "effect sizes" per se have not normally been calculated, because the score scale is constant across studies and the scale itself is familar to most readers. Moreover, although various score adjustments based upon measures of variability in the groups under study might be of theoretical interest to some, the overwhelming practical concern is with absolute changes in the scaled scores themselves.

Cole (1982) estimates that the overall mean gain due to coaching across extant studies is approximately 15 points for the SAT-V or the SAT-M. This represents between one and two items on the SAT. Messick estimates the overall coaching gain from studies having some type of control group to be approximately 9 points on Verbal and 13 points on Math.

Are there characteristics of the instruction or instructional content that systematically covary with coaching gains? Class sizes are rarely below 10 and rarely above 20, so it is not surprising that this variable is unrelated to coaching gains. Messick (1980, 1982) and Messick and Jungeblut (1981) have demonstrated a "law of diminishing returns" for the variable "student contact time." They have shown that student contact time is distinctly *nonlinearly* related to gains from coaching. The relationship, it turns out, is quite linear only after a logarithmic transformation of the time dimension.

When linear equations were fit to the regression of score effects on *log* contact time, the extrapolated predictions for programs of less than 50 hours deviated from the actual coaching gains by less than 5 points for the SAT-V and by 10 points for the SAT-M. If studies without control groups are eliminated from the analysis, the agreement is even closer (between two and three points for the SAT-V and eight points for the SAT-M). This is in contrast with the extreme overprediction of score changes by linear extrapolation (in some cases as much as three times as large).

Rank order correlations of student contact time and program effects for studies with control groups and studies without control groups are on the order of .60 and .75, respectively, for the SAT-V. For the SAT-M, the correlations are between .70 and .75, regardless of the existence or absence of adequate control groups. It should be noted that aggregated correlations generally tend to be higher than individual level correlations, and the difference can often be extreme. But correlations of this magnitude are persuasive, given the approximate nature of the estimates of actual student time on task.

Pike has attempted to relate coaching effects to elements of his score model. With respect to alpha components (1–4), component 1 is, by definition, unlikely to be changed appreciably by brief instructional sessions (under 40 or 50 hours, say). Component 2 (review), however, would appear (in the mathematical domain) to be especially subject to meaningful gains for some individuals, even when the review is brief. For persons not previously well grounded in component 1 abilities, review is an empty exercise both figuratively and literally. Such review would likely heighten math anxiety, as suggested by Dyer's 1953 study. For most individuals, short-term review in the verbal domain would be less likely to produce substantial growth, a fact born out by most relatively brief coaching sessions.

Elements of component 3 (integrative learning, overlearning) are likely not to be a part of most special preparation programs, given that the primary motivation for special instruction is test-specific content and not higher level mathematics or extremely difficult passages with obscure words. In fact, Owen (1985) observes that most commercially available *How to Pass the . . .* books contain words that virtually never appear on admissions tests. It would seem that component 3 instruction is, for now at least, restricted primarily to ordinary higher level courses in secondary schools.

It is difficult to specify the elements of an instructional course that would facilitate increases in component 4 (criterion-relevant, analytic skills such as inference and the ability to identify the main idea in a passage). But Pike cites a hypothetical individual who might benefit from such instruction, were it ever effectively designed: "A student who reads widely and with avid interest . . . but who has not honed his or her analytic skills, could well be such a person" (p. 40).

Components 5–9 have been repeatedly shown to be most relevant for naive test takers. Persons unfamiliar with multiple-choice formats, as many foreign students and some cultural and linguistic subgroups in this country are, would most benefit from instruction in these areas.

The coaching controversy is, as indicated before, both a political and a scientific debate. Some have also contended that it is a moral one as well, a position that would acquire added credibility if it could be demonstrably shown that procedures and techniques exist outside of the regular school experience that foster academic performance but are differentially available to citizens.

Testing organizations, the College Board and Educational Testing Service in particular, insist that all verifiable evidence indicates that abilities measured by the SAT and similar admissions tests develop slowly, are largely insensitive to brief interventions involving drill and practice, and are quite valid for their intended purposes. The majority of the published evidence in the technical literature supports this view. It is unfortunate that the most dramatic claims to the contrary come, with rare exception, from outside the peer review process characteristic of modern scientific practice.

Individual students must inevitably assess the data for themselves. The evidence, by no means conclusive, suggests that not all students benefit equally from special instruction. Highly motivated students, students whose high school record and other accomplishments are inconsistent with their test performance, and students who habitually use inefficient test-taking strategies are likely to benefit most.

Research on the extent to which subgroups in the population benefit differentially from coaching is meager. The two studies devoted exclusively to coaching black students showed the modest coaching gains typically found in studies with white students (Johnson et al., 1985; Roberts & Oppenheim, 1966), as well as some extremely large effects (Johnson et al., 1985). Messick, in analyzing small subsamples from the FTC study, found similarly conflicting effects. More research on this topic is clearly indicated.

There is some suggestion that coaching and sex of subject may interact (Dyer, 1953), but, as is the case with race, it is not sex per se that interacts with coaching. Rather, it is usually a third variable, in this case preparation in mathematics, that is the cause of the interaction.

The coaching debate will probably continue unabated for some time to come. One reason for this, of course, is that, so long as tests are used in college admissions decisions, students will continue to seek a competitive advantage in their attempts to gain admission to the colleges of their choice. A second, more scientifically relevant, reason is that recent advances in cognitive psychology (Glaser & Pellegrino, 1982) have provided some hope of explicating the precise nature of aptitude, how it develops, and how it can be enhanced. This line of research was inspired in part by the controversy surrounding the concepts of aptitude and intelligence and by the felt inadequacy of our understanding of both. Green (1981) has noted that social and political challenges to a discipline have a way of invigorating it, so that the discipline is likely to prosper. So it is with the coaching controversy. Our understanding of human intellectual abilities, as well as our attempts to measure them, is likely to profit from what is both a social and a scientific debate.

REFERENCES

Alderman, D. L. (1980). Critical notes on the FTC coaching study. In S. Messick (Ed.), *The effectiveness of coaching for the SAT: Review and reanalysis of research from the fifties to the FTC* (Research Report 80-8, pp. 75–79). Princeton, NJ: Educational Testing Service.

Alderman, D. L., & Powers, D. E. (1979). The effects of special preparation on SAT verbal scores. *American Educational Research Journal, 17,*239–253.

Allison, D. E. (1970). Test anxiety, stress, and intelligence-test performance, and students who habitually use inefficient test taking strategies. *Canadian Journal of Educational Psychologist, 66*(6), 968–973.

Anastasi, A. (1981). Coaching, test sophistication, and developed abilities. *American Psychologist, 36,* 1086–1093.

Anastasi, A. (1982). *Psychological testing.* New York: Macmillan.

Anastasi, A. (1984). Aptitude and achievement tests: The curious case of the indestructible strawperson. In B. S. Plako (Ed.), *Social and technical issues in testing: Implications for test construction and usage.* Hillsdale, NJ: Lawrence Erlbaum.

Ardiff, M. B. (1965). *The relationship of three aspects of test-wiseness to intelligence and reading ability in grades three and six.* Unpublished master's thesis, Cornell University, Ithaca, NY.

Bangert-Drowns, R. L., Kulik, J., & Kulik, C. (1983). Effects of coaching programs on achievement test performance. *Review of Educational Research, 53,* 571–585.

Bobrow, D. G. (1968). National language input for a computer problem-solving system. In M. Minsky (Ed.), *Semantic information processing.* Cambridge, MA: MIT Press.

Coffman, W. E., & Parry, M. E. (1967). Effects of an accelerated reading course on SAT-V scores. *Personnel and Guidance Journal, 46,* 292–296.

Cole, N. (1982). The implications of coaching for ability testing. In A. K. Wigdor & W. R. Garner (Eds.), *Ability testing: Uses, consequences, and controversies.* Washington, DC: National Academy Press.

College Entrance Examination Board. (1968). *Effects of coaching on Scholastic Aptitude Test scores.* New York: Author.

Cooley, W. W., & Lohnes, P. (1976). *Evaluation research in education.* New York: John Wiley & Sons.

Crehan, K. D., Koehler, R. A., & Slakter, M. J. (1974). Longitudinal studies of test-wiseness. *Journal of Educational Measurement, 11,* 209–212.

Cronbach, L. (1984). *Essentials of psychological testing* (4th ed.). New York: Harper & Row.

Dear, R. E. (1958). *The effects of a program of intensive instruction on SAT scores* (Research Report 58–5). Princeton, NJ: Educational Testing Service.

DerSimonian, R., & Laird, N. M. (1983). Evaluating the effect of coaching on SAT scores: A meta-analysis. *Harvard Educational Review, 53*(1), 1–15.

Diamond, J. J., & Evans, W. J. (1972). An investigation of the cognitive correlates of test-wiseness. *Journal of Educational Measurement, 9,* 145–150.

Downey, G. W. (1977). Is it time we started teaching children how to take tests? *American School Board Journal,* 26–31.

Dyer, H. S. (1953). Does coaching help? *College Board Review, 19,* 331–335.

Evans, F. R., & Pike, L. W. (1973). The effects of instruction for these mathematics item formats. *Journal of Educational Measurement, 10,* 257–272.

Federal Trade Commission, Boston Regional Office. (1978). *Staff memorandum of the Boston Regional Office of the FTC: The effects of coaching on standardized admission examinations.* Boston: Author.

Federal Trade Commission, Bureau of Consumer Protection. (1979). *Effects of coaching on standardized admission examinations: Revised statistical analyses of data gathered by Boston Regional Office of the Federal Trade Commission.* Washington, DC: Author.

Feuerstein, R. (1979). *The dynamic assessment of retarded performers.* Baltimore: University Park Press.

Frankel, E. (1960). Effects of growth, practice, and coaching on Scholastic Aptitude Test scores. *Personnel and Guidance Journal, 38,* 713–719.

French, J. W. (1955a). An answer to coaching: Public school experiment with the SAT. *College Board Review, 27,* 5–7.

French, J. W. (1955b). *The coachability of the SAT in public schools* (Research Report 55–26). Princeton, NJ: Educational Testing Service.

French, J. W., & Dear, R. E. (1959). Effects of coaching on an aptitude test. *Educational and Psychological Measurement, 19,* 319–330.

Gibb, B. G. (1964). Test-wiseness as a secondary cue response. *Dissertation Abstracts International,* (University Microfilms No. 64–7643)

Glaser, R., & Pellegrino, J. (1982). Analyzing aptitudes for learning: Inductive reasoning. In R. Glaser (Ed.), *Advances in instructional psychology: Vol II.* Hillsdale, NJ: Lawrence Erlbaum.

Glass, G. V., McGaw, B., & Smith, M. L. (1981). *Metanalysis in social research.* Beverly Hills, CA: Sage.

Green, B. F. (1981). A primer of testing. *American Psychologist, 10,* 1001–1011.

Greene, K. B. (1928). The influence of specialized training on tests of general intelligence. In *Twenty-seventh Yearbook of the National Society for the Study of Education* (pp. 421–428). Bloomington, IN: Public School Publishing.

Hedges, L. V. (1981). Distribution theory for Glass's estimator of effect size and related estimators. *Journal of Educational Statistics, 6,* 107–128.

Hunter, J. E., Schmidt, F. L. & Jackson, G. B. (1982). *Metanalysis: Cumulating research findings across studies.* Beverly Hills, CA: Sage.

Jackson, R. (1980). The scholastic aptitude test: A response to Slack and Porter's "Critical Appraisal." *Harvard Educational Review, 50,* 382–391.

Jacobs, P. I. (1966). Effects of coaching on the College Board English Composition Test. *Educational and Psychological Measurement, 26,* 55–67.

James, W. S. (1953). Symposium on the effects of coaching and practice in intelligence tests, II: Coaching for all recommended. *British Journal of Educational Psychology, 23,* 155–162.

Jensen, A. (1980). *Bias in mental testing.* New York: Macmillan.

Johnson, S. T., Asbury, C. A., Wallace, M. B., Robinson, S., & Vaughn, J. (1985). *The effectiveness of a program to increase Scholastic Aptitude Test scores of black students in three cities.* Paper presented at the Meeting of the National Council on Measurement in Education, Chicago.

Langer, G., Wark, D., & Johnson, S. (1973). Test-wiseness in objective tests. In P. D. Nacke (Ed.), *Diversity in mature reading: Theory and research: Vol. 1.* (22nd Yearbook of the National Reading Conference). Milwaukee, WI: National Reading Conference.

Lass, A. H. (1958). Unpublished manuscript, Abraham Lincoln High School, Brooklyn.

Levine, R. S., & Angoff, W. H. (1958). The effects of practice and growth on scores on the Scholastic Aptitude Test (Research Report) Princeton, NJ: Educational Testing Service.

Lord, F. M., & Novick, M. R. (1968). *Statistical theories of mental test scores.* Reading, MA: Addison-Wesley.

Marron, J. E. (1965). *Preparatory school test preparation: A special test preparation, its effects on College Board Scores, and the relationship of affected scores to subsequent college performance.* West Point, NY: United States Military Academy, Research Division, Office of Director of Admissions and Registrar.

McClelland, D. (1973). Testing for competence rather than intelligence. *American Psychologist, 29,* 107.

Messick, S. (1980). *The effectiveness of coaching for the SAT: Review and analysis of research from the fifties to the FTC* (Research Report No. 80–8). Princeton, NJ: Educational Testing Service.

Messick, S. (1982). Issues of effectiveness and equity in the coaching controversy: Implications for educational and testing practice. *Educational Psychologist, 17,* 67–91.

Messick, S., & Jungeblut, A. (1981). Time and method in coaching for the SAT. *Psychological Bulletin, 89,* 191–216.

Millman, J., Bishop, H., & Ebel, R. (1965). An analysis of test-wiseness. *Educational and Psychological Measurement, 25,* 707–726.

Moore, J. C. (1971). Test-wiseness and analogy test performance. *Measurement and Evaluation in Guidance, 3*(4), 198–202.

Nickerson, R. S., Perkins, N. O., & Smith, E. E. (1985). *The teaching of thinking.* Hillsdale, NJ: Lawrence Erlbaum.

Oakland, T. (1973). The effects of test-wiseness materials on standardized test performance of preschool disadvantaged children. *Journal of School Psychology, 10,* 355–360.

Owen, D. (1985). *None of the above: Behind the myth of scholastic aptitude.* Boston: Houghton Mifflin.

Pallone, N. J. (1961). Effects of short-term and long-term developmental reading courses upon SAT verbal scores. *Personnel and Guidance Journal, 39,* 654–657.

Pike, L. W. (1978). *Short-term instruction, test-wiseness, and the Scholastic Aptitude Test: A literature review with research recommendations* (CB RDR 77–78, No. 2 and ETS Research Report No. 78–2). Princeton, NJ: Educational Testing Service.

Pike, L. W., & Evans, F. R. (1972). *The effects of special instruction for three kinds of mathematics aptitude items* (Research Report No. 72–19). Princeton, NJ: Educational Testing Service.

Powers, D. E. (1980). Critical notes on the FTC coaching study. In S. Messick (Ed.). *The effectiveness of coaching for the SAT: Review and reanalysis of research from the fifties to the FTC* (Research Report No. 80–8, pp. 81–91). Princeton, NJ: Educational Testing Service.

Powers, D. E. (1982). *Estimating the effects of various methods of preparing for the SAT* (College Board Report No. 82–2). New York: College Entrance Examination Board.

Powers, D. E. (1985). Effects of test preparation on the validity of a graduate admissions test. *Applied Psychological Measurement, 9,* 179–190.

Powers, D. E., & Alderman, D. L. (1983). Effects of test familiarization on SAT performance. *Journal of Educational Measurement, 20,* 71–79.

Powers, D. E., & Swinton, S. S. (1984). Effects of self-study on coachable test item types. *Journal of Educational Psychology, 76,* 266–278.

Pyrczak, F. (1972). Objective evaluation of the quality of multiple-choice test items to measure comprehension in reading passages. *Reading Research Quarterly, 8,* 62–71.

Pyrczak, F. (1974). Passage-dependence of items designed to measure the ability to identify the main ideas of paragraphs: Implications for validity. *Educational and Psychological Measurement, 34,* 343–348.

Roberts, S. O., & Oppenheim, D. B. (1966). *The effect of special instruction upon test performance of high school students in Tennessee* (Research Report No. 66–36). Princeton, NJ: Educational Testing Service.

Rock, D. A. (1980). Disentangling coaching effects and differential growth in the FTC coaching study. In S. Messick (Ed.). *The effectiveness of coaching for the SAT: Review and reanalysis of research from the fifties to the FTC* (Research Report No. 80–8, pp. 123–135). Princeton, NJ: Educational Testing Service.

Rowley, G. L. (1974). Which examinees are favored by the use of multiple-choice tests? *Journal of Educational Measurement, 11,* 15–23.

Slack, W. V., & Porter, D. (1980a). The Scholastic Aptitude Test: A critical appraisal. *Harvard Educational Review, 50,* 154–175.

Slack, W. V., & Porter, D. (1980b). Training, validity, and the issue of aptitude: A reply to Jackson. *Harvard Educational Review, 50,* 392–401.

Slakter, M. J. (1967). Risk taking on objective examinations. *American Educational Research Journal, 4,* 31–43.

Slakter, M. J. (1968a). The effect of guessing on objective test scores. *Journal of Educational Measurement, 5,* 217–222.

Slakter, M. J. (1968b). The penalty for not guessing. *Journal of Educational Measurement, 5,* 141–144.

Slakter, M. J. (1969). Generality of risk taking on objective examinations. *Educational and Psychological Measurement, 29,* 115–128.

Slakter, M. J., Crehan, K. D., & Koehler, R. A. (1975). Longitudinal studies of risk taking on objective examinations. *Educational and Psychological Measurement, 35,* 97–105.

Stricker, L. J. (1982). *Test disclosure and retest performance on the Scholastic Aptitude Test* (College Board Report No. 82–7). New York: College Entrance Examination Board.

Stroud, T. W. F. (1980). Reanalysis of the Federal Trade Commission study of commercial coaching for the SAT. In S. Messick (Ed.). *The effectiveness of coaching for the SAT: Review and reanalysis of research from the fifties to the FTC* (Research Report No. 80-8, pp. 97-121). Princeton, NJ: Educational Testing Service.

Swineford, F. M. & Miller, P. M. (1953). The effects of directions regarding guessing on item statistics of a multiple-choice vocabulary test. *Journal of Educational Psychology, 44,* 185-188.

Swinton, S. S., & Powers, D. E. (1983). A study of the effects of special preparation of GRE analytical scores and item types. *Journal of Educational Psychology, 75,* 104-115.

Vernon, P. E. (1954). Symposium on the effects of coaching and practice in intelligence tests, V: Conclusions. *British Journal of Educational Psychology, 24,* 57-63.

Whimbey, A. (1975). *Intelligence can be taught.* New York: E. P. Dutton.

White, A. P., & Zammarelli, J. E. (1981). Convergence principles: Information in the answer set of some multiple-choice intelligence tests. *Applied Psychological Measurement, 5,* 21-28.

Whitely, S. E., & Dawis, R. V. (1974). Effects of cognitive intervention on latent ability measured from analogy items. *Journal of Educational Psychology, 66,* 710-717.

Whitla, D. K. (1962). Effect of tutoring on Scholastic Aptitude Test scores. *Personnel and Guidance Journal, 41,* 32-37.

Wiseman, S., & Wrigley, J. (1953). The comparative effects of coaching and practice on the results of verbal intelligence tests. *British Journal of Psychology, 44,* 83-94.

Woodley, K. K. (1973). *Test-wiseness program development and evaluation.* Paper presented at the meeting of the American Educational Research Association, New Orleans.

Yates, A. (1953). Symposium on the effects of coaching and practice in intelligence tests: An analysis of some recent investigations. *British Journal of Educational Psychology, 23,* 147-154.

3

Applications

12

Designing Tests That Are Integrated with Instruction

Anthony J. Nitko

School of Education, University of Pittsburgh

This chapter is concerned primarily with the design of tests that are consistent with educators' intentions and the goals of the educational systems within which those tests are used. The discussion is limited to the context of formal instruction and schooling.

It is reasonable to ask why anyone should care about the link between testing and instruction. It is not uncommon, in fact, for both professional educators and laypersons to conclude that, because tests are used in schools, they must measure how well students have learned what they were taught. Considerable evidence exists, however, to support the view that tests created by agencies external to a school inadequately represent the content and skills emphasized by teachers in particular classrooms. Even tests created by classroom teachers frequently seem to inadequately measure the teachers' espoused instructional goals or to contain tasks for which instruction has not been entirely appropriate (although teachers' tests usually do sample adequately the content they teach).

The position taken in this chapter is that appropriately used educational tests, whether created by classroom teachers or other agents, are potent educational tools that enhance the instructional process. In many instances, appropriate test usage means that testing is an integral part of the instructional method or process. As used here, testing is any systematic procedure for observing and classifying students' performance for purposes of obtaining instructionally relevant information, but it is not limited to quantifying observed student performance. Thus, the term *test* includes more procedures than traditional paper-and-pencil instruments. Further, the term *appropriate test usage* means that tests should be linked with or integrated with both instructional materials and procedures.[1]

Among the undesirable consequences of using tests that are inadequately linked or integrated with the instruction received by students are the facts that (a) teachers and students might be inappropriately informed about students' learning progress and learning difficulties; (b) students' motivation for learning could be reduced; (c) critical decisions about students (e.g., whether to award a student a high school diploma) might be made unfairly; (d) the effectiveness of instruction may be evaluated incorrectly. The first two consequences are most likely to result from tests inappropriately created, used, or both, to make day-to-day decisions within a specific instructional system. Tests used primarily to make day-to-day decisions within a particular instructional system are called *internal tests* in this chapter. The last two consequences are most likely to result when tests created by agencies outside a particular school are inappropriately imposed on students in that school. Tests imposed by authorities from outside a particular instructional system are called *external tests* in this chapter.

This chapter discusses instructional linkages for both internal and external tests. There are three major sections: Instructional Design and Its Relation to Instructional Test Design; Linking Internal Tests to Instruction; and Linking External Tests to Instruction. Of particular concern in the first section

---

NOTE: I am very much indebted to the reviewers whose comments on an earlier draft of this chapter helped me to improve it: Peter W. Airasian, Boston College; A. E. Ashworth, University of Malawi; Karen Block, University of Pittsburgh; Thomas M. Haladyna, American College Testing Programs; Tse-chi Hsu, University of Pittsburgh; Boleslaw Niemierko, Wyzsza Szkola Pedagogiczna, Bydgoszcz; Lauren B. Resnick, University of Pittsburgh; and William B. Thomas, University of Pittsburgh. This paper was written, in part, while I was a Fulbright Professor of Education at the University of Malawi.

[1]Surely there are other ways to view educational testing and test usage, many of which have been stated in other chapters of this volume. The point of this paragraph is to set boundaries on the discussion that follows. The volume as a whole presents a comprehensive view of educational testing.

are the instructional design variables that need to be considered when designing and developing tests to be used within any particular instructional system. The second section is organized around four topics: designs of tests to use with learners before new instruction begins, designs of tests used to diagnosis student learning difficulties and to monitor student progress, designs of tests assessing a learner's achievements at the end of an instructional segment, and designs of evaluation systems that motivate pupils to learn. The third section discusses problems associated with the design of tests used for student credentialing and for evaluating instructional systems and schools.

Instructional Design and Its Relation to Instructional Test Design

Instructional Activities Versus Educational Activities

The field of education may be viewed as composed of disciplined inquiry and professional activity in instruction, curriculum, counseling, administration, and evaluation (Reigeluth, 1983b). Instruction, as one professional activity in education, is the means through which educators provide specific conditions and actions that foster changes in the initial cognitive states and behavioral repertoires of learners. Among the activities performed by people concerned with instruction are the following (Reigeluth, 1983b): designing methods of instruction; developing (constructing) methods of instruction; implementing (adapting) methods of instruction; managing (using and maintaining) implemented instructional methods; and evaluating the effectiveness, efficiency, and quality of instructional methods. Each of these may be viewed as an activity of professional practice within instruction, and each may also be viewed as an area for disciplined inquiry (research and scholarship) concerned "with understanding and improving the means to perform each activity with optimal results" (p.7).

Integrating Test Design with Instructional Design

This framework for describing activities in the area of instruction may be used to illustrate the way in which testing needs to be conceptualized in order for it to be appropriately integrated with instruction. Basically, this means that, as a method of instruction is designed, some of the design activities should be concerned with designing testing methods that are optimal for that instructional method. When a teacher (or other instructional developer) is in the process of deciding which instructional method is best for bringing about the desired changes in specific types of students and for a specific course's content, the teacher or developer should also be deciding on the best testing procedures for bringing about these changes. This recommendation goes beyond the usual one of asking teachers and developers to specify the best format for testing students (e.g., essay versus objective items) and includes considering how all of the following contribute to bring about desired changes in students: (a) the types of test materials and their organization, (b) the tasks set by the tests versus the tasks set by the learning materials and procedures, (c) the timing and frequency of testing, (d) the impact of a testing procedure on various students (aptitude-testing program interaction), (e) the usability of test results by the teacher, and (f) the way in which tests and test results will be perceived by students. All of these concerns, and perhaps others, represent professional activities associated with designing tests for instruction. It would be possible to list similar test-instruction considerations for the remaining instruction-related activities in the previously mentioned list (instructional development, implementation, management, and evaluation). This chapter focuses almost exclusively, however, on test-design considerations.

The Need for Prescriptive Theories of Test Design

Traditional approaches to disciplined inquiry in test design have tended to focus on optimizng the measurement efficiency of tests rather than on optimizing their instructional efficacy. One result of this is that the professional activity of designing tests for use in instruction has a rather loosely structured and incomplete knowledge base underpinning it. The professional activities associated with designing tests for use in instruction would benefit from the development of one or more theories of instructional test design, just as the professional practice of instructional design would benefit from prescriptive theories of instructional design (Glaser, 1976; Simon, 1969; Reigeluth, 1983b). The desired outcomes for theories of instructional test design are prescriptions for stating what testing methods to use when the instructional conditions and the desired student outcomes have been specified. Testing methods include format, materials, organizations, administration methods and procedures, scoring procedures, and specific uses of results. Prescriptions about good methods of testing may be viewed as dependent variables that the theory predicts, using as independent variables the instructional conditions, the desired instructional outcomes, and their interactions (cf. Landa, 1983; Reigeluth, 1983b). (This chapter does not describe an instructional test-design theory, but it does consider some of the variables that must be studied if such a theory is to be created.)

Variables Influencing Instructional Test Design

Prescriptions for test designs or for constructing testing methods for any given application are obviously linked to the instructional methods to be employed, to the instructional conditions under which instruction is to occur, and to the instructional outcomes to be expected. Figure 12.1 shows various classes of instructional-method variables and some of the major instructional-condition and outcome variables that influence them. The reader is referred to Reigeluth and Merrill (1979) for details of the variables depicted in the figure. It should be pointed out that the list of condition variables shown in the figure is not complete but is intended to represent the conditions likely to have the strongest influence on instructional-method variables.

FIGURE 12.1 Major categories of instructional condition, method, and outcome variables and their mutual influence.

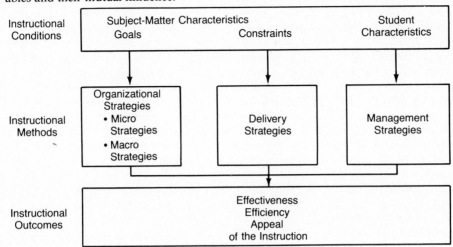

Source: Reigeluth (1983b), p. 19. Reprinted by permission.

INSTRUCTIONAL CONDITIONS

The conditions under which instruction occurs necessarily limit or qualify prescriptions for instructional design and test design. The following conditions represent examples of the variables test designers need to consider.

1. *A pupil's educational and physical development and maturity limit instructional and testing methods that can be used.* This is an obvious point, but as an examination of many operating instructional and testing methods would reveal, it is frequently not taken into account. There are obvious differences between older and younger learners that a test designer needs to consider when deciding how (and even what) to test. Less familiar to some test designers are physical and cognitive factors affecting a handicapped learner's ability to demonstrate what he or she knows. The basic design principle here is that the test should not impede the learner from demonstrating that she or he has acquired the desired behavior or attained the desired cognitive state.

To create effective instruction, it is necessary to have an understanding of the learner's preinstructional cognitive state and the relationship of this state to subsequent learning under each of the options available in, or the constraints of, a particular instructional system (Atkinson & Paulson, 1972; Glaser, 1976, 1982). Designers of effective preinstructional tests need to use both kinds of information.

2. *The way a curriculum is organized restrains the nature of the testing program.* Some curricula, for example, are organized in strictly hierarchical sequences of prerequisite learnings: At each new level of the hierarchy new learning builds on an assumed degree of acquisition of previous knowledge and skill. In such a curriculum, pretests are designed to assure that learners have the necessary prerequisites, and posttests are used to assure that learners have acquired proficiency with the material in the current level of the hierarchy before they are permitted to move forward to a higher level. In such a system few pupil errors are permitted to go forward, because little opportunity for reteaching prerequisites exists at the higher levels. Other curricula are organized in spiral sequences: At the next levels of the sequence, students review and expand their conception of previously taught material, and the system is geared to gradual correction of errors and misconceptions. In this type of curriculum, pretests and posttests check, not so much for initially high levels of mastery, but for the more serious types of errors and to see whether the learner has sufficient grasp of the general process being taught to proceed to a new learning sequence. (Pretests are discussed in more detail in a later section.)

3. *The belief systems of the instruction designer and the test designer are one of the bases for formulating what and how to test.* Curricula differ, not only in organization, but also in how and what they conceptualize as desired learning outcomes, and this naturally shapes and delimits the design of tests linked to instruction. Analyses of performance characteristics and cognitive states of competent persons are important in the instruction-test design process, because one's understanding of these characteristics and states is the basis for formulating desired instructional goals and objectives (Atkinson & Paulson, 1972; Glaser, 1976, 1982). What and how one chooses to teach and to measure are always linked to one's conception of the nature of human intelligence and competence (Wagner & Sternberg, 1984). As more is learned from research on the knowledge structures of competent persons, tests can be created to measure new aspects of competence not previously considered. Because each generation of instructional methods and instructional tests reflects a dominant view of what constitutes competence, there must be a synergy between developments in instructional psychology and developments in testing technology, to assure the integration of testing and instructional procedures.

Although beliefs can be informed or altered by scientific findings, the basic designs of instruction and tests seem to be directed by designers' beliefs. The learning outcomes designers value and believe to be important eventually become the focus of instruction and pupil evaluation. Frequently, test-design considerations must also take into account the beliefs of significant others who have stakes in the educational system (e.g., school board members, teachers, parents, and legislators).

4. *The availability of instructional resources and the mar-*

ketability of an instructional package frequently determine the nature of the tests developed. For tests to be integrated with instruction, ultimately they must be meshed with instructional materials. Currently there are trends toward schools purchasing complete instructional packages that include tests and testlike exercises used for instruction, review, diagnosis, and evaluation. Remedial materials geared to preparing students to pass competency tests depend increasingly on testlike worksheets consisting of multiple-choice tests (Haertel & Calfee, 1983). If a teacher is the instructional deliverer, he or she is more or less committed to using these curricular tests because of the schools' investment, their apparent match to what is taught, and the simplicity of their use. Similarly, others designing instructional approaches might need to take into account the availability, technical quality, and design of commerical materials.

The trend toward the all-encompassing teaching–testing package will accelerate as reasonably priced courseware using technology such as computers, laser discs, and videodiscs begins to supplement print materials. As F. B. Baker (1984) points out, the advances in technology will necessitate a team approach in which instruction, curriculum, textbook, testing, and software designers work together to produce a mixture of conventional and computer-based instructional systems. In Baker's words,

> The testing alternative that I see developing is what can be called nonintrusive testing. Under this approach a student using an instructional software package will not be administered a formal test within the context of computer-based instruction. Instead . . . instructionally relevant data will be collected as the student interacts dynamically with the instructional software. . . . Given these data, evaluation routines embedded within the instructional software can determine the student's instructional status . . . [and] when the desired level of understanding has been reached, the computer simply tells the student he/she knows the material and should move on. From the student's point of view a test was never taken, but from the instructor's point of view the student has been continuously evaluated.

INSTRUCTIONAL METHODS

Instructional designers take into account several types of method variables such as ways of organizing and sequencing instructional events, ways of delivering instruction (e.g., teacher and textbook), and management strategies such as those related to whether or when to individualize instruction. Among the instructional-method variables directly affecting test design are the following.

1. *Types of decisions.* Instructional decisions are points of focus for test design. The form, content, and organization of testing differ, depending on the information and instructional-decision requirements of a particular instructional method. Instructional test designers need to consider both the types of decisions to be made and the critical decision points within a particular instructional method. Some basic types of pupil-oriented instructional decisions can be delineated for those instructional approaches that attempt to adapt to the rate or style of a pupil's learning (Glaser & Nitko, 1971; Nitko, 1969; Nitko & Hsu, 1974).

1. *Placement decisions:* deciding which instructional sequence or at what level in the instructional sequence a learner should begin studies to avoid unnecessarily repeating what is already known and to proceed more rapidly toward the attainment of new goals
2. *Diagnostic decisions:* deciding which learning outcomes a learner has not acquired and the probable cause(s) of the failure to acquire them, in order to remediate and correct incomplete or erroneous prior learning
3. *Monitoring decisions:* deciding whether a pupil is attending to instruction as it is occurring, if the assigned learning activity is working effectively, and whether a different activity should be assigned
4. *Attainment decisions:* deciding, at the end of a particular instructional segment, whether a pupil has attained the desired instructional goals

Although these are fundamental instructional decisions requiring quality information, it does not follow that paper-and-pencil tests are the appropriate means of obtaining the required information or that a test must be administered each time a decision needs to be made. It is likely that the needed information is obtained from both short-term and long-term formal and informal information-gathering procedures that include direct observation of pupils, reviews of daily work, informal discussions with pupils, and general knowledge of pupils' attitudes, interests, typical styles of study, and needs for personal attention (Lindvall & Nitko, 1975).

Airasian and Madaus (1972) describe a general system of evaluation applicable to classroom instructional decisions and suggest ways of integrating these pupil evaluations into instruction through such factors as deciding when evidence is to be gathered and the nature of the evidence to be sampled. Figure 12.2 summarizes their recommendations. It represents one example of how test-design variables and instructional-design variables can be integrated.

2. *Integration of testing with instruction depends on knowledge of the key segments of an instructional model or management strategy.* Instructional models or approaches describe how individual differences in learners are handled and suggest needed instructional resources. Effective instructional test design requires knowing (a) certain key elements in the instructional model being considered for a given decision, (b) the instructional context in which the information is needed, and (c) how the information will be used to arrive at decisions.

Glaser (1977) specifies five strategies that schools have used or could use for adapting to individual pupil differences. Two of these are described briefly here to illustrate how differences in instructional approaches imply different testing strategies.

2A. *Fixed and standard instructional procedures.* In this approach, educational goals and the set of instructional methods available to students are standard and fixed. A pupil new to the system is administered tests to assess her or his initial competence, and a decision is made to enroll the pupil in the fixed, standard instruction or to label the pupil a poor risk or a poor learner. Depending on public policy or the educational setting in which instruction is to occur, poor learners might be entirely excluded from further education, or they might be given an alternate education program, different and

FIGURE 12.2 Four types of classroom decisions and their testing requirements.

	PLACEMENT	FORMATIVE	DIAGNOSTIC	SUMMATIVE

FUNCTION OF EVALUATION	to place students by
	a. determining the degree to which prerequisite entry behaviors or skills are present or absent
	b. determining entering mastery of the course objectives
	c. matching students to alternative teachers or instructional modes according to characteristics known or thought to optimize achievement
		Formative evaluation is contributory. Its functions are
		a. to provide on-going feedback to the teacher for the purposes of
		  1. choosing or modifying subsequent learning experiences
		  2. prescribing remediation of group or individual deficiencies
		b. to provide on-going feedback to the student for the purpose of directing advanced or remedial study
			to recognize psychological, physical, or environmental symptoms manifested by students with extraordinary or recurrent learning and/or classroom problems	to grade, certify, or attest to student learning or teacher effectiveness

TIME OF EVIDENCE GATHERING	prior to entry into an instructional unit	several times prior to the completion of instruction on a predefined segment (unit chapter, etc.) of a course	While a teacher should always be sensitive to the manifestation of symptoms known to be related to learning difficulties he should be particularly attentive to students when classroom or learning difficulties cannot be explained in terms of cognitive or instructional variables.	at the conclusion of a unit, course, or year's instruction
BEHAVIORAL CHARACTERISTICS OF EVIDENCE GATHERED	dependent on the functions stated above: typically cognitive or psychomotor when the function is to determine whether or not prerequisite entry behaviors are present or to determine the student's prior mastery of course objectives; may also be affective when the purpose is to match students to alternative teachers or instructional modes.	cognitive or psychomotor	physical (vision, auditory perception, dominance and laterality, general health, etc.); psychological (intelligence, emotional maladjustment, social maladjustment, etc.); environmental (nutritional, parent-child relationships, peer influences, etc.).	depends on course objectives; higher or lower level cognitive behaviors, affective and/or psychomotor
EVIDENCE GATHERING TECHNIQUES	depend on type of placement sought, but could include: a. commercial tests (Intelligence, achievement, diagnostic, etc.) b. teacher-made instruments (formative, summative, specially designed pre-tests, observation, interviews, checklists, video-tapes, etc.)	a series of teacher-made achievement measures; supply, essay, or selection tests, interviews, video-tapes, checklists, etc.	primarily observational although for certain symptoms general screening techniques to confirm hypotheses may be available to the classroom teacher (e.g. vision). Generally, upon noting symptoms, the teacher forwards his observations to proper agencies, e.g. guidance counselor, nurse, school psychologist, etc.	primarily internally or externally constructed achievement tests

Figure 12.2 *(Continued)*

FIGURE 12.2 *(Continued)*

	PLACEMENT	FORMATIVE	DIAGNOSTIC	SUMMATIVE
SAMPLING CONSIDERATIONS FOR EVIDENCE GATHERING	depend on the functions specified above; evidence must be gathered on a. each prerequisite entry behavior b. a representative sample of course objectives c. those behaviors related to a construct(s) which in turn are known or thought to be related to different types of teachers or to alternative modes of instruction	a. where the objectives of an instructional segment are interrelated (cognitively or sequentially within cognitive levels) the sample should include all objectives in the segment. b. where the objectives of a predefined instructional segment are not interrelated, the determination may depend on such considerations as the use of an objective in subsequent learning; the extent to which an objective integrates or reinforces prior learning, etc.	Sampling in the psychometric sense is not applicable. An ad hoc observational process designed to construct and confirm hypotheses about suspected causes of disorders.	weighted sample of course objectives; weighting may be in terms of teaching emphasis, purpose of evaluation, time spent, transferability of objectives, perceived importance in society, etc.
SCORING AND REPORTING	patterns, profiles, subscores, etc. for all functions except placing students out of a course (where total score may be utilized)	patterns of item responses, abilities mastered or not mastered, etc. All reporting must be free of any intimation of a mark, grade, or certification.	an anecdotal report containing specific behavioral instances forwarded to the appropriate referral agency.	sum of total number of correct responses, either by objective or on total exam; reported as letter or number grade, standard score, percentile, etc.
STANDARDS AGAINST WHICH SCORES ARE COMPARED	predetermined norm or criterion referenced standards	criterion referenced standards	compare manifested behavior against specified abnormal behaviors	almost exclusively norm referenced
RELIABILITY	dependent on the trait measured, and the consequences of the judgments	stability and/or consistency of item response patterns	recurrence of behavior symptoms	internal consistency
VALIDITY	primarily content validity but also construct validity (where students are matched with teachers or instructional strategies)	primarily content validity but also construct validity (where hierarchies of objectives are involved)	face validity	content validity

Source: Airasian and Madaus (1972), pp. 222–223. Reprinted by permission.

away from the mainstream program, because they have been judged unsuitable.

Pupils admitted to the standard program continue to advance through it so long as they can demonstrate satisfactory learning. Otherwise, they repeat the same level of instruction or drop out. This approach uses tests that select, or screen, individuals for their suitability to be instructed. These tests are likely to measure both the degree to which a minimum level of prerequisite knowledge has been attained and the aptitudes that predict success in the particular instructional setting in which an admitted student is expected to learn.

Schwarz (1971) discusses the rationale for identifying and using some of these tests. It is likely that the successful student in this instructional approach is one who can adapt or knows how to learn in the particular fixed instructional context.

Among how-to-learn abilities are the following (Wang & Lindvall, 1984): (a) skill in learning from written materials, (b) study habits and skills, (c) problem-solving strategies, and (d) skill in help seeking. A "job analysis" of a typical instructional setting might help the instructional-test designer identify which of these how-to-learn abilities are required for success, and measures of them could constitute part of the admissions test battery to be constructed and validated. Students' progress and success in learning are judged with the help of achievement tests given at appropriate terminal points in instruction (e.g., end of unit, midterm, and end of course). These tests have been termed *summative evaluation tests* (Bloom, Hastings, & Madaus, 1971).

2B. *Alternative instructional methods to accommodate different learning styles.* Another possible approach provides different methods of instruction, each of which lead to the same instructional objectives. Each method had its own pretest of entry skills and aptitudes, and a student's performance on the pretest(s) determines which method is appropriate. The methods of instruction differ on the basis of learning styles and other learner characteristics. Wang and Lindvall (1984) review the research findings on learner characteristics and their implications for designing methods of instruction that adapt to or accommodate learner differences. They identify three broad categories of variables: (a) students' self-perceptions; (b) abilities and cognitive processes needed to acquire, recall, and use information; and (c) students' temperament patterns and cognitive styles. The measurement requirements of this approach are complex. The specific variables that are measured on the pretests need to be explicitly identified and carefully specified. Frequently these variables are not well defined or operationalized in the research literature, so that a considerable test-design and construct validation effort is required before an operational testing program can be instituted. Assignment to alternate treatments on the basis of measures of learning characteristics requires validation of many aptitide treatment interactions.[2]

INSTRUCTIONAL OUTCOMES

Instructional outcomes include both student variables (achievement, appeal) and system variables (cost-effectiveness, teacher-time allocation). Just as designers prescribe instructional methods, so test designers' prescriptions are optimal for some types of outcomes and not others. Presumably, when testing and instruction are integrated, the desired outcomes are optimized. The following are examples of considerations to keep in mind when seeking optimal instructional-testing methods.

1. *The testing procedures used in the instructional process must measure the student behaviors and cognitive processes that have been stated as desired outcomes of instruction.* Instructional models differ in the ways they conceptualize knowledge and understanding. Testing models similarly differ in the ways knowledge and understanding are conceptualized. This dimension of how knowledge is *conceptualized* is a crucial one to consider when designing tests that are linked to instruction. An example of a lack of congruence between testing procedures and instructional goals is the situation in which the stated goal of instruction is to alter a student's knowledge schema, but the diagnostic tests within the instructional system focus on measuring a student's behavioral manifestations of knowledge rather than on a student's knowledge organization (see the section on diagnostic testing for more details).

2. *Testing procedures used in the instructional process must contribute to the appeal of instruction for students.* Appeal in this context means students' desire to continue learning. The tendency for students to want to continue to learn is re-

lated to both the formal and the informal evaluations that a particular instructional approach imposes (Natriello & Dornbusch, 1984). Thus, one variable for designers to consider in relation to the instructional outcome of appeal is the role of the ensemble of formal and informal tests in the instructional system. Too frequent testing, for example, may lower appeal by increasing students' anxiety or result in students attributing failure to the teacher, rather than to individual effort (see the section on the evaluative role of testing for more details).

Linking Internal Tests to Instruction

This section is concerned with the general nature of instructional test design, emphasizing that the designing of tests and instruction are mutually planned efforts. This section is concerned particularly with types of decisions that occur during the course of instruction and the design of tests that provide information for making these decisions. The section is organized around four topics: Placement and Preinstructional Decisions, Monitoring and Diagnostic Decisions, Attainment and Posttesting Decisions, and The Motivational Role of Pupil Evaluations. Most of the discussion in this section centers on the instructional methods of Figure 12.1, particularly variables associated with instructional management strategies as described by Reigeluth and Merrill (1979).

Placement and Preinstructional Decisions

Earlier in this chapter it was mentioned that the learner's preinstructional state had to be considered when designing effective instruction. This principle has been operationalized in instructional designs emphasizing systematic instruction (Roid & Haladyna, 1982) and by creating placement tests in instructional designs that seek to assign students to one of several courses teaching a particular subject (e.g., different levels of mathematics) (see Figure 12.2). The discussion that follows uses the term *pretest* to describe both of these types of tests, alluding to the time frame in which the tests are administered rather than to the function(s) they serve. Two situations are considered: designing pretests that are used to make decisions about students in relation to the entire course and designing pretests for decision making in relation to a smaller segment of instruction, called a *unit*.

PRETESTS FOR AN ENTIRE COURSE

In some instructional designs, pretests are administered at the start of the course to ascertain whether students have acquired the necessary prerequisites to the course, or have attained knowledge of part or all of the content of the course, or both. Prerequisites can include not only component knowledge and skills, but also the learners' entering knowledge struc-

---

[2]Wagner and Sternberg (1984) identify the following difficulties with ATI research, ATI being the basis of instructional design and testing in this approach: (a) While general scholastic aptitude has been found to interact with different instructional approaches, there is little evidence that specific aptitudes exhibit stable interactions; (b) the generalization of ATIs to conditions beyond the experiment is frequently limited; (c) a great deal of statistical power is required to identify an ATI; and (d) the experiments investigating ATI are frequently weak operationalizations of the theory that spawned them. See also Snow (1980).

ture or schema, which might enhance or inhibit their learning under the planned instructional procedure (for further discussion of this point, see the section on diagnostic assessment).

The presumed advantages of pretests for an entire course are that the instructional system can use pretest information to adjust the instructional content and procedure to be more responsive to students' needs and that some students might have already learned much or all of the course and, hence, could be placed in an advanced or alternate course. A possible additional advantage is that, if the pretest shows students an operational definition of the end-of-course objectives, it might sensitize them to the course goals and enhance learning (Hartley & Davies, 1976). Pretests may be used as a basis for planning group instruction and individualized instruction. In either case, formal course pretesting and placement are most useful when there is little known about the entry-level competencies and abilities of students and when the instructional system can use the information obtained to adapt instruction to subgroups or individuals. If these conditions are not met, course pretesting is not advantageous. If all pupils have essentially the same level of pre-entry knowledge and skill, for example, collecting individuals' pretest data could be unnecessary (group data might be collected on an item-sampling basis). Further, if a teacher has taught many of the individuals previously or if a computer has collected relevant data as the program has interacted with a learner, the preinstructional information needed for effective instruction might already exist, and adding a formal pretest would be unnecessary. When deciding whether to require course pretests in an instructional system, one must keep in mind that the instructional system must be capable of using the pretest information in constructive ways. It must, for example, be capable of allowing students to progress to advanced topics or to skip the course entirely; otherwise there is little use in administering the pretest.

PRETESTS FOR SMALLER INSTRUCTIONAL UNITS

Courses are usually divided into a series of smaller instructional sequences called, as noted, *units.* These units may be arranged in at least a roughly prerequisite order. Pretests for these instructional units have been recommended for some instructional systems, to develop a "unit profile" of a student (see Glaser & Nitko, 1971; Roid & Haladyna, 1982). This profile is frequently of the type that describes which of the within-unit objectives the student has mastered. Instruction is adapted by having students omit instruction covering the mastered objectives.

The practice of unit pretesting must be weighed against its ultimate usefulness in the instructional system. *First,* if the system cannot adapt instruction to pupils who have mastered the material to various degrees, knowing pretest information about each pupil is probably not very useful. *Second,* even if the system is designed to adapt to individuals on the basis of pretest data, pretesting might not be an efficient use of instructional time. A reliable unit pretest is likely to require a considerable number of test items per instructional objective tested. If a unit contains many objectives, the pretest is likely to be lengthy. Further, if many students do not know the material pretested, they are likely to take a long time to respond to the test items. After pretesting, instruction needs to be given. Thus, the total time, pretesting plus instruction, could be inordinately long. It might be entirely more efficient to have all children receive instruction for each unit of the curriculum, instead of pretesting to see if some few children could test out of a unit. Eliminating such pretesting might reduce the amount of time a learner would have to spend in a unit, perhaps from five sessions to three sessions (assuming pretesting takes two instruction sessions).

One principle for designing pretests is to examine the consequences of both pretesting and not pretesting in light of the curriculum, the instructional approach, the resources, and the pupils before planning for them. Unlike a course pretest, where passing the test permits the students to skip over large segments of the course (or the entire course), thus saving student and instructor a large amount of time, a unit pretest can take longer to administer and score than simply providing instruction for all (note that this suggestion is directed to optimizing attainment of the instructional outcome labeled *efficiency* in Figure 12.1). As used here, a unit is rather arbitrary: At some level of education, a unit can represent 4, 6, or 8 weeks of instruction, in which case pretesting out of a unit could save a student considerable time.

Monitoring and Diagnostic Decisions: Tests as Feedback Mechanisms

As instruction proceeds, the teacher and learners need information concerning the degree to which the assigned instructional activity is working effectively and whether a different instructional activity should be considered. If the instructional activity is not effective, the cause of its ineffectiveness needs to be decided, because any new or remedial instructional activity would seek to remedy students' incomplete or erroneous learning. Decisions such as these can be called *monitoring and diagnostic decisions.* In some contexts they are referred to as *formative evaluations* (Airasian & Madaus, 1972; see Figure 12.2). This section discusses the conditions under which tests provide feedback that facilitates learning and instructional efficiency. The next section describes varieties of diagnostic tests and the types of instructional outcomes they foster.

Tests are frequently justified on the grounds that they provide feedback to students and teachers that facilitates learning and instruction. Whether feedback to students facilitates learning is likely to depend on two major aspects of test design: the difficulty of the test tasks for a learner and the utility of test information in confirming a learner's understanding or correcting his or her misunderstanding. A review of the research on feedback in programmed learning indicated that conditions within the learner, and specific to the instructional setting, determine whether feedback is facilitative (Kulhavy, 1977): (a) feedback seems not to be facilitative if a learner knows before responding (before processing the material) what the correct response is, or the nature of the response to be made is beyond the learner's comprehension, so that the learner must guess blindly; and (b) feedback does seem to facilitate learning if the conditions in (a) are absent, the feedback confirms the learner's understanding, and the feedback corrects the learner's misunderstanding.

These conditions for effective feedback seem to be applicable to tests if they are integrated with instruction, in much the same way that response frames are integrated in a segment of programmed instruction. If a student has little comprehension of what is being tested, such as can happen at pretest time, giving test feedback to her or him might have little facilitative effect unless there is further direct instruction. Similarly, if the items are too abstruse or too simplistic, the test is likely to have little facilitative effect. If a test is to serve a learning facilitation function, test designers must (a) attend to the match between items and a learner's instructional experiences, (b) create test reports that convey to students the degree to which they have understood the material or the nature of their misunderstandings, and (c) incorporate into an instructional sequence procedures for learners to review their completed tests.

It would seem logical that, if tests are supposed to function as feedback mechanisms to facilitate teachers' adapting instruction to individual pupils, they should similarly meet the feedback conditions that facilitate learning. The feedback must help a teacher understand each pupil's instructional needs. Standardized testing is frequently justified on the grounds that it facilitates teachers' adaptation of instruction, yet teachers indicate that they find little usefulness from these tests in shaping their daily instructional adaptions (Madaus, 1981; Salmon-Cox, 1981). Madaus's interpretation of these findings would seem to further support the feedback mechanism hypothesis.

> The high congruence between teacher ratings and pupil test performance helps explain why teachers may report that standardized scores are not of great relevance. In competing with other criteria for the teacher's attention and use, standardized tests appear to be in a somewhat anomalous position. If the results of the tests differ greatly from teacher's perceptions, the tests run the risk of being ignored. . . . If, on the other hand, test results correspond quite closely to teacher's perceptions, the test runs the risk of being dismissed on the grounds of redundancy. (p. 635)

Standardized-test publishers do provide various services to schools that are designed to fulfill this feedback function for teachers. Whether and why teachers question the utility of these services is a design topic needing further investigation. Teachers seem to prefer their own informal observations as mechanisms for adapting instruction rather than the use of available appropriate test information (Linn, 1983; Salmon-Cox, 1981; Stake, Easley, et al., 1978).

Monitoring and Diagnostic Decisions:
Approaches to Diagnostic Assessment

In principle, no other area of testing has been viewed as more closely linked to instruction than diagnostic testing. The two major purposes of such testing are to identify which learning goal(s) a learner has not acquired and to point to the probable cause(s) of a learner's failure to acquire them. The first purpose focuses on the content to be learned: manifested behaviors, covert knowledge structures, and covert mental processes. The second purpose focuses on providing specific information needed to identify the instructional procedure to be used with a particular learner to remediate his or her deficit.

Historically, the diagnostic tests proposed in the literature or available in the marketplace, with few exceptions, have been directed primarily toward the first of the two purposes. This section reviews diagnostic tests proposed for instructional usage by classifying them into five categories, each representing a somewhat different approach to the content deficits being diagnosed.

1. The *trait profile differences approach,* in which a deficit is defined as a low standing, relative to peers, in a broad learning outcome area in a subject
2. The *prerequisite knowledge and skills deficits approach,* in which a deficit is defined as failure to acquire necessary preinstructional knowledge and skill
3. The *mastery of behavioral objectives approach,* in which a deficit is defined as failure to master one or more end-of-instruction objectives
4. The *erroneous behavior identification approach,* in which a deficit is defined as a learner's having acquired specific types of inappropriate (erroneous) responses
5. The *knowledge structure approach,* in which a deficit is defined as an inappropriate or incorrect cognitive organization of concepts and their interrelationships

Each of these approaches will be described. Certain technical test-design issues associated with each are discussed, and each is evaluated in terms of how well it meets the second purpose of diagnostic testing: identifying probable causes of learners' deficits. Table 12.1 illustrates each of the first four approaches with a specific example and serves as a device with which the reader can compare the approaches. The section concludes by suggesting a fifth approach to diagnostic testing that is more in line with cognitively oriented instructional psychology and discusses a few of the potential uses of computer-oriented technology in diagnostic testing.

Trait Profile Differences

Description. This approach stems from the tradition of differential, or trait-factor, psychology. Score interpretation is based almost entirely on norm referencing. A school subject, say, elementary arithmetic or elementary reading, is subdivided into areas, each of which is treated as a separate trait or ability. *KeyMath Diagnostic Arithmetic Test* (Connolly, Nachtman, & Pritchett, 1976), for example, divides primary school arithmetic into 14 areas (numeration, fractions, addition, subtraction, etc.) and measures a student in each area with latent-trait-calibrated items. Results are reported as a profile of strengths and weaknesses over the 14 areas. As is typical of tests in this category, strength and weakness have norm-referenced interpretations (e.g., weakness means being significantly below the norm; with grade-equivalent scores and percentiles ranks used as the primary interpretive mechanisms).

Technical issues. To build diagnostic tests of this type, more or less traditional procedures are followed. Items written for each content area to be diagnosed should represent a single trait, and, thus, the area subtest should have high internal con-

TABLE 12.1 Examples of How Different Diagnostic Approaches Interpret the Same Student Response Data

ILLUSTRATIVE TEST ITEMS ALONG WITH POSSIBLE RESPONSES OF A STUDENT

(a)	(b)	(c)	(d)	(e)	(f)	(g)	(h)	(i)
19	16	33	522	542	31	45	631	452
−11	−15	−11	−111	−430	−27	−36	−427	−361
8	1	22	411	112	✓ 16	✓ 11	✓ 216	✓ 111

Total score = 5/9 or 56%. Percentile rank = 20.

Trait profile approach. The total score on the subtraction test is compared to the total scores on other subtests (addition, multiplication, etc.) and a profile of strengths and weakness developed.

Example. Items such as (a) through (i) may constitute the test and the total score and norm-referenced score determined.

Possible interpretation of example. The student is weak in subtraction.

Prerequisite hierarchy approach combined with behavioral objectives approach. The items are associated with behavioral objectives and the objectives are organized into a prerequisite sequence. If a higher-level objective is failed, testing identifies which prerequisite objectives are known and unknown.

Example. The objectives below are in a prerequisite hierarchy and each is measured by the items above as shown in brackets next to each objective. Each objective is scored separately (Objectives adapted from Ferguson, 1969).

Objectives	*Score*
(4) . . . subtracts 3-digit numbers requiring borrowing from either tens' or hundreds' place. [Items (h) and (i)]	0/2 or 0%
(3) . . . subtracts 2-digit numbers with borrowing from tens' place. [Items (f) and (g)]	1/2 or 50%
(2) . . . subtracts two 2-digit and two 3-digit numbers when borrowing is not required. [Items (c), (d), and (e)]	3/3 or 100%
(1) . . . subtracts two 2-digit numbers when number is less than or equal to 20. [Items (a) and (b)]	2/2 or 100%

Possible interpretation. The student has not mastered Objective (4) and Objective (3). Prerequisite Objectives (1) and (2) have been mastered. Begin instruction with Objective (3).

Error classification approach. Student's erroneous responses are studied and categorized according to type. The report is in terms of the error category.

Example. The responses to Items (f), (g), (h), and (i) are wrong so these are targeted for study and error identification.

Possible interpretation. The student fails to rename (or regroup) from tens' to units' or from hundreds' to tens'.

Erroneous process identification approach, using student's knowledge structure. Student's erroneous and correct responses are studied in order to identify a consistent process a student uses that accounts for the observed responses. Identification of the algorithm used by the student may necessitate knowing how the student conceptualizes the problems. The student's erroneous (or "buggy") algorithms are reported along with an explanation of how the student may have come to use it.

Example. Items (a) through (i) are studied to see if one or more consistent rules (algorithms) have been used by the student to obtain the responses shown.

Possible interpretation. The student appears to be using the following rule consistently: "Subtract the smaller digit from the larger digit." This rule will work for items (a) through (g), but not for (f) through (i). This incorrect rule may have been learned initially for solving single-digit subtraction problems and is now interfering with learning how to solve more complex problems.

sistency. For maximum profile interpretability, the subtest scores should be highly reliable within subtests and have low correlations between subtests. When either of these conditions is not met, profile reliability is low, and the observed profile differences are likely to be exaggerated or masked by chance errors of measurement. From a strictly psychometric viewpoint, accurate identification of strengths and weakness from profile discrepancies seems highly unlikely (cf. Thorndike, 1972), given the fact that similar skills are often used in two or more subareas of a subject, resulting in at least moderately high subtest correlations.

Evaluation. Diagnosis with such tests is generally rather coarse. Students' profiles in subareas of the subject provide the educational diagnostician with only general information about where their problems lie. It is much like saying "The Holy Grail lies to the North": The information is helpful, but it leaves the seeker with a lot of work to do before the Grail can be found.

An educational diagnostician, however, especially one with training and experience in testing, is not likely to use such a test as the sole basis of diagnostic decisions. The results of these tests are usually supplemented subsequently by more detailed testing and observation students. The initial test results are used to formulate clinical hypotheses concerning students' difficulties. These hypotheses are confirmed or rejected by information subsequently gathered. Thus, although the trait profile is likely to be rather unreliable, the reliability of the final diagnosis is likely to be much higher when it is made by a skilled diagnostician who incorporates into the diagnosis appropriate additional information that is available. This is not to say, however, that the reliability of the profile-generating test should be ignored. Quite to the contrary, a diagnostician wants the initial set of hypotheses to be as focused as possible and does not want to chase a large number of false leads. A test with very low profile reliability is wasteful of the diagnostician's resources.

PREREQUISITE KNOWLEDGE AND SKILL DEFICITS

Description. Trait profile tests focus on broad learning outcome areas in which students have fallen behind their peers. Tests of prerequisites take the diagnostic process one step further by exploring whether students have fallen behind because they have not acquired necessary preinstructional knowledge and skills. Among the approaches relying upon identification of learning prerequisites is Gagné's learning hierarchies (Gagné, 1962, 1968; Gagné, Major, Garstens, & Paradise, 1962; Gagné & Paradise, 1961). The first step in creating a hierarchy is to analyze an instructional objective the learner must be able to perform, identifying which other behaviors are prerequisite to it. For each prerequisite behavior so identified, the same analysis is performed, generating a hierarchy of objectives. This backward analytic procedure provides a way to identify critical prior behaviors, the lack of which could impede subsequent learning. A number of instructional programs have incorporated such learning hierarchies and used tests to diagnose students' knowledge of prerequisites within the hierarchical framework, for example, Primary Education Program (Wang & Resnick, 1978), Individually Prescribed Instruction (Lindvall & Bolvin, 1967; Ferguson, 1970), and Adaptive Learning Environments Program (Wang, Gennari, & Waxman, 1983).

Prerequisite diagnostic tests may follow a nonhierarchical model. For example, Hunt and Kirk (1974) surveyed teachers of Head Start classes to identify the kinds of entry-level knowledge and skill they expect of pupils in the four areas of color, position, shape, and quantity. Using this information, they built a diagnostic readiness test to assess pupils' ability to identify, name, hear, and communicate concepts in each of the four areas. The resultant profile of prerequisite strengths and weaknesses is used as a basis of instruction by a classroom teacher.

The *Metropolitan Readiness Tests* (Nurss & McGauvran, 1976) are an example of a set of commercially available readiness tests that seek to identify a student's command of knowledge and skills needed to learn in a standard traditional classroom. Among the skills tested are short-term auditory memory; auditory discrimination of phonemic word components; identification of letters via their names; visual matching of letters, numerals, and forms; comprehension of spoken standard American English; and comprehension of quantitative concepts. Norm-referenced profiles are used to interpret pupil performance on these subtests.

Technical Issues. In a continuous-progress curriculum, there is no division between prerequisites and curriculum topics. The distinction between prerequisites and "regular learning" is rather arbitrary, being based more or less on instructional convenience. The learning theory underlying these types of diagnostic tests views learning as strictly cumulative. The corresponding instructional theory assumes that learning proceeds best by first teaching these prerequisites. This is a building-block approach, in which prerequisite informational units build one on another to facilitate the learning of a new method.

The validation of diagnostic tests of prerequisites requires support from experiments, rather than from the correlational studies reported in some readiness test manuals. Data from experiments must demonstrate that students instructed on the particular prerequisite knowledge and skills appearing in the test are better able to learn the new material than students who, although equally deficient, were not explicitly taught these prerequisites. As mentioned in the discussion on instructional models, it might be necessary to analyze the demands the instructional situation places on the learner, as a first step in the test-design process.

Evaluation. Tests of this kind cannot be better than the analyses of the curricular learning requirements on which they are based. Prerequisite tests of the type described provide information about the content (knowledge and skills) students need to learn, but this type of content-based information gives little direction to the teacher concerning how instruction should be designed to overcome the deficiencies. Prerequisites derived from logical analyses of behavioral objectives have at least two negative features that make it difficult to design remedial instruction. They fail to identify certain types of knowledge and skills necessary for learners to acquire new material, and they fail to provide information about the way students organize or structure their partial knowledge about the content to be learned and behavior (cf. Champagne, Klopfer, & Gunstone, 1983). Champagne, Klopfer, and Gunstone reviewed the instructional design implications of the findings of cognitive researchers in the areas of problem solving, semantic memory, and knowledge acquisition, especially as these findings relate to the teaching of principles of Newtonian mechanics. They found that logical analysis of behavioral statements of physics learning outcomes failed to identify (a) the ways in which students who were entering a physics course organized and understood mechanical principles in everyday experience, (b) the fact that students need to be taught how to qualitatively analyze problems before attempting to solve them quantitatively (i.e., before applying an equation), and (c) the fact that one goal of instruction is to change students' entering knowledge schema, so that they approach the schema of experts. Diagnostic tests of prerequisites consistent with these findings would probably be quite different in focus from prerequisite tests based on analyses of content statements or end-of-instruction behavioral objectives. As the Champagne et al. review points out, frequently it is not simply the students' lack of knowledge that is the primary cause of learning difficulty but also the conflicts between the students' preconceptions of the organization of the concepts in the subject and the official (canonical) organization of the concepts they are supposed to learn.

Tests of prerequisite knowledge and skills are advantageous when the teacher knows very little about the pupils, especially in instructional situations in which large variations in individual differences in mastery of prerequisites are expected.

As previously mentioned, there is little need to pretest an individual's command of prerequisites if it is already known that all students lack the important prerequisites to approximately the same degree or that the instructional situation does not allow adaptation to individual differences in prerequisite knowledge. Further, when the instructional sequence is spiral (i.e., when a topic is taught several times throughout the course with increasing elaborations each time, pupils' prerequisite skill profiles may be accommodated differently from their accommodation in situations in which strictly hierarchical instructional sequences face the pupils. This means that tests of prerequisites must be designed for use with particular curricula and with particular types of instructional models in mind, to optimize instructional outcomes.

MASTERY OF BEHAVIORAL OBJECTIVES

Description. This approach has become the dominant one for diagnosing subject matter learning deficits. It is frequently advocated as the method of choice for classroom teachers, as well as for more specialized educational diagnosticians. In spite of the diversity of ways and potential uses of criterion referencing (Nitko, 1980), for many educators, diagnosis, behavioral objectives, and criterion referencing are inseparable concepts, as the following extract illustrates:

> Diagnosing and monitoring student learning progress has become an operating feature of programs aimed at adapting instruction to student differences. A key component of such programs is the use of criterion-referenced assessments, that is [tests] designed to determine the presence or absence of certain specific competencies, providing teachers with the necessary information to determine skills and knowledge already possessed by students so that their appropriate entrance into the learning sequence can be insured. Furthermore, the use of such clear-cut descriptions of the students' capabilities insures that they neither repeat tasks they have already mastered nor work on objectives for which they lack critical prerequisites. (Wang, 1980, p. 5)

The ideal of directing instructional efforts to student acquisition of specific learning objectives is not recent. It dates back at least to the seminal work of Waples and Tyler (Tyler, 1934; Waples & Tyler, 1930). Teachers, however, generally did not write statements of behavior or develop diagnostic tests based on them.

The current widespread popularity of objectives-based testing and instruction is principally a result of the commercial availability of integrated sets of objectives, texts, and tests. Publishers moved toward such integrated materials in the late 1970s and early 1980s, after educators enthusiastically greeted the concept of criterion-referenced testing (Glaser, 1963) and the prototypic instructional methods of the 1960s and early 1970s that integrated objectives, learning material, and diagnostic tests. The principal prototypes were the mastery learning model (Bloom, 1968; Carroll, 1963), Individually Prescribed Instruction (Glaser, 1968; Lindvall & Bolvin, 1967), Program for Learning in Accordance with Needs (Flanagan, 1967, 1969), Individually Guided Instruction (Klausmeier, 1975), and Personalized System of Instruction (F. S. Keller, 1968; F. S. Keller & Sherman, 1974).

To implement the behavioral-objectives approach, one lists the important specific behaviors students are expected to learn after studying a particular subject. The total pool of objectives within a subject area is usually subdivided into topical areas (e.g., decoding, work knowledge, comprehension). Short tests are then developed to measure each objective. For administrative convenience, objectives close together in the instructional sequence are sometimes measured in the same test. If each objective is measured by a separate test, the test is typically 5 to 8 items long. When several objectives are measured in one test

to be administered in a single sitting, there are usually fewer items, perhaps 1 to 3, per objective.

Technical issues. Although the tripartite congruence between the intent of instruction, the statements of the objectives, and the items created for the tests are important concerns for all instructional tests, this congruence is especially important for objectives-based diagnostic tests, because each objective is directly instructed. Written statements of behavior are frequently too ambiguous to guarantee this tripartite congruence (e.g., E. L. Baker, 1974; Popham, 1972, 1984; Roid & Haladyna, 1982).

One solution to the problem is to institute formal systematic methods of logically reviewing items, objectives, and instruction (Roid & Haladyna, 1982). Logical reviews can be analytic or holistic. One analytic reviewing method is the Instructional Quality Inventory (IQI) that was developed for U.S. military trainers (Ellis, Wulfeck, & Fredericks, 1979; Fredericks, 1980; Merrill, Reigeluth & Faust, 1979; Ellis & Wulfeck, 1978; Wulfeck, Ellis, Merrill, Richards, & Wood, 1978) but has also been applied to educational programs (Roid & Haladyna, 1982). With this method, objectives, tests, and instructional procedures are all reviewed for consistency with, and adequacy of, meeting the intent of instruction. From the viewpoint of diagnostic test design, the critical judgements in the IQI are (a) the adequacy of the statement describing the behavior (e.g., whether the statement is worded properly, can be classified into a content-by-type-of-task taxonomy, and expresses the main intent of the instruction); (b) the congruence of each item with the instructional objective; and (c) the technical adequacy with which the items have been written. Another analytic method was proposed by Mager (1973), which dissects the statement of the behavioral objective into the behavior stated or implied, the conditions of its performance, and the criterion by which performance of the objective will be judged. Test items are similarly analyzed to see if they correspond in each of these three areas. If not, items, objectives, or both are revised.

Holistic methods ask for overall judgements about whether objectives and items match or are congruent. Frequently, holistic judgements of degree of congruency are pooled over judges. Rovinelli and Hambleton (Hambleton, 1980; Rovinelli & Hambleton, 1977) provide an index of item-objective congruency when all items are crossed with all objectives. Nitko and Hsu (1984) provide a set of microcomputer (Apple® II/IIe) programs to assist teachers in conducting and summarizing the tripartite congruence for both holistic and analytic reviews.

Objectives-based diagnostic tests are generally plagued with measurement error, principally because the tests tend to have too few items per objective. When a diagnostic test is used to decide whether a student has "mastered" an objective, indexes of decision consistency are more informative of the effects of measurement error than are traditional individual-differences reliability coefficients. Decision consistency indexes describe the extent to which students are likely to be classified the same, when either the same test form is readministered or an alternate form of the test is administered. Consistency of classification (i.e., of mastery or nonmastery) is the main focus, rather than consistency of students' standard scores (z scores) in repeated testing. Traditional reliability coefficients reflect consistency of z scores. Although the two types of indexes present somewhat different information, they are related: Decision consistency increases when reliability increases. However, decision consistency also reflects both the base rate of mastery in the group and the magnitude of the cutoff score that is set. Indexes of decision consistency and their applications are reviewed by Berk (1980, 1984), Brennan (1984), and Subkoviak (1984) (see also Feldt and Brennan, this volume).

Although indexes of decision consistency provide an assessment of the overall rate of correct decisions in diagnosing a group of students with respect to an instructional objective, they do not estimate the chances of misdiagnosing an individual student. Empirically or theoretically developed expectancy tables could be used by test publishers for such purposes. Or the tables (method) developed by Novick and Lewis (1974) could be used to estimate these misclassification chances. The tables were developed by using Bayesian statistical techniques, assuming that test items are independent random samples from an infinite pool of items and that the binominal distribution is appropriate. As an illustration of the magnitude of classification error that is possible with objectives-based diagnosis, the Novick and Lewis tables tell us that, for a mastery criterion of 80%, a student whose true level of mastery is 70% of the large pool of items has a 1 in 3 chance of passing a 7-item test (when the minimum passing score is 6 items correct) simply because the random sample of items contains a sufficient number the student knows. Similarly, a student whose true level of mastery is 80% has a 2 in 5 chance of being misclassified as a nonmaster by scoring less than 6 on the 7-item test because of an unlucky draw of items.

Classification errors are likely to be less when tests are built by using a within-objective stratified sampling plan. Further, some domains of items implied by objectives could be so highly intercorrelated that rates of errors of classification are less than the binomial model would predict. It is not unusual, however, to have heterogenious item domains for an objective (Mcready & Merwin, 1971) (see Forsyth, 1976, for a discussion of which types of objectives would be expected to imply highly intercorrelated item domains).

Some investigators have attempted to increase within-objective item homogeneity by establishing standardized item-writing and item classifying rules. Numerous techniques have been proposed: prose transformation (Bormuth, 1970; Conoley & O'Neil, 1979; Finn, 1975; Roid, 1979, 1984; Roid & Finn, 1978; Roid, Haladyna, Shaughnessy & Finn, 1979); item forms (Hively, 1974; Hively, Patterson, & Page, 1968; Millman, 1980; Millman & Outlaw, 1978; Osburn, 1968); elaborated descriptions of behaviors and stimuli (E. L. Baker, 1974; Popham, 1972, 1978, 1984); mapping sentences (Berk, 1978; Engel & Martuza, 1976; Guttman, 1970); concept analysis (Anderson, 1972; Tiemann & Markle, 1978); logical operations generation rules (Williams & Haladyna, 1982); and application of the IQI. Summaries of these techniques and examples of how to apply them are found in Berk (1984), Popham (1978), and Roid and Haladyna (1982).

Evaluation. Diagnostic tests based on objectives are appealing because they (a) focus on specific and limited things to teach, (b) communicate the goals of instruction in an easily understood form, and (c) center a teacher's attention on visible (overt) student learning. These features greatly facilitate testing, instructional decision making, teaching, and public accountability.

The behavioral-objectives approach to diagnostic testing has serious limitations, however. The information obtained from such tests is limited to only one aspect of diagnosis and testing: the overt behavioral manifestation of what is to be learned. This information provides insufficient help to teachers concerning the nature of the instructional treatment to remediate the deficits discovered. To know that a student has not mastered an objective does not provide enough guidance for remediation. Like the trait profile and learning prerequisite tests, behavioral-objectives-based tests are not fully diagnostic.

The behavioral-objectives approach can also be criticized for implying an inappropriate theory of how knowledge and skill are acquired, one that views a learner's knowledge base as a simple sum of previously learned specific behaviors. Further, critics point to behavior-based tests as failing to assess knowledge schema, problem-solving abilities, and the ability to think in new real-world contexts (e.g., Haertel & Calfee, 1983). Recent work in instructional and cognitive psychology has stressed the importance to knowledge acquisition of a learner's internal representation (or schema) of knowledge, the relationships a learner knows between knowledge elements, and the knowledge-processing skills of which a learner has command (Glaser, 1982, 1984; Greeno, 1976).

IDENTIFICATION OF ERRONEOUS BEHAVIOR

Description. This approach uses test performance to identify and classify a pupil's *in*correct response(s), rather than simply making a dichotomous decision about whether a pupil can or cannot perform a particular behavioral objective. Typically, this approach centers on the learner's overt manifestations of error. It classifies each error a pupil makes into one or more categories that implies a particular fault. Examples of the errors are failure to regroup when "borrowing" in subtraction, improper pronunciation of vowels when reading, reversing *i* and *e* when spelling, and producing a sentence fragment when writing. Once errors are identified and classified, teachers attempt to provide instruction to remediate (eliminate) them.

The error classification approach is exemplified by techniques such as the "Tab-item" (Glaser, Damrin, & Gardner, 1954), the Computer Help in Learning Diagnosis in Arithmetic (Nesbit, 1966), computer-assisted diagnostic testing in Individually Prescribed Instruction (Binstock, Pingel, & Hsu, 1975; Ferguson & Hsu, 1971; Hsu & Carlson, 1972), the *Monroe Diagnostic Reading Examination* (Spache, 1976), and the Buggy model (Brown & Burton, 1978). Because error identification and classification require considerable skill, these tests are frequently administered by a subject matter specialist, by an educational diagnostician, or by a computer, rather than by a classroom teacher.

Technical issues. Tatsuoka and Tatsuoka (Birenbaum & Tatsuoka, 1983; Tatsuoka & Tatsuoka, 1981, 1982) have developed computer programs that identify plausible procedures (solution algorithms) a student might have used to create a given error in solving mathematical problems. Many pupil errors, however, are best discovered by asking them to explain how they solved particular problems and why they answered as they did. If a multiple-choice item is built so that incorrect alternatives represent popular errors, classroom teachers can summarize the frequency of each error type and use this summary as a basis of lesson planning. (Creating such multiple-choice items requires teachers to have considerable subject matter knowledge and test-construction skill, however.) Nitko and Hsu (1984) provide microcomputer (Apple® II/IIe) programs to assist classroom teachers in compiling these summaries once the items have been written.

If diagnosis is made only on the basis of a student's answer to a problem, it could be well off the mark, because several different types of errors can cause the same answer to be produced. The test-design task is to create a set of items that can be used to elicit nearly all possible errors on the problem and that enables the diagnostician to distinguish all of the error types. Burton (1982) describes DEBUGGY, an off-line diagnostic computer program that includes a means of measuring the error diagnostic properties of subtraction tests and of helping to create better tests. In this context, three test-design problems are being certain that (a) if a student uses a particular erroneous subtraction procedure ("bug" in the Brown and Burton language), it can be distinguished from answers of students using different erroneous procedures; (b) if a student has a propensity to use a particular erroneous procedure, the items elicit that erroneous response frequently enough to observe its consistency; and (c) if a student's erroneous procedure is compound (consists of using one or more subskills erroneously), the items should permit the measurement of subskills separately without interfering with an erroneous response in another subskill (Burton, 1982). The computer-aided tests constructed via DEBUGGY permit the test developer to create relatively short tests (12 to 20 items) that solve all three of these design problems for the subtraction domain involving borrowing.

Related to the error classification approach are methods that analyze complex performance into two or more component performances. If a student cannot perform the entire complex performance, diagnostic testing is used to identify which component behaviors are lacking. Resnick and her associates (Resnick, 1975, 1976; Resnick, Wang, & Kaplan, 1973), for example, analyzed complex preschool mathematics objectives into their component behaviors and into the sequence in which contiguous components were to be performed. (This type of analysis differs from the learning hierarchy approach. The analysis in the latter leads to a learning sequence, whereas the analysis in the former identifies a performance sequence.) Burton (1982) and associates do this analysis by identifying all the subskills needed for a student to solve a problem correctly. The measurement of each of these less complex subskills in isolation is the basis of diagnosis. Gagné (1970a, 1970b) proposed a two-stage testing procedure to identify why a pupil fails to solve problems involving the application of two or more principles. Given the failure to solve the problem presented, a second-stage test is used to determine which, if any, of the principles the pupil knows, whether each of the principles is known, and whether the pupil understands how to combine them.

Evaluation. The principal advantage of the error classifica-

tion approach over the behavioral objectives approach is that the teacher knows, not only that a behavior cannot be performed, but also which aspects of the behavior are flawed. This narrows a teacher's search for possible causes of poor performance. A skilled teacher can use this information to quickly identify one or more instructional procedures that have previously worked (remediated the error) with similar students. The computer programs of Burton (1982) also have this capacity, to a limited extent.

Error classification procedures have serious drawbacks, however. There are several practical problems. Many different kinds of errors are made by pupils, and these are difficult to classify and to keep in mind while analyzing a pupil's performance: frequently pupils demonstrate the same erroneous overt behavior for different reasons, so remedial instruction could be misdirected; and the amount of individual testing and interpretation required seems prohibitive, given the amount of instructional time available. Some of these practical problems could be addressed by using "intelligent" computer-assisted testing, in which the programs present the tasks, identify and classify the errors, describe the probable causes of the errors, and suggest remedial instructional procedures. Perhaps statistical models could be incorporated into such a system whereby the program would receive feedback on the success of its recommended remediation, match this with student and teacher characteristics, and revise its future recommendations in light of past experience. (Such programs currently do not exist, however.)

More serious than practical problems of implementation, however, is the problem that, if diagnosis only classifies errors, it still fails to identify the cognitive procedures and processes a learner has used to produce the errors observed and to give teachers insight into the appropriate knowledge structures and cognitive processes a learner needs to acquire to reach the desired outcome. As Bejar (1984) points out, error enumeration and classification focus on the negative aspects of performance and are insufficient for understanding why learners produce errors. Of course, cognitive analyses could be incorporated into error diagnostic procedures. It is to this possibility that we turn next.

KNOWLEDGE STRUCTURE:
AN ALTERNATIVE APPROACH
TO DIAGNOSTIC ASSESSMENT

A shortcoming of the diagnostic testing approaches mentioned, with the possible exceptions of the limited Buggy model and the DEBUGGY program, is their strong ties to the surface features of subject matter information and problem-solving competence that constitute the goals of instruction. Diagnosis should focus on how a learner perceives the structure or organization of that content (the learner's knowledge structures) and processes information and knowledge to solve problems. As Sternberg has pointed out in other contexts (Sternberg, 1984; Wagner & Sternberg, 1984), behavioristic and psychometric approaches are not exactly wrong, but they are incomplete. What is needed is an approach that describes the mental processes that mediate changes in the learner. Information about knowledge structures and psychological processes can form the basis of specifications for instructional objectives, identification of a learner's initial state of competence, and identification of why a learner is failing to acquire the desired instructional objectives (Glaser, 1982).

The difference between specifying instructional goals by the now common behavioral objectives approach and the approach implied by recent cognitive research is illustrated by Champagne and Klopfer (no date) and is reproduced here as Figures 12.3 and 12.4. The objectives in Figure 12.3 show the results of a traditional analysis of the content of a course that focuses on the overt behaviors intended as student outcomes of instruction in a science unit covering the topic of sound. Figure 12.4 represents another approach to articulating an outcome goal of this same science unit. It shows a desired declarative knowledge structure about sound concepts and principles that a student's learning should approximate. The structure illustrated in Figure 12.4 does not encompass every desired outcome of this unit (e.g., problem-solving strategies are not represented), but it does represent the knowledge structure of experts (or the "current paradigm") in the field. The diagram illustrates that, for a person who is knowledgeable, basic physics concepts of sound (e.g., *simple wave* and *sinusodial*) are linked to each other. These links form relational propositions (e.g., "is a," "has," "identifies"). (Follow the paths and their branches to see how experts define concepts and relate them.) Each concept has many links to other concepts in an expert's knowledge schema. The scheme of all links, concepts, and relations forms the knowledge structure or organization depicted by the figure. Students' knowledge structures are found

---

FIGURE 12.3 Traditional statements of instructional objectives for a unit on the physics of sound

---

After completing this unit, the student should be able to:

Describe how waves are created and how they transfer energy.

Discuss the meaning and relationships of the following quantities: wavelength, frequency, period, amplitude, displacement, phase, reflection, refraction, diffraction, interference.

Distinguish between longitudinal and transverse waves.

Use Huygens' principle to predict wave behavior.

Cite experimental evidence that sound energy is transferred by waves.

Describe the waveforms of sounds as shown on the screen of a
    cathode ray
    oscilliscope.

Measure the approximate speed of sound in air.

Set up standing waves in a long spring and observe similar waves in a guitar string.

Describe how sounds are created, how they travel, and how sound differences are related to wave form.

Discuss the physical and psychological characteristics of sound waves.

Source: Adapted from Hill and Stolberg, 1975, as cited in Champagne and Klopfer, n.d.

to be quite different from experts' (or "masters") structures (e.g., Champagne, Klopfer, & Gunstone, 1982; Hewson & Hamlyn, 1984).

Figure 12.3 is, more or less, an example of the currently prevailing conception of how learning outcomes should be stated. Diagnosis (and other forms of testing) are directed toward assessing the presence or absence of each behavior and identifying and categorizing errors a learner makes when trying to perform a behavior (e.g., using "Huygen's principle" to predict wave behavior). The implications of Figure 12.4 are quite different, however, implying that diagnosis should focus on identifying a learner's extant knowledge organization and identifying which links are missing or malformed. Not shown in Figure 12.4, but important for understanding what needs to be diagnosed and taught, is the procedural knowledge structure of experts; that is, how they approach and solve a problem.

A test designer's understanding of the meaning and structure of the knowledge a student brings to the instructional system is important for building diagnostic tests. Tests of prerequisites should focus on these aspects of the preinstructed learner. Frequently, students' everyday understandings of terms and phenomena are at odds with the experts' canonical understandings. These conflicts can interfere with instruction directed toward acquisition of canonical knowledge, unless students' knowledge schema are explicitly addressed in the course of teaching (e.g., Champagne & Klopfer, & Gunstone, 1982). Further, students' everyday understanding of technical and nontechnical concepts varies from culture to culture, so that instruction geared to canonical forms of knowledge might need to be adapted to different settings. (Urevbu, 1984, for example, discusses culturally linked schemas and their relation to science instruction in Africa.) Diagnosis should inform the instructional process about such within- and between-culture differences in knowledge schema. For example, students' understanding of *heat* is frequently nearer to Lavoisier's 1789 proposal (heat as a caloric fluid) than to the present prevailing understanding of heat as a form of kinetic energy (Harris, 1981). This prevailing caloric concept of heat has been found in studies of children from a number of Western countries, for example, from Canada (Erickson, 1980), from England (Schayer & Wylam, 1981), from France (Tiberghien, 1980), and from the United States (Albert, 1978), but it was not found to prevail among children and adults of the Sotho People in Southern Africa (Hewson & Hamlyn, 1984). Hewson and Hamlyn postulate that this Southern African group, and perhaps others, because of their prevailing cultural metaphor concerning heat, "may be at a relative advantage in learning about heat when compared to their Western counterparts" (p. 261).

Hewson and Hamlyn's testing techniques, although qualitative, are worthy of further study as possible devices identifying student's knowledge schema for diagnostic purposes. A Concept Profile Inventory (CPI) was developed for eliciting and categorizing subjects' methaphoric and physical conceptions. This should allow easy comparison of canonical and everyday conceptions of terms. They also used a standard format (template) for depicting each subject's knowledge network, thus allowing easy comparison of experts' and students' schema. Figure 12.5 shows two such templates. Panel A depicts the contemporary scientific conception of heat as kinetic en-

FIGURE 12.4 Knowledge structure instructional goal for physics of sound.

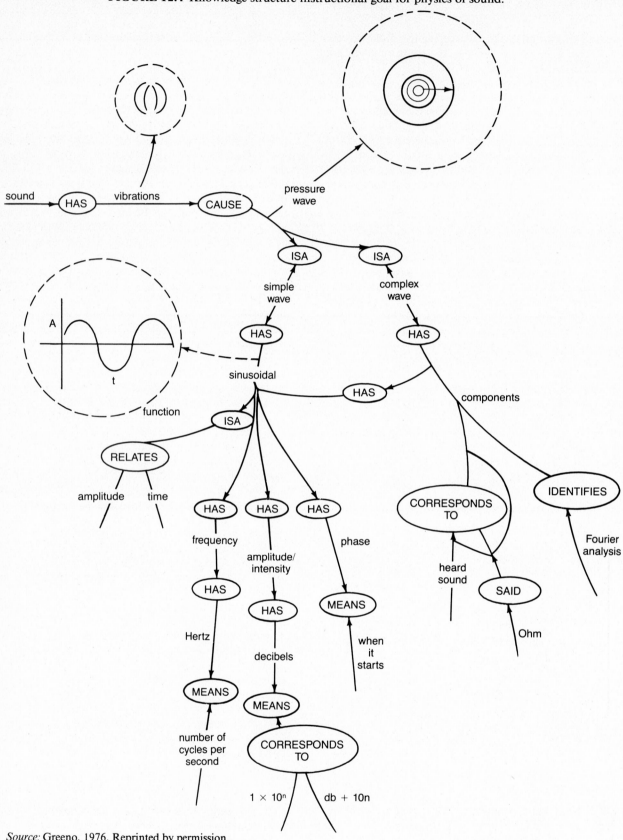

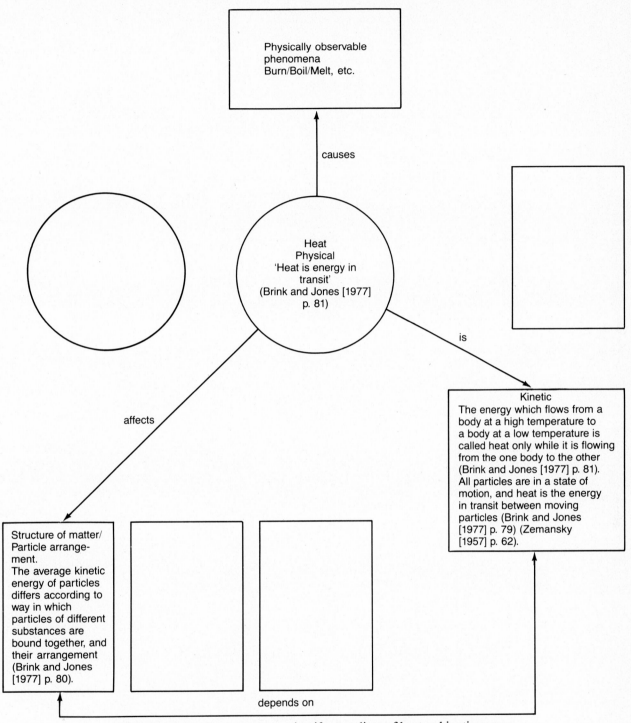

FIGURE 12.5A Contemporary scientific paradigm of heat as kinetic energy.

ergy. Panel B depicts the conceptual network of one subject. In the templates, "the arrangement of conceptions in each network is the same. Each conception appears in a rectangle. It is coded with a CPI number, and includes quotations from original transcripts [of interviews with subjects]. The connections between conceptions are labelled. The subjects' definitions of

heat are in a circle, as are the metaphorical heat conceptions" (p. 252). Haertel and Calfee (1983) suggest testing students by having them both describe the general schema they have of a particular content area and use the schema to solve problems posed by the examiner.

There is considerable evidence that a person's knowledge

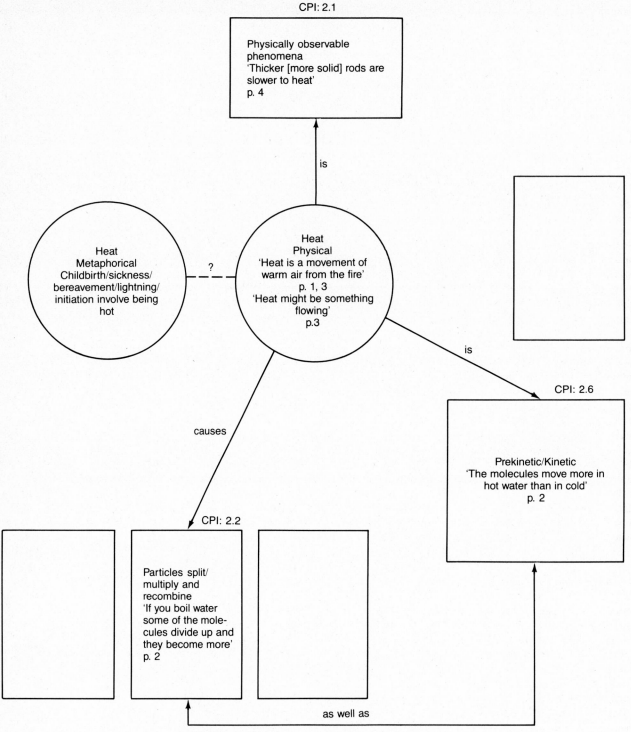

FIGURE 12.5B One person's conception of heat.

structure is important to cognitive performance (Anderson, 1977, 1984; Kintsch, 1974; Prichert & Anderson, 1977; Shank & Ableson, 1977; Shavelson, 1985). Glaser (1984) reviewed the evidence from developmental studies, problem-solving studies of novices and experts, and process analyses of aptitude and intelligence tests. This research documents the role of knowl-

edge structures for recalling information, reasoning, acquiring understanding, representing problems, and identifying clues, heuristics, and constraints in solving problems.

Cognitive researchers have experimented with several methods for assessing students' knowledge structures. These methods share the common perspective that as individuals become more proficient, their knowledge becomes more inter-connected, more deeply organized, and more accessible. The assessment of knowledge organization has a long history in learning research, where studies of "chunking" first used free recall and later used word association (Preece, 1976, is one example). Other methods include free sorting of cards (e.g., Hambleton & Sheehan, 1977); similarity rating (e.g., Johnson, 1967); tree or hierarchical graph building (e.g., Fillenbaum & Rapoport, 1971; ordered tree hierarchy recovery (e.g., Reitman & Rueter, 1980); modified ordered tree (MOT) hierarchy recovery (e.g., Naveh-Benjamin, McKeachie, Lin, & Tucker, 1986); analysis of protocols (e.g., Greeno, 1976, 1978; Hewson & Hamlyn, 1984); mapping tests (e.g., Surber & Smith, 1981; Surber, 1984); structure formation (SLT) (e.g., Ballstadt & Mandle, 1985); and concept structuring analysis (conSAT) (e.g., Champagne & Klopfer, 1980). These techniques vary in theoretical perspective and the type of knowledge organization being represented. Those with similar assumptions about the theoretical constructs underlying knowledge structure and how it is reflected in task performance have convergent validity sufficient for assessment purposes (Shavelson & Stanton, 1975; Champagne, Hoz, & Klopfer, 1984).

Especially important to classroom practice, however, are the practical and instructional features of an assessment procedure. Can the procedure accommodate typical numbers of students? Is it easy for teachers to use? Can it give quick results to guide instruction? Will teachers agree that the theoretical concept of knowledge structure reflects the key understandings they are teaching? Can knowledge structure assessment help explain individual differences? Can these assessments identify misunderstandings needing to be corrected?

From the perspective of practical classroom utility and potential instructional meaningfulness, three of the experimental knowledge structure assessment techniques—MOT, SLT, and conSAT—appear appropriate for teachers. MOT is an efficient way to identify the hierarchical organization in a person's knowledge structure. This technique minimizes student's memory retrieval difficulties, which might mask the underlying organization of key subject-matter concepts. However, how a student understands the relationships among these concepts cannot be assessed by MOT. Both SLT and conSAT permit the latter assessment, but presently do so using time-consuming interviews with skilled interviewers. Perhaps these three techniques could be combined into a single assessment tool which, through microcomputer assistance, would preserve much of the richness of students' cognitive organizations, be instructionally meaningful, and still be practical. Computer-assisted, interactive assessment using cognitive science principles holds the promise for a practical solution to implement knowledge structure assessment at the classroom level.

COMPUTER-ASSISTED DIAGNOSTIC TESTING

The availability of microcomputers in schools, the ability to network these microcomputers, and the linkage of smaller computers to larger computers have raised the hope that educational diagnosis could be assisted by computers. There is some feeling that the complex diagnosis discussed in the preceeding section on cognitive research findings can be handled effectively only with computer assistance. It should be remembered, however, that one of the issues in testing, as well as in instruction, is the availability of conceptually sound software, hardware not being an issue.

Among the advantages computers offer to the diagnostic process are the following (Bejar, 1984): (a) Measurement precision can be improved because the computer can assist in the selection of more technically appropriate items: (b) the computer can measure and incorporate into the diagnostic process response latency and other speed-related variables; (c) computer programs can be written to interact with an examinee, to administer test tasks, and to change or adapt those tasks according to an examinee's responses; (d) computer programs can effectively and consistently search through and use information from a learner-referenced data base to identify plausible, and eventually the most probable, hypotheses explaining the causes of a learner's deficit. To this list add (e) the ability of a computer to create and rapidly update a spatial representation of an examinee's knowledge organization.

The discussion of computer-assisted testing is necessarily brief in this chapter, because chapter 10 is entirely devoted to the topic. Further excellent reviews of current practices are found in the *Journal of Educational Measurement* (Volume 21, Issue 4) and *Educational Measurement Issues and Practice* (Volume 4, Issue 7). There have been prototypic examples of the use of computers to administer each of the types of diagnostic approaches previously described. For example, Weiss and colleagues (Bajar & Weiss, 1978; Weiss, 1974) have developed adaptive tests that measure a student's mastery of subareas (or content strata) within a broad content area, yielding a profile of strengths and weaknesses with as much accuracy as traditional paper-and-pencil-tests, but with fewer items. The testing procedure was dubbed *stradaptive testing*. A number of researchers have used computers to measure mastery of both single behavioral objectives and a hierarchically arranged sequence of objectives (e.g., Ferguson & Hsu, 1971; Hsu & Carlson, 1972; Kingsbury & Weiss, 1979) Computers have been used to identify and classify the errors students make when responding to test items, especially in the areas of arithmetic and mathematics (e.g., Al Daimi & Burghes, 1984; Brown & Burton, 1978; Brown & Van Lehn, 1980; Burton, 1982; Birenbaum & Tatsuoka, 1983; Hsu & Carlson, 1972; Tatsuoka & Tatsuoka, 1981, 1982). It should be remembered, however, that one issue in testing, as well as in instruction, is the availability of conceptually sound software, hardware, as mentioned, not being an issue.

Attainment and Posttesting Decisions

This section is limited to a discussion of testing attainment at the end of an instructional unit, because other sections of this chapter and of this book deal with measuring student attainment in more broadly defined contexts. The most frequently encountered instructional approach in which unit posttesting is described has been called *systematic instruction* (Roid & Haladyna, 1982). The model follows this pattern: pretest → prescription → instruction → posttest → remediate, if necessary, otherwise proceed to new material.

Individually Prescribed Instruction (Glaser, 1968; Lindvall & Bolvin, 1967) is one example of an instructional model that followed the systematic approach.

In the systematic instruction context, pretests and posttest are conceptualized as equivalent forms of the same test: Both cover the terminal learning objectives of a unit of instruction. This is not necessarily a good instructional practice. In the section of this chapter on preinstructional decisions, it was argued that pretesting might be inefficient or unnecessary, wasting valuable instructional time. Unit posttests, however, are likely to be more necessary for providing information to an instructional decision-making process than their preinstructional counterparts. The primary reason is that the major learning objectives of any particular unit are likely to be prerequisites to learning new material in subsequent units (or courses) in the sequence. In a series of sequential units, the posttests function as pretests for subsequent units.

Posttests have typically focused on a subset of important but specific terminal behavioral objectives. However, recent research in instructional psychology indicates that the ways in which students mentally represent knowledge are as important for the development of students' problem-solving skills and for advanced learning as the ways in which they manifest their knowledge behaviorally (these findings are discussed in the section on diagnostic testing). These findings imply that posttests might have to probe more deeply into a student's knowledge base than has traditionally been the case. Practical means of measuring students' knowledge structures are not readily available, but suggestions for the directions these efforts could take are presented in the section on diagnostic assessment, in connection with the discussion on possible new approaches to assessment.

Glaser, Lesgold, and Lajoie (1987) reviewed cognitive psychology research and identified several achievement related variables that could be measured when assessing a learner's proficiency in a domain. These variables include the degree to which a learner's (a) knowledge of a domain is organized, (b) representations of problems in a domain go beyond simply representing surface features, (c) mental modeling of phenomena in a domain is appropriate for representing task complexity, (d) access to knowledge in a domain is efficient, (e) problem-solving strategies in a domain are efficient, (f) knowledge includes the conditions under which specific strategies may be used for solving problems in a domain, (g) knowledge of a domain is amenable to reorganization, and (h) solutions to problems in a domain utilize appropriate metacognitive strategies. The point is that posttests that report only a pass–fail judgment of mastery may be providing inappropriate descriptions of a learner's end-of-unit cognitive state.

Motivational Role of Pupil Evaluations

Little systematic research has been done on specific testing characteristics that relate to how instructional testing might motivate students' efforts in learning situations. From the viewpoint of instructional-design theory, little integrative work has been done on designing motivational strategies for teaching cognitive objectives (Reigeluth, 1983a). Pupil motivation

in the instructional context could be related to both pupil and environmental inputs (J. M. Keller, 1983). Environmental inputs include teachers, teaching materials, teaching strategies, and testing strategies. J. M. Keller's (1979) theory is one approach that attempts to integrate personal and environmental influences on motivation and on cognitive performance of learners. Figure 12.6 is a schematic diagram of these relationships. Details of Keller's theory will not be presented here, but the point should be made that Figure 12.6 suggests that instructional test designers might profit from studies of how instructional usage of tests can influence student effort (engaging in learning activities), performance (actually learning instructional objectives), and consequences (emotional responses, social rewards, and material rewards). One can envision adapting J. M. Keller's (1983) instructional development approach to test materials by considering how test design and usage improve (a) students' interest in learning, (b) students' perceptions of the relevance of what they are learning to their needs and motives, (c) students' perceptions of how well they can expect to learn from a sequence of instruction, and (d) students' intrinsic and extrinsic satisfaction with instruction. Surely the tests students take during the course of study have impact on these motivational variables. Two questions to be researched are: What test design variables relate to each motivational variable and in what ways, and what prescriptions for practical test design are implied by motivational variables?

The role of formal and informal teachers' evaluations in stimulating student effort and motivation has been investigated from a sociological perspective in a series of empirical and theoretical studies by Dornbusch and associates (Dornbusch & Scott, 1975; Natriello & Dornbusch, 1984). Their work, based on a theory of evaluation and authority in organizations, suggests several conditions that must be designed into student evaluation systems if they are to stimulate student effort.

1. *Centrality of evaluations.* Students perceive the rewards and penalities of evaluations as important in their lives. Importance is linked to students' perceptions of the relationship between their school work evaluation and their future success (e.g., world of work) and the social influence of significant others (friends, parents, teachers).
2. *Influence of evaluations.* Students must perceive that there is a direct linkage between the rewards and penalities they receive and their evaluations. Students who perceive a close link between school evaluations and future success and immediate social sanctions are expected to exert more effort. The perception of the influence of evaluation is related to caring about the evaluation (e.g., the test), the evaluator (e.g., the teacher), and the task being evaluated (e.g., the topic being studied).
3. *Links to individual effort.* Even if students perceive evaluations as important and linked to rewards, they will not put forth study efforts unless they perceive a direction connection between those study efforts and their evaluations. Natriello and Dornbusch call this a perception of the degree of soundness of the evaluations. The student must believe that judgements of the quality of perform-

FIGURE 12.6 Keller's model of motivation, performance, and instructional influence.

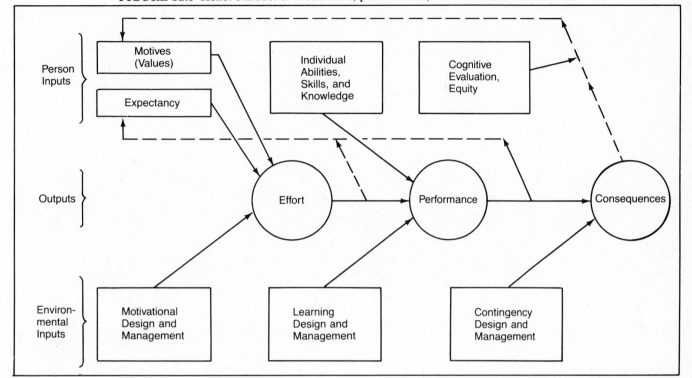

Source: Keller (1983), p. 293. Reprinted by permission.

ance are directly linked to effort and that those performances they view as better are evaluated more highly. If students perceive evaluations as soundly based, these evaluations are perceived as important, and this increases student effort. Dweck's (1975) research in applying attributional theory to mathematics instruction also seems to support this finding.

4. *Reliability of evaluations.* Students must perceive that the same evaluative standards are applied reliably and fairly for all students for the same level of performance. Similar performance by other students on the same task should receive essentially the same evaluation. Natriello and Dornbusch speculate that evaluation reliability enhances students' perceptions of the importance of the authority system of the school (instructor) and, in turn, their efforts to learn.

5. *Norm referencing of evaluations.* This condition relates to the context in which learners receive evaluations and their perceptions of the amount of effort they are putting forth, as well as to perceptions of the worth of the evaluations they receive. Importance, worth, and perceived effort are viewed as socially determined, so that some students might perceive their efforts as exceptionally high in their social context, but, in a broader social perspective, these efforts might be insufficient for ultimate success. A student might believe, for example, that doing ½ hr of homework is a large effort, when that student's peers do no homework. Yet ½ hr might be an insufficient effort in the broader norms of schooling in a nation. Natriello and Dornbusch argue that appropriate

broad social norms of performance and effort help to shape students' local study efforts appropriately.

6. *Frequency and challenge of evaluations.* Teacher behaviors that communicate evaluations must be directed toward reasonably high standards of performance and occur frequently in the course of instruction. Teachers' evaluative behaviors in this context refer to praise, criticism, friendliness, warmth, diffuse responsiveness, academic responsiveness, and standard setting. Natriello and Dornbusch found that the "source of problems in encouraging student effort in school, appears to lie much more within the control of educators. . . . The most pervasive source of problems in the evaluation system . . . is the lack of frequent and challenging teacher evaluations of students' academic work. Students who put forth more effort on school tasks are those who are exposed to more frequent and more challenging evaluations from teachers. Even students with low levels of skill seem to profit from more frequent and challenging evaluations. (p. 1440)

Among the implications of the Natriello and Dornbusch research for designing instructional tests to enhance student study efforts are the following. (a) Instructional test designers would profit from viewing instructional tests, as well as other types of student evaluation, as vehicles for motivating student effort and communicating worth (cf., Messick, 1981b). (The Natriello and Dornbush studies viewed student evaluation more broadly than as paper-and-pencil tasks with scores.) (b) It is difficult to design a single test, or other evaluative procedure, to be challenging without frustrating some students. From this, one can argue that tailored testing should be a motivating mechanism in the instructional process. This hypothesis should be tested in a test-design research program. (c) The frequency of testing and the difficulty level of tests are relevant instructional variables that should be manipulated as part of instructional test-design practice and studied as part of instructional-test design research programs. (d) Teachers tend to use informal evaluations of students frequently, and these evaluations are less reliable than formal evaluations. There needs to be more systematic study of informal evaluation, and its reliability needs to be improved, because students' perceptions of evenhanded teacher evaluations are related to enhanced student effort (Natriello & Dornbusch, 1984). (e) The manner and content of communicating test results to students, as well as results from other types of evaluations, constitute a variable to be considered when designing testing systems that are integral to instruction. Communication of results has a bearing on how students perceive evaluations and on the resultant study efforts they exhibit. (f) The total instructional-test system should include provisions for helping students appropriately reference their evaluations to both within-school and broader national contexts. This means that instruction should be designed so that it includes norm-referenced evaluations as one aspect of anchoring students' perceptions and efforts to realistic social contexts. This does not argue against the use of criterion referencing for instructional purposes, nor does it argue for the use of currently available standardized tests. Nevertheless, appropriate norm referencing seems necessary for pupil development. (g) The techniques and procedures teachers employ for evaluating pupils need to be continually monitored, to assure that teachers are presenting frequent and challenging evaluations to all socioeconomic, gender, and intellectual levels of students (Natriello & Dornbusch, 1984).

Linking External Tests to Instruction

Thus far this chapter has been concerned primarily with what and how to test in a particular instructional context in order to facilitate student learning. One of the important uses of achievement tests not yet discussed is that of externally imposed tests, primarily standardized tests, to inform decisions having a direct bearing on the well-being of individuals and the continued existence of specific instructional programs. These decisions include certifying students for secondary school diplomas, evaluating individual schools and school districts, and evaluating the effectiveness of particular instructional programs. These and similar test uses are of immense importance, and two chapters of this volume (13–14) are devoted to discussing them. The comments about the use of externally imposed tests in this section, therefore, will necessarily be brief and quite limited in scope.

Designing Tests to Evaluate Schools and Instructional Programs

Tests designed to measure individuals and to facilitate their learning within a given instructional program are not necessar-

ily best for measuring the accomplishments of a particular school or program. The following are some of the major design variables that need to be taken into account when designing any achievement test but that become of special importance when the tests are to be used in the context of instructional evaluations that generalize across schools and programs (Airasian & Madaus, 1983): (a) the ability of the test to detect differences among groups of students (e.g., classes, schools, and programs); (b) the representativeness and relevance of the content–behavior–process complex sampled by the test items; (c) the congruence of the response formats and mental processes learned during the instruction, with the responses and processes required to solve test tasks; (d) the properties of the scores to be obtained and the way in which they will be summarized and reported; and (e) the validity of the inferences about school and program effectiveness that could be made from the test results.

Experience indicates that tests are unlikely to detect differences among schools and programs when total scores are bases for comparisons and when the subject matter tested is related more to home background (e.g., reading) than to schooling (e.g., chemistry) (Airasian & Madaus, 1983; Harnisch & Linn, 1981). Further, the sensitivity of test items for detecting school and program differences appears to be related more to the specific knowledge and skills measured by the individual items than to the statistical screening of items. Airasian and Madaus report that items distinguishing schools and programs in their research were as likely to come from criterion-referenced tests as from norm-referenced tests. (The former types of tests tend to be constructed without the benefit of empirical tryout and item-analysis procedures.) This finding poses interesting questions for item-analysis research in the content of instructional design.

It is platitudinous to assert that a test's content should represent a content domain. The issue in the evaluation context is: What is the appropriate domain to represent? Conflicts arise over what to include on tests because different agents, who might or might not be associated with a particular instructional effort, apply different social criteria for judging the importance of content. Because there are no uniform standards of importance and because many tests used in the evaluation context are created for (or by) agents unfamiliar with the specific day-to-day operations of the instruction students are receiving, what is judged to be important and is included on a particular test might not match the content coverage and emphasis delivered to students. Even if test designers wish to include both instruction-specific and broader content, time constrains the testing, and decisions must be made about relative emphasis.

One can identify three major types of domains from which content to be covered can be drawn (Schmidt, 1983): a priori domains, curriculum-specific or learning-material-specific domains, and instructional delivery domains. Agents not associated with local schools or particular programs (e.g., citizens' committees, state commissions, publishers' test department staff) define a priori domains by using social criteria to judge what is important for all to learn. Test exercises and tests for the National Assessment of Educational Progress, various state assessment programs, and commercially available standardized test are examples of assessment instruments built from a priori domains, because they specify content to be included without linking that content to specific instructional material or specific instructional events. Standardized achievement tests, perhaps the most widely used instruments in the evaluation context, not only are nonspecific to local curricula, but also differ widely among each other in their content emphasis, even within the same subject area and the same grade level (e.g., Freeman, Kuhs, Knappen, & Porter, 1982; Hoepfner, 1978). This makes test selection by local authorities a difficult and critical process. Evaluation data that are aggregated from different sites using different tests are extremely difficult to interpret.

Each instructional program or local school has an explicit and an implicit curricular domain from which content could be drawn and tested. The explicit domain is derived from the stated goals, objectives, and syllabi. Additionally, the instructional materials and textbooks that are used define a more implicit curricular domain, one not articulated in detail by a school's published statements. In the United States, where local school authorities decide on which curricular materials to use, there are wide variations among districts in knowledge and skills covered by and emphasized in instruction.

Yet a third domain can be used as a source of test-content coverage and emphasis. Each teacher is more or less free to ignore, to emphasize, and otherwise to implement certain aspects of the local curriculum, so long as he or she works within certain broad, administratively approved, parameters. Thus, the instruction actually delivered to students, all of whom can be classified under the same programmatic title, differs from teacher to teacher within a school.

Each of these domains is not only a basis for defining test-content coverage but also a potential target for defining what instructional outcomes should be. A problem arises for test interpreters when there is lack of congruency among domains and when a test built from specifications derived from one of the domains is used to infer the effectiveness of a school or a program on another domain (e.g., a state assessment might be used to infer that a local school's instructional program is ineffective). Schmidt (1983) refers to the lack of correspondence between a specific test and the intended domain of inference as *content bias*. A test might be biased when used for inferences in one domain but unbiased when used for inferences in another. As a means of understanding the nature of the testing-instruction linkage, some researchers (e.g., Hardy, 1984; Schmidt, 1983) have suggested computing indexes of test-curricular materials congruence or test-instructional delivery congruence.

Questions about the appropriateness of inferences based on test scores fall under the rubric of *construct validity* as it has been articulated in recent psychometric writings (Cronbach, 1971; Guion, 1974; Messick, 1981a, 1981b; see also chapter 2). Some writers, however, refer to these test-to-domain congruence concerns as content validity (match to an a priori domain), curricular validity (match to local curriculum and materials), or instructional validity (match to what has been delivered to the student) (e.g., Airasian & Madaus, 1983; Freeman et al., 1983; Hardy, 1984).

Frequently a school or program is legally or politically committed to using a standardized achievement test that has a less than desirable degree of congruence with the objectives of the local curriculum. Several practical solutions have been proposed to cope with the situation, two of which are to report separately students' performance on items not congruent with the local curriculum (e.g., Wilson & Hiscox, 1984) and to create and administer a supplementary test covering local curricular objectives not tested by the standardized test (e.g., Jolly & Gramenz, 1984). Similar procedures can be used at the classroom level (e.g., Hardy, 1984, Kowal, 1975; Lindquist & Hieronymus, 1964).

Another design variable to consider in the context of building a test able to detect school and program effectiveness is the degree of specificity of the achievement to be measured. Students require more time to acquire global skills and to grow in general educational development than to learn specific knowledge and skills. This means that tests measuring the former are less sensitive to measuring short-term instructional effects than tests measuring the latter (Cole & Nitko, 1981). Test architects designing tests to serve program evaluation purposes need to consider treatment duration: A test might be appropriate for measuring the effectiveness of treatments implemented for certain durations but not for others. Again, this appears to be a construct validity problem.

Still another aspect of construct validity for test used in schools and in program evaluation contexts is the extent to which inferences of effectiveness must be tempered by considerations of extra-school factors that affect test scores. Tests that are influenced greatly by extraschool factors are likely to mislead, giving interpreters the false impression that a particular instructional effort has had little or no impact on students.

When a program is evaluated with an achievement test, it is important to identify classroom variables that are most closely correlated with test scores. There is likely to be large within-program variability associated with test performance of classrooms (e.g., Berliner, 1979; Cooley, 1977). Unless specific program variables are linked to performance on a standardized test, inappropriate evaluative inferences are likely to be made about the program from the test (e.g., condemning or praising the entire program, when one or two variables are responsible for lowered or raised level of test performance). Leinhardt (Leinhardt, 1980; Leinhardt & Seewald, 1981) describes several within-school, program, and classroom variables that are important to program evaluators and how to measure them. Mehrens and Phillips (Mehrens, 1984; Mehrens & Phillips, 1986; Phillips & Mehrens, 1988), however, found no significant differences on standardized tests resulting from the use of different textbooks and different degrees of curriculum–test overlap when previous achievement and socioeconomic status of pupils are controlled statistically.

Designing Tests to Credential Students

Issues of test design are crucial when there is the potential to permanently harm a student or to force a student into a predicament from which it is difficult to recover. Credentialling tests, such as minimum competency and school certificate examinations, tend to be of this type because the consequences of failing have serious effects on individuals. The quality of the tests used for school and program evaluations can be judged by using what has been referred to as *institutional decision criteria*

(Cronbach & Gleser, 1965). The utility of a test for an institution or a state is based on the average rate of correct and erroneous decisions in relation to the cost-benefit ratio of those decisions. For example, although individual students within a school might have received more or less of the intended instructional treatment, a test for evaluating program effects could have positive utility for a school or government agency if it were able to detect average differences among schools or programs (Airasian & Madaus, 1983), even though it did not reliably identify individual pupil successes (provided it didn't cost very much). Schools try to minimize testing costs by using the same test to evaluate both students and programs, but a single test might not be optimal for both purposes.

As compared with tests serving institutional decisions, tests serving individual decisions are evaluated on somewhat different criteria. An individual student usually cannot average her or his test-bound misclassifications or can average them only at great personal cost (e.g., by repeating an entire term or year of instruction). The individual student cannot reasonably be held accountable for instruction that was not delivered to him or her or that was delivered poorly, even though, on the average, instruction was adequate.

A critical test-design variable for minimum competency and school certificate examinations, therefore, is the degree to which the instruction actually delivered to the student corresponded to the content on the test. The closer this correspondence, the fairer the certification decision to the individual. If students have not had the opportunity to learn how to perform the tasks that appear on the certification test, either because a specific school lacked the necessary resources or a particular teacher did not deliver appropriate instruction, the test-based certification process seems inherently unjust.

A resolution of the conflict between what has been taught and what can justifiably appear on the test is not easy to achieve. If one postulates that a student is accountable for what has been taught, an operational definition of *instruction* or *teaching* is necessary (e.g., Is a student accountable for material on a reading list that was not "taught," even though the student's peers, having had another teacher, did have the material explained to them?) Some writers have suggested that "opportunity to learn" might have to be determined separately for each individual before the process can be said to be fair (Airasian & Madaus, 1983).

Even if this could be done, the matter of what and how to test and to instruct is not resolved. When a society's learning goals include the ability to apply knowledge to new situations, to solve new problems, and to exhibit creativity, the tests holding students accountable for these goals must include items containing a certain degree of unfamiliarity or novelty for students. This novelty of testing material is frequently accomplished by creating test materials in formats different from those constituting instruction or by alternating specific content features of the materials used during instruction. The closer the test materials come to duplicating the instructional materials, the less likely the tests will measure these higher order learning goals desired by society (e.g., Anderson, 1972; Linn, 1983). Both fairness to students and fidelity to the measurement of important abilities need to be incorporated into test-design procedures, pointing again to the necessity of incorporating instructionally linked variables into the process of designing educational measurements.

Summary

This chapter examined test design and instructional design as highly related and integrated processes. Many of the categories of variables that are considered when designing instructional methods need to be considered when designing instructionally linked tests. Certain instructional conditions such as the type of goals to be learned, the maturity and educational level of the students, the curriculum organization, and the available resources set limits within which both test designer and instruction designer must work. The instructional methods used in any given situation are influenced by instructional conditions, but these instructional methods also define and delimit test designs. Different instructional methods are likely to vary in the way they emphasize different types of instructional decisions and in the location of crucial instructional points for which test information is needed. Instructional methods lead both to pupil outcomes such as achievement and motivation and to system outcomes such as costliness and efficient use of time and resources. Different instructional methods emphasize different types of achievement and have differential effects on student motivation. Testing programs can enhance or detract from the outcome goals espoused by an instructional designer, so that carefully designed testing and instructional linkages are necessary.

One can delineate general categories of instructional decisions and use these categories as a framework for examining the kinds of variables instructional-test designers need to consider. Among the categories of instructional decisions are these: placement and preinstructional, monitoring and diagnostic, attainment and posttesting, and motivational. The types of tests used to provide information for each category of decision have been discussed, and designs have been suggested for improving their instructional usefulness. Pretests are seen as frequently unnecessary and wasteful of students' instructional time. Tests that monitor the instructional process and student learning are often justified on the basis that they provide feedback to students and teachers, which in turn enhances learning and instruction. The conditions under which these sought-after enhancements are likely to result have been examined. Diagnostic tests should provide information to identify students' learning deficits and to suggest the kinds of instructional treatments necessary to remediate them. Four categories of diagnostic tests were reviewed and evaluated. All provide information about deficiencies but each does so in a different way. Few, if any, of the diagnostic assessment methods reviewed, however, give teachers direct suggestions about the types of instructional treatments needed for remediation. Some recent developments in cognitive instructional psychology seem to offer promise of helping teachers identify the nature of instruction needed for remediation, but these methods are not ready for immediate practical application.

Students are motivated by tests used during the instructional process, but little work has been done to identify the test-design characteristics that encourage or enhance student motivation in school. Important test-design variables to consider can be deduced from theories of motivational design of instruction and from sociological research on the relationship of students' evaluations to their perceptions of authoritarianism.

The final issues considered in the chapter relate to the use of externally imposed tests to evaluate instructional programs and to credential students. In both usages, the primary problem is one of matching the content the students were actually taught with the content that appears on a test. Suggestions in the literature for identifying the degree of linkage or overlap of the content domains were reviewed.

The chapter did not provide a prescriptive theory of instructional test design, but the need for such an integrative theory is apparent. The instructional test-design variables identified in this chapter are suggestive of the variables that should be incorporated in such a theory. The theory would predict which test design would be most appropriate in a particular instructional procedure under given instructional conditions and for specified instructional outcomes. Research would investigate these predictions, and the predictions that were verified could become the basis of practical prescriptions for test designers seeking to improve education through better integration of testing and instruction.

REFERENCES

Airasian, P. W., & Madaus, G. F. (1972). Functional types of student evaluation. *Measurement and Evaluation in Guidance, 4,* 221–233.

Airasian, P. W., & Madaus, G. F. (1983). Linking testing and instruction: Policy issues. *Journal of Educational Measurement, 20,* 103–118.

Al Daimi, K. J., & Burghes, D. N. (1984). Microcomputer-aided differentiation of polynomials and powers of X. *International Journal of Mathematical Education in Science and Technology, 15,* 461–477.

Albert, E. (1978). Development of concepts of heat in children. *Science Education, 62,* 389–399.

Anderson, R. C. (1972). How to construct achivement tests to assess comprehension. *Review of Educational Research, 42,* 145–170.

Anderson, R. C. (1977). The notion of schemata and educational enterprise: General discussion of the conference. In R. C. Anderson, R. J. Spiro, & W. E. Montague (Eds.), *Schooling and the acquisition of Knowledge.* Hillsdale, NJ: Lawrence Erlbaum.

Atkinson, R. C., & Paulson, J. (1972). An approach to the psychology of instruction. *Psychological Bulletin, 78,* 49–61.

Baker, E. L. (1974). Beyond objectives: Domain-referenced tests for evaluation and instructional improvement. In W. Hively (Ed.), *Domain-referenced testing.* Englewood Cliffs, NJ: Educational Technology Publications.

Baker F. B. (1984). Technology and testing: State of the art and trends for the future. *Journal of Educational Measurement, 21,* 399–406.

Bejar, I. I. (1984). Educational diagnostic assessment. *Journal of Educational Measurement, 21,* 175–189.

Bejar, I. I., & Weiss, D. J. (1978). *A construct validation of adaptive achievement testing* (Research Rep. No. 78–4). Minneapolis: University of Minnesota, Department of Psychology.

Berk, R. A. (1978). The application of structural facet theory to achievement test construction. *Educational Research Quarterly, 3,* 62–72.

Berk, R. A. (1980). A consumer's guide to criterion-referenced test reliability. *Journal of Educational Measurement, 17,* 323–349.

Berk, R. A. (1984). Selecting the index of reliability. In R. A. Berk (Ed.), *A guide to criterion-referenced test construction* (pp. 231–266). Baltimore: Johns Hopkins University Press.

Berk, R. A. (1984). *A guide to criterion-referenced test construction.* Baltimore: Johns Hopkins University Press.

Berliner, D. (1979). Tempus educare. In P. L. Peterson & H. J. Walberg (Eds.), *Research on teaching: Concepts, findings, and implications.* Berkeley, CA: McCutchan.

Bernard, J. E., & Bright, G. W. (1984). Student performance in solving linear equations. *International Journal of Mathematical Education in Science and Technology, 15,* 399–421.

Binstock, L., Pingel, K., & Hsu, T. C. (1975). *The design of a computer-assisted mastery testing model for diagnosing inaccurate use of processes underlying problem solutions.* Unpublished manuscript, University of Pittsburgh, Learning Research and Development Center, Pittsburgh.

Birenbaum, M., & Tatsuoka, K. K. (1983). The effect of scoring based on algorithms underlying the students' response patterns on the dimensionality of achievement test data of the problem solving type. *Journal of Educational Measurement, 20,* 17–26.

Bloom, B. S. (1968). Learning for mastery. *Evaluation Comment, 1,* 1–12.

Bloom, B. S., Hastings, J. T., & Madaus, G. F. (1971). *Handbook of formative and summative evaluation of student learning.* New York: McGraw-Hill.

Bormuth, J. R. (1970). *On the theory of achievement test items.* Chicago: University of Chicago Press.

Brennan, R. L. (1984). Estimating the dependability of the scores. In R. A. Berk (Ed.), *A guide to criterion-referenced test development* (pp. 292–334). Baltimore: The Johns Hopkins University Press.

Brown, J. S., & Burton, R. R. (1978). Diagnostic models for procedural bugs in basic mathematical skills. *Cognitive Science, 2,* 155–192.

Brown, J. S., & Van Lehn, K. (1980). *Repair theory: A generative theory of bugs in procedural skills.* Palo Alto, CA: Xerox Palo Alto Science Center.

Burton, R. R. (1982). Diagnosing bugs in a simple procedural skill. In D. Sleeman & J. S. Brown (Eds.), *Intelligent tutoring systems* (pp. 157–183). New York: Academic Press.

Carroll, J. B. (1963). A model of school learning. *Teachers College Record, 64,* 723–733.

Champagne, A. B., Klopfer, L. E., & Gunstone, R. F. (1982). Cognitive research and the design of science instruction. *Educational Psychologist, 17,* 31–53.

Champagne, A. B., & Klopfer, L. E. (no date). *Research in science education: The cognitive perspective.* Pittsburgh, PA: Unpublished manuscript, University of Pittsburgh.

Cole, N. S., & Nitko, A. J. (1981). Instrumentation and bias: Issues in selecting measures for educational evaluations. In R. A. Berk (Ed.), *Educational evaluation methodology: The state of the art.* Baltimore: Johns Hopkins University Press.

Connolly, A. J., Nachtman, W., & Pritchett, E. (1976). *KeyMath diagnostic arithmetic test.* Circle Pines, MI: American Guidance Service.

Conoley, J. C., & O'Neil, H. F., Jr. (1979). A primer for developing test items. In H. F. O'Neil, Jr. (Ed.), *Procedures for instructional systems development.* New York: Academic Press.

Cooley, W. W. (1977, August). *Program evaluation in education.* Invited paper presented at the meeting of the American Psychological Association, San Francisco.

Cronbach, L. J. (1971). Test validation. In R. L. Thorndike (Ed.), *Educational measurement* (2nd ed.). Washington, DC: American Council on Education.

Cronbach, L. J., & Gleser, G. C. (1965). *Psychological tests and personnel decisions* (2nd ed.). Urbana, IL: University of Illinois Press.

Dornbusch, S. M., & Scott, W. R. (1975), *Evaluation and the exercise of authority.* San Francisco: Jossey-Bass.

Dweck, C. S. (1975). The role of expectations and attributions in the alleviation of learned helplessness. *Journal of Personality and Social Psychology, 31,* 647–695.

Ellis, J. A., & Wulfeck, W. H. (1978). *The instructional quality inventory: Vol. IV. Job Performance Aid.* San Diego: Navy Personnel Research and Development Center.

Ellis, J. A., Wulfeck, W. H., & Fredericks, P. S. (1979). *The instructional quality inventory: Vol. II. User's Manual.* San Diego: Navy Personnel Research and Development Center.

Erickson, G. (1980). Children's conception of heat. *Science Education, 64,* 323–338.

Ferguson, R. L. (1970). A model for computer-assisted criterion-referenced measurement. *Education, 81,* 25–31.

Ferguson, R. L., & Hsu, T. C. (1971). *The application of item generators for individualizing mathematics testing and instruction* (Publication No. 1971/4). Pittsburgh: University of Pittsburgh, Learning Research and Development Center.

Finn, P. J. (1975). A question writing algorithm. *Journal of Reading Behavior, 4,* 341–367.

Flanagan, J. C. (1967). Functional education for the seventies. *Phi Delta Kappan, 49,* 27–32.

Flanagan, J. C. (1969). Program for learning in accordance with needs. *Psychology in the Schools, 6,* 133–136.

Forsyth, R. A. (1976). *Describing what Johnny can do* (Iowa Testing Program Occasional Paper No. 17). Iowa City, IA: University of Iowa.

Fredericks, P. S. (1980). *The instructional quality inventory: Vol. II. Training workbook.* San Diego: Navy Personnel Research and Development Center.

Freeman, D. J., Belli, G. M., Porter, A. C., Floden, R. E., Schmidt, W. H., & Schwille, J. R. (1982). The influence of different styles of textbook use on instructional validity of standardized tests. *Journal of Educational Measurement, 20,* 259–270.

Freeman, D. J., Kuhs, T. M., Knappan, L. B., & Porter, A. C. (1982). A closer look at standardized tests. *Arithmetic Teacher, 29,* (7), 50–54.

Gagné, R. M. (1962). The acquisition of knowledge. *Psychological Review, 69,* 355–365.

Gagné, R. M. (1968). Learning hierarchies. *Educational Psychologist, 6,* 1–9.

Gagné, R. M. (1970a). *The condition of learning* (2nd ed.). New York: Holt, Rinehart & Winston.

Gagné, R. M. (1970b). Instructional variables and learning outcomes. In M. C. Wittrock & D. Wiley (Eds.), *Evaluation of instruction.* New York: Holt, Rinehart & Winston.

Gagné, R. M., Major, J. R., Garstens, H. L., & Paradise, N. E. (1962). Factors in acquiring knowledge of a mathematical task. *Psychological Monographs, 76,* (7, Whole No. 578).

Gagné, R. M., & Paradise, N. E. (1961). Abilities and learning sets in knowledge acquisition. *Psychological Monographs, 75* (14, Whole No. 578).

Glaser, R. (1963). Instruction technology and the measurement of learning outcomes. *American Psychologist, 18,* 519–521.

Glaser, R. (1968). Adapting the elementary school curriculum to individual performances. *Proceedings of the 1967 Invitational Conference on Testing Problems* 3–36. Princeton, NJ: Educational Testing Service.

Glaser, R. (1976). Components of a psychology of instruction: Toward a science of design. *Review of Educational Research, 46,* 1–24.

Glaser, R. (1977). *Adaptive education: Individual diversity and learning.* New York: Holt, Rinehart & Winston.

Glaser, R. (1982). Instructional psychology: Past, present, and future. *American Psychologist, 37,* 292–305.

Glaser, R. (1984). Education and thinking: The role of knowledge. *American Psychologist, 39,* 93–104.

Glaser, R., Damrin, D. E., & Gardner, F. N. (1954). The tab item: A technique for the measurement of proficiency in diagnostic problem solving tasks. *Educational and Psychological Measurement, 14,* 283–293.

Glaser, R., & Nitko, A. J. (1971). Measurement in learning and instruction. In R. L. Thorndike (Ed.), *Educational measurement* (2nd ed., 625–670). Washington, DC: American Council on Education.

Greeno, J. G. (1976). Cognitive objectives of instruction: Theory of knowledge for solving problems and answering questions. In D. Klahr (Ed.), *Cognition and instruction.* Hillsdale, NJ: Lawrence Erlbaum.

Greeno, J. G. (1978). Nature of problem-solving abilities. In W. K. Estes (Ed.), *Handbook of learning and cognitive processes:* Vol. 5. Hillsdale, NJ: Lawrence Erlbaum.

Guion, R. M. (1974). Open a new window: Validities and values in psychological measurement. *American Psychologist, 29,* 287–296.

Haertel, E., & Calfee, R. (1983). School achievement: Thinking about what to test. *Journal of Educational Measurement, 20,* 119–131.

Hambleton, R. K. (1980). Test score validity and standard-setting methods. In R. A. Berk (Ed.), *Criterion-referenced measurement: The state of the art.* Baltimore: Johns Hopkins University Press.

Hardy, R. A. (1984). Measuring instructional validity: A report of an instructional validity study for the Alabama High School Graduation Examination. *Journal of Educational Measurement, 21,* 291–301.

Harnsih, D. L., & Linn, R. L. (1981). Analysis of item response patterns: Questionable test data and dissimilar curriculum practices. *Journal of Educational Measurement, 18,* 133–146.

Harris, W. F. (1981). Heat in undergraduate education: Or isn't it time we abandoned the theory of caloric? *International Journal of Mechanical Engineering Education, 9,* 317–321.

Hartley, J., & Davis, I. K. (1976). Preinstructional strategies: The role of pretests, behavioral objectives, overviews, and advance organizers. *Review of Educational Research, 46,* 239–265.

Hewson, M. G. A. B., & Hamlyn, D. (1984). The influence of intellectual environment on conceptions of heat. *European Journal of Science Education, 6,* 245–262.

Hill, F. F., & Stollberg, R. L. (1981). *Physics fundamentals and frontiers.* Boston: Houghton Mifflin.

Hively, W. (Ed.) (1974). *Domain-referenced testing.* Englewood Cliffs, NJ: Educational Technology Publications.

Hively, W., Patterson, H. L., & Page, S. A. (1968). A "universe-defined" system of achievement tests. *Journal of Educational Measurement, 5,* 275–290.

Hoepfner, R. (1978). Achievement test selection for program evaluation. In M. J. Wargo & D. R. Green (Eds.), *Achievement testing of disadvantaged and minority students for educational program evaluation.* Monterey, CA: CTB/McGraw-Hill.

Hsu, T. C., & Carlson, M. (1972). *Computer-assisted testing.* Unpublished manuscript, University of Pittsburgh, Learning Research and Development Center, Pittsburgh.

Hunt, J. McV., & Kirk, G. E. (1974). Criterion-referenced tests of school readiness: A paradigm with illustrations. *Genetic Psychology Monographs, 90,* 143–182.

Jolly, S. J., & Gramenz, G. W. (1984). Customizing a norm-referenced achievement test to achieve curricular validity: A case study. *Educational Measurement: Issues and Practices, 3,* (3), 16–18.

Keller, F. S. (1968). Goodbye Teacher . . . *Journal of Applied Behavior Analysis, 1,* 79–89.

Keller, F. S., & Sherman, J. G. (1974). *PSI: The Keller Plan handbook.* Menlo Park, CA: Benjamin-Cummings.

Keller, J. M. (1979). Motivation and instructional design: A theoretical perspective. *Journal of Instructional Development, 2,* 26–34.

Keller, J. M. (1983). Motivation design of instruction. In C. M. Reigeluth (Ed.), *Instructional-design theories and models: An overview of their current status* (pp. 386–434). Hillsdale, NJ: Lawrence Erlbaum.

Kingsbury, G. G., & Weiss, D. J. (1979). *An adaptive testing strategy for mastery decisions.* (Research Rep. No. 79–5) Minneapolis: University of Minnesota.

Klausmeier, H. J. (1975). IGE: An alternative form of schooling. In K. Talmage (Ed.), *Systems of individualized education.* Berkeley, CA: McCutchan.

Kowal, B. (1975). *Location in a curriculum hierarchy and performance on three standardized achievement tests.* Unpublished master's thesis, University of Pittsburgh, Pittsburgh.

Kulhavy, R. W. (1977). Feedback in written instruction. *Review of Educational Research, 47,* 211–232.

Landa, L. N. (1983). Descriptive and prescriptive theories of learning and instruction: An analysis of their relationships and interactions. In C. M. Reigeluth (Ed.), *Instructional-design theories and models: An overview of their current status* (pp. 55–73). Hilldale, NJ: Lawrence Erlbaum.

Leinhardt, G. (1980). Modeling and measuring educational treatment in evaluation. *Review of Educational Research, 50,* 393–420.

Leinhardt, G., & Seewald, A. M. (1981). Overlap: What's tested, what's taught? *Journal of Educational Measurement, 18,* 85–96.

Lindquist, E. F., & Hieronymus, A. N. (1964). *Teacher's manual: Iowa tests of basic skills.* Boston: Houghton Mifflin.

Lindvall, C. M., & Bolvin, J. O. (1967). Programmed instruction in the schools: An application of programming principles in "Individually Prescribed Instruction." In P. Lange (Ed.), *Programmed instruction: 66th Yearbook, Part II*, (pp. 217–254). Chicago: National Society for the Study of Education.

Lindvall, C. M., & Nitko, A. J. (1975). *Measuring pupil achievement and aptitude* (2nd ed.) New York: Harcort, Brace Jovanovich.

Linn, R. L. (1983). Testing and instruction: Links and distinctions. *Journal of Educational Measurement, 20*, 179–189.

Macready, G. B., & Merwin, J. C. (1971). Homogeneity within item forms in domain referenced testing. *Educational and Psychological Measurement, 33*, 351–360.

Madaus, G. F. (1981). Reactions to the "Pittsburgh Papers." *Phi Delta Kappan, May*, 634–636.

Mager, R. F. (1973). *Measuring instructional intent: Or got a match?* Belmont, CA: Leer Silgler/Fearon.

Mehrens, W. A. (1984). National tests and local curriculum: Match or mismatch? *Educational measurement: Issues and Practice, 3* (3), 9–15.

Mehrens, W. A., & Phillips, S. E. (1986). Detecting impacts of curricular differences in achievement test data. *Journal of Educational Measurement, 23*, 185–196.

Merrill, M. D., Reigeluth, C. M., & Faust, G. W. (1979). The instructional quality profile: A curriculum evaluation and design tool. In H. F. O'Neil, Jr. (Ed.), *Procedures for instructional systems development*. New York: Academic Press.

Messick, S. (1981a). Constructs and their vicissitudes in educational and psychological measurement. *Psychological Bulletin, 89*, 575–588.

Messick, S. (1981b). Evidence and ethics in the evaluation of tests. *Educational Researcher, 10* (9), 9–20.

Millman, J. (1980). Computer-based item generation. In R. A. Berk (Ed.), *Criterion-referenced measurement: The state of the art*. Baltimore: Johns Hopkins University Press.

Millman, J., & Outlaw, W. S. (1978). Testing by computer. *Association for Educational Data Systems Journal, 11*, 57–72.

Natriello, G., & Dornsbusch, S. M. (1984). *Teacher evaluative standards and student effort*. New York: Longman.

Nesbit, M. Y. (1966). *The CHILD program: Computer help in learning diagnosis of arithmetic scores* (Curriculum bulletin 7-E-B). Miami, FL: Dade County Board of Public Instruction.

Nitko, A. J. (1969). A description of the Individually Prescribed Instruction Project. In A. N. Hofstetter (Ed.), *Leadership for curriculum development: Vol. 1* (Seminar and Conference Report and Proceedings Series). Morgantown, WV; West Virginia University.

Nitko, A. J. (1980). Distinguishing the many varieties of criterion-referenced tests. *Review of Educational Research, 50*, 461–485.

Nitko, A. J. (1983). *Educational tests and measurement: An introduction*. San Diego: Harcourt, Brace Jovanovich.

Nitko, A. J., & Hsu, TC. (1974). Using domain-referenced tests for student placement, diagnosis, and attainment in a system of adaptive, individualized instruction. In W. Hively (Ed.), *Domain-referenced testing*. Englewood Cliffs, NJ: Educational Technology Publications.

Nitko, A. J., & Hsu, T. (1984). A comprehensive microcomputer system for classroom testing. *Journal of Educational Measurement, 21*, 377–390.

Novick, M. R., & Lewis, C. (1974). Prescribing test length for criterion-referenced measurement. In C. W. Harris, M. C. Alkin, & W. J. Popham (Eds.), *Problems in criterion-referenced measurement*. Los Angeles: University of California, Center for the Study of Evaluation.

Nurss, J. R., & McGauvran, M. E. (1976). *Metropolitan readiness tests* (Levels I and II, Forms P and Q). New York: Harcourt, Brace Jovanich.

Osburn, H. G. (1968). Item sampling for achievement testing. *Educational and Psychological Measurement, 28*, 95–104.

Phillips, S. E., & Mehrens, W. A. (1988). Effects of curricular differences on achievement test data at item and objective levels. *Applied Measurement in Education, 1*, 33–51.

Popham, W. J. (1972). *Developing IOX Objectives-Based Tests: Procedure guidelines* (Tech. Rep. No. 8). Los Angeles: The Instructional Objectives Exchange.

Popham, W. J. (1978). *Criterion-referenced measurement*. Englewood Cliffs, NJ: Prentice-Hall.

Popham, W. J. (1984). Specifying the domain of content or behaviors. In R. A. Berk (Ed.), *A guide to criterion-referenced test construction* (pp. 29–48). Baltimore: Johns Hopkins University Press.

Prichert, J. W., & Anderson, R. C. (1977). Taking different perspectives on a story. *Journal of Educational Psychology, 69*, 309–315.

Reigeluth, C. M. (1983a). Foreword. In C. M. Reigeluth (Ed.), *Instructional-design theories and models: An overview of their current status* (p. 385). Hillsdale, NJ: Lawrence Erlbaum.

Reigeluth, C. M. (1983b). Instructional Design: What is it and why is it? In C. M. Reigeluth (Ed.), *Instructional-design theories and models: An overview of their current status* (pp. 3–36). Hillsdale, NJ: Lawrence Erlbaum.

Reigeluth, C. M., & Merrill, M. D. (1979). Classes of instructional variables. *Educational Technology, March*, 5–24.

Resnick, L. B. (1975). *The science and art of curriculum design* (Publication No. 1975/9) Pittsburgh: University of Pittsburgh, Learning Research and Development Center.

Resnick, L. B. (1976). Task analysis in instructional design: Some cases from mathematics. In D. Klahr (Ed.), *Cognition and instruction*. Hillsdale, NJ: Lawrence Erlbaum.

Resnick, L. B., Wang, M. C., & Kaplan, J. (1973). Task analysis in curriculum design: A hierarchically sequenced introductory mathematics curriculum. *Journal of Applied Behavior Analysis, 6*, 679–710.

Roid, G. H. (1979). The technology of test-item writing. In H. F. O'Neil, Jr. (Ed.), *Procedures for instructional systems development*. New York: Academic Press.

Roid, G. H. (1984). Generating the test items. In R. A. Berk (Ed.), *A guide to criterion-referenced test construction* (pp. 49–77). Baltimore: Johns Hopkins University Press.

Roid G. H., & Finn, P. J. (1978). *Algorithms for developing test questions from sentences in instructional materials* (NPRDC Tech. Rep. No. 78–23) San Diego: Navy Personnel Research and Development Center.

Roid, G. H., & Haladyna, T. M. (1982). *A technology for test-item writing*. New York: Academic Press.

Roid, G. H., & Haladyna, T. M., Shaughnessy, J., & Finn, P. J. (1979). *Item writing for domain-referenced tests of prose learning*. Paper presented at the meeting of the American Educational Research Association, San Francisco.

Rovinelli, R. J., & Hambleton, R. K. (1977). On the use of content specialists in the assessment of criterion-referenced test items validity. *Dutch Journal for Educational Research, 2*, 49–60.

Salmon-Cox, L. (1981). Teachers and standardized achievement tests: What's really happening. *Phi Delta Kappan, May*, 631–634.

Schmidt, W. H. (1983). Content bias in achievement tests. *Journal of Educational Measurement, 20*, 165–178.

Schwarz, P. A. (1971). Prediction instruments for educational outcomes. In R. L. Thorndike (Ed.), *Educational measurement* (2nd ed.). Washington, DC: American Council on Education, pp. 303–331.

Shayer, M., & Wylam, H. (1981). The development of concepts of heat and temperature in 12–13 year olds. *Journal of Research in Science Teaching, 18*, 419–434.

Simon, H. A. (1969). *The science of the artificial*. Cambridge, Mass.: The M.I.T. Press.

Snow, R. E. (1980). Aptitude and achievement. In W. B. Schrader (Ed.), *Measuring achievement: Progress over a decade. New directions for testing and measurement (No. 5)* (Proceedings of the 1979 ETS Invitational Conference). San Francisco: Jossey-Bass.

Spache, G. D. (1976). *Diagnosing and correcting reading disabilities*. Boston: Allyn & Bacon.

Stake, R. E., & Easley, J. A., Jr., et al. (1978). *Case studies in science education, booklet XIII, findings III*. Urbana, IL: University of Illinois at Urbana-Champaign, Center for Instructional Research and Curriculum Evaluation and Committee on Culture and Cognition.

Sternberg, R. J. (1984). Preface. In R. J. Sternberg (Ed.), *Mechanisms of Cognitive Development*. San Francisco: W. H. Freeman.

Subkoviak, M. J. (1984). Estimating the reliability of mastery-nonmastery classifications. In R. A. Berk (Ed.), *A guide to criterion-*

referenced test construction (pp. 267–291). Baltimore: Johns Hopkins University Press.

Tatsuoka, K. K., & Tatsuoka, M. M. (1981). *Spotting incorrect rules in signed-number arithmetic by the individual consistency index* (Research Rep. No. 81–4) Urbana, IL: University of Illinois, Computer-Based Education Research Laboratory.

Tatsuoka, K. K., & Tatsuoka, M. M. (1982). Detection of aberrant response patterns and their effect on dimensionality. *Journal of Educational Statistics, 7,* 215–231.

Thorndike, R. L. (1972). Dilemmas in diagnosis. In W. H. MacGinitie (Ed.), *Assessment in reading.* Newark, DE: International Reading Association.

Tiberghien, A. (1980). Modes and conditions of learning—an example: The learning of some concepts of heat. In W. F. Archenbold, R. Driver, A. Orton, & C. Wood-Robinson (Eds.), *Cognitive development and research in science and mathematics.* Leeds, England: University of Leeds Printing Service.

Tieman, P. W., & Markle, S. M. (1978, March). *Domain referenced testing in conceptual learning.* Paper presented at the meeting of the American Educational Research Association, Toronto.

Tyler, R. W. (1934). *Constructing achievement tests.* Columbus, OH: Ohio State University.

Urevbu, A. O. (1984). School science curriculum and innovation: An African perspective. *European Journal of Science Education, 6,* 217–225.

Wagner, R. K., & Sternberg, R. J. (1984). Alternate conceptions of intelligence and their implications for education. *Review of Educational Research, 54,* 179–223.

Wang, M. C. (1980). Adaptive instruction: Building on diversity. *Theory into Practice, 19,* 122–128. (Reprinted as *Report to Educators 5.* Pittsburgh: University of Pittsburgh, Learning Research and Development Center.)

Wang, M. C., Gennari, P., & Waxman, H. C. (1983). *The Adaptive Learning Environments Model: An innovative variation on a recurrent theme.* Pittsburgh: University of Pittsburgh, Learning Research and Development Center.

Wang, M. C., & Lindvall, C. M. (1984). Individual differences and school learning environments. In G. E. Gordon (Ed.), *Review of research in education, 11,* 161–225.

Wang, M. C., & Resnick, L. B. (1978). *The primary education program: Manuals 1–8.* Johnstown, PA: Mafex Associates.

Waples, D., & Tyler, R. W. (1930). *Research methods and teacher problems.* New York: Macmillan.

Weiss, D. J. (1974). *Strategies of adaptive ability measurement.* (Research Rep. No. 74–5). Minneapolis: University of Minnesota, Department of Psychology.

Williams, R. G., & Haladyna, T. M. (1982). Logical operations for generating intended questions (LOGIQ): A typology for higher level test items. In G. H. Roid & T. M. Haladyna (Eds.), *A technology for test-item writing.* New York: Academic Press.

Wilson, S. M., & Hiscox, M. D. (1984). Using standardized tests for assessing local learning objectives. *Educational Measurement: Issues and Practices, 3,* 19–22.

Wulfeck, W. H., Ellis, J. A., Merrill, M. D., Richards, R. E., & Wood, N. D. (1978). *The instructional quality inventory: Vol. I. Introduction and overview.* San Diego: Navy Personnel Research and Development Center.

13

Administrative Uses of School Testing Programs

Joy A. Frechtling

Montgomery County (MD) Public Schools

The purpose of this chapter is to discuss the ways in which administrators use test data, describing both current practices and, where relevant, current pitfalls. The focus is on administrators working in local school systems, primarily those in public school systems with districtwide responsibilities extending beyond an individual school.

Tests are clearly more prevalent and more visible in U.S. education today than they were 20 years ago (Resnick, 1981). The changes that have occurred have resulted not only in a proliferation of instruments but also in an expansion and realignment of the uses of these instruments.

There is no established scheme for categorizing the varied possible uses, and attempts at categorization have varied in the emphasis placed on historical, functional, and psychometric issues. Resnick (1981), for example, looks at test usage from a historical perspective, linking differences to long-standing features of U.S. society. The present discussion is more functionally oriented, with tests being considered tools for

1. Reporting to the public on student achievement
2. Evaluating program or curricular effectiveness
3. Enforcing educational accountability

Each of these functions, and some of the problems posed by them, is described briefly.

The reporting function is, at the same time, one of communication and one of public relations. Test scores provide a quick and apparently easily understood indicator of how much students have learned. Over the years, the public reporting of such data has greatly increased, and, as frequently happens, there has also been an increase in the problems posed by both the misreporting and the misuse of such data. The section on the use of test scores for reporting to the public will discuss

these problems and suggest ways for administrators to handle them.

The program-evaluation function, probably the most familiar of the three discussed, uses test data for examining program effects. This use is based on the assumption that test scores provide an indicator not only of what a student knows or has learned but also of how effective a program or curriculum has been in supporting such learning. Tests, in this context, are used as feedback indicators, the purpose of which is to signal whether programs have been successful or whether revisions need to be made. Although the question of whether or not a program works appears, on the surface, to be fairly straightforward, experience shows that this is not the case. In the discussion on administrators' use of tests for program evaluation, a number of complexities in interpretation will be discussed that all too often make the task extremely difficult.

The third function is that of educational accountability. Increasingly, test scores are also being used to judge the quality of the educational system and those who work for it. This usage goes well beyond the previous one, as its intention is less the provision of corrective feedback than of a public evaluation of whether or not standards are being met. Drawing inferences from test scores about the effectiveness of an individual or an institution, however, presents some serious logistical and conceptual problems. These will be discussed in the final section on test usage.

Reporting to the Public

Administrators use test scores to report to parents and the public on student achievement. Scores are used to provide a status report on what the community's children know and, when norm-referenced tests are employed, on how this knowledge compares with that of a similar age group of students across the nation.

In the late 1970s, the practice of releasing test scores to the public was not common. A study by the Educational Research Service conducted during the 1973–1974 school year showed that only 52% of the school systems enrolling 12,000 or more pupils released standardized test scores to the press (Educational Research Service [ERS], 1974). Today the situation is quite different. For example, within one day of the release of the Scholastic Aptitude Test scores for 1984, all major newspapers in the Washington, DC area, as well as the radio and TV networks, were announcing the national trends and comparing scores in local jurisdictions. Administrators have become accustomed to the fact that test scores are public information, and the release of such scores to the public is a carefully orchestrated event. This change in attitude toward the public release of test scores is largely a result of increased demand, which has been fueled by the actions of both governmental bodies and educational institutions.

First, at the governmental level, legislation targeted directly or indirectly at educational practices has elevated the importance of standardized test scores and convinced the public of its need and right to have access to these data. For example, efforts of the federal government to enhance the learning of low-achieving students from low-income homes stressed the importance of test scores as the central measure of program success (see the discussion regarding the use of test scores for assessing program and curricular effectiveness for a more detailed consideration of the role of the federal government in this area). This action served to greatly enhance the credibility of test data as a, if not *the*, major tool for measuring educational success. In addition, legislation such as the Family Education Rights and Privacy Act (the Buckley Amendment) and the "truth in testing" laws convinced the public of its right to be informed of test scores and led to the belief that failure to provide such information was prima facie evidence of a problem. Tests and test data, previously the property of experts, became part of the public domain.

Second, the educational establishment further legitimized and reinforced the importance of test data by increasingly attributing educational decisions to performance on standardized tests. And recent years have seen an expanded use of standardized test data for placing students in special programs or selecting students for postsecondary institutions. For example, formalized screening procedures for programs with limited access, such as gifted and talented or honors programs, almost always include standardized test scores as a major screening criterion. In addition, educational institutions reacted to the demand for test scores by responding enthusiastically to the call for public disclosure. Especially in districts where students were doing well, the political value of publicizing test scores was quickly seen, and annual reporting of test scores soon became an established procedure. Between those districts who wanted to release publicly their test scores and those who had to, the practice soon became widespread.

In addition to those mentioned, there is one further factor that must be noted as contributing to the increased demand for test information. The language used to report test results, which makes the numbers deceivingly interpretable, increased community desire for these statistics. From the point of view of the public or the parent seeking information about school quality, test scores seemed to be informative and easy to understand. This fact, that test scores appeared easily understandable to most laypersons, facilitated their adoption and contributed to their general acceptance. Had test results been couched in more obscure language, relying more heavily on technical terms, the public's enchantment with test information might well have faded more rapidly. However, test results were reported in deceptively simple language, and the majority of the public felt comfortable hearing and acting on the data.

However, experience with reporting test scores to the public has shown that, even in the best of circumstances, the task is not a simple one and that, all too frequently, the data are misinterpreted or only partially understood. Bunch, Haenn, and Mengel (1983), in their discussion of the state of the art in test reporting, conclude that the misinterpretation of test results by well-meaning individuals leads to the greatest misuse of test results. Discussed next are some of the issues that administrators must keep in mind when presenting test reports to the public. Included are concerns regarding the unit for reporting, the type of metric to use, the provision of comparative data, the significance of change, and the format for test reporting.

Unit for Reporting

In the reporting of test results to the public, a number of decisions have to be made regarding what the appropriate unit of reporting is to be. There are four primary institutional levels of aggregation: student level, classroom level, school level, and district level. Most districts that provide reports to the public focus on two of those levels, the district level and the individual school level. Sometimes, however, institutional boundaries are crossed, and reports include data for participants by special program such as Chapter I or programs for limited-English-proficiency students. In addition, where test results are used to address policy issues, such as ones related to educational equity, reporting by selected demographic subgroups is also found. Use of demographic data, however, is currently rather uneven. Although provision of information on test scores by gender is fairly commonplace, presentation of data by other demographic indicators such as racial or ethnic group membership or socioeconomic status is found with far less frequency (Myerberg & Frechtling, 1984).

The issue of whether to present data by these latter indicators raises some important sociopolitical and educational questions. Many school systems have avoided the problem by not carrying out the analyses. Others conduct the analyses but avoid public disclosure unless forced by a freedom-of-information request or court order. The reasons for being cautious about such information are twofold. On the one hand, the primary motivation is often self-serving. Administrators may wish to avoid presenting breakdowns showing a particular group or groups to be performing less well than others, knowing the possible political repercussions of such data. On the other hand, the decisions may be well intentioned. Many argue against the presentation of data by socioeconomic status on the grounds of its potential for misinterpretation. Although they agree that such data are useful in providing a partial explanation of why some students are doing more poorly than others, they fear that such data will be used to prove their failure to educate all students adequately (Frechtling & Myerberg, 1983). This is clearly an issue that must be given careful thought, considering both the value of including socioeconomic information and the possible misuses to which such data might be put.

Type of Metric to Use

A second question concerns the type of metric to be used. Norm-referenced tests, especially, offer a wide choice of metrics for reporting purposes. Results can be reported in terms of stanines, grade equivalents, percentiles, and normal curve equivalents. A somewhat less precise measure, the percentage of local students scoring above a given point, say the national 50th percentile, is also sometimes used.

Each of these alternatives has strengths and weaknesses of which the administrator needs to be aware. Grade equivalents, for example, are frequently used, as they appear to be the easiest to understand; however, they turn out to be the most misunderstood. All too often, the grade-equivalent score is interpreted as being an indicator of the level at which a student is performing, when, in fact, it estimates the grade level at which a student receives a given raw score. Percentile ranks are preferable, as their meaning is far less prone to distortion. Nonetheless, problems arise when people try to assess gains directly from percentiles or to make other types of comparative judgments, as it is not well understood that such scores should not be added or subtracted. Normal curve equivalents have an advantage when comparisons are at issue, as they can be used in ways that percentiles cannot. However, this metric poses a communication problem because the term *normal curve equivalent* is unfamiliar to most laypersons and could sound intimidating. Stanines are also a useful metric (although actually defining what a stanine means is far from a simple task) because they communicate well and can be manipulated to draw most required comparisons. Stanines, however, provide a fairly gross measure of performance, rendering it difficult to show change in performance levels.

Whatever measure is selected, administrators are wise to make sure that any reporting of test scores includes a definition of what the test scores actually mean. Also, it would probably be prudent to provide interpretive cautions, based on commonly observed misinterpretations, with the release of the test scores themselves.

Provision of Comparative Data

Reporting of test scores is commonly done on an annual basis, with the focus of the report being on the most current findings. However, to understand these findings better, administrators are frequently called upon to interpret test scores in terms of what they imply either for the efficacy of instruction at various grades levels or the trends in performance over time. Selecting a method for comparison poses some serious problems, and approaches that at first glance seem reasonable might, after greater consideration, turn out to be highly questionable.

One fairly common approach, comparing performance across grade levels for any one testing year, frequently results in misleading and incorrect conclusions. For example, declining test scores from the 1st through the 12th grades have been interpreted as providing support for the charge that educational institutions are less effective in the higher grade levels.

Although this interpretation has face validity, it is not necessarily correct, and considerably more data are required before such a conclusion can be drawn. There are several reasons for this. *First,* such a comparison involves the assumptions that the cohorts of students are similar in characteristics correlated with achievement and that any differences found in performance reflect the contribution of instructional processes. This is a very shaky assumption. *Second,* such a comparison also presumes that the norm group for the tests at each level were of equal ability. This might not be the case. *Finally,* such an interpretation assumes that the tests themselves provide equally good measures of instruction across grade levels. This, again, in an assumption to be seriously challenged. The procedures for test development and norming do not include steps that assure such comparability across grade levels. In fact, comparative analyses of tests across grade levels suggest just the opposite, indicating that there are grade-level-related differences in how well tests measure what is taught (Stenner, Hunter, & Bland, 1978). Given these problems, it appears that comparison of performance across grade levels can best be made when the same students are studied over time, as is frequently done in curricular evaluations (Smith-Burke & Ringler, 1986). However, this approach provides only a partial solution, as the possibility of the effect of differences in the test instruments themselves cannot be rejected.

Similar difficulties can be cited in attempting to assess trends over time, for example, in comparing the performance of the most current third-grade class with that of third-grade classes of previous years. In addition, attempts to use such data to draw some conclusions regarding the changing merits of an educational system must be viewed with caution. Aside from the fact that it is always questionable to infer that a score on a test that measures student achievement is, in fact, a measure of educational quality (Mehrens, 1984), the comparisons that result from historical tracking suffer from the weakness noted earlier of failing to take into account cohort differences. Where cohort differences are ignored, educational institutions might take the blame when scores decrease, or the credit when scores increase, for changes that could legitimately be attributed to population change.

A preferable approach to providing comparative analyses over time is the use of longitudinal data that show the trend in scores across 2 or more years for only those students tested in all years (Frechtling & Myerberg, 1984). These longitudinal analyses allow firmer conclusions to be drawn about the effects of the educational process. And, as data are accumulated on successive cohorts of students, the sorting out of any cohort effect from an institutional effect becomes increasingly feasible. A second advantage to this approach comes from the additional information provided by the test scores of the group excluded from the longitudinal analyses. Examination of trends over time for these nonlongitudinal students provides another source of valuable data, at least for the administrator, if not for the public. These data are a good source of information on population changes within the district, showing how the "leavers" and "newcomers" compare to each other and to the more stable population in achievement level.

The Significance of Change

A related issue in drawing comparisons is that of setting a standard for determining when a change is important and when it is trivial. Although one could easily adopt traditional standards of statistical significance for this purpose, and this is frequently the approach utilized, the wisdom of doing so must be seriously questioned. Given the influence of sample size in determining statistical significance, use of a strictly statistical criterion might not be educationally advisable. On the one hand, in districts where a grade cohort numbers several thousand students, a change of one percentile point could be statistically significant. On the other hand, where the student population is more limited, enormous gains might be needed for a change to be considered significant from a statistical point of view.

There is no simple solution to this problem. Clearly, what one is ultimately interested in is determining the educational significance of any change that occurs. Although a change of a third of a standard deviation on a given test instrument has frequently been taken to define educational significance, it must be admitted that such a standard is somewhat arbitrary. Administrators reporting test results must recognize that no simple formula can be relied upon, and they must proceed cautiously before sounding alarms or celebrating success related to test-score changes.

Format for Test Reporting

Although test scores are probably most frequently seen as newspapers present them, as a listing by school of average test performance, there are a number of different ways in which such data can be, and are, reported. Formal reports, printouts, simple brochures, and slide and tape presentations are all viable alternatives for communicating with the public.

Experience in presenting test-score data has shown that no single medium or approach is effective with all audiences. The public has a number of different faces, from the school board member to the general taxpayer to the concerned parent. Although it might seem time consuming, the development of alternative formats to meet the needs of differing audiences is very important (Bunch et al., 1983; Frechtling & Myerberg, 1983). Further, tailoring the content of a report to match a group's particular interests can be beneficial. For example, parents are most interested in receiving information on their own children's performance, with data providing comparison to some outside standard. Unless these same parents are house hunting or in the real estate profession, they are probably less interested in receiving a complete enumeration of the scores for each of the district's schools. Reports to parents that include support materials in the form of question-and-answer letters or brochures describing the program and suggesting ways to interpret individual scores have been found to be very successful (Bunch et al., 1983). Reports to school board members, in contrast, are typically more formal and focus on districtwide

and individual school results. Here, explanatory materials should address the comparison of scores across schools.

One final note with regard to the issue of communication. Increasingly, schools are serving populations whose first language is not English and whose familiarity with English is limited. This increased heterogeneity of clientele has given rise to the need to present reports of test scores in other languages. This is a new concern for the American educational system, with some possible far-reaching political and legal implications. For example, with many states requiring that students pass some sort of competency test for graduation, will it become a legal requirement that parents be informed of a student's status in her or his primary language? Will failure to do so be sufficient cause to cite a state for lack of due process? These are questions yet to be addressed fully.

Evaluating Program or Curricular Effectiveness

When administrators want to know whether a special program or curriculum is working, it has become standard practice to use test scores as a primary indicator of success or failure. Although perceptions of staff, students, and parents are also frequently tapped as information sources, test scores are typically considered the all-important bottom line on which judgments are ultimately based.

Today's administrators are certainly not unique in their reliance on test scores as a measure of program or curriculum effectiveness. But the importance accorded to norm- or criterion-referenced test scores over other indicators clearly appears to have increased, and this increase can be tied directly to broader educational changes that occurred during the 1960s and to the prominence accorded to testing in monitoring these changes.

Specifically, during the 1960s special programs such as Head Start and Title I of the Elementary and Secondary School Education Act were initiated, in large part because of documented disparities between racial or ethnic groups in school achievement and economic success later in life. The avowed educational purpose of these programs was to enhance instructional opportunities for low-achieving youngsters, with the long-range goal of improving their earning power and "breaking the cycle of poverty." These programs were outcome oriented, and the outcome of major interest, at least in the short run, was student performance. Central to the present discussion is the fact that this outcome, student performance, quickly became operationalized in terms of how a student scored on standardized achievement tests. Madaus, Airasian, and Kellaghan (1980) suggest several reasons for this practice's being so quickly and widely adopted. These fall into the political, practical, and functional categories.

Politically, the use of these tests to measure program outcomes flowed directly from the rationale used to support the programs in the first place. Just as the problem that federal programs were to address had been defined primarily in terms of differences in test score performance, changes in test scores were seen as the appropriate metric for assessing program impact.

From a practical viewpoint, also, the tests appeared to be the logical choice. They were generally accepted indicators of learning and were readily available for usage. The tests had face validity, as teachers and parents were accustomed to seeing student achievement measured by such indicators. Relatively speaking, they were inexpensive and easy to use. Further, they were the primary tool used by the majority of evaluators called upon to assess program impact. These evaluators had basically been trained as measurement specialists, and they considered standardized tests their stock-in-trade.

Finally, the tests appeared to meet functional needs for interpretability. Because most tests were accompanied by normative data representative of student performance nationwide (at least the norm-referenced tests that were adopted to measure the federal efforts), they provided what can be considered an objective and informative standard against which to assess student progress. The administrator or the evaluator could compare the performance of a particular group of students against these norm data and get what appeared to be a broader perspective on how well a particular group of students was progressing and how they compared with some national average. The end result, that with which administrators are at present coping, is that "standardized tests became the principal measures of the school output in studies of school and program effectiveness" (Madaus et al., 1980, p. 119). And today, assessments of whether a program works must include some sort of standardized test measure if they are to be considered credible.

However, despite the fact that the use of test scores has been institutionalized, problems remain. Although, at first blush, it appears that answering the question of whether a program "works" should be a fairly straightforward task, this is unfortunately far from the truth. *First,* administrators need to be aware of the fact that there are alternative interpretations of what it means to have a program work. *Second,* administrators need to be cognizant of the fact that the answer they receive might be determined, at least in part, by the type and content of the test measure used. *Third,* administrators cannot close their eyes to the fact that the use of test data for making critical decisions about schools and staff can have an important and negative unintended consequence: the manipulation of these outcome measures.

Defining What It Means to Have a Program Work

The first issue that must be addressed in assessing whether or not a program works is the definition of *working.* Roughly speaking, the questions fall into two categories. The first is an implementation question: Is the program actually being delivered as designed? The second is an impact question: What is the effect of this program on student learning? Although it is this latter question that we have referred to as the bottom line that administrators are most interested in, to adequately address the question of impact requires at least some attention to implementation.

The importance of attention to the issue of implementation cannot be overstressed, and the history of evaluation of innovations clearly attests to this fact. Programs do not appear full-blown in schools within the first few months or even the first year of adoption; more often than not, implementation is a slow, piecemeal process. Unless it has been established through some kind of empirical verification that implementation has occurred, the risk of measuring what could be called "a nonevent" and erroneously concluding that a program is or is not working is substantial.

However, even if one is clearly focused on the question of impact and knows that implementation has occurred, there are at least three different questions that can, under different circumstances, be asked, with no one methodology being equally appropriate for addressing all three. The first and most restrictive question is whether the students are acquiring the skills that a program or curriculum is intended to teach. For example, if a reading program, the Instructional System in Reading/Language Arts, is intended to teach objectives *x, y, z,* are these objectives actually learned? Mehrens (1984) refers to this as an "audit" question rather than an evaluation question. The second is whether the program or curriculum is effective in teaching the domain it is intended to address. Does the Instructional System in Reading/Language Arts provide students with comprehension skills? The third question is whether a program or curriculum is more effective in providing this learning than some other alternative. Is the Instructional System in Reading/Language Arts more effective than some basal series in comprehension instruction? Test selection and data interpretation can vary in important ways, depending upon which of these questions the administrator needs to answer.

Selecting a Test

The testing tool selected can have an impact on the degree to which a program or curriculum is judged to be successful. Although we might wish that it were not the case, it is true that tests with the same general name might measure different things in different ways (Frechtling & Myerberg, 1983; Freeman et al., 1983).

One of the much debated issues in selecting a test is whether to use a norm-referenced or a criterion-referenced test instrument. When tests first emerged as the tool for assessing program impact, this issue did not receive much attention, as standardized tests meant norm-referenced tests, at least to the general public and local administrator. Increasingly, however, evaluators and administrators have utilized criterion-referenced measures, and many state and local programs include, or even rely on, them.

The pros and cons of the alternatives are well known and well aired. Administrators like norm-referenced tests because they are relatively brief, inexpensive to use, and well accepted by the public and the media. Even more important is the fact that they provide data comparing local performance to that of a norm group. It must be noted, however, that the usefulness of such normative data has received some vehement challenges. One of the sharpest lines of attack is represented by Williams (1972), who charged that these norms might provide inappropriate standards for assessing the performance of minority students because they are based largely on the performance of white students. This problem has been addressed in more recent test-norming efforts that have sought a more balanced ratio among major ethnic groups, but suspicion remains regarding the appropriateness of the norms for minority students. In addition, even where the majority student is concerned, the representativeness of the norms has been questioned. Simply put, the argument is that the data might not be as representative as one would like, because the sample of districts agreeing to participate in norming activities is likely to differ in some important ways from those who do not. This issue has recently begun to be of increased concern to publishers and school districts alike.

Questions of norming aside, the usefulness of norm-referenced tests has received some more fundamental challenges. It has been argued that these tests are not good measures of school effects. Specifically, it is charged that they are relatively insensitive to the impact of instruction (Madaus et al., 1980), provide information of relatively little use to individual students, and might give very incomplete measures of what is actually being taught.

Criterion-referenced tests, on the other hand, appeal because they can be tailored to match what is actually being taught, they provide diagnostic information useful to the individual student, and they might be more readily translatable into strategies for program improvement. On the debit side, these tests are cited for being too lengthy and demanding of time, too costly and difficult to construct, and too incomplete because of the lack of normative data.

Testing companies have attempted to respond to this problem by providing criterion-referenced scoring and reporting procedures for norm-referenced tests and norm-referenced scoring and reporting procedures for criterion-referenced tests, but these amalgams have not as yet provided an adequate solution (Jolly & Gramenz, 1984). Innovative testing approaches developed by some local school districts have yet to be fully examined (see, for example, Jolly, 1984, regarding the *objective-referenced approach* developed by Palm Beach County, Florida; LeMahieu, 1984, regarding the *edumetric* approach being used in Pittsburgh, Pennsylvania). Computerized adaptive testing, an approach that holds promise of providing both diagnostic and criterion-referenced achievement data in an economic manner, is only beginning to be explored by the public schools. Currently, the administrator wishing to assess program effectiveness still faces a dilemma in test selection that the experts themselves have yet to resolve.

A second issue in selecting a test revolves around the concern for using a test that appropriately matches the content of the program or curriculum being assessed. The question of overlap between test and curricular content has received increasing attention over the last 10 years, and evaluation methodologies have come to be dominated by what can be called the *doctrine of maximal overlap*. Cooley and Leinhardt (1980), in their studies of the effectiveness of Title I programs, found that a critical predictor of achievement was the degree of overlap between test and curricular content. This factor, more than any of the other variables related to instructional practices or techniques, accounted for the greatest amount of variance in end-of-year achievement, once initial achievement was taken into account. They further found that tests differed considerably in the content they covered for any one grade for any one area. Subsequent analyses comparing test content to textbook

content have confirmed the Cooley and Leinhardt findings (Leinhardt & Seewald, 1981).

This has led evaluators to look very closely at the relationship between curricular and test content before selecting an instrument and drawing conclusions regarding whether some practice is working. Preferred is a test whose content matches what has been taught, that contains a minimal number of items addressing areas not covered by the curriculum, and that includes a maximal number of items covering areas the curriculum is intended to address. Presently, the doctrine of maximal overlap is widely embraced by program evaluators and has even been incorporated into some programs aimed at enhancing school effectiveness.

Mehrens (1984) questions, however, whether maximal overlap is, in fact, desirable. Quoting Cronbach (1963), he states, "An ideal evaluation might include measures of all types of proficiency that might reasonably be desired in the area in question, not just selected items to which this curriculum directs substantial attention." Mehrens suggests that a close match between curricular and test content is desirable only if one wishes to make inferences about the specific objectives taught by a specific teacher in a specific school. More commonly, educators and the general public wish to make inferences to a broad domain, whether or not that whole domain has been taught. For those inferences, it is inappropriate to delimit the measuring instrument to a sample of the smaller domain of materials actually taught. Further, even in evaluating the effects of a specific teacher in a specific class, one inference of importance is the degree to which students can generalize from or transfer from specific knowledge taught in class. To make such inferences, one cannot limit the test to material actually taught. Certainly, when curriculum evaluation calls for comparing two different curricula with somewhat different content domains, the inference as to which curriculum is better cannot be made from a test matching only one of the domains.

Again, this discussion points to the importance of being clear about the question that is being addressed. Depending on what the question is, differing degrees of overlap might be optimal.

Manipulating Data

There are several factors besides program effectiveness that can affect how well a group of students performs on a test. One of these, overlap between what is tested and what is taught, has been addressed in some detail already. A second factor that is also well recognized is test-wiseness. All things being equal, a student who has experience in taking tests and who is familiar with the types of questions asked on a particular test is likely to do better on the test than one for whom the situation is unfamiliar and, in all likelihood, anxiety producing. Given these findings, most schools provide test-preparation activities for their students, to minimize the contribution of test-wiseness to the results obtained and to maximize the contribution of learning.

Going further, there are practices that might be called outright cheating that can also be used to make performance appear higher or lower than it normally would. Such activities range from teaching to the exact questions on the test to offering hints and corrections during test taking to changing answers or scores. No one wishes to believe that such cheating occurs on any widespread basis, but experience with programs wherein test performance was used as a basis for allocating resources or evaluating personnel unfortunately indicates that the temptation is too much for some people to bear. As Cooley (1983) points out, there is greater likelihood of an indicator being corrupted if rewards or punishments are associated with extreme values on that indicator than if the indicator is used for guiding corrective feedback.

Depending on how resources are allocated, there might be incentives for both artificially lowering or artificially raising test scores. For example, proposals to allocate Title I funds primarily on the basis of low achievement were considered questionable because of the possible incentives provided for lowering student scores to receive increased funds (Rotberg & Wolf, 1974). In contrast, current efforts devoted to school improvement, in which test scores are used as the principal indicators of school or staff success, might tempt staff to inflate test scores.

Problems like these are not ones that educators would choose to brag about. However, the potential for such abuses cannot be ignored. And, although standardized test instruments might well provide a comparatively objective measure of program effectiveness, some caution in taking this objectivity too seriously is well advised.

Enforcing Educational Accountability

So far, we have discussed administrators' use of test scores for reporting purposes and for assessing the degree to which a program or curriculum is working. Now, we will turn to a use that, although in many ways an extension of the first two, represents what many would consider a quantum jump.

Test scores are increasingly being used as a tool for "educational accountability." This is in large part a result of general dissatisfaction with the American educational system, although, to some extent, it probably also reflects trends toward applying rational management practices found to be effective in business to educational, especially public educational, institutions (Resnick, 1981). Test scores are currently being proposed as both a carrot and a stick for monitoring the performance of educational institutions and educational personnel. The demand for testing is becoming even more widespread, and the decisions made on the basis of test scores are reaching into a wider number of areas of the educational sphere. Further, the consequences of these decisions are taking on increased significance.

The present accountability movement was foreshadowed by the performance-contracting experiments of the 1970s. Performance contracting was an experiment conducted by the Office of Economic Opportunity, whose goals were to find out whether a private educational firm could teach academically underprivileged children to read and write better than the local public schools and how successfully the pecuniary incentive system operates in education (Gramlich & Koshel, 1975). In this experiment, payment for educational services was rendered on the basis of the amount of student gain. Contractors were allowed to choose their preferred approach and were required to meet a standard set by the Office of Economic Opportunity of a gain of one grade equivalent per year. If this standard was not met, no payments would be made. Generally, this experiment failed. It turned out to be harder to meet the proposed standards than many contractors had believed, and few survived the experiment without suffering financial loss. Gramlich and Koshel (1975) suggest a number of reasons for the failure of this effort. Among them are confusion regarding objectives and timing constraints and overreliance on achievement test gains as the sole measure of program success.

More recently, educational accountability has emerged in the guise of the school effectiveness movement and merit pay plans. Whether these will be any more enduring than performance contracting has yet to be determined. However, because these movements clearly have a profound impact on how administrators use test scores (and how test scores are used on administrators!), they will be reviewed briefly here.

The school effectiveness movement and its offshoot, school improvement projects, have grown out of studies of schools that seem to succeed with low-achieving students. Based on the writings of Ron Edmonds and the studies of Weber (1971), Brookover et al. (1978), and Rutter, Maughan, Mortimer, and Oustin (1979), there has emerged a newly consolidated definition of what makes schools more or less effective and a renewed push toward educational changes. The avowed goal of these efforts is to improve the education of students, primarily those from low-income and minority groups.

In this movement, tests and test scores play a critical role. Test performance and differences between groups in test performance are the most common, and too frequently the only, indicator used to measure effectiveness. Test scores, normally scores in the basic-skills areas of reading and mathematics, are considered the primary indicators of whether a particular school is succeeding or failing. Where change or school improvement is the goal, administrators use change in test performance to determine whether schools are making progress.

The movement is extremely widespread and is increasing in popularity. In a study conducted for the National Commission on Excellence, Miles, Farrer, and Neufold (1983) were able to identify 39 school improvement projects covering 875 school districts, ranging in scope from statewide efforts to individual school projects. It is felt, however, that many more projects exist, or are being developed, and that the peak of adoption is yet to be reached.

Although school administrators, as well as the public, have been eager to jump on the effective-schools bandwagon, it is far from clear that this movement is the promising educational enterprise that some have claimed it to be (Cuban, 1984). Close examination of the literature raises some serious questions regarding whether we really know either what an effective school is or how effectiveness should be measured.

Despite the fact that there has been almost universal reliance on test scores for determining school effectiveness, the metric used and the amount of change considered important have varied widely. And the sense of confidence that has emerged in the soundness of the research undergirding the movement and the measures is very much overstated. Some of the problems faced by administrators considering, or being asked to jump on, the bandwagon are summarized next.

First, there is no generally agreed upon measure for determining school effectiveness. Indicators have varied in the metric and the type of test used (Frechtling, 1983). Listed next are the most common variations.

1. Average scores on norm-referenced tests
2. Average gains on norm-referenced tests
3. Passing rates on criterion-referenced tests
4. Gains in passing rates on criterion-referenced tests

Each of these has serious drawbacks. The first and third are flawed because ranking according to absolute scores fails to separate out the effects of school from the effects of background variables. Frequently, the apparently most successful school is that serving the wealthiest students from the best educated families. Schools serving lower income populations, in contrast, might appear ineffective when using this criterion even when they are, in fact, doing a very fine job.

The second and fourth methods, which attempt to control for this problem by taking into account initial achievement, appear more useful but have technical problems of their own. The gain score that is produced has been criticized for being unstable. In analyses conducted in Montgomery County, Maryland, individual school performance has been found to fluctuate more from year to year than would be considered reasonable, given the fact that no major changes occurred in either program or staff; that is, the correlation across years in apparent effectiveness was found to be .24 for reading and .32 for mathematics in a sample of over 100 elementary schools. Researchers at the Far West Educational Laboratory (Rowan, Bossert, & Dwyer, 1982) have reported similar findings and have been unable to eliminate the problem, despite the use of some rather complex regression models. This suggests that either school effectiveness is a very fragile thing or the metric used, the gain score, has some serious problems.

Second, there is no common agreement concerning the amount of gain needed before a school can be considered effective. How much change in percentiles, normal curve equivalents, stanines, percentage of students passing, and so on must be found before effectiveness can be judged to have been achieved? Although, on the surface, this question might appear to be answerable through standard statistical techniques, it is not really a question of statistical significance but one of education meaningfulness, as significance is so closely tied to sample size. Review of the literature indicates that no one standard has been used with any kind of consistency and that guidelines for choosing among the alternatives do not exist. Sometimes, the standard adopted has relied on regression techniques, with schools being considered effective if they gain any more than would be expected. In other cases, a stricter criterion has been adopted, with differences in expectation being required to deviate by some specified magnitude such as a third of a standard deviation before a school can be considered exceptional. A third, somewhat arbitrary, approach has been to set some percentage figure, say 10%, and to consider the top 10% of the gainers effective and the bottom 10% ineffective. Choosing a

standard has, to date, been based more on financial and political concerns than on well-developed models of the phenomena under consideration. Type I and Type II errors clearly abound, but the extent of either is virtually unknown.

Finally, the unit of analysis has also been much discussed. Initially, school effectiveness was judged in terms of average test-score performance, considering all students in a class or grade as the single unit of analysis. Recently, however, concern has been raised that the average score might mask real and important differences in a school's effectiveness for the different populations it serves (Edmonds, 1979). Given this line of thinking, a modified definition of effectiveness has emerged that stresses a school's ability to succeed with initially low- and high-achieving students, students who come from lower and upper socioeconomic backgrounds. This refinement, although probably useful from a conceptual and a sociological viewpoint, does little to overcome the problems associated with measurement.

Taken as a whole, the problems posed by the reliance on test scores for assessing school effectiveness suggest that this manifestation of the accountability movement might give way to other approaches to assuring the quality of education as its limitations become more widely understood. Although the measurement of effectiveness has yet to become as controversial as merit pay (discussed next), the decision to attempt to use test scores for this purpose should not be taken lightly.

Merit pay proposals are another example of educational accountability efforts in which achievement test scores have come to play a critical role, and the focus has turned from educational inputs to educational outputs as indicators of educational quality. Although the idea of merit pay has been debated for nearly three quarters of a century (Robinson, 1983), the idea has been neither totally accepted nor totally rejected, and, recently, interest in the approach has been given renewed attention.

It would be an overstatement to assert that proposed merit pay plans focus solely on achievement test scores. Some emphasize conventional evaluation criteria such as experience, skills in classroom instruction and management, pupil-teacher relationships, and public relations skills. However, these indicators are considered by some to be overly subjective, and they cite the need for more objective measures of educational productivity (Robinson, 1983).

With merit pay, as with the areas already discussed, turning to achievement test scores provides a far less perfect solution than one might originally guess. *First,* there is the question of unit of analysis (Lipsky & Bacharach, no date). Should merit pay be awarded on the basis of the average performance of the class or of some specially targeted group of students? *Second,* there are the questions of effect size and determination of the criteria for being meritorious. Is doing better than average sufficient? On what basis are other cutoffs to be determined? *Third,* there is the issue of the reliability and validity of test instruments. Do the psychometric properties of most tests justify their use for merit pay decisions, especially where relatively fine distinctions need to be drawn? Weissman (1969) suggests that this is a critical problem. *Fourth,* there is the question of impact on the morale of teachers and the climate of the school. If rewards are given on the basis of performance of individual classes, what will this do to the relationships between teachers who do and do not receive bonuses? If whole schools are rewarded on the basis of some average performance score, will teachers whose students show large gains resent carrying those whose students do not perform as well? *Finally,* how does one discourage cheating? The temptation to teach to the test exists when the only reward is a part or the back and a rank in the newspaper. What may happen if financial rewards are also at stake?

Conclusions

This chapter has presented an overview of the differing ways in which local school administrators use test data. For the sake of discussion, current usage has been divided into three general areas, and the specific problems associated with each have received separate attention. It is apparent, however, that a number of the trends or concerns are of general applicability. In concluding this discussion, it seems useful to point out these general trends.

1. The reporting of test scores has become an increasingly public function and is likely to remain so. Whether the test scores are used to describe the achievement level of students, the effectiveness of a program, or the quality of educators, such data are more than likely to be subject to public display and discussion. What was considered information "for internal use only" in the 1960s is now not only public information but also much publicized information.

2. Test scores are increasingly being used as the principal indicator of how well an educational institution or program is functioning. And recent trends suggest that the use of test data for what has been termed *educational accountability* continues to expand. Unfortunately, advocates of this expansion too often fail to acknowledge the shortcomings of most test instruments and act as if such data were both flawlessly accurate and incorruptible.

3. It is very easy to misinterpret test scores and to misuse the information that test performance contains. Basically, a test score provides an estimate of what a student knows. Making the leap from this estimate to a conclusion regarding policies, institutions, or people requires caution and careful consideration of alternative explanations. Too frequently, the complexities of interpretation are overlooked.

REFERENCES

Brookover, W. B., Schweitzer, J. H., Schneider, J. M., Beady, C. H., Flood, P. K., & Wisenbaker, J. M. (1978). Elementary school social climate and school achievement. *American Educational Research Journal, 15,* 301–318.

Bunch, M., Haenn, J., & Mengel, C. W. (1983, December). *The state of the art in test score reporting: Literature review and national survey.* Paper prepared for the Maryland State Department of Education, Baltimore.

Cooley, W. W. (1983). Improving the performance of an educational system. *Educational Researcher, 12,* 4–12.

Cooley, W. W., & Leinhardt, G. (1980). The instructional dimensions study. *Educational Evaluation and Policy Analysis, 2,* 7–25.

Cronbach, L. J. (1963). Evaluation for course improvement. *Teachers College Record, 64,* 672–683.

Cuban, L. (1984). Transforming the frog into a prince: Effective schools research, policy, and practice at the district level. *Harvard Educational Review, 54,* 129–151.

Edmonds, R. (1979). Some schools work and more can. *Social Policy, 9,* 28–32.

Educational Research Service. (1974). *Releasing standardized achievement test scores to the public.* Arlington, VA: Author.

Frechtling, J. A. (1983, April). *Problems in evaluating school effectiveness: A shopping list of dilemmas.* Paper delivered at the meeting of the American Educational Research Association, Montreal.

Frechtling, J. A., & Myerberg, N. J. (1983). *Reporting test scores to different audiences.* Princeton, NJ: (ERIC/TM Rep. 85).

Freeman, D., Belli, G., Porter, A., Floden, R., Schmidt, W., & Schwille, J. (1983). *Consequences of different styles of textbook use in preparing students for standardized tests.* East Lansing, MI: Institute for Research on Teaching.

Gramlich, E. M., & Koshel, P. P. (1975). *Educational performance contracting.* Brookings Institute.

Jolly, J. & Bramenz, G. (1984). Customizing a norm-referenced achievement test to achieve curricular validity a case study. *Educational Measurement: Issues and Practice, 3,* No 3, 16–18.

Leinhardt, G., & Seewald, A. (1981). Overlap: What's tested, what's taught? *Journal of Educational Measurement, 18,* 85–96.

LeMahieu, P. G. (1984). The effects on achievement and instructional content of a program of student monitoring through frequent testing. *Educational Evaluation and Policy Analysis, 6,* 175–188.

Lipsky, D., & Bacharach, S. (no date). The single salary schedule vs. merit pay: An examination of the debate. *Collective Bargaining Quarterly.*

Madaus, G. F., Airasian, P. W., & Kellaghan, T. (1980). *School effectiveness: A reassessment of the evidence.* New York: McGraw-Hill.

Mehrens, W. A. (1984). National tests and local curriculum: Match or mismatch? *Educational Measurement: Issues and Practice. 3,* No. 3, 9–15.

Miles, M. B., Farrar, E., & Neufeld, B. (1983). *The extent of adoption of effective schools programs.* Paper prepared for the National Commission on Excellence in Education, Huron Institute, Cambridge, MA.

Myerberg, N. J., & Frechtling, J. A. (1984, April). *Contents of district test reports.* Paper presented at the meeting of the American Educational Research Association, New Orleans.

Resnick, D. (1981). Testing in America: A supportive environment. *Phi Delta Kappan, 62,* 625–628.

Robinson, G. (1983). *Paying teachers for performance and productivity: Learning from experience.* Arlington, VA: Educational Research Service.

Rotberg, I. C., & Wolf, A. (1974). *Compensatory education: Some research issues.* Washington, DC: National Institute of Education.

Rowan, B., Bossert, S. T., & Dwyer, D. C. (1982). *Research on effective schools: A cautionary note.* San Francisco: Far West Educational Laboratory.

Rutter, H., Maughan, B., Mortimer, P., & Oustin, J. (1979). *Fifteen thousand hours: Secondary schools and their effects on children.* Cambridge, MA: Harvard University Press.

Smith-Burke, T., & Ringler, L. (1986). Star: Teaching reading and writing. In J. Orasanu (Ed.), *A decade of reading research: Implications for Practice.* Hillsdale, NJ: Lawrence Erlbaum. pp. 215–234.

Stenner, A. J., Hunter, E. L., & Bland, J. D. (1978). *The standardized growth expectation: Implications for educational evaluation.* Paper presented at the meeting of the American Educational Research Association, Toronto.

Weber, G. (1971). *Inner-city children can be taught to read: Four successful schools.* (Occasional paper, No. 18). Washington, DC: Council for Basic Education.

Weissman, R. (1969). Merit pay—What merit? *Education Digest, 343,* pp. 16–19.

14

Certification of Student Competence

Richard M. Jaeger

University of North Carolina at Greensboro

CER.TI.FI.CA'.TION (noun). 3. The act of certifying or guaranteeing the truth of anything; attestation. 5. The action of making a (person) certain or sure; assurance. Ref. Bullanger's *Decades* (1592) p. 35 ". . . a certification, as when a thing by perswasions is to beate into our minds, that after that we neuer doubt anye more." (Oxford English Dictionary, 1971, p. 234)
COM.PE.TENCE (noun). 4. Sufficiency of qualification; capacity to deal adequately with a subject.
(Oxford English Dictionary, 1971, p. 719)

From these definitions, it is clear that testing for the purpose of certifying that students are competent is, or ought to be, testing to provide assurance that students are sufficiently qualified to do something, or perhaps, many things. In its current use, competency testing is typically linked to important decisions about students' progress in school, such as high school graduation or grade-to-grade promotion.

Although the second edition of *Educational Measurement* (Thorndike, 1971) has no chapter that parallels this one, suggesting that competency testing is a new phenomenon, Madaus (1981) has amply documented a centuries-old history. He cites a proposal by John Stuart Mill for a law requiring that every citizen be educated to a specific set of standards:

The instrument for enforcing the law could be no other than public examinations, extending to all children and beginning at an early age. An age might be fixed at which every child must be able to read. If a child proves unable, the father, unless he has some sufficient ground of excuse, might be subjected to a moderate fine, to be

worked out, if necessary, by his labour, and the child might be put to school at his expense. Once in every year the examination should be renewed, with a gradually extending range of subjects, so as to make the universal acquisition, and what is more, retention, of a certain minimum of general knowledge, virtually compulsory. (p. 352)

Accountability for students' examination performances is closely linked to competency testing throughout its history, with various individuals or institutions held responsible. Although Mill proposes to hold students' fathers accountable for their test performances, and current U.S. practice appears to hold students accountable, the more common historical trend has been to hold individual teachers or educational institutions themselves responsible.

As Madaus reports (1981, pp. 4–9), in 1444 the town of Treviso, Italy, paid its schoolmaster in proportion to his pupils' performances on tests designed to measure their knowledge of material in a basic grammar. In 1799, a select committee of the Irish Parliament recommended (unsuccessfully) that Irish teachers be "paid by results" (Burton, 1979). The relationships among accountability, testing, and funding were still a matter of debate several centuries later when, in 1941, Irish Prime Minister de Valera spoke in Parliament to support compulsory testing for all sixth-standard pupils (Dail Eireann, 1941). Madaus and Greaney quote de Valera as stating:

if we want to see that a certain standard is reached and we are paying the money, we have the right to see that something is secured for

Note: Four advisors provided excellent suggestions for improvement of this chapter: Ronald Berk, James Impara, George Madaus, and W. James Popham. Their contributions are greatly appreciated. In addition, Cynthia Cole and Donna Sundre, doctoral students at the University of North Carolina-Greensboro, greatly enriched this chapter, and my life, by providing substantial assistance and insightful suggestions. Responsibility for residual shortcomings is, with certainty, mine and not theirs.

that money. The ordinary way to test it and to try to help the whole educational system is by arranging our tests in such a way that they will work in the direction we want. (1983, p. 10)

Though the burden of proving efficacy and the threatened sanction of withholding funds fell on the entire educational system rather than on individual teachers, the Irish National Teachers' Organization adamantly refused to cooperate with the sixth-standard examination program from its inception in 1943 until its abolition in 1967.

In Great Britain, mid-19th-century events laid the groundwork for later extensive testing programs. In a report on the condition of English elementary education, the Newcastle Commission recommended (successfully) that teachers' salaries be based, in large part, on their pupils' examination performances (Lowe, 1861). Madaus (1981, p. 5) cites a report on the ineffectiveness of the system by Sutherland who, in turn, quotes Matthew Arnold (an inspector of schools at the time).

[the system is] . . . a game of mechanical contrivance in which teachers will and must learn how to beat us. It is found possible by ingeneous preparation, to get children through the revised code examination in reading, writing and ciphering, without their really knowing how to read, write and cipher. (1971, p. 52)

British compulsory school attendance legislation, passed in 1880, caused a radical change in the characteristics of the student body to be taught. Teachers and school managers were forced to face the full variety of children's capabilities and conditions (Sutherland, 1984). Because all schoolchildren could no longer be helped to pass their examinations, even by Arnold's "ingeneous preparation," (the 19th century's version of *teaching the test*), various explanations for school failure were advanced. These included poor health, "overpressure," and "feeblemindedness."

In 1905 the Frenchmen Binet and Simon published their first tests, intended to identify children in the "feebleminded" group who could benefit from additional educational help. Mental measurement quickly evolved as the basis for differentiating levels of ability among normal children in the United States and Britain. In Britain, "competitive examinations came to dominate not only secondary school entry but also the relationship between elementary and the other forms of post-elementary education beginning to be developed" (Sutherland, 1984, p. 164).

Competitive examinations were also used in France throughout the first half of the 20th century to screen those students allowed to enter secondary school. Such examinations were abolished in 1959 and replaced by a 2-year period of observation, assessment, and counseling, as part of a general educational reform that, for the first time, expected children to stay in school beyond age 14. Resnick & Resnick (1982) note that in France, as in Great Britain, changes in student population demanded changes in the testing program. They state that

In both [France and England] there is now some movement to provide less demanding examinations so that the academically weaker or less interested students can have some credential when they finish. It is important to note that both countries are considering *extending* exit examinations rather than eliminating them, as a way of serving an expanded school population. (1982, pp. 33–34).

In the United States, minimum competence, rather than excellence, early became the typical focus of testing programs. Horace Mann had introduced basic skills examinations in the Boston Public Schools in 1845 as a device to evaluate the schools' headmasters. Competency testing became widespread, and students' performances were often used to make decisions about grade-to-grade promotions. Tyack (1974) reports an example of this practice in Portland, Oregon, in the late 1800s, where the vast majority of pupils was held back, rather than being promoted. Although this failure rate might have been tolerated in France or Great Britain, the Portland superintendent who initiated this program soon lost his job.

Following the massive influx of immigrants and the rapid growth of the U.S. educational system at the beginning of the 20th century, student failure rates were overwhelming. Educational reformers believed this was due to the failure of the schools to "introduce lower class and immigrant children to American ways" (Wigdor & Garner, 1982). Because of the traditional value placed on universal education, U.S. education agencies have typically adopted examinations designed to preserve minimum, not maximum, standards. Resnick & Resnick (1982) cite the New York Regents examinations (instituted in 1865) and the Advanced Placement examinations of the College Board as the only U.S. examples of external examinations used for the purpose of maintaining high academic standards. They also comment that "Nothing like these minimum competency examination programs exists in other countries. They are a uniquely American response to the question of standards maintenance and improvement" (p. 33).

Some Definitions of Competency Testing

In its principal applications in the United States, the word *minimum* has been added to the competency-testing label. This is because the intent of most competency-testing programs is to determine whether students can demonstrate the least amount of knowledge or skill deemed necessary to certify their competence. Gorth and Perkins (1979a) cite numerous definitions of minimum-competency testing. Six definitions that attempt to specify the essential elements of a competency-testing program follow.

1. [Competency testing programs are] organized efforts to make sure public school students are able to demonstrate their mastery of certain *minimum* skills needed to perform tasks that will routinely confront them in adult life. (American Friends Service Committee, 1978)
2. Minimum competency tests are constructed to measure the acquisition of competency or skills to or beyond a certain defined standard. (Miller, 1978)
3. [Competency testing programs are] testing programs which attempt to learn whether each student is at least "minimally competent" by the time the student graduates from public school. (National School Boards Association, 1978)
4. [Competency testing is] a certification mechanism whereby a pupil must demonstrate that he/she has mastered certain minimal skills in order to receive a high school diploma. (Airasian, Pedulla, & Madaus, 1978)

5. Nearly all minimum competency testing programs seek to define minimum learning outcomes for students in a variety of academic areas and to insure that these standards are satisfied. (Cohen & Haney, 1980)
6. Minimum competency testing involves the administration of proficiency tests in order to certify that minimum competency or proficiency exists with regard to a well-defined set of knowledge or skills. (Beard, 1979, p. 9)

Although these definitions are often circular and differ somewhat in emphasis, two common features emerge.

1. Competency test results are used by institutions to make decisions about the educational future of individual students. Although some competency-testing programs attempt to inform students about their academic strengths and weaknesses, the principal use of competency-test results is to serve institutional purposes such as student placement rather than individual purposes such as student guidance and counseling.
2. Certification requires that test scores be evaluated against a predetermined standard of performance and that a decision be made as to whether each tested student is or is not competent.

The Focus of This Chapter

Certification of student competence is a broad topic that invites a treatise on the whole of educational measurement. This chapter is, appropriately, far narrower in scope and, by implication, relies heavily on many of the other chapters in this volume. In the selection of topics to be discussed, considerable attention has been paid to issues that appear to arise exclusively when the tools of educational measurement are used to certify students' competence or to issues that are central to that application. As a result, a great many measurement issues that are as essential to certifying students' competence as to other common uses of measurement are not considered in this chapter, including estimation of measurement reliability, construct-related evidence of test validity, predictive evidence of test validity, and equating of parallel test forms. These omissions were not intended to suggest that these topics are unimportant to the use of tests to certify students' competence. On the contrary, tests that fail to satisfy fundamental requirements of sound measurement instruments most certainly fail to serve as adequate barometers of students' competence.

Omitted Topics

Chapter 3 of this volume contains a section that describes decision-consistency approaches to assessing test reliability. These approaches should be used to characterize and estimate the reliability of tests used to certify students' competence.

The results of competency testing are typically expressed in terms of decisions about individual students, such as the qualification of students to be awarded a high school diploma or the qualification of students to be promoted to a higher grade in school. In these applications, *qualification* is taken to mean

adequacy of competence. For example, when schools use competency tests to determine the eligibility of students to be awarded a high school diploma, they form two categories of students: those deemed *competent* and those deemed *incompetent*. The fundamental reliability issue in this context is the consistency with which students would be placed in the *same* categories were the decision to be based on their performances on a parallel form of the competency test, perhaps administered at a different time under similar but not identical conditions.

Several indices of the consistency of examinee classification are described in chapter 3 of this volume, as are methods of estimating these indices from data secured in a single administration of a test or in two administrations of a test. Both the indices and the estimation methods are directly applicable when tests are used to certify students' competence, and additional discussion in this chapter would be redundant.

Classification of a student as competent or incompetent involves far more than a judgment of that student's performance on a particular test. Such classification is an *inference* about the student's status with respect to a construct labeled *competence,* as well as a prediction about the student's likely performance in a higher level grade, in a postsecondary educational setting, or in adult society. When tests are used to make inferences such as these, examination of the validity of the inferences is mandatory. Nonetheless, because construct-related evidence of test validity and predictive evidence of test validity are described cogently and completely in Messick's chapter in this volume, these topics are not discussed here. Again, these issues of measurement validity are critical to the responsible use of competency tests. Messick's discussion of validation theory and methods used to secure such validity evidence is directly applicable to tests used to certify students' competence, and it should be studied with great care.

Because competency tests are typically used to make important decisions that profoundly affect the educational and societal futures of individual students, test security becomes a central issue. In addition, responsible use of competency testing demands that students who are initially classified incompetent because they have failed a test be given at least one more (and hopefully many more) opportunities to demonstrate their competence. Both of these issues demand the construction of several alternate forms of each competency test used to classify students.

To ensure equity, students must neither be disadvantaged nor advantaged because they attempted a particular form of a competency test during a particular test administration. Parallel forms of competency tests must be constructed, and these forms must be placed on a common score scale through a procedure known as *test equating*. Lord (1980) has defined equity in test equating as follows: "If an equating of tests x and y is to be equitable to each applicant, it must be a matter of indifference to applicants at every given ability level θ whether they are to take test x or test y" (p. 195).

Methods of constructing comparable, if not parallel, test forms and of equating such forms are described in great detail in chapter 6 of this volume. Many of these methods are required as soon as a competency-testing program moves beyond the initial administration of tests. The equating methods that depend on the use of embedded linking tests (also known as *anchor tests*) should be particularly useful because it is common practice to administer new test items, for tryout purposes, as part of an established operational test form and then to compose new test forms from items that exhibit sound psychometric properties. Refer to chapter 6 herein to learn the important theory underlying their use and how to apply these methods.

Why "Minimum-Competency" Testing?

The focus of this chapter is restricted to minimum-competency testing as it is applied by states and local school systems in the United States. This focus was guided by the reality of competency testing as it is currently practiced, rather than by a judgment on an ideal reality, predictions of what competency testing would be like, or recommendations on what competency testing should be like in future years.

Many have claimed that minimum-competency testing as currently practiced in the United States is seriously flawed. These claims have often been backed by sound logic and occasionally by compelling evidence. At several points in its call for reform of American education, the National Commission on Excellence in Education (1983) questions the value or describes the shortcomings of minimum-competency testing. The commission suggests that expectations for the levels of knowledge, abilities, and skills that high school students should possess are communicated in part "by the presence or absence of rigorous examinations requiring students to demonstrate their mastery of *content* [italics added] and skill before receiving a diploma or a degree" (p. 19). And to clearly indicate that it is not suggesting the proliferation of minimum-competency tests as they existed in 1983 or are now commonly found, the commission states that "'Minimum competency' examinations (now required in 37 states) fall short of what is needed, as the 'minimum' tends to become the 'maximum,' thus lowering educational standards for all" (p. 20).

At the heart of the commission's recommendations on the use of tests in the schools is its proposal for "Five New Basics" that would define the required curriculum for all high school students: 4 years of English, 3 years of mathematics, 3 years of science, 3 years of social studies, and $\frac{1}{2}$ year of computer science. The commission proposes the use of standardized tests of achievement, to be administered

at major transition points from one level of schooling to another and particularly from high school to college or work. The purposes of these tests would be to: (a) certify the student's credentials; (b) identify the need for remedial intervention; and (c) identify the opportunity for advanced or accelerated work. (1983, p. 28)

An essential distinction between the kinds of achievement tests recommended by the commission and the minimum-competency tests commonly in use is in their content. The commission strongly recommends that high school students be tested to determine their mastery of the content of a rigorous high school curriculum. The minimum-competency tests presently used in the United States, with rare exception, test so-called basic skills, many of which are to be imparted through the curriculum of the nation's elementary schools but are found only in the remedial education curricula of our high schools.

The report issued by the National Commission on Excellence was not the only "reform" document brought forward in the harvest of 1983 that suggested alternatives to minimum-competency testing. The Education Commission of the States' Task Force on Education for Economic Growth produced a report entitled *Action for Excellence*. In Action Recommendation 6, suggested to "provide quality assurance in education," the Task Force states:

We recommend that fair and effective programs be established to monitor student progress through periodic testing of general achievement and specific skills. Because the purpose of such testing should be to identify problems and deficiencies promptly, every school system should link its testing program to a carefully designed program of remediation and enrichment for students who need special help. (1983, p. 39)

Once again, the type of testing suggested is achievement testing that is clearly linked to the content of the curriculum being provided to students at the time they are tested, rather than testing of basic skills that derive from a curriculum provided in the elementary schools.

Despite these criticisms, minimum-competency testing is pervasive in U.S. schools, and the measurement issues that are most pertinent to its practice demand careful attention. Hence, the decision to focus on the measurement implications of current practice.

Included Topics

The balance of the chapter consists of four major sections. The next section contains a brief overview of the application of competency testing in secondary education programs in the United States. Some statistics on the use of competency testing in the public schools are supplemented by examples of state-wide competency-testing laws. The setting of standards of competence is the topic of the second major section. In that section, various standard-setting methods are described, and the empirical literature on comparison of the results of using various standard-setting methods is reviewed. The third major section is concerned with the issue of examinees' opportunities to learn the skills assessed by the competency tests they must complete. This issue has been termed *instructional validity* by the courts and in the popular literature. Some researchers have proposed that it is an element of content validity. The nature of the opportunity-to-learn issue is discussed at some length, as are some examples of methods that have been used to demonstrate it.

The penultimate section of the chapter contains a review of legal issues that have arisen in various competency-testing programs and the resolution of those issues in various court proceedings. Competency testing has been challenged in the courts on a variety of grounds including its basic legality, its use with handicapped students, and its fairness to members of legally protected minority groups.

Editorial judgment on the value and worth of competency testing has been left to a concluding section. Although minimum-competency testing is widespread, it is a political phenomenon with largely uninvestigated effects. However, learned commentators on schooling and education have speculated on the impact of competency testing on students, teachers, school curricula, and the very definition of secondary education in the United States. Opinions on the merits of competency testing offered in the concluding section draw heavily on these speculations.

Applications of Competency Testing in the United States

Competency tests have been adopted by hundreds of school systems and dozens of states. Although uniform data on the use of competency tests in school systems are not available, several researchers have compiled statistics on statewide adoptions. Both Baratz (1980) and Gorth and Perkins (1979a) list 31 states as having some form of competency testing in the years their articles were published. Because their lists are not entirely duplicative, they can be concatenated to conclude that 35 states used competency tests as of the 1979–1980 school year. More recently, Pipho (1984) produced an updated listing of competency-testing activity by state. His list indicates that 40 of the 50 states currently use competency tests in at least one grade.

Of the 40 states with some competency testing, statewide standards of performance are imposed in 21 states, standards are determined by local school systems in 10 states, standards are determined by a combination of state and local governments in 7 states, and no uniform standards are imposed in 2 states.

Nineteen of the 40 states mandate the use of competency tests in awarding high school diplomas, and 3 additional states give local school systems the option of using competency-test performance as a high school graduation sanction. Fourteen of the states (more than a third of those using competency tests) use test results in conjunction with remedial education programs.

The range of grades in which competency tests are used by various states covers the full span of elementary and secondary education, from kindergarten through the 12th grade. However, 22 of the states test in grades 11 or 12 or both.

Competency testing in the United States is largely a phenomenon of the 1970s, despite the very early history described previously and the existence of districtwide certification and promotion examinations in a few school systems (e.g., Denver, Colorado) since the 1960s. According to Baratz (1980) and Gorth and Perkins (1979b), only two states had mandated minimum-competency-testing programs as early as 1971. Four more states enacted competency-testing rules in 1972, five more were added in 1975, and four joined the "movement" in 1976. In 1977 and 1978, the ranks of states with competency-testing programs more than doubled, with nine states enacting laws or state board of education rulings during 1977 and eight more doing so in 1978. As the number of states with some form of competency testing increased, the number of additions to the movement decelerated, (as might be expected). Only eight states have enacted competency testing laws and regulations since 1979.

We will describe in some detail the competency-testing programs that have been developed in two states, North Carolina and Oregon. In many ways, these two programs illustrate extremes in the range of state-mandated minimum-competency-testing programs. They differ in such critical factors as locus of control, subject matter scope, underlying philosophy, test content, and locus of responsibility for program development and maintenance. The program in North Carolina is typical of those operating in a majority of the states, in that the state department of education maintains control over the program. In contrast, the program in Oregon is largely controlled by local school systems. School systems determine the competencies to be examined, the methods whereby students demonstrate their competence, and the standards by which competence is judged. The North Carolina program is restricted in subject matter to reading, mathematics, and productive writing skills, whereas the Oregon program is far broader in scope.

North Carolina's Competency-testing Program

The fundamental purposes of the North Carolina competency-testing program are defined by the following legislative citation:

The State Board of Education shall adopt tests or other measurement devices which may be used to assure that graduates of the public high schools supervised by the State Board of Education . . . possess those skills and that knowledge necessary to function independently and successfully in assuming the responsibilities of citizenship. This Article has three purposes: (i) to assure that all high school graduates possess those minimum skills and that knowledge thought necessary to function as a member of society, (ii) to provide a means of identifying strengths and weaknesses in the education process, and (iii) to establish additional means for making the education system accountable to the public for results. (General Assembly of the State of North Carolina, Article 39A, Section 115–320.6 "Purpose," 1977)

These specifications suggest that the legislature believed that high school graduates must possess some definable body of knowledge and skill to "function independently and successfully" in society. The existence of a definable set of survival skills was thus assumed. The legislature also assumed that the existence of a competency-testing program in North Carolina would guarantee that all high school graduates awarded a diploma would have these necessary survival skills. In addition, the legislature specified that the North Carolina competency-testing program would serve a diagnostic purpose. The tests or other measures adopted for use in the program were supposed to help the state's educators "identify strengths and weaknesses in the education process." Finally, the competency-testing program was intended to impose additional state control on public education in North Carolina by "making the education system accountable to the public for results."

As the North Carolina competency-testing program currently operates, all students in the public schools take a reading test and a mathematics test in the fall term of the 11th grade. If these students answer some minimum number of items on each test correctly, they become eligible to receive a high school diploma. To be awarded diplomas, students must also complete all of the attendance requirements and class activities typically required for high school graduation. If students fail either or both of the competency tests, they are given three additional opportunities to pass them prior to or during the spring term of the 12th grade. If a student has not passed both the reading and the mathematics test after four attempts, he or she is given a certificate of completion in lieu of a high school diploma. Students who do not receive regular high school diplomas because they have not passed the competency tests can, if necessary, continue to take the tests each year following the graduation of their high school class, until they reach the age of 21. Upon passing both competency tests, a student can exchange her or his certificate of completion for a high school diploma.

The competency-testing law requires that schools offer remedial instruction to students who have failed the competency tests, including those who are beyond the normal age for high school graduation.

It should be emphasized that passing the high school competency tests in North Carolina is not a sufficient condition for graduation with a regular high school diploma, but it is a *necessary* condition. Thus, a student could satisfy all other graduation requirements (attending all required classes, earning passing grades in all required courses, maintaining a satisfactory attendance record, observing and abiding by all school rules and regulations) and still be denied a regular high school diploma solely because of failure to earn a passing score on one of North Carolina's high school competency tests.

Oregon's Competency Testing Program

In contrast with the development of the competency-testing program in North Carolina, Oregon's State Board of Education adopted broad goals for education and then required local school systems to develop specific competency requirements for graduation. Local school systems were also required to develop and adopt procedures through which students could demonstrate their competence and were required to determine appropriate competency standards.

The administrative rules issued by Oregon's State Board of Education have the force of law, because the Oregon legislature has delegated statutory authority to the board to issue such rules. In effect, then, the State Board of Education established legal requirements that local school boards "shall award a diploma upon fulfillment of all state and local district credit, competency and attendance requirements," and further, that "the local board may grant a certificate identifying acquired minimum competencies to students having met some but not all requirements for the diploma and having chosen to end their formal school experiences" (Oregon Administrative Regulation 581-22-228).

The language of the Oregon regulations is quite technical and includes such terms as *program goals, district goals, performance indicator,* and *planned course statement.* In all, 38 specialized terms are defined in the regulations concerning graduation requirements. In such language the State Board of Education required all local school districts to

establish minimum competencies and performance indicators beginning with the graduating class of 1978; certify attainment of competencies necessary to read, write, speak, listen, analyze and compute beginning with the graduating class of 1978; certify attainment of all competencies beginning not later than with the graduating class of 1981. (Oregon Administrative Regulation 581-22-236)

A performance indicator was defined as being "an established measure to judge student competency achievement," and a competency was defined as "a statement of desired student performance representing demonstrable ability to apply knowledge, understanding, and/or skills assumed to contribute to success in life role functions" (Oregon Administrative Regulation 581-22-200).

By 1981, all school districts were required to record on high school students' transcripts whether or not they had demonstrated competencies necessary to

1. Use basic scientific and technological processes
2. Develop and maintain a healthy mind and body
3. Be an informed citizen in the community, state and nation
4. Be an informed citizen in interaction with the environment
5. Be an informed citizen on streets and highways
6. Be an informed consumer of goods and services
7. Function within an occupation or continue education leading to a career

(Oregon Administrative Regulation 581-22-231)

The State Board expected local school systems to identify specific competencies associated with each of these grandiose goals, to develop performance indicators for each competency, and to establish standards of competence.

The practical problems resulting from Oregon's competency-based high school graduation requirements are well described in a chapter by Herron (1980). He states that effective measures of students' career-development skills and social responsibility were generally unavailable. Some Oregon teachers were unwilling to run the risk of personal liability in certifying that students did or did not possess vaguely defined competencies within elusive domains. Although some local school systems attempted to adopt the "life-skills" goals embodied in statewide graduation requirements, others restricted their attention to the familiar basic school skills. The resulting inconsistencies across school systems created severe problems for transfer students and raised the specter of unequal educational opportunity throughout the state. Herron concludes, nonetheless, that Oregon was unlikely to adopt a statewide minimum-competency-testing program of the sort operating in North Carolina and the majority of other states. W. F. Neuberger (personal communication, November, 1985) confirmed that the problems identified by Herron persist, as does the fundamental design of Oregon's competency-testing program.

In the 6 years following the initial enactment of Oregon's administrative regulations concerning competency-based education and competency testing, the State Board of Education shifted from high school graduation requirements expressed in terms of life skills to a set of requirements expressed in terms of more traditional school skills. Competence requirements exist in the following subject areas: reading, writing, mathematics, speaking, listening, and reasoning. State regulations define the obligation of "helping students achieve the indicators of competence which have been adopted by the school district. Such indicators may be verified by alternative means to meet individual needs as long as the district's standards of performance are not reduced." School districts are empowered to award alternatives to a high school diploma, and three diploma levels are suggested in state regulations: a Diploma, a Modified Diploma, and a Certificate of Attainment (Oregon Administrative Regulation 581-22-316-2). Neuberger reports that denial of a high school diploma solely because a student failed to demonstrate competence in one or more skill areas is extremely rare, and the state does not strictly enforce regulations suggesting the use of differentiated diplomas or alternative certificates.

The competency-testing programs adopted in Oregon and North Carolina exemplify the broad range of such programs operating in many states. North Carolina's program is totally controlled by the state. It includes uniform statewide imposition of competencies, measures, and standards. The state develops and distributes all tests, the state scores students' performances, and the state provides local school districts with information on which students have passed the tests and which students have failed. The North Carolina program is very limited in the scope of its subject matter.

In contrast, the competency-testing program in Oregon is, within very broad and permissive state guidelines, controlled by local school districts. School systems specify competencies, identify indicators of competence, and establish acceptable standards of student performance. All measurement and reporting functions take place in local school districts. The scope of the subject matter of the program is very broad and, as originally conceived, went well beyond the traditional curriculum of the schools.

The ultimate effects of these competency-testing programs on the quality of education in their respective states has been virtually unexplored. In North Carolina, well over 90% of students who remain in high school through the 12th grade pass all competency tests prior to their scheduled high school graduation. Comparable figures for Oregon are not available because methods used to assess students' competence vary across school districts. However, Neuberger's description of program enforcement, noted earlier, suggests that relatively few Oregon students fail to earn a high school diploma because they cannot demonstrate one of the state's competencies.

These results might suggest that competency-testing programs are largely benign in their effects and might be regarded as another form of institutionalized ritual. Further analyses would dispel such conclusions. In states such as North Carolina that maintain statistics on the characteristics of students who fail competency tests, the failure rates of racial minorities are typically found to be 5 to 10 times higher than those of the majority white students. The social and economic consequences of failing to earn a high school diploma are well known, particularly for youths from minority groups (cf., Eckland, 1980).

Minimum-competency-testing programs have been oper-ating long enough now that a sound evaluation of their impact on school curricula, teachers' independence and professionalism, and students' competence and life chances, among other potential outcome variables, would be feasible. Such an evaluation would be complex and, necessarily, of substantial scope. Given the diversity of testing operations labeled *competency-testing programs,* an effective evaluation study would have to examine the programs in place in a number of states. Because many of the social and economic consequences of competency testing are unlikely to manifest themselves in the lives of students for a number of years following high school graduation (or denial of a high school diploma), an effective evaluation would have to be longitudinal in design. Definitive examination of the effects of competency testing on school curricula would have to be conducted retrospectively in many states and longitudinally in others, depending on the length of time states had been operating a competency-testing program. Investigation of the political motivations underlying competency-testing programs, and the political effects of such programs, would require careful analyses of legislative histories, the minutes and records of meetings of state boards of education, and news articles in the public press.

Although many commentators claim that the principal motivation for competency-testing programs is the desire of state legislatures and school boards to wrest control of educational standards from teachers, local school administrators, and local school boards, a careful analysis of the politics of competency testing might reveal a set of motives that are as diverse and complex as the testing programs described earlier. Unfortunately, no major public agency has been willing to invest in the broad and intensive evaluation needed to understand the full effects of competency testing and, as a result, most judgments of the effects of competency testing are based on mere speculation.

Setting Standards of Competence

If the literature on standard setting is conclusive on any point, it is the difficulty of setting defensible standards on competency tests. There is no agreement on a best method, although some procedures are far more popular than others.

Several learned groups and individuals have suggested that competency-testing standards should not be used. In a report to the U.S. Assistant Secretary for Education the Committee on Testing and Basic Skills of the National Academy of Education stated

The NAED Panel believes that any setting of state-wide minimum competency standards—however understandable the public clamor which has produced the current movement and expectation—is basically unworkable, exceeds the present measurement arts of the teaching profession, and will certainly create more social problems than it can conceivably solve. (1978, p. iv)

In an extensive review of the literature on standard-setting methods, Glass (1978) concludes as follows: "To my knowledge, every attempt to derive a criterion score is either blatantly arbitrary or derives from a set of arbitrary premises" (p. 258). In another section of the same paper, he says:

The attempt to base criterion scores on the concept of minimal competency fails for two reasons: (1) It has virtually no foundation in psychology; (2) When its arbitrariness is granted but judges attempt nonetheless to specify minimal competence, they disagree wildly. (p. 251)

Linn, Madaus, & Pedulla (1982) warn against the use of competency tests as sole determiners of student promotion or graduation. A key element in their argument is the seeming arbitrariness of test standards. They cite empirical work by Poggio, Glasnapp, & Eros (1981), showing that test standards depend heavily on the methods used to derive them, and results reported by Jaeger, Cole, Irwin, & Pratto (1980), showing that test standards vary markedly across types of judges used with a single standard-setting procedure. Linn et al. conclude that thousands of students would be declared competent or incompetent in most statewide competency-testing programs on the basis of methodological decisions that have nothing to do with their abilities.

Both Glass (1978) and Shepard (1979, 1980) note that competence is, by virtually all conceptions, a continuous variable. Setting a cutoff score that supposedly divides students into two distinct categories, the competent and the incompetent, is therefore unrealistic and illogical. Shepard argues strongly against the use of any single method of standard setting, and Glass would have us abandon competency testing altogether.

Despite the misgivings of these thoughtful and prudent researchers, the need to determine standards for competency tests is unlikely to disappear. As this is written, competency testing is a widespread and growing movement in the United States. Legislative bodies and policy boards throughout the nation continue to embrace competency-testing programs as a means of righting perceived wrongs of public education and as devices to gain control of the workings of public schools. If competency-testing standards are required, educational measurement specialists should design procedures for establishing them that make the best use of the state of the measurement art.

There is virtually uniform agreement among measurement specialists that standard setting is a judgmental process. Many contributors to the literature echo the conclusion reached by Jaeger that

All standard-setting is judgmental. No amount of data-collection, data analysis and model building can replace the ultimate judgmental act of deciding which performances are meritorious or acceptable and which are unacceptable or inadequate. All that varies is the proximity of the judgment-determining data to the original performance. (1976, p. 2)

Recognition of standard setting as a judgmental process brings to the fore an array of important and interrelated questions. Who should make judgments? How should judgments be elicited? Should judgments be based on information about tests, test items, testing applications, examinee performances, or a combination of these factors? These questions have motivated an extensive set of research studies in recent years. Many questions have not yet been answered conclusively, but the literature is nevertheless informative.

Much early work on standard setting was based on the often unstated assumption that determination of a test standard parallels estimation of a population parameter; there is a "right answer," and it is the task of standard setting to find it. Yet the observations of Glass (1978), Linn et al. (1982), and Shepard (1979, 1980) clearly contravene this view. If competence is a continuous variable, there is clearly no point on the continuum that would separate students into the competent and the incompetent. A right answer does not exist, except, perhaps, in the minds of those providing judgments. This recognition makes the questions just listed of paramount importance.

One could conceive of an ideal scenario for judgment. All persons who had a legitimate stake in the outcome of competency testing would be asked to make judgments on appropriate standards. Each judge would be fully informed of the nature of the competency test, the population of students to be tested, the decisions to be reached on the basis of test scores, and the costs and benefits associated with failing or passing students of various levels of ability. The resulting standard would not be *the* right answer to the standard-setting question. But it could be regarded as the best obtainable answer, given the necessity of setting a standard. One could regard the standard resulting from this idealized scenario as a parameter to be estimated by using a realistic standard-setting procedure. This conception might provide a basis for judging the relative psychometric quality of various standard-setting methods, at least theoretically, if not empirically.

Standard-setting Methods

In a 1980 review of standard-setting methods, Hambleton and Eignor list 18 different procedures. More recent reviews (Berk, 1984; Shepard, 1980) include additional variations on these methods, as well as a few novel proposals (Berk, 1986). In attempting to make sense of the plethora of standard-setting models, various reviewers have proposed classification schemes. Meskauskas (1976) proposed a division into "state models" and "continuum models." State models assume that competence is binary; an examinee either has it or doesn't. Logical use of a state model would require that a perfect score on any valid measure of competence be required of all examinees, provided the measure was totally reliable. Only the acknowledgement of errors of measurement suggests the use of less-than-perfect performance as a criterion of competence. As the label suggests, continuum models are based on the assumption that the trait or construct being assessed is a continuous variable that can assume any value in a prescribed interval. Determining the level of the trait that defines competent performance is the role of these models.

Hambleton and Eignor (1980) further subdivide the continuum models into three categories labeled *judgmental models, empirical models,* and *combination models.* Procedures classified as judgmental models require judgments about the content of competency tests, such as the difficulties of test items. Procedures classified as empirical models require direct judgments about the competence of examinees. Combination models require judgments about the abilities of examinees to perform satisfactorily on the domain of items assessed by a competency test. Although judgments of examinees' abilities are the primary focus of these models, the domains of abilities to be judged are restricted by test content.

STATE MODELS

State models for standard setting such as those proposed by Bergan, Cancelli, & Luiten (1980), Emrick (1971), Knapp (1977), Macready and Dayton (1977, 1980), Roudabush (1974), and Wilcox (1977a, 1977b) have not found wide application in competency-testing programs. Berk (1980, 1986) notes three characteristics of these models that explain their lack of popularity. *First,* several of the models (Knapp, 1977; Roudabush, 1974; Wilcox 1977a, 1977b) pertain to mastery of one or two test items. The domains assessed by most competency tests are typically quite heterogeneous, and sufficiently precise assessment using one or two test items is unobtainable. *Second,* because the models presume that competence is equivalent to absolute mastery of a domain of knowledge or skill, they are only applicable to highly restricted domains. An example would be all two-element, single-digit addition problems, where problems were written in the form $A + B = ?$ Virtually all competency tests are far more heterogeneous in content and in the knowledge and skills they require. *Third,* the models presume that the population of tested students can be described adequately by two levels of competence. Those who are competent are expected to answer all test items correctly and are assumed to have an equal chance of committing an error of omission on an item. Those who are incompetent are not expected to answer all items correctly and are assumed to have an equal chance of answering items correctly due to factors other than their knowledge or skill. Real populations of students in nearly all school contexts are far more heterogeneous in their abilities than these models presume.

In most practical applications, then, choice of a standard-setting method should be restricted to what Meskauskas (1976) terms *continuum models.* Further categorization of these models might be useful, but the labels *judgmental models* and *empirical models* would appear to be more misleading than enlightening, because as noted, all standard setting requires judgment. Only the foci of judgment and the procedures used to elicit judgments differ across models. A more accurate labeling of standard-setting models would divide them into *test-centered models* and *examinee-centered models.* Some of the most widely used test-centered models will be considered first.

A seemingly exhaustive listing of standard-setting models can be found in Berk (1986). The following discussion is restricted to models that have been used to establish standards in one or more statewide competency-testing programs.

TEST-CENTERED CONTINUUM MODELS

Angoff's procedure. Angoff (1971) proposes a simple but elegant standard-setting procedure that he attributes to Ledyard Tucker (Livingston & Zieky, 1983). Angoff's procedure requires that each of a sample of judges examine each item on a competency test and estimate the

probability that the "minimally acceptable" person would answer each item correctly. In effect, the judges would think of a number of minimally acceptable persons, instead of only one such person, and

would estimate the proportion of minimally acceptable persons who would answer each item correctly. The sum of these probabilities, or proportions, would then represent the minimally acceptable score. (p. 515)

To apply Angoff's procedure, it is first necessary to identify an appropriate population of judges and then to select a (hopefully) representative sample from that population. Each judge must then be given some guidance on the conceptualization of a minimally competent examinee. Livingston and Zieky (1982) recommend that this be done by having the judges review what the competency test is supposed to measure and then having a discussion on what constitutes "borderline knowledge and skills." Presumably, the judges can identify the level of knowledge and skills that, in their view, defines the distinction between students who are acceptably competent and those who are not. If agreement on borderline knowledge and skills can be reached, Livingston and Zieky recommend that definitions be written, together with examples of student performance, that are above and below the borderline. Using a test designed to measure the reading comprehension ability of high school students as an example, they suggest that judges might be asked to reach agreement on whether a minimally competent student should be able to, among other things, "find specific information in a newspaper article, distinguish statements of fact from statements of opinion, recognize the main idea of a paragraph, stated in different words, if the paragraph is from a *Reader's Digest* article" (p. 17).

Although the suggestion that minimal competence be clearly defined is obviously sound, in following a procedure of the sort recommended by Livingston and Zieky, it would be essential to insure that the skills used to distinguish between competent and incompetent examinees were representative of the domain from which the competency test was constructed. If that domain were heterogeneous in content, the task of defining a minimally competent examinee might be impossible, or at least redundant with the standard-setting method proposed by Angoff.

It should be noted that very little is known about the sensitivity of judges' conceptions of a minimally competent individual to the procedures used to train judges in formulating those conceptions, or to the standard-setting procedures through which judges must apply those conceptions. At least one doctoral dissertation lurks in the corners of this area of research.

Once judges understand their task clearly, Angoff's procedure has them consider each item on a competency test individually and decide for that item the probability that a minimally competent examinee would be able to answer it correctly.

To compute a recommended test standard, the probabilities proposed by each judge are summed. The sum for a particular judge is treated as that judge's estimate of the total score that would be earned on the examination by a minimally competent examinee. In statistical terms, if a judge's estimated probabilities corresponded to the true probabilities of success of a population of minimally competent examinees, the sum of the estimated probabilities would correspond to the expected value (mean) of the score that would be earned on the examination by the population of minimally competent examinees.

Because the final step in Angoff's procedure is to average the sums of probabilities across all sampled judges, the outcome of the procedure can be regarded as a subjective estimate of the mean score on the competency test that would be earned by a population composed of examinees who were minimally competent.

Modified Angoff procedures. Angoff's standard-setting procedure has been modified prior to its use in several studies. When used by Educational Testing Service to establish passing scores on the subtests of the National Teacher Examinations (NTE) in South Carolina, a multiple-choice format was used to elicit judges' estimates of the probabilities that minimally competent examinees could answer each test item correctly. That is, for each item, judges were given a list of specific probability values and asked to choose the one that most closely approximated their subjective estimates. This procedure greatly simplifies the processing of data that result from a standard-setting study, in that judges' responses can be collected on mark-sense forms that can be read through automated equipment. However, Livingston and Zieky (1982, p. 25) objected to the modification because they felt that use of an asymmetric distribution of probability values might bias judges' responses. A simple experimental study would surely resolve this question and, in the interim, the problem raised by Livingston and Zieky can be avoided by using a symmetric distribution of probability values that covers the full range from 0 to 1 (cf. Cross, Impara, Frary, & Jaeger, 1984).

Additional modifications of Angoff's procedure include the use of an iterative process in which judges are given the opportunity to discuss their initial choices of probability values and then modify those choices. This process is in keeping with recommendations proposed by Jaeger (1978) and Livingston and Zieky (1982) and used by Cross et al. (1984). Cross et al. found the effects of iteration, coupled with the use of normative information on examinees' actual test performances, to be substantial. The mean standards recommended by judges for two NTE subtests were markedly lower at the end of a second judgment session than at the end of the first session. However, when a similar procedure was applied to eight subtests of the New NTE Core Battery by Jaeger and Busch (1984), the results were mixed. Mean recommended standards were higher at the end of a second judgment session than at the end of the first session for four subtests, but they were lower for the remaining four subtests. In no case did the means shift substantially from the first session to the second. However, for all subtests, there were notable reductions in the variability of the distributions of recommended standards, together with attendant increases in the reliabilities of recommended test standards. This finding alone would seem to suggest the use of iteration with Angoff's standard-setting procedure.

Ebel's procedure. Another standard-setting method that requires judgments about test items is proposed by Ebel (1972, pp. 492–494). Just as in Angoff's method, a population of judges must be identified first, and then a sample of judges must be drawn. Also in keeping with Angoff's method, the judges must conceptualize a minimally competent or borderline examinee.

Ebel's method involves three steps. First, judges would establish a two-dimensional taxonomy of the items in the competency test. Ebel labeled one of these dimensions *difficulty* and the other *relevance*. He suggests using three levels of difficulty—easy, medium, and hard—and four levels of relevance — essential, important, acceptable, and questionable. However, different numbers of categories and different labels could be used, depending on the configuration and content of the competency test and the preferences of the judges. Once the taxonomy of items had been established, judges would assign each item in the competency test to one of the resulting categories. Thus Item 1 might be judged of medium difficulty and an essential item; Item 2 might be judged of easy difficulty and a questionable item in terms of relevance. The judges' final task would be to answer the following question for each category of items: If a borderline test taker had to answer a large number of questions like these, what proportion would he or she answer correctly?

The standard computed by using Ebel's method is a weighted average of the proportions recommended by the judges for each category of items. That is, the proportion recommended for each cell is multiplied by the number of items in that cell, and the products are then summed. This sum of products is divided by the total number of items on the test, to produce a weighted average percentage.

Livingston and Zieky (1982, pp. 26–29) provide step-by-step recommendations on the application of Ebel's method. Although their suggestions make good sense and would be expected to increase the consistency and plausibility of standards produced by Ebel's method, they have not been subjected to empirical verification. In several studies, discussed later, Ebel's method has resulted in extreme recommended standards or standards that varied widely and inexplicably across the subtests of a test battery. Research by Poggio et al. (1981) suggests that school personnel are not capable of making reasonable judgments of the sort required by Ebel's method.

Jaeger's procedure. An item-based standard-setting procedure that has been applied in several statewide competency testing programs (Cross et al., 1984; Jaeger, 1982) was proposed by Jaeger in 1978. With Jaeger's procedure, each of a sample of judges must answer the following yes–no question for each item on a competency test: Should *every* examinee in the population of those who receive favorable action on the decision to be based on test performance (e.g., every student who receives a high school diploma in the state that administers the competency test) be able to answer the test item correctly? In contrast with the Angoff and Ebel procedures, this method does not require judges to conceptualize or define a minimally competent examinee.

As is true for the Angoff and Ebel procedures, with Jaeger's procedure it is first necessary to identify a population of judges and then to select a sample from this population. Jaeger's procedure is somewhat more demanding than alternative procedures in this regard, because it requires sampling of several populations of judges. Jaeger defines the ideal situation as sampling all populations that have a legitimate interest in the outcomes of competency testing.

Jaeger's procedure is iterative, in that judges are given several opportunities to reconsider their initial judgments. Prior to reconsidering their recommendations, judges are given data on the actual test performances of the examinees under consideration, in addition to information on the recommendations provided by their fellow judges.

At each stage in the iterative process, the standard recommended by a judge is computed as the number of items for which that judge has answered yes to the question posed earlier. The test standard for a sample of judges is computed as the median of the standards recommended by all judges in that sample. Data on the standards recommended by all samples of judges are assembled and summary statistics are computed for each sample. The lowest of the median recommended standards is to be used in computing the operational standard.

Because Jaeger's procedure is somewhat more complex than those proposed by Angoff and Ebel, a detailed example of its application might be needed to fully understand its use. When Jaeger's method was used to determine standards on North Carolina's High School Competency Tests (Jaeger, 1982), three populations of judges were sampled: high school teachers, high school principals and counselors, and registered voters. Because the competency test consisted of a lengthy (120-item) reading test and a lengthy (120-item) mathematics test (Gallagher, 1980), separate subsamples of judges were assigned to each subtest.

In the first step of the standard-setting process, each judge completed the test that she or he would later review. Standardized procedures, identical to those used with high school students, were used in administering the tests. The purpose of this activity was to ensure that judges would become familiar with each item on the test they were to review, from the perspective of an examinee. At the conclusion of their final judgment session, judges were given the correct answers to each test item, and their test answer sheets were then shredded in their presence. This ensured the confidentiality of the judges' test performances, a point that was of some consequence to a number of judges.

In each of three rating sessions, judges were told to consider each test item separately, in order of appearance on the test. For each item, they were told to mark a yes or no box on a separate sheet in response to the question: Should every high school graduate in North Carolina be able to answer this item correctly? The instructions given the judges stated: "If you answer 'yes' for an item, you are saying that it tests a very important skill — knowledge that should be required of every regular student who is awarded a high school diploma. If you answer 'no' for an item, you are saying that, although the skill it tests may be important, it is not important enough to require that every high school graduate possess the skill it tests. Or you may be saying that the item is too difficult, poorly worded, redundant, or otherwise inappropriate."

After all judges had provided their initial recommendations, their response sheets were optically scanned, and a graph depicting the cumulative distribution function of recommended standards was produced for each sample of judges.

At the beginning of a second rating session, judges were given the cumulative distribution function of standards recommended by their group; their own rating sheets from the first rating session, with the sum of their yes recommendations clearly marked; and a table containing the percentages of 11th-grade students who had answered each test item correctly when the competency test had last been administered. Instruction on the interpretation and use of these data was then provided.

The balance of the second rating session was identical to the first. Each judge reconsidered his or her initial item-by-item recommendations and completed a new rating sheet on which he or she marked yes or no for each item. The judges' second rating sheets were optically scanned, and a new cumulative distribution function of recommended standards was computed for each sample of judges.

Prior to the final session, judges were given the cumulative distribution function of standards recommended by members of their group during the second rating session, in addition to new data on the actual test performances of 11th-grade students. These new data were in the form of a cumulative relative-frequency polygon of students' total test scores, based on data collected during the last administration of the test. For example, judges who were reviewing the mathematics subtest learned that 64% of the 11th graders would have failed the test if a standard of 110 items correct had been used. Judges were asked to keep data such as these in mind, as they considered the necessity of each test item one last time.

Using judges' responses to the yes–no question during the third rating session, a recommended standard was computed for each judge, and the median of these recommendations was computed for each sample of judges.

Berk (1986) terms Jaeger's procedure an "iterative two-choice Angoff procedure" and notes several disadvantages of the method. The form of the question posed to judges limits their item probability choices to 0 and 1; Berk feels that a "continuum of probabilities is more appropriate for most types of items" (pp. 156–157). He also notes that the method is time consuming and complex and suggests that interpretation of the final standard to laypeople could be difficult. Cross et al. (1984) found that Jaeger's method produced less reliable standards than did Angoff's method and attributed the difference to the two probability values (0 and 1) inherent in Jaeger's method.

Nedelsky's procedure. In the modern literature on standard-setting methods, the oldest procedure that still enjoys widespread use was first proposed by Leo Nedelsky in 1954. The procedure requires judgments about test items and can only be used with items in the multiple-choice format.

As is the case with the standard-setting methods already described, the first step in the Nedelsky procedure is to identify a population of judges and select a sample from this population. Consistent with the Angoff and Ebel procedures, judges using the Nedelsky procedure must conceptualize and define a minimally competent examinee. Judges then predict the behavior of a minimally competent examinee on each option of each multiple-choice test item.

When a judge predicts an examinee's behavior on a test item, she or he is asked to specify which of the response options a minimally competent examinee should be able to eliminate as being incorrect. A statistic that Nedelsky termed the *minimum pass level* is then computed for that item. It is the reciprocal of the number of response options remaining. For example, if, on a four-option test item, a judge decides that a minimally competent examinee should be able to identify two options as being clearly incorrect, the minimum pass level for that item would equal $\frac{1}{(4-2)}$ or $\frac{1}{2}$. To compute the standard recommended by a particular judge, the minimum pass levels for that judge are summed across all test items.

The mean of the standards recommended by a sample of judges is used as the initial value of a test standard. This value is adjusted, following a procedure specified by Nedelsky, in an attempt to control the probability that an examinee with true ability equal to the initial standard would be classified as incompetent because of measurement errors in the competency-testing process. In this process Nedelsky assumes that the standard deviation of the standards recommended by the sample of judges is equal to the standard error of measurement of the competency test. If this assumption were true, and if the distribution of measurement errors on the competency test were of known shape (e.g., normal), one could adjust the recommended standard to control the probability that an examinee with true ability equal to the initial recommended standard would fail, due solely to errors of measurement. For example, if the initial recommended standard were reduced by one standard deviation of the judges' recommended standards, only 16% of examinees with true ability equal to the initial recommended standard would fail. If the initial recommended standard were increased by one standard deviation, 84% of examinees with true ability equal to the initial recommended standard would fail. Use of no adjustment would result in 50% of these examinees being classified as incompetent, due solely to errors of measurement.

The initial recommended standard that results from Nedelsky's procedure is based on the assumption that minimally competent examinees choose at random from among the item options that they cannot identify as being obviously incorrect. This somewhat questionable assumption is equivalent to the assumption that minimally competent examinees do not have and use partial information about the correctness of an item option. That is, they either know the option is incorrect or have no idea as to whether it is incorrect. If these assumptions were correct and if, on average, judges were able to correctly identify the options that minimally competent examinees could eliminate as incorrect, the initial standard produced by the Nedelsky procedure would be an unbiased estimate of the mean score that would be earned by a minimally competent examinee.

However, studies by Poggio et al. (1981) suggest that public school personnel are unable to make the consistent judgments required by Nedelsky's method. In addition, studies by Cross et al. (1984) and Jaeger and Busch (1984) show that the standard errors of measurement of competency tests are likely to differ substantially from the standard deviations of judges' recommended test standards, if item-based procedures, such as those proposed by Nedelsky and Angoff, are used. In both of these studies, the standard errors of measurement of the competency tests under review were far larger than corresponding standard deviations of judges' recommended test standards. If these results could be generalized, the adjustment of the initial standard proposed by Nedelsky would be conservative. That is, adjustment of the initial standard by plus or minus one standard deviation of the judges' recommended standards would result in failing a percentage of examinees with true ability equal to the initial standard that was far closer to 50% than the Nedelsky assumption would predict.

EXAMINEE-CENTERED CONTINUUM MODELS

A number of examinee-centered standard-setting models have been proposed for use in competency-testing programs. Among these models, the *borderline-group procedure* and the *contrasting-groups procedure* have been used most frequently. Because they are practical alternatives that have been widely employed, we will describe these procedures and their application in some detail.

Borderline-group procedure. This standard-setting model was first proposed by Zieky and Livingston (1977). It differs from the procedures discussed earlier in that the judgments required to apply the method focus on the qualifications of examinees, rather than on test items or other elements of a competency test.

The first step in using the borderline-group method is to identify a population of judges and then select a representative sample from that population. As Livingston and Zieky note (1982, p. 31), it is essential that judges know or be able to determine the level of knowledge or skills, in the domain sampled by the competency test, of individual examinees they will be asked to judge. In addition, judges must be able to decide on the requisite level of knowledge or skill an examinee must possess, to designate him or her competent.

Once a sample of judges has been selected, they are asked to define three categories of competence in the domain of knowledge and skills assessed by the competency test: adequate or competent, borderline or marginal, and inadequate or incompetent. Livingston and Zieky suggest that this process be conducted collectively if possible, with discussion among the judges. Ideally, judges would develop and come to agreement on operational examples of examinees at competent, borderline, and incompetent levels of knowledge and skill. However, in many realistic applications, it would not be possible to have judges work together in defining these categories, nor would it be possible to formulate workable operational examples.

The principal act of judgment in the borderline-group procedure is identification by the judges of members of the population of examinees whom they would classify as being borderline or marginal on the knowledge and skills assessed by the competency test.

It is important to realize that placement of examinees in the borderline category must be based on information other than their scores on the competency test. If test scores were used as the sole or primary basis for judgments of competence, the standard-setting procedure would be tautological. In addition, because judgments of the quality of test performance are often normative, and a particular judge is unlikely to know all, or a representative sample of, the population of examinees, judgments based on test scores are likely to result in biased allocation of examinees to the borderline category.

Once a subpopulation of examinees has been classified as borderline or marginal, the competency test is administered. The standard that results from the borderline-group procedure is the median of the distribution of competency-test scores earned by examinees who are classified borderline.

Practical application of the borderline-group procedure requires that judges classify only those examinees whose performances they know or about whom they can learn. In many school-based applications, teachers of subjects within the domain of the competency test would appear to be the most logical candidates for judges. These teachers would be asked to classify only the students they had personally instructed and, among those, only students whose test-related knowledge and skills were familiar.

Unless the test-score distribution of borderline examinees in the population was homogeneous, it would be important to ensure that examinees whose competence was judged constituted a representative sample of this subpopulation. Otherwise, the effects of sampling bias would influence the resulting borderline-group standard.

A major advantage of the borderline-group procedure is its inherent simplicity. Because judging students' levels of competence is a familiar task for teachers, one would expect them to have little difficulty applying the borderline-group procedure. Although the method does require that judges define a minimally competent examinee, it does not require subjective estimates of the test performance of such an examinee. This relatively unfamiliar judgment task would probably be far more difficult for teachers or other education professionals.

As is true of the test-centered standard-setting procedures, the borderline-group procedure is subject to criticism. It is not clear that teachers (or other judges) can successfully restrict their judgment of examinees to the elements of behavior assessed by the competency test. Particularly when judging their own students, teachers are likely to be influenced by cognitive and noncognitive factors that fall outside the domain assessed by the test (halo effect is a well-documented phenomenon in psychological research). In addition, studies involving the use of rating scales suggest frequent use of the middle category by those who have insufficient information or knowledge to provide a fully informed and reasoned response. These studies suggest the possibility that judges might place examinees in the borderline category when they do not have sufficient information or knowledge to make an appropriate decision. Because the test-score distribution of examinees who are appropriately placed in a borderline category should be reasonably homogeneous, it might be possible to detect situations in which the method is not being applied correctly.

Full and complete instructions on the definition, use, and misuse of the borderline category are essential to successful application of the procedure.

Contrasting-groups procedure. This procedure was also proposed by Zieky and Livingston (1977), but it is conceptually similar to a standard-setting method suggested by Berk (1976). Like the borderline-group method, the principal focus of judgment in the contrasting-groups method is on the competence of examinees, rather than on the difficulty of a test or its items.

The first two steps of the contrasting-groups method are identical to those of the borderline-group method. A population of judges must be identified, and a representative sample must be selected from this population. Next, sampled judges must define three categories of competence in the domain of knowledge and skills assessed by the competency test: adequate or competent, borderline or marginal, and inadequate or incompetent.

In the third step of the procedure, judges assign all examinees in the population to be tested (or in a representative sample of that population) to one of the three categories. This is the primary judgmental act required by the procedure.

Once all examinees have been classified, the competency test is administered, and the standard is based on analyses of the test-score distributions of examinees who were judged to be competent or incompetent.

Several methods have been proposed for computing a standard from the distributions of test scores of competent and incompetent examinees. Hambleton and Eignor (1980) suggest that the two score distributions be plotted and that the point of intersection of the distributions be chosen as the standard. This suggestion presumes that the score distributions will not coincide and that they will overlap. Livingston and Zieky (1982) suggest that the percentage of examinees classified competent be computed for each test score (provided sufficient data have been collected to compute these percentages precisely) and that the standard be set at the score value where 50% of the examinees have been classified as competent. In many applications of the contrasting-groups method, the total number of examinees tested would be so small that the percentages of examinees classified as competent would fluctuate substantially across adjacent test scores. In such cases, it would be necessary to compute these percentages for ranges of test scores and, perhaps, to use some form of smoothing procedure to obtain consistently larger percentages for larger test scores. Livingston and Zieky (1982) provide detailed suggestions on alternative smoothing procedures.

Comparability of Standard-setting Results

A large number of empirical studies have addressed the question of whether different standard-setting procedures, when applied to the same competency test, provide similar results. Most research has answered this question negatively. Different standard-setting procedures generally produce markedly different test standards when applied to the same test, either by the same judges or by randomly parallel samples of judges.

The research literature on the comparability of standard-setting procedures is so broad and voluminous that it is difficult to summarize. At the risk of obscuring detailed information, we have constructed a table that summarizes the results of 32 contrasts among methods, reported in 12 different studies (see Table 14.1). For each contrast, we have computed the ratio of the largest test standard to the smallest test standard resulting from the comparison, and, when requisite data were provided, the ratio of the largest examinee failure percentage to the smallest examinee failure percentage resulting from the comparison. For example, in the study by Boykoff, Rindone, & Prowda (1981), four standard-setting procedures are compared. When these procedures were applied to the Connecticut Proficiency Test in language arts, the highest standard (30 items correct) resulted from use of the borderline-group method, and the lowest standard (17.5 items correct) resulted from use of the Nedelsky method. The ratio of the larger to the smaller of these two recommended standards is 30.0/17.5 =

TABLE 14.1 Comparability of the Results of Using Different Standard-setting Methods with the Same Tests, Under Similar Conditions

STUDY	TEST	STANDARD-SETTING METHODS	STANDARDS RATIO	FAILURE % RATIO
Andrew & Hecht (1976)	Profess. Certif. Test	Nedelsky (−)* Ebel (+)	1.39	1.90
Schoon, Gullion, & Ferrara (1979)	Health Credent. Exam	Nedelsky (−) Ebel (+)	1.00	?***
Koffler (1980)	New Jersey Minimum Basic Skills Test Reading Grade 3	Nedelsky (−) Contr. Groups (+)	1.13	1.57
Koffler (1980)	New Jersey Minimum Basic Skills Test Reading Grade 6	Nedelsky (−) Contr. Groups (+)	1.38	4.57
Koffler (1980)	New Jersey Minimum Basic Skills Test Reading Grade 9	Nedelsky Contr. Groups (same standard)	1.00	1.00
Koffler (1980)	New Jersey Minimum Basic Skills Test Reading Grade 11	Nedelsky (+) Contr. Groups (−)	1.58	13.62
Koffler (1980)	New Jersey Minimum Basic Skills Test Mathemat. Grade 3	Nedelsky (+) Contr. Groups (−)	1.05	1.20
Koffler (1980)	New Jersey Minimum Basic Skills Test Mathemat. Grade 6	Nedelsky (+) Contr. Groups (−)	1.08	1.32
Koffler (1980)	New Jersey Minimum Basic Skills Test Mathemat. Grade 9	Nedelsky (−) Contr. Groups (+)	1.66	1.75
Koffler (1980)	New Jersey Minimum Basic Skills Test Mathemat. Grade 11	Nedelsky (+) Contr. Groups (−)	34.00	?
Skakun & Kling (1980)	General Surgery Test, U. of Alberta	Nedelsky (−) Modif. Ebel (difficulty) Modif. Ebel (+) (relevance)	1.08	2.03
Boykoff, Rindone, & Prowda (1981)	Connecticut Proficiency Exam in Math.	Angoff Nedelsky Contr. Groups (−) Border. Group (+)	1.34	3.44
Boykoff, Rindone, & Prowda (1981)	Connecticut Proficiency Exam in Lang. Arts	Angoff Nedelsky (−) Contr. Groups Border. Group (+)	1.71	11.00
Harasym (1981)	Endocrinology Cert. Exam. (1979)	Angoff (+) Nedelsky (−)	1.29	18.00****
Harasym (1981)	Endocrinology Cert. Exam. (1980)	Angoff (+) Nedelsky (−)	1.40	18.00****
Harasym (1981)	Endocrinology Cert. Exam. (1981)	Angoff (+) Nedelsky (−)	1.34	18.00****
Saunders, Ryan & Huynh (1981)	Educ. Research Achievm. Test	Two-categ. Nedelsky (−) Three-categ. Nedelsky (+)	1.02	1.16
Behuniak, Archambault & Gable (1982)	Conn. School System Reading Test	Angoff (+) Nedelsky (−)	1.31	?
Behuniak, Archambault & Gable (1982)	Conn. School System Math Test	Angoff (−) Nedelsky (+)	1.10	?
Poggio, Glasnapp, & Eros (1982)	Kansas Compet. Based Tests Reading Grade 2	Border. Group Contr. Groups (three variations) Angoff Nedelsky (−) Ebel (+)	1.73	?
Poggio, Glasnapp, & Eros (1982)	Kansas Compet. Based Tests Reading Grade 4	Border. Group Contr. Groups (+) (three variations) Angoff Nedelsky (−) Ebel	1.62	?

(Continued)

TABLE 14.1 *(Continued)*

STUDY	TEST	STANDARD-SETTING METHODS	STANDARDS RATIO	FAILURE % RATIO
Poggio, Glasnapp, & Eros (1982)	Kansas Compet. Based Tests Reading Grade 6	Border. Group Contr. Groups (three variations) Angoff Nedelsky (−) Ebel (+)	1.68	?
Poggio, Glasnapp, & Eros (1982)	Kansas Compet. Based Tests Reading Grade 8	Border. Group Contr. Groups (+) (three variations) Angoff Nedelsky (−) Ebel	1.82	?
Poggio, Glasnapp, & Eros (1982)	Kansas Compet. Based Tests Mathemat. Grade 2	Border. Group (+) Contr. Groups (−) (three variations) Angoff Nedelsky Ebel	42.00	?
Poggio, Glasnapp, & Eros (1982)	Kansas Compet. Based Tests Mathemat. Grade 4	Border. Group Contr. Groups (+) (three variations) Angoff Nedelsky (−) Ebel (+)	1.62	?
Poggio, Glasnapp, & Eros (1982)	Kansas Compet. Based Tests Mathemat. Grade 6	Border. Group Contr. Groups (three variations) Angoff Nedelsky (−) Ebel (+)	1.57	?
Poggio, Glasnapp, & Eros (1982)	Kansas Compet. Based Tests Mathemat. Grade 8	Border. Group Contr. Groups (+) (three variations) Angoff Nedelsky (−) Ebel	1.71	?
Halpin, Sigmon & Halpin (1983)	Missouri College English Test	Angoff Ebel (+) Nedelsky (−)	1.47	4.83
Mills (1983)	Louisiana Grade 2 Basic Skills Test—Lang. Arts	Angoff (−) Contr. Groups (quad. discr.) Contr. Groups (−) graphical) Border. Group (+)	1.44**	3.51**
Mills (1983)	Louisiana Grade 2 Basic Skills Test—Mathem.	Angoff Contr. Groups (quad. discr.) Contr. Groups (−) (graphical) Border. Group (+)	52.00**	29.75**
Cross, Impara, Frary & Jaeger (1984)	NTE Area Test Mathemat.	Angoff (iterative) Jaeger (+) (modified) Nedelsky (iterative) Nedelsky (−) (iterative and corrected for guessing)	1.70	1.95
Cross, Impara, Frary & Jaeger (1984)	NTE Area Test Elementary Education	Angoff (iterative) Jaeger (+) (modified) Nedelsky (iterative) Nedelsky (−) (iterative and corrected for guessing)	2.31	5.36

* (−) Denotes the standard-setting method that resulted in the smallest recommended standard; (+) denotes the method that resulted in the largest recommended standard.
** These ratios are the largest out of six trials.
*** "?" Indicates that the statistic could not be calculated from the data provided.
**** These ratios are averages across three years of data.

1.71. Had the standard resulting from the borderline-group method been applied, 33% of the examinees would have failed. Application of the standard resulting from the Nedelsky method would have produced a failure rate of only 3%. The ratio of these two failure rates is $33/3 = 11$.

From Table 14.1 we can see that, at best, the ratio of the largest recommended standard to the smallest recommended standard was 1.00, indicating identical standards resulting from different methods. At worst, the recommended standard resulting from one method was 42 times as large as that resulting from another method. The median of ratios of recommended standards, across all 32 contrasts listed in Table 14.1 was 1.46, the average was 5.30, and the standard deviation of such ratios was 12.42. Although there was wide variation in the ratios when several standard-setting methods were applied to a variety of tests in diverse standard-setting situations, it is sobering to realize that, at the median, the least stringent standard was about one and one-half times as large as the most stringent standard, and, on average, the least stringent standard was over five times as large as the most stringent standard, when different methods were applied to the same test under supposedly identical conditions.

Ratios of the percentages of examinees who would fail under the least stringent and most stringent standards were computable for 18 of the 32 contrasts reported in Table 14.1. The smallest ratio was 1.00, indicating identical failure rates using all standard-setting methods compared, but the largest ratio was 29.75, indicating that almost 30 times as many examinees would fail when using one standard-setting method as would fail using another. The median of these ratios was 2.74 across 18 contrasts, the average was 5.90, and the standard deviation of the ratios was 7.62. Here again, there is little consistency in the results of applying different standard-setting methods under seemingly identical conditions, and there is even less consistency in the comparability of methods across settings.

The results summarized in Table 14.1 show that choice of a standard-setting method is critical. As Hambleton (1980), Koffler (1980) and Shepard (1980, 1984) suggest, it might be prudent to use several methods in any given study and then consider all of the results, together with extrastatistical factors, when determining a final cutoff score.

Opportunity to Learn

Among other provisions, the Fourteenth Amendment to the United States Constitution affords the following guarantees:

No State shall make or enforce any law which shall abridge the privileges or immunities of citizens of the United States; nor shall any State deprive any person of life, liberty, or property, without due process of law; nor deny to any person within its jurisdiction the equal protection of the laws.

These constitutional provisions have been held by legal scholars and the courts to provide various protections to students for whom competency tests are used to make educational decisions. Details of those protections and a discussion of the holdings of various court cases are presented in a later section of this chapter. In this section, legal findings are considered only as they apply to requirements that states using competency tests provide students with an adequate opportunity to learn the skills assessed by those tests.

Two topics are discussed in this section. *First,* the genesis of the opportunity-to-learn issue is reviewed, together with some associated definitional controversies. *Second,* is a review of the efforts of states and school systems to collect evidence in support of their claim that they have provided students with an adequate opportunity to learn the skills that their competency tests assess.

Opportunity to Learn: The Nature of the Issue

McClung (1978a, 1978b, 1979) first proposed that Fourteenth Amendment guarantees of due process and equal protection would be violated if examining agencies (states or school systems) that used students' competency-test performance as a high school graduation criterion did not provide those students with adequate instruction in the skills assessed by those tests. McClung's proposal was applied by the Middle District Court in Florida in the 1979 *Debra P.* v. *Turlington* case, a decision that is discussed at some length in a later section of this chapter. McClung (1978a, 1978b, 1979) is credited with introducing the terms *curricular validity* and *instructional validity* in his discussion of students' opportunities to learn what the states were testing.

Even if the curricular objectives of the school correspond with the competency test objectives, there must be some measure of whether the school district's stated objectives were translated into topics actually taught in the district's classrooms. While a measure of curricular validity is a measure of the theoretical validity of the competency test as a test instrument to assess the success of students, instructional validity is an actual measure of whether the schools are providing students with instruction in the knowledge and skills measured by the test. (1979, pp. 682–683)

Madaus (1983) cited a statement of the Middle District Court in the 1979 *Debra P.* case in which McClung's proposals were applied but were confused by the court because it linked them to the content validity of a competency test. The statement cited is clear in its intent but unfortunately opaque in its confusion of the terms *curricular validity, instructional validity,* and *content validity:* "an important component of content validity is curricular validity defined by defendant's expert Dr. Foster[sic] as 'things that are currently taught'" (p. 25). This statement of the court has spawned great debate among measurement experts on the meaning of the validity terms used and on the basic definition of test validity. However, throughout the debate, the obligation of the state to provide students with an opportunity to learn that which it tests has been generally endorsed.

At the heart of the debate is the question of whether curricular validity and instructional validity, as proposed by McClung (1978a, 1978b) and adopted by the courts, are really types of validity at all. A secondary question, assuming the first were to be answered affirmatively, is whether curricular validity and instructional validity are components of content validity.

The concept of test validity, although fundamental to educational measurement, does not enjoy a universally accepted definition. Indeed, the definition has evolved over a period of 6 decades and is still in flux. Cronbach's (1971) recommendations, presented in the previous edition of this volume, have been very influential and have shaped the debate since the late 1970s. He proposes that the often used phrase "validating a test" incorrectly suggests that the test itself is the object of validation. Instead, he states that *validation is the process of examining the accuracy of a specific prediction or inference made from a test score*" (p. 443).

In the 1974 *Standards for Educational and Psychological Tests* (American Psychological Association [APA]), the definition of content validity is stated as follows: "To demonstrate the content validity of a set of test scores, one must show that the behaviors demonstrated in testing constitute a representative sample of the behaviors to be exhibited in a desired performance domain" (p. 28).

The 1985 *Standards for Educational and Psychological Testing* (APA, American Educational Research Association [AERA], & National Council on Measurement in Education [NCME]) amplify and reinforce this definition in several ways. The more recent *Standards* states that "content-related evidence [of validity] demonstrates the degree to which the sample of items, tasks, or questions on a test are representative of some defined universe or domain of content" (p. 10). And Standard 8.4, although not definitional, is particularly applicable when tests are used to certify students' competence.

When a test is to be used to certify the successful completion of a given level of education, either grade-to-grade promotion or high school graduation, both the test domain and the instructional domain at the given level of education should be described in sufficient detail, without compromising test security, so that the agreement between the test domain and the content domain can be evaluated (*Primary*). (p. 54)

The definition of content validity provided in the 1974 *Standards* and the definition of content-related validity evidence contained in the 1985 *Standards* suggest that such validation consists of an examination of sampling adequacy. That is, to demonstrate the content validity of a test one would (a) identify a domain of behaviors that the test was intended to represent; (b) analyze the structure of that population of behaviors, to the point that its major strata were well identified and operationally defined; (c) describe the set of student behaviors elicited by the items on the test to be validated; and (d) determine the degree to which the set of behaviors elicited by the items on the test was proportionally representative of the population of behaviors that composed the "desired performance domain."

It is important to recognize that this process of validation at no point involves the formulation of predictions or inferences about examinees' present or future performances on the basis of their test scores. Thus, according to Cronbach's 1971 definition of test validation, content validity is not an element of validity at all. This interpretation has been advanced by some of our most eminent measurement scholars, including the author of the major chapter on validity in this volume. As cited by Yalow and Popham, Messick in 1975 stated "Call it 'content

relevance,' if you will, or 'content representativeness,' but don't call it 'content validity,' because it doesn't provide evidence for the interpretation of responses or scores" (1983, p. 11). In a later essay, Messick (1981) suggests that an investigation of the representativeness of the content coverage of a test has more to do with test construction than with content validity, in keeping with his earlier assertions. And Guion (1980) suggests that content validation is, when viewed as an examination of the representativeness of content sampling, "distinguishable from [his] broader concept of validity" (p. 393).

The assertion that content validity is not a legitimate form of test validity is not universally shared. Although they recognize the arguments reviewed here, Yalow and Popham suggest the existence of an implicit score-based inference that is inherent in content validation.

to the extent that a test's content is a representative sample of behaviors to be exhibited in a desired performance domain . . . is it not true that there is an *implicit inference* to be made? This inference-in-waiting concerns the meaning that test users can ascribe to an examinee's score. If a test is constructed so that it constitutes a representative sample of the domain of interest, then we expect that an examinee's score on the test reflects how the examinee will perform on the domain of interest. Although content validation of a test does not explicitly produce such an inference, the inference is ready to be drawn. (1983, p. 11)

Yalow and Popham's position is, therefore, that assertion of a test's content validity implies a prediction (hence, an inference) that examinees would exhibit about the same level of performance on the domain of behaviors the test purportedly represents that they exhibit on the test itself. Operationally, one might consider the proportion of test items answered correctly as an estimate of the proportion of items in the domain that an examinee would answer correctly, were it possible to administer the entire domain.

This argument invites debate. First, and foremost, as Yalow and Popham note, the claim of sampling adequacy that is at the heart of content validation does not *require* any prediction about the performance of examinees on any larger domain of test items; the predictive inference is merely implicit. *Second*, it is the examinees' *behaviors* elicited by the test items that must be representative of the performance domain, not the test items per se, to sustain a claim of content validity. As Madaus (1983) notes, a given test item might present different behavioral stimuli to different examinees. For example, an item on a history test about the causes of the U.S. Civil War might require rote recall from an examinee who had studied the period extensively, but it might require deductive logic from an examinee who had little exposure to U.S. history in the mid 1800s, despite a good background in economics and European history. It might be difficult, if not impossible, to identify the behaviors elicited by a test item, and, of greater consequence, those behaviors might be examinee specific. In the latter case, content validity would be examinee specific too.

In the second argument that Yalow and Popham (1983) advance in support of the legitimacy of content validity, they note the general agreement of measurement experts on the importance of test-content representativeness. They then suggest that calling content representativeness content validity enhances its prestige, and, without that prestigious title, content representativeness would frequently be ignored. They might be correct, but the claim is surely testable, and its legitimacy would probably depend on the requirements of future editions of the test *Standards.*

Content validity has been discussed at some length because the courts, and several measurement theorists, have suggested that curricular validity and instructional validity are conceptually similar and, in fact, aspects of content validity. Madaus (1983) presents a history of the definition and conceptual underpinnings of content validity in which he illustrates that many early definitions of content validity contained an instructional component. Madaus cites Ruch (1929) as follows: "validity is in general the degree to which a test parallels the curriculum and good teaching practice" (p. 27). In their 1972 edition of *Education and Psychological Measurement and Evaluation,* Stanley and Hopkins describe content validation as a logical examination of test items "in relation to the objectives and instruction [to] make the following professional judgments:

1. Does the test content parallel the curricular objectives in content and processes, and
2. Are the test and curricular emphasis in proper balance?" (p. 102).

Madaus cites 16 additional measurement specialists who incorporated curricular validity in their definitions of content validity and often also included instructional validity (Cureton, 1951; Ebel, 1956; Furst, 1958; Greene, Jorgensen, & Gerberich, 1943, 1954; Lee, 1936; Noll, 1957; Odell, 1938; Ross & Stanley, 1954; Woody & Sangren, 1933; Wrightstone, Justin, & Robbins, 1956). Madaus concludes

In summary, early conceptualizations of the validity of achievement tests clearly included "curricular" validity. Curricular validity is not a recent concept and it certainly is not unique to the Fifth Circuit decision. Over the past fifty years or so, this concept can be found throughout the literature on achievement testing, . . . more often than not, explicit mention was also made of the match between what was tested and what was taught in a particular course — what McClung (1978, 1979) calls instructional validity. (p. 29)

The conceptual parallelism of content validity, curricular validity, and instructional validity was also advanced by Schmidt, Porter, Schwille, Floden & Freeman (1983). In fact, a major section of their paper is headed "Three Types of Content Validity." Using the definition of content validity contained in the 1974 *Standards* (APA), Schmidt et al. merely modify the specification of the "desired performance domain" when addressing content validity, curricular validity, and instructional validity. For content validity, they view the skill objectives that inevitably underlie the development of a competency test as the desired performance domain. For curricular validity, they ask whether the competency test is "also consistent with the curricular materials used in the school system wherein it is to be administered" (p. 134). For instructional validity, the desired performance domain becomes the "instructional content actually taught to the students" (p. 134). They term these three domains *the objectives domain, the curricular materials domain,* and the *instructional content domain.*

Although the parallel structure proposed by Schmidt et al. is convenient, it has several shortcomings. The authors recognize and discuss the difficulty caused by the concept of representative sampling of the desired performance domain that is essential to content validity. Representative sampling is not a critical element of curricular validity and instructional validity, as it is of content validity. Because most school curricula contain topics and concepts that go well beyond the development of so-called "minimum skills and knowledge," and most competency tests are restricted to assessment of students' achievement of these minima, development of a minimum-competency test that provides a representative sample of the curriculum is impractical. In truth, most minimum-competency tests administered in U.S. high schools assess skills and knowledge that students are expected to learn in elementary school. The same problem is noted by the authors when the instructional content domain is to be sampled.

A more fundamental problem that Schmidt et al. ignore is lack of parallelism in the direction of the inferences implicit in content validation, curricular validation, and instructional validation. When content validation is considered, there is, as Yalow and Popham (1983) assert, an implicit inference from the sample of behaviors provided by an examinee's test performance to a population of behaviors that would be elicited by the tasks in the desired performance domain. When either curricular validity or instructional validity is considered, the direction of inference is reversed. In the case of curricular validity, the principal question at issue is whether the behaviors necessary to answer the test items correctly are likely to have been developed through study of the curricular materials. In the case of instructional validity, the principal question is whether the behaviors necessary to answer the test items correctly are likely to have been developed through the instruction provided examinees. In both cases, the domain to be represented is defined by the test. The issue of sampling adequacy is markedly different from the principal question posed in content validation. The test is the domain, and ideal representation requires that *all* behaviors demanded by the test be present in the domain of curricular materials (for curricular validity) or in the domain of instructional content (for instructional validity).

Historical precedents and convenience notwithstanding, the author is not convinced that curricular validity and instructional validity are components of content validity or of the parallelism of the concepts. Further, the author agrees with Yalow and Popham (1983) that "adequacy-of-preparation is an issue related to the use of test results and the events leading up to the examinee's performance. Although of substantial significance, these notions have nothing to do with a test's validity" (p. 13). Thus the author would argue that *curricular validity* and *instructional validity* are misnomers. Because no score-based inferences are associated with the questions posed by these issues and they can, in fact, be assessed quite apart from the test performances of examinees, they are not issues of test validity. It would be preferable to use the umbrella expression *opportunity to learn* to encapsulate both of these issues and, perhaps, *curricular coverage* and *instructional preparation* to identify them individually.

Opportunity to Learn: Measurement Practice

As noted, Florida's effort to demonstrate that the state had provided the students subject to its high school competency test an adequate opportunity to acquire the skills demanded by that test was stimulated by the Fifth Circuit Court of Appeals (*Debra P.,* 1981). The evidence provided by the state was accepted by the district court in the 1983 *Debra P.* case. The decisions in these cases are discussed in a later section of this chapter, headed *Competency Testing and the Law,* as are those of related cases. As of this writing, only one other sequence of court cases has examined evidence in support of the curricular validity and instructional validity of a competency test. In the *Anderson* v. *Banks* cases (1981, 1982), evidence about curricular validity was offered through the direct testimony of school officials, and evidence about instructional validity was offered through the direct testimony of classroom teachers. The school system's claims were ultimately accepted by the court.

In response to the 1981 *Debra P.* decision, the state of Florida conducted a massive study of the correspondence between the curricula offered by its schools, the instruction provided by its teachers, and the skills required by its high school competency test (originally called the Functional Literacy Test because the enabling legislation mandated a demonstration of students' competence in functional literacy, and later, in response to the prospect of stigma identified by the court, renamed the State Student Assessment Test, Part II). The design of that study is described in a report to the Florida Department of Education prepared by Popham and Yalow (1982), briefly in a paper by Fisher (1983), and in greater detail in a paper by Fisher and Smith (1984). The design of the Florida study will be described in some detail, because it provides the only available example of a statewide instructional validity study that has received final adjudication. However, this attention to the Florida study should not be interpreted as an endorsement of its design or its procedures. Sound measurement practices are not necessarily coincident with procedures that are found acceptable by the courts.

The Florida study had four major components: (a) a survey of all regular classroom teachers in grades 2 through 12, (b) a report on instructional practice and curricular offerings prepared by all school systems in the state, (c) a survey of students in selected 11th-grade classes, and (d) reports by teams of state and school system personnel who visited each Florida school system.

All full-time regular teachers in the Florida schools were asked to complete survey questionnaires that were distributed by the principals in their schools. A full-time secondary teacher was defined as one who had taught at least two courses during either semester of the 1981–1982 school year or during the summer of 1982. A full-time elementary schoolteacher was defined as one who had taught at least 1.5 hours per day during either semester of the 1981–1982 school year or during the summer of 1982. Only teachers of exceptional students were excluded. Of 65,000 survey questionnaires distributed, somewhere between 45,000 (Fisher & Smith, 1984) and 47,000 (*Debra P.* v. *Turlington,* 1984) were completed, so the survey response rate was close to 70%.

Florida's State Student Assessment Test (SSAT), Part II, contains multiple-choice test questions designed to assess 24 skills, 13 in mathematics and 11 in communications. For each of the mathematical skills, teachers were given a skill title, a brief description of the skill, and an example of a test item used to assess the skill. For each of the communication skills, teachers were given a skill title, a brief description of the skill, and a description of a typical test item. Using these stimulus materials, teachers were asked to provide answers to two questions for each of the 24 skills. The first question was as follows: "During the previous instructional year [the 1981–1982 academic year, the summer of 1982, or both] did you provide instruction which specifically prepared students for this SSAT-II skill?" If teachers provided an affirmative response to the first question for any of the skills, they were asked to answer the following question for that skill: "Did you provide your students with sufficient instruction so that they *should be able to* demonstrate mastery of this skill on the SSAT-II?" Teachers were told that

> instruction which specifically prepares students for a skill consists of instructional activities directly focused on preparing students for (1) an actual SSAT-II skill, or (2) a skill so similar that students can transfer what they have been taught to the SSAT-II skill as tested. (Popham & Yalow, 1982, p. 3)

Basic instruction in mathematics or reading that would enable students to gain the skills assessed by the SSAT-II was not included in the definition of *specific instruction* that prepared students for the SSAT-II. If potentially relevant instruction was limited to such basic skills, teachers were told to answer no to the first question.

Assuming they had answered yes to the first question, teachers were given the following instructions for responding to the second question:

> Question Two requires you to make a professional judgment about whether your students received sufficient instruction from you so that, if your students had expended reasonable effort during the instructional process, they would be able to demonstrate mastery of that skill on the SSAT-II. If so, you should answer *YES* to Question Two. (Popham & Yalow, 1982, p. 4)

Madaus (personal communication, November, 1984) notes the incongruity of the state legislature's mandating the use of minimum-competency tests as a high school graduation sanction, presumably because it did not trust the judgments of Florida's teachers in identifying students who were competent to be awarded a high school diploma, and then appropriating funds to support a validation study that rested, in large part, on teachers' judgments of the adequacy of their teaching to prepare students to pass the tests.

The second component of the Florida study was a census of school districts that requested information on each district's instructional activities in support of the skills assessed by the SSAT-II. District personnel completed six forms in this component of the study. The first form was a Skills-by-Grade Summary that sought answers to the following two questions:

> During the 1981–1982 academic year and the 1982 summer session, at what grades did most of the students in your district receive

instruction which specifically prepared them for each of these SSAT-II skills?

By what grade have most of the students in the regular instructional program in your district been provided with sufficient preparation to demonstrate mastery of each of these SSAT-II skills? (Popham & Yalow, 1982, Appendix B, p. 1)

The definitions of *specific instruction* and *sufficient preparation* used with the survey of teachers were either used verbatim or were adapted for use in the district reports.

The second form that district personnel completed requested information on major variations in the regular instructional programs offered by schools in the district. Presumably this form was used to detect variations from the districtwide instructional information requested on the first form. The second form provided limited space for describing variations in instructional programs, together with the names of schools in which these variations were offered, applicable grade levels, and numbers of students enrolled in the variant programs.

The third form sought information on remedial instructional programs operated by the school district. District personnel were requested to indicate, for each remedial program offered, the title of the program, the methods used to select students for the program, the methods used to monitor students' progress through the program, evidence of the program's success, differences in the way the program was conducted in different schools within the district, the grade levels of students enrolled in the program, the types of instructional personnel used by the program, when the program was offered, and any other information they considered important in describing the program.

The fourth form was used to secure information on staff development activities used by the district to promote instructional mastery of the skills assessed by the SSAT-II. District personnel were asked to describe any such activities, to list the academic year each activity was provided, to describe the type of participants in the activity, to list the number of participants, and to list the duration of the activity.

The fifth form required an extensive tabulation of the instructional materials used by the district's schools, in an attempt to assess the curricular validity of the SSAT-II. District personnel were asked to provide a listing of relevant instructional materials for each of the 24 skills assessed by the SSAT-II. Materials were described by author, title, and other standard identifying data if they were published and as "local" if they were locally developed. In addition, the grade levels in which the materials were used, in either regular or remedial instructional programs, were listed. Finally, the numbers of pages containing material pertinent to the SSAT-II skills were listed.

The sixth and final form requested information on "additional instructional activities directed specifically at aiding district students [in] pass[ing] the SSAT-II since 1977" (Popham & Yalow, 1982, Appendix B, p. 5). Examples of such activities included "parent participation programs," "special tutorial programs," "recognition activities for success," and "special motivational activities." District personnel were asked to indicate whether activities were offered districtwide or at certain schools, the grade levels of students affected by the activities,

and the school years during which the activities had been conducted.

The third component of the Florida study was a survey of 11th-grade students designed to determine whether or not they remembered having been taught the skills assessed by the SSAT-II. The survey was administered in sampled 11th-grade English or social studies classes by members of District Site Visit Teams (site visits are described later).

Half the students in each sampled class were given a questionnaire that sought their recollection of mathematics instruction, and the other half were given a questionnaire that sought their recollection of communication skills instruction. Each questionnaire contained a separate page for each SSAT-II skill that listed the skill title and then displayed between two and four test items that presumably assessed that skill. Correct answers to the test items were indicated.

Students were asked to review the test items provided for each skill, together with the correct answers, and then to answer the following question: "Have you been taught in school how to answer these types of test questions?" Students were told not to indicate their names of their schools and that their anonymity would be protected. They were also told to answer no if they could not remember having been taught how to answer the test questions or if they did not know how to answer them. Responses to this survey were gathered from about 3,200 students (*Debra P.* v. *Turlington,* 1984, at 2839).

The fourth component of the Florida study consisted of site visits to all 67 of the state's school districts. The purposes of the site visits were to

(a) judge the accuracy of the district's self-report regarding the preparation of students for the SSAT-II;
(b) determine if there was evidence of instruction on the skills taking place, and
(c) provide any impressions gained during the visit about the quality of the district's SSAT-II preparation efforts. (Fisher & Smith, 1984, p. 4)

Each site-visit team was chaired by a curriculum consultant from the Florida Department of Education. The two additional team members were educators from school systems other than the one being visited. The site-visit teams gathered information by interviewing district-level school personnel and then visiting schools in the district. During their school visits, team members interviewed principals or their designees, then interviewed teachers individually and in groups. Team members who visited high schools also administered the student survey described earlier.

The school district site visits were highly structured. Each team member received eight pages of instructions on required activities, and the chair of each team completed a log that listed the nature, time, and date of each activity that took place during the team's 2-day visit to a school district. In addition, team members prepared a report on their findings that was summarized by the team chair. The final report on each team's findings was approved by each team member.

The schools visited by the teams were selected through a stratified random sampling procedure by the study administrators. However, the high school classrooms used for administration of the student survey were selected by team members, using unknown criteria. At least 5 schools were visited in each Florida school district, and in districts with more than 30 schools, 15% of the schools were visited.

Fisher and Smith (1984, p. 8) report that the Florida study had a total out-of-pocket cost in excess of $100,000, not including the expenses of local school districts and excluding state-level personnel costs. The state's personnel investment was estimated to be three person-years.

The efforts of the Florida Department of Education to demonstrate the fairness of the SSAT-II testing program were accepted by the Middle District Court in *Debra P.* v. *Turlington* (1983) and, following appeal, were upheld by the 11th Circuit Court of Appeals in *Debra P.* v. *Turlington* (1984). The details of the latter trial and the evidence that was found to be particularly compelling by the court are discussed in the next section of this chapter. Although procedures found to be convincing by the court are of obvious interest to those who design and operate competency-testing programs, such procedures must never be accepted unquestioningly as exemplars of sound measurement practice.

Hardy (1984) conducted a study to determine whether students required to take the Alabama High School Graduation Examination (AHSGE) were given sufficient opportunity to acquire the skills assessed by the test. To gather evidence on this question, Hardy surveyed random samples of 7th- through 10th-grade teachers in Alabama.

The AHSGE is administered to students beginning with the 10th grade, and satisfactory performance is a high school graduation requirement. The test assesses students' skills in reading, language arts, and mathematics. The 18 language arts skills assessed by the AHSGE range from proper use of pronouns to writing an appropriate business letter. Its 16 reading skills include knowledge of reference sources and understanding of the main idea in a passage. The test assesses 30 mathematics skills including students' abilities to read and write numerals, calculate the cost of credit, and transform units of measurement.

To determine whether Alabama students had been afforded an adequate opportunity to learn the skills (competencies) measured by the AHSGE, Hardy asked sampled teachers to estimate three quantities for each of the skills assessed by the AHSGE: (a) the proportion of their students who were taught the competency at their current grade level, (b) the proportion of students who were not taught the competency at their current grade level because the competency was too difficult or not yet reached, and (c) the proportion of students who were not taught the competency at their current grade level because it was too easy or because the teacher assumed that the students had mastered the competency in an earlier grade. Teachers were told that these three proportions should sum to 1 (or, in terms of percentages, to 100%) for each competency.

Hardy used a three-stage stratified random sampling procedure to select the teachers he surveyed. He first drew a stratified random sample of Alabama's 127 school districts. Next, he selected random samples of schools within sampled districts. Finally, he stratified teachers by grade level and subject taught and selected stratified random samples of teachers of reading, language arts, and mathematics in grades 7 through 10.

Teachers constituted tertiary sampling units and were drawn only from sampled schools.

In total, Hardy sampled 555 Alabama teachers and received questionnaires from 452. His response rates varied from 72% in Grade 10 to 88% in Grade 7. However, because a number of responses were unclear or obviously inaccurate, percentages of usable questionnaires varied from a low of 54% in Grade 10 to a high of 70% in Grade 8.

When analyzing his data, Hardy created an index that he termed P_{7-10} for each competency assessed by the AHSGE. This index was based on the average proportions of students who were taught a tested skill in their current grades, as reported by teachers of students in Grades 7, 8, 9, and 10. In creating the index, Hardy reasoned that the proportions reported by teachers in different grades were statistically independent, and he then applied the multiplicative law of probability. The multiplicative law states that the probability of the simultaneous occurrence of two independent events equals the product of their individual probabilities. In the Alabama study, Hardy calculated the probability that students would have been taught a given competency in at least one of Grades 7 through 10 as the converse of the probability that they would not have been taught the competency in any of those grades. The resulting formula for the P_{7-10} index is as follows:

$$P_{7-10} = 1 - [(1 - P_7)(1 - P_8)(1 - P_9)(1 - P_{10})],$$

where P_7 represents the average of the proportions of students who were taught the competency at their current grade level, as estimated by teachers of seventh graders. P_8 through P_{10} are defined analogously, for Grades 8 through 10, respectively (Hardy, 1984, p. 295).

When teachers' reports were analyzed, the P_{7-10} index was found to range between 0.97 and 0.99 for the 18 language arts competencies assessed by the AHSGE, between 0.89 and 0.99 for the 16 reading competencies, and between 0.75 and 0.99 for the 30 mathematics competencies. However, the range is not representative of results for the mathematics competencies, because the second smallest value of the index was 0.91.

Hardy also computed "adjusted P_{7-10}" indices that were designed to adjust for teacher nonresponse. He multiplied each of the values P_7 through P_{10} by the response rate of teachers of courses in the competency area in each respective grade, before computing the P_{7-10} index for a given competency. For example, the P_7 value for a reading competency was multiplied by the response rate of seventh-grade reading teachers. Hardy reasoned that the adjusted P_{7-10} indices represented "worst cases," under the assumption that nonresponding teachers would estimate 0 for the proportion of students taught the competency in their respective grade levels.

Whether the approach Hardy used to gather evidence on the instructional validity of the AHSGE will withstand legal challenge has yet to be determined. However, it is not difficult to anticipate arguments based on (a) the cross-sectional nature of its index, (b) the lack of evidence on the adequacy or extensiveness of instruction, (c) the total reliance on the judgments and estimates of classroom teachers, and (d) the extensive time between students' receiving instruction and having to demonstrate competence in many of the skill areas tested.

Schmidt et al. (1983) have developed detailed taxonomies

of objectives covered by mathematics textbooks and standardized achievement tests that are widely used in the elementary grades. Their system of measuring curricular congruence revealed that about one-half to three-fourths of the mathematics content of five popular standardized tests was covered by three popular textbooks intended for use in the same grades. The curricular validity of these tests, assuming the schools' mathematics curriculum was dictated by one of these three textbooks was, thus, far from perfect (pp. 143–144).

Schmidt et al. (1983) suggest that the most accurate way of assessing instructional validity is to gather observational data in teachers' classes. However, these authors recognize the difficulty and expense associated with the collection of extensive observational data, and they propose the use of teacher diaries and logs as an alternative. In some experimental research that was under way at the time their article was written, Schmidt et al. found that teachers were able to "keep fairly accurate logs" (p. 146). When teachers kept logs of the time they devoted to specific content topics, their errors tended to cancel out over a period of days. It is interesting to note that the accuracy of teachers' self-reports through surveys, the mode of data collection used in the Florida and Alabama studies, has not been subjected to experimental validation.

Research by Schmidt et al. has clearly demonstrated the unacceptability of data on curricular coverage as a substitute for instructional preparation. They report the results of collecting data on the instructional practices of seven teachers in three school districts that used common, mandated curriculum materials. In one school district, the teachers were required to follow a detailed system of management by objectives in which they kept records on the objectives that students had mastered; used pretests, locater tests, and mastery tests; and taught under sanctions that included the threat of being dismissed if they failed to teach the mandated curriculum. In every case, teachers adapted the curricular materials and failed to cover the entire curriculum embodied in the prescribed materials. Several teachers added objectives outside the prescribed textbooks, and others covered only parts of the prescribed materials. After analyzing their data, Schmidt et al. concluded as follows:

> Some theoreticians might maintain that an analysis of the curricular materials tells us what is covered in the schools. Current research suggests that this is far from true. Teachers in the United States generally operate as fairly autonomous decision-makers in defining the content of their instruction. They are influenced by many sources other than curricular materials, such as tests, school administrators, and other teachers. It is for this reason that curricular validity should not be used when attempting to establish the instructional validity of a certification test. (p. 151)

In summary, establishment of the instructional validity of a certification test to the satisfaction of a court will be difficult, and the outcome of any effort to do so will be somewhat unpredictable. Florida used a wide variety of evidence collected at great cost in time and dollars, which a district court and a circuit court of appeals found to be acceptable. Evidence collected by the state of Alabama was far more modest in scope but has yet to be challenged in court. A far richer legal history than presently exists is needed to determine the kinds of validity evidence the courts will find minimally sufficient. Although

evidence on curricular congruence advanced in the *Debra P.* case carried some weight, the extent of that weight is not clear. It is likely that the testimony of informed experts would denigrate the significance of evidence of curricular validity as an indicator of instructional validity, if offered in future court cases. In addition, the measurement community has barely entered the debate on what would constitute appropriate or sufficient evidence of students being provided an adequate opportunity to learn or on the procedures that should be used to accumulate such evidence.

Competency Testing and the Law

Because competency tests are used to make important educational decisions, such as whether students will be granted a regular high school diploma or whether students will be assigned to remedial instructional classes, it is not surprising that competency-testing programs have been challenged in the courts. Significant operational principles have emerged from these court decisions that will likely guide the development and use of competency tests for years to come.

Competency Tests Are Constitutionally Permitted

The right of school officials to use competency tests in making educational decisions concerning individual students has been upheld in all relevant court decisions. As noted by Cannell (1983), in *Brookhart* v. *Illinois Board of Education* (1982), the federal district court held as follows:

> The court is satisfied that local boards of education and their staffs have the right, if not a positive duty, to develop reasonable means to determine the effectiveness of their education programs with respect to all individual students to whom they issue diplomas, and the minimum competency testing program here is a reasonable means.

Citron (1983a, 1983b), following a review of recent court cases, concluded that the courts had found appropriate use of competency tests to be constitutional. In fact, she found that courts lauded school districts that attempted to ensure the value of their high school diplomas by requiring students to demonstrate minimal competence. In support of her conclusions, Citron cites *Debra P.* v. *Turlington* (1981) and the most recent appeal of the *Board of Education of the Northport–East Northport Union Free School District* v. *Ambach* (1982). Melvin (1983) notes a similar conclusion in *Wells* v. *Banks* (1981). In the *Ambach* appeal case, the court stated: "the protection of the integrity of a high school diploma is both a legitimate State interest and one to which the competency testing program is reasonably related" (at 689). Use of the word *appropriate* is near universal in the courts' approval of competency-testing programs. Although they have affirmed the state's right to use competency tests, the courts have imposed a number of procedural sanctions on sponsors of such programs.

Requirement of Adequate Notice

In *Debra P.* v. *Turlington* (1979), the court affirmed students' property right to graduation from high school with a regular diploma, provided they have fulfilled requirements for graduation other than completion of a competency test. In addition, the court affirmed students' liberty interest in being free of the stigma associated with receiving a certificate in lieu of a high school diploma. These rights and interests are protected under the due process and equal protection clauses of the Fourteenth Amendment to the Constitution.

An important element of due process requires that students be given adequate notice that they will be required to earn a passing score on a test to receive a high school diploma. This constitutional principle has been addressed in numerous court cases concerning the use of competency tests in schools (Cannell, 1983; Citron, 1982, 1983a, 1983b; Melvin, 1983; Pullin, 1982).

In the original *Debra P.* v. *Turlington* case (1979), the court found that 2 years' notice was inadequate, because there was not a uniform statewide curriculum in Florida and students had not been informed, at the time of instruction, that they would be required to learn the skills being taught prior to high school graduation. In both the original *Board of Education* v. *Ambach* case (1981) and the appeal case (1982) and in *Brookhart* v. *Illinois State Board of Education* (1983) the court found similarly. However these cases concern the use of competency tests with handicapped students, and, in all three, the court ruled that handicapped students must be afforded especially long notice that their high school diplomas depend on their competency-test performance. In *Board of Education* v. *Ambach,* 2 years' notice was found to be inadequate; in *Brookhart,* 18 months' notice was at question.

Although it would appear that students must be given at least 2 years' notice that a competency test will be used in determining their eligibility to receive a high school diploma, the courts have not specified a minimally sufficient time. In *Anderson* v. *Banks* (1981), 2 years' notice was found to be adequate, in contrast with the cases cited earlier.

Freedom from Past Discrimination

When Florida first administered its statewide Functional Literacy Test in 1977, 77% of black students and 24% of white students failed to achieve the arbitrarily imposed standard of 70% correct. After three attempts to pass the test, 1.9% of white students and 20% of black students in Florida's high school classes of 1979 still failed to do so. Because of this disparate racial impact of the competency test, a principle of strict scrutiny was applied by the court in the original *Debra P.* v. *Turlington* case (1979). Under this principle, the state was required to demonstrate that the disparate test results were not caused by the effects of past unlawful racial discrimination in the schools. Because Florida had, in the past, operated racially dual school systems, the state was enjoined from using the Functional Literacy Test as a diploma criterion until all students who had been subjected to those discriminatory practices had graduated. The judgment of the court on this point is well summarized as follows:

In the Court's opinion, punishing the victims of past discrimination for deficits created by an inferior educational environment neither constitutes a remedy nor creates better educational opportunities. (474 F. Supp. [M. D. Fla. 1979] at 257)

Whenever a testing program produces differential racial impact, the courts will apply the principle of strict judicial scrutiny and view such impact as sufficient to cause the testing program to be reviewed for discriminatory intent. However, discriminatory intent, as in the case of Florida's racially dual school systems, has been found necessary to substantiate a claim of constitutionally unlawful racial effect.

Opportunity to Learn

Without doubt, the most difficult court-imposed principle faced by educators who would operate competency-testing programs is the requirement that they demonstrate that students have been given an opportunity to learn the material that is tested. As noted, this has been labeled *content validity* (Citron, 1982, 1983a), *curricular validity* (McClung, 1978a) and *instructional validity* (Fisher, 1983; McClung, 1978a), and the issue concerns the correspondence between students' instructional exposure and the demands placed on them by a competency test.

From the first of the *Debra P.* v. *Turlington* cases (1979) through the fourth (1984), the issue of students' opportunity to learn has been paramount. Originally, the court held that the state could not deny students a high school diploma solely because they failed the Florida Functional Literacy Test unless it could be proven that they were actually taught the material covered on the test (474 F. Supp. at 266). Although the court did not specify the methods to be used in providing an adequate demonstration, Pullin (1982) notes several relevant principles in her review of the case:

Students must be told the specific objectives that will be covered on the test used as a graduation requirement. This announcement must occur at the time of instruction in the objective. (474 F. Supp. at 264).

The curriculum offered the students must include instruction in the objectives covered by the test. (474 F. Supp. at 264).

The acquisition of skills is a cumulative process. Students must be offered instruction in a rational and orderly sequence which can afford them an opportunity to acquire proficiency through an appropriate developmental process. (474 F. Supp. at 264).

The amount of time spent on instruction of a particular skill or unit of knowledge is important. (474 F. Supp. at 264).

The timing of the instruction received by students is important. In addition to receiving sufficient instruction in a skill, students must be provided instruction, or a review of prior instruction, at a time just prior to administration of the test. (474 F. Supp. at 264).

The teaching process must include some mechanism for identifying whether objectives are being learned by individual students, since teaching and learning are not always coterminus. (474 F. Supp. 264).

Students must be offered an opportunity for remedial instruction if they have not mastered an objective. (474 F. Supp. at 264). (p. 28)

Use of these principles as a guide to court-acceptable practice is tempting. However, the original findings in *Debra P.* have been remanded, vacated, and affirmed, in part, in succeeding *Debra P.* cases and, in related cases, the courts have imposed their historic posture of judicial restraint in addressing procedural issues that they view as the appropriate province of school boards and school officials.

Although the plaintiffs in the first appeal of *Debra P.* (1981) argued that the state must demonstrate that the content of the competency test was actually taught in all schools in the state, the court has not, so far, upheld that view. In *Anderson v. Banks* (1982), the court accepted the testimony of school officials that the content of the school district's competency test was included in students' curricula, together with the testimony of teachers that they actually taught the material, as sufficient evidence of the content validity of the test. Although the general instructional validity requirements of *Debra P.* were applied by the court in the *Anderson* v. *Banks* cases, the presiding judge did this with some reluctance. This is evident in the transcripts of the original (1981) and appeal (1982) cases. In the findings of the original case, the judge wrote "The Court is curious as to whether the ruling in *Debra P.* will mean that in the future any diploma determinative test, perhaps a final examination in senior English, will require this justification by school authorities" (520 F. Supp. at 509 n. 11). And in the findings of the appeal case the court held that

> To require school officials to produce testimony that every teacher finished every lesson and assigned every problem in the curriculum would impose a paralyzing burden on school authorities and hamper them in constructing an academic program which they believe most effectively meets the needs of their students. (540 F. Supp. at 765–766)

In its response to the 1981 ruling of the Fifth Circuit Court of Appeals, the state of Florida conducted a massive study (described earlier in this chapter) designed to convince the court that students had been given an adequate opportunity to learn the skills tested on its competency test (Fisher, 1983). The study had six components: (a) a survey of all junior and senior high school principals in the state, to determine whether they had incorporated the skills measured by the test in their curricula; (b) a survey to determine the type and amount of remedial instruction provided students who had failed the test on one or more of up to five attempts; (c) a multi-part survey of all school districts in the state, to determine the methods they had used to provide instruction in the skills assessed by the test; (d) a survey of all teachers of students in grades 2 through 12, to determine whether they had taught the skills assessed and to secure their judgments on whether their instruction would enable students to master the skills; (e) visits to schools by state and local education officials, to judge the accuracy of the school districts' reports of their instructional activities and to gather evidence on instruction in the skills assessed by the test; and (f) a survey of students to determine whether they felt they had received instruction in the skills assessed by the test. Although in 1983 *Debra P.* case was appealed, the district court accepted the evidence offered by the state that it had provided students with an adequate opportunity to learn, and it permitted the use of Florida's competency test in denying high school diplomas to those who had failed. The appeals court also supported this action, pending further litigation.

The series of *Debra P.* cases finally came to a close in 1984, 5 years after the first case had been heard. In its final ruling, The Eleventh Circuit Court of Appeals upheld the finding of the district court that the state of Florida had demonstrated the fairness and validity of the SSAT-II. Although the evidence offered by the state in support of its claim to instructional validity was circumstantial and alleged by the plaintiff to be hearsay, the cumulative weight of the evidence was found by the circuit court and the appeals court to be compelling.

The appeals court noted the extensiveness of the state's effort to gather evidence in support of the instructional validity of the SSAT-II, including its survey of teachers, school districts, students, and site visits to verify the accuracy of data provided by school districts. Objections of the plaintiff concerning the quality of evidence submitted by the state were not held to limit the admissibility of the evidence. In the 1983 trial, the state held that students had been given an adequate opportunity to learn the material tested by the SSAT-II, and it introduced a Mastery Exposure Index that purportedly represented the average number of times students had been given an opportunity to master SSAT-II skills. One witness testified that the index equaled 2.7 and that a single opportunity was adequate for the purpose.

In counterargument, a witness for the plaintiff asserted that the index was based on a cross-sectional study of the 1981–1982 school year and, therefore, did not represent the learning opportunities afforded the 1983 graduating class in Florida through 12 cumulative years of schooling. The appeals court acknowledged this argument but discounted it on several bases including testimony asserting that instruction in the Florida schools had probably not changed materially since the SSAT-II requirement had been introduced in 1977, testimony on the relative importance of instruction during the later years of schooling in passing the SSAT-II, and testimony on the effectiveness of Florida's remedial instructional programs. In its positive ruling on adequacy of preparation, the court also relied on the findings of the state's student survey, in which 90% to 95% of responding students reported that they had been taught the skills assessed by SSAT-II items.

The ultimate passing rates on the SSAT-II were also noted by the appeals court as convincing evidence that students had been afforded an adequate opportunity to learn the material tested. After four attempts, 99.84% of the 1983 graduating class had passed the communications portion of the SSAT-II, and 97.23% had passed the mathematics portion.

In the final appeals case, witnesses for the plaintiff argued that the state's instructional-validity study should have focused on students who consistently failed the SSAT-II, rather than focusing on all students. The court rejected this argument because

> None of the experts at trial suggested that an instructional validity study must focus on students who have failed the test. The experts conceded that there are *no accepted educational standards for determining whether a test is instructionally valid* [italics added]. (at 2840)

In another challenge to the trustworthiness of the evidence offered by the state, witnesses for the plaintiff argued that respondents to the teacher survey were probably biased, because they knew the purposes of the study and that the study was conducted by the state. The court rejected this argument on the grounds that teachers responded to the survey anonymously and school districts were told that their responses would be verified by on-site visitors. In addition, those visitors were told that *their* reports were subject to follow-up audits.

Although the courts have affirmed a clear due process requirement that students be provided instruction in the content assessed by a competency test prior to their assessment, they have not provided clear specifications for evidence that would be regarded as minimally sufficient. Madaus (1983) defines a broad set of responsibilities that he would have all sponsors of competency-testing programs assume. These include traditional content validation; demonstration of the correspondence between test content, curriculum content, and instructional content; detailed definition of the domain assessed by the competency test and widespread dissemination of a description of this domain; criterion-related validation of the competency test; test bias analyses; and provisions for post hoc disclosure of test content and student review of their test performance. Although these responsibilities define sound measurement practice, the cases that have been heard to date suggest that court-imposed requirements will be far narrower in scope and far less stringent. Because both the elaborate empirical studies of the state of Florida and the testimony of local educators were found by different courts to provide sufficient evidence of students' opportunities to learn, an adequate response to legal requirements is not yet evident.

Use of Competency Tests with Handicapped Students

In addition to the protections provided under the Fourteenth Amendment to the Constitution, handicapped students are afforded protection under the Education for All Handicapped Children Act (PL 94–142) and Section 504 of the Rehabilitation Act. Each of these has been used as a basis for suits brought on behalf of handicapped children who were denied a high school diploma because they had failed a competency test.

The basic issues in cases brought on behalf of handicapped students have involved the fairness both of competency tests and procedures used when the tests were applied (Cannell, 1983). Although the courts have ruled that fair competency tests must be applied in a fair and equitable manner, they have repeatedly affirmed the right of states and local school systems to apply the same competency requirements to handicapped and nonhandicapped students (*Board of Education* v. *Ambach.*, 1981, 1982; *Anderson* v. *Banks,* 1982).

In imposing due process and equal protection requirements for testing of handicapped students, the courts have held that standard conditions of testing must be modified so that these students do not fail just because of their handicapping conditions. Modifications include provision of adequate notice of test requirements (*Brookhart* v. *Illinois Board of Education,* 1982), provision of large-print materials for visually impaired examinees, provision of Braille materials for blind examinees, and provision of persons to record the responses of examinees who are physically unable to do so (Cannell, 1983).

Cannell (1983) notes that the standard of strict judicial scrutiny applied by the courts in cases that allege racial discrimination in competency testing will not be applied to cases that allege discrimination against handicapped students. The courts will, instead, apply a "rational basis" standard that shifts the burden of proof of procedural discrimination to the plaintiffs.

The argument that was, for a time, successfully advanced in the *Debra P.* cases, (that students had not been given an opportunity to learn the material tested) has not been upheld in cases

involving handicapped students. In *Anderson* v. *Banks* (1982) and in *Board of Education* v. *Ambach* (1981), the right of handicapped students to a "free and appropriate education" was not found to include the right to receive instruction necessary to pass a high school competency test. None of the constitutional or statutory provisions that protect the rights of handicapped students has been interpreted to guarantee such students specific educational outcomes, such as a high school diploma.

Some Conclusions and Commentary

Testing for certification of student competence is a well-entrenched practice in the public schools of the United States. Although some of the goals and objectives that motivated the current spate of competency testing have also been espoused by educators in Britain and Europe, minimum-competency achievement testing is a uniquely American phenomenon (Resnick & Resnick, 1982).

The description of the nature and status of competency testing provided earlier in this chapter emphasized the role of legislative bodies and lay boards of education in mandating the use of such tests. Competency tests have been proposed by legislators and laypersons, not by educators, as effective means of curing the perceived ills of U.S. education. The expectations of such persons are great and many. Following a review of enabling legislation and actions of state boards of education, Gorth and Perkins (1979a) summarized the assertions of these policymakers. Proponents of competency testing believed it would "(1) restore confidence in the high school diploma, (2) involve the public in education, (3) improve teaching and learning, (4) serve a diagnostic, remedial function, and (5) provide a mechanism of accountability" (p. 12).

Curricular Consequences of Competency Testing

As opposed to public policymakers, many educators either questioned the effectiveness of competency testing from the outset or warned of its dangers. Perrone (1979) cites the early history of the New York State Regents Testing Program in noting that external tests often determine the curriculum of the schools. He states

> The evidence is that the tests influenced significantly what was taught. The diaries of early twentieth-century teachers were filled with accounts of the long periods in which they prepared students for the state examinations, giving up in the process what they considered to be more engaging for the students. (p. 5)

And, in their review of the influence of external tests on the curricula provided in the schools of several nations, Madaus and Airasian (1978) concluded "most studies have found that the proportion of instructional time spent on various objectives was seldom higher than the predicted likelihood of their occurrence on the external exam" (p. 21).

Is the influence of external tests on the content of the high school curriculum necessarily bad? When the external tests are the minimum-competency achievement tests commonly used in the schools of the United States, the problem is apparent.

The only available review of the content of statewide competency tests was prepared by Gorth and Perkins (1979b). These authors report that the competency tests used by over half the states were composed solely of items that assessed students' skills in reading, mathematics, and writing. Moreover, these tests typically demanded nothing more than recognition of basic subject matter mechanics or the application of basic mechanics to so-called "life skills" situations. In one state, a mathematics test question listed the price of various restaurant menu items, and required examinees to *recognize* the correct sum of the prices of three menu items, among the four values given. Skills such as these are expected to result from effective instruction in the elementary school curriculum and surely should not dictate the content of the high school curriculum.

Because it adopted minimum-competency testing earlier than other states, Florida's Functional Literacy Test has been subjected to considerable attention. Commenting on the apparent influence of this test on the high school curricula of that state, Tyler (1979) notes "We were told that many teachers interpreted the emphasis on basic skills to mean that they must devote most of their attention to routine drill" (p. 30). In a thematically similar vein, Broudy (1980), bemoans the shallow interpretation of the requirements of functional literacy evidenced in the content of commonly used minimum competency tests

> Mechanical identification of printed words with their phonetic equivalents and their standard referents is not what is ordinarily meant by reading comprehension, let alone *functional* literacy. Whoever doubts this conclusion need only hand a non-English-speaking reader a dictionary and ask him to be functionally literate about the locution: "They worked around the clock." The point is that *other strands of the curriculum* are needed to provide context-building resources that make literacy possible, in save the barest mechanical sense. If acquisition of these resources is restricted, even intensive instruction in the mechanics will not produce literacy. (p. 113)

Societal Effects of Competency Testing

Evidence accumulated from statewide assessment programs, nationwide studies of student achievement, and minimum-competency achievement testing programs of several states strongly suggests that children of poor parents fail competency tests far more frequently than children of rich parents. The same can be said of black children, when compared with white children. Coleman et al (1966) reports average achievement test scores for black children that were one standard deviation below averages for white children throughout the grade span tested and in all tested subjects. Statistics resulting from the initial administration of North Carolina's High School Competency Tests are equally sobering: Almost 25% of black students and less than 4% of white students failed the reading test; almost 34% of black students and less than 7% of white students failed the mathematics test. It must be noted that opportunities for retesting greatly diminish overall student failure rates in virtually all statewide competency-testing programs, and indeed, well over 90% of North Carolina's high school students currently pass that state's competency tests.

However, the rate of failure among black students is still many times higher than that of white students.

Statistics such as these suggest several issues. Do competency tests serve to protect the public from high school graduates without viable survival skills who would otherwise be a drain on society? What is the effect on students who fail high school competency tests and are therefore denied a high school diploma? Evidence bearing on both issues is sparse, but tentative conclusions can be based on analyses of data collected in the National Longitudinal Study (NLS) of the High School Class of 1972.

As a part of this study, basic skills tests similar in content to high school competency tests used by many states were administered to a nationally representative sample of 18,000 high school seniors throughout the United States. Eckland (1980) completed several analyses of these data that provide partial responses to the questions just raised. The NLS tests consisted of a mathematics test and a reading test. The mathematics test was composed of items that required fundamental computation and the application of basic computation skills to simple word problems. The reading test was composed of comprehension and vocabulary items.

If passing scores on these tests had been set at the 20th percentile of the score distributions of the 18,000 high school seniors who completed them, just over 13% of white students, but almost 50% of black students, would have failed the mathematics test. Comparable failure rates on the reading test would have been 13% for white students and 51% for black students; thus black students would have failed at four times the rate of white students.

Because these tests were not used as a high school graduation sanction, it can safely be assumed that most of the tested students were awarded high school diplomas. What happened to students who did not enter college? Eckland (1980) reports that rates of unemployment following high school graduation among white students who did not enter college were virtually unrelated to their performances on these tests. Among black students who did not enter college, the unemployment rate for those who scored in the lower half of the score distribution on the mathematics test was about twice as high as the rate for those who scored in the upper half of the distribution. In contrast, the reading-test performance of black students was only slightly related to their employment immediately following high school graduation. For students of either race, performance on the reading and mathematic tests was virtually unrelated to rates of part-time employment immediately after high school. And among students of either race who gained full-time employment shortly after high school graduation, weekly income was negligibly related to performance on the tests.

It would appear that performance on minimum-competency tests is not a good predictor of a young person's ability to obtain employment or to earn money, provided that person is awarded a high school diploma. The diploma is critical. In 1978 the unemployment rate of members of the labor force in the age range 16–21 who did not have a high school diploma was more than twice as high as the unemployment rate of high school graduates in the labor force (U.S. Bureau of the Census, 1979, p. 148).

A 4-year follow-up study of NLS high school graduates who

did not attend college was reported by Peng and Jaffe (1978). Their findings on relationships between students' competency-test performances and their economic well-being included the following: (a) Four years after high school graduation, 4.5% of students who scored in the top quarter of the NLS test-score distributions were unemployed and seeking employment; (b) among students who scored in the bottom quarter of the NLS test score distributions, the corresponding figure was 6.8%; (c) four years after high school graduation, the average weekly earnings of students who scored in the top quarter of the NLS test score distributions were $175; (d) the corresponding figure for students who scored in the bottom quarter of the NLS test score distributions was $173.

It would appear that having a high school diploma, rather than having the skills assessed by a minimum-competency test, largely determines whether a young person can obtain employment and earn money, as well as the amount of money earned. It is by denying students a high school diploma, rather than failing to assure their possession of the skills assessed by minimum-competency tests, that our schools endanger students' economic survival.

When minimum-competency tests are used as a high school graduation sanction, black students who aspire to attend college are also likely to be affected to a far greater extent than are white students with similar aspirations. Eckland (1980) reports that 54% of white students in the NLS sample enrolled in college at some time during the 4 years following their high school graduation. The corresponding figure for black students in the NLS sample was 48%. If states were to use the 20th percentiles of the overall NLS test-score distributions as passing scores and were to deny a high school diploma to students whose scores fell below these percentiles on the mathematics test or the reading test, the college-attendance rate of white students would be expected to fall by a negligible amount, from 54% to 52%. However, the corresponding reduction in the college-attendance rate of black students would be from 48% to 31%. Instead of a difference in college-attendance rates of 6%, imposition of this competency-testing policy would result in a difference in college-attendance rates of 21%. The economic value of college attendance is well documented. It is clear that use of minimum-competency tests as a high school graduation sanction, as they are currently used in nearly half the states, disproportionately affects the economic well-being of black students who aspire to attend college.

Responsibilities of the Measurement Profession

As noted in the Standards for Educational and Psychological Testing (APA, AERA, NCME, 1985), "Educational and psychological testing involves and significantly affects individuals, institutions, and society as a whole" (p. 1). With certainty, this statement applies to testing for certification of student competence. If they are to act as responsible professionals, measurement specialists must recognize not only the technical issues that competency testing brings to the fore but also the educational and societal implications of these issues.

Perhaps the principal responsibility of the measurement profession is to question the validity of inferences derived from competency-test results and to promote the use of measurement practices that increase the validity of such inferences. To the extent that invalid inferences are exposed, and measurement practices that reduce validity are eliminated, the value of competency testing can be increased and societal damage resulting from competency testing can be minimized.

To this end, several measurement topics central to the use of competency tests have been discussed in this chapter. Because the use of competency tests requires the establishment of test standards, it is essential that such standards be determined through methods that are replicable, reliable, and equitable. Although the measurement literature does not recognize one best standard-setting procedure, some methods are clearly more defensible than others. Measurement professionals should ensure that effective standard-setting procedures are used; that the procedures are carefully and responsibly applied; and, in keeping with the Standards (in particular, Standard 6.10), that the use of standard-setting procedures is fully documented.

Students whose educational and societal futures are determined by their competency-test performances must be assured an adequate opportunity to learn the skills and acquire the knowledge on which they are tested, and they must be given an adequate opportunity to demonstrate their knowledge and skills through several test administrations (see Standards 8.7 and 8.8). Responsible measurement professionals must strive to enforce these standards and to assure that sound measurement methods are used to assess students' opportunities to learn.

Whether measurement professionals bear a disproportionate burden of responsibility for society's use of competency tests is subject to debate. That they bear primary responsibility for defensible measurement practice within these programs is unquestionable. It is hoped that the measurement considerations discussed here will assist professionals in meeting these important responsibilities.

REFERENCES

Airasian, P., Pedulla, J., & Madaus, G. F. (1978). *Policy issues in minimal competency testing and a comparison of implementation models.* Boston, MA: Heuristics.

American Friends Service Committee. (1978). *A citizen's introduction to minimum competency testing programs for students.* Columbia, SC: Southeastern Public Education Program.

American Psychological Association. (1974). *Standards for educational and psychological tests.* Washington, DC: Author.

American Psychological Association, American Educational Research Association, National Council on Measurement in Education. (1985). *Standards for educational and psychological testing.* Washington, DC: Author.

Anderson v. Banks, 520 F. Supp. 472, 512 (S. D. Ga. 1981).

Anderson v. Banks, 540 F. Supp. 761 (S. D. Ga. 1982).

Andrew, B. J., & Hecht, J. T. (1976). A preliminary investigation of two procedures for setting examination standards. *Educational and Psychological Measurement, 36,* 45–50.

Angoff, W. H. (1971). Scales, norms, and equivalent scores. In R. L. Thorndike (Ed.), *Educational measurement* (2nd ed., pp. 508–600). Washington, DC: American Council on Education.

Baratz, J. C. (1980). Policy implications of minimum competency testing. In R. M. Jaeger & C. K. Tittle (Eds.), *Minimum competency achievement testing: Motives, models, measures, and consequences.* Berkeley, CA: McCutchan, 49–68.

Beard, J. G. (1979). Minimum competency testing: A proponent's view. *Educational Horizons, 58,* 9–13.

Behuniak, P., Jr., Archambault, F. X., & Gable, R. K. (1982). Angoff and Nedelsky standard setting procedures: Implications for the validity of proficiency score interpretation. *Educational and Psychological Measurement, 42,* 247–255.

Bergan, J. R., Cancelli, A. A., & Luiten, J. W. (1980). Mastery assessment with latent class and quasi-independence models representing homogeneous item domains. *Journal of Educational Statistics, 5,* 65–81.

Berk, R. A. (1976). Determination of optimal cutting scores in criterion-referenced measurement. *Journal of Experimental Education, 15,* 4–9.

Berk, R. A. (1980). A framework for methodological advances in criterion referenced testing. *Applied Psychological Measurement, 4,* 563–573.

Berk, R. A. (1984). *A guide to criterion-referenced test construction.* Baltimore, MD: Johns Hopkins University Press.

Berk, R. A. (1986). A consumer's guide to setting performance standards on criterion-referenced tests. *Review of Educational Research, 56,* 137–172.

Board of Education of the Northport–East Northport Union Free School District v. Ambach. (1981). Sup. Ct. NY, Albany County, Slip Opinion. Printed at 3 *Education of the Handicapped Law Report,* 552:282.

Board of Education of the Northport–East Northport Union Free School District v. Ambach, 458 N.Y.S. 2d 680 (A. D. 1982).

Boykoff, J. B., Rindone, D. A., & Prowda, P. (1981, April). *Will the "real" proficiency standard please stand up?* Paper presented at the meeting of the New England Educational Research Association, Lenox, MA.

Brookhart v. Illinois Board of Education, 534 F. Supp. 126 (C. D. Ill. 1982).

Brookhart v. Illinois Board of Education, 697 F. 2d 179 (7th Cir. 1983).

Broudy, H. S. (1980). Impact of minimum competency resting on curriculum. In R. M. Jaeger & C. K. Tittle (Eds.), *Minimum competency achievement testing: Motives, models, measures, and consequences* (pp. 108–117). Berkeley, CA: McCutchan.

Burton, E. F. (1979). Richard Lowell Edgeworth's education bill of 1799: A missing chapter in the history of Irish education. *Irish Journal of Education, 13,* 24–33.

Cannell, J. E. (1983). Denial of standard diploma to handicapped students. In T. N. Jones & D. P. Semler (Eds.), *School law update — 1982* (pp. 13–23). Topeka, KS: National Organization on Legal Problems of Education.

Citron, C. H. (1982). Competency testing: Emerging principles. *Educational Measurement: Issues and Practice, 1,* 10–11.

Citron, C. H. (1983a). Courts provide insight on content validity requirements. *Educational Measurement: Issues and Practice, 2,* 6–7.

Citron, C. H. (1983b). *Legal rules for student competency testing* (Issuegram No. 36). Denver, CO: Education Commission of the States.

Cohen, D., & Haney, W. (1980). Minimums, competency testing, and social policy. In R. M. Jaeger & C. K. Tittle (Eds.), *Minimum competency achievement testing: Motives, models, measures, and consequences* (pp. 5–22). Berkeley, CA: McCutchan.

Coleman, J. S., Campbell, E. Q., Hobson, C. J., McPartland, J., Mood, A. M., Weinfeld, F. D., & York, R. L. (1966). *Equality of educational opportunity.* Washington, DC: U. S. Government Printing Office.

Cronbach, L. J. (1971). Test validation. In R. L. Thorndike (Ed.), *Educational measurement* (2nd, ed.). Washington, DC: American Council on Education.

Cross, L. H., Impara, J. C., Frary, R. B., & Jaeger, R. M. (1984). A comparison of three methods for establishing minimum standards on the National Teacher Examinations. *Journal of Educational Measurement, 21,* 113–130.

Cureton, E. E. (1951). Validity. In E. F. Lindquist (Ed.), *Educational measurement.* Washington, DC: American Council on Education.

Dáil Éireann. (1941). Vote 45 - office for the Minister for Education. *Dáil Debates,* May 28, 1941, col. 1119, Dublin.

Debra P. v. Turlington, 474 F. Supp. 244 (M. D. Fla. 1979).

Debra P. v. Turlington, 633 F.2d 397 (5th Cir. 1981).

Debra P. v. Turlington. Case 78-792, Memorandum Opinion and Order (M. D. Fla., May 4, 1983).

Debra P. v. Turlington. Case 83-3326 (11th Cir. C. App., April 27, 1984).

Ebel, R. L. (1956). Obtaining and reporting evidence on content validity. *Educational and Psychological Measurement, 16,* 294–304.

Ebel, R. L. (1972). *Essentials of educational measurement.* Englewood Cliffs, NJ: Prentice-Hall.

Eckland, B. K. (1980). Sociodemographic implications of minimum competency testing. In R. M. Jaeger & C. K. Tittle (Eds.), *Minimum competency achievement testing: Motives, models, measures, and consequences* (pp. 124–135). Berkeley, CA: McCutchan.

Education Commission of the States. (1983). *Action for excellence* (Report of the Task Force on Education for Economic Growth). Denver: A. B. Itinschfeld Press.

Emrick, J. A. (1971). An evaluation model for mastery testing. *Journal of Educational Measurement, 8,* 321–326.

Fisher, T. H. (1983). Implementing an instructional validity study of the Florida High School Competency Test. *Educational Measurement: Issues and Practice, 2,* 8–9.

Fisher, T. H., & Smith, J. (1984). *Implementation of an instructional validity study in Florida.* Paper presented at the meeting of the American Educational Research Association, New Orleans.

Furst, E. J. (1958). *Constructing Evaluation Instruments.* New York: Longmans Green.

Gallagher, J. J. (1980). Setting educational standards for minimum competency: A case study. In R. M. Jaeger & C. K. Tittle (Eds.), *Minimum competency achievement testing: Motives, models, measures, and consequences,* (pp. 239–257). Berkeley, CA: McCutchan.

Glass, G. V (1978). Standards and criteria. *Journal of Educational Measurement, 15,* 237–261.

Gorth, W. P., & Perkins, M. R. (1979a). *A study of minimum competency testing programs* (Final program development resource document). Amherst, MA: National Evaluation Systems.

Gorth, W. P. & Perkins, M. R. (1979b). *A study of minimum competency testing programs* (Final typology report). Amherst, MA: National Evaluation Systems.

Greene, H., Jorgensen, A. & Gerberich, J. (1943). *Measurement and evaluation in the secondary school.* New York: Longmans Green.

Greene, H., Jorgensen, A., & Gerberich, J. (1954). *Measurement and evaluation in the secondary school* (2nd. ed.). New York: Longmans Green.

Guion, R. M. (1980). Content validity — the source of my discontent. *Applied Psychology, 11,* 385–398.

Halpin, G., Sigmon, G., & Halpin, G. (1983). Minimum competency standards set by three divergent groups of raters using three judgmental procedures: Implications for validity. *Educational and Psychological Measurement, 43,* 185–196.

Hambleton, R. K. (1980). Test score validity and standard-setting methods. In R. A. Berk (Ed.), *Criterion - referenced measurement: The state of the art.* (pp. 80–123). Baltimore, MD: Johns Hopkins University Press.

Hambleton, R. K., & Eignor, D. R. (1980). Competency test development, validation, and standard setting. In R. M. Jaeger & C. K. Tittle (Eds.), *Minimum competency achievement testing: Motives, models, measures, and consequences* (pp. 367–396). Berkeley, CA: McCutchan.

Harasym, P. H. (1981). A comparison of the Nedelsy and modified Angoff standard-setting procedure on evaluation outcome. *Educational and Psychological Measurement, 41,* 725–734.

Hardy, R. A. (1984). Measuring instructional validity: A report of an instructional validity study for the Alabama High School Graduation Examination. *Journal of Educational Measurement, 21,* 291–301.

Herron, M. D. (1980). Graduation requirements in the state of Oregon: A case study. In R. M. Jaeger & C. K. Tittle (Eds.), *Minimum competency achievement testing: Motives, models, measures, and consequences.* Berkeley, CA: McCutchan.

Jaeger, R. M. (1976). Measurement consequences of selected standard-setting models. *Florida Journal of Educational Research, 18,* 22–27.

Jaeger, R. M. (1978). *A proposal for setting a standard on the North Carolina high school competency test.* Paper presented at the meeting of the North Carolina Association for Research in Education, Chapel Hill, NC.

Jaeger, R. M. (1982). An iterative structured judgment process for establishing standards on competency tests: Theory and application. *Educational Evaluation and Policy Analysis, 4,* 461–476.

Jaeger, R. M., & Busch, J. C. (1984). *A validation and standard-setting study of the General Knowledge and Communication Skills Test of the National Teacher Examinations — final report.* Greensboro, NC: University of North Carolina at Greensboro, Center for Educational Research and Evaluation.

Jaeger, R. M., Cole, J., Irwin, D., & Pratto, D. (1980). *An iterative structured judgment process for setting passing scores on competency tests: Applied to the North Carolina high school competency tests in reading and mathematics.* Greensboro, NC: University of North Carolina at Greensboro, Center for Educational Research and Evaluation.

Knapp, T. R. (1977). The reliability of a dichotomous test item: A "correlation-less" approach. *Journal of Educational Measurement, 14,* 237–252.

Koffler, S. L. (1980). A comparison of approaches for setting proficiency standards. *Journal of Educational Measurement, 17,* 167–178.

Lee, J. M. (1936). *A guide to measurement in the secondary school.* New York: D. Appleton Century.

Linn, R. L., Madaus, G., & Pedulla, J. (1982). Minimum competency testing: Cautions on the state of the art. *American Journal of Education, 91,* 1–35.

Livingston, S. A., & Zieky, M. J. (1982). *Passing scores: A manual for setting standards of performance on educational and occupational tests.* Princeton, NJ: Educational Testing Service.

Livingston, S. A., & Zieky, M. J. (1983). *A comparative study of standard-setting methods* (Research Report No. 83-38). Princeton, NJ: Educational Testing Service.

Lowe, R. (1861). *Royal commission on the state of popular education in England.* Newcastle, England: Newcastle Commission.

Macready, G. B., & Dayton, C. M. (1977). The use of probabilistic models in the assessment of mastery. *Journal of Educational Statistics, 2,* 99–120.

Macready, G. B., & Dayton, C. M. (1980). The nature and use of state mastery models. *Applied Psychological Measurement, 4,* 493–516.

Madaus, G. F. (1981, October). *Minimum competency testing: A critical overview.* Paper presented at the Education Conference of the Educational Records Bureau, New York.

Madaus, G. F. (1983). Minimum competency testing for certification: The evolution and evaluation of test validity. In G. F. Madaus (Ed.), *The courts, validity, and minimum competency testing.* Hingham, MA: Kluwer-Nijhoff.

Madaus, G. F., & Airasian, P. (1978, May). *Measurement issues and consequences associated with minimum competency testing.* Paper presented at the National Consortium on Testing, New York.

Madaus, G. F., & Greaney, V. (1983). Competency testing: A case study of the Irish primary certificate examination. Unpublished manuscript.

McClung, M. S. (1978a). Are competency testing programs fair? Legal? *Phi Delta Kappan, 59,* 397–400.

McClung, M. S. (1978b). *Developing proficiency programs in California public schools: Some legal implications and a suggested implementation schedule.* Sacramento, CA: California State Department of Education.

McClung, M. S. (1979). Competency testing programs: Legal and educational issues. *Fordham Law Review, 47,* 652–712.

Melvin, L. D. (1983). Legal aspects of pupil evaluation. In T. N. Jones & D. P. Semler (Eds.), *School law update — 1982* (pp. 89–116). Topeka, KS: National Organization on Legal Problems of Education.

Meskauskas, J. A. (1976). Evaluation models for criterion-referenced testing: Views regarding mastery and standard-setting. *Review of Educational Research, 45,* 133–158.

Messick, S. (1975). The standard problem: Meaning and values in measurement and evaluation. *American Psychologist, 30,* 955–966.

Messick, S. (1981). Evidence and ethics in the evaluation of tests. *Educational Researcher, 10,*(9), 9–20.

Miller, B. S. (Ed.). (1978). *Minimum competency testing: A report of four regional conferences.* St. Louis: CEMREL.

Mills, C. N. (1983). A comparison of three methods of establishing cut-off scores on criterion-referenced tests. *Journal of Educational Measurement, 20,* 283–292.

National Academy of Education. (1978). *Improving educational achievement* (Report of the National Academy of Education Committee on Testing and Basic Skills to the Assistant Secretary for Education). Washington, DC: U.S. Government Printing Office.

National Commission on Excellence in Education (1983). *A nation at risk: The imperative for educational reform.* Washington, DC: U.S. Government Printing Office.

National School Boards Association. (1978). *Minimum competency* (Research report). Denver: Author.

Nedelsky, L. (1954). Absolute grading standards for objective tests. *Educational and Psychological Measurement, 14,* 3–19.

Noll, V. H. (1957). *Introduction to educational measurement.* Boston: Houghton Mifflin.

Odell, C. W. (1938). *Traditional examinations and new type tests.* New York: D. Appleton Century.

Oxford English Dictionary (1971). The Compact Edition. Oxford, England: Oxford University Press.

Peng, S., & Jaffe, J. (1978, September). *A study of highly able students who did not go to college* (Tech. Rep.). Research Triangle Park, NC: Research Triangle Institute.

Perrone, V. (1979). Competency testing: A social and historical perspective. *Educational Horizons, 58,* 3–8.

Pipho, C. (1984). *State activity: Minimum competency testing* (unpublished table). Denver, CO: Education Commission of the States.

Poggio, J. P., Glassnapp, D. R., & Eros, D. S. (1981, April). *An empirical investigation of the Angoff, Ebel, and Nedelsky standard-setting methods.* Paper presented at the meeting of the American Educational Research Association, Los Angeles.

Poggio, J. P., Glassnapp, D. R., & Eros, D. S. (1982, March). *An evaluation of contrasting-groups methods for setting standards.* Paper presented at the meeting of the American Educational Research Association, New York.

Popham, W. J., & Yalow, E. S. (1982). *Study design: Determining the instructional validity of the SSAT-II.* Culver City, CA: IOX Assessment Associates.

Pullin, D. (1982). *Minimum competency testing, the denied diploma and the pursuit of educational opportunity and educational adequacy* (CSE Report No. R-180). Los Angeles: University of California, Center for the Study of Evaluation.

Resnick, D. P. (1981–1982). Educational reform: Recent developments in secondary schooling. *Contemporary French Civilization, 6,* 133–151.

Resnick, L. B., & Resnick, D. P. (1982). *Standards, curriculum and performance: An historical and comparative perspective* (Report to the National Commission on Excellence in Education). (ERIC Document Reproduction Service No. ED 227 104).

Ross, C. C., & Stanley, J. C. (1954). *Measurement in today's schools* (3rd. ed.). New York: Prentice-Hall.

Roudabush, G. E. (1974, April). *Models for a beginning theory of criterion-referenced tests.* Paper presented at the meeting of the National Council on Measurement in Education, Chicago.

Ruch, G. M. (1929). *The objective or new type examination: An introduction to educational measurement.* Chicago: Scott, Foresman.

Sanders, J. C., Ryan, J. P., & Huynh, H. (1981). A comparison of two approaches to setting passing scores based on the Nedelsky procedure. *Applied Psychological Measurement, 5,* 209–217.

Schmidt, W. H., Porter, A. C., Schwille, J. R., Floden, R. E., & Freeman, D. J. (1983). Validity as a variable: Can the same certification test be valid for all students? In G. F. Madaus (Ed.), *The courts, validity, and minimum competency testing.* Hingham, MA: Kluwer, Nijhoff.

Schoon, C. G., Gullion, C. M., & Ferrara, P. (1979). Bayesian statistics, credentialing examinations, and the determination of passing points. *Evaluation and the Health Professions, 2,* 181–201.

Shepard, L. A. (1979). Setting standards. In M. A. Bunda & J. R. Sanders (Eds.), *Practices and problems in competency based instruction.* Washington, DC: National Council on Measurement in Education.

Shepard, L. A. (1980). Technical issues in minimum competency testing. In D. C. Berliner (Ed.), *Review of research in education: Vol. 8* (pp. 30–82). Washington, DC: American Educational Research Association.

Shepard, L. A. (1984). Setting performance standards. In R. A. Berk (Ed.), *A guide to criterion-referenced test construction* (pp. 169–198). Baltimore: Johns Hopkins University Press.

Skakun, E. N. & Kling, S. (1980). Comparability of methods for setting standards. *Journal of Educational Measurement, 17,* 229–235.

Stanley, J. C., & Hopkins, K. D. (1972). *Educational measurement and evaluation.* Englewood Cliffs, NJ: Prentice-Hall.

Sutherland, G. (1971). *Elementary education in the 19th century.* London: London Historical Association.

Sutherland, G. (1984). *Ability, merit and measurement.* Oxford: Clarendon Press.

Thorndike, R. L. (Ed.). (1971). *Education measurement* (2nd ed.). Washington, DC: American Council on Education.

Tyack, D. B. (1974). *The one best system.* Cambridge, MA: Harvard University Press.

Tyler, R. W. (1979). The minimal competency movement: Origin, implications, potential and dangers. *National Elementary Principal, 58,* 29–30.

U.S. Bureau of the Census. (1979). *Statistical abstract of the United States* (100th edition). Washington, DC: Author.

Wells v. Banks, 266 S. F. 2d 220 (GA. Ct. App. 1981).

Wigdor, A. K. & Garner, W. R. (Eds.). (1982). *Ability testing: Uses, consequences, and controversies: Part I. Report of the committee* Washington, DC: National Academy Press.

Wilcox, R. R. (1977a). New methods for studying equivalence. In C. W. Harris, A. P. Pearlman, & R. R. Wilcox (Eds.), *Achievement test items: Methods of study* (CSE Monograph Series in Evaluation No. 6, pp. 66–76). Los Angeles: Center for the Study of Evaluation.

Wilcox, R. R. (1977b). New method for studying stability. In C. W. Harris, A. P. Pearlman, & R. R. Wilcox (Eds.), *Achievement test items: Methods of study* (CSE Monograph Series in Evaluation No. 6, pp. 45–65). Los Angeles: Center for the Study of Evaluation.

Woody, C., & Sangren, P. V. (1933). *Administration of the testing program.* New York: World Book.

Wrightstone, W. J., Justmen, J., & Robbins, I. (1956). *Evaluation in modern education.* New York: American Book.

Yalow, E. S., & Popham, W. J. (1983). Content validity at the crossroads. *Educational Researcher, 12* (8), 10–14, 21.

Zieky, M. J., & Livingston, S. A. (1977). *Manual for setting standards on the basic skills assessment tests.* Princeton, NJ: Educational Testing Service.

15

Educational Admissions and Placement

Douglas R. Whitney
American Council on Education

Distinguishing clearly between educational admissions and educational-placement uses of test data is difficult because institutions often use data from the same tests for both types of decisions. However, because the aims, strategies, timing, and procedures differ, each merits separate consideration. For this discussion, these two uses of test data are distinguished as

Educational Admissions: Measurements contributing data to institutional decisions about whether, and on what basis, to admit students for study in an institution, college, or program

Educational Placement: Measurements contributing data to institutional and student decisions about course enrollment or credit for students already admitted for study

When considering these uses of test data, it is important to recognize that both types of decisions are far more complex than is often acknowledged. It is both simplistic and inaccurate to assume that most institutions use admissions-test scores to rank applicants and then admit those with the highest scores. In fact, when making admissions and placement decisions, institutional officials nearly always consider a number of relevant nontest measures such as prior grades and courses, expressed educational needs, and background characteristics. It is also incorrect to assume that most placement decisions are made by simply using an established cutoff score on some valid test to assign students to alternative courses such as "advanced" or "introductory." The institution is also usually concerned with the prior academic record and study goals of the

student. These, in turn, must be related to the institution's resources and requirements. Accordingly, simple analytical procedures often fail to assist institutions in developing appropriate policies. The complexities of the decisions and the elaborate statistical modeling that is required for thorough study and effective use of the data are discussed herein.

In this chapter, discussion is limited to undergraduate, graduate, and professional-education programs at postsecondary educational institutions. Because practices vary considerably, even among institutions of the same type, size, and location, the issues, procedures, and analytical techniques discussed here do not apply equally to all institutions.

Educational Admissions

Until about 1926, most colleges and universities used locally developed tests (usually essay tests) to evaluate their applicants' readiness to undertake and successfully complete collegiate study. Responding to the need for more efficient and standardized testing procedures, the College Entrance Examination Board introduced the battery now known as the Scholastic Aptitude Test. For the first time, officials at participating colleges were able to obtain comparable data for all applicants. Perhaps because many of the original College Board institutions were small private colleges of outstanding reputation with far more applicants than they could admit, the public perception of the admissions process evolved as one in which a small number of applicants earning high scores on the tests were selected for admission. The use of admissions-test data for

NOTE: The suggestions and comments by Franklin R. Evans, Richard L. Ferguson, Andrew G. Malizio, and Wayne M. Patience contributed significantly to the development of this chapter.

selection certainly continues, but it is only one use. Today, only a relatively small number of institutions use test scores to make selective admissions decisions (College Entrance Examination Board [CEEB], 1980b, p. 18).

Developments following World War II gave rise to a second major use of admissions-test data: evaluation of the readiness of large numbers of applicants with diverse educational experiences. The tests came to be used somewhat later to identify applicants who were at least minimally qualified to begin college work. More recently, admissions-test scores have been used in programs to recruit students.

In all these uses, admissions-test scores serve as a kind of "common metric" for expressing student ability or preparedness on a common scale. Whether used to select, evaluate, or recruit, admissions-test scores serve a number of roles and are interpreted in many ways.

Adjusting for Differences in Educational Programs

Because a relatively high proportion of today's high school graduates and college graduates go on to further study, admissions officials review transcripts from many schools and colleges whose educational programs are of varying quality, whose grading practices differ considerably, and whose institutional emphases are dissimilar. Admissions-test scores, in this context, present relevant student achievement data on a scale that is common across educational institutions.

Similarly, because high school and college graduation requirements are usually stated only in general terms, graduates often complete quite different programs of study, even within a single institution. In the evaluation of the effectiveness of each applicant's program of prior study, admissions-test results reflect the educational outcomes on a common scale across varying programs of study.

Admissions officials are not likely to be equally familiar with all applicants' high schools and colleges; they are likely to be familiar with only the major feeder schools for their institution and with schools having a national reputation. Thus, admissions-test results can facilitate accurate and equitable appraisal of students' academic abilities even when those students come from schools not well known to the admissions decision makers. The educational qualifications of adult applicants who have only recently completed high school programs or who completed them many years ago can be similarly evaluated. The experience after World War II, when thousands of veterans sought admission to universities and law schools, illustrates this use of admissions-test data.

Which use of admissions-test data is most important, at any time, depends upon the needs of the institutions. When the number of student applicants exceeds the openings available, test results are used to help institutions select and admit the students most likely to succeed. When institutional resources are underutilized, test results are used to help identify students with the potential for success. At any given time, some institutions and some programs are likely to be limiting enrollments, and other institutions and programs are going to be actively seeking students. For this reason, no broad generalizations can

be made about the uses of admissions-test data in postsecondary educational institutions.

The Educational Admissions Process

Institutional admissions procedures are diverse. A fairly recent survey documents the varying admissions procedures, policies, and data used in 1,463 American colleges and universities (CEEB, 1980b). Despite the diversity, however, there are some common characteristics of the admissions process, such as the facts that

1. Institutions generally consider admissions a faculty responsibility.
2. Broad guidelines are usually set by faculty action; specific policies are developed and implemented by an administrative staff.
3. Admissions policies are affected by enrollment limitations and shortfalls in projected applications.
4. Admissions decisions are shaped and constrained by institutional values, governing board policies, and public laws.

Within these commonalities, however, three distinct levels of admissions decisions are made within comprehensive universities and colleges.

GENERAL ADMISSIONS

At nearly every undergraduate institution, students apply for general admission. Institutions usually establish and publish a few minimum admissions criteria, which might include test scores. Most institutions also consider nontest data. The admissions decision-making process is generally assigned to an administrative office and conducted according to the pre-established and published criteria. At public institutions, admissions criteria can differ for resident and nonresident applicants. The most frequent criteria include test scores, high school or college grades, and rank in class. Some institutions also have a general admissions policy for admitting students to graduate study.

PROGRAM ADMISSIONS

For undergraduates, general admissions may not be sufficient for enrollment in some programs of study. Graduate programs nearly always involve program-level admissions decisions, and some bypass the general-admissions stage altogether. These program-level admissions processes, ordinarily conducted by departmental faculty, can occur at the time of initial enrollment or after some general study has been completed. Program-level decisions are usually based on course work successfully completed, in either high school or college, in conjunction with admissions-test data. For example, admission to teacher-training programs often requires some satisfactory college study.

PROFESSIONAL SCHOOL ADMISSIONS

Admission to study in a professional program (e.g., dentistry, law, medicine, nursing) is usually determined by the program faculty, rather than by institutional officials. Although minimum grades and test scores may be used, students who meet these criteria are usually not automatically admitted. Often there are far more applicants who meet the minimum criteria than can be accepted, so scores above the minimum might be required, and additional nontest data might be considered in making the final decisions.

At each admissions level, the decisions are often ongoing, and they differentiate (a) a group of applicants ("presumptive-admit") whose qualifications are so outstanding that they are immediately admitted; (b) a group ("presumptive-deny") whose qualifications are so clearly inadequate that they are immediately denied admission; and (c) a group ("hold") whose qualifications call for more detailed study before a decision can be made (Skager, 1982, pp. 290–291). To understand the ways in which test data are used in these admissions decisions, the reader must recognize that institutions have many admissions processes and that these processes involve the use of different data, are conducted at different levels within the institution, and usually involve decisions made on a more-or-less continuous basis throughout the year (Willingham & Breland, 1982), with the criteria for immediate acceptance and denial changing during the year. It should therefore be expected that test-score data are more valid for one level of the process, or for some schools or programs, than for others.

Selective Admissions

The process of admission to an institution, or a program of study, is often selective. One measure of selectivity is the ratio of applicants to openings for study in the institution or program. A program that annually receives 1,000 applications but can admit only 100 (10:1) is considered relatively selective in its admissions process. It has long been recognized that the degree of selectivity is an important consideration in evaluating the validity of test data in the admissions process (Taylor & Russell, 1939). Criterion-related validity evidence (e.g., correlations between test scores and postenrollment criteria) must be judged in light of the selection ratio. A predictive correlation supporting the use of the test data in one situation might be inadequate evidence in another. Further, any improvements in the predictive correlations resulting from adding other relevant predictors might be of greater significance in less selective situations than in highly selective situations (Whitney & Boyd, 1971).

Institutional decisions that lead to limiting enrollment (i.e., to greater selectivity) usually arise from resource limitations and institutional policies intended to maintain enrollment at desired levels. Some generalizations can be made about the relative degree of selectivity in the admissions processes.

1. Undergraduate admissions processes are usually more selective at 4-year institutions than at 2-year institutions.
2. Undergraduate admissions processes are usually more selective at private 4-year institutions than at public 4-year institutions.
3. Undergraduate-program admissions processes are usu-

ally more selective in programs with high student demand than in those with lower demand. Levels of program demand, however, can change quickly, because they often reflect current job markets.
4. Graduate admissions processes are usually more selective than undergraduate processes at the same institution.
5. Professional-education admissions processes are usually highly selective.

There are, however, many exceptions to these generalizations. Changing funding and enrollment patterns lead to frequent modifications in the selectivity of programs and institutions. Thus, analysis of the utility of test data in these decisions must be viewed as a very dynamic area of study. Local program-validity studies often become quickly outdated. In contrast, institutionwide study results tend to be relatively stable over periods of 3 or 4 years (Sawyer & Maxey, 1979). Additionally, changes in the criterion (e.g., college grades) can alter the predictive value of the test scores (Bejar & Blew, 1981).

The warnings of test specialists (American Psychological Association [APA], 1985, p. 54) and test publishers (e.g., American College Testing Program [ACT], 1979, p. 5) against relying exclusively on test results when making educational decisions could be at odds with the desire of admissions decision makers for "hard" criteria that can be used in highly selective processes. An extremely high ratio of applicants to openings for some institutions and educational programs, as well as the amount of time required to process applications, appears almost to dictate that decisions be made on test scores and grades alone, with little attention given to other possibly relevant applicant experiences or characteristics. Selective admissions processes are a major challenge for those who would attend to the pragmatic considerations of evaluating the qualifications of large numbers of applicants and attend to professional standards and guidelines for the use of test data in those processes.

Admissions Tests

At the undergraduate level, the tests most commonly used in making general admissions decisions are the Scholastic Aptitude Test and the American College Testing Program assessment (Skager, 1982). Although test use varies according to geographic location and type of institution, most 4-year institutions require or accept scores from one or both for use in the admissions process. They are less frequently used by 2-year colleges than by 4-year institutions. In addition to the test portions of the batteries, both include extensive questionnaires completed by the examinees. These questionnaires collect biographical information, self-identified educational needs and experiences, choice of career and major field information, and other data elements. Information from these tests, along with high school grade and rank data, are used in many institutional admissions processes. Summary descriptive statistics for admitted students are also sometimes published, as an aid in the choice of an appropriate college (CEEB, 1984b). Both testing programs offer participating institutions a variety of local validity study services.

At the graduate level, the Graduate Record Examination is often required for admission to institutions or graduate programs. The Miller Analogies Test is also occasionally used for this purpose. The GRE includes an examinee questionnaire and an optional set of achievement tests that are sometimes required by graduate admissions programs. For graduate study in business, the Graduate Management Admission Test is frequently used to admit students.

The larger professional-education programs have developed specialized test batteries for their use. These include the Medical College Admission Test and the Law School Admission Test. Each is unique in its makeup, though used for similar purposes by the respective professional-education programs. These testing programs also gather nontest data that are used in admissions and placement decisions. For example, the Law School Data Assembly Service develops local prediction equations using Law School Admission Test scores and undergraduate grade point averages.

Selecting Statistical Models for Admissions Studies

Many institutional validity studies employ statistical models to evaluate local admissions processes. Although such studies are recommended, it should be recognized that the choice of a statistical model has a pronounced effect on the nature of the evaluation that emerges from the study. Because admissions processes are rather complex and data are often numerous and diverse, the danger lies in choosing a model that does not reflect the key variables in the decision process. A review of the research in this area identifies two simple statistical models that have been used regularly; unfortunately, few examples of models that fully address the complexity of the processes can be found. In the choice of an appropriate statistical model, a number of factors must be considered, some of which are discussed next.

NATURE OF AVAILABLE DATA

In most admissions processes, scores are available from a test administered especially for that purpose. In addition, however, prior grades, class rank, or both are also commonly available. Many validity studies use only these data. In actual practice, admissions decisions might also involve data on the student's program of study (courses or classes taken), geographic location, race, gender, age, and life experiences. Unless these are modeled, the statistical procedures can yield unrepresentative or misleading results (Linn, 1973; Linn & Hastings, 1984). If special educational support services are available to high-risk students, participation in these services should also be included in the model, or data for these students should be analyzed separately (Abrams & Jernigan, 1984). In addition, most admissions programs make extensive use of nontest data (Willingham & Breland, 1982, pp. 58–61). These data, too, should be used in the statistical model, if useful study results are to be obtained.

Because criterion data are not available for persons who were not admitted, and because admissions decisions for the study group usually involve test scores, high school perform-

ance data, or both, results are usually affected by restriction in range on the predictor variables. Accordingly, whether the restriction occurs as a result of implicit or explicit selection, the resulting predictor–criterion correlations tend to underestimate the actual validities (Gulliksen, 1950).

Though often overlooked by institutional researchers, the choice of the criteria to be used in predictive validity studies is a critical one. This is particularly true at the graduate and professional levels, as noted by Hartnett and Willingham (1979). Criterion reliability, intrinsic validity, and restrictions in range often limit the usefulness of institutional validity studies and can result in severe understatement or distortion of the criterion-related validities of test scores and other predictive data. Studies using multiple criteria are strongly recommended.

ENROLLMENT LIMITATIONS

For a few admissions processes, a clear enrollment limitation, or quota, exists. In these instances, only a certain number of applicants can be accepted for study. In other instances, the practical limitations on enrollment are unlikely to be reached. Still others have only a general range within which the number of students accepted can fall. Any limits on enrollment should be built into the statistical model employed. The statistical models should include explicit attention to the selection ratio (e.g., as suggested by Thomas, Owen, & Gunst, 1977).

Fixed-quota models can be quite simple, inasmuch as they require only that the applicants be ranked from high to low on a composite of the predictor measures. The highest ranked applicants are then admitted. This simple model implies that all data for all applicants is available at the same time. As noted later, this might not be a realistic assumption.

Quota-free models, on the other hand, involve choosing a threshold ability level on the composite scale and admitting all applicants whose scores exceed this level. In these situations, the major research interest lies in setting the threshold level(s). Considerable attention has been given since the mid 1970s to the issues involved in such decisions (e.g., Burton, 1978; Glass, 1978) and to the methods that can be used to arrive at a defensible threshold standard (e.g., Livingston & Zieky, 1982; Petersen, 1976).

DATA AVAILABILITY

Because the admissions process often continues on a year-round basis, with institutional officials eager to reach valid decisions upon receipt of each applicant's papers, it might be impossible to simply rank applicants according to some criterion for the cohort class. Instead, rank in a prior group of applicants is often used. Most validity studies assume that the results from a prior applicant group can and will be used with current applicants. Major program changes, of course, could quickly render such data inapplicable. To fully reflect the dynamism of many admissions processes, the statistical model should allow for sequential decision making; no admissions studies using a sequential model were located.

PREFERENCES AND LIMITATIONS

Although it may appear to be a purely objective process to the public, an educational admissions process involves sets of values held by the institution or program, the applicants, and society. Some of these act as constraints in the process; others serve as forces that influence the procedures and data used in the process. In addition, for public institutions, laws and administrative regulations often play a major role in the process.

Most admissions processes involve certain institutional and program goals and preferences (e.g., a desired mix of resident and nonresident students or a preference for the former; a desired mix of geographical origins; a desired increase in the number of minorities or women admitted). Adequate statistical modeling requires the use of rather complex models that account for policy preferences and limitations. At a minimum, the model should allow for analyses at a subgroup level, as well as for the entire applicant pool (APA, 1985, p. 17; see, for example, Goldman & Widawski, 1976). If subgroup quotas exist either as limitations or goals, these should be reflected in the model (e.g., Lunneborg, 1982). Because of the need to conduct analyses at the subgroup level, problems arise, due to small sample sizes and, consequently, unreliable predictive results. The recent works of Linn and Dunbar (1986) and Novick, Jackson, Thayer, and Cole (1972) describe ways in which generalizations can be made across "similar" admissions situations and suggest that interinstitutional studies offer promise in this area. Some of these preferences and limitations involve the facts that

1. Selective institutions and programs generally want to admit those applicants with the best potential for success; less selective ones want to admit all students with a reasonable chance of success.
2. Applicants want to be admitted to the school or program of their choice. They want to succeed at the school and also want their application to be judged by fair methods.
3. Society desires that a high proportion of the citizenry participate in postsecondary education. Education is seen as a primary means of upward mobility, and there is a desire for equal opportunity throughout education. Education is further seen as a means of assuring national security (broadly defined) and as a societal economic asset ("investment in America's future"). More recently, a desire has emerged to screen out applicants lacking the requisite skills as a means of improving the perceived quality of education.
4. Governing boards often desire a geographical mix of students and encourage preference for relatives of alumni.
5. For public institutions, legislative actions have resulted in preference or guaranteed admissions for in-state residents and routing of certain students to 2-year and 4-year colleges.
6. Public policy decisions have established a variety of affirmative action programs.

Because of these many influences, constraints, and limitations on the admissions processes, it is probably impossible to literally quantify all relevant variables in the statistical modeling. At the very least, one should develop a statistical model for *each* subgroup of applicants, a model that involves the major variables of interest (e.g., Hogrebe, Ervin, Dwinell, & Newman, 1983).

COMMON STATISTICAL MODELS

The most common statistical model used in studying the admissions process is multiple regression. Frequently, this model is applied to the pre-enrollment data (admissions-test scores, high school grade or rank data, student subgroup, and other relevant data) and uses first-semester or first-year college grades as the criterion. Occasionally, a dichotomous measure of college success (e.g., Did the student earn a *C* average?) is used as the criterion. Other studies have used graduation (or not) as the criterion measure. In studies using a dichotomous criterion, methodological modifications such as those described by Dagenais (1984) and Kolen and Whitney (1978) are recommended.

Another common statistical model employs multiple cutoffs on several pre-enrollment measures including test scores and uses college grades or graduation as the criterion. These models less frequently appear in the research literature, although they represent decision-making strategies commonly used in the admissions process.

Institutional Validity Studies

Most admissions-testing programs offer a set of standard validity study services to participating institutions and programs. These studies generally require institutional officials to identify the test-taking applicants who were enrolled and to provide local grade data. Using these data, publishers prepare expectancy tables, prediction equations, and other information for use by the schools. Because this service is convenient, the number of local admissions validity studies each year is large — more than a thousand at the undergraduate level alone. Many institutional research offices conduct similar studies. Some of these studies involve the development of prediction equations and estimation of regression coefficients; more, however, aim to update expectancy tables used in admissions decisions and to examine existing admissions data in relation to various college study criteria.

Except for those appearing in *College and University* and in the Validity Studies section of *Educational and Psychological Measurement,* few institutional study results are published; most are reported only locally. However, testing organizations often summarize results from local studies, as an aid in interpreting the validity of the admissions uses of their tests (ACT, 1973; Breland, 1979). More recently, Linn (1982) has summarized the available institutional studies of the predictive and differential validity of admissions tests. Certain problems arise, however, in conducting and interpreting such studies, such as in the

1. Selection of appropriate criteria (Should they include first-semester or first-year grades? Grades for specific courses?)
2. Presence of explicit selection in the predictor measures (where test scores and grades or both were used in admitting the study group) and criterion data for enrolled students (where failing students are often not included because they do not complete the term)

3. Presence of implicit selection in the predictor and criterion measures (due to self-selection and counseling)
4. Definition of appropriate student subgroups for analysis
5. Limitations due to missing or sparse data, particularly for subgroup analyses

Use of Test Data in Admissions Decisions

Despite the many difficulties and complexities cited, it is still possible to offer some generalizations and recommendations about the use of test results in admissions decisions and about the conduct of local validity studies. Interested readers should also consider the relevant recommendations of the Committee on Ability Testing (Wigdor & Garner, 1982, pp. 201–202).

GENERALIZATIONS

1. At the undergraduate level for general-admissions purposes, both prior academic record (e.g., high school grades) and admissions-test scores are useful in predicting college grades, with neither consistently better than the other. The combination of scores and prior grades yields more accurate predictions of college grades than does either alone.
2. At the professional-education level, perhaps because of high applicant–openings ratios and extreme degrees of self-selection, test scores are often better predictors than grades. A composite, however, is still preferred.

RECOMMENDATIONS

1. Institutions and programs should not use test scores alone for admissions decisions unless local, group-specific, validity studies provide overwhelming evidence to support the practice.
2. Institutions and programs should conduct validity studies to develop differential predictive equations by race, sex, age, or other relevant student characteristics. Predictive accuracy is usually improved for all applicants, although the use of differential prediction equations for admissions decisions might not be adopted. The aim here is to develop a better understanding of the relevance, or lack of it, that test scores and other data have for each subgroup.
3. Institutions should try to develop systematic ways of obtaining and using nontest data in admissions decision making (e.g., Willingham & Breland, 1982).
4. Validity studies should reflect the utilities involved if the results are to be used in future admissions decisions (see Hills, 1971).
5. Institutional validity studies should be conducted at least every other year; program-level studies should be conducted at least every 2 or 3 years, with data pooled to obtain adequate sample sizes. When possible, common data elements should be used in the periodic studies, and interinstitutional studies should be conducted (e.g., Dallam, Sjoblum, & Wielenga, 1984).

Additional Uses of Admissions Test Data

In addition to their use in admissions decision making, test results are often used to identify students for remedial classes or tutoring, to award scholarships and assistantships, to counsel students about course choices, and to plan and manage institutional needs. The validities of the test data for each of these additional uses must be demonstrated. This might require significant additions to the institution's validity study plan. The many uses of admissions-test data cited do not imply that the test scores will prove adequate for these uses.

Issues in the Use of Admissions Tests

There are a number of significant issues related to the development and use of admissions tests that must be addressed when evaluating their usefulness. Attention has been given to most, but clear satisfactory solutions and resolutions have not yet been reached.

TEST AND SELECTION BIAS

The recent attention given to the analysis of test-item data for possible differential difficulty levels (bias) has resulted in a number of methodological advances (e.g., Berk, 1982). Testing organizations have reported increased efforts to remove stereotyping and biased content from their tests at the development stage (AMEG Commission on Sex Bias in Measurement, 1977; Educational Testing Service [ETS], 1980). However, the degree to which subjective reviews can anticipate differential response patterns (Shepard, 1981) remains to be settled. The larger issues of whether the analytical procedures simply identify outcomes of different or differentially effective educational programs (Pallas & Alexander, 1983) and whether the bias identified in the analytical studies of admissions tests is also present in the criterion measures (e.g., faculty tests and grades) have not yet been thoroughly addressed.

Bias due to the choice and application of selection methods remains a serious problem in educational admissions, although infrequently the focus of public attention. Some much needed clarification was achieved in a special issue of the *Journal of Educational Measurement* (Jaeger, 1976), but the selection models described by the various authors are not yet widely used in institutional validity studies.

TEST DISCLOSURE LEGISLATION

The 1979 New York legislation (S. B. 5200-A and subsequent amendments to Article 7-A of the New York Education Law) requiring most admissions-testing programs to make available copies of their tests shortly after use has resulted in a number of publications containing copies of recent tests (e.g., CEEB, 1983). The legislation has clearly increased the public's access to accurate examples of admissions-test content. The major aims of the legislation, however, were to insure that the tests were developed in a sound manner and to assist students in seeing that their tests were graded accurately and fairly. To date, only a few highly publicized item ambiguities have been noted (e.g., Wainer, Wadkins, & Rogers, 1984). The early results (Greer, 1983, pp. 60–61) suggest that relatively few students have taken advantage of the opportunity to check their test results.

An unintended effect of the legislation has been to encourage admissions-testing programs to develop new ways of scaling new test forms, because prior forms were no longer secure and available for use in random group equating procedures (Marco, 1981). The large number of recent studies involving item response theory applied to test scaling and equating problems can be attributed, in part, to this legislation.

Although many other test-disclosure bills have been introduced, few have been passed by the state legislatures, and none has had an effect comparable to that of the New York law. It remains to be seen whether additional legislation will significantly affect educational testing methodology.

COACHING

Whether or not admissions-test performance can be significantly improved as a result of short-term instruction (coaching) has for some time been a concern of researchers. Claims of large gains by publishers of commercial test-preparation programs have been countered by studies reporting much smaller gains. Although it has become clear that some gains are to be expected from short-term instruction (Messick, 1980), this issue remains clouded by differences in terminology and differences in the interests of the researchers involved. The magnitude of the gains clearly depends on the nature of the instruction, as well as on the characteristics of the students (Cole, 1982; Sesnowitz, Bernhardt, & Knain, 1982). More research is needed; the simplistic formulation of the original question (Does coaching significantly improve test performance?) and initial answers are inadequate. Additional meta-analysis studies of particular components of short-term instruction (e.g., Kulik, Kulik, & Bangert, 1984), will assist in clarifying the effectiveness of specific short-term instructional activities.

ADMISSIONS AS "GATEKEEPER"

Because admission to professional-education programs in law, medicine, and other areas involves the use of admissions-test data and because graduation from such programs is often required for subsequent certification to practice, it has been suggested that educational admissions tests serve indirectly to limit practice opportunities (Nairn & Associates, 1980, chap. 6). Increasing attention is being given to licensing tests, and the focus of certification test content appears to be moving away from the educational setting and toward the relevant-practice settings (e.g., California Department of Consumer Affairs, 1983). Significant changes have also been made in the Medical College Admission Test and the Law School Admission Test since the mid 1970s. It has not been clearly established, however, that admissions tests do (or did) represent an unfair obstacle to professional practice. Clearly, economic rewards are gained by those who are permitted to practice these professions; here, the role of admissions tests is not yet clearly understood. Additional research is needed, but useful research must include consideration of the broad social issues as well as the narrower psychometric issues.

ATHLETES AND ADMISSIONS TESTS

At various times, admissions-test results have been used by the postsecondary institutions affiliated with the National Collegiate Athletic Association (NCAA) to determine student athletes' eligibility for scholarships. Beginning in 1966, admissions-test scores and high school grades were used in prediction equations for these athletes. From these, a predicted college grade average of 1.60 was required to be eligible for a scholarship (NCAA, 1971). This requirement was abolished in 1973, but recent NCAA actions (Zingg, 1983) have reintroduced test scores into the arena. Much of the concern about using test scores in this way arises from validity issues. The use of test scores is said to enable schools to award scholarships to only those athletes with a reasonable chance of succeeding in the college they will attend. Initial studies, however, demonstrate that a high proportion of athletes now competing would have been denied a scholarship if admissions-test scores had been used as now embodied in NCAA rule 48 (*Study of freshman eligibility standards,* 1984). Such a rule would be expected to differentially affect white and black athletes. Concern is also expressed about the quality of the academic program for many athletes who might complete their eligibility with course work that does not represent a significant, coherent, college-level program. Test-scores requirements might also address this concern. We can expect to hear much more on this issue; detailed institutional and inter-institutional validity studies appear likely to shed some much needed light on the issues involved in this use of admissions-test data.

Educational Placement

Educational-placement tests have been used for many years to help assign new students to the courses best suiting their educational skills and experiences. Placement testing and advising is generally intended to let well-qualified students bypass redundant courses and begin their study in areas and at levels representing new knowledge and skills for them. In this sense, placement testing is clearly related to the goals of equitable and efficient course planning. Willingham (1974) provides a very thorough description of educational-placement models and strategies. Aleamoni (1979) recommends and illustrates a series of activities used in developing and validating placement policies.

We usually think of educational placement as involving student enrollment in one of several courses existing in some hierarchical sequence. Optimal placement results when students begin with the courses for which all important prior learning outcomes have been satisfied and few important course outcomes have been mastered. Foreign language and mathematics courses are two of the areas of study in which a hierarchy is at least arguably present. Where no clear hierarchy exists among a set of courses, the goal of the placement process becomes muddled, with the optimal placement for each student more likely to be a matter of student interest, faculty priorities, and available course options.

One common variant in educational placement is the credit-by-examination program (CEEB, 1980a). The placement goal is modified because the credit-by-examination program aims to identify those courses or areas of study for which the student has already achieved a satisfactory level of proficiency in the designated competencies. Academic credit is ordinarily awarded upon successful completion of the examination, whether or not any advanced courses are to be taken. Many institutions conduct local studies related to their credit-by-examination programs (Druesne, 1982).

Relationship of Placement Testing to Admissions Testing

One might expect that admissions-test data would be quite useful in placement decisions. For example, low admissions-test scores might suggest placement into remedial courses; high admissions-test scores might suggest advanced placement, credit by examination, or both. Although it is often the case that admissions data are used to help identify students for placement testing, admissions-test data are not often used alone for such decisions. Test data from the ACT or SAT tests are often used for undergraduate placement decisions in only a few areas of study (e.g., for initial sectioning placements in the English or mathematics sequences). These test batteries also include "needs" and "experiences" sections, in part to facilitate the use of test results in placement.

Placement testing is generally conducted by the educational institutions after admission; admissions tests are usually administered by the test publisher and are taken prior to acceptance. There is much greater dependence on locally developed tests for educational placement than for admissions. Exceptions include the College Board Advanced Placement tests and national credit-by-examination test series such as the College-Level Examination Program, the American College Testing Proficiency Examination Program, and the military's Defense Activity for Non-Traditional Education Support Subject Standardized Tests programs (Cangialosi, 1981). Local curriculum reform and revision more often lead to placement test revision, revalidation, or both than to changes in the institution's admissions tests.

The Educational Placement Process

Unlike the undergraduate admissions process, which is often under the aegis of a central administrative office, the educational placement process frequently occurs at the departmental level. Students might first be identified for placement testing during the admissions process by high admissions-test scores, advanced high school courses, or extensive related work experience. Institutional practices vary, but many colleges include placement testing as part of a pre-enrollment orientation program for new students. Placement testing, in such cases, occurs prior to the students' first registration.

Placement testing occurs chiefly at the undergraduate level for most institutions. Placement programs are usually limited to introductory sequences in foreign languages, English, and mathematics. Credit-by-examination programs, in contrast, often apply to a wider variety of introductory courses. Advanced placement is generally not available for upper level undergraduate classes or in a student's major field. Unlike admissions programs, however, placement programs seldom restrict the number of students who can qualify for advanced placement or credit by examination.

Constraints and Values in the Educational Placement Process

Placement programs are shaped by institutional values; these values serve to expand or contract students' opportunities. For example, many faculty believe that class participation is uniquely valuable over and above course content. They judge that policies that prevent poorly prepared students from obtaining undeserved advanced placement or credit are needed; relatively little concern is shown for deserving students who might be denied advanced placement or credit (that is, in their view, false passes are far worse than false fails). Accordingly, placement test cut-scores are often set relatively high. For a similar reason, faculty may limit the total number of academic credits that can be earned by testing, to insure that credentials are based on significant in-class experience. Too, some faculty might fear the loss of enrollment in first-level courses if extensive placement and credit-by-examination testing occurs.

Students' values, in contrast, tend to favor expanded placement and credit-by-examination testing options. For example, students generally want to bypass unneeded or redundant courses, to shorten their time to graduation, and to reduce their tuition expenses. For that reason, they judge false fails to be worse than false passes; they would prefer relatively low placement-test cut-scores. A few students may, however, wish to improve their grade averages by taking courses for which they have already mastered most of the content and, so, are not interested in credit or advanced placement opportunities.

Governing boards and legislatures wishing to reduce or limit expenditures for undergraduate postsecondary education sometimes establish placement and credit-by-examination programs as a means to this end. In addition, there is probably general public support for the idea that students should be permitted and encouraged to progress as rapidly as possible to graduation. Together, these forces act to expand placement-testing opportunities. The nature of these forces, however, is often not clear. One set of policies or laws, for example, might constrain the placement process by withholding credit-by-examination awards until students have completed one semester at the institution; another might expand opportunities by requiring all new students to be tested, so that all who need help can be identified and assigned to needed remedial courses.

Validation and Standard Setting in Educational Placement

It is nearly universally acknowledged that faculty are responsible for participating in the content validation of educational-placement tests. Because local courses and sequences must be suitably articulated with any placement tests, this faculty role is clearly established for these programs. Even for the credit-by-examination programs, the faculty generally identify those external tests for which credit should be awarded.

Faculty often set score requirements for tests used in placement decisions and credit-by-examination awards. As a general rule, standards for the cut-scores used in placement and credit-by-examination programs should be based on the demonstrated achievement of local or national student groups tested near the completion of appropriate courses. Even for external tests, the performance of local students on the tests is often obtained, to set appropriate cut-scores (e.g., Appenzellar & Kelley, 1982). Such studies usually result in the estimation of correlations between course grades and test scores; these correlations generally range from .30 to .70 (CEEB, 1984a). Correlations near 0 suggest that the correspondence between course and test content is insufficient to recommend that the test be used in the institution's placement or credit-by-examination program. Local standard-setting studies often result in ambiguous results requiring that a considerable degree of judgment be used in setting standards. Although not often treated explicitly in the setting of standards, *utility* is clearly involved in these processes.

Recommendations for institutional standards have been developed by the American Council on Education for most tests used in credit-by-examination programs (Whitney & Malizio, 1987), although such recommendations are not available for most placement tests. The Council's recommended standards are set by panels of college and university faculty specially constituted to review the tests. These recommendations are then often used as the basis of local standards, at least until local standard-setting administrations can be arranged.

Issues in Placement Testing

Except for foreign languages and mathematics (and possibly English), few hierarchical course sequences exist in our colleges. The traditional placement goals apply, therefore, to only a relatively few areas of study. In other areas, the placement process focuses on whether a student has acquired sufficient knowledge to be "passed out" of a number of introductory courses, and a series of tests resembling comprehensive final examinations for a course is often used for placement decisions. It is difficult to validly place a student into a course sequence with a single test. Rather, the process might involve a rather extensive committment of student time to testing, particularly for the exceptionally well-prepared student. The absence of strong standardized tests for this purpose, perhaps because of the lack of standardized course definitions, means that local tests are often the only resource available. Many local placement tests are quite sound, but many others are probably not, because the resources needed to establish a quality comprehensive placement program are missing. Even the most active university testing offices can complete only a few local standard-setting and validation studies in a given year. Few inter-institutional studies have been completed, despite the considerable value of combining data and resources in this manner.

Publishers of tests used in credit-by-examination programs usually obtain normative data for groups of students completing college courses whose content is similar to that of the tests. It is sometimes difficult to identify appropriate courses and even more difficult to obtain institutional and faculty participation in such norming studies. Unless sound normative data are available, the standard-setting procedures have to rely more extensively on judgmental approaches than is desirable. It would appear to be in the best interests of institutions to participate in such studies, but many decline the opportunity, perhaps because of the need to persuade faculty to commit class time for this purpose.

The Future of Admissions and Placement Testing

Changes in admissions and placement testing can be expected to arise from three distinct advances: in measurement practices, in computers and associated technology, and in public policy decisions. The likely effects of each are discussed next.

Measurement Practices

Recent advances in measurement practices could well benefit admissions and placement tests in a number of ways. For example, identifying and removing possible biasing effects in test items could result in slightly improved admissions tests and, accordingly, tests more useful for evaluating the potential of minority students for undergraduate, graduate, and professional study. The possibilities seem limited here, however, because few studies have found significant numbers of admissions-test items with differential item difficulty levels.

Recent attention to the direct measurement of writing ability and advances in scoring methodology (Womer, 1984) might lead to improved admissions and placement tests, if it results in writing samples being added to the tests now constituted exclusively of multiple-choice items. Essays have long been used, on an optional basis, in the College Level Examination Program and the Proficiency Examination Program series. The existence of the essay option, whether or not it actually adds to the validity of the tests, certainly can be expected to reduce faculty resistance to the use of these tests. In fact, a number of states have recently added writing requirements to their high school graduation requirements (Williams, 1984); colleges can be expected to urge that such sections be added to admissions tests.

Recent advances in item response theory are already being used in admissions-test equating and pre-equating, although usefulness could be limited because of the multi-dimensional nature of many of the batteries and tests. Item response theory, as currently understood, will probably have little impact on placement testing (other than as part of an adaptive testing scheme, as noted later) and none on credit-by-examination testing, because of the nature of these tests. Advances in these areas would require a significant extension of the test theory and completion of studies that apply the extended theory to the kinds of content-based tests normally used in these programs.

Greater attention to the relationship between curriculum and test content will improve the usefulness of credit-by-examination tests. Extensive efforts are now being made to obtain a more thorough and representative sampling of course content across institutions. Similar local efforts would improve placement tests, but there does not appear to be a clear institutional commitment to this goal.

Computers and Associated Technology

Computers have rapidly been introduced into many aspects of our lives, so it is not surprising that the availability of affordable computers will have an effect on admissions and placement testing. Computer-administered testing, whether adaptive or sequential, might have a greater effect on local placement testing than on national tests in the admissions and placement areas. Although not publicized at this writing, there are, no doubt, local projects of this sort under way today; some will no doubt receive widespread attention in the future. As some institutions have moved to require their entering students to purchase or lease personal computers, a campuswide computer-administered placement-testing system seems one of the natural applications of this technology. Work on computerized adaptive testing holds significant promise of improving placement-testing procedures, because it can permit a significant reduction in testing time, when compared with pencil-and-paper tests. Unfortunately, however, the financial and technical resources required to develop, test, and validate the adaptive systems appear beyond the levels most institutions would be willing or able to devote to improving their placement-testing program. Perhaps in the next decade a farsighted test publisher will step in to link the adaptive technology with locally identified course outcomes. At least one testing organization is making initial efforts in this direction (Ballas, 1983).

Public Policy Decisions

Public policy discussions and changes can also be expected to affect institutional testing programs. For example, recent public policies aimed at holding institutions more clearly accountable for demonstration or documentation of the educational competencies of their graduates might result in short-term increases in admissions-test-score requirements (Bennett, Miller, Schwartz, & Whitney, 1984). In the longer run, however, this public attention can be expected to result in a significant increase in the number of institutions and systems that introduce institutional graduation and advancement testing requirements. Such tests, upward extensions of current high school certification examinations, will need to be clearly articulated with institutional placement and admissions-testing efforts.

REFERENCES

Abrams, H. G., & Jernigan, L. P. (1984). Academic support services and the success of high-risk college students. *American Educational Research Journal, 21*, 261–274.

Aleamoni, L. M. (1979). *Methods of implementing college placement and exemption programs.* New York: College Entrance Examination Board.

AMEG Commission on Sex Bias in Measurement. (1977). A case history of change: A review of responses to the challenge of sex bias in career interest inventories. *Measurement and Evaluation in Guidance, 10*, 148–152.

American College Testing Program. (1973). *Assessing students on the way to college: Technical report for the ACT assessment program: Vol. 1.* Iowa City, IA: Author.

American College Testing Program. (1979). *Statement of policies.* Iowa City, IA: Author.

American Psychological Association. (1985). *Standards for educational and psychological testing.* Washington, DC: Author.

Appenzellar, A. B., & Kelley, H. P. (1982). *Re-evaluation of decision scores used in course placement and credit by examination in Spanish at U.T. Austin: The Spanish validity study of 1981* (Report No. RB-82-4). Austin, TX: University of Texas Austin. (ERIC Document Reproduction Service No. ED 228 269).

Ballas, M. S. (Ed.). (1983). Entry-level placement test in the works. *ETS Developments,* (Autumn), 1, 3.

Bejar, I. I., & Blew, E. O. (1981). Grade inflation and the validity of the Scholastic Aptitude Test. *American Educational Research Journal, 18*, 143–156.

Bennett, J., Miller, J., Schwartz, J., & Whitney, D. (1984). Academic progression tests for undergraduates: Recent developments. *Educational Record, 65*(1), 44–48.

Berk, R. A. (Ed.). (1982). *Handbook of methods for detecting item bias.* Baltimore: Johns Hopkins University Press.

Breland, H. M. (1979). *Population validity and college entrance measures* (Research Monograph No. 8). New York: College Entrance Examination Board.

Burton, N. W. (1978). Societal standards. *Journal of Educational Measurement, 15*, 263–271.

California Department of Consumer Affairs. (1983, December). *What a licensing board member needs to know about testing.* Sacramento, CA: Author.

Cangialosi, J. (1981). Credit-granting practices for extrainstitutional learning in postsecondary education institutions: Report of a survey. *College and University, 57*, 39–60.

Cole, N. S. (1982). The implications of coaching for ability testing. In A. K. Wigdor & W. R. Garner (Eds.), *Ability testing: Uses, consequences, and controversies: Part II* (pp. 389–414). Washington, DC: National Academy Press.

College Entrance Examination Board. (1980a). *Credit by examination comes of age.* New York: Author.

College Entrance Examination Board. (1980b). *Undergraduate admissions: The realities of institutional policies, practices, and procedures.* New York: Author.

College Entrance Examination Board. (1983). *10 SATs.* New York: Author.

College Entrance Examination Board. (1984a). *CLEP technical manual.* New York: Author.

College Entrance Examination Board. (1984b). *The college handbook 1984–85* (22nd ed.). New York: Author.

Dagenais, D. L. (1984). The use of a probit model for the validation of selection procedures. *Educational and Psychological Measurement, 44*, 629–645.

Dallam, J. W., Sjoblum, J. V., & Wielenga, J. L. (1984). Persistence at the regents' universities of Iowa: A summary of four studies covering twenty years. *College and University, 60*, 5–20.

Druesne, B. (1982). *What 200 studies reveal about CLEP.* New York: College Entrance Examination Board.

Educational Testing Service. (1980). *An approach for identifying and minimizing bias in standardized tests: A set of guidelines.* Princeton, NJ: Author.

Glass, G. V. (1978). Standards and criteria. *Journal of Educational Measurement, 15*, 237–261.

Goldman, R. D., & Widawski, M. H. (1976). An analysis of types of errors in the selection of minority college students. *Journal of Educational Measurement, 13*, 185–200.

Greer, D. G. (1983). *"Truth-in-testing legislation": An analysis of political and legal consequences, and prospects* (Monograph 83-6). Houston, TX: University of Houston, Institute for Higher Education Law and Governance.

Gulliksen, H. (1950). *Theory of mental tests.* New York: John Wiley & Sons.

Hartnett, R. T., & Willingham, W. W. (1979). *The criterion problem: What measure of success in graduate education?* (GRE Board Research Report No. 77-AR). Princeton, NJ: Educational Testing Service.

Hills, J. R. (1971). Use of measurement in selection and placement. In R. L. Thorndike (Ed.), *Educational Measurement* (2nd ed., pp. 680–732). Washington, DC: American Council on Education.

Hogrebe, M. C., Ervin, L., Dwinell, P. L., & Newman, I. (1983). The moderating effects of gender and race in predicting the academic performance of college developmental students. *Educational and Psychological Measurement, 43*, 523–530.

Jaeger, R. M. (Ed.). (1976). On bias in selection. *Journal of Educational Measurement, 13*(1).

Kolen, M. J., & Whitney, D. R. (1978). Methods of smoothing double-entry expectancy tables applied to the prediction of success in college. *Journal of Educational Measurement, 15*, 201–211.

Kulik, J. A., Kulik, C. C., & Bangert, R. L. (1984). Effects of practice on aptitude and achievement test scores. *American Educational Research Journal, 21*, 435–447.

Linn, R. L. (1973). Fair test use in selection. *Review of Educational Research, 43*, 139–161.

Linn, R. L. (1982). Ability testing: Individual differences, prediction, and differential prediction. In A. K. Wigdor & W. R. Garner (Eds.), *Ability testing: Uses, consequences, and controversies: Part II* (pp. 335–388). Washington, DC: National Academy Press.

Linn, R. L., & Dunbar, S. B. (1986). Validity generalization and predictive bias. In R. A. Berk (Ed.), *Performance assessment: Methods and applications*. Baltimore: Johns Hopkins University Press, pp. 203–236.

Linn, R. L., & Hastings, C. N. (1984). Group differentiated prediction. *Applied Psychological Measurement, 8*, 165–172.

Livingston, S. A., & Zieky, M. J. (1982). *Passing scores: A manual for setting standards of performance on educational and occupational tests*. Princeton, NJ: Educational Testing Service.

Lunneborg, C. E. (1982). Testing in college admissions: An alternative to the traditional predictive model. *Educational Evaluation and Policy Analysis, 4*, 495–501.

Marco, G. L. (1981). Equating tests in an era of test disclosure. In B. F. Green (Ed.), *Issues in testing: Coaching, disclosure, and ethnic bias* (pp. 105–122). San Francisco: Jossey-Bass.

Messick, S. (1980). *The effectiveness of coaching for the SAT: Review and reanalysis of research from the fifties to the FTC*. Princeton, NJ: Educational Testing Service.

Nairn, A., & Associates. (1980). *The reign of ETS: The corporation that makes up minds*. Washington, DC: Ralph Nader.

National Collegiate Athletic Association. (1971). *Procedure manual for implementation of the 1.600 rule* (6th ed.). Kansas City, MO: Author.

Novick, M. R., Jackson, P. H., Thayer, D. T., & Cole, N. S. (1972). Estimating regressions in M-groups: A cross-validation study. *British Journal of Mathematical and Statistical Psychology, 25*, 33–50.

Pallas, A. M., & Alexander, K. L. (1983). Sex differences in quantitative SAT performance: New evidence on the differential coursework hypothesis. *American Educational Research Journal, 20*, 165–182.

Petersen, N. S. (1976). An expected utility model for "optimal" selection. *Journal of Educational Statistics, 1*, 333–358.

Sawyer, R., & Maxey, J. (1979). The validity of college grade prediction equations over time. *Journal of Educational Measurement, 16*, 279–284.

Sesnowitz, M., Bernhardt, K. L., & Knain, D. M. (1982). An analysis of the impact of commercial test preparation courses on SAT scores. *American Educational Research Journal, 19*, 429–441.

Shepard, L. A. (1981). Identifying bias in test items. In B. F. Green (Ed.), *Issues in testing: Coaching, disclosure, and ethnic bias* (pp. 79–104). San Francisco: Jossey-Bass.

Skager, R. (1982). On the use and importance of tests of ability in admission to postsecondary education. In A. K. Wigdor & W. R. Garner (Eds.), *Ability testing: Uses, consequences, and controversies Part II* (pp. 286–314). Washington, DC: National Academy Press.

Study of freshman eligibility standards. (1984, August). Reston, VA: Advanced Technology, Inc., Social Sciences Division.

Taylor, H. C., & Russell, J. T., Jr. (1939). The relationship of validity coefficients to the practical effectiveness of tests in selection. *Journal of Applied Psychology, 23*, 565–578.

Thomas, J. G., Owen, D. B., & Gunst, R. F. (1977). Improving the use of educational tests as selection tools. *Journal of Educational Statistics, 2*, 55–77.

Wainer, H., Wadkins, J. R. J., & Rogers, A. Was there one distractor too many? *Journal of Educational Statistics, 9*, 5–24.

Whitney, D. R., & Boyd, N. W. (1971). Limiting effect of predictive validity on the expected accuracy of admissions decisions. *College and University, 46*, 180–190.

Whitney, D. R., & Malizio, A. G. (Eds.). (1987). *Guide to educational credit by examination*. (2nd ed.) Washington, DC: American Council on Education/Macmillan.

Wigdor, A. K., & Garner, W. R. (Eds.). (1982). *Ability testing: Uses, consequences, and controversies: Part I. Report of the committee*. Washington, DC: National Academy Press.

Williams, P. L. (1984, April). *Direct writing assessment: The state of the states*. Paper presented at the meeting of the National Council on Measurement in Education, New Orleans.

Willingham, W. W. (1974). *College placement and exemption*. New York: College Entrance Examination Board.

Willingham, W. W., & Breland, H. M. (1982). *Personal qualities and college admissions*. New York: College Entrance Examination Board.

Womer, F. B. (Ed.). (1984). Writing assessment [Special issue]. *Educational Measurement: Issues and Practice, 3*(1).

Zingg, P. J. (1983). No simple solution: Proposition 48 and the possibilities of reform. *Educational Record, 64*(3), 6–12.

16

Counseling

Lenore W. Harmon

University of Illinois at Urbana-Champaign

The purpose of this chapter is to discuss and illustrate some measurement applications to counseling and issues related to such applications. It is impossible to discuss counseling without discussing educational measurement. They are inextricably linked by history and by the definition of counseling.

History

In discussing the history of counseling psychology, Whiteley (1984) lists five major formative influences in the early period from 1908 to 1950. Three of them involve the relationship between counseling and measurement. The first was the vocational guidance movement, which began with the work of Frank Parsons (1909). Because of the diversity of choices available to young people entering a labor market that was changing rapidly as a result of the industrial revolution, Parsons identified a need to help assess individual aptitudes and interests in relation to the requirements of available jobs. Thus a need for assessment techniques was recognized very early in the 20th century.

This need was addressed by a second formative influence on counseling psychology, the psychometric movement and the study of individual differences that it made possible. For readers of this book, it is probably not necessary to trace the history of mental measurement from Binet (Binet & Henri, 1895), who worked on measuring intelligence on an individual basis, through the 1920s and 1930s, when a number of psychologists learned to measure a great variety of psychological traits on both an individual and a group basis. It is important to note that the application of psychometric procedures and the study of individual differences to human problems was hastened by certain world events.

Indeed, the third of the early formative influences mentioned by Whiteley that is relevant to the relationship between counseling and testing is the effect of "social and economic forces and developments in society" (p. 8). Some of the earliest uses of the new measurement techniques were in the service of individuals and groups of individuals who had been uprooted from their normal lives by social and economic forces over which they had no control (the two world wars and the Great Depression). Another use of the new measurement techniques was in the service of those facing unprecedented educational and vocational opportunity (secondary education early in the century and the GI Bill after World War II). When these applications were made, they were made by psychologists, and, by the mid-1940s, these psychologists had come to call themselves *counselors*. They worked in educational institutions and in Veterans Administration hospitals, using measurement techniques to assess the intellectual, emotional, and attitudinal readiness of their clients to make various educational, vocational, and personal decisions and adjustments.

Definitions of Counseling

Many definitions of counseling have been proposed, and it has been difficult to obtain professional consensus over the years (Whiteley, 1980). A recent collaborative attempt to characterize counseling psychology by a committee of members of the Division of Counseling Psychology of the American Psychological Association includes a fairly broad definition.

> Counseling psychology is a specialty whose practitioners help people improve psychological well-being, resolve crises, and increase ability to solve problems and make decisions. . . . Counseling psychologists conduct research, apply interventions, and evaluate services in order to stimulate personal and group development and to prevent and remedy developmental, educational, social, and/or vocational problems. (Fretz, 1984, p. 38)

Although it is clear that the functions of the counselor have expanded considerably since the profession was founded on

527

the bases of the guidance movement, the measurement movement, and social needs, the authors of the definition cited refer to "assessment, evaluation, and diagnosis" as one of the services provided by counseling psychologists. Procedures used in performing these services

> may include but are not limited to, behavioral observation, interviewing, and administering and interpreting instruments for the assessment of educational achievement, academic skills, aptitudes, interests, cognitive abilities, attitudes, emotions, motivations, psychoneurological status, personality characteristics, or any other aspects of human experience and behavior that may contribute to understanding and helping the user. (American Psychological Association [APA], 1981)

Thus, although not all counselors currently specialize in dealing with problems that lead them to use measurement techniques for assessment, evaluation, and diagnosis, these techniques are seen as services commonly offered by counselors. In fact, it is expertise in measurement techniques that sets the counselor off from the social worker on the one hand and the psychiatrist on the other.

The types of clients typically seen by counselors also serve to define counseling to some extent. In general, counselors see relatively normal clients with normal developmental problems that are not so severe as to be totally debilitating. This is important because it places the counselor in the role of collaborator with the client in a process of exploration and change most often initiated by the client. Sometimes preventive programming is initiated by counselors working in educational and agency settings. When measurement techniques are used under these circumstances, the results are often of considerable interest and use to the clients, as well as to the counselor. For purposes of this chapter, it is important to note that counselors define themselves as professionals who sometimes use measurement techniques to help their clients resolve problems and make decisions.

Applications of Measurement in Counseling

Counselors use techniques of assessment based on measurement principles when they help clients explore educational plans, career plans, life plans, and their personal development. They also use measurement techniques to implement their own research and theory building. These topics will be discussed in detail here. In addition, counselors use measurement techniques when they engage in formal assessments of clients that will be used by schools and agencies to make decisions about the clients and when they serve as consultants on admissions and administrative matters. Because these topics are covered elsewhere in this book and do not represent the situation, unique to counseling, in which the individual client defines the problem to be addressed and makes direct personal use of the results obtained from measurement procedures, they will not be discussed here.

Educational Planning

Counselors are often asked to help individuals decide whether they should pursue specific educational goals. These goals can be broad, such as obtaining a college degree or technical training, or quite narrow, such as whether they should enroll in the more or the less difficult course in a certain subject. In either case the decision to be made has important implications for the individual. It could well influence what further educational doors are opened or closed and contribute to the development of the self-concept of the individual as academically successful or unsuccessful.

In contemplating any educational plan of action, there are two questions that must be answered before one can arrive at a decision as to whether the proposed plan is feasible. The first is whether the individual has the appropriate background knowledge and skills to begin the program. The second is whether the individual has the ability to complete the program. Evidence bearing on the first question can be gathered by obtaining scores on appropriate achievement tests, whether they be normed or criterion referenced. Evidence bearing on the second question can be gathered by obtaining scores on appropriate aptitude tests, providing there are some available that have been validated against the criterion of success in the type of educational program being contemplated. Unfortunately, achievement tests measuring exactly the type of background knowledge necessary for a specific educational course are not always available, and there are those who believe they do not contribute much beyond what is already available from intelligence tests or tests of academic aptitude. Some reviewers of the Sequential Tests of Educational Progress (Rosenbach, 1978; Schutz, 1978), one of the best of the achievement batteries, note this problem although not all reviewers of the battery agree that it is a problem (Floden, 1985). Because the evidence bearing on the questions of readiness to undertake some educational course of action and ability to complete it can be highly correlated, the counselor must select measures carefully, as will be discussed later.

It might appear that, if appropriate and well-developed tests are available, the decision facing the individual could be easily made. However, there are two circumstances under which the task of the counselor is quite difficult and only one under which it is quite uncomplicated. If the results of testing support the proposed plan and the individual is not considering any alternatives, a rather happy conclusion can be reached relatively simply. Unfortunately this is rarely the case. Often testing suggests that an individual has only a marginal chance of succeeding in the educational plan she or he is considering, and the counselor has the task of communicating what is essentially bad news. This must be done in a way that is not damaging to the individual's feelings of general competence and control. Expectancy tables relating the probability of success in an educational program to scores on predictive measures are often ideal for this purpose, because they illustrate the face that the probability of success is rarely 0, no matter how low one's scores on the predictor. Figure 16.1 is an example of a fictitious expectancy table in which scores on a fictitious academic aptitude test, the Harmon Academic Aptitude Inventory, are related to grades at a specific college, the College of Hard Knocks.

Note from this figure that the College of Hard Knocks seems to enroll the majority (2/3) of its students from among those scoring between the 51st and the 80th percentiles on national norms for college-bound students. Students scoring

FIGURE 16.1 Chances in 100 of Receiving Various Grade Point Averages at the College of Hard Knocks based on Various Percentile Scores on Harmon's Academic Aptitude Inventory.[a]

PERCENTILE ON HAAI[c]	GPA[b]			
	0–.99	1.00–1.99	2.00–2.99	3.00–4.00
91–100 (200)[d]	3	2	5	90
81–90 (800)	4	1	25	70
71–80 (1500)	10	20	30	40
61–70 (1500)	15	15	40	30
51–60 (1000)	22	23	47	8
41–50 (500)	25	30	40	5
31–40 (300)	35	33	30	2
0–30 (200)	54	25	20	1

[a] Based on 6,000 freshmen at College of Hard Knocks, 1975–1985 1st year grades.
[b] Based on a 4-point scale.
[c] Percentiles based on a nationally representative sample of college-bound high school seniors, N = 15,000.
[d] N in the percentile range.

between the 51st and the 60th percentiles have a .53 probability of obtaining an average of C or better and only a .08 probability of obtaining a B average or better, whereas those scoring between the 61st and the 80th percentiles have a .70 probability of obtaining a C average or better and a .40 probability of obtaining a B average or better. Note also that a few individuals scoring in the highest percentile category did not obtain a C average (probability = .05), whereas some people scoring in the lowest percentile category did obtain a C average or better (probability = .21). It is clear that such expectancy tables must be specific to the education program undertaken. They require some time and effort to develop. However, they are useful counseling tools because they leave the question of whether the client might be one of those who will succeed despite the predictions open for further discussion and ultimately one for the client to decide. Whether a given client can or will put in the time and effort required to make up a skills deficiency, for instance, depends on the unique personality, ability, and socioeconomic circumstances of that client.

At other times the results of testing undertaken to gather evidence for educational planning and decision making present the client with too much good news. The client appears to have so many possibilities for success that they are confusing. Then the counselor must help the client explore the long-range implications of each decision and consider how it relates to the individual's values and personal style. The uses of measurement in exploring these issues will be discussed in subsequent sections. With the type of client who has too many options, it is important for the counselor to attempt to help that individual organize these options into a manageable number of categories and to assess what steps can be taken to keep the maximum number of educational doors open. It is often possible to take initial steps that lead toward two different educational outcomes of the same general type (for instance, taking biology and physics, which can contribute to premedical or predental studies). It is even possible to take initial educational steps that allow for different educational outcomes of different types in some cases. For instance, taking calculus does not preclude eventually majoring in history, but not taking cal-

culus precludes majoring in mathematics or computer science.

Thus, counseling for educational planning and decision making often rests on a foundation of appropriate measurement techniques but must usually go beyond the results of their use to help clients make sound educational decisions. In a broader perspective, the relationship of these educational decisions to career planning must also be considered.

Career Planning

Measurement techniques can be useful in several ways to the counselor and the client engaged in a discussion of career planning. They can be used to assess the readiness of the client for various career planning activities and to assess the barriers to individual career planning and choice, as well as in the more traditional assessment of interests, needs, and values.

READINESS AND BARRIERS

Developmental theories of vocational behavior hold that the individual goes through a series of stages, each associated with appropriate developmental tasks (Ginzberg, Ginsburg, Axelrad, & Herma, 1951; Levinson, Darrow, Klein, Levinson, & McKee, 1978; Super, 1957). There is an implication, not explicit in all theories of this type, that the stages are hierarchical, that is, that it is necessary to go through the lower stages to reach the higher ones. Validation of hierarchical developmental theories presents some problems that have not been totally resolved (Nesselroade & Baltes, 1979), and the empirical evidence for hierarchical stages in career development is not impressive. Nevertheless, the idea that people go through a series of stages that build on each other in their career development over the life span is so intuitively appealing that it has been accepted by most career counselors.

A number of measures of vocational maturity have been developed (Crites, 1978; Super, Thompson, Lindeman, Jordaan, & Myers, 1981; Westbrook & Mastie, 1974), although none of them covers the complete life span. Although they can be used in counseling to get a general idea of the degree of vocational maturity possessed by an individual client in comparison with an appropriate norm group, it is not possible to assess the stage of career development of an individual or exactly what developmental tasks have been accomplished by that person. It is possible to make some assumptions about the stages of development and tasks accomplished by the norm group on the basis of the age, grade, or employment status of its members in conjunction with theoretical expectations. These considerations make it possible to use measures of career maturity to make rather gross determinations about whether an individual client is similar to others of the same age or grade in vocational maturity. Smith (1976, 1983) holds that these measures are not appropriate for many minority group members. When sex differences in career maturity are found, they usually favor women, but the documented behavior of women in the labor force, where they take low-paying jobs in a limited number of fields (U.S. Department of Labor, 1980), makes this finding enigmatic.

Super (1980) points out that there are many important decision points within the general process of career development. He even suggests that there is considerable similarity between the concepts of career maturity and career decision making. Some counselors (Harren; 1979, Heppner & Petersen, 1982) suggest that a knowledge of the client's decision-making or problem-solving style and skills is important in the counseling process, and they have developed measures for assessing aspects of the decision-making process. For instance, Harren postulates three decision-making styles: the rational, the intuitive, and the dependent. He seems to believe that the rational decider is best equipped to make career decisions, whereas the dependent decider is the most poorly equipped to make career decisions. Subsequent research has suggested that decision-making style might interact with the style of intervention used in career decision making to produce different outcomes. Rubinton (1980) found that rational decision makers increased their career maturity most when exposed to a career decision-making course utilizing a rational systematic program, whereas intuitive decision makers increased their career maturity most when exposed to a career decision-making course utilizing fantasy and attention to feelings. This study used Harren's measure to assess decision-making styles. The author concludes that knowledge of decision-making styles was potentially helpful in planning counseling interventions. At any rate, exploration of decision-making skills and styles of clients is a promising application of measurement to counseling for career planning.

Inability to make vocational decisions among clients who are in appropriate life- and career-development stages to make such decisions has been of long-standing concern to counselors. Salomone (1982) reviews the history of this concern and suggests that there are probably two continua involved. One is decided–undecided, and the other is decisive–indecisive. The undecided client might have a number of reasons for being undecided, but they generally involve not being ready to make a choice at a given time or in a given situation. The indecisive client has not made a choice because of a significant level of anxiety and self-doubt. Salomone characterizes indecisiveness as an "emotional-psychological issue" and reserves the label for adults past the age of 25. His discussion highlights the fact that a counselor would probably treat an undecided client quite differently from an indecisive one.

Some attempts have been made to measure career decidedness in students (Hartman & Hartman, 1982; Holland & Holland, 1977; Osipow, Carney, Winer, Yanico, & Koschier, 1976). Understanding the reasons for a particular client's problem with vocational decision making would aid the counselor considerably in planning the process of counseling with that individual. Slaney, Palko-Nonemaker, and Alexander (1981) explored two measures of career indecision (Holland & Holland, 1977; Osipow et al., 1976). Both measures differentiated between decided and undecided students, but the factor structure of the two measures differed. Osipow, Carney, and Barak (1976) found a factor structure for the Career Decision Scale that seemed to suggest a factor associated with choice anxiety, a factor associated with external barriers to choice, and a factor associated with approach–approach conflict among several attractive alternatives, but Slaney, Palko-Nonemaker, and Alexander found a somewhat different factor structure. As useful as it might be to counselors to score the inventory for these factors, Osipow (1980) recommends against it because of the lack of stability of the factor structure.

As in the case of the concept of career maturity, the measurement of vocational indecision lacks some of the sophistication and differentiation that the practicing counselor could use. Nevertheless this is an area of much current attention. Evidence that supports the use and valid interpretation of either existing measures or new measures should be forthcoming.

In 1979, Engen, Lamb, and Prediger (1982) surveyed secondary schools and found that 93% of them used career guidance tests or inventories and that 73% of them tested 90%–100% of the students in at least one class with such instruments. This study underscores the fact that inventories of vocational interests or aptitudes are greatly used in our society. For the most part, schools responding to that study reported using traditional paper-and-pencil inventories, reporting scores normed on some identified group of students or employed adults. However, Zytowski and Borgen (1983) list among the newest developments in vocational assessment the use of such assessment devices as the Self-Directed Search (Holland, 1985, 1987) and the Occupational Orientation Inventory (Hall, 1976) as intervention strategies. The client's responses are scored idiographically in both cases, not normatively, and the results are used to generate exploratory behavior on the part of the client.

For instance, the Self-Directed Search helps the test taker generate a three-letter Holland Code, which can be used to enter the *Occupations Finder* (Holland, 1986) to explore occupations compatible with the Holland Code or the *College Majors Finder* (Rosen, Holmberg, & Holland, 1987). The code is based on six occupational types defined by Holland (1985): the realistic, the investigative, the artistic, the social, the enterprising, and the conventional. Empirical evidence shows that these types can be arranged in a hexagon so that adjacent types are more closely related than distant types. See Holland, 1985, pp. 94–97, for a discussion of the accumulated evidence for the hexagonal structure since it was first proposed by Holland, Whitney, Cole, and Richards in 1969. Figure 16.2 shows this hexagonal arrangement. The correlations represent the relationships between pairs of types "for a 10% sample of 1,234 out of 12,345 male two year college students in 65 colleges. A sample of 796 out of 7,968 females in the same colleges produced similar results" (Holland et al., 1969, p. 16). Using it, a client who has a code of ACI, with artistic, conventional, and investigative interests predominating, in that order, understands why there are no occupations utilizing the artistic and conventional codes as the top two interests listed in the Occupations Finder. Artistic and conventional interests, the latter of which include clerical and office tasks, rarely come together in an occupation. The individual has to assess the relative strengths of his or her artistic and conventional interests, as well as the realities of the labor market, to find an occupation. The Self-Directed Search, used with the Occupations Finder, might help such an individual explore occupations that correspond to all possible combinations of A with I or C with I. The type of validity information appropriate for measurement techniques designed as interventions to increase career exploration will be discussed later in this chapter.

Another form of vocational assessment that may be seen as an intervention is the vocational interest or values inventory contained in a computerized system of career guidance such as

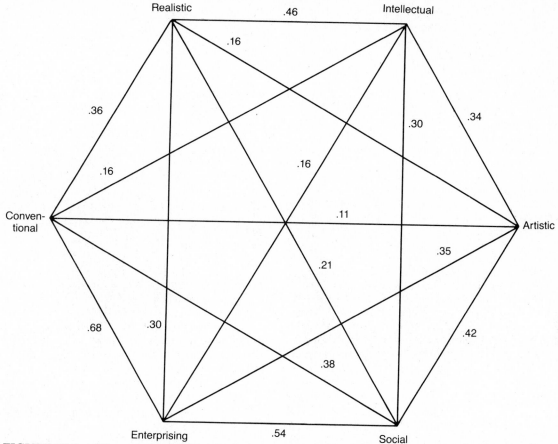

FIGURE 16.2 A Hexagonal Model for Interpreting Interclass Relationships. Copyright © The American College Testing Program. All rights reserved. Reprinted with permission.

SIGI (Katz, 1980) or DISCOVER (Harris-Bowlsbey, Rayman, & Bryson, 1976). Katz and Shatkin (1983) point out that such systems can help a client articulate what her or his self-perceptions are and assess the potential of various occupations for providing satisfaction. Harris-Bowlsbey (1983) points out that they can teach decision-making concepts and concepts about the world of work. Figure 16.3 shows a printout from the DISCOVER system illustrating how the computer can be used to encourage exploration in a career area. It is evident that the measurement of interests, values, and needs is increasingly being incorporated into the larger scheme of career decision making.

Life Planning

Some writers (Super, 1980; Tittle, 1981) have indicated that career planning is only one important segment of a larger process called *life planning* that includes consideration of how the roles one plays over the life span interface with one another. For instance, how do the roles of worker, spouse, and parent relate to one another for individuals and for members of the same family? Although the earliest discussion of these issues focused on the home–career conflict of women (Harmon, 1970; Hoyt & Kennedy, 1958; Rand, 1968) or the work–nonwork conflict of men (Dubin & Goldman, 1972), recent discussions have focused on intraindividual allocations of time and resources to various roles, regardless of the sex of the indi-

vidual (Super, 1980), and on the interaction of these roles in family systems (Bernard, 1981; Richardson, 1981). Measurement techniques to assess the strength of various values and motivations relevant to life planning have begun to appear.

The simplest of these are measures of commitment to work such as those of Eyde (1968) and Greenhaus (1971, 1973). They are important because they rest on the assumption that commitment to work is not to be taken for granted and recognize that some individuals have competing values. For instance, Greenhaus includes one item for which respondents ranked family, career, religion, leisure, local community activity, and national political activity, as well as a set of items that formed a factor he calls the "relative priority" of work. Career salience was demonstrated to be positively related to the degree of congruence between the self-concept and traits perceived as necessary for success in a chosen occupation for males (Greenhaus, 1971). However, this finding was not related to the relative priority factor but to the factor called "general attitudes toward work." More recent measures have targeted work and family roles for special attention (Coombs, 1979; Spence & Helmreich, 1978; Super & Culha, 1976). Perhaps the most sophisticated approach to measuring the importance of various life roles for individuals is reported by Super and Nevill (1984). They used the Salience Inventory (Super & Nevill, 1985) to measure participation, commitment, and values expectation for the roles of student, worker, citizen, homemaker, and leisurite. Super & Neville found that their measure of com-

FIGURE 16.3 A Screen from Discover for Minicomputers.

ANOTHER WAY TO LOOK AT YOUR INTEREST SCORES

YOU HAVE LEARNED THAT YOUR PRIMARY INTEREST RELATES
TO OCCUPATIONS THAT REQUIRE WORKING WITH IDEAS.

SO FAR YOU HAVE LEARNED HOW YOUR INTERESTS RELATE TO
WORK TASKS AND REGIONS IN THE WORK WORLD. IT IS ALSO
POSSIBLE TO RELATE YOUR INTERESTS TO SIX CLUSTERS OF
OCCUPATIONS.

THEN YOUR LEVEL OF INTEREST IN EACH OF THESE CLUSTERS
CAN BE COMPARED TO THAT OF A NATIONAL NORM GROUP.
THE GRAPH ON THE NEXT DISPLAY SHOWS YOU HOW YOUR
INTERESTS COMPARE WITH THOSE OF MORE THAN A MILLION
STUDENTS WHO TOOK THE INTEREST INVENTORY LAST YEAR.
YOU MAY WANT TO PRINT THE NEXT DISPLAY AND DISCUSS IT
WITH YOUR COUNSELOR.

mitment to work was related to career maturity and predicted
scores on a career-planning measure, a decision-making measure, and a measure of knowledge of the world of work. The
scale for commitment to homemaking contributed less to predicting such career maturity components and was significantly
related to sex of high school students. More evidence of validity
is needed.

Measures of this type show great promise for counseling
individuals about life planning. Unfortunately, most of these
measures are unpublished and of limited availability for use in
counseling. They have all been used only in research.

Personal Development

It is not unusual for the problem that brings the client to
counseling to be related directly or indirectly to the personal
characteristics of the individual. Either these characteristics
interact with a decision to be made (e.g., does this person have,
or can he or she develop, the ego strength necessary to implement and gain satisfaction from a very risky or nontraditional
career choice?) or forms part of the problem to be solved (e.g.,
what can the person do about his or her shyness?). Assessment
can be helpful to the counselor in understanding clients and to
clients in understanding themselves. The nature of the clients'
problems should dictate whether client characteristics should
be measured in an ipsative or normative format and whether a
comprehensive inventory of personality traits should be used
in preference to an inventory of one or two traits. Comprehensive inventories are usually well developed and researched, but
they might not measure the exact concept or concepts the
counselor would like to assess in a given therapeutic situation
and nearly always measure more than either client or counselor is interested in knowing in relation to specific counseling
problems. On the other hand, measures of specific concepts
such as anxiety level, self-concept, and coping skills are more
likely to be experimental in nature and infrequently used in
counseling applications.

As in the measurement of interests or values, the measurement of the personal characteristics of individuals for counsel-

ing purposes can rest on the assumption that what is being
measured is a set of relatively fixed traits with which the individual must live from now on. This historical viewpoint has
been challenged by those who view the human experience as a
process of influencing and creating the future (Tyler, 1978). In
assessing the personal characteristics of an individual client, it
is important to keep in mind the delicate and illusive balance
between what is present and what is possible, what is developed
and what is undeveloped. Two approaches have utilized the
concept of change in ways that could be useful in counseling.
The first is the measurement of developmental stage. The second is the measurement of readiness for change.

The personal characteristics of individuals at various stages
of development have most often and most fruitfully been explored in relationship to some specific aspect of development.
Thus, cognitive development (Knefelkamp & Slepitza, 1976;
Perry, 1970; Piaget, 1954), ego development (Loevinger,
1976), identity development (Marcia & Friedman, 1970), and
moral development (Kohlberg, 1981) have all been measured
for research purposes. Assessing the stage of development of an
individual in each of these areas can clearly be relevant to some
of the concerns that bring clients to counseling. An individual
with low levels of cognitive development, ego development,
and moral development would certainly be a poor candidate
for making any important decision except commitment to personal growth. Most of the developmental measures are tied to
particular theories that suggest the conditions under which
growth can occur. Unfortunately, the measures themselves are
often unwieldy and subjectively scored, rendering them of little
use to counselors, who could surely use manageable and well-
developed measures of development stages of various types.

Because there are never enough counselors to see all the
clients who would like help even under expanding economic
conditions, counselors and other psychologists have attempted
to use measurement techniques to assess who is most likely to
continue in counseling or to change in a positive direction as a
result of counseling. Measures used include the Minnesota
Multiphasic Personality Inventory (Hathaway & McKinley,
1967) and various anxiety, depression, and ego strength scales.
Garfield (1978) notes that the results of such efforts are mixed
and attributes the blurred picture to problems in defining populations, treatments, and outcomes uniformly. Earlier, Garfield (1971) suggests that attempts to predict which clients
would continue and profit from psychotherapy are not very
useful unless they are situation specific.

It seems clear that the measures of personal or affective
characteristics that would be of most use to counselors have yet
to be developed in a form that would serve them well. In addition, there is a realm of counselor judgment involved in assessing whether an individual is still developing or can develop
further that is very important in utilizing measures of personal
characteristics, even those with ideal psychometric and theoretical characteristics.

Research and Theory Building

It should be apparent from the foregoing that psychologists
and counselors have made considerable use of psychological

measurements in operationalizing theoretical constructs that describe clients. Most of the examples cited do not have the impact on practice that counselors would like them to have. The picture is not all bleak, however. For example, two theories of vocational behavior have been of considerable use to counselors because they attempt to define individuals and vocational environments in comparable terms and to provide measures of both people and environments. They are the theory developed by John Holland (1973, 1985) and the Work Adjustment Theory developed by Lofquist and Dawis (1969; Dawis & Lofquist, 1984). The measures associated with these theories are published and available for counseling use. Another theorist who has been successful at developing and publishing some of the measures associated with his theory is Donald Super (Super, 1970; Super et al., 1981). It is interesting to note that Super's theory (1957) emphasizes development more than those of Holland or Lofquist and Dawis. He postulates that the individual goes through a series of stages as she or he attempts to implement a self-concept through choosing a career. Consequently, the measures associated with his theory are also developmentally oriented. For instance, the Career Development Inventory (Super et al., 1981) is a measure of various aspects of career maturity that can be used with high school students.

Counselors have always been interested in how the counseling process produces results. Consequently, they have used measurement to help operationalize concepts having to do with client variables, counselor variables, interactional variables, and outcome variables in the counseling process. Kiesler (1973) collected a number of measures used in studying the therapeutic process. Garfield and Bergin (1986) have edited a volume on psychotherapy and behavior change that contains chapters detailing how these variables have been studied.

Counselors make many uses of measurement that are not detailed here because they are related to noncounseling functions. They are discussed in other chapters of this book. We turn now to a discussion of the issues involved in the use of measurement in counseling.

Issues in the Use of Measurement in Counseling

The use of measurement techniques as aids in the counseling process does present the counselor with problems and responsibilities. As a result, some counselors have given up the use of tests and inventories. This appears to be an overreaction, to this author. Tests and inventories must be chosen and used carefully. If they are, they have the potential to be extremely useful in the counseling enterprise, as indicated in the previous section. This section will review some specific issues that the counselor who uses tests and inventories must deal with to use them effectively and ethically.

Culturally Based Assumptions

The counselor must constantly be alert to the assumptions on which a given test or inventory or its use is based. The most difficult assumptions to recognize are those most common to our culture. Achievement tests are sometimes used on the assumption that young people in our society experience rather similar educational experiences at each level of the educational system. However, the average child who has been educated in a school system that has very little money to spend on each pupil will probably score quite differently on a set of achievement tests than the average child who has been educated in a very affluent school system. The assumption that they should score equally well is unfounded. The resulting discrepancy in scores might still be interpretable, but it should not be interpreted as a clear indication that one child has a greater capacity to benefit from instruction than another. It might, however, mean that the high-scoring child is more knowledgeable than the low-scoring child.

The assumption that some occupations are appropriate for men and others are appropriate for women was prevalent when measures of vocational interests were first developed. Some interest inventories had different item sets, scales, norms, and profiles for males and females (Harmon, 1973). The interpretive materials associated with interest inventories until the late 1960s or early 1970s encouraged both counselors and clients to view the world of work as sex segregated. Interest inventories were only one of a number of influences that perpetuated that view. Changes were finally made in interest inventories to reduce or eliminate the effect of assuming sex segregation in the world of work (AMEG Commission, 1973; Tittle & Zytowski, 1978), but there is no way to calculate the loss of human potential that might be attributed to career counseling based on instruments with a built-in bias.

These two examples show how easy it is for the counselor to assume that scores from a test or inventory developed by competent psychologists can be accepted without question. It is important for the counselor to discern what the assumptions of the test developers were and what the assumptions about the use of the test are. In both cases cited, the problems were recognized by the public at least as early as they were recognized by the counselors. It is desirable for counselors to be aware early on of potential problems with the assumptions on which a test is based or used, preferably before the test or inventory is adopted for use. However, once the instrument is in use, the public or clients who have experienced the measurement should be considered allies of the counselor in detecting faulty assumptions. If many clients experience the results of a specific test or inventory as alien to their own self-knowledge or as unfair, the counselor should begin to question the assumptions on which the measure is based. As indicated in the discussion about interest inventories, changes can be made once faulty or dysfunctional assumptions are detected.

Relationship Between Construct Definition and Measurement

Once a test has been developed and named, it is very tempting for the counselor to assume that the test measures the concept it is designed to measure, as he or she defines the concept. Tests can be constructed so that responses can be considered either signs or samples of some behavior or characteristic of interest. In either case, they never measure all the potentially relevant behavior of the test taker. Neither do they measure everything that a theory builder means when she or he defines a construct such as intelligence or anxiety.

Tryon (1979) defines the "test-trait" fallacy, which is using an unsound set of assumptions to imply that test scores reflect enduring personal traits. When the counselor decides to test a client or a group of clients, the first thing to be done is define as clearly as possible exactly what one wants to test. Only then is it appropriate to begin looking for an instrument that will do the job. It is not enough to look for an instrument whose title is the same as the name one gives to what one wants to measure. A careful reading of the test manual, with attention to items, the way scales are formed, and the purposes of the test developer, is imperative. Usually this procedure leaves the counselor with the task of deciding whether to use a measure that does not completely measure the concept he or she wants to measure. The decision must rest on the potential practicality of using the measure in relation to its cost in terms of time and money. Clearly, the counselor who makes careful use of tests must consult references like the *Mental Measurements Yearbook* (Mitchell, 1985), Mitchell's *Tests in Print III* (1983), *Test Critiques* (Keyser & Sweetland, 1986), *Tests* (Sweetland & Keyser, 1986), and individual manuals. Westbrook and Mastie (1983) present a practical guide for evaluation of tests by practitioners. Kapes and Mastie (in press) have edited a useful guide to vocational guidance instruments that critically reviews 40 instruments of the types often used by counselors. It was developed to help counselors choose appropriate measures.

Being sure to measure what the counselor means to measure is a time-consuming process, but well worth the required effort. It is only one of the issues he or she must address before actually selecting a test or inventory to use. To the extent that test developers provide good evidence supporting the validity of the construct interpretation of their tests, this job is made easier.

Appropriate Evidence of Validity

Construct-related evidence of validity is always important, and, in cases where measurement techniques are used in counseling to assess the current level of knowledge or skill of an individual or group of individuals, content-related evidence of validity is important. In general, when tests and inventories have been used to make decisions about future actions, predictive evidence has been considered important. Messick (1980) has argued that, in addition to these traditional evidential bases for test use, we should be concerned about the social consequences of test use. Because the use of tests in counseling is normally part of a decison-making process, both the evidential basis and the social consequences of their use are important.

For example, predictive evidence for empirically developed interest scales that were developed and normed using males in traditionally male occupations is available (Strong, 1955; Zytowski, 1976). The use of these scales has clearly helped males

find their way into such occupations. Unfortunately, one concomitant effect of their use was to point out to women that such scales were not available for women test takers and to imply that women did not belong in male-dominated occupations. This problem has been resolved in recent years by the development of new scales for nontraditional occupations for men and women. As noted earlier, the assumptions underlying measurement can provide us with clues as to why particular measures are unfair to, or are perceived as unfair by, some groups. There are clearly important social consequences.

The temptation, in those instances where the use of some tests and inventories produces negative social consequences, is to develop tests and inventories designed to reverse the negative social consequences without at the same time paying careful attention to the evidential bases of validity. At best, the users of such instruments are participants in a natural experiment designed to develop evidence of the validity of the instruments. One could argue that all instrument development proceeds in this way. At worst, clients are not informed of the experimental nature of the instruments upon which they are depending for information to be used in decision making, or they are not even part of a systematic long-term inquiry designed to gather validity evidence, or both. In this case, the social values of counselors and test developers can be highly creditable, but their goals are frustrated by their own failure to attend to *both* evidence and social consequences, as suggested by Messick's model (1980). This is not easy, because there is often an interaction between the two that makes it difficult to draw conclusions.

For example, Holland (1975) calls attention to the treatment effects of the use of interest inventories, and Tittle (1978) introduces the term *exploration validity* to describe the amount of exploration stimulated by an interest inventory. For homogeneous interest scales, those developed by a content-based clustering of items, Holland (1975) presents evidence that using same-sex norms (a treatment designed to increase exploration) reduces predictive validity for women. Tittle (1978) recognizes that attempts to increase exploration validity will probably decrease predictive validity. Despite considerable controversy over the treatment effect of using same-sex norms in reporting scores on interest inventories (Gottfredson & Holland, 1975; Keeling & Tuck, 1978; Prediger, 1980), no one has yet designed a study to compare the long-term treatment effects of empirical and homogeneous interest scales in terms of both exploration validity and vocational outcomes. It is possible that the interest inventory that is designed to increase vocational exploration could result in vocational outcomes with either more or less predictive validity than an interest inventory not designed to do so. Or it could fail to influence vocational outcomes, while having more or less predictive usefulness than an instrument not designed to increase vocational exploration. Other influences on both exploration and prediction of eventual vocational behavior could include the interpretive materials available, the counselor's interpretation, and the test taker's ability to assimilate the interpretation.

At a minimum, then, the type of validity evidence claimed for a given measure should be stated. It is also highly desirable to show how other types of validity are effected.

Training Counselors

Counselors need to be firmly grounded in applied psychometrics to make the right choices. Some graduate programs for counselors allow students to get the idea that measurement is an outmoded fashion they don't need to know much about. When graduates of such programs enter the professional world, they often find they are called upon to use psychological measurement when they are ill prepared to do so. Getting to the basic informatin about a test or inventory in a market flooded with products designed to make a profit is not always easy for a counselor who is well trained in measurement. One who is poorly trained might give up too easily, without using the inquiring attitude that is necessary to make good selections or to refrain from making any selection at all. In a very real sense, tests cannot be abused in counseling unless counselors abuse them. Inadequate measures need not be used, and adequate measures need not be used for the wrong purposes or with the wrong populations.

Most counselors become counselors because they want to help people solve their problems. One of the most common errors of the beginning counselor is to try to solve the client's presenting problem as quickly and as logically as possible. In most cases, tests and measurements appear more scientific and reliable than they are. They can provide a kind of prop for the counselor who wants to be sure to be objective, accurate, and helpful. Counselors must be trained to let clients explore their problems fully before they begin to explore solutions. Counselors must learn to expect solutions to be made of a complex set of emotions, cognitions, and behaviors that are unique to a given individual and her or his problem. Information from tests or measures can only provide a small and tentative part of the picture. Any counselor who is not well trained in using test results in this way could turn out to be a counselor who abuses test use.

Legal Issues in the Use of Tests in Counseling

Surprisingly, there are few legal restrictions on the use of tests in counseling. Because of the voluntary and cooperative nature of the counseling enterprise, the tests used are usually completed with the cooperation and consent of the client or the client's agent such as a parent. In some educational settings, results of tests taken for other purposes, such as admission or placement, are available to the counselor. To the extent that these are obtained in an ethical manner and used in the counseling process for the information of the client, there is no legal issue involved. Thus, there are no legal restrictions on the use of tests in counseling comparable to those applied in employment settings under the Uniform Guidelines on Employee Selection Procedures of the Equal Employment Opportunity Commission or those applied in educational placement settings under Title IX of the Education Amendments Act of 1972. Counselors in institutions covered by Title IX are enjoined by the regulations not to use test materials that are different for men and women unless the differential materials are essential to the elimination of bias.

If a counselor misuses or abuses tests in his or her counseling practice, he or she can be charged with unethical behavior under state licensing or certification statutes or investigated by the ethics committees of professional organizations such as the APA, if a member. This type of charge is rarely made, because it is very difficult to document the fact that a counselor exceeded her or his expertise in using tests. In addition, the kinds of harm done by misuse of tests in counseling is also subtle and difficult to document. One type of misuse that can sometimes be documented is failure to respect the confidentiality of test data and to obtain proper authorization to release such information to individuals other than the client. In settings where tests are taken by groups of people and might be put to multiple uses such as educational placement and counseling, it is important that the test taker know of all such potential uses at the time tests are administered.

The fact that counselors operate with very few restrictions in using tests in counseling suggests that individual counselors must be personally responsible for upgrading their knowledge in the field as necessary and making good judgments about when testing is indicated and when it is not. A counselor who is not willing to spend a considerable amount of time researching the tests being considered for use should not use them. This is more of an ethical issue than a legal one, however.

Computerized Testing in Counseling

Counselors today have computerized systems available for administering, scoring, and interpreting tests. The Committee on Professional Standards and the Committee on Psychological Tests and Assessment of the APA have published *Guidelines for Computer-Based Tests and Interpretations* (APA, 1986). There are many issues associated with the use of computerized testing, but just three will be highlighted here.

If a test or inventory is to be administered by computer for use in counseling, the counselor is responsible for making sure that the computerized administration of the test is comparable to the paper-and-pencil administration on which the test was normed or standardized, unless the test has been restandardized by using computerized administration. Certain groups of individuals who are not disadvantaged by paper-and-pencil administration might be disadvantaged by computer administration. The elderly and people with certain visual impairments probably fall into this group.

Computers make quick and accurate scoring possible. They also make it possible to combine scores from individual scales in various ways. These combinations do not directly take on the psychometric characteristics of their component parts. Instead, the psychometric characteristics of the composites must be directly explored. For example, the UniAct inventory, which is part of the ACT Assessment Program (American College Testing, 1981), is used to obtain six interest scores, which are used in a weighted combination to plot an individual's location on two dimensions (Data–Ideas and People–Things) that combine to provide a location on the World of Work Map (Prediger, 1981). Figure 16.4 is an illustration of the World of

FIGURE 16.4 World of Work Map (Second Edition)

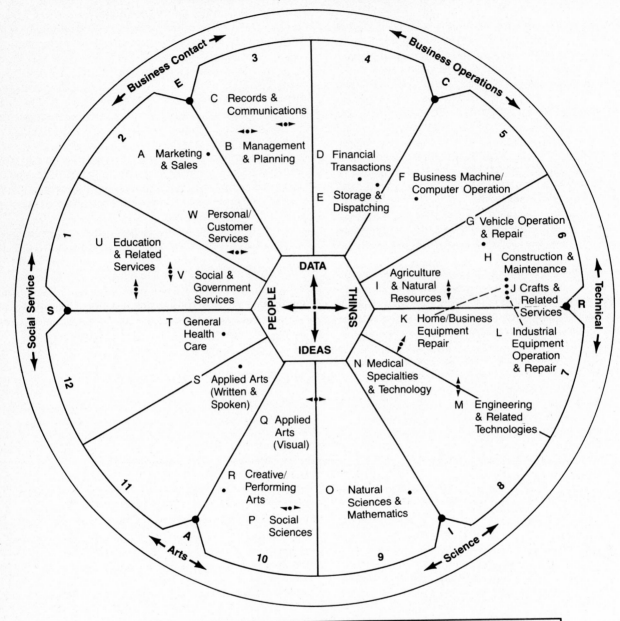

About the Map

- The World-of-Work Map arranges job families (groups of similar jobs) into 12 regions. Together, the job families cover all U.S. jobs. Although the jobs in a family differ in their locations, most are located near the point shown.

- A job family's location is based on its primary work tasks—working with DATA, IDEAS, PEOPLE, and THINGS. Arrows show that work tasks often heavily involve both PEOPLE and THINGS (◄•►) or DATA and IDEAS (⬍).

- Six general areas of the work world and related Holland types are indicated around the edge of the map. Job Family Charts (available from ACT) list over 500 occupations by general area, job family, and preparation level. They cover more than 95% of the labor force.

Work Map, and Figure 16.5 shows the report a test taker receives.

There is evidence that the World of Work Map describes the world of work accurately (Prediger, 1982), but Latona, Harmon, & Hastings (1987) present evidence suggesting that it is no more accurate in locating college students in the correct region for their intended careers than the six individual scores on which it is based. Consequently, the question arises as to whether the test takers would be better served in terms of understanding their interests if they received the six original scores that are comparable to Holland types of their Data–Ideas and People–Things scores than if they received their World of Work Map region. This is especially true because many students do not have an opportunity to discuss their score reports individually with a counselor.

Note also in Figure 16.5 that ability, preference, and interest inventory data collected in a paper-and-pencil format are used to give individualized information about abilities and interests in relation to appropriate norm groups. They are also used to give students information about their preferred colleges in a way that should help in assessing whether the colleges are likely to be appropriate choices for these individuals. Although students might be given the reports with very little counselor explanation, the computer is used to generate individualized reports to provide direct help to them. Although this might not be an optimal situation, it reflects the reality of the students' experiences and makes a good attempt to deal with it. The report contains several warnings designed to keep students from making common misinterpretations of the information they receive.

If a test or inventory is to be interpreted by computer, the counselor's task is to determine whether the computerized interpretive statements provided are valid for the population from which his or her clients are drawn.

Additional examples of inventories for which extensive interpretive statements can be generated for each individual are the Strong–Campbell Interest Inventory (Strong, Campbell, & Hansen, 1981), the Harrington–O'Shea Career Decision Making System (Harrington & O'Shea, 1982), and the Career Assessment Inventory (Johansson, 1978). These examples are all from the career-interest domain. Examples are also available from the personality domain. Figure 16.6 contains a portion of a computerized interpretive report for the 16PF (Sixteen Personality Factor Questionnaires) by the Institute for Personality and Ability Testing (1978). The figure is actually an adaptation from the manual for the Personal Career Development Profile for the 16PF (Walter, 1985). It is of special interest because it shows a portion of the interpretive report for Mr. Sample, as well as some observations that a typical counselor might make about the report while studying it in preparation for discussing it with Mr. Sample. The manual for the Personal Career Development Profile explains which portions of the 16PF are used to derive each of the sections of the report, which goes part way toward solving one of the major problems of using computerized interpretations.

It is difficult for the counselor to make judgments about validity evidence in using computerized interpretations, because interpretive statements are based on combinations of scores that are the trade secrets of the scoring services. Without knowing the algorithms on which the interpretive statements are based, the counselor cannot judge their adequacy; yet the scoring services have not provided data on the validity of the statements. These computerized interpretive statements seem impressive, and they could be. Unfortunately, it could be the least well-trained counselor who is most likely to use them without more evidence than is usually available.

The question of whether these interpretive statements are understood and utilized appropriately by the test taker has not been addressed specifically. It would appear that computerized interpretations might lead some test takers to the same uncritical acceptance they show for test scores. As a matter of fact, Myers (1983) has pointed out that computerized guidance systems have been enthusiastically accepted by students and their parents. He also notes several concrete positive results of the use of these systems, such as a greater awareness of the need to plan and an inclination to consider more options. Although this evidence is tangential to the question of user response to specific interpretive reports, it does suggest that it is feasible and useful to collect such evidence.

In summary, there are issues associated with using tests in counseling. They include the culturally biased assumptions on which some tests are based, the establishment of appropriate validity for tests used in counseling, the adequate training of counselors in the use of tests, and the use of computerized methods in test administration and interpretation. None of these issues is easily resolved.

Conclusions

It is clear that testing can be of considerable use in counseling, whether educational planning, career planning, life planning, or personal growth is being discussed. It is also clear that the use of tests in counseling does not provide all the help that counselors or clients might like. This chapter will conclude, then, with a summary of what advances in testing counselors might use to do a better job of using tests in counseling and a summary of what clients should look for in trying to identify a counselor who uses measurement well in counseling. These suggestions should be viewed as optimistic predictions of the future use of measurement by counselors. In the words of the author of the chapter on counseling in the first edition of *Educational Measurement* (Darley & Andersen, 1951), "Admittedly more needs to be done, but counseling psychology has come a long way from the days of Frank Parsons because of developments in psychometrics" (J. G. Darley, personal communication, October 18, 1984).

What Counselors Need

Many of the things counselors need for more effective testing have not yet been made available by theorists and researchers. Some new measures and new evidence about existing measures are needed. There is a need for published measures of life planning that provide indications of the strength of attraction of such life roles as worker, homemaker, and leisurite in comparable terms, so that they can be con-

TRACY ARTHUR C
7852 W 46TH ST
WHEAT RIDGE CO 80033

ACT.

392-11-1985
HSC 067-890

1985-86 ACT ASSESSMENT STUDENT REPORT

YOUR ACT TEST SCORES   Your 10/85 ACT scores, listed below, provide one way to estimate your level of educational development. The percentile ranks show how your scores compare with those of college-bound students who take the ACT nationwide. For instance, your ENGLISH score is 25, which has a percentile rank of 92. This means that you scored higher than 92% of the college-bound students taking the ENGLISH test. The percentile rank of your Composite score indicates that your overall educational development probably ranks in the top quarter of college-bound students. Compared with all high school students (not just college-bound), your percentile ranks would be higher.

To emphasize that test scores are only estimates of your educational development, ranges (dotted lines) are shown with your percentile ranks. If the dotted lines for two subject areas overlap (for example, MATH and NATURAL SCIENCES), your ranks in those areas are probably similar. If they do not overlap (for example, ENGLISH and MATH), your ranks probably differ.

SUBJECT AREA	SELF-REPORTED H.S. GRADES	ACT SCORES	NATIONAL PERCENTILE RANKS OF YOUR ACT SCORES						
			1	10	25	50	75	90	99
ENGLISH	A	25						----+-92-----	
MATH	C	19				----+56-----			
SOCIAL STUDIES	A	26					-----86--+--		
NATURAL SCIENCES	B	22				----+56-----			
COMPOSITE		23					--+76---		

Your Composite score indicates that you can probably do well in a wide variety of colleges and programs. You may want to consider several options before making a final choice.

For more information about the meaning of your ACT scores, see Section 1 of Using Your ACT Assessment Results.

> The STATE PERCENTILE RANK of your ACT Composite score is 70 (among ACT-tested students in Colorado).

YOUR COLLEGE PLANNING   Admissions standards differ among colleges and, sometimes, among programs of study within a college. Your class rank and ACT Composite score are most like those of students who enter colleges with a traditional or selective admissions policy (see description on back). Remember, however, that many colleges with less selective admissions policies offer opportunities for a good education.

The table below gives information about the colleges you listed when you registered for the ACT. For example, UNIVERSITY OF OMEGA has a traditional admissions policy. Your ACT Composite score is estimated to rank in the middle half of entering students. The average high school GPA for freshmen is 2.7--lower than the 3.2 for the grades you reported. Students with ACT scores and grades like yours, if admitted to this college, would have about 6 chances in 10 of earning a "C" average or higher during the freshman year. The program of study you listed at ACT registration (POLITICAL SCIENCE) is available. The approximate cost of tuition/fees is $1200/year. Financial assistance is offered to 67% of freshmen with judged need.

FIGURE 16.5 1985–86 ACT Assessment Student Report

trasted within an individual at a given time. There is also a need for published measures of several types of developmental stage (cognitive, moral, ego) that are objectively scored. New measures of developmental stage, as well as existing measures (career maturity measures, for instance), would be most useful if they gave an indication of which stage the respondent was most likely to have attained.

Several types of existing measures (career indecision, career maturity, career decision styles) need greater evidence of construct-related validity to inform the user about just what aspects of the construct are being measured. Counselors also need evidence on the relationship between exploration validity (the breadth of exploration encouraged by the use of a test or inventory) and predictive validity for a given instrument used with a specific population. Where combined scores are used, evidence of their psychometric properties is needed. To the

extent that they use computerized interpretations, counselors need evidence of the validity of the interpretive algorithms used beyond the validity of the test scores on which they are based, as well as evidence regarding how clients utilize this information.

Finally, counselors need solid training in the use of measurement techniques. They need to be taught to use good judgment and ethical principles, as well as technical expertise.

What Clients Need

Clients who are asked to spend their time and, in some settings, money on testing have the right to ask some questions before agreeing to the procedure. Clients should look for evidence that the counselor is

FIGURE 16.5 (Continued)

COLLEGE CODE AND NAME	ADMISSIONS POLICY	ESTIMATED RANK OF YOUR ACT COMPOSITE SCORE (ENROLLED FRESHMEN)	H.S. AVERAGE (ENROLLED FRESHMEN)	CHANCES IN 10 OF "C" OR HIGHER	YOUR PROGRAM OF STUDY AVAILABLE	APPROX. YEARLY TUITION & FEES (minus room/board)	PERCENT ACCEPTED FRESHMEN WITH NEED OFFERED FIN. AID
0521 UNIVERSITY OF OMEGA	Trad	Middle Half	2.7	6	Yes:4-yr Degree	1200	67
7111 ALPHA UNIVERSITY	Sel	Middle Half	3.1	5	Yes:4-yr Degree	4500	85
7222 BETA JUNIOR COLLEGE	Open	Upper Quarter	2.4	9	Yes:2-yr Degree	700	58

A dash (—) means ACT has no information available. See *Using Your ACT Assessment Results* for an explanation of program of study and tuition/fees categories

Remember that test scores and past grades do not guarantee success or failure in college. Other factors, such as program of study and motivation, count too. Most colleges have special programs for students wanting help in particular areas. You reported that you would like help with educational or vocational plans and mathematics. Check with your high school counselor, the college catalog, or the college admissions office to learn whether this special help is available at the college of your choice.

Section 2 of *Using Your ACT Assessment Results* provides more information about choosing a college. If you have not yet decided on a college, ACT's *College Planning/Search Book*, which lists colleges by geographical region and admissions policy, may be helpful. (If this book is not available in your library or guidance office, you'll find ordering instructions in *Using Your ACT Assessment Results*.)

YOUR EDUCATIONAL/OCCUPATIONAL PLANNING   Since many people consider several possibilities before making definite career plans, ACT has grouped similar occupations and programs of study into "families" as a career exploration aid. For example, the program of study you indicated (POLITICAL SCIENCE) is in Career Family P (SOCIAL SCIENCES) and the occupational choice you indicated (LAW) is in Career Family S (APPLIED ARTS, WRITTEN AND SPOKEN). If you would like to identify other careers in these families, check the Career Family List on the back of this report.

Occupations differ in how much they involve working with data (facts, records); ideas (theories, insights); people (care, services); and things (machines, materials, lab equipment). Your responses to the ACT Interest Inventory indicate that you might enjoy opportunities to work with PEOPLE and ideas. Career Families S, T, and U include many occupations and programs of study which emphasize these "work tasks." If you scan these families, you may find additional career possibilities that you would like to explore. You can identify other Career Families emphasizing people and ideas "work tasks" by using the World-of-Work Map (found in Section 3 of *Using Your ACT Assessment Results*). See, especially, Map Regions 11 and 12. Remember, however:

*Occupations within each family differ in the proportion of time spent with each of the work tasks.
*Interest scores, like other test scores, are estimates; also, interests may change with experience.
*Interests and abilities may differ; consider both in your educational/occupational planning.
If you will now turn to Section 3 of *Using Your ACT Assessment Results*, you will find a list of activities that can help you identify and explore career options.

392-11-1985

1. well trained in the use of tests. This usually requires that the counselor be trained at the master's degree level in psychology or educational psychology, at least. Practitioners in the ministry, social work, and psychiatry might have attained such training, either in their academic programs or on their own, but psychological testing is the unique contribution of psychology and is most likely to be taught to psychologists.

2. clear about the purpose for which test results will be used. The counselor should be able to tell the client whether the results are potentially useful in promoting exploration, promoting understanding, suggesting a course of action, or eliminating alternatives.

3. relatively certain about what the test will measure and how that measurement will be useful in helping the client.

4. concerned about whether or not the test is fair to women and minority group members. This is a complex question with several potential answers, depending on the viewpoint from which it is asked, but it cannot be answered at all unless it is asked.

5. careful to set the results of testing in proper perspective. Test results are never the sole source of information bearing on a problem or decision. They are rarely the definitive piece of information. They should be used as one of a set of pieces of information.

The use of tests in counseling is a cooperative effort between the counselor and the client, but the counselor needs increasingly effective measurement tools with which to work. The needs of the counselor can inform the theoretician and the test developer. The needs of the client can inform those who train counselors to use tests and measures.

PERSONAL-CAREER DEVELOPMENT PROFILE

John Sample   ID Number 9184-9 -
Sex M   Age 47   9/ 9/1985

ORIENTATION TO THE 16PF QUESTIONNAIRE   **Distortion high.**

    Mr Sample seems to have been highly concerned and motivated to
answer a good number of questions in the inventory in terms of what
people see as socially acceptable responses. As a result, some of
the information that follows in this report has been changed so as to
describe his characteristics more accurately and realistically. The
narrative reported, therefore, will be most useful if it is read in
light of what is actually known about his personal career life-style
patterns.

                                    Don't put him in a spot that
                                    requires precision, planning,
PROBLEM-SOLVING PATTERNS   **or dependability.**

    Mr Sample functions quite comfortably with problems which involve
abstract reasoning and conceptual thinking. He is quite able to
integrate detail and specifics into meaningful, logical wholes. He
is very alert mentally. He sees quickly how ideas fit together and
is likely to be a fast learner. If Mr Sample feels like doing it,
he shows about average interest in the kind of controlled learning
activities which formal university training offers.

    Mr Sample's approach to tasks is usually balanced between getting
things done efficiently and having an awareness of the often hidden
steps and outcomes that are part of the process of getting things
done. Mr Sample is sometimes so sure that he can easily handle most
any problem that comes up that he may not do enough planning and
preparing for thoroughness. He is prone to act on the spur-of-the-
moment without taking the needed time to prepare himself to decide
and act on important issues. As a result, his decisions and actions
tend to be rather risk-seeking and with the expectation that somehow
luck will intervene. Mr Sample sticks mostly to practical methods as
he deals with life and its problems. He usually pays attention to
the everyday aspects and requirements of situations.

PATTERNS FOR COPING WITH   **Trouble with showing, chan-**
STRESSFUL CONDITIONS   **neling feelings?**

    For the most part, Mr Sample seems to be well-adjusted. He does
not usually show signs of tension and worry, even when he is under a
lot of pressure. Nevertheless, Mr Sample is likely to show his
emotions, feelings and worries in situations that he finds upsetting
to him. However, he may have various ways of showing his emotions or
concerns, and as a result, others may find them hard to understand or
predict. He tries to be calm and even-tempered most of the time.
He rarely allows his emotional needs to get in the way of what he
does or tries to do in situations or relationships. He seems to be
quite casual in the way he reacts to most circumstances and
situations. He usually follows his own urges and feelings. He
seldom gives much attention to controlling his behavior and sometimes
finds it hard to consciously discipline himself. Generally, when
Mr Sample is faced with conflict or disagreement from others, he
likes to challenge those who differ with him and to clearly state

FIGURE 16.6 Personal Career Development Profile

FIGURE 16.6 *(Continued)*

```
John Sample                    - 2 -                    9/ 9/1985
```

his views on the subject. However, if pushed far enough, he is
likely to either give in or to break off the conversation --
whichever seems to be best for him.

PATTERNS OF INTERPERSONAL INTERACTION

     Most of the time, Mr Sample tends to pay rather close attention
to people around him and to their concerns and problems. He seldom
spends a lot of effort and time being overly concerned about himself
or his own problems. He likes to put forth a feeling of warmth and
easygoingness when interacting with others. He is a good natured
person and one who generally prefers participation in group
activities. He is generally very forward and bold when meeting and
talking with others. Mr Sample may sometimes want to get others to
do something so much that he may try too hard, and as a result, he
could run the risk of coming across as overly pushy and demanding in
such instances. Nevertheless, he appears to relate to most people
with ease and comfort.

                              **Socially skilled; if any nega-
                              tive, it's being on the pushy
                              side or not sensitive enough
                              to feelings of others.**

     Mr Sample is normally inclined to state his desires and needs
clearly and quite forcefully. He likes to have things his way most
of the time and prefers freedom from other people's influence.
Although Mr Sample usually likes to be free from other people's
influence, he can easily adjust his manner and he can be thoughtful
of other people and their concerns or needs when it is important to
do so. He normally feels closest to people who are competitive and
who understand the importance of being in firm control of their lives
and what they do to reach their goals. Sometimes, Mr Sample may be
in such a hurry to get things done that he tends to forget how others
may be affected by his actions and how others may feel about matters
that are important to them. Mr Sample seems to have a sharp sense of
what is socially necessary, and he is usually aware of the right
thing to say and do in social get togethers with others. For the
most part, he tries to be accepting of people since he tends to be
trusting and accepting of himself and what he does in life.
Mr Sample tends to gain his greatest satisfaction in life from being
involved in activities that have chances for personal achievement
while competing with others. When things are going well between
himself and others, he likes to have influence over other people as
he faces and meets difficult challenges.

ORGANIZATIONAL ROLE AND WORK-SETTING PATTERNS

     Mr Sample tends to experience considerable satisfaction when he
is given the chance to be in a position of leadership in
organizational settings. He likes to be in charge of others,
particularly a group of friends or co-workers. He usually feels
comfortable in situations which require him to provide direction over
others. His group members, too, are likely to respond favorably to
his leadership patterns. Mr Sample generally attempts to influence
others by directing, persuading and challenging them to get things
done. He seems to truly enjoy talking and interacting with people to
get them to agree with his points-of-view when it's important to him.
Mr Sample generally prefers to build feelings of mutual respect and

REFERENCES

AMEG Commission on Sex Bias in Measurement. (1973). Report on sex bias in interest measurement. *Measurement and Evaluation in Guidance, 6,* 171–177.

American College Testing Program. (1981). Technical report for the unisex edition of the ACT Interest Inventory (UNIACT). Iowa City: Author.

American Psychological Association. (1981). Specialty guidelines for the delivery of services by counseling psychologists. *American Psychologist, 36,* 652–663.

American Psychological Association, Committee on Professional Standards & Committee on Psychological Tests and Assessments. (1986). *Guidelines for computer-based tests and interpretations.* Washington, DC: Author.

Bernard, J. (1981). Societal values and parenting. *Counseling Psychologist, 9* (4), 5–11.

Binet, A., & Henri, V. (1895). La psychologie individuelle. *Année Psychologique, 2,* 411–463.

Coombs, L. C. (1979). The measurement of commitment to work. *Journal of Population, 2,* 203–223.

Crites, J. O. (1978). *Theory and research handbook for the Career Maturity Inventory.* Monterey, CA: CTB/McGraw-Hill.

Darley, J. G., & Anderson, G. V. (1951). The functions of measurement in counseling. In E. F. Lindquist (Ed.), *Educational measurement.* Washington, DC: American Council on Education.

Dawis, R. V., & Lofquist, L. H. (1984). *A psychological theory of work adjustment: An individual difference model and its applications.* Minneapolis, MN: University of Minnesota Press.

Dubin, R., & Goldman, D. R. (1972). Central life interests of American middle managers and specialists. *Journal of Vocational Behavior, 2,* 133–142.

Engen, H. B., Lamb, R. R., & Prediger, D. J. (1982). Are secondary schools still using standardized tests? *Personnel and Guidance Journal, 60,* 287–290.

Eyde, L. D. (1968). Work motivation of women college graduates: Five year follow-up. *Journal of Counseling Psychology, 15,* 199–202.

Floden, R. E. (1985). Review of Sequential Tests of Educational Progress, Series III. In J. V. Mitchell, Jr., Ed. *The ninth mental measurement yearbook.* Lincoln, NE: Buros Institute of Mental Measurements, 1363–1364.

Fretz, B. R. (1984). Perspective and definition. In J. M. Whiteley, N. Kagan, L. W. Harmon, B. R. Fretz, & M. F. Tanney (Eds.), *The coming decade in counseling psychology.* Monterey, CA: Brooks/Cole.

Garfield, S. L. (1971). Research on client variables in psychotherapy. In A. E. Bergin & S. L. Garfield (Eds.), *Handbook of psychotherapy and behavior change* (pp. 271–298). New York: John Wiley & Sons.

Garfield, S. L. (1978). Research on client variables in psychotherapy. In S. L. Garfield & A. E. Bergin (Eds.), *Handbook of psychotherapy and behavior change* (2nd ed., pp. 191–232). New York: John Wiley & Sons.

Garfield, S. L., & Bergin, A. E. (Eds.). (1978). *Handbook of psychotherapy and behavior change* (2nd ed.). New York: John Wiley & Sons.

Ginzberg, E., Ginsburg, S. W., Axelrad, S., & Herma, J. L. (1951). *Occupational choice: An approach to a general theory.* New York: Columbia University Press.

Gottfredson, G. D., & Holland, J. L. (1975). Vocational choices of men and women: A comparison of predictors from the Self Directed Search. *Journal of Counseling Psychology, 22,* 28–34.

Greenhaus, J. D. (1971). An investigation of the role of career salience in vocational behavior. *Journal of Vocational Behavior, 1,* 209–216.

Greenhaus, J. D. (1973). A factorial investigation of career salience. *Journal of Vocational Behavior, 3,* 95–98.

Hall, L. G. (1976). *Occupational Orientation Inventory* (3rd ed.). Bensenville, IL: Scholastic Testing Service.

Harmon, L. W. (1970). Anatomy of career commitment in women. *Journal of Counseling Psychology, 17,* 77–80.

Harmon, L. W. (1973). Sexual bias in interest measurement. *Measurement and Evaluation in Guidance, 5,* 496–501.

Harren, V. (1979). A model of career decision making for college students. *Journal of Vocational Behavior, 14,* 119–133.

Harrington, T. F., & O'Shea, A. J. (1982). *Harrington–O'Shea Career Decision Making System.* Circle Pines, MN: American Guidance Service.

Harris-Bowlsbey, J. (1983). The computer and the decider. *Counseling Psychologist, 11* (4), 9–14.

Harris-Bowlsbey, J., Rayman, J. R., & Bryson, D. L. (1976). *DISCOVER: A computer-based guidance and counselor-administrative support system (Field trial report).* Westminster, MD: DISCOVER Foundation.

Hartman, B. W., & Hartman, P. T. (1982). The concurrent and predictive validity of the Career Decision Scale adapted for high school students. *Journal of Vocational Behavior, 20,* 244–252.

Hathaway, S. R., & McKinley, J. C. (1967). The Minnesota Multiphasic Personality Inventory: Manual for administration and scoring. New York: Psychological Corporation.

Heppner, P. P., & Petersen, C. H. (1982). The development and implications of a personal problem solving inventory. *Journal of Counseling Psychology, 29,* 66–75.

Holland, J. L. (1973). *Making vocational choices: A theory of careers.* Englewood Cliffs, NJ: Prentice-Hall.

Holland, J. L. (1975). The use and evaluation of interest inventories and simulations. In E. E. Diamond (Ed.), *Issues of sex bias and sex fairness in career interest measurement,* pp. 19–44. Washington, DC: National Institute of Education.

Holland, J. L. (1985a). *The Self-directed search.* Odessa, FL: Psychological Assessment Resources.

Holland, J. L. (1985b). *Making vocational choices: A theory of vocational personalities and work environments* (2nd ed.). Englewood Cliffs, NJ: Prentice-Hall.

Holland, J. L. (1986). *Alphabetized occupations finder.* Odessa, FL: Psychological Assessment Resources.

Holland, J. L. (1987). *Manual supplement for the self-directed search.* Odessa, FL: Psychological Assessment Resources.

Holland, J. L., & Holland, J. E. (1977). Vocational indecision: More evidence and speculation. *Journal of Counseling Psychology, 24,* 404–414.

Holland, J. L., Whitney, D. R., Cole, N. S., & Richards, J. M., Jr. (1969). *An empirical occupational classification derived from a theory of personality and intended for practice and research* (ACT Research Report No. 29). Iowa City, IA: American College Testing Program.

Hoyt, D. P., & Kennedy, C. E. (1958). Interest and personality correlates of career-motivated and homemaking-motivated college women. *Journal of Counseling Psychology, 5,* 44–48.

Institute for Personality & Ability Testing. (1978). *16 PF* (Sixteen Personality Factor Questionnaries). Champaign, IL: Author.

Johansson, C. B. (1978). *Career Assessment Inventory.* Minneapolis: NCS Scoring Systems.

Kapes, J. T., & Mastie, M. M. (Eds.). (in press). *A counselor's guide to vocational guidance instruments* (2nd ed.). Alexandria, VA: National Career Development Association.

Katz, M. (1980). SIGI: An interactive aid to career decision making. *Journal of College Student Personnel, 21,* 34–39.

Katz, M. R., & Shatkin, L. (1983). Characteristics of computer assisted guidance. *Counseling Psychologist, 11* (4), 15–31.

Keeling, B., & Tuck, B. F. (1978). Raw scores versus same-sex normed scores: An experimental study of the validity of Holland's SDS with adolescents of both sexes. *Journal of Vocational Behavior, 13,* 263–271.

Keyser, D. J., & Sweetland, R. C. (1986). *Test critiques, Volume V.* Kansas City, MO: Test Corporation of America.

Kiesler, D. J. (1973). *The process of psychotherapy: Empirical foundations and systems of analysis.* Chicago: Aldine.

Knefelkamp, L. L., & Slepitza, R. A. (1976). Cognitive developmental model of career development and adaptation of Perry's scheme. *Counseling Psychologist, 6* (3), 53–58.

Kohlberg, L. (1981). *The philosophy of moral development.* New York: Harper & Row.

Latona, J. R., Harmon, L. W., & Hastings, C. N. (1987). Criterion-related validity of the UNIACT with special emphasis on the World of Work Map. *Journal of Vocational Behavior, 30,* 49–60.

Levinson, D. J., Darrow, C. N., Klein, E. B., Levinson, M. H., &

McKee, B. (1978). *The seasons of a man's life.* New York: Ballantine.

Loevinger, J. (1976). *Ego development.* San Francisco: Jossey-Bass.

Lofquist, L. L., & Dawis, R. V. (1969). *Adjustment to work.* Englewood Cliffs, NJ: Prentice-Hall.

Marcia, J. E., & Friedman, M. L. (1970). Ego identity status in college women. *Journal of Personality, 38,* 249–263.

Messick, S. (1980). Test validity and the ethics of assessment. *American Psychologist, 35,* 1012–1027.

Mitchell, J. V. (1983). *Tests in print III.* Lincoln, NE: University of Nebraska, Buros Institute of Mental Measurements.

Mitchell, J. V., Jr. (Ed.). (1985). *Ninth mental measurements yearbook.* Lincoln, NE: The University of Nebraska, Buros Institute of Mental Measurements.

Myers, R. A. (1983). Computerized approaches to facilitating career development. In L. W. Harmon (Ed.), *Using information in career development.* Columbus, OH: Ohio State University, National Center for Research in Vocational Education, ERIC Clearinghouse on Adult, Career, and Vocational Education.

Nesselroade, J. R., & Baltes, P. B. (1979). *Longitudinal research in the study of behavior and development.* New York: Academic Press.

Osipow, S. H. (1987). *Career Decision Scale Manual* (2nd ed.). Odessa, FL: Psychological Assessment Resources.

Osipow, S. H., Carney, C. G., & Barak, A. (1976). A scale of educational vocational undecidedness: A typological approach. *Journal of Vocational Behavior, 9,* 223–243.

Osipow, S. H., Carney, C. G., Winer, J., Yanico, B., & Koscheir, M. (1976). *The career decision scale* (3rd ed.). Odessa, FL: Psychological Assessment Resources.

Parsons, F. (1909). *Choosing a vocation.* Boston: Houghton Mifflin.

Perry, W. (1970). *Forms of intellectual and ethical development in the college years.* New York: Holt, Rinehart & Winston.

Piaget, J. (1954). *The construction of reality in the child.* New York: Basic Books.

Prediger, D. J. (1980). The determination of Holland types characterizing occupational groups. *Journal of Vocational Behavior, 16,* 33–42.

Prediger, D. (1981). Mapping occupations and interests: A graphic aid for vocational guidance and research. *Vocational Guidance Quarterly, 30,* 21–36.

Prediger, D. (1982). Dimensions underlying Holland's hexagon: Missing link between interests and occupations? *Journal of Vocational Behavior, 21,* 259–287.

Rand, L. (1968). Masculinity or feminity? Differentiating career-oriented and homemaking-oriented college freshmen women. *Journal of Counseling Psychology, 15,* 444–450.

Richardson, M. S. (1981). Occupational and family roles: A neglected intersection. *Counseling Psychologist, 9* (4), 13–23.

Rosen, D., Holmberg, K., & Holland, J. L. (1987). *The college majors finder.* Odessa, FL: Psychological Assessment Resources.

Rosenbach, J. H. (1978). Review of sequential tests of educational progress. In O. K. Buros (Ed.), *The Eighth Mental Measurements Yearbook:* Vol. 1 (pp. 91–95). Highland Park, NJ: Gryphon Press.

Rubinton, N. (1980). Instruction in career decision making and decision making styles. *Journal of Counseling Psychology, 27,* 581–588.

Salomone, P. R. (1982). Difficult cases in career counseling: II–The indecisive client. *Personnel and Guidance Journal, 60,* 496–500.

Schultz, R. E. (1978). Review of Sequential Tests of Educational Progress. In O. K. Buros (Ed.), *The Eighth Mental Measurements Yearbook:* Vol. 1 (pp. 95–96). Highland Park, NJ: Gryphon Press.

Slaney, R. B., Palko-Nonemaker, D., & Alexander, R. (1981). An investigation of two measures of career indecison. *Journal of Vocational Behavior, 18,* 92–103.

Smith, E. J. (1976). Reference group perspectives and the vocational maturity of lower socioeconomic black youth. *Journal of Vocational Behavior, 8,* 321–336.

Smith, E. J. (1983). Issues in racial minorities' career behavior. In W. B. Walsh & S. H. Osipow (Eds.), *Handbook of vocational psychology:* Vol. 1. Hillsdale, NJ: Lawrence Erlbaum.

Spence, J. & Helmreich, R. (1978). *Masculinity and femininity: Their psychological dimensions, correlates, and antecedents.* Austin, TX: University of Texas Press.

Strong, E. K. (1955). *Vocational interests 18 years after college.* Minneapolis: University of Minnesota Press.

Strong, E. K., Jr., Campbell, D. P., & Hansen, J. C. (1981). *Strong–Campbell Interest Inventory.* Stanford, CA: Stanford University Press.

Super, D. E. (1957). *The psychology of careers.* New York: Harper & Row.

Super, D. E. (1970). *Work Values Inventory.* New York: Houghton Mifflin.

Super, D. E. (1980). A life-span life-space approach to career development. *Journal of Vocational Behavior, 16,* 282–298.

Super, D. E., & Culha, M. (1976). *The Work Salience Inventory.* Unpublished manuscript.

Super, D. E., & Nevill, D. D. (1984). Work role salience as a determinant of career maturity. *Journal of Vocational Behavior, 25,* 30–44.

Super, D. E., & Nevill, D. D. (1985). *The salience inventory.* Palo Alto, CA: Consulting Psychologists Press.

Super, D. E., Thompson, A., Lindeman, R., Jordaan, J., & Myers, R. (1981). *Career Development Inventory.* Palo Alto, CA: Consulting Psychologists Press.

Sweetland, R. C., & Keyser, D. J. (1986). Tests: *A comprehensive reference for assessments in psychology, education, and business* (2nd ed.). Kansas City, MO: Test Corporation of America.

Tittle, C. K. (1978). Implications of recent developments for future research in career interest measurement. In C. K. Tittle & D. G. Zytowski (Eds.), *Sex-fair interest measurement: Recent research and implications* (pp. 123–128). Washington, DC: National Institute of Education.

Tittle, C. K. (1981). *Careers and family: Sex roles and adolescent life plans.* Beverly Hills, CA: Sage.

Tryon, W. W. (1979). The test-trait fallacy. *American Psychologist, 34,* 402–406.

Tyler, L. E. (1978). *Individuality.* San Francisco: Jossey-Bass.

U.S. Department of Labor. (1980). *Job options for women in the 80's.* Washington, DC: Author, Women's Bureau.

Walter, V. (1985). *Personal Career Development Profile.* Champaign, IL: Institute for Personality and Ability Testing.

Westbrook, B., & Mastie, M. (1974). The Cognitive Vocational Maturity Test. In D. E. Super (Ed.), *Measuring vocational maturity for counseling and evaluation.* Washington, DC: American Personnel and Guidance Association.

Westbrook, B. W., & Mastie, M. M. (1983). Doing your homework: Suggestions for the evaluation of tests by practitioners. *Educational Measurement: Issues and Practice, 26,* 11–14.

Whiteley, J. M. (Ed.). (1980). *The history of counseling psychology.* Monterey, CA: Brooks/Cole.

Whiteley, J. M. (1984). Counseling psychology: A historical perspective. *Counseling Psychologist, 12* (1), 3–10.

Zytowski, D. G. (1976). Predictive validity of the Kuder Occupational Interest Survey: A 12 to 19 year follow-up. *Journal of Counseling Psychology, 23,* 221–233.

Zytowski, D. G., & Borgen, F. H. (1983). Assessment. In W. B. Walsh & S. H. Osipow (Eds.), *Handbook of vocational behavior:* Vol. 2. Hillsdale, NJ: Lawrence Erlbaum.

17

Identification of Mild Handicaps

Lorrie A. Shepard

University of Colorado-Boulder

The purpose of this chapter is to describe methods and issues in the identification of mildly handicapped children. The chapter is not primarily a measurement treatise, although it will consider both conceptual and technical principles governing assessment. To focus on scientific measurement issues presupposes one view of identification. In fact, there are competing paradigms invoked as children are classified mildly mentally retarded, learning disabled (LD), or emotionally disturbed (ED).

The scientific measurement model that uses test scores and signs to infer an underlying trait differs from, and sometimes conflicts with, the service-delivery model that governs identification in schools. Specialists in schools are more often concerned with practical matters such as a child's academic deficiencies, parents' demands for services, and availability of programs than with the technical match between test scores and constructs. Policymakers might seek to improve scientific validity but only because they are concerned with containing costs and wish to emphasize the distinction in entitlement between the handicapped and other remedial populations. Special educators are in sharp disagreement about which conceptual model should prevail.

Ironically, there has been so much attention focused on the debate about how children should be identified to receive special education services that very little attention has been given in the professional literature to measurement for research purposes. The Education for All Handicapped Children Act of 1975 (PL 94-142) took poorly formed, consensual definitions of vaguely understood concepts and made them the basis of entitlements. Scientific understanding of the disorders has not progressed much since then. The research definitions that might have been refined by subsequent studies were frozen by legal requirements and government regulations. The professional literature on definition and assessment has evolved since

the law was enacted, but to respond to the practical problems of allocating special education resources rather than to gain new scientific insights. Attempts to examine the nature of the original constructs and their indicators were outweighed by issues of fairness and utility. People became preoccupied with whether the conceptual distinctions were even necessary for effective intervention to take place. Some basic research has continued, examining, for example, constellations of symptoms, etiology of subtypes, and distinctive learning processes. But classification for research purposes disappeared into the background and has often been confounded by misidentified subjects. Only recently has some attention been given to the harm done to research by using grab-bag school-identified populations such as in the area of learning disabilities (see Kavale & Nye, 1981; Keogh, Major-Kingsley, Omori-Gordon, & Reid, 1982; D. D. Smith et al., 1984).

The chapter is divided into five major sections. Section 1 elaborates on several competing perspectives, especially the difference between what I call the *construct diagnosis* and school placement paradigms. These two perspectives are then used to organize the remainder of the chapter. Other conflicts in terminology and ideology are also presented in section 1, to set the stage for arguments developed later.

Section 2 summarizes issues affecting the identification of children as handicapped, including the positive and negative consequences of identification, bias in assessment, and specific issues related to early identification. These discussions establish the organizing themes for the subsequent sections on the mildly mentally retarded (section 3), the learning disabled (section 4), and the emotionally disturbed (section 5). A brief concluding section includes implications for research and for policy-making. These include the lesson that what is good for research is not necessarily good for school practice (and the converse).

Contradictory Traditions and Their Consequences

The literature on identification of mild handicaps is confusing because authors often do not signal to the reader which perspective they are advancing, nor do they specify which problem they are addressing, although one can usually assume it is the school placement problem. Authors of major position papers rarely cite who it is that they are directly refuting. Those who are thoroughly familiar with the various points of view might immediately know which conceptual orientation is implied when the authoritative references are Becker (1963), Hallahan and Kauffman (1976), or Mercer (1970). The uninitiated reader needs a conceptual map. Section 1 is intended to provide such a guide.

The scientific and service-delivery models are the two predominant views of identification. In this section, several more contrasts in meaning are considered, beginning with the contrast between the terms *handicapped* and *special education* and the conflict between due process and entitlement. Then, the scientific (or construct-based) model and the school placement model are defined. Last, the medical model is defined, in contrast with social deviance theory, and the disjuncture is explained between mild handicap and moderate, severe, and profound handicaps. These distinctions could help to clarify implicit contradictions in the literature.

Handicapped versus Special Education

Words carry meanings that cannot easily be altered by legislation or by new, enlightened attitudes. A *handicap* is a disability serious enough to hinder normal physical or mental activities. *Disabilities* or *impairments* become handicaps when they cannot be overcome in particular situations. The term *handicapped* derives its connotative meaning from crippling physical disabilities. In 1958 English and English included the following definitional elements: "The usual reference is to a person physically handicapped, i.e., who has a specific anatomical or physiological deficiency. . . . But it may also apply to the mentally deficient. It is less often used for the maladjusted or the educationally retarded individual" (p. 236). They go on to contrast a handicapped person, who has reduced capabilities, with a cripple, who is entirely unable to perform certain tasks. However, they acknowledge, "this useful distinction is not always observed" (p. 236).

Handicapped implies a disjuncture, or distinction, from normal children. It is this differentness that not only entitles children to *special* education but also warrants a label with strong connotations. A recognized handicap connotes seriousness, inherentness, pervasiveness, and permanence. As will be examined in sections 3, 4, and 5, each of these connotations conflicts with current understandings of the mild forms of the respective disorders. Ironically, this ordinary understanding of *handicap* was frozen in law and regulation at the same time that the movement toward normalization should have made the handicapped less different and less separate. Parents and educators who believe that negative stereotypes come only from the medieval attitudes of legislators and the lay public should recognize that these meanings were an accepted part of

scientific understandings as recently as 1970 and that the "crippled" metaphor is often perpetuated by the political rhetoric of advocacy groups. Parents of learning-disabled children, not previously called handicapped, formed a coalition with other groups and took on the language of physically observable disabilities, to gain services for their children.

For some, *handicapped* is synonymous with the need for special education. Although the right to special education follows by law from the determination of a handicap, ambiguous definitions have reversed the reasoning: If a child needs special education, she or he must be handicapped. This inverse is not logically defensible, as the following example illustrates. Although children who speak a language other than English or who are below average in achievement would benefit from educational services not available in the regular classroom, they would not properly be called handicapped, unless one ignores the meanings of that term. This argument about whether to be cognizant of both the denotative and connotative meanings of the overarching term is discussed in later sections, in the context of specific mild handicaps.

PL 94-142: Due Process versus Entitlement

The landmark educational rights law, as well as prior court decisions and legislation, seems entirely coherent and internally consistent, if one envisions a seriously impaired child who had previously been kept out of school. Two important provisions of the law now guarantee such a child the right to a free and appropriate public education and to due process. The handicapped child must now be educated in the public schools at public expense and in the least restrictive environment, that is, in a setting as normal as possible. The due process provision holds that the school cannot deny these rights without involving the parents, a comprehensive and unbiased assessment, and, if necessary, specialists of the parents' choosing.

The intent of PL 94-142 is less consistent internally, when one considers a potentially handicapped child who had hitherto been treated as normal by the school. For such a child, the right to be identified and served is at cross-purposes with due process requirements intended to prevent false identification. Due process refers to neutral procedural fairness; however, for minority children, and especially for stigmatizing labels, the onus is against misidentifying a child as handicapped when he or she is not. If the due process portion of the law only were attended to, a child would be considered normal unless proven otherwise, that is, unless the evidence of a handicap were unequivocal. But ambiguous and mixed signs of a potential disorder may be taken as sufficient evidence, if the emphasis is on providing the entitled service. This conflict even in legal intent is central to the practical problem of identifying mildly handicapped children who otherwise would be called normal. How the dilemma is resolved in individual cases depends on more important nontechnical issues such as beliefs about the effects of labeling and the effectiveness of programs. Thus, the positive and negative effects of identification are discussed in section 2 as necessary background to later discussions of fair assessment and placement procedures for each of the handicapped categories.

Construct Diagnosis versus School Placement

Psychological constructs are inferred attributes of people that explain, at least in part, certain aspects of observed behaviors. Constructs, lawful relationships among constructs, and the relations among constructs and observables are the elements of scientific theories. Theories, in turn, are the means by which current understandings are described and subjected to further testing. This paradigm of hypothesis testing and theory building is basic to social science research and borrows its metaphors from the natural sciences, especially physics (for example, see Hull, 1943 MacCorquodale & Meehl, 1948).

Measurement of postulated constructs is imperfect, both because the underlying scientific understandings are incomplete and because the observable signs are limited proxies for the full concepts. In their seminal paper on construct validity, Cronbach and Meehl (1955) explain that "since the meaning of theoretical constructs is set forth by stating the laws in which they occur, our incomplete knowledge of the laws of nature produces a vagueness in our constructs"(p. 293). Because neither the theory nor the measures are complete and exact, their mutual validity evolves slowly as evidence accumulates. To counteract the fallibility of a single measure, we seek confirmation from several indicators that have the concept in common but that have different sources of error. E. J. Webb, Campbell, Schwartz, and Sechrest (1966) called this "triangulation," again after the physical sciences.

Construct diagnosis of a mild handicap answers the question, Does the child have the signs of a particular disability as we understand it? In a research context, a conscientious effort to make a valid categorization is essential, if knowledge is to be advanced. The bootstrapping strategy of testing theory and measurement validity simultaneously allows for some invalid cases, but, if the assignment rule is nearly random, there can be too many confounding factors (too much noise) to learn about causes, secondary characteristics, or efficacious treatments. If a construct definition is not adhered to, the findings from one study will not generalize to the next, because the populations change in unknown ways.

The field of special education has been strongly influenced by behavioral psychology. Many of the changes in expectations about the limitations of the handicapped that led to PL 94-142 grew out of the impressive successes of behavioral interventions with many profoundly and severely retarded or disturbed patients. Behaviorists prefer to deal only with observed behaviors and not make inferences about internal, unseen processes. They could be correct in holding that theoretical constructs are unnecessary for generic educational interventions or when behavior modification is the only treatment considered. However, construct diagnosis as used here is essential to research, even if it only describes important subgroups of individuals for whom different treatments are recommended; that is, if one ever wished to choose between a behaviorist approach and some other treatment. Certainly if causes are to be understood, especially if they are not obvious and do not explain all instances in a category, constructs are needed to embody the conceptual distinctions on which theories are built.

Even with our most refined conceptual understandings, the retarded, emotionally disturbed, and learning disabled are each extremely heterogeneous populations. In the respective sections of the chapter, the need is emphasized for the purposes of research to carry the principle of construct definition even further and to identify more homogeneous subgroups within each population.

The opposite of construct diagnosis for the purposes of research is categorical placement for the purposes of funding and educational services. Professionals making placement decisions are more likely to gather data to answer the question, Does the child require the services normally associated with this category of handicap?

Because political and value questions are involved in the allocation of services in schools, professionals hold differing views about how much attention to pay to legal and scientific definitions. One position still separates identification from instructional prescription: identification still involves comparing a child's characteristics to a construct definition. Additional assessment is then needed to determine what instructional interventions to recommend. From advocates of this view in the respective literatures, efforts to improve but reaffirm conceptual definitions of a category will be seen. Others argue that, because categorical distinctions have no implications for differential educational treatment, identification should start and stop with assessment aimed at determining instructional deficits. From advocates of this position come undifferentiated category labels (e.g., *educationally handicapped* for all forms of mild handicap) and recommendations for noncategorical funding of special education. The policy implications of these proposals are discussed in the final section of this chapter.

The Medical Model versus Social Deviance Theory

Psychologists reject the medical model. The rejection is long-standing, originating from the natural resentment of psychologists at the hegemony of doctors and psychiatrists in the field of mental disorders. The references to the "medical model" is so commonly used and its negative valence so much presumed that many authors do not define the model or its particular harmful features. By inference, it is clear that different special education experts have different quarrels with the medical model but that rejection of the medical model is essential to the definition of various alternative paradigms.

The medical model refers to the diagnostic process whereby an individual's physical symptoms are used to deduce the presence of underlying disease or pathology. As noted by Phillips. Draguns, and Bartlett (1976), the model may be used either literally or metaphorically; that is, to seek a biological disorder or to follow parallel reasoning processes to uncover a deficit that has social causes. Some specialists find the medical model dysfunctional because it presumes, they believe, that the cause of a disorder must necessarily be organic or because, regardless of the nature of the cause, the model overemphasizes etiology and medical treatment, ignoring educational interventions. For many, aversion to the medical model is a moral issue because the model implies that clients are sick or diseased. The locus of the disability is believed to be in the child and creates a pessimistic view of how successful intervention efforts are likely to be. The problems of social stigma and self-fulfilling prophecy associated with the diagnosis of illness are discussed in the section on labeling. It is important to understand these characterizations of medical diagnosis, which pervade the special education literature, to understand the competing positions taken regarding the identification of mild handicaps. This oversimplified view is not intended to describe actual medical practice.

Several theoretical positions contrast with the medical model. According to *social deviance theory* (Becker, 1963; Lemert, 1967) and the labeling perspective, exceptional children are labeled deviant, not because of their inherent biological or psychological defects, but because they are perceived to be in violation of social norms (Rains, Kitsuse, Duster, & Freidson, 1976). Although the most extreme propositions of labeling theory have been disputed (Gove, 1980), professional conceptions of mental retardation have changed over the years in response to the realization that an individual's competence depends in part on differences in expectations from one social system to another (Farber, 1968; Mercer, 1970). Similarly, in the field of mental health Maslow (1960) and others reject diagnostic labels because of their dehumanizing effects. The *ecologists* (e.g., Rhodes, 1967, 1970; Swap, 1974) borrowed not only from social deviance theory but also from community psychology, in which interventions are based on an individual's family and community environment. They argue that disordered behavior is a function of a child's interaction with her or his social system; the behavior is not disturbed, but it is disturbing to those with discordant expectations.

Various theoretical models set up in contradistinction to the medical model share a conception of exceptionality that emphasizes external causes. This orientation goes hand in hand with the emphasis in special education on educational interventions without regard for intrinsic causes or constructs.

Most writing about assessment and identification in special education approaches these topics from within one theoretical frame of reference, with few authors allowing for some elements from the medical model and from some other perspective [Mercer's pluralistic model (1979b) with elements from both medical and social systems models is an exception]. In this chapter it is argued that both causes, whether biological or the accumulated consequences of environment, and current context are important. It is essential to have learned from labeling theory about the issues of social control and status differentiation. Indeed, ecologists and behaviorists might have provided the most constructive and optimistic approach to intervention. It is foolish, however, to throw out biology; just because the causes of the most obvious and severe forms of mental retardation, for example, are already known does not mean there is nothing left to be uncovered. Even if the discoveries of neurophysiology and genetics did not have immediate implications for intervention, they would still be worth knowing.

To a certain extent, the dichotomy between the medical model and the social systems models corresponds to the difference in purpose between research and educational placement. However, even in practice, one has to be concerned about theoretical conceptions that locate the problem outside the child. A handicap does not have to be a disease, but it does have to be a characteristic of the child. In fact, when discussing fair assessment procedures such as the National Academy of Sciences Panel on Selection and Placement of Students in Programs for the Mentally Retarded recommendations for the mentally retarded (Heller, Holtzman & Messick, 1982), it is essential to rule out situationally induced learning problems. If a change of teachers or instructional materials removes the problem, then, by definition, the child is not handicapped.

Mild versus Moderate, Severe, and Profound Handicaps

Mild, moderate, severe, and *profound* describe the degree of severity of a handicap. These adjectives originated with classifications of the mentally retarded (see Grossman, 1973) but are also applied to the emotionally disturbed (Hallahan & Kauffman, 1982). Although many regard learning disabilities as only a mild disorder, there are more extreme instances of dysfunction that can be characterized as severe (Poplin, 1981).

Children with the same handicap but different degrees of impairment have some characteristics in common. As stated by Gast and Berkler (1981), "the problems of the severely/profoundly handicapped differ in degree, not in kind, from the problems of other child populations. That is, it is the extent of the handicaps that results in the child's classification, and not the type of handicap" (p. 433). Conceptually, then, the more extreme and less ambiguous forms of a disorder can be used definitionally to remind us of a construct's meaning. Children with mild forms of the disorder should resemble more extreme cases on salient definitional characteristics, whether intellectual or behavioral, but their symptoms should be less serious, probably also less frequent. When our purpose is construct diagnosis, we harken to more serious examples of the disability, to check our understanding of signs and manifestations.

From the foregoing perspective, the important disjuncture on relevant performance dimensions should be between handicapped and normal; that is, handicapped children in a particular category are more like each other than they are like normal children. This view is consistent with the connotative meaning of handicapped discussed earlier. There is a competing point of view, however, that draws important distinctions between mild and other levels of handicap. Reschly (1982), for example, suggests that it might have been a mistake for the American Association on Mental Deficiency (AAMD) to place all levels of mental deficiency on the same continuum. Although, he said, "the principle underlying this scheme of low intellectual performance is sound" (p. 219) (the common characteristic), the continuum obscures the important differences between mild and other levels of retardation. Reschly emphasizes that mild retardation, unlike more severe categories of retardation, is not attributable to biological anomaly, is not comprehensive (is manifest only in the public school setting), and is not necessarily permanent.

This chapter acknowledges the changing definitions of constructs that in some instances make mild handicaps different from more severe disorders (and less compatible with the connotative meanings of handicapped). For example, quite apart from new attitudes in special education, the entire discipline of psychology has changed its conception of intelligence from "innate capacity" to "developed abilities"(Anastasi, 1981). This trend is consistent with the position that apparent disorders need not be permanent, inherited, or pervasive. However, I do not go so far as to say that the mildly handicapped are whoever the schools say they are. The definitional orientation in this chapter is conservative and restrictive, whether for scientific or public policy purposes. The mildly handicapped have less severe impairments, but are recognizably different from, normals. As stated previously, the handicap is a characteristic of the individual (whether caused or exacerbated by the environment), and it is relatively enduring, that is, not altered by simple remedies such as a change of classroom.

Issues Affecting Identification

Most researchers and practitioners recognize the difficulty of assigning a given person to a particular category. Differences of opinion regarding identification sometimes arise from differences in theoretical constructions. For example, the legal definition of a learning disability excludes children whose problems in school might be attributable to cultural or economic disadvantage. In contrast, Kavale (1980) argues that malnutrition and the culture of poverty could both explain a higher incidence of learning disabilities among those who are economically deprived. The greatest controversy occurs, however, not because of theoretical differences per se, but because of strongly held beliefs about the positive or negative consequences of identification. To those who see special education (or psychotherapy or medical interventions) as helpful and benevolent, the ambiguities of definition and assessment mean one thing. For others, who have found the labels destructive and the interventions ineffective, the potential consequences of misidentification have quite different meanings. These issues affecting identification are reviewed in the following sections because they largely explain the impetus for inclusive or exclusive (generous or restrictive) definitions of each disorder.

Positive Consequences of Identification

Special education costs more money per pupil than regular education. It is intended to be a benefit, an extra resource to the children who receive it. But is there research evidence of the efficacy of special education placements? Both Reschly (1982) and the National Academy of Sciences committee (Heller et al., 1982) have pointed out that, if the benefits of special education were more obvious, there would be much less concern about misidentification.

In the spirit of normalization, researchers in the late 1960s compared regular and special education classes and found a dismal picture. Teachers were not better trained (Dunn, 1968; Jones & Gottfried, 1966), curricula were watered-down versions of regular programs (MacMillan, 1977), classes were overpopulated by minority children (Johnson, 1969; Mercer, 1973), and achievement gains were less than in regular classrooms. Although much of this research was later disputed because of methodological inadequacies (e.g., the controls in regular classes were systematically more able students) (Kirk,

1964; Robinson & Robinson, 1976; Semmel, Gottlieb, & Robinson, 1979), the spirit of these findings continued to be a major impetus for the safeguards enacted in PL 94-142. Balanced reviews of the literature comparing self-contained separate class placements with regular classrooms report contradictory results (Finn & Resnick, 1984; Heller, 1982). Some, more recent, well-controlled studies have replicated the harmful effects of special classes (Calhoun & Elliott, 1977); others find no differences. In a metanalysis of 50 studies comparing special class students with equivalent students who remained in regular classrooms, the overall effect was negative for the special class (ES = $-.12$); that is, on average, children in special classes were about one-eighth of a standard deviation behind their counterparts in regular classes (Carlberg & Kavale, 1980).

The details of the Carlberg and Kavale research synthesis suggest why special education is still believed to be a benefit, and for which type of student. The overall effect size for special versus regular placement was broken down by student characteristics and revealed a positive effect for learning-disabled and emotionally disturbed children (ES = .29); a slight negative effect for lower IQ, retarded students (IQ 50–75, ES = $-.14$); and a more seriously negative effect for slow learners classified as mildly retarded (IQ = 75–90, ES = $-.34$) (Carlberg & Kavale, 1980). Thus, we could argue that the group that was the most ambiguously identified as handicapped, the slow learners, was also the group that was clearly harmed by full-time special education placement. Because almost all of the studies integrated by Carlberg and Kavale were done before 1975, the groups called LD or ED were decidedly more seriously handicapped than children given those labels today; the full-time placement is consistent with this inference. Thus, one could argue that, the more extreme the problem, the more likely that full-time special education is a positive benefit. Other reviewers have also noted the difference in efficacy for mentally retarded students with high and low IQ scores (Heller et al., 1982; Madden & Slavin, 1983). This interpretation, that extremeness is the key to differential efficacy, is consistent with the "least restrictive environment" provision of PL 94-142.

In other words, the handicapped are entitled to be educated in as normal a setting as possible. The finding of benefit for more severe groups explains why we still have some separate special education classes: They are a benefit to those whose impairments are serious enough to preclude progress in the regular classroom. But, because the evidence suggests that special classes are harmful to marginally identified children, special education placement should be a last resort. It is not an unequivocal benefit to be dispensed indiscriminately.

Are there benefits of special education for the mildly handicapped, those not severe enough for self-contained programs? Since 1975, in response to the least-restrictive-environment provision of PL 94-142, most mildly, and even some moderately, handicapped children have been *mainstreamed,* meaning that they spend at least part of their day in regular classrooms. The special program for these students is typically part-time placement in a resource room where instruction can be tailored to provide more intensive help on a child's specific learning problems. Although evidence from research on the effects of part-time resource placements is sparse (see Madden

& Slavin, 1983), the following generalizations seem warranted.

First, as with other treatment in the social sciences, variability is greater than effect. Interventions that are successful in some studies are not in others. And we are not yet privy to the subject or situational factors that explain differential effects (Glass, 1983; Kavale & Glass, 1982). Thus, appropriate policies are those that acknowledge uncertainty about benefits.

Second, there have been a few confirmed failures in special education treatments, namely in psycholinguistic training and perceptual-motor training aimed at remediating the underlying perceptual or psychological processes typically associated with learning disabilities (Hammill & Larsen, 1974; Kavale & Mattson, 1983). Even if some Illinois Test of Psycholinguistic Abilities (ITPA) subskills are trainable (Kavale, 1981b), there is no evidence of transfer to academic skills. These programs had in common an attempt to "fix" an underlying disorder that was poorly understood while they took time away from remedial instruction. A good lesson to learn from these negative experiences is that special programs should not reduce the level of academic help unless there is evidence of transfer of benefits to the original school problem. To the extent that these programs persist, resource room placements could be detrimental.

Third, recent reviewers concur that the classroom setting is not so important in predicting academic or social outcomes as are the particular qualities of instruction (Finn & Resnick, 1984; Heller, 1982; Heller et al., 1982; Madden & Slavin, 1983). The features of effective instruction for the handicapped are likely to be the same as those for other children. The most effective approaches involve direct teaching of basic skills, frequent assessment of progress, process monitoring to increase time on task, and some sort of contingent reward system to enhance motivation (see Heller et al., 1982 p. 81).

Fourth, it is logically appealing to assume that part-time resource room placements provide the optimal combination of normal classroom interactions and specially tailored programs to overcome achievement deficits. We know that one-on-one tutoring might be one of the most potent educational interventions for normal children, achieving as much as a standard deviation effect in mathematics (see Glass, 1984; Hartley, 1977). And it is known that smaller class size raises achievement (Glass, Cahen, Smith, & Filby, 1982). It is assumed that the reduced pupil–teacher ratio in resource rooms automatically produces corresponding educational gains. However, the benefits of very small classes do not occur automatically, without the specific features of effective instruction described previously. For example, Thurlow, Ysseldyke, Graden, and Algozzine (1983) found that learning-disabled students had more individualized reading instruction in the resource room but were just as distracted (i.e., had equally poor time on task) as in the regular classroom.

In addition to potential instructional benefits, other positive consequences of identification include the nonnegligible psychological benefit that parents and teachers feel that something is being done about the problem (Scriven, 1983). Special educators also recognize that the identification of specific disabilities elicits sympathy and political power that garner otherwise unattainable resources (Gallagher, 1972). For some specific subgroups of the mildly handicapped, *diagnosis* also means a match with effective noneducational treatments such as drug treatment of hyperactivity (Kavale, 1981a; Weiss & Hechtman, 1979) and psychotherapy (M. L. Smith, Glass, & Miller, 1980).

Negative Consequences of Identification

The labels that entitle children to special services might themselves be a source of harm. Social deviance theory suggests that social organizations create deviance by specifying rules whereby individuals are identified as different (Becker, 1963; Schur, 1971). From this perspective, individuals labeled abnormal are the victims of social sanctions, rather than possessing an intrinsic abnormality. Especially when deviant behaviors are observed in both the labeled and normal populations, deviance theorists look to the perceptions and motives of the labelers for an explanation as to why particular individuals are singled out for deviant roles.

At the extreme, deviance or labeling theory has been discredited or refuted by demonstrating that the problems of severe, institutionalized populations are serious and not dependent on isolated or self-serving normative comparisons. For example, Edgerton (1970) found social recognition of mental incompetence in all societies, even primitive cultures. Gove (1970) found that the public conception of mental illness was so negative that family and community members worked to deny that an individual was ill, rather than seizing upon isolated deviant behaviors to designate an individual as abnormal.

Labeling theory is clearly indefensible as the sole explanation for severe retardation or psychotic disorders. For milder and more ambiguously defined disorders, however, labeling theory might still be relevant for explaining why some individuals are identified as abnormal and others with similar characteristics are not. For example, Rist and Harrell (1982) use a labeling perspective to examine the social processes involved in calling a child learning disabled.

Although most theorists are willing to acknowledge that there could be prior behaviors in the mentally retarded or emotionally disturbed that cause them to be identified as different, a separate claim made by social deviance theory is that the label has its own effects. *Handicapped, retarded,* or *disturbed* are derogatory names that become more potent when they are confirmed by the system. For example, Edgerton (1967) observed that deinstitutionalized mentally retarded individuals devoted a great deal of time and energy to denying the accuracy of their labeled retardation. Research studies intended to test the effects of special education labels have been unable to demonstrate whether labeling lowers self-esteem or motivation, principally because it is impossible to disentangle the effects of the prior condition from those of the label per se MacMillan, Jones & Aloia, 1974; MacMillan & Meyers, 1979). Thus, there remains concern, rather than demonstrated fact, that labels have debilitating effects on the children to whom they are applied.

At the same time, handicapped labels are believed to change the behavior of those who interact with the child so labeled. Several negative aspects of classification were summarized by Goldstein, Arkell, Ashcroft, Hurley, and Lilly (1976). For example, categorical labels are likely to be reified. The label becomes the explanation for observed behavior: "He cannot read because he is learning disabled." Reification becomes tautological, and, at the very least, the observer is excused from looking any deeper for an understanding of the problem. Also, by focusing on the child's inadequacies, classification systems ignore the interactive nature of classroom problems and tend to blame the child for what might be instructional inadequacies (see also Coles, 1978).

Another negative consequence is that labeling encourages stereotyping of the handicapped. The label, such as *disturbed,* becomes a shortcut summary for a child. Instead of noticing unique strengths and weaknesses, a teacher might rely on a stereotyped view of the handicapped category as a description of the child's capabilities. Generally, expectations are lowered and opportunities are reduced; less challenging work is presented, and there is less teacher pressure for academic progress (Hobbs, 1975). Research into whether a teacher's expectations create a self-fulfilling prophecy that can alter achievement has been equivocal and never so compelling as the original study (Rosenthal & Jacobsen, 1968). There is evidence, however, that negative behaviors are associated in people's minds with handicapped labels and that abnormal behaviors are falsely imputed to normal individuals when they are labeled (G. G. Foster, Ysseldyke, & Reese, 1975; Salvia, Clark, & Ysseldyke, 1973). Although there is no proof that these unfair or overgeneralized attributions actually lower the performance of handicapped individuals, subtle negative effects of this kind, together with the influence of classmates, remain plausible explanations for the negative outcomes that have been documented for special education placements.

Research on the effects of labeling is equivocal. The sides taken are better explained by beliefs than by proofs from the data. MacMillan and Meyers (1979) generally believe that, when properly exercised, categorical labeling "provides benefits that outweigh costs" (p. 188). They summarize the trade-offs thus:

> While we agree that labels may not be worn as a badge of distinction, we are in most cases considering a series of unattractive options: The child can wallow along in general education making little, or no progress and avoid labeling or can be delivered services that are designed to promote more successful achievement, which still requires some form of labeling. (p. 189)

In visible class-action suits, however, parents of minority children have sought to prevent the placement of their children in special education classes (*Larry P. v. Riles,* 1979; Parents in Action on Special Education v. Hannon, 1980). These groups were not persuaded that benefits of placement exceeded harm. Although the debate is unresolved, there is general agreement that policies governing identification should acknowledge the potential for dead-end placements and stigmatizing labels and should weigh intended benefits against these possible costs (see Heller, 1982).

There is another negative consequence of identification of which there is little awareness. Even with the safeguards of PL 94-142, any classification necessarily results in overidentification of normal children as handicapped, because each of the

various disorders is relatively rare. Most people understand that there will be some classification errors, given fallible tests and fallible clinical judgments. But, their intuition is to expect that the number of misclassified normal children will be small, compared with the number of validly identified handicapped children. In fact, even with reasonably valid measures, the identifications will be about equally divided between correct decisions and false-positive decisions.

The basis of this situation has long been recognized in the psychometric literature: Population base rates, as well as the validity of clinical indicators, affect the accuracy of selection decisions (Meehl & Rosen, 1955). Suppose, for example, that the true incidence (base rate) of learning disabilities is 5% and that we therefore choose to classify 5% of schoolchildren as learning disabled. (The problem would be even greater for clinical types of rarer frequency).

Figure 17.1 is the familiar crosstabulation of clinical classification decisions against true characteristics. This example was constructed from the bivariate selection tables given by H. C. Taylor and Russell (1939), assuming a validity coefficient of .75, which is probably generous, given the ambiguity of signs for diagnosing LD. Although 94% of the decisions made in this situation were accurate, the crucial comparison is among the 5% of children who were classified LD. Over half of the children labeled LD were actually normal. In a group of 1,000 children classified LD, only 400 would actually have the disorder. If, instead, the validity of clinical evidence were .5, only one-quarter of those labeled LD would actually be learning disabled. This discouraging picture occurs without bias or any other nefarious influence, as an inevitable consequence of attempting to detect a rare phenomenon using fallible criteria. Note that the same validity coefficient of .5 would lead to two-thirds (compared with one-quarter) correct identifications if we were trying to detect something that occurred in 50% of the population. Thus, misidentification is an omnipresent and substantial problem whenever we are trying to diagnose rare mild handicaps.

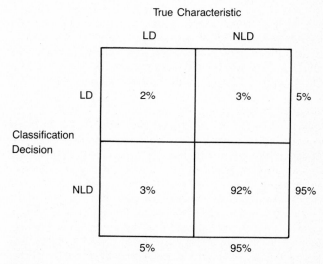

FIGURE 17.1 Crosstabulations of clinical classification decisions against true characteristics.

A final negative cost of identification is the expense of the assessment process. For more severely handicapped children, the initial cost of assessment and staffing is quite small relative to the total cost of special services devoted to that child. For mildly handicapped children, however, it is often true that a substantial part of the special education resources available are expended in identification procedures. In a study involving 81 school districts, Shepard and Smith (1983) found that, on average, more than $500 out of every $1,200 available annually for learning disabled students was spent on assessment and staffing. M. L. Smith (1982) reported the per pupil cost for identification as $1,000, sometimes followed by a low intensity treatment of 3 hours per week in a resource room. Due process requirements, typically involving six or seven professionals, explain the high costs. In this respect, special education placements are fundamentally different from remedial programs, which spend almost nothing on the selection or identification decision. Furthermore, there is no direct benefit to the child of the diagnostic assessments because they are mainly aimed at the question of eligibility and have no immediate implications for instruction.

Bias in Assessment

The overrepresentation of minority children in special education classes has been alleged to be the result of biased tests, especially IQ tests. The issues and relevant literature on test bias are discussed by Cole and Moss in this volume.

In the past, there have been egregious examples of racial (ethnic) prejudices acted out in the misinterpretation of intelligence tests. Goddard (1917) tested foreign-speaking immigrants arriving at Ellis Island and concluded that the majority were feebleminded. Essentially the same misuse was demonstrated in *Diana v. State Board of Education* (1970), which dealt with Mexican-American children who had been placed in special classes on the basis of English IQ tests and who gained a standard deviation when retested on Spanish-language versions. More recently, however, numerous studies and reviews (Bond, 1981; Jensen, 1980; Reynolds, 1982) have failed to demonstrate that educational and psychological tests (administered in the appropriate language) are biased against blacks or other minority groups. The change has occurred not so much because of changes in the tests (although they have improved) but because of changes in the inferences.

Psychologists have always understood that intelligence could be influenced by environment, even if there is sharp disagreement as to the relative contribution of genetic and environmental factors. For example, heritability coefficients range from .9 to 0 (see Jensen, 1980; H. F. Taylor, 1980). The public persists in believing that intelligence is largely inherited. In the early 1970s, attacks on IQ testing were fueled by the angry response to Jensen's (1969) claim of genetic differences between races. The uproar has caused psychologists to be more cautious about what tests can be said to measure. For example, intelligence tests are called measures of "developed abilities," to remind the public of a more appropriate meaning for test scores. As noted by Jensen (1980), "the terms 'capacity' and 'potential' have gone out of favor in modern psychometrics, and for good reason. . . . Tests obviously measure what the individual can do at the time of taking the test and not what he was born with" (p. 242). In the special education literature, it has been argued that IQ tests should be called *tests of academic aptitude* (Reschly, 1979) or *tests of school functioning level* (Mercer, 1979). Given this understanding of intelligence, the tests are equally good as predictors of school success in minority and majority groups; hence the finding of no bias in most studies.

It is now clear that IQ tests do not measure innate potential. They do not assess how a child would have done in school if he or she had been born into a different family or had enjoyed a different set of early school experiences. But, even if specialists hold this more defensible meaning, controversy still exists, because it is not easy to change public conceptions. Once again, interpretation of the facts depends on values. One side might say that intelligence and achievement tests are accurate indicators of existing deficits for which special education is a remedy. Others would say that accepting a stigmatizing label with the connotation of biological inferiority is too big a price to pay for services of questionable efficacy. Notice that neither side says that IQ tests do in fact measure innate capacity. The debate is focused on the social and psychological meanings of the school labels, apart from their professional meanings. So long as some audiences continue to think that IQ tests measure only inherited ability, there will be objections to the tests for being biased and insidious.

Placement practices have had racist overtones; children with similar learning difficulties might be called LD or EMP, depending on socioeconomic class (Franks, 1971). But the greatest overinclusion of minority children occurred, not because of racist intent or biased tests, but because of an expansionist movement in special education. In the early 1960s, before people were concerned with labeling issues and ineffective placements, the definition of EMR was expanded to include those with "borderline" IQs (70-84) in provided services (Robinson & Robinson, 1976). This definition necessarily captured many poor and minority children who were behind in school. Today, in response to discrimination suits and greater awareness of racial issues, there is evidence that, among black and white children with the same assessed characteristics, black children are less likely to be placed in special classes (Frame, 1979; Matuszek & Oakland, 1979; Reynolds, 1982).

Although psychologists today have a more appropriately limited view of what IQ and other tests can measure, some explicit safeguards have also been legislated to prevent overreliance on a single test in making diagnostic classifications. The definition of mental retardation has been restricted and requires evidence of depressed intellectual functioning on both academic and nonschool tasks. Tests must be administered in a child's native language. More than one test and more than one professional must be involved in the assessment (these safeguards contribute to the cost of the identification process).

Preschool Screening and Early Identification

The goal of early identification is prevention. If a child's disability inhibits learning or normal maturation, early attention to the problem could assist her or him in making slow but steady gains. If the problem is ignored until after the child has failed in school, he or she can never hope to catch up, even with intervention. In addition, the experience of failing could have caused permanent injury to self-esteem and motivation. The argument for early identification thus seems unassailable. Indeed, for the seriously handicapped, there is no question about the need for early and continuous help. But extending the argument to include the mildly handicapped ignores the problem of valid identification at an early age.

Obstacles to early diagnosis are usually recognized as being of two types: Reliability and validity of signs are weaker at young ages, and, by definition, certain types of learning disorders are not manifested outside of school. Measures of intellectual and emotional development cause greater problems of stability and validity for the growing child, because the underlying trait is confounded with differences in maturational rates. In their discussion of preschool assessment of learning disabilities, Karnes and Stoneburner (1983) reviewed the predictive validity of several variables such as auditory and visual perception, fine-motor development, neurological signs, cerebral dominance, and general intelligence. Many purported indicators have very weak correlations with later school performance. The best predictor is measured IQ; yet before age 5, IQ is correlated only .5 with later IQ (see Sattler, 1982) and presumably less with later achievement. The impact of a modest validity coefficient on identification of a rare phenomenon has already been discussed; With an r of .5, 75% of the children identified as handicapped would be falsely labeled. Another way to keep the problem in perspective is to realize that children's IQs in the early elementary years are correlated .5 to .6 with parents' IQs (Hopkins & Stanley, 1981). Should a child be singled out for special programs on the basis of her or his father's or mother's IQ? To do so would seem ridiculously unfair, but parent's IQ would be as accurate as the seemingly more relevant clinical tests.

We do not have to conceive of the school system as vicious or destructive to imagine that academic tasks in school would place greater cognitive demands on children. In responding to the discovery of the "6 hour" retarded child (President's Committee on Mental Retardation, 1970), Reschly (1982) argues that it should not be a surprise that mildly retarded children are retarded only in the school setting. The president's committee considers it an abuse that diagnosis could be so much in the eyes of the beholder that a child could function adequately at home but be called retarded at school. Changes since the mid 1970s in response to labeling issues have made the definition of retardation more restrictive and have served to reduce the numbers of 6 hour retarded children. Nevertheless, mild retardation as a concept still leads us to expect that these children are behind their age mates in development but might not be distinguishable from other slow developers until they get to school. Similarly, except for extreme cases (with probably other signs of pathology), children with learning disabilities should not be discernible until they fail at school learning. Even in the case of milder forms of behavior disorders, which are not directly tied to academic achievement, we can imagine that school has an effect, whether it elicits new feelings or is less tolerant of existing behaviors.

Even if the impediments to valid early identification are insurmountable, special educators still seem compelled to try. Because of their intention to help, they are likely to minimize the problems of misidentification, labeling, and lowered expectations. One safeguard usually invoked is the fact that large-scale screening efforts (such as developmental checklists in the pediatrician's office) are followed by more intensive assessment. But it is the validity of the in-depth evaluations that have been described as inadequate in this chapter. Thus, it is argued here that early identification should not be sought for very mild and questionably handicapped children. This position is analogous to Heller's (1982) recommendation that, for ambiguous cases, the burden of proof (of benefits over potential stigma) rests with those proposing special education placement (p. 291).

More sensible alternatives to early identification of mild handicaps are general educational interventions aimed at entire populations at risk, without singling out those "who will be disabled." Programs such as Head Start, targeted toward economically disadvantaged children, provide the same types of enrichment activities without categorical labels.

Mild Mental Retardation

Identification is a larger project than assessment. In a research context, identification involves definition of the construct, observation of the signs, and colligation of evidence to support on inference. Identification in school includes the entire process whereby children are referred, assessed, staffed, and placed in special education. The following discussion of mild retardation is divided into separate analyses of these distinct processes of construct diagnosis and school placement.

Construct Diagnosis

DEFINITION

"Mental retardation refers to subaverage general intellectual functioning resulting in or associated with concurrent impairments in adaptive behavior and manifested during the developmental period." This is the most widely used definition, given by the American Association on Mental Deficiency in its most recent revision (Grossman, 1983, p. 1). Originally the concepts of extremely low intellectual ability and social incompetence were synonymous. In the extreme, mentally deficient individuals are recognized by all cultures as those who cannot learn enough even to care for themselves. Doll's early definition (1941) of mental retardation emphasized social incompetence caused by mental subnormality.

Ironically, the more that assessments of retardation became dependent on IQ tests, the more intellectual functioning was separated from social adaptation. Certainly it was not Binet's intent to make this distinction. Rather, Binet believed that

> The most general formula we can adopt is this: An individual is normal if he is able to conduct his affairs of life without need of supervision of others, if he is able to do work sufficiently remunerative to supply his own personal needs and finally if his intelligence does not unfit him for the social environment of his parents. (Coulter, 1980, p. 67)

However, Binet also set out to construct a measure of intelligence that would predict whether a child could benefit from schooling. This focus led inevitably to a narrowing of the conception of intelligence to higher level reasoning abilities. The manifestation of intelligent behavior in social roles or in coping with everyday problems was ignored.

After 50 years of intelligence testing, it was necessary to formally reintroduce the concept of adaptive behavior. The 1959 revision of the AAMD definition of mental retardation (Heber, 1959) added the criterion of impaired adaptive behavior to that of low IQ. It is important to remember that the inclusion of adaptive behavior corrected a limited view of intelligence. Although complex problem-solving and reasoning tasks are necessary to assess higher levels of intelligence, there are more basic skills that do involve learning and distinguish degrees of intellectual competence at the low end of the scale. If one thinks of intelligence as broader than school aptitude, the debate about whether adaptive behavior should be unrelated to IQ seems silly. Both IQ and adaptive behavior reflect learning ability, but in different domains. We would expect them to have some discriminant validity from each other (i.e., to be distinguishable in the pattern of intercorrelations), but they should still be modestly correlated with each other because they both reflect mental ability.

Mild mental retardation refers to less severe forms of impairment that are nonetheless different from normal mental development. Both the AAMD and the American Psychiatric Association's *Diagnostic and Statistical Manual of Mental Disorders* (1980) (DSM-III) consider IQs from about 50–55 to approximately 70 to be in the mildly retarded range of intellectual functioning. Given adequate opportunity and motivation to learn, retarded individuals would still be expected to have difficulty learning and being able to abstract or generalize from learning that did occur. R. M. Smith, Neisworth, and Greer (1978) listed the following performance problems associated with mild retardation: paying attention to a stimulus, using abstractions in problem solving, seeing similarities and differences, discerning cause, remembering what has been said or heard, developing verbal communication skills, being sensitive to incidental cues from surroundings, and reacting with appropriate speed. It is as if, they said, "such children continually operate without having gained much from their previous experiences with the environment" (p. 173).

For most children who are mildly retarded, there is no known biological cause; that is, they do not have chromosomal abnormalities, gestational disorders, or brain diseases. Instead, their limited intellectual functioning is believed to be the result of some complex interaction between genetic potential and deprived environmental stimulation. Mental retardation of this type is usually referred to as the cultural-familial type, or, more recently, it is attributed to "psychosocial disadvantages." These terms are catchall phrases that are meant to include both the physical effects of poverty, malnutrition, and the like and the psychological effects such as inadequate child-rearing practices and limited exposure to language. This focus on nonbiological etiology is, however, presumptive.

The consideration of environment as one of the contributing factors in mental retardation has had important implications for our beliefs about the permanence of the disorder. The AAMD definition was self-consciously made a description of current status or functioning. For children whose disability is not organic and severe there is "no connotation of chronicity or irreversibility" (Grossman, 1983, p. 15). If the observed deficits are the result of missed early learning opportunities, there might be hope that later remediation could correct the inadequacies. This optimism is more a matter of principle than of fact. In reality, mild retardation can be transitory only if both unusual motivation and extraordinarily effective treatment change the child's status. We also think of mild retardation as impermanent because the cognitive demands of adult life must no longer call as much attention to the individual's limitations. However, it should also be made clear that mental functioning is not infinitely malleable. Not all damage from early deprivation can be redeemed later. A deaf child who later hears might never develop normal language. Similarly, learning processes that are not acquired at the appropriate early stage could be irretrievable. A promising example to the contrary is the training of cognitive processes in adolescents (Feuerstein, Rand, Hoffman, Hoffman, & Miller, 1979).

ASSESSMENT

Limited intelligence is still the central feature of the mental retardation construct, and individual IQ tests are still the preferred means of assessing intellectual functioning. The tests with the best psychometric credentials are the Stanford–Binet and the Wechsler Intelligence Scale for Children—Revised (WISC-R) or, for pre-school-age children, the Wechsler Preschool and Primary Scale of Intelligence. These tests include a variety of knowledge, reasoning, and psychomotor tasks. The WISC-R, for example, is composed of subtests that measure acquired facts, ability to follow verbal directions, recognition of abstract similarities, arithmetic problem solving, vocabulary, memory for digits, recognition of relationships and sequencing, spacial relations, and psychomotor coding speed. Representative national norms permit the interpretation of performance in relation to children of the same age.

The use of IQ tests remains controversial despite the assurance that they are not presumed to measure innate capacity and despite the lack of evidence that scores are substantially affected by cultural bias. Thoughtful clinicians will continue to administer IQ tests as standardized stimuli but will less frequently make the mistake of interpreting a single score as an absolute and immutable indicator of intellectual ability.

One way to think about the clinician's task is to recall that IQ tests are intended to be maximal performance measures. Inferences about results are only warranted if a child is indeed doing his or her best. Even at the risk of compromising standardized administration procedures, psychologists should satisfy themselves that a child is clear on what she or he is being asked to do and is actively trying to respond. At the most simplistic level, this means administering the test in the child's native language. For many Hispanic children, however, it is not easy to establish dominance in Spanish or English. Many children who are poor have limited exposure to both languages. The examiner might try repeating directions in both Spanish and English, a condition more like the child's typical mixed-language experience. This suggestion has nothing to do with arbitrary cutoff scores and precise interpretations of norms; it is in keeping with the goal of finding out how maximally proficient a child can be under optimal circumstances. Following the same rationale, examiners can improve validity by spending more time establishing rapport with possibly handicapped youngsters. In an experiment by Fuchs, Fuchs, Power, and Dailey (1985), familiarity with the clinician did not affect the test scores of normal children, but it did raise the performance of handicapped children.

Nonverbal IQ tests have less cultural loading but are also less predictive of school performance. The WISC-R is the preferred instrument to use with minority populations, because it provides a separate reading on verbal and performance ability. If the two scores are quite discrepant, one suggesting retarded functioning and the other not, the conclusion that the child is retarded is not warranted. (Some would argue that depressed verbal IQ is sufficient to demonstrate need for special education.) For purposes of the construct, we are looking for congruent evidence of limited mental ability. The Ravens Progressive Matrices Test and the Porteus Maze Test are other nonverbal reasoning measures that can be used to triangulate the meaning of IQ tests.

Another proposed solution to the problem of cultural bias has been the creation of group-specific norms for interpreting test performance (Mercer, 1979b). It is argued that, because children from minority cultures have not had the same opportunity to learn as children from the white middle class, performance should only be interpreted in relation to others with the same background experiences. Although this tactic might be a procedural answer to the value question of placing minority children in special education, it is out of place for purposes of scientific diagnosis. Separate norms have the effect of requiring that all groups be equal in mean test performance. This assumption is untenable because ethnic groups in the United States have had very different socioeconomic backgrounds that have had real effects on the development of abilities measured by the tests. The clinician's responsibility is to try to find out whether the child has skills that he or she is unable to demonstrate because of the test format or the testing situation. But, in the absence of such evidence, the clinician should not presume that abilities exist and award extra IQ points (see Grossman, 1983, p. 47–51).

Adaptive behavior refers to an individual's ability to meet the demands of everyday living in her or his social environment. It includes age-appropriate skills in self-care, independence, and interpersonal relationships. Mercer (1979b) emphasized that adaptive "fit" depends on both an individual's ability to meet social expectations and a negotiated accommodation between the child and the social system. It is very clear that a child can be adaptive in one context and not in another.

Major reviewers (Coulter & Morrow, 1978; Heller et al., 1982; Reschly, 1982) acknowledge two primary measures of adaptive behavior suitable for making classification decisions that function in the range that distinguishes normal from retarded children: the AAMD Adaptive Behavior Scale—Public, School Version (Lambert & Windmiller, 1981), and the Adaptive Behavior Inventory for Children (ABIC) (Mercer & Lewis, 1977). The former might, however be more appropriate for more moderately retarded children (Bailey & Harbin,

1980; Reschly, 1982). These and other measures of everyday functioning depend on "informants," who know the child, to indicate what things the child can do. ABIC items, for example, that reflect normative expectations of 5-year olds are the following: takes phone messages, handles sharp or hot things, makes up rhymes, jokes, plays across the street, and tracks future events. The AAMD instrument asks the teacher, the ABIC requires an in-depth home interview, usually with the mother. Each method is vulnerable to some subjectivity and bias. Teachers are likely to guess about home behaviors they are unable to observe. Even without an inclination to "fake good," mothers from within the same culture might still apply different standards to the interpretation of behavior. Both of the two named measures were normed only on state samples. Both rater variability and nonrepresentative norms argue against rigid normative interpretations from these measures (i.e., it would be unwise to set a strict cutoff comparable to an IQ of 70).

The renewed emphasis on assessment of adaptive behavior has been in response to the disproportionale number of minority children in special classes who have appeared to be retarded only in school (Mercer, 1973). Use of dual IQ and adaptive behavior criteria indeed reduces disproportional representation of minority groups but also has the systematic effect of declassifying large numbers of the mildly retarded from all groups. Reschly (1981) estimates that the combined effect of adaptive behavior indexes and group-specific norms would reduce the mildly retarded population to .5% (compared with prevalence figures of 2% or 3%). In fact, the number of mildly retarded children has been sharply curtailed, and, as a consequence, the cases identified tend to be more severe (Polloway & Smith, 1983). The evidence suggests, however, that these changes are the result not so much of the adaptive behavior criterion but of the lowered cutoff on IQ and implicit racial quotas under the scrutiny of the Office of Civil Rights (J. D. Smith & Polloway, 1979; M. L. Smith, 1982).

The extent to which children are included or excluded in the mildly retarded category depends on the relative weight given to IQ and adaptive behavior. To the extent that debate on this question has been motivated primarily by value and policy issues, it is more appropriate to address the question of overidentification in the later section on school placement. Conceptually, intellectual functioning is still the most central element of the retardation construct. As has been said, adaptive behavior expands the domains in which learning ability is assessed and helps to make discriminations along the low end of the continuum. In normal individuals, a great deal of within-person variation on different cognitive dimensions is expected; in the profoundly retarded, there is more nearly uniform deficiency. Moving up the scale from severe retardation, more intraperson variation in proficiency is expected, but there should still be generalized inadequacy. A child with an averaged IQ score near the cutoff (IQ = 70) and age-appropriate adaptations would be called normal. A child with slightly lower intellectual functioning (e.g., IQ = 65) and significantly below-average adaptive behavior would be called mildly retarded.

Medical evaluation should always be an adjunct to the diagnosis of mild mental retardation. Medical screening has an entirely different goal for research purposes, however, than for school identification. For educational decisions and labeling, one is interested in ruling out other explanations for poor school performance. In a research context, one is interested in adding to the knowledge of clinical subtypes. Sometimes diagnoses of biological subtypes have implications for treatment, as when heavy metals are removed by chelation. Usually, however, identification of subtypes furthers our understanding of cause and prevention.

A final area to consider for the future identification of mild retardation is direct assessment of learning ability. Instead of inferring that individuals are incapable of learning because they have not learned, Feuerstein and others have proposed that learning potential be measured as the outcome of controlled, intensive instruction (Feuerstein, Rand, & Hoffman, 1979; Haywood, Filler, Shifman, & Chatelanat, 1975). In the past, research on the cognitive abilities of the retarded has been merely descriptive of limited capabilities; those with retarded functioning especially tend not to be able to generalize or to monitor their own learning. Presently, we are fast leaving the nature–nurture argument behind, as cognitive psychologists and behavioral geneticists discover how reciprocally entwined are brain functioning and learned learning processes. In the future, we should expect to understand a great deal more about language and meta-cognitive processes, not only to assess degree of retardation but also to plan remediation of teachable mental strategies.

School Placement

For research purposes we are interested in identifying a population of subjects who are believably retarded, given the congruence of several indicators. We may be especially interested in distinguishable subgroups that share particular patterns in neurochemistry or family background. We might even be interested, if, for example, we were investigating the modifiability of cognitive processes, in studying a sample of very low IQ, poor, black children who were not labeled retarded in school. To gain new insights into such subgroups, it is important that the study sample homogeneously meet the defining rules, a reasonable criterion when classification errors can be avoided by eliminating cases of uncertain diagnosis from the study.

For the purpose of decisions about educational placement, the definition of mental retardation remains essentially the same. The assessment instruments, IQ tests, adaptive behavior measures and biomedical indicators are the same. However, school placement is entirely different from research diagnosis. The questions answered by the assessment are different, and the valence attached to misidentification is different. For real-life decisions, we need to be reminded of the full meaning of test validity. Validity does not inhere in a test; the inference that a test is valid for a particular use depends on the consequences of test-based decisions (Cronbach, 1980; Messick, 1980). In the school context, it is relevant to ask about the efficacy of special programs. Do the tests (or tests plus clinical judgment) match a deficient child with a beneficial educational program? In the single most comprehensive treatment of current placement issues, the National Academy of Sciences Panel (Heller et al., 1982) emphasized educational utility, in addition to psychological validity. In summarizing their work, Messick stresses that

> (M)easures are to be included because of their educational relevance and utility and are to be evaluated for placement purposes not just in terms of predictive, content, and construct components of psychometric validity but also in terms of the educational consequences of their use. (1984, p. 6)

For school decisions the question, Is this child retarded? is replaced by the question, Should this child be placed in special education?

Mercer (1979b) makes an important distinction about attitudes toward classification errors under the medical model, as opposed to the social deviance model. In medicine, the goal of diagnosis is to detect pathology. If the clinical signs are ambiguous, the physician is motivated by the rule that the worst possible mistake would be to ignore a real deficit. In contrast, from a social system perspective, there is no such thing as an undetected disability. To the extent that deviance or retarded behavior are created when an individual runs afoul of society's normative expectations, an unperceived disability doesn't exist. Furthermore, from the social deviance perspective, the potential for stigma and the uncertain effect of treatment assign greater weight to false-positive errors, or, calling a normal child handicapped. The application of these values makes special education the placement of last resort; ambiguity is always resolved in favor of the child's being normal.

To illustrate how these values should alter the weighing of measurement data, consider this summary of the assessment model recommended by the National Academy of Sciences Panel (Heller et al., 1982). The panel recognized the basic conflict between equal protection and entitlement. As stated, their solution was to insure equity, not by arbitrarily reducing the number of minorities, but by setting up obstacles to facile placement. Furthermore, the assessment stage was made more relevant to "functional needs," so that, by better informing subsequent instruction, there is a better chance the teaching will be effective.

The most striking characteristic of the panel's assessment model is that, in the first phase, the student's learning environment is the objective of assessment: "only after deficiencies in the learning environment have been ruled out, by documenting that the child fails to learn under reasonable alternative instructional approaches, should the child be exposed to the risks of stigma and misclassification inherent in referral and individual assessment" (Messick, 1984, p. 5). Evaluation of the learning environment would usually be made by a consulting teacher or by a school psychologist observing in the classroom. He or she would look for evidence that adequate efforts are actually being made to teach the child. For example, is a child who is clearly functioning below grade level provided with appropriate materials or made to struggle with the regular text? Is the curriculum appropriate for the child's linguistic background? Is there evidence that the child is attending class and that reasonable alternative strategies have been tried? Is the conclusion that the child has not learned what was taught based on curriculum-specific measures? The specialist not only observes but also actively suggests changes in materials or teaching method. In some cases it might be advisable to try a new teacher.

In the second phase, the panel's recommendations for individual evaluation are similar to the earlier discussion of construct diagnosis. However, to answer the placement question and to focus subsequent instruction, there is the additional need to assess educational deficits. Normative achievement measures are not directly part of the retardation construct but address the severity of educational need. The greater the disparity between a child's academic skills and those of other slow learners in the same class, the greater the argument for at least part-time special help. Because achievement tests also reflect intellectual functioning (given opportunity to learn), one should expect scores to be congruent with identified retardation. There is even evidence that, in true clinical cases, because of poor intrinsic motivation or deficient acquisition of cognitive structures, achievement is normatively even further behind measured IQ (Haywood, Meyers, & Switzky, 1982). Conversely, clinicians should be wary of instances in which achievement is enough below grade level to prompt a referral but is significantly above measured IQ. Such a pattern suggests that the child can learn, has learned, and should not be a candidate for a separate classroom. Use of the assessment of functional needs to guide intervention also applies to the domain of adaptive behaviors or, more specifically, maladaptive behaviors. Behaviors that are not conducive to individual learning or that are disruptive in the regular classroom can be modified, and that should be the immediate goal of short-term placement in special education. Consistent with their attitude toward the initial identification decision, the panel also suggested exit criteria that place the burden of proof on the school to justify continued placement.

The weighing of negative effects over benefits that is implicit in the panel's recommendations accurately reflects the current view of mental retardation identification. Mild or educable mental retardation is becoming a more sever category (Polloway & Smith, 1983). For research, such changing characteristics make it even more imperative that features of a particular group be well defined. For school policy, there is an increasing problem of how to deal with children who are failing but are not mentally retarded. These children turn up in the discussion of misidentified LD cases and in the final policy section on noncategorical placement.

Learning Disabilities

The field of learning disabilities presents many sharp contrasts to that of mental retardation. It will again be useful to make the parallel distinction between construct diagnosis and school placement, but here the school identification controversy has a completely different tone. This is the benevolent category of handicap that many believe carries neither stigma nor blame for the child. If this is so, why not open the doors to everyone who needs special help? The section on the construct reviews the original understandings of these disorders. The subsequent discussion of school placement issues summarizes the conflict between those who wish to preserve the unique meaning of the handicap and those who would create a generic service population.

Construct Diagnosis

DEFINITION

The following definition of learning disability is given in PL 94-142:

"Specific learning disability" means a disorder in one or more of the basic psychological processes involved in understanding or in using language, spoken or written which may manifest itself in an imperfect ability to listen, think, speak, read, write, spell, or to do mathematical calculations. The term includes such conditions as perceptual handicaps, brain injury, minimal brain dysfunction, dyslexia, and developmental aphasia. The term does not include children who have learning problems which are primarily the result of visual, hearing, or motor handicaps, of mental retardation, of emotional disturbance, or of environmental, cultural, or economic disadvantage. (Federal Register, 1977, p. 65083)

The term *learning disabled* was introduced (Kirk, 1963) as a more educationally relevant and less pejorative label for children who had previously been called brain-injured, neurologically impaired, or perceptually handicapped or who were said to suffer minimal brain dysfunction. Historically, understanding of this type of disorder derived from the resemblance between certain children's learning problems and brain injury or aphasia in adults. Werner and Strauss (1940) first compared mentally retarded children who were brain injured with those with endogenous causes (genetically determined). The concept of brain injury was later generalized to normal children who had an inexplicable learning problem or whose behavior resembled the behavior profile associated with brain injury, that is, they exhibited distractibility, perseveration, and hyperactivity. Note that, in most cases, the diagnosis was based on observed behavior patterns rather than on certain knowledge about actual brain insult. As part of a long series of name changes to better reflect the nature of the inference and to avoid negative connotations of irreversible tissue damage, the term *brain-injured* was replaced by *minimal brain injury* and later *minimal brain dysfunction*. The final shift to the designation *learning disabilities* was also more inclusive of a wider range of problems and presumed etiologies including, for example, dyslexia, which Orton (1928) believed was due to incomplete hemispheric specialization.

The element central to the definition of LD is the idea of anomalous or discrepant learning proficiency. The concept of a specific learning disorder is in contradistinction to mental retardation, which reflects more pervasively depressed intellectual functioning. The inability to learn in a particular area is "surprising" or discordant, given other evidence of the individual's intellectual functioning. Striking examples of LD are often cited in basic textbooks: a successful engineering student who literally cannot read even street signs, and Nelson Rockefeller, vice president of the United States, who had great difficulty reading. (The author knows of no evidence to substantiate the claim that Albert Einstein was learning disabled except that he was naughty in school, a fact that could as easily be explained by his brilliance and sense of fun.) These pure types, with obviously above-average intelligence, convey the essential element of LD but could oversimplify the construct. More often, children with severe and creditable learning disorders have below-average IQs (because the disability affects IQ tasks), but they are not called retarded because their deficiencies are more specific and isolated.

Learning disability has also been called the handicap defined by exclusions. It refers to learning difficulties that are not caused by physical or emotional handicaps or by environmental, cultural, or economic disadvantage. The reasoning is similar to the National Academy of Sciences Panel's strategy for ruling out competing explanations before labeling a child mentally retarded (Heller et al., 1982). This is not just a political ploy to avoid stigmatizing labels but also a definitional element that preserves the fidelity of the construct. It is thus inconsistent with what we mean by LD to infer a disorder if a child cannot see the blackboard or has been excessively absent from school. Of course such children need remedial instruction, but this redefinition of LD is discussed in the subsection on school placement.

The exclusion of causes due to environmental, cultural, or economic disadvantage is more troublesome. As discussed in the context of mental retardation, it is no longer believed that the source of mental processes can be divided neatly into environmental and hereditary "lumps." The two interact in complex and compounding ways. Extremes of environmental deprivation, whether nutritional or in the lack of constructive stimulation, can impede the development of mental processes. These processes become the individual's learning repertoire and are as much a part of brain functioning as if they had been biochemically "determined." Hallahan and Cruikshank (1973), Kavale (1980), and others have argued that we should expect a greater incidence of learning disabilities from conditions of poverty. To acknowledge the entanglement of environment and biology does not mean, however, that all school failure is attributable to learning disabilities. Learning disability is called a handicap and should be distinguishable, at least in terms of severity, from below-average school achievement. It should also be distinguishable in the definitional sense from ignorance (in Mercer's terms, 1979a), from bad attitude, and from bad teaching.

The purpose of the more recent definition by the National Joint Committee for Learning Disabilities is to reaffirm the unique meaning of learning disability as a subset of school failure. The key phrase in this definition states that, "These disorders are intrinsic to the individual and presumed to be due to central nervous dysfunction" (Hammill, Leigh, McNutt, & Larsen, 1981, p. 336). Regardless of our inability to measure brain functioning directly, this statement emphasizes the meaning of the construct.

It should be obvious that LD refers to an unusually heterogeneous set of dysfunctions. If nothing else, think of the plausible causes of LD—brain insult, fetal anoxia, inadequate acquisition of processes—and multiply these by the numerous specific higher order brain functions: memory, language comprehension, visual-spatial representation, and so on. There might even be a unique disorder for each type of specific dysfunction. Of course, the localization, or deficit, model of LD is only one explanatory view. There is equally strong evidence to support a maturational delay model (see Dalby, 1979) including such inferences as incomplete lateralization.

The first priority of LD research is to identify meaningful subtypes that should first be homogeneous with respect to behavioral symptoms, especially the learning problem. For example, "attention deficit disorder with hyperactivity" (American Psychiatric Association, 1980) is certainly distinct from isolated dyslexia. Children in the first group are characterized by inappropriate inattention, impulsivity, and hyperactivity (see Ross & Pelham, 1981); indeed, their discrepancies in performance occur from day to day or from situation to situation, rather than in a specific subject area. Children in the reading-disabled group show normal learning ability in other areas but, even with concerted effort, seem unable to acquire reading skills. Eventually, each subtype should be defined by shared etiology and responsiveness to treatment. For example, the fact that some hyperactive children are responsive to stimulant drugs not only provides an effective short-term treatment but also suggests a better understanding of the underlying pathology.

The predominant mode of research in which some unspecified group of learning-disabled children is compared with normal peers will have to change before much new can be learned about these disorders. Recognizing that contradictory results from study to study could easily be due to unknown differences in population, the Council on Learning Disabilities Research Committee (D. D. Smith et al., 1984) recently established guidelines for the adequate description of LD samples used in group research. The committee's recommendations might be useful for characterizing group differences due to variations in criteria from state to state or among individual school districts. However, despite their continued assertion that the learning disabled are a heterogeneous population, the committee did not propose a solution that would deal effectively with the heterogeneity within a given sample. What does it mean if, on average, the LD group has achievement scores, say, one-third of a standard deviation below that expected for their IQs? Considering errors of measurement, this difference is not great. Are all discrepancies of this magnitude? How many might have no discrepancy or one in the wrong direction? (Reported ranges help but do not distinguish problems that differ in type rather than degree.)

Some attempts have been made to identify subgroups (Boder, 1973; Fisk & Rourke, 1979; Satz & Morris, 1981; Shepard, Smith, & Vojir, 1983), but these efforts do not characterize the great mass of studies done on the learning disabled. In fact, there is some sentiment for ignoring differentiations among the educationally handicapped, if there is no immediate implication for instruction. Past failures to find significant aptitude-by-treatment interactions should not discourage future research, because, in the past, LD samples were nearly always conglomerates of mildly retarded, clinically LD, hyperactive, significant reading failures, and naughty boys and average children in high socioeconomic districts (Shepard et al., 1983). Effective research designs should address either one subtype at a time, such as severe dyslexia without other achievement deficits, attention deficits, short-term memory deficits (Torgesen, 1982), or learning disabilities accompanied by motor problems (Das, Mulcahy, & Wall, 1982), or they should test the generalizability of a study's findings across recognizable subgroups within the sample.

ASSESSMENT

The first datum contributing to the assessment of a learning disability is nearly always a teacher's referral; even a serious learning disorder might not be discernible until a child starts school. Referral for special education assessment is itself a signal that a child is not meeting normative expectations. However, teachers have different thresholds for individual differences. The propensity for some teachers always to refer the lowest child (and the next lowest, etc.), whereas others handle wide ranges of proficiency, suggests that teachers' judgments of academic progress should not be taken at face value. As Gerber and Semmel (1984) acknowledge, referral is a valid indicator that a child is likely to be unteachable by the referring teacher, but it need not indicate an intrinsic disorder.

If LD is an inexplicable inability to learn, an effective assessment strategy is to start with the evidence of inadequate learning and test for other explanations of the problem. The first task is to distinguish between learning problems and teaching problems, but this issue is better discussed later, in the context of school placement. Hearing and vision screening and a medical checkup should be done to rule out obvious physical causes. The exclusion clause of the definition also disallows learning problems that are primarily the result of mental retardation or emotional disturbance. Of course, evaluating the distinctions among these handicaps can be ambiguous. Children in these diagnostic categories nearly all have trouble learning, and they share many disturbing behavior patterns. The distinction between mental retardation and learning disability depends on the pervasiveness of depressed intellectual functioning.

The choice between these two constructs would be more straightforward if it were not confounded by the policy issue of using *good* and *bad* labels, and if it were more widely understood that most individuals, including the mildly retarded, exhibit considerable within-person variation on cognitive dimensions. Furthermore, emotional disturbance is usually distinguished from LD in terms of severity. If a child is naughty in class, we infer that behavior problems are secondary to the learning disorder, but, if the child's aggressive or withdrawn behavior is more extreme and pervasive, the learning difficulty is attributed to the behavior disorder.

A rationale has already been given against presuming that an economically disadvantaged child cannot be learning disabled. How should this conclusion govern assessment? For research purposes, the researcher must have some theoretical understanding of how conditions of poverty or linguistic differences might influence identification of a subtype. If the criteria for group membership seem relatively impervious to cultural bias, for example, they include extreme cognitive discrepancies plus hard neurological signs, the confounding effects of race or socioeconomic status can safely be ignored. If, for another subtype, the lack of opportunity to learn might be confused with valid instances of the disorder, the researcher always has the option of controlling for confounding effects by eliminating ambiguous cases or by studying one ethnic group

at a time. Conversely, if the nature of a disorder such as inadequate acquisition of cognitive processes is believed to be associated with a particular home background, the researcher might select only those cases with a precisely defined "cultural disadvantage"; for example, alingual children who have severely retarded language development in both Spanish and English and whose family members have similarly limited language functioning. Obviously, theoretically guided decision rules ignore the question of what to do with economically disadvantaged children who need special help but do not match a restrictive definition of learning disability.

An intelligence test, usually the WISC-R, is an essential component of assessment for learning disability. The standardized IQ tasks are used to establish that a child's intellectual functioning is normal, not retarded. In keeping with the concept of a specific learning deficiency, however, a learning-disabled child might exhibit very low scores on two or three related subtests. These areas of deficiency should, in turn, be consistent with reported school problems. Because anomaly and discrepancy are the hallmarks of learning disability, there have been many attempts to create scoring rules for judging within-test variability as evidence of learning disability. For example, LD children might have significant verbal-performance discrepancies or exaggerated subtest scatter. Bannatyne (1974) regrouped the WISC subtests and proposed a gradient of difficulty for LD children. None of these rules has been shown to have diagnostic validity. That is, the hypothesized pattern does not characterize the majority of LD cases and occurs reasonably often in the non-LD population (see Kaufman, 1981). Nevertheless, a remarkably discrepant pattern of intellectual abilities might contribute to the diagnosis of LD, so long as it is truly extraordinary and logically consistent with other evidence of the specific type of dysfunction. In the past, clinicians have interpreted verbal-performance discrepancies or subtest scatter without recognizing how frequently the same results occur in normal children (Kaufman, 1976a, 1976b). Once again the burden is on the researcher–clinician to propose how specific deficits in IQ should map with the character of a particular subtype.

In addition to reports of classroom failure, assessment of LD requires standardized achievement tests in school subjects to corroborate the extremeness of the learning inadequacy and its specificity. Given that children whose achievement is at the national median are sometimes diagnosed LD in high-achieving districts (Shepard et al., 1983), external normative data are essential for judging the seriousness of the learning problem in relation to other same-grade children and in relation to IQ. Although it would be best to reserve comments about identification problems in the school context for the section on school placement, it is necessary to caution that achievement testing should not be a "shotgun" search for a significant discrepancy. As noted by the Work Group on Measurement Issues in the Assessment of Learning Disabilities (Reynolds et al., 1984, published as Reynolds, 1984–1985), it is sometimes the habit of professionals in the field to administer several achievement subtests, compare them to several IQ scores, and take any one discrepancy as evidence of a learning disability. If diagnosis is to stay conceptually grounded, rather than service oriented, the achievement discrepancy should be in the same area as the classroom deficiency (say, reading or both reading and spelling) and should be consistent if tested by more than one instrument.

Clinicians have been indoctrinated to avoid group-administered tests for potentially handicapped children. Indeed, if scores are extremely depressed on group achievement tests, an individual test should be given, to permit maximal performance. However, if group tests given as a regular part of a district testing program show adequate performance in relation to IQ, they should be believed. Group tests do not inflate scores, and normal achievement on standardized tests should direct attention back to the classroom for an explanation of the learning problem.

From the inception of the LD category, special educators have sought a formula for quantifying the discrepancy between achievement and intellectual potential. The earliest methods were borrowed from the reading disability literature and had serious technical problems. As noted by several reviewers, the old computations attempted to convert from IQ into expected grade equivalents, using IQ as if it were a ratio scale and ignoring the changing variance of achievement across grade levels (Cone & Wilson, 1981; McLeod, 1979; Shepard, 1980). Early formulations also ignored the regression of achievement on IQ; thus, clinicians who tried to use these statistical identification rules would erroneously expect a child's achievement to be as extreme (above or below the mean) as his or her IQ score. Because of regression to the mean, this expectation would necessarily be too low for low-ability examinees and too high for high-ability examinees.

The Work Group on Measurement Issues (Reynolds et al., 1984) provides the most thorough treatment of the statistical issues involved in determining a severe discrepancy. They recommended that discrepancy scores between achievement and ability be computed by using a simple prediction or regression model. Achievement (the Y variable) is regressed on IQ (the X variable. Then, rather than obtaining a simple difference between X and Y, the important discrepancy is between observed achievement and expected achievement ($\hat{Y}$), based on X:

$$\hat{D} = Y - \hat{Y}$$

When both X and Y are expressed in z-score units, predicted achievement is a simple function of the correlation between X and Y,

$$z_{\hat{y}} = r_{xy}z_x$$

To judge the magnitude of a child's discrepancy, the individual $Y - \hat{Y}$ is compared with the distribution of residual scores. The standard deviation of this distribution is the standard error of estimate. Again, when X and Y are expressed as z-scores, the standard error is

$$s_{y\cdot x} = \sqrt{1 - r_{xy}^2}$$

A cutoff score defining a severe discrepancy can then be selected from the table of normal deviates. For example, children whose achievement is more than 1.65, or 2 standard errors below ability, are said to be among the 5% or 2% most discrepant cases. Note that Reynolds (1984–1985) recommends a one-tailed cutoff rule, because only negative instances are being sought. Indeed, children are referred because an achieve-

ment deficit is suspected. The formula for severe discrepancy can be written as follows:

$$\text{Severe Discrepancy} \leq z_\alpha s_{y\cdot x}$$

A child's negative residual must be greater than this value to be considered severe (i.e., $\dfrac{Y - \hat{Y}}{s_{y\cdot x}} \leq z_\alpha$).

Reynolds goes on to propose a further refinement of the prediction model, taking into account the reliability of $Y - \hat{Y}$. However, so long as relatively extreme cases are being sought, as in the examples just given, the discrepancy will automatically be large enough to be considered a reliable difference. To be a valid sign of a learning handicap, a child's deficiency should be very extreme or unusual. By focusing directly on the validity issue, rather than on reliability, some conceptual errors that clinicians have made in the past can be avoided. For example, Kaufman (1976b) found that clinicians were interpreting, as signs of pathology, WISC-R verbal-performance discrepancies that occurred in fully one-third of the normative population. These clinicians made the mistake of believing that reliable, or "significant," discrepancies represented important, large, and unusual differences in performance.

Since obviously inadequate formulas for significant discrepancy have been discarded, the only serious alternative to the simple prediction model has been the true-score regression model or, more properly, regression estimates of true discrepancies. Reynolds (1984–1985) gives the formulae for this procedure, which the Work Group referred to as *Model Four*. *Regression estimation* in this context means that observed IQ and achievement scores are regressed to their respective means, based on errors of measurement in both X and Y. The true-score regression method does not take the regression between achievement and IQ into account. For this reason, it is not an acceptable method for LD identification. By not allowing for the empirical relation between the two measures, the formulation assumes that the true scores are perfectly correlated (or that the regression line is a 45° line). Practically, this means that high-IQ children have a greater probability of being identified as learning disabled. With a much steeper implicit regression line than the actual regression slope, it is easier for students above the mean on IQ to appear to be significantly below the regression line. Conversely, students with below-average IQs whose achievement is relatively even lower than their ability do not appear discrepant. Conceptually, the true-score regression model is flawed, because it treats the X and Y measures as if they were estimators of the same underlying ability. This contradicts our understanding of LD as specific learning deficits that are distinct from general intellectual functioning.

Many believe that the ideal statistical approach would compare achievement and ability after correcting for both measurement error and the regression of achievement on IQ. Such a formula, to estimate true residual change or true residual difference, is available in the classic paper by Cronbach and Furby (1970, Equation 23). The development of that equation will not be repeated here, nor is its use recommended over the simple prediction model. In practice, it is very unlikely that the necessary studies would have been done to provide estimates of the appropriate reliability coefficients. Furthermore, unless there is some nonarbitrary and absolute basis for interpreting a severe discrepancy, the true-score prediction model and the simple prediction model identify the same cases. The 5% who are the most extreme from the regression slope of observed scores are also the most extreme when true scores are regressed on true scores, because both the scores and slope are adjusted by the same linear transformation. Effort spent trying to improve statistical identification procedures would more profitably be invested in implementing a multivariate prediction model (Cronbach & Furby, 1970, Equation 24) in which the assessment of IQ and achievement are improved by multiple measures of each.

Although discrepancy is the key to the LD construct, too much attention given to statistical formulae could be misguided. A prediction equation, or even tables suggesting the normal range of achievement for a given IQ, can improve diagnostic practice, especially when clinicians have very poor instincts about how big a difference must be before it is both reliable and unusual (Shepard, 1983). But neither the presence nor the absence of a statistically severe discrepancy is diagnostic by itself. Severe language disorders or attentional disorders that are part of the disability could depress measured IQ, thus obscuring a discrepancy. Nonetheless such cases should be distinguishable, by a combination of other signs, from retarded or slow learners. Conversely, many children have quantifiable discrepancies for reasons other than an intrinsic learning disorder, including English as a second language, poor motivation, and missed curriculum because of excessive absences or moves from school to school. Rigid adherence to statistical criteria would miss a few, rare instances of extreme and believable disorders. At the same time, a large percentage of false-positive errors would be guaranteed because of the base-rate problem described earlier and the fallibility of measures.

What other signs make it plausible that a child has an intrinsic disorder, some inferred dysfunction in the central nervous system? If the learning problem is localized, assessment evidence should help identify the within-brain discrepancy. For example, a child might be able to remember facts presented orally that were not learned from text. Or, from a more developmental perspective, a child might be able to solve inaccessible problems if told the intermediate steps. Understanding of these internal processes is the goal of learning research and is central to the problem of defining and explaining learning disorders. At present, there is no instrument that can unambiguously pinpoint the source of difficulty.

Old measures of assessing internal mental processes were notably unsuccessful. Instruments such as the Frostig Developmental Test of Perception, the Purdue Perceptual Motor Survey, and the Illinois Test of Psycholinguistic Abilities were based on the authors' hypotheses about intermediate brain processes. If children had intact senses and motor responses but could not meet normative standards on perceptual or language tasks, it was presumed they were not processing information accurately, that they had a perceptual or language-processing deficit. These assessment devices were accompanied by training materials intended to remedy the deficient mechanisms. Unfortunately, the various psychological processing instruments tended not to have discriminant validity

from IQ. Thus, what appeared to be a profile of intact versus impaired functions could instead be the ordinary within-person pattern for a below-average learner. Although these measures had modest or low correlations with school achievement, they did not have diagnostic or construct validity (see reviews by Arter & Jenkins, 1979; Coles, 1978). That is, these processing tests could not reliably distinguish learning-disabled from normal learners. As cited earlier, the literature on the effectiveness of these intervention techniques was also discouraging. Even if performance on the processing task could be improved through training, there was no evidence of transfer to academic skills.

Today's models of cognition are more sophisticated and better grounded in empirical work. There is increasing interest in neuropsychological measures intended to link observed learning behavior to brain structure and organization. An entire issue of the *School Psychology Review* (1981) was devoted to the use of neuropsychological models to understand children's learning disorders. This heightened interest in internal processes is consistent with the reaffirmation by the National Joint Committee on the Learning Disabilities that learning disabilities are presumed to be associated with central nervous system dysfunction. Models of brain functioning such as Luria's (1966) paradigm of simultaneous and successive processing can be used to generate measures and expected subtypes. Or, starting empirically, clusters of LD cases can be identified by using neuropsychological measures, suggesting differences in location and extent of dysfunction. For example, Petrauskas and Rourke (1979) and Fisk and Rourke (1979) found three subgroups among retarded readers: (a) those with deficits in concept formation, word blending, verbal fluency, and sentence memory; (b) those with deficits in visual-spatial abilities and verbal comprehension and verbal coding; and (c) those with impairment in sequencing, linguistic abilities, and finger localization.

The best known neuropsychological batteries are the Luria–Nebraska Neuropsychological Battery for Children and the Halstead–Reitan Batteries (see an extensive review by Hartlage (1982)). The batteries must be comprehensive because they seek to avoid the confounding effects of global IQ by providing discrete tests of many separable lower and higher order cognitive skills. The Reitan–Indiana Neuropsychological Test Battery for children ages 5 to 8 includes a category test, a blindfolded block test with dominant and nondominant hand, a finger-tapping task, a matching pictures test, a copying and visual-spatial matching test, a gross-motor marching test, a progressive figures abstraction test, a color form test, a memory-for-figures test, and a complete aphasia screening test of receptive and expressive language. Originally, the measures were developed and validated for brain-damaged populations. They were used with children recovering from brain surgery or with recognized brain lesions, to determine the extent of impairment or to monitor the course of brain disease.

It should be emphasized that, regardless of the current enthusiasm for these types of measures in guiding research programs, they do not have established validity for making diagnoses in a milder and more ambiguously defined school population. For example, on the basis of a half dozen studies with very mixed results, the authors of the Kaufman Assessment Battery for Children were forced to conclude that the Simultaneous and Sequential Processing subtest differences were "less sensitive than we had anticipated as a potential diagnostic indicator of learning disabilities" (Kaufman & Kaufman, 1983, p. 139).

Although advocates are careful to say that the neuropsychological paradigm is merely a heuristic (Reynolds, 1981) and that there is no one-to-one correspondence between any of the tests and valid diagnoses, it is still questionable whether these batteries should be disseminated for use in the schools. This risks prematurely selling the promise of these techniques, as was done earlier with the perceptual processing models. Sandoval and Haapmanen (1981) criticize the use of neuropsychology in schools because it depends too much on the localization hypothesis and generalizes too much from knowledge of adult brain function. Furthermore, its efficacy, if any, for guiding instruction is not yet established. Even its proponents emphasize that use of the relevant techniques requires training and knowledge of brain physiology not typically accessible to school psychologists. A final point has not been made before: True LD children with cerebral dysfunction are relatively rare; thus, the search for neurological explanations in the majority of referred children could be fruitless or produce many false-positive errors. Again, what is good for research is not necessarily good for school practice.

The assessment of learning disability is a struggle. It is fraught with all the problems inherent when a psychological theory and measurements are tested and developed concurrently. There is no well-developed theory of learning or brain functioning to guide the interpretation of signs. Nonetheless, some diagnoses are more obvious than others. Both the researcher and the clinician should be reminded that, the more extreme the symptoms, the more valid the identification. Also, the more congruent the evidence, the more valid the diagnosis. If each measure if fallible, more than one sign must converge on the same conception of disability, before a disability can be inferred.

School Placement

Before learning disabilities were officially recognized as a category of handicap by PL 91-230 and PL 94-142, far fewer children were so identified, and their characteristics were more severe. In the late 1960s, children with minimal brain dysfunction or perceptual handicaps constituted about 1% of the school-age population. Although the prevalence estimates of experts differed wildly, the consensus at the time PL 94-142 was enacted was that 2% of the population were LD and should be served by special programs. Today 4% of schoolchildren are labeled LD, a tripling of incidence since 1976 (Reynolds et al., 1984).

Because of definitional confusion, poor measurements, and the desire to provide needed services, many children have been identified as LD whose characteristics do not resemble the construct as described previously. In the early Child Service Demonstration Centers, the tendency was to serve low IQ or "culturally handicapped" inner-city pupils (Kirk & Elkins, 1975; Mann, Davis, Boyer, Metz, & Wolford, 1983; Norman & Zigmond, 1980). Ysseldyke and his colleagues found school-

labeled LD children indistinguishable from other low-achieving pupils (Ysseldyke, Algozzine, Shinn, & McGue, 1982). In Colorado, Shepard and Smith (1983) analyzed a large, representative sample of LD cases and found that fewer than half (43%) met clinical or statistical definitions of LD. An additional 10% of the cases had other handicapping conditions; primarily they were EMR or emotionally disturbed. The remaining half of the school-identified population was more accurately described by the following subtypes: Children with second-language interference, slow learners, those with minor behavior problems, and average learners in above-average school districts. But should we be surprised that the school populations do not conform to theoretical definitions? Barbara Keogh (1983) argued that there are three primary purposes to LD classification: to provide a focal point for private and governmental advocacy, to create a mechanism for providing services, and to provide a system for organizing research. She was not surprised that the schools served such a hodge-podge of pupils as LD. "The CSDCs were set up to provide services, not to solve the scientific riddle of learning disabilities. For the purposes of classification for advocacy and for delivery of services they did their jobs" (Keogh, 1983, p. 25).

Misidentification is like the misuse of language: an error made often enough is eventually incorporated into the language. The original inclusion of low-achieving non-LD pupils in the category of LD may not have been intentional, but now there are strong arguments to change the definition so it will describe the population being served. For example, Hallahan & Bryan (1981) used the low IQs reported for LD children by Kirk & Elkins (1975) to argue that the majority of LD children have low IQs and hence are indistinguishable from the mentally retarded—another demonstration that advocates of a more generic definition often do not distinguish between research and school definitions.

Perhaps the best known spokespersons for the "school problems" definition of LD are Hallahan and Kauffman (1976). For them the concept of learning disabilities is "a term indicating learning problems in one or more areas of development or ability, and this definition is common to ED, LD, and EMR alike" (p. 41). Their view is well grounded in the behaviorist tradition and is supported by the following arguments (as recapitulated by Hallahan & Bryan, 1981): First, the influence of theories based on neurological impairment is useless and potentially harmful to children because there is no one-to-one correspondence between behavioral characteristics and evidence of brain dysfunction, and the diagnosis has no implications for treatment. Furthermore, the use of the term *minimal brain dysfunction* focuses attention on unalterable characteristics rather than emphasizing factors that clinicians can change (Kauffman & Hallahan, 1979). The exclusion rule, discussed earlier, falsely treats lower-class and middle-class children with the same problem as if they were different. Finally, they argue, it is impossible to identify behavioral characteristics that will reliably distinguish among mildly retarded, mildly disturbed, and learning disabled children (especially, one might add, if one tried to do so with the school-identified populations). Children in all three groups show academic performance behind their mental ages and have numerous social and emotional problems.

Gerber and Semmel (1984) use a similar theme when they propose that handicaps are created by the failure of schools to tolerate or accommodate individual differences rather than by deviations within the individual. The federal psychometric assessment model is misguided, they argue, because it presumes that reliable and valid tools exist to confirm a real and intrinsic disorder. If we realize, however, that teachers typically give more attention to slower students but not to the very slowest learners, then it is rational for teachers to seek assistance for children they find they cannot teach (Gerber & Semmel, 1984, p. 141). From this perspective, referrals are reliable indicators of the learning problem and should be regarded as a legitimate request for help. Bureaucratic controls under this system would be governed not by the characteristics of the child but by the number of children school administrators were willing to treat as handicapped. If schools were allowed to control their own resources, problem-solving teams could work with classroom teachers to implement alternative strategies before deciding that the extra resources of special education were warranted.

A school definition of LD has several implications for assessment. Most important, there is no longer a need to sort out teaching and learning problems. In Australia, for example, the term *learning difficulties* was adopted to include all needy children explicitly because "in practice, it is difficult to decide whether a child's problems relate to intrinsic deficits, instructional inadequacies, or a lack of match between the child and the instruction he has received" (Select Committee, 1976, p. 10). There is much less need to assess intellectual functioning (except to satisfy legal requirements) or to make inferences about neuropsychological processes.

When school failure is the construct, then the severity of the problem can be measured entirely in terms of academic achievement. While those who are still interested in diagnosing "true" LD would use achievement measures at the instructional prescription stage, the needs-based definition would use achievement deficits as both the diagnosis and the prescription. Criterion-referenced achievement tests that provide detailed information about instructional strengths and weaknesses are emphasized because they have immediate implications for remedial instruction. Ysseldyke and Bagnato (1976), for example, argue that because efforts to train internal abilities had failed, assessment should be focused on task analyses of prerequisite skills needed for desired academic tasks. Although arbitrary cut-off rules can be established to limit the number of children identified by this method (e.g., Marston, Tindal, & Deno, 1982), it should be obvious that there is no implicit limit to the number of low-achieving children who could be labeled LD under this model.

Abandoning the internal construct of LD is controversial. Is there a reason to preserve the original meaning in the school context? Advocates for a needs-based definition tend to believe that only bureaucratic gate-keepers try to maintain a stricter interpretation of LD. A number of professionals, however, hold a different *value* regarding special education policy, not just an anachronistic scientific conception. For them, one negative consequence of the "catch-all" definition of LD is that more severely disabled children, those who are aphasic or hyperactive — who would have been identified before the term

LD was coined — are ignored (Poplin, 1981). The new NJCLD definition (Hammill et al., 1981) was motivated by the participants' desire to emphasize that learning disabilities are handicaps inherent in the individual. Many, like Kirk and Kirk (1983), believe that if the category continues to be a "dumping ground" for all educational problems a political backlash will occur, jeopardizing special programs for more severely affected children.

None of the perspectives on LD identification reflects much concern about the effects of labeling. The placement is viewed as an unambiguously positive benefit for the child — typically more individualized attention in a resource room for a few hours per week. (More severely impaired children might be in a full-time special class, but represent less than 10% of the current LD population.) Factors that might mitigate against placement are system level constraints, usually implicit quotas on the total number classified as handicapped. Thus, a two-stage assessment process is increasingly popular even if its purpose is not to ward off a debilitating label. Ysseldyke and Thurlow (1984) describe an assessment model that is similar to the National Academy's proposal for assessing mental retardation. "Instructional diagnosis" and "pre-referral interventions" are key aspects of their approach. Even Gerber and Semmel's (1984) proposal, which appears to take teacher-defined LD at face value, incorporates intervention strategies prior to applying the special education label.

The prevailing practice in schools is to label children who need special help as LD. Shepard and Smith (1981) conclude that only half of LD cases could reasonably be said to be handicapped, but they also state that 80% of the sample had special educational needs not currently being met in the regular classroom. When Pugach (1985) examined teachers' reasons for referring pupils to special education, she found the need for one-to-one instruction cited in over half of the cases. From teachers' descriptions of how referrals and resource rooms functioned, Pugach concluded that "In effect, special education services were redefined as general remedial services — which better met the instructional needs of many students and teachers" (p. 135). From the school-needs perspective, assessment rests on teacher referral and achievement tests. Because LD, by this definition, could include 10%, 30%, or 50% of the school population who are not conceptually distinguishable, this model invites more and more bureaucratic structures to keep the number of children who are labeled handicapped in bounds.

Emotional Disturbance

This discussion of the identification of the emotionally disturbed begins with a conundrum. Emotional disturbance is treated here and by most special educators as a category of mild handicap, yet federal legislation specifically includes only the "seriously emotionally disturbed." Like everything else in this confusing literature, the contradiction can be explained by the influence of at least two schools of thought.

Emotional disturbance is viewed as a mild handicap because it is not a physical handicap; it is one of those "soft," subjectively determined disorders. Furthermore, except for the very extreme and rare instances of psychosis, emotionally disturbed children have symptoms and educational needs that are not easily distinguished from those of LD and EMR children (Hallahan & Kauffman, 1976). Thus, the move toward noncategorical programming and the parallels with other mild categories create the impression that ED is a mild handicap.

Many special educators attribute the restrictiveness of the ED category to the stinginess and conservatism of legislators and bureaucrats. However, it might also be that emotional disturbance was more clearly recognized by lawmakers as an ambiguous handicap defined by degree. As will be seen, many unusual behaviors are exhibited by normal children and become abnormal only when extensive and debilitating. Of course, mental retardation and learning disabilities are also defined by degree, but it might have been believed for those categories that deviation from normal could be determined with assurance by appropriate tests. Because the identification of ED depends more obviously on clinical judgment, the restrictiveness was affirmed in the definition rather than in the assessment rules. The limitation of ED to those who are seriously impaired makes this category more consistent with the public and, hence legislative, view of the term *handicapped*.

Construct Diagnosis

DEFINITION

Public Law 94-142 states, in part,

Seriously emotionally disturbed is defined as follows: (i) The term means a condition exhibiting one or more of the following characteristics over a long period of time and to a marked degree, which adversely affects educational performance: (a) an inability to learn which cannot be explained by intellectual, sensory, or health factors; (b) an inability to build or maintain satisfactory interpersonal relationships with peers and teachers; (c) inappropriate types of behavior or feelings under normal circumstances; (d) a general pervasive mood of unhappiness or depression or (e) a tendency to develop physical symptoms or fears associated with personal or school problems. (ii) The term includes children who are schizophrenic or autistic. The term does not include children who are socially maladjusted, unless it is determined that they are seriously emotionally disturbed. (*Federal Register*, 1977, p. 42478)

Emotionally disturbed children exhibit excessive deviant behavior that is either hyperactive and impulsive or depressed and withdrawn (Haring, 1963). A disturbed child's actions are distressing to parent and teacher and are destructive to the child's own learning and development. Disturbed children appear to have emotional reactions that are out-of-control and inappropriate; might have temper tantrums or be aggressive toward others; and might be withdrawn, fearful, or highly anxious. Often their behaviors such as crying or hitting playmates would not be bizarre in much younger children. Physical symptoms include enuresis, encopresis, obesity, and illness in response to stress. Severely and profoundly disordered children have excessive maladaptive behaviors and no positive social or self-help skills.

Because emotional disturbance is characterized by disordered behavior, the two terms are often used interchangeably. Historically, these labels implied the distinction that emotional disturbances were more serious disabilities, believed to be caused by intrapsychic disturbances (Hewett & Taylor, 1980). Behaviorists preferred and promulgated the term *behavior disorder* because it focused on what was observable and alterable, rather than on any underlying construct. Indeed, the labels more often reflect this theoretical difference in taste than any meaningful distinction among the characteristics of disturbed children (see the survey of professional journals in Wood & Lakin, 1982). Because the labels are unreliable for making distinctions in the population, *behavior disorders* and *emotional disturbance* are treated as synonyms. However, one connotative difference lingers. Disordered behaviors (rather than children) refer to milder and more temporary deviant actions that might be problem behaviors but are not sufficiently serious to classify their owners as disturbed.

The definition in PL 94-142 was taken nearly verbatim from a definition developed by Bower and Lambert (1971), who emphasized, as does the law, that abnormal behaviors of the types enumerated must be manifested to a marked degree over a prolonged period of time. Basically, unless the problems are serious and pervasive across time and situations, it is not clear that one could recognize emotional disturbance. Because most normal individuals exhibit problem behaviors from time to time, pathology can be discerned only in the extreme.

The most controversial aspect of the federal definition is the clause excluding the socially maladjusted, the only significant departure from the Bower and Lambert (1971) description. Considering the seriousness of the problems of children who are socially maladjusted and delinquent, Kauffman (1980) complains that the exclusion makes the definition "nonsensical by any conventional logic" (p. 524). Kauffman and Kneedler (1981) argue that this last clause gives too much authority to the medical model and to psychiatric opinion, because "'emotional disturbance' is given an intrapsychic connotation by its distinction from 'social maladjustment'" (p. 167). However, even psychiatrists recognize pervasively disturbed behavior as a mental disorder, specifically called a *conduct disorder*. Quoting from the DSM-III Training Guide, "This disorder is characterized by a repetitive and persistent pattern of conduct which violates the rights of others or age appropriate societal norms or rules" (L. J. Webb, DiClemente, Johnstone, Sanders, & Perley, 1981, p. 52). The issue is not to rule out a particular subclass of antisocial behavior or to demand allegiance to a psychodynamic interpretation but, again, to emphasize extremity and seriousness. From the DSM-III, a conduct disorder should not be diagnosed unless the behavior is "more serious and more intense than the ordinary mischief of children and adolescents" (p. 52).

SUBTYPES

Work on subcategorizing the emotionally disturbed population is more advanced than are efforts to find important subtypes among the mildly retarded or the learning disabled. Although differences in biological eitology are certainly known for more moderate and severe forms of retardation, the milder cases are undifferentiated, as evidenced by their having been called garden variety retarded. Subtypes of learning disabilities are still unique to each researcher. Identification of ED subgroups is fostered partly because they are obviously found at opposite extremes of normal behavior. The psychiatric profession also has a longer history of recognizing the need for common terminology to guide clinical practice and research. Hence, there is greater commitment in that group to seeking consensus definitions and criteria (e.g., in DSM-III), however imperfect, and to being governed by them when filling out insurance claim forms or publishing research.

The APA diagnostic system is multidimensional and includes physical conditions, psychosocial stressors, and prognosis factors, as well as clinical "syndromes," or, diagnostic categories. Although any of the major classifications could be relevant for a given child, most childhood disorders are included in the grouping called "Disorders Usually First Evident in Infancy, Childhood or Adolescence." Primary subdivisions within this class include mental retardation and attention deficits (a subset of learning disabilities), which have already been discussed. Other subtypes are conduct disorders; anxiety disorders; other disorders of emotion including schizoid disorders (inability to develop social relationships and oppositional disorder), extreme negativism, and provocative opposition to authority; and physical disorders such as anorexia nervosa. A final and usually severe subclass called *pervasive developmental disorders* is further subdivided into *infantile autism* and *childhood onset* (similar disturbance but beginning after 30 months of age).

The DSM-III is an improvement over previous versions because there is more empirical support for the reliability of the classes in clinical practice and because specific criteria are given for inclusion in a subtype. For example, the diagnostic criteria for "conduct disorder, undersocialized, nonaggressive" are as follows:

A. A repetitive and persistent pattern of nonaggressive conduct in which either the basic rights of others or major age-appropriate societal norms or rules are violated, as manifested by any of the following:
  (1) chronic violations of a variety of important rules (that are reasonable and age-appropriate for the child) at home or at school (e.g., persistent truancy, substance abuse)
  (2) repeated running away from home overnight
  (3) persistent serious lying in and out of the home
  (4) stealing not involving confrontation with a victim
B. Failure to establish a normal degree of affection, empathy, or bond with others as evidenced by no more than one of the following indications of social attachment:
  (1) has one or more peer-group friendships that have lasted over six months
  (2) extends himself or herself for others even when no immediate advantage is likely
  (3) apparently feels guilt or remorse when such a reaction is appropriate (not just when caught or in difficulty)
  (4) avoids blaming or informing on companions
  (5) shows concern the welfare of friends or companions
C. Duration of pattern of nonaggressive conduct of at least six months.
D. If 18 or older does not meet the criteria for antisocial personality disorder. (American Psychiatric Association, 1980, p. 48–49)

The stipulation that there be no more than one characteristic in category B is arbitrary but helps to separate isolated problem behaviors from a diagnosis of disorder. The duration require-

ment likewise emphasizes seriousness and, by implication, that the child has been unresponsive to ordinary intervention and remonstrance.

There are several other categorization schemes. One of the most popular in the education literature is Quay's (1972, 1979) behavioral subtypes identified by factor analysis of self-report and observer questionnaire data. Quay's four patterns of behavior are conduct-disorder, anxious–withdrawn personality, socialized aggression, and immaturity. In addition to the first two, dominant, classes, which map exactly with DSM-III, socialized aggression is the delinquency category and, in DSM-III, a subtype of conduct disorder. Quay's immaturity, characterized by poor attention, boredom, passivity, drowsiness, and lack of perseverance, is not recognized as a disorder in DSM-III unless the symptoms are so extreme as to indicate a developmental disability. Clearly this one difference of opinion raises important questions about whether children with these characteristics should be called emotionally disturbed. Although the clinician should be able to make at least the distinctions represented by Quay's major subtypes, the more detailed subclassifications represented by DSM-III are at a level more profitable for research on causes or effects.

ASSESSMENT

It should be obvious that assessment of emotional disturbance relies almost entirely on clinical judgment. Measurement techniques consist mainly of strategies for collecting direct evidence of behavior patterns. Personality "tests" and measures of self-concept might be relevant, but they are not primary diagnostic indicators. Once a reliable picture of behavior and changes in behavior across situations and time has been established, the process of diagnosis rests on normative comparisons and the ruling out of competing explanations. Formal checklists or observation schedules do not make the clinician more insightful about what behaviors to observe, but they are helpful if they provide a basis for judging how extreme a pattern is in relation to the normal range of individual differences.

Behavioral assessment refers to the systematic gathering of behavioral data. Measurement in the behavioral domain could conceivably be approached from any conceptual framework. In fact, however, the term is owned by the behaviorists and is used by them in contrast with traditional psychometric assessment, which makes more assumptions about intrapsychic constructs. Regardless of competing psychological theories, the most important contribution of behavioral assessment is the focus on observable characteristics that are most relevant to the diagnosis. Rather than trying to detect pathology by ink-blot responses or WISC-R profiles, which have only the weakest validity correlations (known groups), they attend instead to the deviant behaviors. Appropriate and commonsense data sources are parents, teachers, classmates, direct observers in the classroom, and the child herself or himself. These methods have been known, of course, to traditional school psychologists but probably have been used only tangentially to more formal tests because they lacked respectability. Extensive reviews of behavioral assessment methods are given by Evans and Nelson (1977), Kratochwill (1982), and Nelson and Hayes (1979).

Behavioral assessment has also improved our appreciation

for authenticity or representativeness of the sampled behaviors. Much greater emphasis is placed on data gathered in a naturalistic setting. The clinical interview is one context in which to test the generalizability of a behavior pattern, but it is inaccurate if it is the only situation in which behavior is observed. If a child is said to be abusive to peers, does this behavior happen only on the playground or also in the classroom? Is the frequency bimonthly or weekly? Is the behavior deviant in the eyes of the clinician or only those of the teacher?

Ironically, behavioral therapists have had such distaste for traditional psychometric models that they have been loath to apply basic principles of reliability and validity to the assessment procedures. Therefore, it is safe to say that they potentially have had the best raw data but impoverished methods of summarizing and interpreting the evidence. Only relatively recently have proponents of behavioral assessment acknowledged the need to consider the psychometric properties of behavioral data (Evans & Nelson, 1977; Goldfried & Linehan, 1977). For example, validity is threatened if parents have selective perceptions or other biases when recalling significant events; and the presence of the observer can increase or decrease the frequency of target behaviors. At a minimum, behavioral data should satisfy requirements for interrater reliability.

There are limits, of course, to the merging of a behavioral perspective and traditional psychometric theory. Behavioral therapists are especially interested in establishing how an individual's response pattern differs from situation to situation (Nelson & Hayes, 1979), because these differences could reveal the variables that control behavior. Thus, it is essential to distinguish real instability in behavior from measurement error and not lump them together in one reliability coefficient.

Construct validity is an issue for behaviorists when separate countable behaviors (e.g., being out of the seat and staring out the window) are used to draw an inference about a global behavioral characteristic. For example, S. L. Foster and Ritchey (1979) discovered that "social competence" could not be reduced to a specific list of desirable behaviors. Instead, the judgment of competence required an inference about the appropriateness of a response in a specific context. Behaviorists are thus freshly discovering what educational researchers using observational data have known for some time: discrete, countable occurrences can be coded with the greatest reliability, but composite impressionistic ratings might have greater meaning (validity) for explaining events (e.g., individual distress and classroom disruption). Such inferences, even if they are not intraperson explanations, require empirical test and validation.

Personality measures are also often used to assess emotional disorders. Anxiety scales and self-concept tests especially, are structured ways for a child to report fears or negative feelings about himself or herself. In the past there has been an elaborate mystique surrounding projective techniques and tests that could uncover aspects of personality, even if the client was unwilling (or unable) to reveal them. The Rorschach, the Thematic Apperception Test, and human figure drawing tests have very weak validity. Although extremely disordered patients tend to have bizarre test profiles, it does not follow that, on the margin, measures such as these can distinguish normal and disordered responses. It is especially difficult to establish discriminant validity from IQ for children on these measures. Clinicians cling to such tests because they symbolize professional expertise and "because they are good for generating hypotheses." Nevertheless, it is well to remember that these tests cannot be interpreted with certainty except in cases in which the disturbance is so grave that it could have been detected without the tests.

To interpret behavioral data, including test responses, the clinician must bring two perspectives to bear: age-appropriate norms and the child's unique context, or ecology. Many behaviors that signify disturbance would not be abnormal in a younger child; for example, under most circumstances, a 6-year-old should not cry and become anxious when separated from her or his mother, but 2-year-olds often respond this way. Normative comparisons are essential but do not imply that every child must be average. If children of a given age could be ranked on some maturational or social-competence dimension, we would expect considerable variation. Many 5-year-olds act like the average 4-year-old. It would only be the child who was consistently at the first or second percentile among age-mates who would appear to be disturbed.

The extremeness of the ED handicap is central to the distinction between naughty, disruptive behavior and the persistent problems of a disturbed child. If serious emotional disturbance has a prevalence of 1% a teacher with a class of 25 would on average encounter only one emotionally disturbed child every 4 years.

The behaviorists and ecologists have taught school-based professionals to be more aware of the contextual variables that impinge on a child's behaviors. From these perspectives, the emphasis in assessment has been on identifying the reinforcers or situational demands that have implications for intervention. However, understanding the ecology also has important implications for identification. Also, both duration and pervasiveness are essential to the diagnosis of disturbance. For most disorders, the DSM-III criterion is arbitrarily set at 6 months. Beyond this, the clinician must be well enough informed about home and school situations to rule out a temporary response to a traumatic episode. The pervasiveness criterion, especially, requires that the reported disturbing behaviors not be unique to one teacher's classroom.

School Placement

The topic of emotional disturbance sets the stage for another battle between the service providers and the defenders of a conservative definition of handicap. For LD, if one gave up the narrow definition of the construct, everyone with serious school problems would be learning disabled. For ED, it is clear that many more children have behavior problems than are emotionally disturbed.

Many special educators believe that the government's estimate of 2% grossly underestimates the true numbers in need. In their review, Kauffman and Kneedler (1981) cited estimates as high as 30% of the school-age population. It is farily clear, however, that, the more inclusive the count, the more mild and vague the implied definition of problem behavior. In one survey, only 41% of the children (over a 3-year period) were *never* identified by their teachers as having behavior problems. Thus, as Kauffman and Kneedler (1981) conclude,

> Although "behavior problem" may not mean the same thing as "emotionally disturbed," there are good reasons to believe that a sizable proportion of school children—probably 7.5 to 10%—exhibit behavior consistently perceived by teachers as disordered enough to warrant special attention or intervention. (p. 168)

A service orientation also raises the issue of screening. Following the same reasoning as early identification programs, behavioral screening is intended to identify problems before they are of such severity that treatment might not be effective. As Mercer (1979a) explains, screening efforts conform to the medical model's presumption of an underlying pathology that is as yet undetected. The concept of an invisible disorder, however, contradicts the normative definition of emotional disturbance. If we cannot see it, cannot recognize it as deviant, how can it exist? More pragmatically, among apparently normal children it is impossible to distinguish the rare child who is "about to become disturbed" from the 30% of the cohort who are at the naughty or immature end of the normal behavioral continuum. The only legitimate use of behavioral screening arises when working with groups of normal, healthy children, and that is to capitalize on strengths and remediate weaknesses. Labeling or categorical diagnosis would not be warranted if screening measures uncovered previously unrecognized problems.

If educational need is substituted for the construct definition of emotionally disturbed, teachers' reports of disturbing behavior become salient in the assessment process. The arguments of Gerber and Semmel (1984) apply to behavioral disorders as well as learning disabilities. A teacher's referral is essentially a statement that the child's behavior is beyond the limits of tolerance and that learning will not take place without special help.

Assessment data gathered by the clinician are essentially the same for school decisions as for research and clinical categorization. Differences in identification practices reflect differences in values more than differences in definition, psychological models, and psychometric techniques. If one believes that labeling a child emotionally disturbed could be harmful, one is likely to use the designation sparingly. If one's professional orientation is to help the child and the teacher (believing that the labels serve only funding purposes), one will be inclined to verify that a child with milder problems needs services. As the low incidence of ED suggests, however, emotional disturbance is not so popular a category as LD. The current number being served is only .8%, rather than the estimated 2% or more. For many, ED is still a pejorative label, which mitigates against the pressure to place a child to receive services.

Although it has not been discussed directly in the literature on emotional disturbance, an effective identification model is still one that makes special education the last resort. From the ecological perspective, the goal of data gathering should be to document the appropriateness of behaviors in various settings. Then, following the National Academy of Sciences model or that of Gerber and Semmel (1984), strategies for improving the interactions between teacher and child should be tried and monitored before ascribing the problem to the child. Especially if the severe behavior problems seem to originate with a given teacher in a given year, it would be important to try a different teacher before calling the child disturbed.

Conclusions

This chapter appears in a volume on educational measurement. Yet, in addressing the identification of the mildly handicapped, the author has given only passing attention to assessment and testing. For the purposes of research, an understanding of the intended construct is more important than a single sign or psychometric device. For the purposes of school placement, both the constructs and the trait validity of the tests have become nearly irrelevant. In schools the compelling issue is how to provide services for children who are failing and placing too great a demand on regular classrooms. My opinion is that children should not have to be labeled *handicapped* to receive remedial help. But this is a matter of values, and my beliefs are not necessarily widely shared. Elsewhere it has been argued that treating these problems as if they were amenable to technical solution not only misses the point but can also actually be harmful, such as by adding to the already excessive cost of assessment without increasing validity (Shepard, 1983).

By focusing on the issues more than on the measures, I have taken an ecological approach. Just as we should examine a child's situation, as well as a child's characteristics, so should we consider the ecology of the identification problem. This broader view is consistent with the expanding conception of test validity. Cronbach (1980) has convinced us that empirical facts cannot be neatly detached from value judgments. Deciding which facts to honor as evidence of validity is itself value laden. In identifying the handicapped, the value choice is between validity evidence that demonstrates a match with the construct, on the one hand, and educational utility that furthers an effective instructional program, on the other.

Research Implications

The single most important conclusion to draw for any of the categories of mild handicap is that school-identified populations cannot be trusted as the basis of scientific inquiry. More than half of the LD cases in school do not match clinical definitions and are indistinguishable from other low achievers who are not in special education (Shepard & Smith, 1983; Ysseldyke et al., 1982). The school ED and EMR populations are generally more severe than the LD but vary tremendously from district to district. Some ED and EMR cases are labeled LD.

For research, identification should be aimed at important subpopulations. Researchers have the luxury, not available in school practice, to exclude cases that do not meet definitional criteria unambiguously. The search for subtypes is essential, whether the goal is to find new biological causes for a subgroup of EMR, LD, or ED or to discover aptitude–treatment interactions whereby children of a certain type benefit more from a particular strategy of instruction. It is essentially a measurement task to identify the characteristics of children that make them more homogeneous with respect to treatment effects or etiology.

Policy Implications

The National Academy of Sciences Panel's recommendations for the mentally retarded reflect the growing trend in special education toward noncategorical placements. The panel concluded that there was little empirical support for differential instructional treatment of the mildly retarded, the learning disabled, or the children receiving compensatory education. Furthermore, it is not necessary to use the label *mentally retarded,* with all of its connotations of inability to learn. Instead, a label might be selected to "describe the type of special instruction that is provided, and thus focus attention on the school program and away from the deficits of the child" (Finn & Resnick, 1984, p. 11). Under this model the purposes of assessment are to verify first that every possible effort has been made, short of special education, and to determine the functional needs of the child, to guide instruction. Similar noncategorical placements have been urged for the learning disabled and the emotionally disturbed.

There are several obstacles to sensible implementation of these recommendations that the panel failed to address. First, the panel was silent about whether children in these generic programs should be called handicapped. If they are, the issue of labeling remains. If children in these programs are not labeled, will the rights guaranteed by the PL 94-142 still be assured? Special educators who want to have it both ways rarely face up to this choice. The panel also addressed neither the prevalence nor the cost implications of their recommendations. If the population to be served by noncategorical programs is an undifferentiated mix of low achievers or children with problem behaviors, the eligible population could easily be 30% of school-age children. Assessment could be quite simple; for example, it could be by teacher nomination or by standardized achievement tests, as is typical for Chapter I programs. Except, however, if the children are called handicapped, identification is, and should continue to be, governed by elaborate due process protections. The now institutionalized safeguards of PL 94-142 are excessively costly; for example, it costs $600 to identify a child as LD, versus $5 for Chapter I (see Shepard, 1983). The inordinate cost of identification is caused by continued efforts to try to make the school decision-making process resemble construct diagnosis. Hence, numerous professionals administer countless tests (Shepard & Smith, 1983), even though more than half the time the placement decision is made on the basis of educational need rather than on insight about an underlying handicap.

Nearly everyone agrees that current practice in identifying the mildly handicapped is inadequate. There is sharp disagreement, however, about what should be done to improve the situation. In fact, the competing paradigms have given us the worst of two worlds. The strict constructionists have driven up the cost of identification without improving validity. The advocates of an educational-needs definition of *handicapped*

have created a growing service population, without regard for the huge difference in cost between remedial and special education.

The only reasonable solution is one that accepts the dominant service-oriented model *but at the same time sets limits on the size of the special education population.* (The number identified as handicapped can be constrained by both consideration of teaching interventions prior to child assessment and use of explicit quotas.) To attempt to enforce scientific definitions for school placement purposes is not a realistic option. Evidence from the field clearly indicates that arbitrary criteria such as IQ cutoffs and discrepancy formulas will be subverted, if professionals are in agreement that a child needs help (Pugach, 1985; M. L. Smith, 1982). When local-level professionals translate the identification problem from, Is the child handicapped? to, Does this child need special services? they are making an adaptive response to the demands and constraints of the local school environment (see Lipsky, 1976; Weatherly's 1979 analyses of street-level bureaucrats). The service-oriented model also has its own scientific legitimacy in the traditions of behavioral psychology, (in eschewing intrapsychic explanations and equating diagnosis with prescription).

In rare instances, special education experts have recommended that an instructional-needs identification model be combined with a quota on the number to be served. For example, Gerber and Semmel (1984) acknowledge that political and economic factors would determine which at-risk pupils identified by their teachers could be treated as "handicapped (p. 146). More explicitly, Edgar and Hayden (1984–1985) analyze prevalence data and propose the following:

> An intellectually honest approach is to identify the 2% with quantifiable handicaps; accept a reasonable percent (2%) for speech-only handicapped children; and then predetermine a further percentage of the total school-age population defined as low achieving who will receive assistance by special education and another (higher level) group to receive additional services (remedial programs) from regular education. (p. 536)

Similarly, Pugach (1985) suggests policy alternatives to the use of special education as the primary option for support services. Either evidence must be gathered to document intensive interventions before referral to special education or general remedial programs should be developed "to service students who may need small instructional settings but who are not *handicapped* as such" (p. 136).

These proposals are consistent with the National Academy of Sciences Panel's model but are more explicit about excluding some children currently being served in special education from the handicapped rolls. Perhaps because they were addressing the shrinking category of mental retardation, the panel could expect that an instructional-needs model of assessment would not inflate the numbers called handicapped, especially because other aspects of their identification model were clearly intended to reserve special education as a last resort. If the panel's model is applied to the LD category, however, it is obvious that, without a quota, the instructional-needs model gives permission to professionals to call anyone who needs help handicapped.

Quotas are policy devices seemingly remote from issues of

validity or effective intervention. Yet, in the research on identification practices, it was found that the school districts with the highest percentages of valid LD cases were those with more alternative programs, short of special education, and strict state-scrutinized ceilings on the number of handicapped (Shepard, 1983; Shepard & Smith, 1981). It was also noted from surveys of professionals' knowledge, as well as pupil case files (Davis & Shepard, 1983; Shepard & Smith, 1983), that clinicians were more accurate in ranking the severity of learning problems than in drawing a line between normal and handicapped. Thus, quotas, combined with professional judgment, would have a high probability of identifying the children with the most serious problems as those who are handicapped.

NOTE. This chapter was written in 1985.

REFERENCES

American Psychiatric Association (1980). *Diagnostic and statistical manual of mental disorders* (3rd ed.). Washington, DC: Author.

Anastasi, A. (1981). Coaching, test sophistication, and developed abilities. *American Psychologist, 36*, 1086–1093.

Arter, T. A., & Jenkins, J. R. (1979). Differential diagnosis—prescriptive teaching: A critical appraisal. *Review of Educational Research, 49*, 517–555.

Bailey, D. H., Jr., & Harbin, G. L. (1980). Nondiscriminatory evaluation. *Exceptional Children, 48*, 590–595.

Bannatyne, A. (1974). Diagnosis: A note on recategorization of the WISC scaled scores. *Journal of Learning Disabilities, 7*, 272–273.

Becker, H. S. (1963). *Outsiders: Studies in the sociology of deviance,* New York: Free Press.

Boder, E. (1973). Developmental dyslexia: A diagnostic approach based on three atypical reading-spelling patterns. *Developmental Medicine and Child Neurology, 15*, 663–687.

Bond, L. (1981). Bias in mental tests. In B. F. Green (Ed.), *Issues in testing: Coaching, disclosure, and ethnic bias.* San Francisco: Jossey-Bass.

Bower, E. M., & Lambert, N. M. (1971). In-school screening of children with emotional handicaps. In N. Long, W. Morse, & R. Newman (Eds.), *Conflict in the classroom.* Belmont, CA: Wadsworth.

Calhoun, G., & Elliott, R. (1977). Self-concept and academic achievement of educable retarded and emotionally disturbed pupils. *Exceptional Children, 44*, 379–380.

Carlberg, C., & Kavale, K. (1980). The efficacy of special versus regular class placement for exceptional children: A meta-analysis. *Journal of Special Education, 14*, 295–309.

Coles, G. S. (1978), The learning disabilities test battery: Empirical and social issues. *Harvard Educational Review, 48*, 313–340.

Cone, T., & Wilson, L. (1981). Quantifying a severe discrepancy: A critical analysis. *Learning Disability Quarterly, 4*, 359–371.

Coulter, W. A. (1980). Adaptive behavior and professional disfavor: Controversies and trends for school psychologists. *School Psychology Review, 9*, 67–74.

Coulter, W. A., & Morrow, H. W. (1978). *Adaptive behavior: Concepts and measurements.* New York: Grune & Stratton.

Cronbach, L. J. (1980). Validity on parole: How can we go straight? In W. B. Schraeder (Ed.), *New directions for testing and measurement (No. 50—Measuring achievement: Progress over a decade).* San Francisco: Jossey-Bass.

Cronbach, L. J., & Furby, L. (1970). How should we measure "change"—or should we? *Psychological Bulletin, 74*, 68–80.

Cronbach, L. J., & Meehl, P. E. (1955). Construct validity in psychological tests. *Psychological Bulletin, 52*, 281–302.

Dalby, J. T. (1979). Deficit or delay: Neuropsychological models of developmental dyslexia. *Journal of Special Education, 13*, 239–264.

Das, J. P., Mulcahy, R. F., & Wall, A. E. (Eds.). (1982). *Theory and research in learning disabilities.* New York: Plenum Press.

Davis, W. A., & Shepard, L.A. (1983). Specialists' use of tests and clinical judgment in the diagnosis of learning disabilities. *Learning Disability Quarterly, 6*, 128–138.

Doll, E. A. (1941). The essentials on an inclusive concept of mental deficiency. *American Journal of Mental Deficiency, 46*, 214–219.

Dunn, L. M. (1968). Special education for the mildly retarded: Is much of it justified? *Exceptional Children, 35*, 5–22.

Edgar, E., & Hayden, A. H. (1984–1985). Who are the children special education should serve and how many children are there? *Journal of Special Education, 18*, 521–539.

Edgerton, R. (1967). *The cloak of competence: Stigma in the lives of the mentally retarded.* Berkeley, CA: University of California Press.

Edgerton, R. B. (1970). Mental retardation in non-Western societies. In H. C. Haywood (Ed.), *Social-cultural aspects of mental retardation.* New York: Appleton-Century-Crofts.

English, H. B., & English, A. C. (1958). *A comprehensive dictionary of psychological and psychoanalytical terms: A guide to usage.* New York: David McKay.

Evans, I. M., & Nelson, R. D. (1977). Assessment of child behavior problems. In A. R. Ciminero, K. S. Calhoun, & H. E. Adams (Eds.), *Handbook of behavioral assessment.* New York: John Wiley & Sons.

Farber, B., (1968). *Mental retardation: Its social context and social consequences.* Boston: Houghton Mifflin.

Federal Register, 42 (163) 42474-42518, 1977). Regulations implementing Education for All Handicapped Children Act of 1975 (PL 94-142).

Feuerstein, R., Rand, Y., & Hoffman, M. B. (1979). *The dynamic assessment of retarded performers: The learning potential assessment device: Theory, instruments, and techniques.* Baltimore: University Park Press.

Feuerstein, R., Rand, Y., Hoffman, M., Hoffman, M., & Miller, R. (1979). Cognitive modifiability of retarded adolescents: Effects of instrumental enrichment. *American Journal of Mental Deficiency, 83*, 539–550.

Finn, J. D., & Resnick, L. B. (1984). Issues in the instruction of mildly mentally retarded children. *Educational Researcher, 13*, 9–11.

Fisk, J. L., & Rourke, B. P. (1979). Identification of subtypes of learning-disabled children at three age levels: A neuropsychological, multivariate approach. *Journal of Clinical Neuropsychology, 1*, 289–310.

Foster, G. G., Ysseldyke, J. E., & Reese, J. H. (1975). I wouldn't have seen it if I hadn't believed it. *Exceptional Children, 41*, 469–473.

Foster, S. L., & Ritchey, W. L. (1979). Issues in the assessment of social competence in children. *Journal of Applied Behavior Analysis, 12*, 625–638.

Frame, R. (1979, September). *Diagnoses related to school achievement, client's race, and socio-economic status.* Paper presented at the meeting of the American Psychological Association, New York.

Franks, P. (1971). Ethnic and social status characteristics of children in EMR and LD classes. *Exceptional Children, 37*, 537–538.

Fuchs, D., Fuchs, L. S., Power, M. H., & Dailey, A. M. (1985). Bias in the assessment of handicapped children. *American Educational Research Journal, 22*, 185–198.

Gallagher, J. J. (1972). The special education contract for mildly handicapped children. *Exceptional Children, 38*, 527–535.

Gast, D. L., & Berkler, M. (1981). Severe and profound handicaps. In A. E. Blackhurst & W. H. Berdine (Eds.), *An introduction to special education.* Boston: Little, Brown.

Gerber, M. M., & Semmel, M. I. (1984). Teacher as imperfect test: Reconceptualizing the referral process. *Educational Psychologist, 19*, 137–148.

Glass, G. V (1983). Effectiveness of special education. *Policy Studies Review, 2*, 65–78.

Glass, G. V (1984). *The effectiveness of four educational interventions* (Project Report No. 84-A19). Stanford, CA: Stanford University, Institute for Research on Educational Finance and Governance.

Glass, G. V, Cahen, L. S., Smith, M. L., & Filby, N. N. (1982). *School class size: Research and policy.* Beverly Hills, CA: Sage.

Goddard, H. M. (1917). Mental tests and the immigrant. *Journal of Delinquency, 2*, 243–277.

Goldfried, M. R., & Linehan, M. M. (1977). Basic issues in behavioral assessment. In A. R. Ciminero, K. S. Calhoun, & H. E. Adams

(Eds.), *Handbook of behavioral assessment*. New York: John Wiley & Sons.

Goldstein, H., Arkell, C., Ashcroft, S. C., Hurley, O. L., & Lilly, M. S. (1976). Schools. In N. Hobbs (Ed.), *Issues in the classification of children*. San Francisco: Jossey-Bass.

Gove, W. R. (1970). Social reaction as an explanation of mental illness. *American Sociological Review, 35,*873–884.

Gove, W. R. (Ed.). (1980). *The labelling of deviance: Evaluating a perspective (2nd ed.)*. Beverly Hills, CA: Sage.

Grossman, H. (Ed.). (1973). *Manual on terminology and classification in mental retardation*. Washington, DC: American Association on Mental Deficiency.

Grossman, H. J. (1983). *Classification in mental retardation*. Washington, DC: American Association on Mental Deficiency.

Hallahan, D. P., & Bryan, T. H. (1981). In J. M. Kauffman & D. P. Hallahan (Eds.), *Handbook of special education*. Englewood Cliffs, NJ: Prentice-Hall.

Hallahan, D. P., & Cruickshank, W. M. (1973). *Psychoeducational foundations of learning disabilities*. Englewood Cliffs, NJ: Prentice-Hall.

Hallahan, D. P., & Kauffman, J. M. (1976). *Introduction to learning disabilities*. Englewood Cliffs, NJ: Prentice-Hall.

Hallahan, D. P., & Kauffman, J. M. (1982). *Exceptional children: Introduction to special education*. Englewood Cliffs, NJ: Prentice-Hall.

Hammill, D. D., & Larsen, S. C. (1974). The effectiveness of psycholinguistic training. *Exceptional Children, 41,* 5–14.

Hammill, D. D., Leigh, J. E., McNutt, G., & Larsen, S. C. (1981). A new definition of learning disabilities. *Learning Disability Quarterly, 4,* 336–342.

Haring, N. (1963). The emotionally disturbed. In S. Kirk & B. Weiner (Eds.), *Behavioral research on exceptional children*. Washington, DC: Council for Exceptional Children.

Hartlage, L. C. (1982). Neuropsychological assessment techniques. In C. R. Reynolds & T. B. Gutkin (Eds.), *The handbook of school psychology*. New York: John Wiley & Sons.

Hartley, S. S. (1977). *Meta-analysis of the effects of individually paced instruction in mathematics*. Unpublished doctoral dissertation, University of Colorado, Boulder.

Haywood, H. C., Filler, J. W., Jr., Shifman, M. A., Chatelanat, G. (1975). Behavioral assessment in mental retardation. In P. McReynolds (Ed.), *Advances in psychological assessment*. San Francisco: Jossey-Bass.

Haywood, H. C., Meyers, C. E., & Switzky, H. N. (1982). Mental retardation. *Annual Review of Psychology, 33,* 309–342.

Heber, R. F. (1959). *A manual on terminology and classification in mental retardation*. Washington, DC: American Association on Mental Deficiency.

Heller, K. A. (1982). Effects of special education placement on educable mentally retarded children. In K. A. Heller, W. H. Holtzman, & S. Messick (Eds.), *Placing children in special education: A strategy for equity*. Washington, DC: National Academy Press.

Heller, K. A., Holtzman, W. H., & Messick, S. (Eds.). (1982). *Placing children in special education: A strategy for equity*. Washington, DC: National Academy Press.

Hewett, F. M., & Taylor, F. D. (1980). *The emotionally disturbed child in the classroom* (2nd ed.). Boston: Allyn & Bacon.

Hobbs, N. (1975). *The futures of children: Categories, labels, and their consequences*. San Francisco: Jossey-Bass.

Hopkins, K. D., & Stanley, J. C. (1981). *Educational and psychological measurement and evaluation, (6th ed.)*. Englewood Cliffs, NJ: Prentice-Hall.

Hull, C. L. (1943). *Principles of behavior*. New York: Appleton-Century.

Jensen, A. R. (1969). How much can we boost IQ and scholastic achievement? *Harvard Educational Review, 39,* 1–123.

Jensen, A. R. (1980). *Bias in mental testing*. New York: Free Press.

Johnson, J. L. (1969). Special education and the inner city: A challenge for the future or another means for cooling the mark out? *Journal of Special Education, 3,* 241–251.

Jones, R., & Gottfried, N. (1966). The prestige of special education teaching. *Exceptional Children, 32,* 465–468.

Karnes, M. B., & Stoneburner, R. L. (1983). Prevention of learning disabilities: Preschool assessment and intervention. In J. D. McKinney & L. Feagans (Eds.), *Current topics in learning disabilities:* Vol. 1. Norwood, NJ: Ablex.

Kauffman, J. M. (1980). Where special education for disturbed children is going: A personal view. *Exceptional Children, 46,* 522–527.

Kauffman, J. M., & Hallahan, D. P. (1979) Learning disabilities and hyperactivity (with comments on minimal brain dysfunction). In B. B. Lahey & A. E. Kazdin (Eds.), *Advances in clinical child psychology:* Vol. II. New York: Plenum Publishing.

Kauffman, J. M., & Kneedler, R. D. (1981). Behavior disorders. In J. M. Kauffman & D. P. Hallahan (Eds.), *Handbook of special education*. Englewood Cliffs, NJ: Prentice-Hall.

Kaufman, A. S. (1976a). A new approach to the interpretation of test scatter on the WISC-R. *Journal of Learning Disabilities, 9,* 160–168.

Kaufman, A. S. (1976b). Verbal-performance IQ discrepancies on the WISC-R. *Journal of Consulting and Clinical Psychology, 44,* 739–744.

Kaufman, A. S. (1981). The WISC-R and learning disabilities assessment: State of the art. *Journal of Learning Disabilities, 14,* 520–526.

Kaufman, A. S., & Kaufman, N. L. (1983). *KABC: Kaufman Assessment Battery for Children: Interpretive Manual*. Circle Pines, MN: American Guidance Service.

Kavale, K. A. (1980). Learning disability and cultural-economic disadvantage: The case for a relationship. *Learning Disability Quarterly, 3,* 97–112.

Kavale, K. (1981a). The efficacy of stimulant drug treatment for hyperactivity: A meta-analysis. *Journal of Learning Disabilities, 15,* 280–289.

Kavale, K. (1981b). Functions of the Illinois Test of Psycholinguistic Abilities (ITPA): Are they trainable? *Exceptional Children, 47,* 496–510.

Kavale, K. A., & Glass, G. V (1982). The efficacy of special education interventions and practices: A compendium of meta-analysis findings. *Focus on Exceptional Children, 15,* 1–14.

Kavale, K., & Mattson, P. D. (1983). "One jumped off the balance beam": Meta-analysis of perceptual-motor training. *Journal of Learning Disabilities, 16,* 165–173.

Kavale, K., & Nye, D. (1981). Identification criteria for learning disabilities: A survey of the research literature. *Learning Disability Quarterly, 4,* 383–388.

Keogh, B. K. (1983). Classification compliance, and confusion. *Journal of Learning Disabilities, 16,* 25.

Keogh, B. K., Major-Kingsley, S., Omori-Gordon, H., & Reid, H. P. (1982). *UCLA marker variable project*. Syracuse, NY: Syracuse University Press.

Kirk, S. A. (1963). Behavioral diagnosis and remediation of learning disabilities. In *Conference on exploration into the problems of the perceptually handicapped child*. Evanston, Ill.: Fund for the Perceptually Handicapped Child.

Kirk, S. A. (1964). Research in education. In H. A. Stevens & R. Heber (Eds.), *Mental retardation: A review of research*. Chicago: University of Chicago Press.

Kirk, S. A., & Elkins, J. (1975). Characteristics of children enrolled in the Child Service Demonstration Centers. *Journal of Learning Disabilities, 8,* 630–637.

Kirk, S. A., & Kirk, W. D. (1983). On defining learning disabilities. *Journal of Learning Disabilities, 16,* 20–21.

Kratochwill, T. R. (1982). Advances in behavioral assessment. In C. R. Reynolds & T. B. Gutkin (Eds.), *The handbook of school psychology*. New York: John Wiley & Sons.

Lambert, N. M., & Windmiller, M. (1981). *AAMD Adaptive Behavior Scale, School Edition* (3rd ed.). Washington, DC: American Association on Mental Deficiency.

Larry, P. v. Riles, 495 F. Supp. 926 (N. D. Calif. 1979) (decision on merits).

Lemert, E. (1967). *Human deviance, social problems, and social control*. Englewood Cliffs, NJ: Prentice-Hall.

Lipsky, M. (1976). Toward a theory of street-level bureaucracy. In W. D. Hawley & M. Lipsky (Eds.), *Theoretical perspectives on urban politics*. Englewood Cliffs, NJ: Prentice-Hall.

Luria, A. R. (1966). *Human brain and psychological processes.* New York: Harper & Row.

MacCorquodale, K., & Meehl, P. E. (1948). On a distinction between hypothetical constructs and intervening variables, *Psychological Review, 55*, 95–107.

MacMillan, D. (1977). *Mental retardation in school and society.* Boston: Little, Brown.

MacMillan, D. L., Jones, R. L., & Aloia, G. F. (1974). The mentally retarded label: A theoretical analysis and review of research. *American Journal of Mental Deficiency, 79*, 241–261.

MacMillan, D. L., & Meyers, C. E. (1979). Educational labeling of handicapped learners. In D. C. Berliner (Ed.), *Review of research in education.* Washington, DC: American Educational Research Association.

Madden, N. A., & Slavin, R. E. (1983). Mainstreaming students with mild handicaps: Academic and social outcomes. *Review of Educational Research, 53*, 519–569.

Mann, L., Davis, C. H., Boyer, C. W., Metz, C., & Wolford, B. (1983). LD or not LD, that was the question: A retrospective analysis of Child Service Demonstration Centers' compliance with the federal definition of learning disabilities. *Journal of Learning Disabilities, 16*, 14–17.

Marston, D., Tindal, G., & Deno, S. L. (1982). *Eligibility for learning disability services: A direct and repeated measurement approach* (Research Report No. 89). Minneapolis: University of Minnesota, Institute for Research on Learning Disabilities. (ERIC Document Reproduction Service No. ED 226 047).

Maslow, A. (1960). Resistance to being rubricized. In B. Kaplan & S. Wapner (Eds.), *Perspectives in psychological theory.* New York: International Universities Press.

Matuszek, P., & Oakland, T. (1979). Factors influencing teachers' and psychologists recommendations regarding special class placement. *Journal of School Psychology, 17*, 116–125.

McLeod, J. (1979). Educational underachievement: Toward a defensible psychometric definition. *Journal of Learning Disabilities, 12*, 42–50.

Meehl, P. E., & Rosen, A. (1955). Antecedent probability and the efficiency of psychometric signs, patterns, or cutting scores. *Psychological Bulletin, 52*, 194–216.

Mercer, J. R. (1970). Sociological perspectives on mild mental retardation. In H. C. Haywood (Ed.), *Social-cultural aspects of mental retardation.* New York: Appleton-Century Crafts.

Mercer, J. R. (1973). *Labelling the mentally retarded.* Berkeley, CA: University of California Press.

Mercer, J. R. (1979a). In defense of racially and culturally non-discriminatory assessment. *School Psychology Digest, 8*, 89–115.

Mercer, J. R. (1979b). *Systems of Multicultural Pluralistic Assessment (SOMPA): Technical Manual.* New York: Psychological Corporation.

Mercer, J. R., & Lewis, J. F. (1977). *Adaptive Behavior Inventory for Children, Parent Interview Manual:* System of Multicultural Pluralistic Assessment. New York: Psychological Corporation.

Messick, S. (1980). Test validity and the ethics of assessment. *American Psychologist, 35*, 1012–1027.

Messick, S. (1984). Assessment in context: Appraising student performance in relation to instructional quality. *Educational Researcher, 13*, 3–8.

Nelson, R. O. & Hayes, S. C. (1979). The nature of behavioral assessment: A community. *Journal of Applied Behavior Analysis, 12*, 491–500.

Norman, C. A., & Zigmond, N. (1980). Characteristics of children labeled and served as learning disabled in school systems affiliated with Child Service Demonstration Centers. *Journal of Learning Disabilities, 13*, 16–21.

Orton, S. T. (1928). Specific leading disability: Strephosymbolia. *Journal of the American Medical Association, 90*, 1095–1099.

Parents in Action on Special Education (PASE) v. Hannon. 506 F. Supp. 831 (N. D. Ill. 1980).

Petrauskas, R. J., & Rourke, B. P. (1979). Identification of subtypes of retarded readers: A neuropsychological, multivariate approach. *Journal of Clinical Neuropsychology, 1*, 17–37.

Phillips, L., Draguns, J. G., & Bartlett, D. P. (1976). Classification of behavior disorders. In N. Hobbs (Ed.), *Issues in the classification of children:* Vol. I. San Francisco: Jossey-Bass.

Polloway, E. A., & Smith, J. D. (1983). Changes in mild mental retardation: Population, programs, and perspectives. *Exceptional Children, 50*, 149–159.

Poplin, M. S. (1981). The severely learning disabled: Neglected or forgotten? *Learning Disability Quarterly, 4*, 330–335.

President's Committee on Mental Retardation. (1970). *The six-hour retarded child.* Washington, DC: U.S. Government Printing Office.

Pugach, M. C. (1985). The limitations of federal special education policy: The role of classroom teachers in determining who is handicapped. *Journal of Special Education, 19*, 123–137.

Quay, H. C. (1972). Patterns of aggression, withdrawal, and immaturity. In H. C. Quay & J. S. Werry (Eds.), *Psychopathological disorders of childhood.* New York: John Wiley & Sons.

Quay, H. C. (1979). Classification. In H. C. Quay & J. S. Werry (Eds.), *Psychopathological disorders of childhood* (2nd ed.). New York: John Wiley & Sons.

Rains, P. M., Kitsuse, J. I., Duster, T., Freidson, E. (1976). The labeling approach to deviance. In N. Hobbs (Ed.), *Issues in the classification of children:* Vol. I. San Francisco: Jossey-Bass.

Reschly, D. (1979). Nonbiased assessment. In G. Phye & D. Reschly (Eds.), *School psychology: Perspectives and issues.* New York: Academic Press.

Reschly, D. J. (1981). Evaluation of the effects of SOMPA measures on classification of students as mildly mentally retarded. *American Journal of Mental Deficiency, 86*, 16–20.

Reschly, D. J. (1982). Assessing mild mental retardation: The influence of adaptive behavior, sociocultural status, and prospects for nonbiased assessment. In C. R. Reynolds & T. B. Gutkin (Eds.), *The handbook of school psychology.* New York: John Wiley & Sons.

Reynolds, C. R. (1981). Neuropsychological assessment and the habilitation of learning: Considerations in the search for the aptitude and treatment interaction. *School Psychology Review, 10*, 343–349.

Reynolds, C. R. (1982). The problem of bias in psychological assessment. In C. R. Reynolds & T. B. Gutkin (Eds.). *The handbook of school psychology.* New York: John Wiley & Sons.

Reynolds, C. R. (1984–1985). Critical measurement issues in learning disabilities. *Journal of Special Education, 18*, 451–476.

Rhodes, W. C. (1967). The disturbing child: A problem of ecological management. *Exceptional Children, 33*, 449–455.

Rhodes, W. C. (1970). A community participation analysis of emotional disturbance. *Exceptional Children, 36*, 309–314.

Rist, R. C., & Harrell, J. E. (1982). Labeling the learning disabled child: The social ecology of educational practice. *American Journal of Orthopsychiatry 52*, 146–160.

Robinson, N. M., & Robinson, H. B. (1976). *The mentally retarded child* (2nd ed.). New York: McGraw-Hill.

Rosenthal, R., & Jacobsen, L. (1968). *Pygmalion in the classroom.* New York: Holt, Rinehart & Winston.

Ross, A. O., & Pelham, W. E. (1981). Child psychopathology. *Annual Review of Psychology, 32*, 243–278.

Salvia, J., Clark, G. M., & Ysseldyke, J. E. (1973). Teacher retention of stereotypes of exceptionality. *Exceptional Children, 39*, 651–652.

Sandoval, J., & Haapmanen, R. M. (1981). A critical commentary on neuropsychology in the schools: Are we ready? *School Psychology Review, 10*, 381–388.

Sattler, J. M. (1982). *Assessment of Children's Intelligence and Special Abilities* (2nd ed.). Boston: Allyn & Bacon.

Satz, P., & Morris, R. (1981). Learning disabilities subtype: A review. In F. J. Pirozzolo & M. C. Wittrock (Eds.), *Neuropsychological and cognitive processes in reading.* New York: Academic Press.

School Psychology Review (1981). *10*, 321–409.

Schur, E. M. (1971). *Labeling deviant behavior.* New York: Harper & Row.

Scriven, M. (1983). Comments on Gene Glass. *Policy Studies Review, 2*, 79–84.

Select Committee on Specific Learning Difficulties of the Australian House of Representative. (1976). *Learning difficulties in children and adults.* Canberra: Australian Government Publishing Service.

Semmel, M. L., Gottlieb, J., & Robinson, N. M. (1979). Mainstreaming: Perspective on educating handicapped children in the public schools. In D. C. Berlinger (Ed.), *Review of research in education:* Vol. 7, Washington, DC: American Educational Research Association.

Shepard, L. (1980). An evaluation of the regression discrepancy method for identifying children with learning disabilities. *Journal of Special Education, 14,* 79–91.

Shepard, L. (1983). The role of measurement in educational policy: Lessons from the identification of learning disabilities. *Educational Measurement: Issues and Practice, 2,* 4–8.

Shepard, L., & Smith, M. L. (with Davis, A., Glass, G. V, Riley, A., & Vojir, C.). (1981). *Evaluation of the identification of perceptual-communicative disorders in Colorado.* Boulder, CO: University of Colorado.

Shepard, L. A., & Smith, M. L. (1983). An evaluation of the identification of learning disabled students in Colorado. *Learning Disability Quarterly, 6,* 115–127.

Shepard, L. A., Smith, M. L., & Vojir, C. P. (1983). Characteristics of pupils identified as learning disabled. *American Educational Research Journal, 20,* 309–331.

Smith, D. D., Deshler, D., Hallahan, D., Lovitt, T., Robinson, S., Voress, J., & Ysseldyke, J. (1984). Minimum standards for the description of subjects in learning disabilities research reports. *Learning Disability Quarterly, 7,* 221–225.

Smith, J. D., & Polloway, E. A. (1979). The dimension of adaptive behavior in mental retardation research: An analysis of recent practices. *American Journal of Mental Deficiency, 84,* 203–206.

Smith, M. L. (1982). *How educators decide who is learning disabled: Challenge to psychology and public policy in the schools.* Springfield, IL: Charles C Thomas.

Smith, M. L., Glass, G. V, & Miller, T. I. (1980), *The benefits of psychotherapy.* Baltimore: Johns Hopkins University Press.

Smith, R. M., Neisworth, J. T., & Greer, J. G. (1978). Classification and individuality. In J. T. Neisworth & R. M. Smith (Eds.), *Retardation: Issues, assessment and intervention.* New York: McGraw-Hill.

Swamp, S. (1974). Disturbing classroom behaviors: A developmental and ecological view. *Exceptional Children, 41,* 163–172.

Taylor, H. C., & Russell, J. T. (1939). The relationship of validity coefficients to the practical effectiveness of tests in selection: Discussion and tables. *Journal of Applied Psychology, 23,* 565–578.

Taylor, H. F. (1980). *The IQ game: A methodological inquiry into the heredity-environment controversy.* New Brunswick, NJ: Rutgers University Press.

Thurlow, M. L., Ysseldyke, J. E., Graden, J. L., & Algozzine, B. (1983). What's "special" about the special education resource room for learning disabled students? *Learning Disability Quarterly, 6,* 283–288.

Torgesen, J. K. (1982). The use of rationally defined subgroups in research on learning disabilities. In J. P. Das, R. F. Mulcahy, & A. E. Wall (Eds.), *Theory and research in learning disabilities.* New York: Plenum Press.

Weatherly, R. A. (1979). *Reforming special education: Policy implementation from state level to street level.* Cambridge, MA: MIT Press.

Webb, E. J., Campbell, D. T., Schwartz, R. D., & Sechrest, L. (1966). *Unobtrusive measures.* Chicago: Rand McNally.

Webb, L. J., DiClemente, C. C., Johnstone, E. E., Sanders, J. L., & Perley, R. A. (1981). *DSM-III Training Guide.* New York: Brunner/Mazel.

Weiss, G., & Hechtman, L. (1979). The hyperactive child syndrome. *Science, 206,* 309–14.

Werner, H., & Strauss, A. A. (1940). Causal factors in low performance. *American Journal of Mental Deficiency, 45,* 213–218.

Wood, F. H., & Lakin, K. C. (1982). Defining emotionally disturbed/behaviorally disorderd populations for research purposes. In F. H. Wood & K. C. Lakin (Eds.), *Disturbing, disorderd or disturbed? Perspectives on the definition of problem behavior in educational settings.* Reston, VA: Council for Exceptional Children.

Ysseldyke, J. E., Algozzine, B., Shinn, M. R., & McGue, M. (1982). Similarities and differences between low achievers and students classified learning disabled. *Journal of Special Education, 16,* 73–85.

Ysseldyke, J. E., & Bagnato, S. J. (1976). Assessment of exceptional students at the secondary level: A pragmatic perspective. *High School Journal, 59,* 282–289.

Ysseldyke, J. E., & Thurlow, M. L. (1984). Assessment practices in special education: Adequacy and appropriateness. *Educational Psychologist, 9,* 123–136.

18

Testing of Linguistic Minorities

Richard P. Duran

Graduate School of Education
University of California, Santa Barbara

Introduction

The testing of persons with non-English backgrounds has become an increasing concern among educators and the public at large since the last edition of *Educational Measurement*. The 1970s and 1980s have seen a rise in educational programs targeted toward persons who are less than totally proficient in English and who have a native background in a non-English language. Educators such as Sanchez (1932, 1934) were quick to note early on some of the problems inherent in testing children and adults in their less familiar language, but research and assessment progress in this area has not been as rapid and successful as in other areas of assessment. As the reader will learn from the discussion provided in this chapter, the adaption and implementation of valid testing practices for persons with non-English backgrounds is a complicated matter; it is linked intrinsically to the population validity of tests and to the legitimacy of test-development and test-administration practices.

Following an orienting discussion concerning language, culture, and testing, the chapter overviews samples of progress in five important application areas in the testing of persons with non-English backgrounds. These areas were selected because they represent important arenas within which the use of tests has been coupled with significant developments in educational policy and with scientific analyses of assessment issues. The areas are

1. Language proficiency assessment
2. Cognitive assessment
3. Assessment of school achievement
4. Special education assessment
5. Assessment for college admissions

Consideration of studies for review has been selective, but an attempt has been made to cite studies that exemplify progress toward resolution of significant problems in the field. Emphasis has been given to studies explicitly addressing questions of language proficiency and its effects on assessment.

On practical grounds, only limited attention is given to the large and interesting body of studies focused on ethnic subgroup differences in test performance and only indirectly given to language-related influences on test performance. Apart from the sheer volume of such studies (often involving a small number of subjects), the treatment of this body of research is limited here, because, typically, the studies do not conduct a formal assessment of the language proficiency or other specific language characteristics of subjects. Because of this lack of information, the studies are unable to directly investigate relationships between test performance and the language characteristics of subjects. Nonetheless, some citation of this work is essential. Some studies, for example, have produced evidence of disparities between verbal and nonverbal test performance that implicate language proficiency as a factor affecting test performance. The last portion of the chapter draws attention to conclusions that might be made about the status of testing of persons with non-English backgrounds and areas of future research that appear to be the most promising for the resolution of unresolved scientific questions and questions regarding the best, most valid methods of assessment.

Linguistic and Cultural Influences on Test Behavior

Cultural Influences on Thinking

Assessment of persons with non-English backgrounds is difficult because of the confound existing among culture, language, and thought. Contemporary cross-cultural research suggests that there are intimate connections among the ways people perceive the nature of problem-solving situations, problem-solving tasks, the language surrounding tasks, and sociocultural experiences. The display of intended skills in assessment situations requires an aptitude itself seldom studied: the ability to understand the nature of assessment tasks and the nature of appropriate performance. Everyday familiarity with the language in which assessment tasks are stated might not be adequate to ensure that individuals understand tasks. Scribner (1979), for example, found that the Kpelle African tribespeople were incapable of performing simple acts of deductive inference when reasoning problems involved statements that were not connected to their real experiences, echoing a similar finding by Luria (1976) in his early research on the inference skills of unschooled citizens in the Soviet Union. Scribner and others, such as Cole (1985), point out that the modes of thinking associated with Western formal schooling are products of social experiences and of the learning of values placing importance on these styles of thought. To perform as expected on tasks, persons have to first understand the social and cultural context of assessment situations, the modes of thinking expected, and the ways in which language is used in an assessment context. Thus, analysis of issues affecting the testing of language-minority persons is ultimately not totally reducible to consideration solely of how lack of familiarity with a language affects test performance.

Because language-minority persons reflect a different social and cultural heritage from that of mainstream American English speakers, there is always a possibility that unrecognized differences in the backgrounds of examinees might violate assumptions about the nature of the population under assessment. The challenge faced by assessment specialists and educators is to explore and understand how cultural and linguistic factors influence assessment, rather than to deny that such influences might readily exist. The challenge is to understand both the strengths and the limits of assessment.

Language Proficiency

In the field of human assessment, the construct *language proficiency* refers to a person's learned, functional capability to use a language system. Most typically, the construct is conceived of as unitary, though assessment researchers have called attention to skills in different modalities of language use: speaking, writing, oral comprehension, and reading. Native speakers of a language are assumed to be proficient in that language by virtue of their acquisition of the language during childhood. The term *language proficiency* usually is applied only to nonnative speakers of a language. Historically, and in contrast, researchers have used the term *verbal ability* to refer to the language abilities of native speakers of a language.

In recent years (see, e.g., Canale & Swain, 1980; Rivera 1983, 1984a, 1984b), language-assessment researchers have begun to distinguish multiple language competencies underlying the construct of language proficiency that add to the complexity of language assessment. Canale and Swain (1980) and Canale (1984), for example, consider language skill in terms of four underlying competencies: grammar, discourse, sociolinguistic abilities, and strategic abilities.

A debate exists in the field regarding the number of assessment dimensions underlying language proficiency. Researchers on language proficiency assessment such as Oller (1979) argue that empirical evidence suggests that only a single general proficiency factor is required to explain language proficiency, whereas researchers such as Bachman and Palmer (1981) present data supporting a multiple-competence model of language proficiency. Oller, citing numerous studies and his own research, concludes that there is a strong association among performance on language proficiency tests, performance on intelligence tests, and performance on other cognitive abilities tests. He argues that these associations reflect a true overlap of language skills and general intelligence. Research to be cited later in this chapter, however, has found that performance on cognitive tasks can be depressed or made statistically unreliable by low proficiency in a language.

The point to this introductory discussion of language proficiency is that there is not total universal scientific agreement on what the term means and, hence, that there is some conceptual variability in our understanding of how language skills affect test performance. Despite theoretical disagreements on how to best define language proficiency, there is a convergence of research evidence suggesting that limited familiarity with a language used in testing can affect test performance and, hence, the ability to draw valid inferences about the meaning of test performance. As will be pointed out in the conclusion to the chapter, improved measurement procedures and research on these procedures are critical to advances in the valid testing of linguistic minority individuals.

Language Minority Groups

Although there are large numbers of people with non-English backgrounds residing in the United States, assessment research has tended to focus only on certain groups that have a significant numerical representation in American education. The groups primarily considered in this chapter are identified on the basis of ethnic origin or by institutional participation. They are Asians, Hispanics, college students of foreign origin, and children in bilingual education and English as a Second Language (ESL) programs. These groups will be given the most attention in this chapter though exceptions will be made. In particular, some significant studies concerning bilingual (English, non-English) populations outside the United States will be mentioned. Discussion will now turn to assessment research in the five issues areas cited earlier.

Language Proficiency Assessment

The field of language proficiency assessment has grown considerably since the late 1960s. This growth has two major foci: *first,* the call for tests of English-language and non-English-language proficiency for use in identification and placement of language minority children in language-based educational programs and, *second,* the use of tests of English-language proficiency in the admission of foreign students to U.S. colleges. Spolsky (1981) overviews the history of the field, noting the evolution that has been taking place in the theories underlying assessment practices. Over the years, investigators have increasingly been discovering that it is difficult to get an accurate assessment of language skills if the language stimuli found on tests and the skills elicited by test items are of a highly restricted and artificial nature. Researchers such as Oller (1979) and Bachman and Palmer (in press) discuss the importance of having the language tasks in proficiency tests resemble authentic language use. Bachman and Palmer (1981) suggest that multitrait–multimethod assessment procedures be used in investigating the construct validity of proficiency tests that utilize different forms of assessment for the same language proficiency constructs.

To overview the nature of proficiency tests, it is helpful to offer some characterizations of tests extant in the field. Most researchers on language proficiency assessment distinguish between *direct* and *indirect* methods of assessment and, separately, whether a test utilizes *discrete-point* or *integrative* approaches to assessment. In direct proficiency assessment, examinees are tested for their ability to understand and produce language much as it occurs in real-world criterion settings. Direct methods involve language use situations such as examinees in face-to-face interviews with an examiner, examinees listening to recordings or an oral lecture and answering questions based on it, examinees taking dictation of recorded discourse, and examinees writing essays. In contrast, indirect methods of assessment utilize language tasks that are readily identified as being of an artificial nature. These tasks are selected because they are convenient to administer in such contexts as multiple-choice testing.

Discrete-point proficiency tests can involve direct or indirect assessment. They are designed to present examinees with many separate independent language tasks or items, and they are intended to test examinees' control of specific language features, such as the ability to recognize the need for agreement between subject and verb in an indirect test of grammatical skills or the ability to distinguish a question from a request in a direct test of conversational ability. Because of their emphasis on the assessment of ability to control specific language features across a number of test items, discrete-point tests most often utilize indirect testing procedures.

Integrative language proficiency tests require examinees to understand or produce more extensive stretches of language than typically occur in discrete-point tests. Such tests require simultaneous control of many separate skills in working test tasks or items correctly. The scoring of performance on an integrative test can be either *discrete* or *holistic*. Discrete scoring of performance is based upon scoring of specific responses made by an examinee in performing an integrative language task. Holistic scoring is based upon ratings or judgmental classifications of examinees' language performance along one or more dimensions. A reading comprehension cloze test that requires examinees to fill in missing words in a paragraph is an example of an integrative and indirect proficiency test that utilizes discrete-point scoring of performance. Performance on such a test is scored on the basis of the discrete responses examinees make in a task requiring the integration of many language skills related to text comprehension. Such a test is indirect because the language task faced by examinees only partially resembles an everyday reading task.

In contrast with the foregoing examples, an integrative and direct proficiency test is exemplified by an oral interview session between an examinee and an examiner. In this context, an examinee is required to understand and produce language on the basis of many integrated skills, and further, the language-testing context bears high authenticity to natural language use. Scoring of performance on such a test can be either discrete or holistic, depending on the test.

Although there are theoretical grounds supporting preference for the use of direct, integrative language proficiency tests, use of such tests is not widespread in practice. Discrete-point, indirect, language proficiency tests or integrative, discrete-scored proficiency tests are most used because such instruments are easiest to develop, administer, and score. Development of items for such tests can be based, a priori, on a set of test specifications that provide details on the desirable or permissible characteristics of items and the particular language skill that must be tested by them. Such tests can often be administered to groups, rather than to individuals, utilizing objective response methods such as multiple choice. Finally, use of objective scoring procedures for such tests permits efficient and timely scoring of test performance, utilizing electronic devices or scoring by humans with little training. A further important advantage of these types of tests is that their use of independently constructed items and mass administration facilitates investigation of the psychometric reliability and validity characteristics of items and tests and, in some cases, the equating of test forms. Studies of the psychometric characteristics of direct tests of language proficiency are desirable, but they are harder to undertake because of the amount of effort needed to collect sufficient data. They are practical only for large-scale testing programs.

Recent major summary descriptions of proficiency tests and abstracts of published research on proficiency tests are included in materials by Lange and Clifford (1980); Pletcher, Locks, Reynolds, and Sisson (1978); Stansfield (1981); Thorum (1981); and Wildemuth (1981). Collections of papers in volumes by Dieterich and Freeman (1979), Rivera (1983, 1984a, 1984b), Seidner (1982, 1983), and Silverman, Noa, and Russell (1978) review the status of proficiency testing of language-minority children. Papers in Erickson and Omark (1981) also provide reviews of this topic, and, in addition, they detail the strengths and weaknesses of particular tests for language-minority children.

Research on proficiency testing of language-minority children has tended to concentrate on oral language proficiency tests in English and Spanish involving discrete-point scoring of performance, though there has been research on other test types and research on tests in other languages. Table 18.1 identifies some of the tests cited and reviewed in the references. Of necessity, this list is abbreviated, and the reader is referred to the original references for a complete listing of tests and their characteristics.

A careful review of the literature regarding tests of proficiency for language-minority children indicates that norming studies of performance are not always undertaken. Further, internal consistency and test–retest reliability and validity research are sparse or nonexistent for most tests. The proficiency test guide by Pletcher et al. (1978) is valuable because, as of late 1984, it covered descriptions of more proficiency tests for language-minority children than any other reference. It also contains brief summaries of information on the norming of tests and the reliability and validity of tests offered by test publishers.

In examining the published research literature on language proficiency tests for language-minority children, it is apparent that little, if any, research exists investigating whether performance on given language proficiency tests has had the expected associations with authentic language behavior in criterion settings. Existing validity studies are useful but tend to be limited to two types of studies. One type examines the concurrent or construct validity of instruments. This type of study examines associations between scores on a criterion proficiency test and scores on other proficiency tests in the same language. A second type of study is concerned with the predictive validity of scores on a proficiency test. In this type, proficiency test scores are used to predict a school achievement criterion such as grades in courses.

This latter type of study is often misconceptualized and misinterpreted by investigators. All too often, investigators fail to make a distinction between assessment of the language skills of examinees and assessment of the academic aptitudes of examinees. Ability to perform academic tasks can be considered distinct from ability to use a language. If a prediction of academic achievement is desired, it is most appropriate, on measurement grounds, to test academic aptitude and its possible relationships to achievement, as moderated by language proficiency. This suggestion is sound, even though some investigators such as Oller (1979) theorize that a close connection must exist between intellectual capacity and proficiency.

At present, significant problems exist in establishing objective criteria for use of language proficiency test scores in educational decision making. This problem is most apparent when practitioners are required to use language proficiency tests for identification of children who might benefit from bilingual education and training programs in English. In one major

TABLE 18.1 Some Tests of Language Minority Children's Language Proficiency Reviewed in References Cited

TEST	LANGUAGE(S)
James Language Dominance Test	English, Spanish
Language Assessment Scale	English
Dos Amigos Verbal Language Scales	English, Spanish
Short Tests of Linguistic Skills	English, Spanish, and nine other languages
The Boehm Test of Basic Concepts	English, Spanish
Test of Auditory Comprehension of Language	English, Spanish
Basic Inventory of Natural Language	English, Spanish, Portuguese, Italian, and other languages
High/Scope Instruments	English
Bilingual Syntax Measure	English, Spanish
Caso Test of Non-English-Speaking Students Language Assessment Battery	English

study, conducted in the state of California, involving three proficiency tests of English, Ulibarri, Spencer, and Rivas (1981) found serious inconsistencies in the classification of 1,100 Hispanic first-, third-, and fifth-grade children into one of three state-mandated English language proficiency categories: Non-English Speaking (NES); Limited English Speaking (LES); and Fluent English Speaking (FES). The three tests examined were the Language Assessment Scale (LAS), the Bilingual Syntax Measure (BSM), and the Basic Inventory of Natural Language (BINL). The students tested were identified as coming from language-minority backgrounds, on the basis of responses to a home language survey. The publisher of each of the three tests in question had developed recommendations on test cutoff scores for use by appropriate school staff in the classification of examinees into the three categories NES, LES, and FES.

The LAS test classified 44% of first-grade children as non-English speaking, 26% of first-grade children as limited English speaking, and 30% of first-grade children as fluent English speaking. In contrast, the BSM test classified the same group of first-grade children very differently: 8% NES, 79% LES, and 13% FES. The classifications provided by the BINL test for first-grade children were yet again different: 16% NES, 26% LES, and 58% FES. Similar but less marked discrepancies were noted in the classification of Grade 3 and Grade 5 children into the same language proficiency categories. Ullibari, Spencer, and Rivas conducted nonparametric analyses of variance with pairwise contrasts of these differences across groups. Based on these analyses, they concluded that there were statistically significant discrepancies in classification among all tests at Grade 1 and between the LAS and the BSM and the BSM and the BINL for Grade 5. A more detailed examination of the classification data indicated that LAS and BSM classifications were the most consistent for the same children across grades and, further, that more agreement would be reached between these two tests if the classification cutoff criteria procedures for each test were readjusted by adding or subtracting a constant number to cutoff scores. The findings of this study illustrate some of the technical problems in the valid use of proficiency tests in the classification of language-minority children that are in need of intensive research.

Attention will now be turned to proficiency testing of the English-language skills of foreign students attending North American colleges. This area of concern has spawned much research literature, occasionally motivated by theoretical models of language proficiency. Examples of research based on theoretical models of language proficiency are found in original works and collections of papers by Briere and Hinofotis (1979); Clark (1978); Duran, Canale, Penfield, Stansfield, and Liskin-Gasparro (1985); Hale, Stansfield, and Duran (1984); Oller (1979); Oller and Perkins (1978, 1980); Palmer, Groot and Trosper (1981); and Stansfield (1986). Among the most available and used tests in this area are the Test of English as a Foreign Language (TOEFL) (Educational Testing Service, 1983), the Michigan Test of English Language Proficiency, the English proficiency test of the American Language Institute at Georgetown University, and the Comprehensive English language test for Speakers of English as a Second Language. The Foreign Service Institute Oral Interview has been one of the most widely used and well-known tests of oral proficiency. A new version of this test, known as the Interagency Language Roundtable scale, is now in use. This test is used by U.S. federal agencies in assessment of candidates for service in foreign countries. Research on the earlier foreign service instrument is described in Clark (1978).

In addition to these tests, there are a number of locally developed tests of English-language proficiency that are used by those assessing the English-language skills of incoming foreign students. Also, there are a large number of experimental tests of proficiency for this same population resulting from dissertation studies. Hale et al. (1984) provide summaries of published research on the TOEFL during the period 1963–1982; these summaries include references to a number of other proficiency tests involved in studies.

One of the key debates in the testing of English as a foreign language is whether proficiency in English is best conceived of as a unidimensional trait or as a complex of multidimensional traits. As mentioned earlier, positions on this debate have been affected by the development of theories of language proficiency and by the emergence of contrasting empirical evidence. For example, one study involving a factor analysis of 22 English-language proficiency tests of both productive and receptive language skill (Scholz, Hendricks, Spurling, Johnson, & Vandenburg, 1980) found that a single factor accounted for 51.4% of the common variance among scores on instruments. Attempts to fit four oblique factors to the intercorrelations among test scores did not lead to evidence suggesting that there were separate factors representing speaking, listening, writing, and reading abilities. The four-factor solution accounted for only 6% more of the variance among test scores.

In contrast with this sort of finding, other studies have supported a conclusion that multiple dimensions of proficiency in English exist. Swinton and Powers (1980), for example, found factor-analytic evidence that the TOEFL assessed separate, but correlated, traits. These traits were interpreted to involve listening comprehension, reading comprehension and grammatical knowledge, and vocabulary. Bachman and Palmer (1981) conducted a factor analysis of intercorrelations among scores on six tests of speaking and reading, which resulted in a separation of reading and speaking factors. In addition to these two trait factors, they found evidence of other factors that distinguished the methods of testing: interview, translation, and self-rating.

Evidence informing the debate on the number of factors underlying proficiency in English is difficult to interpret. The number of examinees involved in studies in some cases is too small to justify use of a particular factor-analytic technique, and, further, studies do not usually take into account estimates of the measurement error present in test scores.

One important question encountered in the use of tests of proficiency in English with foreign students concerns the population validity of these tests for students from different language backgrounds. Research conducted by the TOEFL program on the TOEFL item performance of more than 12,000 examinees from six language groups (African, Arabic, Chinese, Germanic, Japanese, and Spanish) found significant differences across groups in the propensity to select correct answers for approximately seven-eighths of all items considered (Alderman & Holland, 1981). Items from the Reading Comprehension and Vocabulary sections of the TOEFL showed the greatest sensitivity.

There is no reason to believe that results of this sort are unique to the TOEFL; other examinations of proficiency in English for foreign students would be likely to lead to similar affects. Proficiency tests of English for incoming foreign students are designed to assess skills in English as it is used in American colleges. Foreign candidates for study in U.S. colleges might or might not have come from countries and educational systems that utilized English as a medium of instruction. For example, English is used to varying extents in the educational systems of a number of African and Asian countries and in Latin America. Previous exposure to English and contact with English speakers, based on country of origin and language background, could thus lead to systematic differences in performance on tests of proficiency in English. Such differences need not be thought of as reflecting population bias, if it is assured that the English language used on test items and the linguistic proficiency points tested by items are reflective of the English that foreign students need to command when matriculating in U.S. colleges. The fact that population differences in performance on items and tests exists, however, means that extreme care needs to be exercised by proficiency test developers when undertaking equating procedures for test forms. Variation in the national origins of test takers across test administrations used for equating purposes could affect the outcome of equating procedures.

Another significant question regarding use of tests of proficiency in English with foreign students concerns the interpretation of college admissions test scores, given students' proficiency test scores. This matter is addressed in a later section of this chapter.

Cognitive Assessment

Intelligence testing of language-minority persons in the United States has a long and controversial history, which has been reviewed extensively by Diaz (1983), Hakuta (1986), and Padilla (1979). A collection of many of the seminal empirical papers in this area is provided by Cordasco (1978). Research in the period 1910–1962 focused on evidence that immigrants to the United States and native blacks and Hispanics scored lower on intelligence tests than U.S.-born nonminority persons. Gould (1981) reviews much of this work, citing analytic and methodological flaws in the research designs. He also discusses ways in which beliefs about racial and social equality and inequality were likely to have contributed to the design of research studies and to the conclusions drawn from them.

Early studies of the connections between language-minority status and intelligence test scores made no attempts, or only very limited attempts, to control for the educational and social background characteristics of individuals studied. Hence, performance differences on English-language intelligence tests across monolingual English-speaking and language-minority groups were probably seriously confounded with differences in the background characteristics of the groups compared. Language-minority groups almost invariably came from backgrounds reflecting less socioeconomic well-being and less formal education than those of monolingual English-speaking groups. A common conclusion drawn was that bilingualism had a detrimental effect on intellectual functioning.

Peal and Lambert (1962) question this point, citing lack of control in research studies for background and personal characteristics. They also cite a few isolated studies indicating superior performance of bilinguals on intelligence tests. They go on to describe their own research on the verbal and nonverbal intelligence test scores of Canadian French–English bilinguals, which did control for important background and personal characteristics between a group of these individuals and a monolingual comparison group. Peal and Lambert found that a bilingual group of 10-year-old children outperformed the comparison group of 10-year-old monolingual English speakers on both verbal and nonverbal intelligence tests. Peal and Lambert's work is important because it leads to further research premised on the possibility that, under some circumstances, bilingualism might be associated with enhancement of cognitive abilities rather than with retardation of them.

Lambert (1977) reviewed studies subsequent to 1962 that sought to investigate connections between proficiency in two languages and thinking abilities. Rather than focusing on general intelligence alone as an indicator of cognitive aptitudes, many studies after about 1962 began to focus on specific sorts of cognitive skills in bilinguals. Lambert cites six studies during the period 1964–1973 that were judged to include proper controls in research design, given their research hypotheses. The findings of all of these supported a conclusion that bilingualism was associated with enhanced cognitive abilities relative to the cognitive abilities shown by control-group monolinguals. The skills investigated across the studies included cognitive flexibility, creativity, and capacity for divergent thought. Interestingly, the studies involved a number of different nations, geographical locales, and non-English languages: Singapore (Torrance, Gowan, Wu, & Aliotti, 1970); Switzerland (Balkan, 1970); South Africa (Ianco-Worral, 1972); Israel and New York (Ben-Zeev, 1972); western Canada (Cummins & Gulutsan, 1973); and Canada (Scott, 1973).

More recently, in the United States De Avila and Duncan (1978) investigated the cognitive abilities of 204 Grade 1 and Grade 3 Hispanic children drawn from the United States and Mexico. The results of the study showed that children who were classified as high in proficiency in both English and Spanish earned higher scores on the Children's Embedded Figures Test and the Draw-a-Person Test than control-group children who were monolingual and matched on socioeconomic background. The construct measured by these tests was degree of field independence.

Cummins (1978) reports the performance of 80 Grade 3 and 26 Grade 6 English–Irish bilingual children on tasks requiring metalinguistic awareness. Bilingual and monolingual groups of children were matched on IQ, socioeconomic status, gender, and age. The findings showed that children classified bilingual showed a greater aptitude than monolingual children in working problems involving reasoning with words given artificial meanings and in spotting contradictions between linguistic statements about the characteristics of objects and their characteristics as actually perceived.

Cummins (1978), De Avila and Duncan (1978), and Ferdman and Hakuta (1985) suggest that there is likely to be an important connection between children's cognitive development and their language skills development. Cummins (1984), for example, has postulated that there might exist two threshold levels of language proficiency associated with children's cognitive development. The first corresponds roughly to Piaget's preoperational development stage, whereas the second threshold level is associated with the development of children's ability to use a language in cognitively demanding problem-solving situations. In these latter situations the context of language use involves written language as it appears in textbooks or oral language in which reference is made to ideas and facts not in the immediate sensory environment. Cummins and others have theorized that bilingual children's development of academic skills in a second language might critically depend on initial development of academic language skills in the first language. It is hypothesized that the failure of many bilingual children to progress normally in their schooling via a second language can be explained by the premature transition of developmentally unprepared children into cognitively demanding second-language classroom learning situations.

A recent study by Hakuta (Hakuta & Diaz, 1984) suggests support for the positive influence of bilingual programs consistent with these views. This research involved 392 children enrolled in grades K–6 of a bilingual education program in an east coast community with a high density of Hispanics. Statistically significant relationships were found between measures of children's degree of bilingualism and their scores on the Raven's Coloured Progressive Matrices test, after controlling for the influence of students' age. The study also found that the correlation between measures of children's proficiency in English and Spanish increased across the school grades. This finding is supportive of the contention that bilingual schooling experience strengthens students' verbal skill development in both languages.

De Avila and Havassy (1976), in earlier work, cite their own research findings, suggesting that interpretation of standardized intelligence test scores of children from ethnic minority backgrounds can be problematic when the children's development level is not assessed. As an alternative to intelligence tests, they advocate neo-Piagetian tests of developmental level. Such instruments would involve culturally familiar material and would address children's aptitude in performing specific kinds of cognitive operations associated with a developmental level. In fairly recent years, researchers and educators such as Feuerstein (1979) have advocated, in a similar vein, an assessment of specific information-processing skills in children from minority backgrounds. According to these views, the assessment of aptitudes should be specific in terms of the skills assessed, and it should probe the capability of children to generalize and to combine the skills they already possess into new units of cognitive ability. Further discussion of information-processing skills of bilinguals in their two languages is given at a later point in this section.

As mentioned earlier, a good deal of research exists on minority children's standardized intelligence test performance that implicates, but does not directly investigate, the impact of children's English-language proficiency and cultural background upon test performance. Figueroa (1983), for example, investigated the WISC-R item performance of moderately large groups of 7½ through 10½-year-old Hispanic children. Children were categorized *monolingual Spanish, bilingual,* or *monolingual English* on the basis of ratings of parents' preferred language at the time of administration of the System of Multicultural Pluralistic Assessment (SOMPA) sociocultural scales to parents. Figueroa was interested in learning whether he could replicate evidence of lack of ethnic subgroup bias in WISC-R verbal item performance.

Previous research by Jensen (1974) and Sandoval (1979) on the Peabody Picture Vocabulary Tests, the Raven's Progressive Matrices Test, and the WISC-R, among others, had utilized an ethnic-group-by-test-item analysis-of-variance (ANOVA) procedure to detect evidence of test-item bias. Bias would exist if there were statistically significant interactions among levels of an ethnic group membership factor and an items factor. The studies cited found very little evidence of test bias, using this procedure. In his study, Figueroa used a variant methodology. He found that the ordinal difficulty of items from three WISC-R verbal item types was virtually identical among children categorized monolingual Spanish, bilingual, or monolingual English. Figueroa had expected that inconsistencies in the ordinal difficulty of items would emerge across the groups, given the extreme differences in their cultural and language backgrounds. He commented that the depressed performance of Hispanic children across items, regardless of language background, might stem from general dissimilarities between the sociocultural background of the Hispanic and Anglo children tested. This latter discrepancy would make verbal items more difficult for Hispanic children than for Anglo children.

Mercer (1984) presents an extensive and expanded discussion of this sort of possibility. She reviews her own research with the WISC-R as part of the SOMPA test battery for the purpose of assessing black, Hispanic, and white children of 6, 8, and 10 years of age. In summarizing her data, she states that

It seems clear . . . (1) that there are large and statistically significant socioculturally differences in three ethnic groups studied; (2) that the average scores in the WISC-R and the individual items consistently discriminate in favor of whites; and (3) that there is a significant amount of variance in the WISC-R scores, especially the Verbal subtests, that can be explained by sociocultural factors. (p. 348)

Going beyond this immediate conclusion, she comments that the WISC-R might not possess normative validity for use with minority children when it is used as the sole measure of aptitude. She indicates that the use of the WISC-R should be coupled with other measures such as those found in the SOMPA that assess a larger range of aptitudes and behaviors and, in addition, with measures of children's social and familial backgrounds relevant to their development. Thus, she proposes methods that rely on multiple indicators of children's ability extending beyond use of intelligence tests.

Alan Kaufman (1979), in a comprehensive review of research on the WISC-R, comments explicitly on difficulties in using the instrument with bilingual children. He also comments on the value of examining various factor scores, based on a factor analysis of scores obtained on WISC-R subtests. His views are similar to those of Figueroa and Mercer. He states

When the WISC-R is deemed an appropriate instrument for use with a bilingual child [cf. Oakland and Matuszek, 1977; Tucker, 1977, for appropriate guidelines], the examiner is advised not to compute or interpret the Full Scale IQ. The fact that all three WISC-R IQs, including Full Scale IQ, were found to be quite reliable for a sample of Mexican American children (Dean, 1977) does not alter the inadvisability of computing an overall IQ for bilingual youngsters. The Perceptual Organization and Freedom from Distractability factors should be stressed for estimating their intellectual functioning and school related potential. (pp. 33–34)

In his summary of research on the use of the WISC-R with bilingual children, Kaufman calls attention to findings suggesting that nonverbal intelligence measures are better predictors of many Hispanic children's school achievement than are intelligence measures assessing verbal ability (Mishra & Hurt, 1970; Phillipus, 1967; Shellenberger, 1977). He cautions, accordingly, that users of the WISC-R with bilingual children need to be alert to differences in performance on the test, as against verbal scores, of children of bilingual backgrounds.

A body of cognitive research exists investigating ways in which proficiency in two languages affects problem solving on specific tasks. Most of this research relies on experimental methodology, but some also relies on psychometric assessment of cognitive and linguistic skills. Fairly recent reviews and theoretical analysis of this cognitive research on bilingualism are provided by Dornic (1980), Duran (1978 and 1985), McCormack (1977), and McLaughlin, Rossman, and McLeod (1983). A major finding of this research has been that bilinguals process information more quickly and accurately in their more familiar language. There is some evidence of a speed–accuracy trade-off in problem solving. For example, d'Anglejan, Gagnon, Hafez, Tucker, and Winsberg (1979) and Duran (1985) report that bilinguals' accuracy in solving syllogism problems of identical form in their two languages tends to be the same, though performance is significantly slower in the less familiar language. McLaughlin et al. (1983) and Duran (1985) suggest that bilinguals, who must attend carefully to an analysis of language in their problem solving in a less familiar language, might need to martial attention in a very different way from when they are solving problems in a native language. When working verbal problems presented in the less familiar language, bilinguals must juggle their attention, dividing their time and attention between the task of decoding the linguistic statement of a problem and applying cognitive strategies and previous knowledge to the interpretation and solution of a problem. When problems are being worked in the more familiar language, there is less attentional demand placed on decoding of language, and hence, attention can be focused more on the conceptual substance of a problem and ways to solve it.

One area of bilingual cognitive research that has been researched intensively concerns whether a single long-term memory store for conceptual information underlies the meanings of words in the two language systems of bilinguals. Hines (1978), Lopez (1977), and McCormack (1977), among others, have reviewed previous research on this question. Research findings have supported both the hypothesis of a single conceptual memory store in bilinguals and the hypothesis of separate long-term memory stores for conceptual information in each language for bilinguals. On the basis of the pattern of existing findings, parsimony, and current cognitive theories of language processing (Clark & Clark, 1978; MacLeod, 1976; Goldman, Reyes, & Varnhagen, 1984), the single-store model of semantic memory in bilinguals seems more defensible, though this view might not be comprehensive enough to account for all the findings.

Assessment of School Achievement

Assessment of language-minority children's success in elementary and secondary school has received increasing attention in the 1970s and 1980s. The conduct of major national education surveys has permitted examination of the achievement patterns and schooling outcomes of this population. Important survey sources include the Survey of Income and Education (SIE) of 1976; the National Assessment of Educational Progress (NAEP) in 1979–1980, 1983–1984, and 1985–1986; the High School and Beyond (HS&B) longitudinal survey of 1980; and the Sustaining Effects Study of Title I Progress (1977). Each of these surveys has assessed the language background of respondents and permitted study of patterns of schooling outcome in light of students' English-language and non-English-language backgrounds. The NAEP and HS&B surveys are especially noteworthy because they have administered school achievement test items to children. Each of the surveys has differed somewhat in its criteria for identifying language-minority status, and, hence, precise comparisons and interpretation of data and data analyses cannot be made across surveys; nonetheless, there is some noteworthy convergence of results of studies on these survey data bases.

The most general question asked in studies is whether there exists an association between school achievement and school attainment indexes and language-minority status. In the case of the Survey of Income and Education, the High School and Beyond, and the Sustaining Effects surveys, it has been possible to use regression analysis to investigate the degree to which language characteristics contribute to educational attainment or achievement test scores, controlling for the contribution of other background and personal measures to the prediction of achievement test scores.

In the SIE survey, the term *non-English-language background* identified persons who used a non-English language as their usual or second household language. If persons were over 14 years of age, they were also classified as being from a non-English background, if they indicated that they had a non-English mother tongue. The National Center for Education Statistics (Silverman, 1976) reported that children of non-English backgrounds enrolled in grades 5–12, who usually spoke their native languages, were more than three times as likely to be two or more grades below the grade levels expected for their ages as children from English-only language backgrounds. These effects were most pronounced among persons who identified themselves as Hispanics usually preferring Spanish. The survey data also indicated that children from non-English backgrounds whose usual language was not English were three

to four times more likely not to be attending school as other children.

Utilizing the SIE data, Veltman (1981) investigated the propensity for Hispanic children to fall behind expected grade, as predicted by a number of personal and background variables. These predictor variables included children's age, U.S. geographical region of residence, population density of place of residence, parental education level, place of birth and its language characteristics, and Hispanic subgroup identity. Veltman found that children's age, parental education level, and native or nonnative birth language characteristics were significant predictors of their propensity to be enrolled in the expected school grade. Older children tended to be behind their school grades, and, the higher the education level of parents, the more likely children were to be in a school grade appropriate for their age. Among students in the age range 6–13 years, birth outside of the United States and Spanish-language dominance coupled with U.S. birth were negatively related to progress in school. Among older students, aged 14–17 years, Spanish-language dominance regardless of birth place was most related to being behind expected school grade.

The NAEP (1982) reported on the educational attainment and reading achievement levels of children of non-English backgrounds who were 9, 13, and 17 years old in 1979–1980. Children were classified as *other language dominant* (OL), *shared-language dominant* (SL) if they only used the non-English language sometimes, and *English language dominant* (EL). Data analysis indicated that OL students were more likely than SL and EL students to be a grade behind their age cohorts. At age 9, almost one-third of OL students were below their modal grade, compared with about one-fifth of EL students. At age 13, 28% of OL students were behind in grade, as compared with 23% of EL students. At age 17, 20% of OL students were behind, as compared with 11% of EL students. The trend for these recidivism rates to become lower as age increases probably reflects the fact that some students are dropping out before reaching the higher grades.

The NAEP reading performance data for 1979–1980 indicated that children who were classified as OL solved 6% to 8% fewer reading achievement items than SL and EL children at all three NAEP age levels. Whereas EL children solved proportionately more reading items correctly than SL children, the discrepancy was relatively small; it ranged from less than 1% to 3%.

Research on the relationship between language characteristics and achievement test scores in the HS&B survey of 1980 has concentrated on Hispanic students. Nielsen and Fernandez (1981) used regression analysis to predict Hispanic students' mathematics, reading, and vocabulary achievement test scores and measures of school delay and aspirations. These criterion variables were predicted from background and personal characteristic variables including information on language characteristics. They found that achievement test scores, school delay, and aspiration measures were related in the obvious directions to level of family income. Interestingly, family length of residence in the United States was found to be a negative predictor of achievement measures, that is, the longer families had resided in the United States, the lower achievement test scores tended to be. In addition, Hispanic students' judgements of English-language proficiency and Spanish-language proficiency were found to contribute significantly and positively to prediction of achievement test scores and, to some extent, to measures of educational aspirations and ability to avoid school delay. Self-judged Spanish-language proficiency contributed positively to prediction of measures of school achievement, but greater reliance on *oral use* of Spanish was associated with delay in schooling. The results of data analyses indicated that self-judged English-language and self-judged Spanish-language proficiency remained significant positive predictors of achievement test scores, even after controlling for the influence of oral reliance on Spanish, the measures of socioeconomic status, and the Hispanic subgroup identity.

In a followup study, Nielsen and Learner (1982) examined over 21,000 1980 HS&B Hispanic high school seniors' achievement test scores, aspirations levels, and grade point averages. They used confirmatory factor-analytic methods to investigate correlations among measures of achievement, aspirations, and grade point average measures and measures of English and Spanish usage; exposure; and self-judged proficiency. The outcome of their analysis supported the hypothesis that three correlated factors accounted for the observed correlations. These factors were described as Hispanicity, English Proficiency, and Ability. The Hispanicity factor loaded on measures reflecting self-judged proficiency in Spanish, preference for use of Spanish, and exposure to Spanish. The English-proficiency factor loaded on measures of self-judged proficiency in English and achievement test measures. The Ability factor loaded on measures of self-judged proficiency in Spanish and English and on achievement test scores.

So and Chan (1984) investigated the prediction of reading achievement test scores from language measures and socioeconomic background variables among Hispanics and nonminority white students participating in the HS&B survey. The results of separate regression analyses for Hispanics and whites indicated that socioeconomic level, based upon a composite scale involving responses to HS&B background items, was a much more important contributor to whites' reading achievement test scores than to Hispanics' scores. Using an analysis procedure based on Duncan (1969), So and Chan concluded that socioeconomic status and ethnic identity accounted for only about half of the 15-point reading achievement test score difference between Hispanics and whites. They argue that a major proportion of the remaining difference in reading achievement performance could be accounted for by differences in the language characteristics of Hispanics and whites. A similar finding is reported by Rosenthal, Baker, and Ginsburg (1983) in their reanalysis data from the Sustaining Effects Study of Title I programs.

Special Education Assessment

Tests play a central role in the field of special education, and, over the past 15 years, concern has been evident over the valid use of testing for these purposes among language-minor-

ity children. Shepard provides an extensive discussion of this matter in chapter 17 of this volume.

Concern about assessment of language-minority children for special education was stimulated in the 1970s by a class action suit filed on behalf of Mexican-American children in the state of California *(Diana v. State Board of Education)*. The *Diana* suit claimed that there were too many Hispanic children in EMR classes, given the proportional representation of Hispanics in school districts, and that misuse of intelligence tests contributed to this misrepresentation. The suit claimed that Hispanic children came predominantly from Spanish-speaking backgrounds. Because of this, the verbal intelligence test scores of Hispanics were lower than would be expected, given children's scores on performance-based intelligence tests. A formal decision was not rendered in the case. Instead a series of stipulated agreements was negotiated to resolve the suit. The history of the *Diana v. State Board of Education* case from 1970 to 1983 and a summary of the board's compliance with the agreements negotiated during this period are given in California State Department of Education (1983b).

Figueroa (1980) and the California State Department of Education, Office of Special Education (1983b) cite a number of needed improvements in special education assessment practices for Hispanic children stemming from attempts to resolve the *Diana* case. These needs include routine assessment of the English-language and Spanish-language proficiency of children, to determine the appropriate language for intelligence testing. Attention is also called to the need for test administrators to be familiar with the language and social background of children and the need for administrators to call on this knowledge in interpreting children's test performance. Another improvement concerns the need to evaluate the translation procedures and psychometric properties of tests translated from English to Spanish. Mention is also made of the need to develop documentation regarding the findings of studies evaluating the suitability of translated tests.

Cummins (1984) presents a major review of issues pertaining to special education assessment of language-minority children in Canada and the United States. He discusses a number of alternative models of assessment that are applicable to language-minority children and that could supplement or replace the use of intelligence tests for special education purposes. He cites, for example, the System of Multicultural Pluralistic Assessment (Mercer, 1979), the task analysis model of assessment (Mercer & Ysseldyke, 1977), the Cartoon Conservation Scales (De Avila & Havassy, 1976), the Kaufman Assessment Battery for Children (Kaufman & Kaufman, 1982), and the Learning Potential Assessment Device (Feuerstein, 1979).

According to Cummins, each of these assessment systems can supply information on language-minority children's cognitive abilities, to supplement information provided by existing intelligence tests. He notes, however, that the valid use of supplemental procedures requires that assessment administrators understand the language and cultural background of children and the language proficiency characteristics of the children assessed. This knowledge needs to be utilized in interpreting children's assessment performance. Care must be taken to avoid falsely concluding, on the basis of performance on verbal tests of reasoning in the nonnative language, that bilingual children are learning disabled or mentally retarded. Children might have limited proficiency in the language when it is used in cognitively demanding tasks involving reading and writing. Evidence of this limited proficiency might be masked by the appearance of sufficient oral skills in the language to support participation in everyday social interaction. Thus, teachers and other school staff face the risk of falsely identifying bilingual children as mentally retarded or learning disabled when limited proficiency in the language of assessment is responsible for children's depressed assessment performance. Use of multiple assessments, some involving nonverbal tests, and possible tests in the native language can help avoid this problem. As research progresses, new assessment techniques will also be of value in avoiding the problem.

Innovative assessment techniques such as Feuerstein's Learning Potential Assessment Device (Feuerstein, 1979) and cognitive training methods such as Instrumental Enrichment (Feuerstein, 1980) are currently drawing much attention among special education staff and school psychologists. The term *dynamic assessment* has been applied to assessments designed to measure students' ability to learn new skills and new knowledge. Much of the work in the area draws on the Vygotskian notion of "zone of proximal development" (Vygotsky, 1978). According to this notion, the purpose of dynamic assessment procedures is to systematically probe students' ability to accomplish tasks that cannot be accomplished without assistance. Students are provided hints and other advice, to ascertain whether such mediation is sufficient to allow successful completion of tasks.

Cognitive psychology research on dynamic assessment has begun, and investigators have encountered some success in operationalizing this notion in terms of observable performance measures (Campione & Brown, 1987; Vye, Burns, Delclos, & Bransford, in press). Psychometric research on dynamic assessment measures has just begun. Embretson (in press) discusses some of the major measurement issues that need to be treated. Dynamic assessment techniques tend to be viewed currently within the province of special education, and their use could eventually spread to mainstream educational programs and bilingual education or ESL programs. Adaptation of these techniques for use with U.S. children of non-English backgrounds has not been investigated and merits intensive attention. Cummins (1984) provides a preliminary review of this issue in light of research on bilingualism.

Assessment for College Admissions

In recent years information has begun to accumulate on connections between students' proficiency in English and their college admissions test scores. Data on SAT test takers summarized annually by the College Board indicates that students who judge themselves more proficient in a non-English language earn lower verbal and mathematics test scores. For example, in 1983 SAT examinees who indicated on the College Board background questionnaire that English was not their best language, earned a median SAT Verbal score of 310, compared with a median Verbal score of 428 for all other examinees. Differences in median SAT Mathematics scores were less pronounced for the two groups. Examinees who reported that English was not their best language earned median SAT Mathematics scores of 438, whereas other examinees earned median Mathematics scores of 468 (Ramist & Arbeiter, 1984).

Rock and Werts (1979) investigated the internal construct validity of SAT Verbal and Mathematics subtests across samples of Native American, black, Mexican-American, Puerto Rican, and white students. Subjects in this study were not classified according to characteristics of English proficiency. Analysis of covariance structure methodology was used to investigate intercorrelations among subtest parcels consisting of items drawn from the same subtest. The results of this study supported the conclusion that SAT Verbal and SAT Mathematics items were measuring the same skills across populations, though there were differences across groups in mean levels of performance on the two subtests. Rock and Werts, however, suggest that the pattern of results raises the possibility that the test performance of Hispanics and Asians from non-English backgrounds might have been affected by English-language proficiency.

Alderman (1982) studied the influence of English-language proficiency upon prediction of Puerto Rican college candidates' SAT Verbal and Mathematics scores from scores of the same type on the Prueba de Aptitud Académica (PAA). Three hundred forty-four candidates were involved in the study. The PAA college aptitude test was developed and normed by the Puerto Rico Office of the College Board, for use with Latin American, native Spanish-speaking, college candidates. English proficiency in the Alderman study was assessed by performance on the TOEFL, the English as a Second Language Achievement Test, and the Test of Standard Written English. Inclusion of any one of these measures of proficiency in English singly in regression prediction equations significantly contributed to improvement of prediction of SAT subscores from PAA subscores of the same type. Prediction was improved further, and significantly, by additional inclusion of an interaction term involving scores of proficiency in English and PAA subscores. Alderman concluded that level of proficiency in English acted as a moderator variable in the prediction of college aptitude in English from a measure of college aptitude in Spanish, the native language of examinees. Similar studies involving other non-English candidate populations would be valuable to conduct. The findings of the Alderman study are consistent with the claim that the English language college aptitude scores of students with non-English backgrounds vary in their validity as a function of candidates' proficiency level in English. The academic aptitudes of candidates with low proficiency in English are likely to be underestimated or estimated inaccurately on the basis of candidates' English-language college aptitude scores.

Breland (1979) reviewed predictive validity studies using SAT or ACT test scores and high school rank in class or high school grade point average to predict early college grades of white, black, and Hispanic students. Some evidence suggested less accurate prediction of Hispanics' college grades relative to non-Hispanics in the same institutions. Breland, however, did not find evidence of consistent over- or underprediction of Hispanics' college grade point average. Duran (1983) examined predictive validity studies involving Hispanic college students, which included and supplemented the studies reviewed earlier by Breland. Duran's conclusions were consistent with Breland's, but the expanded review of studies led to evidence of somewhat lower associations between admissions test scores and college grade point averages of Hispanic students. Duran also found a somewhat higher association between high school rank in class, or high school grade point average, and college grade point average than did Breland. Hispanics' college grade point average across studies had a median correlation of .30 with high school rank in class, a median correlation of .25 with verbal test scores, a median correlation of .17 with quantitative test scores, and a median multiple correlation of .38 when predictors were combined.

Follow-up examinations of regression studies reviewed by Duran indicated that the lower associations between predictor measures and college grade for Hispanics was not induced by restrictions in the range of predictor measures. Hispanics' test scores and high school grades tended to show consistently larger variances than comparable measures for non-Hispanics in the same studies. These differences in variance might have reflected the liberalized admissions policies of institutions and their decision to promote admission of selected Hispanics earning low high school grade and admissions test scores relative to the norm for entering students as a whole. Entrance requirements for non-minority students at the same institutions might have been more stringent. Duran (1983) speculated that Hispanic college students might show more variability than non-Hispanic students in personal and background characteristics influencing college performance. This increased heterogeneity, for example in English-language proficiency, could affect the accuracy of high school grades and admissions test scores as predictors of Hispanics' college grades.

Duran (1983) notes that the fact that Hispanics earn lower SAT verbal and mathematical scores than whites cannot be explained entirely by limitations in Hispanics' familiarity with English. As with other minorities, Hispanics' lower test scores also reflect inequities in the education they receive. This fact is well-documented in the educational survey literature and in analysis of minorities' educational attainment in the United States.

Breland and Duran (1985) reported results of a study investigating prediction of Hispanic college candidates' scores on an essay portion of the College Board English Composition Test (ECT). The results of this study suggested that heterogeneity in the English-language and Spanish-language proficiencies of Hispanics is related to accuracy of prediction of their English writing skills for college. The study involved 742 Mexican-Americans and 369 Puerto Ricans who judged that English was their best language, plus an additional 236 Puerto Ricans who judged that English was not their best language. Data analyses indicated that the ECT essay-writing scores of Hispanics, as a whole, tended to be overestimated by scores on a separate multiple-choice portion of the ECT test that indirectly assessed English-writing ability. However, evidence emerged indicating a very different pattern of prediction for some students. The essay-writing scores in English among students who indicated that Spanish was their best language and who also scored high on the multiple-choice portion of the ECT test were underpredicted, rather than overpredicted.

A recent study by Duran, Enright, and Rock (1985) investigated the value of language background and language proficiency survey questions as predictors of Hispanic students' SAT scores and TSWE scores. This study involved over 700 Hispanic college freshmen enrolled in 17 institutions. Two subsets of language survey questions stood out as especially effective predictors of test scores. These questions asked students to rate their ability to use English well in their academic work and to rate their global proficiency in speaking, orally comprehending, reading, and writing English. The responses to these questions correlated between .26 and .45 with student's SAT Verbal and TSWE scores. Stepwise regression analyses showed that the academic questions on proficiency in English tended to predict as much as 18% more variance in SAT Verbal scores than could be predicted on the basis of answers to a simple question asking whether English was a student's best language or not. Other language questions included in the survey were found to be less useful in predicting students' SAT and TSWE scores. These questions asked students about their Spanish skills, first language, preference for language in social activities, educational experiences in English and Spanish, and judgments of instructors' attitudes toward the English spoken and written by them.

The findings of the study appeared robust across various Hispanic subgroups: Cuban-Americans, Mexican-Americans, Puerto Ricans, and other Hispanics, with the exception that questions about general proficiency in English were more useful for predicting test scores of Puerto Rican and other Hispanic students. The findings of the study suggest that Hispanic students with non-English backgrounds are reasonably sensitive to their proficiency in English-language skills for academic study and that their judgments of English skills are corroborated by their performance on verbal portions of college admissions and placement tests.

Although the research studies discussed here stem primarily from selected research conducted at ETS, a number of additional investigations of connections between college candidates' English skills and academic aptitudes of students are surveyed by Hale et al. (1984). This compendium of summaries was referenced at an earlier point in this chapter; all of these studies involved use of the TOEFL and students from a wide variety of international backgrounds. The results of these studies indicate that it can be difficult to assess college candidates' academic skills accurately when students' proficiency in English is limited and that the validity of college aptitude tests in English increases as students' proficiency in English increases.

Conclusion

The research described in this chapter is indicative of intense current interest in the development of valid assessment procedures for students with non-English backgrounds. As mentioned at the outset, the issues and research reviewed here were drawn selectively from material available in the field. The studies that have been reviewed are a sample of those available that explicitly look at the effects of language background and language proficiency on the validity of test use in education. Excluded from extensive review were studies examining the broader question of ethnic-group differences in test performance. These studies are growing rapidly in the educational research literature, and they deserve a separate and detailed treatment of their own. There is no doubt that a review of this broader domain of studies would give attention to many of the issues discussed here, though the coverage of topics would probably also be broader.

This caveat in coverage aside, it seems clear that much of the interest in the testing of students with non-English backgrounds will continue to be driven by practical policy questions faced by educators as they cope with the changing demographic characteristics of U.S. students. In particular, the school-age population of children with non-English backgrounds and limited proficiency in English is expected to continue growing throughout the remainder of the century at a pace exceeding the growth of the general population at large (Oxford et al., 1981). This pattern of growth will have a long-term impact on school systems' personnel needs, and it will continue to increase pressures on schools to provide useful and valid assessment services for language-minority students. Public and interest-group sentiments toward the responsibilities of schools in providing specialized services to children from non-English backgrounds is subject to change as political movements come and go. In the long run, however, the sheer growth rate of the population with non-English backgrounds is likely to force schools and communities to rely even more on testing and assessment as a critical tool in making decisions about which educational services to offer these students.

There are certain frontiers in measurement research that might contribute in an important fashion to progress in assessment in this area. Pennock-Roman (1986a, 1986b) provide a useful preview of some of this additional psychometric research. Among other things, she calls attention to the need for item performance studies that carefully explore connections between an examinee's language proficiency and ethnolinguistic group membership. As part of such a program, she calls for studies that would systematically vary the content and format of items so as to investigate how examinees' performance on items interacts with their language and cultural backgrounds. Such studies would employ modern item response theory techniques. Pennock-Roman also advocates many cross-language validity studies, in particular predictive validity studies that would employ empirical Bayesian and other estimation techniques useful with small samples. This advice is sound, given the fact that small samples often occur in studies involving language-minority students enrolled in particular educational institutions. She also suggests that future predictive validity studies at the college level should pay more attention to models of college achievement that include measures beyond college grades as criterion variables.

Another interesting and promising area of research is suggested by Hulin, Drasgow, and Parsons (1983). These investigators describe the use of item response theory to study performance on tests translated from one language to another. This research provides valuable measurement insights into the difficulties of creating translation-equivalent tests in two lan-

guages. The reported results indicate that the design of test translations needs to be specific to a target population for assessment. Target groups for assessment can vary considerably in their familiarity with dialects and varieties of English and non-English languages. Familiarity with the variety of a language embodied in test items can affect test performance and, correspondingly, estimates of item parameters and item-characteristic curves. In controlling for the variety of language used in test items, item response theory has an important use. It can be used to verify that performance on translated items is invariant across languages for specified target groups of students.

In closing, it is important to note that research can inform, but not govern, assessment practice. Significant progress in the valid assessment of students with non-English backgrounds will continue to depend critically upon test developers' and test users' sensitivity to professionally sound testing practices. The 1985 Standards for Educational and Psychological Testing developed by the American Psychological Association, the American Educational Research Association, and the National Council on Measurement in Education, include explicit reference to such sound testing practices in the assessment of language-minority students.

Standard 13.1	For non-native English speakers or for speakers of some dialects of English, testing should be designed to minimize threats to test reliability and validity that may arise from language differences. (Primary)
Standard 13.2	Linguistic modifications recommended by test publishers should be described in detail in the test manual. (Primary)
Standard 13.3	When a test is recommended for use with linguistically diverse test takers, test developers and publishers should provide the information necessary for appropriate test use and interpretation. (Primary)
Standard 13.4	When a test is translated from one language or dialect to another, its reliability and validity for the uses intended in the linguistic groups to be tested should be established. (Primary)
Standard 13.5	In employment, licensing, and certification testing, the English language proficiency level of the test should not exceed that appropriate to the relevant occupation or profession. (Primary)
Standard 13.6	When it is intended that the two versions of dual-language tests be comparable, evidence of test comparability should be reported. (Primary)
Standard 13.7	English language proficiency should not be determined solely with tests that demand only a single linguistic skill. (Primary). (pp.74-75)

The designation *Primary* attached to each standard means that a standard "should be met by all tests before their operational use and in all test uses, unless a sound professional reason is available to show why it is not necessary, or technically feasible, to do so in a particular case. Test developers and users and, where appropriate, sponsors, are expected to be able to explain why any primary standards have not been met" [pp. 2–3].

Depending on the characteristics of an assessment context, adherence to these standards might require that test users pursue a number of test-administration and test-interpretation strategies. These strategies might include use of appropriately translated tests, use of language interpreters in administering tests, use of nonverbal measures of aptitude, and use of supplemental assessments of value in interpreting test scores of interest.

REFERENCES

Alderman, D. (1982). Language proficiency as a moderator variable in testing academic aptitude. *Journal of Educational Psychology, 74,* 580–587.

Alderman, D. L. & Holland, P. W. (1981). *Item performance across native language groups on the Test of English as a Foreign Language* (TOEFL Research Rep. No. 9). Princeton, NJ: Educational Testing Service.

American Psychological Association, American Research Association, National Council on Measurement in Education (1985). *Standards for educational and psychological testing.* Washington, DC: American Psychological Association.

Bachman, L. F., & Palmer, A. S. (in press). *Basic concerns in language test validation.* Reading, MA: Addison-Wesley.

Bachman, L. F., & Palmer, A. S. (1981). A multitrait-multimethod investigation into the construct validity of six tests of speaking and reading. In A. S. Palmer, P. M. Groot, & G. A. Trosper (Eds.), *The construct validation of tests of communicative competence* (pp. 149–165). Washington, DC: Teachers of English to Speakers of Other Languages.

Balkan, L. (1970). *Les effects du bilinguisme français-anglais sur les aptitudes intellectuelles.* Brussels: Aimav.

Ben-Zeev, S. (1972). The influence of bilingualism on cognitive development and cognitive strategy. Unpublished doctoral dissertation, University of Chicago.

Breland, H. (1979). *Population validity and college entrance measures* (Research Monograph No. 8). New York: College Entrance Examination Board.

Breland, H., & Duran, R. P. (1985). Assessing English composition skills in Spanish-speaking populations. *Educational and Psychological Measurement, 45,* 309–318.

Briere, E. J., & Hinofotis, J. B. (Eds.) (1979). *Concepts in language testing: Some recent studies.* Washington, DC: Teachers of English to Speakers of Other Languages.

California State Department of Education. (1983a). Improving special education for minority students (A task force report prepared for James R. Smith, Deputy Superintendent of Curriculum and Instructional Leadership). Sacramento, CA: Author.

California State Department of Education. (1983b). *A status report on Diana et. al.* Sacramento, CA: Author.

Campione, J. C., & Brown, A. L. (1987). Linking dynamic assessment with school achievement. In C. S. Lidz (Ed.), *Dynamic assessment: An interactional approach to evaluating learning potential* (pp. 82–115). New York: Guilford Press.

Campione, J., Brown, A., Ferrara, R. A. (1982). Mental retardation and intelligence. In R. J. Sternberg (Ed.), *Handbook of human intelligence* (pp. 392–490). New York: Cambridge University Press.

Canale, M. (1984). A communicative approach to language proficiency assessment in a minority setting. In C. Rivera (Ed.), *Communicative competence approaches to language proficiency assessment: Research and application* (pp. 107–122). Avon, England: Multilingual Matters.

Canale, M., & Swain, M. (1980). Theoretical bases of communicative approaches to second language teaching and testing. *Applied Linguistis, 1,* 1–47.

Clark, J. L. D. (Ed.). (1978). *Direct testing of speaking proficiency: Theory and application.* Princeton, NJ: Educational Testing Service.

Cole, M. (1985). The zone of proximal development: Where culture and cognition create each other. In J. V. Wertsch (Ed.), *Culture, communication, and cognition: Vygotskian perspectives* (pp. 146–161). Cambridge: At the University Press.

Cordasco, F. (Ed.). (1978). *The bilingual-bicultural child and the question of intelligence.* New York: Arno Press.

Cummins, J. (1978). Bilingualism and the development of metalinguistic awareness. *Journal of Cross-Cultural Psychology, 9*(2), 131–149.

Cummins, J. (1984). Bilingualism and Special Education. In C. Rivera (Ed.), *Language proficiency and academic achievement* (pp. 71–76). Avon, England: Multilingual Matters.

Cummins, J., & Gulutsan, M. (1973). Some effects of bilingualism on cognitive functioning. Mimeo. Edmonton, Alberta: University of Alberta.

d'Anglejan, A., Gagnon, N., Hafez, M., Tucker, R., & Winsberg, S. (1979). *Solving problems in deductive reasoning: Three experimental studies of adult second language learners* (Working Papers on Bilingualism No. 17). Montreal: University of Montreal.

Dean, R. S. (1977). Reliability of the WISC-R with Mexican-American children. *Journal of School Psychology, 15,* 267–268.

De Avila, E. A., & Duncan, S. E. (1978). Bilingualism and the metaset. In R. P. Duran (Ed.), *Latino languages and communicative behavior* (pp. 337–355). Norwood, NJ: Ablex.

De Avila, E. A., & Havassy, B. (1976). The testing of minority children: A neo-Piagitian approach. *Today's Education.*

Diaz, R. M. (1983). Thought and two languages: The impact of bilingualism on cognitive development. In E. Gordon (Ed.), *Review of research in education, 10.* Washington, DC: American Educational Research Association.

Dieterich, T. G., & Freeman, C. (1979). *Language in education: Theory and practice, 23.* Arlington, VA: Center for Applied Linguistics.

Dornic, S. (1980). Information processing and language dominance. *International Review of Applied Psychology, 29,* 119–141.

Duncan, O. T. (1969). Inheritance of poverty or inheritance of race? In D. P. Moynihan (Ed.), *On understanding poverty.* New York: Basic Books.

Duran, R. P. (1978). Reading comprehension and the verbal deductive reasoning of bilinguals. In R. P. Duran (Ed.), *Latino language and communicative behavior* (pp. 311–336). Norwood, NJ: Ablex.

Duran, R. P. (1983). *Hispanics' education and background: Predictors of college achievement.* New York: College Entrance Examination Board.

Duran, R. P. (1985). Influences of language skills on bilinguals' problem solving. In J. W. Segal, S. F. Chipman, & R. Glaser (Eds.), *Thinking and Learning Skills: Research and Open Questions,* (pp. 187–207). Hillsdale, NJ: Lawrence Erlbaum.

Duran, R. P., Canale, M., Penfield, J., Stansfield, C., & Liskin-Gasparro, J. E. (1985). *TOEFL from a communicative viewpoint on language proficiency: A working paper* (TOEFL Research Report No. 17). Princeton, NJ: Educational Testing Service.

Duran, R. P., Enright, M. K., & Rock, D. A. (1985). *Language factors and Hispanic freshmen's student profile* (College Board Report No. 85-3). New York: College Entrance Examination Board.

Educational Testing Service. (1983). *Test and score manual, 1983 Edition.* Test of English as a Foreign Language Program. Princeton, NJ: Author.

Erickson, J. G., & Omark, D. R. (Eds.). (1981). *Communication assessment of the bilingual bicultural child.* Baltimore: University Park Press.

Ferdman, B., & Hakuta, K. (1985). *A population perspective on bilingualism in Puerto Rican children.* Paper presented at the meeting of the Society for Research in Child Development, Toronto.

Feuerstein, R. (1979). *The dynamic assessment of retarded performers: The Learning Potential Assessment Device, theory instruments and techniques.* Baltimore: University Park Press.

Feuerstein, R. (1980). *Instrumental Enrichment: An Intervention Program For Cognitive Modifiability.* Baltimore: University Park Press.

Figueroa, R. A. (1980). Intersection of special education and bilingual education. In J. E. Alatis (Ed.), *Georgetown University roundtable on languages and linguistics 1980* Washington, DC: Georgetown University Press.

Figueroa, R. A. (1983). Test bias and Hispanic children. *Journal of Special Education, 17,* 431–440.

Goldman, S. R., Reyes, M., & Varnhagen, C. K. (1984). Understanding fables in first and second languages. In E. E. Garcia (Ed.), *NABE*

Journal, 8(2), 35–67. Washington, DC: National Association for Bilingual Education.

Gould, S. J. (1981). *The mismeasure of man.* New York: W. W. Norton.

Hakuta, K. (1986). *Mirror of language: The debate on bilingualism.* New York: Basic Books.

Hakuta, K., & Diaz, R. (1984). The relationship between the degree of bilingualism and cognitive ability: A critical discussion and some longitudinal data. In K. E. Nelson (Ed.), *Children's language: Vol. 5.* Hillsdale, NJ: Lawrence Erlbaum.

Hale, G. A., Stansfield, C. W., & Duran, R. P. (1984). *TOEFL research reports: Summaries of studies involving test of English as a foreign language, 1963–1982* (TOEFL Research Report No. 16). Princeton, NJ: Educational Testing Service.

Hines, T. M. (1978). *The independence of language in bilingual memory.* Unpublished doctoral dissertation, University of Oregon, Eugene.

Hulin, C. L., Drasgow, F., & Parsons, C. K. (1983). *Item response theory. Application to psychological measurement.* Homewood, IL: Dow Jones-Irwin.

Ianco-Worrall, A. D. (1972). Bilingualism and cognitive development. *Child Development* (pp. 43, 1390–1400).

Jensen, A. R. (1974). How biased are culture loaded tests? *Genetic Psychology Monograph, 90,* 185–244.

Kaufman, A. S. (1979). *Intelligent testing with the WISC-R.* New York: Wiley.

Kaufman, A. S., & Kaufman, N. L. (1982). *Kaufman Assessment Battery for Children: Interpretive Manual.* Circle Pines, MN: American Guidance Service.

Lambert, W. E. (1977). The effects on bilingualism on the individual: Cognitive and sociocultural consequences. In P. A. Hornby (Ed.), *Bilingualism: Psychological, social, and educational implications.* 15–27. New York: Academic Press.

Lange, D. C., & Clifford, R. T. (1980). *Language in education: Theory and practice, 24.* Arlington, VA: Center for Applied Linguistics.

Lopez, M. (1977). Bilingual memory research: Implications for bilingual education. In J. L. Martinez (Ed.), *Chicano psychology* (pp. 127–140). New York: Academic Press.

Luria, A. R. (1976). Towards the problem of the historical nature of psychological processes. *International Journal of Psychology, 6,* 259–272.

MacLeod, C. M. (1976). Bilingual episodic memory: Acquisition and forgetting. *Journal of Verbal Learning and Verbal Behavior, 15,* 347–364.

McCormack, P. D. (1977). Bilingual linguistic memory: The independence-interdependence issue revisited. In P. A. Hornby (Ed.), *Bilingualism: Psychological, social, and educational implications* (pp. 57–67). New York: Academic Press.

McLaughlin, B., Rossman, T., & McLeod, B. (1983). Second language in learning: An information-processing perspective. *Language Learning, 33*(2), 135–159.

Mercer, J. R. (1979). System of Multicultural Pluralistic Assessment *(SOMPA): Technical Manual.* New York: Psychological Corporation.

Mercer, J. R. (1984). What is a racially and culturally nondiscriminatory test? A sociological and pluralistic perspective. In C. R. Reynolds & R. T. Brown (Eds.), *Perspectives on bias in mental testing* (pp. 293–356). New York: Plenum Press.

Mercer, J., & Ysseldyke, J. (1977). Designing diagnostic-intervention programs. In T. Oakland (Ed.), *Psychological and educational assessment of minority children* (pp. 70–90). New York: Brunner/Mazel.

Mishra, S. P., & Hurt, M., Jr. (1970). The use of Metropolitan Readiness Tests with Mexican-American children. *California Journal of Educational Research, 2l,* 182–187.

National Assessment of Educational Progress. (1982). *Students from homes in which English is not the dominant language: Who are they and how well do they read?.* Denver: Author.

Nielsen, F., & Fernandez, R. M. (1981). *Hispanic students in American high schools: Background characteristics and achievement.* Washington, DC: National Center for Education Statistics.

Nielsen, F., & Learner, S. J. (1982). *Language skills and school achievement of bilingual Hispanics.* University of North Carolina at Chapel Hill.

Oakland, T., & Matuszek, P. (1977). Using tests in nondiscriminatory assessment. In T. Oakland (Ed.), *Psychological and educational assessment of minority children.* (pp. 52–69). New York: Brunner/Mazel.

Oller, J. W. (1979). *Language tests at school.* London: Longman Group.

Oller, J. W., & Perkins, K. (1978). *Language in education: Testing the tests.* Rowley, MA: Newbury House.

Oller, J. W., & Perkins, K. (1980). *Research in language testing.* Rowley, MA: Newbury House.

Oxford, R., Poll, L., Lopez, D., Stupp, P., Gendell, M., & Peng, S. (1981). Projections of non-English background limited English proficient persons in the United States to the year 2000: Educational planning in the demographic context. *NABE Journal, 5* (3), 1–30.

Padilla, A. M. (1979). Critical factors in the testing of Hispanic Americans: A review and some suggestions for the future. In R. W. Tyler & S. H. White (Eds.), *Testing, teaching and learning* (pp. 219–243). Washington, DC: National Institute of Education.

Palmer, A. S., Groot, P. J. M., & Trosper, G. A. (Eds.). (1981). *The construct validation of tests of communicative competence.* Washington, DC: Teachers of English to Speakers of Other Languages.

Peal, E., & Lambert, W. E. (1962). The relation of bilingualism to intelligence. *Psychology Monographs,* 1–23.

Pennock-Roman, M. (1986a). Fairness in the use of tests for selective admissions of Hispanics. In M. A. Olivas (Ed.), *Latinos in Higher Education.* (pp. 246–277). New York: Teachers College Press.

Pennock-Roman, M. (1986b). New directions for research on Spanish-language tests and test-item bias. In M. A. Olivas (Ed.), *Latinos in Higher Education.* (pp. 193–220). New York: Teachers College Press.

Phillipus, M. J. (1967). *Test prediction of school success of bilingual Hispano-Americano children.* Denver: Denver Department of Health and Hospitals. (ERIC Document Reproduction Service No. ED 036 577)

Pletcher, B. P., Locks, N. A., Reynolds, D. F., & Sisson, B. G. (1978). *A guide to assessment instruments.* Northvale, NJ: Santillana.

Ramist, L., & Arbeiter, S. (1984). *Profiles college-bound Seniors, 1983.* New York: College Entrance Examination Board.

Rivera, C. (Ed.). (1983). *An ethnographic/sociolinguistic approach to language proficiency assessment.* Avon, England: Multilingual Matters.

Rivera, C. (Ed.). (1984a). *Communicative competence approaches to language proficiency assessment: Research and application.* Avon, England: Multilingual Matters.

Rivera, C. (Ed.). (1984b). *Language proficiency and academic achievement.* Avon, England: Multilingual Matters.

Rock, D., & Werts, C. (1979). *Construct validity of the SAT across populations: An empirical confirmatory study* (College Entrance Examination Board Report No. RDR 78–79, No. 5). Princeton: Educational Testing Service.

Rosenthal, A. S., Baker, K., & Ginsburg, A. (1983). The effect of language background on achievement level and learning among elementary school students. *Sociology of Education, 56,* 157–169.

Sanchez, G. I. (1932). Scores of Spanish-speaking children on repeated tests. *Journal of Genetic Psychology, 40*(1).

Sanchez, G. I. (1934). Bilingualism and mental measures: A world of caution. *Journal of Applied Psychology, 18.*

Sandoval, J. (1979). The WISC-R and internal evidence of test bias with minority groups. *Journal of Consulting and Clinical Psychology, 47,* 919–927.

Scholtz, G., Hendricks, D., Spurling, R., Johnson, M., & Vandenburg, L. (1980). Is language ability divisible or unitary? A factor analysis of 22 English language proficiency tests. In J. W. Oller & K. Perkins (Eds.), *Research in Language Testing* (pp. 24–34). Rowley, MA: Newbury House.

Scott, S. (1973). The relation of divergent thinking to bilingualism: Cause or effect. Unpublished research report, McGill University.

Scribner, S. (1979). Modes of thinking and ways of speaking: Culture and logic reconsidered. In R. O. Freedle (Ed.), *New direction in discourse processing* (pp. 223–243). Norwood, NJ: Ablex.

Seidner, S. S. (Ed.). (1982). *Issues of language assessment: Foundations and research.* Evanston, IL: Illinois State Board of Education.

Seidner, S. S. (Ed.). (1983). *Issues of language assessment: Vol. 3. Language assessment and curriculum planning.* Evanston, IL: Illinois State Board of Education.

Shellenberger, S. (1977). *A cross-cultural investigation of the Spanish version of the McCarthy Scales of Children's Abilities for Puerto Rican children.* Unpublished doctoral dissertation, University of Georgia, Athens.

Silverman, L. J. (1976). The educational disadvantage of language-minority persons in the United States. *NCES Bulletin, B-4.*

Silverman, R., Noa, J., & Russell, R. (1978). *Oral language tests for bilingual children.* Portland, OR: Northwest Regional Education Laboratory.

So, A. Y., & Chan, K. S. (1984). What Matters? A study of the relative impact of language background and socioeconomic status on reading achievement. *NABE Journal, 8*(3), 27–40.

Spolsky, B. (1979). Linguistics and language testers. In B. Spolsky (Ed.), *Advances in language testing.* Washington, DC: Center for Applied Linguistics.

Stansfield, C. (1981). The assessment of language proficiency in bilingual children: An analysis of theories and instrumentation. In R. V. Padilla (Ed.), *Ethnoperspectives in bilingual education research: Bilingual education technology* (pp. 233–248). Ypsilanti, MI: Department of Foreign Languages and Bilingual Studies.

Stansfield, C. (1986). *Toward communicative competence testing: Proceedings of the Second TOEFL Invitational Conference* (TOEFL Research Report No. 21). Princeton, NJ: Educational Testing Service.

Swinton, S. S., & Powers, D. E. (1980). *Factor analysis of the test of English as a foreign language for several language groups* (TOEFL Research Report No. 6). Princeton, NJ: Educational Testing Service.

Thorum, A. R. (1981). *Language assessment instruments: Infancy through adulthood.* Springfield, IL: Charles C Thomas.

Torrance, E. P., Gowan, J. C., Wu, J. M., & Aliotti, N. C. (1970). Creative functioning of monolingual and bilingual children in Singapore. *Journal of Educational Psychology.*

Tucker, J. A. (1977). Operationalizing the diagnostic-intervention process. In T. Oakland (Ed.), *Psychological and educational assessment of minority children.* New York: Brunner/Mazel.

Ulibarri, D. M., Spencer, M. L., & Rivas, G. A. (1981). Language proficiency and academic achievement: A study of language proficiency tests and their relationship to school ratings as predictors of academic achievement. In R. L. Lignt (Ed.), *NABE Journal, 5*(3), 47–80.

Veltman, C. J. (1981). Relative educational attainment of Hispanic-American children, 1976. *Metas, 2*(1), 36–51.

Vye, N., Burns, S., Delclos, V., & Bransford, J. (in press). Dynamic assessment of intellectually handicapped children. In C. S. Lidz (Ed.), *Dynamic assessment: Foundations and fundamentals.* New York: Guilford Press.

Vygotsky, L. S. (1978). *Mind in society: The development of higher psychological processes* (ed. and trans. by M. Cole, V. John-Steiner, S. Scribner, & E. Souberman). Cambridge, MA: Harvard University Press.

Wildemuth, B. M. (1981). *Testing Spanish speaking students.* Princeton, NJ: Educational Testing Service.

Index

589